MW00991235

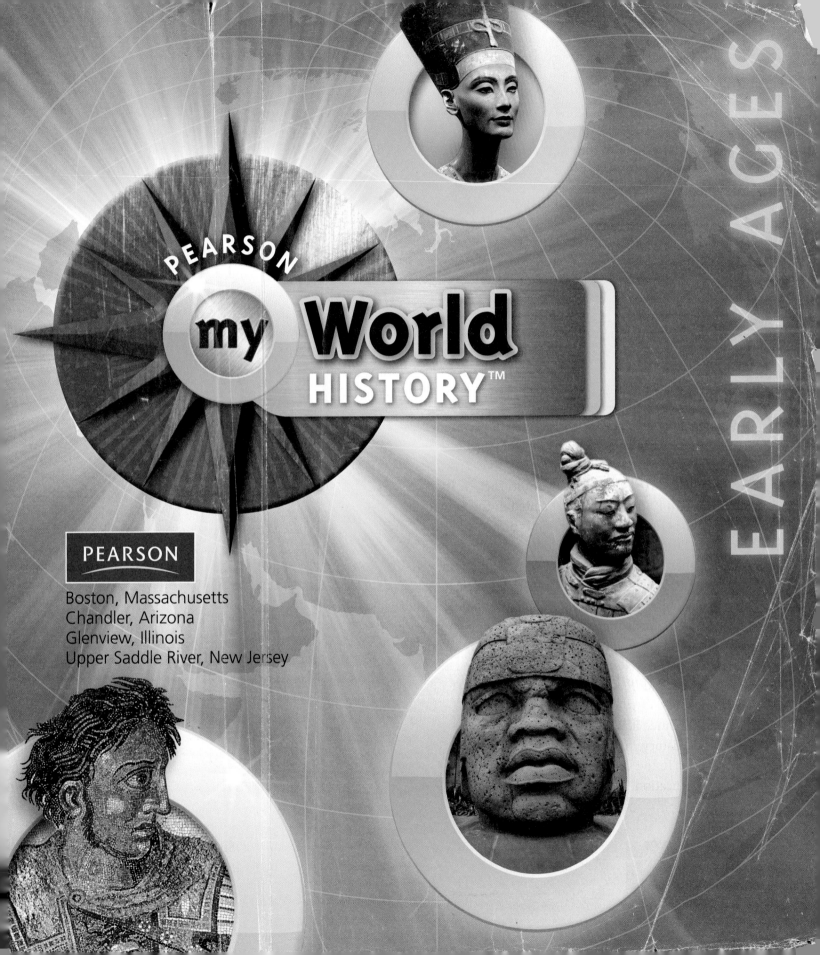

PEARSON

my World HISTORY™

EARLY AGES

PEARSON

Boston, Massachusetts
Chandler, Arizona
Glenview, Illinois
Upper Saddle River, New Jersey

Acknowledgments appear on pages 850–856, which constitute an extension of this copyright page.

Copyright © 2012 Pearson Education, Inc., or its affiliates. All Rights Reserved. Printed in the United States of America. This publication is protected by copyright, and permission should be obtained from the publisher prior to any prohibited reproduction, storage in a retrieval system, or transmission in any form or by any means, electronic, mechanical, photocopying, recording, or likewise. For information regarding permissions, write to Pearson Curriculum Group Rights & Permissions, One Lake Street, Upper Saddle River, New Jersey 07458.

Pearson, Prentice Hall, Pearson Prentice Hall, myWorld History, and Success Tracker are trademarks, in the U.S. and/or other countries, of Pearson Education, Inc., or its affiliates.

ISBN-13: 978-0-13-372697-8
ISBN-10:   0-13-372697-5
8 9 10 V063 14 13

Program Authors

Frank Karpiel teaches at the Citadel Military College in South Carolina and earned his Ph.D degree in history from the University of Hawaii. His focus of study is world history and how cross-cultural interactions shape present-day human society. In addition to writing articles on a variety of historical topics for academic journals, newspapers, and magazines, he has helped develop Web sites focusing on comparative cultural history/geography.

Kathleen Krull received a B.A. in English from Lawrence University in Appleton, Wisconsin. Today she is well known for her innovative approach to biographies for young readers. Her recent books include *Lincoln Tells a Joke: How Laughter Saved the President (and the Country)* (Harcourt); *Lives of the Pirates: Swashbucklers, Scoundrels (Neighbors Beware!)* (Harcourt); *The Brothers Kennedy: John, Robert, Edward* (Simon & Schuster); *The Boy Who Invented TV: The Story of Philo Farnsworth* (Knopf); and more as featured at www.kathleenkrull.com. Forthcoming books include *Charles Darwin,* next in her "Giants of Science" series (Viking) and *Kubla Khan: The Emperor of Everything* (Viking). Kathleen lives in San Diego, California, with her husband, children's book writer and illustrator Paul Brewer, and from there travels frequently to speak about the craft and pleasures of writing biographies.

Program Consultant

Grant Wiggins is the President of Authentic Education in Hopewell, New Jersey. He earned his Ed.D. degree from Harvard University and his B.A. from St. John's College in Annapolis, Maryland. Wiggins consults with schools, districts, and state education departments on a variety of reform matters; organizes conferences and workshops; and develops print materials and Web resources on curricular change. Over the past 20 years, Wiggins has worked on some of the most influential reform initiatives in the country, including Vermont's portfolio system and Ted Sizer's Coalition of Essential Schools. He is the coauthor, with Jay McTighe, of *Understanding by Design* and *The Understanding by Design Handbook,* the award-winning and highly successful materials on curriculum published by ASCD. He is also the author of *Educative Assessment* and *Assessing Student Performance*, both published by Jossey-Bass.

Academic Reviewers

Barbara B. Brown
African Studies Center
Boston University
Boston, Massachusetts

Christopher Key Chapple
Department of Theological
    Studies
Loyola Marymount University
Los Angeles, California

J. P. Dessel
Department of History
University of Tennessee
Knoxville, Tennessee

J. Michael Francis
Department of History
University of North Florida
Jacksonville, Florida

Judy E. Gaughan
Department of History
Colorado State University
Fort Collins, Colorado

Brent Isbell
Department of Religious Studies
University of Houston
Houston, Texas

Geoffrey Koziol
University of California
Department of History
Berkeley, California

Huping Ling
Department of History
Truman State University
Kirksville, Missouri

Gordon Newby
Department of Middle Eastern
    and South Asian Studies
Emory University
Atlanta, Georgia

Thomas J. Sanders
Department of History
United States Naval Academy
Annapolis, Maryland

Douglas Skopp
Department of History
State University of New York at
    Plattsburgh
Plattsburgh, New York

David Webster
Department of Anthropology
Pennsylvania State University
University Park, Pennsylvania

Contents

Core Concepts Handbook

Master Teachers and Contributing Authors

George F. Sabato
Past President, California Council for
the Social Studies
Placerville Union School District
Placerville, California

Michael Yell
Past President, National Council for
the Social Studies
Hudson Middle School
Hudson, Wisconsin

Teacher Reviewers

Maureen Andreadis
School for Creative and
Performing Arts
Cincinnati, Ohio

Richard Coop
Shadow Ridge High School
Las Vegas, Nevada

Doug Fillmore
Bloomington Junior High School
Bloomington, Illinois

Marc Fleming
Greece Central School District
North Greece, New York

Kristin Fox
Bernards Township Public
Schools
Bernards Township, New Jersey

Marla Horwitz
Carl Sandburg Junior High
Rolling Meadows, Illinois

Lauryn Humphris
Jackson Middle School
Villa Park, Illinois

Bonnie Lock
La Center School District
La Center, Washington

Lester Lurie
Casey Middle School
Boulder, Colorado

Charles Ogdan
Sycamore Junior High
Cincinnati, Ohio

Janie Phelps
Orange County Public Schools
Orange County, Florida

Tiferet Reilly
Parkland Magnet Middle School
Rockville, Maryland

Chuck Schierloh
Lima City Academy of Learning
Lima, Ohio

Patricia Shelton
Odle Middle School
Bellevue, Washington

Chris Taylor
Liberty Elementary School
Boise, Idaho

Amy Thornhill
Parkway School District
Saint Louis, Missouri

Chuck Triplett
Lindbergh School District
Saint Louis, Missouri

PEARSON

my World HISTORY™

EARLY AGES

PEARSON

Boston, Massachusetts
Chandler, Arizona
Glenview, Illinois
Upper Saddle River, New Jersey

Acknowledgments appear on pages 850–856, which
constitute an extension of this copyright page.

**Copyright © 2012 Pearson Education, Inc., or its
affiliates.** All Rights Reserved. Printed in the United
States of America. This publication is protected by
copyright, and permission should be obtained from
the publisher prior to any prohibited reproduction,
storage in a retrieval system, or transmission in
any form or by any means, electronic, mechanical,
photocopying, recording, or likewise. For
information regarding permissions, write to Pearson
Curriculum Group Rights & Permissions, One Lake
Street, Upper Saddle River, New Jersey 07458.

Pearson, Prentice Hall, Pearson Prentice Hall,
myWorld History, and Success Tracker are
trademarks, in the U.S. and/or other countries, of
Pearson Education, Inc., or its affiliates.

ISBN-13: 978-0-13-372697-8
ISBN-10:   0-13-372697-5
8 9 10 V063 14 13

Program Authors

Frank Karpiel teaches at the Citadel Military College in South Carolina and earned his Ph.D degree in history from the University of Hawaii. His focus of study is world history and how cross-cultural interactions shape present-day human society. In addition to writing articles on a variety of historical topics for academic journals, newspapers, and magazines, he has helped develop Web sites focusing on comparative cultural history/geography.

Kathleen Krull received a B.A. in English from Lawrence University in Appleton, Wisconsin. Today she is well known for her innovative approach to biographies for young readers. Her recent books include *Lincoln Tells a Joke: How Laughter Saved the President (and the Country)* (Harcourt); *Lives of the Pirates: Swashbucklers, Scoundrels (Neighbors Beware!)* (Harcourt); *The Brothers Kennedy: John, Robert, Edward* (Simon & Schuster); *The Boy Who Invented TV: The Story of Philo Farnsworth* (Knopf); and more as featured at www.kathleenkrull.com. Forthcoming books include *Charles Darwin*, next in her "Giants of Science" series (Viking) and *Kubla Khan: The Emperor of Everything* (Viking). Kathleen lives in San Diego, California, with her husband, children's book writer and illustrator Paul Brewer, and from there travels frequently to speak about the craft and pleasures of writing biographies.

Program Consultant

Grant Wiggins is the President of Authentic Education in Hopewell, New Jersey. He earned his Ed.D. degree from Harvard University and his B.A. from St. John's College in Annapolis, Maryland. Wiggins consults with schools, districts, and state education departments on a variety of reform matters; organizes conferences and workshops; and develops print materials and Web resources on curricular change. Over the past 20 years, Wiggins has worked on some of the most influential reform initiatives in the country, including Vermont's portfolio system and Ted Sizer's Coalition of Essential Schools. He is the coauthor, with Jay McTighe, of *Understanding by Design* and *The Understanding by Design Handbook*, the award-winning and highly successful materials on curriculum published by ASCD. He is also the author of *Educative Assessment* and *Assessing Student Performance*, both published by Jossey-Bass.

Academic Reviewers

Barbara B. Brown
African Studies Center
Boston University
Boston, Massachusetts

Christopher Key Chapple
Department of Theological
    Studies
Loyola Marymount University
Los Angeles, California

J. P. Dessel
Department of History
University of Tennessee
Knoxville, Tennessee

J. Michael Francis
Department of History
University of North Florida
Jacksonville, Florida

Judy E. Gaughan
Department of History
Colorado State University
Fort Collins, Colorado

Brent Isbell
Department of Religious Studies
University of Houston
Houston, Texas

Geoffrey Koziol
University of California
Department of History
Berkeley, California

Huping Ling
Department of History
Truman State University
Kirksville, Missouri

Gordon Newby
Department of Middle Eastern
    and South Asian Studies
Emory University
Atlanta, Georgia

Thomas J. Sanders
Department of History
United States Naval Academy
Annapolis, Maryland

Douglas Skopp
Department of History
State University of New York at
    Plattsburgh
Plattsburgh, New York

David Webster
Department of Anthropology
Pennsylvania State University
University Park, Pennsylvania

Unit 1   Origins

Unit 2 The Ancient Near East

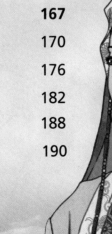

Unit 3 Ancient India and China

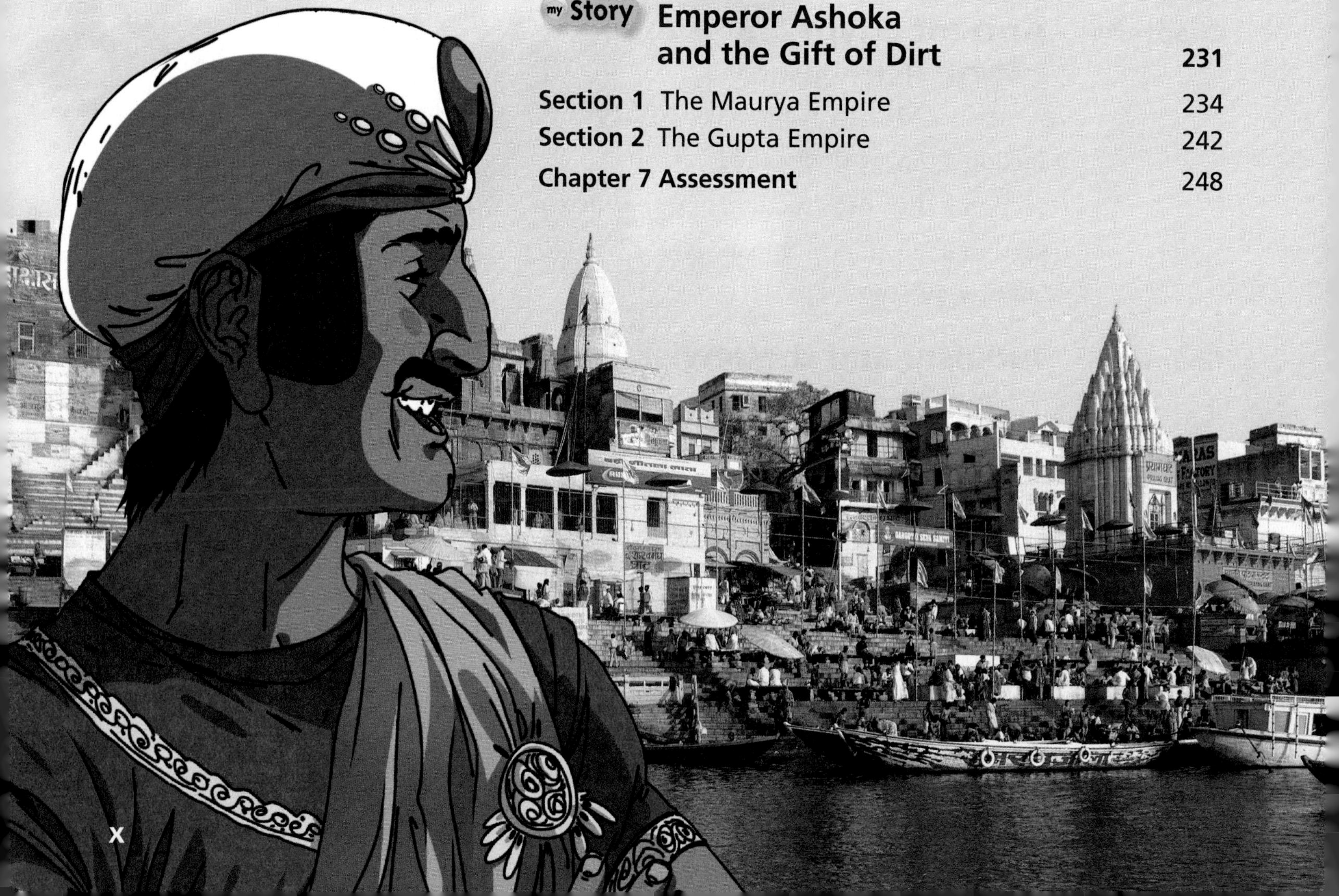

Unit 4 Ancient Greece

Unit 5 Ancient Rome

Unit 6 The Byzantine Empire and Islamic Civilization

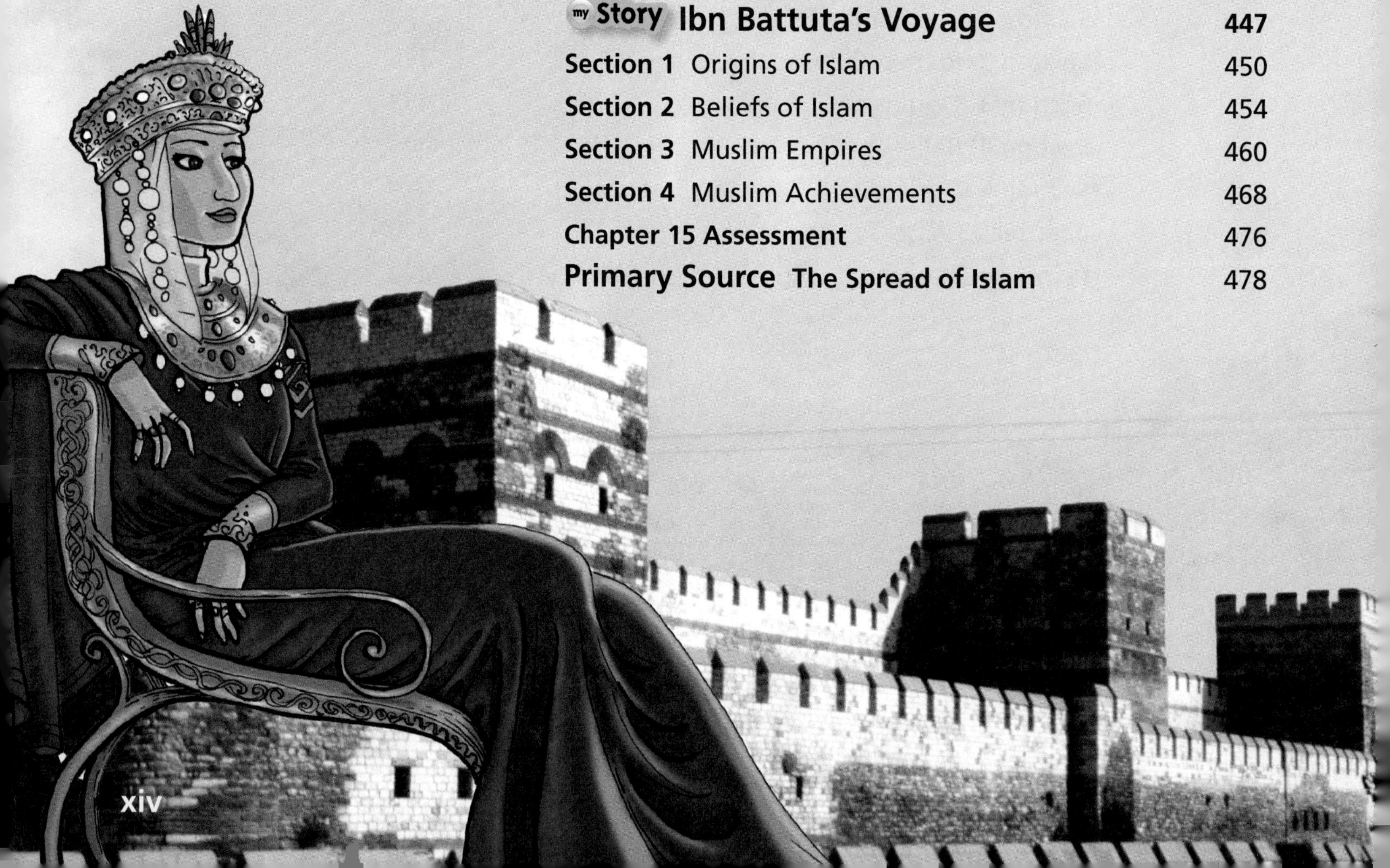

Unit 7　African and Asian Civilizations

Unit 8 Civilizations of the Americas

Unit 9 Europe in the Middle Ages

Unit 10   The Rise of Europe

my Story

Connect to stories of historical figures throughout the ages. my worldhistory.com ➔

Scenes from *Joan of Arc: Voices of Victory*

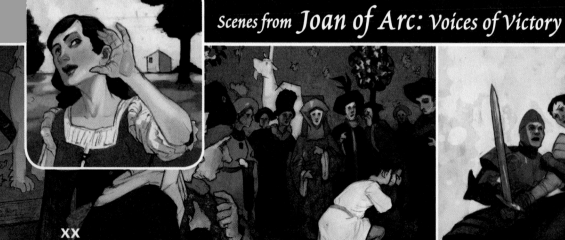

21st Century Learning

Learn new skills through interactive activities. my worldhistory.com

Closer Look

Photographs, maps, charts, illustrations, and text help you take a closer look at the world.

Primary Sources

Compare viewpoints through eyewitness accounts and documents.

Diagrams

Colorful diagrams help you visualize history. my worldhistory.com

Charts, Graphs, and Tables

Data in charts, graphs, and tables help you visually access important information.

Primary Source Quotations

Quotations from important primary sources connect you directly to the people who made and witnessed history (my)worldhistory.com →

Primary Source Quotations *(continued)* my worldhistory.com

Maps

Interactive maps help you actively understand your world. my worldhistory.com

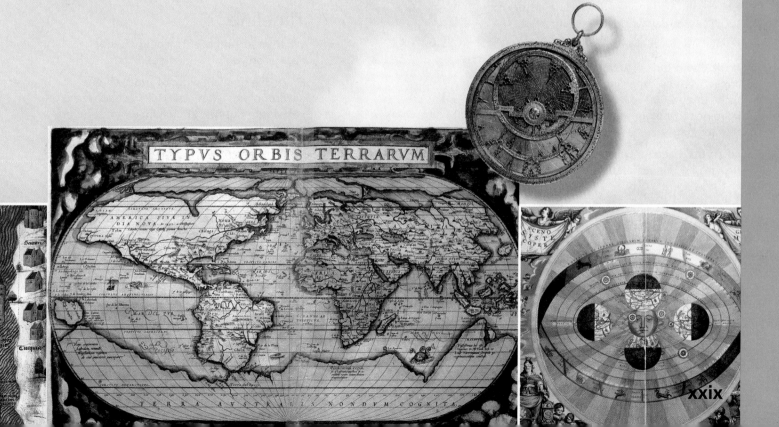

TYPVS ORBIS TERRARVM

CONNECT

EXPERI

Prepare for your *myWorld* travels by exploring the features of your textbook through the following fun activities.

myStory

If your life story was made into a graphic novel, what would it look like?

FIND: Which **my Story** links the Essential Question, *"What are the consequences of technology?"* and Cyrus the Great?

HINT: The beginning of the Table of Contents shows what is in each unit. Following these pages is a special Table of Contents that quickly identifies where you can find the **my Story** and more exciting features.

Essential Questions

Each chapter begins with an essential question which helps you connect and relate history to your present-day world. One example is:

"What are the consequences of technology?"

Think about today's technology. How does it impact your everyday life? Now, think about technology 4,000 years ago. It may be hard to imagine technology was present in the world that long ago.

FIND: The Essential Question for the chapter titled "The Fertile Crescent."

HINT: The Essential Question appears on the first page of the chapter.

Timeline

What important events would appear on your life timeline?

FIND: The timeline with information on anthropologist Mary Leakey. She discovered the remains of the first known member of *Homo habilis*, which means "Handy Man" in Latin.

HINT: Timelines are found on unit openers and Mary Leakey's unit is titled "Origins."

UNDERSTAND ENCE

Key Ideas and Key Terms

How do you begin a project? Do you list important words and ideas or pull your knowledge together in a graphic organizer?

FIND: Key ideas and terms for the Hunter-Gatherer Societies section. How do they impact your thoughts on the Essential Question, *"What are the consequences of technology?"*

HINT: Key ideas and Terms are on the first page of every section. The Hunter-Gatherer Societies section is found in the same chapter as Mary Leakey.

Closer Look

If someone was to take a close look at your life what would they find?

FIND: The Closer Look on Uncovering the Past. How does the technology of archeologists uncover the technology of the past?

HINT: Check out the Special Table of Contents to find the list and page numbers of Closer Looks.

Culture Close Up

Are there any gardens in your neighborhood? What would it have been like to live near the Hanging Gardens of Babylon?

FIND: The Hanging Gardens of Babylon Culture Close-Up.

HINT: The Special Table of Contents includes a list of Culture Close Ups.

Primary Sources

In 100 years, do you think people will remember what you thought and said?

FIND: The Primary Source that references the invention of the wheel. What was the consequence of this invention? How many times a day do you use something that involves a wheel?

HINT: Check the special Table of Contents for this Primary Source titled "Digging for Clues."

21st Century Learning Activity

Are you prepared to be successful in the 21st century?

FIND: The 21st Century Learning Activity titled "Debate the Digital Future". What are the consequences of the type of technology discussed?

HINT: Look on page xxi to find the list of 21st Century Learning Activities. The skill that refers to *Debate the Digital Future* is *Solve Problems.*

Core Concepts Handbook

The three Core Concepts parts that follow will introduce you to basic concepts in history, geography, government, economics, and culture. They will help you understand material that follows in the rest of the book.

The fundamental social studies skills and concepts taught in this handbook are central to understanding the world around you. After you have read the Core Concepts, you will be able to make sense of a highway map, compare systems of government, explain how banks work, and understand different cultures.

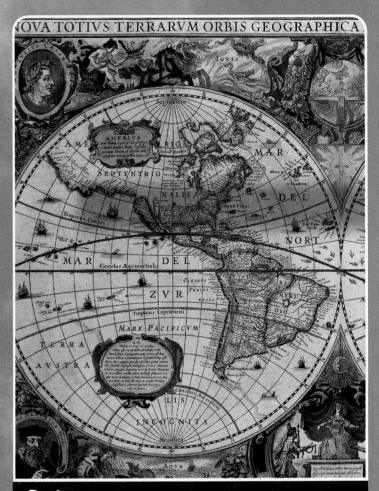

Part

1 History and Geography

Examine the ways in which people study history and understand our planet, Earth. Connect to the content by reading about Brian McCray, a young archaeologist who helped examine the remains of the Incan empire.

page 2

History and Geography

Inca ruins in Peru

An archaeologist sketches a dig in Lima, Peru.

2

Part

2 Citizenship and Economics

Learn how people organize governments, what governments do, and how people make economic decisions. Connect to the content by reading about Anne Marie Sutherland, who worked as an intern for a United States senator.

page 18

Part

3 Culture

Understand how the practices of a people make up their culture, and how culture can change over time. Connect to the content by reading about Joanna Baca, a young Navajo woman who works to preserve her traditions.

page 40

Archaeologists at a dig

Brian McCray

Digging for Clues

Story by Miles Lemaire for myWorld History

Brian McCray likes to dig in the dirt. But Brian isn't just playing around. He's an archaeologist who has traveled around the world to dig up objects from the past and learn more about the people who made them.

Carrying out an archaeological dig isn't as simple as picking a location, grabbing a shovel, and starting to dig, Brian says. He spends weeks or months researching the history of the dig's location before a shovel goes into the ground. Brian will study maps, look at photographs, and read written descriptions of the area. He wants to know as much as possible about the site before he begins to explore it.

Once an archaeological dig begins, archaeologists like Brian carefully examine all the objects found at the site. Then they record and save the objects for future research. Keeping good records is very important. All archaeological sites are drawn and mapped carefully, with detailed information about where each object was found. It can take months or years to fully examine all of the artifacts, or objects made by people, found at an archaeological site.

"The things that are deeper in the ground are, in most cases, older than the things closer to the surface," says Brian. "We keep track of every layer of soil and what we find there."

Brian's research has allowed him to travel throughout the Americas. He has studied sites in the northern United States, the Caribbean, and western South America. Brian has worked with the Digital Archaeological Archive of Contemporary Slavery. This research has helped historians learn more about the lives of enslaved Africans in North America and the Caribbean. But his most interesting discovery was in the Andes Mountains in South America. In the Andes, Brian studied something that researchers still don't fully understand.

"It was actually what appears to be a swimming pool," Brian says. "It was constructed by the Incas at the very end of the Incan empire." That was almost 500 years ago.

What was the "pool" used for? "Who knows?" Brian says. "It was a big sunken court with really amazing cut-stone masonry and five or six canals bringing water down into it from up the hill … It's way too cold up there for anyone to want to swim all that often."

But although Brian and his fellow archaeologists don't yet know why the Incas built this pool, you can be sure that they'll keep digging to find out the answer. Who knows? Maybe Brian will be the one to finally uncover the truth.

Measuring Time

Key Ideas
- Throughout history, societies and cultures have organized time in different ways.
- People have used a number of different calendars to measure time.

Key Terms • historian • timeline • chronology • period • prehistory

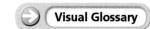 Visual Glossary

It can be hard to describe the concept of time. But **historians**—people who study events in the past—know that organizing time is important if we want to understand past events.

Using a Timeline

Historians use timelines as a tool. A **timeline** is a line marked off with a series of events and dates. Historians use timelines to put events in a **chronology,** a list of events in the order in which they occurred.

A timeline is flexible. It can cover a day, a year, a decade (ten years), a century (one hundred years), a millennium (one thousand years), or any other period in history. A **period** is a length of time singled out because of a specific event or development that happened during that time. A period is also known as an era or an epoch. Historians use periods and eras to organize and describe human activities.

The timeline on this page shows watershed events—important points in history. The period 1940–1949 is an example of a decade, or a period of ten years. Below, a Sumerian writing tablet. ▼

3200 B.C. Sumerians develop the earliest known form of writing.

A.D. 1945 World War II ends.

| 1940 | 1941 | 1942 | 1943 | 1944 | 1945 | 1946 | 1947 | 1948 | 1949 |

| 3000 B.C. | 2000 B.C. | 1000 B.C. | A.D. 1 | A.D. 1000 | A.D. 2000 |

1766 B.C. China's Shang dynasty begins.

A.D. 250 Maya Classic period begins in Mexico and Central America.

A.D. 1492 Christopher Columbus sails to the Americas.

Organizing Time

The past is often split into two parts, prehistory and history. **Prehistory** is the time before humans invented writing. *History* refers to written history, which began about 5,200 years ago.

We can also organize history by beginning with a key event from the past. Today much of the world uses the believed birthdate of Jesus as a key event. Years before that event are labeled B.C., for "before Christ," or B.C.E., for "before common era." Years after Jesus's birth are labeled A.D., meaning *anno Domini*, Latin for "in the year of our Lord." These years are also known as C.E., for "common era."

The Jewish calendar counts the years since the creation of the world, according to Jewish tradition. The Islamic calendar is dated from the year that the prophet Muhammad moved to the city of Medina.

Throughout history, societies have used different calendars. Maya and Aztec priests made calendars for farming and religious purposes. Today much of the world uses the Gregorian calendar, which has a 365- or 366-day year. It is based on the movement of Earth around the sun. The Jewish year, based on both sun and moon, varies from 353 to 385 days to adjust to the solar year. The Islamic year, however, is based on the cycles of the moon and lasts about 354 days.

Calendar Systems

Calendars are based on the movements of Earth, the moon, the stars, or a combination. Throughout history, people have used different methods to create calendars. The objects shown here were all different ways of measuring the passage of time.

Astrolabe This astrolabe was used by Muslim astronomers to calculate the positions of the sun, moon, planets, and stars. ▶

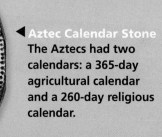

◀ **Aztec Calendar Stone** The Aztecs had two calendars: a 365-day agricultural calendar and a 260-day religious calendar.

Roman Calendar Early Roman calendars were based on the movements of the moon and had 10 months and 304 days. Later, the calendar had 12 months and 355 days. ▶

MENSIS
OCTOBER
DIES·XXXI
NONAE
SEPTIMAN
DIES
HOR·X S=
NOX
HOR·XIII=
SOL
LIBRA
TVTELA
MARTIS
VINDEMIAE

MENSIS
NOVEMBER
DIES·XXX
NON·QVINT
DIESHOR·VIIII
NOX·HOR·XIII
SOL
SCORPIONE
TVTELA
DEANAE
SEMENTES
TRITICARIA
ITHORDIAR
SCROBATIO
ARBORVM
IOVIS

MENSIS
DECEMB
DIES·XXXI
NON·QVINT
DIESHOR·VIIII
NOX·HOR·XV
SOL·SAGITT
TVTELVESTAE
HIEMIS·NITIV
SIVETROPAE
CHIMERIN
VINEAS·STERC
FABA·SERINS
MATERIAS
DEICIDITES
OLIVALEGENT

Assessment

1. How do people organize time?

2. If you created a timeline of everything you did yesterday, what would you choose to be the first event? What would be the last event? How would you decide which events are important enough to include on the timeline?

Historical Sources

Key Ideas
- Historical sources can provide important information.
- Historians must evaluate the accuracy and reliability of sources.

Key Terms • primary source • artifact • secondary source • bias

Visual Glossary →

Historians try to accurately understand and describe the past. To understand past events, historians study historical sources.

Primary and Secondary Sources

A **primary source** is information that comes directly from a person who experienced an event. It consists of what the person writes, says, or creates about the event. Primary sources include letters, diaries, speeches, and photographs. Artifacts are also primary sources. An **artifact** is an object made by a human being, such as a tool or a weapon. We use primary sources to understand events from the points of view of people who lived at the time in which they happened.

Books, articles, movies, and other sources that describe or make sense of the past are secondary sources. A **secondary source** is information about an event that does not come from a person who experienced that event.

This U.S. poster created during World War II is an example of a primary source. ▼

Primary Sources

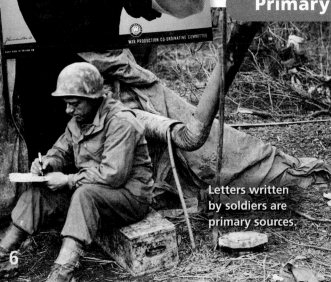

Letters written by soldiers are primary sources.

66 Yesterday, December 7, 1941—a date which will live in infamy—the United States of America was suddenly and deliberately attacked by naval and air forces of the empire of Japan . . . No matter how long it may take us to overcome this premeditated [planned] invasion, the American people in their righteous might will win through to absolute victory. 99

—President Franklin D. Roosevelt, December 8, 1941

Evaluating Historical Sources

Historical sources do not always give a true account of events. Even primary sources can be wrong or misleading. An author's personal opinions may have influenced what he or she recorded. Sometimes the author may not remember the event accurately. A historian must decide what, if anything, to trust in a primary source.

A historian must also be cautious when using secondary sources. Not all secondary sources are equally reliable. For example, the Internet includes millions of well-researched articles, books, and other reliable secondary sources. However, any Internet search will also find many inaccurate Web sites.

Historians and students of history—like you—must evaluate a source to determine its reliability. When you examine primary and secondary sources, ask yourself questions like these:

- Who created the source material? A witness to an event may be more trustworthy than someone looking back at the event from a later time. However, a scholar or publication with a good reputation is also a reliable source. For example, a college professor who specializes in Chinese history would be a reliable source on China.
- Is the information fact or opinion? A fact is something that can be proved true or false. An opinion is a personal belief. Opinions are valuable not as a source of facts but as a clue to the author's judgments or feelings.
- Does the material seem to have a bias? A **bias** is an unfair preference for or dislike of something. Biased material often leaves out facts that do not support the author's point of view.

The painting and article below are secondary sources. ▼

Secondary Sources

66 Japanese planes attacked the U.S. naval base at Pearl Harbor, Hawaii, on December 7, 1941. . . . This disaster caused the American public to support an immediate American entry into the war. 99

—*History of Our World*, Prentice Hall, 2008

Assessment

1. What is a primary source?

2. How does the secondary source quoted above help you understand the primary source quoted at the left?

Archaeology and Other Sources

> **Key Idea**
> - Archaeology and other historical sources offer clues to what life was like in the distant past.

Key Terms
- archaeology
- oral tradition
- anthropology

 Visual Glossary

Machu Picchu, Peru, is an Incan city abandoned in the 1500s and largely forgotten until the 1800s.

Archaeologists Louis and Mary Leakey found many fossil remains of human ancestors in Africa's Olduvai Gorge.

The Temple of Inscriptions in Palenque, Mexico, contains the tomb of the Maya ruler Pakal, who died in A.D. 683. ▼

8

Over time, much of the ancient world has disappeared. Large cities have collapsed into ruins. Buildings are buried under layers of soil and sand or covered by thick forests. The artifacts that show what life was like in ancient times are often buried or hidden. The science of archaeology aims to uncover this hidden history. **Archaeology** is the scientific study of ancient cultures through the examination of artifacts and other evidence.

Archaeologists and Anthropologists

Archaeologists are part treasure hunters and part detectives. They explore the places where people once lived and worked, searching for artifacts such as tools, weapons, and pottery. Archaeologists study the objects they find to learn more about the past.

Artifacts can help us identify the resources available to ancient people. They can help us understand how these people used technology and how they adapted to their environment.

Anthropology also helps historians understand the past. **Anthropology** is the study of humankind in all aspects, especially development and culture. Anthropologists seek to understand the origins of humans and the ways humans developed physically. This field often involves studying fossils—bones and other remains that have been preserved in rock.

Anthropologists also try to determine how human cultures formed and grew. Clues to the past can come from a culture's oral traditions. **Oral tradition** is a community's cultural and historical background, passed down in spoken stories and songs.

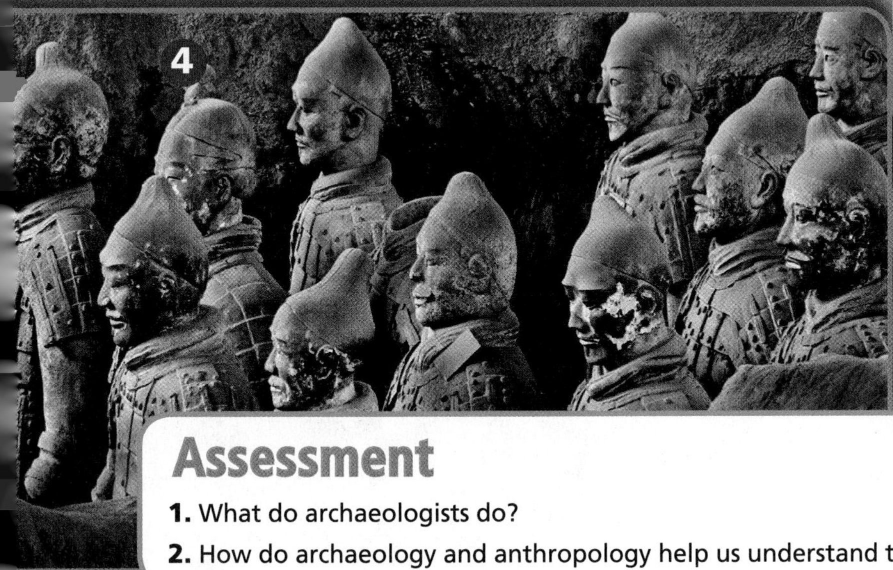

New Zealand's Maori people have passed down many aspects of their culture through oral tradition. ▼

Thousands of clay statues were buried in the tomb of China's first Qin emperor in 210 B.C.

4

5

Assessment

1. What do archaeologists do?

2. How do archaeology and anthropology help us understand the past?

Geography's Five Themes

Key Ideas
- Using five themes can help you make sense of geography.
- The theme of location is used to describe where a place is found, while the other themes describe features of a place.

Key Terms
- absolute location
- relative location
- place
- region
- movement
- human-environment interaction

Visual Glossary ➔

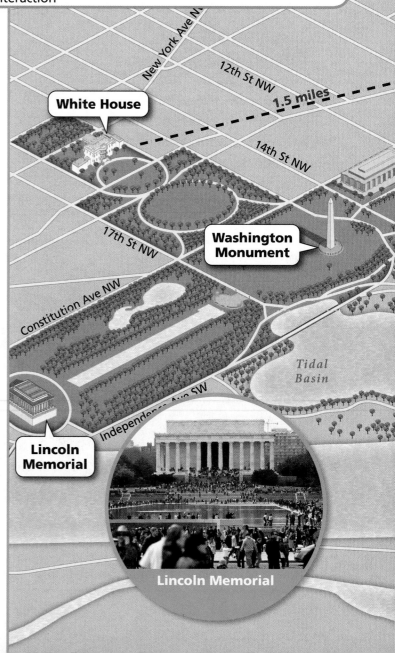

White House

1.5 miles

Washington Monument

Lincoln Memorial

Tidal Basin

Lincoln Memorial

The study of the human and nonhuman features of Earth is called geography. To study geography, we use five different themes, or ways of thinking. These are location, place, region, movement, and human-environment interaction. They help answer two basic questions: Where are things located? Why are they there? You can understand the themes by looking at the example of our nation's capital, Washington, D.C.

Location

Geographers begin to study a place by finding where it is, or its location. There are two ways to talk about location. **Absolute location** describes a place's exact position on Earth in terms of longitude and latitude, imaginary lines drawn around Earth to help geographers describe places. Lines of latitude are east-west, while lines of longitude are north-south. Using these lines, we can describe the absolute location of the center of Washington, D.C., which is at the intersection of the 38°54′ north latitude line and the 77°2′ west longitude line. **Relative location,** or the location of a place relative to another place, is another way to describe location.

Place

Geographers also study place. **Place** refers to the mix of human and nonhuman features at a given location. For example, you might talk about how many people live in a place and the kinds of work they do. You might mention that a place is hilly or that it has a wet climate. As a place, Washington, D.C., is on the Potomac River. It has a humid climate with cool winters and hot summers. It is a major city and the center of government for the United States.

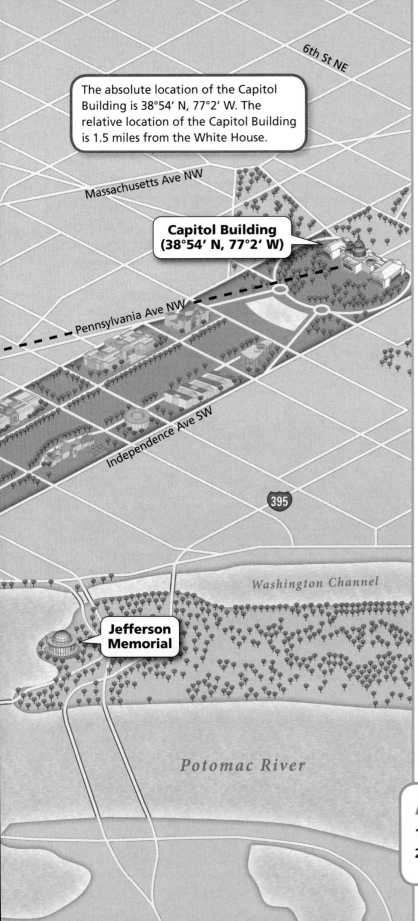

The absolute location of the Capitol Building is 38°54' N, 77°2' W. The relative location of the Capitol Building is 1.5 miles from the White House.

6th St NE

Massachusetts Ave NW

Capitol Building (38°54' N, 77°2' W)

Pennsylvania Ave NW

Independence Ave SW

395

Washington Channel

Jefferson Memorial

Potomac River

Region

Geographers use the theme of region to group places that have something in common. A **region** is an area with at least one unifying physical or human feature such as climate, landforms, population, or history. Washington, D.C., is part of a region called the Washington Metropolitan Area, which includes the city of Washington and its suburbs. This region shares a job market and a road and rail network. New technology, such as high-speed railroads, may give places new unifying features and connections. This can change the way people see regions.

Movement

The theme of **movement** explores how people, goods, and ideas get from one place to another. A daily movement of trucks and trains supplies the people of Washington with food, fuel, and other basic goods.

Human-Environment Interaction

The theme of **human-environment interaction** considers how people affect their environment, or their natural surroundings, and how their environment affects them. The movement of water from the Potomac River into Washington's water system is an example of human-environment interaction.

Assessment

1. What are the five themes of geography?
2. What is the difference between your hometown's location and your hometown as a place?

11

Understanding Maps

Key Ideas	• Maps have parts that help you read them. • Though different maps show different things about a place, you can use the same tools to help understand them.

Key Terms • key • locator map • scale bar • compass rose

 Visual Glossary

Look at the maps on these two pages. One is a physical map of the state of Colorado. The other is a road map of Colorado. These maps cover the same area but show different kinds of information. Despite their differences, both maps have all of the basic parts that you should find on any map.

The map has a title that tells you the subject of the map.

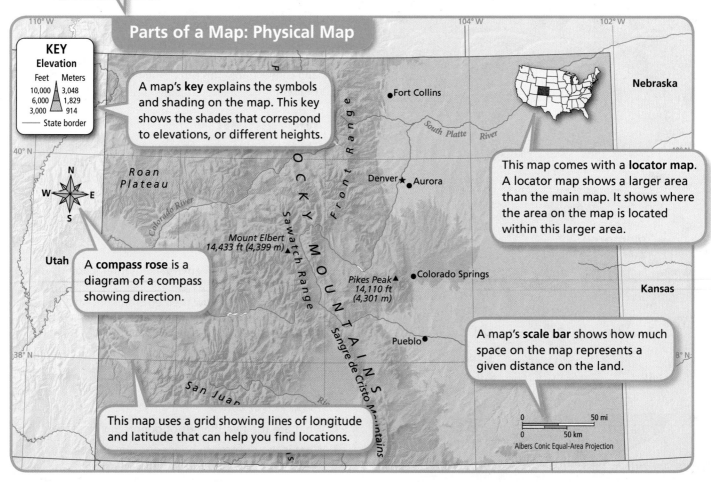

Parts of a Map: Physical Map

A map's **key** explains the symbols and shading on the map. This key shows the shades that correspond to elevations, or different heights.

This map comes with a **locator map**. A locator map shows a larger area than the main map. It shows where the area on the map is located within this larger area.

A **compass rose** is a diagram of a compass showing direction.

A map's **scale bar** shows how much space on the map represents a given distance on the land.

This map uses a grid showing lines of longitude and latitude that can help you find locations.

KEY
Elevation

Feet		Meters
10,000		3,048
6,000		1,829
3,000		914

—— State border

Mount Elbert 14,433 ft (4,399 m)
Pikes Peak 14,110 ft (4,301 m)

Fort Collins, Denver, Aurora, Colorado Springs, Pueblo

Nebraska, Kansas, Utah

Roan Plateau, Colorado River, South Platte River, Front Range, Rocky Mountains, Sawatch Range, Sangre de Cristo Mountains, San Juan

0 — 50 mi
0 — 50 km
Albers Conic Equal-Area Projection

Reading a Map

Look at the map below. It is a highway map of the state of Colorado. This map looks different from the physical map of Colorado that you have just studied. However, it has the same parts that can help you read it. In fact, you can read most maps using the key, scale bar, and other map tools that you have learned about.

Find the key on this map. Using the key, can you find the route number of the Interstate highway that connects Denver and Colorado Springs, Colorado? Using the scale bar, estimate the number of miles between these two cities. Using the compass rose, find the direction that you would need to travel from Denver to Colorado Springs. Now you have learned to read a highway map!

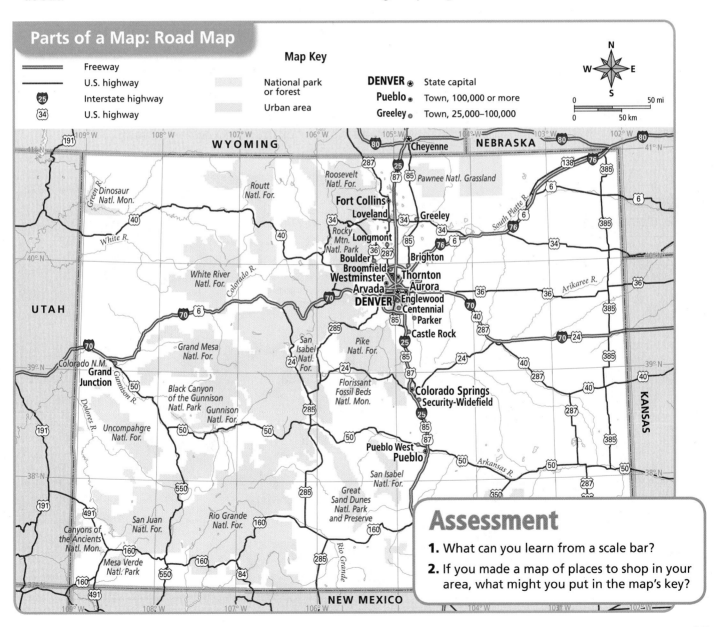

Parts of a Map: Road Map

Freeway
U.S. highway
25 Interstate highway
34 U.S. highway

Map Key

National park or forest
Urban area

DENVER ⊛ State capital
Pueblo ◉ Town, 100,000 or more
Greeley ◎ Town, 25,000–100,000

Assessment

1. What can you learn from a scale bar?
2. If you made a map of places to shop in your area, what might you put in the map's key?

13

Historical Maps

Key Ideas
- Historical maps offer visual representations of historical information.
- Historical maps show information about places at certain times.

Key Term • historical map

Visual Glossary

When you read about a historical event like an important battle, it can be hard to get a clear picture of what really happened. You may have to understand how landforms like rivers and hills affected the battle. Or perhaps the location of a nearby town, railroad, or road influenced the fighting. Sometimes the best way to learn about a historical event or period is by examining a historical map.

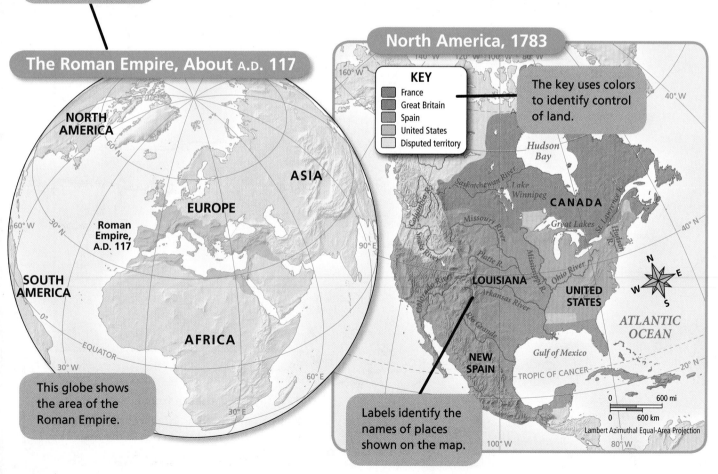

The title identifies the map's subject and time period.

The Roman Empire, About A.D. 117

NORTH AMERICA

ASIA

EUROPE

Roman Empire, A.D. 117

SOUTH AMERICA

AFRICA

This globe shows the area of the Roman Empire.

North America, 1783

KEY
- France
- Great Britain
- Spain
- United States
- Disputed territory

The key uses colors to identify control of land.

Hudson Bay

CANADA

Great Lakes

LOUISIANA

UNITED STATES

ATLANTIC OCEAN

NEW SPAIN

Gulf of Mexico

TROPIC OF CANCER

Labels identify the names of places shown on the map.

0   600 mi
0   600 km
Lambert Azimuthal Equal-Area Projection

A **historical map** is a special-purpose map that provides information about a place at a certain time in history. Historical maps can show information such as migration, trade patterns, or other facts.

Historical maps have similar features. Most have a title and a key. Most use colors and symbols to show resources, movement, locations of people, or other features. Use the following four steps to become familiar with historical maps.

1. Read the title. Note the date, the time span, or other information about the subject of the map. If the map includes a locator map, examine it to see what region is shown.

2. Study the map quickly to get a general idea of what it shows. Read any place names and other labels. Note any landforms.

3. Examine the map's key. Pick out the first symbol or other entry, read what it stands for, and find an example on the map. Repeat this process for the remaining key entries until you understand them all.

4. Study the map more thoroughly. Make sure you have a clear understanding of the picture the map presents. If you need help, reread the related section of your textbook or examine the map again.

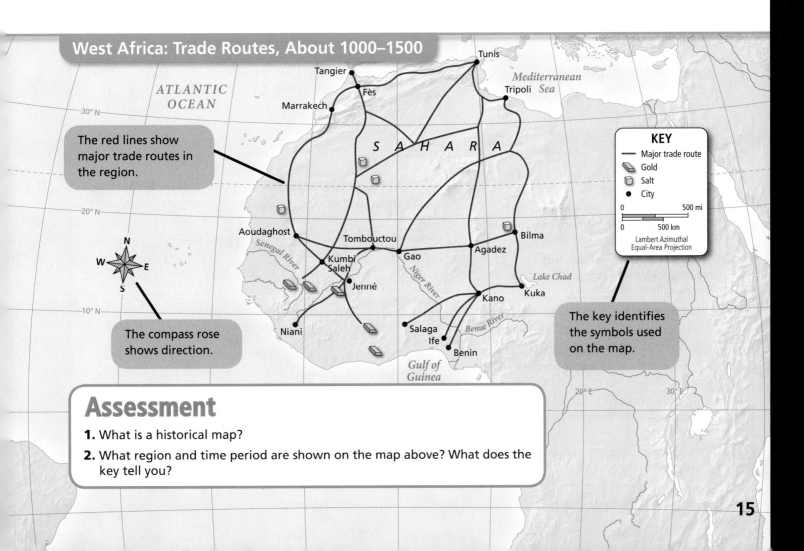

West Africa: Trade Routes, About 1000–1500

The red lines show major trade routes in the region.

The compass rose shows direction.

The key identifies the symbols used on the map.

KEY
- ⎯ Major trade route
- Gold
- Salt
- ● City

0   500 mi
0   500 km
Lambert Azimuthal Equal-Area Projection

Assessment

1. What is a historical map?

2. What region and time period are shown on the map above? What does the key tell you?

Part 1 Assessment

Key Terms and Ideas

1. **Describe** What are some features of the geographic themes of **place** and **region**?

2. **Summarize** What is **archaeology**?

3. **Identify** When a person who did not experience an event describes the event, is the description a **primary source** or a **secondary source**?

4. **Recall** What are the basic parts of a map and what does each part show to readers?

5. **Identify Cause and Effect** What do archaeologists do with **artifacts**?

6. **Discuss** What does the **scale bar** of a map show?

7. **Synthesize** How do **timelines** show historical events or periods?

Think Critically

8. **Make Decisions** Think about creating a map that will show ancient trade routes. Name three things you might include in the map's key.

9. **Draw Conclusions** How do you think the work of archaeologists and anthropologists can help present and future generations?

10. **Draw Inferences** Why do you think so many different calendars still exist today?

11. **Categorize** Match each feature to the correct theme of geography: very flat landscape, four trains in and out of town every day, factory waste enters a local river, large Hispanic population across three states, and 42° S 147° E.

Identify

Answer the following questions based on the map.

12. Which area of the United States is shown on this map? Where can you find this information?

13. What do the light yellow dots represent? Where can you find this information?

14. What time period is shown on the map?

15. What color dots represent hurricanes with the highest wind speeds?

16. What large body of water borders Texas and Louisiana?

17. Is Georgia north or south of Florida? What part of the map helps you figure this out?

18. How many category 5 hurricane strikes are shown on the map?

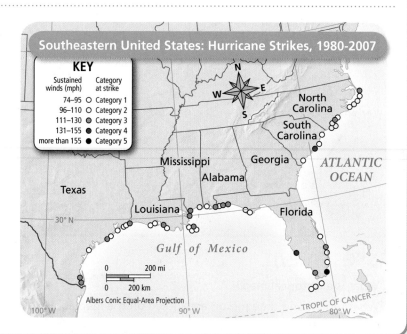

Southeastern United States: Hurricane Strikes, 1980-2007

KEY

Sustained winds (mph)	Category at strike
74–95	○ Category 1
96–110	○ Category 2
111–130	◑ Category 3
131–155	● Category 4
more than 155	● Category 5

Journal Activity

Fill in the graphic organizer in your Student Journal.

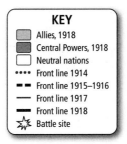 **Demonstrate Your Understanding** Complete the Sum-It-Up activity in your journal to demonstrate your understanding of history and geography. After you complete the activity, discuss your plan for using historical resources with a small group. Be sure to support your plan with information from the lessons.

21st Century Learning

Develop Cultural Awareness

Oral tradition remains an important part of many cultures. Research a song or story still passed on by oral tradition today, either in your own culture or in another. Then share the song or story with the class. Be sure to address the following topics:
- Origins of the song or story
- Cultural significance of the song or story

Document-Based Questions

Online at myworldhistory.com

Use your knowledge of history and geography and Documents A and B to answer questions 1–3.

Document A

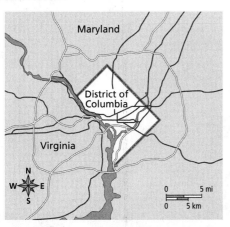

Document B

KEY
☐ Allies, 1918
☐ Central Powers, 1918
☐ Neutral nations
•••• Front line 1914
▬ ▬ Front line 1915–1916
—— Front line 1917
▬▬ Front line 1918
✸ Battle site

1. Which of the five themes of geography is best represented by this map?

   A location

   B place

   C region

   D human-environment interaction

2. Document B is a key to a historical map showing Europe during World War I. What information does this map not give you?

   A location of front line in 1917

   B locations of battles

   C members of the Central Powers in 1918

   D outcome of World War I

3. **Writing Task** If you were making a map of your school, what items would you list in the key? Explain your answer in complete sentences.

my worldhistory.com   Self-Test

Citizenship and Economics

Supporters hold campaign signs.

A group of congressional interns

Voters in the 2008 presidential election

Anne Marie Sutherland

Serving Her Country

Story by Miles Lemaire for myWorld History

Anne Marie Sutherland has been trying to get people to vote since before she was old enough to join them at the polls.

Anne Marie is the daughter of a high school government teacher. She became interested in politics as a child. Her first experience with a political campaign was the U.S. presidential election in 1996, when she was just nine years old. "[M]y friends and I made some signs and walked up and down the street with them before the election," Anne Marie says. "We started talking to people, and we stayed up all night to see who would win."

As Anne Marie grew older, her interest in the political process increased. In 2000 and 2004, she worked as a volunteer on George W. Bush's presidential campaigns. In the 2008 presidential primaries, she helped manage candidate Mitt Romney's campaign in Atlanta, Georgia.

"We did lots of grassroots work," Anne Marie says about her work with the Romney campaign. "We were talking to different folks, getting signs out, working on some strategies for the area."

When Romney failed to win the Republican nomination for president, Anne Marie worked for 2008 Republican nominee John McCain. She looks back on her work with the Romney and McCain campaigns as a great learning experience. Most of all, she loved discussing political issues with people.

"What I took away from that opportunity was working directly with voters," Anne Marie says. "That's not something that you get to do for very long in politics [before] you move up and start taking on larger roles."

Anne Marie soon began taking on larger roles herself, winning an internship with U.S. Senator Saxby Chambliss. As part of her internship, Anne Marie helped other young people achieve their own goals. As she explains, "Every year a senator appoints a certain number of graduating [high school] seniors to the United States military academies. ... so I put most of my energy into working on that process.

"I love doing that," she says, "because what I'm able to do is [to help] prepare our future military leaders at such a young age. ... [S]ometimes when I'm working with them, I honestly think, 'This young student could really be our future president, or could be leading us in a major war, or could be the leader of any one of the branches of the military.' You never know."

Now 22 years old, Anne Marie is about to graduate from college with a degree in political science. She isn't content with helping other people achieve their dreams. "Maybe there is a campaign of my own in the future," she says. "I'd do anything I can to serve my country."

Foundations of Government

Key Ideas
- Governments are created to keep order in a society and provide for the people's common needs.
- A government's powers are either limited or unlimited.

Key Terms • government • constitution • limited government
• unlimited government • tyranny

Visual Glossary

Hammurabi's Code is a set of laws created in ancient Babylon—now Iraq—around 1760 B.C. The code was carved onto a large stone slab, below. The photo at the bottom of the page shows the ruins of ancient Babylon. ▼

A **government** is a group of people who have the power to make and enforce laws for a country or area. The basic purpose of government is to keep order, to provide services, and to protect the common good, or the well-being of the people. Governments make and enforce laws to keep order. Protecting the common good can include building roads and schools or defending the country from attack. Governments also collect taxes, or required payments, from people and businesses. Governments use these taxes to pay for the goods and services they provide. The purpose of government has not changed much throughout history.

Origins of Government

Long before modern governments existed, people lived together in groups. These groups often had leaders who kept order and made decisions for the group. This was a simple form of government.

More complex governments first appeared in Southwest Asia more than 5,000 years ago. By that time, groups of people had begun to settle down. Villages grew into cities. People found that they needed an organized way to resolve problems and oversee tasks such as repairing irrigation canals and distributing food. They formed governments to manage those tasks.

Powers of Government

Today, most governments have a constitution. A **constitution** is a system of basic rules and principles by which a government is organized. A constitution also identifies the powers a government has. A government's powers are either limited or unlimited.

Limited Government

People gather in front of the U.S. Capitol.

Today, most constitutions call for limited government. **Limited government** is a government structure in which government actions are limited by law. Limited governments work to protect the common good and provide for people's needs.

In the United States, government actions are limited in order to protect people's individual freedoms. Generally, people in a limited government may gather freely to express their opinions and work to change government policies.

Unlimited Government

Chinese police arrest a protester.

Unlimited government is a government structure in which there are no effective limits on government actions. In an unlimited government such as China, a ruler or a small ruling group has the power to make all decisions for a country or society. This much power can lead to **tyranny,** which is the unjust use of power.

Unlimited governments often do not protect citizens' basic rights. They may censor, or restrict, citizens' access to the Internet and other forms of communication technology.

Assessment

1. How do constitutions limit the powers of government?

2. How do limited and unlimited governments differ?

Political Systems

> **Key Ideas**
> - Types of states have varied throughout history.
> - There are many different kinds of government.
>
> **Key Terms** • state • city-state • empire • democracy • nation-state
> • monarchy • authoritarian • communism
>
> → Visual Glossary

A man votes in Kenya's 2007 presidential election.

A **state** is a region that shares a common government. The first real states—called city-states—developed in Southwest Asia more than 5,000 years ago. A **city-state** is an independent state consisting of a city and its surrounding territory. Later, some military leaders conquered large areas and ruled them as empires. An **empire** is a state containing several countries. Geographic features such as rivers and mountains sometimes helped governments control territory by protecting against invasion.

Democracy

Examples Direct democracy: ancient Athens; representative democracy: United States

- **Democracy** is a form of government in which citizens hold political power; citizens are the ultimate source of government power and authority.

- In a direct democracy, citizens come together to pass laws and select leaders.

- In a representative democracy, citizens elect representatives to make government decisions.

- The powers of a democratic government are usually limited.

Queen Elizabeth II of the United Kingdom

BALLOT BOX

Nation-States

Today, most states are nation-states. A **nation-state** is a state that is independent of other states. The United States is an example of a nation-state. We often use the general words *nation* or *country* to refer to nation-states.

All nation-states have some common features. For example, nation-states have specific territory with clearly defined borders. Nation-states have governments, laws, and authority over citizens. Most are divided into smaller states or provinces that contain cities and towns.

Forms of Government

Each state has a government, but there are many different kinds of government. Throughout history, most states were autocracies (ruled by a single person) or oligarchies (ruled by a small group of people). Today, however, many states have some form of democracy in which citizens hold political power.

A large statue of former leader Kim Il Sung stands above people in communist North Korea.

Monarchy

Examples Absolute monarchy: Saudi Arabia; Constitutional monarchy: United Kingdom

- A monarchy is a form of government in which the state is ruled by a monarch.
- A monarch is usually a king or queen.
- Power is inherited by family members.
- Absolute monarchs have unlimited power.
- Monarchs in constitutional monarchies are limited by law and share power with other branches of government.
- The powers of a monarchy can be limited or unlimited.

Authoritarian Government

Examples Nazi Germany, Cuba, North Korea

- An **authoritarian** government is one in which all power is held by a single person or a small group.
- Government may control all aspects of life.
- One of the common forms of authoritarian government is **communism,** a political and economic system in which government owns all property and makes all economic decisions.
- The powers of an authoritarian government are unlimited.

Assessment

1. What are states, city-states, and nation-states?
2. Which form of government relies most on its citizens? Explain your answer.

Political Structures

Key Ideas
- Political structures help governments operate in an organized way.
- The U.S. government follows basic democratic principles.

Key Terms • unitary system • federal system

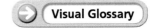
Visual Glossary

Central Government

Central governments are responsible for national affairs.

U.S. Capitol

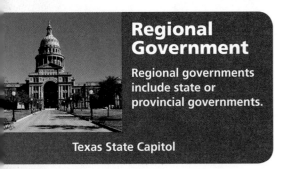

Regional Government

Regional governments include state or provincial governments.

Texas State Capitol

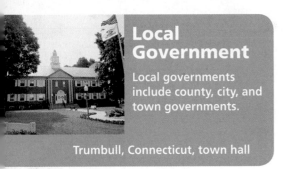

Local Government

Local governments include county, city, and town governments.

Trumbull, Connecticut, town hall

Countries distribute power between the central government and smaller units of government. We can learn more about how a government functions by examining its structure and principles.

Systems of Government

Governments can distribute power in three basic ways: the unitary system, the federal system, and the confederal system. In a **unitary system,** a central government makes all laws for the entire country. In a **federal system,** power is divided among central, regional, and local governments. In a confederal system, a group of independent states join together and give limited powers to a common government. Most countries have a unitary system. The United States and some other countries have a federal system. The confederal system is rare.

Principles of Government

Every government has basic principles that affect the way it serves its people. Authoritarian governments may seek to control all aspects of society, even people's actions and beliefs. For example, some authoritarian governments limit citizens' use of communications technology such as the Internet. Most democratic governments act to protect individual rights and the common good.

In the United States, government follows basic democratic principles. For example, government follows the rule of law. That is, government powers are defined by laws that limit its actions. Also, government decides issues by majority rule. A law cannot pass unless the majority—most—representatives vote for it. At the same time, the majority may not take away the basic rights and freedoms of minority groups or individuals. In other words, government must balance majority rule with minority rights.

Branches of Government

Under the U.S. Constitution, power is divided among the three branches of government: the legislative, executive, and judicial branches. This division is called separation of powers. The Constitution also establishes a system of checks and balances that limits each branch's power. Each branch has some power to change or cancel the actions of the other branches.

Legislative Branch

The legislative branch establishes laws. In a representative democracy like the United States, citizens elect legislative representatives to make decisions for them. The legislative branch also imposes taxes, or required payments. Taxes are used to pay for government services and public goods such as roads, parks, fire departments, and national defense. Public goods are owned by everyone in the country.

U.S. Congress

Executive Branch

The executive branch carries out, or enforces, the laws. It also provides for the country's defense, conducts foreign policy, and manages day-to-day affairs. The United States and some other countries have a presidential system with an elected president as the head of the executive branch. Other democracies, such as the United Kingdom, have a parliamentary system. In this system, the parliament, or legislative branch, chooses a prime minister as chief executive.

U.S. President Barack Obama

Judicial Branch

The judicial branch makes decisions about disputes. It does this through courts of law. These courts can range from local criminal courts to the highest court in the land. In the United States that court is called the Supreme Court. Among other things, the Supreme Court interprets the law. That is, it judges how a law should be applied and whether the law violates the Constitution.

U.S. Supreme Court

Assessment

1. What are the three branches of government?

2. What are three key democratic principles?

Citizenship

Key Ideas
- Citizens have basic rights, but those rights come with responsibilities.
- Rights and responsibilities can vary widely in different countries.

Key Terms • citizen • civic life • civic participation • political party • interest group

 Visual Glossary

The United States is a representative democracy. In a democracy, all political power comes from citizens. A **citizen** is a legal member of a country. In the United States, most people become citizens by being born on U.S. territory. Immigrants to the United States can become citizens through a legal process known as naturalization.

Rights and Responsibilities

Citizens' rights and responsibilities can come from a number of sources. These sources include constitutions, cultural traditions, and religious laws.

Americans' basic rights are protected by the Bill of Rights, a part of the U.S. Constitution. The Bill of Rights and other laws protect rights such as freedom of speech and freedom of religion. If the government violates these rights, citizens can fight the injustice in court. For the most part, these rights are also guaranteed to noncitizens.

Immigrants to the United States become citizens at a naturalization ceremony. ▼

Americans also have responsibilities. For example, we have the right to speak freely, but we also have the responsibility to allow others to say things we may not agree with. Our responsibilities include a duty to participate in government and **civic life,** or activities having to do with one's society and community. Voting is both a right and a responsibility for U.S. citizens.

Rights and responsibilities can vary widely in different countries and societies. Although most democratic governments protect basic human rights, nondemocratic governments often do not. Citizens who live in autocracies or oligarchies usually cannot take part in government or express their views openly.

Citizenship Worldwide

Ideas about rights and responsibilities can change over time. Many countries have become democracies over the past 200 years. These democracies now protect basic human rights such as freedom of expression and freedom from unfair imprisonment. Some of these countries did not protect these rights in the past or did not protect these rights for all people.

Today, international trade, transportation, and communication have linked the world's people. As a result, some people think that we should consider ourselves to be citizens of a global community. They believe that we are responsible for supporting human rights and equality for all people around the world.

Assessment

1. What is the main source of American citizens' basic rights?

2. How do the roles and responsibilities of citizens vary between democratic and nondemocratic countries?

Civic Participation

Voting is one type of **civic participation**, or taking part in government. Here are some others:

Keeping informed about local, state, and national issues

Contacting an elected representative, such as a state legislator or member of Congress

Voicing opinions at town meetings

Taking part in public gatherings, protests, or demonstrations

Signing a petition, a formal request for government to do something

Running for public office

Getting involved in a political party— a group that supports candidates for public offices

Joining an interest group—a group that seeks to influence public policy on certain issues

Economic Basics

> **Key Ideas**
> - People make choices about how to meet their wants and needs.
> - Economies bring together people and businesses that make, sell, and buy goods and services.
>
> **Key Terms** • economics • scarcity • opportunity cost • demand
> • supply • producer • consumer • incentive
>
> → Visual Glossary

Economics is the study of how people meet their wants and needs. People must answer three basic economic questions:

1. What goods and services should be produced?
2. How should goods and services be produced?
3. Who uses or consumes those goods and services?

The resources people use to make goods and services are called factors of production. The three main factors are land, labor, and capital. Geographers study where the factors of production are located.

Making Choices

There is no limit to the things that people want, but there are limits to what can be created. This difference between wants and reality creates **scarcity,** or having a limited quantity of resources to meet unlimited wants. Since people have limited money and time, they have to choose

Factors of Production

Entrepreneur
A person known as an entrepreneur combines resources to create new businesses.

Land, Labor, Capital
The three main factors of production are land and resources; human labor; and capital, or human-made goods like tools and buildings.

Goods and Services
Entrepreneurs use the factors of production to produce goods and services.

what they want most. Making a choice involves an **opportunity cost,** or the cost of what you have to give up.

Economics also involves demand and supply. **Demand** is the desire for a certain good or service. **Supply** is the amount of a good or service that is available for use. Demand and supply are connected to price. As the price of a product increases, people will buy less of it. That is, demand will decrease. If the price of the product decreases, demand will increase.

Supply functions in a similar way. If the price of a product increases, companies will make more of it. If the price of the product decreases, companies will make less of it. The price at which demand equals supply is the market price, or the market-clearing price.

Basic economic choices have influenced world events. For example, high demand for resources such as gold or oil has led to exploration and colonization.

Making Goods and Services

Economies bring together producers and consumers. **Producers** are people or businesses that make and sell products. **Consumers** are people or businesses that buy, or consume, products. Producers try to win consumers' business by offering better products for lower prices than other producers. If they sell more products, they

Supply and Demand of Apples

usually increase production. But producers will not make more products if the sale price is less than the marginal cost. Marginal cost is the cost of making one more unit of the product. Therefore, the marginal cost for the producer sets a minimum price for the product.

Businesses make products because of economic incentives. An **incentive** is a factor that encourages people to act in a certain way. Money is an incentive. The desire to earn money gives most producers an incentive to make and sell products. The incentive to save money leads most consumers to look for lower prices.

Assessment

1. On the line graph on this page, what is the market-clearing price?

2. How might a change in the price of one good or service lead to changes in prices of other goods or services?

Economic Process

Key Ideas
- Producers and consumers exchange goods and services in a market.
- Competition is a key part of the economic process.
- Economic activity occurs at four levels.

Key Terms
- market
- profit
- revenue
- specialization
- competition
- inflation
- recession

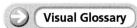
Visual Glossary

The economic process is complicated, but its basic idea is simple: Producers and consumers exchange goods and services in a market. A **market** is an organized way for producers and consumers to trade goods and services.

Exchanging Goods and Services

Throughout history, people have often engaged in barter, the trading of goods and services for other goods and services. Today, the means of exchange in a market is usually money. Modern governments issue money in the form of currency, or paper bills and metal coins. Different countries use different currencies. As a result, countries must establish the relative values of their currencies in order to trade. They must also establish a system for exchanging different currencies.

Businesses and the Economic Process

Businesses want to make a profit. **Profit** is the money a company has left after subtracting the costs of doing business. To make a profit, companies try to reduce expenses and increase revenue. **Revenue** is the money earned by selling goods and services. The price of resources affects revenue and profit. If resources become more expensive, the cost of making goods with them will also increase. Businesses' profits will drop.

Companies can increase profit and revenue through **specialization,** the act of concentrating on a limited number of goods or activities. Specialization allows people and companies to use resources more efficiently and to increase production and consumption.

Companies' profits are affected by **competition,** which is the struggle among producers for consumers' money. If one company raises the price of its products, another company may sell similar goods

Economists divide economic activity into four levels, as you can see in this table. ▼

Levels of Economic Activity	
Primary Industry	Collects resources from nature. Examples: farming, mining
Secondary Industry	Uses raw materials to create new products. Example: manufacturing
Tertiary Industry	Provides services to people and secondary industries. Examples: banking, restaurants
Quaternary Industry	Focuses on research and information. Example: education

Competition in the Market

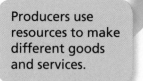

Producers use resources to make different goods and services.

Buyers and sellers interact to trade goods and services in a market.

Competition between buyers and between sellers affects product price, quality, and marketing.

for a lower price to win more business. Companies use advertising to help increase demand for their products and to compete with other companies.

Nonprofit organizations are businesslike institutions that do not seek to make a profit. Nonprofit organizations can include churches, museums, hospitals, and other bodies.

A healthy economy grows as companies produce and sell more goods and services. In a growing economy, prices may increase over time. This general increase in prices is called **inflation.**

Economies do not keep growing forever. Eventually, economic activity falls as production slows and consumers buy fewer goods and services. This lack of demand for goods and services can lead to increased unemployment. A decline in economic growth for six or more months in a row is known as a **recession.**

Assessment

1. Does a person always need money to obtain goods or services?

2. How does competition affect producers and consumers?

Economic Systems

Key Ideas
- Different societies have different types of economic systems.
- Most societies have economic systems with some element of government control.

Key Terms • traditional economy • market economy • command economy • mixed economy

Visual Glossary

Every society has an economic system in which people make and distribute goods and services. There are four basic economic systems: traditional, market, command, and mixed. The roles of individuals, businesses, and government vary in each system. Economic goals, incentives, and government regulations can also vary.

Traditional Economies

A **traditional economy** is an economy in which people make economic decisions based on their customs and habits. They usually satisfy their needs and wants through hunting or farming, as their ancestors did. People in traditional economies usually do not want to change their basic way of life. Today, traditional economies are not common.

The Fulani people in Niger are livestock herders. ▶

Market Economies

A **market economy** is an economy in which individual consumers and producers make economic decisions. This type of economy is also called capitalism, or a free market. Market economies encourage entrepreneurs to establish new businesses by giving them economic freedom.

A consumer makes a purchase at a grocery store. ▶

Command Economies

A **command economy** is an economy in which the central government makes all economic decisions. This kind of system is also called a centrally planned economy. In a command economy, individual consumers and producers do not make basic economic decisions.

◄ In North Korea, government leaders make most economic decisions.

Circular Flow in a Mixed Economy

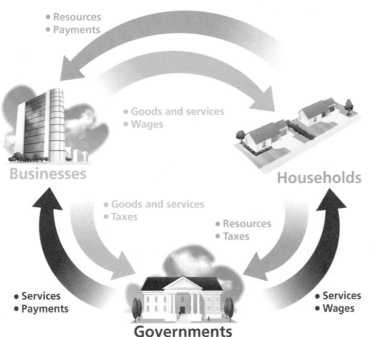

- Resources
- Payments

- Goods and services
- Wages

Businesses

Households

- Goods and services
- Taxes

- Resources
- Taxes

- Services
- Payments

- Services
- Wages

Governments

Mixed Economies

In reality, pure market or command economies do not exist. Most societies have mixed economies with varying levels of government control. A **mixed economy** is an economy that combines elements of traditional, market, and command economic systems. The diagram at left shows the circular flow of economic activity in a mixed economy.

Countries such as the United States and Australia have mixed economies that are close to pure market economies. In these countries, government makes some economic decisions. For example, government passes laws to protect consumers' rights. Government spending and taxation provide jobs and services and influence economic growth.

Countries such as North Korea and Cuba have mixed economies that are close to pure command economies. In these countries, government owns and controls most businesses.

Assessment

1. What are the differences among traditional, command, and market economies?

2. What are some possible advantages of the free-market system used in the United States and other countries?

Core Concepts 2.8

Trade

Key Ideas
- Individuals and countries trade with one another to get the things they need and want.
- Many countries are working toward the removal of trade barriers.

Key Terms • trade • export • import • tariff • trade barrier • free trade

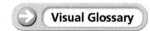 Visual Glossary

In the past, most people grew or hunted their own food. They made their own clothing. They built their own homes. In short, people did nearly everything for themselves. Today, however, most people depend on others to supply the goods and services they need. Our world is interdependent. That is, people and countries depend on one another for goods and services.

Trade and Geography

To get the products we need and want, we engage in trade. **Trade** is the exchange of goods and services in a market. When individuals engage in trade, they do so because they gain from that trade. In other words, trade benefits both the buyer and the seller.

Geographic location can give a country or region advantages in trade. For example, a region that is close to an ocean can more easily ship goods overseas. On the other hand, a manufacturing plant located far away from a market will need to add transportation costs to its products, making them higher in price.

Container ships, such as the ones in this photo, carry most of the world's goods from one port to another. ▼

Types of Trade

All of the buying and selling that takes place within a country is known as domestic trade. Domestic trade involves producers and consumers located inside the same country.

Domestic producers and consumers can also engage in international trade, or trade with foreign producers and consumers. International trade involves exports and imports. **Exports** are goods and services produced within a country and sold outside the country's borders. **Imports** are goods and services sold in a country that are produced in other countries. International trade requires a system for exchanging types of currency.

Trade Barriers and Free Trade

If imported goods are cheaper than domestic goods, consumers will usually buy more of them. These lower prices can harm domestic producers by reducing their sales. Governments sometimes try to protect domestic producers through tariffs. A **tariff** is a tax on imports or exports. Tariffs are an example of trade barriers. A **trade barrier** is a government policy or restriction that limits international trade.

Today, many countries are working toward **free trade,** or the removal of trade barriers. Free trade gives consumers lower prices and more choices. However, domestic producers can suffer if consumers prefer cheaper imported goods.

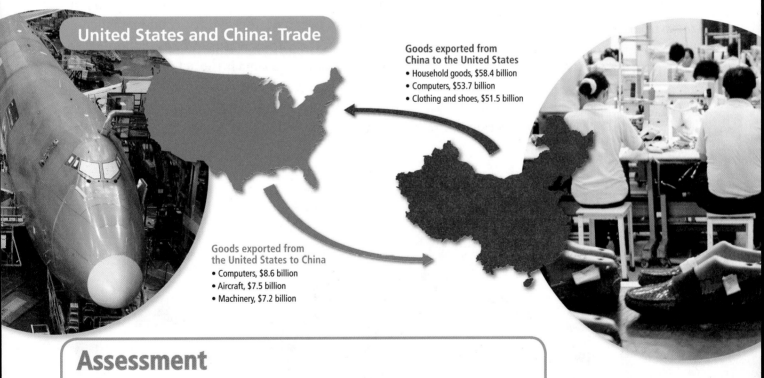

United States and China: Trade

Goods exported from China to the United States
- Household goods, $58.4 billion
- Computers, $53.7 billion
- Clothing and shoes, $51.5 billion

Goods exported from the United States to China
- Computers, $8.6 billion
- Aircraft, $7.5 billion
- Machinery, $7.2 billion

Assessment

1. How might geography affect the locations of economic activities?

2. How might scarcity encourage international trade and make countries interdependent?

Money Management

Key Ideas
- People must manage money to have enough for their needs and wants.
- Many people save and invest money.

Key Terms • budget • saving • interest • credit • investing • stock • bond

→ (Visual Glossary)

Money is anything that is generally accepted as payment for goods and services. Money is a scarce resource that people must manage to have enough for their needs and wants. Because people's needs, wants, and incomes can change, it is important to plan ahead.

Budgeting, Saving, and Lending

A key tool in money management is a budget. A **budget** is a plan that shows income and expenses over a period of time. A budget's income should be equal to or greater than its expenses. A budget should also include money reserved for saving. **Saving** is the act of setting aside money for future use. Many people save by using banks. A bank is a business that keeps money, makes loans, and offers other financial services. Credit unions are nonprofit banks owned by their members.

A man uses an automated teller machine (ATM) to access his bank account. ▼

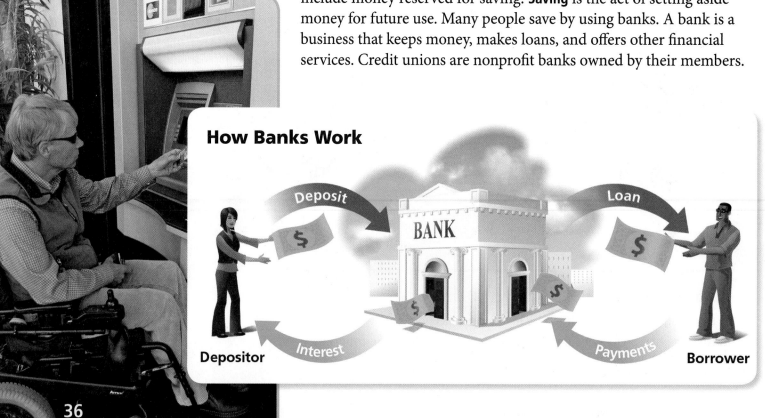

How Banks Work

Deposit — BANK — Loan

Depositor — Interest — Payments — Borrower

Many people who save money in banks do so using checking or savings accounts. Banks may pay interest on money deposited in these accounts. **Interest** is the price paid for borrowing money. Interest is an incentive for people to save money.

Banks use deposits to make loans to people and businesses around the world. These loans help people buy houses or make other large purchases. They help businesses get started or grow. As a result, banks are a big part of economic growth.

Loans are a form of credit. **Credit** is an arrangement in which a buyer can borrow to purchase something and pay for it over time, such as by using a credit card. Banks and other lending organizations charge borrowers interest on loans. As a result, it costs more for a borrower to purchase a good using credit than to pay cash for the good at the time of purchase.

Investing

Investing is the act of using money in the hope of making a future profit. Some people invest in stocks, bonds, or mutual funds. A **stock** is a share of ownership in a company. A **bond** is a certificate issued by a company or government promising to pay back borrowed money with interest. A mutual fund is a company that invests members' money in stocks, bonds, and other investments.

▲ Stock brokers buy and sell stocks and bonds for investors at places such as the New York Stock Exchange.

Investments offer different levels of risk and return—the amount of money an investor might earn. In general, the safest investments offer the lowest rates of return. For example, a savings account is very safe, but it pays a relatively low rate of interest. Stocks are riskier but can earn a great deal of money for an investor if they increase in value. On the other hand, stocks can decline in value and become worth less than the stockholder paid. Bonds are less risky than stocks, but they usually offer a lower rate of return.

Assessment

1. How do banks function?

2. Why do people invest money in stocks, bonds, and mutual funds?

Part 2 Assessment

Key Terms and Ideas

1. **Recall** There are two types of democracy: direct and representative. What kind of **democracy** is the United States?

2. **Identify** What level of economic activity includes mining? What level includes manufacturing?

3. **Compare and Contrast** How are the powers of an **unlimited government** different from those of a **limited government**?

4. **Describe** How does the U.S. government balance legislative, executive, and judicial power?

5. **Paraphrase** Explain the relationship among **revenue, profit,** and the costs of doing business.

6. **Identify Cause and Effect** What role does risk play in investment?

7. **Identify** Name two ways American **citizens** can participate in the political process.

Think Critically

8. **Draw Inferences** Consider that you can freely read about your government's actions and policies on the Internet. How might Internet access differ in a country with an authoritarian government?

9. **Draw Conclusions** Who do you think is more likely to speak out against the government: a citizen in a limited government or a citizen in an unlimited government? Explain.

10. **Decision Making** How do societies organize and make decisions about the production of goods and services?

11. **Summarize** How do government policies affect free market economies such as the U.S. economy?

Identify

Answer the following questions based on the map.

12. Which country is the westernmost member of the European Union?

13. Which EU members border Latvia?

14. List the EU members with territory located to the north of 60° N latitude and to the east of 0° longitude.

15. Which EU members border Slovenia?

16. How many members made up the European Union in 2009?

17. What sea do Spain and Greece border?

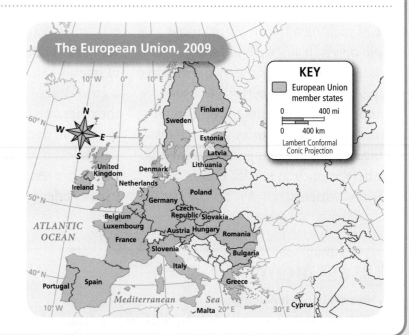

The European Union, 2009

KEY

European Union member states

0   400 mi

0   400 km

Lambert Conformal Conic Projection

Journal Activity

Fill in the graphic organizer in your Student Journal.

Demonstrate Your Understanding Complete the Sum-It-Up activity in your journal to demonstrate your understanding of citizenship and economics. After you complete the activity, discuss your answers with the class. Be sure to support your answers with information from the lessons.

Analyze Media Content

Authoritarian governments usually allow little media freedom. Find political news articles from authoritarian and democratic countries. Then compare and contrast them in a short essay. Remember to
- include excerpts from a variety of articles.
- discuss how the government might influence what is published.

Document-Based Questions

Success Tracker™ Online at myworldhistory.com

Use your knowledge of citizenship and economics and Documents A and B to answer questions 1–3.

Document A

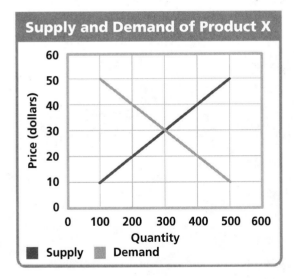

Supply and Demand of Product X

Document B

" It is not from the benevolence [kindness] of the butcher the brewer, or the baker that we expect our dinner, but from their regard to their own interest. We address ourselves, not to their humanity, but to their self-love, and never talk to them of our own necessities [needs], but of their advantages."

—Adam Smith, *The Wealth of Nations*

1. Examine Document A. Which of the following statements is true?

   A As the price of Product X increases, demand for it decreases.

   B As the price of Product X decreases, its supply increases.

   C As the price of Product X increases, demand for it increases.

   D As the price of Product X decreases, its supply does not change.

2. Read Document B. Why does Adam Smith believe people do business with one another?

   A because they stand to gain from trading

   B because they are forced to by the government

   C because it is the right thing to do

   D because they are interested in business

3. **Writing Task** Do you agree or disagree with Adam Smith? Write a short essay in which you respond to Smith. Explain your position clearly, supporting it with information from the lessons.

Culture

Tepees at a Native American powwow

Native American dancers

Joanna Baca (at right) dances at a powwow.

Joanna Baca

EXPLORING CULTURE THROUGH DANCE

Story by Miles Lemaire for myWorld History

When Joanna Baca and her family moved to Las Vegas, Nevada, from the Native American Navajo reservation in Shiprock, New Mexico, she looked for things that reminded her of home—and her Navajo culture.

"Most of our family stayed back home," Joanna says. "After we first moved here [Las Vegas], we didn't think there was anyone out here that was Native American, and it actually took us a while to find someone we knew."

In an effort to make their new city feel like home, Joanna and her family looked for community organizations that promoted Native American culture. Joanna eventually discovered the Las Vegas Indian Center. Among other things, this organization helps Native American high school students apply to and get accepted at colleges.

"[The Center helps] Native American kids find out what colleges are good for them," Joanna says. "They teach us that college is possible for Native American kids, not just for the kids that live on the reservation, but for kids who live in the city, too."

The more time Joanna spent with the organization, the closer she felt to her Navajo culture. She decided that she wanted to get involved in more aspects of Native American culture, especially traditional forms of dance.

Joanna had grown up going to powwows with her family. A powwow is a gathering where Native American people dance, sing, and honor Native American cultures. "I'd just see all the dancers there and how beautiful they were," Joanna remembers. She decided that she wanted to learn more about Native American dance. "I did ballet, jazz, and hip-hop before, and I thought they were fun," she says, "but I wanted to do something cultural, because dancing is a big part of my culture."

It has been several years since Joanna first started studying and performing Native American dances. She loves how these traditional forms of dance help her connect to her culture. But she also thinks dance is a wonderful way for non-Native American people to learn more about native culture.

"We go to events where they have dancers from all over the world, and they'll have a bit of everyone's culture in this one little get-together," Joanna says. "So we shared food, we were part of the dancing there, and a lot of people were like, 'Oh that's nice, I've never seen that type of dance before, what kind is that?' We'd tell them that it's Navajo, or native and . . . it got them very interested. Some of those people would come to the show again just to see our part of the performance and to see what it was all about."

What Is Culture?

Key Ideas
- Every culture has a distinctive set of cultural traits.
- Earth has thousands of different cultures.

Key Terms
- culture
- cultural trait
- norm
- culture region
- cultural landscape

 Visual Glossary

All people have the same basic needs and wants, such as food, clothing, and shelter. But different cultures respond to those needs and wants in different ways. **Culture** is the beliefs, customs, practices, and behaviors of a particular nation or group of people.

Where Culture Comes From

The features that make up a culture are known as cultural traits. A **cultural trait** is an idea or way of doing things that is common in a certain culture. Cultural traits include language, laws, religion, values, food, clothing, and many other customs. Children learn cultural traits from their parents and other adults. People also learn cultural traits from the mass media and from organizations such as schools, social clubs, and religious groups. Common cultural traits are called norms. A **norm** is a behavior that is considered normal in a particular society.

French Quebec Culture Region

CANADA
Quebec
UNITED STATES

0   500 mi
0   500 km
Lambert Azimuthal
Equal-Area Projection

120° W   110° W   100° W   90° W   80° W   70° W
50° N
40° N
30° N

Culture Regions

A **culture region** is an area in which a single culture or cultural trait is dominant. In Canada, French Canadian culture dominates much of the province of Quebec. The people of Quebec who have this culture identify themselves as French Canadian or Québécois (kay bek WAH).

Cultural Landscapes

Human activities create **cultural landscapes,** or geographic areas that have been shaped by people.

◀ Bolivia

Left, Egypt; below, Ukraine

Some cultural traits remain constant over many years. But culture can change over time as people adopt new cultural traits. For example, the way Americans dress today is very different from the way Americans dressed 100 years ago.

The environment can also affect culture. For example, the environment of a region influences how people live and how they earn their living. Humans can also shape their environment by creating cultural landscapes. The cultural landscape of a place reflects how its people meet their basic needs for food, clothing, and shelter. These landscapes differ from one culture to another.

Culture and Geography

Earth has thousands of different cultures and culture regions. In a specific culture region, people share cultural traits such as religion or language.

Culture regions are often different from political units. Occasionally, a culture region may cover an entire country. In Japan, for example, nearly everyone speaks the same language, eats the same food, and follows the same customs. A country may also include more than one culture region. For example, the French Canadian culture region of Quebec is one of several culture regions in Canada.

Culture regions can also extend beyond political boundaries. For example, many of the people who live in Southwest Asia and northern Africa are Arab Muslims. That is, they practice the religion of Islam. They also share other cultural traits, such as the Arabic language, foods, and other ways of life. This region of Arab Muslim culture covers several countries.

Clothing

Styles of clothing vary in different cultures.

A Spanish-born Swedish woman practices flamenco, a traditional Spanish dance. ▶

▲ A Saudi Arabian woman

Weddings in Japan (above) and Indonesia (left)

Assessment

1. Does every country form a single culture region? Explain.

2. What are some elements of the cultural landscape in the area where your school is located?

Food

People in different cultures eat different types of food.

◀ A man in Saudi Arabia sells vegetables.

Women in Ukraine selling potatoes and other produce

43

Core Concepts 3.2

Religion

Key Ideas
- Religious beliefs play an important role in shaping cultures.
- The world has many different religions.

Key Terms • religion   • ethics

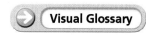 Visual Glossary

Judaism

Judaism is based on a belief in one God, whose spiritual and ethical teachings are recorded in the Hebrew Bible. It began in the Middle East around 2000 B.C. By A.D. 100, Jews were scattered across Europe, Southwest Asia, and North Africa. The Jewish state of Israel was established in 1948. There are about 14 million Jews.

Christianity

Christianity is based on the teachings of Jesus, who Christians believe was the son of God. The Christian Bible is their sacred text. Christianity began in Southwest Asia around A.D. 30 and spread to Europe and Africa. It later spread to the rest of the world. There are about 2 billion Christians.

Islam

Islam is based on the Quran, a sacred text. The Quran contains what Muslims believe is the word of God as revealed to Muhammad beginning in A.D. 610. Islam spread quickly across Southwest Asia and North Africa, then to the rest of the world. There are about 1.25 billion Muslims.

An important part of every culture is religion. **Religion** is a system of worship and belief, including belief about the nature of a god or gods. Religion can help people answer questions about the meaning of life. It can also guide people in matters of **ethics**, or standards of acceptable behavior. Religious beliefs and values help shape cultures.

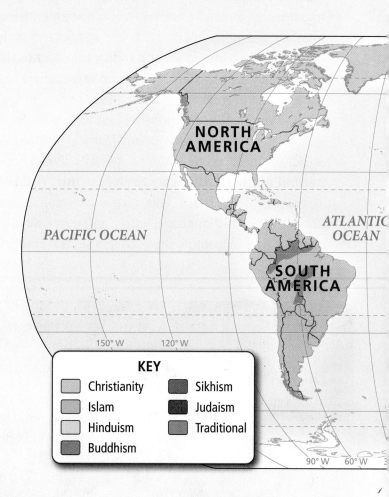

KEY
- Christianity
- Islam
- Hinduism
- Buddhism
- Sikhism
- Judaism
- Traditional

The world has many religions. Jews, Christians, and Muslims believe in one god. Members of other religions may believe in several gods.

All religions have prayers and rituals. Followers also observe religious holidays. For example, Jews celebrate the new year on Rosh Hashanah and their escape from slavery in Egypt on Passover. On Yom Kippur, Jews make up for their sins. Christians celebrate Jesus' birth on Christmas and his return to life on Easter. For Muslims, the holy month of Ramadan is a time to avoid food during daytime, to pray, and to read the Quran.

The world's major religions began in Asia. Hinduism, Buddhism, and Sikhism first developed in India. Judaism, Christianity, and Islam began in Southwest Asia before spreading throughout the world.

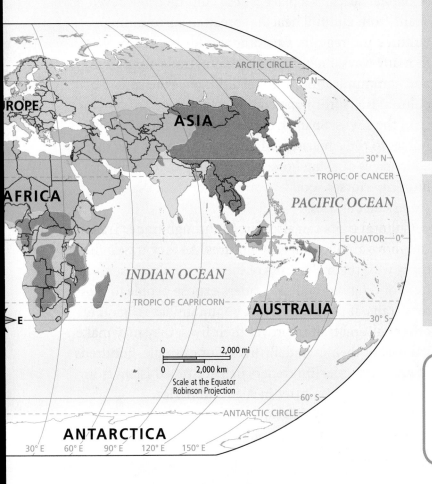

Hinduism

Hinduism evolved gradually over thousands of years in South Asia. It has several sacred texts. Hindus believe that everyone in the universe is part of a continuing cycle of birth, death, and rebirth. There are about 837 million Hindus.

Buddhism

Buddhism is based on the teachings of Siddhartha Gautama, known as the Buddha, who was born in India about 563 B.C. The Buddha's teachings include the search for enlightenment, or a true understanding of the nature of reality. There are about 400 million Buddhists.

Sikhism

Sikhism is based on the writings of several gurus, or religious teachers. Guru Nanak founded Sikhism about A.D. 1500 in South Asia. Sikhism's teachings include the cycle of rebirth and the search for enlightenment. There are about 24 million Sikhs.

Traditional Religions

Traditional religions include thousands of distinct religions. These religions tend to be passed down by word of mouth instead of through sacred texts. Each has its own set of beliefs. Examples include many African religions.

Assessment

1. How does religion help shape a culture?
2. What does the map tell you about the major religion where you live?

Cultural Diffusion and Change

Key Ideas
- Cultures change over time.
- Cultural traits can spread from one culture to another.

Key Terms • cultural hearth   • cultural diffusion   • diversity    Visual Glossary

Chinese people in France celebrate the Chinese New Year.

All cultures change over time. That is, their cultural traits change. In general, for a new cultural trait to be adopted by a culture, it must offer some benefit or improvement over an existing trait.

How Cultural Traits Spread

A **cultural hearth** is a place where cultural traits develop. Traits from cultural hearths spread to surrounding cultures and regions. Customs and ideas can spread in many ways, including settlement, trade, migration, and communication. **Cultural diffusion** is the spread of cultural traits from one culture to another.

In the 1500s, Spanish explorers and settlers brought horses to the Americas. Many native peoples saw the advantages of using horses for moving quickly and for hunting. Horses soon became part of some Native American cultures.

Cultural traits can also spread through trade. Traders can move among different cultures. As they travel, they carry with them elements of their own culture, such as food or religious beliefs. Traders expose people to these new traits. If people find that an unfamiliar religion or other cultural trait improves their lives, they may make it a part of their own daily lives. For example, hundreds of years ago, Muslim traders helped spread Islam from Arabia to other cultures in Asia and Africa.

In a similar way, migrants spread cultural traits. Migrants bring cultural traditions with them to their new homelands. Over time, many migrants, or immigrants, have come to the United States. Immigrants have brought with them foods, languages, music, ideas, and other cultural traits. Some of these new ways of doing things have become part of American culture.

Technology and Culture

Technology also helps spread culture. The Internet, for example, has made instant communication common. Today, Americans can find out instantly what people in places such as Peru, India, or Japan are wearing, eating, or creating. If we like some of these traits, we may borrow them and make them a part of our culture.

Rapid transportation technologies, such as airplanes, make it easier for people to move all over the world. As they travel, people may bring new cultural traits to different regions.

Cultural change has both benefits and drawbacks. If customs change too quickly, people may feel that their culture is threatened. Some people worry that rapid communication is creating a new global culture that threatens diversity. **Diversity** is cultural variety. These people fear that the things that make people and cultures unique and interesting might disappear. They worry that we might end up with only a single worldwide culture.

Assessment

1. Why do cultures change?
2. What cultural traits have you borrowed in the last few years?

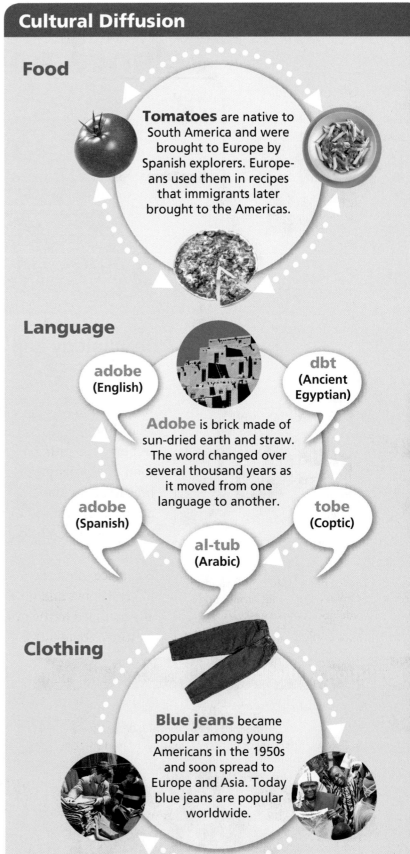

Cultural Diffusion

Food

Tomatoes are native to South America and were brought to Europe by Spanish explorers. Europeans used them in recipes that immigrants later brought to the Americas.

Language

adobe (English)

dbt (Ancient Egyptian)

Adobe is brick made of sun-dried earth and straw. The word changed over several thousand years as it moved from one language to another.

adobe (Spanish)

tobe (Coptic)

al-tub (Arabic)

Clothing

Blue jeans became popular among young Americans in the 1950s and soon spread to Europe and Asia. Today blue jeans are popular worldwide.

Science and Technology

Key Ideas	• Cultures often develop along with science and technology.
	• Technological advances have greatly changed human life.

Key Terms • science • irrigate
• standard of living

 **Visual Glossary**

Science and technology are important parts of culture. **Science** is the active process of acquiring knowledge of the natural world. Technology is the way in which people use tools and machines.

Technology and Progress

Early humans made gradual advances in technology. About 3 million years ago, people first learned how to make tools and weapons out of stone. They later discovered how to control fire.

Technological advances changed cultures. Early humans were hunters and gatherers who traveled from place to place to find food. Later, people discovered how to grow crops. They learned how to adapt plants to make them more useful. They tamed wild animals for farming or used them as food. Over time, people began to rely on agriculture for most of their food.

Agriculture provided a steady food supply and let people settle in one place. As settlements grew and turned into cities, people began to create laws and governments. They developed writing. These advances led to the first civilizations, or societies with complex cultures, about 5,000 years ago.

The Roman empire's thousands of miles of roads let armies and trade goods move easily.

Evolution of the Wheel

The wheel transformed culture. Below, the Sumerian Standard of Ur, about 2600 B.C., showing chariots pulled by donkeys; at right, a covered wagon from the 1800s

Early civilizations developed new technologies that allowed people to grow more crops. People invented tools such as the plow to help increase food production. They built canals and ditches to **irrigate,** or supply water to, crops. Cultures that lacked writing developed more slowly. Over time, agriculture and civilization spread across the world.

Modern Technology

Beginning around 1800, people developed new technologies that used power-driven machinery. This was the Industrial Revolution. It led to the growth of cities, science, and many new businesses. Eventually, people developed even more advanced technologies such as automobiles, airplanes, computers, and space travel.

All of these advances in science and technology have greatly changed people's lives and raised their standard of living. **Standard of living** is the level of comfort enjoyed by a person or a society. Modern technology also helps to connect people, products, and ideas.

Political decisions and belief systems can affect the use of technology. For example, the Chinese government has limited Chinese citizens' use of the Internet. This is an attempt to control discussion of government policies and other issues. Many religions have used technology as part of their practices. For example, religious groups have used the printing press to print the Hebrew Bible, the Christian Bible, the Quran, and other holy writings. Today, some religious organizations use radio, television, and the Internet to broadcast their beliefs.

Technology and Culture

Technological Advances	Effects on Culture
Control of fire	Allowed humans to cook food, have light, protect themselves from animals
Irrigation	Increased food production; allowed people to do jobs other than farming; led to growth of cities
Wheel	Led to improved transportation in the form of carts and carriages; eventually led to trains, cars, and other vehicles
Printing press	Allowed the mass production of books; spread knowledge and ideas, increasing the number of educated people
Steam engine	Steam-powered machines performed work once done by hand; people moved to cities to find work in factories.
Refrigeration	Kept food fresh and safe longer; allowed food to be shipped over long distances from farms to cities

Assessment

1. What are science and technology?
2. How do you think technology might change culture in the future?

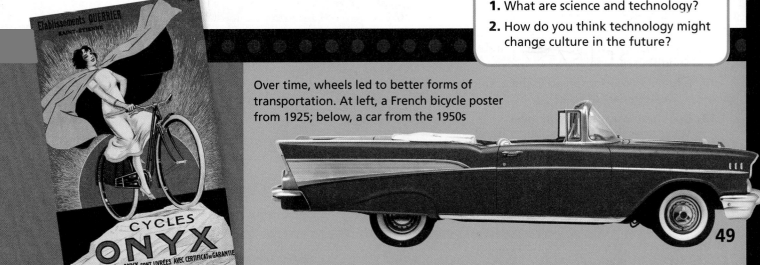

Over time, wheels led to better forms of transportation. At left, a French bicycle poster from 1925; below, a car from the 1950s

49

Part 3 Assessment

Key Terms and Ideas

1. **Define** What is **culture**?
2. **Recall** What is **religion**?
3. **Recall** What do all religions have in common?
4. **Summarize** Does migration cause **cultural diffusion**? Explain why or why not.

5. **Connect** What role did **cultural hearths** play?
6. **Connect** Are all **cultural traits** also **norms**? Explain.
7. **Sequence** Explain the relationship between technology and a **standard of living**.

Think Critically

8. **Draw Inferences** As technology makes it easier for people to travel to different countries, how might world culture regions change?
9. **Make Decisions** What other aspects of culture might link people in a country who practice different religions?

10. **Identify Evidence** Give two examples of ways in which today's cultures are influenced by past cultures.
11. **Draw Conclusions** How do you think ethics guide a country's laws?

Identify

Answer the following questions based on the map.

12. What does this map show?
13. Name one mostly Christian country.
14. What is the majority religion in most of India?
15. What does the color orange represent on the map?
16. Is the majority religion in Saudi Arabia Buddhism or Islam?
17. Is Islam more widespread in the eastern or western part of Asia?
18. Buddhism was founded in India. What does this tell you about cultural diffusion?

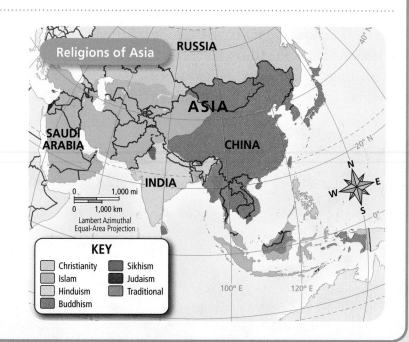

Religions of Asia

RUSSIA

ASIA

SAUDI ARABIA

CHINA

INDIA

0   1,000 mi
0   1,000 km
Lambert Azimuthal
Equal-Area Projection

KEY

- Christianity
- Islam
- Hinduism
- Buddhism
- Sikhism
- Judaism
- Traditional

Journal Activity

Fill in the graphic organizer in your Student Journal.

Demonstrate Your Understanding Complete the Sum-It-Up activity in your journal to demonstrate your understanding of culture. After you complete the activity, discuss your drawing with a partner. Be sure to support your answers to the questions with information from the lessons.

21st Century Learning

Work in Teams

Working with a partner choose a country that is not familiar to anyone in your group. Then research and create an illustrated informational brochure about the country's culture. Be sure to
- provide examples of the country's art.
- identify and describe the country's major religions and languages.

Document-Based Questions

Success ⭐ Tracker™
Online at myworldhistory.com

Use your knowledge of culture and Documents A and B to answers questions 1–3.

Document A

Main Language Spoken in U.S. Homes, 1980–2000

SOURCE: U.S. Census Bureau ▨ English ■ Other

Document B

" The printing press certainly [began] an "information revolution" on par with the Internet today. Printing could and did spread new ideas quickly and with greater impact."

—Historian Steven Kreis

1. Examine Document A. Which of the following statements is probably true?

   A Cultural diffusion is decreasing in the United States.

   B Cultural diffusion is increasing in the United States.

   C Cultural diffusion is unrelated to the decrease in English use at home.

   D Cultural diffusion is no longer taking place in the United States.

2. Read Document B. Which of the following statements would Steven Kreis most likely agree with?

   A The printing press was not an important invention.

   B The printing press is more important than the Internet.

   C The printing press was important because it helped new ideas spread.

   D Technological change does not affect people's lives.

3. **Writing Task** Think about recent technological advances and how they have spread. Pick which one you think is the most important and write a paragraph justifying your choice.

my worldhistory.com
Self-Test

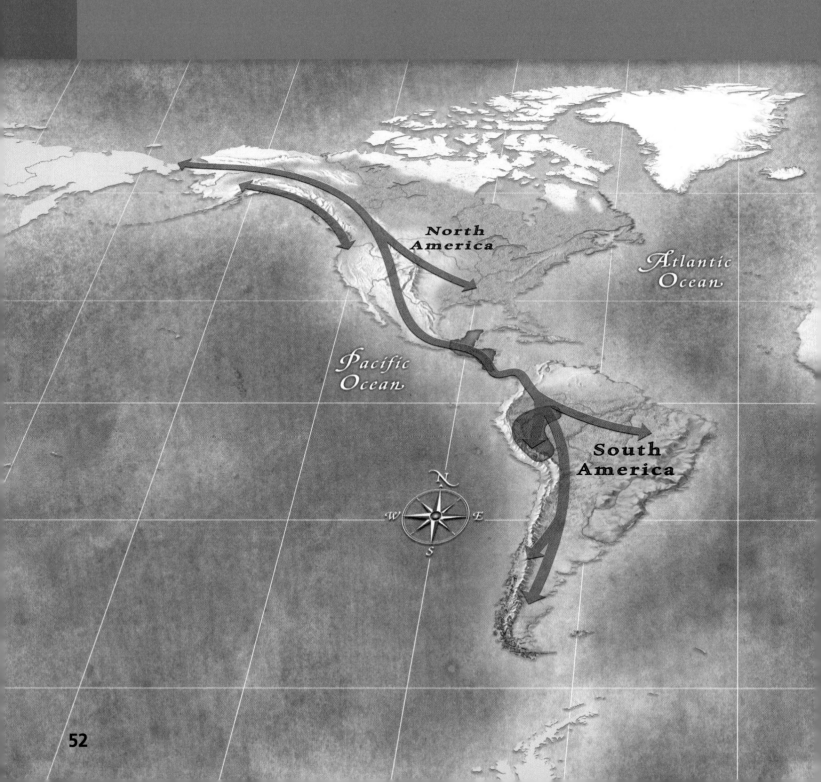

Unit 1

Origins

North
America

Atlantic
Ocean

Pacific
Ocean

South
America

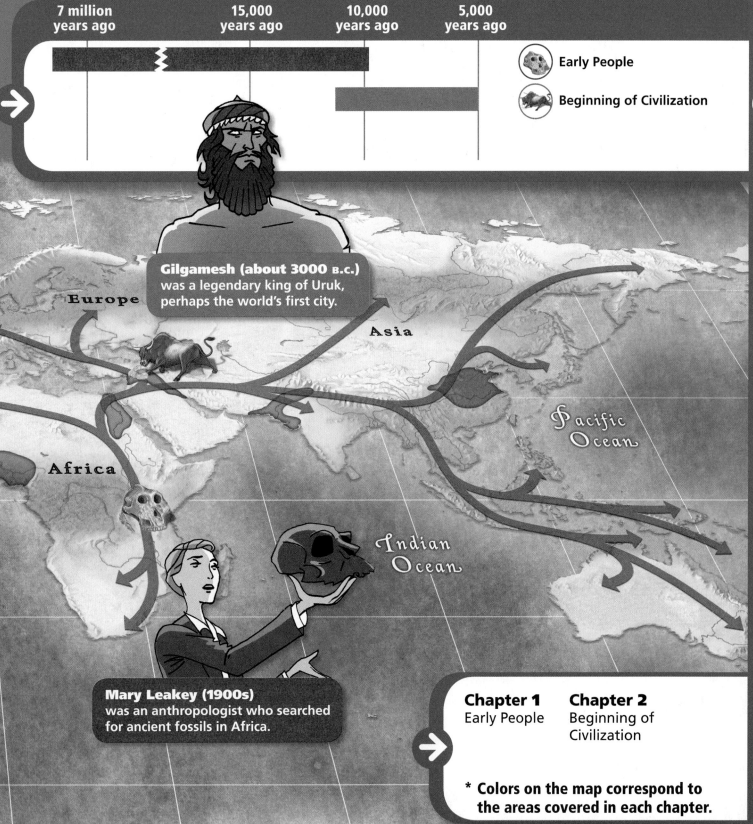

7 million years ago 15,000 years ago 10,000 years ago 5,000 years ago

Early People

Beginning of Civilization

Gilgamesh (about 3000 B.C.) was a legendary king of Uruk, perhaps the world's first city.

Europe

Asia

Pacific Ocean

Africa

Indian Ocean

Mary Leakey (1900s) was an anthropologist who searched for ancient fossils in Africa.

Chapter 1
Early People

Chapter 2
Beginning of Civilization

* Colors on the map correspond to the areas covered in each chapter.

Chapter 1

Early People

Essential Question

What are the consequences of technology?

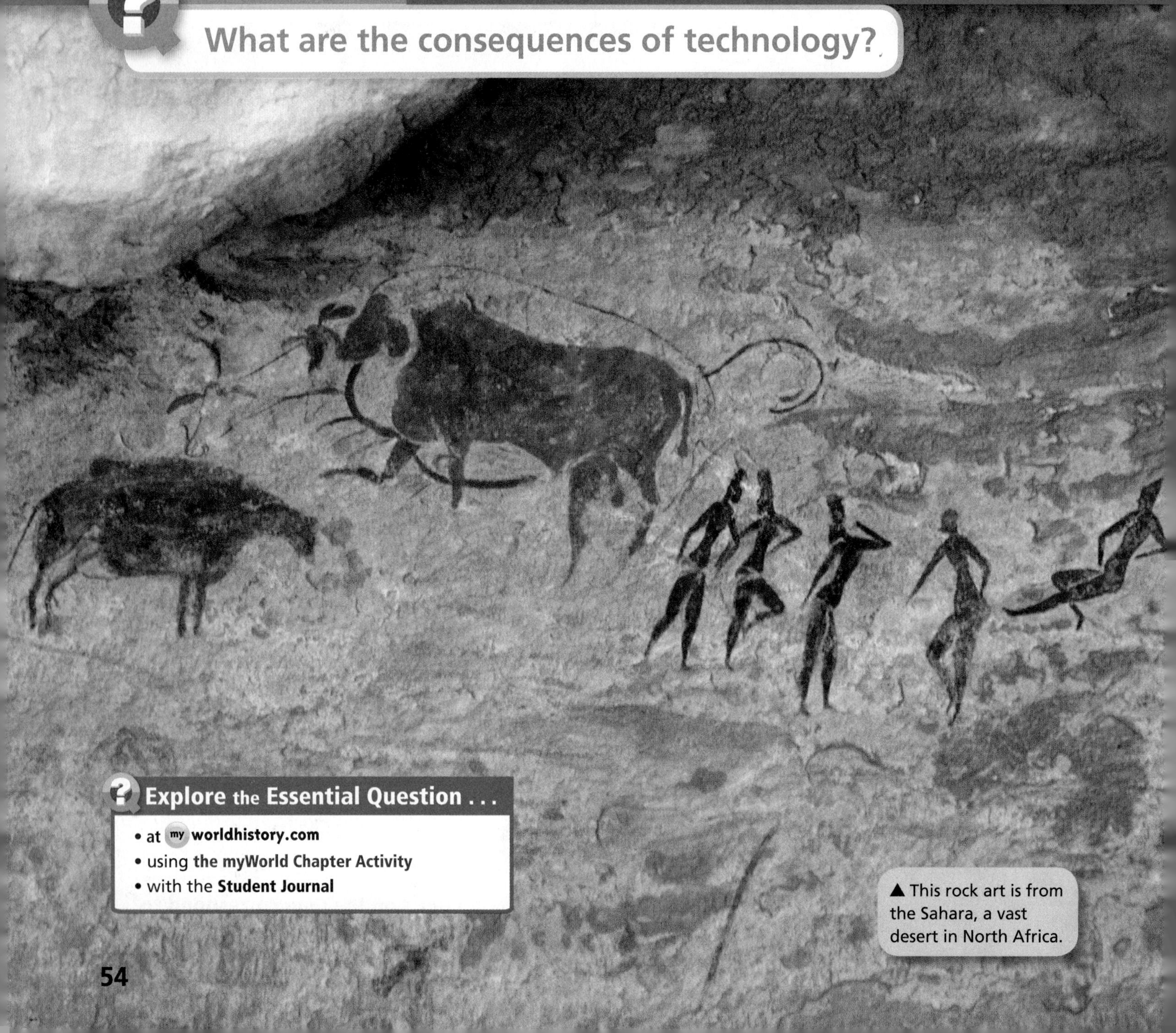

Explore the Essential Question . . .

- at myworldhistory.com
- using **the myWorld Chapter Activity**
- with the **Student Journal**

▲ This rock art is from the Sahara, a vast desert in North Africa.

Human Life in the Stone Age

People make stone tools; Paleolithic Age begins.	Neanderthals appear.	Modern humans appear.	Last ice age begins.
2.5 million years ago	**200,000 years ago**	**100,000 years ago**	**70,000 years ago**

Mary Leakey:
Exploring the Stone Age

Young Mary Nicol was not a typical English schoolgirl. The daughter of an artist, she loved to draw. She was also obsessed with prehistory. When she was 12, she was fascinated by the amazing cave paintings that she saw in southwest France. Some were more than 10,000 years old! As a teen, she earned her first money by sketching prehistoric tools. Still, she found life in England rather stuffy. "Given the chance," she said, "I'd rather be in a tent than in a house."

She got her wish when she married Louis Leakey, an anthropologist who worked in remote areas of Africa. In a most unlikely career choice for a woman of her day, she joined him in his work, making many discoveries with him and on her own. Mary Leakey also became one of the world's foremost experts at drawing and classifying ancient stone tools.

myworldhistory.com

Timeline / On Assignment

Mary Leakey and her team look for signs of early humans in Olduvai Gorge. They spend hours each day carefully digging under the blazing African sun.

Surrounded by spectacular scenery, Mary Leakey oversaw the excavation site at Olduvai Gorge on the Serengeti Plain in Tanzania, East Africa. The vast savanna shimmered and changed colors as the sun rose and set, while in the distance roamed leopards, lions, giraffes, elephants. Working with her own staff, as well as her three young sons, she was on

Back in the lab, Mary watches as her husband Louis examines the latest finds of bones and stone tools.

Life at the camp is not all work. Mary relaxes by playing with her three sons, their dogs, and the various wild animals the family had befriended.

the hunt for the early humans. Under the boiling hot sun, they chipped at the dirt with ice picks, and sifted through the ashes of long-extinct volcanoes to find fossilized bones.

The work was worth it. One day in 1960, they found the remains of the first known member of *Homo habilis*, which means "Handy Man." The Leakeys determined that *Homo habilis* lived between 1.8 and 1.2 million years ago.

Other evidence suggested that *Homo habilis* used tools. No anthropologist before the Leakeys had ever found such an early tool user. The tools, formed by hitting one stone against another, allowed these early people to scrape meat from the carcasses of dead animals. Now humans could add meat to their diet. But *Homo habilis* was prey as well as hunter. They were a regular part of the diet of large carnivores such as leopards and lions.

Earlier scientists had differing ideas about where and when human life began. Now, thanks to the Leakeys and others who followed, scientists think that around the time of *Homo habilis*, early humans began to move from the central region of Africa into Europe and Asia. As people slowly moved into different environments, they invented more and better tools.

Tools made by *Homo habilis* were exciting to find, but scarce. They probably took much less time to make than Mary Leakey and her staff took searching for them. When she was not working, Mary and her sons would play with her pack of beloved Dalmatians as well as the monkeys and other wild animals that roamed the camp.

Researchers—including her own son Richard—continued her investigations and made new discoveries. But there is no doubt that Mary Leakey changed the way we think about human origins. "Basically, I have been compelled by curiosity," she said. The excitement of discovery kept her wanting to find out more and more.

Based on this story, why do you think Mary Leakey's discoveries caused so much excitement? As you read the chapter ahead, think about what Leakey's story tells you about the search for early humans.

myStory Video

Learn more about the discoveries of Mary Leakey and her family.

Section 1

Studying the Distant Past

Key Ideas

- Scientists use fossils and artifacts to draw conclusions about early humans.
- Archaeological evidence indicates that human life began in Africa.

Key Terms • anthropology • archaeologist • prehistory • fossil • geologist • artifact

 **Visual Glossary**

 Reading Skill Identify Main Ideas and Details Take notes using the graphic organizer in your journal.

Scientists study fossils like this skull to learn about early human life. ▼

We are all interested in people. But certain people, called anthropologists, have made a science out of studying people. **Anthropology** is the study of how human beings behave, how they act together, where they came from, and what makes one group of people different from another.

In this section, we will look at the work of a particular group of anthropologists, known as archaeologists. **Archaeologists** study human life in the past by examining the things that people left behind.

Study of Early Humans

Learning about early humans is not easy. Until about 5,000 years ago, people had no way to write things down. To study **prehistory,** or the time before written records, archaeologists look for the places where people may have lived.

Hunting for Fossils To learn about the earliest humans, archaeologists depend mainly on fossils. **Fossils** are hardened remains or imprints of living things that existed long ago. These remains may include plants, feathers, bones, and even footprints that are millions of years old.

Fossils form in several ways. For example, after a living thing dies, it may quickly become covered by sand or mud. Once covered, the soft parts of the plant or animal rot away.

58

The harder parts, such as bones, teeth, or woody stems, last much longer. Over many years, minerals from the soil slowly replace this once-living material. What remains is a rocklike copy of the original.

Fossilized bones of early humans are rare. A complete fossil skeleton is even rarer. Fossil hunters usually find a bone here or a tooth there. Still, studying a tooth can show what kind of food early people ate. Bones tells us about the size and structure of an early human's body.

Dating Ancient Remains Archaeologists use several methods for determining the ages of fossils and other prehistoric objects. In this work, they get valuable information from **geologists,** scientists who study the physical materials of Earth itself, such as soil and rocks.

One dating method is to compare objects found in similar layers of rock or soil. Objects found in lower layers are generally older than those found in upper layers. Archaeologists may also compare an object with a similar fossil or artifact whose age is already known.

Radioactive dating is another method for determining the age of very old objects. Both living things and rocks contain radioactive elements that decay, or break down, over time. By measuring the amount of radioactive material left, scientists can tell when an object was formed.

In recent years, scientists have developed other methods to study fossils. They use DNA to compare human remains from the past with people living today. Genetic evidence has uncovered new information about how people changed and how they moved from place to place.

Searching for Artifacts The earliest humans lived millions of years ago. To study prehistoric people who lived more recently, archaeologists look for old settlements, such as villages or campsites. Such sites often lie buried beneath layers of dirt. Archaeologists must carefully excavate, or uncover, these sites to learn about the people who once lived there.

Thanks to advanced technology, such as radioactive dating, figuring out the ages of fossils and other remains is not just guesswork. ▼

This one's old, that one's really old... oh, and that one there is really super old.

Rock Historian

my World
CONNECTIONS

Cutting tools
and arrowheads
made of flint
are the most
common
Native American
artifacts found
in America.

As archaeologists dig up a site, they look for artifacts such as tools, pottery, or weapons. **Artifacts** are objects made and used by humans. They then try to identify patterns, examining what artifacts are found together in the same spot. Artifacts found in an ancient campsite can help archaeologists understand how the people who once camped there hunted for food or what they ate.

Some questions, however, are difficult to answer by studying artifacts. For example, archaeologists excavating old campsites have found animal bones carved with strange designs. Archaeologists can identify the animals from which the bones came and describe the tools used to carve the designs. But they cannot explain why people created these fascinating artifacts.

Reading Check What types of objects do archaeologists study to learn about the past?

The Hunt for Early Humans

Where did people first appear on Earth? For a long time, scientists could not agree on an answer.

Then, in 1960, British archaeologists Mary and Louis Leakey discovered a piece of a human-like skull at Olduvai Gorge in East Africa. As you read, the Leakeys called their find *Homo habilis* ("handy man") because <u>evidence</u> showed that these early humans made and used tools. Tests showed that the *Homo habilis* fossils were at least 1.75 million years old. From that point on, the search for the origins of humankind has largely focused on Africa.

evidence, *n.,* something that can be used as proof

African Beginnings On November 30, 1974, American fossil hunter Donald Johanson made a discovery that helped shape how scientists view early human history. For three years, Johanson had been searching for evidence of early humans in Ethiopia, a country in East Africa. Johanson later recalled,

❝ We had found fossilized remains of all kinds of animals. Elephants, rhinos, gazelles, monkeys, and so on. But our main goal, of course, was to find as many human ancestor fossils as we could.... On this November morning, it was about noon, I was heading back to my Land Rover to drive back to camp. And I happened to look over my right shoulder. And as I did so, I saw a fragment of a bone which I recognized as coming from the elbow region in a skeleton.... There was a piece of a leg, there was a piece of a pelvis, there was a piece of a jaw, there was a piece of a skull. And I realized almost instantaneously that we had part of a skeleton. Normally, we are happy to find a fragment of jaw, a few isolated teeth, a bit of an arm, a bit of a skull. But to find associated body parts is extremely rare. ❞
— Donald C. Johanson, achievement.org, January 25, 1991

After two weeks of careful searching, Johanson and his team had uncovered hundreds of pieces of bone. They decided that all the bones belonged to one individual because they did not find two examples of any one type of bone. They determined that she was a 3.5-foot-tall woman. Johanson named her "Lucy" after a song by the Beatles.

60

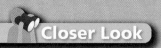
Closer Look

UNCOVERING THE PAST

On an archaeological dig, people must often work in cramped conditions. They map the site, dividing into grids. Then, they patiently sift through layers of soil, and preserving and sketching what they find. The big find for the day may be a fragment of a pot. But every find tells us a little more about the past.

THINK CRITICALLY Why is it important for archaeologists to make detailed maps of the site? What activities can you see going on in this illustration?

Using a brush, the archaeologist carefully removes the dirt around an artifact.

Brushes, chisels, and picks are important parts of an archaeologist's toolkit.

my worldhistory.com   Primary Source

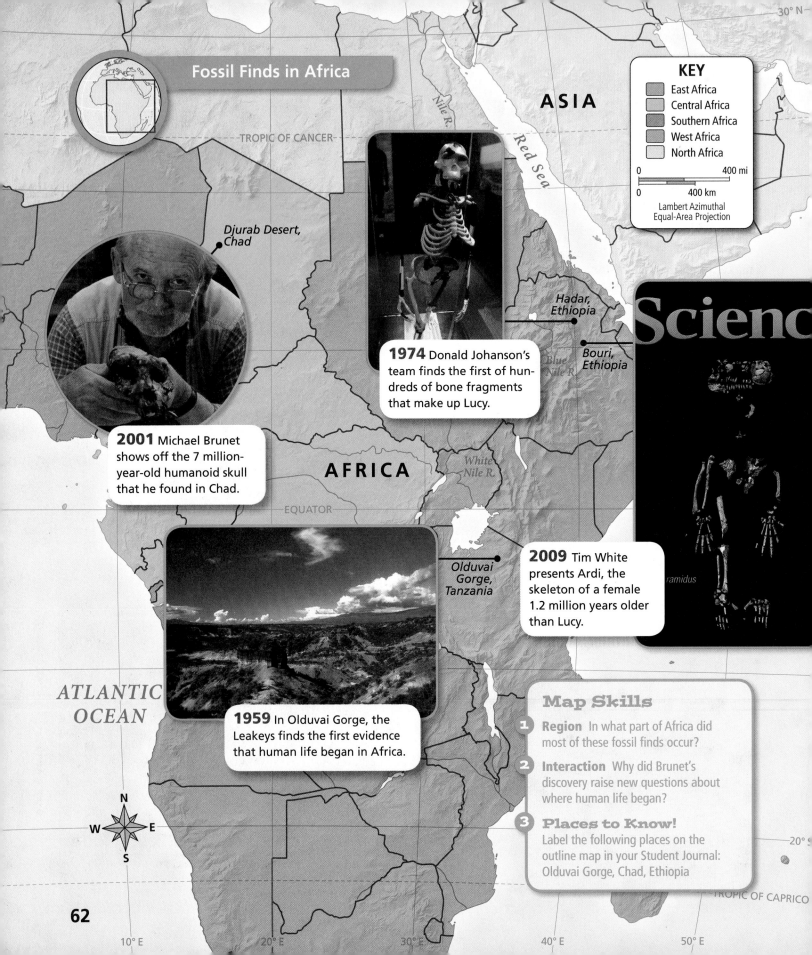

Fossil Finds in Africa

ASIA

Nile R.

TROPIC OF CANCER

Red Sea

KEY

East Africa
Central Africa
Southern Africa
West Africa
North Africa

| 0 | 400 mi |
| 0 | 400 km |

Lambert Azimuthal
Equal-Area Projection

Djurab Desert, Chad

Hadar, Ethiopia

Bouri, Ethiopia

Scienc

1974 Donald Johanson's team finds the first of hundreds of bone fragments that make up Lucy.

Blue Nile R.

2001 Michael Brunet shows off the 7 million-year-old humanoid skull that he found in Chad.

AFRICA

White Nile R.

EQUATOR

ramidus

Olduvai Gorge, Tanzania

2009 Tim White presents Ardi, the skeleton of a female 1.2 million years older than Lucy.

ATLANTIC OCEAN

1959 In Olduvai Gorge, the Leakeys finds the first evidence that human life began in Africa.

Map Skills

1. **Region** In what part of Africa did most of these fossil finds occur?

2. **Interaction** Why did Brunet's discovery raise new questions about where human life began?

3. **Places to Know!** Label the following places on the outline map in your Student Journal: Olduvai Gorge, Chad, Ethiopia

N W E S

20° S

TROPIC OF CAPRICO

10° E   20° E   30° E   40° E   50° E

Johanson's team found some 40 percent of Lucy's skeleton. The bones of her legs, pelvis, ankle, and spine suggest that, like us, she walked upright on two legs. However, she lived 3.2 million years ago.

Since then, even older fossils have been found in Africa. In 1992, American anthropologist Tim White found remains of humans who lived in Ethiopia at least 4.4 million years ago. Beginning with a single tooth, White's team uncovered more fragments. Finally, in 2009, White unveiled a nearly complete skeleton of a female that he named "Ardi." More than a million years older than Lucy, Ardi was taller and heavier. She probably walked upright, but slowly and awkwardly.

Search for the "Oldest One" Discoveries such as Lucy and Ardi have led most scientists to <u>conclude</u> that humankind began in East Africa about 4.5 million years ago. But not everyone agrees. Some argue that human life may have developed separately in different parts of the world. Others agree that human life started in Africa, but in a different region.

French fossil hunter Michael Brunet is one of those who believes that human life started elsewhere in Africa. In 2001, Brunet found a brown, humanlike skull in the country of Chad. Tests showed the skull to be nearly 7 million years old. That makes it, says Brunet, "the oldest one."

Brunet's discovery has raised many questions. Chad is in Central Africa. Did humankind begin there rather than in East Africa? The skull Brunet found is much older than all the other human fossils discovered so far. Does this mean that humankind is older than scientists once thought? The skull found in Chad looks more apelike than other early human skulls. Does this mean that it may not be an early human skull at all?

Scientists will continue to look for answers to questions like these. Meanwhile, the search for ancient human fossils continues. "This is the beginning of the story," says Brunet of his work in Chad, "just the beginning."

Reading Check Where do most scientists believe that human life began?

myWorld Activity
Spread the News!

conclude, *v.,* to decide as a result of thinking or reasoning

Section 1 Assessment

Essential Question
What are the consequences of technology?

Key Terms

1. For each key term, write a sentence explaining its importance to the study of human life in the past.

Key Ideas

2. How do scientists date fossils and artifacts?

3. How do archaeologists look for evidence about early people?

4. Why are the discoveries of the Leakeys and Donald Johanson considered important?

Think Critically

5. **Identify Evidence** Which evidence do you think is more reliable, artifacts or written records? Explain.

6. **Draw Inferences** Why do you think scientists are trying to find out more about how and where early humans lived?

7. Modern archaeologists make use of both hand tools and advanced scientific equipment. Why do you think both types of technology are necessary? Go to your Student Journal to record your answer.

myworldhistory.com

Places to Know

Hunter-Gatherer Societies

Key Ideas
- The development of new skills allowed hunter-gatherer societies to survive.
- Modern humans and Neanderthals both appeared late in the Stone Age.

Key Terms • hunter-gatherer • technology • culture • nomad

 **Visual Glossary**

 Reading Skill Analyze Cause and Effect Take notes using the graphic organizer in your journal.

The scenes below and on the next page are from museum displays. Although they are based on archaeological evidence, we cannot be sure what Stone Age people really looked like. We do know that they learned to make and use fire. ▼

Early humans were **hunter-gatherers,** which means that they lived by hunting small animals and gathering plants. In this section, you will read about the societies that these people formed and the developments that improved their chances for survival.

How Early Hunter-Gatherers Lived

Archaeologists know very little about how early hunter-gatherers such as Lucy lived. But they do know that their lives were often harsh. Many groups appeared for a time and died out. To survive and grow, early humans developed **technology,** tools and skills that people use to meet their needs and wants.

The Development of Tools About 2.5 million years ago, early humans learned how to make tools out of stone. This technology was so important to human survival that archaeologists call this period the Paleolithic Era, or the Old Stone Age. (The word *Paleolithic* comes from Greek words meaning "old" and "stone.") The Paleolithic Era lasted from about 2.5 million to 10,000 years ago.

At first, the tools made by early humans were simple. Toolmakers split stones to make cutting tools for chopping down small trees, cutting meat, or scraping animal skins clean.

▲This museum display shows a band of hunter-gatherers preparing to cook a deer.

Over time, toolmakers became more skillful, making thinner and sharper stone blades. Some blades were used to tip spears and arrows. Toolmakers also began making weapons from bones and antlers. As their skills and weapons improved, Paleolithic hunters were able to turn from hunting small animals to hunting larger animals such as deer.

The Use of Fire At some time during the Paleolithic Era, people also learned how to use fire. Making fire was a technology that had many different uses. With fire, people could have light on dark nights. They could cook meat and plants, and use flames to scare off dangerous animals.

Making fire also had important long-term effects. Here, a British archaeologist explains why learning to control fire was an important step in human development. (Like many earlier writers, the archaeologist uses the term *man* to refer to humankind):

66 The control of fire was presumably the first great step in man's [freedom] from the bondage of his environment…. Man is no longer restricted in his movement to a limited range of climates, and his activities need not be entirely determined by the sun's light. But in mastery of fire man was controlling a mighty physical force. 99

—V. Gordon Childe, *Man Makes Himself*

Fire made it possible for hunter-gatherers to live in places where it would have otherwise been too cold to survive.

▲ Early stone tools were very simple, but they helped hunter-gatherers survive. These tools may have been used to scrape flesh off animal bones.

65

Wandering Bands The culture of early societies was simple. **Culture** includes the many different <u>elements</u> that make up the way of life of a people. Elements of culture include social and family organization, beliefs and values, technology, shelter and clothing, common activities, storytelling, rituals, and art.

Stone Age hunter-gatherers lived in small groups, or bands. A typical band included ten or twelve adults and their children. Many of these people were **nomads,** people who move from place to place with the seasons. After gathering as much food as they could in one area, they moved on to a new campsite. These wandering bands sometimes used caves as shelters. More often, they built temporary huts out of branches or tents from animal skins, another major advance in technology.

Hunter-gatherers spent many hours each day looking for food. Men and boys generally did the hunting. Women and girls usually gathered fruit, grains, seeds, and nuts. They collected eggs and honey and caught small animals such as lizards or fish. They also may have picked herbs for medicine.

Reading Check What technology helped Paleolithic humans survive?

Later Stone Age Peoples

Toward the end of the Paleolithic Era, two groups of larger-brained humans appeared. Both groups had more developed cultures than earlier peoples. However, only one of these groups would survive past the Stone Age.

▲ **Neanderthal skull** ▲ *Homo sapiens* **skull**

Neanderthals vs. *Homo Sapiens*

Homo sapiens and Neanderthals both

- made hunting tools
- used fire
- buried their dead
- had large brains
- lived in the same regions about 30,000 to 40,000 years ago

Neanderthals	Homo sapiens
• first appeared about 200,000 years ago	• first appeared about 100,000 years ago
• had short, sturdy skeletons	• had taller, slimmer bodies
• had only very simple language skills	• had complex language skills
• made no art or music	• made art and music
• had simple burial practices	• had more complex burial practices

Neanderthals A group known as Neanderthals appeared in Europe and parts of Asia about 200,000 years ago. Their name comes from the Neander Valley in present-day Germany, where their fossil remains were first found.

Some archaeologists believe that the Neanderthals were the first people to bury their dead. Remains of flowers and other objects in burial sites may be evidence that Neanderthals carefully buried bodies and may have believed in life after death. Other archaeologists, however, disagree. Even if Neanderthals did bury their dead, their burial practices were much simpler than those of later people.

Modern Humans About 100,000 years ago, the last new group of humans appeared. The scientific name of this group is *Homo sapiens,* which means "wise people." *Homo sapiens* were the first modern humans—or people like us.

These people were like Neanderthals in some ways. Both groups made tools, used fire, and hunted animals. But modern humans were taller and less muscular. They also developed a powerful new skill—<u>complex</u> language.

The ability to form words is probably not a skill that Neanderthals had. One scientist who has studied the remains of Neanderthals claims they made a sound resembling a frog's croak or a burp. *Homo sapiens,* on the other hand, did have the ability to form words. Having a shared language gave them a great advantage in the struggle to survive. They could organize a hunt, warn of danger, or pass knowledge and skills on to their young.

For thousands of years, Neanderthals and modern humans lived near each other, but the Neanderthals eventually disappeared. Some archaeologists believe they fought with the newcomers and lost, while others think the groups mixed together. Whatever the cause, there is no fossil evidence of Neanderthals in Europe after about 28,000 years ago.

Reading Check What skill gave modern humans an advantage over Neanderthals?

complex, *adj.,* having many related parts; not simple

myWorld Activity
Get Yours Now

Section 2 Assessment

Key Terms

1. How did early hunter-gatherers get what they needed to survive?

2. Give two examples of Paleolithic technology.

3. What are some of the elements that make up a culture?

Key Ideas

4. How did the Paleolithic Era get its name?

5. How was Paleolithic society organized?

6. How did Neanderthals and *Homo sapiens* differ from earlier people?

Think Critically

7. **Draw Conclusions** What do you think was the most important skill developed by hunter-gatherers? Explain your answer.

8. **Solve Problems** How might Neanderthals have communicated without the ability to speak?

Essential Question

What are the consequences of technology?

9. Choose one technological advance from this section. How did that technology benefit Stone Age people? How could that technology have unexpected results? Go to your Student Journal to record your answer.

Populating the Earth

Key Ideas

- Over time, modern humans populated most regions of the world.

- As they migrated, humans learned to adapt to various environments.

- Art and other evidence reveals that human societies became more complex and developed religious beliefs.

Key Terms • populate • migration • environment • adapt • clan • animism

→ **Visual Glossary**

→ **Reading Skill Sequence** Take notes using the graphic organizer in your journal.

Over millions of years, many groups of early humans appeared and then died out. *Homo sapiens,* or modern humans, were the last of these groups to appear. As you will read, scientists still have much to learn about the development of the first modern humans. But one fact is clear: These large-brained "wise people" were often on the move. Over many thousands of years, they spread out to **populate,** or become inhabitants of, almost every land area of the world.

▼ These modern-day Mongolians are nomads who migrate from place to place with the seasons.

The Human Migration

Most archaeologists agree that *Homo sapiens* have walked on Earth for only about 100,000 years. But they do not agree on where modern humans came from or how they spread around the world. In search of answers, they have studied both fossils and genetic information, or the physical qualities that living things pass from one generation to the next. They have developed two main theories, or possible explanations, about the movement of early humans.

Two Theories About Migration Some scientists think that *Homo sapiens,* like other early humans, originated in Africa. From there, they argue, *Homo sapiens* began a long migration to other regions of the world. A **migration** occurs when people leave their homeland to live somewhere else. Scientists who support the "out of Africa" theory suggest that as modern humans migrated from Africa to new places,

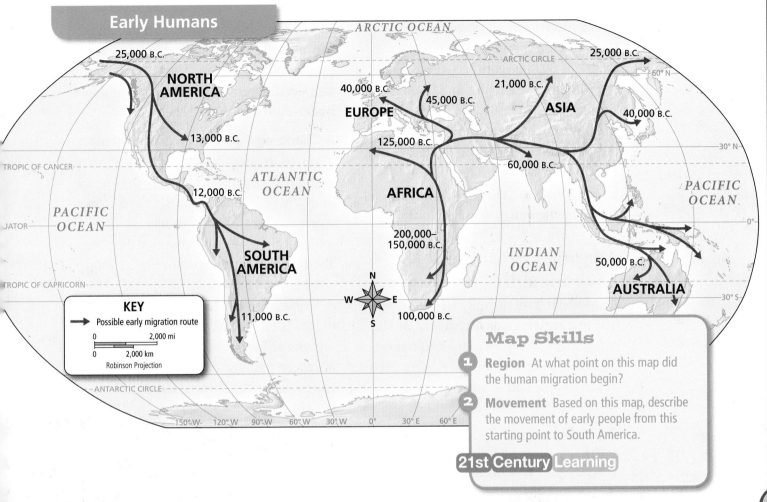

Early Humans

ARCTIC OCEAN

25,000 B.C.

NORTH AMERICA

ARCTIC CIRCLE

25,000 B.C.

60° N

13,000 B.C.

40,000 B.C.

45,000 B.C.

EUROPE

21,000 B.C.

ASIA

40,000 B.C.

125,000 B.C.

30° N

TROPIC OF CANCER

ATLANTIC OCEAN

12,000 B.C.

60,000 B.C.

AFRICA

PACIFIC OCEAN

PACIFIC OCEAN

JATOR

0°

200,000–150,000 B.C.

INDIAN OCEAN

50,000 B.C.

SOUTH AMERICA

N

TROPIC OF CAPRICORN

W E

S

AUSTRALIA

30° S

KEY

→ Possible early migration route

11,000 B.C.

100,000 B.C.

0   2,000 mi

0   2,000 km

Robinson Projection

ANTARCTIC CIRCLE

150° W   120° W   90° W   60° W   30° W   0°   30° E   60° E

Map Skills

1 **Region** At what point on this map did the human migration begin?

2 **Movement** Based on this map, describe the movement of early people from this starting point to South America.

21st Century Learning

they gradually replaced the older groups who were already living there.

Not all scientists agree that modern humans migrated from Africa. Some argue that large-brained humans developed separately in many different parts of the world. These scientists believe that as regional populations mixed together, the different groups eventually became the one group known today as *Homo sapiens*.

New Evidence For years, there was little fossil evidence to support either theory. In recent years, however, new evidence has emerged. In 2007, scientists analyzed a fossil skull that had been found in South Africa. Tests showed that the skull

was about 36,000 years old. It was the same as skulls found in Europe from the same period. This similarity suggests that humans were already in their modern form when they migrated from Africa.

In 2008, scientists completed a genetic study of nearly a thousand people around the globe. Scientists found the greatest genetic variety in communities closest to Africa. This finding supports the idea that, as people migrated away from Africa, groups branched off to populate new areas. The new evidence gives a boost to the "out of Africa" theory. Still, many questions about human migration remain unanswered.

Wherever *Homo sapiens* first appeared, they eventually spread across Earth. By about 30,000 years ago, these modern humans were living in Africa, Asia, Europe, and Australia. Evidence suggests that modern humans were already living as far south as central Chile by about 12,500 years ago.

Reading Check What two theories do scientists have about early migration?

Adapting to Varied Environments

As modern humans migrated, they settled in a variety of **environments,** or surroundings. Each new place had its own climate, plants, and animals. With each move, people had to **adapt,** or change their way of life, to suit their new environment. They had to find out which plants could be eaten. They had to learn to hunt different animals and to find new materials for tools and shelters.

A Changing Climate Over time, people also had to adapt to changes in the world's climate. During the past two million years—including most of the Stone Age—the Earth has experienced four long ice ages. The last great Ice Age began about 70,000 years ago, soon after modern humans appeared.

During the last Ice Age, thick sheets of ice, called glaciers, spread across large regions of Earth. Glaciers covered the northern parts of Europe, Asia, and North America. Parts of the Southern

Ice Age Hunters

Simulation

Prehistoric hunters carved these pieces of mammoth ivory in the shape of flying birds. ▶

◀ Larger, stronger spearheads like this one made it possible to hunt big prey.

▲ How could Ice Age hunters bring down prey as large as a mammoth? This painting shows three advantages people had. First, hunters worked together. Second, they developed strong, sharp weapons. Finally, they used their intelligence to set traps.

myWorld Activity
What Do I Need?

Hemisphere were also under ice. Moving glaciers created many of the world's mountains, lakes, and rivers.

With so much of Earth's water frozen in the glaciers, rainfall decreased. Areas that had once been well-watered grasslands became deserts. Sea levels dropped, exposing "land bridges" where ocean waters had once been. Because of these changes, many animals had to migrate to find food. The people who depended on those animals for food had little choice but to follow the herds.

Staying Warm Ice Age hunter-gatherers adapted to climate change in many ways. As winters grew longer, people learned to use whatever materials they could find to build warm shelters. In Eastern Europe,

for example, people built huts out of mammoth bones. Mammoths were huge furry animals, related to elephants, that lived during the Ice Age. To keep out the winter wind and snow, hunters covered these huts with animal skins.

People also found other ways to stay warm. Using bone needles, they sewed snug clothing from animal skins and furs. They kept fires burning in their hearths day and night.

Forming Larger Communities Some groups adapted to change by forming larger communities. In larger groups, hunters could work together to kill animals such as mammoths. They could also better defend their communities from attack by other nomadic groups.

Most mammoth bones have been found in Siberia and the northern parts of North America. However, they have also been found as far south as California.

Frozen for 37,000 years, this baby mammoth was uncovered in Russia in 2007. It is the best-preserved mammoth ever found.

network, *n.,* a closely interconnected group of people or things

Growing communities might be organized into **clans,** or groups of families with a common ancestor. A clan would be made up of perhaps 25 to 50 people. Clan leaders took on decision-making roles, such as organizing hunts. Everywhere human society developed, <u>networks</u> of clans or families played a vital role in creating strong communities.

In time, Stone Age communities began to trade with one another for special stones or shells. They likely also traded information about finding food during hard times.

Reading Check How did the environment in which people lived change during the last Ice Age?

Developing Complex Cultures: The Evidence of Art

Over the course of the Ice Age, the culture of Paleolithic communities became more and more complex. One of the most important signs of a complex culture is the existence of artwork such as painting and statues.

potential, *n.,* possibility to grow or change in the future

Paintings in Caves In 1940, four French teenagers and their dog made a remarkable discovery. The boys were exploring a cave near Lascaux in southern France. By the dim light of their lamps, they were amazed to see that the walls were covered with paintings of horses, bison, bulls, and other prehistoric animals. Other paintings in the cave showed human figures or abstract designs.

Scientists later determined that the Lascaux cave paintings dated back about 16,000 years, to the time of the last Ice Age. Some images were carved into the stone, but most were painted. The artists made pigments by grinding up minerals of various colors.

Even older cave paintings have been found elsewhere in France, as well as in Spain. Examples of cave and rock art have also been discovered in many other parts of the world where early people lived. For example, the rock paintings shown at the beginning of this chapter are from the Sahara, a vast desert in North Africa.

Stone Age artists also carved small statues. Like the cave paintings, many of these carvings represent animals. Others depict pregnant women.

What Do They Tell Us? Early works of art such as these show that Stone Age people were capable of complex thoughts and actions. After visiting one French cave, an archaeologist commented,

66 The mark of human genius is here, full-blown, with its immense and eternal mystery, and with all its <u>potential</u> for hope in the success of the adventure of modern man. We become modest in these surroundings; a great feeling of timelessness [comes] from them. When we return to the surface, we can't help but question the motivations that lie behind the creation of all those frescoes. To imagine the unimaginable. In any case, in contemplating them we feel the presence ... of an intense, enormous will to create. 99

—Robert Begouën,
The Cave of Chauvet-Point-D'Arc

Closer Look

The Caves at Altamira

In 1868, a hunter stumbled upon paintings in the Altamira cave in Spain. They were the first Paleolithic cave paintings discovered in modern times. The paintings depict wild animals and human hands. Scientific tests done in 2008 showed that the paintings are from 25,000 to 35,000 years old. The magnificent paintings influenced famous artists like Pablo Picasso and even inspired a Spanish comic book.

THINK CRITICALLY At first, most experts refused to believe that the Altamira paintings were really the work of prehistoric people. Why do you think this might have been?

▲ This powerful bison is the most famous image from Altamira.

▲ Most of the paintings are found close to the entrance to the caves.

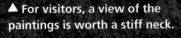

▲ For visitors, a view of the paintings is worth a stiff neck.

We do not know the exact reasons Stone Age people created these works of art. Perhaps hunter-gatherers believed that creating an image of an animal would give them power over that animal during the hunt. Statues of pregnant women may have been intended to bring good luck to women about to give birth.

Reading Check What subjects did Stone Age people show in their art?

Developing Complex Cultures: Religious Beliefs and Practices

Cave paintings and other art provide strong evidence that the cultures of Stone Age people became more complex over time. Another sign of a more complex culture is the development of religious beliefs and practices. Many of these practices involve death and burial.

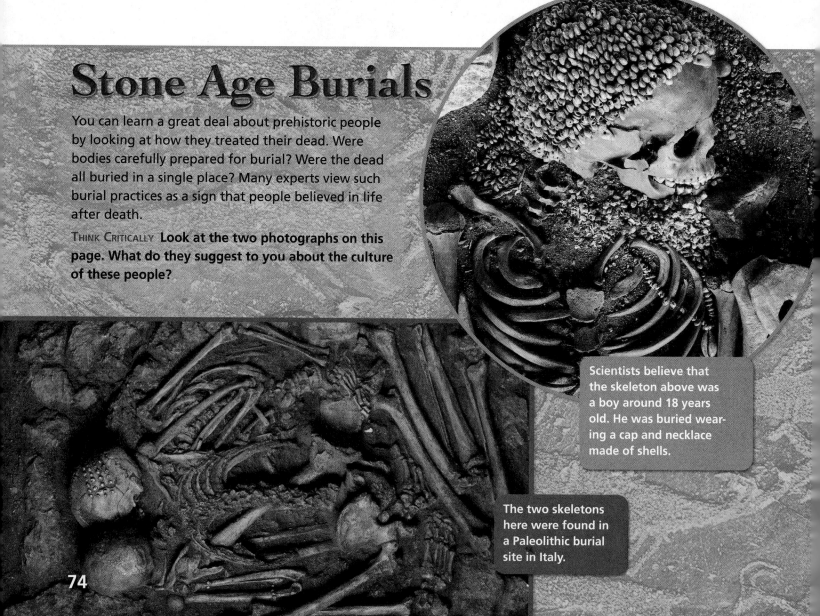

Stone Age Burials

You can learn a great deal about prehistoric people by looking at how they treated their dead. Were bodies carefully prepared for burial? Were the dead all buried in a single place? Many experts view such burial practices as a sign that people believed in life after death.

THINK CRITICALLY **Look at the two photographs on this page. What do they suggest to you about the culture of these people?**

Scientists believe that the skeleton above was a boy around 18 years old. He was buried wearing a cap and necklace made of shells.

The two skeletons here were found in a Paleolithic burial site in Italy.

Burial Practices Scientists have found much evidence to show that Ice Age people buried their dead. One grave found in present-day Russia contained the bodies of two children, a boy about 13 years old and a girl about 8 years old. Both children were covered with thousands of ivory beads. On his chest, the boy wore an ivory pendant carved in the shape of an animal. The girl wore a bead cap and an ivory pin at her throat.

Early Religious Practices Discoveries such as cave paintings, statues, and burial sites may suggest how early humans reacted to what they thought were mysterious and powerful forces. These rituals and symbols were an important part of early culture. They go beyond survival, and express deeper meanings of the natural and social world.

The evidence suggests that these early people believed that the natural world was filled with spirits, a belief known as **animism**. To early humans, there were spirits in the animals they hunted. There were also spirits in the trees, rocks, water, and weather around them. Prehistoric people may have painted pictures of animals, such as bison or deer, to honor the spirits of those animals and to ask forgiveness for having to kill them.

The Next Big Change By the end of the Paleolithic Era, human beings occupied many regions of the world. They had developed complex spoken language, learned to make a variety of tools and weapons, and adapted to different environments. Yet, in many important ways, their lives had not changed. They still lived in relatively small groups as hunter-gatherers, following the herds of animals that they depended on for survival.

Then, around 10,000 years ago, humans learned a new skill that forever changed how they would live. This development marked the end of the Paleolithic Era, and the beginning of what we call the Neolithic Era, or New Stone Age. In the next chapter, you will learn about the birth of farming.

Reading Check What religious beliefs did Stone Age people develop?

Section 3 Assessment

Key Terms

1. Describe the "out of Africa" theory of human migration.

2. What are some of the things that make up a person's environment?

3. What linked families who were members of the same clan?

Key Ideas

4. What kinds of evidence do scientists use to study early migration?

5. How did forming larger communities help people survive?

6. What are two signs that people who lived during the Ice Age developed more complex cultures?

Think Critically

7. **Draw Inferences** What skills and tools would be needed to make cave paintings? What does this suggest about the people who created them?

8. **Predict** How do you think farming might have changed human life?

Essential Question

What are the consequences of technology?

9. What technology helped people adapt to the last Ice Age? What other skills and tools would have helped Ice Age people survive? Go to your Student Journal to record your answer.

Chapter Assessment

Key Terms and Ideas

1. **Explain** How do **archaeologists** and **geologists** help us learn about the past?

2. **Recall** What discoveries did Mary Leakey, Donald Johanson, and Michael Brunet make?

3. **Describe** How did **hunter-gatherers** of the Paleolithic Era survive?

4. **Compare and Contrast** Identify two ways that Neanderthals differed from modern humans.

5. **Recall** What evidence supports the theory that the **migration** of modern humans began in Africa?

6. **Describe** How did people **adapt** to changing climate conditions during the last Ice Age?

7. **Explain** What is **animism**?

Think Critically

8. **Ask Questions** You are an anthropologist working in a part of Africa where no human fossils have ever been found. You discover bones that might be human. List three questions you would want to answer as you study the bones.

9. **Analyze Primary and Secondary Sources** Reread the quotation from Robert Begouën in Section 3. What experience is he describing? What emotions did he feel? What conclusions did he draw about Stone Age people?

10. **Compare and Contrast** Based on what you have read, how do you think Stone Age people differed from us? How were they similar?

11. **Core Concepts: Science and Technology** An old saying states, "Necessity is the mother of invention." Restate this saying in your own words. Then, give two examples from this chapter that fit the saying.

Analyze Visuals

Look at the cartoon and answer the following questions.

12. Who are the men in the cartoon? What are they doing?

13. Where is this scene probably taking place?

14. Why does one man think that this find is "suspicious"?

15. Based on your reading, what would a genuine find probably look like?

"IT'S A WONDERFUL FIND, AND YET THERE'S SOMETHING SUSPICIOUS ABOUT IT."

Essential Question
myWorld Chapter Activity

Archaeological Mysteries Conference Follow your teacher's instructions to role-play archaeologists at a conference. Work in teams to examine an artifact from early human society. Draw the artifact and then discuss how early humans might have used it. Make a poster to show your findings to other archaeologists at the conference.

21st Century Learning
Search for Information on the Internet

Use the Internet to find information about an important archaeological find of the past or present. Create a fact sheet that answers the following questions: **Who** was the main archaeologist? **When** was the discovery made? **Where** was the discovery made? **How** did the team work? **What** did they find? **Why** was it important?

Document-Based Questions

Success Tracker™
Online at myworldhistory.com

Use your knowledge of the Paleolithic Era and Documents A and B to answers Questions 1–3 below.

Document A

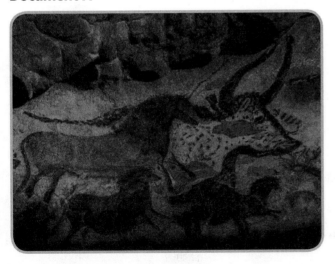

Document B

" As many as 1,700 visitors traipsed through Lascaux every day, but by the late 1950s, the presence of so many carbon dioxide-exhaling, warm-blooded bodies had altered the cave's climate to the point where calcite deposits and lichen were threatening the paintings. . . . The threat of permanent damage had grown so acute that [France's] Minister of Culture ordered the cave closed."

—James Graff, "Saving Beauty,"
Time, May 7, 2006

1. This cave painting from Lascaux is evidence that Paleolithic people
   - **A.** hunted horses and bulls for food.
   - **B.** rode horses when they hunted.
   - **C.** were skilled artists.
   - **D.** migrated from Africa.

2. Why were the caves at Lascaux closed?
   - **A.** The paintings had been destroyed.
   - **B.** Tourists affected the climate of the caves.
   - **C.** France did not care about preserving the caves.
   - **D.** People lost interest in visiting the caves.

3. **Writing Task** Why do you think so many people visited Lascaux? Write a paragraph giving reasons for and against closing the caves to the public.

my worldhistory.com Self-Test

Beginning of Civilization

Essential Question

What should governments do?

The remains of an
ancient city in the
Indus River valley ▼

Explore the Essential Question . . .

- at **my worldhistory.com**
- using the **myWorld Chapter Activity**
- with the **Student Journal**

From Agriculture to Civilization

Last ice age ends.		Oldest known farming village in Turkey is settled.		Uruk, the first city, is settled in Southwest Asia.	
12,000 years ago	**10,000 years ago**	**8,000 years ago**	**6,000 years ago**	**4,000 years ago**	

People learn to farm; Neolithic agricultural revolution begins.

The Story of Gilgamesh

Nearly 3,000 years ago, a writer inscribed clay tablets with a story about Gilgamesh, the legendary king of Uruk. Uruk was a real city in the ancient Middle East. And there probably was a real king named Gilgamesh who once ruled Uruk.

But the Gilgamesh described in the clay tablets was no ordinary king, and no ordinary man. He was two parts god and one part mortal, and he stood well over 10 feet tall.

The writer of the tablets tells us that no man was as strong or handsome as Gilgamesh, and no city was as great or beautiful as Uruk. Uruk was surrounded by a defensive wall six miles long, and inside the city walls were all the riches and art of the civilized world—and Gilgamesh, mighty Gilgamesh, ruled over it all.

But Gilgamesh was a cruel and selfish king. To construct the magnificent public buildings of Uruk he forced men to work until they dropped dead of exhaustion—and he did not care. He left families grief-stricken and let the people of Uruk live in constant ear.

And he did not care.

One day the citizens of Uruk asked the gods to do something, anything, about Gilgamesh. "Help us!" they pleaded. "Our king is ruining our lives!"

my worldhistory.com

Timeline / On Assignment

79

The mighty Gilgamesh forces his people to build the great city of Uruk.

The people of Uruk ask their gods for protection from their cruel king, Gilgamesh.

The storyteller writes that the gods were sympathetic to the people of Uruk. They decided that Gilgamesh needed a companion who was his equal in strength, appetite, and thirst for adventure. Once Gilgamesh had a friend, the gods hoped, he would leave his people alone.

So the gods created Enkidu. Like Gilgamesh, Enkidu was not an ordinary man. He was wild. He was huge. He was covered with hair. He lived with the animals roaming the

countryside. Gradually, however, Enkidu left his wild ways and entered civilization. He began helping shepherds on the outskirts of Uruk by guarding their sheep at night. Prowling tigers and wolves were no match for the mighty Enkidu.

One day Enkidu heard that Gilgamesh was going to take the bride of an Uruk citizen. Enkidu was appalled. He swore he would prevent Gilgamesh from mistreating his own subjects. When Enkidu confronted Gilgamesh, they immediately began fighting. Gilgamesh

Gilgamesh and Enkidu do battle as soon as they meet. Later, though, they will become friends.

Gilgamesh mourns the death of his friend Enkidu.

had never been challenged by anyone as strong as Enkidu. It took all of Gilgamesh's strength to defeat Enkidu—and Gilgamesh was part god! Deep down, Gilgamesh knew that Enkidu, who was *not* part god, was his equal. After their fight, Gilgamesh and Enkidhu respected each other, and they became inseparable friends.

Then, the storyteller writes, Gilgamesh and Enkidu had many adventures. They felled Humbaba, a fierce giant. One day Gilgamesh angered the goddess Ishtar, so she sent the Bull of Heaven after him. The bull could kill 600 soldiers with just one snort of its fiery breath. Yet Gilgamesh and Enkidu slew the beast. Every day, Gilgamesh and Enkidu became better friends and tackled bigger and bigger foes. They were unstoppable . . . almost.

One day the gods decided Enkidu must die. Soon, Enkidu became ill. Over several days he grew weaker and weaker. Enkidu was angry that he was not dying a heroic death, but his anger could not change his fate.

Gilgamesh was grief-stricken at his friend's death. If someone as strong as Enkidu could die, then surely that meant that one day *he* might die!

Gilgamesh did not want to die. He wanted to live forever, so he traveled to the ends of the earth in search of immortality. But on his quest he began to accept that even he, mighty Gilgamesh, would eventually die.

The storyteller's clay tablets tell us that on his return to Uruk, Gilgamesh was a humbler ruler who no longer mistreated his citizens. He had learned an important lesson. He understood that immortality would not come from escaping death. Instead, he would live on in the city of Uruk and in its people. The true way to achieve immortality was by being remembered well by his subjects.

Thus ends the legend of Gilgamesh. Or does it? The magnificent city of Uruk is now only a ruin. But the clay tablets that tell the story of mighty Gilgamesh survive. In the art of a story that has existed for thousands of years, Gilgamesh lives on.

In this section, you read about a legendary king of the city of Uruk. What does this story suggest about government and religion in ancient times? As you read the chapter ahead, look for ways that the story illustrates some features of early civilizations.

 myStory Video

Learn more about the legend of Gilgamesh.

Early Agriculture

Key Ideas
- Human life changed dramatically when people learned to farm and to domesticate animals.
- Farming enabled people to settle in one place and develop specialized skills.

Key Terms • revolution • domesticate • surplus • specialization

 Visual Glossary

Reading Skill Analyze Cause and Effect Take notes using the graphic organizer in your journal.

About 9,000 years ago, people began raising cattle. ▼

People of the Paleolithic Era, or Old Stone Age, lived as hunter-gatherers. They could not have imagined many of the things that we now take for granted. People often had to follow herds of animals, so they were unable to settle for long in one place. People could own few possessions—only what they could easily carry. Food supplies were uncertain. Life was short and dangerous. Survival was a full-time job.

About 10,000 years ago, life began to change. The changes occurred in many places over a 2,000- to 4,000-year period. We call this period the Neolithic Era, or "New" Stone Age. (The prefix *neo-* means "new".) During this period, people learned how to farm.

In time, most hunter-gatherers stopped wandering in search of food and settled in one place. Life was still difficult, and survival was still the main concern. But with people staying in one place, the world began to take on many features we recognize today. In fact, the shift from hunting to farming was so important that historians call it the Neolithic Agricultural Revolution. A **revolution** is a complete change in ways of thinking, working, or living.

The Birth of Farming

The last Ice Age ended about 12,000 years ago. Slowly, temperatures increased and rainfall patterns changed. Glaciers that had covered so much of Earth began to shrink. As the ice from the glaciers melted, ocean levels rose.

Most plants and animals adapted to these changes. Fir trees, which could survive cold weather, spread north into once-icy regions. Some large Ice Age animals did not adapt to a warmer world, and many species died out. People who had hunted some of these animals for food had to find something else to eat. Some people adapted to these changes by searching for new sources of food. They found smaller animals to hunt. People living near rivers or lakes began to depend more on fishing.

Modifying the Environment Others learned to modify or change their environment so that it would provide more food. For example, people cleared trees and bushes by setting them on fire. The grasses that grew back attracted grazing animals such as deer.

People may also have noticed that, if seeds were scattered on the ground, new plants grew there the next year. This discovery led them to find ways to encourage the growth of wild food plants.

Domesticating Plants and Animals Over time, people learned to domesticate plants and animals, especially those that they used for food. To **domesticate** means to change the growth of plants or behavior of animals in ways that are useful for humans. Widespread domestication marked the birth of farming.

Even before the Agricultural Revolution, wild wolves developed into dogs, which humans then domesticated. Dogs provided help in the hunt, as well as companionship and protection.

History of Domestication

When	What
20,000–15,000 years ago	Dogs
11,000 years ago	Fig trees, Rice
10,500–10,000 years ago	Sheep, Goats, Barley, Wheat
9,000 years ago	Pigs, Cattle
8,000 years ago	Chickens, Millet
7,000 years ago	Potatoes, Avocados, Maize, Chickpeas
6,000 years ago	Donkeys, Chili peppers, Watermelons, Guinea pigs
5,500–5,000 years ago	Horses, Camels, Llamas, Cats, Silkworms, Honeybees, Pomegranates

reliable, *adj.*,
dependable; steady;
not risky

Domesticated plants, or crops, became a nutritious and <u>reliable</u> source of food. Grains such as wheat, rice, or maize became chief food sources for entire societies. Many animals also provided food—not only meat, but eggs, milk, and even honey. Horses and oxen became work animals. Sheep and llamas had coats of hair that were used to make clothing.

At first, there was little difference between wild and domesticated breeds. But over time, people selected the seeds of the plants that produced the best crops to sow again. As a result, domesticated plants began to produce more abundant food of higher quality. A wild tomato, for example, is the size of a cherry, but a domesticated tomato is the size of an orange. By contrast, some breeds of domesticated goats, pigs, and cattle are smaller than their wild ancestors. Smaller animals may have been easier to manage.

New Tools Farmers invented new tools. They used axes to cut down trees for farmland and sickles to harvest grain crops. The grain was then ground into flour with stone querns, or hand mills.

All of these tools were at first made out of stone. As later people developed new technologies, they created more efficient tools from materials such as bronze and iron. That is why historians refer to different stages of early history as the Stone Age, the Bronze Age, and the Iron Age.

Reading Check **Why was domestication of plants and animals important?**

This painting shows Egyptian farmers using sickles to harvest wheat. ▼

The earliest sickles were made of stone or flint.

Bronze sickles were lighter than stone sickles and had a sharper cutting edge.

The development of iron allowed farmers to make even stronger sickles.

Evolution of
Farming Tools

Ancient farmers developed tools to cut cereal crops such as wheat and barley. The tools became more efficient over the centuries, but the job remained the same.

Today's mechanical reapers do the same job as the sickles above. ▼

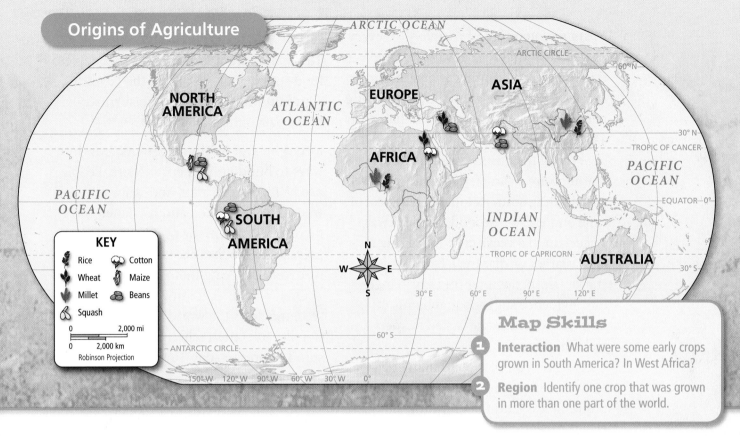

Origins of Agriculture

KEY

Rice
Wheat
Millet
Squash
Cotton
Maize
Beans

0   2,000 mi
0   2,000 km
Robinson Projection

Map Skills

1 **Interaction** What were some early crops grown in South America? In West Africa?

2 **Region** Identify one crop that was grown in more than one part of the world.

The Spread of Farming

No one knows for sure where people first began to plant seeds for food. Still, archaeologists have found evidence to suggest where farming began and how it spread. They have also learned something about the way people lived in early farming communities.

The First Centers of Agriculture Most historians believe that about 10,000 years ago, southwestern Asia became the first center of agriculture. There, scientists have unearthed seeds from domesticated wheat plants that were buried long ago. The seeds are similar to wild varieties of wheat that still grow in the area.

As the map above suggests, farming may then have spread from southwestern Asia westward into Africa. It may also have spread northward into Europe and eastward into the Indus River valley of South Asia.

The map also shows that other centers of agriculture appeared independently in different areas of the world. In southwestern Asia for example, farming began when people started to plant wheat and barley. These crops then spread to Egypt. In the southern part of present-day China, farming began with the domestication of rice. Farther to the north, a grain called millet was the first crop to be domesticated.

Farming in the Americas started with the domestication of gourds in present-day Mexico. In South America, people learned to grow potatoes, beans, and squash. In Africa, farming began with crops such as sorghum and yams.

Costs and Benefits of Farming In every place that agriculture developed, the transition from hunting and gathering to farming took place gradually, over a long period of time. Each way of life had costs as well as benefits.

Some of the costs of shifting to agriculture were clear. First, planting crops and herding animals took a great deal of time and energy. Second, farming was uncertain. If a year's crop failed due to bad weather or disease, a family might starve. Third, farming could be dangerous. Evidence suggests that bands of nomads sometimes attacked farmers and stole their food.

Agriculture also offered many benefits. Farming produced more food and required less land than hunting and gathering. An early farm family might need only 6-7 acres of land to raise enough wheat or maize to feed themselves for a year. In contrast, a hunter-gatherer family needed about 20,000 acres on which to find enough food for a year.

As a result of agriculture, more people were able to build permanent homes and farming villages. Farming also provided new sources of material for clothing. (Later in this section, you will read more about the new types of shelter and clothing that were invented during the Neolithic Era.)

Some groups tried farming for a time and then returned to hunting and gathering. But in the end, most people chose to remain farmers.

Reading Check **Where did farming begin and how did it spread?**

▲ Archaeologists found this statue in the ruins of Çatalhöyük.

New Ways of Living

The first effect of farming was on people's food supply. But over time, the Neolithic Agricultural Revolution transformed every part of human culture.

New Kinds of Shelter Farmers found ways to build permanent shelters. People used a mixture of mud and straw to form walls. The sun baked and hardened the mixture. People made roofs by placing poles and branches across the tops of walls and covering them with mud.

One of the oldest known farming settlements in the world is a village called Çatalhöyük (chah tahl hyoo YOOK). It stood in present-day Turkey more than 8,000 years ago.

At its height, a few thousand people may have lived in Çatalhöyük. The environment provided sources of water and building materials. A British archaeologist described the two-story homes that made up the settlement:

66 The houses of Çatalhöyük were so tightly packed together that there were few or no streets. Access to interior spaces was across roofs—which had been made of wood and reeds plastered with mud—and down stairs. People buried their dead beneath the floors. Above all, the interiors were rich with artwork—mural paintings, reliefs, and sculptures, including images of women that some interpreted as evidence for a cult of a mother goddess. 99

— Ian Hodder, "This Old House"

Each home had its own kitchen and food storage area. The people grew grains and raised flocks of sheep and goats.

Çatalhöyük

Located in southern Turkey, Çatalhöyük is the largest and best-preserved Neolithic village in the world. The settlement is made up almost entirely of private dwellings. There are no large public buildings.

THINK CRITICALLY **How could living close together in this way benefit the people of Çatalhöyük?**

Closer Look

Many dwellings have wall paintings like these. Scientists are unsure what they mean.

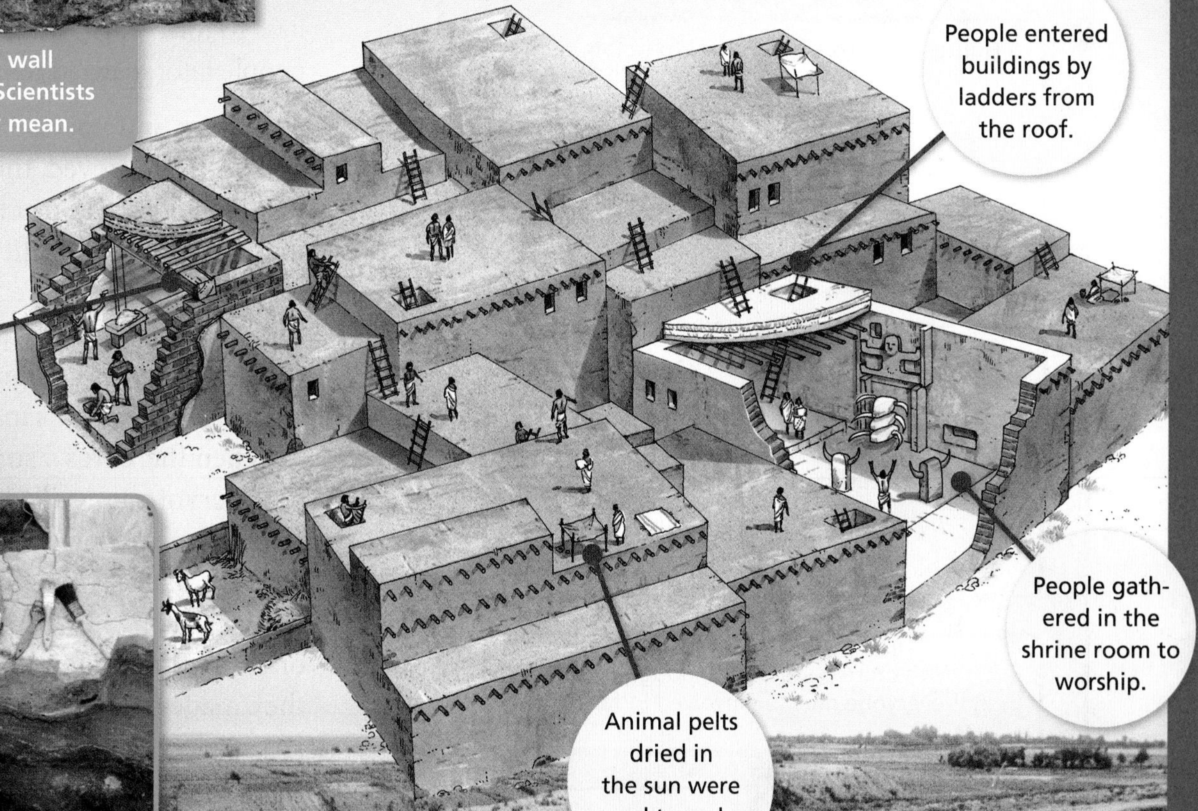

People entered buildings by ladders from the roof.

Roofs were made from poles covered by layers of mud and reeds.

People gathered in the shrine room to worship.

Animal pelts dried in the sun were used to make clothing.

Archaeologists digging in Çatalhöyük have found human remains buried in pits beneath the floors of people's homes.

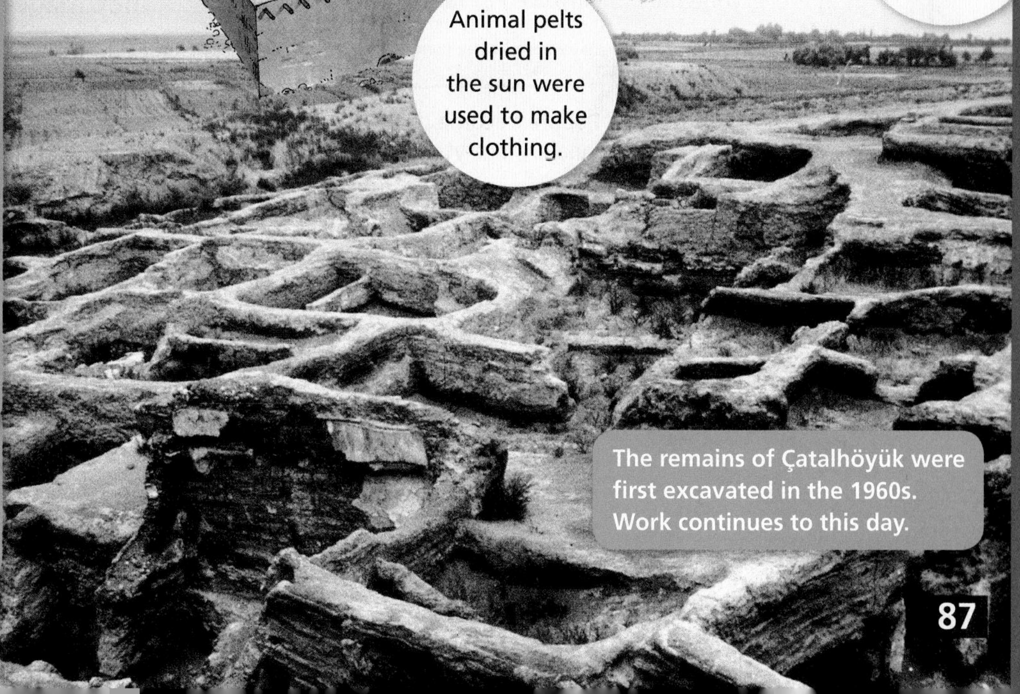

The remains of Çatalhöyük were first excavated in the 1960s. Work continues to this day.

87

myWorld Activity
When I Grow Up

New Kinds of Clothing Agriculture also changed the way that people dressed. For hunter-gatherers, the most important materials for clothing were animal hides and furs. Farming provided new materials that were lighter and easier to work with. From Egypt and India to the Americas, farmers domesticated the cotton plant. They learned to weave cloth from the plant fibers. Another plant, flax, became a source of linen.

Domesticated animals such as sheep and yaks also provided clothing materials. People used wool and other animal hair to form yarn or thread. In China, people later learned to breed silkworms.

Surpluses and Specialization As crops and herds improved, the amount of food that farmers could produce each year increased. Some families were able to raise a **surplus,** or more than they needed to feed themselves. Surplus food could support a growing population. The size of farming villages thus increased.

When there was a surplus of food, not everyone in a village needed to farm. Some people could specialize. **Specialization** occurs when people spend most of their time working at a single job or craft. They could then trade the goods they made for the surplus food grown by farmers. Skilled toolmakers turned stone into polished axes and knives. Potters shaped clay into bowls. Weavers wove sheep's wool into cloth. A few people also became skilled at metalworking. Early metalworkers heated ore to extract, or remove, such metals as copper and tin.

Social Organization Early farming communities remained small. Like hunting, farming required close cooperation among members of the community. Heads of families consulted to make

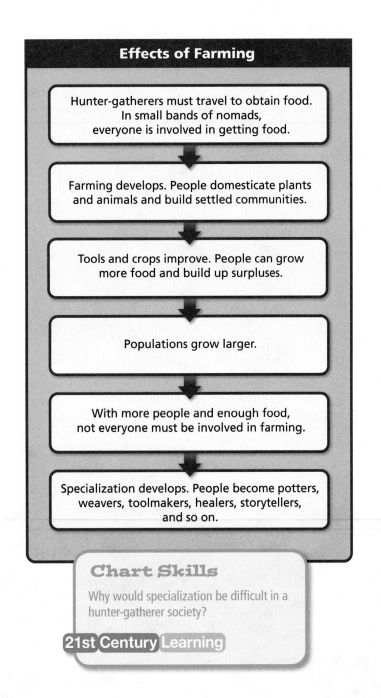

Effects of Farming

Hunter-gatherers must travel to obtain food. In small bands of nomads, everyone is involved in getting food.

↓

Farming develops. People domesticate plants and animals and build settled communities.

↓

Tools and crops improve. People can grow more food and build up surpluses.

↓

Populations grow larger.

↓

With more people and enough food, not everyone must be involved in farming.

↓

Specialization develops. People become potters, weavers, toolmakers, healers, storytellers, and so on.

Chart Skills

Why would specialization be difficult in a hunter-gatherer society?

21st Century Learning

important decisions. They might discuss when to plant and harvest crops, what to do with food surpluses, or how to protect the community from outside dangers.

Archaeologists have uncovered the remains of several Neolithic villages, such as Skara Brae in Scotland (right). In these villages, all homes were more or less the same size. Some historians believe this means that great differences in social standing did not yet exist.

Still, having a permanent place to live meant that people could own more possessions. Early farmers filled their homes with furniture, tools, clay pots, and other goods. These items would have been too heavy to move from one campsite to another. Over time, some families accumulated more possessions than others.

As surpluses increased and people began to specialize, greater social differences emerged. You will read more about this development in the next section.

Reading Check How did farming lead to specialization?

▲ The village of Skara Brae was made up of one-room houses like this one.

Section 1 Assessment

Key Terms

1. For each key term, write a sentence explaining its relationship to the development of farming in the Neolithic Era.

Key Ideas

2. What new skill made agriculture possible?

3. Identify one cost and one benefit of farming for early people.

4. How did farming change the kinds of communities people lived in?

Think Critically

5. **Categorize** Make a list of domesticated animals and classify them according to how people use them. Some animals may fit in more than one category.

6. **Draw Conclusions** What are some of the benefits and drawbacks of job specialization?

? Essential Question

What should governments do?

7. How do you think decision making would change as people moved from hunter-gather bands to larger farming communities? Go to your Student Journal to record your answer.

my **worldhistory.com**

21st Century Learning

Section 2
Cities and Civilizations

Key Ideas
- As populations grew, farming villages developed into cities.
- In several fertile river valleys, cities gave rise to the world's first civilizations.
- Early civilizations all had certain features in common.

Key Terms
- economy
- civilization
- resource
- religion
- social class

 **Visual Glossary**

 Reading Skill Summarize Take notes using the graphic organizer in your journal.

This statue was found in the remains of the ancient city of Uruk. ▼

As farming spread, many small settlements appeared. In time, some villages grew into cities. In this section, you will read about early cities and how they led to the rise of early civilizations.

The First Cities

The world's first cities began as farming villages in the Middle East. As the villages grew, they began to trade with one another. Trade, like farming, became an important source of wealth.

The City of Uruk At the beginning of this chapter, you read a story about the ancient city of Uruk. Although the story is a legend, the city was real. In fact, many historians consider Uruk to be the world's first city. It was founded around 6,000 to 7,000 years ago.

Uruk was different from Çatalhöyük and older farming villages. One difference was Uruk's size. Çatalhöyük covered about 32 acres and was home to no more than 6,000 people. In comparison, when Uruk was at its height, more than 40,000 people lived there. Uruk covered an area of nearly 1,000 acres and had houses, gardens, and large public buildings such as temples.

Another difference was Uruk's form of government. Villages such as Çatalhöyük had little need for complex government. People acted and made decisions according to ancient village customs. A village council settled most disputes. A city such as Uruk was too large to manage that way. Uruk had a strong, well-organized government. The city's first rulers were probably temple priests. Later, powerful military leaders ruled Uruk as kings. These rulers had far more power than a village council did.

Centers of Wealth A city such as Uruk also had a more complex economy than did early farming villages. An **economy** is the system that a community uses to produce and <u>distribute</u> goods and services. The economy of a society or nation is defined by how it answers three basic questions. What goods and services should be produced? How should goods and services be produced? Who should get and use goods and services?

In the earliest human communities, the answers to these three economic questions were fairly simple. Each group produced those goods and services that were necessary for its survival. The group produced these goods and services by hunting and gathering. The goods and services were then shared by the members of the community.

Çatalhöyük's economy was based mainly on farming. By contrast, Uruk's more complex economy was based on both farming and trade. Workshops that produced all kinds of goods lined the city's streets. Traders from Uruk traveled widely. Archaeologists have found pottery and other trade goods from Uruk in many places in the Middle East.

The wealth of Uruk and other early cities attracted many newcomers. People began to move from the countryside into the cities. Many early cities built walls to protect themselves from raiders. Uruk, for example, was surrounded by a thick wall that stretched for 6 miles around the city. This wall was a sign that Uruk was a wealthy city worth protecting.

Reading Check Where did the earliest cities appear?

distribute, *v.,* to divide and give out

Even the ruins of Uruk give a hint of the great city it was 7,000 years ago. ▼

EARLY CIVILIZATIONS

The earliest civilizations rose in four fertile river valleys in Asia and northeastern Africa. The first to emerge were the city-states of Sumer in the region we call Mesopotamia.

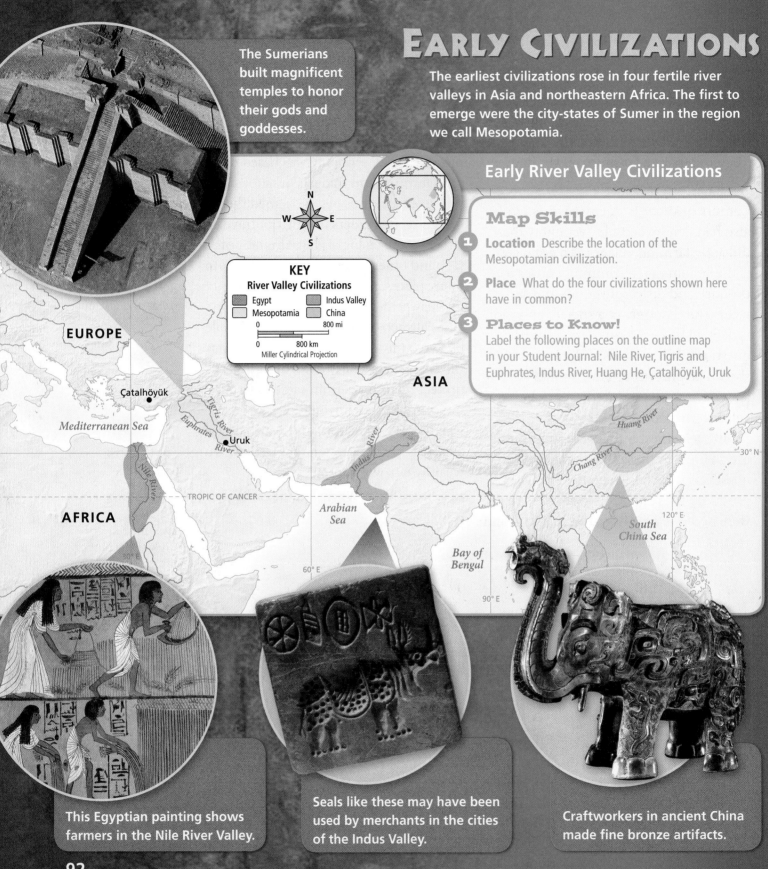

The Sumerians built magnificent temples to honor their gods and goddesses.

Early River Valley Civilizations

Map Skills

1 **Location** Describe the location of the Mesopotamian civilization.

2 **Place** What do the four civilizations shown here have in common?

3 **Places to Know!**
Label the following places on the outline map in your Student Journal: Nile River, Tigris and Euphrates, Indus River, Huang He, Çatalhöyük, Uruk

KEY
River Valley Civilizations
- Egypt
- Indus Valley
- Mesopotamia
- China

0   800 mi
0   800 km
Miller Cylindrical Projection

EUROPE

Çatalhöyük

Mediterranean Sea

Tigris River

Euphrates River

Uruk

Nile River

TROPIC OF CANCER

AFRICA

ASIA

Indus River

Huang River

Chang River

30° N

Arabian Sea

Bay of Bengal

South China Sea

120° E

60° E

90° E

This Egyptian painting shows farmers in the Nile River Valley.

Seals like these may have been used by merchants in the cities of the Indus Valley.

Craftworkers in ancient China made fine bronze artifacts.

The Rise of Civilizations

As early cities grew in size and power, some of them became centers of civilizations. A **civilization** is a complex society that has cities, a well-organized government, and workers with specialized job skills. The word *civilization* comes from the Latin word *civis*, meaning "resident of a city."

The Importance of Resources The rise of early civilizations depended on the creation of a food surplus. Creating that surplus, in turn, depended on the ability of people to manage their resources well. A **resource** is a supply of something that can be used as needed.

The most important resources that people needed were fertile soil, fresh water, and seeds. However, these resources were worth little if people could not provide the labor and tools needed to produce enough food. Managing these resources well required a level of planning and organization that marked a new stage in human society.

Settings of Early Civilizations Like the earliest villages, the earliest civilization also appeared in southwestern Asia, in the city-states of Sumer. (You will read more about Sumerian civilization in Chapter 3.) In time, other civilizations appeared in different parts of the world.

Four of these early civilizations developed in the fertile valleys surrounding major rivers: the Nile in northeastern Africa; the Tigris and Euphrates in southwest Asia; the Indus in South Asia; and the Huang River in China. (You can see the locations of these river valley civilizations on the map on the opposite page.)

River valleys provided a good setting for permanent settlements. Each year, the rivers rose and flooded the nearby land. When the floodwaters went down, a fresh layer of fertile soil remained that farmers could use to grow crops.

Not all early civilizations began in river valleys, however. Greek civilization, for example, emerged on a rocky peninsula in southeastern Europe and a series of islands in the eastern Mediterranean Sea. The Maya civilization started in the rain forests of present-day Mexico and Central America. The Inca civilization began in the Andes Mountains of South America.

Reading Check Why did many early civilizations arise in river valleys?

Features of Civilizations

The civilizations that arose in different parts of the world differed in many ways. Still, all of them had certain things in common. Early civilizations shared eight basic features: cities; organized governments; established religion; job specialization; social classes; public works; arts and architecture; and a system of writing.

Cities The first of these features was cities. Early cities emerged near farming centers. As food surpluses led to rapid population growth, villages grew into cities. They served as centers of religion, government, and culture. A few ancient population centers, such as Damascus, Syria, are still major cities today.

my World CONNECTIONS

Many American cities such as Boston, New York, and New Orleans grew as ports for sea or river trade.

my worldhistory.com

Places To Know

Organized Governments The second feature of early civilizations was a well-organized government. One role of government is managing society's resources so that people get those things they need to survive. A strong government can also form and train an army to defend a society from attack or to expand its borders.

As populations grew, government became more difficult. Rulers came to rely on large numbers of public officials who handled different duties.

Established Religion A third common feature of a civilization was an <u>established religion,</u> or a set of shared beliefs about supernatural powers that created and rule the world. Religion was often linked to government. Rulers of early civilizations usually claimed that their right to rule came from the gods. In China, for example, emperors were called "Sons of Heaven."

In most early civilizations, people believed in many gods and goddesses that controlled most events in their lives. People feared their gods, but also hoped that the gods would protect them from harm. To keep their gods and goddesses happy, priests offered sacrifices and led prayers. This prayer is from the civilization of ancient Sumer:

> 66 May the wrath of the heart of my god be pacified!
> May the god who is unknown to me be pacified!
> May the goddess who is unknown to me be pacified!
> May the known and unknown god be pacified!
> May the known and unknown goddess be pacified!
> The sin which I have committed I know not. . . .
> My god, my sins are seven times seven; forgive my sins!
> My goddess, my sins are seven times seven; forgive my sins! 99

— "Penitential Psalms," translated by Robert F. Harper

established, *adj.,* set up officially

Chart Skills

Which feature do you think was the most important to a successful civilization? Why?

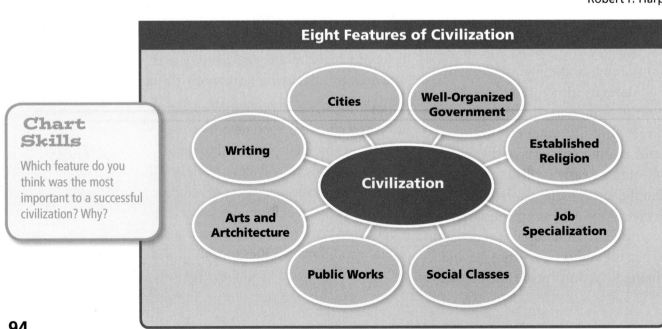

Eight Features of Civilization

- Cities
- Well-Organized Government
- Writing
- Established Religion
- Civilization
- Arts and Artchitecture
- Job Specialization
- Public Works
- Social Classes

From earliest times, religion included beliefs about life after death. People also looked to their religion for rules about how to treat one another and how to live moral lives.

Job Specialization Job specialization was a fourth feature that was common to civilizations. Most people in early civilizations were farmers. They produced enough food to support many kinds of specialized workers, such as priests, rulers, soldiers, craftworkers, and others. Priests specialized in religious activities. Rulers and soldiers specialized in keeping order in a society and protecting it from outside threats. Skilled craftworkers specialized in producing goods. Traders and merchants specialized in buying and selling goods. Job specialization allowed people within a society to develop the many skills and talents needed to create and maintain a civilization.

Social Classes A fifth feature of early civilizations was a system of social classes. **Social classes** are groups of people that occupy different ranks or levels in society. Class structures resembled pyramids, with the smallest number of people at the top and the largest number at the bottom.

The highest social class in most early societies was made up of priests and rulers. The people at these ranks had the most power and wealth.

The social classes in the middle included farmers, merchants, and skilled workers. Members of these classes varied in wealth and status from one society to another. In many societies, slaves made

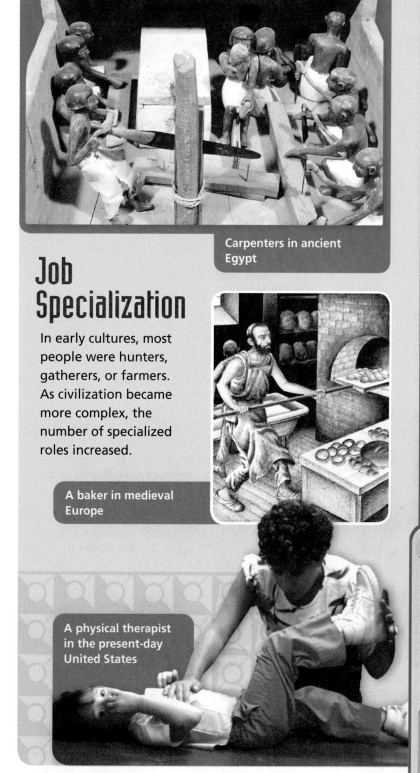

Carpenters in ancient Egypt

Job Specialization

In early cultures, most people were hunters, gatherers, or farmers. As civilization became more complex, the number of specialized roles increased.

A baker in medieval Europe

A physical therapist in the present-day United States

my worldhistory.com

Primary Source

up the lowest class. Slaves were often prisoners captured in war or poor people who sold themselves to pay their debts.

Public Works Public works were a sixth feature of civilizations. Governments organized workers to build large-scale projects such as roads, water systems, city walls, and granaries where food was stored after harvesting. Building these public works was costly, time-consuming, and often dangerous. Often, workers were injured or killed. Still, public works benefited the society as a whole.

Arts and Architecture Architecture was closely related to public works. Early people built and decorated magnificent temples, tombs, and palaces. Many of these buildings served a public function, but they were also objects of beauty.

Early civilizations developed other forms of art as well. In this chapter, you can see a number of examples of statues and paintings that date back thousands of years. Skilled craftworkers also produced fine luxury items for the upper classes, such as gold jewelry and perfume boxes. Music and literature, too, enriched the lives of early people and became a mark of advanced civilization.

Public Works

Large-scale projects are generally organized and built by a government for the benefit of society.

→ Culture Close-Up

A modern American public school

Part of the Incan road system in South America

A public bath in the Indus Valley city of Mohenjo-Daro

Writing

Every civilization has evolved a system for keeping written records.

Inscriptions on a bone from ancient China

A medieval Arabic book written and illustrated by hand

A book on a modern electronic reader

System of Writing The final common feature of civilizations was a system of writing. Forms of writing varied, from picture writing to symbols representing sounds and letters.

In some early societies, writing was first developed mainly to record numbers, such as the amount of grain harvested. Eventually, however, people used writing to preserve all kinds of information. They recorded laws, wrote down prayers to the gods, and described the mighty deeds of rulers.

Historians have learned much about early civilizations from the written records that they left behind. With the development of writing, we pass from prehistory to recorded history.

Reading Check What are the eight basic features of civilization?

myWorld Activity
Pass the Civilization Test

my worldhistory.com

Culture Close-Up

Section 2 Assessment

Essential Question

Key Terms

1. What three questions define the economy of a society?

2. What is the first feature that all civilizations have in common?

3. What social classes were common in most early civilizations?

Key Ideas

4. How did Uruk differ from earlier farming communities?

5. How were natural resources linked to the growth of civilization?

6. What are public works? Give two examples.

Think Critically

7. **Draw Inferences** Why do you think people in early cities began to trade with other cities?

8. **Synthesize** How was job specialization linked to the emergence of social classes?

What should governments do?

9. How was a strong government linked to public works? Do you think organizing such projects was a necessary job for early governments to do? Go to your Student Journal to record your answers.

Chapter Assessment

Key Terms and Ideas

1. **Summarize** What was the Neolithic Agricultural **Revolution**?

2. **Recall** What region do historians think was the first center of agriculture?

3. **Explain** How did farming lead to food **surpluses**?

4. **Describe** Why do historians consider Uruk to be the first city?

5. **Recall** What are the eight basic features of a **civilization**?

6. **Explain** In early civilizations, how was government connected to **religion**?

Think Critically

7. **Make Decisions** If you were an early human, would you have preferred living as a nomadic hunter-gatherer or as a settled farmer? Give reasons for your answer.

8. **Analyze Cause and Effect** How did the birth of farming allow people to own more possessions? How do you think possessions were related to the development of social classes?

9. **Analyze Cause and Effect** Do you think there could have been civilization without the development of agriculture? Explain.

10. **Core Concepts: Foundations of Government** What happened to governments as people moved from hunter-gatherer groups to farming communities to civilizations? How is government related to decision making?

Analyze Visuals

For each river valley civilization, write the letter from the map that shows its location.

11. Egyptian civilization (Nile River)

12. Chinese civilization (Huang and Chang Rivers)

13. Indus Valley civilization (Indus River)

14. Mesopotamian civilization (Tigris and Euphrates rivers)

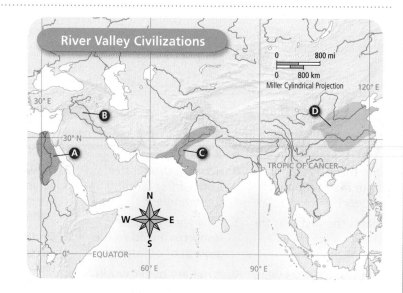

River Valley Civilizations

0   800 mi
0   800 km
Miller Cylindrical Projection   120° E

30° E

30° N

B

A

C

D

TROPIC OF CANCER

N
W   E
S

0°   EQUATOR
60° E   90° E

Essential Question

myWorld Chapter Activity

The Road to Civilization Follow your teacher's instructions to study early human cultures. Role-play a scribe to record and analyze clues about a culture and decide when it existed. Then work in a team to draw conclusions and construct a living timeline that sequences several different cultures in time

21st Century Learning

Solve Problems

Divide into small groups. Each group is an early farming community faced with one of these problems: (1) Nomadic bands are raiding your crops. (2) There is a shortage of water nearby. (3) Your land produces wheat in the fall, but not in the winter. Create a plan to solve the problem. Consider what technology or skills you can develop and how your people can best work together.

Document-Based Questions

Success Tracker™
Online at myworldhistory.com

Use your knowledge of the Neolithic Era and Documents A and B to answers Questions 1-3 below.

Document A

Document B

" Chickens were selected to be larger, wild cattle (aurochs) to be smaller. . . . Most domestic animals . . . have smaller brains and less acute sense organs than do their wild ancestors. Good brains and keen eyes are essential to survival in the wild, but represent a . . . waste of energy in the barnyard, as far as humans are concerned."

—Jared Diamond, *Nature*, August 8, 2002

1. Why do you think the wild pig on the left looks different from the domesticated pig on the right?

   A. People bred pigs to have more meat.

   B. Larger pigs were easier to domesticate.

   C. Larger pigs are less expensive to feed.

   D. Wild and domesticated pigs are not related.

2. According to Document B, animals were domesticated in certain ways in order to

   A. be larger.

   B. have keener senses.

   C. be more useful to people.

   D. survive better in the wild.

3. **Writing Task** Document B explains how chickens and cattle were bred. How did this benefit humans? Write a paragraph describing how people today benefit from domestication of animals.

myworldhistory.com

Self-Test

Digging for Clues

Key Idea
- Archaeologists interpret evidence based on clues and discoveries about different peoples and civilizations.

When studying the origins of humans, historians must rely on clues, as primary sources do not exist from prehistoric times. Remember, a primary source is a firsthand account of an event. Since early humans had no system of writing, they left behind no written records. The first excerpt describes how archaeologists must use detective work to find and interpret clues about early peoples and civilizations. The second excerpt provides an example of the kind of information that archaeologists can obtain from their studies.

An archaeologist uncovers an artifact.

Read the text on the right. Stop at each circled letter. Then answer the question with the same letter on the left.

Ⓐ Draw Inferences Why is "comprehensive documentation" so important for archaeologists?

Ⓑ Analyze Primary Sources Why do you think the author includes the phrase "creating light where there was darkness"?

Ⓒ Summarize In what way are archaeologists like detectives?

criminology, *n.,* the scientific study of crime

incontrovertible, *adj.,* not open to question

material, *adj.,* physical

trace, *n.,* a sign or evidence of some past thing

Archaeologists as Detectives

❝ It has often been argued that the archaeologist works like a detective. . . . Both archaeology and <u>criminology</u> draw on seemingly <u>incontrovertible</u> <u>material</u> evidence, which is taken to provide significant clues as to what has really gone on. These clues are often provided by telltale <u>traces</u> left on the site. As anything might be significant, comprehensive
Ⓐ documentation is of the utmost importance. . . . Archaeologists are trained and experienced in recording, studying, and interpreting such traces and routinely integrate the results of expert analysis. . . .

The archaeologist is thus the detective of the past. Like the detective the archaeologist solves mysteries and is often
Ⓑ portrayed as creating light where there was darkness by
Ⓒ finding clues and revealing truths. ❞

—Cornelius Holtorf, *From Stonehenge to Las Vegas: Archaeology as Popular Culture,* 2005

Read the text on the right. Stop at each circled letter. Then answer the question with the same letter on the left.

D **Identify Details** What evidence of early wheeled transport did archaeologists discover?

E **Identify Main Ideas** How does this passage describe the invention of the wheel?

F **Analyze Cause and Effect** What effects did the wheel have on trade and culture?

millennium, *n.,* a period of 1,000 years

evolution, *n.,* a process of continuous change

unprecedented, *adj.,* new, unique, occurring for the first time

diffusion, *n.,* the state of being diffused; spread

The Invention of the Wheel

&& The question of the origins of wheeled transport requires an analysis of the history of transportation. . . . The appearance of wheeled transport . . . is documented by the discoveries of wheels, fragments of vehicles, models of vehicles, and pairs of
D draft cattle. . . .

The invention of the wheel is one of the most important
E discoveries in the history of humankind. For five <u>millennia</u> it has largely determined the <u>evolution</u> of our civilization. The use of wheeled transport considerably increased labor productivity both in farming . . . and in livestock herding, where it allowed herdsmen to follow their cattle in pursuit of new pastures. . . . But first and foremost, it furthered the <u>unprecedented</u> expansion of exchange, which in turn promoted cultural contacts between remote regions and accelerated the <u>diffusion</u> of ideas,
F and consequently led to great historical change. Therefore, studying the evolution of wheeled transport is of considerable scientific interest. 99

— E. E. Kuzmina, *The Prehistory of the Silk Road,* 2008

Analyze the Documents

1. **Draw Conclusions** Using evidence from the text, explain how the first quotation relates to the second quotation.

2. **Writing Task** Suppose that you are an archaeologist who has just discovered a wheel made thousands of years ago in the Middle East. In a letter to another archaeologist, explain your thoughts about the long-term effects of the invention of the wheel.

The wheel, shown in this ancient Egyptian artifact, had an important influence on early cultures.

Hold an Agricultural Fair

Your Mission On the Internet, research the development of agriculture. Then present your findings at a class agricultural fair. Divide into four groups to research one of these topics: domestication of plants and animals, early tools and technology, early farming and village life, and modern farming techniques. Work as a group to plan your information booth for the fair.

Studying early peoples and the farming tools and technologies they used can give us clues about their development. For example, early people domesticated animals so that they could produce their own food instead of hunting for it. As people began to stay in one place to farm, villages and cities developed.

Use the Internet to find facts about the development of agriculture from ancient times to today. In your search, use words or phrases that relate to your topic. (Put the phrases inside quotation marks to get more specific results.) During your research, think of ways to present the information at the agricultural fair. As a group, design a booth for the fair that includes a display about your topic.

STEP 1

Research Your Topic.

With your group, develop a list of questions or ideas about your topic that your research needs to answer. Then ask your teacher for a list of reliable Web sites that might be good sources for your group's topic. As you search for information online, think about any possible questions your audience might ask you during the agricultural fair. Be sure to find answers for those questions.

STEP 2

Compile Your Findings.

Once you've found the answers to your questions, organize your group's information about your topic. Decide what information is the most important—and most interesting—for your audience to learn.

STEP 3

Prepare and Present.

Plan how you will effectively present facts about your topic. You might illustrate facts using photos, charts, graphs, or timelines. You may wish to choose one or two members of your group as presenters. Be prepared to answer questions from your audience. When you visit other groups' information booths, write down any questions you might have, and ask them when the presentation is finished.

my worldhistory.com

21st Century Learning

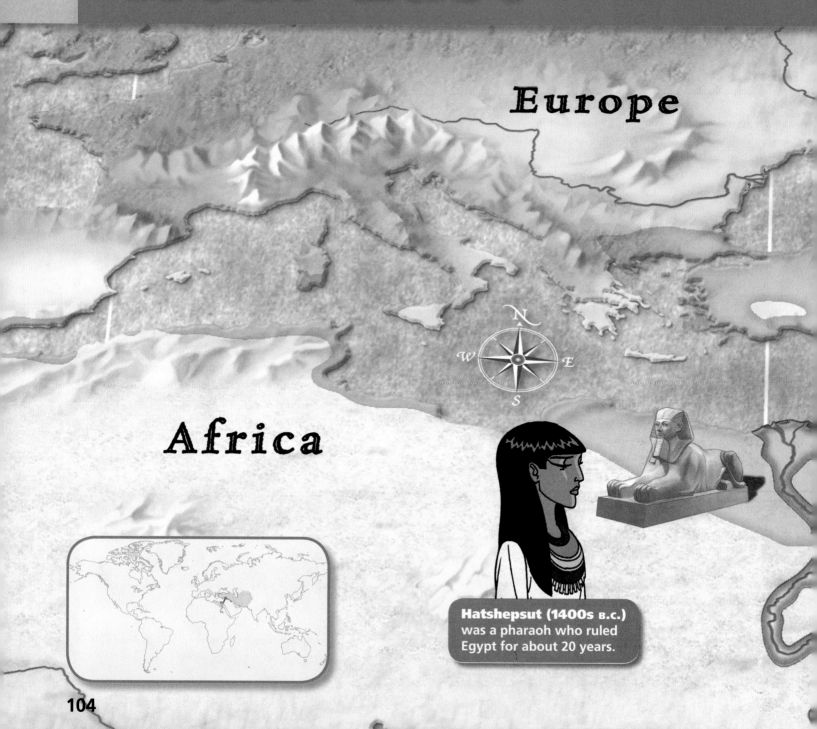

The Ancient Near East

Europe

Africa

Hatshepsut (1400s B.C.) was a pharaoh who ruled Egypt for about 20 years.

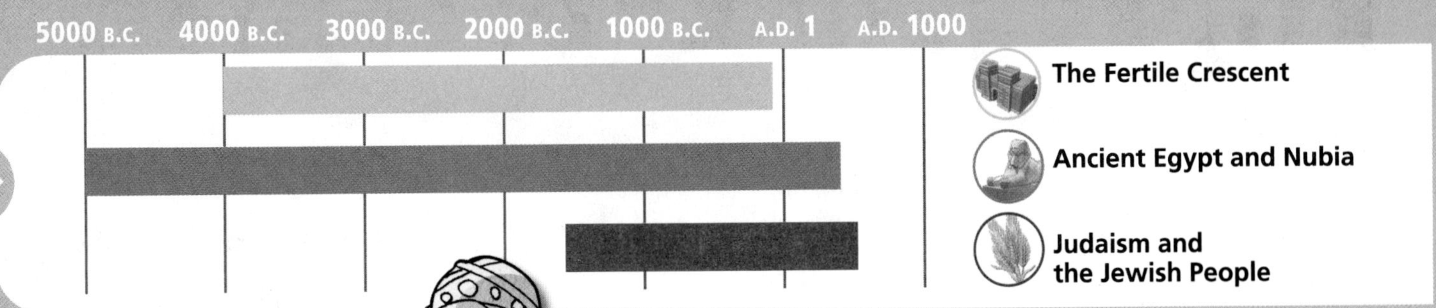

5000 B.C.   4000 B.C.   3000 B.C.   2000 B.C.   1000 B.C.   A.D. 1   A.D. 1000

The Fertile Crescent

Ancient Egypt and Nubia

Judaism and
the Jewish People

Asia

Cyrus the Great (500s B.C.)
was a powerful leader who built
Persia into the largest empire the
world had ever seen.

Ruth (about 1000s B.C.),
a central figure in the Bible's
book of Ruth, converted to
Judaism and journeyed to
Bethlehem.

Chapter 3
The Fertile
Crescent

Chapter 4
Ancient Egypt
and Nubia

Chapter 5
Judaism and
the Jewish People

* **Colors on the map correspond to
the areas covered in each chapter.**

The Fertile Crescent

? Essential Question

What are the consequences of technology?

Ruins at the palace of Darius the Great, the ruler of the Persian empire, in Persepolis, Iran

? Explore the Essential Question . . .

- at my worldhistory.com
- using the **myWorld Chapter Activity**
- with the **Student Journal**

Mesopotamian Empires

3500 B.C. Sumerian city-states form.	2750 B.C. Phoenician civilization begins.		539 B.C. Persian empire begins.
3500 B.C.	**2500 B.C.**	**1500 B.C.**	**500 B.C.**
	2334 B.C. Akkadian empire begins.		934 B.C. Assyrian empire begins.

Cyrus the Great: King of the World

This myStory is a fictionalized account of events in the life of a real person from this chapter.

In 539 B.C., Cyrus the Great declared that he was the king of the world. Few people would have dared to disagree with him. Cyrus was the ruler of the mighty Persian empire, and his troops had just conquered Babylon (BAB uh lahn), the greatest city of the time period. Within 50 years, the Persian empire grew to cover nearly 3 million square miles. It was the largest empire the world had ever seen.

Like other rulers, Cyrus used his army to expand his territory. But he also used his wits. He used one clever strategy when he attacked the rich kingdom of Lydia, in what is now Turkey. Cyrus knew that horses are often frightened by the smell of camels. He had his soldiers collect all of the camels the Persian army had used to carry supplies, and bring them to the front lines.

At night, Cyrus has his soldiers dig trenches to drain water from the Euphrates River.

The level of the river drops low enough for the Persian army to march across it into Babylon.

Once the Lydian horses saw and smelled the camels, they ran away in terror. As a result, the Persians quickly defeated the Lydian army, doubling the size of the Persian empire.

The conquest of Babylon was one of Cyrus's most brilliant triumphs. Babylon was a fabulously wealthy city-state located just south of present-day Baghdad, Iraq. Its engineers were skilled at new building technologies. They built tall towers and great palaces and temples, surrounded by walls covered with colorful tiles. To support their agriculture, Babylonians used a system of canals to bring water from the Euphrates River.

Thousands of Persian troops follow Cyrus through the Ishtar Gate into Babylon.

Babylonian people bow to Cyrus, their new ruler.

The Babylonian people were unhappy with their current ruler, so Cyrus thought it would be easy to win their support once he took power. But first he had to get into the city. Babylon was partly protected by a branch of the Euphrates River that was filled with strong currents and dangerous rapids. The Persian army would not be able to enter Babylon—unless Cyrus could figure out a way to cross the river safely.

Cyrus organized his troops into several units. As darkness fell, he had each unit secretly dig a narrow trench. These trenches allowed water to drain from the Euphrates into an old empty reservoir outside the city walls. That night, while the city's residents were busy celebrating a Babylonian festival, the Euphrates slowly emptied.

When the river dropped to thigh level, Cyrus ordered his soldiers to march across the water into Babylon. The Persian invaders entered without a fight, quickly capturing the city. Mighty Babylon had fallen, thanks to Cyrus's clever use of technology to drain the river.

Days later, Cyrus made a triumphant entrance into Babylon. He rode in through Babylon's immense Ishtar Gate, more than 40 feet tall and decorated with colorful tile and brick images of dragons and bulls. After him came thousands of Persian soldiers, armed with swords and lances.

Cyrus announced to the Babylonians that he had been chosen as their ruler by Marduk, the highest Babylonian god. He proclaimed his victory on clay tablets that read: "I am Cyrus, king of the world, the great king, the mighty king, king of Babylon, king of Sumer (soo mur) and Akkad (AK ad), king of the [four corners of the world]." Of course, Cyrus did not actually control the entire world. But on that day when Babylonians bowed down before him at the Ishtar Gate, he must have felt like the most powerful person in the world.

Based on this story, how do you think Cyrus's use of technology affected his conquest of Babylon? As you read the chapter ahead, think about what Cyrus's story tells you about life in the Fertile Crescent.

 **myStory Video**

Learn more about the life of Cyrus the Great.

myworldhistory.com   myStory Video

Section 1
The Civilization of Sumer

Key Ideas
- Fertile land between the Tigris and Euphrates rivers supported the earliest known civilization.
- Priests and kings held great power in the city-states of Sumer.
- Sumerian achievements included new technology, a written language, and epic poetry.

Key Terms • Fertile Crescent • Mesopotamia • irrigate • city-state • barter • polytheism • ziggurat • cuneiform

→ (**Visual Glossary**)

Reading Skill Identify Main Ideas and Details Take notes using the graphic organizer in your journal.

A Sumerian bronze sculpture of a bull's head ▼

The **Fertile Crescent** is a region of the Middle East that stretches in a large, crescent-shaped curve from the Persian Gulf to the Mediterranean Sea. The Fertile Crescent includes **Mesopotamia** (mes uh puh TAY mee uh), a wide, flat plain in present-day Iraq. This plain lies between two great rivers, the Tigris (TY gris) and the Euphrates (yoo FRAY teez). In fact, *Mesopotamia* means "land between the rivers" in Greek. Here, thousands of years ago, the world's first civilization began to form. This was the civilization of Sumer (SOO mur).

110

Agriculture in Mesopotamia

As its name suggests, the Fertile Crescent's soil is rich and fertile. Some of the most productive land in the region is in Mesopotamia. This rich soil allowed Sumerian farmers to grow many grains and vegetables. They also raised sheep, goats, and cattle.

Geography of Mesopotamia Northern Mesopotamia includes the foothills of the Taurus and Zagros mountain chains. To the south, these foothills flatten into plains that stretch southeast toward the Persian Gulf.

Southern Mesopotamia is a hot, dry region with little rainfall. At first glance, the land looks like a desert. But the soils are not desert soils. In fact, they are rich with nutrients.

The southern part of Mesopotamia owes its good soil to the Tigris and Euphrates rivers. These rivers begin in the mountains of southeastern Turkey and flow south and east, through present-day Iraq. The rivers unite in southern Iraq and continue to the Persian Gulf as a single waterway known as the Shatt-al-Arab.

For many years, the Tigris and Euphrates have carried fine, fertile soil called silt down from the mountains. Each spring, the rivers flood their banks, spreading floodwaters and silt across the plain. When the floods end, they leave behind a fresh layer of moist, fertile earth that is perfect for growing crops.

But Mesopotamia's geography also gave Sumerian farmers many challenges. The heavy spring floods could wash away crops and even whole villages. During the summer, the hot sun baked the ground rock hard. With little rain for months, plants died.

Farming the Land Despite these challenges, the Sumerians used technology to turn Mesopotamia into productive farmland. Remember that technology is the practical application of knowledge to accomplish a task.

my World CONNECTIONS

The Fertile Crescent's major crops were barley and wheat. Both are grown today in the United States, primarily in the Great Plains.

The Tigris and Euphrates rivers are a key part of life in the Fertile Crescent. ▼

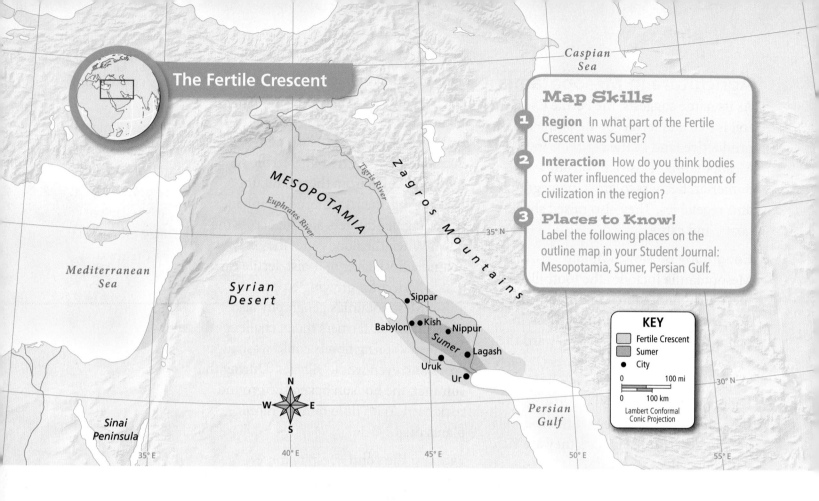

The Fertile Crescent

Map Skills

1 **Region** In what part of the Fertile Crescent was Sumer?

2 **Interaction** How do you think bodies of water influenced the development of civilization in the region?

3 **Places to Know!** Label the following places on the outline map in your Student Journal: Mesopotamia, Sumer, Persian Gulf.

KEY

Fertile Crescent
Sumer
• City

0   100 mi
0   100 km

Lambert Conformal
Conic Projection

The Sumerians used technology to **irrigate,** or supply water to, their crops. They dug many miles of irrigation canals to bring water from the rivers to their fields. With irrigation, crops could still get water during the hot, dry summer.

Sumerians also developed a new way of planting crops. Earlier farmers had used a plow pulled by oxen to cut a long furrow, or trench, in the soil. Then the farmers dropped seeds into the furrow by hand. But Sumerian farmers developed a seed funnel that they attached to their plows. As the plow moved forward, seeds automatically dropped from the funnel into the soil. This made planting faster and easier.

Reading Check **How did geography affect the Sumerians?**

City-States of Sumer

Better agricultural techniques helped the Sumerians produce more food. With a dependable food supply, the population of villages began to grow. Around 3400 B.C., cities started to form in southern Mesopotamia.

Cities Emerge The first Mesopotamian city was Uruk, which you read about in Chapter 2. Uruk had a population of more than 40,000 people. Other early cities were Ur, Lagash, and Nippur. Some cities grew large and powerful. They became the world's first city-states. A **city-state** is an independent state that includes a city and its surrounding territory. Each Sumerian city-state had its own government and laws, and each had its own main god.

Mesopotamian traders used boats to ship goods to and from city-states such as Uruk (background).

my worldhistory.com

Places to Know

Trade Each city-state was also a center of trade. Although southern Mesopotamia had fertile soil, it had little wood or stone and no metal ores. Sumerians traveled far to find these important resources and bring them back to their cities. Most trade was done by barter. **Barter** is a trading system in which people exchange goods directly without using money.

Early traders often used the rivers and major canals to transport their goods. They loaded goods onto barges, or large rafts. Workers on land used ropes to pull the barges along the water.

As they had done with agriculture, the Sumerians used new technologies to make widespread trade easier. For example, they used wheels on their carts. They used sails on their boats. With wheeled carts and sailboats, Sumerians could more easily transport barley, wheat, dates, and cloth to faraway lands. They could also bring home trade goods like lumber, metals, and precious stones.

Social Classes The Sumerians developed a social order with three classes. People of each class had <u>distinct</u> roles within Sumerian society. The upper class included the ruler, his top officials, powerful priests, wealthy merchants, and owners of large plots of land. Farmers and skilled workers made up the middle class. The lowest class was mostly slaves. The city-states' governments and Sumerian religious beliefs, which were firmly connected, helped support this social order.

Reading Check **Why was trade important to Sumerian city-states?**

distinct, *adj.*, separate, different

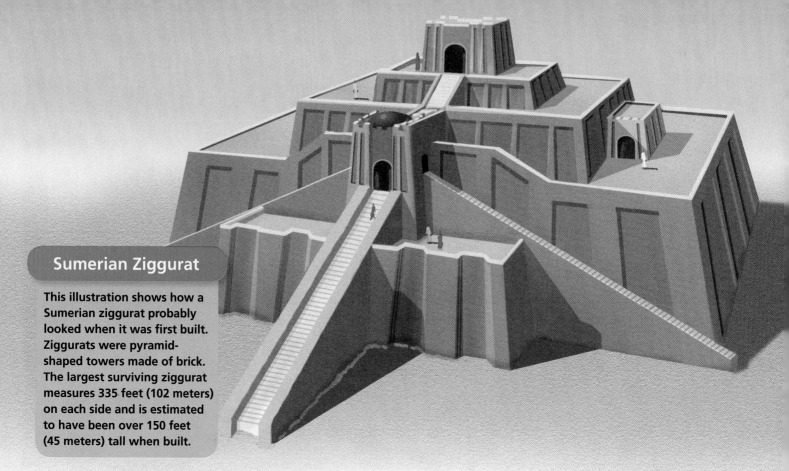

Sumerian Ziggurat

This illustration shows how a Sumerian ziggurat probably looked when it was first built. Ziggurats were pyramid-shaped towers made of brick. The largest surviving ziggurat measures 335 feet (102 meters) on each side and is estimated to have been over 150 feet (45 meters) tall when built.

Sumerian Religion

Like most ancient peoples, the Sumerians practiced **polytheism,** the belief in more than one god. Sumerians believed these gods controlled every aspect of life, including rain, wind, and other elements of nature. Some gods represented agriculture or other activities.

Sumerians believed that the gods behaved much like people. They thought that the gods ate, drank, slept, and married. However, Sumerians also believed that the gods lived forever and had great power. If the gods were happy with people's prayers and offerings, they might bring good fortune to the city. If not, they might bring war, floods, or other disasters. As a result, Sumerians felt that they needed to keep the gods happy in order for their cities to grow and <u>prosper</u>.

prosper, v., gain in wealth

Sumerians believed that only priests knew how to communicate with the gods. They depended on priests to tell them what the gods wanted. As a result, priests had an important role in Sumerian society. Priests lived in and ran the temples in which people worshiped the gods.

In larger Sumerian cities, temples were pyramid-shaped brick towers known as **ziggurats** (ZIG oo rats). The largest ziggurats were seven stories tall. They rose upward in steps, with each level smaller than the one below. Some were filled with beautiful paintings and statues.

The area around a temple often included large areas of farmland controlled by the temple. Priests kept grain and other goods belonging to temples in large storehouses.

Reading Check What made priests powerful in Sumerian society?

Sumerian Writing

Sumerian priests needed a system to keep track of their stored goods. At first they drew pictographs on clay. Pictographs are simple pictures that represent objects. To record the number of fish given to a temple, for example, Sumerian priests drew a fish. Then they added marks to represent the number of fish. In time, this way of keeping records developed into the world's first system of writing.

Cuneiform By 3400 B.C., Sumerian priests had created a new writing system called cuneiform. **Cuneiform** is a system of writing that uses triangular-shaped symbols to stand for ideas or things.

Cuneiform involved pressing wedge-shaped marks into clay tablets. By combining the marks in different ways, Sumerians could create thousands of symbols.

Epic of Gilgamesh Cuneiform was originally used to record sales, taxes, and agreements. Later, Sumerians began to use writing for more than recordkeeping. Around 2000 B.C., the long poem known as the *Epic of Gilgamesh* appeared. This poem tells about the adventures of a Mesopotamian hero named Gilgamesh. The first tablet introduces Gilgamesh:

> 66 Supreme over other kings, lordly in appearance, he is the hero, born of Uruk, the . . . wild bull. He walks out in front, the leader, and walks at the rear, trusted by his companions. Mighty net, protector of his people, raging flood-wave who destroys even walls of stone! 99
>
> —from the *Epic of Gilgamesh*, translated by Maureen Gallery Kovacs

Closer Look

Cuneiform

Ancient Sumerians developed a writing system called cuneiform. Sumerian scribes—people who could write—used a pencil-like writing instrument called a stylus to make wedge-shaped marks in wet clay. These marks stood for words, concepts, or sounds. The Sumerians eventually developed thousands of different symbols.

THINK CRITICALLY Why was the development of cuneiform an important achievement?

A Sumerian cuneiform tablet ▶

◀ This ancient Greek sculpture shows a scribe using a stylus to write.

◀ The *Epic of Gilgamesh* was written in cuneiform on 12 clay tablets.

▲ The Standard of Ur is a mosaic from about 2500 B.C. This section shows Sumerian leaders holding a feast to celebrate a military victory.

myWorld Activity
Standard for Modern Times

The stories about Gilgamesh are myths, or made-up tales of gods and heroes. However, some scholars believe that Gilgamesh may have been a real king. These scholars think that he ruled the Sumerian city-state of Uruk sometime after 3000 B.C.

Reading Check How did Sumerian writing develop?

Sumerian Government

The first leaders of Sumerian city-states were priests, not kings. But when conflicts arose among city-states, the way cities were ruled began to change.

Development of Kingship As city-states grew, people in different cities began to argue with one another over the control of land and water. These conflicts sometimes led to war.

In times of war, priests helped choose the best person to lead the city-state into battle. After the war was over, this leader was expected to give up his power and return to normal life. But some of these military leaders kept control of the city-states even after war ended. These military leaders became the first kings.

Kings and Priests To stay in power, kings needed the support of the priests. So kings were careful to respect the priests' rights and powers. In turn, priests declared that the gods had sent the king to rule the city. This idea that kings were chosen by the gods became common in Sumer. Together, kings and priests created religious ceremonies that supported royal power.

Sumerian kings eventually took over many jobs the priests once did. They hired workers to build new canals, temples, and roads. Each king also served as the city's chief lawmaker and judge.

Written Laws Some rulers collected city laws into a law code, or a written set of laws. The earliest known law code was issued around 2100 B.C. by Ur-Nammu (uhr NAHM oo), the king of Ur. The Ur-Nammu law code included laws about marriage, slavery, and causing harm to other people. One law read, "If a man knocks out the eye of another man, he shall weigh out half a mina of silver." (A mina is a unit of weight that varied over time but was approximately one pound.)

Achievements Under the rule of priests and kings, Sumerians produced many advances in technology. You have already read about the Sumerians' improvements to the plow and their use of irrigation, the wheel, and the sail. Through trade, many of these Sumerian advances spread to other lands.

Another important advance in technology was the development of bronze. The Sumerians were one of the first cultures to make bronze by mixing copper and tin. Bronze is a harder metal than copper, so it is better for making tools and weapons. Bronze weapons would later play an important role in the growth of cities into large, powerful states.

Reading Check How did kings replace priests as rulers of Sumerian city-states?

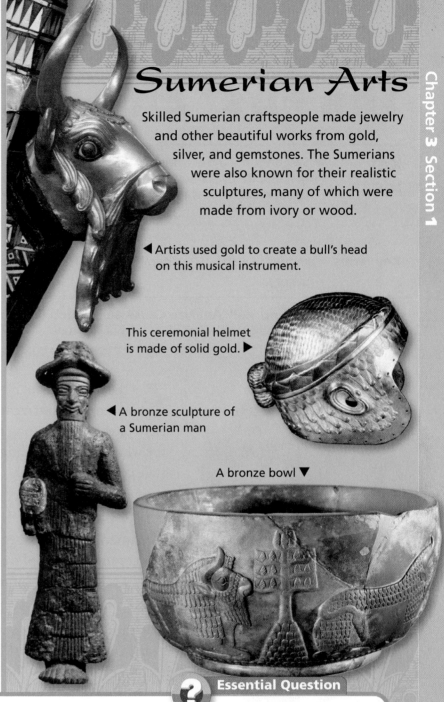

Sumerian Arts

Skilled Sumerian craftspeople made jewelry and other beautiful works from gold, silver, and gemstones. The Sumerians were also known for their realistic sculptures, many of which were made from ivory or wood.

◄ Artists used gold to create a bull's head on this musical instrument.

This ceremonial helmet is made of solid gold. ►

◄ A bronze sculpture of a Sumerian man

A bronze bowl ▼

Section 1 Assessment

Key Terms

1. What is polytheism?
2. What is a city-state?
3. What shape is used to create cuneiform?

Key Ideas

4. Which people held the most power in Sumer?
5. What is the area between the Tigris and Euphrates rivers called?
6. Name two advances that helped Sumerian civilization expand.

Think Critically

7. **Identify Evidence** How did the priests and kings of Sumer support one another?
8. **Draw Conclusions** How did irrigation affect Sumer?

? Essential Question

What are the consequences of technology?

9. How did technology help Sumerian civilization develop? Go to your Student Journal to record your answer.

The First Empires

Key Ideas

- Sargon formed the world's first empire by conquering the Sumerian city-states.

- The Babylonian emperor Hammurabi created an important legal code.

Key Terms • empire • ally • cultural trait • Hammurabi's Code • rule of law

 **Visual Glossary**

Reading Skill Analyze Cause and Effect Take notes using the graphic organizer in your journal.

▲ A copper bust of Akkadian ruler Sargon

As the independent city-states of Sumer grew in size, power, and wealth, they often came into conflict. For hundreds of years, the city-states fought among themselves. In time, strong rulers conquered the whole region, creating the world's first empires. An **empire** is a state containing several countries or territories.

The Conquest of Sumer

As Sumerian kings struggled for power, fighting between city-states was common. Years of frequent fighting made Sumerian city-states grow weaker. This eventually led to the conquest of Sumer.

Conflict in Sumer The fighting between the city-states of Umma and Lagash is one example of the widespread conflict in Sumer. For many years, Umma and Lagash and their allies fought to control a fertile region on their shared border. An **ally** is an independent state that works with other states to achieve a shared military or political goal.

Around 2450 B.C., armies from Umma and Lagash met in a major battle. Soldiers used bronze axes and long spears with sharp metal points. Thousands of troops died in the fighting before Lagash won the battle. To celebrate their victory, Lagash soldiers looted and burned Umma. They captured prisoners from Umma to be sold as slaves.

It took years for Umma to recover from the defeat. Around 2375 B.C., a powerful king of Umma finally defeated Lagash and several other Sumerian city-states. But his rule soon came to an end.

Sargon Builds an Empire While the Sumerian city-states struggled for power, a new society arose in Mesopotamia. The Akkadian people lived to the northwest of Sumer, but they were not related to Sumerians. Akkadians spoke a different language and had different customs.

During the 2300s B.C., an Akkadian man named Sargon became king of the Sumerian city-state of Kish. He changed the language used by the government to Akkadian. Under Sargon's rule, the Akkadian army conquered other Mesopotamian city-states. He placed loyal Akkadians in important government and religious positions. For example, he chose his daughter to be a high priestess in the city-state of Ur. These moves helped him solidify his power. Then Sargon united much of Mesopotamia under his rule, creating the world's first empire: the Akkadian empire.

Akkadian Culture The Akkadians and Sumerians shared some cultural traits. A **cultural trait** is an idea or way of doing things that is common in a certain culture. For example, the Akkadians and Sumerians had similar religious practices, and both societies used the cuneiform system of writing.

As Sargon's troops moved throughout the Fertile Crescent, they brought their cultural traits with them. Furthermore, Akkadians began to trade with people as far away as the Indus Valley in modern-day Pakistan. As a result, Akkadian and Sumerian ways of doing things spread throughout the region.

The Akkadian Empire Ends To control such a large empire, Sargon appointed local rulers. Each local ruler served as king of the land he oversaw. Sargon was able to control the Akkadian empire for more than 50 years.

A bronze mace, or club, covered with spikes ▼

War in Sumer

War was common in Sumer as rival city-states fought for power and territory. The background image shows a carving of soldiers made to celebrate the victory of Lagash over Umma around 2450 B.C. The ceremonial gold dagger at left was buried with a Sumerian queen around 2500 B.C.

Empires Rise and Fall

Over time, powerful rulers built mighty empires in the Fertile Crescent. But each empire eventually collapsed as invading peoples battled to control the region's rich city-states. This pattern of empires rising and falling continued over hundreds of years.

◄ Akkadian empire
This carving of an Akkadian military victory shows the king Naram-Sin, Sargon's grandson, standing on his defeated enemies. But the Akkadian empire soon collapsed.

Lagash ►
Sumerian city-states grew strong as the Akkadian empire fell apart. This statue shows Gudea, the king of Lagash, around 2100 B.C.

After Sargon's death in 2279 B.C., the Akkadian empire faced a growing number of rebellions and invasions. Within 100 years, the empire had collapsed. Warriors from the Zagros Mountains, east of the Tigris River, eventually took control of the region.

Around 2100 B.C., Sumer was united again, this time by Ur-Nammu, the ruler of Ur. As you read in Section 1, Ur-Nammu issued the world's first known law code. Ur prospered for about 100 years under Ur-Nammu and later rulers. Then, an uprising of rebels from the east managed to destroy Ur and capture its ruler. This ended Ur's rule over Sumer. Once again, the Sumerian city-states fought over power.

Reading Check Why did Sargon put Akkadians in important positions?

The Babylonian Empire

After the destruction of Ur, many groups invaded Sumer. One of them, the Amorites, came from northern Mesopotamia. The Amorites took control of several Sumerian cities, including Babylon (BAB uh lahn). At the time, Babylon was a small, unimportant city on the Euphrates River near present-day Baghdad, Iraq. But under a king named Hammurabi (hah muh RAH bee), Babylon became the center of a new Mesopotamian empire.

The Empire Forms Around 1792 B.C., Hammurabi became king of Babylon. For 30 years, he solidified his power and built up his army. Then he launched a series of attacks against other Mesopotamian city-states. Within a few years he had united southern Mesopotamia into what we now

Old Babylonian empire
After hundreds of years of struggle among Mesopotamian city-states, Hammurabi (at right) united much of the region under the control of Babylon (far right). He created a code of laws to govern his empire.

call the Old Babylonian (bab uh LOH nee uhn) empire, or Babylonia.

Hammurabi was an excellent military leader, and he was also a skilled ruler. Like Sargon, after Hammurabi built his empire he had to create a government strong enough to hold it together. He sent his own governors, tax collectors, and judges to rule distant cities. He spread out his well-trained troops over the empire. Hammurabi also oversaw a number of public building projects and encouraged the growth of trade.

Hammurabi's Code Today, Hammurabi is best remembered for his creation of **Hammurabi's Code,** a set of laws that governed life in the Babylonian empire. Many of these laws had existed since Sumerian times, but Hammurabi wanted to make sure everyone in Babylonia knew the laws they were expected to live by. In the introduction to his code, Hammurabi wrote that he wanted to

> 66 bring about the rule of righteousness in the land, to destroy the wicked and the evil-doers; so that the strong should not harm the weak—so that I should . . . further the well-being of mankind. 99
>
> —Hammurabi's Code

Hammurabi's Code includes nearly 300 laws. Some of these laws have to do with crimes such as robbery and murder. Hammurabi's Code sets out specific punishments for these crimes. For example, one law reads, "If a man put out the eye of another man, his eye shall be put out." Although some of the punishments may sound cruel by modern standards, they did encourage social order.

Hammurabi's Code:
An Eye for an Eye

The best surviving example of Hammurabi's Code is carved onto a piece of basalt stone that stands over seven feet tall. At the top, a carved image shows Hammurabi (standing) receiving the laws from Shamash, the god of the sun and of justice. Below this image is the text of 282 laws carved in cuneiform in the Akkadian language. Each law follows the same basic pattern, first describing an offense and then listing the punishment.

Think Critically How does Hammurabi's Code tell us about life in Babylonia?

If any man, without the knowledge of the owner of a garden, fell a tree in a garden he shall pay half a mina in money.

If a man put out the eye of another man, his eye shall be put out.

If any one hire oxen and kill them by bad treatment or blows, he shall compensate the owner, oxen for oxen.

If any one is committing a robbery and is caught, then he shall be put to death.

If he break another man's bone, his bone shall be broken.

If a builder build a house for some one, and does not construct it properly, and the house which he built fall in and kill its owner, then that builder shall be put to death.

122

Other laws in Hammurabi's Code dealt with private matters such as business contracts, taxes, marriage, and divorce. Many of these laws treated various groups of people differently. For example, the penalty for harming someone of the same rank in society was greater than harming someone of lower rank, such as a slave.

Hammurabi's Code was more detailed than the Ur-Nammu law code. In fact, it was the first major attempt to organize and write down all the laws that <u>governed</u> a society. It established and enforced the **rule of law,** or the idea that all members of a society—even the rich and powerful—must obey the law. This idea is a key part of modern democratic principles.

Daily Life in Babylonia Hammurabi's Code and other Babylonian writings give historians a great deal of information about life in Babylonia. Most people's lives revolved around agriculture. Food had to be grown and distributed. Irrigation canals had to be kept clear of silt. Wool had to be collected and woven into textiles, or cloth.

In the cities, some people bought and sold goods. They used new technologies to make tools, weapons, pottery, perfumes, and medicines. Babylonian artists were known for their stone and bronze sculptures. They also used gold and precious stones to make jewelry.

Legacy of Sumer Sumerian culture stayed alive in Babylonia, just as it had in the Akkadian empire under Sargon. But despite Hammurabi's efforts to build a strong government, the Babylonian empire eventually collapsed after his death in 1750 B.C. In the years that followed, the once-great civilization of Sumer slowly faded away.

Sumer's influence, however, did not disappear. The many peoples who had come into contact with Sumerian civilization learned from it. They brought ideas and customs from Sumer back to their homelands. In this way, Sumerian advances in technology, farming, writing, learning, and the law lived on.

Reading Check What was Hammurabi's Code?

myWorld Activity
An Eye for an Eye

govern, v., to control or strongly influence

Section 2 Assessment

Essential Question

Key Terms

1. What Sumerian cultural traits did Akkadians share?

2. Who created Mesopotamia's first empire?

3. What is the rule of law?

Key Ideas

4. How was the Akkadian empire formed?

5. Why was Hammurabi's Code important?

6. How is Hammurabi's Code similar to modern laws?

Think Critically

7. **Draw Conclusions** How did Sumerian culture influence later peoples?

8. **Compare and Contrast** How did Sargon and Hammurabi keep control of large empires?

What are the consequences of technology?

9. How do you think Sumerian technologies might have helped later empires form and expand? Go to your Student Journal to record your answer.

The Assyrian and Persian Empires

Key Ideas

- Assyrian armies conquered a vast empire that stretched from Mesopotamia southwest into Egypt.

- The Persian empire balanced local self-government with central power.

- The cultures of Mesopotamia created a rich artistic tradition.

Key Terms • cavalry • standing army • tribute • currency • stele

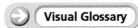 **Visual Glossary**

 Reading Skill Summarize Take notes using the graphic organizer in your journal.

This ivory carving of a woman's head was probably a gift given to an Assyrian king around 700 B.C. ▼

Invaders swept into Mesopotamia after Hammurabi's death in 1750 B.C. Hundreds of years passed before the Assyrians, a people of northern Mesopotamia, united the region again. In time, the Assyrian empire gave way to the powerful Persian empire.

The Assyrian and Neo-Babylonian Empires

Assyria (uh SEER ee uh) lay north of Babylon, along the Tigris River. Like much of Mesopotamia, it fell under the influence of Sumer. Later, Assyria was part of the Akkadian and Babylonian empires.

A Military State After Babylonia fell, the Assyrians fought against a steady stream of invaders. Some of those invaders conquered Assyria, but for long periods the Assyrians stayed free.

This frequent conflict led the Assyrians to become fierce warriors. Assyria's armies included some of the world's earliest **cavalry,** or soldiers who fight while riding horses. Assyrians used iron weapons and tools, which were far stronger than the bronze weapons and tools used by earlier peoples. Assyrians learned ironworking from the Hittites, a people who had invaded Mesopotamia from Asia Minor.

The Assyrians built up a strong military state by the mid-800s B.C. Within 200 years, they turned that state into an empire. By the mid-600s B.C., the Assyrian empire stretched north from the Persian Gulf across the entire Fertile Crescent and southwest into Egypt.

Governing the Empire Like Sargon and Hammurabi, Assyrian rulers found that controlling a large empire was difficult. The Assyrians divided the empire into about 70 smaller units of government called provinces. They assigned a governor to each province. Each governor reported directly to the Assyrian ruler. This helped the ruler keep control of distant lands.

An Assyrian ruler named Ashurbanipal made the city of Nineveh his capital. There, he built a library and filled it with cuneiform tablets. These tablets were mainly texts and letters from Sumer and Babylonia on subjects such as law, literature, mathematics, and science. Some 20,000 of these tablets survive today. They are an important source of knowledge about Mesopotamian history.

Babylon Restored After Ashurbanipal's death, civil war and enemy attacks weakened the Assyrian empire. In 604 B.C., Nebuchadnezzar (neb yuh kud NEZ ur) II became king of Babylon. He expanded his power as far west as Egypt. He also captured Jerusalem, destroyed the Jewish Temple, and exiled many Jews to Babylon. Nebuchadnezzar's empire is known as the Neo-Babylonian empire.

Nebuchadnezzar spent much money on large building projects in Babylon. He built great walls, gates, and temples. His most famous project was the Hanging Gardens of Babylon. The Hanging Gardens were elaborate gardens built on a series of stone terraces.

Reading Check How did the Assyrians organize their government?

An 1853 illustration shows what Nineveh may have looked like in Ashurbanipal's time.

125

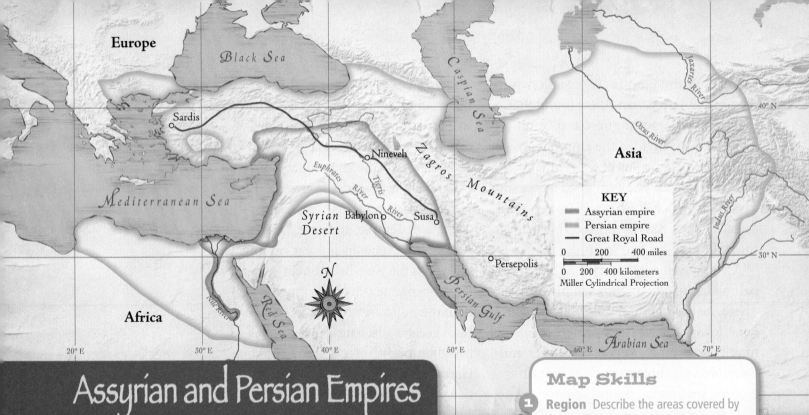

Europe

Black Sea

Sardis

Mediterranean Sea

Syrian Desert

Nineveh

Zagros Mountains

Euphrates River

Tigris River

Babylon   Susa

Caspian Sea

Asia

Oxus River

Jaxartes River

Indus River

Persepolis

Persian Gulf

Arabian Sea

Red Sea

Nile River

Africa

N

40° N
30° N
20° E   30° E   40° E   50° E   60° E   70° E

KEY
Assyrian empire
Persian empire
Great Royal Road

0   200   400 miles
0   200   400 kilometers
Miller Cylindrical Projection

Assyrian and Persian Empires

Assyria's strong armies built an empire across the Fertile Crescent. Later, the Persian empire became the largest the world had ever seen.

Map Skills

1 **Region** Describe the areas covered by the Assyrian and Persian empires.

2 **Interaction** How do you think the Great Royal Road helped connect people throughout the Persian empire?

Persia A gold drinking cup in the shape of a winged lion

Persia A sculpture of a bull's head from the palace of Darius the Great at Persepolis

Assyria A reconstructed gateway to the ancient city of Nineveh

Assyria The powerful Assyrian military used war chariots against their enemies in battle.

Assyria An ivory carving of an Assyrian warrior

Rise of the Persian Empire

Babylon's thick walls and strong gates were not able to keep out new conquerors. In 539 B.C., Babylon and the rest of Mesopotamia fell under the control of the powerful Persian empire. Within a few decades, the Persian empire became the largest the world had ever seen.

Cyrus the Great Persia formed to the east of Mesopotamia, in what is now Iran. For years, the Persians had been ruled by their neighbors to the north, a people called the Medes. The Medes controlled an empire stretching from what is now Iran northwest across the Zagros Mountains. But in 550 B.C., Cyrus the Great led the Persians to victory over the Medes. By conquering the Medes, the Persians won an empire.

Cyrus dreamed of building an even larger empire. He began in Asia Minor, in what is now Turkey, where he went to war with the kingdom of Lydia. He defeated Lydia's rich king, Croesus (KREE sus). Then Cyrus pushed south into Ionia, a region settled by Greeks. One by one, he conquered Ionia's city-states. Later, Cyrus expanded Persia's border in the east, toward India. At that point the Persian empire reached deep into Asia.

Persia's rapid growth was due to its large and highly skilled standing army. A **standing army** is a permanent army of professional soldiers. The core of this army was a force of 10,000 <u>elite</u> soldiers known as the "Immortals."

Conquest of Babylon As you read at the beginning of this chapter, Cyrus and the Persian army captured Babylon in 539 B.C.

Under his rule, Babylon grew into the wealthiest province of the Persian empire. In general, Cyrus treated the Babylonians and other conquered peoples well. He allowed them to keep their own customs and religions rather than forcing them to adopt Persian ways. For example, when Cyrus conquered Babylon he allowed the Jewish people to return to Jerusalem and rebuild their Temple.

Further Expansion Cyrus died in a battle in 530 B.C. But his son Cambyses (kam BY seez) II continued his father's dream of increasing the size of the Persian empire. First, Cambyses moved his troops into northeast Africa and conquered Egypt. From there, he traveled south to try to capture Kush.

The invasion of Kush was a failure. Cambyses marched the Persian army through the desert with little food or other supplies. Soon his men were forced to kill and eat their pack animals. Many Persians died of starvation before Cambyses ended the disastrous invasion.

After Cambyses died, Darius (duh RY us) took the throne by force. Under his rule, Persia grew even larger, and Darius became known as Darius the Great. He extended Persian rule east to the Indus Valley. In the west, the Persian army defeated Thrace, which was the first Persian victory in Europe. But later campaigns against Greece ended in Persia's defeat at the Battle of Marathon. You will read more about Darius and the wars between Persia and Greece in a later chapter.

elite, *adj.,* representing the best

Reading Check Which Persian leader conquered Babylon?

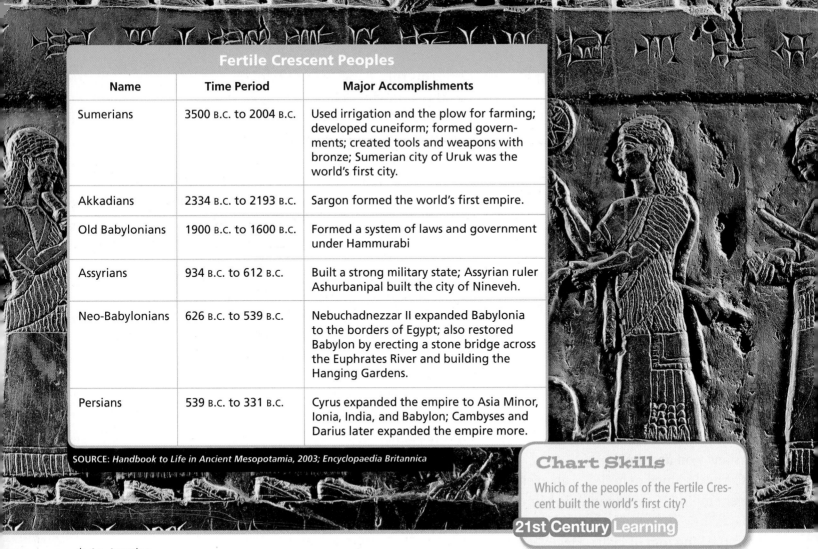

Fertile Crescent Peoples		
Name	**Time Period**	**Major Accomplishments**
Sumerians	3500 B.C. to 2004 B.C.	Used irrigation and the plow for farming; developed cuneiform; formed governments; created tools and weapons with bronze; Sumerian city of Uruk was the world's first city.
Akkadians	2334 B.C. to 2193 B.C.	Sargon formed the world's first empire.
Old Babylonians	1900 B.C. to 1600 B.C.	Formed a system of laws and government under Hammurabi
Assyrians	934 B.C. to 612 B.C.	Built a strong military state; Assyrian ruler Ashurbanipal built the city of Nineveh.
Neo-Babylonians	626 B.C. to 539 B.C.	Nebuchadnezzar II expanded Babylonia to the borders of Egypt; also restored Babylon by erecting a stone bridge across the Euphrates River and building the Hanging Gardens.
Persians	539 B.C. to 331 B.C.	Cyrus expanded the empire to Asia Minor, Ionia, India, and Babylon; Cambyses and Darius later expanded the empire more.

SOURCE: *Handbook to Life in Ancient Mesopotamia, 2003; Encyclopaedia Britannica*

Chart Skills

Which of the peoples of the Fertile Crescent built the world's first city?

21st Century Learning

▲ An Assyrian carving

reform, *v.*, to improve

Persia's Government and Religion

The vast Persian empire included peoples with many different cultures. Persian rulers had to find a way to unify the empire. They might have tried to force people to follow the same customs and obey the same laws. But the Persians took a different approach. Darius created a political structure that gave local people some control over their own government.

Local Self-Government Darius divided his empire into satrapies, or provinces, and chose a leader for each one. These leaders had a great deal of independence. Darius allowed them to keep their local laws and traditions and make many of their own decisions.

Central Control Darius also <u>reformed</u> the empire's central, or overall, government. First, he improved its finances. Conquered peoples had always sent tribute to the Persian ruler. **Tribute** is payment made to show loyalty to a stronger power. But the amount of tribute was often set by the ruler with no concern for what a region could really afford to pay. Darius created a fairer system in which each province paid according to its wealth.

Next, Darius created a common currency. **Currency** is money that is used as a medium of exchange, usually bills or coins. Darius introduced gold coins—printed with an image of himself—that would be accepted across the Persian empire as payment for goods. The currency helped unify the Persian economy by making it easier for distant provinces to trade with one another.

New Roads Darius used some of Persia's great wealth to build roads across the empire. Trade goods and tribute traveled on these roads. So did armies, government officials, and royal messengers.

The Persians set up postal stations along the 1,500-mile-long Great Royal Road. Messengers on horseback brought messages from one station to the next. It took three months for a message to travel from one end of the road to another. Still, the Persian system was the fastest communication system in the ancient world. The Greek historian Herodotus wrote

> 66 Nothing mortal travels so fast as these Persian messengers. . . . [T]hese men will not be hindered from accomplishing at their best speed the distance which they have to go, either by snow, or rain, or heat, or by the darkness of night. 99
> —from *The Persian Wars* by Herodotus, translated by George Rawlinson

Religion In ancient times, most people worshiped many gods. But beginning around 600 B.C., a Persian man known as Zoroaster (zoh roh AS tur) taught that there was one supreme god, Ahura Mazda, who has an evil opponent. Over time, Zoroaster's beliefs developed into the religion Zoroastrianism. Zoroastrianism eventually became the official religion of the Persian empire.

The sacred text of Zoroastrianism is the Avesta, which includes prayers, hymns, and other writings. Zoroastrianism's central belief is that the universe is in a state of struggle between the forces of good and evil. Zoroastrians believe that people have an important role to play in this conflict by working for good. They also believe in the existence of an afterlife. Historians believe that these teachings of Zoroastrianism later influenced Judaism, Christianity, and Islam.

Reading Check How did Darius change the Persian empire?

A carving of the Zoroastrian god Ahura Mazda ▼

The ancient Persian capital of Persepolis, in what is now Iran, includes many detailed carvings. Below, people bring tribute to Persian ruler Darius the Great. ▼

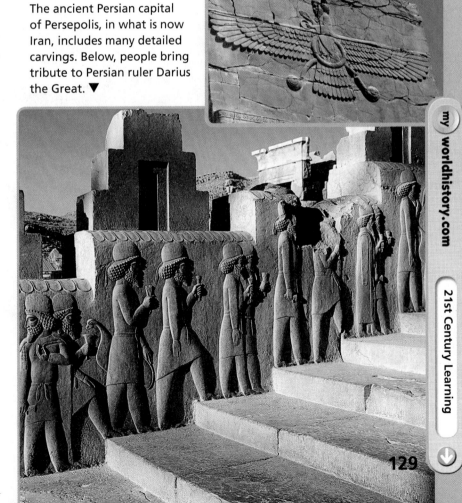

The Hanging Gardens of Babylon

According to ancient Greek writers, the wealthy city of Babylon had beautiful terraced gardens filled with exotic plants. An elaborate system of irrigation watered the plants. This illustration shows what the Hanging Gardens of Babylon may have looked like.

Culture Close-Up

Babylonians used a system of buckets and pulleys to bring water from wells up to the top level of the gardens.

Well

Canals brought water from the Euphrates River to the base of the terraces. Steps led from one terrace to the next.

Canals connected to the wells watered the plants on the terraces. Waterfalls allowed water to flow down to lower terraces.

Arts of Mesopotamia

Unlike art produced by earlier world cultures, the arts of ancient Mesopotamia give us a glimpse of daily life. They show people and activities from a number of Mesopotamian societies.

Seals The Sumerians often used carved stone seals to identify the owner of an object, especially before the development of cuneiform writing. A seal left the owner's personal mark—such as an animal or a geometric shape—stamped in clay. For example, a sack containing trade goods might be tied closed with a string. Then the owner would cover the knot with wet clay and stamp the clay with the seal.

Some seals were shaped like cylinders, or tubes. When rolled over wet clay, the seals left the image of an entire scene.

Sculptures Sumerians also carved statues of people that, for the first time in history, looked like real humans. Other peoples created a form of sculpture known as relief. In relief sculpture the scene sticks out from the surface of the base material.

One place a relief sculpture may be found is on a stele (STEE lee). A **stele** is a carved stone slab or pillar that stands on end. A famous example is the stele of Hammurabi, seen in Section 2. At the top of this stele is a relief showing Hammurabi and the Babylonian god Shamash. Below the relief is Hammurabi's Code, carved in cuneiform in the Akkadian language.

The Assyrians created large, colorful reliefs on the sides of buildings. They decorated structures such as Babylon's Ishtar Gate with colorful tiles and bricks that formed elaborate patterns and images of cattle, dragons, and other animals. Assyrians also decorated walls with cone-shaped pieces of baked clay painted in white, black, and red.

Reading Check **What was the purpose of a stone seal?**

myWorld Activity
Rebuilding Babylon

A lion made of colored bricks, from Babylon's Ishtar Gate. ▼

my worldhistory.com

Culture Close-Up

Section 3 Assessment

Key Terms

1. How did Darius change the Persian system of tribute?
2. What is a standing army?
3. What is cavalry?

Key Ideas

4. How did the Assyrians create an empire?
5. How did Darius unify the Persian empire?
6. Describe a relief.

Think Critically

7. **Summarize** How did Persian leaders treat conquered peoples?
8. **Analyze Cause and Effect** How might an effective system of communication benefit a nation?

Essential Question

What are the consequences of technology?

9. How did Assyrian, Babylonian, and Persian rulers use technology to expand and unite their empires? Go to your Student Journal to record your answer.

Section 4
The Phoenicians

Key Ideas

- The Phoenicians were ocean traders who spread their culture over a wide area.
- The most lasting contribution of the Phoenicians was the development of the alphabet.

Key Terms • import • export • navigation • colony • cultural diffusion • alphabet

Visual Glossary

Reading Skill Summarize Take notes using the graphic organizer in your journal.

A statue of a Phoenician god, about 700 B.C. ▼

The Mediterranean Sea forms the western boundary of the Fertile Crescent. The Phoenician (fuh NISH un) civilization began here, on a thin strip of land along the Mediterranean coast. Like Sumer, Phoenicia consisted of city-states. Although Phoenicia was small in size, it had an important influence on the region's history.

The Phoenician People
The Phoenicians were fearless sailors who guided ships full of trade goods through ocean waters. For hundreds of years, they dominated sea trade across the Mediterranean, just as the earlier Greek Minoan people had done.

Origins Phoenician society developed from the earlier Canaanites (KAY nun ites). The Canaanites were a people who lived in parts of what are now Israel, Jordan, Lebanon, and Syria. Nearby Egypt had a strong influence on Canaan. In fact, Egypt controlled parts of Canaan off and on for many years beginning around 1500 B.C.

Egyptian rule ended around 1150 B.C., and Phoenician society began to emerge. The independent Phoenician city-states soon prospered. In general, the rulers of Phoenician city-states were priest-kings. But each priest-king shared government power with leading merchant families and a citizen assembly.

Farming and Manufacturing Geography greatly influenced Phoenicia's development. The Lebanon Mountains formed Phoenicia's eastern border. These heavily-forested mountains sloped down close to the Mediterranean coast, leaving little flat land for farming.

Phoenicians manufactured a number of goods. Weavers created cloth that they colored with a rare purple dye made from tiny sea snails. They sold this purple cloth for high prices. Skilled Phoenician craftsworkers made pottery and glass and metal objects. They also used trees to make wood furniture and other items.

Phoenician Traders Because Phoenicia had few natural resources of its own, the Phoenicians traded with other cultures for resources and goods. Phoenician traders brought back many imports. An **import** is a good or service sold within a country that is produced in another country. Most Phoenician imports were raw materials, including gold, silver, tin, copper, iron, ivory, and precious stones.

Phoenician craftsworkers used the raw materials they imported to make many different items, such as bronze and silver bowls, iron tools and weapons, and gold jewelry. Traders shipped these goods—as well as pine and cedar logs, wine, olive oil, salt, fish, and other goods—as exports to ports across the Mediterranean. An **export** is a good or service produced within a country and sold outside the country's borders.

Reading Check What goods and materials did the Phoenicians trade?

Phoenician craftsworkers made beautiful glass vases. ▼

Phoenician Trade Routes

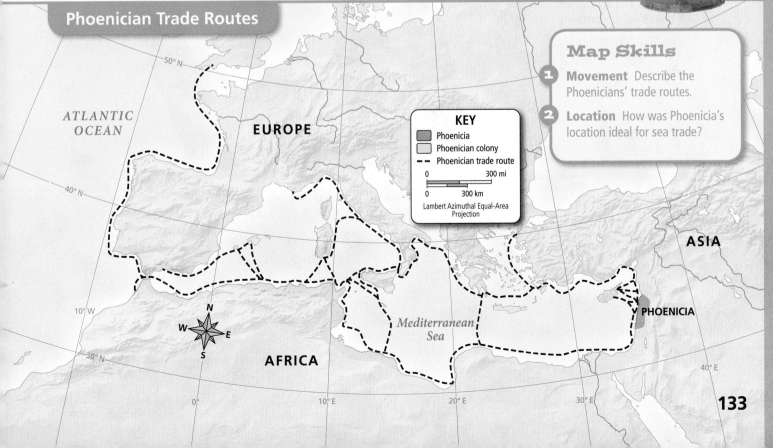

KEY
- Phoenicia
- Phoenician colony
- - - Phoenician trade route

0 ___ 300 mi
0 ___ 300 km
Lambert Azimuthal Equal-Area Projection

Map Skills

1. **Movement** Describe the Phoenicians' trade routes.

2. **Location** How was Phoenicia's location ideal for sea trade?

ATLANTIC OCEAN

EUROPE

ASIA

Mediterranean Sea

AFRICA

PHOENICIA

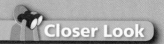

A PHOENICIAN TRADE SHIP

Phoenician sailors steered ships full of trade goods from western Asia throughout the Mediterranean region. Some Phoenicians traveled into the Atlantic and sailed north along the European coast, or south to West Africa. Their ships varied in size but could be as much as 60 feet long.

THINK CRITICALLY Why did many people in Asia and the Mediterranean region come to depend on the Phoenicians for trade?

Phoenician ships could be powered by a sail or by rowers using oars.

Phoenician sailors were skilled navigators with great knowledge of wind and ocean patterns.

Pine and cedar wood, purple cloth, and fish were common trade goods.

Phoenicians shipped wine in large ceramic vases called *amphoras*.

Phoenicians and the Sea

Phoenicia's location was ideal for trade. It lay on the western edge of Asia, within sailing distance of Europe and Africa. Several overland trade routes from the east ended in Phoenicia. As a result, many peoples came to depend on the Phoenicians to ship their trade goods across the Mediterranean Sea.

Navigation Because of Phoenicia's location between the Mediterranean and the Lebanon Mountains, Phoenicians turned to the sea to trade. They became experts at **navigation,** or the art of steering a ship from place to place. Phoenician sailors developed a thorough knowledge of wind patterns and ocean currents.

Phoenician sailors are believed to be the first people to use the North Star to guide their voyages. In the Northern Hemisphere, the North Star seems to remain still while other stars appear to move across the sky. Phoenician sailors used the North Star's position to calculate their location.

Exploring Unknown Waters From Phoenicia, the Phoenicians sailed south and west past Egypt and along the North African coast. Others traveled north and west past the Balkan and Italian peninsulas. They explored the Mediterranean islands of Sicily and Sardinia. In time, the Phoenicians reached Iberia, at the western end of the Mediterranean Sea. Today this land includes Spain and Portugal.

After passing the southern tip of Iberia, Phoenician sailors left the Mediterranean for the Atlantic Ocean. Some sailed north along the Iberian coast, and a few traveled all the way to Britain. Others headed south to West Africa.

Phoenician sailors showed great courage by sailing far into unknown waters. But why did they keep traveling ever farther from home? Some historians think that the Phoenicians were driven to find precious metals. Indeed, the Phoenicians traded for silver in Iberia and gold in West Africa. An ancient Greek historian described how Phoenicians <u>profited</u> from the silver trade:

> 66 Now the natives were ignorant of the use of the silver, and the Phoenicians . . . purchased the silver in exchange for other [goods] of little if any worth. And this was the reason why the Phoenicians, as they transported this silver to Greece and Asia and to all other peoples, acquired great wealth. 99
>
> —Diodorus Siculus, *Library of History*

profit, *v.*, to make a gain

Colonies and City-States Phoenician sailors found many sheltered harbors along the Mediterranean coast. At first these places served only as trading stations. There, ships stopped to pick up water, food, and other supplies.

Areas with fertile land or other resources attracted Phoenician farmers and other settlers. Those settlements grew into colonies. A **colony** is an area ruled by a distant country. When Phoenicia came under attack by Assyrians and others starting in the 800s B.C., many Phoenicians left Phoenicia. They migrated to their colonies for safety.

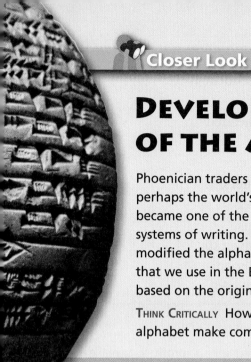

DEVELOPMENT OF THE ALPHABET

Phoenician traders developed what is perhaps the world's first alphabet. It quickly became one of the world's most widely used systems of writing. Over time, other peoples modified the alphabet. Today, the 26 letters that we use in the English language are based on the original Phoenician alphabet.

THINK CRITICALLY How would a widely used alphabet make communication easier?

▲ Phoenician writing evolved from cuneiform (shown at far left).

Phoenician Alphabet Characters

✝	٩	٦	△	٦	Y	ㄥ
*	B	G	D	H	W	Z
ᚻ	⊕	٦	⅄	ㄥ	ᛘ	ㄚ
H	T	Y	K	L	M	N
‡	O	٦	ᚹ	φ	٩	W	✝
S	*	P	S	Q	R	SH	T

* No equivalent letter in English
SOURCE: BBC Online

A few Phoenician colonies developed into wealthy city-states. One was Carthage, on the North African coast. Carthage eventually became rich and powerful, setting up its own colonies and fighting three wars against the powerful Romans. In the last of these wars, the Romans destroyed Carthage. Over time, the Roman empire took over all of the Phoenician city-states and colonies.

Reading Check Why was Phoenicia's location perfect for trade?

Legacy of the Phoenicians

Although Phoenicia did not survive, some of its achievements did last. Greece and Rome absorbed key elements of Phoenician culture in a process known as cultural diffusion. **Cultural diffusion** is the spreading of cultural traits from one region to another. The Phoenicians' legacy included the spread of its culture and a new way of writing.

Spread of Culture Through trade, the Phoenicians linked the diverse peoples and cultures around the Mediterranean region and beyond. In the process, Phoenicians helped ideas spread. They passed parts of their culture on to the Greeks. For example, the Greeks used the Phoenician standard of weights and measures. Greek culture later spread throughout the entire Mediterranean region, and its influence continues today.

The Alphabet The Greeks also adopted the Phoenician way of writing. Before the Phoenicians, the main writing system in the ancient Near East was cuneiform. In cuneiform, symbols represent syllables or whole words. In order to write, a person had to know hundreds of symbols.

The Phoenicians developed an alphabet. An **alphabet** is a small set of letters or symbols, each of which stands for a single sound. The Phoenician alphabet had 22 symbols. Each symbol stood for a

The Greeks modified the Phoenician alphabet, adding vowels (left). Later, the Roman alphabet made even more changes (below).

◀ The letters we use today in English are based on the Phoenician alphabet.

consonant sound. Now, instead of having to memorize hundreds of different symbols, a person only had to know 22 symbols in order to write. This alphabet made writing much easier.

People who traded with the Phoenicians learned their alphabet in order to communicate with them. By 750 B.C., the Greeks had begun using the Phoenician alphabet. Around 500 B.C., the Greeks added letters to represent vowels. They also gave the letters names. The word *alphabet* comes from the first two letters in the Greek alphabet—alpha and beta.

Around 100 B.C., the Romans adopted the Greek alphabet. The Romans changed some letters. The result was an alphabet that looks much like ours today.

Reading Check What was the cultural impact of the Phoenicians?

myWorld Activity
A Sound Alphabet

Section 4 Assessment

Key Terms

1. How did the Phoenicians use imports?

2. Where does the word alphabet come from?

3. What is cultural diffusion?

Key Ideas

4. How did geography affect the development of Phoenician civilization?

5. How did the Phoenicians influence later peoples?

6. How did the Phoenicians trade with other peoples?

Think Critically

7. **Draw Inferences** How would the fact that the North Star appears to remain still make ocean navigation easier?

8. **Synthesize** Why might Egyptians be eager to buy logs from Phoenicia?

Essential Question

What are the consequences of technology?

9. How did the Phoenician economy depend on technology? Go to your Student Journal to record your answer.

Chapter Assessment

Key Terms and Ideas

1. **Summarize** Why is **Mesopotamia** an appropriate name for the place where the civilizations of the Fertile Crescent first began?

2. **Discuss** How did **Hammurabi's Code** establish the **rule of law**?

3. **Describe** What is a **stele**?

4. **Recall** Name three Phoenician **imports** and three Phoenician **exports.**

5. **Describe** What is **cuneiform**?

6. **Summarize** How did Sargon create the Akkadian empire?

7. **Explain** Why was Persia's **standing army** an important factor in Persia's rapid growth?

Think Critically

8. **Draw Inferences** Why do you think the Phoenicians were better than other civilizations at ocean navigation and trade?

9. **Sequence** Put the following peoples in chronological order, beginning with the earliest: Akkadians, Assyrians, Sumerians, and Persians.

10. **Draw Conclusions** Why did the Phoenician alphabet make writing easier and more efficient than cuneiform?

11. **Core Concepts: Historical Sources** Why do archaeologists and historians try to find artifacts and writings from ancient civilizations?

Analyze Visuals

12. Which civilization shown on the map covered the largest area?

13. Compare and contrast the size and location of the Babylonian empire and Phoenicia.

14. How do you think the location of rivers in the Fertile Crescent influenced the founding and growth of Sumer?

15. How did Phoenicia differ from the other civilizations shown on this map?

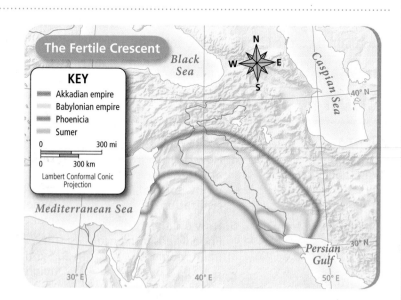

The Fertile Crescent

KEY
- Akkadian empire
- Babylonian empire
- Phoenicia
- Sumer

0   300 mi
0   300 km
Lambert Conformal Conic Projection

Black Sea

Caspian Sea

Mediterranean Sea

Persian Gulf

Essential Question
myWorld Chapter Activity

Mesopotamian Trade and Transport Follow your teacher's instructions to investigate and describe ancient Mesopotamian trade in the role of either a merchant or journalist. Work with your group to collect and organize information about trade and transportation. Then write and present the script for a documentary film about a Mesopotamian marketplace.

21st Century Learning
Search for Information on the Internet

On the Internet, find and print out a political outline map showing Southwest Asia. Fill in the names of the modern countries. Then find historical maps showing Sumer, Akkadia, Babylon, Assyria, and Persia. On your outline map, use a different color or pattern to mark the location of each ancient civilization. Compare maps with a partner and explain any differences you notice.

Document-Based Questions

Success Tracker™ Online at myworldhistory.com

Use your knowledge of the Fertile Crescent and Documents A and B to answer Questions 1–3.

Document A

" Of all the powers in Asia, the kingdom of Cyrus showed itself to be the greatest and most glorious. On the east it was bounded by the Red Sea, on the north by the Euxine, on the west by Cyprus and Egypt, and on the south by Ethiopia. And yet the whole of this enormous empire was governed by the mind and will of a single man, Cyrus: his subjects he cared for and cherished as a father might care for his children, and they who came beneath his rule reverenced him like a father."

—Xenophon, *Cyropaedia: The Education of Cyrus*, about 370 B.C.

Document B

" [T]hen [the gods] Anu and Bel called by name me, Hammurabi, the exalted prince, who feared God, to bring about the rule of righteousness in the land, to destroy the wicked and the evil-doers; so that the strong should not harm the weak; . . . to further the well-being of mankind."

—Introduction to Hammurabi's Code, about 1780 B.C.

1. In Document A, what does the author suggest about Cyrus's relationship with the peoples he conquered?

   A He ignored them and concentrated only on people who lived in his capital city.

   B He was a cruel ruler.

   C He had little power over their lives.

   D He cared for the conquered peoples and ruled them kindly.

2. According to Document B, what are Hammurabi's main reasons for publishing his code of laws?

   A improve trade

   B end wicked behavior and protect the weak

   C expand Babylonian territory

   D describe the history of Babylon

3. **Writing Task** Did Cyrus and Hammurabi have similar beliefs about a ruler's responsibility to the people? Explain your answer in a short paragraph.

my worldhistory.com

Self-Test

Chapter 4

Ancient Egypt and Nubia

Essential Question

How much does geography affect people's lives?

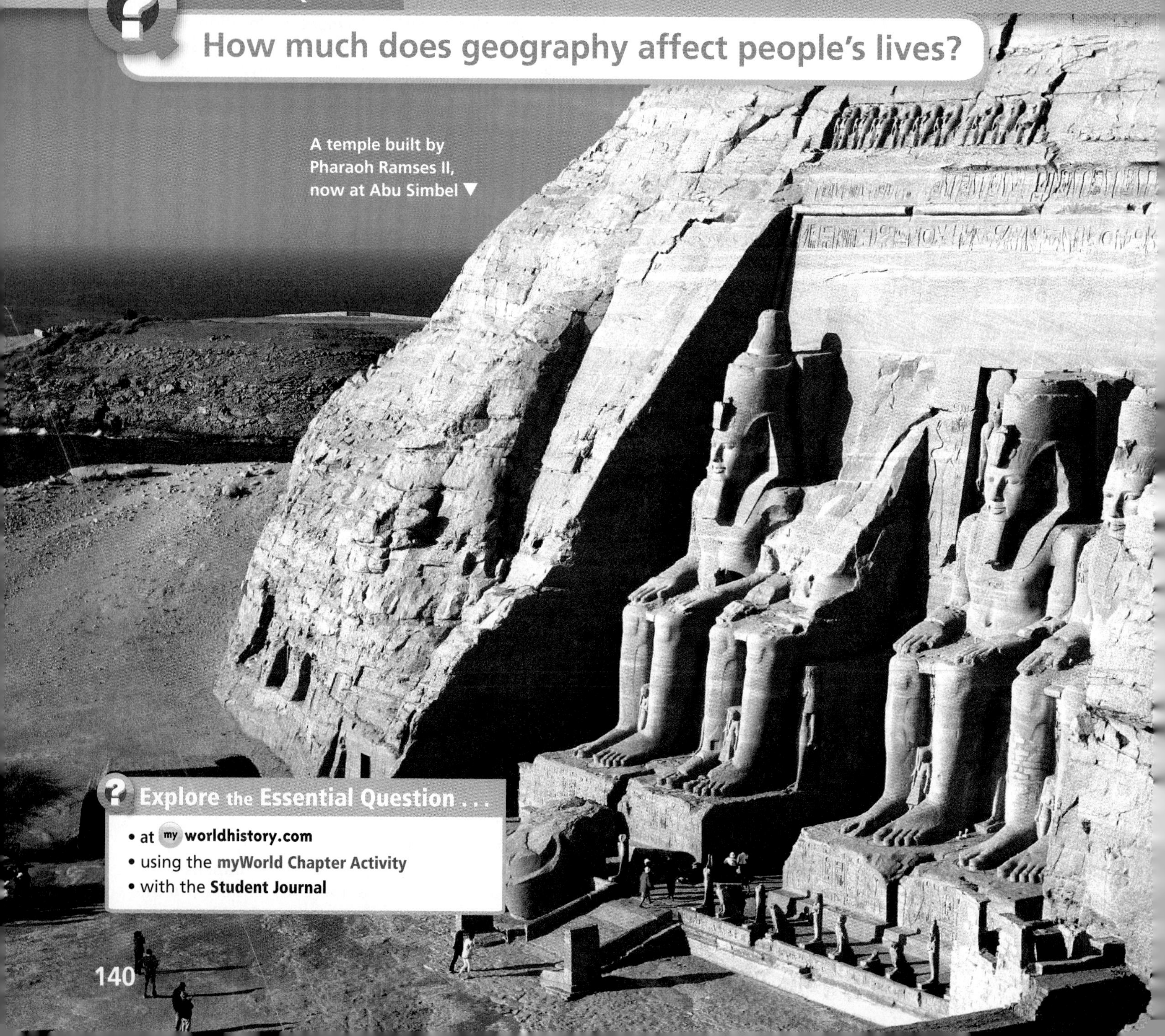

A temple built by Pharaoh Ramses II, now at Abu Simbel ▼

Explore the Essential Question . . .

- at my worldhistory.com
- using the **myWorld Chapter Activity**
- with the **Student Journal**

The Rise and Fall of Ancient Egypt

3100 B.C. Egypt's first pharaoh unites Upper and Lower Egypt.

1475 B.C. Hatshepsut becomes pharaoh.

343 B.C. Persian invaders defeat the last Egyptian pharaoh.

4000 B.C. **3000** B.C. **2000** B.C. **1000** B.C. **1** B.C.

2450 B.C. The Great Pyramid of Giza is built.

730 B.C. A Nubian pharaoh conquers Egypt.

HATSHEPSUT:
Taking Power With Style

This is a fictionalized account of events in the life of Hatshepsut, a real Egyptian pharaoh.

More than 3,000 years ago, when she was about 30 years old, Hatshepsut (haht SHEP soot) had herself crowned king, or pharaoh, of Egypt in a lavish ceremony.

She had no choice about her male title. There wasn't even a word in ancient Egyptian for a female pharaoh, although women had occasionally ruled as pharaohs before.

Because few women had ruled Egypt before her, she had few role models. But once she put on the heavy red-and-gold double crown of the two Egypts—Upper and Lower Egypt—she knew just what to do. She had learned from watching her three brothers, all dead now, train to be pharaohs.

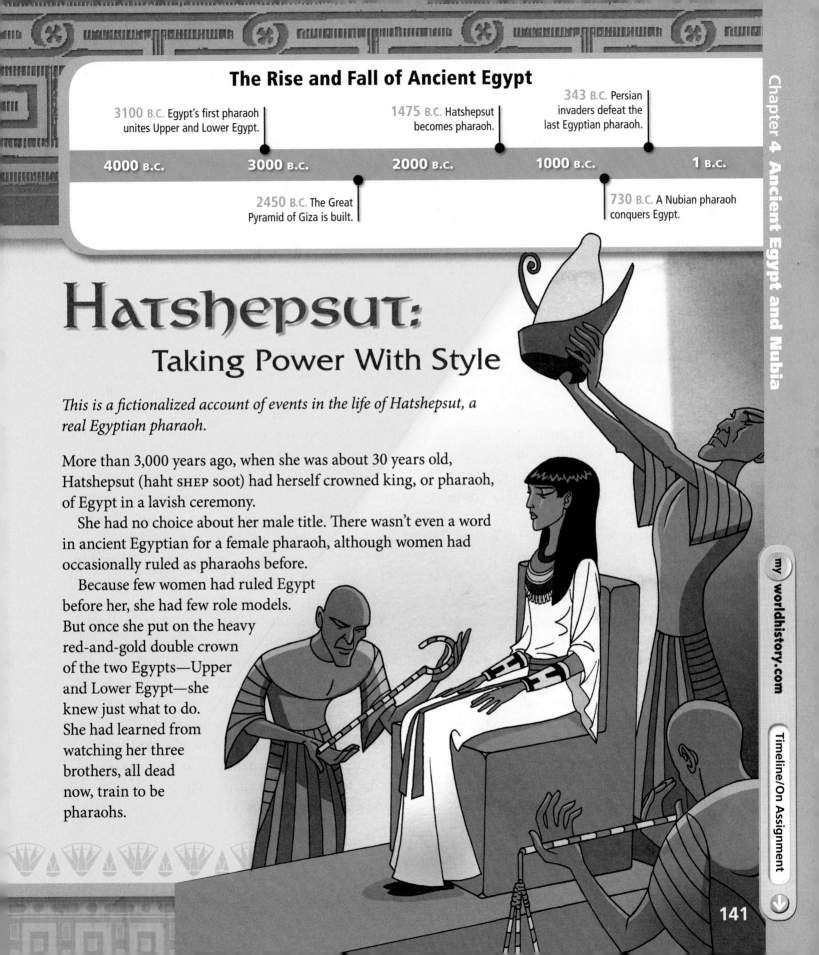

Hatshepsut and her scribe think up grand statements praising her. She will have these statements carved on monuments around Egypt.

Hatshepsut sees herself as Sekhmet, the lion-headed goddess of war.

She quickly called her favorite advisor, Senenmut, a famous scribe, her good friend, and her daughter's tutor. Egyptians believed that the pharaohs were the representatives of Egyptian gods, so she needed to create a myth to explain her link to the gods.

She had Senenmut write statements supposedly from the god Amon for her many monuments to herself: "Welcome my sweet daughter, my favorite, the King of Upper and Lower Egypt, Maatkare, Hatshepsut. Thou art the pharaoh, taking possession of the Two Lands."

Hatshepsut also linked herself to goddesses. This was something a male pharaoh couldn't have done. She liked the lioness image of Sekhmet, the goddess of war.

She stopped wearing the long, narrow dresses that restricted women's movement, and in public always wore the traditional king's outfit of a skirt and broad collar. Like male pharaohs, she wore a fake beard, woven with gold thread, attached with a chin strap. She still wore jewelry, makeup, and exotic perfumes, but so did all wealthy Egyptians, male and female.

Life in the desert was difficult and fragile. Her most important job, something only a pharaoh

could do, was to preserve *ma'at* (mah AHT)—the Egyptian sense of order in the universe, established by the gods. To avoid chaos, Hatshepsut performed all the necessary rituals. She prayed for the Nile River, Egypt's source of life-giving water, to flood its banks every year to supply the water needed for crops. She appeared on every major holiday, riding in a golden chariot drawn by a team of horses.

With a knack for self-promotion, she carved praise of herself everywhere, sometimes referring to herself as a man, sometimes as a woman: "To look upon her was more beautiful than anything. . . . Her fragrance was like a divine breath . . . her skin is made of gold, it shines like the stars." Hatshepsut claimed credit, like pharaohs before her, for actions taken by others. She built gigantic obelisks, tipped with gold, in her own honor.

She personally chose officials to handle the big jobs in her government, and rewarded them richly with silver and gold—unless they proved disloyal. Then they might disappear suddenly.

She kept Egypt strong and avoided costly wars. Instead, as a more efficient way to stay in power, she set out to make Egypt richer than ever. Already she had her eye on precious frankincense and myrrh

Hatshepsut appears in public, driven in a chariot, wearing the beard and collar of a male pharaoh.

Hatshepsut has a disloyal scribe taken away, never to be seen again.

trees in other countries. She had them transplanted to Egypt to provide a source of heavenly incense and perfumes. She took up an ambitious building program, including a magnificent temple on the west bank of the Nile at Luxor.

She promoted trade with other countries. She exchanged Egypt's rich grain supplies for products Egypt couldn't produce, such as wood and precious gems and metals.

Right after she became pharaoh, she also began detailed preparations for her own burial, as other pharaohs had. She planned a most stylish tomb, full of riches, amid the sheer cliffs of the Valley of the Kings. There she would become one with the gods.

Death wouldn't come for another 20 or so years, but it was not going to take this powerful, practical woman by surprise.

What connections do you see in this story between geography and the lives of ancient Egyptians? As you read the chapter ahead, think about what Hatshepsut's story tells you about life in ancient Egypt.

 myStory Video

Join Hatshepsut as she takes charge of Egypt.

Hatshepsut views her tomb under construction.

Egypt Under the Pharaohs

Key Ideas
- Egypt's unique geography helped shape its civilization and farming methods.
- Pharaohs belonging to dynasties ruled Egypt and were seen as gods.
- Egyptians worshiped many gods.

Key Terms • cataract • delta • artisan • pharaoh • dynasty • bureaucracy • mummy

Visual Glossary

Reading Skill Identify Main Ideas and Details Take notes using the graphic organizer in your journal.

Coffin mask of Pharaoh Tutankhamen ▼

Like the Fertile Crescent, Egypt was home to one of the world's first great civilizations. As in the Fertile Crescent, Egypt's civilization developed in a river valley with rich soil. However, Egypt's geography and culture differed in many ways from those of the Fertile Crescent.

The Nile River Valley

The ancient Egyptians treasured the Nile River. They knew that without the Nile, their land would be nothing but a sun-baked desert of bright blue skies and dry sand.

The World's Longest River The Nile is the world's longest river. It begins in East Africa and flows about 3,500 miles north to the Mediterranean Sea.

This great river has two main sources—the White Nile and the Blue Nile. The White Nile flows from Lake Victoria. The Blue Nile rushes down from the highlands of present-day Ethiopia. The two rivers meet in present-day Sudan. In ancient times, northern Sudan was known as Nubia, or Kush.

In Nubia and Egypt, the Nile flows through the Sahara, a vast desert that stretches across most of northern Africa. Before reaching Egypt, the river in ancient times roared through six **cataracts,** or groups of rocky rapids. The rocky cataracts made it impossible for people to travel by ship upstream from Egypt.

Upper and Lower Egypt Below the cataracts, the Nile flows through a narrow valley lined with cliffs. This region is known as Upper Egypt because it is upstream from the Mediterranean Sea.

The river carries silt—fine mineral particles that can form fertile soil—from its sources in East Africa. Near the end of its journey, the Nile slows down and fans out into many streams and marshy areas. As it slows, the river drops its silt. Over thousands of years, this silt has built up to form a large river delta. A **delta** is an area of sediment—soil or minerals carried by water—deposited at the mouth of a river. The Nile delta forms the region known as Lower Egypt.

Floods and the Black Land A narrow strip of fertile soil lines both banks of the Nile and covers its delta. This rich, dark soil was so important to the Egyptians that they called their country *Kemet*, which means "the Black Land."

The yearly flooding of the Nile created the Black Land. Each summer, heavy rainfall in East Africa poured into the Nile's sources. Flood waters surged through Egypt. When the flood waters drained away, they left behind a layer of fresh soil.

However, the Nile floods were unpredictable. If too much water came, the floods could be a natural disaster that swept away soil. If too little water came,

Egypt could suffer a drought, or a shortage of water. Droughts could bring hunger by causing crops to fail.

The Red Land On either side of the Black Land lay vast deserts. Egyptians called these deserts "the Red Land." Unlike the Black Land, the Red Land was a deadly place of hot, burning sands.

Reading Check What are the sources of the Nile River?

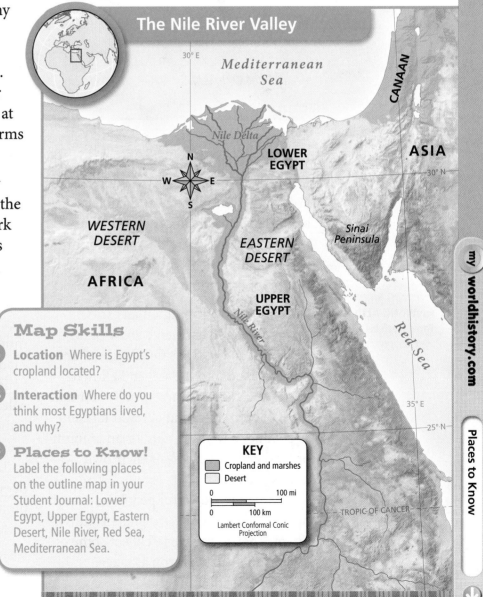

The Nile River Valley

Mediterranean Sea

30° E

Nile Delta

LOWER EGYPT

CANAAN

ASIA

30° N

WESTERN DESERT

AFRICA

EASTERN DESERT

Sinai Peninsula

UPPER EGYPT

Nile River

Red Sea

35° E

25° N

TROPIC OF CANCER

Map Skills

1. **Location** Where is Egypt's cropland located?

2. **Interaction** Where do you think most Egyptians lived, and why?

3. **Places to Know!** Label the following places on the outline map in your Student Journal: Lower Egypt, Upper Egypt, Eastern Desert, Nile River, Red Sea, Mediterranean Sea.

KEY

Cropland and marshes

Desert

0   100 mi

0   100 km

Lambert Conformal Conic Projection

Nile Valley croplands during the yearly flood

The same croplands after the flood

Civilization Develops

More than 7,000 years ago, people began growing grains in the fertile soil left behind by the Nile floods. Over time, Egypt's farmers were able to grow more and more food. This food supported a growing population.

myWorld Activity
Farm Fresh Lyrics

Growing a Surplus Egyptian farmers learned to build earthen walls around fields to trap the Nile's flood waters. The water soaked into the soil and allowed grains such as wheat to grow. This simple form of crop irrigation allowed farmers to produce a food surplus, or an amount of food greater than their their own family's needs.

Meanwhile, powerful people and families gained control over regions within Egypt. They were able to collect some of the farmers' surplus crop as taxes.

The Birth of Cities These local rulers used this surplus to buy rich cloth, jewelry, and luxury goods. These were supplied by merchants and **artisans,** or skilled workers who practice a handicraft.

Farmers' production of a surplus supported these artisans. Some became full-time artisans, such as weavers or potters. Skilled artisans' products were much more advanced than similar products made by farmers. Artisans and merchants began to settle around the homes of local rulers. In time, these settlements grew into cities.

Egypt's cities brought together wealthy and skilled people. They became centers of culture and power. Skilled architects built impressive buildings. Artists created great works of art to decorate them.

Reading Check Why could some Egyptians take jobs other than farming?

146

The Kingdoms of Egypt

During the 3000s B.C., two kingdoms developed in Egypt. The kings of Upper Egypt wore white crowns. The kings of Lower Egypt wore red crowns.

Uniting Egypt Legends say that Narmer united the two kingdoms in about 3000 B.C. This made him the first **pharaoh,** or king, of a united Egypt. He wore a double crown of red and white and founded Egypt's earliest dynasty. A **dynasty** is a ruling family.

Normally, control passed between members of a dynasty. Sometimes, however, a new dynasty gained power. Historians divide Egypt's history into periods based on kingdoms and dynasties.

The Old and Middle Kingdoms
Historians call the period from about 2686 B.C. to 2125 B.C. the Old Kingdom. Like later kingdoms, the Old Kingdom was a period of prosperity, political strength, and cultural achievement.

After a period of civil wars, the Middle Kingdom began. It lasted from about 2055 B.C. to 1650 B.C. Pharaohs of the Middle Kingdom dealt with one of Egypt's major <u>environmental</u> challenges—the Nile floods. They built a system of canals that could drain dangerous flood waters and irrigate new farmland.

High Point and Decline The New Kingdom followed more civil wars and invasions. The New Kingdom lasted from about 1550 B.C. to 1070 B.C. New Kingdom pharaohs conquered lands in Asia and Africa. This was the high point of ancient Egyptian power and prosperity.

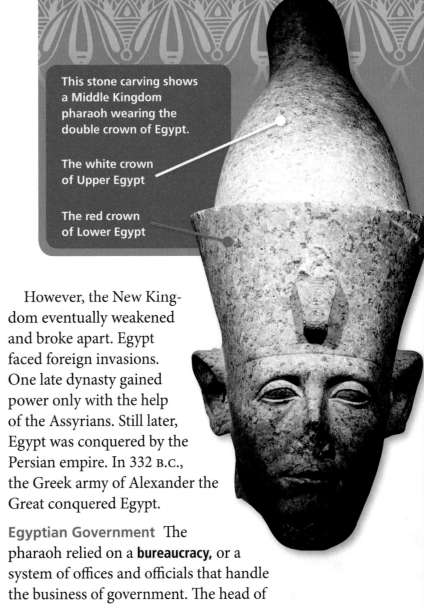

This stone carving shows a Middle Kingdom pharaoh wearing the double crown of Egypt.

The white crown of Upper Egypt

The red crown of Lower Egypt

However, the New Kingdom eventually weakened and broke apart. Egypt faced foreign invasions. One late dynasty gained power only with the help of the Assyrians. Still later, Egypt was conquered by the Persian empire. In 332 B.C., the Greek army of Alexander the Great conquered Egypt.

Egyptian Government The pharaoh relied on a **bureaucracy,** or a system of offices and officials that handle the business of government. The head of Egypt's bureaucracy was an official called the vizier. The bureaucracy collected taxes from farmers. Farmers paid these taxes mainly in the form of surplus crops.

The bureaucracy took some of this surplus for itself. It distributed the rest to priests, to the pharaoh, and to artisans and merchants who worked for the pharaoh. Egypt's bureaucracy and system of taxation were a model for later governments, including those of today.

Reading Check Which of Egypt's kingdoms was the most powerful?

environmental, *adj.,* having to do with natural surroundings

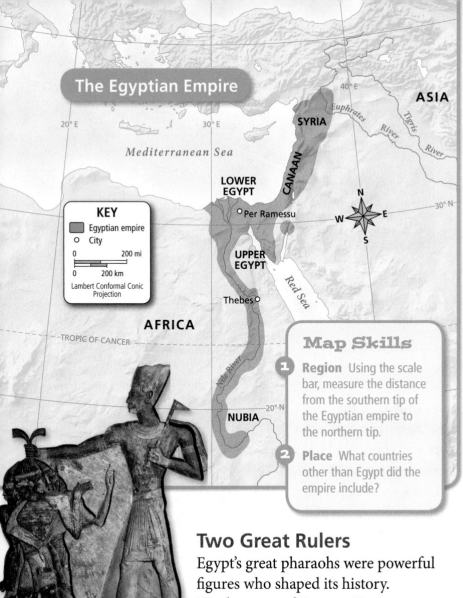

The Egyptian Empire

KEY

▢ Egyptian empire
○ City

0   200 mi

0   200 km

Lambert Conformal Conic Projection

SYRIA

CANAAN

LOWER EGYPT

○ Per Ramessu

UPPER EGYPT

Thebes ○

Red Sea

AFRICA

TROPIC OF CANCER

NUBIA

Nile River

Euphrates River

Tigris River

ASIA

Mediterranean Sea

40° E

20° E   30° E

30° N

20° N

Map Skills

1 **Region** Using the scale bar, measure the distance from the southern tip of the Egyptian empire to the northern tip.

2 **Place** What countries other than Egypt did the empire include?

▲ Pharaoh Ramses II defeating Egypt's enemies

Two Great Rulers

Egypt's great pharaohs were powerful figures who shaped its history. Hatshepsut and Ramses II were two famous New Kingdom pharaohs.

Hatshepsut In the story at the beginning of this chapter, you learned about Hatshepsut, one of the few women to rule Egypt. She was the daughter of one pharaoh and the wife of another. When her husband died, he left a son who was too young to rule. So Hatshepsut decided to make herself Egypt's new pharaoh.

Some Egyptians did not want to bow to a woman. To gain their support, Hatshepsut carried out all of the rituals expected of a king. Her statues showed her dressed as a king. She even wore the false beard that was a symbol of the pharaoh's power. Although she was a woman, most Egyptians came to accept her rule:

> 66 [T]he god's wife Hatshepsut executed the affairs of the Two Lands according to her counsels. Egypt worked for her, head bowed . . . 99
>
> —From "The 18th Dynasty Before the Amarna Period," by Betsy M. Bryan, in *The Oxford History of Ancient Egypt*

Hatshepsut's rule was peaceful. Hatshepsut built Egypt's wealth and power through trade. She sent traders by sea to a land called Punt in East Africa. They returned with precious wood, ivory, gold, and perfumes. Hatshepsut recorded the story of their journey on the stone walls of an enormous temple that she built.

Ramses II Ramses II, who ruled about 200 years after Hatshepsut, was a different kind of pharaoh. What Hatshepsut had tried to do through trade, Ramses chose to do through war. He spent the first half of his time as pharaoh fighting in Canaan and Syria, in the Fertile Crescent.

In 1275 B.C., Ramses II led his army against the powerful Hittites. The two armies fought in a place called Kadesh in present-day Syria. In fact, Ramses II lost many soldiers to the Hittites in the battle of Kadesh. He later made peace with the Hittites by agreeing on a border.

Ramses II was a great builder. During his reign, he built more monuments than any other pharaoh.

Reading Check How did Hatshepsut gain power?

Egyptian Society

To control Egypt, pharaohs needed the loyalty and labor of the people. Egypt's social order provided both.

Egyptian society was shaped like a pyramid. The pharaoh was at the top of that pyramid. Egyptians believed that gods controlled everything. The pharaoh controlled Egypt, so people saw him as a god-king who deserved loyalty.

Just below the pharaoh were nobles, priests, and officials. They helped the pharaoh govern Egypt. So did scribes, who kept records for its bureaucracy.

Merchants and artisans made up a middle level. In Egypt, painters, stonecutters, and builders spent their entire lives working on temples and tombs.

Farmers were lower on the social pyramid. By far, most of the people of ancient Egypt were farmers. During the growing season, farmers raised Egypt's food. For the rest of the year, many worked as laborers on the pharaoh's building projects. Most did so willingly out of religious <u>devotion</u>. They believed that if they helped the god-king, they would be rewarded after death.

Slaves were at the bottom of the social pyramid. Many were prisoners of war or debtors who were freed from slavery after serving for a period of time. Slaves were the property of their owners and had to do forced labor.

Reading Check Why were Egyptians loyal to the pharaoh?

devotion, *n.,* a strong feeling of love, loyalty, or commitment

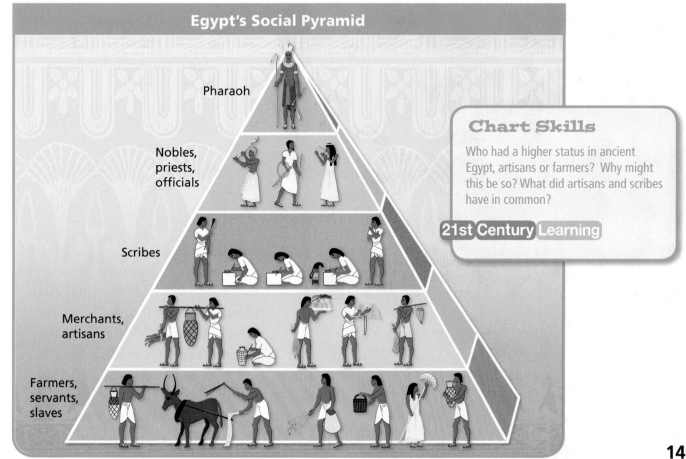

Egypt's Social Pyramid

Pharaoh

Nobles, priests, officials

Scribes

Merchants, artisans

Farmers, servants, slaves

Chart Skills

Who had a higher status in ancient Egypt, artisans or farmers? Why might this be so? What did artisans and scribes have in common?

21st Century Learning

Mummies and Mummification

For ancient Egyptians, it was very important to preserve the body so that it could be a home for a person's spirit after death. The Egyptians preserved bodies through a process called mummification—making mummies, or preserved bodies.

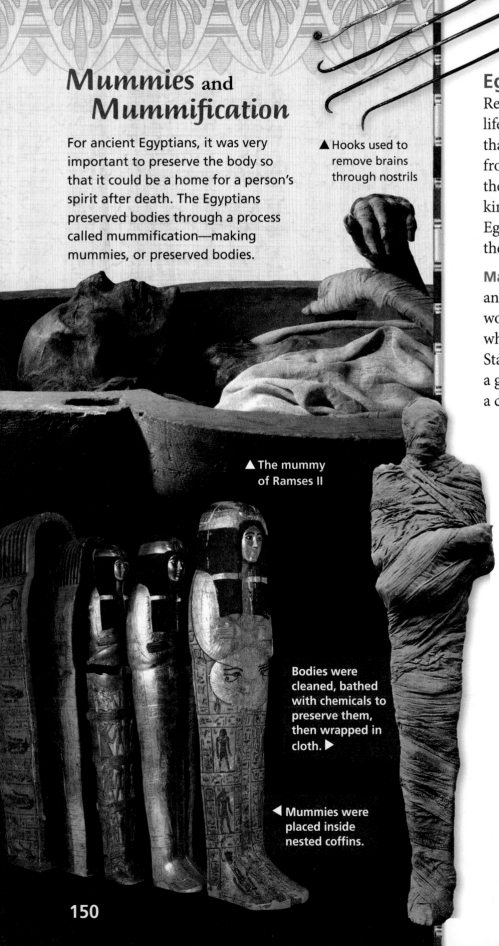

▲ Hooks used to remove brains through nostrils

▲ The mummy of Ramses II

Bodies were cleaned, bathed with chemicals to preserve them, then wrapped in cloth. ▶

◀ Mummies were placed inside nested coffins.

Egyptian Religion

Religion played an important role in the life of the people of Egypt. They believed that their gods controlled everything from the flooding of the Nile River to the death of a child. Their gods could be kind or dangerous. To please the gods, Egyptians built them temples and offered them prayers and gifts.

Many Gods Like the Sumerians, ancient Egyptians were polytheists. They worshiped hundreds of gods, many of whom were associated with animals. Statues or other works of art often show a god with the head or body of a lion, a crocodile, or some other creature.

Egyptians believed that gods shared the qualities of these animals, such as their strength, speed, or bad temper.

One of the most important gods was Amon-Re, the sun god. Egyptians believed that Amon-Re made a daily journey across the sky. Each night, he died in the west as the land grew dark. Each morning, he was reborn in the east as the sun rose.

Osiris was the god of the under-world, or the world of the dead. According to Egyptian legend, Osiris was killed and chopped into pieces by a rival god named Seth. Isis, the wife of Osiris, was the mother goddess of Egypt. She moved heaven and earth to help her husband. Isis found the pieces of Osiris's body and brought her husband back to life.

Isis represented love, caring, and protection. Egyptians looked to Isis for protection in both life and death.

Horus was the son of Isis and Osiris. Egyptian legends tell of great battles between Horus and Seth. When Horus defeated Seth, he united the two lands of Egypt. As a result, every pharaoh was thought to be Horus in human form.

Religion and Society The belief that the pharaoh was a god on Earth contributed to the power of the pharaoh. People obeyed the pharaoh and his officials for fear of angering a god. Priests were also powerful, because Egyptians thought priests could help a person gain favor with the gods. The priests of the Temple of Amon-Re in the city of Thebes were especially powerful.

Preparing for the Afterlife Egyptians believed that they, like Osiris, could overcome death. Life on Earth could lead to an afterlife, or life after death. However, this required preparation.

The first way to prepare for the afterlife was to live a good life. Egyptians believed that Osiris decided who would have an afterlife. Those who had lived good lives would be allowed to live forever, but the sinful would be destroyed.

Preserving the Dead The second way that Egyptians prepared for the afterlife was by having their bodies preserved after death. Egyptians believed that they needed to preserve their body to have an afterlife. They believed that, after death, their spirit would need to recognize their preserved body and use it as a home.

Egyptians went to great efforts to preserve the bodies of their dead. Poor people were buried in the desert, where the hot, dry sand quickly dried out their bodies. Wealthy Egyptians had their bodies made into mummies. A **mummy** is a body preserved by a special process. The knowledge of this process was one of ancient Egypt's great achievements. From mummies, scientists have learned much about life and death in ancient Egypt.

Reading Check Why were priests powerful?

▲ Thoth, the baboon-headed Egyptian god of thought and morality

Section 1 Assessment

Key Terms

1. Define the words *pharaoh, dynasty,* and *bureaucracy.*
2. Describe the Nile's cataracts and delta.
3. Use the words *artisan* and *mummy* in a sentence.

Key Ideas

4. How did Egypt's geography affect its farming methods?
5. How did dynasties affect Egyptian government?
6. Describe the importance of the god Osiris in the religion of ancient Egypt.

Think Critically

7. **Draw Inferences** Explain how ancient Egyptian religion supported the power of the pharaoh.
8. **Compare and Contrast** Compare and contrast the ways in which farmers, artisans, and scribes contributed to the civilization of ancient Egypt.

Essential Question

How much does geography affect people's lives?

9. Which aspects of ancient Egyptian civilization were based on its geography? Which were not? Go to your Student Journal to record your answer.

Art, Architecture, and Learning in Egypt

Key Ideas

- Egyptians developed one of the first systems of writing and some of the world's earliest literature.
- Egyptians built impressive pyramids and produced beautiful works of art.
- Egyptians were accomplished mathematicians and scientists.

Key Terms • hieroglyphic • papyrus • pyramid • sculpture • anatomy

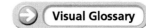 **Visual Glossary**

Reading Skill Summarize Take notes using the graphic organizer in your journal.

An Egyptian scribe writing on papyrus, about 2500 B.C. ▼

Like the Sumerians, the ancient Egyptians were great inventors. In writing, literature, art, architecture, mathematics, and science, the Egyptians made advances that paved the way for later civilizations.

Writing and Literature

The ancient Egyptians developed one of the world's first writing systems. Egyptian writing preserved some of the world's oldest records and works of literature.

Hieroglyphic Writing Ancient Egyptians developed early forms of writing by 3200 B.C. At around the same time, Sumerians were developing their own system of writing. Scholars aren't sure who developed writing first. They also don't know if one group borrowed the idea of writing from the other, or if each people came up with the idea separately.

However, Egyptian writing was unlike Sumerian cuneiform. Egyptian writing used hieroglyphics. A **hieroglyphic** is a drawing or symbol that represents a word or a sound. Most ancient Egyptians did not know how to write. Scribes, or officials who knew how to write, were valued for their knowledge. With writing, Egyptians could share and preserve knowledge. This ability made its complex civilization and advanced technology possible.

Papyrus Egyptians invented a material very similar to paper. This material is called **papyrus** (puh PY rus) and was made from the papyrus reed that grew along the Nile. Our word *paper* comes from the word *papyrus*. Scribes wrote in ink on papyrus sheets. This was much easier than pressing letters into wet clay as the Sumerians did. Papyrus sheets were also easier to transport than pieces of clay.

Papyrus sheets had another important quality. They could last a very long time in the dry environment of Egypt. Many documents written on papyrus—including medical books, calendars, stories, poems, and prayers—have survived to the present. Wall paintings may show us how Egyptians lived; however, written records give us a fuller sense of what was in their hearts and minds.

Egyptian Literature Ancient Egyptian literature included teachings, stories, poems, religious texts, and histories. Egyptian literature was written on sheets of papyrus, carved on stone monuments, and painted on the coffins of mummies.

One famous text, *The Book of the Dead,* is a guide to the afterlife for dead souls. *The Tale of Sinuhe* tells the tale of an Egyptian official. Hearing that the pharaoh has been killed, he flees Egypt out of fear that he will be blamed for the crime:

> “My heart staggered, my arms spread out;
> trembling fell on every limb.
> I removed myself, leaping,
> to look for a hiding place.”
>
> —From *The Tale of Sinuhe,* translated by R. B. Parkinson

survive, *v.,* to continue to live, continue to exist

Reading Check Why were scribes valued?

Hieroglyphics on the wall of an Egyptian tomb

Egyptian Writing

The ancient Egyptian writing system was complex, with over 800 different hieroglyphics. The represented words, ideas, or sometimes sounds. Egyptian hieroglyphics are the ancestors of many of the letters in our alphabet.

This Egyptian hieroglyphic was used for the Egyptian word *det* or “hand” and for the *D* sound that begins that word.

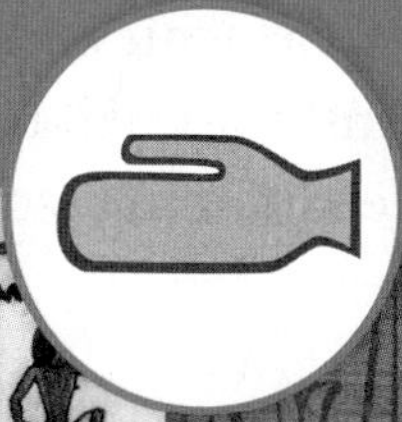

The Phoenician letter *kaph*, or “hand,” used for the *K* sound, took its shape from the Egyptian hieroglyphic for “hand.”

The hieroglyphic for “hand” and the Phoenician letter *kaph* are the basis for our letter *K*.

K

▲ To write on papyrus, Egyptians used more flowing forms of writing, such as the demotic script shown here.

my worldhistory.com
Primary Source

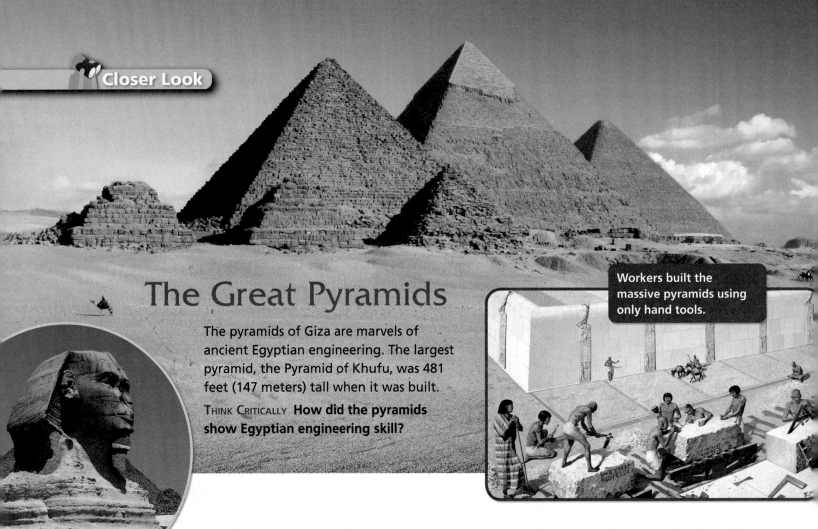

The Great Pyramids

The pyramids of Giza are marvels of ancient Egyptian engineering. The largest pyramid, the Pyramid of Khufu, was 481 feet (147 meters) tall when it was built.

THINK CRITICALLY **How did the pyramids show Egyptian engineering skill?**

Workers built the massive pyramids using only hand tools.

▲ The Great Sphinx is a massive sculpture guarding the pyramids of Giza.

myWorld Activity
Math and
the Pyramids

Architecture and Art

The Egyptians created temples for their gods and tombs for their pharaohs. The temple complex at Karnak contains the ruins of the world's largest temples, built with massive blocks of stone. These great buildings, and the art they contain, continue to inspire artists to this day.

The Pyramids Tombs of early rulers were underground chambers, or rooms. The burial chamber contained items that the ruler might want in the afterlife.

An architect named Imhotep designed a new kind of tomb for his pharaoh, with six stone mounds, one on top of the other. The result is known as a step

pyramid. Later architects made the sides smoother to create a true **pyramid,** or structure with triangular sides.

During the Old Kingdom, three enormous pyramids were built at Giza for King Khufu, his son Khafre, and his grandson Menkaure. The largest is the Great Pyramid of Khufu. For nearly 4,000 years, this pyramid was the world's tallest building. Nearby stands the Sphinx, a famous statue. The Sphinx guarded the road to Khafre's pyramid.

When they were built, these pyramids were the largest structures on Earth. They were a great achievement. They show Egyptians' command of mathematics and advanced building techniques.

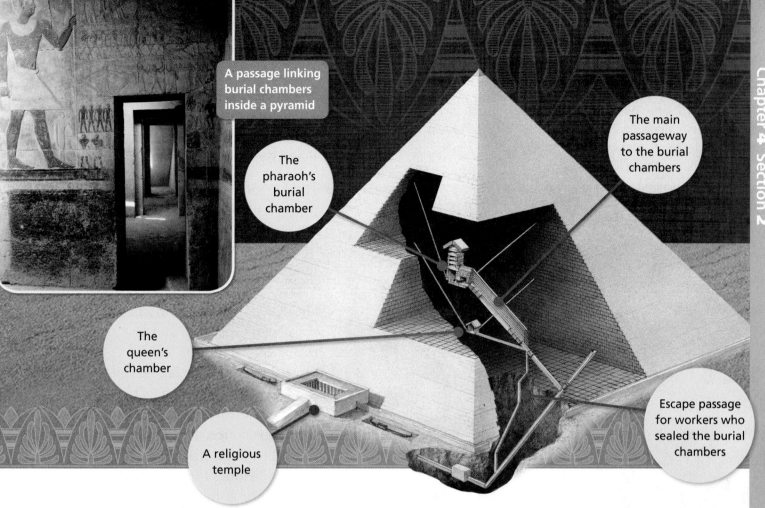

A passage linking burial chambers inside a pyramid

The pharaoh's burial chamber

The main passageway to the burial chambers

The queen's chamber

A religious temple

Escape passage for workers who sealed the burial chambers

Building the pyramids also required the labor of thousands of workers. Workers cut and placed the huge stones by hand. Scholars once thought that slaves had built the pyramids. They now think that the workers were not slaves.

The great age of pyramid building ended about 2200 B.C. Pharaohs who ruled after that time carved massive tombs from the cliffs at the edge of the Nile Valley. Egypt's massive tombs and temples show that Egyptians valued monuments to the gods, including pharaohs.

Painting and Sculpture Egyptians were skilled artists as well as builders. Much of what we know about life in Egypt comes from paintings found on the walls of tombs. Although these paintings show Egyptians at work and at play, their purpose was not decoration. The paintings were created to provide the person buried in the tomb with all of the objects and pleasures shown on the walls.

Egyptian artists also created wonderful sculptures. A **sculpture** is a statue or other free-standing piece of art made of clay, stone, or other materials. Colossal statues of gods stood in temples. Egyptians placed smaller statues of people in tombs along with their mummies. If a mummy was destroyed, the statue could replace it as a home for the dead person's spirit.

Reading Check Why did ancient Egyptians create paintings in tombs?

my World CONNECTIONS

The Great Pyramid was **481** feet tall when it was completed. The tallest building in the United States is **1,730** feet tall.

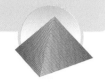

The Egyptian Calendar

The Egyptians developed two different calendars. A solar calendar, with 12 months and 365 days, was a model for our modern calendar. An older lunar calendar was based on observation of the sky.

Each figure around the edge of this solar calendar represents one month.

Ancient Egyptians used a tool called a merkhet to observe stars and other objects in the sky. The line and weight allowed them to measure angles.

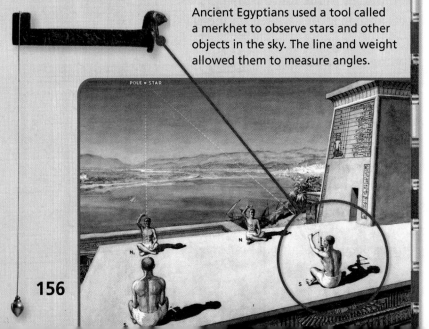

POLE ★ STAR

Science and Mathematics

The Egyptians made many great discoveries in science, mathematics, and technology. Later civilizations built on these discoveries.

The Egyptian Calendar Like most early peoples, prehistoric Egyptians probably measured time by the cycles of the moon. The result would have been a lunar, or moon-based, year of about 354 days.

Over the years, the seasons would run ahead of such a calendar, since the seasons follow a solar, or sun-based, year of 365.2422 days. The ancient Egyptians wanted to keep the calendar linked to the seasons to help farmers plan when to plant and harvest crops. The ancient Egyptians noticed that, each year, a bright star called Sirius first appeared above the horizon before sunrise about the same time of year as the Nile floods. Mindful of this, they watched carefully for the appearance of Sirius.

Sometimes the first appearance of Sirius came too close to the end of the lunar year. So, the Egyptians added an extra month to that year so that the year could catch up to the seasons.

However, this meant that each year had a different number of days. That made record keeping and planning difficult. So the ancient Egyptians developed a solar calendar with exactly 365 days. They used this calendar for official record keeping.

The seasons still slowly shifted through this solar calendar, too, so the ancient Greeks added leap years when they ruled Egypt in the 200s B.C. Our modern calendar was modeled after this solar calendar.

Mathematics The ancient Egyptians developed a solid understanding of mathematics. Their ability to <u>construct</u> the great pyramids proves their command of arithmetic, or addition, subtraction, multiplication, and division. It also shows their skill in geometry, or the measurement of dimensions.

Science, Technology, and Medicine
Ancient Egyptians also made advances in science, technology, and medicine. As you have learned, the Egyptians knew that the star Sirius first appeared in the early morning sky at the same time of year as the Nile flood. This was part of their advanced knowledge of astronomy—the study of the stars and other objects in the sky.

The construction of the great pyramids shows the ancient Egyptians' mastery of engineering. No other civilization had been able to plan and build structures so large or so perfectly shaped.

The ancient Egyptians also made many of the earliest discoveries in chemistry.

These discoveries led to many new inventions. These included the earliest forms of glass, mortar for setting stones and bricks, and many kinds of cosmetics.

The great pyramids were not the only example of Egyptian engineering. To bring the water of the Nile River to their fields, the ancient Egyptians developed complex systems of irrigation, or ways of watering land.

The Egyptians had the most advanced medical knowledge of their time. From their work with mummies, for example, they learned much about human anatomy. **Anatomy** is the study of the structure of the body and its organs. The ancient Egyptians were skilled surgeons. Egyptian doctors also studied diseases and developed effective medicines to treat or cure them.

Reading Check How did mummies help advance Egyptian medicine?

construct, v., to build or put together

Tools used by Egyptian surgeons ▼

Section 2 Assessment

Key Terms

1. Describe how Egyptians used hieroglyphics and papyrus.

2. Use the words *pyramid* and *sculpture* in a sentence.

3. How might a knowledge of anatomy help doctors?

Key Ideas

4. How did Egyptian writing differ from Sumerian writing?

5. Why are the pyramids considered one of ancient Egypt's greatest achievements?

6. Describe some of ancient Egypt's achievements in mathematics, science, and technology.

Think Critically

7. **Draw Inferences** How did the invention of writing help make other Egyptian achievements possible?

8. **Identify Evidence** What do the different calendars developed by ancient Egyptians reveal about their interests and abilities?

Essential Question

How much does geography affect people's lives?

9. What was the connection, if any, between Egypt's geography and its achievements? Go to your Student Journal to record your answer.

Egypt and Nubia

Key Ideas
- Trade led to cultural diffusion between Egypt and neighboring lands.
- Nubia had a close relationship with Egypt and shared elements of its culture.
- Nubia was also a unique African civilization with its own accomplishments.

Key Terms • commerce • ivory • interdependence • Meroitic script • ebony

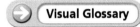 **Visual Glossary**

 Reading Skill Analyze Cause and Effect Take notes using the graphic organizer in your journal.

S outh of Egypt, farther up the Nile River, was a land that the Egyptians called Kush. We know this region today as Nubia. Today, Nubia extends from southern Egypt into northern Sudan. Trade brought Egypt and Nubia together.

Nubian princes and their servants bring gold to Egypt. ▼

Trade in Ancient Egypt

Egypt was rich in sunshine and fertile soil, but it lacked the forests, minerals, horses, and other useful natural resources found in Nubia and other countries. The people of ancient Egypt had to get these resources through trade, or commerce, with neighboring countries. **Commerce** is the buying and selling of goods and services.

As their country grew in wealth, Egyptians also wanted to buy luxury goods from other lands. Luxury goods are expensive goods that are not needed, but that make life more enjoyable. Egyptian luxury goods included precious stones and perfumes. Trade gave Egypt access to goods it would not otherwise have.

Trade in the Eastern Mediterranean The pharaohs sent merchants and officials to other lands to promote trade. As early as the Old Kingdom, a pharaoh named Snefru promoted trade with lands on the eastern Mediterranean Sea.

The area of modern Lebanon in the eastern Mediterranean had forests that Egypt lacked. The Egyptians were eager to buy its cedar wood. In other Mediterranean lands, they bought olive oil and metals such as tin and copper.

Trade in the Nile Valley Snefru also boosted trade between Egypt and Nubia. Under later dynasties, trade between Egypt and Nubia increased.

The most valuable goods that Egyptians bought in Nubia were gold and elephant tusks, which were a source of **ivory,** a hard white material made from these tusks. In return, the Egyptians sold grain, cloth, papyrus, glass, and jewelry.

Egypt <u>relied</u> on Nubia's gold, and Nubia relied on Egypt's grain. Trade created **interdependence,** or dependence by each country or group on the other.

Trade brought the Nubians into closer contact with ancient Egypt. Over time, the Nubians adopted elements of Egyptian culture, including Egyptian religion.

Reading Check Why did Egyptians want to trade with Nubia?

rely, v., to depend, trust

A model of an Egyptian seagoing ship ▶

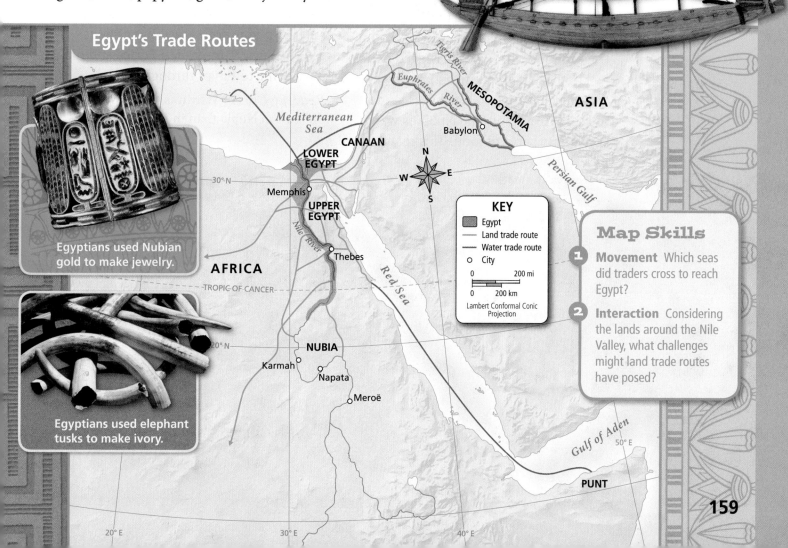

Egypt's Trade Routes

Mediterranean Sea

Tigris River

Euphrates River

MESOPOTAMIA

ASIA

Babylon

CANAAN

LOWER EGYPT

30° N

Memphis

N
W E
S

Persian Gulf

UPPER EGYPT

Nile River

KEY
Egypt
Land trade route
Water trade route
○ City
0   200 mi
0   200 km
Lambert Conformal Conic Projection

AFRICA

Thebes

Red Sea

TROPIC OF CANCER

Egyptians used Nubian gold to make jewelry.

20° N

NUBIA

Karmah

Napata

Meroë

Egyptians used elephant tusks to make ivory.

Gulf of Aden

50° E

PUNT

Map Skills

1 **Movement** Which seas did traders cross to reach Egypt?

2 **Interaction** Considering the lands around the Nile Valley, what challenges might land trade routes have posed?

20° E   30° E   40° E

The Land of Nubia

Like Egypt, Nubia had an ancient culture. Nubia's geography was similar to Egypt's in some ways and different in others.

The Geography of Nubia Like Egypt, Nubia received very little rainfall. Deserts surrounded Nubia's Nile Valley. Like Egypt, Nubia depended on the Nile River and its annual floods. Its people farmed a narrow ribbon of fertile land along the Nile River. Their farming methods <u>generated</u> a surplus, though a smaller one than Egypt's. This surplus supported cities with artisans and merchants.

However, the Nile's cataracts lay within Nubia. While Egyptians used boats, cataracts made it impossible to travel very far by boat in Nubia. Instead, people had to travel on foot through the rugged desert.

Another difference from Egypt was that the Nubians had much less land to farm. As a result, the Nubians were sometimes short of food. This made them eager to trade gold, iron, and other products for Egypt's grain.

Nubia was also in closer contact than Egypt with the peoples of Africa south of the Sahara. The Nubians traded goods and ideas with these peoples just as they did with the Egyptians.

Sources of Information About Nubia Scholars have used both historical records and archaeological evidence to learn about Nubia. Written records in Egypt document trade with Nubia. They also describe a powerful kingdom in Nubia modeled on the kingdom of Egypt.

Some of the evidence of trade with Egypt comes from archaeology. Archaeologists have also found that the Nubians and Egyptians both saw kings as gods. This idea was common in Africa and may have come to Egypt through Nubia.

Reading Check Why was travel more difficult in Nubia than in Egypt?

generate, *v.,* to produce, create

A thin strip of fertile land borders the Nile at Napata, the first capital of Nubia. ▼

Simulation

160

Nubia and Egypt

Through trade, the Egyptians discovered that Nubia was rich in resources, including gold. The Egyptians realized that the more gold they had, the more wood and other resources they could buy from the eastern Mediterranean.

Egypt Conquers Nubia To gain more control over Nubia's riches, Egypt conquered most of Nubia for a time during the Middle Kingdom, and then again during the New Kingdom. The conquered Nubians had to pay tribute to the pharaoh. One year's tribute to the pharaoh Thutmose III included hundreds of pounds of gold, cattle, slaves, ivory, and ostrich feathers from Nubia.

After the rule of Ramses II, Egypt weakened, and the New Kingdom ended. Rival leaders in different cities fought for control of Egypt. Meanwhile, Nubia became an independent kingdom ruled by Nubian kings.

Nubia Conquers Egypt In the mid-700s B.C., a Nubian king conquered the Egyptian city of Thebes. The next ruler of Nubia, a king named Piye (PEE yeh), or Piankhi, expanded the Nubian empire by conquering one Egyptian city after another. Finally, Piye declared himself pharaoh of a united Egypt and Nubia.

> 66 O mighty, mighty Ruler, Piankhi, O mighty Ruler, [you come] having gained the dominion of the Northland. . . . [You are] unto eternity, [your] might endure[s], O Ruler, beloved of Thebes. 99

—Inscription from the victory monument of Piye, translated by James Henry Breasted

A modern painting of a Nubian pharaoh named Taharqa ▶

Pharaohs from Nubia ruled Egypt for almost a hundred years. Nubian rulers promoted the traditional Egyptian ways that they had learned under earlier pharaohs. They built temples to honor Nubian and Egyptian gods.

The rulers from Nubia might have remained in power longer if they had been willing to govern only Egypt. Instead, they tried to expand their power. They went to war with the Assyrians, skillful warriors who had recently conquered the Fertile Crescent. This error in judgment led to the Nubians' downfall. Assyrian troops invaded Egypt around 665 B.C. After losing many battles, the Nubians retreated from Egypt to Nubia.

Reading Check Why did Egypt conquer Nubia?

myWorld Activity
Best Advice

Nubian Art and Architecture

The art and architecture of ancient Nubia reflected its ties with neighboring Egypt and, later, with the Roman empire. However, Nubian art and architecture also had original features.

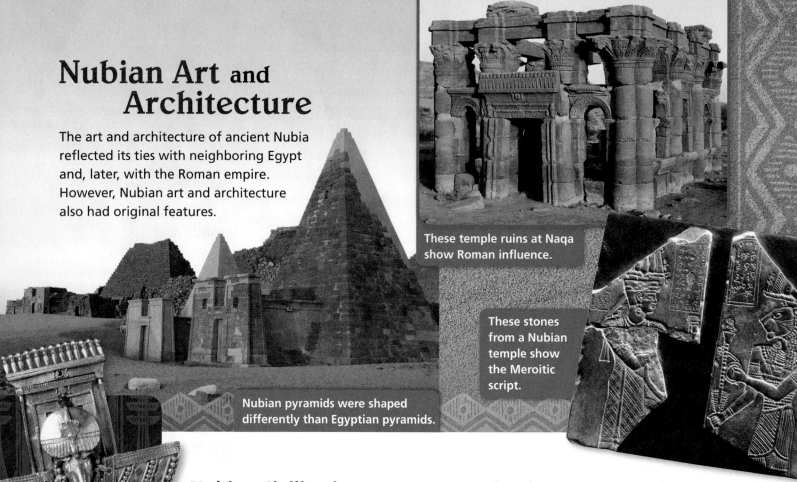

These temple ruins at Naqa show Roman influence.

These stones from a Nubian temple show the Meroitic script.

Nubian pyramids were shaped differently than Egyptian pyramids.

▲ Nubians made beautiful gold jewelry.

Nubian Civilization

Nubia remained an advanced civilization for almost a thousand years after it lost Egypt. It developed its own system of writing, economy, and government.

Independent Nubia In 591 B.C., the Egyptians destroyed Napata, the capital of Nubia. The Nubians moved their capital south to the city of Meroë (MEHR oh ee), which was easier to defend.

Meroë was also located near iron deposits and on a trade route from Central Africa. This region received more rain than did most of Nubia. This rain supported the growth of wood that the Nubians could burn to smelt, or melt out, iron from a rock called iron ore.

The Nubians turned Meroë into Africa's first ironworking center. Nubia's iron tools and weapons were much stronger than Egypt's soft bronze tools. The Nubians continued to make jewelry and other beautiful objects from their gold.

The Nubians built hundreds of pyramids at Napata and Meroë. These pyramids were built at a steep angle. The pyramids held the tombs of the kings and the queen-mothers of Nubia.

The queen-mothers of Nubia are also known by their Roman name—*candaces*. Candaces remained powerful, sometimes more powerful than kings, throughout the history of Nubia.

The Nubians created the **Meroitic script,** one of the world's first alphabets. Scholars have learned to read this alphabet but still don't understand the words of the Meroitic language written in it.

Nubia's Links to Africa and the World

Nubia played an important role in ancient Africa. The kingdom may have controlled an area larger than the Egyptian empire. Nubia had advanced iron-working technology. The Nubians traded iron goods, cloth, and gold with other African peoples. In return, the Nubians bought **ebony,** a black wood from West Africa, and elephant tusks, valued as a source of ivory, from East and Central Africa. The Nubians also sold slaves from other parts of Africa to the Egyptians.

The Nubians also traded with Greek and Roman Egypt. Nubians sold ebony, ivory, gold, and iron goods and bought grains and cloth in Egypt. The Nubians used irrigation to grow more food for their busy cities, but they still had to trade to meet some of their need for food.

The ancient Greeks and Romans knew the Nubians for their metalworking skills, and they valued Nubian iron tools and weapons. Ports on the Red Sea allowed the Nubians to trade with countries as far away as India.

By the A.D. 200s, war with the Roman empire, which controlled Egypt, had weakened Nubia. Meanwhile, desert peoples raided Nubia's cities and disrupted its trade. Finally, in the A.D. 300s, Nubia was conquered by the kingdom of Axum, centered in the present-day country of Ethiopia to the southeast.

Throughout its history, Nubia had linked Africa south of the Sahara with other ancient civilizations. The Nubians created patterns of trade and farming that continued after the conquest by Axum. These traditions have continued in the region to this day.

Reading Check Why did the Nubians move their capital to Meroë?

A Nubian ceramic jug ▼

Section **3** Assessment

Key Terms

1. Explain why commerce was important to the Egyptians.

2. Explain how commerce between Egypt and Nubia led to interdependence.

3. What was different about Nubia's Meroitic script?

Key Ideas

4. How was trade connected to the spread of culture and ideas between Egypt and Nubia?

5. What kinds of similarities were there between the cultures of Nubia and Egypt?

6. How did the accomplishments of Nubian civilization set it apart from Egyptian civilization?

Think Critically

7. **Draw Conclusions** How did trade benefit both Egypt and Nubia?

8. **Draw Inferences** Why might the Nubians have depended more heavily on trade than the Egyptians?

Essential Question

How much does geography affect people's lives?

9. Give examples of how geography helped shape the civilization of Nubia. Go to your Student Journal to record your answer.

Chapter Assessment

Key Terms and Ideas

1. **Define** What are the **cataracts** of the Nile?
2. **Describe** What did **artisans** do?
3. **Recall** Why were Egypt's **pharaohs** seen as gods?
4. **Describe** Use the word **bureaucracy** in a sentence describing ancient Egyptian government.
5. **Discuss** Why were **papyrus** and **hieroglyphics** important in ancient Egypt?

6. **Explain** Which achievements show Egyptians' mathematical abilities?
7. **Define** What is **anatomy**?
8. **Explain** Why is the relationship between Egypt and Nubia described as one of **interdependence**?
9. **Describe** How did the political relationship between Egypt and Nubia change over time?
10. **Define** What is Meroitic script?

Think Critically

11. **Draw Inferences** Why might the ancient Egyptians have wanted to control the Nile's flood waters?
12. **Synthesize** What was the connection between the religion of ancient Egypt and the practice of mummification?
13. **Analyze Cause and Effect** What were the reasons that the ancient Egyptians adopted their two calendar systems?

14. **Compare and Contrast** How was Nubian civilization similar to and different from ancient Egyptian civilization?
15. **Core Concepts: Measuring Time** How do historians divide the history of ancient Egypt into periods?

Analyze Visuals

An Egyptian Tomb Painting

Use the painting at right to answer the following questions.

16. Notice that grain is being cut at the top of this painting. What do you think is in the yellow stacks at the bottom of the painting?
17. Based on what you know about Egyptian society, who are the men dressed in white robes?
18. Name at least two activities that these men appear to be doing.

Essential Question

myWorld Chapter Activity

Water in the Desert Follow your teacher's instructions to write an article or Web site for a geography journal about the impact of geography on ancient Egypt. Make sure your article describes ancient Egypt for a modern reader who knows nothing about it.

21st Century Learning

Work In Teams

Working in teams, make a map that shows Egypt's trade with neighboring countries. Each team member should have a different task. One person could draw the coastlines and the course of the Nile River. Another could use the textbook or the Internet to research goods that the Egyptians traded. A third could draw these objects and place them where they belong on the map.

Document-Based Questions

Success Tracker™
Online at myworldhistory.com

Use your knowledge of ancient Egypt and Nubia and Documents A and B to answer Questions 1–3.

Document A

" Distinguish the superintendent who directs from the workman, for manual labor is little elevated; the inaction of the hands is honorable."

—from "Precepts of Ptah-Hotep, " written by an Egyptian scribe, translated by Charles F. Home

Document B

" The sandal maker is utterly wretched . . . The fowler is utterly weak . . . I mention for you also the fisherman. He is more miserable than one of any other profession. . . . See, there is no office free from supervisors, except the scribe's. He is the supervisor! But if you understand writings, then it will be better for you than the professions which I have set before you."

—from *The Literature of the Ancient Egyptians*, translated by Adolf Erman

1. According to Document A, how did ancient Egyptian scribes view workers?
   A They respected workers.
   B They pitied workers.
   C They thought workers were lazy.
   D They looked down on workers.

2. For whom is Document B most likely written?
   A a king
   B a scribe in training
   C an unhappy sandalmaker
   D a fisherman

3. **Writing Task** Based on Documents A and B, write a paragraph discussing the positions of different social classes in ancient Egypt and relations among them.

myworldhistory.com

Self-Test

Judaism and the Jewish People

? Essential Question

How are religion and culture connected?

יהודה

דן

לוי

זבולון

אשר

בנימין

יד

יוסף

? Explore the Essential Question . . .

- at **my worldhistory.com**
- using the **myWorld Chapter Activity**
- with the **Student Journal**

ראובן

נפתלי

ש מעון

ש שכר

Stained-glass symbols of the 12 tribes of Israel, the ancestors of the Jewish people

Key Dates in Jewish History

About 1700 B.C. God speaks to Abraham, according to the Bible.

About 900 B.C. Israel splits into the kingdoms of Israel and Judah.

586 B.C. Babylonians conquer Judah, exile its people, and destroy the First Temple.

A.D. 70 Romans destroy the Second Temple; many Jews flee the region.

2000 B.C.   **1400 B.C.**   **800 B.C.**   **200 B.C.**   **A.D. 400**

About 1000 B.C. The kingdom of Israel is founded and the First Temple is built.

720s B.C. Assyrians conquer Israel.

538 B.C. Jews return to Judah and build the Second Temple.

The Story of Ruth

This story about Ruth is based on the book of Ruth. This account from the Hebrew Bible, or Tanakh, helps us understand the culture and religion of the Jewish people in ancient times. All direct quotes are taken from Tanakh, *Jewish Publication Society (1985).*

One day, thousands of years ago, Ruth stood crying on a road in Moab, or present-day Jordan. She had been married to her husband for ten years, and now he was dead. So were the husbands of Naomi, her mother-in-law, and Orpah, her sister-in law. The three women faced danger without male protection.

Naomi had a plan. It was a famine in Bethlehem, in the nearby Jewish kingdom of Judah, that had earlier driven Naomi and her husband to Moab. But now Naomi heard that the famine had passed, and she was determined to return to her homeland.

myworldhistory.com

Timeline/On Assignment

167

Ruth says to Naomi, "Wherever you go, I will go."

Ruth and Naomi arrive at the gates of the city of Bethlehem.

Her two daughters-in-law were gentiles, or non-Jews. Naomi was urging them to stay in their own country and find new husbands: "Turn back, each of you to her mother's house. May the Lord deal kindly with you, as you have dealt with the dead and with me. May the Lord grant that each of you find security in the house of a husband!"

She kissed them both good-bye. But, through their tears, the younger women raised their voices: "No, we will return with you to your people."

Naomi insisted, "Turn back, my daughters! Why should you go with me?"

All three of them sobbed as their talk went back and forth. Reluctantly, Orpah made her decision. She gave her mother-in-law one last hug and walked away. But Ruth was still holding Naomi's arm.

"See, your sister-in-law has returned to her people and her gods," said Naomi. "Go follow your sister-in-law."

But Ruth's love and loyalty toward her mother-in-law was too great for her to give in. She chose to leave her parents and people behind and follow Naomi, saying, "For wherever you go, I will go; wherever you lodge, I will lodge; your people shall be my people, and your God my God."

Ruth's willingness to adopt the religion of Naomi touched her deeply. The two women journeyed on to Bethlehem. When they finally arrived, the harvesting of barley had just begun. But the two had no work, no protection, and they were starving.

Ruth meant to take care of them both. She said, "I would like to go to the fields and glean among the ears of grain." She went to work gathering up the grain in the fields of a rich man named Boaz.

That day Boaz said to his servant who was in charge of the men harvesting the grain, "Whose girl is that?"

"She is a Moabite girl who came back with Naomi," said the servant. "She has been on her feet ever since she came this morning."

Boaz gave Ruth extra barley, plus some for Naomi, and offered his protection: "Don't go to glean in another field. Don't go elsewhere, but stay here close to my girls."

Ruth was grateful, but puzzled by his kindness.

Boaz explained, "I have been told of all that you did for your mother-in-law after the death of your husband, how you left your father and mother and the land of your birth and came to a people you had not known before." He added, "May you have a full

Ruth bends in the field to glean, or pick up pieces of grain left behind, after the men have harvested.

Boaz gives Ruth a basket full of grain.

recompense [reward] from the LORD, the God of Israel, under whose wings you have sought refuge!"

In time, Boaz and Ruth married and had a son. This brought joy to everyone—especially to Naomi. For, as the other women pointed out, "He will renew your life and sustain your old age; for he is born of your daughter-in-law, who loves you and is better to you than seven sons."

Most of the figures in the Hebrew Bible are men. But Ruth became one of its heroines, and her story became the book of Ruth. Her self-sacrificing words—"Wherever you go, I will go"—have touched so many people that wedding services often make use of them today.

What connections do you see in this story between religion and the lives of the Jewish people in ancient times? As you read the chapter ahead, think about what Ruth's story tells you about the world of the Jewish people in ancient times.

myStory Video

Join Ruth as she leaves her homeland to live in another country.

The Origins of Judaism

Key Ideas
- The Israelite belief in one God developed into the religion known as Judaism.
- Jews believe that God freed the Israelites from slavery after sending Moses to lead them.
- The Israelites eventually settled in Canaan, their Promised Land.

Key Terms • monotheism • ethics • Torah • covenant • Exodus • commandment

Visual Glossary

Reading Skill Summarize Take notes using the graphic organizer in your journal.

A modern artist's impression of Abraham ▼

Judaism first developed as a religion more than 3,000 years ago in the Fertile Crescent. It was the world's first religion based on one God who set down laws about right and wrong. Judaism has helped shape the religions of Christianity and Islam, as well as modern ideas about law and human rights.

The Early Israelites and the Worship of One God

The Israelites were related to other peoples of the Fertile Crescent, but they developed a unique culture. Although their neighbors worshiped many gods, the Israelites practiced **monotheism,** or the belief that there is only one God. They believed that God created each person in God's image. They believed that God called on them to act based on **ethics,** or ideas of right and wrong. Their teachings and practices became known as Judaism, the religion of the Jewish people. Judaism is one of the world's oldest religions.

Sources Most of what Jews believe about the origins of their religion comes from the Torah (TOH ruh). The **Torah** consists of the first five books of the Hebrew Bible. (These are also the first five books of the Christian Old Testament, which is made up of all of the books of the Hebrew Bible.) The archaeology and history of biblical sites in Egypt and Mesopotamia also help us understand the world of the Torah.

Abraham's Covenant The Torah tells about a man named Abraham, who may have lived about 1700 B.C. He herded flocks of sheep and other animals. His home was Ur in Mesopotamia.

According to the Torah, God told Abraham to leave Ur and travel with his family to a land called Canaan (KAY nun) on the coast of the Mediterranean Sea. The Torah says that God then made a **covenant,** or binding agreement, with Abraham. The land of Canaan would belong to Abraham's descendants, so it became known as the Promised Land.

66 I will maintain My covenant between Me and you, and your offspring to come, as an everlasting covenant throughout the ages, to be God to you and your offspring to come. 99

—Genesis 17:7

The Patriarchs The Torah says that Abraham led his people to Canaan, where they lived for a long time. Abraham, his son Isaac, and Isaac's son Jacob are known as the patriarchs, or the forefathers of the Jewish people.

According to the Torah, Abraham's grandson Jacob had twelve sons. Each of Jacob's sons would become the ancestor of at least one large group of related families called a tribe. Abraham's grandson Jacob was later renamed Israel. As a result, the twelve tribes descended from Jacob became known as the Israelites.

Scholars believe that the stories of the patriarchs were passed along by word of mouth for hundreds of years. Eventually, they were written down in Genesis (JEH nuh sihs), the first book of the Torah.

Reading Check Why did Canaan become known as the Promised Land?

eventually, *adv.,* after a time

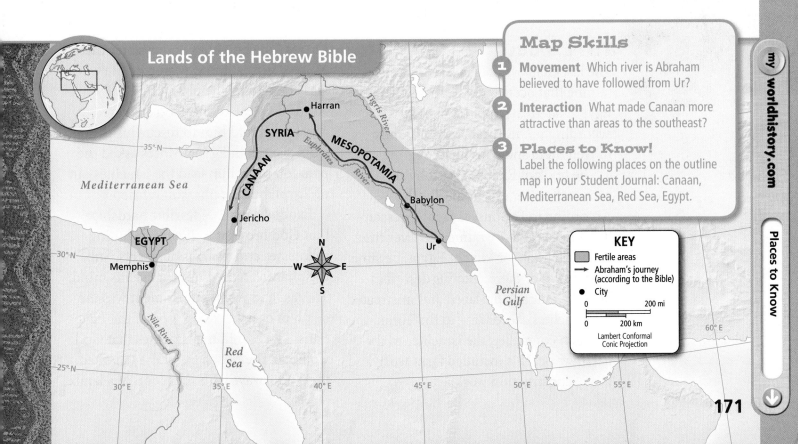

Lands of the Hebrew Bible

Harran

SYRIA

Tigris River

Euphrates River

MESOPOTAMIA

CANAAN

Mediterranean Sea

Jericho

EGYPT

Babylon

Memphis

Ur

Persian Gulf

Nile River

Red Sea

35°N

30°N

25°N

30°E   35°E   40°E   45°E   50°E   55°E   60°E

Map Skills

1 **Movement** Which river is Abraham believed to have followed from Ur?

2 **Interaction** What made Canaan more attractive than areas to the southeast?

3 **Places to Know!** Label the following places on the outline map in your Student Journal: Canaan, Mediterranean Sea, Red Sea, Egypt.

KEY
- Fertile areas
- Abraham's journey (according to the Bible)
- City

0   200 mi
0   200 km
Lambert Conformal Conic Projection

myworldhistory.com

Places to Know

171

The Exodus

According to the Bible, the Israelites spent 40 years traveling from Egypt, across the Sinai Peninsula, to the Promised Land of Canaan. Along the way, Moses received the Ten Commandments at Mount Sinai.

THINK CRITICALLY **How did the Exodus affect the Israelites?**

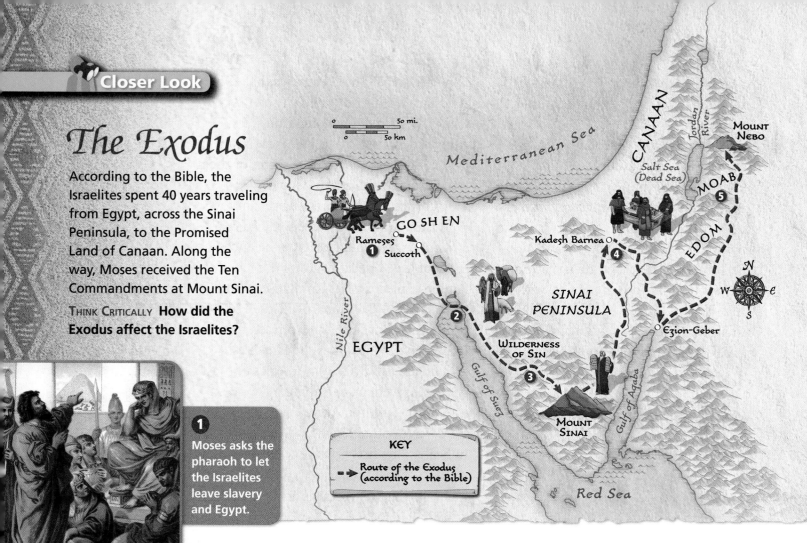

1
Moses asks the pharaoh to let the Israelites leave slavery and Egypt.

KEY

→ Route of the Exodus (according to the Bible)

The Exodus

The last chapters of Genesis describe a famine that occurred in Canaan. Because Egypt had great supplies of grain, according to the Torah, Jacob's family moved there and continued to grow.

The book of Exodus (EKS uh duhs) comes after Genesis in the Torah. According to Exodus, as Jacob's descendants became more numerous over time, a new pharaoh, or king of Egypt, became mistrustful of them. Exodus describes how the pharaoh enslaved and mistreated the Israelites. According to the Torah, the pharaoh <u>compelled</u> the Israelites to do harsh work. This included farm work and heavy construction work.

compel, *v.,* force

Moses The book of Exodus states that Moses (MOH zuhz) was an Israelite who was adopted by the pharaoh's family. According to Exodus, God appeared to Moses and told him to rescue his people from slavery in Egypt. Moses asked the pharaoh to let him lead the Israelites out of Egypt, but the pharaoh refused.

Exodus describes terrible hardships that God brought to Egypt, including sicknesses and swarms of insects. Still, the pharaoh would not change his mind. The last and worst punishment was the death of every firstborn son of the Egyptians. Moses told the Israelites that God would let their sons live if they marked their doorways with the blood of a lamb.

2 The waters of the Red Sea part to let the Israelites escape from Egypt, according to the story in the Bible.

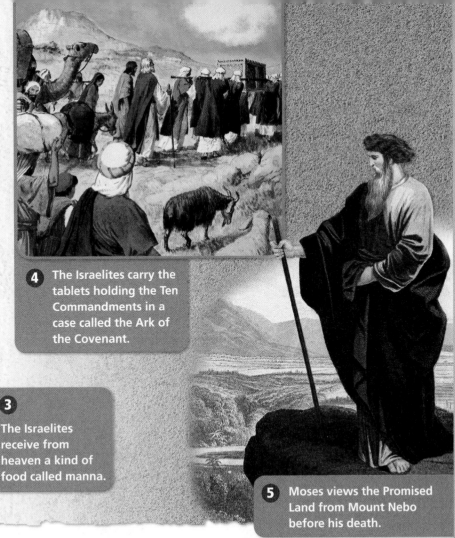

4 The Israelites carry the tablets holding the Ten Commandments in a case called the Ark of the Covenant.

3 The Israelites receive from heaven a kind of food called manna.

5 Moses views the Promised Land from Mount Nebo before his death.

Finally, the pharaoh allowed the Israelites to leave Egypt. Moses led the Israelites to the Sinai (SY ny) Peninsula, out of the pharaoh's reach. The escape of the Israelites from slavery in Egypt is called the **Exodus.** Each year, Jews celebrate Passover to commemorate God's freeing them from slavery in Egypt.

The Desert Experience The Exodus is traditionally believed to have occurred during the 1200s B.C. According to the Torah, after the Israelites left Egypt, they lived in the Sinai desert for 40 years. During this time, God prepared the Israelites for life in the Promised Land. They received a series of instructions from God. They also learned ways to worship God and created important religious objects.

On the journey through the desert to Canaan, according to the Torah, the Israelites faced harsh conditions. Occasionally, the Israelites battled other peoples.

Some Israelites questioned the leadership of Moses or even of God. However, they came to believe that if they obeyed God's commands, God would provide for them. The Torah states that during their journey, God even provided them with water and with food from heaven.

Reading Check What does Passover celebrate?

myWorld Activity
Interviewing Moses

173

The Ten Commandments

According to the Hebrew Bible, God called Moses to the top of Mount Sinai and gave him the Ten Commandments. The text below is a summary of the commandments as Jews group them.

1) I the LORD am your God.

2) Have no other gods besides Me, and do not make idols and worship them.

3) Do not swear falsely by the name the LORD your God.

4) Remember the sabbath day and keep it holy.

5) Honor your father and your mother.

6) Do not commit murder.

7) Do not commit adultery.

8) Do not steal.

9) Do not bear false witness against your neighbor.

10) Do not covet your neighbor's house, wife, or belongings.

The Ten Commandments

Exodus says that during the Israelites' journey, they stopped at the foot of Mount Sinai. Moses went up the mountain to meet with God. God gave Moses laws, including those known today as the Ten Commandments. A **commandment** is an order to do something. The Torah contains many other laws, but the Ten Commandments are the most important.

Laws for Living The Ten Commandments and other laws told the Israelites how to behave toward God and one another. These laws are still important to Jews today. Jewish people believe that they have a covenant with God. This means that they have a sacred duty to follow the ethical teachings of the Torah.

The Impact of God's Laws Because they believe that each person is created in the image of God, Jews have a strong sense of each person's worth. They also believe that each person has a responsibility to do what is right.

The Ten Commandments and other laws deepened the Israelites' relationship with God and one another. According to these laws, behaving well toward one another is a duty to God.

The accounts of Exodus and the Ten Commandments are important to Jews, Christians, and others. For them, the lesson of Exodus is that if people believe in God and obey God's laws, God will protect them and support them.

Reading Check What are the Ten Commandments?

Return to the Promised Land

After the Israelites received the laws from Moses, according to the Torah, they resumed their journey to the Promised Land. Moses himself died before he could enter the Promised Land. After Moses died, his deputy, Joshua, took his place as the leader of the Israelites.

According to the book of Joshua in the Bible, the Israelites entered Canaan from the east under Joshua's leadership. One of the first cities they conquered was the high-walled city of Jericho (JEHR ih koh). After the defeat of Jericho, the Israelites went on to conquer several other kingdoms in Canaan.

Then each of the tribes descended from Jacob's sons settled in a different area. The tribes of Judah, Simeon, and Benjamin settled in the south, near the Dead Sea. The other tribes settled in lands to the north along the Jordan River.

Unlike the Israelites, the Canaanites, or people of Canaan, worshiped many gods. These included the gods Baal and El and the goddess Asherah. The Canaanites worshiped idols, or carved images, of their gods. Some Canaanites might have worshiped just one god but accepted the existence of others.

According to the Bible, the Israelites maintained their identity. They sometimes sinned and were punished, but they always returned to the teachings of the Torah, including the belief in only one God.

Reading Check According to the Bible, who led the Israelites into the Promised Land?

The Bible states that the walls of Jericho crashed down when the Israelites shouted. ▼

Section 1 Assessment

Key Terms

1. Explain the relationship between Judaism and monotheism.
2. Use the words *commandment* and *ethics* in a sentence about Judaism.
3. What is a covenant?

Key Ideas

4. Describe the relationship between the Israelites and their God.
5. What was the lesson of the Exodus, according to the Torah?
6. What did the Israelites do after they reached Canaan?

Think Critically

7. **Draw Conclusions** Explain the connection, according to the Hebrew Bible, between Abraham's covenant with God and the Israelites' belief about Canaan.
8. **Synthesize** What is the connection between Jewish beliefs about individual worth and the modern idea of equality before the law?

? Essential Question

How are religion and culture connected?

9. Explain how religion helped shape the culture of the ancient Israelites, as presented in the Hebrew Bible. Go to your Student Journal to record your answer.

Section 2

The Teachings of Judaism

Key Ideas

- The Hebrew Bible is the basis of Jewish teaching and practice.
- Jewish people give special importance to studying and understanding God's laws.
- The teachings of Judaism deal with how people should relate to God and to one another.

Key Terms • Scripture • prophet • rabbi • Talmud • righteousness • justice • Sabbath

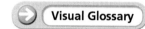 Visual Glossary

Reading Skill **Analyze Cause and Effect** Take notes using the graphic organizer in your journal.

Jews read from the Torah in front of Jerusalem's sacred Western Wall. ▼

God's covenants with the Israelites and his commandments for his people are described in the Torah. They form the basis for the Jewish religion and its teachings. These teachings mainly have to do with how people should relate to God and to one another.

The Hebrew Bible

The written tradition is very important in Judaism. Jews greatly value scholarship and learning. In fact, Jews are often called "People of the Book." The **Scriptures,** or sacred writings, are the source of Jewish teachings. The Jewish Scriptures are also known as the Hebrew Bible, or Tanakh. To Jews, the Bible is not just a history of their ancestors. They believe it reveals God's will as carried out in human events. This shared account unites Jews all over the world with a common set of teachings. The Hebrew Bible also forms the basis for the Christian Old Testament, which includes the books of the Hebrew Bible, but in a different order.

The Hebrew Bible describes events believed to have happened hundreds of years before the Bible was put into writing. By tradition, the books of the Hebrew Bible are divided into three sections.

The Torah As you have learned, the first five books of the Hebrew Bible are called the Torah. The Torah begins by telling the story of God's creation of the world and the first people. It tells of a man named Noah who escaped a great flood on an ark, or boat. It tells of the life of Abraham and God's covenant with him.

The Torah then focuses on Abraham's son Isaac, his grandson Jacob, and Jacob's descendants, the Israelites. The Torah follows their journey from Egypt back to the Promised Land. The Torah is also called the Law of Moses. It contains not only the Ten Commandments but also many other rules and laws.

The Prophets The next section of the Hebrew Bible is called the Prophets. This section contains books by or about Jewish prophets. A **prophet** is a person believed to be chosen by God as a messenger to bring truth to the people. The prophets were preachers, poets, and reformers. They reminded people to obey God's laws. In so doing, they told people how they should relate to God, to other people, to the land in which they lived, and even to themselves.

The Prophets traces the history of Judaism and the Jewish people. Beginning with the book of Joshua, it continues the story of the Israelites from the Torah, describing their arrival in the Promised Land. Other books deal with the creation of the kingdom of Israel, described in Section 3.

The Writings The last section of the Hebrew Bible is the Writings. This section includes great Hebrew literature such as the Psalms (sahmz), the Proverbs, and the Song of Songs. Psalms are poems or songs offering praises or prayers to God. The book of Proverbs contains

wise sayings. Many give advice to young people, such as this example:

> 66 Do not envy a lawless man,
> Or choose any of his ways. 99
>
> —Proverbs 3:31

Other Writings tell about heroes such as Esther, Ruth, and Job (johb). The Writings also contain books, such as Chronicles, a history of the early Jewish people.

Reading Check Which part of the Hebrew Bible covers covenants and laws?

myWorld Activity
Voices From the Bible

Three Prophets

Jews believe that the prophets delivered messages from God. The Hebrew Bible records their messages. These images are artists' impressions of the prophets.

▲ Isaiah (eye ZAY uh) urged people to act morally.

▲ Ezekiel (ih ZEE kee ul) predicted that the Jews would survive hardship.

Jeremiah (jehr uh MY uh) condemned those who were unfaithful to God. ▶

177

▲ This Talmud was written by hand in medieval Europe.

◄ Students traditionally study the Talmud in pairs.

Commandments. Many of these laws give directions for religious rituals. Others describe how to have a fair society, how to help those in need, and even how to protect the health of the community through cleanliness and sanitation.

Many centuries after the time of Moses, prominent Jewish **rabbis** (RAB yz), or religious teachers, recorded oral laws that they believed had come down from the teachings of Moses. Other rabbis discussed how laws should be interpreted in different situations. Eventually, they wrote down their commentaries, or discussions, about the laws. The **Talmud** (TAHL mood), a text finished around A.D. 600, is a collection of oral teachings and commentaries about the Hebrew Bible and Jewish law. Jews still study and discuss it.

The Importance of Law and Learning

commentary, *n.*, a set of comments or a recorded discussion about something

The Hebrew Bible and <u>commentaries</u> on the Bible are vitally important to Jews. They are important because they are the source of Jews' most important teachings, including teachings about ethics.

Laws, the Talmud, and Commentaries Respect for God's laws is basic to Judaism. The great leader Moses is known to Jews as "Moses our teacher." The Torah contains many laws in addition to the Ten

The Need to Study The Hebrew Bible and the Talmud are central to Jewish teaching and practice. As a result, Jewish people value the study of these religious texts. Jewish scholars still write commentaries on the Scriptures today.

The Hebrew Bible is mostly written in the Hebrew language. As a result, many Jewish people try to learn to read Hebrew. Some also learn Aramaic, the language of most of the Talmud.

Reading Check Why do Jewish people value the Hebrew Bible and Talmud?

Basic Teachings

The Jews' idea of God was unique in the ancient world. In other early religions, people worshiped many gods. They had images of these gods made of wood, stone, pottery, or metal. People believed that each god lived in a certain place. In contrast, the God of the Israelites did not live in stones, rocks, or the sea. He did not take a human or an animal form. He was invisible, and yet he was everywhere.

> 66 Am I only a God near at hand
> —says the LORD—
> And not a God far away?
> If a man enters a hiding place,
> Do I not see him?
> —says the LORD—
> For I fill both heaven and earth
> —declares the LORD. 99
>
> —Jeremiah 23:23–24

Ethical Monotheism According to the Bible, in the Sinai desert the Israelites made a covenant with God to follow a code of laws, including the Ten Commandments. Along with the Ten Commandments, Jews follow other teachings from the Torah, as interpreted by the Talmud and other commentaries. Many of these teachings have to do with ethics.

Ethical monotheism is probably the most important teaching of Judaism. This is the idea that there is one God who sets down ethical rules, or rules about right and wrong. Being faithful to God means following these rules.

The Key Teachings of Judaism

The table at right lists key teachings of Judaism. **Which teachings do the photos below illustrate?**

▲ Young American Jews at the sacred Western Wall in Jerusalem

▲ A Jewish volunteer

1. *Ethical monotheism*
   There is only one God. God wants people to lead moral lives. All people are created in the image of God, so everybody is equally important.

2. *Observance of law*
   The Hebrew Bible and Talmud have laws to guide how Jews live and treat other people. Judaism teaches that what you do is more important than what you believe.

3. *Love for others*
   The Hebrew Bible states, "Love your fellow human being as yourself." Jews are expected to help others, for example by fighting discrimination and giving to charity.

4. *Weekly day of rest*
   The idea of a weekly day of rest, or Sabbath, began in Judaism.

5. *Commitment to study and prayer*
   Studying the Hebrew Bible leads to wisdom and good deeds. Knowledge is valuable. People communicate with God through prayer.

6. *Connection to the Land of Israel*
   The Land of Israel, where Judaism and the Jewish people began, has a central role in the Hebrew Bible and is home to Judaism's most sacred sites.

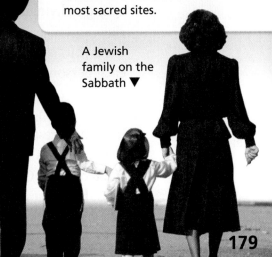

A Jewish family on the Sabbath ▼

Jewish Traditions

Judaism includes traditions that take place both within and outside the home. These include the Sabbath, a special Passover meal, and the Bar or Bat Mitzvah, when a young person becomes a full member of the Jewish community.

▲ A Passover Seder (SAY dur) plate holds foods eaten at this special Passover meal.

◀ A woman lights Sabbath candles.

A Jewish girl reads from the Torah at her Bat Mitzvah.

Culture Close-Up

A Jewish family shares a Passover Seder.

Righteousness and Justice Ethical monotheism calls on Jews to know the difference between right and wrong. For Jews, actions should be based on righteousness and justice. **Righteousness** is acting or living in a way that is ethically right and obeys God's laws.

As you have learned, Jews believe that each person has value and worth because he or she is created in the image of God. Along with <u>individual</u> worth comes individual responsibility to God. Each individual has the responsibility to act righteously in God's eyes.

Righteousness was a key concern of the prophets. For example, they reminded people that they needed to be honest and kind to each other. They criticized rulers who were cruel to the poor and weak. They urged people to work for **justice**— fairness or fair treatment—for everyone. Jewish teachers also expected everyone to help those in need.

Observance of Law The laws and other rules that Jews follow are seen as part of the Jewish people's covenant with God. According to the Torah, God had a special relationship with the Israelites. In return, the Israelites believed that they had a responsibility to obey God's laws and commandments.

individual, *adj.,* having to do with a single person or thing

The Jewish idea of individual responsibility means that these laws and commandments apply equally to every Jewish person. This means that God's laws apply equally to leaders such as Moses and to the ordinary people who follow them. This idea of equality in the eyes of God helped shape modern systems of law.

Love for Others The Hebrew Bible commands, "Love your fellow [human being] as yourself." Jewish people are required to help others. As a result, Jews have been involved in many efforts to fight discrimination. Jewish people also give charity in reponse to this teaching. These ideas have influenced modern thinking about human rights.

Other Key Teachings Another important Jewish teaching is to observe the **Sabbath,** or a weekly day of rest. For Jews, the Sabbath is the seventh day of the week, or Saturday. According to Jewish teachings, this should be a day free from work.

Many nations have adopted the idea of a weekly day of rest.

Jewish teaching also stresses the importance of study and prayer. You have learned about the importance of studying the Scriptures and commentaries on them, such as the Talmud. Jewish people also value prayer as a way of communicating with God.

Jewish teachings also include Jewish people's ties to the Land of Israel. This is the land that was promised to Abraham, according to the Torah. It includes the modern state of Israel. Many Jewish people feel a deep connection to this land because of its place in the Jewish Scriptures and Jewish history.

Reading Check What is ethical monotheism?

A box used by Jews to collect donations for charities ▼

Section **2** Assessment

Key Terms

1. Explain who the Jewish prophets were.

2. Describe the relationships among the Scriptures, the Talmud, and Jewish ideas of righteousness and justice.

3. Which Jewish teaching has to do with the Sabbath?

Key Ideas

4. What are the three main parts of the Hebrew Bible and how do they differ?

5. Why is studying the Hebrew Bible and commentaries such as the Talmud so important to Jews?

6. Explain how Jews follow the teaching "Love your fellow [human being] as yourself."

Think Critically

7. **Summarize** Why might ethical monotheism be considered the most important Jewish teaching, and how is it related to other Jewish teachings?

8. **Synthesize** How are God's covenants with the Jewish people related to Jewish teachings about ethics and justice?

Essential Question

How are religion and culture connected?

9. Give examples of ways in which Judaism as a religion has shaped Jewish culture. Go to your Student Journal to record your answer.

The Jewish People

Key Ideas
- A kingdom emerged in the Land of Israel, but it was later divided and conquered.
- Over time, Jewish communities spread to many different parts of the ancient world.
- The religious and ethical teachings of Judaism influenced later religions and civilizations.

Key Terms • judge • exile • Diaspora • synagogue

Visual Glossary

┼┼┼┼┼┼ **Reading Skill Sequence** Take notes using the graphic organizer in your journal.

A modern artist's painting of King Solomon of Israel at the opening of the First Temple ▼

After the Israelites settled in the Land of Israel, they lived as a group of separate tribes before joining to form a kingdom. After about 70 years, the kingdom split, and the Israelites were later conquered by foreign empires. The descendants of the Israelites, known as Jews, later spread to many parts of the world.

The Kingdom of Israel

Most of what we know of early Jewish history comes from the Hebrew Bible. Archaeologists also have found evidence for some of the events mentioned in the Bible before about 900 B.C. After that date, there is even more evidence from other written sources and from archaeology for events mentioned in the Bible.

The Time of the Judges As you have read, the Hebrew Bible states that Joshua led the Israelites in the conquest of Canaan. After Joshua died, the Israelites remained a group of tribes without a common government. They faced a number of conflicts with other peoples.

In times of distress, the Israelites often rallied around leaders called judges. As the term is used in the Bible, a **judge** was a leader who could rally the Israelites to defend their land. Judges were often warriors or prophets. Judges did not pass leadership to their descendants.

Some women became well known during the time of the judges. The prophet Deborah, who inspired an army to win a great battle, was the only female judge. Another well-known woman was Ruth, whose story you have read. Ruth, who came from Moab, married an

Israelite living in her country. When her husband died, Ruth followed her mother-in-law Naomi back to the Land of Israel. There, she accepted Naomi's religion and became a member of the tribe of Judah.

According to the Bible, the time of the judges ended when the warrior Saul became the first king of Israel.

David and Solomon The Hebrew Bible states that one of Saul's best fighters was David, a young shepherd and musician. David became the next king, about 1000 B.C. David captured the city of Jerusalem and made it his capital. He extended the borders of the kingdom.

David is also believed to have written beautiful psalms—poems or songs in the Bible—such as this one:

◀ King David, as sculpted by Michelangelo

66 The Lord is my shepherd;
I lack nothing. . . .
Though I walk through a valley of deepest darkness,
I fear no harm, for You are with me;
Your rod and Your staff—they comfort me. 99

—Psalm 23:1, 4

David's son Solomon ruled after him. He <u>commissioned</u> the great First Temple in Jerusalem. According to tradition, Solomon wrote many of the wise sayings in the Bible's Book of Proverbs.

commission, *v.,* order the creation of

The Kingdom Divides The kingdom of Israel split into two parts after Solomon died, around 900 B.C. Solomon's descendants ruled the kingdom of Judah in the south. From the name *Judah*, the religion of the Israelites became known as Judaism, and the descendants of the Israelites became known as Jews.

Map Skills

1 **Movement** In which direction would David have traveled from Jerusalem to conquer Aram?

2 **Region** How did the region ruled from Jerusalem change between 966 and 722 B.C.?

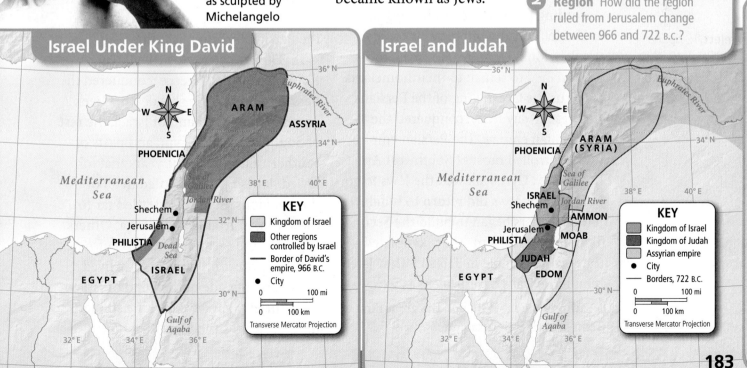

Israel Under King David

ARAM
ASSYRIA
PHOENICIA
Euphrates River
36° N
34° N
38° E 40° E
32° N
Mediterranean Sea
Sea of Galilee
Jordan River
Shechem
Jerusalem
Dead Sea
PHILISTIA
ISRAEL
EGYPT
30° N
Gulf of Aqaba
32° E 34° E 36° E

KEY
☐ Kingdom of Israel
☐ Other regions controlled by Israel
— Border of David's empire, 966 B.C.
• City
0   100 mi
0   100 km
Transverse Mercator Projection

Israel and Judah

Euphrates River
36° N
34° N
ARAM (SYRIA)
PHOENICIA
ISRAEL
Shechem
AMMON
Jerusalem
MOAB
PHILISTIA
JUDAH
EDOM
EGYPT
Mediterranean Sea
Sea of Galilee
Jordan River
38° E 40° E
30° N
Gulf of Aqaba
32° E 34° E 36° E

KEY
☐ Kingdom of Israel
☐ Kingdom of Judah
☐ Assyrian empire
• City
— Borders, 722 B.C.
0   100 mi
0   100 km
Transverse Mercator Projection

183

A rival, or competing, kingdom in the north kept the name of the kingdom of Israel. About 722 B.C., the Assyrian empire conquered the kingdom of Israel. The Assyrians were brutal rulers. Thousands of Israelites were sent to distant parts of the empire. Other Israelites avoided capture by fleeing south to Judah.

One hundred years later, the city-state of Babylon, in present-day Iraq, rebelled against Assyria and began the second Babylonian empire. Babylon's greatest emperor, Nebuchadnezzar (neb yuh kud NEZ ur) conquered Judah. About 587 B.C., the Babylonians destroyed Jerusalem, including Solomon's Temple.

The Babylonian Captivity

The Babylonians took thousands of people from Judah, later known as Jews, to faraway Babylon. Many Jewish prophets urged the Jews to obey the Hebrew Scriptures while living in exile. **Exile** means separation from one's homeland. According to the Bible, some Jews, such as Daniel, became important people in the Babylonian empire. However, most Jews wished to return to their homeland.

Cyrus the Great, king of the Persians (in present-day Iran), conquered the Babylonian empire. The Persian empire now controlled most of Southwest Asia. In 538 B.C., Cyrus allowed the Jews to go home. Many Jews did return to Judah. Jewish leaders began to build the Second Temple in Jerusalem. They completed the Second Temple in 515 B.C. They later rebuilt the walls of Jerusalem as well.

Reading Check Who had the great First Temple built in Jerusalem?

reject, *v.,* decide against, turn away

The Diaspora

The Babylonian Exile was a turning point in Jewish history. Communities of Jews now lived throughout the Babylonian empire, which stretched across the Fertile Crescent. These communities outside the Land of Israel came to be known as the **Diaspora** (dy AS puh ruh), or communities of Jews living outside of their ancient homeland. *Diaspora* is a Greek word meaning dispersion, or scattering.

Lands of the Diaspora After the Persians conquered Babylon, their empire spread across all of Southwest Asia. The Persian empire included the Land of Israel, but it also included Egypt, Asia Minor (present-day Turkey), Mesopotamia, what is now Iran, and parts of Central Asia. Jewish people spread across these regions.

One of the best-known Jewish people in the Persian empire was Esther. According to the Bible, she married the Persian emperor. One of his advisors planned to kill all Jewish people. Esther convinced the Persian king to reject this plan.

In 330 B.C., Alexander the Great, from present-day Greece, conquered the Persian empire. After his death, Greek empires ruled the Land of Israel, the rest of Southwest Asia, Egypt, and parts of southern Europe. In the years that followed, Jewish people settled in all of these regions. Some also settled far to the south, in Arabia and Africa. Others settled to the east in many parts of Asia.

By this time, millions of Jews lived inside and outside of the Land of Israel. Nonetheless, Jews everywhere still looked to Jerusalem as their spiritual home.

Closer Look

The Diaspora

After 725 B.C., a series of empires conquered the Land of Israel. Some Jews moved to other lands in Asia, Africa, and Europe. In modern times, they have moved to other continents.

THINK CRITICALLY Why might Jews have left Europe in modern times?

2 The Great Synagogue in Budapest, Hungary

3 Esther, a queen of ancient Persia

Jewish Migrations

1 Anne Frank, a Jewish girl killed because of prejudice

KEY

→ Jewish migrations

• City

0 ——— 2,000 mi

0 ——— 2,000 km

Miller Cylindrical Projection

NORTH AMERICA

EUROPE

ASIA

ATLANTIC OCEAN

Jerusalem

AFRICA

4 Maimonides, a philosopher in the Middle Ages

PACIFIC OCEAN

SOUTH AMERICA

N W E S

INDIAN OCEAN

EQUATOR

0°

AUSTRALIA

30° S

ATLANTIC OCEAN

30° E   60° E   90° E

7 Albert Einstein, a German-American physicist

6 Temple Emanu-El in New York City

5 The Great Synagogue of Cape Town, South Africa

185

There are about
6.5 million
Jewish people in
the United
States.

New Ways to Worship The Diaspora brought changes in the way Jews worshiped. Many Jews lived too far from Jerusalem to return for worship.

Previously, most Jews could worship at the Temple in Jerusalem. Because of the Diaspora, however, Jews had to practice their faith wherever they were.

Some Jews had already been used to gathering in a **synagogue,** or meeting place. There they could pray and discuss the Scriptures. Often, someone who knew the Scriptures well became the group's rabbi, or teacher. In the Diaspora, synagogues became even more important.

Greek and Roman Rule After the Babylonian Exile ended, Jews in the Land of Israel tried hard to live according to their religion. However, they faced harsh and unfair treatment by rulers of the Greek and Roman empires.

Jews rebelled against harsh Greek rule. During the 100s B.C., a family known as the Maccabees rebelled and won independence from Greek rulers who tried to ban important parts of Judaism. The Jewish holiday of Hanukkah celebrates the victory of the Maccabees and their reclaiming of the Temple.

In A.D. 6, the Land of Israel became part of the Roman empire. By this time, it was called Judaea, or "land of the Jewish people." Disrespect toward Judaism led Jews to rebel against Rome. In response, in A.D. 70, the Romans destroyed Jerusalem, including the Second Temple.

More Dispersions The Romans also killed or enslaved thousands of Jews. Thousands more fled to other lands inside and outside of the empire.

During the war, a teacher from the Second Temple named Yohanan ben Zaccai (YOH hah nahn ben ZAH ky) secretly visited the Roman commander. He received permission to set up a center for Jewish scholars in another part of Judaea. The temple was gone, but learning survived and remained important to Jews.

After another Jewish rebellion, the Romans changed the name of the province in A.D. 135 to Palestine, after the ancient Israelites' enemies the Philistines.

Reading Check Why were synagogues important in the Diaspora?

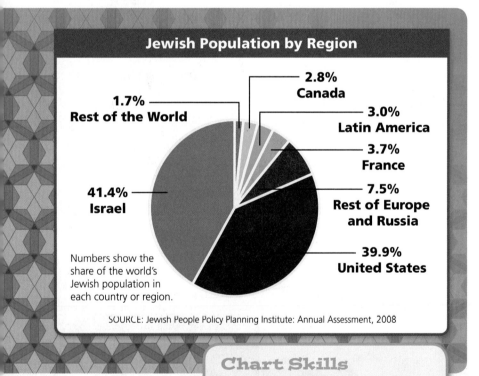

Jewish Population by Region

2.8%
Canada

1.7%
Rest of the World

3.0%
Latin America

3.7%
France

41.4%
Israel

7.5%
Rest of Europe and Russia

39.9%
United States

Numbers show the share of the world's Jewish population in each country or region.

SOURCE: Jewish People Policy Planning Institute: Annual Assessment, 2008

Chart Skills

1 Which country has the most Jewish people?

2 Does the chart show which country has the fewest Jewish people?

21st Century Learning

The Legacy of Judaism

Today, nearly 14 million Jewish people live throughout the world. A large majority of the world's Jewish people live in either the United States or Israel.

Judaism's legacies, or the concepts and values it has given the world, include teachings about one supreme, invisible God who created everything. Christians and Muslims, like Jews, honor Abraham as a founding figure and Moses as a messenger of God. They both share with Jews the belief in a single God. The ethical teachings of Judaism have influenced spiritual leaders in all parts of the world.

The Hebrew Bible is another legacy of Judaism. Its beautiful language makes it a classic of world literature, as do its dramatic stories of unforgettable characters such as Moses, David, and Esther.

One of the greatest legacies of Judaism is the Judeo-Christian tradition. This is the set of values shared by both Judaism and Christianity that are part of a lasting moral and ethical tradition. Judeo-Christian values form a basis for modern democratic societies such as the United States. These values include the equal importance of every individual, individual freedom and responsibility, community responsibility, and the importance of human rights and justice.

Reading Check What is the Judeo-Christian tradition?

myWorld Activity
Exploring Dispersion

Jewish rabbis meet with Christian priests and ministers. ▼

Section 3 Assessment

Key Terms
1. Define the word *judge* as it is used in the Hebrew Bible.
2. Explain what the exile in Babylon was and how it led to the Diaspora.
3. What are synagogues?

Key Ideas
4. What eventually happened to the kingdoms of Israel and Judah and their people?
5. Why did many Jewish people leave the Land of Israel, and where else did they settle?
6. Describe some of the ways in which Judaism has influenced modern democratic societies.

Think Critically
7. Draw Conclusions How did the position of the Land of Israel, in a region conquered by several ancient empires, affect Jewish history?
8. Synthesize How did Jewish people preserve their cultural and religious traditions in the Diaspora?

? Essential Question
How are religion and culture connected?

9. Explain how Judaism shaped the culture of Jews in the Diaspora. Go to your Student Journal to record your answer.

myworldhistory.com 21st Century Learning

187

Chapter Assessment

Key Terms and Ideas

1. **Describe** What was the **Exodus?**

2. **Discuss** What is the connection between the **Torah** and Jewish **ethics?**

3. **Recall** According to the **Torah,** what is the Promised Land?

4. **Define** What is the **Sabbath?**

5. **Discuss** What is the role of the **rabbi** in Judaism?

6. **Explain** Why is study an important part of Judaism?

7. **Describe** What is the focus of the basic teachings of Judaism?

8. **Define** What is the **Diaspora?**

9. **Describe** What happened to the first kingdom of Israel?

10. **List** What are some of the legacies of Judaism?

Think Critically

11. **Synthesize** Why are law and ethics important in Judaism?

12. **Identify Evidence** What is the main source for the basic teachings of Judaism? Support your answer with evidence from the text.

13. **Summarize** What role did covenants play in the development of Judaism?

14. **Analyze Cause and Effect** Why did many Jews leave the Land of Israel after 750 B.C.?

15. **Draw Inferences** How did Jews' movement away from the Land of Israel affect Judaism?

16. **Core Concepts: Religion** What are some similarities and differences between Judaism and other world religions?

Analyze Visuals

Use the map at right to answer the following questions.

17. Where on this map were the Promised Land and the first kingdom of Israel?

18. According to the Hebrew Bible, where on this map were the Israelites kept as slaves?

19. Where on this map did Jewish people live during the Diaspora?

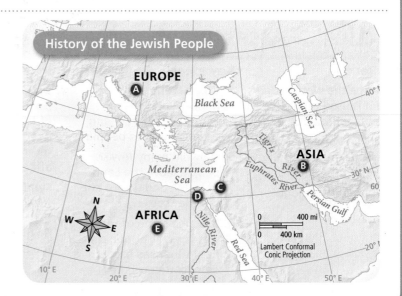

History of the Jewish People

Essential Question
myWorld Chapter Activity

Wall of Fame Follow your teacher's instructions to create posters about five famous Jewish people from history. Your posters will present the world in which each person lived and show why he or she is famous.

21st Century Learning
Develop Cultural Awareness

Form small groups. Following your teacher's instructions, consider and discuss the following questions with your group. Then present your group's findings to the class.
• Identify a Jewish teaching that is similar to an American value.
• Which American value is similar?
• In what ways are they similar?

Document-Based Questions

Success Tracker™
Online at myworldhistory.com

Use your knowledge of Judaism and the Jewish people and Documents A and B to answer Questions 1–3.

Document A

" It is Wisdom calling,
. . . she shouts, . . .
'All my words are just,
None of them perverse or crooked.
All are straightforward to the intelligent man,
And right to those who have attained knowledge.'"

—from Proverbs 8,
Tanakh, The Holy Scriptures.
The Jewish Publication Society

Document B

" Only those who cultivate both religious practices and mathematics, logic, natural science, and metaphysics [thoughts on the nature of existence] are privileged to enter the inner courtyard of God. Only after having thus comprehended Him and His works . . . can man . . . strengthen the bond that links man to Him—namely, human intellect [reason]."

—from Maimonides, *Guide to the Perplexed,* cited in *Maimonides: His Wisdom for Our Time,* Gilbert S. Rosenthal (editor)

1. According to Document A, who can find wisdom?

A those who are perverse

B those who are crooked

C those who have knowledge

D those who are just

2. According to Document B, why is learning important?

A It increases a person's math skills.

B It helps connect a person to God.

C It reveals the nature of existence.

D It increases a person's reasoning skills.

3. Writing Task Based on Documents A and B, write a paragraph discussing the importance of knowledge and learning for Judaism.

myworldhistory.com

Self-Test

Polytheism and Monotheism

Key Idea
- Ancient Egyptian religious beliefs were very different from the ideas expressed in the Hebrew and Christian Bibles.

The Book of the Dead is a collection of spells, prayers, and drawings that ancient Egyptians often buried with their dead. Egyptians believed that these texts would help the dead find happiness in the afterlife. Egyptian religious beliefs are an example of polytheism, or the belief in more than one god. Monotheism, or the belief in one god, is expressed in both the Hebrew and the Christian Bibles, from which the second excerpt comes. In Psalms 23 and 24, the writer compares God to a shepherd watching over his sheep.

Illustrations from the Book of the Dead

Read the text on the right. Stop at each circled letter. Then answer the question with the same letter on the left.

Ⓐ Analyze Primary Sources What words indicate that the speaker believes in more than one god?

Ⓑ Draw Inferences Why do you think the speaker says he has "destroyed wickedness"?

Ⓒ Summarize In your own words, explain the meaning of the last four lines.

homage, *n.,* respect, honor

behold, *v.,* to gaze upon, see, observe

oppressed, *v.,* crushed or burdened by abuse of power

wrought, *v.,* produced, shaped, made

The Book of the Dead

❝ <u>Homage</u> to you, Great God, . . .
I have come to you, my Lord,
I have brought myself here to <u>behold</u> your beauties.
I know you, and I know your name,
Ⓐ And I know the names of the two and forty gods,
Who live with you in the Hall of the Two Truths,
Who imprison the sinners, and feed upon their blood, . . .
Ⓑ And I have destroyed wickedness for you.
I have committed no evil upon men.
I have not <u>oppressed</u> the members of my family.
I have not <u>wrought</u> evil in the place of right and truth.
I have had no knowledge of useless men.
I have brought about no evil. . . .
I have not brought my name forward to be praised.
Ⓒ I have not oppressed servants.
I have not scorned any god. ❞
—*The Egyptian Book of the Dead,* translated by Wallace Budge

Read the text on the right. Stop at each circled letter. Then answer the question with the same letter on the left.

D **Analyze Details** What language in these lines indicates a peaceful tone?

E **Draw Conclusions** What does this passage suggest about the author's view of God?

F **Draw Inferences** What do these lines show about the author's faith and belief in God?

want, *v.,* to fail to possess; lack

anoint, *v.,* to apply oil to as a sacred rite

Psalms of David

❝ The LORD is my shepherd, I shall not <u>want</u>. He makes me lie down in green pastures; he leads me beside still waters; he **D** restores my soul. He leads me in right paths for his name's sake. Even though I walk through the darkest valley, I fear no evil; **E** for you are with me; your rod and your staff—they comfort me. You prepare a table before me in the presence of my enemies; you <u>anoint</u> my head with oil; my cup overflows. Surely goodness **F** and mercy shall follow me all the days of my life, and I shall dwell in the house of the LORD my whole life long.

The earth is the LORD's and all that is in it, the world, and those who live in it; for he has founded it on the seas, and established it on the rivers. Who shall ascend the hill of the LORD? And who shall stand in his holy place? Those who have clean hands and pure hearts, who do not lift up their souls to what is false, and do not swear deceitfully. They will receive blessing from the LORD, and vindication from the God of their salvation. Such is the company of those who seek him, who seek the face of the God of Jacob. ❞

—Psalms 23 and 24, *New Revised Standard Version Bible*

Analyze the Documents

1. **Compare and Contrast** How are the two documents similar and different?
2. **Writing Task** What do the two documents suggest about ancient religious beliefs? Explain your thoughts in a short paragraph.

Creation of the Animals, Jacopo Tintoretto, 1550

Solve a Water Shortage

Your Mission Research past and present irrigation technology used to manage water-shortage problems. In a small group, write a report about how different peoples have handled water shortages. Then brainstorm ideas for a way to deal with a real-life water shortage in the world today. As a class, develop a proposed solution to submit to an organization or person that might be able to help.

Suppose you had to spend most of your day searching for clean water to use for drinking or cooking. In some parts of the world, that is what people must do to survive. Fertile land and sufficient water can support a society, but what happens when clean water runs out? Droughts can wipe out crops and lead to widespread famine and death.

Having too little clean water is a serious problem for many people in the world. Can your ideas be part of the solution?

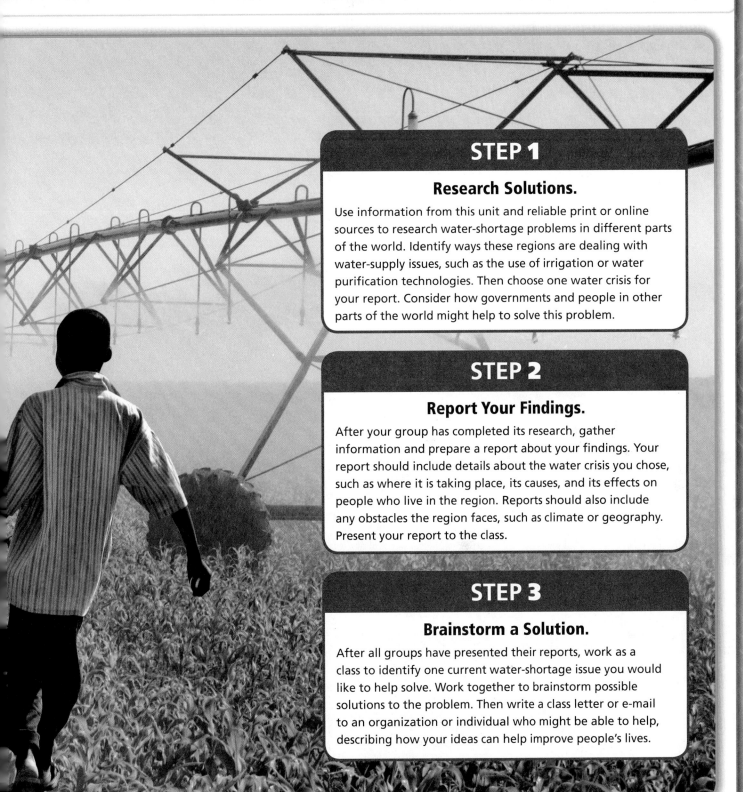

STEP **1**

Research Solutions.

Use information from this unit and reliable print or online sources to research water-shortage problems in different parts of the world. Identify ways these regions are dealing with water-supply issues, such as the use of irrigation or water purification technologies. Then choose one water crisis for your report. Consider how governments and people in other parts of the world might help to solve this problem.

STEP **2**

Report Your Findings.

After your group has completed its research, gather information and prepare a report about your findings. Your report should include details about the water crisis you chose, such as where it is taking place, its causes, and its effects on people who live in the region. Reports should also include any obstacles the region faces, such as climate or geography. Present your report to the class.

STEP **3**

Brainstorm a Solution.

After all groups have presented their reports, work as a class to identify one current water-shortage issue you would like to help solve. Work together to brainstorm possible solutions to the problem. Then write a class letter or e-mail to an organization or individual who might be able to help, describing how your ideas can help improve people's lives.

my worldhistory.com

21st Century Learning

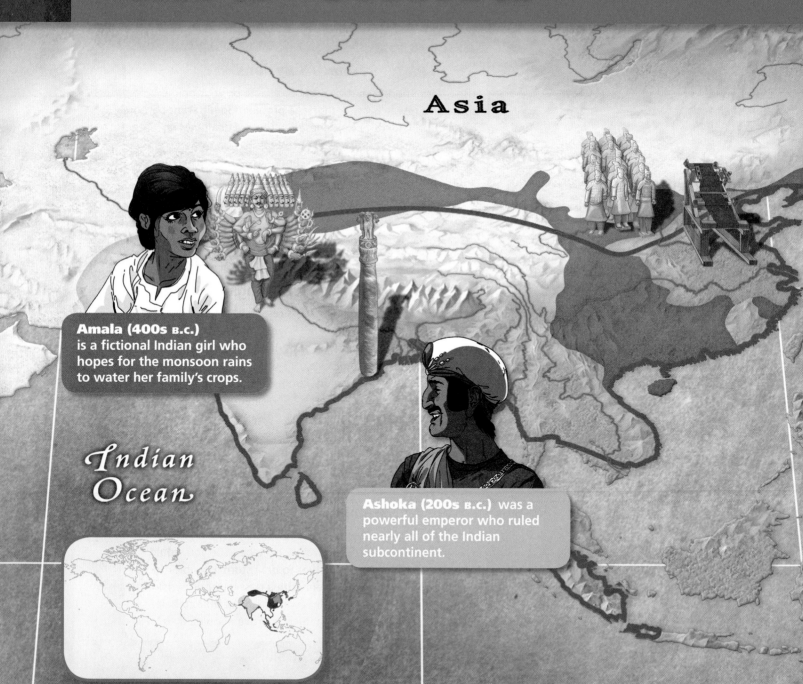

Ancient India and China

Asia

Amala (400s B.C.) is a fictional Indian girl who hopes for the monsoon rains to water her family's crops.

Indian Ocean

Ashoka (200s B.C.) was a powerful emperor who ruled nearly all of the Indian subcontinent.

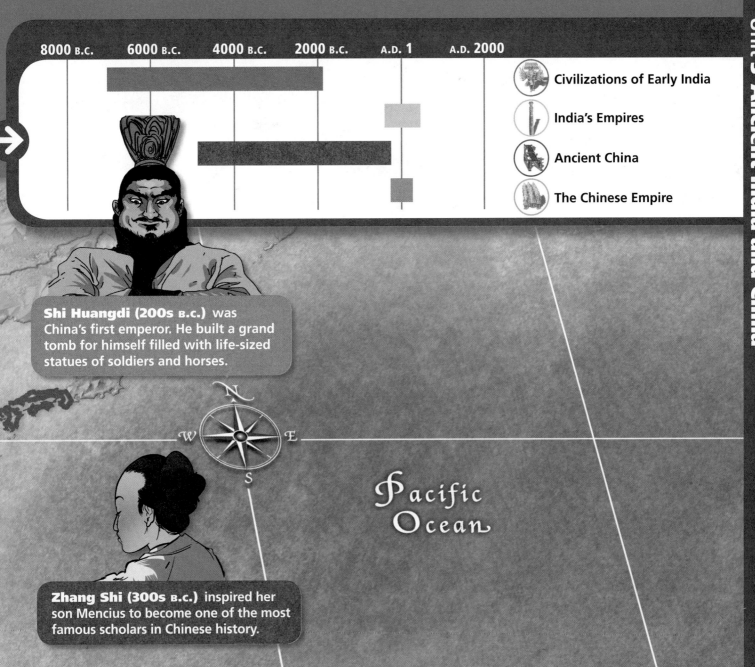

| 8000 B.C. | 6000 B.C. | 4000 B.C. | 2000 B.C. | A.D. 1 | A.D. 2000 |

- Civilizations of Early India
- India's Empires
- Ancient China
- The Chinese Empire

Shi Huangdi (200s B.C.) was China's first emperor. He built a grand tomb for himself filled with life-sized statues of soldiers and horses.

Zhang Shi (300s B.C.) inspired her son Mencius to become one of the most famous scholars in Chinese history.

Pacific Ocean

Chapter 6
Civilizations of Early India

Chapter 7
India's Empires

Chapter 8
Ancient China

Chapter 9
The Chinese Empire

* Colors on the map correspond to the areas covered in each chapter.

Unit 3 Ancient India and China

195

Chapter 6

Civilizations of Early India

Essential Question

How much does geography affect people's lives?

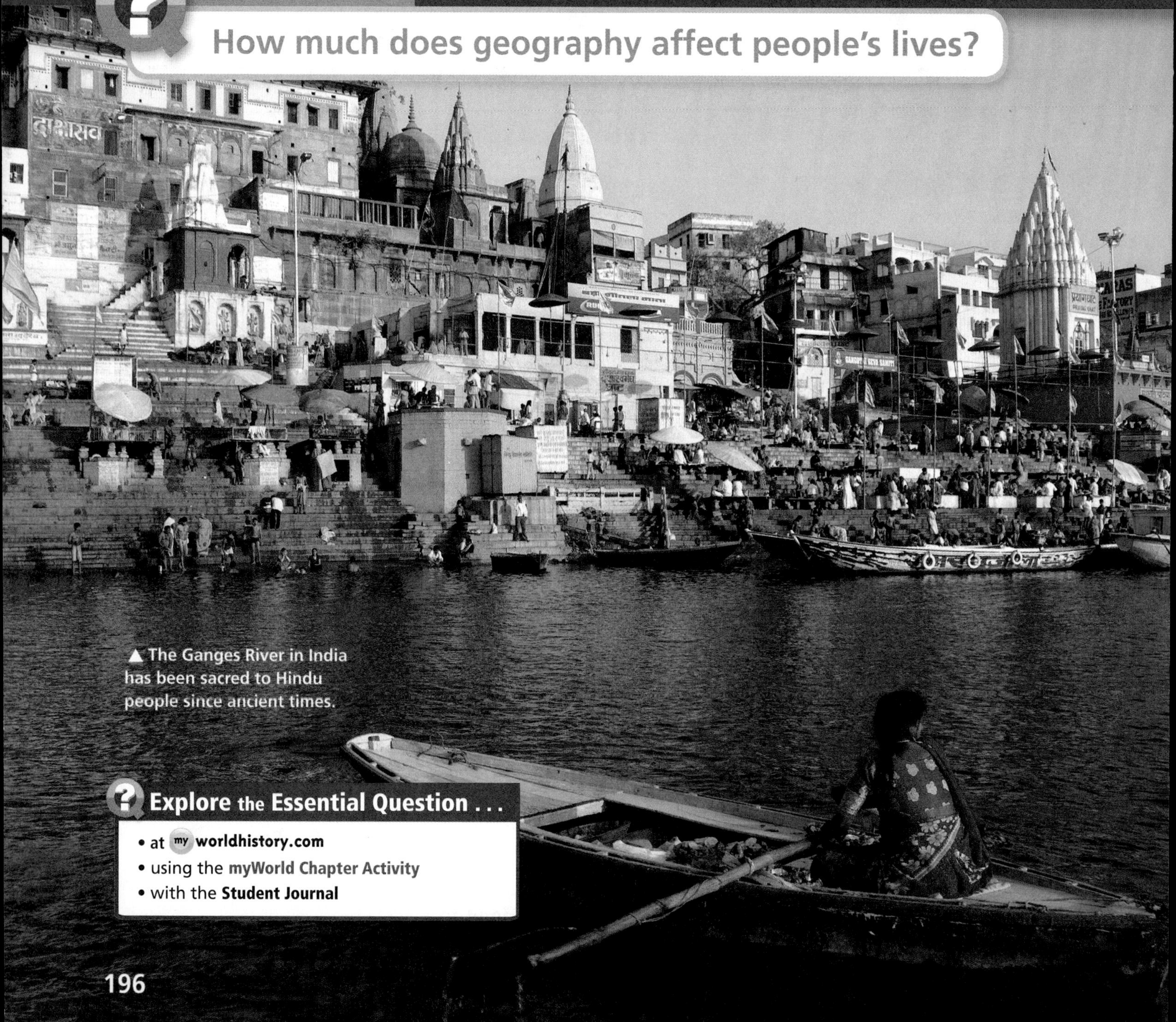

▲ The Ganges River in India has been sacred to Hindu people since ancient times.

Explore the Essential Question . . .

- at myworldhistory.com
- using the **myWorld Chapter Activity**
- with the **Student Journal**

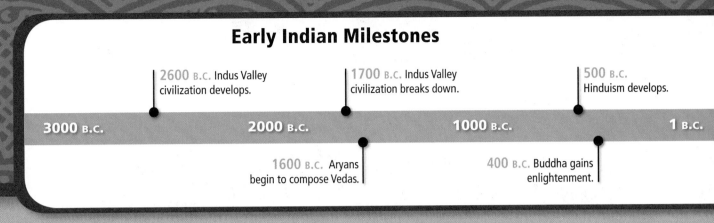

Early Indian Milestones

2600 B.C. Indus Valley civilization develops.

1700 B.C. Indus Valley civilization breaks down.

500 B.C. Hinduism develops.

3000 B.C.   2000 B.C.   1000 B.C.   1 B.C.

1600 B.C. Aryans begin to compose Vedas.

400 B.C. Buddha gains enlightenment.

Amala and Trijata

This is the fictional story of Amala, a young woman living in India sometime after 500 B.C.

One morning Amala's mother had a headache. When thirteen-year-old Amala asked her mother what was wrong, her mother said she was worried that the monsoon rains were not going to come, and that all the valley's crops would dry up and blow away.

Amala did not know what to tell her mother. They sat together in front of their hut, and then Amala's mother asked her to get some river water so she could cool her forehead.

On her way down the hill to the river, Amala walked by the drooping wheat shoots. The plants looked thirsty. The sun beat down on the hard, dry soil. Amala scooped up a handful of dusty dirt. Perhaps her mother was right—perhaps the rains would not come. What would they do then?

my worldhistory.com

Timeline/On Assignment

197

Amala daydreams beneath a tree.

Ravana kidnaps Sita and carries her away in his chariot.

At the edge of the Ganges River, Amala looked up at the foothills of the Himalayas to the north. She remembered her father explaining that the river began in those mountains where the god Brahma washed the feet of the god Vishnu. She also remembered her mother telling her that *Amala* meant "clean and pure," a tribute to the holy Ganges.

Amala looked at her reflection in the Ganges. She was wearing the cotton sari her mother had woven. She stirred the water with her hand. Her reflection blurred in the rippling water and her face became another face—the face of Trijata.

Trijata was Amala's favorite character in the *Ramayana,* the long story her grandfather told while they sat under the stars beside the *yagna,* the community fireplace. The story was about Rama, a human form of Vishnu. Like the river, Rama was calm but very strong. However, Rama had a dreadful enemy.

Rama's enemy was Ravana. Ravana had several heads and arms. He commanded an army of rakshasas, or demons. One day, Ravana kidnapped Rama's beautiful wife Sita. Poor Sita! She was trapped in Ravana's kingdom for so long that she began to lose hope that Rama would ever save her.

Ravana had a niece, Trijata. She was a rakshasa, but she was not like the other rakshasas. They were cruel and bloodthirsty, but Trijata was kindhearted and compassionate. Amala loved the part in the *Ramayana* when Trijata dreams that Rama destroys Ravana and his rakshasa army, demolishes Ravana's kingdom, and saves Sita. When Trijata wakes from her dream, she runs to the courtyard where several rakshasas are terrorizing Sita, threatening to tear her flesh from her bones and eat her piece-by-piece. "Stop!" Trijata demands. "If you do not treat Sita with respect, Rama will destroy you! I have seen this come true in my dream!" Then the other rakshasas back away from Sita, and good-hearted, compassionate Trijata reassures Sita that Rama will indeed come for her.

After facing many challenges, Rama fights Ravana. After two days of battle, Rama calls on God for help. As a result of his prayer, his arrow becomes the missile of Brahma. Rama shoots this weapon, and it flies into Ravana's heart and kills him. Finally, Rama rescues Sita.

Amala watched the river's surface become smooth. Her own face was again sharp in the water. Suddenly, she knew what to tell her mother. She

Trijata warns the other rakshasas to stay away from Sita.

Rama kills Ravana by shooting a mighty arrow into his heart.

would echo the message of Trijata. She would tell her mother that she must not lose hope. She would sprinkle the clean, pure water of the holy Ganges on her mother's forehead, and she would say, "The rain will come, mother. Like Rama to Sita, the rain will come."

In this story, you read about Amala, a fictional character set in the world of early India. Based on this story, how important do you think geography, including climate, was to the people of early India? As you read the chapter ahead, think about what Amala's story tells you about life in early India.

 myStory Video

Join Amala as she learns the importance of hope.

Section 1
Indus Valley Civilization

Key Ideas
- The Indian subcontinent's first civilization grew along the Indus River.
- The Indus Valley civilization had large, well-planned cities, a strong government, and an extensive trade network.
- We do not understand the Indus Valley civilization's writing, so its politics, religion, and history remain a mystery.

Key Terms • subcontinent • river system • monsoon • granary • citadel 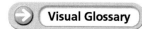 **Visual Glossary**

 Reading Skill Identify Main Ideas and Details Take notes using the graphic organizer in your journal.

The first civilizations arose near rivers. One such civilization was in India. Its people farmed along the Indus River. Farmers grew plenty of food, and populations grew. In time, some of the people settled in towns and cities and formed governments.

The Indian Subcontinent

Geographers divide the continent of Asia into regions. One of those regions is South Asia. It looks like a huge triangle jutting out into the Indian Ocean. Today, it includes the countries of India, Pakistan, Bangladesh, Sri Lanka, Maldives, Nepal, and Bhutan. India is by far the biggest country in the region.

For much of its history, all of South Asia was known simply as India. It is still called the Indian subcontinent. A **subcontinent** is a large landmass that is set apart from the rest of the continent. The Indian subcontinent stretches almost 2,000 miles from north to south. In some places, it is nearly as wide from east to west. The subcontinent is separated from the rest of Asia by the towering Himalayas and Hindu Kush, two mountain ranges to the north.

The Indus Valley civilization developed near the banks of the Indus River. ▼

River Systems The Indus River flows across the northwestern part of the subcontinent. The Indus forms part of a **river system,** or a main river and all of the other rivers and streams that drain into it. These rivers start as melting snow and ice in the mountains and flow to the sea.

India's first civilization grew around the valley of the Indus River. This civilization developed in an area that is dry most of the year. When the river flooded, it left behind rich soil. River water let farmers harvest plentiful crops. These crops fed the cities of the civilization.

To the east of the Indus, the Ganges River flows more than 1,500 miles across the northern part of the subcontinent. Its floods created a huge, fertile plain good for farming. The rich Ganges Plain became the center of another ancient Indian civilization.

Climate Much of the Indian subcontinent has a tropical climate. For much of the year, the land bakes under a high, hot sun. Seasonal winds, known as **monsoons,** help shape life in this region.

In the winter, dry monsoon winds blow from the land to the sea. Little rain falls. In the summer, this pattern reverses. Wet winds from the ocean blow onto the land. They bring rain, which provides water for crops. They also bring a welcome break from the intense heat.

For much of India, agriculture depends on the summer monsoon. If the rains come on time, all is well. If the rains come late or not at all, crops die and people may starve.

Reading Check During which season does most rain fall in the Indian subcontinent?

An Indus Valley man ▶

The Indian Subcontinent

Hindu Kush

Indus River

○ Harappa

H I M A L A Y A S

Mohenjo-Daro ○

Ganges River

Brahmaputra River

TROPIC OF CANCER

Arabian Sea

○ Lothal

20° N

KEY

◻ Indus Valley civilization
2600 B.C.–1900 B.C.

○ City

0   400 mi

0   400 km

Lambert Conformal Conic Projection

Bay of Bengal

INDIAN OCEAN

10° N

60° E   70° E   80° E   90° E   100° E   110° E

Map Skills

1 Location What mountain range lay north and west of the Indus Valley civilization?

2 Place Why might Mohenjo-Daro have been built where it was?

3 Places to Know!

Label the following places on the outline map in your Student Journal: Indus River, Ganges River, Himalayas, Harappa.

my worldhistory.com

Places to Know

201

An Advanced Civilization

Farmers began growing crops in hills near the Indus river system around 7000 B.C. With a steady food supply, the population grew. After 3000 B.C., cities began to develop on the broad plains of the Indus Valley. By about 2500 B.C., these cities were the centers of the advanced Indus Valley civilization. However, by around 1700 B.C., the civilization had largely disappeared.

Archaeologists have discovered most of what we know about the Indus Valley civilization. In the 1920s, they discovered the ruins of two great cities: Harappa and Mohenjo-Daro. Since then, archaeologists have found more than 1,000 other towns and villages from this civilization.

**myWorld Activity
Exploring Harappa**

Technology Indus Valley cities were well planned and organized. The people of the Indus Valley built thick walls around their cities. They also built huge raised mounds of earth and brick in their cities. During times of flooding, these mounds remained above water.

Many houses in these cities had a bathroom and toilet. Wastewater from houses flowed into brick-lined sewage channels. These were the world's first citywide sewer systems. A trash chute in many houses led to a bin in the street.

achievement, *n.,*
a success gained by making an effort

Many of the <u>achievements</u> of the Indus Valley people showed an advanced knowledge of mathematics. Their cities were built with wide, straight streets in a grid pattern. The Indus Valley civilization had an advanced system of weights and measurements using multiples of ten, like the modern metric system.

Farming the Indus Valley The dry Indus Valley could not always depend on the monsoon rains. Therefore, Indus Valley farmers built irrigation channels and ditches. These brought river water to the wheat and barley fields. Some scholars think that these farmers stored their surplus crops in a **granary,** or special building used to hold grain. They may have been the first farmers to grow cotton for making cloth.

Indus Valley farmers also raised cattle, sheep, goats, and chickens for food. They used oxen, or cattle, to pull carts. Animals seem to have been important to the Indus Valley people. They carved wooden animals and painted pictures of animals on pottery.

Trade The Indus Valley environment was rich in resources for trade. Indus Valley jewelers made beautiful jewelry from precious stones. Traders sold this jewelry as far away as Mesopotamia. Traders sold cotton cloth woven in the Indus Valley. They also sold teak, a valuable wood from a tree that grows in India. Indus Valley cities prospered from trade.

Indus Valley traders used stone seals with writing to identify their goods. They stamped their seals on soft clay squares attached to their goods. Accurate weights and measures helped promote trade.

Sumerian writers mentioned trade with people who probably came from the Indus Valley. Trade spread ideas between these two civilizations.

Reading Check What two main economic activities supported the Indus Valley civilization?

Closer Look

Indus Valley
Achievements

The Indus Valley civilization invented some of the most advanced technology of its time. Indus Valley cities like Mohenjo-Daro, whose ruins are shown below, had many features that promoted health.

THINK CRITICALLY   How were Indus Valley cities similar to and different from modern cities?

▲ The world's oldest dice come from the Indus Valley people, who probably invented the game.

▲ The walls in the foreground are part of the ruins of Mohenjo-Daro. The mound in the distance is a later ruin.

▲ These clay seals show examples of Indus Valley writing and art. They were used to stamp trade goods. The writing on each seal may be the name of the person who owned the goods.

▲ This photo shows a well-built sewer, one of the world's first.

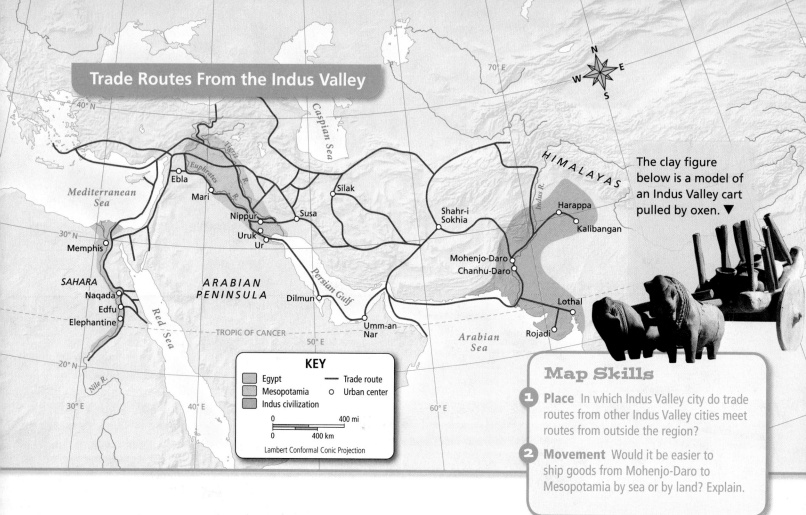

Trade Routes From the Indus Valley

The clay figure below is a model of an Indus Valley cart pulled by oxen. ▼

KEY

Egypt
Mesopotamia
Indus civilization

— Trade route
○ Urban center

0   400 mi
0   400 km
Lambert Conformal Conic Projection

Map Skills

1 **Place** In which Indus Valley city do trade routes from other Indus Valley cities meet routes from outside the region?

2 **Movement** Would it be easier to ship goods from Mohenjo-Daro to Mesopotamia by sea or by land? Explain.

Indus Valley Mysteries

Artifacts and ruins of many buildings have been found in the Indus Valley. They provide a lot of information. But scholars still have many questions about this ancient civilization. They want to know more about its rulers, religion, and writing. They wonder why it disappeared and where its people went.

Government and Religion Clearly, the people of the Indus Valley were well organized. Their cities show a surprising level of planning. They all used a common system of weights and measures. These facts suggest that the Indus Valley people had a strong central government. Yet no royal statues or

tombs have been found. This makes it seem unlikely that kings ruled the Indus Valley. Based on the available evidence, it just isn't possible to know for sure what kind of government the Indus Valley had.

Most cities had a huge **citadel,** or fortified area. The walled citadel was built on a raised platform of earth and brick that could have protected it from floodwaters or attackers. Scholars are not sure, but the citadel may have been a center of government, religion, or both.

Religion is another part of the Indus Valley civilization about which little is known. Scholars have found no obvious temples and no clear sign of priests.

However, some Indus Valley statues look like gods worshiped in Hinduism, a religion that developed later in this region. Also, some Indus Valley carvings look like people meditating, an important practice in Hinduism today.

Writing Scholars have not yet discovered how to read the symbols found on the stone seals and pottery of the Indus Valley. There are too few examples of each symbol to be sure of its meaning. Most experts think that these marks are a form of writing. However, they do not know if these markings are names, records of sales, or something else.

Disappearance The greatest mystery is what caused this civilization to disappear. Sometime before 1700 B.C., the Indus Valley people began to abandon their cities. The civilization declined rapidly after that. No one knows why.

There are many possible explanations. Some <u>evidence</u> suggests that standing water in drains may have bred mosquitos that spread disease and weakened Indus Valley populations. Indus Valley people may also have stripped forests of trees, leaving them without wood for building or fuel. A lack of forest cover could have caused severe floods that damaged Indus Valley cities. Their cattle may have over-grazed the land, leaving bare soil. Smaller herds could have led to starvation.

Some historians think that climate change may have brought an end to the civilization. Years of drought could have made it impossible to feed city dwellers. They would either have starved or moved away. Foreign invasion might also have weakened the civilization. Nobody knows for sure what happened, but it would take a thousand years for a new civilization to appear on the Indian subcontinent.

Reading Check What present-day religion may be related to the Indus Valley religion?

evidence, *n.,* information used to prove something

Section 1 Assessment

Key Terms

1. Explain why India is called a subcontinent.

2. Explain what a granary and monsoon are.

3. Describe the citadels of the Indus Valley civilization and their possible function.

Key Ideas

4. How did ancient farmers use the water of the Indus river system to help grow crops?

5. What were some advanced features of the Indus Valley civilization?

6. Why do archaeologists know so little about the government or religion of the Indus Valley civilization?

Think Critically

7. **Identify Evidence** What kinds of evidence could help prove or disprove the possible causes for the decline of the Indus Valley civilization?

8. **Compare and Contrast** What are some similiarities and differences between the Indus Valley civilization and other ancient river valley civilizations?

Essential Question

How much does geography affect people's lives?

9. Give examples of how geography helped shape the civilization of the Indus Valley. Go to your Student Journal to record your answer.

India's Vedic Age

Key Ideas

- Most historians believe that Indo-Aryan nomads entered the Indian subcontinent over many years and mixed with local people.

- Sacred scriptures known as the Vedas teach us about the Aryan religion and customs.

- A caste system emerged in India dividing Indians into groups based on birth and occupation.

Key Terms   • Veda   • caste   • Brahmin   • Kshatriya   • Vaishya   • Sudra   • Dalit

 **Visual Glossary**

 Reading Skill Summarize Take notes using the graphic organizer in your journal.

The Aryan god Brahma holds a page from the Vedas. ▼

By 1500 B.C., another group of people were living in the Indus Valley. They called themselves Aryans. This meant "the noble ones" in their language. Scholars often call them Indo-Aryans, after the language that they spoke. The Aryans introduced a new social structure. The Aryans also brought a new religion with them that had many gods. They expressed their beliefs in hymns and holy scriptures known as Vedas. For this reason, this period of Indian history is called the Vedic age.

The Origins of the Indo-Aryans

Historians have taken different views on the origins of the Indo-Aryans. In the past, many historians accepted the Aryan invasion theory. This theory held that the Aryans were nomadic warriors who crossed the mountains into India. They rode horse-drawn chariots and used iron weapons to defeat the local people. Then they settled in the Indus Valley and spread to other parts of India.

Others have argued that the Aryans were not invaders. Instead, they believe Aryans were India's original inhabitants. Supporters of this view say that if the Indo-Aryans came from a region outside of India, the Vedas would refer to it. The Vedas, however, do not make any mention of such a place.

Most recent scholars believe that neither of the above theories is correct. These scholars propose a third theory. They suggest that the Aryans were once nomads raising cattle and horses on the dry grasslands of what is now Afghanistan and Central Asia.

Over many years, they migrated into India with their livestock. In India, they mixed with local people and adopted local beliefs. Local people adopted the mixed Aryan language and religion and called themselves Aryans, too. Over time, people across a large part of India came to see themselves as Aryan.

The Vedas After settling in India, the Aryans composed the Vedas. Each **Veda** is a collection of hundreds of sacred hymns.

Priests memorized and sang or chanted these verses during ceremonies. The Vedas called upon people to make offerings to their gods. Typical offerings might be barley, butter, or milk.

For a thousand years, Indians passed the Vedas down by word of mouth. They sang or chanted them in an Indo-Aryan language called Sanskrit, which is a distant relative of English. Today, Sanskrit remains a language of sacred literature. Sanskrit is the ancestor of many modern Indian languages. Around 500 B.C., Indians relearned the art of writing. They began to collect the Vedas and put them into writing.

The best known of the Vedas is the *Rig Veda*. It includes more than 1,000 hymns. Most of them praise Aryan gods and goddesses representing natural forces such as the sky, sun, and fire.

migrate, *v.*, to move from one region to another in order to live there

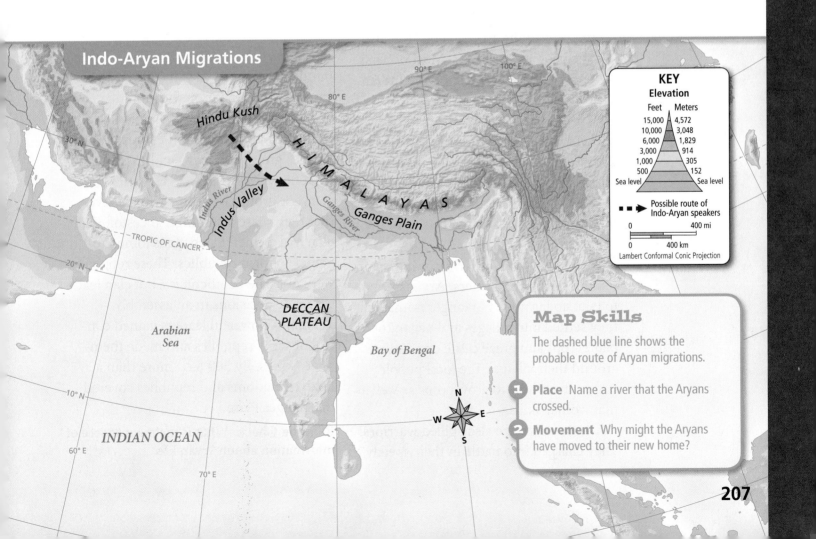

Indo-Aryan Migrations

Hindu Kush

Indus River

Indus Valley

H I M A L A Y A S

Ganges River

Ganges Plain

TROPIC OF CANCER

30° N

20° N

10° N

60° E

70° E

80° E

90° E

100° E

Arabian Sea

DECCAN PLATEAU

Bay of Bengal

INDIAN OCEAN

KEY
Elevation

Feet		Meters
15,000		4,572
10,000		3,048
6,000		1,829
3,000		914
1,000		305
500		152
Sea level		Sea level

Possible route of Indo-Aryan speakers

0 — 400 mi
0 — 400 km
Lambert Conformal Conic Projection

Map Skills

The dashed blue line shows the probable route of Aryan migrations.

1 **Place** Name a river that the Aryans crossed.

2 **Movement** Why might the Aryans have moved to their new home?

N W E S

207

▲ The early Aryans tended flocks of livestock, much like this modern Indian herdsman.

horse-drawn, two-wheeled chariots. They went to war with other nearby peoples. They also fought among themselves.

The Vedas show that the Aryans found joy in their day-to-day lives. They loved music and dancing. They held chariot races and enjoyed gambling. They also had human weaknesses. The following passage from a hymn in the *Rig Veda* describes one family's reaction to a man who gambled too much:

> 66 My wife rejects me; her mother hates me;
> For a man in such trouble there is no pity:
> 'I think a gambling man is no more useful
> Than an old horse that is up for sale.' 99

—*Rig Veda,* adapted from translations by
R.T.H. Griffith and A.A. MacDonell

Aryan Life The *Rig Veda* and the other sacred texts provide a record not only of the Aryans' gods but also of the people themselves. Most of what we know about Aryan life on the Indian subcontinent comes from the Vedas.

The earliest Aryans lived as nomadic herders. They raised cattle, horses, goats, and sheep. Cattle held special importance for them since the herds provided both food and clothing. Early on, the Aryans measured their wealth by the size of their cattle herds.

After many years of living in India and mixing with local farmers, Aryans began to take up farming. No longer nomadic, they settled into villages and began to plant crops and graze cattle on pastures around their villages. The local people taught them how to grow crops as well as many other skills.

The Aryans were also skilled warriors. They charged into battle in their speedy,

The Growth of Vedic Civilization Over hundreds of years, Aryan culture slowly spread eastward across the humid and fertile Ganges Plain. The Aryans carved farms and villages from the forests. Some villages grew into towns and cities.

At first, the Aryans were divided into clans, or groups of people who believe that they share a common ancestor. Each clan had a chief. Later, clans joined together to form republics. These republics were not true democracies, but clan leaders made decisions in an assembly.

Finally, powerful leaders gained control of some republics and made themselves kings. By 500 B.C., more than a dozen kingdoms and republics covered the Ganges Plain.

Reading Check What is the main source of information about Aryan life?

The Caste System

Over time, India developed a social structure based on caste. A **caste** is a fixed social class into which a person is born. People inherited their caste from their parents. They stayed in that caste for their entire lives. Members of different castes did not usually mix socially. They were not allowed to eat together and rarely married across caste lines. This social structure is known as a caste system.

Two Kinds of Caste Indians grouped people into castes in two different ways. The most basic grouping was by occupation. The term for an occupation-based caste is jati, meaning "birth group." Some scholars think that these castes began as extended families who may have had a family business or occupation. There are hundreds of jatis in India today.

These jatis were grouped into large caste groupings. The Vedas identify four varnas, or caste groupings based on religious status. Priests, known as **Brahmins,** were the highest varna. Next came the **Kshatriyas,** or the rulers and warriors. Below them were the **Vaishyas,** or landowners, bankers, and merchants. At the bottom were the **Sudras,** who did farm work and other manual work.

Men in the three highest varnas were considered "twice-born." First, they experienced physical birth. Then, after they had studied Sanskrit and the Vedas, they had a spiritual birth. Being twice-born meant that these men could practice the Vedic religion. They had the right to take part in certain religious ceremonies. This was a great honor.

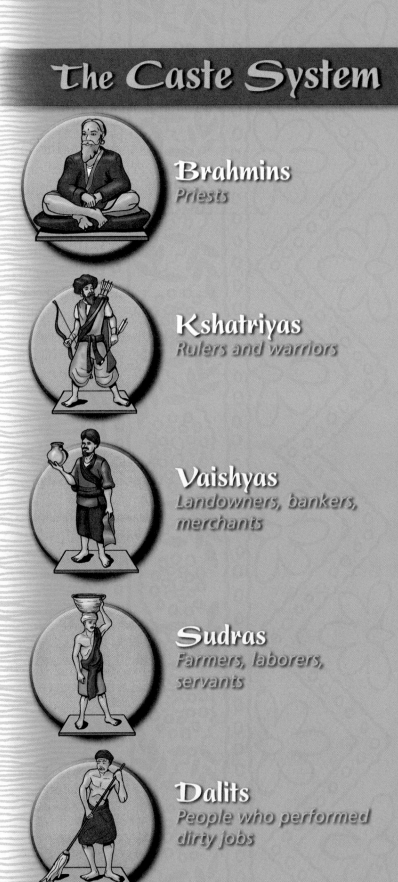

The Caste System

Brahmins
Priests

Kshatriyas
Rulers and warriors

Vaishyas
Landowners, bankers, merchants

Sudras
Farmers, laborers, servants

Dalits
People who performed dirty jobs

The lowest varna was the Sudras. The Sudras worked in the fields tending crops, as laborers, or as servants for people in higher varnas.

Later, a caste grouping below the Sudras developed. People in other castes called its members untouchables. Known today as **Dalits,** these people had to do dirty jobs that no one else wanted, such as cleaning toilets or butchering animals. Members of the higher varnas thought of themselves as "pure." They avoided contact with untouchables for fear of being made unclean. In modern India, treating Dalits as untouchable is against the law.

Evolution of the Caste System Scholars are not sure how the caste system developed. They aren't sure whether the status-based varnas or the occupation-based jatis developed first. The system probably developed over hundreds of years as the Aryans settled into villages. As they settled, they developed specialized jobs for priests, warriors, merchants, and farmworkers.

At first, caste may have been mainly based on a person's occupation or family membership. Children might have been able to move into a different caste than their parents. In time, castes seem to have

Caste and Daily Life

Indians of higher varnas, such as the Kshatriya woman at left, traditionally considered Dalits "impure." Dalits could not use a well like the one below if higher-caste Indians used it. Sudras and Dalits were traditionally forced to do heavy labor, like the women doing road work at right. The woman stacking bricks below right is a Dalit. *Which group would have been most likely to clean the streets?*

become more rigid. Each caste was given a particular status. People were born into a caste and could not leave it.

In <u>theory</u>, Indian castes never gained members except by birth and never lost members except by death. In fact, the evidence suggests that families could sometimes move from one varna to another. Foreign invaders sometimes became Kshatriyas. Marriages across caste lines may also have occurred.

In time, the caste system became the basis for India's social structure. The system brought both costs and benefits. For instance, the system limited people's individual freedom. The patterns of their lives were fixed at birth.

However, some believe that the caste system helped India develop. They feel that it brought stability to Indian society. Indian goods became famous because caste members perfected their skills. The system also allowed different groups to follow their own beliefs.

In India today, the law forbids caste discrimination. People's jobs no longer depend on their caste alone. Brahmins or Kshatriyas may work with their hands. Dalits may work as professionals.

Reading Check What occupations did Kshatriyas traditionally hold?

theory, *n.*, an ideal or proposed explanation or description

K.R. Narayanan, at right, was India's first Dalit president. ▶

Section 2 Assessment

Key Terms

1. Explain why the Vedas are important.
2. Explain the meaning of the term *caste* in Indian history.
3. Describe the different jobs performed by Brahmins, Kshatriyas, Vaishyas, Sudras, and Dalits.

Key Ideas

4. Who were the Aryans and how might they have come to India?
5. What do the Vedas teach us about Aryan culture?
6. How did castes shape the lives of their members?

Think Critically

7. **Identify Evidence** What evidence would offer proof for the different theories about the origins of the Aryans?
8. **Compare and Contrast** What are the similarities and differences between jati and varna?

Essential Question

How much does geography affect people's lives?

9. How did the lives of the Aryans change as they moved from the dry grasslands west of the Indus River to the humid Ganges Plain? Go to your Student Journal to record your answer.

211

Hinduism

Key Ideas

- Hinduism grew out of Brahmanism.

- Hindus believe in a supreme God, Brahman, who is the source of all things.

- Hindus believe that people's actions determine how they are reincarnated.

- Hinduism spread across India and to Southeast Asia and has had a lasting impact on those regions.

Key Terms • Brahmanism • guru • Brahman • reincarnation • karma • dharma • ahimsa • moksha

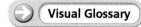 Visual Glossary

Reading Skill Sequence Take notes using the graphic organizer in your journal.

 A Hindu temple in Varanasi, India ▼

Hinduism is one of the oldest religions in the world. It began in India during the Vedic age in a form called Brahmanism. Then it slowly grew and changed into Hinduism.

The Roots of Hinduism

For most of the past 2,000 years, Hinduism has been the main religion of India. In fact, the word *Hinduism* means "the religion of the people of India."

Vedic Age Beliefs and Practices As you have learned, the Vedas are India's oldest religious texts. Brahmins, or priests, in the Vedic age memorized these works and passed them on by word of mouth. Around 500 B.C., they wrote them down.

The Vedas contain hymns to many gods. They also describe rituals to please the gods. These rituals often involved sacrifices, or offerings, of animals or food to specific gods, such as Agni, the god of fire.

Brahmanism Scholars call the religion of the Vedic age **Brahmanism.** Brahmanism was a religion based on priests and rituals, particularly sacrifices to the gods. Brahmins studied the Vedas. Brahmins were also the only ones who were allowed to perform the rituals. They believed that they had to perform rituals perfectly, and that any little mistake would anger the gods. This gave the Brahmins great power in early Indian society.

Reading Check Why was sacrifice important in the Vedic age?

The Evolution of Hinduism

Beginning about 500 B.C., as Indians adapted to town and village life, Indian beliefs began to change. The old gods became less important. People began to doubt that carrying out precise rituals was as important as the priests claimed. Other people began asking questions such as: Why are we born? How should we live? What happens to us when we die? Hinduism evolved from Indians' efforts to answer these difficult questions.

New Teachings To find those answers, thinkers and teachers known as **gurus** left their homes to live in the forest, to think, and to talk about religious ideas. In a sense, these gurus and their students were founders of Hinduism.

Their ideas survive in writings known as the Upanishads (oo PAN uh shadz). The Upanishads made connections between heavenly forces and people's lives. Alongside the Vedas, the Upanishads became Hindu holy scriptures. The oldest Upanishads date to around 800 or 700 B.C. Indian thinkers continued to produce them for several hundred years.

The Upanishads helped connect people to the emerging Hindu religion. Only Brahmins were supposed to interpret the Vedas. But Indians of all castes could study the Upanishads. These sacred writings dealt with questions of life and death or right and wrong that concern all people.

Hindu Worship

While Hinduism deals with deep questions, it also involves acts of worship such as offering candles, as shown here along the Ganges River in India.

A woman making offerings to God in the form of Shiva

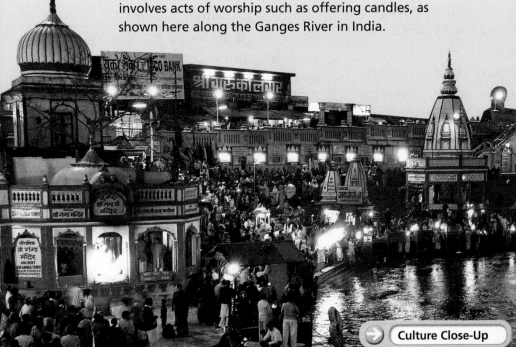

Culture Close-Up

Hindus make beautiful patterns on the ground with colored, powdered rice during the festival of Diwali.

This historic illustration shows a battle scene from the *Mahabharata*. ▶

Epic Poems Everyone could also learn and study two very important epic poems. An epic poem is a long story of heroes told in verse. Both of these poems took shape within a few hundred years of A.D. 1. These epic poems are the *Ramayana* (rah MAH yuh nuh) and the *Mahabharata* (muh hah BAH rah tuh). They helped explain how people should live their lives as Hindus.

The *Ramayana* is the story of a king named Rama and his beautiful wife, Sita. This is the epic remembered by Amala in the story at the beginning of this chapter. Sita is kidnapped by the demon king Ravana. His niece, the demon Trijata, protects Sita. Eventually, Rama rescues Sita. This epic offers moral lessons about right and wrong. One such lesson is the importance of loyalty and respect.

The *Mahabharata* may be the world's longest poem. It is 200,000 lines long. It tells the story of two families at war for control of a kingdom. Like the *Ramayana*, it deals with moral <u>issues</u>. These include the conflict between loyalty to family and duty.

The most sacred section of the *Mahabharata* is the *Bhagavad-Gita* (BUG uh vud GEE tuh). This means "Song of the Lord." Some scholars consider the *Bhagavad-Gita* to be Hinduism's most important religious text.

This text deals with key Hindu beliefs. These beliefs have to do with the nature of the soul, of life, and of God and the importance of various Hindu practices.

Reading Check Who could study the Upanishads?

issue, *n.,* problem or subject to be discussed or decided

Beliefs About God

Hinduism is like a great river. Over thousands of years, many beliefs and traditions have flowed into it. As a result, Hindus may have different practices. But Hindus share certain basic beliefs.

The Upanishads contain two beliefs that lie at the heart of Hinduism. The first is that there is one supreme cosmic consciousness, spiritual force, or God known as **Brahman**. The Upanishads teach that all of the gods that Indians worship are forms of Brahman. Brahman, they say, is the source of all things.

Many Hindus worship individual gods or goddesses as forms of Brahman. Some Hindus worship Brahman as Vishnu. Others worship Brahman as Shiva. Still others worship Brahman as the goddess Shakti. These gods and goddesses may have other named forms. For example, the god Krishna is a form of Vishnu.

The second core Hindu belief is that every person is born with a soul. This soul is also a form of Brahman. According to the Upanishads:

> 66 This soul of mine within the heart is smaller than a grain of rice.... This soul of mine within the heart is greater than the earth,... greater than the sky.... This soul of mine within the heart, this is Brahman. 99

—*The Thirteen Principal Upanishads*

Reading Check What do Hindus believe about their different gods and the soul?

Forms of God

Three of Hinduism's most important gods are Brahma, Vishnu, and Shiva. Hindus see each of these gods as a form of the supreme God, Brahman.

Hindus see Shiva as a god of power, change, creation, and destruction.

For Hindus, Brahma is the creator of the universe and humankind.

Hindus see Vishnu as a god who preserves and maintains creation.

215

Beliefs About Life

Hindu scriptures such as the Upanishads and the *Bhagavad-Gita* also teach important Hindu beliefs about life.

Reincarnation and Karma Hinduism teaches that when people die, most will undergo reincarnation. **Reincarnation** is the rebirth of a soul in a new body.

In the *Bhagavad-Gita*, the god Krishna explains the process of reincarnation to Arjuna, the hero of the *Mahabharata*:

> 66 As a man discards
> worn-out clothes
> to put on new
> and different ones,
> so the embodied self (soul)
> discards
> its worn-out bodies
> to take on other new ones. 99
>
> —*Bhagavad-Gita*

Below, Krishna, whose skin is blue, explains the nature of life and reality, as recorded in the *Bhagavad-Gita.* ▼

The law of karma determines how a person is reborn. **Karma** is the effect of a person's actions in this and in previous lives. Hindus believe that bad karma—evil deeds—will bring rebirth into a lower caste or even as a lower animal. Good karma brings rebirth into a higher caste.

Four Goals Hindus believe that people have four basic goals in life. People should pursue all four. But not everyone achieves all of these goals in one lifetime.

The first goal is doing what is right. For Hindus, **dharma** is a person's duty or what is right for him or her. Dharma includes the duties that come with one's caste or one's age or position in life. Dharma also includes the rule of **ahimsa,** or avoiding doing harm to any living thing. Following dharma brings good karma. Violating dharma brings bad karma.

The second goal is striving for well-being, or earning a livelihood with dignity. This goal can involve making a good living and raising a family. It can involve starting or running an honest business. However, Hindus say, material well-being by itself does not bring true happiness.

The third goal is pleasure. This includes physical pleasures such as eating good food or taking a hot bath. However, seeking nothing but pleasure, Hindus believe, can leave a person feeling empty.

The final goal is **moksha,** or liberation from reincarnation. When this happens, a person's soul becomes one with Brahman. For Hindus, the purpose of human life is to achieve moksha. A soul that achieves moksha is free from want, fear, and pain. It lives forever in a state of joy.

MOKSHA
(liberation)

Rebirth at a
higher level

Good Karma

Follows Dharma

BIRTH

Fails to follow
Dharma

Bad Karma

Rebirth at a
lower level

Chart Skills

1 What do Hindus believe will happen to a person if she follows her dharma?

2 How would this affect her progress toward moksha?

Three Paths to Moksha Hinduism lays out three different paths to moksha. These paths are all forms of yoga, traditionally defined as a way of seeking moksha. The first path is the way of knowledge. The second is the way of works. The third is the way of devotion. Hindus may try to follow all three paths.

Traditionally, Brahmins chose the way of knowledge. For a person following the way of knowledge, moksha comes with a true understanding of one's soul and its oneness with Brahman—or God. The Upanishads say that such understanding does not come easily.

The way of works means carrying out the religious rituals and duties that will improve one's karma. Most Hindus have chosen this path. To follow the way of works, Hindus must carry out duties within their family. They also offer

prayers and food to the gods. Those who do good deeds without expecting any reward are especially praised.

The way of devotion is also known as the path of love. People on this path <u>devote</u> themselves to loving God. For most Hindus, following the path of love means worshiping one of the Hindu gods or goddesses. These gods and goddesses have human forms and personalities. People can love them as they might love a parent or child.

The way of devotion takes many forms. People on this path may repeat their god's name all day long. They may present offerings to their god at a temple. They may travel to sites sacred to their god. In all of these ways, Hindus try to move closer to God in their hearts.

Reading Check What are the three paths to moksha in Hinduism?

devote, v., to set aside for a purpose

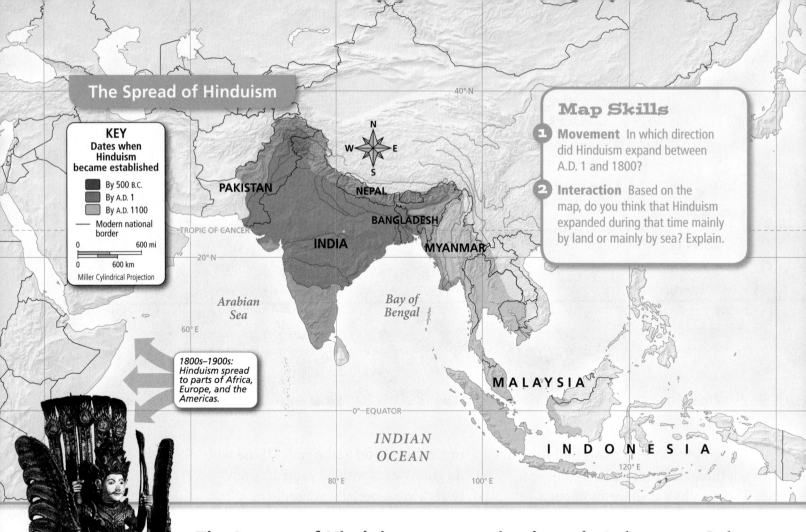

KEY
Dates when Hinduism became established

By 500 B.C.
By A.D. 1
By A.D. 1100
Modern national border

0   600 mi
0   600 km
Miller Cylindrical Projection

PAKISTAN

NEPAL

BANGLADESH

INDIA

MYANMAR

TROPIC OF CANCER

20°N

40°N

60°E

80°E

100°E

120°E

Arabian Sea

Bay of Bengal

0°—EQUATOR

INDIAN OCEAN

MALAYSIA

INDONESIA

1800s–1900s: Hinduism spread to parts of Africa, Europe, and the Americas.

Map Skills

1 **Movement** In which direction did Hinduism expand between A.D. 1 and 1800?

2 **Interaction** Based on the map, do you think that Hinduism expanded during that time mainly by land or mainly by sea? Explain.

▲ This sculpture from Bali in Indonesia shows Vishnu flying on a mythical bird.

The Impact of Hinduism

More than a billion people live in India today. About 80 percent of them follow Hinduism. The rest follow other religions. Hindus also live and worship in many places outside of India. The spread of Hinduism has had a lasting impact on India and on the world.

The Spread of Hinduism Long ago, the people of India lived under many separate rulers. They spoke many different languages. They worshiped many different gods. Yet, most Indians still became Hindus.

Several things helped the growth of Hinduism in India. One was Hinduism's flexibility. Because Hinduism views all gods as forms of a single, supreme God, it can accept the worship of new gods. People did not have to give up their old religion when they became Hindus. Instead, Hinduism adopted their traditions and gods or viewed their gods as forms of existing Hindu gods.

Hinduism also did not require regular attendance at religious services. Instead, Hindus could pray or make offerings to the gods at a local temple during special celebrations or whenever it was convenient. They could also pray or make offerings at shrines in their homes. A shrine is a place of worship that is often dedicated to a sacred object or being. So no matter where Indians went, they could easily practice their religion.

218

Over time, Hinduism spread to other lands. For more than a thousand years after A.D. 1, Indian traders and priests carried Hinduism to Southeast Asia. Hinduism left a lasting influence on countries such as Thailand and Indonesia, where epic poems such as the *Ramayana* remain popular. Today, most people on the Indonesian island of Bali are Hindus.

Indians also took Hinduism with them when they moved across the seas. Many migrated to Great Britain, the United States, and Canada. More than a million Hindus now live in the United States.

Hindu Traditions Today Hindus live in some 150 countries. But most Hindus still live in India. Hindu traditions remain an important part of Indian life. For example, Hindu festivals draw huge crowds. One festival takes place on the Ganges River. It is one of India's holiest sites. Every year, millions of Indians line the banks of the Ganges and bathe in its waters. They believe that those waters can wash away bad karma and cure disease.

Hinduism's openness to all religions has shaped India's political system. It guarantees religious freedom.

Hinduism has also influenced India's art and literature. Beautiful carvings of gods and goddesses decorate the walls of majestic Hindu temples. The temples are places of worship. But they also serve as centers of art, music, and dance.

The *Mahabharata* and the *Ramayana* were India's first great literature. They have inspired other literature for hundreds of years. In India, comic books and movies still retell their stories today.

Reading Check What aspects of Hinduism helped it to spread?

myWorld Activity
Hindu Wall of Words

A woman rows flower candles across the sacred Ganges River in Varanasi, India. ▼

Section 3 Assessment

Key Terms

1. Describe how gurus helped Hinduism to grow from Brahmanism.

2. Explain the meaning of the terms *dharma* and *ahimsa* in Hinduism.

3. Use the terms *Brahman, karma,* and *moksha* to describe Hindu beliefs.

Key Ideas

4. How did the Upanishads and the Hindu epic poems contribute to the growth of Hinduism from Brahmanism?

5. How do Hindus try to achieve moksha?

6. How did Hinduism spread to Southeast Asia?

Think Critically

7. **Draw Conclusions** What features of Hinduism made it more accessible than Brahmanism to people of lower castes?

8. **Synthesize** Why is moral behavior important to Hindus?

9. **Analyze Cause and Effect** Why might a Hindu offer food or flowers to a god such as Shiva?

Essential Question

How much does geography affect people's lives?

10. How important is India's geography to the beliefs of Hinduism? Go to your Student Journal to record your answer.

Section 4

Buddhism

Key Ideas

- The Buddha gave up a life of luxury to seek the truth and eventually found enlightenment.

- Buddhists believe the root of suffering is desire and that, by following an eight-step path, they can end suffering and desire.

- Buddhism spread across Asia and had an impact on other parts of the world.

Key Terms • meditate • enlightenment • nirvana • monastery • Theravada Buddhism • Mahayana Buddhism

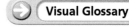 **Visual Glossary**

Reading Skill Compare and Contrast Take notes using the graphic organizer in your journal.

Buddhist monks and a statue of the Buddha near Bodh Gaya, the place in India where they believe the Buddha gained enlightenment ▼

Buddhism, like Hinduism, arose in ancient India. Buddhism is a religion based on the teachings of Siddhartha Gautama (sid DAHR tuh GOW tuh muh), an Indian spiritual leader. Siddhartha became known as the Buddha (BOO duh). We call his followers Buddhists.

The Life of the Buddha

Scholars know few hard facts about the Buddha. The story of his life comes mainly from Buddhist texts. Those texts include the teachings of the Buddha, which his followers memorized and passed down by word of mouth. But they also include many legends.

A Pampered Youth Siddhartha Gautama was probably born during the 400s B.C. in what is now Nepal. A Hindu prince, he was raised in wealth and luxury. According to legend, his mother dreamed that a white elephant came down to her from heaven. Based on the dream, a prophet predicted that the child would grow up to be a wandering holy man. This disturbed Siddhartha's father. He wanted his son to grow up to be a ruler.

To keep Siddhartha from becoming a holy man, his father shielded him from everything unpleasant or disturbing. The prince never saw anyone who was poor, sad, or sick. When he rode out of the palace in his chariot, guards traveled ahead of him to clear beggars and sick people from the streets.

Legends say that one day when Siddhartha was about 29, he rode out of the palace without any guards. During that ride, Siddhartha

220

saw an old, bent, toothless man leaning on a stick. On a second ride, Siddhartha saw a man shrunken by disease. On a third, the prince saw a dead man. Siddhartha was shocked. He realized that he too faced old age, sickness, and death.

A few days later, Siddhartha rode out of the palace again. He came upon a fourth sight, a wandering holy man. The holy man was homeless and owned nothing. Still, he seemed content. Siddhartha decided to search for the same sense of peace that the holy man showed.

A Search for Truth That night, he cut his hair and traded his rich clothing for the simple robe of a religious seeker. He set out to find the truth about life, suffering, and death.

Siddhartha began his search by studying with Hindu gurus. They taught him that life was a cycle of birth, death, and rebirth. Then he joined a band of religious ascetics. Ascetics deny themselves physical comforts to seek a spiritual goal.

For five years, Siddhartha wore scratchy clothes and fasted, or went without food, for long periods. He lost weight and became very weak. After six years of self denial, he realized going to such extremes was not the path to truth.

Finding Enlightenment Siddhartha renewed his search. One day Siddhartha sat down under a fig tree to meditate. To **meditate** means to calm or clear the mind, often by focusing on a single object. The fig tree would come to be known as the Bodhi Tree, or Tree of Knowledge.

According to legend, Siddhartha meditated under the tree for 49 days and nights. During this time, he came to understand the cycle of birth, death, and rebirth. Finally, Siddhartha reached an awareness that freed him from his ties to the world. He entered a new life free of suffering. He had, at last, achieved **enlightenment**—a state of perfect wisdom. Siddhartha had become the Buddha, which means "the Enlightened One."

▲ This Tibetan painting shows the young Siddhartha, seated on a chariot, noticing a dead man by the side of the road.

221

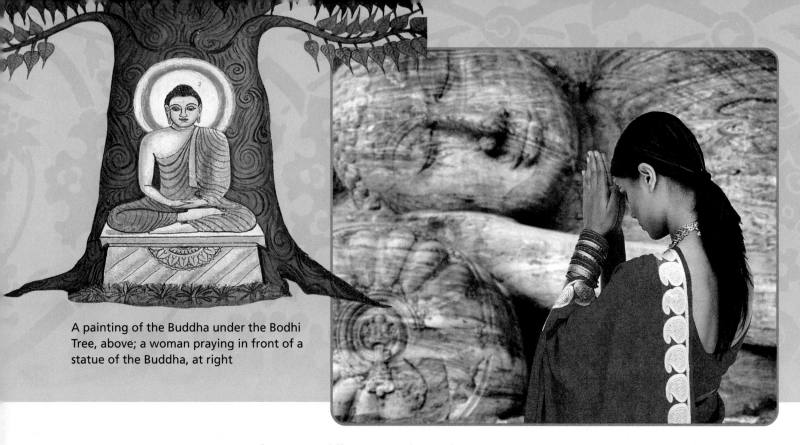

A painting of the Buddha under the Bodhi Tree, above; a woman praying in front of a statue of the Buddha, at right

consequence, *n.*, result of an action, effect

According to Buddhist texts, the Buddha had freed himself from the "wheel of existence." He could have enjoyed freedom from the world's suffering. Instead, he went back into the world to teach others what he had learned.

For the next 45 years, the Buddha traveled across India sharing his message. He attracted many followers and students. He trained some of them to be teachers and religious leaders.

The Buddha died at about the age of 80. According to legend, his dying words to his followers were these:

> 66 This is my last advice to you. All . . . things in the world are changeable. They are not lasting. Work hard to gain your own salvation. 99
>
> –Rev. Siridhamma, *Life of the Buddha*

Reading Check What did Siddhartha hope to find when he left his life of wealth?

Buddhist Beliefs

Buddhists believe that when the Buddha gained enlightenment, he had a flash of insight. He understood why people suffer. He also saw how people could escape the cycle of death and rebirth.

The Buddha accepted the Hindu idea of karma—the idea that a person's actions have <u>consequences</u> in this or in future lives. However, the Buddha did not accept the Hindu idea of a permanent soul. He believed that a "self" might be reborn in a new body, but he thought that the "self" was an illusion. He believed that it would disappear and cease to exist when a person achieved enlightenment.

The Buddha moved even further away from other Hindu beliefs. For example, the Buddha did not believe in the existence of any god. He also did not accept the caste system. The Buddha believed that the good and bad actions of people were more important than caste. The Buddha believed in following what he called the Middle Way.

The Middle Way The Buddha had lived in luxury, as a wealthy prince. He had also lived in poverty, as an ascetic. One was "a life given to pleasures." The other was a life of suffering. Neither way of life had led him to enlightenment. To gain enlightenment, the Buddha advised people to follow a Middle Way. That way of life called for accepting four truths.

The Four Noble Truths These Four Noble Truths were among the insights the Buddha had when he achieved enlightenment under the Bodhi Tree.

The First Noble Truth is that all of life involves suffering. Birth, sickness, old age, and death bring suffering.

The Second Noble Truth is that wanting or desiring things for oneself causes suffering. Not all desires are bad. It is not wrong to desire the happiness of others. However, selfish desires lead to suffering.

The Third Noble Truth is that people can end their suffering. The way to do this is to give up all selfish desires.

The Fourth Noble Truth is that there is a way to overcome selfish desires. The way to overcome those desires is to follow the Eightfold Path.

The Eightfold Path was another of the Buddha's insights. By following this path, he believed, people could end their desires and suffering. The Buddha taught that this path was open to anyone. People of any caste could follow it.

The Four Noble Truths

According to Buddhist tradition, the Buddha discovered the Four Noble Truths. These truths offer Buddhists a way to understand and overcome suffering.

1 **All of life involves suffering.**

2 **Suffering is caused by selfish desires.**

3 **The way to end suffering is to overcome selfish desires.**

4 **The way to overcome selfish desires is to follow the Eightfold Path.**

◄ Prayers are written inside these Buddhist prayer wheels from Tibet. Spinning them is a form of prayer.

223

The Eightfold Path

The first two steps involve preparing one's mind for a new way of life.	
1. Right Belief	The first step is belief in and understanding of the Four Noble Truths.
2. Right Purpose	The second step is to make spiritual growth the purpose of one's life.
The next three steps involve taking charge of one's behavior.	
3. Right Speech	The third task is to become aware of what one says. This means avoiding lies or statements that hurt others.
4. Right Conduct	The next task is to understand one's behavior and work to improve it. Right conduct means not killing, stealing, lying, or hurting others.
5. Right Livelihood	This involves choosing a livelihood, or profession, that supports one's spiritual growth. A person should earn a living in a way that does not harm other living things.
The last three steps help train the mind to gain enlightenment.	
6. Right Effort	The sixth step involves making an effort to avoid bad thoughts and to hold only good thoughts in one's mind.
7. Right Mindfulness	Being mindful means becoming aware of what one thinks and feels. A person who has achieved right mindfulness controls his or her thoughts and emotions rather than being controlled by them.
8. Right Meditation	The last step is to practice the kind of meditation that can lead to enlightenment. Buddhists say that those who complete this step often feel as if they have awakened from a dream to experience a new reality.

Chart Skills

1. Which would Buddhists do first: stop lying or improve their meditation?

2. How might the steps on this path help Buddhists overcome selfish desires?

myWorld Activity
What's My Step?

The Eightfold Path The Eightfold Path takes its name from its eight steps. These steps lead to Three Qualities.

The first two steps are Right Belief and Right Purpose. They involve preparing one's mind for spiritual growth. These steps produce the first of the Three Qualities, wisdom.

The next three steps are Right Speech, Right Conduct, and Right Livelihood (or profession). These steps call for taking charge of one's behavior. They include respect for all living things and compassion for others. These steps produce the quality of morality, or right action.

The last three steps are Right Effort, Right Mindfulness (awareness of one's thoughts), and Right Meditation or Concentration. They help train the mind to gain enlightenment. The third quality is the same as the eighth step—meditation.

Reaching Nirvana The goal of a person who follows the Eightfold Path is to reach nirvana. **Nirvana** is a state of blissful peace without desire or suffering. Those who reach nirvana are at peace with themselves. They are also freed from having to go through reincarnation. A person can reach nirvana without dying but will not be reborn after dying.

Some Buddhists believe that nirvana always brings enlightenment. Others believe that enlightenment is a form of wisdom that sometimes follows nirvana.

Reading Check What are the Three Qualities?

Hinduism & Buddhism

SIMILARITIES

Both religions believe in karma and the cycle of rebirth. Both use meditation—either as a way to bring an end to the illusion of one's self or to unite one's soul with God.

▲ A Buddhist monk praying

▲ A Hindu Brahmin praying

DIFFERENCES

Hinduism	Buddhism
• There are many gods who are forms of Brahman—the supreme God.	• Siddhartha Gautama (the Buddha) is not a god and did not believe in any god.
• The goal is to reach moksha, a state of joy when an individual's soul becomes one with Brahman.	• The goal is to reach nirvana, a state of blissful peace, when one sees that one's self is an illusion and it ceases to exist.
• Hinduism stresses the goals of following one's duty and living a moral life as a way to work toward moksha.	• Buddhism stresses giving up selfish desires and following the moral teachings of the Eightfold Path to achieve nirvana.

THINK CRITICALLY How are moksha and nirvana similar and different? How are these differences connected to other differences between the two religions?

225

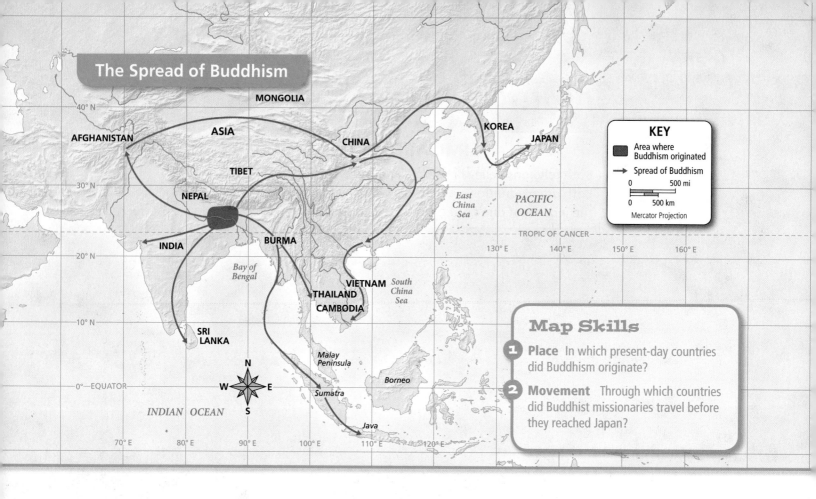

The Spread of Buddhism

Map Skills

1 **Place** In which present-day countries did Buddhism originate?

2 **Movement** Through which countries did Buddhist missionaries travel before they reached Japan?

The Spread of Buddhism

For hundreds of years, the Buddha's followers memorized his teachings. After many years, they wrote those teachings down. Those written teachings make up the sacred scriptures of Buddhism today. Different branches of Buddhism accept different collections of these scriptures. However, all Buddhists acept the Four Noble Truths and the Eightfold Path.

Monasteries and Missionaries As the Buddha preached, he gained many followers. At first they followed him from place to place. After a while, the Buddha found places for them to stay during the rainy season. These became Buddhist **monasteries,** or religious communities.

The most devoted Buddhists lived in monasteries. There they had time to study and meditate.

The Buddha urged his followers to carry his teachings to all corners of Earth. A person who spreads religious ideas is a missionary. After the Buddha died, Buddhist missionaries, or people who seek to spread their religion, first carried Buddhism across India and to Sri Lanka.

Later, missionaries carried his teachings throughout Asia. Some traveled north to Central Asia. From Central Asia, missionaries followed trade routes east into China. From China, Buddhism spread to Korea and Japan. Buddhism arrived later in Tibet.

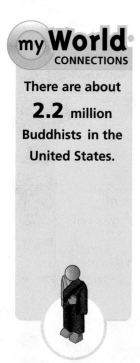

my World CONNECTIONS

There are about **2.2** million Buddhists in the United States.

Two Schools As Buddhism spread, its followers split into two major branches, or sects. The two branches share basic beliefs. But they see the Buddha's life and teachings differently.

One branch is **Theravada Buddhism** (thehr uh VAH duh). This sect focuses on the wisdom of the Buddha. Members think that the Buddha's greatest achievement was his enlightenment and entry into nirvana.

Mahayana Buddhism (mah huh YAH nuh) is the other branch. It focuses on the Buddha's compassion. For its members, the Buddha's greatest achievement was returning from nirvana to share his wisdom out of compassion for others. Its members also revere, or hold sacred, Bodhisattvas (boh dih SUT vuz), or beings who have gained enlightenment and, out of compassion, try to help others.

The Legacy of Buddhism Today, there are about 400 million Buddhists. Most live in Asia. Theravada Buddhism is the main religion of Sri Lanka, Myanmar (or Burma), Thailand, and Cambodia.

Mahayana Buddhism is <u>widespread</u> in Bhutan, Vietnam, China and Taiwan, Mongolia, the Koreas, and Japan.

More than 2 million Buddhists live in the United States. Although few Buddhists remain in India, the religion's birthplace, the Buddha's teachings made a lasting impact on Hinduism.

Buddhism has inspired beautiful art and architecture. It has been a source of wisdom even for some non-Buddhists.

Reading Check What did people do at Buddhist monasteries?

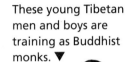

widespread, *adj.*, common, spread across a large area

These young Tibetan men and boys are training as Buddhist monks. ▼

Section **4** Assessment

Essential Question

How much does geography affect people's lives?

Key Terms

1. Use the terms *meditate* and *enlightenment* in a sentence.

2. Explain the meaning of the term *nirvana* for Buddhism.

3. Describe the difference between Theravada Buddhism and Mahayana Buddhism.

Key Ideas

4. Why did Siddhartha Gautama decide to give up his life of luxury?

5. Why do Buddhists try to follow the Eightfold Path?

6. How did Buddhism spread?

Think Critically

7. **Compare and Contrast** How is Buddhism similar to and different from Hinduism?

8. **Synthesize** What are Buddhism's moral teachings, or teachings about right and wrong?

9. Did geography affect the spread of Buddhism? If so, how? Go to your Student Journal to record your answer.

Chapter Assessment

Key Terms and Ideas

1. **Recall** Why were **monsoons** important to early Indian civilizations?

2. **Describe** What do the ruins of Indus cities show about their people's planning and technology skills?

3. **Explain** What are two theories about the decline of the Indus Valley civilization?

4. **Compare and Contrast** How did Aryan culture change over time?

5. **Explain** What are the two kinds of **caste**?

6. **Describe** What two epic poems helped explain how people should live as Hindus, and what lessons did the epics teach?

7. **Summarize** What is the relationship between **dharma** and **karma** for Hindus?

8. **Explain** How are the Four Noble Truths connected to the Eightfold Path?

9. **Explain** How is **meditation** related to **nirvana**?

Think Critically

10. **Draw Conclusions** What two conclusions can you draw about the Indus Valley civilization from the existence of granaries?

11. **Draw Inferences** What can we infer about Aryan society from passages about livestock and horse-drawn chariots in the Vedas?

12. **Categorize** Place the following ways of making a living into the correct varna or caste grouping: landowner, soldier, servant, priest, governor, construction worker, merchant, garbage collector.

13. **Synthesize** In Hinduism, how are karma and moksha related?

14. **Compare Viewpoints** How do Buddhism and Hinduism differ on the idea of a soul?

Analyze Visuals

Use the graph at right to answer the following questions.

15. What percentage of people in the world are Hindus? What percentage are Buddhists?

16. Compare the number of Hindus and Buddhists to those of other religions.

17. What are the world's three largest religions?

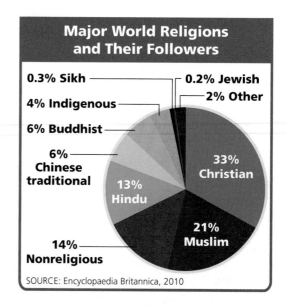

Major World Religions and Their Followers

0.3% Sikh
0.2% Jewish
2% Other
4% Indigenous
6% Buddhist
6% Chinese traditional
33% Christian
13% Hindu
21% Muslim
14% Nonreligious

SOURCE: Encyclopaedia Britannica, 2010

Essential Question

myWorld Chapter Activity

A Trip Through India Create a travel brochure describing five sites related to early Indian civilizations. For each site in your brochure, explain whether geography is important for understanding that site.

21st Century Learning

Develop Cultural Awareness

Describe three characteristics you believe a friend should have. Then search online for Lakshmana or Hanuman, two important characters in the Hindu epic *Ramayana*. Write a paragraph describing the strengths of the character you selected. Explain whether the character's strengths match those you admire in a friend. What does this comparison tell you about Hindu culture?

Document-Based Questions

Success Tracker™
Online at myworldhistory.com

Use your knowledge of the early civilizations of India and Documents A and B to answer questions 1–3.

Document A

" The music of the Frogs comes forth in concert like the cows lowing [mooing] with their calves beside them. When at the coming of the Rains the water has poured upon them as they yearned and thirsted, One seeks another as he talks and greets him with cries of pleasure as a son his father."

—Excerpts from the *Rig Veda*, Hymn CIII

Document B

" She [Kulfi] could hear the sound of cheering from the bazaar [market]. And she watched the children in the streets leap like frogs, unable to keep still in their excitement. . . . Kulfi watched with unbelieving elation [joy] as the approaching smell of rain spiked the air like a flower, as the clouds . . . moved in."

—From Kiran Desai's *Hullabaloo in the Guava Orchard*, 1999

1. According to Document A, why are the frogs making so much noise?

   A. They have found food.

   B. They have been captured.

   C. Cows are entering their field.

   D. Rain has quenched their thirst.

2. Which of these BEST describes why the people described in Document B are so excited?

   A. Rains have flooded the streets.

   B. The monsoons have arrived.

   C. Winter is over.

   D. The Hindu holiday season has begun.

3. **Writing Task** Write a paragraph exploring Indian feelings toward the monsoon and what might explain those feelings.

my worldhistory.com

Self-Test

India's Empires

▲ Emperor Ashoka ordered the construction of this Buddhist shrine in India.

? **Explore the Essential Question . . .**

- at **my** worldhistory.com
- using the **myWorld Chapter Activity**
- with the **Student Journal**

The Maurya and Gupta Empires

321 B.C. Maurya empire is founded.

185 B.C. Last Maurya emperor dies.

A.D. 320 Gupta empire is founded.

| 400 B.C. | 200 B.C. | A.D. 1 | A.D. 200 | A.D. 400 | A.D. 600 |

268 B.C. Ashoka becomes emperor.

A.D. 540 Gupta empire no longer exists.

Emperor Ashoka
and the Gift of Dirt

This is a story about Ashoka, a real emperor who ruled ancient India. Though it is based on legend, this story helps us understand India in the times of Ashoka.

One day Emperor Ashoka was walking through the kingdom of Kalinga, which his army had just completely, utterly destroyed. Ashoka had been emperor for eight years, and Kalinga was his latest conquest. More than 100,000 people had died in his merciless drive to take the kingdom. Finally, he brought Kalinga to its knees. Now everyone and everything in the kingdom belonged to him.

But what exactly did he possess? The earth beneath his feet was stained with blood. The only movement he saw came from vultures circling above, and from smoke rising from smoldering buildings.

Then he noticed women and old men weeping as they searched for the bodies of their husbands, brothers, and sons. He had won a decisive victory, but was the power and territory he had gained worth so much blood and misery?

Vultures circle as Ashoka views the devastation of Kalinga. ▼

myworldhistory.com

On Assignment/Timeline

231

"He's the one!" say the Buddhist monks treating Ashoka. They see him as a reincarnation of a boy named Jaya.

The Buddha shared his teachings. Jaya was in awe. He wanted to give something to the Buddha. He quickly grabbed a handful of dirt.

Suddenly, Ashoka remembered a time several years earlier, when he was still a prince. His father had sent him to a southern province to control an uprising, and he had been injured in battle. While recovering from his wounds at a Buddhist monastery, he began to learn about Buddhism. He also noticed that the monks in the monastery gazed at him and whispered to each other, *"He's the one!"*

When he asked what they meant, he was told that before he was born, he had lived as a boy named Jaya. One day, the great Buddha came to the little boy's village. All the men and women in the village welcomed the Buddha. They listened reverently to everything he said. Jaya listened too, and he was awed to be in the presence of one so calm and wise.

When the Buddha rose to leave the village, all the men and women offered him food and drink to take with him. Jaya wanted to give the Buddha something also, but he couldn't think of an appropriate gift. Eager to show his appreciation, but not knowing what else to do, he scooped up a handful of dirt and put it into the Buddha's wooden bowl. The Buddha smiled at Jaya, for he knew this gift of dirt was a pure expression of the little boy's love and kindness.

Then the Buddha said, "A hundred years after my death, this child will be reborn as the great emperor Ashoka. He will rule the land and will honor the Buddha. His fame will be widespread because of his concern for his people."

That was what the monks meant when they whispered, "He's the one." They meant that he was the rebirth of the little boy, and that one day he would be emperor and would honor the Buddha.

Standing in Kalinga, Ashoka realized that part of the prophecy had indeed come true: He was emperor, and he ruled the subcontinent. But did he honor the Buddha? Was his fame widespread because of his concern for his people—or because of his ruthlessness toward them? Yes, he ruled a vast empire, but had he offered the Buddha a gift of love and kindness as good as Jaya's bowl of dirt?

From that point on, Ashoka threw himself into the study of Buddhism. For the rest of his life he ruled according to the Buddha's teaching of dharma, which emphasizes tolerance, generosity, and good deeds. Instead of warring with neighboring kingdoms, he befriended them. He tried to make life better for all by building roads, digging wells, and planting shade trees. He built hospitals

The Buddha was pleased with Jaya's loving gift. The Buddha predicted that Jaya would be reborn as an emperor.

Looking at the death and destruction he had caused, Ashoka shuddered. His actions were not worthy of the Buddha. He needed to change his ways.

for people and animals. He prohibited hunting and encouraged everyone to treat animals kindly.

He also erected large stone pillars with engraved messages to the people he ruled. On these pillars he publicly apologized for his earlier ways, saying that he felt "deep remorse for having conquered the Kalingas." On these pillars he urged people to be tolerant and to treat one another with respect, regardless of religion or caste. He also stressed that peaceful conquest through dharma was the only conquest that mattered.

Ashoka's story began before he was born, when a child put a handful of dirt in the Buddha's wooden bowl. More than two thousand years later, his story continues. The words he carved into the pillars are still with us, and so is his emblem: the Dharmachakra, or Wheel of Righteous Duty. It adorns the national flag of India, and it is a good reminder of the way history shapes who we are and how we think of ourselves.

As you read this chapter, think about what Ashoka's story tells you about life, religion, and culture in ancient India's empires.

myStory Video

Watch Ashoka as he changes his ways.

The Maurya Empire

Key Ideas

- Chandragupta used military strategy to unite much of India for the first time.

- Chandragupta developed a bureaucracy, a tax system, and a system of spies to help rule his empire.

- The emperor Ashoka turned from war to peace, promoted the growth of Buddhism, and encouraged morality among his subjects.

Key Terms • strategy • province • bureaucracy • subject • tolerance

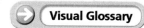 **Visual Glossary**

Reading Skill Analyze Cause and Effect Take notes using the graphic organizer in your journal.

This Indian stamp honors Chandragupta Maurya, the first ruler of all of India. ▼

By the end of the Vedic age, many kingdoms and chiefdoms covered India. The strongest of the kingdoms was Magadha (MUH guh duh). Around 321 B.C., a rebel army overthrew the king of Magadha. The leader of the rebels was a young man named Chandragupta Maurya (chun druh GOOP tuh MOWR yuh).

Chandragupta Unites India

Most of what we know about Chandragupta's life comes from ancient writings, stories, and legends. Some of these legends say that he was born into Magadha's royal family but left with poor farmers when he was young. Others say that he was born into a Kshatriya family west of Magadha. Historians may never know the truth for sure.

321 B.C. Chandragupta conquers Magadha and founds the Maurya empire.

297 B.C. Bindusara becomes emperor and extends the empire south.

268 B.C. Ashoka becomes emperor.

350 B.C.

300 B.C.

250 B.C.

303 B.C. Chandragupta completes his conquest of northwestern India by driving out the Greeks.

260 B.C. Ashoka conquers Kalinga.

256 B.C. Ashoka begins to promote Buddhist values.

Seizing Power As a young man, Chandragupta depended on the advice of an older, educated Brahmin named Kautilya (kow TIL yuh). Legends say that Kautilya had been searching for a leader to drive Greek invaders out of northwestern India. In one story, Kautilya saw Chandragupta playing as a boy and knew that he could be trained as a leader.

Kautilya helped Chandragupta raise an army. He also helped Chandragupta develop a strategy for gaining power. A **strategy** is a long-term plan for achieving a goal. Their strategy was to take control of the northwest from the Greeks and then attack Magadha from the northwest.

Success on the Battlefield Kautilya trained his pupil well. Chandragupta was a brilliant military leader. He armed his men with powerful weapons, including the enormous Indian bow. This bow was as tall as a man. An arrow shot from this bow could pierce a strong shield.

A story says that Chandragupta saw a mother scold her child for starting to eat from the center of the plate. She said the center is too hot. So Chandragupta weakened Magadha by attacking its borders, then moved in to take its capital city.

After Chandragupta conquered Magadha, he moved on to other kingdoms. By 305 B.C., he ruled much of the Indian subcontinent. He had also forced the Greeks out of northwestern India. Chandragupta's Maurya empire stretched from the Bay of Bengal to present-day Afghanistan. For the first time, one state controlled all of northern India.

Reading Check Which part of Magadha did Chandragupta attack first?

Chandragupta's army used elephants to overpower opponents in battle.

232 B.C. Ashoka dies. Weaker emperors rule after him.

250 B.C.　　　　200 B.C.　　　　150 B.C.

185 B.C. The last Maurya emperor is killed.

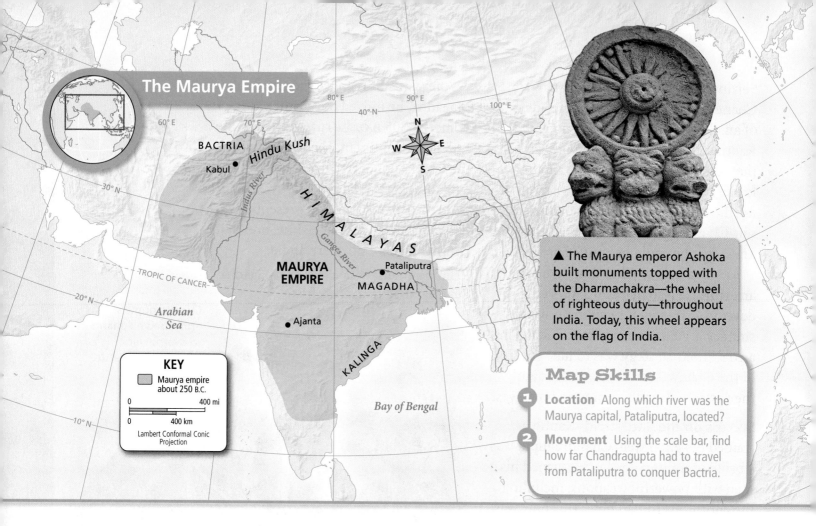

The Maurya Empire

BACTRIA
Kabul
Hindu Kush
Indus River
HIMALAYAS
Ganges River
MAURYA EMPIRE
Pataliputra
MAGADHA
Ajanta
KALINGA
TROPIC OF CANCER
Arabian Sea
Bay of Bengal

KEY

Maurya empire about 250 B.C.

0 _____ 400 mi
0 _____ 400 km
Lambert Conformal Conic Projection

▲ The Maurya emperor Ashoka built monuments topped with the Dharmachakra—the wheel of righteous duty—throughout India. Today, this wheel appears on the flag of India.

Map Skills

1 **Location** Along which river was the Maurya capital, Pataliputra, located?

2 **Movement** Using the scale bar, find how far Chandragupta had to travel from Pataliputra to conquer Bactria.

Ruling an Empire

As emperor, Chandragupta faced the same problem as other empire builders: How could he rule over a large area with many different needs and traditions?

Building a Government Chandragupta solved this problem by dividing his empire into four regions. He divided each region into smaller provinces. A **province** is a region with its own government.

The emperor also set up a **bureaucracy,** or a system of offices that carries out government rules and regulations. Appointed officials in each region, province, and village carried out the emperor's orders. In this way, he was able to control every village in his empire.

Chandragupta also set up a tax system. Tax workers collected 25 percent of the crops raised by farmers. They also collected a sales tax on goods. Chandragupta used the taxes to pay government workers. They also supported a large army and the emperor's costly lifestyle.

This system gave the Maurya empire an efficient government. However, its strength depended on the power and authority of the ruler. The government was only as strong as the emperor.

Subjects and Spies Chandragupta ruled a vast empire, but he lived in constant fear of his enemies. He had servants taste his food for poison. He slept in a different bed every night.

my World
CONNECTIONS

If the Maurya empire were located within the United States, it would stretch from Montana to Pennsylvania to Texas.

To ease his fears, Chandragupta had specially trained female warriors guard his palace. He set up a huge spy network to watch his **subjects,** or people under his rule. He even hired spies to watch other spies. The emperor set aside time every day to receive reports from his spies. Chandragupta's subjects had no right to privacy or freedom of speech.

Slavery existed in Maurya India. Most slaves were prisoners of war or people who could not pay what they owed. Laws protected slaves from harsh treatment in India, unlike in other countries.

Kautilya's Advice Many of Chandragupta's ideas about ruling came from his advisor Kautilya. Kautilya was the author of a book called the *Arthashastra.* The book gives advice on how to be a good ruler. "The primary duty of a king," the *Arthashastra* says, "is the protection of his subjects."

66 In the happiness of his subjects lies the king's happiness. In the welfare of his subjects, his welfare. A king's good is not that which pleases him, but that which pleases his subjects. 99

—Kautilya, *Arthashastra*

welfare, *n.*, well-being, comfort, prosperity

On the other hand, the *Arthashastra* also advises the ruler to do whatever is necessary to keep power. Kautilya says that people cannot be trusted, and he urges severe punishments for crimes.

Reading Check How did Chandragupta get money to pay for his government?

▲ A coin from the Maurya empire

◀ A painting showing a ruler from the Maurya period

237

myWorld Activity
Interview Chandragupta and Ashoka

Emperor Ashoka, whose conquest of Kalinga left many thousand dead ▼

Ashoka Turns to Peace

As Chandragupta grew older, he became a Jain—a follower of Jainism (JY niz um). Jainism is an Indian religion. Like Buddhists, Jains aim for enlightenment. However, they accept the reality of the soul like Hindus. According to legend, Chandragupta gave up being emperor to enter a Jain monastery.

Power passed to his son, Bindusara. Bindusara expanded the Maurya empire farther across India. Then his son Ashoka took power.

Ashoka Rises to Power Ashoka was one of Bindusara's seven sons. Legends say that Bindusara did not like him. As soon as Ashoka was old enough to hold a job, Bindusara sent him away to be the ruler of a faraway province.

When Bindusara died, there was a struggle for the Maurya throne. One legend says that Ashoka killed his own brothers in order to become emperor. After four years of fighting, Ashoka became the third Maurya emperor.

Ashoka spent the next eight years strengthening his hold on power. Then, he went to war again. His target was the kingdom of Kalinga, which had resisted conquest. The war between Maurya and Kalinga was long and terrible. Eventually, Ashoka conquered Kalinga, but at a terrible cost. Thousands of soldiers died.

Ashoka's New Path

Ashoka began his reign as a cruel conqueror and ended as a patron of peace. Few other rulers in history have had such a striking change in attitude.

Ashoka's warriors used huge bows as tall as a man to shoot their arrows far into the enemy's ranks.

Later in life, Ashoka became a follower of the Buddha and the Buddhist Eightfold Path. He rejected violence and called for tolerance.

Another 150,000 people were captured and sent to other parts of the empire.

Ashoka was shocked by the suffering caused by the war. "The slaughter, death, and carrying away of captive people," he later wrote, "is a matter of profound sorrow and regret to His Sacred Majesty."

New Rules for the Empire The suffering that Ashoka saw during the war made him think hard about how he wanted to rule. Ashoka began trying to follow Buddhist values. He turned away from violence. He also rejected some of the harsher teachings of the *Arthashastra*.

Whenever possible, Ashoka replaced rule by force with rule based on dharma, or moral law. His rule of moral law included three principles. The first was the principle of ahimsa, or the belief that one should not hurt any living thing. Ashoka gave up hunting and banned the cruel treatment of animals.

The second principle was tolerance. **Tolerance** is a willingness to respect different beliefs and customs. Ashoka was a Buddhist, but he respected Hinduism, Jainism, and other religions.

The third principle was the people's well-being. Ashoka believed that a ruler must be careful to rule his people well. As a result, Ashoka made many decisions to make his empire a better place to live.

Ashoka's Stone Pillars To share his ideas, Ashoka had stone pillars, or columns, set up across his empire. Each pillar rose 40 feet into the air and weighed 50 tons. Some of Ashoka's stone pillars are still standing today.

These pillars were not just decorative. Ashoka had messages carved into the polished pillars. In some of these messages, he <u>assured</u> his subjects that he was focused on their well-being. He apologized for making war on Kalinga, and he explained his new goals. He urged people to respect their parents and to be generous to other people. He urged respect for all religions. Most of all, Ashoka encouraged people to live moral lives.

assure, *v.*, promise, convince

Buddhism Expands While Ashoka respected all religions, he became a follower of Buddhism. His support for Buddhism helped the religion spread. With Ashoka's backing, Buddhists were able to build monasteries and shrines throughout India.

Buddhists also sent missionaries to neighboring countries, such as Sri Lanka. The support of the powerful Maurya emperor gave the religion prestige. This encouraged other rulers to adopt it.

Reading Check Why did Ashoka turn away from violence?

Ashoka had stone columns like this one built all over India. ▶

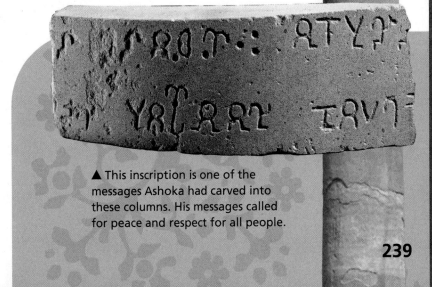

▲ This inscription is one of the messages Ashoka had carved into these columns. His messages called for peace and respect for all people.

239

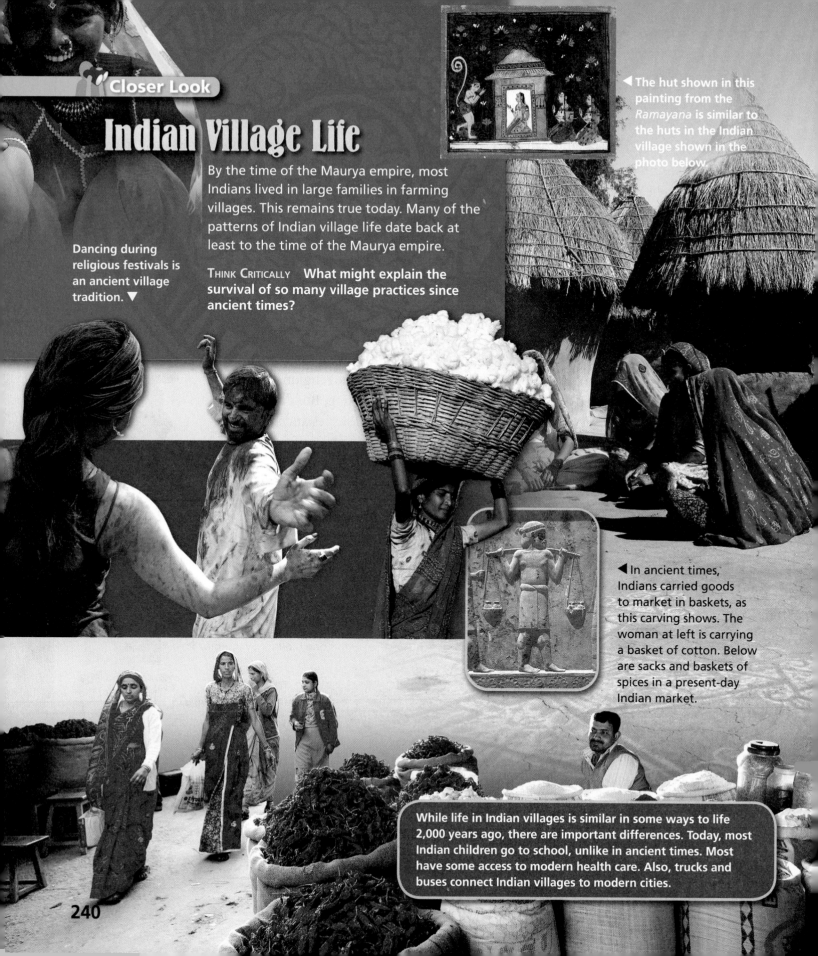

Indian Village Life

By the time of the Maurya empire, most Indians lived in large families in farming villages. This remains true today. Many of the patterns of Indian village life date back at least to the time of the Maurya empire.

THINK CRITICALLY   What might explain the survival of so many village practices since ancient times?

Dancing during religious festivals is an ancient village tradition. ▼

◄ The hut shown in this painting from the *Ramayana* is similar to the huts in the Indian village shown in the photo below.

◄ In ancient times, Indians carried goods to market in baskets, as this carving shows. The woman at left is carrying a basket of cotton. Below are sacks and baskets of spices in a present-day Indian market.

While life in Indian villages is similar in some ways to life 2,000 years ago, there are important differences. Today, most Indian children go to school, unlike in ancient times. Most have some access to modern health care. Also, trucks and buses connect Indian villages to modern cities.

Ashoka's Aftermath

Ashoka ruled India for nearly 40 years. During that time, he did much to improve life for his people. He set up hospitals and dug wells. He built an excellent road system.

The roads promoted trade within the empire. They also increased trade with neighboring lands, such as the Greek-controlled kingdoms of southwest Asia.

The longest of these roads—the Royal Road—stretched more than a thousand miles across northern India. Trees along the road provided shade for travelers. Rest houses offered food and shelter.

As a result of Ashoka's efforts, India prospered. The country was at peace. There was little crime. People could leave their homes unguarded and travel the country without fear.

Ashoka died in 232 B.C. After his death, the Maurya empire struggled. The emperors that followed Ashoka were weak. As you have read, the Maurya government depended completely on the

▲ Ashoka built this road for foot travelers and pack animals.

emperor's ability to make good decisions and command loyalty. As emperors lost control of parts of the empire, they lost support. In 185 B.C., the last Maurya ruler was murdered. After 136 years, the Maurya empire had come to an end.

Reading Check Why did the Maurya empire end?

Section 1 Assessment

Key Terms

1. Use the terms *bureaucracy, subject,* and *tolerance* to describe Maurya government.

2. How did strategy help Chandragupta Maurya's rise to power?

3. Use the term *tolerance* to describe the rule of Ashoka.

Key Ideas

4. How did Chandragupta Maurya conquer Magadha?

5. How did a bureaucracy help the Maurya emperors rule?

6. How did Ashoka's rule promote Buddhism?

Think Critically

7. **Draw Inferences** What was the relationship between the Maurya government and the people it governed?

8. **Compare Viewpoints** Compare the views of Ashoka and Kautilya on the purpose of government.

How are religion and culture connected?

9. What impact did religion have on the Maurya empire? Go to your Student Journal to record your answers.

241

The Gupta Empire

Key Ideas
- The Gupta dynasty created the second major Indian empire.
- The Guptas ruled an India that made advances in the arts, science, and mathematics, including our modern system of numerals.

Key Terms • citizenship   • numeral   • decimal system   • metallurgy

Visual Glossary

Reading Skill Summarize Take notes using the graphic organizer in your journal.

Chandra Gupta II, who ruled the Gupta empire at its height ▼

After the collapse of the Maurya empire, India broke into many small kingdoms. Armies from the north and west invaded India repeatedly. Meanwhile, trade brought Indians into contact with China, Southeast Asia, and the Roman empire. Invaders and traders brought new ideas from the ancient Greeks and other peoples. Indians built on these ideas to make their own advances in art, literature, math, and science.

A New Empire in India

About 500 years after the Mauryas, the Gupta dynasty again united northern India. Chandra Gupta I, the first Gupta ruler, may have been named after the founder of the Maurya empire, Chandragupta. Like the first Maurya emperor, Chandra Gupta I dreamed of building an empire. He gained power over a kingdom in the Ganges Basin and ruled from about A.D. 320 to A.D. 335. He expanded his territory across the Ganges Basin through alliances and wars of conquest.

His son Samudra Gupta conquered most of the remaining small kingdoms of northern India, calling himself the "Exterminator of Kings." Samudra Gupta also conquered lands to the south and west.

Under Samudra's son, Chandra Gupta II, the Gupta empire reached its greatest size. He conquered areas along the west coast. Then, like Ashoka, he tried to bring peace and prosperity to India.

Unlike the Mauryas, the Guptas did not try to rule their entire empire directly. Instead, they left most decisions in the hands of local leaders. Governors controlled provinces. Village and city councils made decisions at the local level.

In each village, the leading families sent representatives to the council. In the cities, guilds, or groups of merchants or craftsmen working in the same line of business, sent representatives to the city council. People living in the Maurya empire were subjects, with a duty to obey. The people of the Gupta empire were also subjects, but some also had a kind of **citizenship,** or a status with political rights and obligations.

A Buddhist monk from China named Fa Xian (fah shen) visited India under the Guptas. He wrote:

66 The people are numerous and happy. . . . If they want to go, they go. If they want to stay, they stay. The king governs without . . . corporal [physical] punishments[.] 99

—Fa Xian, *A Record of the Buddhistic Kingdoms*

Under later Gupta rulers, the empire faced new invaders from the west. Parts of the empire broke away. The last Gupta ruler died around the year 540.

Reading Check How did the Gupta empire come to be?

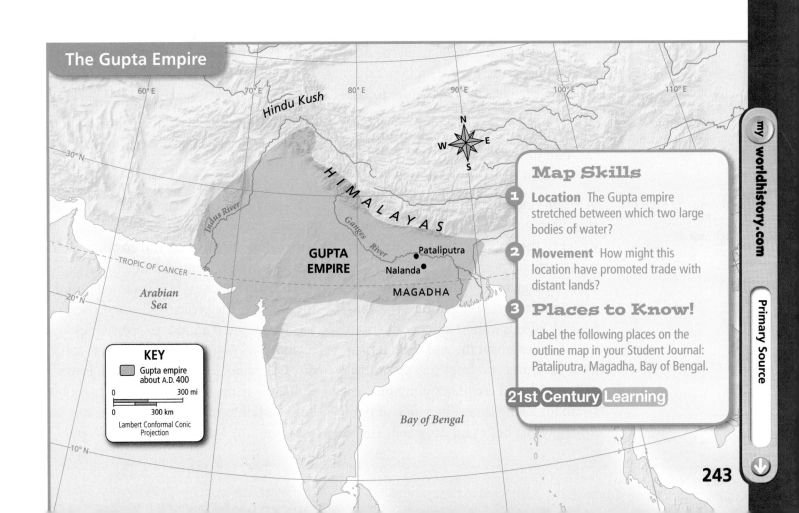

The Gupta Empire

Hindu Kush

H I M A L A Y A S

Indus River

Ganges River

GUPTA EMPIRE

Pataliputra

Nalanda

MAGADHA

Arabian Sea

TROPIC OF CANCER

Bay of Bengal

KEY

Gupta empire about A.D. 400

0   300 mi

0   300 km

Lambert Conformal Conic Projection

Map Skills

1 **Location** The Gupta empire stretched between which two large bodies of water?

2 **Movement** How might this location have promoted trade with distant lands?

3 **Places to Know!**

Label the following places on the outline map in your Student Journal: Pataliputra, Magadha, Bay of Bengal.

21st Century Learning

India has a rich tradition of performing arts. Some of these art forms date back to Gupta times. The historic drawing and the photo at right both show traditional forms of dance.

In traditional Indian dance, hand gestures can have meanings. This woman's gesture means "flag." ▶

Culture Close-Up

▲ Performers of Kathakali (kah tah KAH lee) use makeup to make their facial expressions stand out. This art form combines dance, music, and stories.

drama, *n.*, plays or performances that tell stories

A Rich Culture

Around the time of the Guptas, artists produced great literature, painting, and architecture. The art and literature of the Gupta period still influence Indian culture today.

Much of this art was religious. While Buddhism remained important under the Guptas, the Guptas favored Hinduism.

A Flowering of Literature Under Gupta rule, literature flourished. The greatest writer of the time was the poet Kalidasa, who wrote plays and poetry in the ancient language of Sanskrit.

A popular form of literature was the fable. A fable is a short story with a moral, or lesson, at the end. One Indian fable describes two frogs that fell into a pail of milk and could not jump out. They swam for a long time. Then, one of the frogs gave up hope and drowned. The

other frog kept swimming. Eventually, the swimming frog churned the milk into butter and was able jump out easily. The lesson of this fable is to keep trying even when things look hopeless.

Music, Dance, and Entertainment Music and dance also thrived during the Gupta period. Dancers created works based on Hindu literature. Musicians played stringed instruments and drums.

Some forms of Indian <u>drama</u> combined stories, dance, and music. Performers with elaborate makeup and costumes told stories through song and dance.

The game of chess was invented under the Guptas. The pieces of the first chess sets represented an Indian army. They included a king, war chariots, horse soldiers, elephants, and foot soldiers. From India, the game moved along trade routes both east, into other parts of Asia, and west, into the Middle East and Europe.

Architecture and Painting Hindus and Buddhists built many temples and monasteries during this time. Stonecutters carved some temple buildings from one huge rock in the ground. Architects also built impressive free-standing temples and monasteries. Both rock-carved and free-standing temples show good engineering skills.

Just after the Gupta period, Indians carved temples and monasteries into the rocks of cliffs. In central India, the rock-cut shrines of Ellora contain brilliant sculptures and paintings.

Reading Check What art forms did Indian drama combine?

Mathematics and Science

During the Gupta period, trade and invasion brought the learning of Greece and Persia to India. Indian scholars drew on this learning to make advances of their own in mathematics and science.

The Decimal System One such advance was the development of the concept of zero as a number and as a **numeral,** or a symbol used to represent a number. Probably the greatest advance of Indian mathematicians, though, was the **decimal system,** a counting system based on units of ten. Together these advances were the basis for what we know as the Arabic numerals, in use worldwide today.

This obelisk, or carved pillar, from Ellora is 50 feet (15 meters) tall. It was carved from a single solid rock.▼

▲ This Gupta molded ceramic tile shows a fisherman.

The temples of Ellora were cut into solid rock shortly after the Guptas. Their richly carved stepped towers and pillars are typical of Hindu temples across India.

my worldhistory.com

Culture Close-Up

245

Gupta mathematicians in India developed numerals 1,500 years ago that we still use today. Although the shapes of the numerals have changed over the years, the system remains the same.

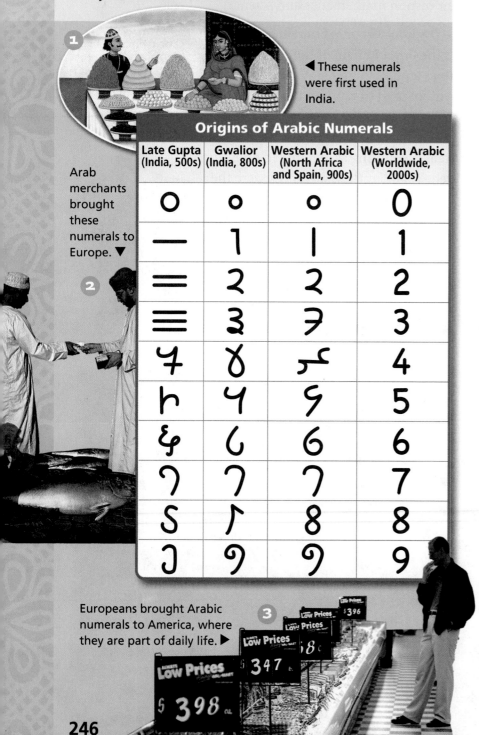

1

◀ These numerals were first used in India.

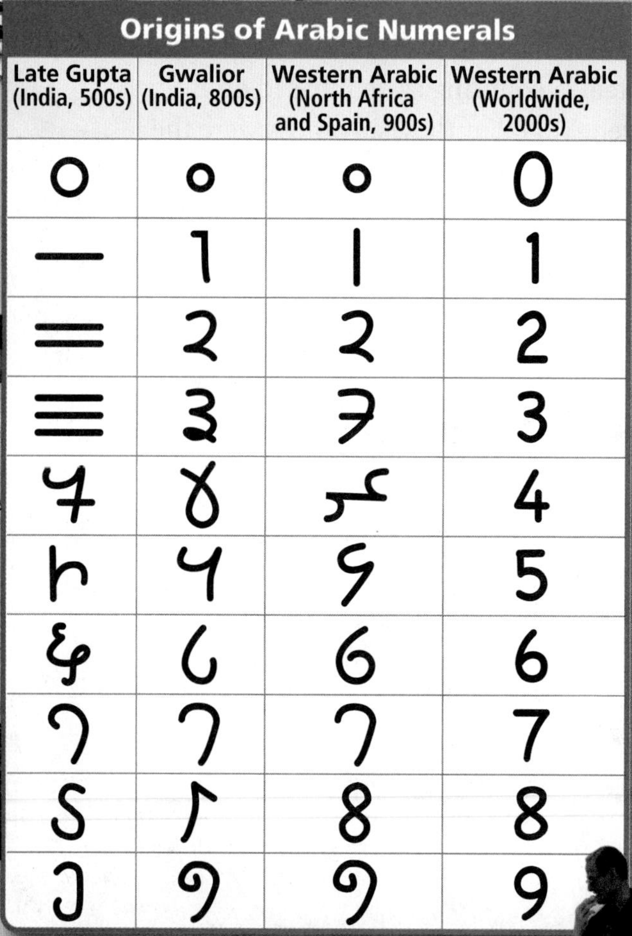

Origins of Arabic Numerals
Late Gupta (India, 500s)
Gwalior (India, 800s)
Western Arabic (North Africa and Spain, 900s)
Western Arabic (Worldwide, 2000s)
0
1
2
3
4
5
6
7
8
9

Arab merchants brought these numerals to Europe. ▼

2

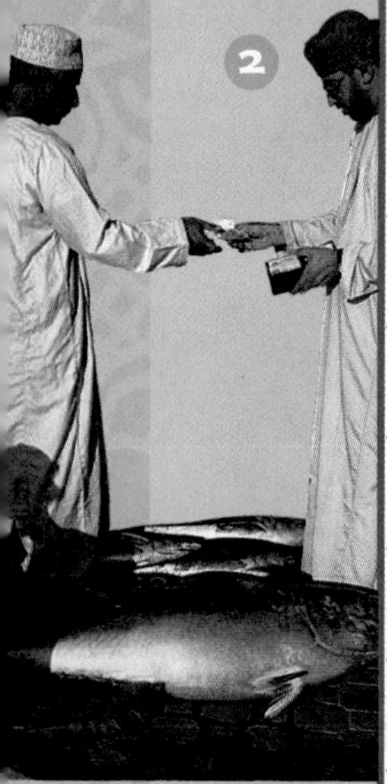

Europeans brought Arabic numerals to America, where they are part of daily life. ▶

3

Low Prices
$ 398
347
Low Prices
Low Prices
$396

A New World of Mathematics

Combining a decimal system with a numeral for zero transformed mathematics. Operations such as multiplication and division were very difficult using earlier systems of numerals, such as Roman numerals. With the new Indian system of numerals, these operations became much easier. This new system opened the way for other advances in mathematics, such as algebra.

Aryabhata (ahr yuh BUH tuh) was an important Indian astronomer and mathematician. In A.D. 499, Aryabhata wrote a book covering the mathematical fields of arithmetic, algebra, and trigonometry. Hundreds of years later, mathematicians in Europe relied on Aryabhata's work to learn how to calculate the area of triangles and the volume of spheres.

Astronomy Aryabhata was the first astronomer to state that the Earth rotates, or spins, on its axis to create day and night. He discovered that eclipses were caused by the motion of Earth and the moon. Aryabhata also discovered that the moon shines because it reflects sunlight.

Medicine Indian doctors made progress in medical science as well. They developed a system of medicine known as Ayurveda.

Ancient Ayurvedic medical textbooks describe more than a thousand different diseases. They explain how to make hundreds of medicines from plants, animal parts, and minerals. The texts also explain how to treat medical problems such as broken bones and blindness.

Achievements of Ancient India
Developed numerals 0 through 9
Created the decimal system
Developed algebra and trigonometry
Explained calculation of area and volume
Discovered that Earth rotates
Explained why the moon shines and the reason for eclipses
Created medicines to treat illnesses
Developed surgical techniques
Had superior metal-working skills

▲ Herbs, fruits, and vegetables used in Indian medicine

myWorld Activity
Book of Gupta Achievements

Chart Skills

1. Which two achievements changed the way we do mathematics?

2. Which achievement changed our view of day and night?

Metallurgy Gupta artisans also made progress in **metallurgy,** the science that deals with <u>extracting</u> metal from ore and using it to create useful objects. These artisans produced metal compounds of great quality. The Iron Pillar of Delhi is a famous example of that skill. This 23-foot-high column was made from a single piece of iron. It has stood outside for more than 1,500 years without turning to rust.

Reading Check What were two key advances in astronomy during the Gupta age?

extract, *v.*, remove, draw out

Section 2 Assessment

Key Terms

1. Use the term *citizenship* in a sentence describing the Gupta system of government.

2. How is a numeral different from a number?

3. Which Gupta advances were related to the decimal system and metallurgy?

Key Ideas

4. How did the Guptas build their empire?

5. Which Gupta traditions continue to influence the art of India today?

6. Explain how the Gupta system of numerals led to other advances in mathematics.

Think Critically

7. **Compare and Contrast** How was the Gupta system of government different from the Maurya system of government?

8. **Analyze Cause and Effect** How did the numeral system developed in ancient India pave the way for modern advances in science and technology?

Essential Question

How are religion and culture connected?

9. Which aspects of Gupta civilization were connected to religion? Which were not? Go to your Student Journal to record your answers.

Chapter **7**

Chapter Assessment

Key Terms and Ideas

1. **Recall** Who was Kautilya, and what was his **strategy**?

2. **Describe** How did Chandragupta conquer Magadha?

3. **Describe** How did Chandragupta's **bureaucracy** work?

4. **Explain** What was Chandragupta's attitude toward his subjects?

5. **Discuss** How did Ashoka try to bring peace and prosperity to his empire?

6. **Explain** What was the impact of Ashoka's rule on Buddhism?

7. **Recall** What improvements did Ashoka make to Indian life?

8. **Explain** What **citizenship** rights did people have in the Gupta empire?

9. **Recall** When and where was our system of numerals invented?

10. **Describe** What information did Gupta astronomers discover?

Think Critically

11. **Solve Problems** Do you think a government needs a bureaucracy? Why or why not?

12. **Analyze Primary and Secondary Sources** Reread the subsection "Kautilya's Advice" in Section 1. With which advice do you agree? With which do you disagree? Why?

13. **Analyze Cause and Effect** Why might Ashoka have stressed tolerance of religions other than Buddhism?

14. **Draw Inferences** How did the Gupta bureaucracy differ from the bureaucracy established by the Maurya emperor?

15. **Core Concepts: Science and Technology** Why would discoveries in metallurgy be important to a civilization?

Analyze Visuals

Use the map at right to answer the following questions.

16. Which empire covered more territory, the Maurya or the Gupta?

17. Why might both empires have wanted coastlines on both the Arabian Sea and the Bay of Bengal?

18. Pataliputra was the capital of both the Maurya and the Gupta empires. How did its location make it a good choice for a capital city?

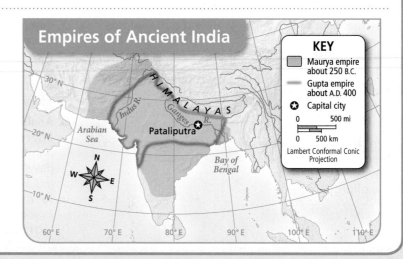

Empires of Ancient India

KEY
- Maurya empire about 250 B.C.
- Gupta empire about A.D. 400
- ✪ Capital city

0   500 mi
0   500 km
Lambert Conformal Conic Projection

Essential Question
myWorld Chapter Activity

Outline a Documentary Follow your teacher's instructions to gather information about five important people from ancient India. Use the information to outline the plot for a documentary about one of these figures. Make sure your documentary addresses your person's relation to India's religions.

21st Century Learning
Solve Problems

Working in small groups, list two benefits and two drawbacks of bureaucracy. Then search online to learn about the bureaucracy of your state government or the bureaucracy of at least one state agency. Suggest ways in which your state or one of its agencies could increase the benefits and reduce the drawbacks of bureaucracy.

Document-Based Questions

Success Tracker™
Online at myworldhistory.com

Use your knowledge of the Maurya empire and Documents A and B to answer Questions 1–3.

Document A

" **The Duties of a King**
When in his court he shall never cause his petitioners [people seeking help] to wait at the door, for when a king makes himself [unapproachable] to his people and entrusts [passes] his work to his immediate officers, he may be sure to [create] confusion in business, and to cause thereby public [hostility], and make himself a prey [victim] to his enemies."

—from Kautilya's *Arthashastra*, Book I, Chapter 19

1. What does Document A advise a king to do?
  A cause people to wait at his door
  B allow people to seek help from him directly
  C create confusion in business
  D entrust his work to immediate officers

Document B

" Father and mother must be hearkened [paid attention] to; similarly respect for living creatures must be firmly established; truth must be spoken. These are the virtues of the Law of Piety [or Dharma] which must be practiced. Similarly, the teacher must be reverenced [respected and valued] by the pupil, and toward relations [relatives] fitting courtesy [politeness] should be shown."

—from Ashoka's Minor Rock Edict II

2. To whom is Ashoka offering advice in Document B?
  A a king
  B parents
  C teachers
  D citizens

3. **Writing Task** Write an edict giving advice that reflects how you believe a leader should govern American society today.

myworldhistory.com

Self-Test

Ancient China

Essential Question

How much does geography affect people's lives?

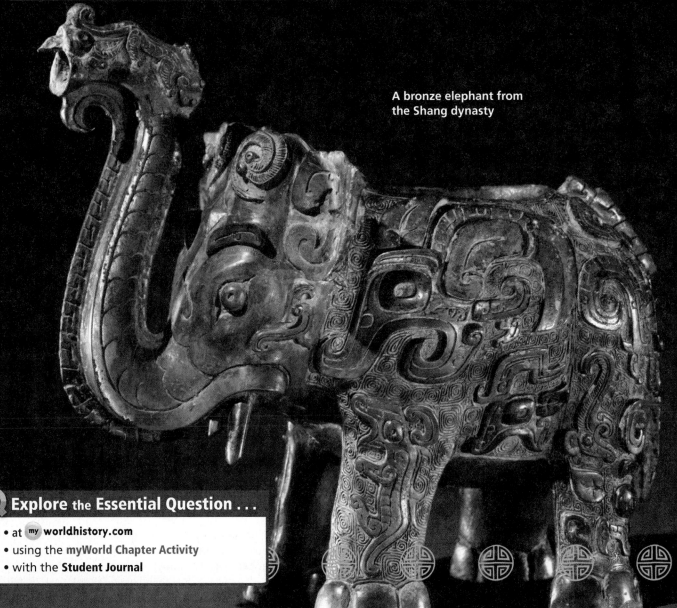

A bronze elephant from
the Shang dynasty

? Explore the Essential Question . . .

- at **my worldhistory.com**
- using the **myWorld Chapter Activity**
- with the **Student Journal**

Shang and Zhou China

about 1800 B.C. The Shang kingdom is founded.	**about 1050** B.C. The Zhou dynasty begins.	**about 500** B.C. The first coins are used in China.	**371** B.C. Mencius is born.

1800 B.C.   **1400** B.C.   **1000** B.C.   **600** B.C.   **200** B.C.

about 1400 B.C. The Shang begin writing oracle bones.	**475** B.C. The Warring States period begins.	**256** B.C. The Zhou dynasty ends.

The Wisdom of Zhang Shi, Mother of Mencius

Mengzi was a famous Chinese scholar who advised kings during the turbulent end of the Zhou dynasty. European historians translated his name to "Mencius." The story below is based on a traditional tale told about Mencius's childhood. Mencius was advised by his mother, Zhang Shi, long before he became a counselor to kings.

Mencius's father died when he was a very young boy. This meant that Zhang Shi (jahng sher) had to figure out how to provide for her young son. One night she went to bed hoping that in the morning she would know what to do. As the sun rose the next morning, she knew what to do—she would weave. That way, she could sell what she made and buy food with the money. Right away she set to work on her loom. As she worked the silk thread through the loom, it occurred to her that she was not weaving a piece of colorful fabric. She was weaving a better life for her son. Day after day she wove, and the whole time she sat at the loom she thought of Mencius. "How happy his father would be," she said to herself, "if one day his son grew up to be a scholar!"

Mencius and his friend copy the workers in the graveyard near Mencius's home.

Mencius and his friend squabble like the merchants in the market.

But one afternoon, she glanced up from her loom to see Mencius playing a disturbing game with his friends. They were digging what seemed to be graves, and they were pretending to be corpses and mourners. Zhang Shi was shocked to see her son playing such a game. Then she realized that the boys were mimicking what they saw in a graveyard near where they lived. She said to herself, "I should not raise my son in such a place as this. I want my son to be a scholar, not a gravedigger!"

That evening she told Mencius they were moving to a place where he would have better influences on his life.

So they moved to a new home, next to a bustling marketplace. Zhang Shi did not particularly like the men who worked in the market, for they often argued and fought with each other over money. But Mencius was happy there, and he made lots of new friends.

Zhang Shi picks up a knife and slashes the cloth that she was weaving.

Zhang Shi packs their belongings to move again.

Mencius works hard at his studies.

For a while, all was well, and when Zhang Shi worked at her loom she again thought to herself how happy her husband would be if his son grew up to be a scholar.

But one afternoon, she looked up from her weaving and saw Mencius and his new friends swearing at each other and punching each other—just like the men who worked in the marketplace! Zhang Shi frowned and immediately began packing.

This time, they moved next to a school. Mencius watched the children learning to read and write, and he asked his mother if he could join them. She smiled. "At last," she said to herself, "I have found a place that is right for my son. Now he can grow up to be a scholar."

Mencius did well in school, and Zhang Shi continued to do well with her weaving. Her pieces were bigger and more beautiful than ever before.

But one afternoon Zhang Shi noticed that Mencius had come home from school earlier than usual. She looked at him carefully and asked what he had learned in school that day.

Mencius blushed. "Not much. Same as yesterday."

Zhang Shi knew Mencius had skipped school. So she picked up a knife and slashed the cloth that she had been weaving. All of her beautiful work fell to the floor in tatters!

"No!" cried Mencius. "What are you doing?"

Zhang Shi said that she had cut her weaving to show him the mistake he was making. "Skipping school is the same as me cutting my weaving. If you do not study and cultivate your character, you will end up a thief or a slave. If I do not weave, I will also end up a thief or a slave. They are the same thing. Do you not see that?"

From that point on, Mencius studied hard in school, and he went on to become one of the most famous scholars in Chinese history. Mencius once said that he who attends to his greater self becomes a great man, and he who attends to his smaller self becomes a small man. Wise words indeed—and a lesson learned from his mother.

Based on this story, how did location influence Mencius? As you read the chapter, think about what Mencius's life tells you about ancient China.

 myStory Video

Learn more about Zhang Shi and Mencius.

Settling Along the Huang River

Key Ideas

- Geographic features isolated ancient China from other early civilizations.
- Farming settlements along the Huang River were the beginning of Chinese civilization.
- Achievements of the Shang dynasty included advanced bronze work and the development of writing.

Key Terms • loess • dike • oracle bones • pictograph

→ **Visual Glossary**

Reading Skill Summarize Take notes using the graphic organizer in your journal.

→ **Culture Close-Up**

Shang artisans created beautiful bronze statues.

Chinese civilization arose along the Huang (hwong) River, also called the Yellow River. By around 5000 B.C., farmers had settled in a number of villages in this river valley. Over time, powerful rulers united these villages to create large kingdoms. Among these, the Shang kingdom rose to become the most influential.

Geography of China

Today, the country of China is a huge land, similar in size to the United States. Much of China is covered by rugged mountains and vast deserts. Despite the challenges of the geography, early people found the resources they needed along China's river valleys.

River Systems Rivers helped China's development, just as they aided the development of civilizations in Mesopotamia, Egypt, and India. China has two main rivers: the Huang and the Chang (chahng). They provide water for farming. People move goods along these waterways.

Both rivers begin in the high mountains of western China. The Chang is China's longest river, but the Huang River was especially important to China's early history. It flows east to the Yellow Sea. Along the way, this river crosses the flat North China Plain.

Winds from the Gobi Desert blow loess (LOH es) onto the Huang River valley. **Loess** is a fine, dustlike material that can form soil. The Huang River cuts through deep deposits of loess and picks it up.

The loess makes the river muddy and turns the river yellow. The name of the Huang River comes from this mud. In Chinese, *huang* means yellow.

When the river overflows its banks, it deposits the loess on the surrounding plain. This fertile soil makes the North China Plain well suited for agriculture. Even with simple tools, ancient farmers could easily plant their crops in the soft soil. It is on this plain that people created the first large settlements in China.

Isolation China is nearly surrounded by physical barriers. Two great deserts, the Taklimakan (tah kluh muh KAHN) and the Gobi, lie to the north and west of China. The towering Himalayas form a wall between China and India. To the south lie more mountains, and to the east stretches the vast Pacific Ocean.

Travel and trade between China and other civilizations was difficult. Some early innovations, such as the domesticated horse and the chariot, may have come to China from western Asia. However, ancient China was largely cut off from other civilizations. It developed its own traditions and way of life.

Reading Check What natural barriers isolated China from other civilizations?

my World CONNECTIONS

The Chang River is almost twice as long as the Missouri River, the longest river in the United States.

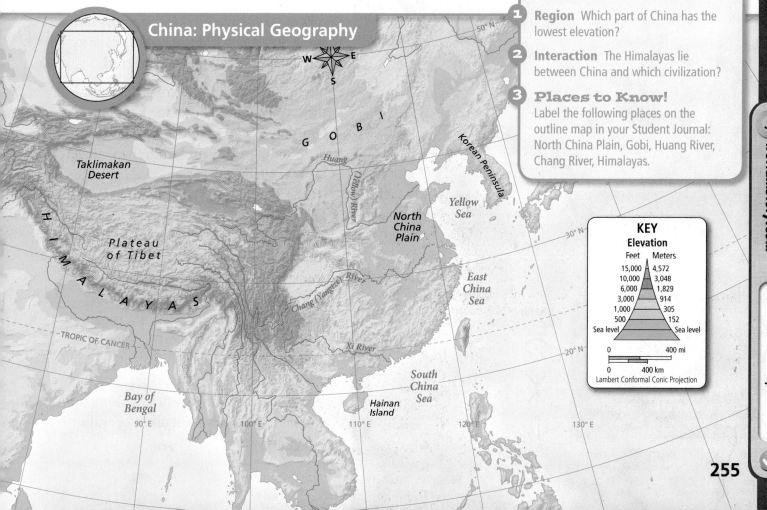

China: Physical Geography

Taklimakan Desert

G O B I

Huang

Huang (Yellow) River

Korean Peninsula

North China Plain

Yellow Sea

H I M A L A Y A S

Plateau of Tibet

Chang (Yangtze) River

East China Sea

TROPIC OF CANCER

Xi River

Bay of Bengal

South China Sea

Hainan Island

50° N

30° N

20° N

90° E   100° E   110° E   120° E   130° E

Map Skills

1 **Region** Which part of China has the lowest elevation?

2 **Interaction** The Himalayas lie between China and which civilization?

3 **Places to Know!** Label the following places on the outline map in your Student Journal: North China Plain, Gobi, Huang River, Chang River, Himalayas.

KEY
Elevation

Feet	Meters
15,000	4,572
10,000	3,048
6,000	1,829
3,000	914
1,000	305
500	152
Sea level	Sea level

0   400 mi

0   400 km

Lambert Conformal Conic Projection

ORACLE BONES

Shang diviners would write questions to the ancestors on an animal bone or turtle shell., They would heat it until it cracked, then interpret the pattern of cracks. One Shang king used this method to divine the outcome of a conflict between two other kingdoms.

THINK CRITICALLY Why might the king want to know the outcome of a conflict between two other kingdoms?

Many modern Chinese characters can be traced to writing on oracle bones. ▶

Chinese Writing

Shang Character	Modern Character	Meaning
𠕲	雨	Rain
米	木	Tree
D	月	Moon

The Shang Dynasty

From the early settlements along the Huang River, the Shang kingdom rose to dominate a large part of the region. The language and culture of the Shang would have a lasting influence on China.

The Shang Rise Farming villages grew along the Huang River. The people used stone tools and made pottery and silk cloth. Some of these villages had chiefs, or rulers, who organized workers and commanded warriors. Strong chiefs led their warriors to take control of nearby villages, creating small kingdoms.

Around 1700 B.C., one of those kingdoms began to expand. A ruler from this kingdom founded the Shang dynasty. A dynasty is a ruling family that holds power for many years. This dynasty lasted some 600 years. It is the earliest dynasty for which we have a written record.

Shang Government Strong rulers ran the government. The Shang kept power within the family. Rule passed from brother to brother and from the youngest brother to his oldest son.

The Shang leaders organized groups of farmers to clear and prepare new land. The result was larger harvests. With extra food, Shang rulers could support many soldiers. They attacked neighboring lands and expanded their territory. Soldiers fought with bows, lances, and bronze axes. Some rode into battle in chariots.

Shang rulers used their wealth to build a number of large walled cities. They also tried to control the floods along the Huang River. They built **dikes,** or walls to hold back water.

Writing The earliest written records from China are **oracle bones** from the Shang dynasty. Oracle bones are animal bones or turtle shells carved with written characters that the Shang kings used to try to tell the future.

Questions were written on the bone, which was then heated until it cracked. The king or a priest would <u>interpret</u> the cracks to get an answer. No one knows exactly how the cracks were read.

At times, the Chinese also used oracle bones to record important events related to their questions. From these written records, scholars have learned much about ancient China and its rulers.

The Shang did not use an alphabet for their written words, which are called characters. Instead, some characters were **pictographs,** that is, pictures that represent words or ideas. Other characters were a combination of symbols. Some symbols stood for the meaning of the word while others represented the sound.

By 1300 B.C., the Shang had a fully developed writing system. Many ancient characters became the writing Chinese people use today. The sound changed, but their meaning can still be understood. Today, written Chinese has many thousands of characters, making it a <u>challenge</u> to learn.

Still, this system is useful in a country where people speak many languages. Spoken Chinese is different across the country, but all Chinese speakers use the same characters. In a sense, Chinese characters are like numbers. A number has the same meaning in many languages even if the spoken word used for that number is different in each of those languages.

Bronze Metalworking Shang artisans created pottery and jade carvings, but they are best known for their bronze metalworking. These objects included finely decorated pots, cups, and weapons.

Most tools used on a daily basis were not made out of bronze. The Shang used the expensive, beautiful bronzes in religious ceremonies. Human and animal sacrifices were prepared with bronze blades. They also offered food and wine to their gods and ancestors in the hope that these spirits would help them.

Reading Check How long did the Shang dynasty last?

challenge, *n.,* something that is difficult or demanding to do

interpret, *v.,* to explain, give the meaning of

myWorld Activity
A Bronze Pot Tells a Story

Section 1 Assessment

Key Terms

1. What is loess?

2. Use the terms *oracle bones* and *pictograph* to describe the Chinese language.

Key Ideas

3. What are the two major rivers in China?

4. What were two accomplishments of the Shang dynasty?

5. How did the leaders of the Shang dynasty increase their power?

Think Critically

6. **Draw Conclusions** Why have scholars studied oracle bones?

7. **Compare and Contrast** How is Chinese different from English?

Essential Question

How much does geography affect people's lives?

8. How did the Huang River affect the lives of the Chinese who settled along its banks? Go to your Student Journal to record your answer.

257

China Under the Zhou Dynasty

Key Ideas

- The Zhou dynasty defeated the Shang dynasty in about 1050 B.C.

- The Zhou developed the idea of the Mandate of Heaven, which explained the rise and fall of dynasties.

- The kings of the Zhou dynasty expanded their empire but had difficulty controlling their large territory.

Key Terms • Mandate of Heaven • warlord • chaos • Warring States period

 Visual Glossary

Reading Skill Identify Main Ideas and Details Take notes using the graphic organizer in your journal.

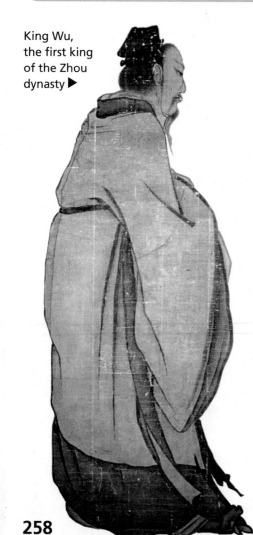

King Wu, the first king of the Zhou dynasty ▶

Around 1050 B.C., a group called the Zhou (joh) attacked the Shang kingdom from the west. They overthrew the Shang ruler and established a new dynasty. The Zhou dynasty ruled for about 800 years. For much of the second half of its rule, however, the Zhou struggled to keep its large kingdom united.

Rise and Fall of the Zhou

Most of what is known about the fall of the Shang comes from sources written during the Zhou. According to these sources, the Zhou gained power because the Shang kings had grown corrupt. The last Shang king governed badly. He cared only about his own enjoyment, and many people came to resent him. When the Zhou attacked the Shang, many Shang warriors refused to fight. They surrendered and accepted the Zhou king as their new ruler.

The Right to Rule After taking power, the Zhou leaders declared that their success proved that they had heaven's support. In their view, heaven was the highest force of nature that gave dynasties the right to rule. They called this right to rule the **Mandate of Heaven.** If a dynasty failed to act properly, it lost this right. This mandate would then pass to a new dynasty. The Mandate of Heaven permitted a leader to seize control by force, if necessary. Victory served as proof that heaven supported the change in leadership.

To stay in power, however, the rulers of the new dynasty would have to act virtuously. They would have to be kind and just and serve the interests of the people. The concept of the Mandate of Heaven became a tradition of Chinese government. Under this tradition, the ruler was called the Son of Heaven. If he performed his role well, there would be harmony between heaven and earth.

One ancient Chinese source, the *Book of History,* explains why the Zhou kings received the Mandate of Heaven:

> 66 . . . our kings of Zhou treated the people well . . . and presided over services to spirits and to Heaven. Heaven therefore instructed the Zhou kings, chose them . . . and gave them the decree to rule. 99
> —*Book of History*

Emperors had to care for their people and stop corruption. Uprisings and natural disasters were seen as possible omens that the current dynasty had lost the Mandate of Heaven.

Governing the Zhou Through conquest, the Zhou expanded its lands. At its height, the Zhou ruled a territory that reached to the Chang River.

This large kingdom included many different cultures. To keep control, the king placed family members in charge of individual regions or states. Over time, the ties between the Zhou king and local nobles weakened.

In 771 B.C., a group of nobles joined with nomadic invaders to try to overthrow the king. With the help of other nobles, the Zhou <u>survived</u> this attack. But the power of the Zhou king decreased. From that point on, the Zhou kings were weak and dependent on the nobles who had helped them to stay in power.

States that had once been tied to the Zhou grew more independent. Fighting broke out between warlords. **Warlords** are military rulers of small states. Although these warlords claimed loyalty to the king, they often really hoped to gain power for themselves.

survive, *v.,* to last, to continue to live

myWorld Activity
Announcement of Power

Shang and Zhou China

KEY

- Zhou civilization, 1000 B.C.
- Core area of Shang dynasty
- ● Last Shang capital
- ○ Last Zhou capital

0   300 mi
0   300 km
Lambert Conformal Conic Projection

Huang (Yellow) River

Anyang

Luoyang

Chang (Yangtze) River

Yellow Sea

East China Sea

PACIFIC OCEAN

30° N

TROPIC OF CANCER

20° N

100° E   110° E   120° E   130° E

Map Skills

1 **Location** Did the Zhou control the core Shang lands?

2 **Place** Why might both the Shang and Zhou capitals have been located along the Huang River?

minor, *adj.*,
not serious, not
important

The Warring States Eventually, <u>minor</u> battles escalated into full-scale warfare. China entered an era of **chaos**—total disorder and confusion. This era, from about 475 B.C. to 221 B.C., became known as the **Warring States period.** Brutal and destructive conflict marked the period. Battles ravaged the countryside. Millions of people died.

Stronger states conquered weaker ones. Over time, a few large states emerged. Loyalty to the Zhou dynasty disappeared. In 256 B.C., the last Zhou ruler was overthrown. Fighting continued for years, however, before a new dynasty managed to unite China.

Reading Check What made governing the Zhou kingdom difficult?

Zhou Society

The Zhou adopted much of Shang culture. They followed the same basic laws, wore similar clothing, and spoke the same language. They produced bronze art that rivaled that of the Shang. However, great changes also occurred in the Zhou dynasty. For example, the Zhou kings gave up the practice of human sacrifice and stopped using oracle bones.

Structure of Society The Zhou kings, just as the Shang rulers before them, occupied the center of government. The Zhou, however, gave more power to individual states and the nobles who led them. Those states set up their own walled capital cities, from which they controlled the lands of lesser nobles. The nobles were expected to serve the king and raise armies to support him.

A new dynasty rises.
• A strong ruler defeats other local rulers.
• The new dynasty expands China's borders.

The new dynasty rules.
• It restores peace.
• It chooses loyal officials.
• It makes reforms.

The dynasty grows weak.
• Large empire difficult to govern.
• Heavy taxes pay for projects and luxuries.
• Officials become corrupt.

The dynasty loses the Mandate of Heaven
• Rebellion and invasion
• Floods, famine, earthquakes
• The dynasty falls.

A period of violence follows.
• Local rulers fight for power.

The Rise and Fall of Dynasties

Many of China's dynasties rose and fell in a similar pattern. The Chinese believed that each dynasty first gained and then lost the Mandate of Heaven.

Chart Skills

1 Why do dynasties become weak?

2 Why do you think Chinese people saw floods and earthquakes as proof that a dynasty had lost the Mandate of Heaven?

21st Century Learning

The majority of people, as in most ancient societies, were peasants. They farmed the land. They also had duties such as serving as soldiers in battles.

In addition, there were a small number of merchants, artisans, and slaves in Zhou society. Some people were sold into slavery when their family fell on hard times. Slavery was also used as a punishment.

Family Relationships The ancient Chinese put a high value on family. Society demanded that individuals show loyalty to their family. Within the family, older family members had more power and privileges than younger ones. As in most ancient societies, men had higher status than women.

Economy and Technology During the Zhou, there were many technological advances. For weapons, one important invention was the crossbow. Artisans learned to make iron, which is stronger than bronze. The Zhou used iron to make weapons.

Innovations also helped strengthen the Zhou economy. Iron was used to make stronger, more effective farm tools. Crop yield also increased as the Zhou used irrigation and fertilizer for more of their farmland. The Zhou built a network of roads, which helped travel and trade. A number of new cities sprang up.

Coins were also used for the first time in the Zhou dynasty. Coins made trade across the large Zhou empire easier.

Cultural Life The Zhou dynasty was also a time of great creative energy. As the leaders of the Warring States vied for influence, they supported poets and artists. They looked for wise men to help them to rule. The writings of thinkers from this time became the foundation of much of Chinese thought for centuries.

Reading Check What were two advances of Zhou society?

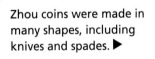

Zhou coins were made in many shapes, including knives and spades. ▶

Section **2** Assessment

Key Terms

1. What is a warlord?

2. Use the terms *chaos* and *Warring States period* to write a sentence about China under the Zhou dynasty.

Key Ideas

3. How did the Zhou dynasty establish its right to rule China?

4. How did the power of the king change during the Zhou dynasty?

Think Critically

5. **Compare and Contrast** How was the Zhou dynasty similar to and different from the Shang dynasty?

6. **Make Inferences** How did the invention of coins help make trade easier?

Essential Question

How much does geography affect people's lives?

7. How did China's geography make it difficult for the Zhou kings to keep their large kingdom united? Go to your Student Journal to record your answer.

Religions and Beliefs of Ancient China

<table>
<tr><td>**Key Ideas**</td><td>● Traditional Chinese beliefs focused on spirits and the importance of ancestors.</td><td>● Confucianism and Daoism were important philosophies developed during the Zhou dynasty.</td></tr>
</table>

Key Terms • philosophy • ancestor worship • Confucianism • filial piety • Daoism

 **Visual Glossary**

Reading Skill Compare and Contrast Take notes using the graphic organizer in your journal.

◄ Noisy firecrackers are believed to drive away bad spirits. The crackle of these fireworks can be heard all night long on New Year's Eve in some Chinese towns.

Isolated by its geography, ancient China had a unique culture. Two important belief systems, Confucianism and Daoism, developed during the Zhou. Each is a **philosophy,** that is, a set of beliefs about the world and how to live. These philosphies influenced all aspects of society. Religious practices, such as the worship of certain gods, became connected to these philosphies. Today, Daoist and Confucian temples are found across China. Before these philosophies appeared, the Chinese followed ancient spiritual traditions.

Spiritual Traditions

Some ancient Chinese viewed Earth as a flat square. Heaven stretched above. Both heaven and Earth were populated by a variety of spirits.

Many Spirits The ancient Chinese viewed heaven as the home of the spirits of the sun, moon, stars, and storms. On Earth, spirits lived in hills, rivers, rocks, and seas. These spirits ruled the daily lives of people. Good spirits made the rains fall and crops grow. They helped sailors travel safely on the ocean. They brought happiness.

Not all spirits were so kind. Harmful spirits made it unsafe to walk the roads at night. They might hide in a house, bringing bad luck to all who lived there. During festivals, people used loud sounds to frighten evil spirits away.

Honoring Ancestors The most important spirits to many ancient Chinese were those of their ancestors. They believed that family members lived on after death in the spirit world. The spirits of those ancestors remained part of the family.

Like any family member, the ancestors had to be supported and cared for. If the living took care of their ancestors, then the ancestors would protect and guide them. But the spirits of ancestors could also cause people trouble. The key to a good relationship was for the living to honor the dead.

Over the centuries, the Chinese developed many rituals to honor their ancestors. Families had shrines with tablets inscribed with ancestors' names. They set out food for their ancestors on special occasions to welcome them home. After paper money came into use, they burned fake "spirit" money to give the ancestors <u>income</u> in the afterlife. Practices of honoring the spirits of the dead are known as **ancestor worship.** Many of these rituals related to ancestor worship are performed at holidays and funerals in China today.

income, *n.,*
payments of money

Reading Check Why was it important to the Chinese to honor their ancestors?

Spirits in the Home

Today, many Chinese think the ancient ideas about spirits are superstitions. However, Chinese decorations show the influence of traditional ideas about good and bad spirits.

Some Chinese decorate their doorways with paintings of a pair of generals. The generals keep evil spirits from entering the home.

The Kitchen God is a friendly spirit who lives in a family's kitchen. He reports to a powerful spirit known as the Jade Emperor. At the New Year, the family will hang an image of the Kitchen God and put honey on his lips so that he will tell the Jade Emperor "sweet" things about their family.

263

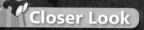

Be Good:
Leading by Example

The thinker Confucius hoped to teach his students to be wise and good. He wanted rulers to follow his advice and become examples of good behavior to their subjects. People would only learn to be good when ruled by a just ruler. Confucius believed that education and ritual were two ways to teach values.

Why did Confucius believe that it was important for rulers to act in a proper way?

66 If the people are led by laws . . . they will try to avoid the punishment but have no sense of shame. If they are led by virtue [goodness] . . . they will have the sense of shame and will become good . 99
—Confucius, *Analects*

Ritual
Confucius felt that following traditional rituals helped people focus on important values. For example, he argued that after a parent died, the child should mourn for three years. During this time, the child lived a more plain life. This ritual was a tribute to the love and care the parent gave the child. Above, mourners burn candles and spirit money at a funeral.

Education
Confucius urged his students to study not only writing and math, but also music. Music was central to Zhou ceremonies. It could fill the listener with feelings of beauty and harmony and inspire good behavior. Left, a musician strikes a bronze bell. Large bronze bells like these were made during the Zhou.

The Teachings of Confucius

Confucianism, the teachings of the thinker Confucius, is one of the most important philosophies that developed in China. Confucius lived just before the Warring States period. The Zhou kings had already grown weak. He and later thinkers at the end of the Zhou dynasty looked for solutions to China's problems. Among these thinkers, Confucius had the greatest effect on Chinese culture. He is known as the "First Teacher" and is honored for his great wisdom.

Life of a Philosopher Confucius was born into a poor family in 551 B.C. He held several low-level jobs in government. He saw for himself some of the problems of his time, such as greed and cruelty. Officials often did not enforce the law. Some took bribes, or illegal payments, to do favors for the rich. Peasants starved while rulers taxed them to pay for wars.

Confucius believed that the cause of the disorder was that the Chinese had turned away from the traditional roles and values of the early Zhou. Only a return to those ideals could bring order to China. Confucius made his life's work teaching the wise ways of the ancestors.

To carry out this work, Confucius started his own school. Students of Confucius collected his teachings in a book called the *Analects*. In later centuries, this book became central to political and ethical thought in China and across East Asia. Chinese students still memorize passages from it today. It is a source of great wisdom. The book includes the following saying:

> 66 What I do not wish men to do to me, I also wish not to do to [other] men. 99
> —Confucius, *Analects*

Confucius never achieved great wealth or influence in his lifetime, but his students, such as Mencius, spread his ideas throughout China.

Five Relationships The heart of Confucianism lay in a vision of a <u>stable</u>, orderly society based on five relationships: (1) ruler and subject, (2) father and son, (3) husband and wife, (4) older and younger brothers, and (5) two friends.

Especially important was the relationship between father and son, or parents and their children. Elders care for and teach younger family members. In return, children respect and obey their elders. The devotion of children to their parents is called **filial piety.** Confucians referred to this as "the source of all virtues."

The relationship between parents and children was the model for the other four relationships. The person of higher status in each of the five relationships, that is, the father, husband, elder, or ruler, must fulfill the responsibilities of their role. The person of lower status, that is, the wife, subject, or younger person, should respect the senior person. Confucius believed order and harmony would come to society once all people acted according to their roles.

Reading Check What is the most important virtue in Confucianism?

stable, *adj.*, able to last, not likely to fall apart

What Do Daoists Do?

Daoists want to connect to the Dao. But how can you do that? The Wudang Mountains are an important Daoist center in China. Here, we can see different ways that Daoism is practiced.

1 Many Daoists worship spirits and important figures, such as Laozi. Many visitors to the Wudang Mountains come to pray at Daoist temples there.

2 Daoist monks and nuns live year-round in the Wudang Mountains. Monks may meditate as a way to follow the Dao.

3 Visitors learn tai chi (ty chee), a slow and graceful form of exercise. According to legend, a Daoist monk developed tai chi in the Wudang Mountains. Tai chi is a balance of yin and yang, rest and activity.

Beliefs of Daoism

Confucius and his students were not the only scholars affected by the chaos in China during the Zhou dynasty. Another group of thinkers saw the disorder and responded differently. Their reaction led to the development of Daoism. **Daoism** is an ancient Chinese way of life that emphasizes a simple and natural existence. It is a philosophy of following the Dao (dow), that is, the natural way of the universe.

The Legend of Laozi According to legend, a man named Laozi founded Daoism. Laozi (LOW dzuh) is known as a sage, or wise person. He is said to have written down his beliefs in a book called the *Dao De Jing* (DOW deh jing).

Historians do not know whether Laozi actually lived. They believe that the *Dao De Jing* was probably written by many people. It is a small book, made up mostly of poems. Here are a few lines:

> 66 In dwelling, live close to the ground.
> In thinking, keep to the simple.
> In conflict, be fair and generous.
> In governing, don't try to control. 99
> —Laozi, *Dao De Jing*

People throughout the world still read the *Dao De Jing* for its wisdom.

Yin and Yang Daoism reflects ancient Chinese beliefs about the world. The ancient Chinese saw quiet order in the changing seasons. They also saw the violence of nature in floods and storms.

They believed that two great forces were at work in nature. These forces are called yin and yang. They are opposites

yet work together. Yin is the female force. It is dark, cool, and quiet. Yang is the male force. It is bright, warm, and active. Chinese thinkers believed balance between yin and yang is key to harmony in the universe.

The Dao Daoists saw the Dao, which means "the way" or "the path," as the source of yin and yang. The Dao is mysterious and impossible to define clearly. However, Daoists felt people should try to understand the Dao. Often, they saw evidence of the Dao in natural things, like water:

> 66 There is nothing in the world more soft and weak than water, and yet for attacking things that are firm and strong, nothing is better than it. . . 99
>
> —Laozi, *Dao De Jing*

Water, through patient effort over time, is even stronger than rock. By acting like water, people are following the Dao.

People can upset order with their actions. Order comes when people keep to a simple life, instead of competing for wealth and power. Daoists believed a good leader took little action, leaving people to live a simple life. Daoists were not concerned with the morals, rituals, and learning that the Confucians valued.

Despite the differences between Confucianism and Daoism, most Chinese thinkers studied both philosophies. They freely used ideas from both. Throughout Chinese history, Confucianism and Daoism influenced Chinese culture even as new ideas came from abroad.

Reading Check What is one difference between Confucianism and Daoism?

This symbol represents yin and yang. It is painted on the door of a temple in the Wudang Mountains. ▶

Section 3 Assessment

Key Terms
1. What is a philosophy?
2. Use the term *filial piety* to describe the ideas of Confucius.

Key Ideas
3. How did people in ancient China believe that spirits influenced their lives?
4. What are the five relationships of Confucianism?

Think Critically
5. **Solve Problems** How did Confucianism and Daoism develop different solutions to the chaos of the Warring States period?
6. **Draw Conclusions** Why did the ancient Chinese place special emphasis on the spirits of their ancestors?

Essential Question
How much does geography affect people's lives?

7. How did Chinese geography have an influence on beliefs in ancient China? Go to your Student Journal to record your answer.

Chapter Assessment

Key Terms and Ideas

1. **Explain** What brought wealth to Shang rulers? How did they use this wealth?

2. **Describe** What type of information was carved on **oracle bones**?

3. **Discuss** How did rulers have to act in order to keep the **Mandate of Heaven**?

4. **Recall** When was the **Warring States period**? What happened during this time?

5. **Explain** How did the ancient Chinese try to protect themselves from harmful spirits?

6. **Discuss** What are some ways the Chinese honor the spirits of their ancestors?

7. **Recall** What problems did Confucius see in Chinese society?

8. **Summarize** What are the basic ideas of **Daoism**?

Think Critically

9. **Analyze Cause and Effect** What is one effect of the mountains, deserts, and oceans around China?

10. **Draw Conclusions** How did the Mandate of Heaven justify rebellion against a ruling dynasty?

11. **Compare and Contrast** What were three differences between the Shang and Zhou dynasties?

12. **Core Concepts: Citizenship** Confucius compares the role of the king to the role of the father in a family. Do you agree that the role of a leader is similar to the role of a parent? Explain why or why not.

Analyze Visuals

Write the name of each of the physical features described below. Match the letters on the map at the right to the features.

13. Chinese civilization arose on this fertile plain.

14. This river is the longest in China.

15. This river carries loess, which makes it yellow.

16. This feature divides China from India.

17. Dust blows from this desert to the North China Plain.

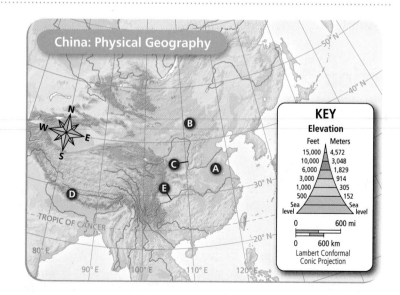

China: Physical Geography

KEY

Elevation

Feet	Meters
15,000	4,572
10,000	3,048
6,000	1,829
3,000	914
1,000	305
500	152
Sea level	Sea level

0   600 mi

0   600 km

Lambert Conformal
Conic Projection

? Essential Question
myWorld Chapter Activity

Clues to Ancient China Follow your teacher's instructions to study artifacts and gather information about life during ancient China. Use the information to create an advertisement for a display "coming soon to a museum near you."

21st Century Learning
Develop Cultural Awareness

List three characteristics you believe a good citizen should have. Then reread the chapter myStory as well as the information about Confucianism and Daoism. In a paragraph, describe whether each of your citizen characteristics more closely matches Confucianism or Daoism and why.

Document-Based Questions

Success Tracker™
Online at myworldhistory.com

Use your knowledge of ancient China as well as Documents A and B below to answer the questions that follow.

Document A

" I will not be afflicted [harmed] at men's not knowing me; I will be afflicted that I do not know men."

" When we see men of worth, we should think of equaling them; when we see men of a contrary [bad] character, we should . . . examine ourselves."

" By extensively studying all learning . . . one may not err [stray] from what is right."

—Confucius, *Analects*

Document B

"Throw away holiness and wisdom, and people will be a hundred times happier.
Throw away morality and justice, and people will do the right thing.
Throw away industry and profit, and there won't be any thieves. . .
Stop thinking, and end your problems."

—*Dao De Jing*

1. Which is the best summary of Confucius's ideas about learning in Document A?

    A Learning makes one richer.

    B Learning leads one to know what is right.

    C Learning must be accompanied by restraint.

    D Learning and suffering go hand in hand.

2. According to Document B, what does wisdom result in?

    A unhappiness

    B harmonious relationships

    C remedies

    D simple happiness

3. **Writing Task** With which document do you most agree? Write a paragraph explaining why.

myworldhistory.com

Self-Test

269

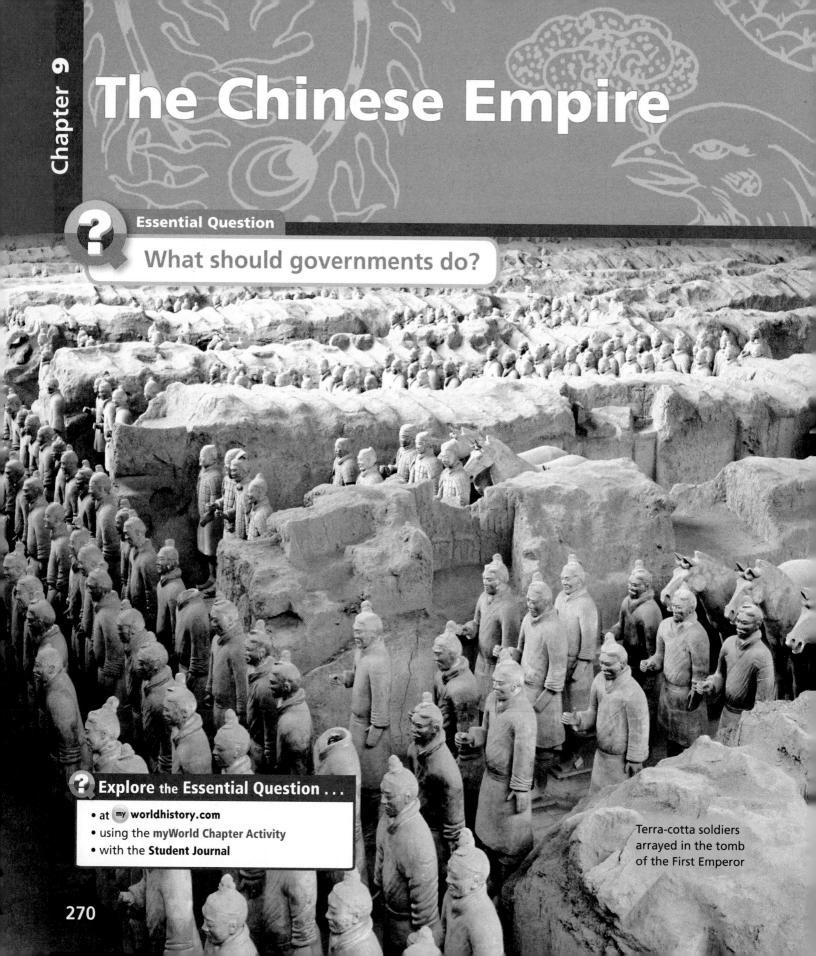

The Chinese Empire

? Essential Question

What should governments do?

? Explore the Essential Question . . .

- at **my** worldhistory.com
- using the **myWorld Chapter Activity**
- with the **Student Journal**

Terra-cotta soldiers arrayed in the tomb of the First Emperor

Qin and Han China

206 B.C.
The Han
dynasty
begins.

221 B.C. The Qin
dynasty begins.

about 138 B.C.
Zhang Qian's expedition
leaves for Central Asia.

A.D. 105 The use of paper
is mentioned for the first
time in a written source.

| 300 B.C. | 200 B.C. | 100 B.C. | A.D. 1 | A.D. 100 | A.D. 200 | A.D. 300 |

210 B.C. The First
Emperor dies.

141 B.C. Emperor
Wudi's reign begins.

A.D. 220
The Han
dynasty ends.

An Emperor in this Life and the Next

This is a fictional account of events in the life of one of China's most important leaders, the emperor Shi Huangdi (shur hwahng DEE).

The First Emperor, Shi Huangdi, peered through the window of his carriage. The sun was just rising that cold, fall morning. Dust swirled across the dry North China Plain. The emperor had not slept much the night before. In the middle of the night, he rose from bed and called for a carriage to take him to the place where his tomb was being built.

His sleep had been disturbed by thoughts of the meteor that had fallen near the Huang River earlier that year. He knew some people saw the meteor as an omen—a message from heaven telling the people that he had lost the Mandate of Heaven. Someone had carved on the meteor "the First Emperor will die and his lands be divided."

When the emperor heard about this, he was enraged. One of the emperor's advisors had described him as having the heart of a tiger or a wolf. No one wanted to face him when he was angry.

myworldhistory.com

Timeline/On Assignment

Shi Huangdi's minister reads the inscription on the meteor.

Shi Huangdi built his empire by attacking and conquering the neighboring kingdoms.

He sent an official to find the person who had written the message. No one would confess, so the emperor executed all the people living near where the meteor had been found.

Despite the fact that work had begun on the emperor's tomb, he clung to the hope that he would not die. After all, he was no ordinary man. He had done something no one had ever done before. He had united the warring kingdoms of China. Ending the conflict that had raged between these kingdoms for hundreds of years was no easy task. The emperor had been ruthless in battle, attacking one kingdom after another until he controlled them all.

He wanted his descendants to rule his empire for 10,000 generations. He built a great wall to protect China from marauding nomads. He standardized weights, measures, and currency so that a sack of rice in the kingdom of Qin weighed the same in Yan, a length of silk in Han measured the same in Zhao, and a coin used in Liadong could also be used in Chu.

The emperor felt that no man had accomplished so much. Perhaps he would also be the first man to find the secrets to immortality. He searched for herbs that could extend his life. He consulted with wise men who told him to move frequently between his palaces to avoid harmful spirits.

Still, Shi Huangdi wanted to be prepared if death did find him. He should have a grand palace for his life in the spirit world. His entourage pulled up to the site of the tomb, and Shi Huangdi stepped out. An official bowed to the emperor before leading him into the tomb. In one room was a model of China, with silver rivers and oceans made from liquid mercury. The ceiling twinkled with pearls depicting constellations in the night sky. Other rooms overflowed with gold and jade.

Shi Huangdi then set out to view the four halls being built east of his tomb. To be a great king in the spirit world, the emperor would need a great army. He had ordered laborers to make thousands of life-sized soldiers and horses of terra cotta.

As the emperor approached these halls, he saw the bustling workers. Some arranged the terra-cotta warriors in neat rows. Others painted the final details on the soldiers' uniforms. When the emperor stepped out of his carriage, all work stopped. The laborers dropped to the ground before the emperor. Many had scars—the emperor kept order through harsh punishments.

Workers toil to build the Great Wall.

Shi Huangdi looks over the model of China in his tomb.

Shi Huangdi scanned the rows of soldiers. Their faces were so lifelike! He felt if he called out "Forward, march!" they would all step forward. In death, these soldiers would be at his command.

As he stepped back into his carriage, he glanced at the bowed heads of the workers. They looked so obedient, but he knew that he could not take any chances. He had many enemies who might disturb his final resting place.

He had already told his closest advisors that anyone who knew about the defenses of the tomb was to be buried alive at his death. Shi Huangdi trusted that this would be done. His word, after all, was law.

Based on this story, what do you think Shi Huangdi thought government leaders should do? As you read the chapter ahead, think about what the First Emperor's story tells you about the Chinese empire.

→ **myStory Video**   Learn more about the First Emperor.

my worldhistory.com

myStory Video

Shi Huangdi Unites China

Key Ideas
- Qin armies united China and founded a powerful new dynasty.
- Emperor Shi Huangdi united China by standardizing many aspects of daily life.
- Emperor Shi Huangdi created a powerful government based on Legalist principles.

Key Terms • Great Wall • standardize • Legalism • censor

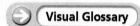 **Visual Glossary**

Reading Skill Identify Main Ideas and Details Take notes using the graphic organizer in your journal.

A warrior from Shi Huangdi's tomb ▼

The Warring States period came to an end when the kingdom of Qin (chin) unified China. King Zheng (jung) of Qin, who became the First Emperor, is remembered as a leader determined to build a great empire. Although his dynasty lost power soon after his death, later dynasties built upon his methods for ruling a large empire.

Unity Under the Qin

Qin was a mountainous kingdom located in northwestern China. Beyond Qin lay the foreign lands of Central Asia. The Qin rulers built a strong kingdom with an efficient government. By the late Zhou dynasty, Qin was the strongest kingdom in western China. Still, King Zheng, who came to power in 247 B.C., thirsted for more power.

Uniting the Warring States King Zheng was skilled and ruthless. Under his leadership, Qin brought down rival kingdoms one by one. In 221 B.C., Qin forces defeated their last enemy. They had united China. Yet many challenges remained. Languages and customs varied from place to place. Rebellion was always a danger, as was invasion by nomads from north and west of China. The king needed to make the Chinese into one people ruled by one government.

The First Emperor The Qin ruler decided that "king" was too small a title for the leader of such a vast empire. He thus declared himself to be Shi Huangdi, or "First Emperor." The word "Huangdi" was tied to the gods and legendary rulers of China's past.

Defending the Empire Before the Qin unification, the many Chinese kingdoms built walls to protect themselves from other kingdoms. Shi Huangdi had these walls torn down to make rebellion more difficult. Without these walls, local leaders could not defend their territory and break away from Qin rule.

The First Emperor also began work on one of the largest public works projects in history—the **Great Wall,** a long wall running east and west along his empire's northern border. The purpose of the wall was to defend the empire from nomads living on the vast grasslands to the north.

The wall went up quickly. Already, there were shorter walls along the border. Workers connected these old walls together, making a huge stone barrier. This achievement came at a cost. Building the wall was hard and dangerous. Many died while working on the wall.

The Great Wall did not always keep nomads out. Determined invaders were able to get around it. Still, the emperors of dynasties that followed the Qin also relied on the wall as a way to protect their northern border. Later emperors made the wall stronger, adding towers in key locations along its length.

Uniform Standards Shi Huangdi knew he needed to standardize many aspects of daily life. To **standardize** is to set rules that make things more similar. He created standards that unified China's economy and culture. Anyone who did not follow the standards was punished as a traitor.

Perhaps most importantly, the Qin government established a single written language with standard characters. These characters are the basis of the written language in China today.

Transportation was also standardized. The government established a standard length for the axles of all vehicles. As a result, all ruts made in Chinese roads by the wheels of carts would be the same width. This made travel between different areas easier. All carts and wagons could travel in the same ruts. The Qin government also created a uniform set of weights and measures for use in trade. It produced uniform coins to be used as <u>currency</u> across China.

Organizing the Empire Shi Huangdi introduced the concept of centralization, or a central governing system. He organized China into 36 provinces.

currency, *n.,* money, something used for exchange

Standard coins and axle widths for carriages helped connect the Chinese through trade and travel.▼

▲ Scholars who disobeyed Shi Huangdi were buried alive. He also had many books burned but preserved those about agriculture and medicine. *Why do you think these books were not burned?*

Rule of the First Emperor

Shi Huangdi is remembered as a cruel leader. He believed strict rules were necessary to end the chaos in Chinese society. The laws that he created helped him unite the empire. However, his harsh rule was also one cause of the fall of the Qin dynasty.

A Legalist Government In the late Zhou, the Qin rulers brought in advisors from other kingdoms to help make Qin stronger. Shang Yang (shahng yahng) was one important advisor. He belonged to a school of thought called Legalism. According to **Legalism,** a strong leader and a strong legal system are needed to create social order.

Following Shang Yang's advice, the Qin kings took more direct control over the common people. Heavy taxes and required labor service increased the wealth of the Qin kings. The kingdom became stronger and more orderly. Shi Huangdi set out to extend this Legalist government over the rest of China.

Harsh Laws Shi Huangdi was especially interested in the teachings of the Legalist Han Feizi (hahn FEY zuh). Han Feizi did not agree with Confucianism. Confucius and his followers believed people could be led by setting a good example. Han Feizi believed people must be forced to be good. This could be done by making laws and enforcing them strictly.

Shi Huangdi made a uniform legal code across his empire. Penalties for breaking a law were severe. For example, a thief could face physical punishment as harsh as cutting off the feet or nose.

Each province was divided into counties. County leaders were responsible to the heads of provinces. Province heads reported to the central government which, in turn, reported to the emperor. The emperor dismissed any official who failed to carry out his policies.

To prevent rebellion, Shi Huangdi forced thousands of noble families to move to the capital. There, government spies could watch over them.

Reading Check Why did Shi Huangdi call himself the First Emperor?

A less serious theft might carry the punishment of hard labor, such as helping to build roads and walls. Other punishments included execution by beheading or cutting the criminal in half. According to one account, the emperor had 460 scholars executed for disobeying an order. Han Feizi explained the reason for these harsh punishments:

> 66 Punish severely light crimes. People do not easily commit serious crimes. But light offenses [crimes] are easily abandoned by people. . . . Now, if small offenses do not arise, big crimes will not come. And thus people will commit no crimes and disorder will not arise. 99

—Han Feizi

Thought Control The First Emperor also tried to control Chinese thought. He decided to **censor**, or ban, ideas he found dangerous or offensive. Censorship took many forms. Debate about the government was banned. People were not allowed to praise past rulers or criticize the present one. The emperor ordered the burning of all books that did not support his policies.

The Fall of the Qin Dynasty These policies were not popular. But they did help create a single nation from China's diverse regions. The First Emperor believed that his dynasty would last forever, but it <u>collapsed</u> about three years after his death.

The Qin Dynasty was undone by its unbending enforcement of its harsh laws. A rebellion was sparked by a soldier named Chen Sheng, who led a band of men north to guard China's border. Along the way, heavy rains delayed the band. Chen knew that the penalty for arriving late would be severe. So he and his men decided that they had nothing to lose by rebelling.

As news of Chen's uprising spread, thousands rose up to support him. Qin generals tried to put down the uprisings, but the rebellions spread rapidly. Knowing the punishments for failure, some generals joined the rebellions. The rebels joined together long enough to overthrow the Qin but then began fighting amongst themselves. China again slid into chaos.

Reading Check How did Shi Huangdi try to stop people from criticizing him?

collapse, *v.,* to break down or fall down

Section **1** Assessment

Essential Question

Key Terms

1. Use the terms *standardize* and *censor* to describe how Shi Huangdi united his empire.

2. Why did Shi Huangdi build the Great Wall?

Key Ideas

3. How did the Warring States period come to an end?

4. What were three things Shi Huangdi did to unify his empire?

5. Why did Shi Huangdi create harsh laws?

Think Critically

6. **Compare and Contrast** How is Legalism different from Confucianism?

7. **Analyze Cause and Effect** What was one cause of the fall of the Qin dynasty?

What should governments do?

8. What did the Legalists think the role of government should be? Go to your Student Journal to record your answer.

Expansion Under the Han Dynasty

Key Ideas
- The Han Dynasty was one of the longest-lasting dynasties in Chinese history.
- The Han supported Confucianism.
- The Han created a civil service of officials who were selected based on merit.
- The Silk Road became an important trade route linking China to kingdoms to the west.

Key Terms • official   • civil service   • Silk Road   • envoy   • cuisine

 Visual Glossary

 **Reading Skill** **Analyze Cause and Effect** Take notes using the graphic organizer in your journal.

Liu Bang, the first emperor of the Han dynasty ▼

Besides founding China's first empire, Shi Huangdi also laid the foundation for a system of government to rule a large empire. The next ruling family was the Han. The Han emperors built on the successes of the Qin to create one of the most influential dynasties in Chinese history.

Government of the Han

The fighting that toppled the Qin dynasty lasted for several years. Finally, a rebel general named Liu Bang (LYOH bahng) gained control of China. In 206 B.C., he founded the Han dynasty. The Han ruled China for about 400 years. Today, the largest ethnic group in China still call themselves the "Han."

Reuniting and Expanding China The first Han emperor came from a poor family. His success was, in part, due to his ability to surround himself with capable advisors. As emperor, he consulted with a Confucian scholar who pointed out that the Qin lost power because of their cruel policies. The emperor encouraged learning, lowered taxes, and ended many of the Qin's harsh rules.

Confucian scholars throughout the Han gave practical advice and encouraged rulers to set an example of mercy and proper behavior. Han emperors kept many of the Qin laws and policies to standardize Chinese life but avoided the harsh rule that had caused unrest.

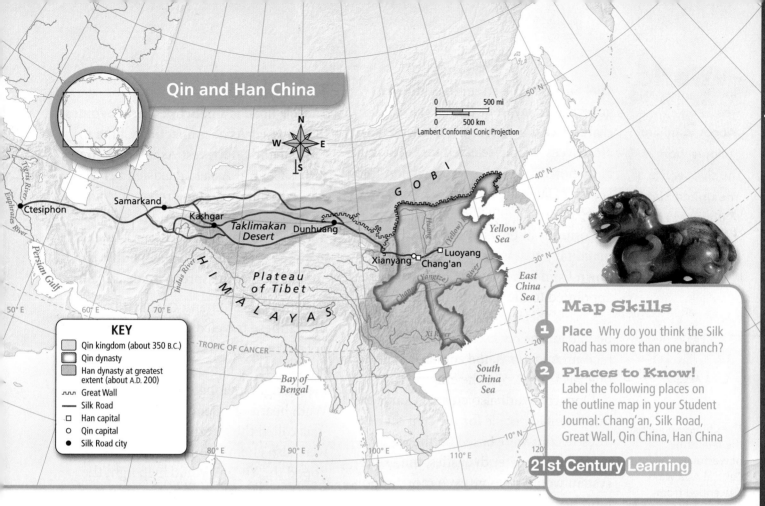

Qin and Han China

0   500 mi
0   500 km
Lambert Conformal Conic Projection

KEY

- ☐ Qin kingdom (about 350 B.C.)
- ☐ Qin dynasty
- ☐ Han dynasty at greatest extent (about A.D. 200)
- ⌁⌁⌁ Great Wall
- — Silk Road
- ☐ Han capital
- ○ Qin capital
- ● Silk Road city

Map Skills

1 **Place** Why do you think the Silk Road has more than one branch?

2 **Places to Know!**
Label the following places on the outline map in your Student Journal: Chang'an, Silk Road, Great Wall, Qin China, Han China

21st Century Learning

The Han not only stayed in power, they expanded China's territory. Much of this expansion took place under the fifth Han emperor, Wudi (woo dee). Remembered as one of the country's greatest emperors, Wudi ruled for more than 50 years. Wudi sent his armies west to conquer lands far into Central Asia. He extended his empire north to the Korean peninsula and south into what is now Vietnam.

The Structure of Government Han emperors followed the example of the Qin by creating a strong central government. In this way, they avoided the problem of disunity that the Zhou dynasty had faced. As the Zhou dynasty had expanded, local noblemen became more powerful than the Zhou king. The Han emperors tried to make sure that local leaders remained too weak to challenge their authority. When the Han emperors conquered new lands, they administered this land directly rather than giving it to a nobleman.

The Han government was organized like a pyramid. The broad base of the pyramid was made up of China's many towns and villages. At the top of the pyramid were the emperor and his chief advisors. Many layers of government lay between the top and bottom of the pyramid. At each level, **officials**, that is, people <u>assigned</u> to a position in the government, took orders from those above them and gave orders to those below them.

myWorld Activity
Join the Han

assign, *v.,* to give as a job or task

my **World**
CONNECTIONS

About **2 million** people work in the civil service of the United States government.

The Chinese believed the beautiful, powerful horses from Central Asia were descended from "heavenly horses." ▼

Civil Service The strength of the Han government lay in its civil service. A **civil service** is a system of government employees mainly selected for their skills and knowledge. In the first two hundred years of Han rule, the civil service grew to more than 130,000 officials.

Positions in the civil service were not hereditary, that is, they were not passed down from father to son. Officials were appointed to their positions. Han emperors asked their officials to recommend people for the civil service. From those recommendations, the emperors selected officials from across the empire.

Emperor Wudi also created exams to find talented people for the civil service. These exams were based on the ideas of Confucius. In later dynasties, the exam system would become even more important for selecting officials.

Han officials enjoyed high salaries and a life of comfort and influence. They wore special clothes that indicated their rank. They collected taxes, organized labor, and enforced laws. They could even force people to move. If there were too many people in one area, officials could relocate them to lands with fewer people.

The Han emperors placed some limits on the powers of officials. For example, officials were not allowed to serve in their home districts. The Han emperors did not want officials to work with family and friends to organize against the emperor. The emperors knew that to rule successfully, they needed their officials' loyalty.

Reading Check What was one of Wudi's accomplishments?

The Silk Road

The **Silk Road** is a network of trade routes that crossed Asia, connecting China to Central and Southwest Asia. Trade routes across Central Asia had existed before the Han, but during the reign of Wudi contact between China and regions to the west increased. Merchants made their fortunes along the Silk Road, but it was also a path for the spread of ideas.

The Journey of Zhang Qian At first, the Chinese traveled to Central Asia not to trade but to seek an ally in their fight against a fierce group of nomads, the Xiongnu (shong noo). Emperor Wudi heard of a people from Central Asia called the Yuezhi (yooeh jur) who were also enemies of the Xiongnu. Wudi hoped the Yuezhi would help fight the Xiongnu. He asked for a volunteer to find the Yuezhi. Zhang Qian (jahng chyen) stepped up to take on this challenge.

Zhang set out to the west. He was captured by the Xiongnu and held prisoner for ten years. He escaped and found the Yuezhi but could not persuade them to ally with the Han against the Xiongnu.

Still, Wudi was interested in Zhang's account of his travels. Zhang described exotic lands where horses sweat blood and "the inhabitants ride elephants when they go into battle." Wudi and later Han emperors sent **envoys,** that is, representatives of the emperor, to create relations with kingdoms to the west. The Han also sent troops to the west. With the Han army protecting the region, trade flourished. Merchants could trade with less fear of being attacked by bandits.

Simulation

An Important Trade Route The name "Silk Road" comes from China's most important export: silk. It is made from the cocoon of a caterpillar called the silk worm. It is strong, soft, and can be dyed many colors. Only the Chinese knew how to make silk. They guarded this secret closely. It was illegal to export silk worms.

The Chinese exchanged silk and other luxury goods for a wide range of other products. The Chinese particularly valued the strong horses of Central Asia. The Silk Road also enriched Chinese **cuisine,** that is, the style of cooking. Grapes, sesame, and onion were all brought into China along the Silk Road. The emperor also <u>obtained</u> rare animals, such as elephants, lions, and ostriches from abroad.

New Ideas: Buddhism Enters China The Silk Road was a path for the exchange of ideas. Chinese inventions, such as paper, spread west along the Silk Road.

Foreign ideas, such as Buddhism, entered China during the Han along these trade routes. The religion of Buddhism started in India and spread into Central Asia. The Chinese, then,

▲ White Horse Temple in Luoyang is one of the earliest Buddhist temples in China.

learned about this religion from Buddhists in Central Asia. Over time, Buddhism became very popular in China. After the Han, Chinese Buddhists traveled to India to study the religion. Chinese Buddhists also brought new ideas and practices to the religion.

Along with Confucianism and Daoism, Buddhism is one of the most influential belief systems in China. Chinese scholars mixed ideas from the three belief systems in their writings and art. Buddhist temples can be found across China today.

Reading Check What was one good that was brought to China along the Silk Road?

obtain, *v.,* to get or to receive something

my worldhistory.com

Simulation

Section 2 Assessment

Key Terms

1. Use the terms *official* and *civil service* to describe the government of the Han.

2. What was the Silk Road?

Key Ideas

3. How did Han emperors support Confucianism?

4. What was tested on the exam for officials created by Wudi?

5. How did the Silk Road influence Chinese culture?

Think Critically

6. **Compare and Contrast** How was the Han dynasty similar to and different from the Qin dynasty?

7. **Solve Problems** How did Emperor Wudi try to solve his conflict with the Xiongnu? What was the result?

Essential Question

What should governments do?

8. You must make an exam for officials in the U.S. government. What knowledge should government officials have? Go to your Student Journal to record your answer.

Section 3

Han Society and Achievements

Key Ideas
- Han society was based on Confucian teachings about order and social relationships.
- Under the Han, China enjoyed a strong economy.
- Han prosperity supported many advances in the arts and technology.

Key Terms • monopoly • calligraphy • lacquer • acupuncture • seismometer

 Visual Glossary

Reading Skill Summarize Take notes using the graphic organizer in your journal.

This dancer from the Han dynasty tosses the long sleeves of her dress. ▼

The Han dynasty was a time of innovation and economic development. The production of many goods increased and trade flourished. More people worked as craftsmen and merchants. Many important inventions also date to this dynasty.

Han Society

Han China was a mixture of peoples and cultures, but the country became more unified during this dynasty. Han emperors continued many of the Qin policies that standardized life in China, such as using a common currency. Shared values also bound the people together.

The Social Order China's social order was based on Confucian values. Confucius and his followers valued mental work more than physical labor. Scholars, therefore, were highly respected. Farmers were also highly respected because they produced the most important and basic goods: food and cloth. Artisans were valued for their skill and hard work.

Confucius and many other early Chinese thinkers had little respect for merchants because merchants do not produce anything. As a result, merchants fell lower in the social order. The government placed restrictions on merchants. They were not allowed to wear fine clothing or own land. Their children could not become officials.

282

Still, many merchants became wealthy and powerful. They lived comfortable lives despite the lack of respect for trade.

At the bottom of the social order were a small number of slaves. When someone committed a serious crime, family members might be punished with slavery. Other people were sold into slavery when their families fell deep into debt.

Family Life Confucian teachings about family loyalty and respect for elders were key values. During the Han, ancestor worship continued. People made offerings to show respect and gain support from their ancestors.

Also, the Han legal code enforced Confucian values. Parents could report children who did not behave with filial piety. Adult children would be punished harshly. Younger children, though, were usually <u>exempt</u> from punishment.

The Role of Women The status of women was generally lower than that of men. Most worked in the home, weaving and caring for their children and elderly family members.

One exceptional woman was Ban Zhao (bahn jow). Unlike most Han women, she received a good education. Ban became a historian in the royal court. She wrote that young women deserved an education. Yet she also accepted the higher status of men in society.

> 66 If a wife does not serve her husband, then the proper relationship between men and women . . . [is] neglected and destroyed. 99
>
> —Ban Zhao, *Lessons for Women*

Reading Check What was one restriction placed on merchants?

exempt, *adj.,* to be free from a punishment or duty

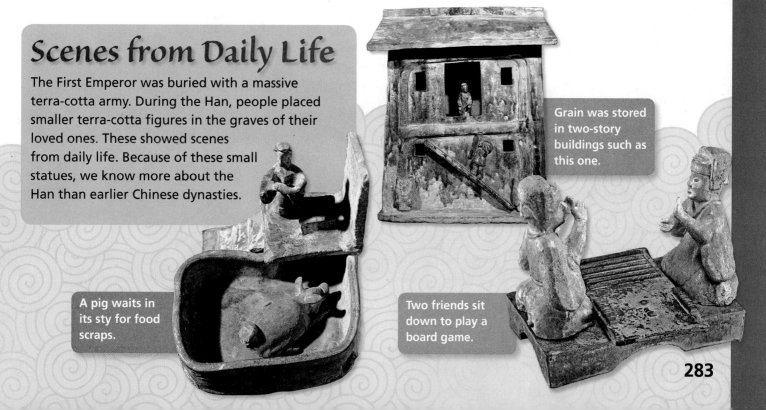

Scenes from Daily Life

The First Emperor was buried with a massive terra-cotta army. During the Han, people placed smaller terra-cotta figures in the graves of their loved ones. These showed scenes from daily life. Because of these small statues, we know more about the Han than earlier Chinese dynasties.

Grain was stored in two-story buildings such as this one.

A pig waits in its sty for food scraps.

Two friends sit down to play a board game.

283

Silk Making

The technique for making silk was developed thousands of years ago in China. For centuries, this process remained a closely guarded secret. It was illegal to share information about silk making with people outside of China. This strong, smooth cloth became one of China's major exports. Production of silk increased during the Han as wealthy people as far away as the Roman empire sought Chinese silk for their clothing.

THINK CRITICALLY Why would the Chinese want to keep the process of making silk a secret?

▲ This silk cloth was found in a Han dynasty tomb.

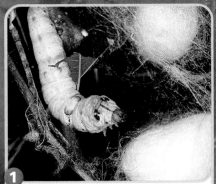

1 Silkworms are fed leaves from the mulberry tree. More than 2,000 silkworms are needed to make a pound of silk.

2 The silkworm cocoon is made of one continuous fiber that is several thousand feet long. Cocoons are boiled to loosen the silk fiber.

3 The cocoon is unwound. Then, several silk fibers are wound together to make a thread.

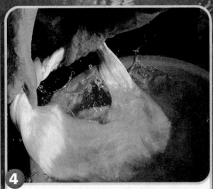

4 The silk thread is cleaned and then dyed.

5 Silk thread is woven into beautiful cloth.

Economic Life

China under the Han was peaceful compared to the chaotic Warring States period. The Han emperors lowered the high taxes that Shi Huangdi had collected. China prospered in this more stable time.

Agriculture Farmers were the backbone of China's economy. They made up about 90 percent of the population. As one Han emperor said,

> 66 Agriculture is the foundation of the world. No duty is greater. 99
> —Emperor Wen, *Hanshu*

Most farms in Han China were small. Farmers grew wheat, millet, barley, beans, and rice. Farmers with more land might also grow fruit or bamboo. Farming families often made their own cloth.

Silk production was especially important as trade along the Silk Road increased. On small farms, the women of the family tended silkworms and wove silk. In wealthy households, the women hired workers to help make silk. Workshops in cities also employed many weavers. Workshops bought silk thread from farms. They specialized in making the most expensive, high-quality cloth.

Industry Industries, such as iron production, also became important. Iron was useful for making tools and weapons. Salt mining was another key industry.

These industries became so important that Wudi turned them into state monopolies. A **monopoly** is when a single group controls the production of a good or service.

The monopolies brought in money. Profits from selling iron and salt helped support Wudi's military adventures.

Controlling Production and Prices Wudi's monopoly was also a way to try to keep important producers and merchants from becoming too powerful. Some producers of salt and iron had become very wealthy. They bought huge areas of land and employed large numbers of people. The Han emperors worried that these producers could become so influential that they could challenge the emperor's power. The emperors also worried that too many farmers were leaving their fields to work for these producers. Without enough farmers, China might face food shortages.

The Han emperors also made policies to try to control prices. For example, in years when crops were good, the government bought up the extra grain. In years when the harvest was bad, the grain harvest decreased and grain became expensive. The government then sold back the stored grain to keep prices lower and avoid a shortage.

Despite the <u>benefits</u> of these policies, there were many problems. Some officials tried to make money by selling stored goods at high prices. Also, there were complaints that iron tools produced by the government monopoly were poor quality. Many emperors after Wudi either changed or gave up these policies.

Reading Check What industries did Wudi control?

▲ A fish merchant displays his wares.

benefit, *n.,* something good or helpful

285

▲ This lacquer box was found in a Han tomb. It is decorated with illustrations of good, filial sons.

myWorld Activity
Continuum of Han Achievements

Han Achievements

The prosperity of Han China helped support many cultural achievements. Artists, writers, and musicians created works of beauty. Scientists and inventors also made important advances.

China's Traditional Arts The traditional arts of China include painting, sculpture, and poetry. Han artists painted colorful murals. Sculptors created beautiful works in stone, clay, and bronze. Poets wrote about the Chinese countryside.

Because Confucius believed that music was good for the spirit, Han rulers created an official Bureau of Music. Musicians played drums, bells, flutes, and harps. Music and dancing were common at public festivals and ceremonies.

Two other traditional arts were garden design and **calligraphy,** the art of beautiful writing. Calligraphers expressed emotions in the way they painted Chinese characters. Garden designers carefully arranged plants, rocks, and water to resemble scenes in nature.

Perhaps the greatest craft of the Han period was lacquerware. **Lacquer** is a protective coating made from the sap of a special tree. Han artists brushed it on wood or metal objects to create a hard finish. The process required many layers of lacquer and many hours of work. When color was added, the lacquerware seemed to glow.

Advances in Science Han China is also known for scientific advances. Astronomers studied the sky and made precise calculations of the length of the solar year.

◄ Acupuncture needles and a small carrying case from a later Chinese dynasty

Han doctors made progress in medicine. They studied ancient texts on medicine and developed new theories to explain and treat illness. Herbal medicines were one important treatment. Another was **acupuncture,** a therapy that uses needles to cure sickness and stop pain.

Chinese Inventions Han inventors produced important new tools. One was the **seismometer,** a tool to detect earthquakes. The seismometer was a metal jar that dropped small balls when a tremor from an earthquake was felt.

Another invention was the wheelbarrow. This human-powered cart appeared in China about 100 B.C. It was so useful for moving heavy loads that it was called the "wooden ox."

Perhaps the most important innovation of the Han was paper. Early paper was made from rags and bark. Paper was probably not widely used at first. Documents continued to be written on more durable wood and silk. In later dynasties, printing on paper became a way to make

cheap books. More people could afford books, and new ideas spread quickly.

Reading Check What is one invention from the Han dynasty?

▲ This is a model of a Han seismometer. A ball drops from a dragon's mouth into a frog's mouth if an earthquake is felt.

Section 3 Assessment

Key Terms

1. What is a monopoly?

2. Use the terms *acupuncture* and *seismometer* to describe the achievements of the Han dynasty.

Key Ideas

3. How did the ideas of Confucius influence Han society?

4. What role did women have in Han society?

5. Why was paper an important invention?

Think Critically

6. Draw Inferences Why was silk an important industry during the Han?

7. Analyze Cause and Effect Why was China's economy better under the Han than during the Warring States period?

Essential Question

What should governments do?

8. One way Han emperors raised money was by taking over the iron and salt industries. What is another way that governments can get funds? Go to your Student Journal to record your answer.

Chapter Assessment

Key Terms and Ideas

1. **Recall** Why were the Qin able to build the **Great Wall** quickly?

2. **Summarize** What are some of the important ideas of **Legalism**?

3. **Explain** Why did Shi Huangdi's harsh rules cause the fall of the Qin dynasty?

4. **Recall** Why is Wudi considered a great ruler?

5. **Describe** Describe the civil service created during the Han dynasty.

6. **Discuss** Why did the Han emperors create a **monopoly** on iron and salt?

7. **Summarize** How did the Chinese begin trading along the **Silk Road**?

8. **Recall** What is **acupuncture**?

Think Critically

9. **Analyze Cause and Effect** What effect did Shi Huangdi's policies have on the culture and government of China?

10. **Compare Viewpoints** Why might a Confucian scholar and Legalist scholar have different viewpoints about Shi Huangdi's policy of censorship?

11. **Draw Conclusions** Why was the seismometer an important invention?

12. **Core Concepts: Cultural Diffusion and Change** Use the example of the Silk Road to explain how trade can lead to cultural change.

Analyze Visuals

These sculptures of horses were found in a grave from the Han dynasty.

13. Do you think these horses were used for farm work? Explain.

14. Many sculptures of horses have been found in the Han dynasty. Why might these sculptures have been popular during this time period?

15. Why might someone have wanted a sculpture of a horse in his tomb?

Essential Question
myWorld Chapter Activity

The Empire Game Create a board game about the Qin and Han dynasties. Create game cards related to the emperors that you have read about in this chapter. Decide whether their actions helped or hindered China. Take turns drawing cards and moving your game piece around the board.

21st Century Learning
Innovate

Inventions from the Han dynasty, such as the wheelbarrow, made daily life easier. What is one chore that you must do? Imagine a robot that could do the chore for you. What would the robot look like? How big would it be? Draw a diagram of your robot that shows its features.

Document-Based Questions

Success Tracker™
Online at myworldhistory.com

Use your knowledge of Qin and Han China and Documents A and B to answer Questions 1–3.

Document A

" . . . the August Emperor [Shi Huangdi] made a new beginning . . . He erases doubt and establishes laws so all will know what to shun [avoid] . . . Evil and wrongdoing are not permitted [allowed]; all practice goodness and integrity . . . All delight in honoring instructions, complete in their knowledge of the laws. . . ."

—From an inscription ordered by the First Emperor

Document B

" Half of all the people passing along the roads had suffered punishment, and the bodies of the daily dead piled up in the market place. Those [ministers] who put the largest number of people to death [as punishment for crimes] were called loyal ministers."

—the historian Sima Qian comments on the reign of Shi Huangdi's son, the Second Emperor

1. Which philosophy is most similar to the quote in the first document?

   A Confucianism

   B Daoism

   C Legalism

   D Buddhism

2. In Document B, what is Sima Qian's criticism of the Second Emperor?

   A The punishments are too light.

   B The laws are not clear.

   C Too many people are being punished harshly.

   D The Emperor is not virtuous.

3. **Writing Task** Sima Qian was a Confucian scholar and historian during the Han dynasty. Why might he have been critical of Shi Huangdi?

myworldhistory.com

Self-Test

The Right Way to Govern

Key Idea
- In both ancient India and China, political thinkers expressed ideas about the right way to govern.

Ancient India's Maurya empire was ruled by the emperor Ashoka, a peaceful leader who supported tolerance and the growth of Buddhism. During his reign, Ashoka worked to improve people's lives. He had stone pillars constructed throughout his empire. The pillars displayed edicts, or rules about morality, respect, and the right way to govern. In ancient China, people were guided by a similar set of rules. The teachings of Confucius gave people values to live by. These teachings were collected in analects, or selected writings, about family, loyalty, respect, and proper conduct. In the second excerpt, "the Master" refers to Confucius.

A relief carving from one of Ashoka's stone pillars

Read the text on the right. Stop at each circled letter. Then answer the question with the same letter on the left.

Ⓐ Draw Inferences What do you think the author means by "at all hours and in all places"?

Ⓑ Summarize In your own words, explain the meaning of this paragraph.

Ⓒ Draw Conclusions What does the author feel is his main purpose?

executed, *v.,* carried out fully

intrusted, *v.,* delivered in trust to

monastic, *adj.,* relating to monasteries, monks, or nuns

dispatch, *v.,* to complete a task

The Edicts of Ashoka

" For a long time past it has not happened that business has been dispatched and that reports have been received at all hours. Now by me this arrangement has been made that
Ⓐ at all hours and in all places . . . the official Reporters should report to me on the people's business, and I am ready to do the people's business in all places. And if, perchance, I personally by word of mouth command that a gift be made or an order <u>executed</u>, or anything urgent is <u>intrusted</u> to the superior officials, and in that business a dispute arises or a fraud occurs among the <u>monastic</u> community, I have commanded that immediate report must be made to me at any
Ⓑ hour and in any place, because I never feel full satisfaction in my efforts and <u>dispatch</u> of business. For the welfare of all folk is what I must work for—and the root of that, again, is
Ⓒ in effort and the dispatch of business. "

—Emperor Ashoka, "The Rock Edicts," about 257 B.C.

Read the text on the right. Stop at each circled letter. Then answer the question with the same letter on the left.

D **Draw Conclusions** Why does the author compare the practice of government to the North Star?

E **Analyze Primary Sources** Why does the author think that leading by virtue will help people "become good"?

F **Summarize** What does the last paragraph reveal about the author's attitude toward leadership?

virtue, *n.,* moral excellence

uniformity, *n.,* the state of being the same

propriety, *n.,* the quality or state of being proper or socially acceptable

reverence, *v.,* to show honor or respect

incompetent, *adj.,* not qualified

Analects of Confucius

❝ The Master said, 'He who exercises government by means of **D** his <u>virtue</u> may be compared to the north polar star, which keeps its place and all the stars turn towards it. . . .

The Master said, 'If the people be led by laws, and <u>uniformity</u> sought to be given them by punishments, they will try to avoid the punishment, but have no sense of shame.

'If they be led by virtue, and uniformity sought to be given them by the rules of <u>propriety</u>, they will have the **E** sense of shame, and moreover will become good.'

The Master said, 'Let him preside over them with gravity;—then they will <u>reverence</u> him. Let him be final and kind to all;—then they will be faithful to him. Let him **F** advance the good and teach the <u>incompetent</u>;—then they will eagerly seek to be virtuous.' ❞

—*Analects of Confucius,* about 400 B.C.

Analyze the Documents

1. **Compare Viewpoints** Identify similarities and differences in these two excerpts about the right way to govern.

2. **Writing Task** Review each quotation and the material in this unit about how ancient India and China were governed. How did each culture's belief in strong morals and values help to stabilize its society? Explain your thoughts in a paragraph.

A portrait of Confucius painted in the 1600s

Plan a
Cultural Web Site

Your Mission The cultural affairs departments of India and China have asked your group to design a cultural Web site that describes ancient India and ancient China. Your job is to show how ancient Indian and Chinese cultures, empires, and dynasties were similar and different.

By designing a Web site about ancient India and China, you can show the importance of each country's ancient empires, including their legacies today. To examine aspects of ancient India and China, you may find it helpful to ask a series of questions. For example, what are each country's achievements? How was each country ruled during ancient times? What conflicts did each country face? What about these two civilizations is similar? What about them is different? Think about ways to make your Web site interesting and informative. Then design and illustrate your Web site on paper or on a board in your classroom.

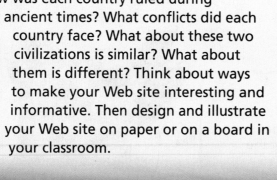

STEP 1

Research Each Country.

Review the chapters about ancient India and China. Using information you have learned in this unit, identify each culture's similarities and differences. Be sure to find answers to the questions asked in the introduction to this activity on the previous page. Think about how you will organize information on your Web site.

STEP 2

Design Your Web Site.

After you have gathered facts about each culture, begin planning your Web site on paper or a classroom board. Think about text, images, and links you might put on your site. For example, you may wish to have a link titled "Ancient Governments" with sublinks titled "Empires" and "Dynasties." You may want to study real-life examples of tourism or government Web sites to see how they present information. Be sure to include at least one page that clearly compares and contrasts the cultures. Review the design of your Web site to ensure information is presented accurately.

STEP 3

Present Your Web Site.

After your group has designed and reviewed its Web site, take the class on a "virtual tour" of your site. Present the Web site as if you were presenting it to the members of the Indian and Chinese cultural affairs departments who asked you to make the site. Be sure to explain each link, the significance of each page, and where other information about each culture can be found.

Ancient Greece

Europe

Atlantic Ocean

Africa

Pericles (400s B.C.) was an Athenian military leader and statesman who, as a teenager, watched the Greek navy fight off Persian invaders.

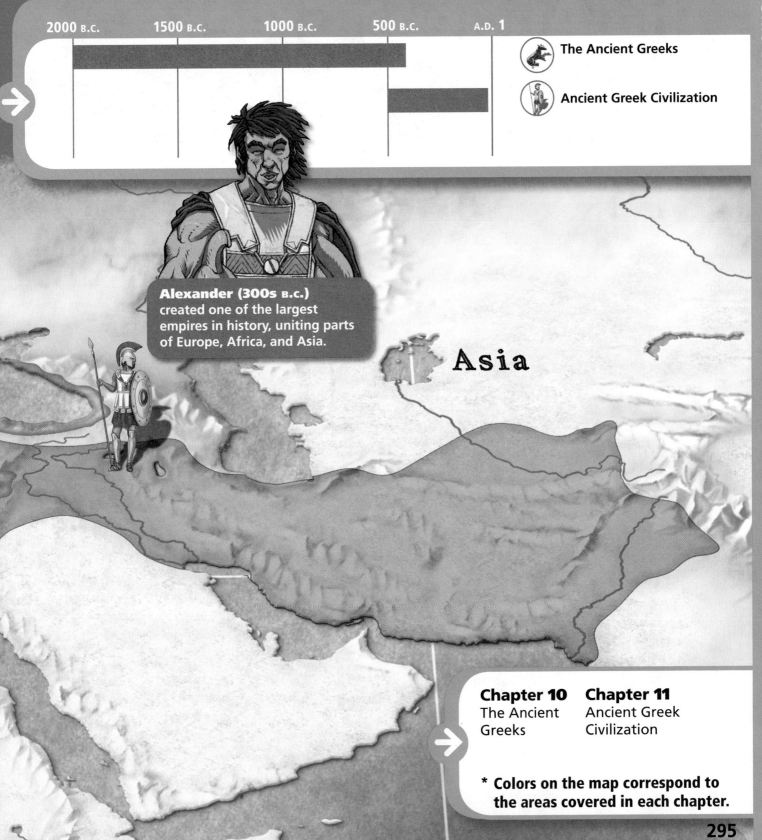

2000 B.C.   1500 B.C.   1000 B.C.   500 B.C.   A.D. 1

The Ancient Greeks

Ancient Greek Civilization

Alexander (300s B.C.) created one of the largest empires in history, uniting parts of Europe, Africa, and Asia.

Asia

Chapter 10
The Ancient
Greeks

Chapter 11
Ancient Greek
Civilization

* Colors on the map correspond to the areas covered in each chapter.

295

Chapter 10

The Ancient Greeks

Essential Question

What is power? Who should have it?

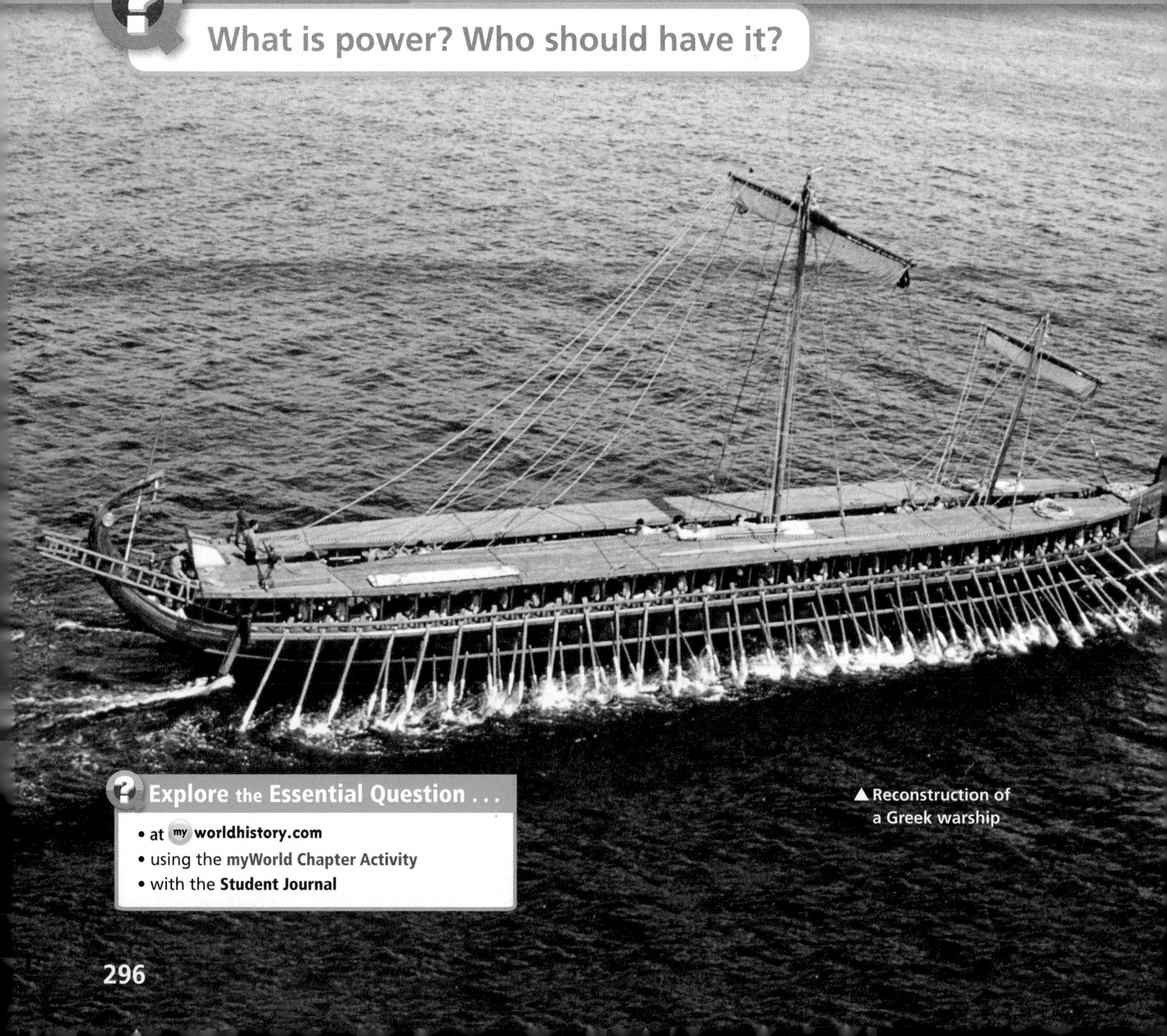

▲ Reconstruction of a Greek warship

Explore the Essential Question . . .

- at myworldhistory.com
- using the myWorld Chapter Activity
- with the **Student Journal**

Ancient Greece and the Dark Age

1450 B.C. Minoan towns are destroyed.

1100 B.C.–750 B.C. The region passes through a dark age.

508 B.C. Democracy develops in Athens.

1400 B.C.　　**1200 B.C.**　　**1000 B.C.**　　**800 B.C.**　　**600 B.C.**　　**400 B.C.**

Around 1100 B.C. Mycenaean kingdoms are destroyed.

700s B.C. Homer shapes the *Iliad*. Greek colonies spread. Trade increases.

Around 650 B.C. Greeks start using coins.

PERICLES
Calm in the Face of Danger

This myStory is a fictionalized account of events in the early life of Pericles, who appears in this chapter.

Young Pericles never forgot the sight of the enemy approaching his city of Athens. He and his dog, Ajax, were up on the hill of the Acropolis, high above the city. From there they could see the huge dust cloud of the advancing Persian army. Some said that the Persians were five million strong. How could tiny Athens resist such a mighty force?

A voice echoed in the city below, calling out the warning to evacuate. All Athenians were to leave their homes at once and proceed to the port of Piraeus, four miles away. Ships there would ferry everyone to safety.

Pericles and Ajax raced home through the crowded streets. They joined their family, who were already rushing to pack up their clothes and evacuate their stately home. Fifteen-year-old

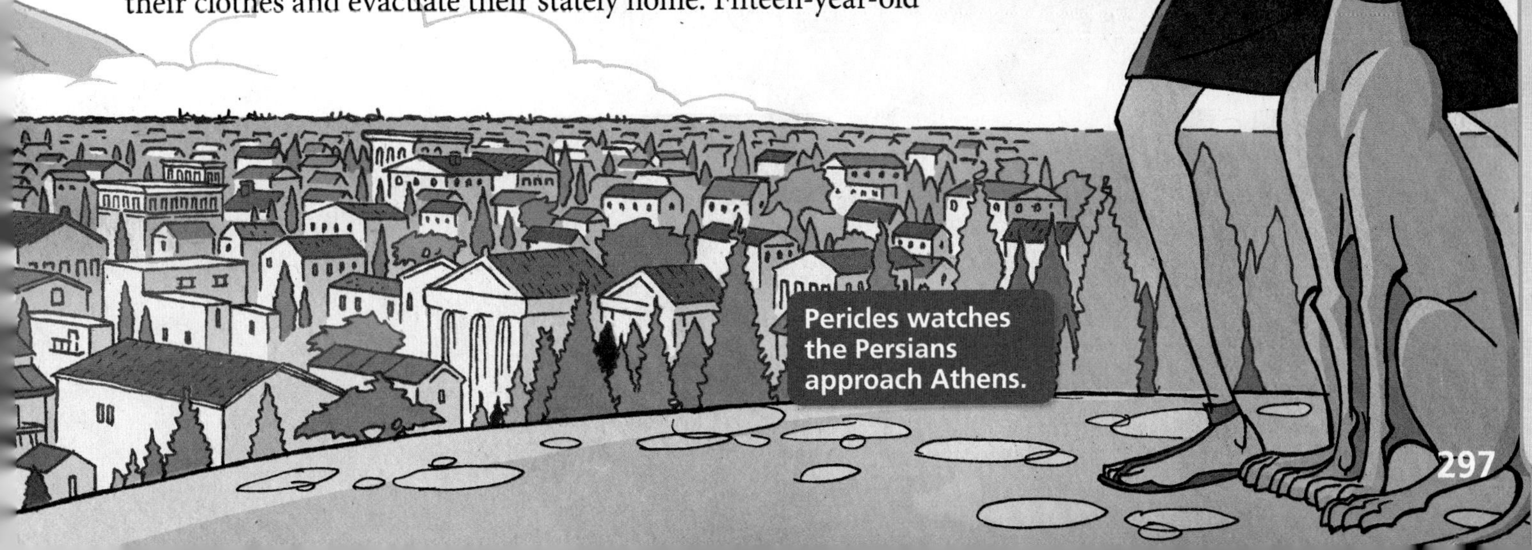

Pericles watches the Persians approach Athens.

my worldhistory.com

Timeline/On Assignment

297

Pericles and Ajax rushed home through crowds of fleeing citizens.

Behind each boat, dozens of dogs were swimming after their masters.

Pericles was scared, angry, and confused, but he didn't show it—he always appeared calm, even in the face of danger. He helped his family lock up the house before heading down to the ships at Piraeus.

At Piraeus, the docks swarmed with panicking crowds. The ships were packed to capacity. Women and children were being sent to a distant coast, while most Athenian men were shipping out to the island of Salamis, a few miles away. At Salamis, the Greeks planned to fight a final naval battle against the Persian fleet.

Along the waterfront, families wept as they were forced to part. But Pericles' family was lucky. Because Pericles' father was an important politician, his entire family was being sent to Salamis. Only one family member would have to stay behind—poor Ajax, their beloved dog.

The ship's officer told them that, without exception, no dogs were allowed on board. As the ships left port, Pericles' family grew silent. Leaving their home was bad enough. Leaving Ajax was unbearable.

Suddenly someone shouted and pointed. Behind each boat dozens of dogs were swimming frantically after their masters. Pericles laughed as he caught a glimpse of Ajax's

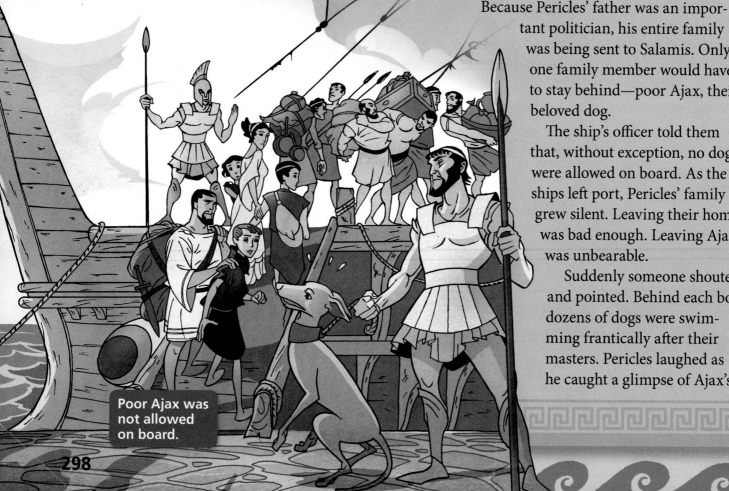

Poor Ajax was not allowed on board.

298

From their safe haven on the island of Salamis, Pericles' family mourned as they watched Athens burn.

The Persian king, Xerxes, reacted with horror as his fleet was destroyed.

head bobbing above the waves. Not even Athenian dogs were willing to live under Persian tyranny—the rule of a king!

It was fear of tyranny that had motivated the Athenians to join other Greeks in resisting the Persian invasion. Like many Athenians, Pericles probably viewed the Persian war in political terms—Athenian democracy against Persian tyranny. After all, he came from a very political family and would grow up to become a leading politician. His father and his mother's uncle were supporters of democratic government in Athens. In Athens, power was shared among all citizens. This was a new approach to political power, quite unfamiliar to the Persians, who simply obeyed their king. Even now, from the ship's deck, Pericles was watching democracy in action—for the decision to evacuate their city and continue fighting had been made by popular vote.

When the family disembarked on Salamis, Ajax bounded in from the sea, drenching them all as he shook himself dry. But the family's laughter was short-lived. They knew that the powerful Persian fleet would soon arrive in hot pursuit. They feared that the next day, when the Greek ships faced the enemy, the entire Greek navy might be destroyed.

That night they saw Athens burning in the distance. They mourned for their home and for the beautiful temples on the Acropolis. All seemed lost.

Yet, the next day, as the battle unfolded, they watched in astonishment as the Athenian and other Greek ships fought back—hard. Slowly the Greeks gained the upper hand. The family celebrated as the last Persian ships fled, giving the Greeks a decisive victory. The naval battle of Salamis, fought in 480 B.C., became a turning point in the war.

When his family returned to Athens, Pericles dedicated his life to restoring the city and strengthening its power. Years later, Pericles helped bring about a golden age in Athens, the world's first democracy. He always remembered the lessons of Salamis—when a tiny democracy stood up to the world's greatest empire.

Based on this story, how do you think the Greeks viewed political power? As you read the chapter ahead, think about what Pericles' story tells you about life in ancient Greece.

→ **myStory Video**

Join Pericles as he watches the battle of Salamis.

The Rise of City-States

Key Ideas
- Physical geography helped shape Greek life and culture.
- The basic political unit of ancient Greece was the city-state.
- Early Greek history was marked by frequent warfare among small city-states.

Key Terms • polis • citizen • acropolis • politics • aristocracy

 **Visual Glossary**

→ **Reading Skill Analyze Cause and Effect** Take notes using the graphic organizer in your journal.

Statue of Athena, the Greek goddess of wisdom and protector of cities. Foreground: temple of Poseidon ▼

ifteen-year-old Pericles, as you read in the story, watched his fellow Greeks defeat Persia, the greatest empire on Earth. The battle of Salamis was a turning point in Greek history. After Salamis, Greek culture reached a peak in art, drama, philosophy, and political science. It helped form Western civilization—the civilization of Europe and the Americas. The Greeks gave us words and traditions such as *democracy, geometry, politics,* and *the Olympic games.* How did the Greeks come to have so much influence on our world?

Geography of the Greek World

In ancient times, there was no country called Greece. Instead, there were communities of Greek speakers scattered across the islands and coasts of the Mediterranean Sea. This early Greek world lay on the fringe of two continents—Europe and Asia. Travelers and traders passed through the region exchanging goods, ideas, and customs.

A Rugged Land Modern Greece occupies a large peninsula that juts into the Mediterranean Sea. A peninsula is a land area almost surrounded by water. A number of other peninsulas also extend from the peninsula of mainland Greece. The largest of them, in southern Greece, is called the Peloponnesian (pel uh puh NEE shun) Peninsula.

About 2000 B.C., Greek-speaking peoples entered these lands from the north. They settled on mainland Greece. A mainland is an area of land that is part of a continent. Greek speakers also settled on the islands of the Aegean [ee JEE un] Sea.

Mainland Greece is divided by mountain ranges. Between these ranges lie narrow valleys and small plains. The mountains were good for grazing sheep and goats, but they were too steep and rocky for farming. Less than one quarter of the land could be used to grow crops. The only fertile land was in the lowland valleys and plains. Here people settled in farming communities.

The mountains isolated these lowland communities. So a fiercely independent spirit developed among the Greeks. They never attempted to unite under a single government. In fact, Greek cities were often at war with one another.

Surrounded by the Sea Although mountain ranges isolated communities, the sea brought contact with the wider world. The Greeks became skillful sailors and merchants. Greek fishing and trading ships crisscrossed the waters of the Mediterranean Sea to the south, the Aegean Sea to the east, and the Ionian (eye OH nee un) Sea to the west. This led to contact with the older, more complex cultures of North Africa and Asia.

A Mediterranean Climate Greece has a Mediterranean climate, with mild, wet winters and hot, dry summers. The lack of rain made it difficult to grow shallow-rooted crops such as grains, which need frequent watering. So the mainland Greeks were always searching for foreign sources of grain. On the other hand, the Mediterranean climate was ideal for growing deep-rooted plants such as olive trees and grape vines. Olive oil and wine became important trade goods and brought in wealth.

Reading Check How did physical geography shape Greek culture?

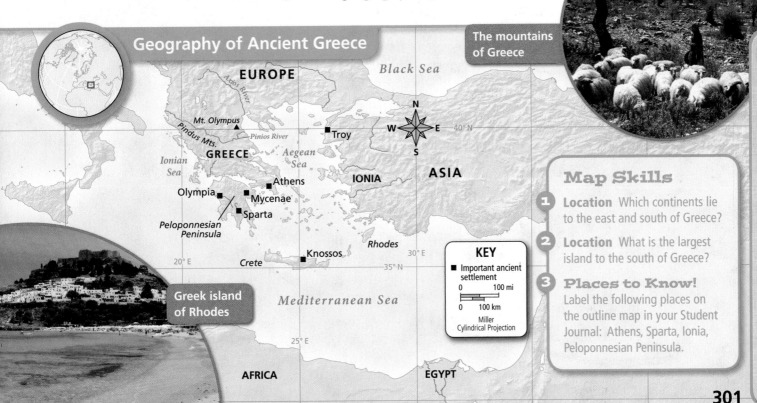

The mountains of Greece

Geography of Ancient Greece

Greek island of Rhodes

Map Skills

1. **Location** Which continents lie to the east and south of Greece?

2. **Location** What is the largest island to the south of Greece?

3. **Places to Know!** Label the following places on the outline map in your Student Journal: Athens, Sparta, Ionia, Peloponnesian Peninsula.

myworldhistory.com

Places to Know

Early Greek History

The Greeks were influenced by an early civilization—the Minoans. Minoan culture developed on Crete, an island south of mainland Greece. It spread across the Aegean islands and influenced mainland Greece around 2000 B.C.

Minoan Civilization Minoan civilization was highly advanced. The Minoans had a writing system and built huge stone palaces with running water, like the one at Knossos (NAH sus). They traded goods throughout the Mediterranean.

Around 1450 B.C., Minoan palaces and towns were mysteriously destroyed. Most historians believe that mainland Greeks were responsible.

The Mycenaeans The Minoans influenced a civilization that developed among Greek speakers on mainland Greece. This civilization, known as Mycenaean [my suh NEE un], developed around 1600 B.C. Each Mycenaean town was governed by a monarchy, a government headed by a king. Mycenaean rulers lived in stone fortresses on hilltops overlooking their towns.

The Mycenaeans made fine bronze weapons and pottery. They traded these goods for copper, ivory, and luxury goods from other lands. Mycenaeans sometimes raided other peoples and one another for gold and other goods.

Eventually, the Mycenaean kingdoms grew weak. Then, around 1100 B.C., this civilization was destroyed by newcomers from the north known as Dorians.

KNOSSOS

The Minoan palace of Knossos was begun around 1700 B.C.

Reconstructed section of the palace ▶

◀ Interior wall paintings reveal the importance of the sea.

The Dark Age With the fall of the Mycenaeans, Greek culture declined. People lost the ability to read and write. The following period, which lasted roughly from 1100 to 750 B.C., has been called a dark age. During these centuries, mainland Greeks migrated across the Aegean, settling the islands and the west coast of Asia Minor, an area that became known as Ionia (eye OH nee a).

The Greeks in Ionia never forgot the "heroic age" of the Mycenaeans. They told and sang stories of the world that existed before the dark age. One of these stories was about the Trojan War.

Reading Check What happened during the dark age?

The Trojan War

In the legend of the Trojan War, warriors from Mycenaean kingdoms sailed across the Aegean to attack Troy, a city in Asia Minor. The ten-year-long conflict ended when the Greeks tricked the Trojans into accepting a "gift" of a large wooden horse. Greeks hiding in the horse crept out and opened the city gates. The Greek army entered and burned Troy to the ground.

For centuries, the stories of the Trojan War were recited or sung, as the Greeks could no longer read or write. Then, in the 700s B.C., the Greeks developed an alphabet based on the Phoenician alphabet. According to tradition, a poet named Homer shaped the stories of the Trojan War into a long epic poem, the *Iliad*. The poem was eventually written down.

The *Iliad* tells of events during the war but stops before the Greeks' <u>eventual</u>

▲ Trojans celebrate the gift of the wooden horse, in this scene from a recent movie.

victory. Homer's *Odyssey* is another epic poem, which describes the adventures of the hero Odysseus on his journey home after the war.

The *Iliad* and the *Odyssey* shaped Greek culture. Students learned the verses by heart. The values expressed in these poems became part of Greek identity. One of those values was courage. In the *Iliad*, the warrior Achilles speaks to his troops before battle:

> 66 Every man make up his mind to fight
> And move on his enemy! Strong as I am,
> It's hard for me to face so many men
> And fight with all at once. . . .
> And yet I will! 99
> —Homer, the *Iliad*

The ancient Greeks tried to live up to the ideals of bravery, strength, and honor expressed in Homer's work.

Reading Check How did Homer preserve the memory of Mycenaean civilization?

eventual, *adj.,* final

my worldhistory.com

Primary Source

303

View of Corinth at the height of its power

The City-State of

CORINTH

Corinth was one of the richest city-states in Greece. The city's economic power grew from its location. Corinth controlled not only the north–south land route across the Isthmus of Corinth, but also the east–west sea route. A special roadway allowed ships to be dragged across the five-mile-wide isthmus.

THINK CRITICALLY **Study the map. Explain why Corinth's location was important to communication and trade.**

KEY
- Territory of Corinth
- • City
- — Trade route

0   100 mi
0   100 km
Miller Cylindrical Projection

40°N
Aegean Sea
Ionian Sea
Gulf of Corinth
Isthmus of Corinth
IONIA
Athens
38°N
Corinth
Peloponnesian Peninsula
Sparta
Mediterranean Sea
24°E
20°E   22°E

N W E S

Emergence of City-States

By the time Homer's epics were composed, each Greek community had begun to organize itself into a **polis,** or city-state. The city-state became one of the most important features of Greek culture. The Greeks created such city-states everywhere they settled.

The Polis A polis was more than just a city. It was a community with its own government. The government of a polis ruled a wide area that included not only the city but its surrounding villages and countryside as well.

Each Greek city-state usually had a marketplace and government center. Here members of the city-state who had legal rights—the **citizens**—would meet to make laws and discuss issues affecting the entire community.

The area and population of a polis were generally small. All the citizens of the polis could gather to make decisions as a single group.

The ruins of ancient Corinth ▼

The High City A typical polis was usually built on two levels. On a high hill stood the **acropolis** (uh KRAH puh lis), a word meaning "high city." Public buildings and marble temples were located in this area. The acropolis also served as a fortress in times of danger. On lower ground, below the hill, lay people's homes, shops, and farms. In Athens, the lower city included the agora, or marketplace. There people gathered to discuss public affairs.

Politics in the Polis The word *polis* gave rise to the term **politics,** the art and practice of government. Each city-state had a different kind of government. Some city-states were monarchies, ruled by a king. In early times the polis was governed by an **aristocracy,** a hereditary class of rulers. Aristocracy meant "rule by the best people."

But in some city-states an extraordinary thing happened—the citizens began governing themselves. Rule by citizens made such Greek city-states unique. By contrast, in most of the world, priests and kings held all the political power.

Even though self-government was a feature of most city-states, not everyone was allowed to participate in making decisions. Women, slaves, and foreigners were all <u>excluded</u> from the process. The polis had three kinds of inhabitants: citizens (who could vote), women and free foreigners (who could not vote), and slaves, who had few rights at all.

Pride in the Polis Citizens felt strong pride and loyalty toward their polis. Greeks believed that a good citizen should always be willing to sacrifice for his city. He should be prepared to die for his polis, if necessary.

As one historian wrote, "The polis was the framework of Greek life." Greeks identified with their city. If their polis was a success, so were they. Throughout the history of ancient Greece, the polis played a key role in Greek life.

Reading Check What was the polis?

myWorld Activity
Polis Timeline

exclude, *v.,* to shut out, keep from participating

Section 1 Assessment

Essential Question

Key Terms

1. Use the following terms to describe the rise of the city-states: polis, citizen, acropolis, politics, aristocracy.

Key Ideas

2. How did the physical geography of Greece encourage the development of the city-state?

3. What kinds of governments ruled Greek city-states?

4. Why was the polis called "the framework of Greek life"?

Think Critically

5. **Synthesize** What changes took place in the Greek world during the dark age?

6. **Compare and Contrast** Compare the advantages and disadvantages for settlers of Greece's physical geography.

What is power, and who should have it?

7. Who held political power in Greek city-states? Go to your Student Journal to record your answer.

Greek Society and Economy

Key Ideas

- Greek society was divided according to wealth and legal status.

- Women had clear roles and few rights in the Greek city-states.

- Geography and limited resources spurred conquest, trade, and colonization.

Key Terms • tenant farmer • metic • slavery

 Visual Glossary

Reading Skill Identify Main Idea and Details Take notes using the graphic organizer in your journal.

Gravestone showing a Greek family ▼

A Greek traveler in ancient times would have felt at home in any Greek port city. Greeks spoke the same language and worshiped many of the same gods. All city-states allowed slavery, and all had a class system. At each city's docks there were similar sights—groups of settlers boarding ships, and merchants inspecting trade goods.

However, our ancient traveler might also have been startled at the differences between city-states. He or she would have observed a variety of governments, economies, and ways of organizing society. Among the city-states, customs and traditions varied.

Women in Ancient Greece

In the Greek world, women had different rights and roles, depending on the city-state. In Sparta, they had a good deal of freedom. However, in city-states such as Athens, they had few rights.

Family Life The typical Greek family consisted of husband, wife, and children. As head of the house, the man had control over his family. Poorer women worked outdoors on farms or sold goods in markets. But in city-states like Athens, women from richer families were expected to stay at home while the men took part in public life. Although women did play public roles in religious ceremonies, for the

 **Culture Close-Up**

most part their lives were restricted. The Greek philosopher Xenophon described Greek gender roles:

> 66 The gods have ordered and the law approves that men and women should each follow their own capacity. It is not so good for a woman to be out of doors as in. And it is more dishonorable for a man to stay indoors than to attend to his affairs outside. 99

—Xenophon, *Economics*

In most Greek homes, women supervised the household, raised the children, kept track of money and spending, and managed the slaves. Many Greek women made most or all of the clothing family members needed. They had to spin wool or flax into yarn, weave fabric, and sew or knit the clothes. Greek women also supervised the preparation of meals.

Spartan Women In Sparta, women enjoyed more rights and freedoms than did women in other city-states. Spartan women could sell their property. Like their brothers, Spartan girls were educated and trained in sports. Such Spartan customs shocked the Greeks of other city-states.

Reading Check How did the lives of women in Athens and Sparta differ?

Greek Society

Ancient Greek society had a complex class system, with rich landowners at the top and slaves at the bottom. Between these two extremes were ranked the small landowners, merchants and artisans, and the landless poor of Greek society.

The Aristocracy Early city-states were controlled by aristocrats or kings. Some aristocrats claimed descent from kings or gods. They believed this gave them the right to hold political power. Their wealth came from owning large plots of land, where they raised crops and livestock.

Slaves did most of the work on these estates. This left aristocrats with free time for politics and leisure activities.

Citizens and Noncitizens Society was divided between citizens (who were all adult males) and noncitizens, whose rights were limited. All citizens had the right to vote.

Farmers who owned large areas of land enjoyed a relatively high status, or rank in society. Although such landowners were rich, they made up only a minority of citizens. Many more citizens were small farmers—farmers who owned smaller plots of land. Small farmers rarely had

myWorld Activity
Taking Sides

Greek vase showing a seated woman and her servants ▼

my worldhistory.com

Culture Close-Up

307

ANCIENT GREEK SOCIETY

People in ancient Greece were ranked according to their social or legal status. The main division was between free people and the enslaved. Of the free, only citizens took part in government. *Did all free Greeks have equal rights?*

FREE

Aristocracy

Small farmers

Tenant farmers (thetes)

Women and children born of citizens

Resident aliens (metics)

CITIZENS

NONCITIZENS

NOT FREE

SLAVES

dent aliens, or **metics**. A metic might be a Greek from another city-state or someone who was not Greek. Metics were noncitizens. Although they were free, they enjoyed fewer rights than the native-born men of the polis.

Slaves The lowest class in Greek society was made up of slaves. **Slavery** is the ownership and control of other people as property. The philosopher Aristotle explained that slavery was a natural condition of some people. "From the hour of their birth," he wrote, "some are marked out for slavery, others for rule."

Slaves were acquired in various ways. Most were prisoners of war. Others were bought from slave traders or sold into slavery by their families. Sometimes parents who could not care for their children abandoned them. These children often become slaves. Many slaves in Greek city-states came from other lands. Some slaves were Greeks themselves.

By the 500s B.C., slavery was widespread in Greece. In some city-states, slaves made up one third of the population. Slaves did many jobs in Greek society. Household slaves cooked, cleaned, and took care of children. Some slaves were teachers. Others worked on farms, ships, or in mines. Their labor helped the Greek economy grow.

Some slaves were treated kindly. A few were even freed. But slaves had no legal rights and could be punished harshly by their owners. Slaves were sometimes worked to death under cruel conditions.

Reading Check What were some social divisions in ancient Greece?

enough land to raise livestock or produce a food surplus. On a lower social scale were the **tenant farmers**—people who paid rent, either in money or crops, to grow crops on another person's land. These tenant farmers were called *thetes.*

Merchants and artisans were often resi-

Greek Economic Expansion

As you have read, the Greeks lacked good farmland and some basic resources. When the population of Greek city-states increased, the Greeks had to find ways of feeding their people.

Conquest Some city-states <u>obtained</u> more land and resources by conquering their neighbors. Sparta, located on the Peloponnesian Peninsula, decided not to depend on trade for growth. Spartan troops conquered the neighboring city-state of Messenia and turned its conquered people into non-free laborers. The Messenians were forced to raise crops for the Spartans.

This captive workforce freed Spartan men from their farming chores. So the Spartans were able to form a professional army that was the most feared in Greece.

By the mid-500s B.C., Sparta controlled most of the Peloponnesian Peninsula.

Colonization Migration—moving to a new area—was another solution to the population problem. Beginning in the 700s B.C., new waves of Greek colonists sailed off to find new places to settle. Leaving home was not an easy decision. Colonists faced danger and uncertainty on the voyage and the challenge of building new homes. As historian Donald Kagan notes, "Only powerful pressures like overpopulation and land hunger" drove people to take such risks.

The ideal site for a colony was on the coast. There, the settlers could anchor their ships. They could also set up a port for trading with other ports. The best spot would have good land for farming. It needed to be near important resources

obtain, *v.,* to gain

THE BEGINNING OF Urban Planning

Miletus, in Ionia, was one of the first Greek cities to be laid out on a grid pattern. For Western civilization, this was the beginning of urban planning—the rational planning of cities. Many modern American cities follow the same kind of grid plan.

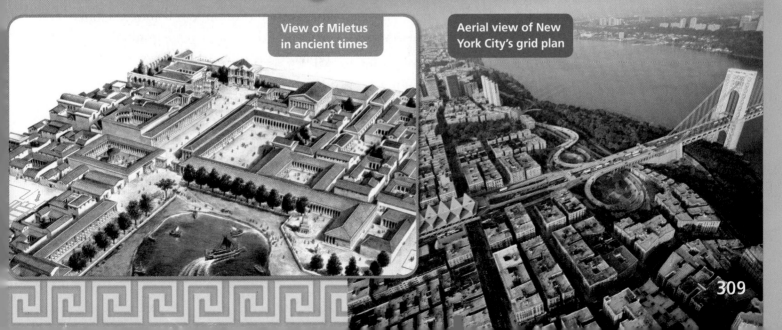

View of Miletus in ancient times

Aerial view of New York City's grid plan

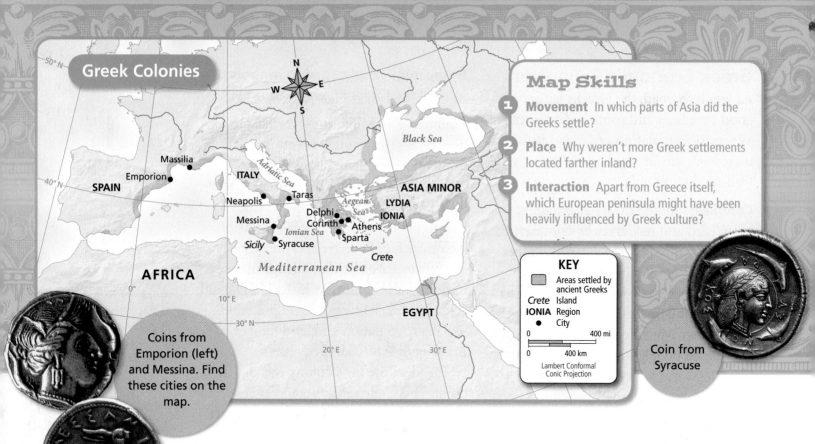

Greek Colonies

Map Skills

1. **Movement** In which parts of Asia did the Greeks settle?

2. **Place** Why weren't more Greek settlements located farther inland?

3. **Interaction** Apart from Greece itself, which European peninsula might have been heavily influenced by Greek culture?

KEY

Areas settled by ancient Greeks

Crete Island

IONIA Region

• City

0 ————— 400 mi

0 ————— 400 km

Lambert Conformal Conic Projection

Coins from Emporion (left) and Messina. Find these cities on the map.

Coin from Syracuse

such as timber or minerals that could be exported. Homer described the founding of a fictional colony:

> 66 So [the founder] led them away, settling them in [a place called] Scheria, far from the bustle of men. He had a wall constructed around the town center, built houses, erected temples for the gods, and divided the land. 99
>
> —Homer, the *Odyssey*

Greek colonists brought a flame from home to light fires in the new colony. This flame <u>symbolized</u> their ties to their old city-state. They often traded with the home city. But most colonists never returned home. They made new lives in their new city-state.

By the 500s B.C., there were hundreds of Greek colonies around the Mediterranean Sea and the Black Sea.

symbolize, *v.,* to represent

They stretched from the shores of what is now Russia all the way west to Spain.

The First Coins Trade led to an important new development. Around 650 B.C., the kings of Lydia began making the world's first gold and silver coins. Lydia was in present-day Turkey, near the city-states of Ionia. Using coins led to a kind of economic revolution. Coins of standard size and value gradually replaced the old bartering system, in which some goods would be traded for other goods. Thanks to the use of coins, trade became easier.

Greeks learned about coins from trading with Lydia. Several city-states set up their own mints, or places where coins are made. Each city-state stamped its coins with symbols of the city or an image of the god or goddess who protected the city. The coins of Athens, for instance, were marked with an owl. This bird was associated with Athena, the goddess for whom Athens was named.

Athens Grows Rich Trade made the city-state of Athens rich. Athens had very little farmland, but it did have an excellent port called Piraeus, three miles away. The Athenians relied on commerce to meet their needs for food and other resources. For example, Athenians came to rely on grain that was shipped from ports on the Black Sea.

To pay for the grain, Athenian workshops produced pottery, jewelry, and other trade goods. These products, along with olive oil and wine, were also shipped to other lands. Ships returned to Athens with timber, minerals, and luxury goods such as ivory, glass, and perfume. Streets and markets bustled with activity.

The Effects of Expansion Greek colonization affected both trade and culture. Just as colonization spread Greek culture and goods across the Mediterranean world, it also drew new customs and ideas back to Greece. As a result, cultural borrowing increased throughout the Mediterranean region. As you have read, the use of coins and the Greek alphabet were both inspired by the cultures of Asia Minor.

The establishment of colonies had economic effects on Greece. Many colonies became prosperous, or successful. The colonies carried on an active trade with Greece. They also introduced mainland Greeks to new goods from foreign lands.

Merchants grew rich from the increased trade. They built large merchant fleets, or groups of ships, that crossed the Mediterranean. As their wealth increased, merchants began to play a greater role in the life of Greek city-states. The new wealth of the city-states also brought about changes in how the city-states were governed, as you will read in the next section.

Reading Check How did Greek city-states gain needed resources when their populations grew?

Some Greek cities exported perfume in bottles like this. ▼

Section 2 Assessment

Key Terms

1. Use the following terms to describe Greek society and economy: tenant farmer, metic, slavery.

Key Ideas

2. Why were some Greeks shocked by the lives of Spartan women?

3. Why were the aristocracy in Greek city-states so wealthy?

4. What effects did colonization have on mainland Greece?

Think Critically

5. **Make Inferences** Why did the physical geography of Greece encourage colonization?

6. **Draw Conclusions** How did the adoption of coins help increase Greek wealth?

? Essential Question

What is power, and who should have it?

7. Who held the most power in the Greek family? Go to your Student Journal to record your answer.

Democracy in Athens

Key Ideas
- Greek city-states experimented with many forms of government, including oligarchy and tyranny.
- In Athens, democracy developed. Citizens participated in lawmaking and the courts.
- Athenian democracy and the responsibilities of citizenship developed gradually over many years.

Key Terms • oligarchy • phalanx • tyranny • democracy • citizenship • direct democracy • representative democracy

Visual Glossary

 Reading Skill Summarize Take notes using the graphic organizer in your journal.

One night in 508 B.C., the sounds of a power struggle echoed through the streets of Athens. Isagoras, the city's leading judge, was trying to crush a movement for democracy. He had invited the Spartans to help him defeat this dangerous new trend. He forced the popular leader Cleisthenes (KLYS thuh neez) to flee the city. Isagoras also exiled 700 families who supported democratic reform.

But now some Athenians were fighting back. They chased Isagoras and the Spartans up into the Acropolis. The Spartans were excellent soldiers, but they were overwhelmed by the Athenian people. After the Spartans surrendered, Cleisthenes returned, and Athens continued building its democracy.

The Parthenon, or temple of Athena, stands on the Acropolis in Athens. ▼

Before Democracy

Isagoras and the Spartans feared the new political trends in Athens. They were trying to keep government in the hands of the aristocrats, a type of government the Greeks called an **oligarchy** (AHL ih gahr kee). In an oligarchy, political power is held by a small group of people.

GREEK PHALANX

The phalanx was a formation of soldiers that might be as deep as eight lines. *How might such a battle formation create a spirit of equality?*

Oligarchies Oligarchies were usually headed by a council of leaders who belonged to the aristocracy. One of these aristocratic leaders was a lawgiver named Draco. He created a legal code that specified harsh punishments for all offenses, from serious to minor crimes. Today, people still use the word *draconian* to describe laws that seem unnecessarily harsh or severe.

The Rise of the Phalanx In many city-states, power began to shift into the hands of more people. This process may have been sparked by a change in the way Greek armies were organized. In earlier times, the outcome of battles depended on fights between individual aristocratic warriors. The aristocrats were the most important soldiers of the state.

Around 700 B.C., a new military formation called the phalanx was introduced. The **phalanx** was a formation of heavily armed foot soldiers who moved together as a unit. Before battle, these citizen-soldiers lined up to form a row of overlapping shields. Each man's shield helped protect his neighbor. He held the shield with his left arm. In his right hand he held a spear or sword. A well-trained phalanx could overcome almost any other force.

As foot soldiers, fighters in a phalanx did not need to be rich enough to buy and <u>maintain</u> a horse. More men could afford the necessary weapons and armor. As city-states came to depend on the phalanx formation for defense, citizen-soldiers may have gained more political power. Some historians believe this gave more men a voice in government. Aristocratic leaders risked losing the support of their army if they did not consider the interests of these men.

Each city-state set up a different form of government. With so many city-states, great political variety characterized the Greek world.

maintain, *v.,* to keep and support

313

▲ Solon frees a debt slave.

myWorld Activity
Report from Athens

Tyranny At first tyrants, or strong leaders, emerged to champion the interests of ordinary citizens. Tyrants were usually members of the aristocracy. But by promising land and other benefits to the poor, they won popular support. Then they were able to set up **tyrannies,** or governments run by a strong ruler.

Tyrants did not allow others to play a significant role in government. Neverthe-less, Greek tyrants were not always bad rulers. In some city-states, they governed fairly and worked to improve life for ordi-nary people.

Many tyrants, however, found that they could not fulfill their promises. Other tyrants ruled harshly. Eventually, other forms of government replaced tyrannies.

Reading Check What were two common types of governments in the early Greek city-states?

Power of the People

Most city-states adopted tyranny, but some moved toward rule by the many. The Greeks called this form of government **democracy,** which means "rule by the people." In these new democracies, large numbers of men participated in civic affairs.

Beginnings of Democracy In the year 594 B.C., the aristocrats of Athens chose Solon to lead the polis. Solon reformed the courts. He ended the practice of selling into slavery poor people who could not pay their debts. He also gave some non-aristocratic men the right to vote for officials. These measures set Athens on the path to democracy.

Later Reforms In 508 B.C., a leader named Cleisthenes gained power in Athens. He made several reforms that reduced the power of the rich. By increasing the number of citizens who could vote, he brought in many new voters from the lower classes. Cleisthenes also increased the power of the assembly, which included all male citizens. The assembly met to discuss political issues and make decisions for the city-state.

Another major reform took place in 461 B.C. In that year, Athens created citizen juries. A jury is a group of people who hear evidence and decide a court case. The new system put legal decisions in the hands of the people.

The Age of Pericles More reforms followed in the 450s B.C. under Pericles (whose youth was described in the myStory for this chapter). His first major change was to pay citizens for participating in jury service and in other civic duties. These payments helped poor people to take part in government. No longer was participation in the legal system restricted only to those who could afford to serve on juries.

These reforms created the world's first democracy. Athenians were proud of what they had achieved. In 431 B.C., during a time of war, Pericles gave a speech honoring Athenians who had died in battle. In it, he talked about the democratic values that made Athens unique:

> 66 When it is a question of settling private disputes, everyone is equal before the law. When it is a question of putting one person before another in positions of public responsibility, what counts is not membership in a particular class, but the actual ability which the man possesses. 99
> —"Pericles' funeral oration"

One factor that encouraged democracy in Athens was the idea of citizenship. **Citizenship** is membership in a community. Citizenship gives a person both rights and responsibilities. Elsewhere in the ancient world, people lived as subjects of a ruler whom they were expected to obey without question. In contrast, the Greeks gave ordinary people the right to help make government decisions.

Education for Democracy Education helped promote the growth of democracy in Athens. The education students received was designed to produce well-rounded citizens who could take part in public life.

Although some girls could probably read and write, most education was reserved for boys. They attended school from the age of seven and studied literature, physical education, and music.

By the 420s B.C., there was also higher education. Traveling <u>lecturers</u> taught various subjects such as mathematics and public speaking.

Reading Check What important political development occurred in Athens?

Athenian Democracy at Work

Political reforms produced a golden age of democracy in Athens. Citizens ran all parts of the government. The most important were the assembly, the council, and the courts.

The Business of Government The main political body of Athens was the assembly, which all free adult male citizens had the right to attend. Meetings took place 40 times a year. Everyone who attended the assembly had the right to speak, from the poorest farmer to the richest aristocrat.

A 500-person council, known as the boule, was the second key component of the Athenian government. The council helped decide which issues should come before the assembly. Members of the council were chosen by lot, or at random, from among the citizens. As a result, every male citizen had a chance of serving on the council.

lecturer, *n.,* person who gives an informative talk to students

Voters could send someone into exile by recording a name on a piece of pottery.▼

315

ATHENIAN DEMOCRACY

Democracy first developed in Athens before spreading to hundreds of other Greek city-states. Here's how Athenian democracy and justice worked.

THINK CRITICALLY **What was the relationship between the assembly and the boule?**

Democracy crowns the people.

Assembly members were chosen for special duties:

Assembly

This main political body was open to all adult male citizens.
- voted on legislation
- determined foreign policy

Citizens

In Athens there were possibly 45,000 citizens in the mid-400s B.C. Out of this pool of citizens, Athenians were chosen for various government positions.

Boule (Council of 500)

- prepared the bills to be voted on by assembly
- enforced assembly decisions

Juries

Jurors were chosen at random. From 201 to more than 1,000 jurors might sit for a trial.

Archons

Nine judges chosen annually at random

Council Subcommittees

- handled finances
- maintained religious rites

The Courts The government's third key component was the court system. Athens had many different courts, each of which decided different types of cases. Juries made up of citizens served in the courts, deciding cases by majority vote.

Juries in Athens were much larger than modern juries. Many people, from several hundred to several thousand, might serve on a single jury! Additional laws were passed to discourage bribery.

As democracy grew stronger in Athens, older governmental bodies lost power. For example, the Areopagus (ar ee OP uh gus), a council of advisers who decided some court cases, lost all its functions except the right to judge murder cases.

A Limited Democracy Athens was not completely democratic. Women could not vote or hold office. Foreigners, even if they came from another Greek city-state, could not be citizens and had no voice in the government. Slaves had no rights.

Athens, then, did not have rule by all the people. Compared to most places in the ancient world, however, Athens included far more people in government.

Direct Democracy Athenian democracy depended on active citizen involvement. A political system in which citizens participate directly in decision making is called a **direct democracy.** Direct democracy worked in Athens because the population of the city-state was small and because of the commitment and hard work of its citizens.

Direct democracy is less practical in large countries like the United States. In countries spread over a wide area of land, citizens live too far apart to meet. In addition, nations like the United States have so many citizens that Athenian-style assemblies would be too big.

For this reason, most democracies today are representative democracies. In a **representative democracy,** citizens elect others to represent them in government. These representatives then make the decisions and pass laws on behalf of all the people. Despite the differences, modern democracies share the Athenian ideal of rule by the people.

Reading Check How did the assembly provide Athenians with a direct role in government decisions?

my World CONNECTIONS

In the United States today, the New England town meeting is an example of direct democracy.

Section 3 Assessment

Essential Question

What is power, and who should have it?

Key Terms

1. Use the following terms to describe government in Athens: oligarchy, phalanx, tyranny, democracy, citizenship, direct democracy, representative democracy.

Key Ideas

2. How did tyrants gain power in the city-states?

3. How did Solon contribute to the development of democracy in Athens?

4. How did Pericles change the practice of government in Athens?

Think Critically

5. **Draw Conclusions** Why did the use of the phalanx affect politics?

6. **Compare and Contrast** What is the difference between direct democracy and representative democracy?

7. How did citizens gain power in Athens? Go to your Student Journal to record your answer.

Oligarchy in Sparta

Key Ideas

● Sparta developed an oligarchic government based on military conquest.

● Sparta differed greatly from Athens in terms of education, citizenship, and women's roles.

Key Terms • ephor • helot • military state • barracks

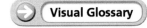 Visual Glossary

Reading Skill Compare and Contrast Take notes using the graphic organizer in your journal.

Statue of the Spartan hero Leonidas ▶

Life was simple in Sparta. Most decisions were made for you. If you were a Spartan boy, the state would take you from your family at the age of seven. You would spend more than 20 years training for and serving in the professional army. If you were a girl, you would be raised for the sole purpose of bearing strong children for the state.

The Spartan State

Other Greeks regarded Sparta with a mix of fear and admiration. Sparta was like a huge army camp. Its government was an odd mixture of monarchy, oligarchy, and democracy. Instead of using coins, the Spartans used iron rods as money. People in city-states such as Athens were amused by Sparta's strange customs. They were also frightened by its growing power.

Government in Sparta As you have read, Sparta was a city-state on the Peloponnesian Peninsula. The center of Sparta was inland, and Sparta was not a sea power. Neither was it a democracy. Sparta was ruled by two kings. The kings served as military leaders. A Spartan army seldom marched into battle without one of its kings as its leader.

The kings headed Sparta's governing body, the council of elders. The council included 28 men over the age of 60. Members were elected for life. This oligarchy was the true government of Sparta.

Sparta did have a democratic assembly made up of some free adult males, but it had only about 9,000 citizens compared to about 45,000 in Athens. The Spartan assembly also had far less power than the

Athenian assembly. It could pass laws, but the council had to approve them.

However, the Spartan assembly did have one important power. It elected five **ephors** (EH forz), who were responsible for the day-to-day operation of the government. They made sure that the kings and the council acted within the limits of Spartan law. Ephors could remove a king who broke the law.

Military Conquests As you have read, to meet its growing need for resources, Sparta turned to conquest.

The Spartans conquered the neighboring city-state of Messenia. Some conquered Messenians became **helots** (HEL uts). The helots belonged not to individual Spartans but to the polis as a whole. They were forced to farm the land and turn over half the food they raised to Sparta. Helots were treated harshly. They were made to wear dogskin caps to show their lowly status.

The helots produced enough food to support the Spartans. As a result, the Spartans did not have to farm for a living. Spartan men were free to become professional warriors.

The Helot Revolts In the early 400s B.C., the helots launched a violent revolt. Although the Spartans put down the revolt, they lived in fear of further unrest. The helots outnumbered them.

The Spartans faced a choice. They could give up control of the helots and the food they produced, or they could strengthen their control by turning Sparta into a military state. A **military state** is a

society organized for the purpose of waging war.

The Spartans chose the second option. Not only did they create a military society, they also tried to control the helots through terror. Every year, the ephors declared war on the helots. This gave any Spartan the right to kill any helot without fear of punishment. At the same time, secret police watched over the helots. Helots who protested might be beaten or even executed.

Reading Check Who were the helots?

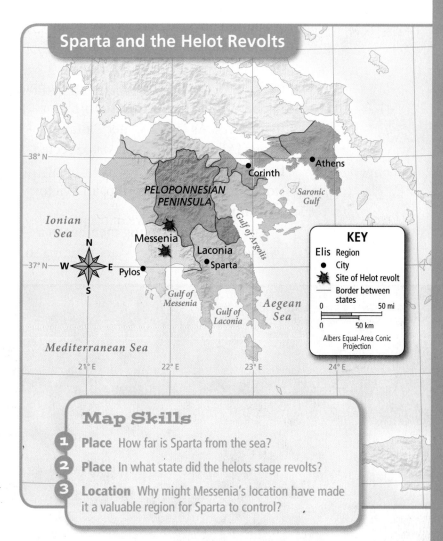

Sparta and the Helot Revolts

Map Skills

1 **Place** How far is Sparta from the sea?

2 **Place** In what state did the helots stage revolts?

3 **Location** Why might Messenia's location have made it a valuable region for Sparta to control?

319

A Disciplined Society

Because of their history of conquest and their need to control the helots, Spartans valued military discipline. Even today, the word *Spartan* means "highly disciplined or lacking in comfort." Unlike Athenians, Spartans did not value luxury goods or beautiful buildings.

Education With the helots working the fields, Spartan males had plenty of time to train for military service. At seven, they were taken away from their homes for schooling at state expense. They lived together in **barracks,** or military housing.

Spartan boys did not receive a well-rounded education. They spent most of their time exercising, hunting, and training with weapons. They were taught to obey orders rather than to think for themselves. As Greek writer Plutarch wrote, "All their education was directed toward prompt obedience to <u>authority</u>, stout endurance of hardship, and victory or death in battle."

At the age of 18, young men began a two-year program of military training to become part of a phalanx. During this time, the trainees could marry, but they were allowed little time for a life at home. Even after the age of 30, when they left the army, they spent most of their time with other men.

Social Classes When they left the school system, Spartan men faced another test. In order to become full citizens, they had to gain entry to a men's club of soldiers. If they failed, they became "inferiors" who would never gain citizenship and would live as outcasts.

Men who won election to a men's club became known as "equals." They had full citizen rights. This included membership in the assembly and the right to a piece of state-owned land worked by helots. At age 60, an equal became a candidate for election to the council of elders.

Role of Women Spartan women were raised to be strong and vigorous. They participated in sports. By staying fit, they could have healthy babies who would grow into good soldiers.

authority, *n.,* people in power

The Pyrrhic Dance
Artist Lawrence Alma-Tadema's painting re-creates a famous Spartan war dance.

320

Spartan women had a good deal of freedom and responsibility because their husbands spent almost their entire lives away at military camp. Spartan women were responsible for raising future soldiers for the state. For these reasons they had greater independence than women had in other Greek city-states.

Sparta and Athens The discipline and training of Spartan life created a powerful army and a stable government. But Spartan society feared individual differences and change. The Spartans valued people who fit in, not those who stood out.

Unlike the Spartans, the Athenians valued individual expression and new ideas. As a result, Athens was open to change. Athenian democracy evolved over time. Sparta's rigid oligarchy and society changed very little. These differences led the Greek historian Thucydides to describe the Athenians as "addicted to innovation." In contrast, he viewed the

Spartans as having "a genius for keeping what you have got." The opposing values of Athens and Sparta helped create tensions between the two city-states. Eventually, their rivalry led to war, as you will read in the next chapter.

Reading Check How did Sparta's rigid society affect the lives of women?

Governments of Athens and Sparta

ATHENS
- Large assembly as main political body
- Members of council chosen at random to serve one-year terms
- Courts run by large citizen-juries

(Overlap)
- Assemblies made up of free adult males
- Governments that included smaller councils

SPARTA
- Government led by two kings
- Smaller and less powerful assembly than in Athens
- Council members elected for life
- Kings and council monitored by ephors

myWorld Activity
Day in Sparta

innovation, *n.*, new ways of doing things

Section 4 Assessment

Essential Question
What is power, and who should have it?

Key Terms
1. Use the following terms to describe government in Sparta: ephor, helot, military state, barracks.

Key Ideas
2. Why did the Spartans fear the Messenians?
3. How was family life different for Spartans and Athenians?
4. What was unusual about Spartan education?

Think Critically
5. **Make Inferences** Why did Sparta become a military society?
6. **Compare Viewpoints** What might have bothered Spartans and Athenians about each other's society?

7. Who held the most power in Spartan society? Go to your Student Journal to record your answer.

Chapter Assessment

Key Terms and Ideas

1. **Summarize** How did physical geography shape early Greek culture?

2. **Discuss** How was the **polis** governed?

3. **Recall** What were some social divisions in Greek society?

4. **Explain** Why did the Spartans need the **helots**?

5. **Summarize** What kind of government developed in Athens?

6. **Compare and Contrast** What is the difference between the **direct democracy** of Athens and the **representative democracy** of the United States?

7. **Explain** What kind of government ruled in Sparta?

8. **Recall** What was the role of the **ephors** in Sparta?

Think Critically

9. **Draw Conclusions** Why did the location of Greek settlements allow contact with other civilizations?

10. **Analyze Cause and Effect** Why did Greek culture spread so rapidly across the Mediterranean Sea and the Black Sea?

11. **Draw Inferences** What conditions allowed the Spartans to create a professional army?

12. **Core Concepts: Migration Basics** How did Greek colonization encourage trade?

Analyze Visuals

13. Study this modern illustration, which shows a politician addressing the Athenian assembly in ancient times. Based on what you have learned about Athenian democracy, explain what is wrong with the picture.

Essential Question

myWorld Chapter Activity

Ask the Oracle Follow your teacher's instructions to take the role of Greek settlers who are migrating to new homes. Using the Activity Cards, along with Sections 1–4 and myworldhistory.com, you will decide where to settle. Then create a skit about taking your plan to the oracle at Delphi to gain approval from the gods.

21st Century Learning

Give an Effective Presentation

With a partner, research Greek colonization. Make a list of which regions were colonized earlier and which regions were colonized later. Then, using a map of the Black Sea and the Mediterranean Sea, explain to the class the different waves of Greek colonization.

Document-Based Questions

Success Tracker™
Online at myworldhistory.com

Use your knowledge of ancient Greece and Documents A and B to answer questions 1–3.

Document A

" It is clear that the polis is a natural growth and that man is by nature a political animal, and a man who is citiless by nature and not by fortune is either low in the scale of humanity or above it, solitary like an isolated piece in chess."

—Aristotle, *Politics*

Document B

" Just because you do not take an interest in politics doesn't mean politics won't take an interest in you."

—Pericles

1. In Document A, the writer believes that
   A human beings do not belong in cities.
   B an individual should not join a group.
   C people are by nature political and belong in communities.
   D it is better to live a solitary life.

2. Document B shows that Pericles believed
   A no one should have political opinions.
   B no one can avoid getting involved in politics.
   C politics has no effect on people's lives.
   D it is better not to take an interest in politics.

3. **Writing Task** What do Documents A and B together reveal about the Greek attitude toward politics?

myworldhistory.com

Self-Test

Ancient Greek Civilization

? Essential Question

How should we handle conflict?

The Parthenon is an ancient Greek temple that overlooks the city of Athens.

? Explore the Essential Question . . .
- at **my worldhistory.com**
- using **the myWorld Chapter Activity**
- with the **Student Journal**

Greek Wars and the Hellenistic Age

490 B.C. Battle of Marathon

431 B.C. Peloponnesian War begins.

334 B.C. Alexander invades Asia.

| 500 B.C. | 450 B.C. | 400 B.C. | 350 B.C. | 300 B.C. |

480 B.C. Battle of Salamis

404 B.C. Athens surrenders, ending the Peloponnesian War.

323 B.C. Alexander dies.

A Prophecy Fulfilled

In 334 B.C., Alexander the Great led his army from Europe into Asia. His troops came from Macedonia and Greece. Alexander wanted to defeat the Persian forces led by Darius III. The two armies met at the Granicus River in present-day Turkey. With 75,000 troops, Darius seemed to have the advantage. Alexander had only 35,000 soldiers. Even so, he felt that he was destined to defeat Darius and conquer Asia. Indeed, his upbringing prepared him to become a great ruler.

Alexander's father was Philip II, the king of Macedonia. His mother was Olympias, a princess from western Greece. Olympias taught Alexander that he was descended from the great warrior Achilles. And Philip convinced his son that Macedonian kings were descended from the god Hercules.

The respected philosopher Aristotle taught the young Alexander. From him, Alexander learned about science, the arts, and politics. While he studied, he also trained in sports and combat. When Alexander's father Philip conquered Greece, Alexander commanded a division in his father's army.

At age 12, Alexander tamed Bucephalus. The name means "ox's head."

myworldhistory.com

Timeline/On Assignment

325

The Greeks perfected the phalanx, a battle formation.

The Persian king Darius faced Alexander in battle three times.

"There is no part of my body remaining free of wounds. I have been wounded with the sword, shot with arrows, and hit with stones for the sake of your lives, your glory, and your wealth."

Philip had wanted to invade Asia, but his plans were cut short when a bodyguard murdered him. So at the age of 20, Alexander became king of Macedonia and Greece. Two years later, he invaded the Persian empire, seeking to be ruler of Asia as well.

At the shores of the Granicus River, Alexander readied his troops for combat. It would be the first of three battles against the Persians. The Greek historian Arrian described how both armies waited at the edge of the river, ready to attack. Alexander inspired his troops, calling for his men to show courage:

66 Alexander leaped upon his steed, ordering those about him to follow, and exhorting [urging] them to show themselves valiant men. 99

The cavalry attacked first, with warriors and horses moving in a phalanx formation. Archers and spear throwers then joined in to support the assault. Next the foot soldiers joined in and dealt the crushing blow. The modern historian Robin Lane Fox describes Alexander's army in combat:

Alexander raised his sword to cut apart the Gordian knot.

Alexander is said to have wept when he looked out over his empire, sad because there were no more worlds to conquer.

66 Nobody who faced them ever forgot the sight; they kept time to their roaring of the Greeks' ancient war cry, Alalalalai; their scarlet cloaks billowed, and the measured swishing of their sarissas [long pikes], up and down, left and right, seemed to frightened observers like the quills of a metal porcupine. 99

The Greeks crushed the Persians. Darius and his troops retreated eastward. Alexander needed more troops, so he set off to find new recruits to join his army. According to legend, on his march Alexander came upon the legendary Gordian knot. This knot was a complex mass of rope that was tied to an ox cart. An ancient prophecy stated that the person who untied the knot would rule Asia. Alexander first tried to undo the huge knot by hand but failed. Frustrated, he drew his sword and quickly cut through the knot with one stroke.

Later, at the battle of Issus, the Greeks were again victorious. Darius escaped, but he offered Alexander a peace treaty. He said he would give Alexander a large sum of money and the Persian lands west of the Euphrates River. Alexander's general Parmenio advised his commander to accept the terms—but Alexander had greater ambitions.

He faced Darius again at Gaugamela. With a third victory here, Alexander took control of much of southwest Asia. It was still not enough—Alexander wanted India.

After eight long years of marching and fighting, the army reached the western border of India. However, by then Alexander's troops had become homesick and wanted to turn back.

Alexander reluctantly agreed to return to Macedonia, but he would not make it home. He died of a mysterious illness at Babylon in 323 B.C.

Alexander's empire stretched from Macedonia and Greece in the west to the borders of India in the east. This region included much of the world that was known to the ancient Greeks. Indeed, from the Greek point of view, the prophecy of the Gordian knot had come true.

Based on this story, how well do you think the Greeks handled conflict? As you read the chapter ahead, think about what Alexander's story tells you about ancient Greek civilization.

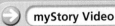
myStory Video

Join Alexander the Great as he conquers a vast empire.

my worldhistory.com

myStory Video

War in Ancient Greece

Key Ideas
- Greek city-states cooperated to defeat a threat from the mighty Persian empire.
- After the Persian Wars, Athens became the dominant Greek city-state.
- Rivalry between Athens and Sparta led to a series of wars that weakened all of Greece.

Key Terms
- Battle of Marathon
- Battle of Salamis
- Delian League
- Peloponnesian League

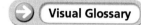 Visual Glossary

Reading Skill Compare and Contrast Take notes using the graphic organizer in your journal.

Warfare was frequent in ancient Greece. The quarrelsome city-states battled one another over land and resources. In addition to all their minor conflicts, the Greeks fought three major wars in the 400s B.C. Twice they united long enough to defeat the Persian empire. But these periods of unity were brief. By the late 400s B.C., the Greeks were fighting a destructive war among themselves.

The Persian Wars

After 546 B.C., Persia conquered the Greek city-states of Ionia in western Asia. The Ionian city-states were used to governing themselves, so they rebelled in 500 B.C. To help them, Athenian soldiers burned the Persian city of Sardis. This enraged Darius, the Persian king. After his troops recaptured the Ionian cities, Darius set out to conquer Greece.

Darius Invades Greece In 490 B.C., about 20,000 Persian soldiers sailed for Greece. They landed by the plain of Marathon, near Athens. This flat plain seemed like the perfect battleground for the Persian cavalry, or soldiers on horseback.

Although Athenian infantry, or foot soldiers, rushed to Marathon, their situation looked hopeless. The Athenians were outnumbered by about two to one. Also, unlike the Persians, they had no archers or cavalry.

A Greek warrior (on the right) defeats a Persian soldier in this scene painted about ten years after the Second Persian War.▼

328

Despite these disadvantages, the Athenians attacked the day after the Persian landing. At dawn, Greek phalanxes raced across the plain, taking the Persians by surprise. In panic, the Persians fled to their ships. The unexpected Greek victory at the **Battle of Marathon** ended the First Persian War. In ancient times, a legend told of a messenger who died after running 26 miles to carry the news of the victory back to Athens. Ever since then, the word "marathon" has been used to describe a challenging footrace.

Xerxes Attacks Darius died before he could launch another attack. But his son, Xerxes (ZURK seez), was determined to defeat the Greeks, and began the Second Persian War.

In 480 B.C., Xerxes assembled an invasion force of about 100,000 men. The Persian empire was the superpower of its day. Because it controlled Egypt, Persia was able to add the Egyptian army to its ranks. Although the Persians did not have a navy, they used the ships of the Phoeni-

cians, who were part of their empire. The Greek historian Herodotus wrote:

> 66 The army was indeed immense—far greater than any other in recorded history. . . . There was not a nation in Asia that he did not take with him against Greece. 99
> —Herodotus, *The Histories*

The Spartans moved north to block the huge army. Led by King Leonidas, a small Spartan force stopped the Persians at a narrow mountain pass called Thermopylae (thur MAHP uh lee). The Spartans held off the invaders for days. Then, a Greek traitor showed the Persians another path through the mountains. Attacked from both sides, the Spartans died heroically, in defense of Greece.

Victory for Athens With no Greek army to stop them, the Persians now advanced on Athens. The Athenian leader Themistocles (thuh MIS tuh kleez) convinced Athenians to flee to nearby islands. When the Persians reached Athens, they found the city almost empty.

Ancient Warriors, a painting by Georges Rochegrosse, shows an attack by Greek soldiers. ▼

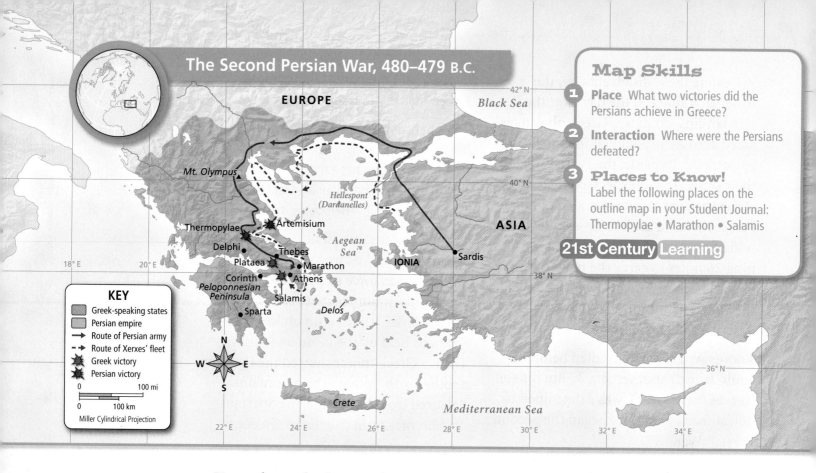

The Second Persian War, 480–479 B.C.

EUROPE

Black Sea

Mt. Olympus

Hellespont
(Dardanelles)

Thermopylae
Artemisium

Delphi

Thebes

Aegean
Sea

ASIA

Plataea

Marathon

Corinth
Peloponnesian
Peninsula

Athens

Salamis

IONIA

Sardis

Sparta

Delos

Crete

Mediterranean Sea

KEY
- Greek-speaking states
- Persian empire
- → Route of Persian army
- ⇢ Route of Xerxes' fleet
- ✹ Greek victory
- ✹ Persian victory

0 — 100 mi
0 — 100 km
Miller Cylindrical Projection

Map Skills

1 **Place** What two victories did the Persians achieve in Greece?

2 **Interaction** Where were the Persians defeated?

3 **Places to Know!** Label the following places on the outline map in your Student Journal: Thermopylae • Marathon • Salamis

21st Century Learning

pursue, *v.,* to chase

Xerxes burned Athens and sent his ships to <u>pursue</u> the Greek navy. The Persians had 1,200 warships—three times more ships than the Greeks. Confident of victory, Xerxes had his throne placed on a hill to watch the naval battle in the Strait of Salamis.

But Themistocles had set a trap. He kept his Greek ships hidden until Persian ships filled the narrow strait. Suddenly, the Greeks attacked. They rammed the crowded Persian ships, splintering their hulls. By nightfall, the strait was clogged with more than 200 broken Persian ships. The Greeks lost only about 40 ships. The **Battle of Salamis** broke Persian naval power. After another defeat for Xerxes on land, the Persians returned home.

Reading Check What naval battle helped end the Second Persian War?

Athens Rivals Sparta

After defeating the Persians at Salamis, Athens enjoyed a "golden age." The Athenian leader Pericles began rebuilding the city, which became famous for its art and learning. The wealth and power of the city increased.

However, trouble was brewing. Greece now had two rival powers—Athens, with the strongest navy, and Sparta, with the strongest army. Each wanted to be the supreme power in Greece. Their rivalry would lead to deadly conflict.

The Delian League Soon after the Persian wars, Athens formed an alliance with other city-states. An alliance is an association of nations formed to achieve a goal. The members of an alliance are called allies. Because Athens and its allies met together on the island of Delos, their alliance was called the **Delian League.** Members promised to protect one another from Persia and provide ships or money for defense. This money was kept in the League's treasury on Delos.

The Delian League had about 150 members. All of the allies were supposed to be equal. However, Athens was by far the most powerful member. Athenian ships protected Greek traders and travelers. By building an alliance of city-states that bordered the Aegean Sea, Athens was able to protect its grain supply that came from the Black Sea.

Athens ran the Delian League as if it were its own empire rather than an alliance of equals. The Athenians brought some cities into the League by force and blocked others from leaving. When Naxos tried to leave, Athens attacked the city-state and forced it to stay.

The arrogant behavior of the Athenians angered other League members. Rather than asking city-states to contribute ships, Athens requested money. Athens used the money to build its navy. It continued to collect these funds even when there was no fighting with Persia. Athens also forced League members to use Athenian <u>currency</u> instead of their own.

In 454 B.C., Athenian leaders moved the League's treasury from Delos to Athens. Soon after, money from League members was used to rebuild Athens. Some of this money went to constructing the Parthenon, the great temple to Athena that stood on the Acropolis. Other members of the Delian League came to resent this use of the League's funds.

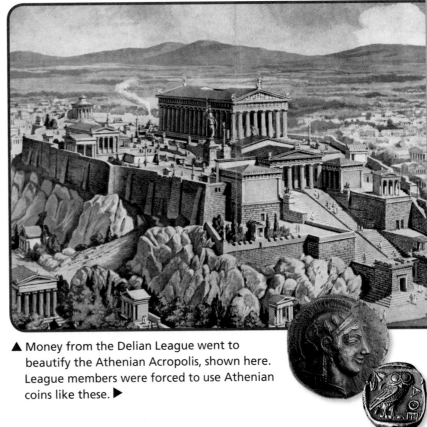

▲ Money from the Delian League went to beautify the Athenian Acropolis, shown here. League members were forced to use Athenian coins like these. ▶

The Peloponnesian League The Spartans had already formed their own alliance on the Peloponnesian Peninsula. It is known today as the **Peloponnesian League.** Like Sparta, other members of the Peloponnesian League feared the power of Athens and its style of government. In contrast to democratic Athens, Sparta and most of its allies were oligarchies.

In 433 B.C., Sparta's Peloponnesian League and Athens's Delian League came into conflict. That year, Athens placed a ban on trade with Megara, a member of the Peloponnesian League. This angered Sparta and its allies, who prepared for war. Athens and its allies did the same. Both sides were confident of a quick and easy victory.

Reading Check Why did Athens form the Delian League?

currency, *n.*, money

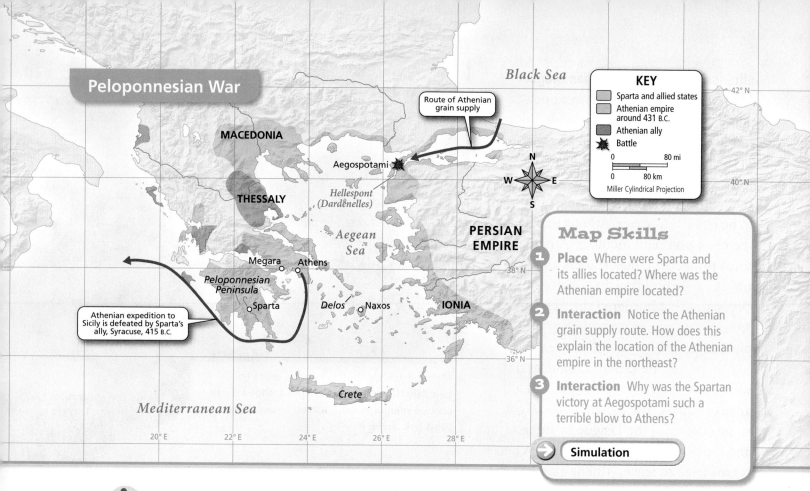

Peloponnesian War

Black Sea

MACEDONIA

Route of Athenian grain supply

Aegospotami

THESSALY

Hellespont
(Dardenelles)

Aegean
Sea

PERSIAN
EMPIRE

Megara   Athens

Peloponnesian
Peninsula

Athenian expedition to
Sicily is defeated by Sparta's
ally, Syracuse, 415 B.C.

Sparta

Delos   Naxos

IONIA

Mediterranean Sea

Crete

20° E   22° E   24° E   26° E   28° E

42° N

40° N

38° N

36° N

KEY

Sparta and allied states

Athenian empire
around 431 B.C.

Athenian ally

Battle

0   80 mi

0   80 km

Miller Cylindrical Projection

Map Skills

1 **Place** Where were Sparta and its allies located? Where was the Athenian empire located?

2 **Interaction** Notice the Athenian grain supply route. How does this explain the location of the Athenian empire in the northeast?

3 **Interaction** Why was the Spartan victory at Aegospotami such a terrible blow to Athens?

→ Simulation

myWorld Activity
Interview a Warrior

The Peloponnesian War

War between the two Greek alliances broke out in 431 B.C. Known as the Peloponnesian War, the conflict lasted on and off for 27 years.

The Siege of Athens The Peloponnesian War began when an army led by Sparta marched into Athenian territory. Pericles, the leader of Athens, instructed farmers living in the Athenian countryside to move inside the walled city for safety.

The Spartans settled down around Athens for a long siege. The goal of a siege is to force the enemy to surrender by cutting off its food and other supplies. Athenians had prepared for just such an event, however. They had built two long walls to line the four-mile road that connected Athens to its port city. While these Long Walls stood, Athenians could receive supplies by sea.

Supplied with food by ship, the Athenians held out for more than a year. Then, a plague, or contagious disease, broke out in the overcrowded city. Thousands of people died in Athens. Among the dead was Pericles, who had led Athens during its golden age. To avoid catching the disease themselves, the Spartans left the region around Athens.

However, the war dragged on. Sparta, with its powerful army, and Athens, with its strong navy, found it difficult to defeat each other. Athens sent ships to attack Spartan-allied cities in Sicily, an island that is now part of Italy. Sparta seemed near defeat until it won some important victories. In 421 B.C., both sides agreed to a truce, or an agreement to stop fighting, while they discussed peace terms.

Athens Surrenders Within a few years, however, the truce was broken. Athens launched another invasion of Sicily. With help from Sparta, the Greeks of Sicily destroyed the Athenian forces. Athens lost a large part of its navy at Syracuse.

Athens was now desperately weakened. The Persians saw a chance to deal Athens a fatal blow. They gave money to Sparta so it could build its own powerful navy. With this new fleet, Sparta defeated the Athenian navy at the Battle of Aegospotami in 404 B.C. After that, the Spartans attacked Athens itself.

Once again, the Athenians resisted. But with its new navy, Sparta was able to keep food from reaching Athens by sea. Without a food supply, the Athenians began to starve. The following year, the city of Athens was forced to surrender.

The peace terms were harsh. The Athenians were forced to demolish the Long Walls. Sparta even made the Athenians give up their democratic government.

Although democracy was soon restored, Athens had lost its power.

The Peloponnesian War hurt all the city-states. Thousands of Greeks were slaughtered. Cities were destroyed. Governments fell. Trade dropped. Yet, the constant feuding of the city-states continued. Throughout the 300s, the Greeks persisted in fighting amongst themselves, ignoring the growing threat of powerful Macedonia—a northern kingdom that would soon unite them by force.

Reading Check **Why did Athens lose the Peloponnesian War?**

Gravestone of a young Athenian soldier. The curved ship's prow suggests he died at sea. ▼

Section 1 Assessment

Essential Question

How should we handle conflict?

Key Terms

1. Use the following terms to describe war in ancient Greece: Battle of Marathon, Battle of Salamis, Delian League, Peloponnesian League.

Key Ideas

2. Why did Persia invade Greece?

3. How did Athens become so powerful?

4. How did Pericles react to the Spartan invasion as the Peloponnesian War began?

Think Critically

5. **Compare Viewpoints** Why did other Greek city-states resent Athens's power?

6. **Draw Conclusions** Why was it so difficult for Athens and Sparta to defeat each other?

7. Why were the Greeks able to unite during the Persian Wars? Go to your Student Journal to record your answer.

Section 2
Alexander's Empire

Key Ideas

- The Macedonian rulers Philip and Alexander conquered the Greek city-states and united Greece.
- Alexander the Great went on to conquer an empire stretching from Egypt to India.
- Alexander's empire helped spread Greek culture across a wide area.

Key Terms • sarissa • Alexandria • Hellenistic

 Visual Glossary

Reading Skill Sequence Take notes using the graphic organizer in your journal.

Alexander and Bucephalus in the midst of a battle, from a mosaic found in the Roman city of Pompeii ▼

The Greeks told a story about Alexander the Great, the young man who set out to conquer the world. The story begins one afternoon as 12-year-old Alexander, the prince of Macedonia, watched his father, King Philip II, barter over a horse. It was a fine black stallion, but it was also angry and unruly. The king decided that the horse could not be tamed. As the king turned away, Alexander grabbed the reins. Alexander sensed that the horse's wildness was caused by fear. He turned the horse to face the sun so that it would no longer be frightened by its own shadow. Alexander quickly calmed and mounted the horse, to everyone's astonishment. The king bought the horse for Alexander, who named him Bucephalus. Bucephalus never allowed anyone else to ride him. He carried Alexander into many battles as the young Macedonian fought for world conquest.

The Rise of Macedonia

Macedonia was a land in the north of the Greek peninsula. The Macedonians had their own traditions, which the Greeks considered old-fashioned. Unlike most Greek city-states, the Macedonians were still governed by kings. Despite their different customs, the Macedonians were influenced by Greek culture.

Philip of Macedonia Macedonia was briefly part of the Persian empire. But after Persia's defeat during Xerxes' invasion of Greece, the Macedonians regained their independence. Their kingdom expanded over the lands north of Greece.

One of the rulers of Macedonia was a brilliant and ambitious leader named Philip. Philip gained power after his brother, the Macedonian king, was killed in battle in 359 B.C. The king's son, who was heir to the throne, was only an infant. So the nobles of Macedonia elected Philip as king.

To strengthen his power, Philip built up a powerful army and developed new tactics. Like the Greeks, Philip organized his infantry into phalanxes. Then he armed each man with an 18-foot-long pike. The Macedonian pike, or **sarissa,** was much longer than the spears used by the Greeks. It gave the Macedonians an advantage in battle, as the Macedonian pikes could be used to keep enemies at a greater distance. Philip also trained his men to change directions in battle without losing formation. Armed with long pikes and fighting with greater discipline, Philip's soldiers were an powerful force.

Philip proved the value of his ideas soon after becoming king. His powerful army defeated the Illyrians, who had won a victory over the Macedonians just a few months before.

Philip Conquers Greece Philip then turned to conquer Greece. First, he tried to win the loyalty of each city-state with diplomacy. When these tactics failed, he went to war.

In 338 B.C., Philip, along with his son Alexander, who led the cavalry, won a decisive battle in central Greece over the combined armies of Thebes and Athens. Philip gained control of all of Greece. The city-states were allowed to keep their governments. However, they were expected to support Philip in his next goal—a war against Persia. But as preparations were being made for the invasion of Asia, Philip was assassinated, or murdered, during his daughter's wedding.

Reading Check How did Philip strengthen his power?

myWorld Activity
Alexander's Bio

Ivory portrait of Philip of Macedonia ▼

Philip's new weapon helped him win battles. The long Macedonian pike meant that the enemy could not easily attack his troops head-on. ▼

335

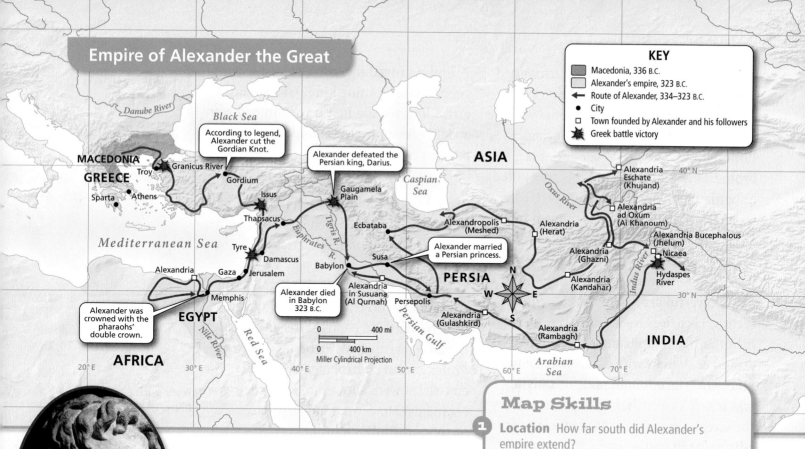

Empire of Alexander the Great

KEY

Macedonia, 336 B.C.

Alexander's empire, 323 B.C.

Route of Alexander, 334–323 B.C.

• City

□ Town founded by Alexander and his followers

✴ Greek battle victory

Danube River

Black Sea

MACEDONIA

GREECE

Troy Granicus River

Gordium

According to legend, Alexander cut the Gordian Knot.

Sparta Athens

Thapsacus

Issus

Alexander defeated the Persian king, Darius.

Gaugamela Plain

ASIA

Caspian Sea

Oxus River

Alexandria Eschate (Khujand)

Alexandria ad Oxum (Ai Khanoum)

40° N

Mediterranean Sea

Tyre

Damascus

Euphrates R.

Tigris R.

Ecbataba

Alexandropolis (Meshed)

Alexandria (Herat)

Alexandria (Ghazni)

Alexandria Bucephalous (Jhelum)

Nicaea

Alexandria

Gaza Jerusalem

Babylon

Susa

Alexander married a Persian princess.

PERSIA

N

Indus River

Hydaspes River

30° N

Alexander was crowned with the pharaohs' double crown.

Memphis

EGYPT

Alexander died in Babylon 323 B.C.

Alexandria in Susuana (Al Qurnah)

Persepolis

Persian Gulf

W E

S

Alexandria (Kandahar)

Alexandria (Gulashkird)

Alexandria (Rambagh)

INDIA

AFRICA

Nile River

Red Sea

0   400 mi

0   400 km

Miller Cylindrical Projection

Arabian Sea

20° E   30° E   40° E   50° E   60° E   70° E

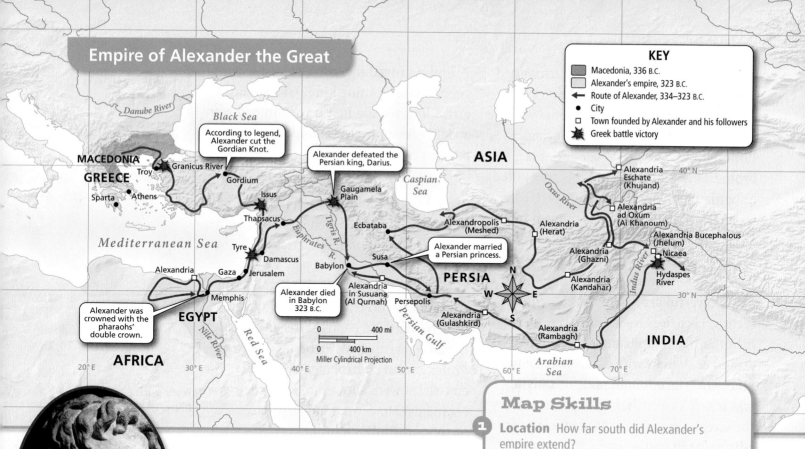

▲ As this portrait shows, Alexander was the first Greek ruler to shave his beard—a fashion that lasted 500 years!

Alexander's Conquests

Alexander, Philip's 20-year-old son, now gained the throne. Alexander was already a military leader. His brilliant mind had been shaped by the famous scientist and philosopher, Aristotle. Alexander was filled with dreams of glory. As a boy, Alexander's favorite book was a copy of the *Iliad* that Aristotle had given to him. Alexander wanted to be like the book's hero, Achilles. This ambition would inspire his spectacular conquests.

Securing Greece Alexander's first task was to secure control of Greece. After Philip's death, some city-states in Greece tried to regain their independence. Alexander quickly crushed these revolts. To discourage future rebellions, he burned Thebes to the ground.

Map Skills

1 **Location** How far south did Alexander's empire extend?

2 **Interaction** Was Alexander ever defeated?

3 **Interaction** Across which three continents did Alexander's empire stretch?

With Greece secure, Alexander turned eastward. In 334 B.C., he took his army of 30,000 foot soldiers and 5,500 cavalry troops into Asia. Alexander inspired fierce loyalty among his soldiers by personally leading them in battle.

World Conquest In Asia, Alexander freed the Ionian city-states from Persian rule. He marched south to capture the cities along the Mediterranean coast. Then the army marched to Egypt. The Egyptians welcomed Alexander for liberating them from the Persians. Before leaving Egypt, he founded the city of **Alexandria** on the edge of the Nile delta.

From Egypt, Alexander headed back toward Persia. By the end of 330 B.C., he had defeated the Persian king.

Alexander was not satisfied with the defeat of the Persian empire. His eyes were fixed on a greater goal—world conquest. He led his army farther east, into Afghanistan and India. These were lands no Greek had ever seen. Because he built a vast empire in only 11 years, people called him "Alexander the Great."

But Alexander's luck was turning. After his last major battle in what is now Pakistan, his beloved horse Bucephalus died of battle wounds. Soon after, his army mutinied and refused to conquer any more lands. The army headed west. In 323 B.C., Alexander died of a fever in Babylon. He was not quite 33 years old.

Alexander's infant son was too young to take control of the empire. So Alexander's generals divided the empire into kingdoms. One kingdom, in Egypt, was ruled by a general named Ptolemy. The family of Ptolemy ruled Egypt for nearly three hundred years. Cleopatra was the last member of this family to rule Egypt.

A New World Alexander founded Greek-style cities everywhere he went. In these cities, Greek customs mingled with the ideas and art of other lands. Out of this exchange emerged a new form of Greek culture called **Hellenistic,** or Greek-like. The word *Hellenistic* comes from the Greeks' word for themselves: Hellenes.

The Hellenistic <u>period</u> lasted from Alexander's time until about 30 B.C. Because of Alexander, Greek culture spread all the way to India. Alexander's empire was short-lived, but the world was forever changed by his conquests.

Reading Check Why was Alexander's empire so short-lived?

period, *n.,* a span of time

In the Hellenistic period, power and wealth shifted to Greek cities like Pergamum in Asia. ▼

Section 2 Assessment

? **Essential Question**

How should we handle conflict?

Key Terms

1. Use the following terms to describe Alexander's empire: sarissa, Alexandria, Hellenistic.

Key Ideas

2. How did Philip reorganize his army?

3. How did Alexander's conquest help create Hellenistic culture?

4. What happened to Alexander's empire?

Think Critically

5. **Draw Inferences** Why did Alexander burn Thebes to the ground?

6. **Draw Conclusions** Why do you think Alexander's empire broke apart so quickly after his death?

7. Why did the Greeks rebel after Philip's death? Go to your Student Journal to record your answer.

Ancient Greek Beliefs and Arts

Key Ideas
- Ancient Greek religion was based on a belief in many gods.
- Greek art and architecture have remained influential to the present day.
- Greek writers contributed to the development of lyric poetry and drama.

Key Terms
- polytheism
- mythology
- Olympic games
- Delphic oracle
- lyric poetry
- chorus

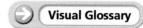 **Visual Glossary**

Reading Skill Identify Main Ideas and Details Take notes using the graphic organizer in your journal.

▲ A furious Athena changes Arachne into a spider.

Greek children grew up hearing many stories about their gods. In one tale, a proud girl named Arachne boasts that her weaving skills are better than those of the goddess Athena. Athena challenges Arachne to a weaving competition. When Arachne creates a tapestry, or cloth with pictures, that mocks the gods, Athena is furious. The goddess changes the girl into a spider, condemned to weave webs forever. The Greeks told the story of Arachne as a warning against the sin of excessive pride.

Greek Religion and Mythology

The ancient Greeks practiced **polytheism,** the worship of many gods, or deities. A deity is a being with supernatural powers. Unlike the gods of Egypt, however, Greek gods looked—and behaved—like human beings.

Greek Mythology Greeks expressed their religious beliefs in their mythology. **Mythology** is the collection of myths or stories that people tell about their gods and heroes.

Some myths explained the changing of the seasons. Others revealed why so much suffering exists in the world. Many myths explained human behavior or taught moral lessons. Some told the stories of heroes, such as Hercules, who had amazing strength.

Greek myths and stories are still read and retold today. The myths reveal important truths about human nature and why people act in certain ways. These ancient stories also describe entertaining adventures.

Many Gods and Goddesses Zeus was the supreme ruler of the gods, as well as the lord of the sky and the god of rain. He lived on Mount Olympus and threw thunderbolts at those who displeased him. His wife, Hera, protected married women and their households.

Zeus had two brothers. The first, Poseidon, was god of the sea. His anger made the earth shake and the seas churn. Zeus's other brother, Hades, did not live on Olympus. He ruled and lived in the underworld, which was inhabited by the souls of the dead.

Other major gods included Apollo, god of the arts, prophecy, and healing, and Ares, god of war. Aphrodite was goddess of love and beauty, and the goddess Demeter oversaw farming and the harvest.

Athena was a popular goddess because, according to one myth, she had given the Greeks the gift of the olive tree. Athena was also the guardian of the city of Athens. When the Greeks fought against other peoples, they believed Athena would appear to help them.

Greek gods and goddesses behaved like human beings. They fell in love, got married, and had children. They liked to celebrate and play tricks. They also felt jealousy and rage.

Greek Religion and Life The Greeks honored their gods with public and private religious rituals. Public meetings began with prayers and animal sacrifices. Women played important roles in some of these public ceremonies. In private homes, families maintained household shrines, where they honored their favorite gods or goddesses.

Each city-state built temples to its patron deity. On holy days, citizens made sacrifices in front of the gods' temples. People offered gold, cakes and wine, or prized animals such as bulls. They asked the gods for favors, such as good crops or good health.

Greek plate showing Apollo or Helios driving the chariot of the sun. ▼

The Twelve Olympian Gods	
Zeus	Father of many of the other gods; bringer of storms; god of justice
Hera	Wife of Zeus and queen of the gods; goddess of marriage
Athena	Daughter of Zeus; goddess of wisdom and protector of cities
Apollo	God of prophecy, music, and poetry; god of light
Artemis	Twin sister of Apollo; goddess of hunting and childbirth
Poseidon	Brother of Zeus; god of the sea
Ares	God of war
Aphrodite	Goddess of love and beauty
Hermes	Messenger of the gods; patron of merchants; protector of travelers
Demeter	Goddess of agriculture and the harvest
Hephaestus	God of fire and of craftworkers
Hestia	Goddess of the hearth

▲ At Olympia, the Olympic flame is passed to a modern athlete, to mark the start of the 2004 Games.

cease, v., to stop

Athletic Contests Some religious festivals included athletic contests. Athletes competed in boxing, wrestling, and running as well as in throwing the javelin and discus. They displayed their skill and strength to honor the gods.

The leading competitions brought together athletes from many city-states. The most famous sports event was the **Olympic games**, which honored Zeus. These games took place every four years. During the games, all conflicts between city-states <u>ceased</u>. Travelers came from all over the Mediterranean to attend the games. The festival site at Olympia was crowded with merchants, food sellers, and artisans. Winners became celebrities, or famous people. Successful athletes were rewarded not with money but with privileges and fame.

Sacred Sites The Greeks considered groves of trees, springs, and other places to be sacred because they were home to a god or spirit. Mount Olympus, in northern Greece, was an important sacred spot. The Greeks believed it was home to the major gods.

Another sacred site was Delphi, on the slopes of Mount Parnassus. Delphi contained many shrines, but the most important building was the holy temple of the god Apollo. The temple of Apollo housed Apollo's priestess, who was known as the **Delphic oracle.** An oracle is someone who predicts what will happen in the future. People traveled to Delphi from all over Greece and other lands to ask the priestess questions about the future. Many left confused, however, because the oracle answered with puzzling statements or riddles that could be interpreted in several ways.

Reading Check Why are the stories of ancient Greece still influential today?

The Arts of Ancient Greece

The Greeks had a strong appreciation of beauty. They expressed this in their painting, sculpture, and architecture. Even ordinary objects such as vases and jugs were carefully designed. Although most of their paintings have not survived, Greek statues and buildings have been admired for generations.

Painting From the descriptions of ancient writers, we know that ancient painting was realistic. Painters created an impression of depth and perspective in their work.

THE ARCHITECTURAL ORDERS

American buildings reveal the influence of ancient Greek architecture. Study the three styles or "orders" below. Then identify which order appears in the Lincoln Memorial (left) and the Supreme Court (right). *Can you think of any buildings in your neighborhood in which these styles appear?*

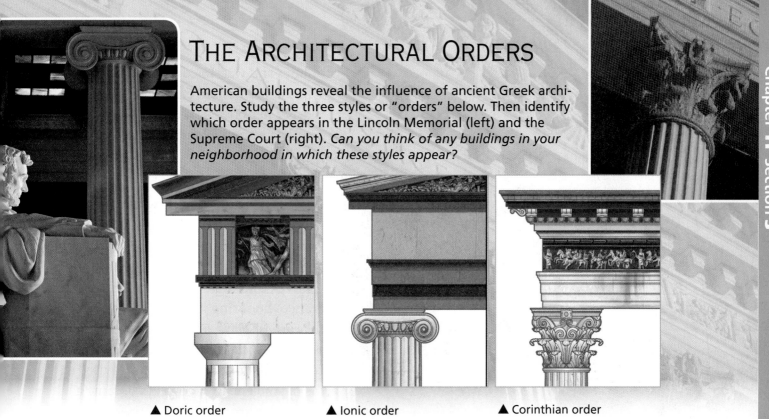

▲ Doric order   ▲ Ionic order   ▲ Corinthian order

Sculpture Early Greek sculpture shows strong Egyptian influence. However, Greek sculptors gradually developed a style that was much more realistic than any other sculpture in the ancient world. At the same time, Greek sculptors created images of humans and deities that seemed to inhabit an ideal world of calm and peace. They often used this ideal style to decorate their temples and gravestones.

The Greeks honored their deities by creating huge statues of gods and goddesses for shrines and temples. They also carved scenes to decorate temple walls.

Architecture Like Greek sculpture, Greek architecture was inspired by the proportions of the human body. Architects also tried to achieve perfection in their work. They created buildings that gave a sense of balance and harmony of parts. The finest example of classical Greek architecture is the temple known as the Parthenon, built to honor Athena. The architects Ictinus and Callicrates designed graceful marble columns to support the roof. Above the columns, bands of sculptures showed images of gods and humans. Inside the temple stood a giant statue of the goddess Athena, designed by the sculptor Phidias.

People today think of Greek buildings and statues as dazzling white marble. In ancient times, however, these works would have been painted. Statues would have had colored eyes, skin, and hair, making them appear startlingly real. Over time, however, the ancient colors have faded.

Reading Check What makes Greek sculpture unique?

my World CONNECTIONS

Ancient Greek architecture has influenced the design of many American government buildings.

▲ In a modern performance of the Greek play *Antigone*, Antigone heroically defies the tyrant of the city.

myWorld Activity
Greek Art Mural

Literature

Like the other arts, Greek literature was linked with religion. Religious festivals often included contests between poets. Others included plays based on myths. The *Iliad* and the *Odyssey*, Homer's great epic poems, reflected the Greeks' belief that the gods controlled human lives.

submission, *n.,* obedience

Lyric Poetry Some Greek poets who came after Homer wrote shorter poems. Performers often sang these poems while playing a stringed instrument known as a lyre. As a result, these poetic songs became known as **lyric poetry.**

Greeks wrote lyric poetry on many different subjects. Pindar praised victorious athletes while Alcaeus wrote about politics and war. In contrast, Sappho wrote about human emotions. Although most of her poetry has been lost, she was greatly admired in ancient times.

Greek Drama The roots of modern Western theater reach back to ancient Greece. The word *drama*, which means a play or performance on stage, is a Greek word. The words *theater, tragedy, comedy,* and *scene* also come from Greek.

Greek drama developed from performances honoring the god Dionysus. In the earliest plays, a few individual actors performed the character roles. The **chorus** commented on the action and advised the characters. In time, plays became a central feature at festivals. Prizes were awarded for the best play, the best chorus, and the best actor.

Greek dramatists wrote two types of plays: tragedy and comedy. The plot of a tragedy often came from mythology or Homer's epics. Tragedies often traced the downfall of heroic figures caught in violent conflict with their family, their city, or the gods. In the tragedy *Antigone* by Sophocles, the chorus offers the audience this advice:

> 66 There is no happiness where there is no wisdom;
> No wisdom but in submission to the gods.
> Big words are always punished,
> And proud men in old age learn to be wise. 99
>
> —Sophocles, *Antigone*

Two other famous authors of Greek tragedies are Aeschylus and Euripides. Theater groups still stage some of the tragedies of these dramatists. In addition, modern playwrights continue to draw inspiration from the plots and themes of ancient Greek tragedies.

Greek comedies ended happily. They dealt with current events and made amusing observations about Greek culture, society, and politicians. Aristophanes was perhaps the most famous comic playwright. Two of his comedies that are still performed today are *The Frogs* and *Lysistrata*.

Aesop's Fables Another lasting form of Greek literature is the fable, a story that teaches a moral lesson. The most famous of these fables are by Aesop. According to some legends, Aesop was a slave who lived on the Greek island of Samos during the 500s B.C. Freed as a reward for his learning, Aesop traveled widely, collecting and retelling his fables.

Many of Aesop's fables are still familiar. Some have even contributed expressions to our language today. One fable told of a boy who falsely claimed many times that a wolf was attacking his sheep. His lies angered his neighbors. When a wolf really did come and the boy called for help, no one rushed to his aid. The moral was to avoid "crying wolf," or spreading false alarms.

Another tale about a tortoise and a hare shows the Greeks' love of athletic competition. In this fable, a hare mocked the slow speed of a tortoise. So the tortoise challenged the hare to a race. The hare was so confident of winning that he took a nap. When he awoke, the tortoise had won. The moral: "Slow and steady wins the race!"

Reading Check **What were the two main types of Greek drama?**

Illustration of one of Aesop's fables, showing the race between the tortoise and the hare ▼

Section 3 Assessment

Key Terms

1. Use the following terms to describe ancient Greek beliefs and arts: polytheism, mythology, Olympic games, Delphic oracle, lyric poetry, chorus.

Key Ideas

2. What human characteristics can you recognize in the ancient Greek gods?

3. What was the most famous sports competition in ancient Greece?

4. How did Greek drama develop?

Think Critically

5. **Synthesize** What were some things that the Greeks admired?

6. **Draw Conclusions** Why are Greek myths and dramas still important to us today?

Essential Question

How should we handle conflict?

7. What sort of conflicts did Greek drama explore? Go to your Student Journal to record your answer.

Ancient Greek Learning

Key Ideas

- Greek scholars made important contributions in both philosophy and history.
- The ancient Greeks pioneered scientific and medical discoveries by examining nature.
- Greek learning continued to grow and spread during the Hellenistic age.

Key Terms • Socratic method • Academy • hypothesis • Hippocratic oath

 Visual Glossary

 Reading Skill Summarize Take notes using the graphic organizer in your journal.

If you had sailed to Alexandria, Egypt, in ancient times, you might have arrived by night. Your ship would have been guided into harbor by the Great Lighthouse, one of the wonders of the ancient world. From the ship's deck, you would have gazed on a coastline of white marble palaces and temples glowing in the moonlight. As you stepped ashore, you might also have glimpsed the roofline of another wonder of the city—the Great Library, the largest library of its time.

Alexandria, founded by Alexander the Great, quickly became the most magnificent city of the ancient world. Its museum and library attracted scholars from many lands. The ancient Greeks had made important advances in many fields of knowledge. The Great Library was built to protect all the progress that had been made in the fields of history, science, mathematics, medicine, and philosophy.

Greek Philosophy

As you read earlier, Chinese thinkers were among the world's first philosophers. Their goal was to pursue wisdom. Greek philosophers had the same goal. In fact, the word *philosophy* comes from Greek words meaning "love of wisdom."

The Importance of Reason The Greeks began their search for wisdom by asking questions similar to those the Chinese asked, such as: "What is the nature of the universe? What is a good life?"

◀ The Great Lighthouse at Alexandria

The Greeks, however, took their search a step further. They also asked: "How do we know what is real? How can we determine what is true?"

The Greeks believed that they could answer these questions by using the human power of reason. Reason is the power to think clearly. To increase their thinking power, the Greeks developed a system of reasoning known as logic. Logic involves a step-by-step method of thinking through a problem or question.

Socrates and Plato Several important philosophers lived in Athens. One of them, Socrates, wandered around the city, drawing other Athenians into discussion. In these discussions, Socrates asked question after question to force his listeners to think more clearly. Today, this question-and-answer method of teaching is called the **Socratic method** and is used to instruct students in a variety of subjects.

Socrates' discussions challenged accepted beliefs. Eventually, this got him into trouble with the leaders of Athens. They charged him with corrupting the young. Socrates was also accused of not believing in the gods that the city recognized. In the trial that followed, Socrates defended himself:

> 66 I have never set up as any man's teacher. But if anyone, young or old, is eager to hear me . . . I never grudge [deny] him the opportunity. . . . If any given one of these people becomes a good citizen or a bad one, I cannot fairly be held responsible. 99
> —Socrates, quoted in Plato's *Apology*

▲ *The Death of Socrates* by Jacques-Louis David shows the execution of Socrates by poison.

Fairly or not, Socrates was found guilty and sentenced to death in 399 B.C.

Plato, a student of Socrates, recorded his teacher's ideas in a series of conversations called dialogues. Plato went on to found a school of philosophy called the **Academy.** Today, the word *academy* often means a school of higher learning. Plato was interested in the nature of reality. He remains one of the most influential thinkers in history.

Stoicism During the Hellenistic period, new philosophies arose. One group, founded by Zeno, was called the Stoics.

To the Stoics, divine reason governed the universe. So people needed to live in harmony with nature. Stoics tried to master their emotions through self-control.

Reading Check What is the Socratic method?

History and Politics

The Greeks' search for wisdom also led them to study the past. Greek historians did more than record events, however. Most importantly, they examined why these events took place.

Greek Historians The Greek writer Herodotus is often called "the father of history" because he asked why certain events happened. Born about 484 B.C., Herodotus lived during the Second Persian War, described in Section 1. The Persian Wars, and the cultures of both peoples, are carefully described in his masterwork, *The Histories.* In this work, he investigates the causes of the conflict between the Greeks and the Persians.

Thucydides, of Athens, was another important Greek historian. Born in 460 B.C., Thucydides lived during the Peloponnesian War. He began writing his history of the war while the events were fresh in people's memories. Before writing about a battle, he would visit the battle site. He would also interview people who had participated in the event. He hoped that his history would be accurate—and that it would help people avoid repeating the mistakes of the past.

Xenophon lived from about 427 B.C. to around 355 B.C. He traveled widely in the Persian empire and Greece. He wrote the first known autobiography in world history. An autobiography is a book about a person's life written by the subject of the book. Xenophon believed that the study of history could teach people how to live moral lives.

Political Thinkers Greek writers also discussed politics and government. For example, Plato wrote a book called *The Republic,* which presented his views about the ideal government. Plato did not approve of the way democracy functioned in Athens. He thought that the ideal city-state would be led by philosopher-kings, who had the wisdom to make the right decisions. Such leaders would not be elected by the people.

The philosopher Aristotle also wrote a book about government, called *Politics.* In this book, Aristotle compared existing governments. He argued that the best government would be a balanced one that avoided extremes. Aristotle also believed that citizens must participate in politics in order to be happy.

Reading Check Why did the Greeks study the past?

Greek historians described battles on land and at sea.▼

◀ Double portrait of the historians Herodotus and Thucydides

Science and Technology

Most ancient peoples associated everyday occurances, like the rising of the sun or common illnesses, with the activities of various gods or spirits. While most Greeks shared these beliefs, some began to look for natural causes of such events.

The Power of Observation Like modern scientists, the Greeks first made observations of nature. They then formed **hypotheses,** or logical guesses, to explain their observations. This way of thinking represented something new in the ancient world. It laid the foundations of modern science, mathematics, and medicine.

The Natural Sciences Greek philosophers began the scientific study of nature. These early scientists believed that natural laws governed the universe. They set out to identify and explain those laws.

One of the first scientific thinkers was a philosopher named Thales of Miletus. Thales was born around 624 B.C. Thales asked questions such as: How big is the Earth? What is its shape? What holds it up in space? In each case, he based his answer on his observations of nature.

These early Greek scientists were not always correct. For example, Thales believed that all things are made of water. Thales also believed that Earth was a disk that floated on water. Even though Thales's ideas were incorrect, he inspired other thinkers to use logic to develop answers. For example, the philosopher Democritus said that the universe was made up of tiny particles that could not be split. He called them "atoms."

Aristotle The most famous natural philosopher was the scholar Aristotle. He was born in 384 B.C. and studied at Plato's Academy. Later, he set up his own school, called the Lyceum.

Unlike Plato, who distrusted the senses, Aristotle sought knowledge through observation. He analyzed data about plants, animals, and rocks. He studied mathematics and logic. He analyzed government and the arts. A modern historian summarized Aristotle's work:

▲ Aristotle realized that the Earth was round by observing the position of the stars as he traveled north.

66 He was a great collector and classifier of data. . . . What he wrote provided the framework for the discussion of biology, physics, mathematics, logic, literary criticism, aesthetics, psychology, ethics, and politics for two thousand years. 99

—J. M. Roberts, *History of the World*

The First Computer?

In 1901, an astonishing machine called the Antikythera mechanism was discovered on the seafloor. The mechanism originally had about 40 gears and was made around 100 B.C. It has been called the first computer, because it was used to predict the positions of the sun, moon, and possibly, the planets. When the mechanism's handle was turned, a series of gears set the main gear wheel in motion. A full turn of the wheel showed the positions of the sun and the moon during the solar year. Other dials indicated when the various Greek games should take place. The Antikythera mechanism is the only surviving astronomical calculator from the ancient world.

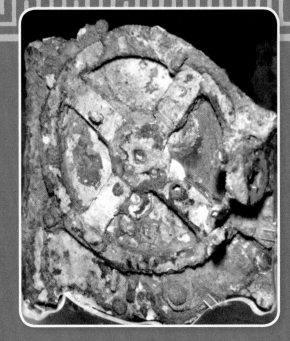

▲ A fragment of the Antikythera mechanism

Technology The Greeks put their powers of observation to practical use as they developed sophisticated technology. From the 400s on, the Greeks invented all kinds of mechanisms, including water clocks, watermills, and locks. They understood the principle of steam power, which they used to operate mechanical statues, gadgets, and toys. The inventor Archimedes is said to have created a weapon that used mirrors to redirect the sun's light to set fire to enemy ships—an early laser!

concept, *n.*, idea

Reading Check How did Greek science develop?

Mathematics and Medicine

Greek thinkers often excelled in many different fields. For example, Thales, the philosopher, was also a leading mathematician. The Greeks also believed that Thales had studied geometry in Egypt. Later, in the Hellenistic period, this kind of cultural exchange helped produce a golden age of Greek mathematics and medicine.

Mathematics The Greeks first discovered many basic <u>concepts</u> in mathematics. Pythagoras of Samos was an early Greek mathematician. Pythagoras thought that numbers were the key to understanding the universe. He developed the idea of "square numbers." Today students of geometry still learn the Pythagorean theorem, which bears his name. A theorem is a statement in mathematics that can be proved to be true.

Medicine The Greeks also made contributions in the field of medicine. Greek doctors looked for natural causes of illnesses instead of blaming them on the gods. Their success at treating patients brought them fame throughout the Mediterranean world. Greek doctors practiced surgery and dentistry.

Hippocrates became the best-known Greek doctor. He also wrote many medical books and ran a school that trained new doctors. Hippocrates taught his students to diagnose patients by asking them questions and making observations so they could learn about their symptoms.

Hippocrates also had his students swear an oath. In this oath, medical students promised to use their knowledge only in ethical ways. The **Hippocratic oath** still guides doctors today.

> 66 I will prescribe treatment for the good of my patients according to my ability . . . and never do harm to anyone. To please no one will I prescribe a deadly drug nor give advice which may cause his death. . . . In every house where I come I will enter only for the good of my patients. . . . All that I learn from my patients . . . I will keep secret. If I keep this oath faithfully, may I enjoy my life and practice my art, respected by all men and in all times. 99
>
> —Hippocrates, from *The Hippocratic Oath*

Greeks and Egyptians The city of Alexandria, Egypt, became an important center for the study of medicine. The Greeks benefited from the medical knowledge of the Egyptians. Egyptian doctors carefully examined patients and recorded their symptoms. But the Greeks went further and sought to understand the reasons for a patient's illness.

Although Greek societies frowned on dissection of the human body, two scientists working in Alexandria, Herophilus and Erasistratus, studied human anatomy. It was in Alexandria that doctors realized that the optic nerve linked the eye to the brain. Ancient Greek doctors also discovered that the brain was the center of thought, and that the pulse sent blood through the arteries.

Reading Check Why were medical students required to take an oath?

myWorld Activity
Identity Challenge

GREEK DOCTORS AND SCIENTISTS

▲ Top right: Carved relief showing a Greek doctor and patient. Top left: The snake and staff on modern ambulances is an old symbol for the Greek god of healing.

Name	Achievement
Aristarchus	First suggested that the Earth revolves around the sun
Aristotle	Realized that the Earth is round
Democritus	First to name "atoms," the particles that form all matter
Eratosthenes	Used geometry to measure the size of the Earth
Hippocrates	Believed that all diseases have natural causes. Created a standard of conduct for doctors

Chart Skills

What do these achievements reveal about Greek scientists' level of knowledge?

349

Uncovering Ancient Alexandria

Ancient Alexandria is slowly being uncovered. Part of the metropolis lies buried under the modern city, while the old seafront is now under water. Divers have begun to explore the palaces and temples that slid under the waves during earthquakes. Recent discoveries confirm what we know from ancient writers—that Alexandria was one of the most magnificent cities of the ancient world.

THINK CRITICALLY Study the map. How can you tell that the city was culturally diverse?

Cleopatra's Needle, which once stood on the seafront of Alexandria, now stands in New York City's Central Park.▼

◄The Great Lighthouse

Ptolemy II and Queen Arsinoe lived in the Royal Palace. ►

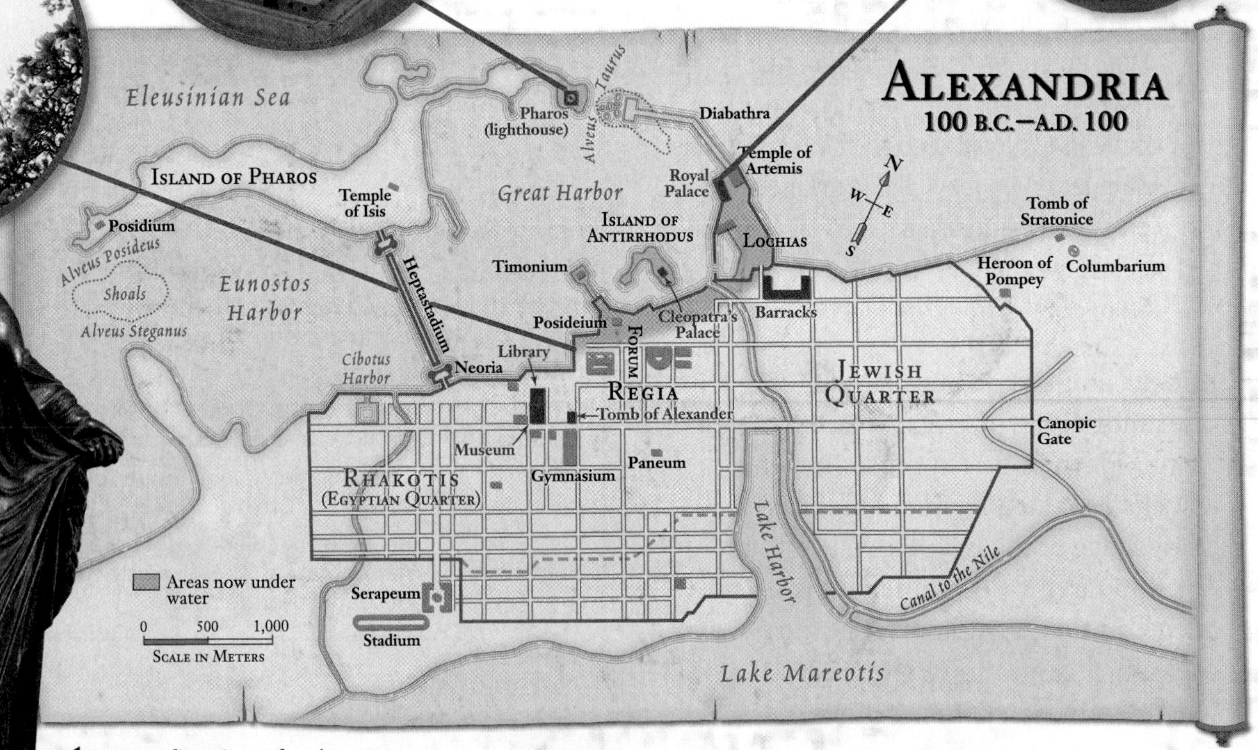

ALEXANDRIA
100 B.C.—A.D. 100

Eleusinian Sea

Pharos (lighthouse)

Alveus Taurus

Diabathra

Temple of Artemis

Royal Palace

ISLAND OF PHAROS

Great Harbor

Temple of Isis

ISLAND OF ANTIRRHODUS

LOCHIAS

N
W E
S

Tomb of Stratonice

Posidium

Heroon of Pompey   Columbarium

Alveus Posideus

Timonium

Eunostos Harbor

Shoals

Alveus Steganus

Heptastadium

Posideium

Cleopatra's Palace

Barracks

Cibotus Harbor

Library

Neoria

F O R U M

REGIA

JEWISH QUARTER

◄—Tomb of Alexander

Canopic Gate

Museum

Gymnasium

Paneum

RHAKOTIS (EGYPTIAN QUARTER)

Lake Harbor

Areas now under water

0   500   1,000
SCALE IN METERS

Serapeum

Stadium

Canal to the Nile

Lake Mareotis

◄Bronze figurine of a dancer. Alexandria, 200s–100s B.C.

Hellenistic Learning

Aristotle's interest in the world deeply impressed his student, Alexander the Great. When Alexander led his army into Asia, he brought scientists to study local plants and animals. Alexander's support for research flourished in one of the cities that he founded—Alexandria, the Greek capital of Egypt.

Alexandria, Egypt Alexandria grew rich from handling the trade between peoples of three continents. The wealth of the city helped fund projects like the Great Library. The Library was founded by the Ptolemies, the Hellenistic rulers of Egypt. Their goal was to <u>acquire</u> a copy of every book in the world. Over the years, the collection grew to about 500,000 book rolls, or scrolls.

City of Scholars Alexandria's library and museum attracted some of the most important scholars in history. It was here that Jewish scholars created the Septuagint, a translation of the Hebrew Bible into Greek. Euclid, an important mathematician, lived in Alexandria about 300 B.C. Euclid brought together all that was known about geometry in his book *Elements.* This work still forms the basis of many modern geometry textbooks.

Although the inventor and mathematician Archimedes spent most of his life in Syracuse, he may have studied in Alexandria. Archimedes created many useful inventions. One of them, the Archimedean screw, is still used to lift water for irrigation or to drain swamps. Archimedes also made important contributions to mathematics.

Greek Culture Spreads Greek culture spread during Alexander's conquests. In Italy, Greek culture influenced the Romans, long before they conquered Greek lands. The union of Greek and Roman culture created what we call Greco-Roman or classical civilization. As you will read in the next chapter, the Romans spread this civilization across even larger parts of the world.

Reading Check How did Alexandria become so rich?

▲ This mosaic shows Alexandria as a goddess.

acquire, *v.,* to get hold of; obtain

Section 4 Assessment

Essential Question

How should we handle conflict?

Key Terms

1. Use the following terms to describe ancient Greek learning: Socratic method, Academy, hypothesis, Hippocratic oath.

Key Ideas

2. Why was Socrates executed?

3. What principle formed the basis of Greek science?

4. Why did the city of Alexandria attract scholars?

Think Critically

5. **Make Inferences** In what ways did Aristotle influence Alexander?

6. **Synthesize** What methods of the early Greek historians might be useful to historians today?

7. Why might Greek historians have written about conflicts? Go to your Student Journal to record your answer.

Chapter Assessment

Key Terms and Ideas

1. **Recall** What was so surprising about the Athenian victory at the **Battle of Marathon**?

2. **Explain** Why did members of the Delian League resent Athens's power?

3. **Describe** Which ruler was able to gain control of Greece?

4. **Compare and Contrast** How did **Hellenistic** culture differ from earlier Greek culture?

5. **Explain** Why were the **Olympic games** held?

6. **Describe** In what ways were the Greek gods different from the gods of other ancient peoples?

7. **Summarize** What is the purpose of the **Socratic method** of teaching?

8. **Discuss** What role did observation play in the work of Greek scientists?

Think Critically

9. **Compare and Contrast** Were Athens and Sparta evenly matched during the Peloponnesian War? Explain your answer.

10. **Identify Evidence** What did the destruction of Thebes reveal about Alexander's character?

11. **Draw Inferences** In what ways did the Great Library at Alexandria symbolize the Greeks' confidence in human achievement?

12. **Core Concepts: Political Basics** How did Macedonia's government differ from the governments of the city-states?

Analyze Visuals

13. The goddess Athena, standing on the far left on this vase painting, is often depicted in armor. Here she is shown delivering a chariot to the warrior who appears on the center of the vase. What does this image reveal about the Greek attitude toward warfare?

Essential Question

myWorld Chapter Activity

Digging the Hellenistic World Follow your teacher's instructions to take the role of archaeologists investigating each site on the activity cards. Study each card, as well as the map, to try to figure out where in the Hellenistic world each object was made. When you have finished, explain your findings to the class.

21st Century Learning

Evaluate Web Sites

With a partner, search the Internet for Web sites on "Ancient Greek Civilization + for kids." Make a table with each Web site listed in a column on the left. Then add headings across the top. The headings can be: visuals, information, reading level, and so on. Then, evaluate each Web site by filling in the table.

Document-Based Questions

Success Tracker™
Online at myworldhistory.com

Use your knowledge of ancient Greece and Documents A and B to answer Questions 1–3 below.

Document A

" It is quite true . . . that we have given up our houses and our city walls, because we did not choose to become enslaved for the sake of things that have no life or soul. But what we still possess is the greatest city in all Greece, our 200 ships of war, which are ready now to defend you, if you are still willing to be saved by them."

—Themistocles

Document B

" At first, indeed, the Persian line held its own; but when the mass of ships was crowded into the narrows and no one could render aid to another, each crashed its bronze-faced beak into another in the line and shattered its oars."

—Aeschylus, *The Persians*

1. In Document A, Themistocles is
   A offering the Athenian army to defend Greece.
   B explaining why the Athenians won't leave Athens.
   C surrendering to the Persians.
   D offering the Athenian navy to defend Greece.

2. Document B shows that during the Battle of Salamis,
   A the Persians were victorious.
   B the Persian ships could not maneuver.
   C the Persians were defeated on land.
   D the Spartans were defeated.

3. **Writing Task** What do Documents A and B together reveal about the Battle of Salamis?

my worldhistory.com

Self-Test

Comparing Athens and Sparta

Key Idea
- Athens and Sparta had different types of governments and societies.

Studying the government and daily life of ancient Greece gives us insight about the roots of modern governments. The Greek city-state Athens had a fair and open democracy that had a lasting impact on Western civilization. The first document, which describes the Athenian government, is from a speech made by the Athenian statesman Pericles honoring soldiers killed in a war between Athens and the rival city-state Sparta. Sparta was a military state in which discipline and physical toughness were prized. In the second document, the Greek philosopher Xenophon describes life in Sparta.

A bust of Pericles

Read the text on the right. Stop at each circled letter. Then answer the question with the same letter on the left.

A Analyze Primary Sources What does Pericles mean by the words "favours the many instead of the few"?

B Identify Details What is Pericles saying about how poor citizens are treated?

C Summarize Explain in your own words what Pericles is saying about citizenship.

---

administration, *n.,* performance of duties

capacity, *n.,* a person's ability or skill

hindered, *v.,* held back

magistrate, *n.,* a government official

statute, *n.,* a law

Government in Athens

66 Our constitution does not copy the laws of neighbouring states; we are rather a pattern to others than imitators
A ourselves. Its <u>administration</u> favours the many instead of the few; this is why it is called a democracy. If we look to the laws, they afford equal justice to all in their private differences; if no social standing, advancement in public life falls to reputation for <u>capacity</u>, class considerations not being allowed to interfere with merit; nor again does poverty
B bar the way, if a man is able to serve the state, he is not <u>hindered</u> by . . . his condition. The freedom which we enjoy in our government extends also to our ordinary life. . . . But all this ease in our private relations does not make us law-
C less as citizens. Against this fear is our chief safeguard, teaching us to obey the <u>magistrates</u> and the laws, . . . whether they are actually on the <u>statute</u> book, or belong to that code which, although unwritten, yet cannot be broken without acknowledged disgrace. 99
—Pericles, "Funeral Oration," about 431 B.C.

Read the text on the right. Stop at each circled letter. Then answer the question with the same letter on the left.

D **Summarize** How were Spartan boys treated?

E **Draw Conclusions** What is Xenophon's point of view in these lines?

F **Identify Evidence** What do these lines tell you about the power of kings in ancient Sparta?

Lycurgos, *n.,* a Spartan lawmaker

muster, *n.,* an act of assembling; inspection

chastise, *v.,* to inflict punishment on

ill-starred, *adj.,* ill-fated, unlucky

descent, *n.,* ancestry

Spartan Society and Government

66 When we turn to <u>Lycurgos</u> (ly KUR gus), instead of leaving it to each member of the state privately to appoint a slave to be his son's tutor, he set over the young Spartans a public guardian . . . with complete authority over them. This guardian was elected from those who filled the highest magistracies. He had authority to hold <u>musters</u> of the boys, and as their guardian, in

D case of any misbehavior, to <u>chastise</u> severely . . . with this happy result, that in Sparta modesty and obedience ever go hand in hand, nor is there lack of either. . . .

Instead of softening their feet with shoe or sandal, his rule was to make them hardy through going barefoot. . . .

It is clear that Lycurgos set himself deliberately to provide all the blessings of heaven for the good man, and a sorry and

E <u>ill-starred</u> existence for the coward. . . .

Lycurgos laid it down as law that the king shall offer on behalf of the state all public sacrifices, as being himself of divine <u>descent</u>, and wherever the state shall dispatch her armies

F the king shall take the lead. 99

—Xenophon, *The Polity of the Spartans,* about 375 B.C.

Analyze the Documents

1. **Draw Inferences** Why do you think Pericles discusses Athenian democracy during a speech to honor Athenian soldiers who died in a war?

2. **Writing Task** In a paragraph, explain how Sparta's government differed from the way Athens's government was run. Use an excerpt from each quotation to support your point.

The Spartans were fierce warriors.

355

Plan a
MUSEUM EXHIBIT

Your Mission Learn more about ancient Greek sculpture, architecture, literature, and other forms of art. Then design a museum exhibit about ancient Greek art that includes a comparison to modern works influenced by Greek culture.

The ancient Greeks left behind a lasting cultural legacy. The realistic depiction of the human body in Greek art had a strong influence on later art. Elements of Greek architecture can be seen in many modern buildings. The plots and themes of ancient Greek tragedies and comedies still influence literature, plays, and movies today.

As you plan your museum exhibit, think about the different aspects of Greek culture and how they affect modern life. Be sure to make your exhibit interesting and engaging.

STEP 1

Research Your Subjects.

Use material from this unit and do Internet research to plan your Greek culture exhibit. Ask your teacher for a list of reliable Web sites to find specific facts about Greek arts. Make a list of the types of objects you want to have on display. Collect or draw images of the objects you want to include in your exhibit.

STEP 2

Plan Your Exhibit.

Think about how to organize your exhibit. For example, you may wish to divide your displays by topic, such as sculpture, architecture, and literature. Or you may wish to divide them by time period according to the date of their creation. Get creative and think about how you can present your objects in an interesting way.

STEP 3

Present Your Exhibit.

Once you have finished designing your exhibit, show your ideas to the class. Answer any questions the class may have about your exhibit, such as why you chose certain objects or why you organized the exhibit the way you did. You may also choose to present a poem, a monologue, or an original artwork modeled after ancient Greek art.

my worldhistory.com

21st Century Learning

Ancient Rome

Europe

Atlantic Ocean

Tullia Ciceronis (70s B.C.–45 B.C.) was the daughter of Marcus Tullius Cicero, one of the leaders of the Roman republic.

Africa

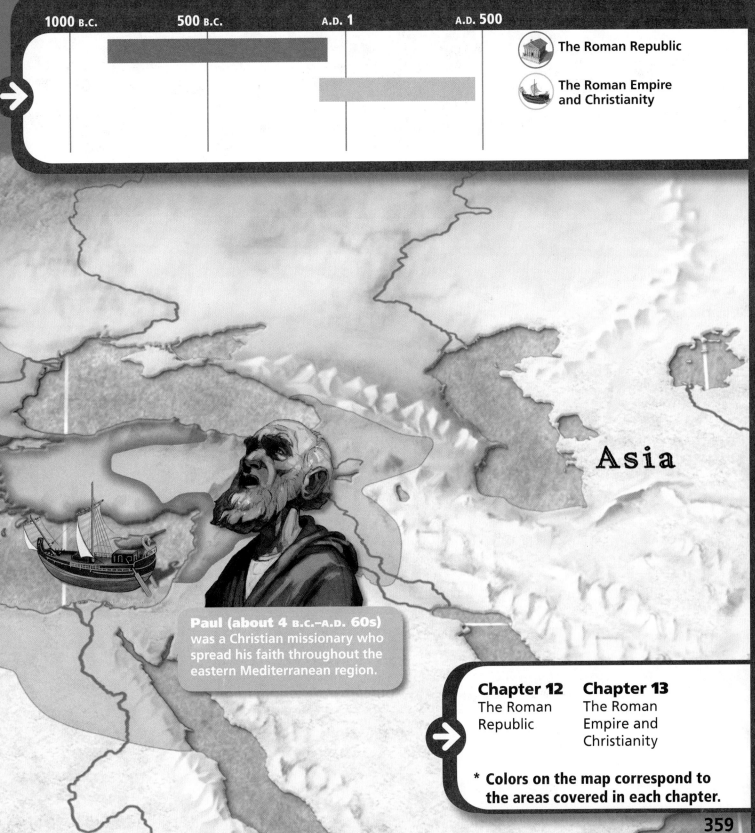

1000 B.C. 500 B.C. A.D. 1 A.D. 500

The Roman Republic

The Roman Empire and Christianity

Asia

Paul (about 4 B.C.–A.D. 60s) was a Christian missionary who spread his faith throughout the eastern Mediterranean region.

Chapter 12
The Roman Republic

Chapter 13
The Roman Empire and Christianity

* Colors on the map correspond to the areas covered in each chapter.

359

The Roman Republic

Essential Question

What should governments do?

An ancient Roman temple that still stands in modern-day France

Explore the Essential Question . . .

- at my worldhistory.com
- using the **myWorld Chapter Activity**
- with the **Student Journal**

The Roman Republic

1100 B.C.	800 B.C.	500 B.C.	200 B.C.	A.D 100

- Around 800 B.C. People first settle in Rome.
- 509 B.C. The Roman Republic is founded.
- 146 B.C. Rome destroys Carthage.
- 44 B.C. Julius Caesar becomes dictator for life.

Tullia's father saves the republic

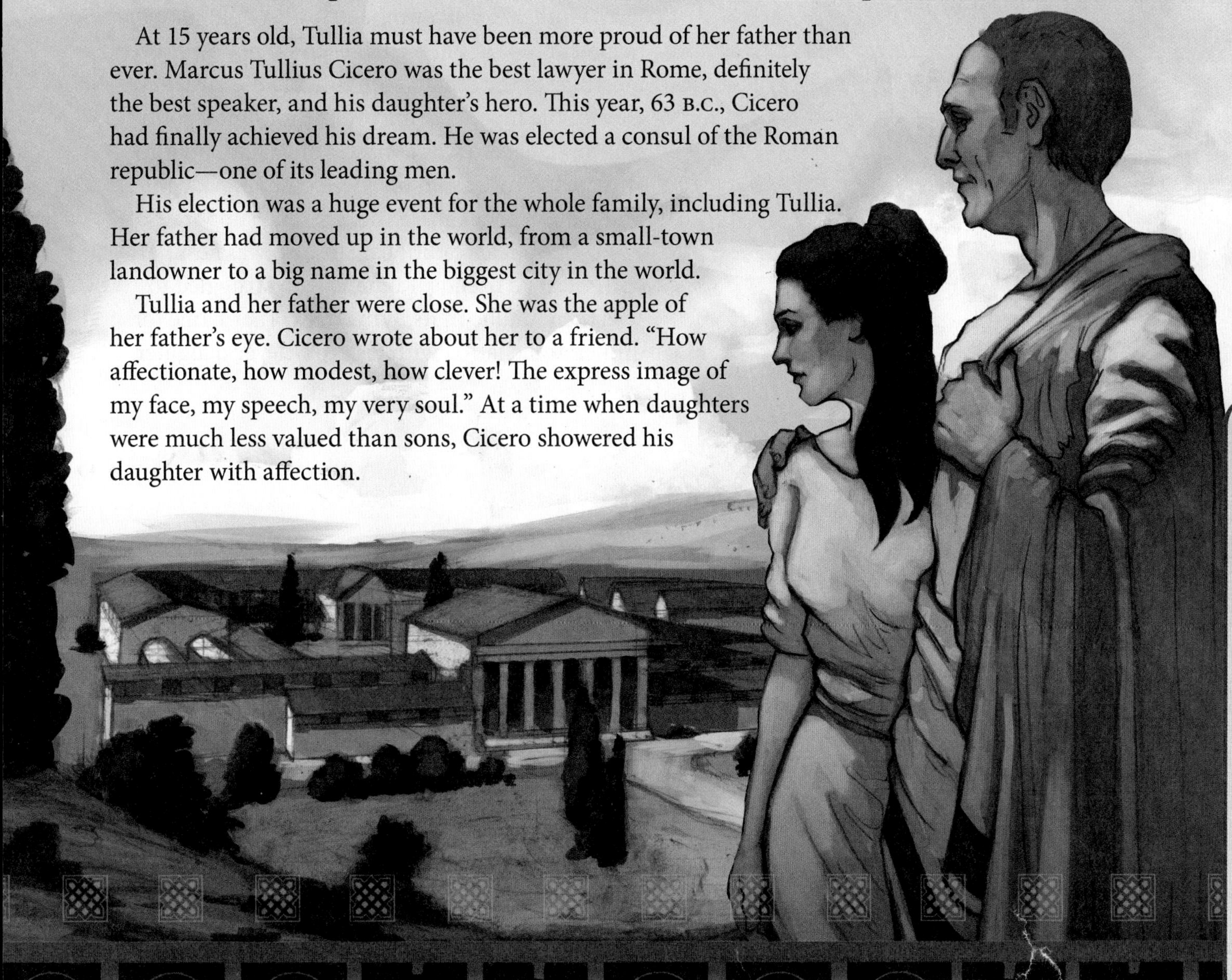

At 15 years old, Tullia must have been more proud of her father than ever. Marcus Tullius Cicero was the best lawyer in Rome, definitely the best speaker, and his daughter's hero. This year, 63 B.C., Cicero had finally achieved his dream. He was elected a consul of the Roman republic—one of its leading men.

His election was a huge event for the whole family, including Tullia. Her father had moved up in the world, from a small-town landowner to a big name in the biggest city in the world.

Tullia and her father were close. She was the apple of her father's eye. Cicero wrote about her to a friend. "How affectionate, how modest, how clever! The express image of my face, my speech, my very soul." At a time when daughters were much less valued than sons, Cicero showered his daughter with affection.

myworldhistory.com

Timeline/On Assignment

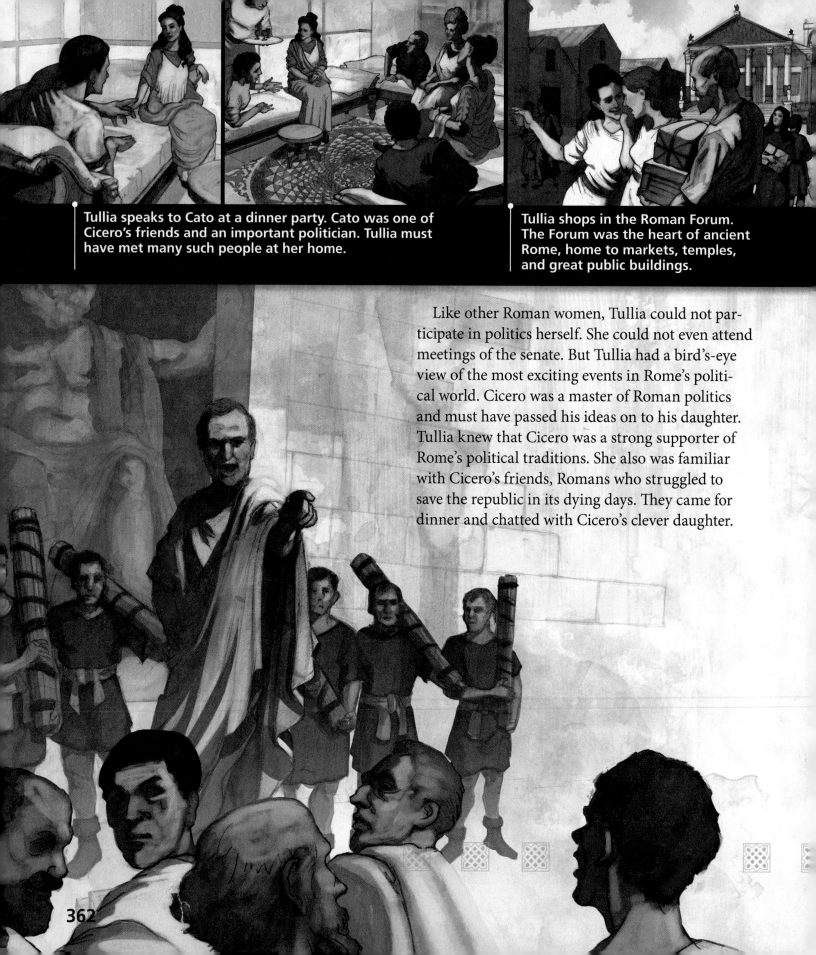

Tullia speaks to Cato at a dinner party. Cato was one of Cicero's friends and an important politician. Tullia must have met many such people at her home.

Tullia shops in the Roman Forum. The Forum was the heart of ancient Rome, home to markets, temples, and great public buildings.

Like other Roman women, Tullia could not participate in politics herself. She could not even attend meetings of the senate. But Tullia had a bird's-eye view of the most exciting events in Rome's political world. Cicero was a master of Roman politics and must have passed his ideas on to his daughter. Tullia knew that Cicero was a strong supporter of Rome's political traditions. She also was familiar with Cicero's friends, Romans who struggled to save the republic in its dying days. They came for dinner and chatted with Cicero's clever daughter.

As consul, Cicero executes men who conspired against the republic. Later, his enemies get revenge. They send him into exile and burn down his house.

After a lonely exile in Greece, Cicero is allowed to come home. Tullia travels 300 miles to meet her father when he first comes ashore in Italy.

Some elite Roman women carved out a role in politics by influencing the men around them. Tullia's mother, Terentia, may have been one of these. An account of the day noted that she "took more interest in her husband's political career than she allowed him to take in household affairs."

Outside of politics, Tullia had more freedom. With an escort, she could visit her friends, catch her favorite show at the theater, shop in the forum, or go to a temple for an important religious ritual.

The year of Cicero's consulship was an exciting one for Tullia's family. Cicero's new office brought power, but also danger. One of the men Cicero had defeated in the election, Catilina, couldn't bear the loss. He plotted to kill Cicero, overthrow the republic, and burn down Rome. He even raised his own army to attack the city.

Cicero denounced his enemy in four magnificent speeches to the senate. Catilina was forced to flee Rome. He fought an army sent out by Cicero and was killed. After consulting with the senate, Cicero executed Catilina's supporters without a trial.

Cicero had saved the day. He was a national hero, at least for now. Crowds cheered him in the streets.

But his glory quickly faded. His enemies turned the people against him. They were angry because Cicero executed Catilina's followers without a trial.

Cicero lost the favor of the Roman people. His enemies forced him into lonely exile in Greece. An angry mob burned down his house. While Cicero was abroad, Tullia and her mother wore black clothes as if they were in mourning. In exile, Cicero worried about his family.

But the family's fortunes suddenly changed once more. Soon enough, Cicero was on his way back to Rome. His powerful friends had him called back from exile. Cicero lived to fight another day. But the sweetest part of his triumph may have been seeing his devoted daughter. Without enough money to travel comfortably or a proper escort, Tullia made the long journey from Rome to southern Italy to greet her father when he returned to his country.

Based on this story, what do you think were some jobs of a consul? As you read the chapter ahead, think about what Tullia's story tells you about life in the Roman republic.

▶ **myStory Video**

Join Tullia as she lives through exciting and dangerous times.

The Rise of the Roman Republic

Key Ideas

- The Italian Peninsula and the area around Rome provided many natural advantages.
- Roman culture was influenced by Etruscan and Greek neighbors.
- The people of Rome overthrew their kings, founded a republic, and conquered Italy.

Key Terms • forum • republic • legion • maniple

 **Visual Glossary**

 Reading Skill Analyze Cause and Effect Take notes using the graphic organizer in your journal.

A Roman coin shows Lucius Junius Brutus. He was one of the Roman republic's first leaders, and helped overthrow the monarchy. He is followed by special bodyguards called lictors. ▼

Around 800 B.C., a small settlement called Rome was built along the Tiber River in present-day Italy. In time, this settlement became the world's largest city and the center of a mighty empire.

The Geography of Italy

Rome lies near the center of the Italian Peninsula. The peninsula extends from Europe into the Mediterranean Sea. A high mountain range called the Alps separates Italy from the rest of Europe. Another range called the Appenines runs down the center of Italy.

Despite its many mountains, Italy has a less rugged landscape than Greece. Soldiers could march from one place to another more easily than in Greece. This made it easier for Rome to unite the peninsula. In addition, Italy has several rivers that ships can use. Since ancient times these rivers have provided water and transportation routes.

Italy has several large, flat plains. These gave it plenty of land suited for farming. The peninsula's volcanoes helped form fertile soil, though they also threatened people's lives and property.

Ancient Rome was part of a region called Latium. This region gave its name to the Latin people. The Latins were the group of people who lived in Rome and in neighboring cities. The language they spoke was also called Latin.

Reading Check What region of Italy was Rome located in?

Rome's Earliest Days

Historians do not know exactly how Rome was <u>founded</u>. The Romans themselves told a legend about the beginning of their city.

According to the legend, Rome was founded by twins named Romulus and Remus. Their mother was a Latin princess. The twins' father was Mars, the god of war. The king, their uncle, was jealous of the twins. He had the babies placed in a basket and thrown into the Tiber. They were saved from death by a she-wolf and raised by a shepherd.

As adults, the twins gathered a group of men to found a new city. However, they quarrelled and Romulus killed Remus. Romulus lived and gave his name to the city he built—Rome.

Historians do not believe this legend. However, we can learn from the story that the Romans believed their city had a special origin and a connection to the gods. A Roman writer made this point.

66 Now, if any nation ought to be allowed to claim a sacred origin and point back to a divine paternity [fatherhood] that nation is Rome. 99
—Livy, *The History of Rome*

Archaeologists have discovered that people first settled in Rome around 800 B.C. They built villages on the tops of seven hills overlooking the Tiber River, near where the river flows into the sea. Over time these villages formed a single town that grew into a small city.

Reading Check Do historians believe the story of Romulus and Remus?

found, *v.*, set up or start

The Tiber River flows through a fertile valley. Rome was founded along the banks of this river. ▼

Italy: Physical

KEY
Elevation

Feet	Meters
6,000	1,829
3,000	914
1,000	305
500	152
Sea level	Sea level

— Region of Etruria
— Region of Latium
○ City
0   100 mi
0   100 km
Azimuthal Equal-Area Projection

Po River, Rubicon River, Arno River, Appennines, Tiber River, Adriatic Sea, Corsica, Rome, Sardinia, Tyrrhenian Sea, Ionian Sea, Sicily, Mediterranean Sea, Carthage, AFRICA

Map Skills
1 Was Latium north or south of Etruria?
2 Find the large area of low elevation in northern Italy. What river runs through it?

21st Century Learning

myworldhistory.com
21st Century Learning

365

The City Grows

The early Romans drained a swampy area between two of the town's hills. This became the Roman Forum.

The Forum A **forum** is an open area in a city filled with public buildings, temples, and markets. The Roman Forum was the center of Rome's government, religion, and economy. When the Romans founded new cities in later years, they usually built a forum at the center.

Natural Advantages Several factors in Rome's geography helped the city grow and prosper. The city's hills gave the Romans a natural defense against attack. Because Rome was located on the Tiber River, it had access to a nearby port. Although the river was shallow, small boats could pass from the city out to the sea. However, the river was too fast and dangerous for large boats, so seagoing ships could not attack Rome.

Rome was also located on key trade routes. The Tiber Valley was a natural east–west route for trade. In addition, several north–south trade routes crossed the Tiber just south of Rome.

Reading Check What natural advantages did the city of Rome enjoy?

consent, *n.*, agreement

A Roman king built this drain, which still keeps the Forum dry. ▼

From Monarchy to Republic

Like Athens and Sparta, Rome began as an independent city-state. Its first form of government was a monarchy.

The Roman Kings In Rome's earliest days, kings ruled the city. The kings had broad powers. They served as head of the army, chief priest, and supreme judge. The Roman kings helped the city grow. They built the first buildings in the Forum and led the Romans in wars against small neighboring villages.

The kings ruled with the <u>consent</u> of Rome's wealthy aristocrats. Older male aristocrats formed a body called the senate. The senate advised the king on important matters. The word *senate* comes from the Latin word *senex*, which means "old man."

The Founding of the Republic Over time, Roman aristocrats grew tired of royal rule. The seventh king of Rome, Tarquin the Proud, mistreated his people. In 509 B.C., leading Romans overthrew the king and formed a **republic**. A republic is a government in which citizens have the right to vote and elect officials.

The word *republic* comes from the Latin term *res publica,* which means "public thing" or "public business." In the Roman republic, all free adult male citizens could play a role in the city's government. You will read more about the government of the republic later in this chapter.

Reading Check What does *res publica* mean?

The People of Italy

When the city of Rome was founded, Italy already had many different cultures. As Roman power grew, the Romans came into contact with different Italian peoples and borrowed from their cultures.

Greek Colonies Many Greeks settled in Italy starting around the 700s B.C. They founded cities in southern Italy. They brought their culture with them. As Rome's power grew, it came into contact with these cities. This contact taught the Romans about Greek culture.

The Greeks of Italy had a strong influence on Roman culture. Romans made Greek mythology their own by <u>identifying</u> their gods with those of the Greeks. For example, the Greek Zeus was identified with Roman Jupiter, Hera with Juno, and Athena with Minerva.

The Romans also adopted Greek legends and heroes as their own. They believed that the ancestor of the Roman people was Aeneas. He was a character in the *Iliad*, a Greek poem. The story of Aeneas was written down by the Roman writer Virgil in a poem called the *Aeneid*.

The Etruscans The Etruscans were the most powerful people in central Italy when Rome was founded. They lived in Etruria, a region just north of Latium. They influenced Roman culture

The Etruscans had an advanced culture. They were skilled artists and builders. They sailed around the Mediterranean as traders. They learned many things from other peoples such as the Greeks and the Phoenicians.

Reading Check How did the Greeks influence the Romans?

myWorld Activity
Location, Location!

identify, *v.*, consider or treat as the same

Rome began in the 800s B.C. as a group of villages on top of hills overlooking the Tiber River. Below you can see a close view of one of the villages.

By the A.D. 300s, Rome was the largest city in the world. The small area in the circle below shows where the hill shown at left was located.

367

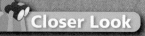

THE ETRUSCANS

Etruscan culture was influenced by the Greeks and Phoenicians. In turn, the Etruscans helped shape Roman culture. For example, Etruscan religion influenced Roman practices. Roman architecture got its start in Etruscan building styles. The Etruscans developed their own alphabet based on Greek. The Romans developed an alphabet for Latin based on the Etruscan model. Today, we use Roman letters to write in English and many other languages.

THINK CRITICALLY How did the Etruscans influence the modern world?

These are the ruins of the Etruscan city of Veii, less than 10 miles from Rome. The Romans conquered it in 396 B.C.▼

Early Alphabets		
Etruscan	Early Latin	Modern Roman
∩	A	A
⊟	H	H
९	P	R

SOURCE: *Blackwell Encyclopedia of Writing Systems*

Above is an Etruscan statue of a chimera. A chimera is a legendary beast with a lion's body, the heads of a lion and a goat, and a tail that ends in snake's head.

A statue of the god Apollo (left) once stood on top of a temple in the Etruscan city of Veii. It was made of terra cotta, or clay, and was originally painted in bright colors. The photo below shows an Etruscan statue with the paint still visible.

Roman Expansion

The Roman people were feared conquerors. They also made skillful use of diplomacy, or managing relationships with other countries. They conquered neighboring peoples and slowly expanded their rule. By the late 200s B.C., Rome ruled all of Italy.

The Legions The basic unit of the Roman army was the **legion** (LEE jun). Each legion had from 4,500 to 5,000 heavily armed soldiers. Most served as infantry, or foot soldiers.

Each legion was broken up into maniples. A **maniple** was a unit of between 60 and 160 soldiers. On flat plains, all the maniples in a legion formed a solid battle line. But in rough country, each maniple could move and fight on its own. This flexibility gave the Roman legions a great advantage over enemies who fought in a single square block, including Greek phalanxes. Phalanxes were less flexible.

The Roman military did not just use Roman innovations. It was open to good ideas wherever they came from. For example, the Romans picked up the gladius, or short sword, from Spain. Maniples were first used by the Samnites, a mountain people who lived in the Appenines in central Italy.

Roman soldiers were builders as well as fighters. When a Roman army was on the move, its soldiers would build a temporary fort every night. Soldiers also built roads and bridges. These helped armies move faster.

Friends and Allies Rome gained power with the help of its allies. The Romans signed treaties with other peoples, often defeated enemies. The treaties required allies to send troops to fight alongside the Romans in their campaigns. Eventually, many loyal allies were given Roman citizenship and the right to vote.

Reading Check What was a maniple?

▲ A Roman soldier carrying a shield, short sword, and spear

Section 1 Assessment

Key Terms

1. What is a republic?
2. What was the role of the Roman Forum?
3. What was the basic unit of the Roman army?

Key Ideas

4. How did Italy's geography help Rome unite the peninsula?
5. What advantages did the Tiber River provide?
6. What powers did the Roman kings have?
7. Where did the Latin alphabet come from?

Think Critically

8. **Compare and Contrast** How was a Roman legion different from a Greek phalanx?
9. **Draw Conclusions** Find evidence to support the idea that the Romans were open to the influences of foreign cultures.

Essential Question

What should governments do?

10. Why did the Romans overthrow their king and form a new system of government? Go to your Student Journal to record your answer.

The Government of the Republic

Key Ideas

- In the Roman republic, power was divided among many different people so that no one person could become too powerful.

- The government of the Roman republic was made up of three separate branches that held different powers.

- The Roman republic influenced later republics, including the United States.

Key Terms • constitution • veto • magistrate • toga • consul

 Visual Glossary

Reading Skill Identify Main Ideas and Details Take notes using the graphic organizer in your journal.

A Roman politician wearing a toga, a symbol of Roman citizenship ▶

The Roman republic was a unique system of government that lasted for 500 years. It led the Roman people from their humble origins to their conquest of the Mediterranean world.

Principles of Roman Government

The ancient historian Polybius said about the Roman republic that "it was impossible even for a native to pronounce with certainty whether the whole system was aristocratic, democratic, or monarchical." Rome's system combined all three forms of government. Strong leaders, wealthy aristocrats, and average citizens all had a role to play.

Rome's Constitution Roman government was structured by a **constitution**. This is a system of rules by which a government is organized. Unlike the United States' consitution, the Roman constitution was unwritten. It was based on tradition and custom.

The Separation of Powers The main idea in Rome's system of government was the separation of powers. This means that power was shared among different people with set roles. After they threw out their last king, the Romans did not want to be ruled by a single man. They built their new system of government to make sure no one person could become too powerful. For centuries, it worked.

A Roman Hero

Roman citizens were expected to fight courageously for their city. One legendary brave citizen was named Gaius Mucius. He tried and failed to assassinate an enemy king to save his city. Captured, he was brought before the king to face torture and death. But Mucius was not afraid. To show the king Roman bravery, Mucius put his own right hand into a fire and said,

> 66 I am a citizen of Rome. Men call me Gaius Mucius. As an enemy I wished to kill an enemy, and I have as much courage to meet death as I had to inflict it. It is the Roman nature to act bravely and to suffer bravely. 99
>
> —Gaius Mucius, quoted by Livy in *The History of Rome*

◄ A painting of Gaius Mucius putting his hand into a fire to show his bravery.

One way in which the Romans limited officials' power was by splitting offices between two or more men. The Romans did not elect one top leader. Instead, they elected two leaders called consuls. They held equal powers. Each could veto the action of the other. To **veto** means to stop or cancel the action of a government official or body. In Latin, *veto* means "I forbid."

The Romans also limited the power of officials by limiting their time in office to one year. Even a powerful official could not do too much harm in that short time.

Checks and Balances Power was also divided among the three branches of government. They were the assemblies, the senate, and the **magistrates,** or elected officials who enforce the law. A government with three parts is called a tripartite government.

Each branch had its own set of powers. They were balanced against the powers of the other branches. One branch could check, or stop, another branch from misusing its power. No one branch could hold total power, though at most times the senate was the most powerful branch.

The Rule of Law Another important principle in Roman government was the rule of law. This means that the law applied to everyone. Even elected officials could be tried for <u>violating</u> the law after their term of office was over.

Reading Check What are checks and balances?

Roman Citizens

Free Roman men were citizens of the Roman republic. Women and slaves were not citizens and had no direct role in government. The symbol of Roman citizenship was the **toga,** a garment that adult men wore wrapped around their bodies. Only citizens could wear togas.

violate, *v.*, break a rule or agreement

my worldhistory.com

Primary Source

The Three Branches of the Roman Government

The Roman government was made up of three branches or parts: the assemblies, the senate, and the magistrates. Each part had its own set of powers. This setup provided checks and balances, meaning that each branch could watch over the activities of the others.

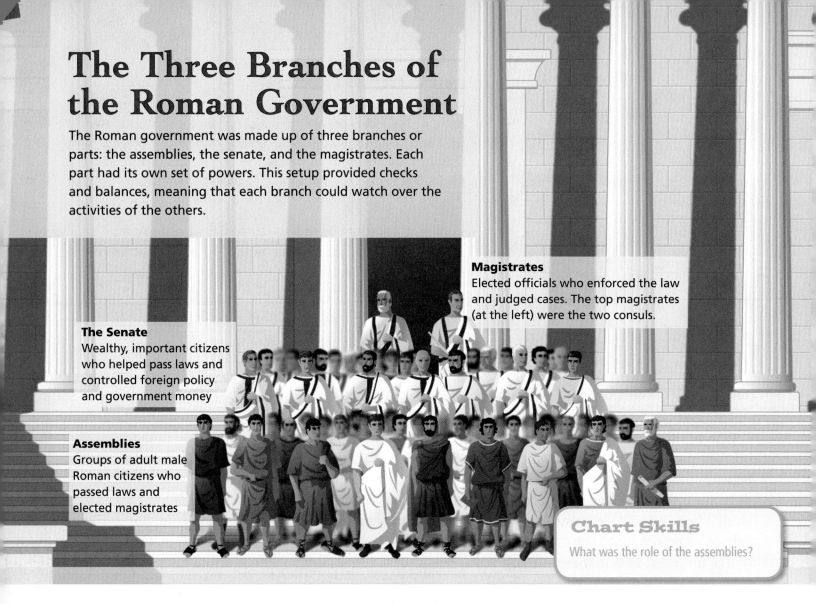

Magistrates
Elected officials who enforced the law and judged cases. The top magistrates (at the left) were the two consuls.

The Senate
Wealthy, important citizens who helped pass laws and controlled foreign policy and government money

Assemblies
Groups of adult male Roman citizens who passed laws and elected magistrates

Chart Skills
What was the role of the assemblies?

Rights and Responsibilities Roman citizens had the right to a trial. Any adult male citizen had the right to vote. He also had the responsibility to serve in the army if he could afford his own armor. Roman culture stressed civic duty, meaning the responsibility of a citizen.

Patricians and Plebeians Roman citizens were divided into two orders. One was the patricians, members of the oldest families in Rome. They were usually wealthy. In the early days of the republic, they may have controlled all government offices.

The other order was made up of the plebeians, who were a majority of Romans. They did not come from famous old families like the patricians. Most were common farmers or artisans. However, some plebeians were wealthy.

The plebeians forced patricians to open up political offices to them. According to Roman tradition, they did so by going on strike. During a war, the plebeians walked out of the city and sat down on a nearby hill. Rome could not fight on without them, so the patricians had to give in.

Reading Check Who had the right to vote?

The Assemblies and Senate

Patricians and plebeians alike had a role to play in Roman government.

The Assemblies Assemblies of Roman citizens were the democratic part of Roman government. All adult male citizens could participate in assemblies, though the votes of the wealthy usually counted for more than those of the poor.

At assemblies, Roman citizens elected officials and passed laws. This was a form of direct democracy, like the assembly in Athens. However, the power of the assemblies was checked by the powers of the senate and of elected officials.

The Senate The senate was the part of Roman government that worked like an oligarchy. It was made up of the wealthiest and best-known older Roman men, often former magistrates. Senators were chosen by an official called the censor. They did not represent the people. They were supposed to guide the state. Rich, older senators were thought to be wiser than other citizens.

The senate advised the assemblies and magistrates. Its advice was almost always followed. It also ran foreign policy and decided how to spend the state's money. It was the most powerful part of the Roman government.

Reading Check **What did the senate control directly?**

Magistrates

The Romans elected a number of powerful magistrates. The power of these high officials made them almost like monarchs. Magistrates were wealthy men. Their ancestors had usually held high offices. For men from elite families, politics was a key part of life.

Politicians usually moved from lower offices to higher offices. This path was called the Race of Honors. It changed over time. But by the later years of the republic, it followed a standard form.

Lower Offices The Race of Honors started with the lowest office, the quaestor (KWY stor). Quaestors were accountants who kept track of the state's money. They also served as assistants to higher officials. If a citizen did well as a quaestor, he might seek election as an aedile (EE dile). Aediles were in charge of holding festivals and maintaining public buildings. These lower offices were stepping-stones to greater power.

policy, *n.*, course of action taken by a government

Fasces

Bundles of rods and an axe were symbols of a high magistrate's power in Rome.

Fasces have been used as symbols of republics throughout history, including in the United States.

But because they represent state power, fasces were also used as symbols by dictatorships in the 1900s. The word "fascism" comes from the fasces. Fascism is a political system in which government has total control over society.

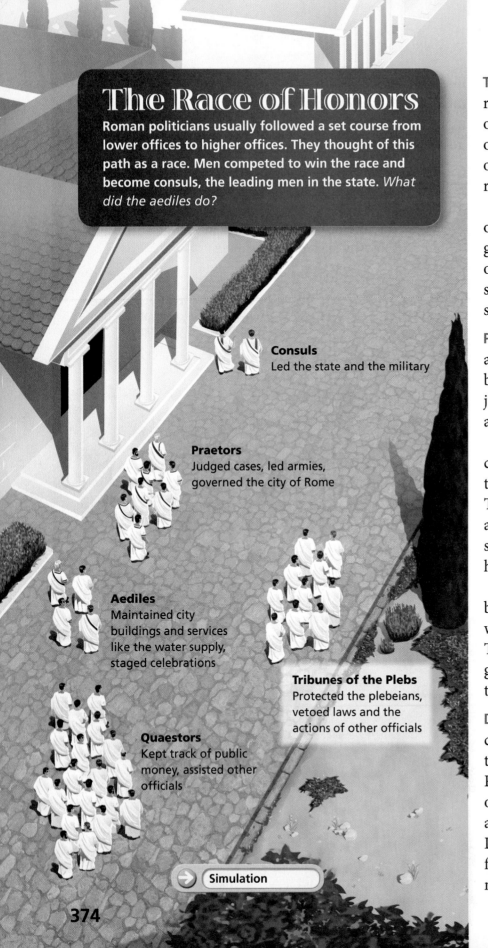

The Race of Honors

Roman politicians usually followed a set course from lower offices to higher offices. They thought of this path as a race. Men competed to win the race and become consuls, the leading men in the state. *What did the aediles do?*

Consuls
Led the state and the military

Praetors
Judged cases, led armies, governed the city of Rome

Aediles
Maintained city buildings and services like the water supply, staged celebrations

Tribunes of the Plebs
Protected the plebeians, vetoed laws and the actions of other officials

Quaestors
Kept track of public money, assisted other officials

→ Simulation

Tribunes of the Plebs Plebeians could run for the powerful office of tribune of the plebs before moving on to higher offices. Tribunes acted as the protectors of the plebeians. Sometimes they took radical or even revolutionary positions.

Tribunes had the right to veto any law, or the action of any magistrate. The veto gave the tribunes great power over all other parts of the government. It was also strictly forbidden to harm a tribune or stop him from doing his job.

Praetors and Consuls After serving as an as an aedile or tribune, men could try to be elected as a praetor (PRY tor). Praetors judged cases, managed the city of Rome, and led armies in times of war.

After serving as a praetor, a politician could be elected consul. The **consuls** were the top officials in the Roman republic. Their most important job was to lead the army. They also presided over the senate and assemblies and were the highest judges.

Consuls and praetors had visible symbols that showed their authority. They wore special togas and sat on ivory chairs. They were followed around by bodyguards called lictors. The lictors carried the consul's or praetor's fasces.

Dictators In the modern world, when we call someone a dictator we usually mean that he is a cruel tyrant. But in ancient Rome, a dictator was an important public official. The senate could vote to name a dictator in times of great emergency. Dictators held complete power, but only for a limited time. They served for a maximum of six months.

A man named Cincinnatus was one famous dictator. Cincinnatus was working his farm when he heard that he had been chosen dictator. He quickly defeated Rome's enemies, resigned his office, and went back to his fields. He was thought of as a model citizen.

Reading Check Who was Cincinnatus?

The Roman Example

The Roman republic was the most successful and long-lasting republic until modern times. The writers of the American constitution knew a great deal about Roman history and government. They followed the Roman example in many areas.

For instance, like Roman citizens, American citizens have the right to vote and stand for office. The United States government has three branches with separate powers, like the Roman republic had. Checks and balances limit the power of each branch. The rule of law applies equally to every American, as it did to every Roman citizen. Like tribunes of the plebs, presidents have the power to veto laws. The United States has a senate, as ancient Rome did.

Still, many parts of American government are different. As you read, the Roman republic did not have a written constitution, while the United States does. Ancient Rome also practiced forms of direct democracy. In contrast, the United States practices representative democracy. Roman citizens voted directly on laws. In the United States, laws are usually passed by representatives elected by the citizens.

In the United States today, women participate equally in the government. In ancient Rome, women did not have a role in politics. While slavery has been illegal in the United States since the 1860s, many people in ancient Rome were slaves who had no political rights.

Reading Check How was a tribune of the plebs like an American president?

my World CONNECTIONS

The Roman Senate had as many as **900** members, all men. The United States Senate has only **100,** both men and women.

myWorld Activity
Who Decides?

my worldhistory.com

Simulation

Section 2 Assessment

Essential Question

Key Terms

1. What is a constitution? Did the Romans write theirs down?

2. What was a toga a symbol of?

3. What do magistrates do?

Key Ideas

4. What were the three branches of Roman government?

5. What is the rule of law?

6. What jobs did a consul do?

7. What are three ways in which Roman government is similar to American government?

Think Critically

8. **Identify Main Ideas** In what ways were the tribunes of the plebs especially powerful?

9. **Compare and Contrast** How is direct democracy in the Roman republic different from representative democracy in the United States?

What should governments do?

10. What are some benefits of dividing the government into three branches with separate or different powers? Go to your Student Journal to record your answer.

Section 3
Roman Society

Key Ideas
- Roman men were the leaders of their families while women had other roles.
- Life was very different for different classes of Romans.
- Religion was important to the Roman people, and the Roman government played a role in it.

Key Terms • patriarchal society • paterfamilias • villa • established religion

 **Visual Glossary**

Reading Skill Compare and Contrast Take notes using the graphic organizer in your journal.

Like other ancient societies, Rome was divided by gender and class. Men and women had their own social roles. The lives of wealthy Romans were very different from the lives of poor Romans and slaves.

Men and Women

Rome was a **patriarchal society.** This means that men ruled their families, and that people traced their origins through male ancestors.

The Power of Fathers The oldest man in a Roman family was called the **paterfamilias,** or head of the household. He owned all the family's property. In theory, a father had absolute, or unlimited, power over his wife, children, slaves, and underage siblings. He could sell his children into slavery. He could even kill them if he chose. In practice, however, a father's power was limited by custom.

The Role of Women Roman women enjoyed more freedom than Greek women. Unlike most Greek women, they could own personal property. Also unlike many Greek women, Roman women took an active role in social life. Women went to parties, enjoyed the theater, and participated in religious rituals. But, as you have read, women could not vote, attend assemblies, or hold public office.

According to the Romans, the most important role of a Roman woman was to bear children and raise them to follow traditions. The ideal woman was a faithful wife and mother, devoted to her family.

Reading Check Could Roman women own property?

A Roman husband and wife ▼

Rich and Poor

Most Romans were poor free people or slaves. A tiny <u>minority</u> were wealthy.

Living the Good Life Most wealthy Romans earned their money from agriculture. They owned huge farms worked by poor Romans or slaves. The landowners grew rich from what these people produced. Other wealthy Romans earned their fortunes through business.

Upper-class Romans lived in one- or two-story houses as large as a city block. These homes had courtyards, gardens, private baths, beautiful decorations, and even running water. Many elite families also owned **villas,** or large country homes.

Wealthy Roman men worked at looking after their business interests and advancing their political careers. Wealthy women supervised the slaves who took care of their homes and their children.

The Common People Life was different for poor Romans. In the city, most poor people lived in cramped apartments without running water. Crime, disease, and fire were serious dangers. Apartment buildings were often badly built, and sometimes collapsed.

Common men and women worked at a variety of jobs. Many were <u>tenant</u> farmers who rented land from wealthy landlords. Others worked as day laborers in construction or at the city docks. Some ran stores, taverns, or restaurants.

Reading Check Were the majority of Romans rich or poor?

minority, *n.*, a group that is less than half of a population

tenant, *n.*, person who rents land or a home

Reconstructed View of the
Villa Rūstica of the *Cornēliī*

Roman Villas
Above is a model of a Roman villa. At the left is a reconstructed bedroom from a villa. Wealthy Romans owned large villas in the country where they could escape the heat, noise, and filth of downtown Rome.

377

Slavery in Rome

In the ancient world, a person could be born into slavery, or become a slave if he or she was captured in a war, kidnapped by pirates or bandits, or fell into too much debt. Slaves came from many different ethnic groups and regions. *How does this change how you think about the ancient world?*

A Roman slave works in a kitchen. ▶

◀ One slave wore this metal collar showing his master's name and address in case he tried to run away.

myWorld Activity
A Day in the Life...

Slavery

Slavery was very common in ancient Rome. As Rome became richer and more powerful, Romans bought or captured increasing numbers of slaves. As many as 40 percent of people in Rome in the year 1 B.C. may have been slaves.

Living Conditions For most of Roman history, slaves had no rights. They were bought and sold as property. They could be beaten or killed by their masters for any reason. Children born to slaves were also slaves. Many slaves worked in mines or on large farms. These slaves often died quickly due to brutal treatment.

Other slaves led easier lives. Some worked in the homes of their wealthy masters. They lived like typical poor Romans or even better, performing housework for their masters.

Some educated slaves worked as secretaries or teachers. These slaves were usually Greeks. Although they lived in much better conditions than other slaves, they could still be treated very cruelly.

Slaves who served loyally could be freed as a reward. They could also save up to buy their freedom. Freed slaves became citizens and had the right to vote.

Fighting Back Some slaves fought back against their masters. One famous fighter was Spartacus, who led an army of rebel slaves in the 70s B.C. They fought the Roman army and threatened to capture Rome before the Romans defeated them.

Reading Check Could slaves become free?

Roman Religion

Religion was an important part of everyday life in ancient Rome.

Origins The Romans worshipped hundreds of gods. Many were adapted from the Greeks or Etruscans. Others came from Latin traditions. Some came from people the Romans conquered.

The Role of Government Rome had an **established religion,** or an official religion supported by the government. Top government officials also served as priests. They often consulted religious experts before making decisions. Romans believed that maintaining good relations with the gods was part of the government's job.

The Romans tried to placate their gods, or keep them happy. They believed that if they did certain things, the gods would give them what they asked for. They prayed, worshiped at home, built temples, offered animal sacrifices, and held games in honor of the gods. Romans like Cicero believed that their success was due to their careful attention to the gods.

> ❝ I am quite certain that . . . [Rome] would never have been able to be so great had not the immortal gods been placated. ❞
> —Cicero

Reading Check Why did the Romans sacrifice to their gods?

Jupiter
Jupiter was the king of the Roman gods. He ruled the sky and thunder.

Juno
Juno was the wife of Jupiter. She was the goddess of marriage and the family.

Minerva
Minerva was the daughter of Jupiter. She was the goddess of wisdom and war.

Jupiter, Juno, and Minerva were the most important Roman gods. In Greek mythology, they were known as Zeus, Hera, and Athena.

Section 3 Assessment

Key Terms

1. In what way was Roman society patriarchal?

2. What class of people owned villas?

Key Ideas

3. What was considered the most important role of a Roman woman?

4. How did most wealthy Romans earn their money?

5. What are some tasks that slaves worked at?

6. What did the Romans do to keep their gods happy?

Think Critically

7. **Compare Viewpoints** How might a wealthy Roman view the growth of Roman power differently from a slave?

8. **Identify Main Ideas** What were three important influences on Roman religion?

Essential Question

What should governments do?

9. What was the role of government in Roman religion? Go to your Student Journal to record your answer.

Section 4

The Republic's Growth and Crisis

Key Ideas
- The Romans fought three wars against Carthage and took control of the Mediterranean region.
- Wealth and power led to problems in Roman society and government.
- The Roman republic was torn apart by civil war and replaced by the rule of the emperors.

Key Terms • empire • province • civil war • Augustus

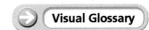 Visual Glossary

Reading Skill Summarize Take notes using the graphic organizer in your journal.

An artist's illustration of a Carthaginian war elephant ▼

Rome began as a small city-state in central Italy. It expanded its power and conquered a large area around the Mediterranean Sea, but its system of government did not survive this change.

The Struggle With Carthage

Rome fought Carthage for control of the western Mediterranean in a series of three wars. These are known as the Punic Wars.

Hannibal's Invasion As you have read, Carthage was a city in North Africa that also controlled parts of Spain and Sicily. The second of Rome's wars with Carthage nearly destroyed the Roman republic. Hannibal, Carthage's most successful general, led his city's troops. In 218 B.C. he launched a daring strike. He marched from Spain into Italy over the Alps mountains with 40,000 soldiers and about 40 war elephants. Despite the dangerous trip, his army reached Italy.

Through clever tactics, Hannibal defeated three armies the Romans sent against him. He probably expected Rome to give up after these crushing defeats. But the Romans desperately kept up the fight, year after year. They wore down Hannibal's men.

In 204 B.C, the Roman general Scipio crossed the sea into Africa. His army attacked Carthage. Hannibal had to sail home from Italy to protect his city. In Africa, Scipio defeated Hannibal and won the war.

The End of Carthage Although Rome had defeated Hannibal, many Romans still feared Carthage. One famous senator ended every speech with the words, "Carthage must be destroyed." Rome attacked Carthage in 146 B.C. Roman troops burned and looted the city. They sold its people into slavery.

Rome now controlled most of the lands along the western half of the Mediterranean Sea. Rome also sent its armies to the east. They conquered Greece and parts of southwest Asia. Rome did not yet have an emperor, but it ruled an **empire,** or a state containing several countries or territories. It was divided into **provinces,** or areas within a country or empire. Roman magistrates were sent out to govern these provinces. Many governors were corrupt and cruel.

Reading Check Who was Hannibal?

Growing Pains

Conquest brought Rome power and wealth. But it also caused problems.

Breaking the Rules In the later years of the republic, magistrates often became very wealthy by stealing from people in the provinces and looting from rich foreign enemies they fought overseas. Wealth made them more powerful at home. Because politicians could become so powerful in this way, they became willing to break the rules of politics or use violence to win elections. Government slowly stopped working.

The Urban Poor Although Rome was growing richer, many Romans were getting poorer. Landowners and employers bought slaves to do work that used to be done by poor Romans. Tenant farmers lost their livelihood. Poor people came to the city in search of work.

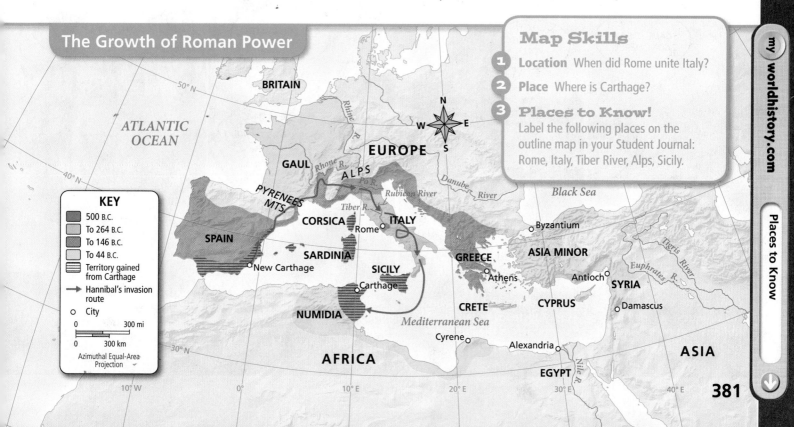

The Growth of Roman Power

Map Skills

1 **Location** When did Rome unite Italy?

2 **Place** Where is Carthage?

3 **Places to Know!** Label the following places on the outline map in your Student Journal: Rome, Italy, Tiber River, Alps, Sicily.

KEY
500 B.C.
To 264 B.C.
To 146 B.C.
To 44 B.C.
Territory gained from Carthage
Hannibal's invasion route
City
0 300 mi
0 300 km
Azimuthal Equal-Area Projection

equipment, n.,
things used for a
specific purpose

professional, adj.,
trained, expert

myWorld Activity
It's Your Call

The government feared that Rome's poor could riot or start a revolution. It gave out free grain to keep the peace. Some politicians supported reforms. They appealed to the poor to win office. More traditional elite politicians opposed them.

Politicians from these two sides supported gangs that fought one another in the streets. In 123 B.C., the tribune Tiberius Gracchus tried to give land to the poor. His opponents killed him. His brother Gaius later died in the same struggle.

The Power of the Army Gaius Marius was a powerful consul. He reformed, or changed and improved, the Roman army. Until around 100 B.C., only citizens who could afford their own armor served in the military. But Marius allowed even the poorest citizens to join. The government paid for their equipment. This made the army larger, and more professional. It also helped the poor.

These new soldiers stayed in the army for many years. When they retired, they needed land to support themselves. They relied on their commander to make the government give it to them. As a result, soldiers became more loyal to their commander than to the government.

Reading Check What did Tiberius and Gaius Gracchus try to do?

From Republic to Empire

The republic's military commanders used their new power. They turned their armies against their rivals and the senate. Rome had its first **civil war,** or war between groups from the same country.

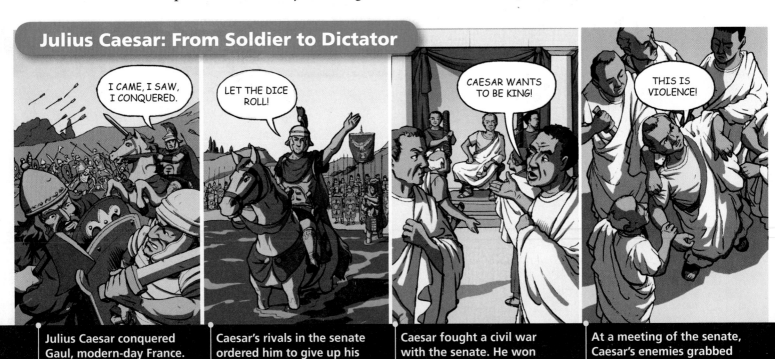

Julius Caesar: From Soldier to Dictator

I CAME, I SAW, I CONQUERED.

LET THE DICE ROLL!

CAESAR WANTS TO BE KING!

THIS IS VIOLENCE!

Julius Caesar conquered Gaul, modern-day France. His conquests made him famous. But they also made his enemies jealous.

Caesar's rivals in the senate ordered him to give up his army. Instead, he led his troops across the Rubicon River into Italy.

Caesar fought a civil war with the senate. He won and became dictator. Some senators said he wanted to be king and plotted to kill him.

At a meeting of the senate, Caesar's enemies grabbed him by his toga and stabbed him 23 times. His death set off more civil wars.

Marius and Sulla In 87 B.C., the commander Sulla was chosen to fight a rich enemy. But an assembly voted to take this position away and give it to Marius. Sulla marched his troops to Rome to get his job back by force. He fought and won a civil war against Marius and his supporters. Sulla ruled as dictator for more than a year before he retired.

Pompey and Caesar New commanders rose up to take Sulla's place. Gnaeus Pompey conquered parts of southwest Asia. Gaius Julius Caesar conquered Gaul. The two men teamed up and used their influence to run the government together, ignoring laws and customs.

But later the two commanders fought. The senate sided with Pompey. It ordered Caesar to give up his legions. But the troops were loyal to Caesar, who marched his army across the Rubicon River into Italy. This began a civil war. Caesar's army defeated Pompey and the senate.

Caesar took control of Rome. He used his power to help the poor. But he also made himself dictator for life. This an-gered many senators, who wanted to keep the republic as it was. A group of senators murdered Caesar on a day called the Ides of March, or March 15, 44 B.C.

The End of the Republic Caesar's death did not save the republic. In his will, Caesar made his teenage relative Octavian his heir. Octavian became a leader of Caesar's many followers. He swore to avenge Caesar's death. He defeated Caesar's murderers in a civil war.

Later, Octavian defeated his main rival Mark Antony, and Antony's ally Cleopatra, the queen of Egypt. By 30 B.C., he ruled Rome. With Octavian's victory, the republic was dead. It was replaced by a monarchy, the Roman empire. Octavian became the first emperor. He took the title **Augustus,** meaning venerable or greatly honored one. It was used by later Roman emperors as well.

Reading Check Why was it important that Caesar crossed the Rubicon?

▲ Pompey

▲ Cleopatra

◄ Marius

Section 4 Assessment

Essential Question

Key Terms

1. What did Marius do to reform the Roman army?

2. Who is involved in a civil war?

Key Ideas

3. How did Rome defeat Hannibal?

4. Why were some Roman politicians afraid of the urban poor?

5. Why did Roman soldiers rely on their generals after Marius's reforms?

6. Who became Rome's first emperor?

Think Critically

7. **Compare and Contrast** Compare the Roman army before and after Marius's reforms. What was the same? What was different?

8. **Identify Main Ideas** What do you think was the main reason why the Roman republic fell?

What should governments do?

9. How did Rome's increasing wealth and power help bring about the collapse of the Roman republic? Go to your Student Journal to record your answer.

Chapter Assessment

Key Terms and Ideas

1. **Recall** How did the Greeks influence Roman religion?

2. **Discuss** How did Rome's allies help it expand?

3. **Recall** Who could wear a **toga**?

4. **Categorize** List two kinds of Roman **magistrates** and the jobs they did.

5. **Compare and Contrast** List one similarity and one difference between the governments of the Roman republic and the United States.

6. **Summarize** What does it mean to say that ancient Rome had an **established religion**?

7. **Analyze Cause and Effect** How did Rome's expansion lead to a rise in the number of slaves owned by Romans?

Think Critically

8. **Analyze Primary Sources** Read the quotation spoken by Gaius Mucius in Section 2. Does this quotation suggest that the Romans believed citizenship was important? Do you think Gaius Mucius was proud to be a Roman? Explain.

9. **Identify Evidence** Defend the statement that the Roman republic was structured to keep a single person from holding too much power. Support your answer with evidence from this chapter.

10. **Ask Questions** Suppose that you could travel back in time to ancient Rome. You want to learn about society. List one question you would ask to each of the following: a man, a woman, a rich person, a poor person, and a slave.

11. **Core Concepts: Foundations of Government** What was the first system of government in Rome? What replaced this system?

Analyze Visuals

Read the timeline and use it to answer the following questions.

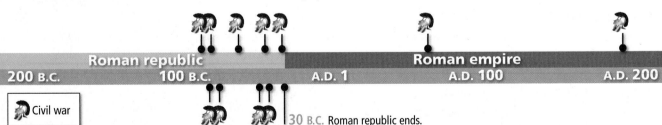

12. How many civil wars took place under the Roman empire before 200 A.D.?

13. Did the Roman republic became more stable or less stable over time?

14. Do you think life improved for ordinary Romans after the Roman republic fell apart and emperors began to rule? Explain your answer. Use evidence from the timeline above and the chapter.

Essential Question
myWorld Chapter Activity

Speech to the Roman Government Imagine that you are a real person who lived in the Roman republic. You will write a speech this person might give to the Roman government asking for a political change to be made. Then you will take on the role of this person and present it to your classmates.

21st Century Learning
Search for Information on the Internet

On the Internet, research one of the following Roman gods or goddesses: Mars, Venus, Neptune, Mercury, or Ceres. Write a paragraph describing your god or goddess. Make sure to include the following information:
- appearance, powers, and role
- name in Greek mythology
- a story about the god or goddess

Document-Based Questions

Online at myworldhistory.com

Use your knowledge of the Roman republic, as well as Documents A and B, to answer Questions 1–3.

Document A

" The three kinds of government, monarchy, aristocracy and democracy, were all found united in the commonwealth [government] of Rome. . . . Such being the power that each part has of hampering the others or co-operating with them, their union is adequate [enough] to all emergencies, so that it is impossible to find a better political system than this."

—Polybius (a historian from the 200s B.C.), *The Histories*

Document B

" There are only Three simple Forms of Government [oligarchy, democracy, and monarchy]. . . . The best Governments of the World have been mixed. The Republics of Greece, Rome, Carthage, were all mixed Governments."

—John Adams (American Revolutionary leader and second President), "Notes for an Oration at Braintree"

1. Why does Polybius believe the Roman constitution worked so well?
   A because it gave all power to a single ruler
   B because different parts of the government balanced one another
   C because it was a pure democracy
   D because one part of the government had total power over all other parts

2. Which sort of government does John Adams support?
   A a monarchy
   B an aristocracy
   C a democracy
   D a republic that mixes elements of all three systems

3. **Writing Task** Based on what you have learned about the Roman constitution, what are the benefits of a government with checks and balances?

myworldhistory.com

Self-Test

385

The Roman Empire and Christianity

Essential Question

Why do people move?

The Colosseum as it appears in modern-day Rome ▼

Explore the Essential Question . . .

- at **my worldhistory.com**
- using the **myWorld Chapter Activity**
- with the **Student Journal**

A Great Empire and a New Faith

27 B.C. Augustus becomes the first Roman emperor.

A.D. 117 The Roman empire reaches its largest extent.

A.D. 313 Emperor Constantine ends the persecution of Christians in the empire.

100 B.C.	A.D. 1	A.D. 100	A.D. 200	A.D. 300	A.D. 400	A.D. 500

Around 1 B.C. Jesus is born, according to Christian tradition.

A.D. 80 The Colosseum is completed.

A.D. 180 The Pax Romana ends.

A.D. 476 The Western Roman empire collapses.

Paul's Shipwreck

Paul's life had been in danger before. For many years he had traveled from place to place across the Roman empire preaching Christianity, a new religion. His message rubbed some people the wrong way. An angry crowd in Jerusalem had almost killed him in A.D. 57. The Romans arrested him, saving his life, but then imprisoned him in Caesarea for two long years. As a Roman citizen, Paul had the right to appeal his case all the way to the emperor, and he did.

Now, in A.D. 59, Paul's life was still in danger—but this time from a sea voyage and not a mob. His journey is described in the Acts of the Apostles, a book that is part of Christianity's scripture.

In Caesarea, Paul got on board a huge ship full of grain, heading west across the Mediterranean Sea. He was going to Rome for trial before Emperor Nero. Grain ships were the largest vessels of the time, bringing food to Rome from Egypt and other provinces. Rome's population was huge and hungry. If the government did not keep the masses fed, they might riot or try to overthrow the emperor. Partly for this reason, the emperors made sure travel by sea was as safe as possible.

ITALY
Rome
GREECE
SICILY
Malta
CRETE
Myra
CYPRUS
MEDITERRANEAN SEA
Alexandria Caesarea Jerusalem

387

Paul boarded a ship at Caesarea bound for Rome. He was escorted by Julius, a Roman centurion. Paul asked Julius to delay the trip, because it was a dangerous time of year for sailing.

Though he treated Paul kindly, Julius ignored Paul's advice and they set to sea. Their ship ran into a storm.

But there was only so much the emperor's soldiers and sailors could do. They could execute as many pirates as they could catch, but winter storms were another matter. Even in the best of times, sailing in the ancient world was a dangerous business.

Paul's escort on his trip was Julius, a centurion, or officer in the Roman army. He was under orders to deliver Paul, along with some other prisoners, to the authorities in Rome. He respected Paul and treated him well, but he decided to travel by sea even though it was late September and the season for safe shipping was just about over.

Many, including Paul, had warned the ship's captain that it was dangerous to travel at that time. The captain insisted he could make it, wanting to squeeze in one last profitable trip. Julius was on the captain's side, and so the ship set sail.

In ancient times, ships normally stayed within sight of land. The captain tried to follow this rule, but he ran into serious trouble once the boat passed the island of Crete. There, northeastern winds drove the ship far away from the coast. The crew lost sight of land, terrifying everyone on board.

The boat tossed and turned in the pounding waves. The crew did their best to lessen the storm's impact. Desperate to lighten the ship, they tossed overboard whatever cargo they could, including most of their food. This dire situation went on for days. Starving and scared, the 276 people on board panicked, certain they were all going to die.

On the fourteenth day, Paul stood on deck and said, "Men, you should have listened to me and not have set sail from Crete and thereby

Paul speaks to a crowd in a market in Malta.

The storm terrified the crew and passengers. They threw cargo overboard to lighten the ship. Paul spoke to them, telling them not to fear.

The ship broke up and ran aground on the island of Malta. Paul and his fellow passengers were safe, but stuck for the winter.

avoided this damage and loss." The listeners probably did not like this "I told you so."

But Paul went on, drawing strength from his faith. "I urge you now to keep up your courage, for there will be no loss of life among you, but only of the ship. For last night there stood by me an angel of the God to whom I belong and whom I worship, and he said, 'Do not be afraid, Paul; you must stand before the emperor; and indeed, God has granted safety to all those who are sailing with you.' So keep up your courage, men, for I have faith in God that it will be exactly as I have been told."

The crew was encouraged by Paul's promise that they would survive. Dawn came, and finally someone sighted land. This was good news, though none of the sailors recognized the coastline. The captain steered the ship into a sandbank, running it aground. Waves battered the ship, and it started to break up. Soldiers yelled for the prisoners to be tossed overboard, to drown rather than escape.

Julius disagreed and protected Paul. Anyone who could swim was urged to jump out and head for shore. The others grabbed pieces of the ship and floated in. Amazingly, everyone survived the wreck.

In the cold and the rain, Paul immediately began gathering wood for a fire. Sailors soon found that they had landed on Malta. An island in the Mediterranean, south of Sicily, Malta was still quite a distance from Rome. But there they would have to stay through the winter.

The people of Malta and their leader, Publius, took care of Paul and his fellow travelers over the next three months. Paul spent his days introducing Christianity to the island. He preached to the people of Malta in the marketplace. He may even have written some of his influential letters there.

In the spring, the group boarded another grain ship bound for Rome. Although Paul's future was still uncertain as he faced trial and possible execution, he must have been proud of his accomplishments. He had spread the word of Christianity to many parts of the Roman empire. He had founded churches and guided them through their difficult early days. And now he had survived a shipwreck!

Based on this story, what was one reason why people traveled in ancient Rome? As you read the chapter ahead, think about what Paul's story tells you about life in the Roman empire and about Christianity.

 myStory Video

Join Paul as he survives a shipwreck.

The Roman Empire

Key Ideas
- Emperor Augustus and his successors helped bring about a long period of peace and prosperity known as the Pax Romana.
- Rome reached new heights in practical technology.
- Long-distance trade helped make the Roman empire wealthy.
- Greco-Roman culture spread across the Roman empire.

Key Terms • deify • Pax Romana • concrete • aqueduct • Greco-Roman

 **Visual Glossary**

Reading Skill Analyze Cause and Effect Take notes using the graphic organizer in your journal.

Augustus, the first Roman emperor ▼

After the fall of the Roman republic, Rome was ruled by emperors. They helped bring about two centuries of peace.

The Emperors and the Roman Peace

In 30 B.C. Octavian took control of the Roman world. He became Augustus, the first and often considered the best Roman emperor.

Augustus After Augustus won the civil wars that had torn apart the Roman republic, he brought peace to the Roman world. He held nearly total power over the empire, although Rome still had a senate.

Augustus made the empire more stable. He shrank the size of the army and raised soldiers' pay. By bringing peace, Augustus gave the economy a boost, improving life for ordinary people. He also fought corruption. He was considered an ideal emperor. After his death he was **deified,** or officially declared to be a god, and worshipped. Most later emperors were also deified, some while they were still alive.

Other Emperors When Augustus died, his stepson Tiberius became emperor. Rome was now clearly a monarchy. The republic was not coming back. Later, a law was passed stating that the emperor had nearly total power, though in fact this had already been the case.

> 66 Whatever he considers to be in accordance with the public advantage and . . . public and private interests he shall have the right and the power to do and to execute, just as had the deified Augustus. 99
>
> —Law concerning the power of Vespasian, from *Ancient Roman Statutes*

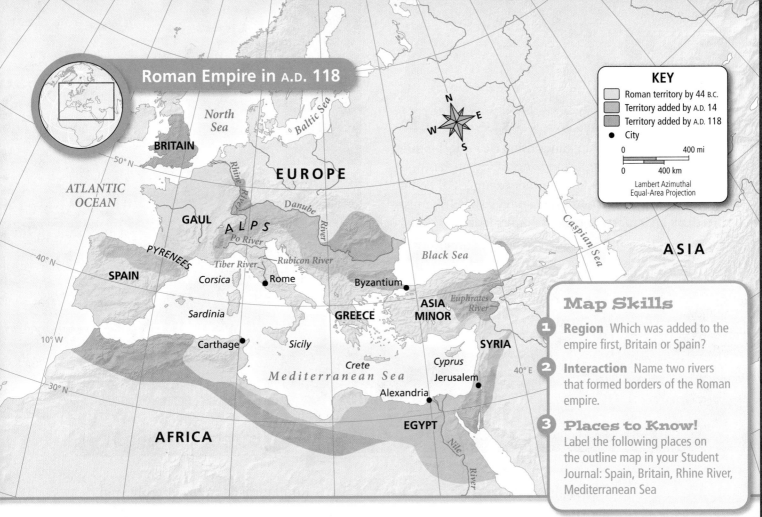

Roman Empire in A.D. 118

North Sea
Baltic Sea
ATLANTIC OCEAN
50° N
EUROPE
BRITAIN
GAUL
ALPS
Rhine River
Danube River
Po River
PYRENEES
40° N
SPAIN
Tiber River
Corsica
Rome
Rubicon River
Black Sea
Caspian Sea
ASIA
10° W
Sardinia
GREECE
ASIA MINOR
Euphrates River
Byzantium
Carthage
Sicily
Crete
Cyprus
SYRIA
40° E
Jerusalem
Mediterranean Sea
Alexandria
30° N
AFRICA
EGYPT
Nile River

KEY
- Roman territory by 44 B.C.
- Territory added by A.D. 14
- Territory added by A.D. 118
- • City

0   400 mi
0   400 km
Lambert Azimuthal Equal-Area Projection

Map Skills

1. **Region** Which was added to the empire first, Britain or Spain?

2. **Interaction** Name two rivers that formed borders of the Roman empire.

3. **Places to Know!** Label the following places on the outline map in your Student Journal: Spain, Britain, Rhine River, Mediterranean Sea

Rome had no formal or set way to choose a new emperor. <u>Succession</u> was a serious problem. Members of the imperial family and other powerful Romans schemed and even killed to become emperor. Sometimes the Roman army made the final decision.

Some of the emperors after Augustus were successful. Trajan conquered new territory for Rome. Hadrian travelled around the empire. He also built walls that separated Roman provinces from non-Roman lands. Marcus Aurelius wrote a famous book of philosophy. Many emperors built aqueducts, public baths, temples, stadiums, and other large buildings in Rome and across the empire.

Other emperors were considered failures. Some are still known for their cruelty. For example, Nero was accused of killing Roman citizens without cause, even his close relatives. He was also was the first emperor to persecute Christians You will read more about Nero later.

Pax Romana Still, Augustus's rule began a long period of peace and prosperity known as the **Pax Romana**, or the "Roman Peace." It lasted from 30 B.C. to around A.D. 180. During that time as many as 65 million people were able to go about their lives in relative peace. No major wars threatened the people of the empire.

Reading Check What was the Pax Romana?

succession, *n.*, one person or thing following another

Roman Architecture

The Romans built sturdy buildings using clever techniques. Some of their buildings still stand, including the Pantheon and many aqueducts. These and other examples of Roman architecture influenced modern building styles. This makes architecture an important part of Rome's legacy.

THINK CRITICALLY **How did aqueducts help cities grow?**

An aqueduct bridge in modern-day France

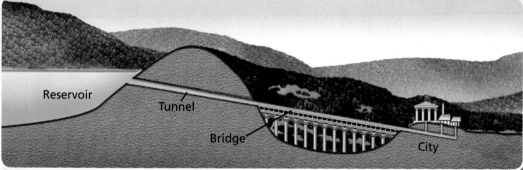

Reservoir

Tunnel

Bridge

City

AQUEDUCTS

Cities cannot grow without water. Aqueducts allowed the Romans to move water across mountains and valleys to supply large cities.

Rome's Practical Achievements

The Romans were a practical people. They excelled at using technology to improve daily life.

Roman Roads "All roads lead to Rome" is an old saying. In ancient Italy, it was true. Major roads extended out from the city like the spokes of a wheel. More than 50,000 miles (80,467 km) of paved roads crisscrossed the Roman empire, linking cities and forts. Roman roads were built to last. Some are still used today.

Roman roads were built mainly so that soldiers could march quickly from place to place. Military engineers traveled with the army. So did architects, stonemasons, and surveyors. Roman soldiers often worked on the roads when not fighting.

Roman roads were superbly engineered. Main roads were hard-paved and well drained. Smooth, all-weather roads were a considerable improvement over dirt paths. They sped up communication throughout the empire. This made government and trade more efficient. Good roads from ports to large inland cities also helped supply food.

Architecture Roman architects devised new building methods and materials, such as concrete. **Concrete** is a building material made by mixing small stones and sand with limestone, clay, and water. The thick, soupy mixture is then poured into molds, where it hardens.

Concrete was lighter and easier to work with than stone. Workers needed less skill to pour concrete than to carve

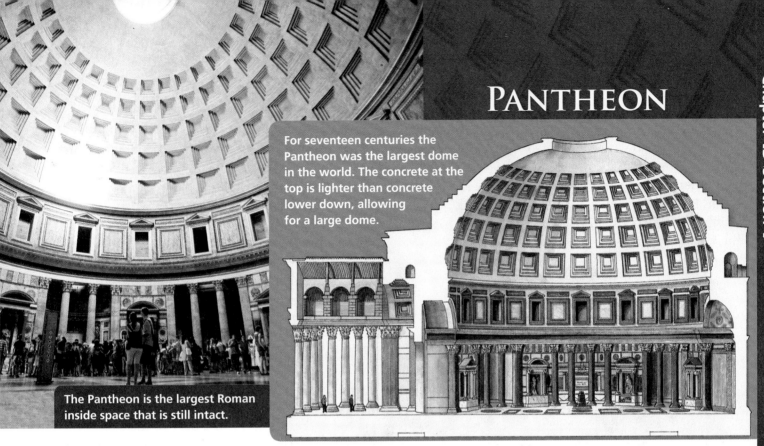

PANTHEON

For seventeen centuries the Pantheon was the largest dome in the world. The concrete at the top is lighter than concrete lower down, allowing for a large dome.

The Pantheon is the largest Roman inside space that is still intact.

stone. Using this new material, workers built large <u>structures</u> covered with domes. The largest dome covered the Pantheon.

In addition to domes, Roman engineers and soldiers also built large, sturdy bridges, supported by rounded, semi-circular arches. Such arches allowed for longer bridge spans. In fact, a rounded arch is the most typical feature of Roman architecture.

Aqueducts and Water A good water supply is as important to city life as are bridges and roads. Roman engineers designed water systems to supply towns with clean water. They built hundreds of miles of aqueducts. An **aqueduct** is a channel that moves water over land.

Roman aqueducts were usually made of stone or concrete channels. They flowed mostly underground. When aqueducts needed to cross valleys, the Romans built long arched bridges to pipe the water along. Some of these bridges still stand today.

In the city, water flowed into public fountains. Some wealthy people had water piped directly into their homes. Aqueducts also supplied public baths. The baths were an important part of the Roman lifestyle and were built in every Roman city. Many Romans went to the baths every day to bathe, exercise, see friends, and even conduct business.

Aqueducts were only part of the water system. Sewers carried waste away from the cities. Roman cities were considered clean by ancient standards. Roman water and sewer systems were not equaled until modern times.

Reading Check Why did Romans visit the public baths?

structure, *n.,* building

Pompeii

The city of Pompeii was destroyed when the volcano Vesuvius erupted in A.D. 79. The ash that covered the city preserved many of its buildings. Today, Pompeii is a valuable source of information about daily life in the Roman empire.

Rome
Mount Vesuvius ▲ ○ Pompeii

Culture Close-Up

The courtyard of a home in Pompeii

A street in Pompeii

After Pompeii's people were buried in volcanic ash, their bodies decayed and left empty spaces. Archaeologists have made plaster casts of these spaces, showing us the way Pompeiians looked as they died.

394

The Roman Economy

Roman roads were usually built for military purposes, but goods also moved across the empire by road. Merchants also traveled by sea. Trade increased across the empire. Cities became centers of industry and commerce.

Trade, Agriculture, and Crafts Before the Romans built a navy, piracy was a problem in the Mediterranean. It made shipping dangerous and expensive. But the Romans cleared the sea of most pirates. This made trade by sea safer. It was also faster and cheaper than travel by land. Ships carried grain, wine, olive oil, and pottery across the empire.

Farming was the base of the Roman economy. The most important crops were grains like wheat. Grain was shipped to Rome to feed its massive population. Imported grain also fed Rome's armies.

In return, money flowed from Rome to the provinces. Provincial farmers grew rich from trade with Rome. Many used their new wealth to help develop their provinces. They built temples, theaters, and public baths. Some wealthy provincial people joined the Roman elite. They became senators and even emperors.

Craft industries were also part of the Roman economy. Skilled craftworkers produced cloth, glass, pottery, metalwork, and ships. The construction industry supplied building projects with marble, terra-cotta tiles, and lead pipes for plumbing.

Currency Economic growth in the empire was helped by a stable currency. A stable currency is a system of money that does not change much in value over time. It is more quickly and widely accepted in trade and commerce. Rome's stable currency made it easier to conduct long-distance trade than in the past.

Reading Check What was the most important good shipped to Rome?

Greco-Roman Culture

You have read that the Romans borrowed from Greek civilization. They adopted Greek cultural practices, and spread their own as well. A combined **Greco-Roman** culture emerged that included Greek and Roman elements. Many people in the empire combined Greco-Roman culture with other local traditions.

Some Roman practices in this joint culture were visiting public baths and worshiping the emperors. Greek traditions included seeing plays by Greek authors, and studying Greek philosophy.

Government and Culture Some actions of the Roman government helped spread Greco-Roman culture. For military purposes, it built roads and founded cities called colonies in the provinces. Roads made it easier to travel and spread ideas. Colonies looked like Rome in many ways. Each had a forum, amphitheater, and baths. Roman culture spread from colonies to nearby lands.

The government also spread Roman culture when it allowed more people to become Roman citizens. By A.D. 212, almost every free person in the empire was a citizen. As citizens, they lived under Roman law. They used Roman courts to settle disputes. Male citizens could serve in the Roman army.

Army Life Roman soldiers helped spread Greco-Roman culture as well. Many soldiers were sent to the far reaches of the empire. They often married local women and settled where they had served. Military outposts on the frontiers grew into towns and cities which introduced the local people to Greco-Roman culture.

Reading Check How did colonies help spread Greco-Roman culture?

my World CONNECTIONS

Like Rome, the United States has a large road system. There are more than **4** million miles of paved roads in the United States today.

myWorld Activity
The Following Announcement . . .

Section 1 Assessment

Key Terms

1. How were aqueducts used?

2. What is concrete made from?

3. What are two Roman elements in Greco-Roman culture?

Key Ideas

4. What were some of Augustus's achievements?

5 Why did the Roman army need good roads?

6. What was the role of farming in the Roman economy?

Think Critically

7. **Analyze Cause and Effect** How did the Pax Romana help economic growth in the empire?

8. **Identify Main Ideas** How did roads, aqueducts, and concrete contribute to city life?

Essential Question

Why do people move?

9. If you traveled to Roman cities all across the empire in A.D 100, what similar buildings would you see wherever you went? Go to your Student Journal to record your answer.

myworldhistory.com

Culture Close-Up

Roman Culture and Its Legacy

Key Ideas

- The Romans made many achievements in art, literature, and science.

- Latin continued to be an important world language long after the fall of the Roman empire.

- The Romans pioneered large-scale public entertainment.

- Roman law influenced the legal systems of many modern countries.

Key Terms • mosaic • Romance languages • oratory • satire • gladiator

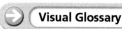 Visual Glossary

Reading Skill Identify Main Ideas and Details Take notes using the graphic organizer in your journal.

The Roman empire may be ancient history, but Roman culture is still with us in many ways. Rome's art, language, entertainment, and law continue to influence the modern world.

A mosaic showing Virgil, a famous Roman poet ▼

Art and Language

The arts flourished in the Roman empire. Roman art is still widely admired. The Latin language also remains important.

The Arts In Roman towns, art filled public buildings and the homes of the wealthy. Colorful mosaics brightened up floors. A **mosaic** is a design formed with small tiles of glass, stone, or pottery. Public buildings and the homes of the wealthy boasted colorful painted murals on the walls and ceilings. These showed beautiful landscapes, events from mythology and history, and scenes from daily life.

The Romans built statues of their gods, great heroes, and important people. They stood in markets, temples, and other public places. Many were copies of Greek originals. But the Romans also developed their own style. Greek sculptors usually idealized their subjects, or made them look like ideal people. Greek sculptures usually show young and beautiful people. In contrast, earlier Roman sculptors usually showed their subjects as they were in real life.

Latin Lesson

Latin may not be spoken by anyone today as a first language, but it is still useful. The chart below shows Latin words and phrases that we use often in English.

Latin Phrases	
carpe diem	seize the day
circa	about, around
caveat emptor	buyer beware
de facto	in reality
et cetera (etc.)	and other things
quid pro quo	something for something

"Salve! Ut vales? Hello! How are you?"

"Valeo, et tu? I am well, and you?"

On the quarter, you can read the United States' Latin motto, "E Pluribus Unum." It means "From Many, One."

Skillful Roman artisans used various materials to make beautiful objects. They crafted vases and jars of blue glass and mirrors of polished silver. Romans wore jewelry made of silver, gold, and gems.

The Influence of Latin Roman soldiers, colonists, and merchants took their language to many parts of Europe. Latin, the Roman language, became the spoken language across much of the western part of the empire. Over centuries, local ways of speaking of Latin changed into new languages, including Spanish, Italian, French, and Portuguese. These are called **Romance languages,** or languages that developed from Latin. Millions of people speak Romance languages today.

English is not a Romance language, but as many as half of all English words may come directly or indirectly from Latin. For example, the word *educate* comes directly from Latin, while *labor* comes indirectly from Latin by way of French.

Latin was the language of education in Europe for many centuries. Scientists still use it to name plants and animals. Latin also served as the language of the Roman Catholic Church. All Catholic services were held in Latin into the 1900s.

Reading Check What were two types of art developed by the Romans?

Literature and Science

The Romans prized literature and science. They built on Greek achievements.

Oratory and Poetry The Romans developed **oratory,** the art of giving speeches. Rome's most famous orator was Cicero. He was a politician during the last days of the Roman republic. Cicero spoke about the great political issues of his time. He used his powers of persuasion to win election to high office. Many of his speeches were written down and used as models by later orators.

achievement, *n.*, accomplishment that requires effort or skill

397

The poet Virgil lived around the same time as Cicero. He wrote the *Aeneid*, an epic poem. It was modeled on Homer's Greek epics, the *Iliad* and the *Odyssey*.

Horace was another famous Roman poet. He is best known for a collection of poems called *Odes*. Some are about friendship and love. Others give advice.

The poet Ovid wrote witty verses. Many of his poems explored the theme of love. Some retold stories from Greek and Roman myths.

Satire The author Juvenal wrote **satires,** works of literature that make fun of their subject. Juvenal mocked Roman life. For example, he complained that the Roman people accepted the rule of the emperors instead of having a republic. He wrote that in his day Roman citizens only wanted free food and entertainment.

> 66 The people that once bestowed [gave out] commands, consulships, legions, and all else, now . . . longs eagerly for just two things—bread and circuses! 99
> —Juvenal, *Satire 10*

Philosophy The Romans also continued developing philosophy, inspired by the Greeks. One famous Roman philosopher was Seneca. He wrote about Stoic philosophy. Stoicism urges people to accept suffering and practice self-control.

Science and Medicine Like philosophy, the Romans also contributed to science and medicine. One important scientist during this period was an astronomer and mathematician named Claudius Ptolemy (KLAW dee uhs TAHL uh mee). He lived in Egypt, which was part of the Roman empire.

Ptolemy wrote a famous book called the *Almagest*. It shaped the way astronomers viewed the universe until the 1400s, although its main idea was wrong. Ptolemy also wrote important works on geography and optics, or the study of light.

The best-known physician in the Roman empire was a Greek named Claudius Galen. Galen carefully dissected, or cut open, animals such as monkeys. He did this to study how bodies work. Galen was the first to discover that arteries and veins carry blood. Earlier, people believed that they carried air. Doctors used Galen's writings for more than a thousand years.

Reading Check What type of writing is Juvenal famous for?

Popular Entertainment

The Greeks staged public entertainments, including plays and athletic events. But the Romans developed a taste for public entertainment on a massive scale. They invented the round amphitheater, and built stadiums across the empire.

Gladiatorial Games The Romans enjoyed fights between **gladiators,** or men who fought one another as part of a public entertainment. They often fought to the death. Fights were held in the arenas such as the Colosseum in Rome.

Gladiatorial matches were first held in southern Italy before Rome existed. Originally, these games were staged at funerals. The death of a gladiator was meant as a sacrifice to the spirit of the person whose death was being mourned. Later, the games lost this connection with funerals and were held just to entertain.

COLOSSEUM
and the Gladiators

The Colosseum is one of the most famous surviving Roman buildings. It was round, but the cut-away illustration below shows how it may have looked inside. As many as 50,000 Romans packed its stands to watch the fights that took place in the arena.

THINK CRITICALLY **How was seating arranged in the Colosseum?**

A gladiator looks to the emperor to decide whether to spare the life of his defeated opponent.

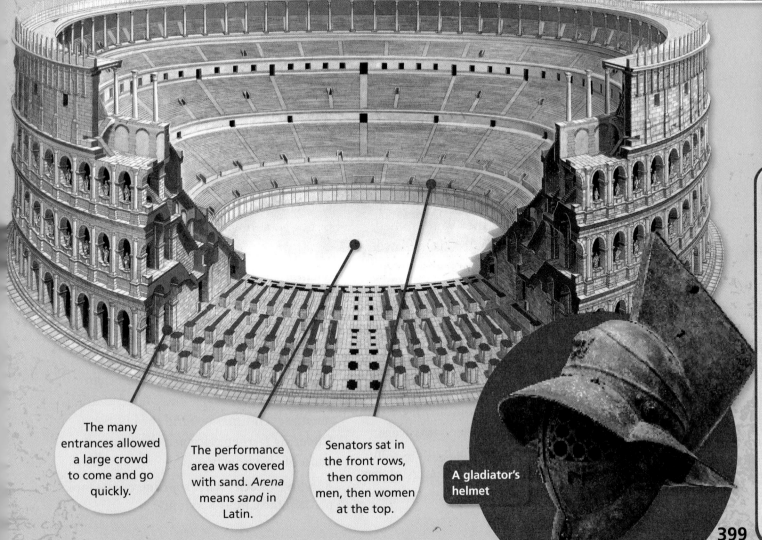

The many entrances allowed a large crowd to come and go quickly.

The performance area was covered with sand. *Arena* means *sand* in Latin.

Senators sat in the front rows, then common men, then women at the top.

A gladiator's helmet

my worldhistory.com

Primary Source

399

CIRCUS MAXIMUS
and the Chariot Races

Chariot racing was extremely popular in ancient Rome. Chariots pulled by teams of horses raced around the track at breakneck speeds to the cheers of fans.

What modern sport is similar to chariot racing?

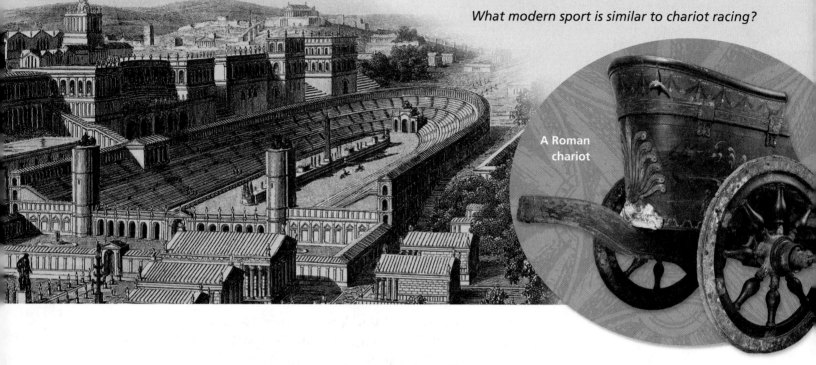

A Roman chariot

The word *gladiator* means swordsman in Latin, though gladiators used a variety of weapons. Gladiators were usually slaves or criminals. They were trained both to fight and to entertain a crowd. Skilled or lucky gladiators who survived many matches could win their freedom. They could even become celebrities.

Sometimes, huge battles between teams of gladiators were staged. Special arenas were flooded so that gladiators could fight one another on boats, recreating famous naval battles from history. Exotic animals like lions and elephants were brought to Rome. Special fighters, condemned criminals, and prisoners of war were made to fight these wild animals.

Emperors or wealthy aristocrats paid for these extravagant games. Expensive events showed off the wealth and power of the person who sponsored them.

Chariot Races One of the most popular event in ancient times was chariot racing. In Rome, chariot races took place at the Circus Maximus. The Circus Maximus was a huge racecourse that could seat as many as 270,000 people.

Races were held far more often than gladiatorial games. Horses pulled charioteers seven times around the course. Cheering fans encouraged their favorite team of charioteers.

Reading Check What sporting events took place in the Circus Maximus?

A charioteer pulled by four horses

Roman Law

You have read that the government of the Roman republic influences governments today. Similarly, Roman law shapes the laws of many modern countries.

The Twelve Tables In the early years of the Roman republic, there were no written laws. Judges decided what the law was in each case. They based decisions on custom and <u>tradition</u>. In the 400s B.C., the Romans wrote down a law code called the Twelve Tables. It set down laws relating to family relations, property, inheritance, and other important issues.

The Influence of Roman Law Roman law lasted longer than the empire itself. It changed a great deal over the centuries. Over time it developed into a system called civil law. Today, civil law is used in many parts of the world. For example, it is used in some countries that were once Roman provinces, such as France, Spain, and Portugal. It is also used in nations that were once colonies of these countries, including Algeria, Mexico, and Brazil. Even today, one American state uses a legal system partly based on civil law. This is Louisiana, which was founded as a French colony.

Reading Check What were the Twelve Tables?

tradition, *n.*, a custom or practice that is handed down over generations

Section 2 Assessment

Key Terms

1. What are mosaics made from?

2. Were gladiators usually slaves or usually free?

3. What is a Romance language? Is English one of these?

Key Ideas

4. How did the Romans affect the languages spoken in Europe?

5. What were two popular types of Roman entertainments?

6. Who was Rome's most famous orator?

Think Critically

7. **Compare and Contrast** How are Cicero's writings different from Juvenal's?

8. **Identify Main Ideas** How is the legacy of the Latin language important to scientists today?

? Essential Question

Why do people move?

9. What important discovery did Galen make about how things move inside people's bodies? Go to your Student Journal to record you answer.

Section 3

Origins of Christianity

Key Ideas
- Many Jews opposed Roman rule in Judea.
- Jesus was an influential Jewish teacher whose followers believed he was the Messiah.
- Jesus' followers founded Christianity and spread it to many people, despite Roman persecution.

Key Terms
- resurrection
- baptism
- crucifixion
- conversion
- martyr

 Visual Glossary

||||||| **Reading Skill Sequence** Take notes using the graphic organizer in your journal.

An early image of Jesus as the Good Shepherd, sacrificing for his flock ▼

You have read that the Roman empire made great strides in technology and culture. Still, many people in the empire opposed Roman rule. A Jewish spiritual leader name Jesus arose during the Pax Romana. He was executed by the Romans. A new religion soon emerged based on his teachings and the writings of his early followers.

Judea Under Roman Rule

In 63 B.C., the Romans took control of the Jewish kingdom of Judea, centered in Jerusalem. A large number of Jews opposed Roman rule.

Zealots Many Jews saw the Romans as foreigners who occupied their land and treated them cruelly. They hoped that God would send a Messiah, or specially chosen king who would save the Jews from oppression. The Messiah would drive the Romans from their homeland. One group of Jews called the Zealots resisted the Romans by force. They refused to pay taxes and killed Roman officials.

Religious Groups Different religious groups existed among Jews during this time. One group was called the Pharisees (FAR uh seez). These were educated people who observed Jewish law. They believed that good people could be resurrected after death. **Resurrection** means coming back to life. Another large group was the Sadducees. They came from the elite and supported the traditions of the temple in Jerusalem. The Sadducees generally cooperated with Roman rule.

Other, smaller, groups of Jews withdrew from society and lived in <u>isolated</u> communities in the desert. Many of these groups practiced ritual cleansing by plunging into water. Christianity later adopted this ritual as **baptism.**

Reading Check Who were the Sadducees?

Jesus' Life and Teachings

During this period of upheaval, a Jewish man named Jesus of Nazareth lived and taught. He attracted a large following.

Early Life Most of what we know about Jesus comes from early Christian writings known as the Gospels. According to the Gospels, Jesus was a descendant of the great Jewish king, David, and his birth was miraculous. According to tradition, Jesus was a carpenter, like his father.

Jesus the Teacher The Gospels tell us that as an adult, Jesus was baptized by a prophet named John in the Jordan River. Afterward, he began teaching from the Hebrew scriptures. For three years, Jesus traveled throughout Judea, telling people that God would soon come to establish his kingdom.

Jesus became known as a champion of the poor and the outcasts of society. Word spread that he could heal sick people who came to him for help. His closest followers began to wonder whether Jesus was the Messiah.

isolated, *adj.,* set away from other people or places

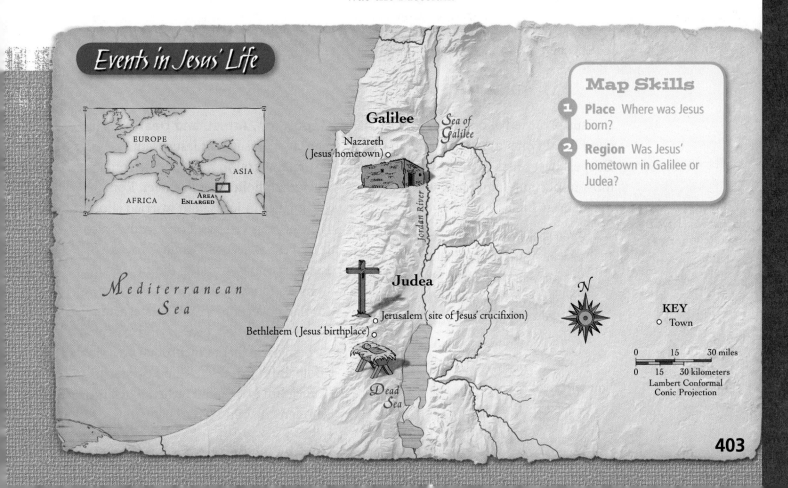

Events in Jesus' Life

EUROPE

ASIA

AFRICA

Area Enlarged

Galilee

Sea of Galilee

Nazareth (Jesus' hometown)

Jordan River

Mediterranean Sea

Judea

Bethlehem (Jesus' birthplace)

Jerusalem (site of Jesus' crucifixion)

N

Dead Sea

Map Skills

1 **Place** Where was Jesus born?

2 **Region** Was Jesus' hometown in Galilee or Judea?

KEY

o Town

0   15   30 miles

0   15   30 kilometers

Lambert Conformal Conic Projection

Early Christian Symbols

Early Christians used different symbols to show their faith. These decorated churches and tombs. Some are still used by Christians today.

The symbol above is called a Chi Rho. It combines two Greek letters that begin the word "Christ."

▲ A fish and a cross, both important Christian symbols.

This jar was used in worship services by early Christians. ▶

The fish, used in the two images at the left, is a major early Christian symbol. Fish are important in the Gospels. For example, Jesus performs a miracle by feeding a large crowd with a few fish. As well, the letters of the word "fish" in Greek can stand for the sentence "Jesus Christ, God's Son, Savior."

Jesus preached about how to live a good life. In one famous passage in the Gospels, Jesus lists what he called the two most important commandments from the Hebrew Bible.

authorities, *n.,* people who have the right to give orders

66 'You shall love the Lord your God with all your heart, and with all your soul, and with all your mind.' This is the greatest and first commandment. And a second is like it: 'You shall love your neighbor as yourself.' 99

—Matthew 22:37–39

You will read more about Jesus' teachings in the next section.

Opposition, Arrest, and Death

The Gospels say that Jesus went to Jerusalem around A.D. 33 to celebrate the Jewish holiday of Passover. Roman <u>authorities</u> in Jerusalem worried about the large holiday crowds. Local leaders also feared trouble. A riot might provoke the Romans into destroying the city.

In response to these concerns, the Roman governor Pontius Pilate, acted. He had Jesus arrested, beaten, and executed by being crucified. **Crucifixion** was a slow and painful Roman method of execution. The victim was nailed or tied to a large wooden cross and left to hang until dead.

The Resurrection After Jesus died, his body was taken down from the cross and laid in a tomb. The Romans sealed the tomb and posted guards around it. According to the Gospels, some of Jesus' followers visited the tomb three days later. They found the guards gone and the tomb empty. They ran to tell the other disciples. Many claimed to have seen him after his death. They believed that God had resurrected Jesus and that he was indeed the Messiah. The Greek word for *Messiah* is "Christ."

Jesus and his early followers were Jews. But those who believed Jesus was the Messiah eventually formed a new religion known as Christianity.

Reading Check What does the word *Christ* mean?

The Spread of Christianity
During his life, Jesus chose twelve trusted followers, called disciples or apostles. After his death, they spread his teachings.

The Early Church When Jesus died, Peter, a key apostle, became a leader of the new church. The word *church* can refer to the community of all Christians, a specific group of Christians, or a building Christians worship in.

Peter and other apostles spread belief in Jesus as the Messiah. They carried their faith to many parts of the world. They visited Europe, Asia, and North Africa.

Christians and Jews The first followers of this new faith still considered themselves Jews. They respected most Jewish laws and traditions. They read the Hebrew Bible and prayed in synagogues.

But differences grew between Jewish followers of Christianity and other Jews. Christians began sharing their beliefs with non-Jews outside of Judea. The apostle Peter even traveled to Rome itself. People from different backgrounds heard the apostles' message. More and more gentiles, or non-Jews, became Christians.

In A.D. 66, the Zealots you have already read about led a huge rebellion against Rome. With difficulty, the Romans defeated them and destroyed the temple in Jerusalem. After a later rebellion, Jews were forbidden to live in Jerusalem. Many left Judea as migrants or were taken away as slaves. They settled around the empire.

The Apostle Paul You have already read about Paul. He helped spread Christianity around the Roman empire. Early in his life he was opposed to Christians. He had an experience that led to his conversion to Christianity. A **conversion** is a heartfelt change in one's opinions or beliefs. Paul believed that Jesus had appeared to him and told him to spread the new faith. Paul is called an apostle, though he was not one of the original twelve.

Paul traveled to Greece and other areas. He founded churches and preached. Paul also wrote letters called epistles to various Christians. He helped spread the belief that non-Jews did not need to follow all Jewish laws to become Christians. They still needed to live moral lives and could not worship other gods. As more gentiles came into the church, Christianity became a separate religion and no longer a part of Judaism.

The cross is the most important and widely recognized symbol of Christianity.

myWorld Activity
Comparing Religions

Reasons for Growth Christianity spread rapidly during the Pax Romana, although it remained a minority faith in the empire for centuries. Several factors helped the new faith grow quickly.

As you read, the Roman government built roads and kept the seas free of pirates. This made travel safer. It allowed Christians to move more easily from place to place, spreading their beliefs. Paul's journeys, for example, might not have been possible in an earlier period.

As well, Greek was widely spoken in the eastern half of the empire, and by educated people everywhere. Christian scriptures were in Greek, so a large number of people could understand them.

The ideas of Christianity also appealed to many people. Many appreciated Christianity's moral teachings and its monotheism, or belief in one god. Some were also attracted by the Christian belief that all people are equal in God's sight, including slaves and women.

Reading Check How did the Greek language help the spread of Christianity?

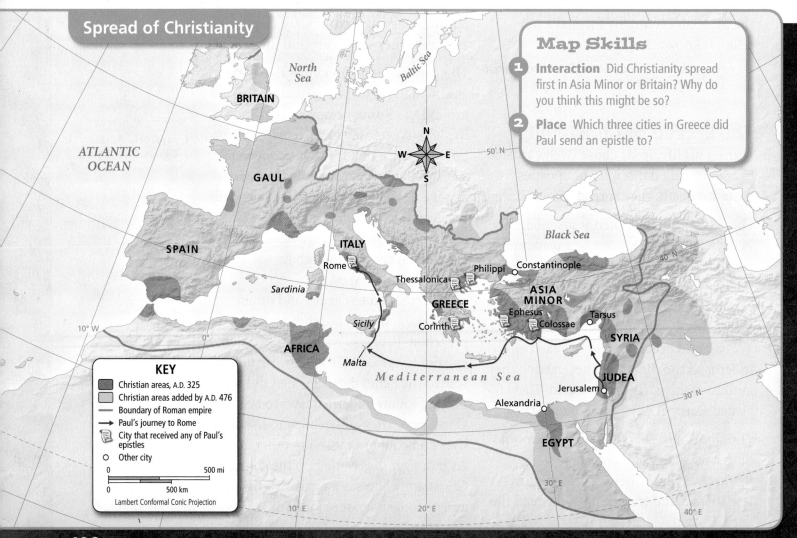

Spread of Christianity

Map Skills

1 **Interaction** Did Christianity spread first in Asia Minor or Britain? Why do you think this might be so?

2 **Place** Which three cities in Greece did Paul send an epistle to?

North Sea
Baltic Sea
BRITAIN
ATLANTIC OCEAN
GAUL
SPAIN
ITALY
Rome
Sardinia
Sicily
AFRICA
Malta
Mediterranean Sea
Thessalonica
Philippi
Constantinople
GREECE
Corinth
ASIA MINOR
Ephesus
Colossae
Tarsus
SYRIA
JUDEA
Jerusalem
Alexandria
EGYPT
Black Sea

50° N
40° N
30° N
10° W
0°
10° E
20° E
30° E
40° E

KEY
- Christian areas, A.D. 325
- Christian areas added by A.D. 476
- Boundary of Roman empire
- Paul's journey to Rome
- City that received any of Paul's epistles
- ○ Other city

0   500 mi
0   500 km
Lambert Conformal Conic Projection

Christianity and the Empire

The growth of Christianity worried Roman officials. They sometimes persecuted, or mistreated Christians.

Toleration The Romans generally allowed people in the empire to worship their own gods, so long as they also worshiped Roman gods and emperors as a sign of loyalty. Most people in the empire already worshiped many gods and did not object to worshiping a few more. Although Jews did not worship Roman gods, this did not greatly bother the Romans. This was because they respected old religious traditions. Jewish traditions forbade worshiping more than one god.

A New Faith But Christianity was a new religion, and the government opposed it. When non-Jews became Christians they stopped worshiping the old gods. Officials feared that Christians refused to worship Roman gods because they were disloyal. Romans also worried that the gods would be angry if people who became Christians stopped worshiping them. It was considered the government's job to keep the gods happy.

Persecution A fire destroyed much of Rome in A.D. 64. Emperor Nero falsely blamed the Christians. Many Christians were killed in the city of Rome. After A.D. 250, emperors persecuted Christians across the empire. Persecution scared some away from Christianity. However, it caused others to bond to their faith. Persecution produced **martyrs,** or people who die for their beliefs. Their courage strengthened the faith of many Christians.

Persecution continued, on and off, until the reign of Emperor Constantine (KAHN stun teen). According to tradition, he had a dream just before a key battle which told him to fight under the sign of the cross. He won the battle. In 313, he ended the persecutions of Christians and eventually became a Christian himself. A later emperor made Christianity the official Roman religion in 380.

Reading Check Which emperor ended the persecution of Christians?

Constantine holding a cross ▼

Section 3 Assessment

Essential Question

Why do people move?

Key Terms

1. What is baptism?

2. What does it mean for someone to be resurrected?

3. How did Christian martyrs help strengthen the faith of other Christians?

Key Ideas

4. How did the Zealots feel about Roman rule in Judea?

5. Summarize the events of Jesus' life according to the Gospels.

6. Why did the Roman government fear the spread of Christianity?

Think Critically

7. **Identify Main Ideas** Why did the Roman government tolerate Judaism but not Christianity?

8. **Analyze Cause and Effect** According to tradition, how did Constantine's dream change the course of Roman history?

9. How did the actions of the Roman government help allow the spread of Christianity and other ideas? Go to your Student Journal to record your answer.

Beliefs of Christianity

Key Ideas

- Early Christians wrote books about the life of Jesus and other topics that form part of Christianity's scripture.

- Most Christians share a core set of beliefs, including faith in Jesus as the son of God and in the Trinity.

- Christians believe that it is important to follow Jesus' ethical teachings.

Key Terms • New Testament • Gospel • parable • epistle • Trinity • ethics • denomination

 **Visual Glossary**

Reading Skill Summarize Take notes using the graphic organizer in your journal.

A Christian man at prayer with a copy of the Bible ▼

In the centuries after the death of Jesus, Christians gathered their sacred writings and developed their faith. Their writings centered on the life of Jesus and the Christian belief in Jesus as the son of God.

The Christian Bible

You have already read about the Hebrew Bible, which contains Jewish history, religious laws, and many other writings. Like Jews, early Christians read the Hebrew Bible as their scripture, or holy writings.

The Old and New Testaments At first, the Hebrew Bible was the Christians' only sacred text. Then they began to add their own body of writings. Jews did not and still do not accept these as scripture. Christians called the Hebrew Bible the Old Testament, and this new body of work the **New Testament**. They read both together as their holy text.

The works that became the New Testament were written down between A.D. 50 and 150. By the 300s they were collected and began circulating in the form that Christians recognize today. Jesus and his early followers probably spoke Aramaic. But the New Testament was written in Greek. Greek was the most widely spoken language in the eastern part of the Roman empire. The New Testament contains 27 separate documents, called books.

The Gospels The first four books of the New Testament are the **Gospels.** They describe the life and teachings of Jesus from four different points of view. The Gospels do not all describe the same events in exactly the same way. Together, however, they create a powerful portrayal of Jesus and his teachings.

Many of Jesus' teachings are presented in the form of **parables,** or stories with a moral. Jesus often used parables to explain important lessons.

Other Books After the Gospels come a number of other books. Most of them are **epistles,** or formal letters. These are letters that apostles and other early leaders wrote to the newly established churches.

Most epistles were written to explain Christian teachings or to solve problems in the church. Paul wrote many of these epistles to churches he had started himself. His letters explained many Christian beliefs in great detail. Paul's life and the lives of other early Christians are described in another book in the New Testament, the Acts of the Apostles.

The last book of the New Testament is the Book of Revelation. It is written like an epistle, but makes predictions about future events. It uses complicated images to predict Jesus' return to Earth and a final battle between good and evil.

Reading Check What are the first four books of the New Testament called?

The Good Samaritan

This painting shows the parable of the Good Samaritan, which appears in the Gospel of Luke. In this story, a man is robbed and beaten. As he lies in the road, two wealthy, well-connected people pass by and ignore him. Finally, a Samaritan, a member of a disliked ethnic group, comes by. He stops and helps the man who has been attacked. Jesus praises the Samaritan. By telling this story, Jesus is saying that people must treat one another kindly, and that we should judge others based on their actions, not their ethnicity. Today, the phrase "a Good Samaritan" means a person who helps a stranger in need.

Beliefs About God

Christians use the New Testament as a source for their teachings. Throughout the centuries, Christians have disagreed about some parts of their faith. But most Christians today share many basic beliefs in common.

The Son of God The Gospels refer to Jesus not only as the Messiah, but also as the Son of God. Christian belief holds that Jesus was God in human form. To the early Christians, Jesus' death proved he was human. His resurrection proved that he was divine, or godlike. For some, the idea of Jesus as both human and divine was puzzling or <u>controversial</u>. But Christians could have faith that they, too would be resurrected after death. Christians believe that by believing in Jesus, they will be rewarded with eternal, or endless, life in the presence of God.

The Soul and Salvation Christians believe that everyone has a soul, or spirit. To a Christian, what happens to the soul after death depends on how that person has lived and whether that person believes in Jesus. Christians believe that people need God to forgive their sins, or wrongdoings, so that their souls can live on in the presence of God after death. They believe that God may forgive people who are truly sorry for their sins and choose to follow Jesus.

Many Christians view Jesus' death and resurrection as key to forgiveness. In the ancient world, some peoples atoned, or made up for sins, by offering animal sacrifices to their gods. Many Christians

controversial, *adj.*, something that people disagree or argue about

Sermon on the Mount

The Sermon on the Mount is one of the most famous parts of the New Testament. It is a speech given by Jesus on a mountain. Its words continue to guide and inspire Christians today.

believe that Jesus, by being crucified, became the sacrifice for everyone's sins.

The Trinity   Like Jews, Christians are monotheists. As you have read, this means that they worship one god. Most Christians, however, believe that God exists as three forms, called persons. Together, these three forms are known as the **Trinity**. The Trinity includes God the Father, Jesus the Son, and the Holy Spirit.

Christians believe that God the Father created the universe. They believe that Jesus is God's son. He is God in human form. The Holy Spirit, also called the Holy Ghost, is described as the power of God as experienced on Earth. To early Christians, the Holy Spirit allowed them to sense the presence of God after Jesus was no longer with them.

Reading Check   How did people in the ancient world atone for sins?

Practicing Christianity

In daily life, Christians try to follow Jesus' teachings. Most Christians also observe similar rituals and holidays.

Following Jesus' Teachings   Much of Jesus' teaching has to do with **ethics,** or issues of right and wrong and how to treat people. Christians today try to live according to Jesus' ethical teachings. Jesus urged his followers to treat others as they would like to be treated. This is called the "Golden Rule."

> 66 In everything, do to others as you would have them do to you. 99
>
> —Matthew 7:12

Jesus also showed great concern for poor and humble people. He accepted even those with the lowest social standing among his followers.

myWorld Activity
Do the Right Thing

Jesus may have given the Sermon on the Mount on a hill overlooking the Sea of Galilee, below. ▼

Blessings

> 66 Blessed are the poor in spirit, for theirs is the kingdom of heaven. Blessed are those who mourn, for they will be comforted. Blessed are the meek, for they will inherit the earth. Blessed are those who hunger and thirst for righteousness, for they will be filled. 99
>
> —Matthew 5:3–6

Teachings

> 66 You have heard that it was said, 'You shall love your neighbor and hate your enemy.' But I say to you, Love your enemies and pray for those who persecute you, so that you may be children of your Father in heaven. 99
>
> —Matthew 5:43–44

Christianity Today

Christianity is the world's largest religion. There are about 2 billion Christians in the world. They are divided into thousands of **denominations,** or religious groups. Different groups share some beliefs and rituals but disagree about others. The largest single groups are Roman Catholicism and Eastern Orthodoxy. Protestantism is a large family of groups. Some Protestant denominations are the Baptist, Methodist, Lutheran, Presbyterian, Pentecostal, and Episcopalian churches.

THINK CRITICALLY **What is the largest Christian group?**

21st Century Learning

Christians working in a soup kitchen ▼

Pope Benedict XVI, the leader of the Roman Catholic Church, greets worshipers. Roman Catholicism is the largest Christian group.

Protestant Christians pray at church in Africa. Christianity is growing rapidly on that continent.

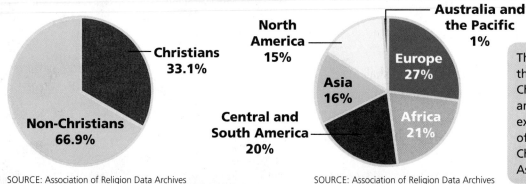

Christians in the World

- Christians 33.1%
- Non-Christians 66.9%

SOURCE: Association of Religion Data Archives

Where Christians Live

- North America 15%
- Australia and the Pacific 1%
- Europe 27%
- Asia 16%
- Africa 21%
- Central and South America 20%

SOURCE: Association of Religion Data Archives

The circle graph at the left shows how Christians are divided among regions. For example, 16 percent of the world's Christians live in Asia.

As well as following Jesus' teachings, most Christians believe religious faith is also important. To most Christians, Christianity means believing in Jesus, in his sacrifice for other people's sins, and in his resurrection.

Rituals and Holidays Many practices are shared by nearly all groups of Christians. Most Christians observe Sunday as the special day of rest and prayer. At worship services many Christians participate in a ritual meal called a Holy Communion or Eucharist. This usually includes bread and wine or grape juice. Many Christians are baptized, either as infants or adults.

Christmas and Easter are two important holidays for most Christians. Christmas celebrates the birth of Jesus, a miracle according to Christian tradition. Easter celebrates Jesus' resurrection.

Reading Check What event is marked by Easter?

The Judeo-Christian Tradition

Judaism and Christianity are separate religions. They have many important differences. But the two faiths also have much in common. Both Jews and Christians worship one God. Both read the Hebrew Bible (Old Testament) as scripture. They share a similar ethical tradition. Members of both groups respect the Ten Commandments.

Together, the common <u>elements</u> of Judaism and Christianity are called the Judeo-Christian tradition. This tradition has helped shaped much about life in Europe, the Americas, and other areas. It has contributed to art and literature. For example, stories from parts of the Bible read by members of both faiths are common themes in art. The tradition also helps shape law. For example, it teaches the equality of all people before the law.

Reading Check What is one element that Judaism and Christianity have in common?

element, *n.*, part

Section 4 Assessment

Key Terms

1. When was the New Testament written down?

2. Who do Christians believe are the members of the Trinity?

Key Ideas

3. Which part of the New Testament was partly written by the apostle Paul?

4. Do most Christians believe that Jesus was human, divine, or both?

5. What is the "Golden Rule"?

6. What two faiths make up the Judeo-Christian tradition?

Think Critically

7. **Analyze Primary Sources** In the Sermon on the Mount, what sorts of people did Jesus say are "blessed"? What does this say about how Christians believe people should act?

8. **Identify Main Ideas** What do Christians believe about atonement, or making up for sins?

Essential Question

Why do people move?

9. Do more Christians today live in Asia, where Christianity was founded, or on other continents? Go to your Student Journal to record your answer.

Decline of the Roman Empire

Key Ideas

- Problems including civil wars and foreign invasions led to the decline of the Roman empire.

- The Roman empire was divided into eastern and western halves, each with its own emperor.

- The western half of the Roman empire collapsed while the eastern half survived.

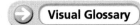 **Visual Glossary**

Key Terms • inflation   • barbarian   • mercenary   • orthodoxy

 Reading Skill Analyze Cause and Effect Take notes using the graphic organizer in your journal.

Marcus Aurelius, the last great emperor of the Pax Romana ▼

For centuries, the Roman empire ruled the Mediterranean region. In the A.D. 200s, however, Rome began to decline.

The End of the Pax Romana

In A.D. 180, the emperor Marcus Aurelius died. He was the last of five powerful emperors who had kept the empire strong and united for many years. His death marks the end of the Pax Romana. Over the next 300 years, the empire slowly declined and finally collapsed.

The peace of the Roman empire depended on one emperor following another without violence. Starting in the late A.D. 100s, military commanders began to challenge emperors, hoping to become emperor themselves. Civil wars broke out more frequently. A series of wars broke out after Marcus Aurelius's son Commodus was assassinated.

A general named Septimius Severus briefly restored peace. Severus became emperor after winning a civil war. He was able to hold on to power. He understood that he was emperor because the army supported him, not because the people liked him. His strategy for holding on to power was blunt and simple. He said, "Enrich the soldiers, scorn all other men." While many earlier emperors had tried to win over the people and the senate, later emperors cared less for their opinions and focused on the military.

Reading Check Who was Septimius Severus?

The Imperial Crisis

Severus's successors lost power. The empire soon fell again into civil wars. The years A.D. 235 to 284 are called the Imperial Crisis. During the crisis, Rome was torn apart by civil wars and even split into pieces. Generals quickly became emperor one after another. Each killed or defeated the previous emperor.

Economic Problems Civil wars created massive economic problems. Wars were expensive. Men who wanted to be emperor needed to convince soldiers to support them. They increased soldiers' pay or gave them bribes. Emperors raised taxes to support these expenses. That hurt common people and the economy.

Emperors also tried to get the money they needed by debasing the currency. That means making coins with less gold or silver and more copper or other less valuable metals. When merchants realized that coins had less precious metal than before, they raised their prices. This caused **inflation,** or a general rise in the cost of goods.

Wars also hurt the economy by making trade dangerous. The trade networks that had made Rome wealthy were disrupted.

Foreign Invasions During this period, Rome's foreign enemies became more dangerous. Roman armies were often tied up fighting civil wars. Troops were pulled away from the borders.

As Romans fought other Romans, people from outside the empire took advantage of the bad situation. They raided Roman lands more often.

Persians, Goths, and Huns

As Rome grew to become a great empire, it defeated many rivals. In its later years, it faced new enemies. The Persians in the east, and the Goths and Huns in the north, were some of Rome's most serious challengers.

Persians

The Sassanian Persian emperor Shapur I captured the Roman emperor Valerian in battle. The relief at the right shows Shapur sitting on a horse holding Valerian by his wrists. A second Roman emperor kneels before Shapur.

Goths

Unlike the Persians and the Huns, the German Goths settled down inside Roman territory and became Christians. The set of Gothic crowns and jewelry at the right includes a cross, showing this fact.

Huns

The Huns were one of the most fearsome enemies Rome ever faced. As in the image at the left, they were skilled riders who could use spears and even shoot arrows from horseback.

415

Late Roman Empire

The Roman empire did not collapse all at once. It declined slowly over 300 years. This timeline shows some of the most important events during that period.

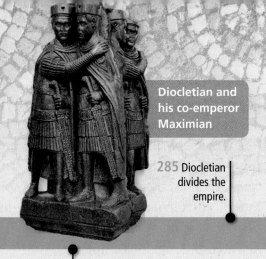

Diocletian and his co-emperor Maximian

180 The Pax Romana ends.

285 Diocletian divides the empire.

100

200

235–284 Imperial Crisis occurs.

communication, *n.,* way of passing on information

The empire's size made it hard to defend the borders. Despite good roads, <u>communication</u> and travel were much slower than they are today. Troops could not be moved quickly to fight invaders. It took a long time to bring word of an invasion to the emperor.

In the 200s, the Sassanian empire rose up in Persia. The Sassanian Persians took advantage of Roman civil wars to raid Roman lands. In 260, they captured and executed the Roman emperor Valerian.

The Germanic Tribes The Romans called the people who lived across the empire's northern borders Germans. They were made up of many different groups. Some were the Franks, Vandals, and Goths.

Like the Persians, the Germans also raided Roman territory more often during the Imperial Crisis. They saw Rome as a rich, easy target. Many Germans also wanted to settle in the empire. Living conditions were often better there.

Romans called the Germans **barbarians**. This is the word Greeks and Romans used for all people who did not share their cultures. They believed that barbarians were savage or uncivilized.

In fact, many Germans adopted parts of Greco-Roman culture. They lived in or near the empire for generations. After Rome became Christian, many Germans converted as well. During and after the Imperial Crisis, tens of thousands of Germans joined the Roman army. By the end of the empire, Germans had become leading Roman generals.

Reading Check Who were the Sassanians?

The Late Empire

The Roman empire did not recover from its crisis until the late 200s. A man named Diocletian (dy uh KLEE shun), a military leader, became emperor in 284. For the first time in decades, a single man ruled the whole empire. He held on to power for many years.

Diocletian During his rule, Diocletian tried to make Rome more stable. He reorganized the imperial government. He sent troops to restore peace to frontier regions. Diocletian also persecuted Christians, since many Romans believed that Christians had made the gods angry and that this had caused their problems.

Emperor
Constantine

The ruins of the
Roman Forum

312 Constantine
converts to
Christianity.

410 Goths sack Rome.

476 Roman Empire
in the west ends.

300

400

500

Diocletian's most important contribution was to divide the empire into two halves. He chose a co-emperor to help him manage the empire. Diocletian ruled over the eastern part of the empire, while Maximian ruled in the west.

Diocletian also appointed two junior emperors. They were meant to take power after senior emperors died or retired. This step was intended to prevent civil wars. If this system had worked, one emperor could have followed another peacefully.

Constantine But Diocletian's effort failed. After his death, military leaders again fought for power. In time, a man named Constantine defeated his rivals and became emperor. As you read, Constantine converted to Christianity and made it a legal religion in the empire.

In 324, Constantine began work on an impressive new capital for the eastern half of the empire. He built his "New Rome" in what is now Turkey. It was on the site of an old Greek city called Byzantium. After his death, the city was called Constantinople, city of Constantine.

Reading Check What does *Constantinople* mean?

Collapse of the West

Despite Constantine's work, Rome's decline continued after his death. The empire's enemies took advantage of its weakness and caused it to <u>collapse</u>.

The Huns Arrive Nomads from the plains of Central Asia, known to the Romans as the Huns, triggered a crisis along the empire's northern borders. They were fierce warriors who moved into Europe in the 300s. Later, in the 400s, they attacked Rome under their leader Attila. The Romans defeated that invasion at the battle of Châlons. But the arrival of the Huns was still dangerous. As they thundered across the continent, Germans fled ahead of them into Roman lands.

The Germans Invade By 376, some Germans had reached the Danube River, the border of the empire. The German Goths crossed the river. They entered the empire, looking for refuge from the Huns.

The Romans attacked the Goths and tried to control them, but the Goths defeated them at the battle of Adrianople. Gothic invasions followed. Goths and other Germans crossed into the empire.

myWorld Activity
Tonight's Guest Is . . .

collapse, *v.,* fall apart, break into pieces

417

Fall of the ROMAN EMPIRE

Political problems and civil wars helped seriously weaken the Roman empire. Foreign enemies invaded, and economic problems sapped Rome's prosperity. These and other problems caused the western half of the Roman empire to collapse.

THINK CRITICALLY How did civil wars encourage foreign invasions?

Causes and Effects

Civil wars

Foreign invasions

Economic problems

End of the western Roman empire

Foreign Invasions

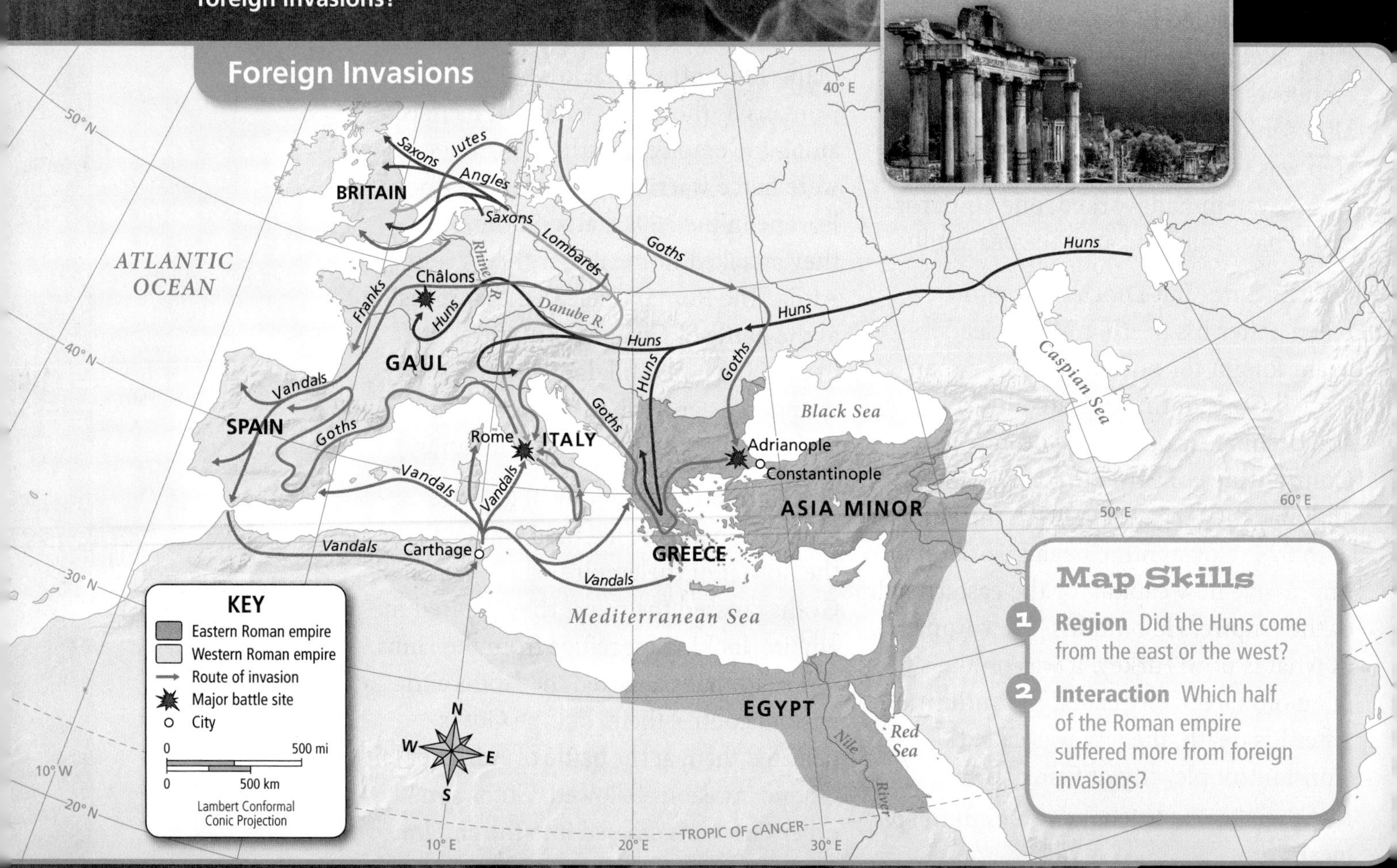

ATLANTIC OCEAN

Saxons Jutes
Angles
BRITAIN
Saxons
Lombards
Goths
Huns

Franks
Châlons
Huns
Rhine R.
Danube R.
Huns
Huns
Goths

GAUL
Vandals
Huns
Goths

SPAIN
Goths

Rome ITALY
Vandals
Vandals

Black Sea
Caspian Sea

Adrianople
Constantinople

ASIA MINOR

Vandals Carthage
GREECE

Vandals
Mediterranean Sea

EGYPT
Nile River
Red Sea

KEY

- Eastern Roman empire
- Western Roman empire
- → Route of invasion
- ✸ Major battle site
- ○ City

0   500 mi
0   500 km

Lambert Conformal Conic Projection

N W E S

Map Skills

1 **Region** Did the Huns come from the east or the west?

2 **Interaction** Which half of the Roman empire suffered more from foreign invasions?

The Romans tried to pay some tribes of Germans to fight others. They hired Germans as **mercenaries,** or soldiers who fight for pay rather than for their country. But these mercenaries were not always loyal. They sometimes turned against the empire. Rome failed to stop the invasions.

The emperor Theodosius took over after the disaster at Adrianople. He was the last person to rule both the eastern and western halves of the Roman empire. Theodosius became a strong supporter of Christian **orthodoxy,** meaning traditional or established religious beliefs. He made Christianity the official Roman religion.

After Theodosius's death, the situation went from bad to worse in the western empire. German tribes began to seize whole provinces. In 410, Roman troops pulled out of Britain. They abandoned the province to German invaders.

As the western empire fell apart, German generals dominated western Roman emperors from behind the scenes. The emperors lost power.

The Fall of Rome In time, the city of Rome itself was attacked. Goths captured Rome in 410 and looted the city. In 455, the Vandals plundered Rome.

Rome never recovered from these attacks. The western Roman empire ended in 476. In that year, a German general named Odoacer deposed, or removed from power, Romulus Augustus, the last western Roman emperor. Odoacer became king of Italy.

As the government of the western Roman empire collapsed, cities came under attack. People moved from the cities to the country for safety. Trade and learning declined.

The Roman empire survived in a smaller form in the east, however. Eastern emperors held on to power. Eastern cities continued to prosper. The eastern Roman empire survived for almost 1,000 years after the western empire fell. Modern historians know the eastern Roman empire as the Byzantine empire.

Reading Check Who won the battle of Adrianople?

Section 5 Assessment

Essential Question
Why do people move?

Key Terms

1. When inflation occurs, do prices rise or fall?

2. Why do mercenaries fight?

Key Ideas

3. Whose support did a man need most to become emperor?

4. How did the emperors cause inflation?

5. Why did Diocletian divide the empire?

6. How did the Western Roman empire finally end?

Think Critically

7. **Analyze Cause and Effect** How did civil wars lead to economic problems?

8. **Identify Main Ideas** What changes did Diocletian make to try to solve the Roman empire's succession problem?

9. How did the movement of the Huns affect the Roman empire? Go to your Student Journal to record your answer.

Chapter Assessment

Key Terms and Ideas

1. **Compare and Contrast** How was the government of the Roman empire different from the government of the Roman republic?

2. **Recall** What do the words "**Pax Romana**" mean in Latin?

3. **Summarize** What is the purpose of **satire**?

4. **Categorize** List two everyday situations in which a person would have to think about **ethics**.

5. **Analyze Cause and Effect** What caused **inflation** in the Roman empire?

6. **Discuss** How did Diocletian try to solve the problem of choosing a new emperor? Did he succeed?

7. **Recall** What are two important ways in which Constantine changed the Roman empire?

Think Critically

8. **Analyze Primary Sources** Find the quote by Juvenal in Section 2. What is Juvenal's complaint about the Roman people?

9. **Make Inferences** In what ways did the Roman government help the spread of Christianity, despite its persecution of Christians?

10. **Sequence** Put the following three emperors in order from earliest to latest: Diocletian, Constantine, Augustus. Write one sentence about the main contribution of each emperor.

11. **Core Concepts: Religion** What is the importance of Christmas and Easter in Christianity?

Analyze Visuals

The statue to the right sits in front of the United States Supreme Court building. The Latin word on the scroll is *lex*, which means "law."

12. Why do you think this particular statue has Latin writing on it?

13. What does the fact that this statue has a Latin word on it tell you about the legacy of ancient Rome in the modern world?

Essential Question

myWorld Chapter Activity

A Moving Experience Follow your teacher's instructions to explore the spread of Roman culture to different parts of the empire. Using the Activity Cards, along with Sections 1–5 and myworldhistory.com, you will role-play a Roman moving to a distant province. You will record your experiences in diary entries and then discuss those experiences to connect immigration long ago with immigration today.

21st Century Learning

Give an Effective Presentation

Use the Internet or your library to find information about a Roman emperor of your choosing. Give a presentation to your class about your emperor. Include the following information:
- Dates ruled
- Accomplishments and interesting facts
- Your opinion: was this emperor successful or unsuccessful?

Document-Based Questions

Success Tracker™
Online at myworldhistory.com

Use your knowledge of the Roman empire, as well as Documents A and B to answer questions 1–3.

Document A

" Aqueducts which have crumbled through age, I have restored. . . . I have given gladiator exhibitions; in these exhibitions about 10,000 men have fought. . . .
I have cleared the sea from pirates. . . .
I added Egypt to the Empire of the Roman People."

—The Deeds of the Divine Augustus, Emperor Augustus

Document B

" If a man were called to fix the period in the history of the world, during which the condition of the human race was most happy and prosperous, he would, without hesitation, name [the Pax Romana]. . . . The vast extent of the Roman empire was governed by absolute power, under the guidance of virtue and wisdom."

—*The History of the Decline and Fall of the Roman Empire*, Edward Gibbon, 1776

1. In Document A, Augustus listed his major accomplishments. Of the following, which is not something Augustus considered important enough to list?
   A adding new lands to the empire
   B building improvements to Rome
   C protecting people's rights
   D staging public entertainments

2. According to Document B, what did Edward Gibbon believe?
   A The Pax Romana was a difficult period.
   B The Roman empire mistreated its subjects.
   C The Pax Romana was a happy period.
   D Absolute, or unlimited rule is a bad form of government.

3. **Writing Task** Do you agree with Edward Gibbon about life during the Pax Romana? Write a paragraph explaining your answer.

myworldhistory.com

Self-Test

421

The Spread of Christianity

Key Idea
- Christianity spread despite persecution by the Roman government.

During the Roman republic and the Roman empire, Roman religious beliefs included the worship of multiple gods. The Roman government often persecuted, or mistreated, Christians for refusing to worship the Roman emperor. This intolerance is shown in the first document, a letter written by the Roman governor Pliny to Emperor Trajan. But as the Roman empire weakened, Christian practices and beliefs spread. Under the emperor Theodosius, who ruled from A.D. 379 to 395, Christianity became the official religion of the Roman empire.

A painting from the 1800s showing the burial of an early Christian killed by Roman persecution

Read the text on the right. Stop at each circled letter. Then answer the question with the same letter on the left.

A Identify Details What punishment is given to those who do not confess to being Christians?

B Draw Inferences How does this passage reveal Pliny's point of view?

C Summarize In your own words, what is Pliny describing in the last paragraph?

denounced, *v.,* accused publicly
interrogated, *v.,* questioned formally
creed, *n.,* a set of beliefs
obstinacy, *n.,* stubbornness
folly, *n.,* lack of good sense
check, *v.,* to slow or stop

Pliny's Letter to Emperor Trajan

66 [I]n the case of those who were <u>denounced</u> to me as Christians, I have observed the following procedure: I <u>interrogated</u> these as to whether they were Christians; those who confessed I interrogated a second and a third time, threatening them with punishment; those who persisted I **A** ordered executed. For I had no doubt that, whatever the nature of their <u>creed</u>, stubbornness and inflexible <u>obstinacy</u> **B** surely deserve to be punished. There were others possessed of the same <u>folly</u>; but because they were Roman citizens, I signed an order for them to be transferred to Rome. . . .

[T]his superstition has spread not only to the cities but also to the villages and farms. But it seems possible to <u>check</u> it. It is certainly quite clear that . . . the established religious **C** rites, long neglected, are being resumed. 99
—Pliny the Younger, *Letters,* about A.D. 111–113

Read the text on the right. Stop at each circled letter. Then answer the question with the same letter on the left.

D **Summarize** Explain in your own words what Theodosius is saying in the first sentence.

E **Identify Details** What does Theodosius mean by belief in "one deity"?

F **Draw Inferences** What do you think might happen to people who refuse to become Christians?

clemency, *n.,* an act of leniency, mercy

apostolic, *adj.,* of or relating to an apostle

deity, *n.,* a god or goddess

ignominious, *adj.,* dishonorable, humiliating

heretic, *n.,* person who contradicts established religious beliefs

conventicle, *n.,* a religious assembly

condemnation, *n.,* blame

Theodosian Code

66 It is our desire that all the various nations which are subject to our <u>clemency</u> and moderation, should continue to the profession of that religion which was delivered to the Romans
D by the divine Apostle Peter. . . . According to the <u>apostolic</u> teaching and the doctrine of the Gospel, let us believe in the
E one <u>deity</u> of the father, Son and Holy Spirit, in equal majesty and in a holy Trinity. We authorize the followers of this law to assume the title Catholic Christians; but as for the others, since in our judgment they are foolish madmen, we decree that they shall be branded with the <u>ignominious</u> name of <u>heretics</u>, and shall not presume to give their <u>conventicles</u> the
F name of churches. They will suffer . . . divine <u>condemnation</u> and the . . . punishment of our authority, in accordance with [what] the will of heaven shall decide to inflict. 99
—Theodosius, A.D. 380, from *Documents of the Christian Church,*
edited by Henry Bettenson and Chris Maunder

Analyze the Documents

1. **Compare and Contrast** How are these two documents similar? How are they different?
2. **Writing Task** Using these two documents to support your thoughts, write a paragraph giving your opinion about the following statement: Religious tolerance is needed to maintain a peaceful society.

Constantine I was the first Christian emperor of Rome.

Produce a **Roman Newscast**

Your Mission Your class will create and present a newscast about life in ancient Rome. Divide into teams to focus on four different parts of the newscast: news, sports, special reports, and editorial segments. Work together as a class to perform the newscast.

Over time, Rome grew from a small town to the center of a huge, diverse empire. As you plan your newscast, think about events from Roman history that your viewers would find interesting. For example, you might choose to include a story about the political influence of key Roman leaders, or about construction projects during the Pax Romana. A sports story might describe an event held in the Colosseum. A special report on culture might include information about Roman arts, religious beliefs, or educational practices. Be sure to use interesting visuals in your reports.

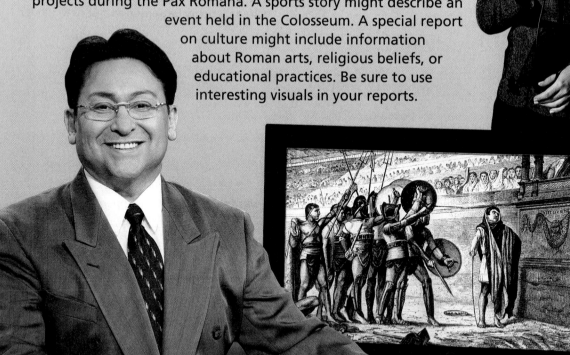

STEP 1

Gather the News.

Begin by using your textbook, your school library, and the Internet to gather information about your assigned topic. News teams should collect facts about ancient Rome's politics and wars. Sports teams should find information about Roman athletic events. Special reports teams might focus on topics such as science, economics, religion, or medicine. Editorial teams should take a stand on an important issue in Roman history.

STEP 2

Write Your Reports.

After you have gathered facts for your part of the newscast, write a report about your topic. Be sure to address any questions that a viewer might have about the topic, such as what happened and why it was important. If you have time, your team may wish to produce a commercial for a product or service that existed in ancient Rome. Choose one or two students from your group to be the newscasters who will read the reports to the class.

STEP 3

Present Your Newscast.

Your newscast should present the facts clearly and concisely. Rewrite any sentences that may be too long and check that you are pronouncing words correctly. Rehearse with your team by reading each report aloud. Each team's segment should be about five minutes long, so use the classroom clock to time your stories. Above all, make sure that your information is accurate! Invite another class to view the presentation of your newscast and commercials.

The Byzantine Empire and Islamic Civilization

Atlantic Ocean

Europe

Africa

Theodora (500s), a Byzantine empress, was a skilled politician and a powerful leader.

Ibn Battuta (1300s) was a Moroccan man who traveled widely throughout Africa and Asia.

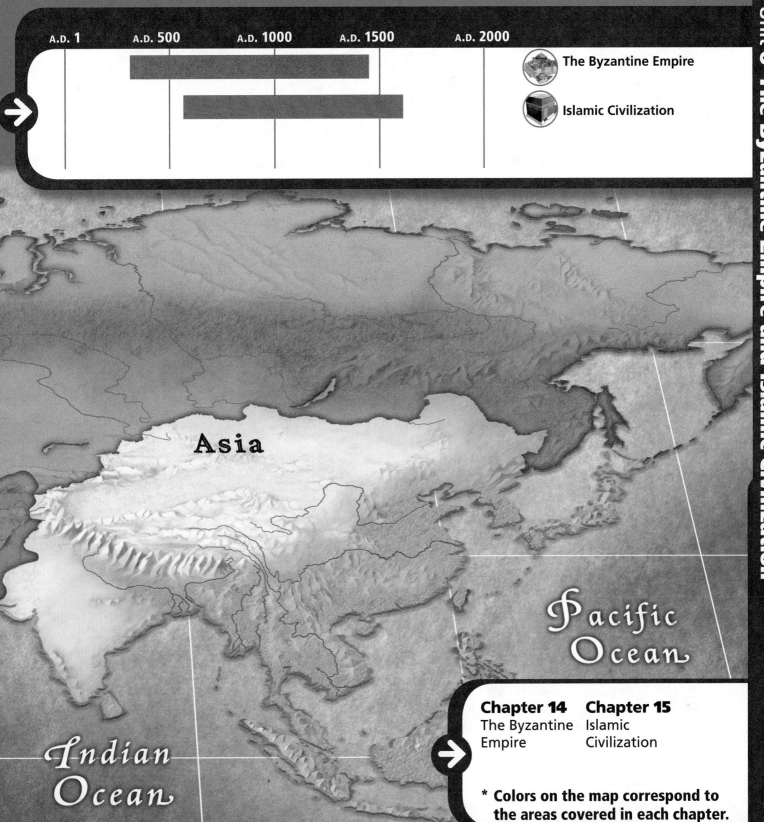

A.D. 1   A.D. 500   A.D. 1000   A.D. 1500   A.D. 2000

The Byzantine Empire

Islamic Civilization

Asia

Pacific Ocean

Indian Ocean

Chapter 14
The Byzantine
Empire

Chapter 15
Islamic
Civilization

* Colors on the map correspond to
the areas covered in each chapter.

The Byzantine Empire

? Essential Question

What distinguishes one culture from another?

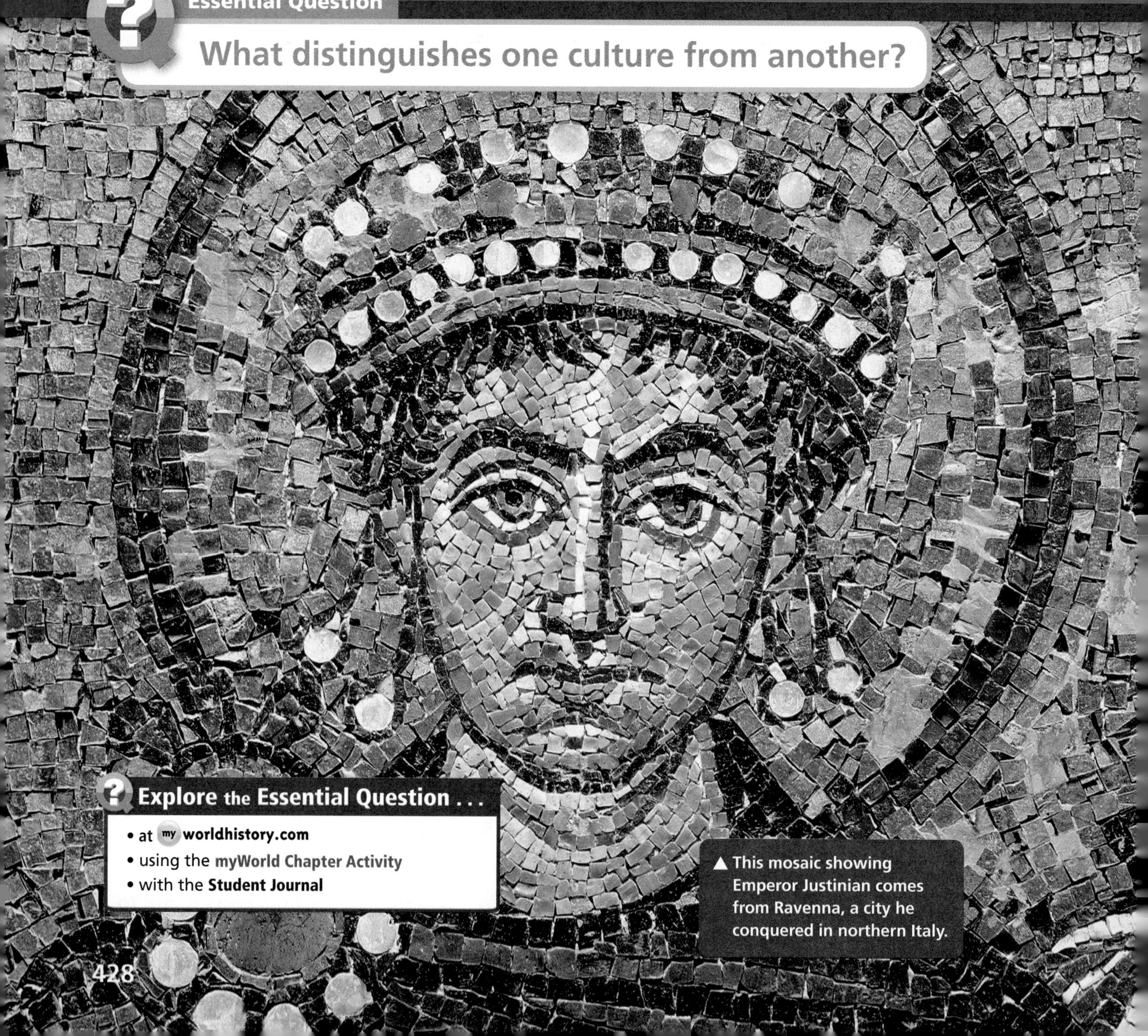

? Explore the Essential Question . . .

- at **my worldhistory.com**
- using the **myWorld Chapter Activity**
- with the **Student Journal**

▲ This mosaic showing Emperor Justinian comes from Ravenna, a city he conquered in northern Italy.

1000 Years of Byzantine History

324 Constantinople is founded.

527 Justinian becomes emperor.

1054 Great Schism divides Eastern Orthodox and Roman Catholic churches.

A.D. **300**   A.D. **600**   A.D. **900**   A.D. **1200**   A.D. **1500**

476 Western Roman empire collapses.

630s Arab Muslims conquer much of the Byzantine empire.

1453 Constantinople falls to the Ottoman Turks. Byzantine empire ends.

THE NIKA RIOT:
Theodora's Great Victory

Although she was the empress, Theodora knew as well as any commoner how passionate the people of Constantinople were about their chariot races. She had practically grown up in the Hippodrome, Constantinople's massive racecourse. Her father used to take care of the trained bears whose performances entertained the crowd between races.

The chariot races combined heart-pounding sports action with imperial politics. The teams represented different political and religious groups. Fans were fiercely loyal to their teams, especially the dominant Blues and Greens. Fans of the Blues tended to be landowners, while fans of the Greens were typically artisans and traders. The city buzzed with their intense rivalry, which often broke out into street violence.

A riot broke out one day in A.D. 532, not long after Theodora and her husband Justinian came to power. Usually, fans fought the fans of an opposing team, but this time was different. Anger at Justinian brought fans of the Blues and Greens together.

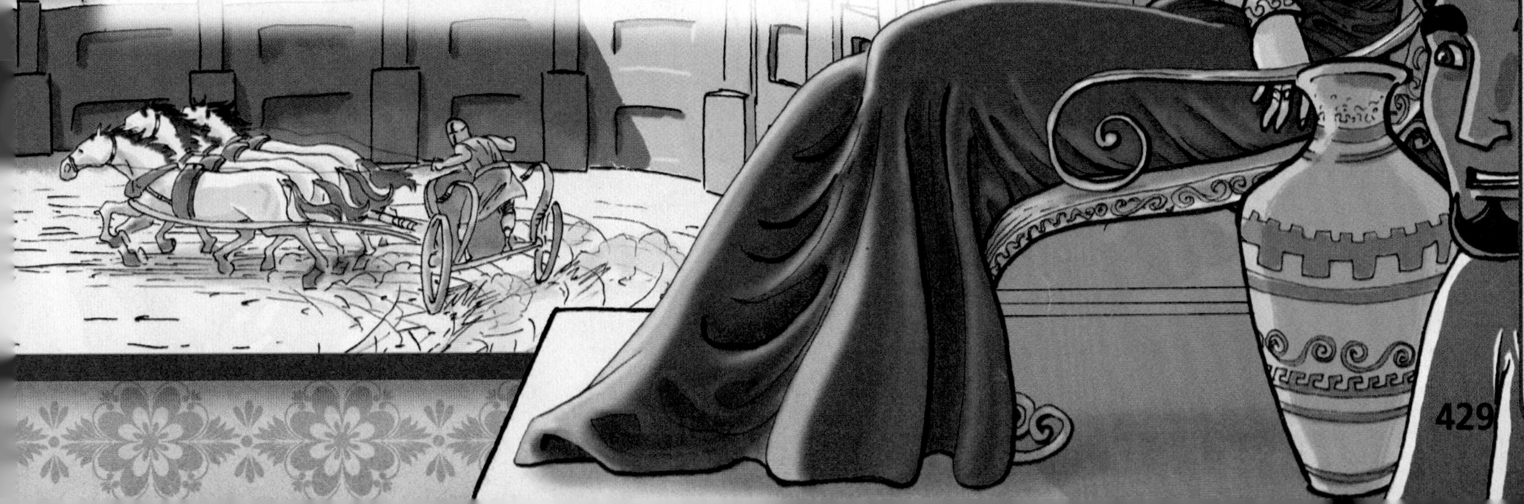

my worldhistory.com

Timeline/On Assignment

429

Anger at Justinian and Theodora boiled over at the Hippodrome. Fans attacked soldiers and began a riot. Some aristocrats supported the mob.

Justinian could not decide what do to. He feared the worst. Mobs rioted throughout the city and even burned down the main church.

"...for one who has been an emperor it is unendurable to be a fugitive."

Earlier, Justinian had executed fans of both teams who had fought one another in a violent riot. This enraged other fans. United by their hatred of the emperor, thousands screamed: "Nika! Nika! Nika!" (which means "Victory! Victory! Victory!")

The rioting fans swelled into an angry mob that took over the Hippodrome. Constantinople had no police force to stop them. The mob took over the city, burning and looting. They had the support of many aristocrats, who hated Justinian and his high taxes. Many of them hated Theodora, too, a former lower-class actress who had risen up in the world. The aristocrats did not consider actors and actresses to be good people. They thought such people should not have power in the government.

The rioters and their supporters crowned one aristocrat as their new ruler. They went on to torch almost half the city, including the great church called Hagia Sophia (AH ye uh suh FEE uh), which means Holy Wisdom.

Theodora's speech inspired the emperor. He sent his army into the Hippodrome. Soldiers killed thousands of rioters.

The riot was put down and order was restored. Justinian rebuilt the great church Hagia Sophia. It still stands today.

And where was Justinian during this chaos? As his rule collapsed, he cowered in his palace. He and his advisors were paralyzed with fear. Should they send the army to fight the mob? Should they grab all the money they could and flee the city by boat?

When they failed to decide, Theodora rose to address the court. Theodora was her husband's partner in his rule. She advised him on many important issues. Now, dressed in her fine robes of imperial purple, she gave a stirring speech urging Justinian to fight for his throne.

She couldn't stand the idea of fleeing. According to a historian of her day, she said, "For one who has been an emperor it is unendurable to be a fugitive."

Theodora refused to give up power, symbolized by her purple imperial robes. A historian recorded her words, "May I never be separated from this purple, and may I not live that day on which those who meet me shall not address me as mistress [ruler]."

She taunted her husband, saying he could flee if he wanted to, though he would regret it later on. And if he did go, he was on his own. Theodora preferred to die rather than lose power. "If, now, it is your wish to save yourself, O Emperor, there is no difficulty. For we have much money, and there is the

sea, here the boats. However, consider whether it will not come about after you have been saved that you would gladly exchange that safety for death. For myself, I approve a certain ancient saying that royalty is a good burial-shroud."

Her dramatic words won over Justinian. Energized, he ordered his generals to attack the mob. Soldiers entered the Hippodrome and killed thousands of rioters. The Nika riot was over.

With his wife's help, Justinian went on to have a long and successful reign. One of his proudest achievements was rebuilding the Hagia Sophia church with its massive golden dome. It still stands today, a symbol of the wealth and power of the Byzantine empire, and of the determination of its greatest emperor and empress.

Based on this story, why do you think Theodora was so successful as empress? As you read the chapter ahead, think about what Theodora's story tells you about life in the Byzantine empire.

 myStory Video

Join Theodora as she helps put down the Nika riot.

Survival of the Eastern Empire

Key Ideas

- Now known as the Byzantine empire, the eastern half of the Roman empire survived until A.D. 1453.

- The emperor Justinian tried to reconquer areas of the western Roman empire that had been lost.

- The Byzantine empire declined slowly as parts of it were conquered by Slavs, Arabs, and Turks.

Key Terms • Byzantine • strait • moat • Greek fire

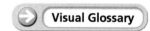 **Visual Glossary**

Reading Skill Analyze Cause and Effect Take notes using the graphic organizer in your journal.

▲ Constantine, founder of Constantinople

By the year A.D. 500, the western Roman empire had collapsed. But the eastern Roman empire lasted almost one thousand years more.

The New Rome

During the later years of the Roman empire, power shifted from the western part of the empire to its east and the empire changed. Emperor Constantine built Constantinople as a new capital for the empire.

Who Were the Byzantines? The people of this empire did not call themselves "Byzantines" (BIZ un teens.) They thought of themselves as Romans. But their empire became different from the ancient Roman empire. Most of the time, it did not control the city of Rome. Most of the empire's people were Christians, unlike people in the early Roman empire. They also spoke Greek, not Latin.

Because of these and other differences, historians needed a separate name for this empire. They called it the **Byzantine** empire because its capital, Constantinople, was built at a place called Byzantium.

The City's Location Constantine built his new capital on the Bosporus Strait. A **strait** is a narrow body of water that cuts through land, connecting two larger bodies of water. The Bosporus and other waterways link the Black and Mediterranean seas. On one side of the Bosporus is Asia. On the other side is Europe.

Defense and Trade Constantinople was easier to defend than Rome. It was built on a peninsula. The city was surrounded on three sides by water. Two rings of thick walls and a **moat,** or trench filled with water, protected the city on land.

Constantinople's strategic location and good harbors made it an ideal trading center. Merchants brought spices from India, furs from Russia, silk from China, and grain from Egypt. Traders from Western Europe came to Constantinople to buy products from Asia. Trade made Constantinople rich.

Reading Check Where was Constantinople located?

Justinian and Theodora

One great Byzantine emperor was Justinian, who ruled for nearly 40 years, from A.D. 527 to 565. He and his wife, Theodora, were a colorful and unusual royal couple.

Justinian was born to a family of peasants. His uncle Justin began his career as an impoverished soldier. He worked his way up through the army to the throne. Justinian was his <u>successor</u>. Theodora also came from a lower-class family. Her father worked as a bear trainer at the circus. When she grew up, she became an actress. Both Justinian and Theodora were intelligent, bold, and ruthless.

successor, *n.,* person who follows another in an office or role

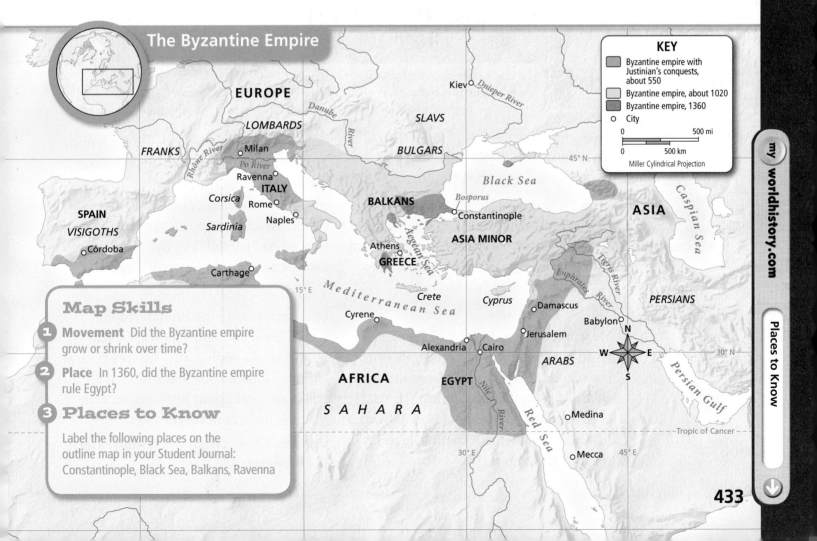

The Byzantine Empire

KEY
- Byzantine empire with Justinian's conquests, about 550
- Byzantine empire, about 1020
- Byzantine empire, 1360
- ○ City

0   500 mi
0   500 km
Miller Cylindrical Projection

Map Skills

1 Movement Did the Byzantine empire grow or shrink over time?

2 Place In 1360, did the Byzantine empire rule Egypt?

3 Places to Know
Label the following places on the outline map in your Student Journal: Constantinople, Black Sea, Balkans, Ravenna

Fortress Constantinople

Constantinople's defenses helped it stand against attackers for hundreds of years. The city's location made it a magnet for invaders, but in its history only two were able to capture the city. Constantine built the city's first defenses, and later emperors improved on them.

A Byzantine ship shoots Greek fire at its enemy. ▼

A clay hand grenade that would have been filled with Greek fire and thrown at the enemy ▶

▲ Above: a part of Constantinople's walls that still stands today Below: An artist's illustration of the moat and one of the walls as they looked in Byzantine times

Justinian's Conquests Justinian dreamed of restoring Rome's lost empire. He wrote,

66 We have good hopes that [God will help us to establish] our empire over the rest of those whom the Romans of old ruled from the boundaries of one ocean to another and then lost by their negligence. 99

—Justinian

He worked for more than 30 years trying to do just that. Justinian's generals won back lands around the Mediterranean, such as Spain, Italy, and North Africa. He even recaptured the city of Rome. During Justinian's reign, the Byzantine empire reached its greatest size.

Justinian's many wars, however, left the empire with money problems. Disease broke out across the empire as he was trying to complete his conquests. After his death, invaders chipped away at the territory he had gained. The Byzantine empire lost the areas he conquered.

Justinian's Legacy Although Justinian could not restore the Roman empire, he did leave an important legacy. He rebuilt Hagia Sophia, the empire's central church. He also collected a law code. You will read more about Justinian's accomplishments later in this chapter.

Reading Check What was Justinian's goal in his conquests?

The Shrinking Empire

After the death of Justinian, the Byzantine empire slowly shrank. Over the next 800 years, it declined and fell.

Foreign Invaders Many outside groups took parts of the empire. Germans took lands in the west that Justinian had conquered. Slavic peoples invaded from the north. Arab Muslim invaders conquered Syria, Egypt, and North Africa. The Turks, a Muslim Central Asian people, seized much of modern-day Turkey and other areas from the Byzantines.

However, the Byzantine emperors kept control of the <u>core</u> of their empire, modern-day Greece and western Turkey. They also continued to rule Constantinople. Toward the end, they controlled little else. The empire was more like a city-state. The once powerful emperors had to hire Italian ships and soldiers to help defend their capital.

Constantinople's Defenses Invaders often tried to capture the city of Constantinople. Nearly all failed. Those who attacked by land could not get past the city's strong walls. Those who came by sea were stopped by a heavy chain across the city's harbor. The Byzantines also used a secret weapon against ships. This was **Greek fire,** a chemical mixture that burned furiously, even in water. The Byzantines shot Greek fire at enemy ships or against troops attacking the city walls. The result was terrible to see.

The Defenses Fail Still, Constantinople could not hold out forever. In 1204, soldiers from Western Europe called *crusaders* took the city. They looted it and did great damage. You will read more about the crusaders later. The Byzantine empire eventually retook its capital.

The final attack came from the Turkish Ottoman empire. Constantinople's walls were built in an age before gunpowder. The Ottomans used cannons that helped them break down the walls. In 1453, Constantinople fell to the Ottomans. The Byzantine empire was no more.

Reading Check Who attacked Constantinople in 1204?

myWorld Activity
Put It Here

core *n.,* center, most important part

The Ottomans used cannons like this one in the siege of Constantinople. ▼

Section 1 Assessment

Essential Question

What distinguishes one culture from another?

Key Terms
1. What is a strait?
2. How might a moat help someone defending a city?

Key Ideas
3. What lands did Justinian try to conquer?
4. Which foreign power finally destroyed the Byzantine empire?

Think Critically
5. **Identify Evidence** Why might Justinian be considered a successful emperor? Why might he be considered a failure?

6. How was the Byzantine empire different from the ancient Roman empire? Go to your Student Journal to record your answer.

Section 2

The Division of the Christian Church

A Byzantine icon showing Jesus ▶

Key Ideas
- Bishops and patriarchs governed the early Christian church.
- Christians disagreed over church organization, the use of icons, and other issues.
- Eventually divisions between East and West led to a permanent split between the Roman Catholic and Eastern Orthodox churches.

Key Terms • creed • icon • iconoclast • pope • Great Schism

 Visual Glossary

Reading Skill Compare and Contrast Take notes using the graphic organizer in your journal.

A Byzantine icon showing the archangel Michael with a sword ▼

By the late 300s, Christianity was the official religion of the Roman empire. However, various groups of Christians held different religious beliefs and views about important issues. Christianity split into two churches, Roman Catholic and Eastern Orthodox.

Religious Differences

As Christianity grew, Christians began to argue about the beliefs of their faith. These arguments divided Christians into different groups.

The Nicene Creed Early Christians disagreed over exactly who Jesus was. Some argued that he was fully human. Others believed that he was fully divine, or that he was both human and divine. The emperor Constantine called a council of bishops in 325. They met in the city of Nicea (ny SEE uh) and adopted a statement of beliefs, or a **creed,** called the Nicene Creed. It said that Jesus was both human and divine. Most Christian groups accepted it. But over time, Eastern and Western Christians came to disagree over the creed's exact wording.

The Controversy Over Icons Christians also argued over the use of icons. An **icon** is a holy image, usually a portrait of Jesus or a saint. Many Christians displayed icons in their homes and churches. For them, honoring an icon was a pathway to God. But to others, praying to icons seemed like worshiping objects, which is forbidden in the Bible.

In the 700s, several Byzantine emperors tried to stop icon use. People who opposed icons were called **iconoclasts,** meaning "image-breakers." They went into churches and smashed icons. Violence broke out between iconoclasts and their opponents.

Attacks on icons angered Christians in Western Europe. There, Church leaders saw holy images as a way to teach people about God, not as objects of worship. Eventually, Byzantine emperors who opposed the iconoclasts took power. Today, icons are an important part of worship in Eastern Orthodox churches. But the issue left bitterness between Eastern and Western Christians.

Reading Check Who were the iconoclasts?

Church Organization

Christianity spread and grew in part because of its strong organization. But Christians came to disagree about who should lead the Church.

Bishops and Patriarchs The most important Christian leaders were called bishops. In early days each church was led by its own bishop. Later, a single bishop took charge of all the churches in a city, aided by members of the community. Eventually, bishops gained <u>authority</u> over all the churches in a region. The bishops of the five most important cities were known as patriarchs. These cities were Constantinople, Rome, Alexandria, Antioch, and Jerusalem.

authority, *n.,* power, control

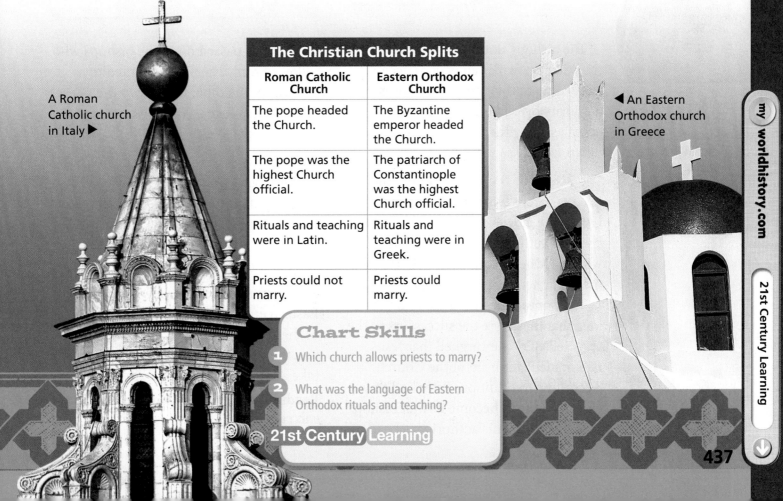

◄ A Roman Catholic church in Italy ▶

◄ An Eastern Orthodox church in Greece

The Christian Church Splits

Roman Catholic Church	Eastern Orthodox Church
The pope headed the Church.	The Byzantine emperor headed the Church.
The pope was the highest Church official.	The patriarch of Constantinople was the highest Church official.
Rituals and teaching were in Latin.	Rituals and teaching were in Greek.
Priests could not marry.	Priests could marry.

Chart Skills

1 Which church allows priests to marry?

2 What was the language of Eastern Orthodox rituals and teaching?

21st Century Learning

my worldhistory.com

21st Century Learning

The Eastern Orthodox World

ESTONIA
LATVIA
LITHUANIA
Baltic Sea
RUSSIA
BELARUS
POLAND
CZECH REPUBLIC
SLOVAKIA
UKRAINE
MOLDOVA
AUSTRIA
HUNGARY
SLOVENIA
CROATIA
ROMANIA
BOSNIA AND HERZEGOVINA
SERBIA
KOSOVO
ITALY
MONTENEGRO
ALBANIA
BULGARIA
MACEDONIA
GREECE
RUSSIA
KAZAKHSTAN
Black Sea
TURKEY

KEY

Majority Eastern Orthodox Country

Large Eastern Orthodox Minority

0   200 mi
0   200 km
Miller Cylindrical Projection

Map Skills

1 **Place** Does Greece have a majority Orthodox population?

2 **Region** Italy was once part of the Byzantine empire. Does it have an Eastern Orthodox majority?

▲ Above: the onion domes of a Russian Orthodox church in Moscow Below: a Greek Orthodox priest

The bishops' authority was based on a tradition known as apostolic succession. According to this tradition, Jesus gave authority over his Church to the original apostles. They then passed this authority down to each generation of bishops.

The Power of the Pope At first, the five patriarchs were equal in authority. Over time, however, the bishop of Rome claimed authority over Christians everywhere. He began to be called **pope**, which means father, or head, of the Church.

The popes based their claim on the idea that they were the successors to the apostle Peter. They argued that Jesus had made Peter head of the Church. According to tradition, Peter had traveled to Rome to become its first bishop. After his death, his authority as head of the Church passed on to the bishops who followed him. The popes pointed to a passage in the Bible to back up their case. Here, Jesus spoke to Peter, whose name means "rock" in Greek.

66 You are Peter, and on this rock I will build my church. . . . I will give you the keys of the kingdom of heaven, and whatever you bind on earth shall be bound in heaven. 99

—Matthew 16:18–19

Eastern patriarchs and the Byzantine emperors rejected this view of the pope. Eastern emperors wanted to be in charge of the church in their empire. If the pope was the head of the Church, this would take away from their authority.

Reading Check What is apostolic succession?

The Great Schism

Over time, differences between the Eastern and Western churches grew. Two religious traditions developed. In 1054, these two traditions formally split. The split is known as the **Great Schism** (SIZ um). The word *schism* comes from a Greek word meaning split, or division.

Two Christian Churches The Eastern branch of the church came to be called the Eastern Orthodox Church. *Orthodox* means following established beliefs.

In the Eastern Orthodox tradition, the Byzantine emperor was head of the Church. Patriarchs handled the churches' day-to-day affairs. They were all equals, though the Patriarch of Constantinople was considered first among equals. The Byzantine emperor had the power to <u>remove</u> a patriarch if he chose to.

The Western tradition became known as the Roman Catholic Church. *Roman* refers to the fact that it was based in Rome. *Catholic* means universal, or concerned with all people. This church shaped the culture of Western Europe.

The pope was the head of the Roman Catholic Church. As the spiritual leader of the Church, the pope claimed authority over all secular, or nonreligious, rulers. He did not take orders from any secular ruler, including the Byzantine emperor. This was the most important issue dividing the Eastern Orthodox and Roman Catholic churches.

Different Traditions There were other differences between the two churches. The language of the Eastern Orthodox Church was Greek. The language of the Roman Catholic Church was Latin. Orthodox priests were allowed to be married. Catholic priests were not. The churches also differed in some rituals.

Today there is no Byzantine emperor. Eastern Orthodox churches in different countries are led by their own patriarchs. Eastern Orthodox Christians still do not recognize the pope's power. Since 1054, the two churches have been separate. Recently, relations between the churches have improved, but the division remains.

Reading Check What does the word *schism* mean?

my World
CONNECTIONS

There are at least

233

million Eastern Orthodox Christians in the world.

remove, *v.,* move, take away, send away

myWorld Activity
Can We Talk?

Section 2 Assessment

Essential Question

What distinguishes one culture from another?

Key Terms

1. Why did iconoclasts oppose the use of icons?

2. Which city has the pope for its bishop?

Key Ideas

3. How did Roman Catholic and Eastern Orthodox Christians disagree over church organization?

4. Which church was headed by the the Byzantine emperor?

Think Critically

5. **Compare and Contrast** List three differences between the Roman Catholic and Eastern Orthodox churches.

6. What is one way in which culture set the Eastern Orthodox and Roman Catholic churches apart? Go to your Student Journal to record your answer.

Byzantine Civilization

Key Ideas
- The Byzantine empire developed its own culture while maintaining the Greco-Roman legacy.
- Justinian's Code preserved Roman law.
- Byzantine culture and Eastern Orthodox religion spread to Eastern Europe and Russia.

Key Terms • Justinian's Code • missionary • Cyrillic alphabet

Visual Glossary

Reading Skill Summarize Take notes using the graphic organizer in your journal.

▲ A fresco from the wall of a Byzantine-style church in southern Italy

Although the Byzantine empire shrank in size throughout its history, its people produced a great civilization. In this section, you will study Byzantine civilization and especially its influence on Eastern Europe and Russia.

A Unique Culture

The people of the Byzantine empire maintained some of the Greco-Roman traditions you read about in the last chapter. But their society was also strongly shaped by Eastern Orthodox Christianity. The result was a cultural blend that was unique, or distinct from other cultures.

Architecture and Literature Byzantine civilization produced its own styles of architecture. The most famous example is Justinian's church, Hagia Sophia, which you have already read about. It was the model for many buildings in other places. Similar domes can be seen on churches and other houses of worship in southern Europe and the Middle East.

Byzantine librarians and monks copied and preserved the manuscripts, or handwritten documents, of ancient Greece and Rome. The works saved included Homer's epics and writings by Greek and Roman philosophers. Many of these works would have been lost if Byzantine librarians and monks had not preserved them.

Organizing Roman Law You have read about Roman law and its later influence. It was preserved and updated in the Byzantine empire. This effort was largely the work of the emperor Justinian.

Closer Look

Hagia Sophia

The beautiful Hagia Sophia church was built on a cross-shaped floor plan. It is topped by an enormous dome, rising 185 feet above the floor. Windows and hanging lamps fill the church with light. When the Ottomans conquered Constantinople, they turned the church into a mosque, or Islamic house of worship. They built the towers that stand around the building, as you can see below. Today the building is a museum.

THINK CRITICALLY **Why might Justinian have rebuilt Hagia Sophia?**

▲ Hagia Sophia's massive dome makes the building spacious. Its windows allow in natural light.

Above: Hagia Sophia as it appears today.

Justinian found the vast legal legacy he inherited from Rome to be a confusing jumble of local laws, imperial decrees, and judges' decisions. He ordered a group of lawyers to organize this material. He had them produce a <u>unified</u> code, or systematic body of law. His code brought order to the system of Roman law.

Justinian's Code was published in 529. It gave great power to the emperor. The code said "that which seems good to the emperor has the force of law."

The code reveals ways people were treated in the empire. For example, the code <u>discriminated</u> against Jews and other non-Christians. On the other hand, it allowed women to inherit property and protected some individual rights.

Reading Check How did Justinian help preserve Roman law?

discriminate, *v.,* treat some people differently or worse

unified, *adj.,* joined together as a single whole

Cyril and Methodius

The Byzantine missionaries Cyril and Methodius are still revered as saints in the Eastern Orthodox church. They were missionaries who brought Orthodox Christianity to the Slavs, and invented an alphabet that is still used today.

◀ Cyril and Methodius

A sample of the Cyrillic alphabet ▶

The Empire's Influence

The politics of the Byzantine empire were often violent. The imperial court was known for its plots and power struggles. Some rulers were blinded or poisoned by rivals hoping to take power. Even so, the Byzantine empire was so wealthy and its culture was so attractive that its influence spread far beyond the empire's borders.

The Lure of Constantinople Byzantine culture spread in two ways. One was by attracting visitors to Constantinople. Merchants came to trade. Scholars came to study. Artists came to work. Visitors were amazed by what they saw.

Byzantine leaders showed off their wealth. They impressed their visitors with elaborate ceremonies, glittering jewels, and rich clothing. One visitor was impressed by Byzantine religious practices.

myWorld Activity
Spread the Word

66 We knew not whether we were in heaven or on earth. For on earth there is no such splendour or such beauty, and we are at a loss how to describe it. We know only that God dwells there among men, and their service [ceremony] is fairer than the ceremonies of other nations. 99
—Russian chronicle

The visitors took ideas home with them. Many Eastern Europeans adopted parts of Byzantine culture.

Spreading the Faith Byzantine culture was spread in another way by Eastern Orthodox missionaries. A **missionary** is someone who tries to convert others to a particular religion. Beginning in the late 800s, Eastern Orthodox missionaries began to travel among non-Christians in southeastern Europe. This area was the home of people called Slavs.

Byzantine missionaries converted many Slavs to Christianity. As a result many Eastern Europeans practice Eastern Orthodox Christianity to this day.

The best-known Eastern Orthodox missionaries were two brothers named Cyril and Methodius. They came from a noble family but gave up their wealth to become priests. They made a major contribution to Slavic culture. Cyril and Methodius invented the **Cyrillic alphabet** (suh RIL ik), which allowed the Slavs to write down their language. It was based on the letters of the Greek alphabet. Today it is used mostly for Slavic languages like Russian and Bulgarian.

Reading Check What contribution did Cyril and Methodius make to writing?

Early Russia

The early history of Russia was strongly influenced by the Byzantine empire. The first large state in what would become Russia and Ukraine was the Kievan Rus (KEE eh vun ROOS). It was based in the city of Kiev, and founded by a people called the Rus. The Rus were Vikings, a people from northern Europe. The Rus joined with local Slavs to form a powerful state. They controlled trade routes along Russia's rivers south to Constantinople.

Trade made the Kievan Rus rich. It also brought Russians into contact with the Byzantines. Eventually the rulers of the Rus converted to Eastern Orthodox Christianity and spread that religion.

As in the Byzantine empire, icons were very important to Russian Christians. Russian architecture was influenced by Byzantine building styles.

Over time, the power of Kiev declined just as the Byzantine empire was also declining. Although the Byzantine empire fell in 1453, in time a new Russian empire developed. The Russian empire considered itself the "third Rome," taking up the legacy of ancient Rome and the Byzantine empire. Russian emperors even took the title *tsar*, the Russian version of *caesar*, a title used by Roman and Byzantine emperors.

Reading Check How did Kiev become wealthy?

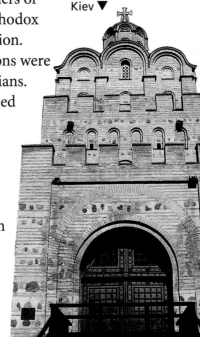

The Golden Gate of Kiev ▼

Culture Close-Up

myworldhistory.com

Culture Close-Up

Section 3 Assessment

Key Terms

1. What did Justinian's code say about the role of the emperor?

2. What does a missionary do?

Key Ideas

3. How did the Byzantine empire help preserve Greco-Roman culture?

4. Who founded the Kievan Rus?

Think Critically

5. Identify Main Ideas Which two influences helped shape Byzantine culture?

Essential Question

What distinguishes one culture from another?

6. How did the Byzantine empire change the cultures of the Slavic peoples of Eastern Europe? Go to your Student Journal to record your answer.

Chapter Assessment

Key Terms and Ideas

1. **Recall** Did the people of the **Byzantine** empire call it "Byzantine"?

2. **Summarize** What made Constantinople a good location for a new city?

3. **Discuss** What were the most important accomplishments of Emperor Justinian?

4. **Sequence** Is this statement true or false: "The Byzantine empire began as a small country and grew slowly over time." Explain your answer.

5. **Analyze Cause and Effect** How did the Ottomans cause the end of the Byzantine empire?

6. **Summarize** What did **iconoclasts** believe about icons?

7. **Compare and Contrast** In Byzantine times, what aspects of the **pope's** powers did Roman Catholic and Eastern Orthodox Christians disagree about?

8. **Categorize** Which two groups were divided by the **Great Schism**?

Think Critically

9. **Make Inferences** How did the appeal of Constantinople help spread Byzantine culture?

10. **Analyze Primary Sources** Find the quote from the biblical book of Matthew in Section 2. What does this statement have to do with the popes?

11. **Core Concepts: Religion** Why did Western Christians oppose the iconoclasts?

Analyze Visuals

The illustrated map at the right shows the city of Constantinople. It was made during the Byzantine period.

12. What about Constantinople's location makes it easy to defend?

13. What did the Byzantines build that made Constantinople even more secure?

14. Constantinople was built on a narrow body of water that cuts through land, connecting two larger bodies of water. What is this geographic feature called?

Essential Question
myWorld Chapter Activity

Put the Pieces Together Follow your teacher's instructions to plan, write, and illustrate a mosaic poster about a topic related to the Byzantine empire. Throughout your work, focus on the importance of this topic to the Byzantine empire. Take turns presenting your mosaic's topic and learning about the topics shown on your classmates' mosaic posters.

21st Century Learning
Develop Cultural Awareness

Reread the information in this chapter about Byzantine culture. Then think about your own culture. Write a paragraph comparing the two. Make sure to discuss the following aspects:
• Government
• Religion
• Entertainment
• Architecture

Document-Based Questions

Success Tracker™
Online at myworldhistory.com

Use your knowledge of the Byzantine empire as well as Documents A and B to answer Questions 1–3.

Document A

" We have found the entire arrangement of the law which has come down to us from the foundation of the City of Rome and the times of Romulus, to be so confused that it is extended to an infinite length and is not within the grasp of human capacity; and hence We [worked to] make them more easily understood."

—Justinian's Code

Document B

" The circumference of the city of Constantinople is eighteen miles; half of it is surrounded by the sea, and half by land, and it is situated upon two arms of the sea. . . . It is a busy city, and merchants come to it from every country by sea or land, and there is none like it in the world except Baghdad, the great city of Islam."

—Benjamin of Tudela

1. Why does Justinian say he created his law code?
   A because he wanted to give himself more power
   B because Roman law had become too confusing to be understood
   C to help him recapture the western Roman empire
   D to support Eastern Orthodox Christianity

2. In what way was Constantinople like Baghdad?
   A Both cities were located near the sea.
   B Both cities were part of the Byzantine empire.
   C Both cities lived under Justinian's law code.
   D Both cities were busy and full of merchants.

3. **Writing Task** Pretend that you work for Emperor Constantine. Write him a letter arguing in favor of building a capital city at Constantinople. Use evidence in the chapter to prove your point.

my worldhistory.com

Self-Test

Islamic Civilization

? Essential Question

How are religion and culture connected?

? Explore the Essential Question . . .

- at **my** worldhistory.com
- using the **myWorld Chapter Activity**
- with the **Student Journal**

Muslim pilgrims circle the Kaaba in Mecca, the holiest place according to their religion.

Islamic Civilization

610 According to Islam, Muhammad receives his first revelations.

622 Muhammad and his followers move from Mecca to Medina. This journey is called the Hijra.

1258 Mongols destroy Baghdad.

1501 Safavid empire founded.

600 **800** **1000** **1200** **1400** **1600**

630–640 Arab Muslims conquer much of North Africa and Southwest Asia.

762 Baghdad founded as capital of Arab Muslim empire.

970 Al-Azhar University, a center of Islamic learning, founded.

1453 Ottoman Turks conquer Constantinople.

Ibn Battuta's *Voyage*

This myStory is a fictionalized account of events in the life of Ibn Battuta, a real person who appears in this chapter.

The lone traveler walked toward Tangier, Morocco, his hometown. He was called Ibn Battuta (IB un bat TOO tah). He had left Tangier in 1325, when he was around 20—more than half his life ago. He remembered the day he left as if it were yesterday. A devout Muslim, or follower of the religion of Islam, he decided to go on a hajj. *Hajj* is the Arabic term for the pilgrimage, or journey to a holy place, that every able Muslim must make to the city of Mecca, in Arabia. On that late spring day so long ago, Ibn Battuta had wept as he said goodbye to his parents and friends. He then set out on his 3,000-mile trip.

EUROPE
Central Asia
ASIA
Spain
Asia Minor
Tangier
Persia
North Africa
Cairo
Egypt
Jerusalem
Red Sea
Arabia
Mecca
China
West Africa
AFRICA
Arabian Sea
India
Bay of Bengal
Southeast Asia
East Africa
Indian Ocean

— First pilgrimage to Mecca
— Later travels

my worldhistory.com — On Assignment/Timeline

Ibn Battuta traveled across the vast deserts of North Africa on his way to Egypt. He went with a group of travelers headed in the same direction.

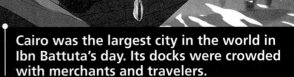

Cairo was the largest city in the world in Ibn Battuta's day. Its docks were crowded with merchants and travelers.

But this pilgrimage had turned into a journey of 24 years and around 75,000 miles. After he completed his hajj, he just kept on going. He remembered the generosity and hospitality of his fellow Muslims who had kept him fed and sheltered during his years of traveling. He had visited every Muslim-ruled area in the world, and traveled to many other regions as well. He had met famous scholars, holy men, kings, sultans, and emperors.

He closed his eyes. How lonely he had been when he first left Tangier! But his loneliness had given way to amazement at the wonders of the world—the ancient lighthouse at Alexandria, the mighty Nile River, and magnificent Cairo, such a vast city! He later wrote describing it as "the mother of cities . . . whose throngs surge as the waves of the sea and can scarce be contained in her for all her size and capacity. It is said that in Cairo there are twelve thousand water-carriers who transport water on camels, and thirty thousand hirers of mules and donkeys, and that on the Nile there are thirty-six thousand boats."

Cairo was not just a huge and impressive city. It was also a major religious center. Ibn Battuta had toured Cairo's mosques and described the communities of religious scholars who lived there. He had

also visited the beautiful graves in the city's cemetery, where "the people build beautiful pavilions surrounded by walls, so that they look like houses."

If Ibn Battuta had not been on the hajj, it would have been easy to settle in Cairo, with its many mosques, brilliant scholars, lovely promenades, and busy bazaars. But he continued on towards Mecca.

After leaving Cairo, Ibn Battuta had gone to Jerusalem, a city holy to Jews, Christians, and Muslims. He described it according to its place in Islam as the city "third in excellence after the two holy shrines of Mecca and Medina." In Jerusalem, he had prayed at the Dome of the Rock—the spot where, according to Islamic tradition, the Prophet Muhammad ascended to heaven and returned one night in A.D. 620. He had also paid his respects to Christian sites, such as the spot where Christians believe Jesus was crucified. At that time, Christians and Jews were allowed to practice their religions freely in Muslim countries, though they had to pay a special tax and faced other restrictions.

From Jerusalem, Ibn Battuta had made his way to the ancient city of Damascus, once the capital of the Arab Muslim empire. Then he had journeyed south through the desert to Medina to pray at the tomb of Muhammad, the prophet of Islam.

Cairo was also a major religious center. Ibn Battuta studied there with famous Islamic scholars.

Jerusalem is a holy city to Muslims, as it is to Jews and Christians. When he visited the city, Ibn Battuta prayed at the Dome of the Rock mosque.

At last, he reached Mecca. As he entered the holy city, he and his companions prayed "What is Thy command? I am Here, o God!" He had been traveling for more than a year by then. He did not know at the time that he would travel for 23 years more.

That first hajj was so long ago! He had made six more since then, but his very first memories of Mecca were still fresh in his mind. He remembered putting on the snow-white, two-piece garment worn by pilgrims to symbolize their purity and piety. He remembered praying at the Kaaba, the square building covered with a black cloth in the sacred area of Mecca. Muslims believe that the Kaaba was built by Abraham, who they believe was Muhammad's ancestor. All Muslims, no matter where they are, face the Kaaba when they pray.

Of course, the first hajj wasn't the end of Ibn Battuta's journey. He went on to Persia, East Africa, the Byzantine empire, Central Asia, India, Southeast Asia, China, and West Africa before returning home to Tangier. But as he returned, it was the memories of Cairo, Jerusalem, Medina, and Mecca that filled the old traveler's heart with joy.

Based on this story, how do you think religion and culture were connected in Islamic civilization in Ibn Battuta's time? As you read the chapter ahead, think about what Ibn Battuta's story tells you about life in Islamic civilization during this period.

myStory Video

Join Ibn Battuta as he travels to Mecca.

myworldhistory.com

myStory Video

449

Origins of Islam

Key Ideas

- People began practicing Islam in Arabia, a large peninsula covered mostly by harsh desert.

- The prophet of Islam was Muhammad, who preached his beliefs to the people of Mecca, his hometown.

- Muhammad moved from Mecca to the city of Medina, where he built up the Muslim community.

Key Terms • oasis • Bedouin • Hijra • Kaaba

 Visual Glossary

Reading Skill Identify Main Ideas and Details Take notes using the graphic organizer in your journal.

A traditional building in Mecca, Islam's birthplace ▼

Arabia has one of the harshest climates in the world. In its vast deserts water is scarce, and temperatures can soar to more than 120 degrees Fahrenheit (49 degrees Celsius). The religion of Islam arose in this difficult region in the A.D. 600s. Today, Islam is the world's second-largest faith.

Arabia Before Islam

Arabia is a huge peninsula. It is nearly twice the size of Alaska. It lies south of modern-day Iraq and across the Red Sea from eastern Africa. The geography of Arabia influenced its history and culture.

A Harsh Environment Arabia is extremely dry. It receives little rain and has no permanent rivers. Much of Arabia is covered by desert. The Rub' al-Khali or "Empty Quarter" desert covers much of the peninsula. Summer temperatures in these arid lands are some of the hottest in the world. The peninsula's harsh environment helped keep foreign invaders out of Arabia for most of its history.

Arabia's difficult climate limited the region's population. The people of Arabia depended on oases (oh AY seez) for water. An **oasis** is a place in a desert where water can be found, usually from a spring. In the past, most settlement occurred around oases in the Hijaz, a mountainous region along the western coast of Arabia. Many people also lived in the southwestern corner of the peninsula. This is today's Yemen. There, enough rain falls to support agriculture.

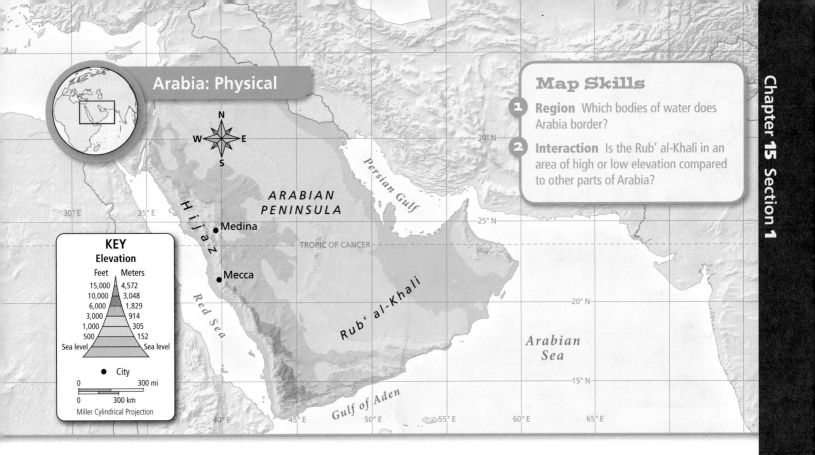

Arabia: Physical

Map Skills

1 **Region** Which bodies of water does Arabia border?

2 **Interaction** Is the Rub' al-Khali in an area of high or low elevation compared to other parts of Arabia?

ARABIAN PENINSULA

Hijaz

Medina

Mecca

Persian Gulf

Red Sea

Rub' al-Khali

Arabian Sea

Gulf of Aden

TROPIC OF CANCER

30° E   35° E   40° E   45° E   50° E   55° E   60° E   65° E

30° N   25° N   20° N   15° N

KEY
Elevation

Feet	Meters
15,000	4,572
10,000	3,048
6,000	1,829
3,000	914
1,000	305
500	152
Sea level	Sea level

● City

0   300 mi
0   300 km
Miller Cylindrical Projection

As a peninsula, Arabia is surrounded on three sides by water. Arabian sailors crossed the seas around them to trade with East Africa, India, and China. Traders also traveled north across the desert into Mesopotamia and areas beyond it.

Living in Arabia The Arabs, the people of Arabia, practiced two different ways of life in ancient times. Some were nomads. They had no fixed homes. Others were sedentary, or settled. Both nomadic and settled Arabs belonged to tribes. Their loyalty lay mainly with tribe and family rather than with any larger nation. They worshiped many gods and tribal spirits.

Arab nomads, known as **Bedouins**, lived in rural desert areas. They herded sheep, goats, and camels. They traveled from oasis to oasis with their flocks. Bedouins were skilled warriors. They raided other tribes for animals and goods.

Sedentary Arabs lived as farmers and merchants. Farmers tended fields watered by oases. Merchants set up shop in oasis towns along Arabia's main trade route. This route passed along the western coast of Arabia, through the Hijaz. Camel caravans carrying trade goods stopped at these towns for water, food, and supplies.

Trade brought wealth and attracted settlers. Jews and Christians moved to towns in the Hijaz. The largest town, Mecca, became a trading center. It was there, around 570, that Muhammad (moo HAM ud) was born. Muhammad was the first person to preach the religion of Islam.

Reading Check What two different ways of life did the people of ancient Arabia follow?

myWorld Activity
Living in Arabia

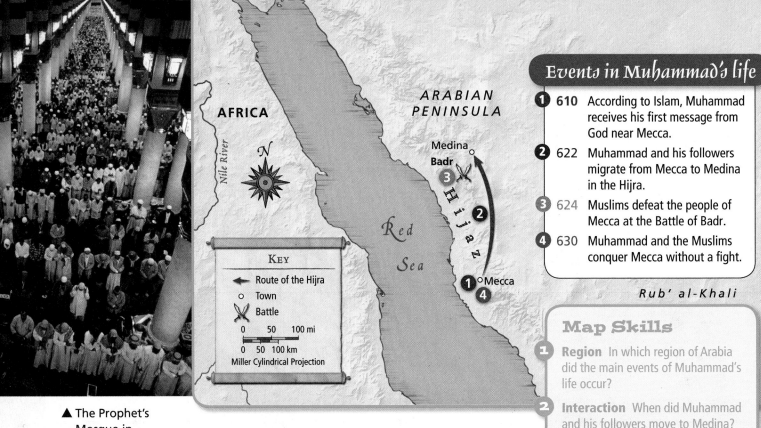

Events in Muhammad's life

1. **610** According to Islam, Muhammad receives his first message from God near Mecca.
2. **622** Muhammad and his followers migrate from Mecca to Medina in the Hijra.
3. **624** Muslims defeat the people of Mecca at the Battle of Badr.
4. **630** Muhammad and the Muslims conquer Mecca without a fight.

Map Skills

1. **Region** In which region of Arabia did the main events of Muhammad's life occur?

2. **Interaction** When did Muhammad and his followers move to Medina?

▲ The Prophet's Mosque in Medina was built on the site of Muhammad's home in that city. It contains his tomb.

The Rise of Islam

Muslims, people who practice Islam, consider Muhammad the prophet of their religion. Muslims believe that he was the messenger of God.

Mecca As you read, Muhammad was born in Mecca, a town in the Hijaz. At the time of Muhammad's birth, Mecca was a religious center. It had an important shrine called the Kaaba where Arabs came to worship their gods. Every year, a religious fair attracted thousands of people.

Muhammad's Early Life Muhammad was orphaned at an early age. He was raised by close relatives. At 25, he married a wealthy, widowed merchant named Khadija. Muhammad prospered in business. But he was critical of Meccan society. All around him, he saw greed, corruption, and violence.

Seeking peace of mind, Muhammad often retreated to a cave outside Mecca to pray and reflect. Muslims believe that one night, in 610, the angel Gabriel appeared before Muhammad in the cave. Gabriel told him to recite, or say out loud, messages from God.

> 66 Recite in the name of your Lord who created—created man from clots of blood.
>
> Recite! Your Lord is the Most Bountiful One, who by the pen taught man what he did not know. 99
>
> —Quran 96:1–5

Muslims believe that Gabriel brought more messages from God. Muhammad passed these on to his followers. They later wrote them down in the Quran (koo RAHN), Islam's holy book.

Preaching a New Message Muhammad began to preach in the streets of Mecca. He told Arabs to worship only one God and to change many of their behaviors. He said that he had received <u>revelations</u> from God. He said this was the same God who had spoken to Abraham, Jesus, and prophets and religious figures of Judaism and Christianity. Muhammad respected those religions. But Muslims believe he was the final prophet. He said he had the responsibility of clarifying God's truth.

Muhammad began to win believers. But many Meccans opposed Islam. The Meccans feared that the beliefs preached by Muhammad would reduce their status and wealth as keepers of the Kaaba. They also feared he would anger the gods they worshiped. They began to persecute Muhammad and other Muslims.

The Hijra In 622, Muhammad and his fellow Muslims fled Mecca. They moved to the town of Medina, about 275 miles to the north. The move to Medina was called the **Hijra,** which is the Arabic word for <u>migration</u>.

In Medina, Muhammad continued his preaching. He became Medina's political and military leader. The Muslims of Medina fought with the people of Mecca. The Meccans tried to conquer Medina but Muhammad defeated them. After several key Muslim victories, Mecca's resistance crumbled.

In 630, Muhammad returned to Mecca as its ruler. He banned worship of the old gods and organized the Muslim community. Muhammad destroyed statues of the gods at the Kaaba and rededicated it as an Islamic holy site. The **Kaaba** became a place for Muslim pilgrims, or people who travel for religious reasons, to visit.

Quickly, the Muslims united most of Arabia under their rule. Muhammad died, but his death did not halt the spread of his faith. United by Islam, Arabs preached their religion and expanded their rule across Southwest Asia and to many other parts of the world.

Reading Check How do Muslims believe Muhammad was different from earlier prophets?

revelation, *n.,* message, usually one believed to come from God

migration, *n.,* moving to a new place

Section 1 Assessment

Key Terms

1. What is an oasis?

2. What is special about the way in which nomads live?

3. What religion do Muslims practice?

Key Ideas

4. Describe Arabia's climate.

5. According to Muslims, what happened to Muhammad in a cave outside Mecca in 610?

6. Why did Muhammad and his followers flee from Mecca?

Think Critically

7. **Compare and Contrast** How is Islam different from the religion practiced by Arabs in earlier times?

8. **Summarize** Describe what happened to the Muslim community in the years after the Hijra.

Essential Question

How are religion and culture connected?

9. How did the coming of Islam change what religious activities took place at the Kaaba? Go to your Student Journal to record your answer.

Beliefs of Islam

Key Ideas

- The main sources of Islamic teachings are the Quran and the Sunnah.
- Islam is a monotheistic religion that requires believers to perform five basic duties known as the Five Pillars of Islam.
- Prayer and right conduct are important parts of Islamic teaching.

Key Terms • Quran • Sunnah • hajj • mosque • Sharia

 Visual Glossary

Reading Skill Summarize Take notes using the graphic organizer in your journal.

A Muslim woman praying ▼

If you were visiting any Muslim city in the world, you would likely wake up at dawn hearing the call to prayer chanted from one of the city's houses of worship. In Arabic, you would hear "God is great. I bear witness that there is no God but God. I bear witness that Muhammad is the messenger of God. Come to worship." This call contains the most important beliefs of Islam—belief in one all-powerful God, and belief that Muhammad was God's final messenger to human beings.

Sources of Islamic Teachings

The **Quran** is Islam's holy book. It is also the main source of Islamic teaching.

The Quran Muslims believe that the Quran is the record of God's revelations to Muhammad over a period of nearly 23 years. Those revelations began in a cave outside Mecca in the year 610. They continued for the rest of Muhammad's life, until his death in 632.

According to Islamic tradition, Muhammad recited the words that had been revealed to him. His followers memorized what Muhammad told them and wrote his messages down. They compiled them into a book called the Quran not long after Muhammad's death. It has remained unchanged since then.

The Quran consists of 114 chapters in verse form. The verses discuss the nature of God, creation, and the human soul. They also address moral, legal, and family issues. Much of the Quran's language is written in a poetic style that many Arabic speakers find beautiful.

To Muslims, the Quran is the word of God. They recite its passages during daily prayers and on special occasions. They believe that it must be studied in Arabic, the language in which it is written. Muslims throughout the world recite the Quran only in Arabic. Although most Muslims are not Arabs, the Arabic language of the Quran unites all Muslims.

Muslims treat the Quran with great devotion. They take special care of copies of the book. They commit passages to memory. Children often first learn reading and writing from the Quran.

The Sunnah Another key source of Islamic thought is the **Sunnah** (SOON ah), or traditions of Muhammad. The Sunnah refers to the words and actions of Muhammad. He is considered the best role model. The Sunnah provides Muslims with guidelines for living a proper life. It also helps believers <u>interpret</u> difficult parts of the Quran.

The Sunnah is based on accounts from people who knew Muhammad during his lifetime. They recorded his sayings and actions in a collection of writings called the Hadith. The Hadith is the written record of the Sunnah. Many of its passages deal with Islamic law. Others promote moral or ethical concepts. Here is one example:

> 66 He who eats his fill while his neighbor goes without food is not a believer. 99
>
> —Hadith

Reading Check What is the original language of the Quran?

interpret, *v.,* give the meaning of

A copy of the Quran written in Arabic

A Muslim boy studying the Quran

Beliefs About God

A number of core beliefs are central to Islam. They are stressed in the Quran and in Islamic tradition.

Monotheism The principal belief of Islam is that there is only one God. He created the universe and all things in it. Muslims believe this is the same God that Jews and Christians worship. Muslims usually refer to God as *Allah,* which is simply the word for "God" in Arabic.

Muslims also believe that Muhammad was a prophet, God's messenger, but that he had no divine, or godlike, power himself. Muslims believe that important Jewish and Christian religious figures like Abraham, Moses, and Jesus were also prophets and that Muhammad is part of this tradition.

Unlike Muslims, Jews and Christians do not believe that Muhammad was a prophet. Unlike Christians, Muslims view Jesus as a human prophet. Most Christians believe Jesus was both God and man.

Submission to God's Will The word *Islam* means "submission" in Arabic. A Muslim is one who has submitted to God's will. This means trying to please God by following his teachings.

The Soul and Afterlife Like Christianity, Islam teaches that each person has a soul that keeps living after a person dies. Each person also has the freedom to choose between good and evil. The choices a person makes in life affect what happens to his or her soul after death.

Reading Check What is the principal core belief of Muslims?

submission *n.,* giving control over yourself to someone else

The Five Pillars of Islam

Muslims have five key religious duties. These are known as the Five Pillars.

- **Belief** The first pillar is stating a belief that "there is no god but God and Muhammad is the messenger of God."
- **Prayer** The second pillar is prayer. It is a religious duty for Muslims to pray five times a day. You will read more about Islamic worship later.
- **Charity** The third pillar of Islam is giving charity to the needy. Muslims must share their wealth with the less fortunate. Devout Muslims give 2.5 percent of their wealth each year, though many give more.
- **Fasting** The fourth pillar is fasting during Ramadan, a month on the Islamic calendar. Fasting means not eating or drinking for a period of time. During Ramadan, Muslims fast between daybreak and sunset. Fasting tests Muslims' commitment to God and reminds them of the hunger of the poor. The end of Ramadan is marked by Eid al-Fitr (eed al fitter), or Festival of the Breaking of the Fast. This is an important holiday.
- **Pilgrimage** The fifth pillar is the **hajj,** or pilgrimage to the holy city of Mecca. A pilgrimage is a journey to a sacred place or shrine. The Quran instructs every Muslim to make the hajj at least once, if possible. By bringing Muslims from all parts of the world together every year, the hajj strengthens the global community of Muslims.

Reading Check What event does Eid al-Fitr celebrate?

456

Closer Look

The Five Pillars of Islam

The Five Pillars are the main religious duties of every Muslim. Along with other Islamic practices, they help shape the daily lives of Muslims. Following the Five Pillars is part of living life with a purpose and staying committed to Islam's teachings about God and the proper way to live.

THINK CRITICALLY How do these Five Pillars affect daily life?

1 Belief
The Islamic declaration of faith in a single God and in Muhammad as his messenger is painted above.

2 Prayer
Muslims pray five times daily. They may sometimes pray in a mosque.

3 Charity
Muslims give part of their income to care for the poor.

4 Fasting
After fasting on a day during the month of Ramadan, Muslims break the fast with a special meal known as iftar, as above.

5 Pilgrimage
Muslims travel to worship in the holy city of Mecca (behind) at least once in their life if able.

Islam Today

Today Islam is the world's second-largest religion. Although Islam began among Arabs, most Muslims are not Arabs. South Asia—India, Pakistan, Bangladesh, and neighboring countries—has the largest Muslim population of any region.

Students reading the Quran in Pakistan

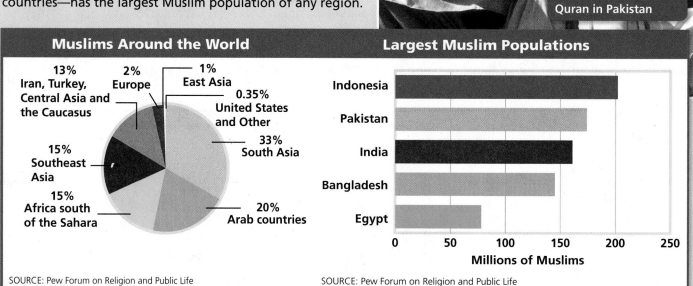

Muslims Around the World

- 13% Iran, Turkey, Central Asia and the Caucasus
- 2% Europe
- 1% East Asia
- 0.35% United States and Other
- 33% South Asia
- 15% Southeast Asia
- 15% Africa south of the Sahara
- 20% Arab countries

SOURCE: Pew Forum on Religion and Public Life

Largest Muslim Populations

Indonesia
Pakistan
India
Bangladesh
Egypt

0   50   100   150   200   250
Millions of Muslims

SOURCE: Pew Forum on Religion and Public Life

▲ This chart shows what percentage of the world's Muslims lives in each region.

Chart Skills

Which country has the largest Muslim population in the world? Using the atlas at the back of this book, describe the location of this country.

Prayer, Pilgrimage, and Law

Islam plays a large role in the daily lives of Muslims. It helps shape society in Muslim-majority nations.

Worship Prayer and worship are key elements of daily life for Muslims. At five specific times each day, Muslims stop what they are doing to pray. Before praying, Muslims remove their shoes and wash their hands and feet. This is called an ablution. They may bow several times. Then, facing in the direction of Mecca, they kneel and pray.

A Muslim house of worship is called a **mosque**. At a mosque, the community participates in group prayer and other religious activities. Mosques are usually found at the heart of Muslim-majority towns or cities. Their features may differ, but all mosques contain a prayer hall facing in the direction of Mecca. They usually include a special place for the imam, or religious leader, to stand to give sermons. A minaret is attached to most mosques. Minarets are towers from which a man called a muezzin sings the call to prayer. On Fridays, Muslims may gather at a mosque for group worship and to hear a sermon.

The Hajj As you read, the hajj is a pilgrimage to Mecca. During the hajj, pilgrims take part in many rituals. The most important is walking in a circle around the Kaaba. The Kaaba is a cube-like building in the courtyard of the Grand Mosque in Mecca. Muslims believe that in ancient times, Abraham and his son Ishmael built the Kaaba as a place to worship God. During the hajj, Muslims also visit the place where Muhammad gave his last sermon. The hajj reminds Muslims of Abraham, Ishmael, and Muhammad. It connects Muslims to their religious history.

Law Muhammad taught that everyday life was no different from religious life. Living a proper life meant following God's laws as revealed in the Quran and the Sunnah. These laws are collected in the Islamic law code known as the **Sharia**. The Arabic word *Sharia* means "the way," as in the right way to act.

The Quran and the Sunnah served as sources for the Sharia. But those sources could not cover every situation that might come up. Religious scholars used reason to judge new situations.

By the 900s, Muslim scholars had established the Sharia as a fixed set of laws. In this form it was used by Muslim societies for centuries. In the 1800s, however, governments in some Muslim lands began replacing parts of Sharia law with law codes based on European models. Other parts of the Sharia were reformed. Today, law codes in some Muslim nations are closely based on Sharia. Others are more secular, or nonreligious.

Rules of Proper Conduct The Sharia provides Muslims with specific rules of personal conduct. The most important rules concern the basic duties of every Muslim—the Five Pillars of Islam. Other rules list things that Muslims should not do. For example, the Sharia forbids Muslims from gambling, stealing, eating pork or drinking alcohol. The Sharia also includes rules for resolving family issues and for doing business ethically.

Reading Check What does a muezzin do?

my **World**
CONNECTIONS

Between **2** and **5** million Muslims live in the United States. California has the largest Muslim population of any state.

Section **2** Assessment

Key Terms	Key Ideas	Think Critically	Essential Question
1. What is the Quran? What do Muslims believe about it?	**5.** What are the two main sources of Islamic teaching?	**8. Draw Inferences** What are the Five Pillars of Islam? List them, and explain their role in a Muslim's life.	**How are religion and culture connected?**
2. Who must go on the hajj?	**6.** What does the word *Islam* mean in Arabic?	**9. Identify Main Ideas** What is the central Muslim belief about God?	**10.** How does the hajj help strengthen the community of Muslims around the world? Go to your Student Journal to record your answer.
3. What happens at a mosque?	**7.** What are some rules of conduct contained in the Sharia?		
4. What is the role of the Sharia?			

Muslim Empires

Key Ideas

- After converting to Islam, the Arabs conquered many lands and built a huge empire in a very short span of time.

- Muslims became divided over the issue of who should follow Muhammad as the leader of the Muslim community.

- After the Arab Muslim empire collapsed, Muslim empires including the Ottoman, Safavid, and Mughal empires rose up.

Key Terms • caliph • Sunni • Shia • sultan

→ Visual Glossary

□→□ **Reading Skill Sequence** Take notes using the graphic organizer in your journal.

A painting showing the founder of the Ottoman empire ▼

At the time of Muhammad's death in A.D. 632, many tribes of Bedouin warriors had converted to Islam. United by devotion to Islam, these Arab tribes formed a powerful and skilled army. They began an expansion of Arab Muslim rule across three continents.

The Arab Muslim Empire and the Spread of Islam

Arab Muslim armies began to conquer new territory in Arabia itself. After Muhammad's death, some Arab tribes rebelled against Muslim rule, but the Muslims were able to defeat them.

Early Conquests After securing their hold on Arabia, Arab Muslim soldiers defeated larger rivals in nearby lands. In the 600s, these soldiers conquered the Persian empire and much of the Byzantine empire. Arab Muslims took Mesopotamia, Palestine, Syria, Egypt and Persia. Then they moved into Afghanistan and northern India. They conquered North Africa and Spain. By A.D. 800, the Muslims ruled a vast empire.

Islam Spreads As the Arab Muslims built their empire, Islam spread peacefully both inside the empire and to the lands beyond its borders. This happened at different speeds in different regions. For example, most western North Africans were quick to convert to Islam, while most Egyptians remained Christian for centuries. Along with Islam, the Arabic language spread to many parts of the empire.

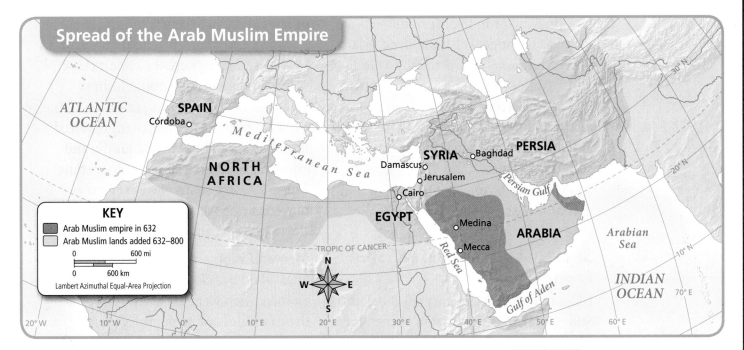

Spread of the Arab Muslim Empire

KEY

Arab Muslim empire in 632

Arab Muslim lands added 632–800

0   600 mi

0   600 km

Lambert Azimuthal Equal-Area Projection

ATLANTIC OCEAN

SPAIN

Córdoba

Mediterranean Sea

NORTH AFRICA

SYRIA   Baghdad   PERSIA

Damascus

Jerusalem

Cairo

EGYPT

Persian Gulf

Medina

Mecca

Red Sea

ARABIA

Arabian Sea

INDIAN OCEAN

TROPIC OF CANCER

Gulf of Aden

N S E W

Merchants traveled outside the empire to many new lands. They carried their faith with them. Missionaries spreading Islam often accompanied traders to preach their faith. Over time, many people in South Asia, Southeast Asia, and Africa turned to Islam.

Reasons for Success Early Arab Muslims built a massive empire in a short period of time. Several factors led to Muslim success. One was the decline of the Persian and the Byzantine empires. Years of warfare had left those large empires weak and vulnerable.

A second factor was the ability and <u>devotion</u> of Muslim warriors. They had the fighting skills needed to win battles. Their religious faith gave them a special edge. They believed that God was on their side.

Religious toleration also helped the Arab Muslim empire expand. Muslims

Map Skills

1 Location Which cities were part of the Arab Muslim empire before 632?

2 Interaction What are three regions conquered by early Arab Muslims?

3 Places to Know!

Label the following places on the outline map in your Student Journal: Mecca, Medina, Arabia, Damascus, Baghdad, Red Sea.

conquered lands where large numbers of Jews and Christians lived. In many of these areas, Christians remained a majority for centuries, and Jews also remained a large presence. Muslims did not force their religion on these groups.

This policy made conquered peoples less likely to rebel. It also set the Arab Muslim empire apart from the Byzantine empire, which persecuted Jews and non-Orthodox Christians.

devotion, *n.,* dedication, loyalty

my worldhistory.com

Places to Know

461

A final factor in the Muslims' success was the appeal of Islam itself. Islam offered followers a direct path to God and salvation. It emphasized the equality of all believers. It stressed fairness and justice in human affairs. For these reasons and others, many non-Muslims chose to convert to Islam.

Reading Check Why did Islam appeal to non-Muslims?

Society in the Arab Muslim Empire

Islam stressed the equality of all believers. Still, social divisions existed in the Arab Muslim empire.

Social Divisions In the early days of the Arab Muslim empire, Muslim society was split into four main groups. Arab Muslims were at the top. Next came non-Arab Muslims. The third group consisted of Jews and Christians, although some Jews and Christians rose to high positions in society. Slaves were the lowest class.

Slaves were usually non-Muslims captured in war. They did not have all the rights of free people, but Islam required that they should be treated kindly and encouraged freeing slaves. Under some Muslim rulers, many slaves served as soldiers or key government officials. Some slaves even became rulers themselves.

Men and Women The Quran and the Sharia laid out clear roles for men and women. Men were expected to support their families and to conduct their business in public. Women customarily stayed at home, although some women rose to important positions. In general, however, women had fewer rights than men and occupied an inferior position.

Still, overall, Islam improved conditions for women. Before the development of Islam, Arab women had virtually no rights. Under the Sharia, women and men had religious equality.

Jews and Christians The Arab Muslim empire was generally tolerant towards Jews and Christians. Because Muslims regarded Jewish and Christian scriptures as sacred, they respected Jews and Christians as "People of the Book." Jews and Christians in Muslim lands were allowed to practice their faiths and govern themselves. Still, they had to pay a special tax and faced other restrictions.

Reading Check What was the role of men in Muslim society?

Muslims today hold different views about what clothing is appropriate to wear in public. These women are wearing two different types of head coverings.▼

The Caliphs

As you read, Muhammad was the first Muslim leader. After he died, rulers called **caliphs** (KAY lifs) led the Muslim community and then the empire. In Arabic, *caliph* means "successor," as in the successor of Muhammad. A government run by a caliph is called a caliphate.

The Question of Succession But who was to be the first caliph? Who could follow a man who for Muslims was the messenger of God? This difficult issue split Muslims into two competing groups.

Most Muslims believed that the community needed a leader with political skills. They supported Muhammad's main advisor, Abu Bakr, who became the first caliph. Members of this group became known as **Sunnis** (SOO neez) because they hold the Sunnah in high regard.

A minority of Muslims believed that only Muhammad's relatives should become caliph. They supported Ali, Muhammad's cousin and son-in-law. They were called **Shias** (SHEE uz), which means supporters, because they supported Ali.

The split between Sunnis and Shias still exists today. Most Muslims— at least 85 percent—are Sunnis. Shias are the largest minority Islamic group. There are some differences in ritual and observance between the two groups. Despite this division, Muslims around the world share most of the same basic beliefs.

The "Rightly Guided" Caliphs Four caliphs ruled the Arab Muslim empire during its earliest years. Each had close ties to Muhammad. Each was guided by

▲ Umar, the second caliph, was assassinated by a Persian slave.

Muslim principles. For these reasons, Sunni Muslims came to refer to these leaders as the "rightly guided caliphs." They ruled the growing empire from the city of Medina, in Arabia.

Muhammad's cousin Ali, favored by Shias, finally became the fourth caliph in 656. But by then, he had many enemies. In the fifth year of his reign, he was assassinated. After that, the caliphate passed to the powerful Umayyad family.

The Umayyad Dynasty The Umayyads founded the first Muslim dynasty. A dynasty is a family that passes down political power from one relative to another. The Umayyads moved the empire's capital from Medina to Damascus, an ancient city in Syria.

Muslim Dynasties

Many dynasties and empires ruled Muslim lands over the centuries. The early empires were dominated by Arabs. Later states were mostly run by non-Arabs, including Persians, Turks, and Mongols. The dynasties and empires listed on this page and the following two pages were some of the larger and more powerful Muslim states.

Which dynasties were ruled by Arabs? Which by non-Arabs?

▲ **The Umayyad Dynasty 661–750**
The Umayyad caliphs ruled an empire stretching from Spain to Persia. They built this mosque in Damascus, Syria, an early capital of the Arab Muslim empire.

▲ **The Abbasid Dynasty 750–1258**
The Abbasids seized the caliphate from the Umayyads in 750. They built the spiral minaret above in Samarra, near their new capital of Baghdad, in Iraq.

Under the Umayyads, the Arab Muslim empire reached its greatest size. Muslim armies conquered North Africa and Spain. Expansion brought Arabs into contact with other cultures. Many non-Arabs adopted Islam and some began to speak Arabic. In turn, non-Arab cultures influenced the Arab conquerors. Over time, a distinct Muslim civilization emerged that blended these influences.

The Abbasid Dynasty In 750, rebel Arab forces overthrew the Umayyads and installed a caliph from the Abbasid family. The Abbasids built a new capital called Baghdad, in present-day Iraq. Baghdad became the center of a golden age of art, science, and learning.

But as Islamic civilization flourished, the Abbasids were losing control of their empire. In 756, Spain became an independent Muslim state under its own caliphs. Later, the Shia Fatimid dynasty seized control of Egypt. They founded Al-Azhar university in Cairo. Al-Azhar is still a center of Muslim learning.

Power slowly passed from Arabs to non-Arabs. Starting in the 900s, Turks migrated into Muslim lands. The Turks were a nomadic people from Central Asia who became Muslims. The Abbasid caliphs hired Turks as soldiers. Eventually, a group of Turks gained control of Baghdad. They allowed the Abbasid caliphs to remain on the throne but stripped them of all real power.

In the 1250s, the Mongols invaded Muslim lands. They destroyed the city of Baghdad in 1258. There, they slaughtered tens of thousands of people and killed the Abbasid caliph.

Reading Check Into what two groups did Muslims split after Muhammad's death?

▲ **Ottoman Empire 1299–1923**
The Ottoman empire was the largest and most powerful of all the non-Arab empires that followed the Arab Muslim empire. Above are marching janissaries, the fearsome soldiers in brightly colored uniforms who helped the Ottomans conquer their vast empire.

▲ **The Safavid Dynasty 1502–1736**
The Safavid dynasty arose in Persia and fought with the Ottomans. The painting above shows the sport of polo, popular in the Safavid empire.

Non-Arab Muslim Empires

The Mongol invasion ended the caliphate and the golden age of Islamic civilization. But individual Muslim states survived, ruled by non-Arab dynasties. The leaders of many of these states called themselves **sultans,** or rulers of Muslim states.

The Ottoman Empire The largest of these states became the Ottoman empire, which lasted into the 1900s. The Ottomans were a Turkish dynasty. They founded their empire in Asia Minor, part of the country now called Turkey.

Beginning in the 1300s, the Ottomans attacked the Byzantine empire in Asia and in Europe. Ottoman troops captured Constantinople in 1453. From there, Ottoman armies conquered an empire that included southeastern Europe, Arabia, and northern Africa.

The Ottoman empire was powered by a strong military, particularly the janissary corps. Janissaries were boys taken from the Christian provinces of southeastern Europe, raised as Muslims, and trained as elite soldiers. A visitor to the empire compared the janissaries favorably with European soldiers of his day.

> ❝ It is the patience, self-denial and thrift of the Turkish soldier that enable him to face the most trying <u>circumstances</u> and come safely out of the dangers that surround him. What a contrast to our [European] men! ❞
>
> —Ogier Ghiselin de Busbecq

circumstance, *n.,* condition

The Safavid Empire In the 1500s, the powerful Safavid empire rose up in Persia and challenged the Ottomans.

You have already read about the rich culture of the ancient Persian empire.

465

The Mughal Empire 1526–1858
The Mughal emperor Shah Jahan built the stunning Taj Mahal as a tomb for his wife Mumtaz Mahal.

myWorld Activity
Who Was When?

Persian culture continued to develop after the ancient Persian empire fell. After the Arab conquest, most Persians converted to Islam but kept the Persian language. Persian culture survived. Persians remained proud of their ancient heritage.

The Safavid dynasty took power in Persia in the 1500s. They claimed Ali, Muhammad's cousin, as an ancestor. They were Shias and made Shia Islam the official religion of Persia. Today, Persia is called Iran, and it remains a majority Shia country.

Under the Safavid dynasty, Persian painting, architecture, carpet weaving, and metalwork all blossomed. So did astronomy and mathematics.

Reading Check Which Muslim state captured Constantinople?

Islam in India

Traders introduced Islam to India as early as the 700s. Some 200 years later, Turks invaded northern India, beginning a long period of Muslim rule.

The Delhi Sultanate In 1206, a Turkish leader formed the Delhi sultanate in the north of India. During the next 300 years, many Indians converted to Islam. The Delhi sultanate ruled much of India. But Hindu rebellions and Mongol invasions took their toll. One Mongol leader named Timur destroyed Delhi, the capital.

The Mughal Empire In 1526, a group of Muslim Mongols and Turks overran what remained of the Delhi sultanate. Their leader, Babur, founded the Mughal empire. (*Mughal* is another word for "Mongol.") Mughal emperors expanded

Muslim rule over nearly all of India. They oversaw a great flowering of culture. Scholars, writers, and artists migrated to India from the west, especially Persia.

The Founding of Sikhism In Mughal India in the 1500s, a new religion called Sikhism developed. It was influenced by both Hinduism and Islam. Like Islam, Sikhism teaches monotheism. Like Hindus, Sikhs believe in reincarnation.

The founder of Sikhism was a guru, or religious teacher, named Nanak. Guru Nanak declared that "there is neither Hindu nor Muslim." Nine gurus followed him. The Sikh holy book, the Guru Granth Sahib, is considered the final teacher of the community.

The Sikh community fought the Mughals. In 1801, the Sikhs founded a powerful kingdom in northern India under the rule of Maharaja (king) Ranjit Singh. It lasted until 1849. Today, there are about 24 million Sikhs in the world, mostly in India.

Reading Check Who were the Mughals?

▲ A Sikh man stands in front of the Golden Temple, a major Sikh holy place in Amritsar, India.

▲ Guru Nanak, the founder of Sikhism

Section **3** Assessment

? Essential Question

How are religion and culture connected?

Key Terms

1. What does the word *caliph* mean?

2. Are Sunnis or Shias a majority in the Muslim world?

Key Ideas

3. Which two large empires did the Muslims defeat soon after Muhammad's death?

4. What issue divided Muslims into Shia and Sunni groups?

5. Which dynasty made Persia, present-day Iran, a Shia state?

Think Critically

6. Categorize Under the early caliphate, what were the main social groups in Muslim society?

7. Compare and Contrast How was the early caliphate different from later Muslim states like the Ottoman and Mughal empires?

8. What changed about life in Persia after the Arab Muslim conquest of Persia? What did not change? Go to your Student Journal to record your answer.

Muslim Achievements

Key Ideas
- Cities were central to the economies of Muslim empires, which grew through trade.
- Art, architecture, and literature flourished under the Muslim empires.
- Muslims made important advances in mathematics, philosophy, science, and other fields of learning.

Key Terms • textile • Sufism • Arabic numerals • calligraphy

 Visual Glossary

Reading Skill Analyze Cause and Effect Take notes using the graphic organizer in your journal.

A Persian carpet, one of many beautiful products produced in Islamic civilization before modern times

As Islam spread to many different lands, a distinctive Muslim culture developed. Muslims in different regions combined Arab culture and Islam with the Persian, Byzantine, Indian, and other cultures that existed before the coming of Muslim rule.

Growth of Cities and Trade

The expansion of Muslim rule and the spread of Islam united many peoples. Under the protection of a strong central government, trade flourished and cities grew. Even after the end of the Arab Muslim empire, cities continued to play an important role in maintaining a flourishing Islamic civilization.

An Urban Economy By 1000, Muslim culture thrived in cities such as Mecca, Medina, Damascus, and Baghdad. Other cities also prospered. Córdoba was the largest city in Muslim Spain. Cairo, Egypt, was the most important urban center in Africa. Outside of China, the Muslim empires had the largest, most developed cities in the world.

Without a strong economic foundation, Muslim cities could not have grown so rapidly. Farms supplied food, wool, and other basic goods. Traders brought more exotic goods, such as fine silks, from distant lands. Cities produced a wide range of trade goods.

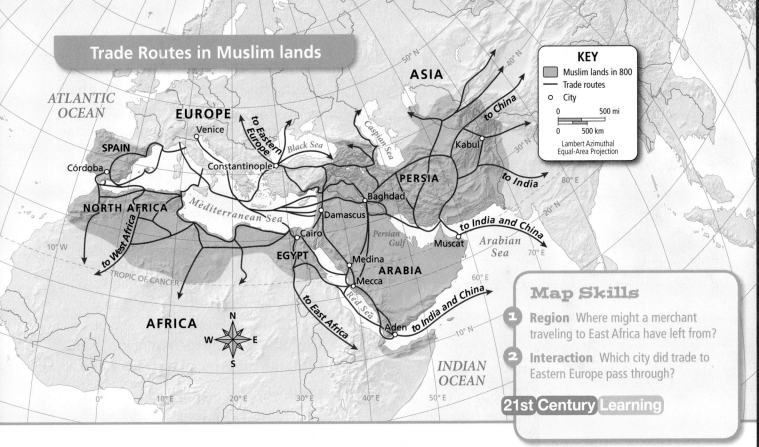

Trade Routes in Muslim lands

KEY

Muslim lands in 800
Trade routes
○ City

0   500 mi
0   500 km

Lambert Azimuthal
Equal-Area Projection

ATLANTIC OCEAN
EUROPE
Venice
SPAIN
Córdoba
Constantinople
Black Sea
NORTH AFRICA
Mediterranean Sea
to Eastern Europe
to West Africa
TROPIC OF CANCER
AFRICA
to East Africa
Cairo
EGYPT
Medina
Mecca
Red Sea
Aden
to India and China
ASIA
Caspian Sea
Kabul
to China
PERSIA
Baghdad
Damascus
Persian Gulf
Muscat
to India
to India and China
ARABIA
Arabian Sea
INDIAN OCEAN

Map Skills

1 **Region** Where might a merchant traveling to East Africa have left from?

2 **Interaction** Which city did trade to Eastern Europe pass through?

21st Century Learning

Muslim civilization gained fame for its fine **textiles,** or woven fabric. These valuable goods included cotton cloth from Egypt and beautiful wool carpets from Persia. Artisans also produced finely crafted steel swords in Damascus, and beautiful leather goods in Córdoba.

Trade and Trade Routes Geography helped make the lands ruled by Muslims a center for trade. Muslim lands included parts of Asia, Europe, and Africa. Muslim traders had access to the Mediterranean Sea and the Indian Ocean. Overland routes to and from East and South Asia passed through Muslim territory. As Muslim merchants traveled by land and sea, they created a network of trade routes that linked three continents.

Muslim traders traveled in two main ways. They crossed the seas in small sailing ships called dhows. Dhows sailed from Arabia south to Africa and east to India. On land, merchants traveled by camel caravan. The most famous overland caravan route was the Silk Road. It linked Baghdad to distant China.

As a result of trade, goods flowed into Islamic cities from three continents. From Asia came Chinese silk and dishes as well as Indian spices, gems, coconuts, and tropical woods. Gold and salt came from Africa. Amber and furs arrived from northern Europe.

Ideas and inventions also spread along the trade routes. For example, Muslim traders brought back inventions such as the Chinese compass and the technique of making paper. In turn, traders spread Muslim culture and learning as well as Islam to other lands.

my worldhistory.com   21st Century Learning

Ibn Sina wrote *The Canon of Medicine*, a medical textbook, in 1025. This copy shows illustrations of the heart, lungs, and other organs.

Philosophy and Medicine

Muslim rulers prized learning. They built libraries and academies where scholars could study and exchange ideas. Muslim scholars collected and translated great works of Greek, Persian, and Indian thinkers. They merged ideas from these cultures with their own knowledge. They also created original works.

Philosophy Islamic civilization produced a number of brilliant philosophers. Some of these scholars, such as Ibn Rushd, studied the ideas of Aristotle and other Greeks. They worked to combine Islamic faith with the principles of Greek logic.

Medicine Muslim physicians, too, studied works by ancient Greek scholars. They improved on Greek medical practices. Muslims also made their own contributions to medical science.

The greatest Muslim doctor was Ibn Sina, known in Europe as Avicenna. A Persian physician, he wrote many books on medicine, philosophy, and other topics. His most famous work was a medical encyclopedia. This book covered every disease and treatment known at that time. It became the standard medical text in Europe for hundreds of years.

Hospitals were built throughout the Arab Muslim empire. Separate areas within these hospitals were set aside for people with different diseases. Hospitals also had pharmacies in which medicines could be prepared. Skilled Muslim doctors performed difficult operations, including cancer and brain surgeries.

Reading Check Who was Ibn Rushd?

Importance of Merchants Merchants played a key role in the urban economy. Some merchants' lives centered on the *souk*, the Arabic word for "marketplace." Here, merchants bought and sold goods from around the empire. Other merchants traveled along well-worn trade routes, carrying manufactured goods to distant Muslim lands and beyond.

Muslim societies honored their merchants. In Muslim lands, successful merchants had great social mobility. Social mobility is the ability to move up in society. Many merchants became important figures in Muslim lands.

Reading Check What key role did merchants play in the urban economy?

Literature

As with medicine, Islamic culture put a high value on literature. Literacy, or the ability to read, spread through religion. Many Muslims learned to read in order to study the Quran. Some Muslim writers wrote down folk tales. Others wrote lyrical poetry about love and nature.

History and Geography Muslim scholars wrote about history and geography. The author Ibn Khaldun wrote a famous history of the world that tried to explain the rise and fall of dynasties. You have already read about Ibn Battuta. He wrote an account of his travels around many Muslim countries.

Folk Tales Muslim folk tales came from a long tradition of storytelling. Some tales featured animals. Others described great heroes and their adventures. Many of these tales appeared in a book titled *The Thousand and One Nights.* This collection includes romantic stories as well as fables that teach lessons.

It is popular around the world. These stories have also provided scholars with helpful information about life in early Muslim times, a period described in many of these stories.

Poetry Like folk tales, Muslim poetry began as an oral art form. Arab nomads used spoken verse to praise their tribes and mock their enemies. Poetry was central to early Arab culture. This oral tradition gave rise to many written forms.

The Persians, like the Arabs, also had a long tradition of writing poetry. One of the most famous Muslim poets was a man named Rumi who came from a Persian family. He often wrote about religious themes.

Rumi practiced **Sufism,** an Islamic lifestyle that <u>emphasizes</u> controlling one's desires, giving up worldly attachments, and seeking nearness to God. Poetry served as a way for Sufis to express their connection with God.

emphasize, *v.,* stress, mark as important

Reading Check What does Sufism teach?

Poetry

Rumi's poems are still widely read in many countries. Like much of Rumi's work, the beautiful poem below has a religious theme.

❝ What God said to the Rose
And caused it to laugh in full blown beauty,
He said to my heart
And made it a hundred times more beautiful. ❞

—Rumi, "The Rose"

◀ The poet Rumi

A manuscript copy of one of Rumi's poems ▼

471

Mathematics and Science

Muslim scholars made important advances in various fields of science. Some of their main contributions were in mathematics and astronomy.

Mathematics Arab mathematicians used a decimal system based on Indian numerals (sometimes called Hindu numerals). This system included the <u>concept</u> of zero.

concept, *n.*, idea

A book by the Muslim mathematician al-Khwarizmi introduced that number system to Europe. We call the symbols that we use for numbers today (0, 1, 2, 3, . . . 9) **Arabic numerals** because it came to Europe from the Arab world. Previously, Europeans used Roman numerals, but Arabic numerals are easier to work with.

Al-Khwarizmi also made groundbreaking advances in the field of algebra. Algebra is a kind of mathematics in which letters are used to stand in for unknown numbers, allowing people to solve complex problems.

In fact, the word *algebra* comes from Arabic. Another word that came to English through Arabic is *chemistry*, a field in which Muslim scientists made advances.

Astronomy Muslim astronomers built observatories, or buildings for viewing and studying the stars. They created charts that showed the positions of stars and planets. They also measured the size of Earth and developed precise calendars.

Reading Check What Muslim mathematician helped advance algebra?

Math and Science

Muslim thinkers made great contributions to math and science. The images on this page show tools used by astronomers in Muslim lands.

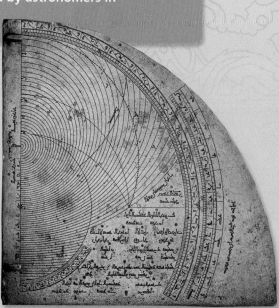

This astrolabe quadrant tracked the movement of the planets. It allowed religious leaders to determine correct time for prayers, and also allowed sailors to navigate more accurately. ▶

▲ In this painting, you can see a Muslim astronomer studying the movements of the sun.

Art and Architecture

You have read that Muslims valued learning. They also placed a high value on the arts. A Hadith says, "God is beautiful and loves beauty." This ideal inspired the creation of beautiful and influential works of art and architecture.

Design and Calligraphy Before Islam, Arabs worshiped images of their gods. Islam opposed the worship of images and discouraged art that showed humans or animals. In time, some painting of images was allowed, but it never became as important as the decorative arts in Islamic civilization.

Decorative designs appeared on everything from colorful tiles to finely woven carpets to the domes of mosques. One of the most popular designs, the arabesque, consists of a pattern of curved shapes and lines resembling flowers or vines.

In Islamic civilization, calligraphy merged art and religion. **Calligraphy** is the art of decorative writing. Using this art form, artists recreated verses from the Quran. They wrote them in decorated books, carved them on walls, painted them on tiles, and wove them into textiles.

Through trade and travel, the various Muslim decorative styles found their way to Europe. In the 1300s in Italy, a new artistic age began. Artists there applied Muslim styles and techniques to glassware, metalwork, and other forms of art.

▲This arched doorway has an arabesque pattern carved into it. It comes from the Alhambra, a large and elaborately decorated palace built in Muslim Spain.

The Arts

On this page you can see some examples of Islamic art. Decorative forms of art, such as the tile and vase below, were particularly important in Islamic civilization before modern times.

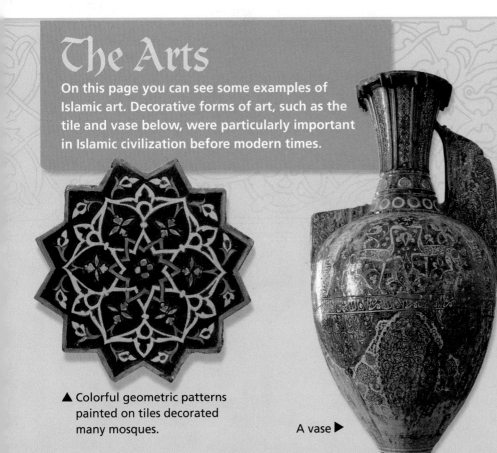

▲ Colorful geometric patterns painted on tiles decorated many mosques.

A vase ▶

▲ Calligraphy made writing beautiful. It was written on paper manuscripts or even carved onto buildings.

473

Islamic Architecture

The four mosques below come from different countries and use different styles. As you read in Section 2, mosques around the world contain many of the same features. Which common part of a mosque can you see on two of the buildings below? Which architectural feature is common to all four?

→ Culture Close-Up

The Blue Mosque in Istanbul, Turkey, was built in a Byzantine-influenced style, typical in the Ottoman empire.

The Imam Mosque in Esfahan, Iran, features a tall dome covered with mosaic tiles. This is common in Iranian mosques.

Black Sea

Mediterranean Sea

| 0 | 1,000 mi |
| 0 | 1,000 km |

Miller Cylindrical Projection

ASIA

AFRICA

ARABIAN PENINSULA

Red Sea

INDIAN OCEAN

ATLANTIC OCEAN

The Dome of the Rock, in Jerusalem, features a striking gilded dome that sparkles in the sunlight.

The Badshahi Mosque in Lahore, Pakistan, was built by a Mughal emperor. The small domes on its minarets were influenced by Hindu architecture.

myWorld Activity
Time for Class

Architecture Muslim architects built striking mosques, fountains, gates, gardens, baths, and palaces. Domes and arches were common features used in Muslim architecture.

Islamic civilization included many cultures that had long histories before the coming of Islam. The influences of these cultures are clearly visible in the buildings designed by Muslims. Byzantine and Roman influences were very strong, especially in western Muslim lands that were once ruled by the Byzantine and Roman emperors. Persian (Iranian) styles were also influential. They spread to many Muslim lands, including India and East Africa.

Reading Check What are arabesques? How are they used?

Preserving Ancient Cultures

Muslims helped preserve Greek and Roman cultural achievements. They passed these advances on to later European civilizations, who benefited from them as they benefited from Muslim advances in mathematics, chemistry, and other fields.

Many areas ruled by Muslims had been influenced by Greco-Roman culture. Muslim rulers and scholars gathered the works of famous authors such as Aristotle. They translated them into Arabic, studied them, made their own advances, and preserved many original texts.

After the fall of the western Roman empire, many of these works had been forgotten in Europe. Muslim scholars wrote about these works, and their writings were translated into Latin. This made them accessible to Europeans. The works of Muslim scholars helped spark a new European interest in the Greeks and Romans and their cultures.

Reading Check Which ancient cultures did Muslims help preserve?

Section 4 Assessment

Key Terms

1. What are textiles? What is one example of a textile product that was produced in early Islamic civilization?

2. Where did the system of Arabic numerals come from originally? To what regions did it spread after al-Khwarizmi wrote his book on the subject?

Key Ideas

3. Name three large cities in Islamic civilization.

4. Identify one idea that passed through Islamic civilization on trade routes.

5. What was the role of poetry in early Arab culture?

6. How did Muslims help preserve ancient cultures?

Think Critically

7. **Analyze Cause and Effect** How did Ibn Sina use Greek learning? What was the effect of his book in Western Europe?

8. **Draw Inferences** What can you infer about Muslim learning considering that the words *algebra* and *chemistry* both come through Arabic?

Essential Question

How are religion and culture connected?

9. How did religion help increase literacy in Islamic civilization? Go to your Student Journal to record your answer.

myworldhistory.com

Culture Close-Up

Chapter Assessment

Key Terms and Ideas

1. **Recall** In which modern-day country is the Hijaz located?

2. **Summarize** What is the significance of the **hajj?** What set of religious duties is the hajj a part of?

3. **Compare and Contrast** What divides **Sunnis** and **Shias**? What do they have in common?

4. **Compare and Contrast** How are the **Quran** and the **Sunnah** similar? How are they different?

5. **Categorize** How do Judaism, Christianity, and Islam differ in their views of Muhammad? How do Muslims and Christians differ in their views of Jesus?

6. **Recall** Where was the religion of Sikhism founded? Who was its founding leader?

7. **Analyze Cause and Effect** Islam discourages art that shows humans or animals. What was the effect of this rule on art in Islamic civilization?

Think Critically

8. **Sequence** Put the following dynasties, rulers, and empires in order from earliest to latest: Abbasid dynasty, Muhammad, Mughal empire, "Rightly Guided Caliphs," Umayyad dynasty.

9. **Draw Inferences** What do you think were the long term effects of the Mongol invasion of Muslim lands?

10. **Analyze Primary Sources** Find the quote from the Hadith in Section 2. According to this quote, how should people treat their neighbors?

11. **Core Concepts: Religion** Do most Muslims live in Arab countries?

Analyze Visuals

At the right is the flag of Saudi Arabia. The writing on it means "There is no God but God and Muhammad is the messenger of God."

12. What pillar of Islam does this line refer to?

13. Saudi Arabia is the country where Mecca is located. Its people are almost all Muslims. Why do you think this line might appear on its flag?

The Flag of Saudi Arabia

Essential Question

myWorld Chapter Activity

Islamic Community Center Follow your teacher's instructions to participate in a meeting at an Islamic Community Center. Exchange information about the way Islam is practiced in different countries. Then write a letter to your character's home country to share what you have learned.

21st Century Learning

Search for Information on the Internet

On the Internet, research one of the following Muslim dynasties or empires: Seljuk, Nasrid, Ghaznavid, Mamluk. Write a short paragraph listing the following:
- Dates and how dynasty began and ended
- Area ruled
- Cultural achievements
- information about a famous ruler

Document-Based Questions

Success Tracker™
Online at myworldhistory.com

Use your knowledge of Islamic civilization, as well as Documents A and B, to answer Questions 1–3.

Document A

" O people, listen to me in earnest, worship God, say your five daily prayers, fast during the month of Ramadan, and give your wealth in zakah [charity]. Perform Hajj if you can afford to. You know that every Muslim is the brother of another Muslim. You are all equal."

—Muhammad, farewell sermon

Document B

"[God has] given mankind in this Quran all manner of parables, so that they may take heed: a Quran in the Arabic tongue [language], free from any flaw, that they may guard themselves against evil."

—Quran, 39:28

1. What does Muhammad urge Muslims to do in Document A?

   A Practice the Five Pillars of Islam, and respect the equality of all Muslims.

   B Obey political leaders.

   C Remember that some Muslims are better than others because of their nationality.

   D Never drink alchohol or eat pork.

2. What does Document B tell Muslims?

   A that they must only speak Arabic

   B that the Quran is not an accurate guide to life

   C that the Quran does not have any flaws

   D that the Quran is written in direct language

3. **Writing Task** Write a paragraph summarizing the teachings of Islam. Use examples from these two documents to support your statements.

my worldhistory.com

Self-Test

The Spread of Islam

Key Idea
- Migration, trade, conflict, and pilgrimages spread the Muslim faith. Islam spread throughout Southwest Asia, the Mediterranean region, and northern Africa.

In the years after Muhammad's death in 632, Islam spread rapidly from its origins in Arabia to Southwest Asia, North Africa, and Spain. Muslim soldiers, merchants, pilgrims, and migrants brought their faith with them as they traveled to new lands. The first excerpt describes the enormous markets in the city of Thessalonica (thes uh LAHN ih kuh), Greece, which attracted Muslim and other merchants from all over the world. The second excerpt was written by Ibn Jubayr, a Spanish Muslim. It describes his pilgrimage in the 1180s to the Muslim holy city of Mecca, in what is now Saudi Arabia.

An illustration from the 1800s of Muslim traders

Read the text on the right. Stop at each circled letter. Then answer the question with the same letter on the left.

A Analyze Details What does this description of the fair suggest about the extent and impact of trade?

B Summarize What do these lines say about travel by land and sea?

C Draw Inferences From this description of the animals, what do you think the fair was like for traders and shoppers?

Boeotia, *n.,* a region in ancient Greece

Peloponnese, *n.,* a large peninsula and region in southern Greece

Euxine, *n.,* the Black Sea

assailed, *v.,* attacked, overwhelmed

The Great Fair at Thessalonica

66 [T]here was every kind of material woven or spun by men or women, all those that come from <u>Boeotia</u> (bee OH shuh) and the <u>Peloponnese</u> (pel uh puh NEES), and all that are brought in trading ships from Italy to Greece. Besides this, Phoenicia furnishes numerous articles, and Egypt, and Spain, and the

A pillars of Hercules, where the finest coverlets are manufactured. These things the merchants bring direct from their respective countries to old Macedonia and Thessalonica; but the <u>Euxine</u> (YOOK suhn) also contributes to the splendour of the fair by sending across its products to Constantinople,

B whence the cargoes are brought by numerous horses and mules. . . . I was struck with wonder at the number and variety of the animals, and the extraordinary confusion of their noises which <u>assailed</u> my ears—horses neighing, oxen low-

C ing, sheep bleating, pigs grunting, and dogs barking, for these also accompany their masters as a defence against wolves and thieves. 99

—anonymous, *Timarion*, probably 1100s

Read the text on the right. Stop at each circled letter. Then answer the question with the same letter on the left.

D **Summarize** In your own words, explain the scene that Ibn Jubayr is describing.

E **Analyze Details** What does the description of the crowd tell you about how the observer feels about the pilgrimage?

F **Draw Conclusions** Why do you think the author uses images of light to describe the travelers?

Emir, *n.,* a ruler, chief

multitude, *n.,* a great number

teeming, *v.,* to be present in large quantity

giddily, *adv.,* dizzily

billows, *n.,* waves

litter, *n.,* covered couch used to carry a single passenger

Pilgrimage to Mecca

66 This assembly of 'Iraqis, together with the people from . . . other lands who were united in the company of this <u>Emir</u> (e MIR) of **D** the Pilgrimage, formed a <u>multitude</u> whose number only God Most High could count. The vast plain was <u>teeming</u> with them, and the far-extending desert could barely contain them. You could see the earth shake <u>giddily</u> because of them, and form waves through their great number. You might behold them as a sea of swollen <u>billows</u>; its waters the mirage, its ships the mounts, and its sails the raised canopies. . . . Like piled up clouds they moved along. . . . He who has not witnessed this **E** journeying of the 'Iraqis has not seen one of those wonders of time that are discussed amongst men. . . . [These] marvels are such that a description cannot comprehend them. . . .

By night they march by lighted torches held in the hands of footmen, and you can see no <u>litter</u> that is not led by one, so that the people march between wandering stars that lighten the **F** darkness of the night, while the earth vies in splendour with the stars of the sky. 99

—Ibn Jubayr, about 1185, from *The Travels of Ibn Jubayr*, translated by Roland Broadhurst

A woven tapestry showing pilgrims at Mecca

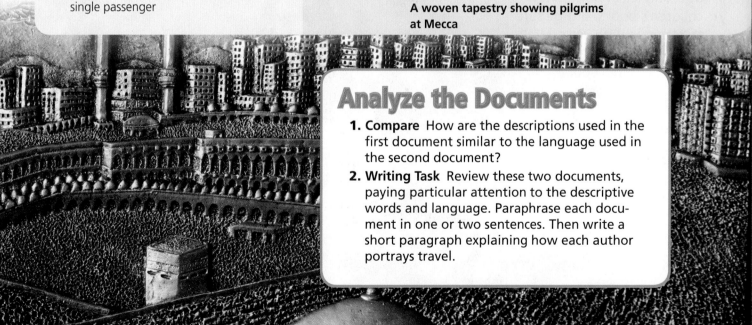

Analyze the Documents

1. **Compare** How are the descriptions used in the first document similar to the language used in the second document?

2. **Writing Task** Review these two documents, paying particular attention to the descriptive words and language. Paraphrase each document in one or two sentences. Then write a short paragraph explaining how each author portrays travel.

Design a

Children's Book

Your Mission Working in teams, you and your classmates will write and illustrate a children's book about a topic from this unit that could be used to teach younger students about the topic. After completing your book, your team will present it to the class.

In this unit, you learned that after the fall of the western Roman empire, new cultures and belief systems formed and spread in the Byzantine empire and throughout Muslim civilization.

Work as a team to pick a topic from the unit. The topic could be large, such as the origins of Islam, or more narrowly focused, such as the history of Hagia Sophia. You might choose to write a biography of a leader or to tell the stories of a number of different people. You may want to look at examples of nonfiction children's books, but be sure to come up with your own ideas. Try to visualize the best way to tell your story. How can you make a book that will interest and educate young children? Be creative!

Go to myWorldHistory.com for help with this activity.

 STEP 1

Choose and Research Your Topic.

Review unit content to choose a topic for your book. After your team picks a topic, gather important facts to present in your book. Research images to use when you create illustrations. As you research, be sure to think about how you will present your topic. For example, if you choose to write about Constantinople, you may want to include a timeline of important events in the city's history. If you write about the spread of Islam, you may want to include a map of its spread.

 STEP 2

Write and Design Your Book.

Choose members of your team to do specific tasks, such as writing, designing, or illustrating. As you create the book, think about your intended audience. The story and the book's design need to be clear and logical. Use simple words that young students can understand. Use illustrations that show the information you want your readers to learn.

STEP 3

Present Your Story.

After your team has written and designed its book, practice reading it aloud. Revise sentences to make them clear and accurate. Make sure that you think about any questions your young readers might have, and try to answer those questions in the book. Then read your book to your classmates and accept their feedback and criticism. Make any necessary revisions they suggest. If possible, invite a younger class of students to listen to your books.

Unit **6** 21st Century Learning

my worldhistory.com

21st Century Learning

African and Asian Civilizations

Europe

Mansa Musa (1300s), the greatest ruler of the rich kingdom of Mali, made a famous pilgrimage to Mecca.

Atlantic Ocean

Africa

N

W · E

S

2000 B.C.   1000 B.C.   A.D. 1   A.D. 1000   A.D. 2000

Early African Civilizations

China in the Middle Ages

Japan Before Modern Times

Murasaki Shikibu (1000s), the lady-in-waiting to the Japanese emperor's wife, was the author of the world's first novel.

Kublai Khan (1200s) was the ruler of the mighty Mongol empire who welcomed foreign visitors to his court.

Pacific Ocean

Indian Ocean

Chapter 16 Early African Civilizations

Chapter 17 China in the Middle Ages

Chapter 18 Japan Before Modern Times

* **Colors on the map correspond to the areas covered in each chapter.**

Early African Civilizations

Essential Question

What are the consequences of trade?

Explore the Essential Question . . .

- at ᵐʸ worldhistory.com
- using the **myWorld Chapter Activity**
- with the **Student Journal**

Bronze plaque of African warriors from Benin, about 1550–1650

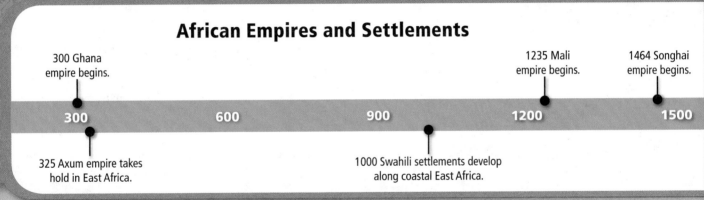

African Empires and Settlements

300 Ghana empire begins.

1235 Mali empire begins.

1464 Songhai empire begins.

300   600   900   1200   1500

325 Axum empire takes hold in East Africa.

1000 Swahili settlements develop along coastal East Africa.

Mansa Musa: The Lion of Mali

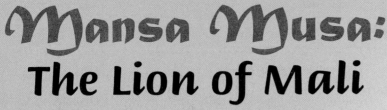

This myStory is a fictionalized account of real-life events experienced by the people named in this chapter.

In 1324, Mali emperor Mansa Musa stopped his caravan outside of Cairo. There had never been a larger caravan in the world. Thousands had joined him on his hajj (religious journey) to the Muslim city of Mecca. Many were soldiers wearing chain mail. Most were slaves wearing the finest silk; hundreds carried solid gold staffs. There were thousands of camels and donkeys. About 80 camels carried bags of gold.

By the time the caravan had reached Cairo, word had spread of Mansa Musa. It was said that every Friday during his hajj, he ordered a new mosque built so that Islam could spread throughout Africa. It was also said that he gave gold dust to nearly everyone he met on his hajj.

my worldhistory.com

Timeline/On Assignment

485

About 60,000 followers joined Mansa Musa on his hajj. When they reached Cairo, the sultan sent a messenger to invite Mansa Musa to a meeting.

It did not take long for the sultan of Cairo to send a messenger to Mansa Musa. "The sultan wishes to meet you," the messenger said.

Mansa Musa sighed. To appear before the sultan was a distraction from his spiritual pilgrimage to Mecca. But Mansa Musa decided he did not want to offend the sultan. To do so could disrupt trade between Mali and Egypt. He told the messenger that he and his advisors would visit the sultan.

In the sultan's palace, the messenger announced Mansa Musa to the sultan. The sultan sat upon a large throne. He did not move. Neither did Mansa Musa. The messenger said to Mansa Musa, "All who appear before the sultan must fall to their knees."

Mansa Musa frowned. He did not want to kneel before the sultan. In Mali, when people came before him, they first sprinkled dust on their heads to express humility and respect. Mansa Musa whispered to an advisor, "I do not understand. Should not the sultan fall to his knees before me? After all, who controls the salt and the gold trade routes throughout West Africa?"

"You do, Your Highness," whispered his advisor.

"Who has united his kingdom and made it orderly and just? Who has spread Islam throughout his empire?"

"None other than you, Your Majesty."

"Who travels among the world's largest caravan across the Sahara?"

"You do, Your Excellency."

Mansa Musa glanced at the sultan, who waited for his guest to kneel. A tremor ran through all in attendance. Nobody had ever refused to kneel before the sultan and lived to tell of it.

The advisor whispered in Mansa Musa's ear. "Your Majesty, you are indeed more powerful than the sultan. But who is more powerful than you?"

"Only God," said Mansa Musa.

"Then, perhaps, rather than submit to the sultan, you should submit to God."

Mansa Musa nodded at his advisor, then dropped to his knees to bow. "I bow before God who created me," he said.

The sultan smiled. He rose and beckoned Mansa Musa to sit with him. Through his translator he told Mansa Musa how much he respected him. "You found a solution that saved us both from humiliation and its terrible consequences. To honor your dignity and our mutual faith of Islam, I will give you horses, slaves, and provisions for your hajj."

"And I," said Mansa Musa, "will give you gold beyond your wildest dreams."

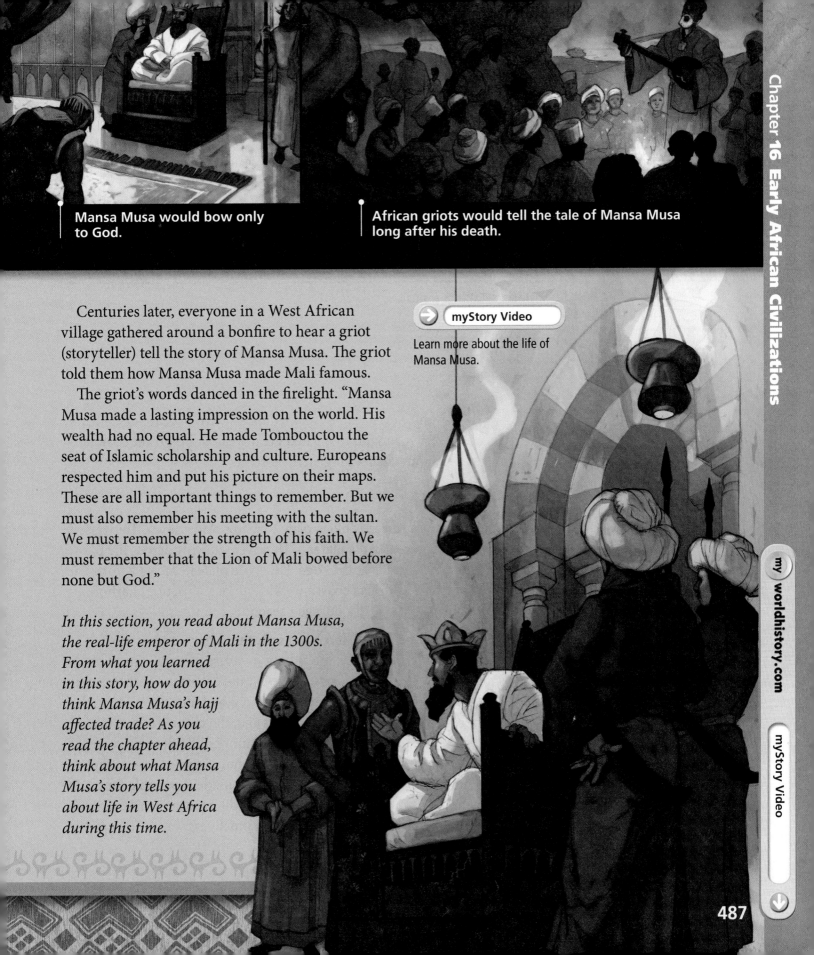

Mansa Musa would bow only to God.

African griots would tell the tale of Mansa Musa long after his death.

Centuries later, everyone in a West African village gathered around a bonfire to hear a griot (storyteller) tell the story of Mansa Musa. The griot told them how Mansa Musa made Mali famous.

The griot's words danced in the firelight. "Mansa Musa made a lasting impression on the world. His wealth had no equal. He made Tombouctou the seat of Islamic scholarship and culture. Europeans respected him and put his picture on their maps. These are all important things to remember. But we must also remember his meeting with the sultan. We must remember the strength of his faith. We must remember that the Lion of Mali bowed before none but God."

In this section, you read about Mansa Musa, the real-life emperor of Mali in the 1300s. From what you learned in this story, how do you think Mansa Musa's hajj affected trade? As you read the chapter ahead, think about what Mansa Musa's story tells you about life in West Africa during this time.

→ myStory Video

Learn more about the life of Mansa Musa.

my worldhistory.com

myStory Video

A Trading Empire

Key Ideas
- Africa is a continent with diverse land and rich natural resources.
- Ironworking and the gold–salt trade helped the development of African empires.
- Trade wealth helped rulers in Ghana create a powerful West African empire.

Key Terms
- plateau
- savanna
- natural resources
- labor specialization
- trans-Saharan

 Visual Glossary

 Reading Skill Summarize Take notes using the graphic organizer in your journal.

Camels allowed African traders to cross the Sahara. ▼

Africa's unique geography shaped the growth of African civilizations. Early kingdoms earned great wealth and power by adapting to a rich but challenging environment.

The African Landscape

The interior of Africa is like a plate turned upside down. This raised but flat region is called a **plateau**. The rivers flowing across the plateau fall as waterfalls at the edge. Here, the plateau meets a thin strip of coastal plain. Africa's coastline, with its lack of natural harbors and many waterfalls, discouraged seagoing trade.

The Sahara The world's largest desert, the Sahara, covers most of northern Africa. Today, the Sahara measures about 3.5 million square miles. In ancient times, however, the desert was not so large. Thousands of years ago, rivers, trees, and grasslands covered much of the region. Then, about 6,000 years ago, the climate began to get drier. Travel across the Sahara grew more difficult as the years passed. About 2,000 years ago traders began to use camels, rather than horses, for the long, dry trip. Camels made it possible for trade to occur between West Africa and the Mediterranean world. Camels can travel much farther than horses on much less water. They can also cross sandy areas more easily.

Vegetation Zones Rain is critical to life in Africa. People tend to live where rain falls the most. Africa consists of several vegetation zones, or bands of plant life. Each zone has its own climate.

Rain in Africa is most common along the equator. This is the rain forest zone. It is hot and wet year-round. Thousands of different insects, plants, and animals live here. Some of the rain forest has been cut down to make way for towns and cities. In other places, the land has been cleared for farming.

Above and below the equator is a zone called the **savanna**, a broad grassland with scattered trees. Some grasslands support herds of animals, such as giraffe and antelope, as well as livestock, such as cattle, sheep, and horses. Tropical savannas have wet and dry seasons.

North and south of the savanna are the deserts such as the Sahara. Few people live there due to a lack of food.

At the northern tip of Africa is the Mediterranean zone. Here summers are warm and dry, and winters are rainy.

Some variations can be found within these seemingly similar zones. The oceans affect local climates, as do cooler highland regions.

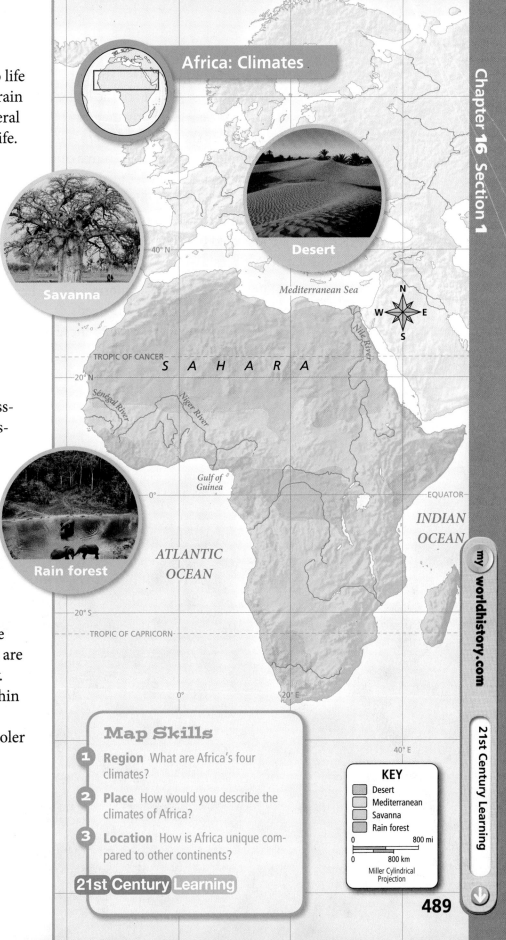

Africa: Climates

Savanna

Desert

Rain forest

Mediterranean Sea

Nile River

SAHARA

TROPIC OF CANCER

Sénégal River

Niger River

40° N

20° N

Gulf of Guinea

0°

EQUATOR

INDIAN OCEAN

ATLANTIC OCEAN

20° S

TROPIC OF CAPRICORN

0°

20° E

40° E

KEY
- Desert
- Mediterranean
- Savanna
- Rain forest

0   800 mi

0   800 km

Miller Cylindrical Projection

Map Skills

1 **Region** What are Africa's four climates?

2 **Place** How would you describe the climates of Africa?

3 **Location** How is Africa unique compared to other continents?

21st Century Learning

The Niger and Senegal Rivers The two largest rivers of West Africa are the Niger (NY jur) and the Senegal. Early civilizations formed near these rivers. Rivers provided people with a reliable source of water in a dry region. They let farmers grow crops even in years with little rainfall. Boats could travel rivers most of the year. People used the rivers to travel and trade across West Africa.

Natural Resources Natural materials that people can use to meet their needs are called **natural resources**. Some of these materials include land used for farming or grazing; trees that provide fuel or building material; and minerals such as gold, copper, and salt.

Some natural resources made valuable trade items. Prized items like gold, along with agricultural wealth, gave rise to powerful trading empires. Trade brought Africans into contact with one another and with people and ideas from other parts of the world.

Reading Check What is a vegetation zone?

Rise of Ghana
Learning to work with metals was an important step in the development of West African civilizations and empires. Metal tools and weapons were stronger than those made of stone, wood, or bone. People with metalworking skills had an advantage over their neighbors.

The Niger River
This great river supported the early African civilizations. Below, the Niger flows along the shores of Djenné, Mali.

Iron-Working Technology By 350 B.C., West Africans began making iron tools in a place called Nok. Iron was much harder than other materials used. With the help of iron tools, the people of West Africa could grow more food. As food supplies increased, so did the population. Iron-working technology then spread throughout West and Central Africa.

Ancient Ghana As the population of West Africa grew, governments were formed to keep order. Around A.D. 300, the Soninke people founded a kingdom between the Niger and Senegal rivers. As food supplies grew, not everyone had to grow food. Some could become experts in things like government or crafts. The division of jobs and skills in a society is called **labor specialization**.

Families were very important in Ghana. Each clan, or group of related families, specialized in a craft or trade. The Sisse clan, for example, formed the ruling class. Its members became Ghana's kings and officials. Other clans specialized in trades such as fishing, cloth making, or cattle raising.

The Soninke benefited from the use of iron. They had iron swords and spears, while their enemies still used wooden clubs. Over time, they used their superior weapons to control others. The kingdom grew into an empire known as Ghana. (The modern African nation of Ghana is named after this ancient empire, but it is in a different part of West Africa. See the map on page 496.) Like many ancient empires—including Greece and Rome—

Ghana enslaved people in its wars of con-quest. Ghana traded slaves for salt and other goods offered by Berber merchants.

Reading Check What is labor specialization?

A Powerful Empire

By the 700s, Arab and Berber traders of northern Africa regularly traveled across the Sahara. They traded salt, horses, cloth, swords, and books for gold and ivory. Ghana was located across trade routes. It acted as a go-between for the North African traders and the producers of gold and ivory in the south.

Gold–Salt Trade **Trans-Saharan** trade (trade across the Sahara) relied heavily on gold and salt. North Africans wanted gold to make into coins, since most states

conquest, *n.,* capturing something, especially in war

myWorld Activity
A Trading Empire

The Nok civilization was among the first to use iron. Below are stone sculptures from the Nok culture. ▼

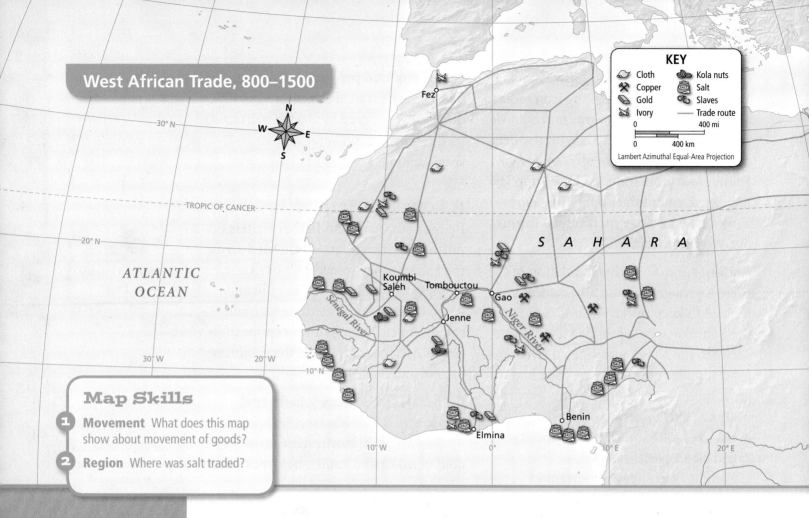

West African Trade, 800–1500

KEY

Cloth		Kola nuts	
Copper		Salt	
Gold		Slaves	
Ivory		Trade route	

0   400 mi
0   400 km
Lambert Azimuthal Equal-Area Projection

SAHARA

ATLANTIC OCEAN

Fez

Koumbi Saleh

Tombouctou

Gao

Jenne

Benin

Elmina

Senegal River

Niger River

TROPIC OF CANCER

Map Skills

1 **Movement** What does this map show about movement of goods?

2 **Region** Where was salt traded?

Salt was critical to African trade. Below are salt mounds in Senegal. ▼

in the area based their currency on gold. West Africans were rich in gold, but they needed salt—a mineral necessary for good health. Miners removed slabs of salt from ancient sea beds in the Sahara. North African traders loaded salt onto camels and crossed the desert to West Africa to trade the salt for gold.

Wealthy Rulers Kings of Ghana grew rich from the gold–salt trade. They taxed gold producers and every load of goods that entered or left Ghana. Ghana's rulers also controlled the gold supply. They knew that if the supply grew too large, its price would fall. Gold taken from the ground became the king's property. This law removed much gold from the market,

keeping the price high. It also made the kings rich. It was said that one king had a gold nugget weighing 30 pounds!

In 1067, a Spanish Muslim scholar described a king's court:

66 He sits in a pavilion around which stand ten horses with gold-embroidered trappings. Behind the king stand ten pages holding shields and gold-mounted swords; on his right are the sons of princes of his empire, splendidly clad and with gold plaited [braided] in their hair. . . . The door of the pavilion is guarded by dogs of an excellent breed . . . who wear collars of gold and silver. 99

—Al-Bakri, from *African Kingdoms* by Basil Davidson, 1966

492

Invasion and Decline For centuries Ghana prospered. Its rulers welcomed North African traders, who brought Islam to West Africa. Ghana kept its traditional religions. However, Ghana was known for its religious tolerance and welcomed Muslims. Ghana's leaders borrowed and used Islamic administrative and legal practices.

However, Ghana eventually began to decline. Among the reasons are overpopulation, food shortages, and an overdependence on trade. To make matters worse, around 1060 the Almoravids, a group of Berbers from northwest Africa, expanded their empire into Ghana. They were religious reformers who wanted to purify the Islamic practices of Muslims in Ghana and spread their own interpretation of Islam. They also wanted greater control of the gold trade.

Although the Almoravid invasion failed in the end, it disrupted trade and weakened the monarchy. The Almoravids brought with them large flocks of animals that took over much farmland. Soon, Ghana had trouble supporting its population. Ghana never returned to its <u>prosperity</u> after the Almoravid invasion.

prosperity, *n.,* economic well-being

Reading Check What two goods were most important to trans-Saharan trade?

Gold was a key trade item. It was mined (inset) or panned.

Section 1 Assessment

Key Terms

1. How is a plateau described in this section?

2. What is a savanna?

3. How does labor specialization help a society?

Key Ideas

4. How have natural resources affected West African history?

5. Why were some kings of Ghana so wealthy?

6. Why was salt so valuable in West Africa?

Think Critically

7. **Summarize** Explain how ancient Ghana became powerful and then declined.

8. **Identify Main Ideas and Details** Describe how the Sahara and regions south of the Sahara differ from each other.

? Essential Question

What are the consequences of trade?

9. The Sisse clan became rulers of the Soninke. Explain whether this is an example of labor specialization. Go to your Student Journal to record your answer.

493

Muslim Empires of West Africa

Key Ideas

- Mali was the second West African empire to prosper from the gold–salt trade.

- After its rulers converted to Islam, Mali became a center of Muslim culture.

- Under the Songhai empire, Islam and the Arabic language spread across West Africa.

Key Terms • caravan • scholarship • griot

 Visual Glossary

┼┼┼┼┼┼ **Reading Skill Sequence** Take notes using the graphic organizer in your journal.

Sundiata Keita is believed to be the founder of Mali. *What does this picture tell you about him?* ▼

conduct, *n.,* the way that one acts

Rise of Mali

After Ghana fell, the small kingdoms it once ruled competed for power. In about 1203, a ruler named Sumanguru took over what was left of the old empire. He ruled over many small kingdoms that had been under the control of Ghana. One of these was the home of the Malinke people.

Triumph of Sundiata According to oral history, the Malinke tired of Sumanguru's cruel rule. They asked Sundiata (soon JAH tah), the son of a Malinke ruler, to free their kingdom. In 1230 Sundiata led a rebellion with the help of Malinke kings. By 1235 he ruled over a new empire, Mali. It took over all the former territory of Ghana, and added more. Sundiata became Mali's national hero and remains honored by the Malinke.

A New Empire Sundiata proved to be a wise ruler. He called himself mansa, or emperor. He ruled with an assembly of kings. At their first meeting, the assembly put forth a set of laws. The laws dealt with the social classes, property rights, the environment, and personal <u>conduct</u>. Passed by word of mouth, they became the law of the land. The rules divided responsibilities and privileges among the clans. The laws allowed women to serve in government on rare occasions.

Under Sundiata, Mali gained control of the gold-producing regions and trade routes, and grew wealthy from trade. It traded items like gold, salt, cloth, books, and copper with Egypt and North Africa.

Reading Check Who was Sundiata?

Mali at its Height

Mansa Musa, emperor from 1312–1337, ruled Mali during its most prosperous period. He made the empire larger. By embracing Islam, he changed the empire into a center of Muslim learning and art.

Mansa Musa's Hajj A hajj, or religious journey to the holy city of Mecca, is one of the duties of a faithful Muslim. In 1324 Mansa Musa made a great hajj. He set off from Mali with a **caravan,** which is a large group that travels together. Twelve thousand officials and slaves and more than 80 camels loaded with bags of gold dust traveled with him across the desert. Arab writers at the time were amazed by Mansa Musa's great wealth. It was reported that he spent so much gold in Cairo that he upset the economy of Egypt for years. His great hajj brought world attention to the empire. North Africans, Arabs, and Europeans began to understand just how wealthy and advanced the empire had become. The Arab historian Ibn Khaldun wrote

66 The authority of the people of Mali became mighty. All the nations of the Sudan stood in awe of them, and the merchants of North Africa traveled to their country. 99

—from *West Africa before the Colonial Era: A History to 1850* by Basil Davidson

Muslim Culture in Mali Mansa Musa returned home from his hajj with Muslim scholars, artists, and teachers. One such person was a famous poet, scholar, and architect called As-Saheli. Mansa Musa had As-Saheli build great mosques in the cities of Gao and Tombouctou (also spelled Timbuktu). Tombouctou became a center for Islamic **scholarship,** or formal study and learning. Students and teachers from North Africa and the Middle East traveled to Tombouctou to study.

my World CONNECTIONS

Many African nations mine gold. More than **80** countries mine it worldwide. The U.S. produces about **10%** of the world's supply.

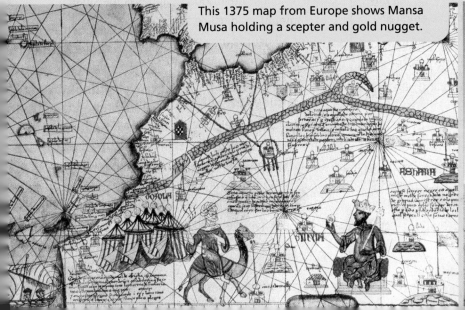
This 1375 map from Europe shows Mansa Musa holding a scepter and gold nugget.

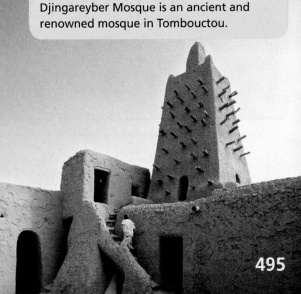
Djingareyber Mosque is an ancient and renowned mosque in Tombouctou.

495

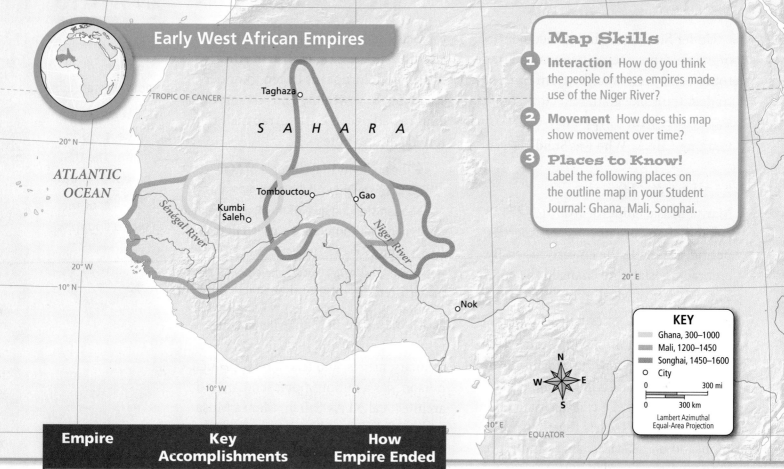

Early West African Empires

TROPIC OF CANCER

Taghaza

SAHARA

20° N

ATLANTIC OCEAN

Senegal River

Kumbi Saleh

Tombouctou

Gao

Niger River

20° W

10° N

20° E

10° E

Nok

20° W

10° W

0°

20° E

10° E

EQUATOR

KEY

Ghana, 300–1000
Mali, 1200–1450
Songhai, 1450–1600
○ City

0   300 mi
0   300 km

Lambert Azimuthal
Equal-Area Projection

Map Skills

1 **Interaction** How do you think the people of these empires made use of the Niger River?

2 **Movement** How does this map show movement over time?

3 **Places to Know!** Label the following places on the outline map in your Student Journal: Ghana, Mali, Songhai.

Empire	Key Accomplishments	How Empire Ended
Ghana	Ghana worked with iron and prospered from the gold-salt trade.	Almoravids from northwest Africa invaded, disrupting the empire.
Mali	Mali created a code of laws, made Tombouctou the center of Islamic scholarship, expanded its empire to 50 million people, and prospered from trade.	Poor leadership resulted in loss of control of Gao, and then the rest of the empire.
Songhai	Songhai maintained a strong military, established a government system, and became the largest of the West African empires.	Soldiers from Morocco invaded and overpowered Songhai.

Chart Skills

Which empire do you think did the most to advance trade? Explain.

A great traveler of the time was Ibn Battuta (IB un bat TOO tah) of Morocco. In 1352, he spent many months in Mali. Battuta described Mali as peaceful.

" Amongst their good qualities is the small amount of injustice amongst them, for of all people they are the furthest from it. Their sultan [Mansa Musa] does not forgive anyone in any matter to do with injustice. Among these qualities there is also the prevalence of peace in their country, the traveller is not afraid in it nor is he who lives there in fear of the thief or of the robber by violence. "

—*Ibn Battuta in Black Africa*
by Said Hamdun and Noël King, 1995

myWorld Activity
Creating Paper-Plate
Leaders

Expansion of Mali During Mansa Musa's long rule, he extended Mali's territory westward to the Atlantic Ocean and northward, creating one of the largest empires of its time. At its height Mali covered an area about the size of Western Europe. It supported a population of roughly 50 million. Some think that the people of Mali may have explored the ocean at this time, but there is no evidence to support this claim.

Reading Check What is a hajj?

Rise of the Songhai Empire

In the 1300s, Mali controlled trading cities along the Niger River. One of these cities was Gao, the capital of the Muslim kingdom of Songhai. Rulers of Mali following Mansa Musa began losing control of the empire in the 1400s. When they lost control of Gao, Songhai grew in power. Under a Muslim leader named Ali, it became the center of a new empire.

Conquests of Ali In 1464, Ali Ber became king of Songhai, taking the title *sunni*. (*Ali Ber* means "Ali the Great.") Sunni Ali was a great military leader. He kept mounted warriors to protect the land. He also had a fleet of war canoes patrolling the Niger River. This extended Songhai's empire along the great bend of the Niger River.

Once in power, Ali wanted to gain control of Tombouctou, a center of the gold-salt trade. At that time a nomadic people called the Tuareg controlled the city. In 1468, Ali's well-equipped army drove the Tuareg out of Tombouctou. Ali next captured Djenné, another wealthy trading city. With the successful capture of Djenné, Songhai controlled the trans-Saharan trading routes.

The Largest Empire Later rulers conquered still more territory, making Songhai the largest of West Africa's trading empires. The greatest of these rulers was Askia Muhammad. A successful military leader, he used a well-trained army to control the empire. He was an even better administrator. The government system he set up brought the region together. Business ran smoothly with the help of highly trained administrators. The system of weights and measures Muhammad established helped ensure the wealth of the empire.

Islamic Law and Scholarship Askia Muhammad strengthened the influence of Islam within the empire. He appointed Muslim judges to enforce laws. These laws were based on the Quran, the holy book of Islam. Since the Quran was written in Arabic, Songhai's laws were written in Arabic also.

Muhammad further promoted scholarship as well. Songhai's scholars learned to read and write Arabic to study the Quran. They copied old manuscripts and wrote new books in Arabic. These books focused on topics of advanced human thought, such as biology, medicine, law, ethics, agriculture, mathematics, and astronomy. The books, which were sold at great expense, demonstrate the advanced society of Tombouctou at the time.

my worldhistory.com

Places to Know

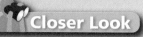
Closer Look

Muslim Scholarship in Tombouctou

An old saying from West Africa tells us, "Salt comes from the north, gold from the south, and silver from the country of the white men, but the word of God and the treasures of wisdom are only to be found in Tombouctou." This points out the fame of the city as a center of both Islam and of learning. As many as 25,000 scholars at one time studied there. Arabic was and remains the language of scholarship for millions of people throughout the Muslim world.

THINK CRITICALLY **Why is a stable society needed for scholarship to thrive?**

Sankore Mosque in Tombouctou

Man and child outside of Djingareyber Mosque

▲ Manuscript in Arabic

◄ Children sit in a class reading Arabic.

498

Arabic also assisted trade. It provided a common language for traders in West Africa and traders from Arab regions to set up deals and keep records. Tombouctou's <u>commercial</u> success soared to new heights through the use of a common language.

Decline of Songhai When Askia Muhammad could no longer rule due to his health, his sons competed to take over their father's lands. As a result, the empire slowly began to weaken.

Songhai's era came to a close in 1591. In that year, soldiers from Morocco invaded Songhai. Armed with guns, the Moroccan forces overpowered the Songhai warriors and captured Tombouctou and other cities.

A historian from Tombouctou described the effects of the invasion:

66 From that moment on, everything changed. Danger took the place of security; poverty of wealth. Peace gave way to distress, disasters, and violence. 99
—Abd al-Rahman al-Sadi

The invasion caused the Songhai empire to collapse. Its once-thriving cities fell into ruin.

Reading Check Why were Songhai's laws written in Arabic?

Legacy of Empires

The powerful empires of Ghana, Mali, and Songhai are long gone, but their <u>legacy</u> remains. Millions of Africans speak the languages of Mali and Songhai. **Griots,** professional storytellers and oral historians who are the keepers of West African history, still sing about the achievements of great kings like Sundiata.

Family, Agriculture, and Religion Families form the basis of modern African society, as you will learn in the next section. Likewise, markets and farming remain key parts of the economy. Islam continues to be a major influence in West African life, along with many traditional religions.

Reading Check What is a legacy?

commercial, *adj.,* having to do with trade and business

legacy, *n.,* an influence from the past

Section 2 Assessment

Essential Question
What are the consequences of trade?

Key Terms

1. How did Mansa Musa's hajj and caravan show he was a great leader?
2. Why was Tombouctou a great center of scholarship?
3. Why were griots important before writing was adopted in West Africa?

Key Ideas

4. Why was Sundiata a national hero in Mali?
5. Describe two ways Mali became a center of learning.
6. Why do so many people still speak the languages of Mali and Songhai?

Think Critically

7. **Draw Inferences** How did controlling the gold–salt trade make Songhai the largest empire in West Africa?
8. **Identify Bias** Sundiata called himself mansa, or emperor. Why do you think he did so?

9. When Songhai became powerful, what do you think happened to the people of Ghana? Go to your Student Journal to record your answer.

East African Civilizations

Key Ideas
- After the fall of Kush, Axum became an important trading kingdom.
- Ethiopia became a center of Christianity in East Africa.
- East African city-states played a key role in ocean trade.

Key Terms • stele • Greco-Roman • monk • dynasty • stonetown

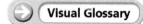 **Visual Glossary**

 Reading Skill Analyze Cause and Effect Take notes using the graphic organizer in your journal.

A Christian Orthodox priest in Ethiopia

Early civilizations often formed near rivers or larger bodies of water. The East African civilizations were no different. The Nile River and the Red Sea made East Africa an ideal location for settlement because these bodies of water made trade, farming, and transportation easier.

The Kingdoms of Kush and Axum

The area along the Nile River south of the Egyptian empire was called Nubia. Desert covered much of the region. The Nile, however, created fertile land along its banks. A civilization formed there around 2000 B.C. This civilization was known as Kush (also called Kerma). The people of Kush tapped into the trade routes of the Red Sea and the Nile River. Kushite merchants traded heavily with Egypt, who wanted Kush's gold. By the late 1400s B.C., however, Egypt took direct control of Kush.

Decline of Kush Over the years, Egypt lost its hold over Kush. By the 1000s B.C. Kushite kings again ruled. After many generations, however, the kingdom began to fail. By A.D. 150 Kush was too weak to defend itself from invaders from the highlands.

Axum: A Great Trading Kingdom In 325 A.D. King Ezana of Axum took over Kush. Axum replaced Kush as the commercial center of northeast Africa. Axum now controlled the trade routes to Roman Egypt, southern Arabia, and Asia. Most trading along the Red Sea took place in the port city of Adulis. Goods from the interior, such as glass, copper, brass, gold, and slaves were traded for textiles, tools, jewelry, and steel.

Axum's wealth and power can be seen in its huge monuments. Great stairways led to altars honoring Axum's gods. A kind of grand stone pillar, called a **stele,** marked each grave of Axum's rulers. Each stele looked like a skyscraper. It had false doors and windows carved into the stone. Beneath the stele lay royal burial tombs and chambers.

Reading Check Why was the city of Adulis important?

Christianity in East Africa

In the 300s, the Red Sea was bustling with trading activity. **Greco-Roman** (Greek and Roman) trading settlements dotted the region. Christianity had been spreading in this region. Christian merchants and traders interacted daily with the people of Axum. They introduced Axum to a type of Christianity from the eastern shores of the Mediterranean. Before long, Christian churches began to appear alongside the stelae along the coast of East Africa. The Church of Saint Mary, built in the 300s, was probably the earliest. A member of the Portuguese embassy, Francisco Alvarez, visited the church in the 1520s.

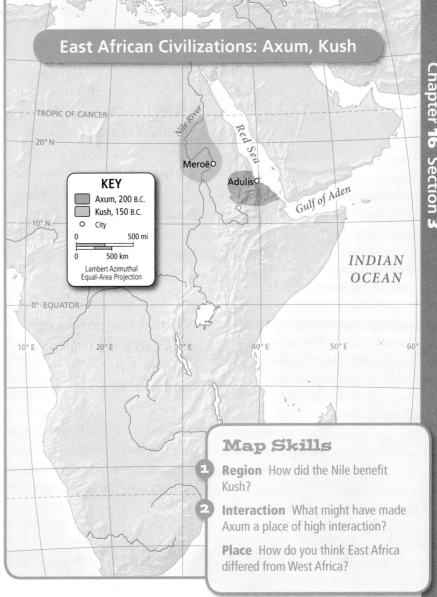

East African Civilizations: Axum, Kush

KEY

- Axum, 200 B.C.
- Kush, 150 B.C.
- ○ City

0 ——— 500 mi
0 ——— 500 km

Lambert Azimuthal Equal-Area Projection

Map Skills

1 **Region** How did the Nile benefit Kush?

2 **Interaction** What might have made Axum a place of high interaction?

Place How do you think East Africa differed from West Africa?

He described this grand church:

66 This church is very large. . . . It has seven chapels, all with their backs to the east, and their altars well placed. . . . This church has a large enclosure, and it is also surrounded by another larger enclosure, like the wall of a large town or city. . . . Inside this large enclosure there are two palaces, one on the right hand and the other on the left, which belong to two rectors [directors] of the church. 99

—Francisco Alvarez

501

Christianity in Axum Christianity grew significantly after 340. Around this time, two Syrian brothers on their way to India were shipwrecked in Axum. They were captured and put to work in the king's court. One brother, Frumentius, became a trusted civil servant. Frumentius was a Christian. Under his influence, King Ezana became a Christian. Monks continued to establish Christianity throughout the kingdom. **Monks** are men who dedicate themselves to worshiping God.

tradition, *n.,* a long-established custom or practice

Ethiopia, a Christian Kingdom Axum slowly began to weaken in the 600s due to economic problems. Another factor was the spread of Islam to the area. Eventually a new **dynasty** (ruling family), called the Zagwe, emerged in what is now Ethiopia. The Zagwe rose to power in the mid-1000s, and continued the Christian tradition. They replaced officials with those who were Christian. They also traded successfully with the Muslim world.

Zagwe rulers saw Ethiopia as a Christian holy land. They carved huge churches out of solid rock. The religious literature and music produced during the Zagwe period are still used in the Ethiopian Christian church.

Reading Check What did the Zagwe do with Christianity in Ethiopia?

East African City States

Trade brought distant peoples together. The contact between cultures created unique societies along the East African coast. Between the 800s and the 1400s Arab and Persian immigrants blended with the local communities. They formed more than three dozen city-states along the coast of present-day Somalia, Kenya, Tanzania, Mozambique, and Madagascar.

East African traders sailed to India for items such as grain (below), cotton cloth, oil, and sugar. ▼

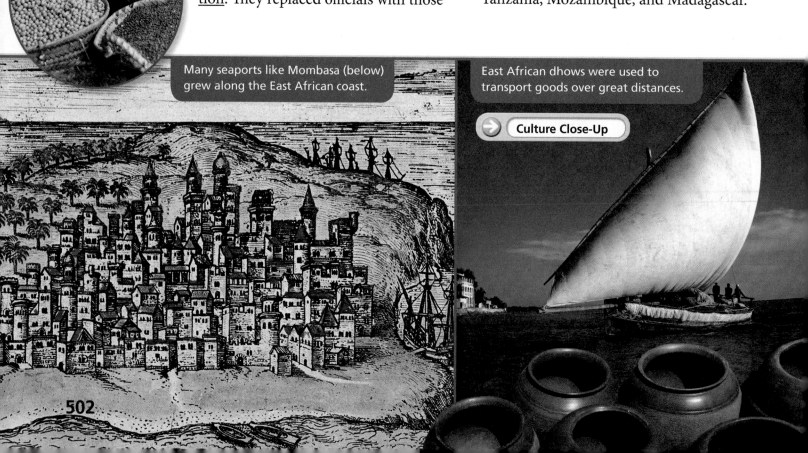

Many seaports like Mombasa (below) grew along the East African coast.

East African dhows were used to transport goods over great distances.

Culture Close-Up

myWorld Activity
People, Places, and
Things Charades

Indian Ocean Trade Routes The peoples of East Africa, the Mediterranean, and India traded with each other as early as A.D. 100. Traders sailed to western India for cotton cloth, grain, oil, sugar, and ghee (strained butter). Others sailed down the coast of the Red Sea in search of cloaks, tunics, copper, and tin. They traded gold, tortoiseshell, ivory, timber, and slaves in return. From about 700, Arab traders exchanged metal weapons and iron tools for raw materials such as tortoiseshell, rhinoceros horn, ivory, and coconut oil.

The Swahili Culture Over time a new culture, Swahili, formed in trading towns along the coast of East Africa. This African culture was primarily Muslim. The Swahili imported ceramics, glassware, silver and copper jewelry from the Middle East, and Chinese silk. They adopted Islam by the 700s, which had been brought to the area by Muslim traders, immigrants, and teachers of Islam.

Blending of Cultures By the 1000s, Swahili settlements had grown into city-states, called stonetowns. **Stonetowns** were named for the multistoried stone houses built there. These houses often served as custom houses for foreign traders. Through trade, cultural contact spread among the East Indies, China, India, Arab lands, Persia, and East Africa.

The Swahili imported trade goods from the interior of East Africa to be traded for goods from distant lands. In the interior, wealth was based on control of resources. For example, the cattle-based kingdom of Bunyoro arose in the Great Lakes region (an area with several large lakes in east-central Africa). Other kingdoms grew wealthy from their control of copper and gold mines or grazing land.

Contact through trade brought a multicultural mix to the East African coast. Swahili, for example, became a language that includes words from trade languages spoken on the coast of the Indian Ocean. Islam was the shared religion, but the East African version of Islam included parts of folk religions from the region.

Reading Check What was the Swahili culture?

Section 3 Assessment

Key Terms
1. What is a stele?
2. What did monks of the Zagwe help do?
3. What is a stonetown?

Key Ideas
4. Where was Axum located?
5. How did Ethiopia become a center of Christianity?
6. How was the Swahili culture like many East African cultures?

Think Critically
7. Draw Conclusions Why are port cities important for trade?
8. Compare and Contrast How were Kush and Axum alike and different?

Essential Question
What are the consequences of trade?
9. How might the lack of natural resources affect a region's ability to trade? Go to your Student Journal to record your answer.

Section 4

Society and Culture

Key Ideas
- Society in West Africa was based on kinship and caste.
- African religions varied from place to place, but shared certain features.
- Oral tradition played a key role in preserving African history and culture.

Key Terms
- caste
- kinship
- lineage
- ethnic group
- oral tradition
- proverb
- polyrhythmic drumming

 Visual Glossary

 Reading Skill Sequence Take notes using the graphic organizer in your journal.

Ancient West African village economies were based on producing food, a tradition that still exists in parts of Africa. Here a woman carries millet in Mali. ▼

West African empires of Ghana, Mali, and Songhai had organized societies. There were large empires, but also cities, towns, and villages. Throughout the empires, societies had complex, family-based relationships. "Kings may come and go," observed a popular saying from Mali, "but the family endures."

Society in West African Empires

Little is known about how a person spent time in past civilizations. Throughout the West African empires, most positions of leadership were reserved for men. Men also took part in warfare and Islamic learning. In later African societies, women farmed and took care of the family. Early West African society was organized by a ranking of social classes. In West Africa a person's social class, or **caste,** determined that individual's place in the social structure. A person's caste was established by the family he or she was born into.

Social Structure The emperor ruled each empire. He had the most power and the highest status, or social rank. All who appeared before him had to bow. In Mansa Musa's kingdom, some had to sprinkle dust on themselves to acknowledge his superiority.

The nobility and kings formed the next-highest caste. Nobles helped the emperor govern the various parts of the empire and lead its armies. They paid tribute to the emperor.

Below the noble families were traders and free people of the towns. They ran the businesses and farms. Next down the rung of the

504

social ladder were the skilled workers. Each trade formed a different caste. For example, one caste might specialize in iron working, but another might work as musicians.

Slavery in West Africa Enslaved people made up the lowest level of society. People were enslaved for different reasons. Some people were born into slavery. Often, however, war captives, political prisoners, and kidnap victims were enslaved. Slaves performed many tasks. In the Songhai empire they served as soldiers, farm workers, and servants. In Mali, slaves served in the royal court and in the government.

Some slaves had rights in West African society. Some could marry, and families could not be separated. Slaves were also protected from harsh punishment. They could earn money and buy their freedom. One enslaved person even became an emperor of Mali.

Importance of Kinship In West Africa, family members shared a strong sense of **kinship,** or connection based on family relationships. Families were not just made up of parents and children. They included grandparents, aunts, uncles, and cousins. These large families formed lineages. A **lineage** is a group of people descended from a common ancestor. Often the head of a lineage controlled the family members and property.

Lineages were the building blocks of West African society. Each lineage was part of a clan, or larger group of related families. In turn, West African clans formed even larger groupings. Several closely related clans lived together in a village. Many villages shared a distinct culture, language, and identity. Such a social unit is called an **ethnic group**. The West African empires included many ethnic groups, each with its own way of life.

Relationships in West African Families

Traditional family structure in Africa is complex. Villages are made up of clans. Each clan has lineages descended from a common ancestor. This structure fosters strong kinship.

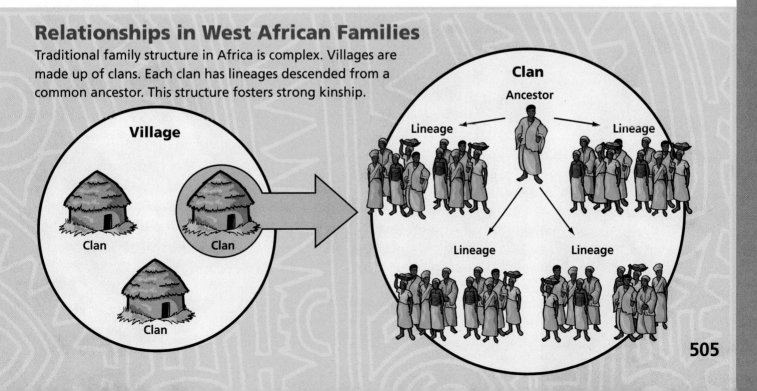

Village

Clan

Clan

Clan

Clan

Ancestor

Lineage

Lineage

Lineage

Lineage

505

City and Village Life West African families grouped together in cities, towns, and villages. In many urban areas, Arabic was the main language of trade and Islamic worship and teaching. In rural villages, families spoke languages of their ancestors and worshiped ancient gods.

Village economies were based on producing food. Villagers developed tools for farming. Farmers grew crops such as rice, yams, and beans. Herders raised animals such as cattle for meat, milk, and skins. Villagers traded in markets.

diversity, *n.,* variety

City economies were based on trade. Markets offered goods brought on the caravan routes. City dwellers could count on a varied and steady supply of food. They could also buy finely crafted goods. A leading Muslim scholar of the time described the city of Djenné.

66 Djenné is one of the great markets of the Muslim world. There one meets the salt merchants from the mines of Teghaza and merchants carrying gold from the mines of Bitou. . . . Because of this blessed city, caravans flock to [the area] from all points of the horizon. 99

—Abd al-Rahman al-Sadi, from *African Civilizations* by Graham Connah

Thousands lived in large cities such as Djenné, Gao, and Tombouctou.

Reading Check What is a clan?

African Religions

A great <u>diversity</u> of ethnic groups populated West Africa. Although Islam and Christianity were practiced to a great extent in early Africa, some people followed traditional religions. These traditional religions shared some common characteristics. Many African religions

This is a buffalo mask and vegetable fiber costume from an African agricultural festival. ▼

This West African memorial screen is used to honor the dead.

Rituals are still an important part of African life. This shows a "praise song" at a wedding in Bamako, Mali.

506

had religious leaders to guide prayers, and followers prayed on a daily basis. Most traditional religions also involved religious rituals, and promoted the honoring of ancestors. Many Muslims also practiced rituals and ancestor worship.

Religious Rituals People engaged the gods on a daily basis. They attended shrines to pray, get advice, and make offerings. Religious officials helped people communicate with the gods. Rituals reinforced the social and moral values represented by the gods. Following religious teachings helped keep society functioning smoothly.

Honoring Ancestors Africans also honored their ancestors. Upon death, they believed a person became a spirit and joined the spirits of ancestors. Some families created shrines to their ancestors, so that they could remain in touch with them. Rituals and spiritual mediums helped some people seek ancestors' help with their problems, much like the gods.

Reading Check How did West Africans treat their ancestors?

Cultural Legacy

The Arabic language allowed for more learning and teaching within the African empires. Many Africans also had a strong **oral tradition**. That is, they used oral history, poetry, folk tales, and sayings both to teach and to entertain. The societies of West Africa were also rich with music, dance, and art. These artistic traditions helped to pass on each group's history and culture.

A Rich Oral Tradition Storytelling was a part of daily life. Families shared folk tales at home. A popular fable, still shared today, told how Ananse the Spider gave people wisdom.

> 66 . . . Ananse did indeed finish collecting the world's wisdom. He packed all this in a gourd and began to climb a tall palm. Halfway to the top he got into difficulties. He had tied on the gourd in front of him, and it hampered his climbing. At this point his son, Ntikuma . . . called in a shrill young voice: 'Father, if you really had all the wisdom in the world up there with you, you would have tied that gourd on your back.' This was too much even for Ananse, who was tired from long labor. He untied the gourd in a fit of temper and threw it down. It broke and the wisdom was scattered far and wide. After a while people who had learned their lesson came and gathered in their own gourds whatever each could find; it is this that explains why a few people have much wisdom, some have a little, but many have none at all. 99
>
> —African folk tale

Proverbs, or wise sayings, provided a quicker way to share wisdom. For example, the proverb "Every time an old man dies, it is as if a library has burnt down" reminds us to value our elders. Such sayings were passed down through countless generations.

Professional storytellers and oral historians, the griots, served African kings and nobles in some areas of Africa. Griots memorized and told stories of famous events and people.

myWorld Activity
Oral Storytelling
Telephone Game

myworldhistory.com

Primary Source

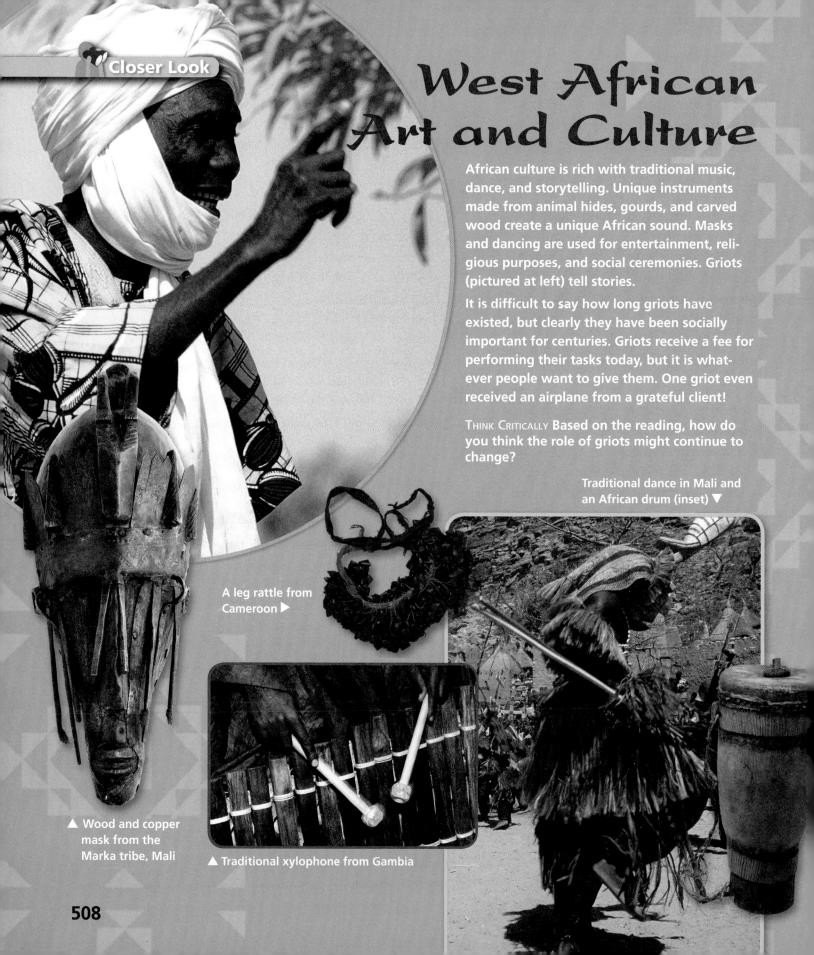

West African Art and Culture

African culture is rich with traditional music, dance, and storytelling. Unique instruments made from animal hides, gourds, and carved wood create a unique African sound. Masks and dancing are used for entertainment, religious purposes, and social ceremonies. Griots (pictured at left) tell stories.

It is difficult to say how long griots have existed, but clearly they have been socially important for centuries. Griots receive a fee for performing their tasks today, but it is whatever people want to give them. One griot even received an airplane from a grateful client!

THINK CRITICALLY **Based on the reading, how do you think the role of griots might continue to change?**

Traditional dance in Mali and an African drum (inset) ▼

A leg rattle from Cameroon ▶

▲ Wood and copper mask from the Marka tribe, Mali

▲ Traditional xylophone from Gambia

Ibn Battuta described griots at a festival in Mali, where griots stood before the ruler in a "costume made of feathers." When they recited their poetry, he wrote, it was like "a kind of preaching." The griots urged their leaders to rule fairly. Their main job, however, was the <u>transmission</u> of their people's history and culture. "Without us the names of kings would vanish," explains a modern-day griot.

The tradition of griots and griottes (female storytellers) remains today. Their role has changed with time and circumstance. It will continue to change as griots accompany Africans wherever they live.

Music, Dance, and Art West Africans' lives were filled with dance and music. Mothers lulled babies to sleep with soothing songs. Young people learned songs that taught them adult responsibilities. They also learned certain dances when they became adults. Dance and music marked many important stages in people's lives. Dancers celebrated births and marriages and performed at funerals.

West Africans created many musical instruments. The most widely used instrument was the drum. African drummers created polyrhythmic music. **Polyrhythmic drumming** combines two or more different rhythms at the same time. Dancers performed complex movements to match the drummers' polyrhythms. Dancers' feet might follow one rhythm, while their hands or hips moved to another. Dancers performed during festivals and religious ceremonies. The dancers acted out stories of gods or ancestors.

Dancers wore masks of gods and spirits carved by skilled artists. West African artists created art for many purposes. Art was used in everyday life to express people's beliefs. For example, people honored the dead with carved wooden images of their ancestors. Emperors used art to show off their wealth and power. In the kingdom of Benin, sculptors made metal plaques and figures to record important events and people. In Mali, artists crafted clay soldiers in fine detail.

Reading Check What is a griot?

transmission, *n.*, the passing on of something, such as stories or history

Section **4** Assessment

? **Essential Question**

What are the consequences of trade?

Key Terms

1. What is a lineage?

2. Why is an oral tradition important?

3. Which musical instrument is the most used in West Africa?

Key Ideas

4. Describe the social structure of West African society.

5. How are West African traditional religions like Islam?

6. What was the purpose of griots?

Think Critically

7. **Compare and Contrast** How do you think slavery in West Africa compared to slavery in the United States?

8. **Draw Inferences** Why do you think the story about Ananse is included in this section?

9. Are art and trade related? Explain. Go to your Student Journal to record your answer.

509

Chapter **16**

Chapter Assessment

Key Terms and Ideas

1. **Compare and Contrast** What is the difference between a **caste** and an **ethnic group**?

2. **Summarize** What was the gold–salt trade?

3. **Discuss** How did Mansa Musa's hajj affect Egypt?

4. **Recall** Who was considered the greatest emperor of Songhai? Why?

5. **Explain** What is **scholarship**?

6. **Describe** What was the role of monks in Axum?

7. **Explain** Why was the **oral tradition** important before the development of writing?

Think Critically

8. **Draw Inferences** In ancient Africa, the gold–salt trade made empires wealthy. In today's world, what type of trade might make a country or empire wealthy? Explain.

9. **Sequence** Put the following terms in chronological order: Almoravids, Ghana, Mali, Songhai, and Zagwe.

10. **Draw Conclusions** How does honoring one's ancestors contribute to a stable society?

11. **Core Concepts: Trade** How would you describe the trade system of early Africa? Was this a free trade system? Explain why or why not.

Analyze Visuals

For each place shown on the map, write the letter from the map that shows its location.

12. Tombouctou

13. Sahara

14. Songhai empire

15. Ghana empire

16. Mali empire

17. Gao

18. Using the map scale, estimate about how far apart Tombouctou and Gao are.

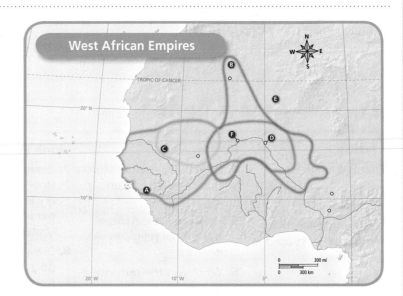

West African Empires

Essential Question

myWorld Chapter Activity

African Museum Tour Guide Create a script for an African museum tour, supposing you are the tour guide. In your script, focus your tour on African artifacts and convey the importance of early African trade.

21st Century Learning

Analyze Media Content

Use the Internet to find information about modern-day griots in Africa. Find at least two sources from reliable organizations or media outlets. Then decide whether griots today perform the same functions as in ancient Africa. Write a paragraph on how their role has changed over time.

Document-Based Questions

Success Tracker™
Online at myworldhistory.com

Use your knowledge of the empires of ancient West Africa and Documents A and B to answer Questions 1–3.

Document A

Document B

" While Europe was torn by the Hundred Years' War [1337–1453], scholars were writing books in comfort and security at Sankore University in Timbuktu. . . . Timbuktu was a cosmopolitan city . . . where Arabic was widely spoken, written, and read."

—from *The Royal Kingdoms of Ghana, Mali, and Songhai* by Patricia and Fredrick McKissack

1. Which of the following would be the most accurate caption for Document A?

   A "Arabic: The Language of Islam"

   B "Christian Scholarship"

   C "Personalized Education at Your Fingertips"

   D "Tombouctou: An Islamic Center of Learning"

2. In Document B, why does the author mention the Hundred Years' War?

   A to show that Arabic was a peaceful language

   B to show that West Africa was ahead of Europe

   C to show that Europe was ahead of West Africa

   D to prove that Europeans eventually would declare war on West Africa

3. **Writing Task** Write a promotional brochure to convince students to come to Tombouctou to study at Sankore University.

my worldhistory.com

Self-Test

China in the Middle Ages

Essential Question

What are the consequences of technology?

The Great Wall was
rebuilt during the
Ming dynasty. ▼

 Explore the Essential Question . . .

- at **my** worldhistory.com
- using the **myWorld Chapter Activity**
- with the **Student Journal**

Chinese Dynasties

618 Tang dynasty unites China.

960 Song dynasty begins.

1368 Ming dynasty is founded by a rebel general.

600   800   1000   1200

1271 Kublai Khan declares the Yuan dynasty.

Kublai Khan: How to Make an Impression

In 1274, Kublai Khan seemed comfortably on his way to ruling the entire world. He had inherited the mighty Mongol empire built by his grandfather Genghis Khan and, for 14 years, Kublai had busied himself with extending it. There had never been an empire larger than his. The Khan considered China to be the jewel in his crown. When he controlled most of it, he declared himself the first emperor of a new dynasty.

The Khan could be cruel and he conquered people by force, but he also put many good ideas into action. He improved the safety of the fabled Silk Road to make it easier to transport ceramics, silk, carpets, precious stones, medicines, spices, and other valuable products for sale. He encouraged foreign merchants to come to China. Under his wise rule, trade flourished and his empire prospered.

myworldhistory.com

Timeline/On Assignment

Mongols ruled from Russia to China. They protected the traders who carried goods and ideas along the Silk Road.

Kublai Khan threw extravagant parties at his palaces in Mongolia and in China.

One of the Khan's strategies was being unusually friendly to foreign visitors. Sometimes he even hired them to work for him. He did it partly for the thrill of having them travel—sometimes for years—to bow before him, partly to promote trade, and partly because he didn't trust the ethnic Chinese.

So, in 1274, the Emperor of China was pleased to welcome the Venetian adventurer Marco Polo into his court. The Khan set out to make a great impression on Polo with his extravagant lifestyle.

He had a lavish reception hall at his palace in Khanbaliq, the city now called Beijing. All around were decorations of dragons and phoenixes, and precious furnishings made of silk and jade. According to Polo, the walls in the Khan's sleeping quarters were lined with the skins of ermines.

Extravagant feasts took place on the Khan's

Marco Polo pays respect to Kublai Khan.

Guests dined on foods from across the empire.

Merchants in China used paper money to pay for goods like porcelain.

birthday and at any other opportunity. He hosted thousands of guests, with much singing, dancing, and loud shouting. Fabulous meals featured foods and drinks from countries he'd conquered—rare spices from the Middle East, raw vegetables sprinkled with precious saffron and wrapped in pancakes, scented fish in rice wine, goose with apricots, and lotus seed soup.

Not content with one palace, the Khan had another in Mongolia, called Shangdu, to which he retreated in the summers. There he kept ten thousand special white horses. Only he and those he rewarded for acts of valor were allowed to drink their milk.

In Khanbaliq, he liked to be reminded of the Mongol ways. He stalked deer in the private hunting grounds he had built near the capital. The gigantic park even included fountains and streams.

But Kublai Khan did not try to make China just like Mongolia. He was interested in learning from other people. In the same year he declared his dynasty, he brought Persian and Arab astronomers to his court to study the stars. He welcomed Muslim doctors and European missionaries. He enjoyed Chinese theater and painting so much that he paid artists to work at the palace.

The Khan's court dazzled his visitors and he took pleasure in their wonder. To Polo, he showed off fancy restaurants, teahouses, and theaters. And then there was the technology! The Chinese printed books and made fireworks with gunpowder. These were unknown in Europe during Polo's time.

Polo was also impressed by paper money, which printing made possible. Europeans still used heavy coins or bartered when they bought and sold goods. Polo must have been fascinated that simple paper could be made valuable.

Marco Polo stayed in China for 17 years—nearly half of his life to that point—before he returned to Europe. Later, he recounted his adventures to a writer who recorded his tales, some about Kublai Khan. It became a bestseller.

In this section, you read about Kublai Khan, a legendary but real-life ruler of China. Based on this story, how do you think trade and technology affected China? As you read the chapter, think about what Kublai Khan's story tells you about China.

 myStory Video

Learn more about Kublai Khan.

Tang and Song China

Key Ideas

- The Tang dynasty was marked by political unity and a flowering of the arts.
- The Song dynasty rulers strengthened government based on the civil service system.
- Advances in farming and trade led to great prosperity in Tang and Song China.

Key Terms • bureaucracy • scholar-official • merit system • urbanization • money economy • porcelain

 **Visual Glossary**

 Reading Skill Identify Main Ideas and Details Take notes using the graphic organizer in your journal.

Tang Taizong ▼

More than a thousand years before Kublai Khan's reign, the Han dynasty made China into a vast empire. The fall of the Han in A.D. 220 left China divided. It later reunited and experienced a golden age under two strong dynasties, the Tang and the Song.

The Tang Dynasty

For hundreds of years after the fall of the Han dynasty, several kingdoms competed for power. The short-lived Sui dynasty reunited China between 581 and 618. The next dynasty, the Tang, reigned for nearly 300 years. Tang rulers built a strong central government and expanded the nation's borders.

Tang Rule The military leader Tang Gaozu founded the Tang dynasty. He and his son led the armies that finished reuniting China. His son, Tang Taizong, became emperor in 626. Other strong rulers followed.

Taizong made the government stable by reviving China's official bureaucracy. A **bureaucracy** is a system of government with many departments and bureaus led by appointed officials. Each official has a rank and fixed responsibilities. In setting up this bureaucracy, Taizong wanted to create a government that was efficient. The departments created under Taizong remained the core of Chinese government until the early 1900s.

Under Tang rulers, China grew to its largest size up to that time. The strong military expanded the borders and protected the growing population. In the late 600s, Wu Zhao (woo jow) became the only woman to rule China on her own. Empress Wu was capable and ruthless. She argued that an ideal ruler cares for the people as a mother cares for her children.

A Flourishing Capital The Tang capital was Chang'an (chahng ahn). Under Tang rule, it became the largest city in the world. In 742, more than a million people lived within the city walls. 700,000 more lived just outside.

Chang'an may also have been the largest planned city ever built. Its walls formed a rectangle that measured five miles from north to south and six miles from east to west. Great homes, temples, gardens, and the imperial palace stood inside the walls. A wide, tree-lined avenue led to the main gate, impressing visitors.

Sitting at one end of the Silk Road, Chang'an was a thriving cultural and <u>commercial</u> center. Turks, Indians, Jews, Koreans, Persians, and other visitors filled its streets and markets. Camels carried goods into and out of the city. Musicians, actors, and other performers provided public entertainment. People practiced many different religions.

Chang'an was welcoming to foreigners, though they lived in their own sections of the city. Chinese nobles used foreign goods, adopted foreign fashions, learned to play new instruments, and borrowed other parts of foreign cultures.

Reading Check Who lived in Chang'an?

commercial, *adj.,* relating to the buying and selling of goods

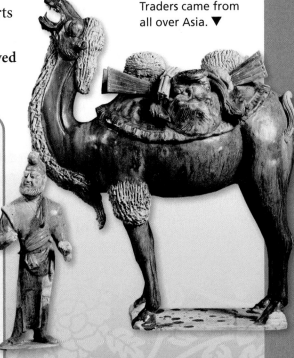

Traders came from all over Asia. ▼

Map of Chang'an

Imperial Park

Daming Palace

Imperial Park

West Market

Imperial City

Chengtian Gate

Administrative City

Jinguang Gate

Chunming Gate

East Market

Yanping Gate

Yanxing Gate

Hibiscus Garden

Mingde Gate

0   0.5 mi
0   0.5 km

◀ Court ladies played polo, a Persian game.

City of *Chang'an*

The streets of Chang'an were laid out in a grid. Each section of the city was walled off, including the two large markets. The East Market was for Chinese merchants and the West Market was for foreign merchants.

517

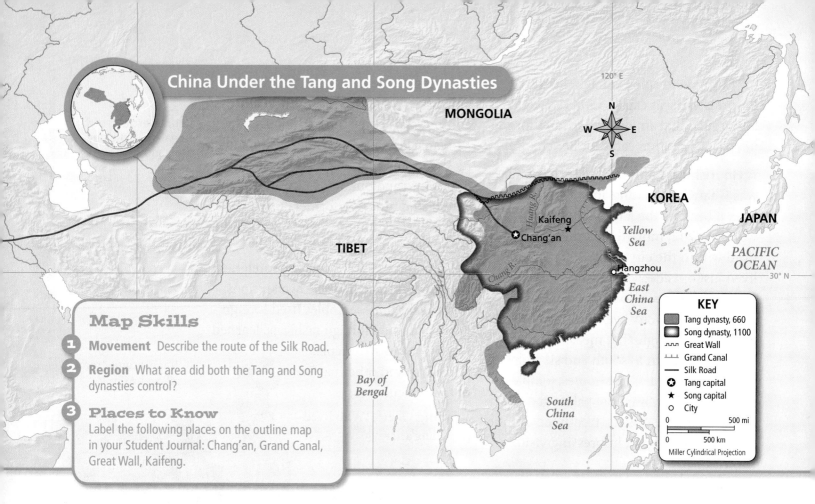

China Under the Tang and Song Dynasties

MONGOLIA

KOREA

JAPAN

TIBET

Huang R.

Kaifeng
Chang'an

Yellow
Sea

PACIFIC
OCEAN

Chang R.

Hangzhou

East
China
Sea

Bay of
Bengal

South
China
Sea

KEY

- Tang dynasty, 660
- Song dynasty, 1100
- Great Wall
- Grand Canal
- Silk Road
- ✪ Tang capital
- ★ Song capital
- ○ City

0   500 mi
0   500 km

Miller Cylindrical Projection

Map Skills

1 **Movement** Describe the route of the Silk Road.

2 **Region** What area did both the Tang and Song dynasties control?

3 **Places to Know**
Label the following places on the outline map in your Student Journal: Chang'an, Grand Canal, Great Wall, Kaifeng.

Rise of the Song Dynasty

eventually, *adv.,* at a later time

Eventually, the Tang dynasty fell. After a period of unrest, a new dynasty arose.

Fall of the Tang For much of Tang rule, China was at war with neighboring peoples. This allowed military leaders to gain power. Drought, famine, and high taxes led to problems at home. In the late 700s, several military leaders rebelled.

Although the government survived, it had less control. Military and local leaders took power. Neighboring peoples attacked and often took land. Revolts became more common. In 907, a military leader overthrew the last Tang emperor.

A New Dynasty Rises For more than half a century, China had no clear ruler.

Different people ruled parts of China and neighboring peoples took more land.

In 960, a military leader united much of China and began the Song dynasty. It ruled China from 960 to 1279.

To protect the empire, Song rulers kept a huge army. But they did not want the military to have too much power, so they gave control to government officials who were not in the military. Sometimes they tried to buy peace with neighboring peoples who threatened China by making payments to them. At other times, Song rulers made agreements with one outside group to fight another.

Reading Check How did Song rulers prevent the military from becoming too strong?

The Examination System

Civil service examinations are tests required for people to work for the government. The Han dynasty introduced these tests in China. The Tang and Song expanded their use. The highly educated men who passed the civil service examinations were known as **scholar-officials.** They qualified for government jobs.

The examinations were based on teachings of Confucius. They were difficult, and few students passed. Wealthy men were most able to spend years studying. During the Tang, some officials earned positions through the the exam system. However, the majority still received positions because of family connections.

During the Song dynasty, the tests became part of a merit system. In a **merit system,** people are hired and promoted based on talent and skills, rather than wealth or social status. The government opened schools that even poor students could attend. Passing higher-level exams could lead to promotions, but scholar-officials also had to perform their jobs well to move higher in the bureaucracy.

By preventing corruption and promoting the best officials, Song rulers tried to maintain good government. Officials were supposed to act honestly and efficiently.

A later dynasty, the Ming, made new rules for officials. They could not serve in their home district, where they might do favors for family and friends. They also changed jobs every three years, so that they could not build up too much power.

Reading Check How did Song rulers achieve good government?

Scholar-Officials

Scholars studied for official exams in several subjects. The highest-level exams required students to know the teachings of Confucius, write poetry, and write calligraphy. Scholars often studied for more than 20 years, even though the chances of passing were small. *Why did people spend years studying for exams?*

▲ Students take a civil service exam.

▲ In later dynasties, officials wore badges to show their rank.

A painting of a scholar studying ▼

519

Tang and Song Prosperity

The Tang and Song eras were times of great prosperity in China. It experienced good government, growth in the economy, and advances in farming.

The Emperor and the Officials The emperor ruled under the Mandate of Heaven. In theory, this meant that he was all-powerful and had heavenly support. In practice, most early emperors needed the backing of nobles and warlords to stay in power.

Song rulers changed that. By giving more power to the scholar-official class, emperors developed a base of loyal supporters. Meanwhile, scholar-officials rose in power and influence. They pushed aside the noble families to become the highest-ranking group in Chinese society.

China experienced great economic growth during the Song dynasty. Along with economic growth came **urbanization,** or the growth of cities. By 1100, China had several large cities that were home to hundreds of thousands of people. Many of these cities were in southern China, south of the Chang River, which is also known as the Yangtze.

The Song Dynasty Shifts South The Song dynasty became weak over time. The foreign Jin kingdom took control of northern China in 1127. The Song rulers withdrew from the north and focused on southern China.

This period is called the Southern Song. The port of Hangzhou (hahn JOH) became the capital. A European visitor wrote that Hangzhou was "the first, the biggest, the richest, the most populous, and altogether the most marvelous city that exists on the face of the earth."

Land Tenure Patterns of land ownership changed during the Tang dynasty. Since the Han, the Chinese government had owned all farmland. Farmers received equal shares of land. The Tang government changed this system.

Under the Tang, rich families bought much of the good farmland. Most peasants worked the land as tenant farmers. Tenant farmers rent the land they farm.

Population Shifts

Yellow Sea

Huang R. ✪ Kaifeng

Chang'an ●

100° E

Hangzhou ✪

30° N

East China Sea

Chang River

40° N

KEY

- ☐ Song empire, about 1100
- ☐ Southern Song empire, about 1140–1150
- ☐ Jin kingdom
- ☐ Xi Xia empire
- └┴┘ Grand Canal
- ➡ Population shift
- ✪ Capital city
- ● Other city

0 — 400 ml
0 — 400 km
Lambert Conformal Conic Projection

90° E

TROPIC OF CANCER

South China Sea

20° N

120° E

110° E

10° N

N W E S

Map Skills

1 **Movement** In what direction did people move during the Song dynasty?

2 **Place** What was the capital of the Southern Song empire?

Advances in Farming Chinese farming changed under the Tang and Song. The population of southern China grew rapidly. Meanwhile, the population in the north shrunk. New farming methods and technology allowed farmers to feed more people.

During this period, rice became China's most important crop. In the past, farmers had grown mostly dry-land crops like wheat and barley. These grew well in the dry north, but not in the humid south. The south, however, was perfect for rice farming. It was warmer and had more rainfall than the north.

Rice grows in flooded fields called paddies. To keep their rice paddies wet, Chinese farmers developed irrigation systems such as pumps and other water-control <u>devices.</u> They also developed new strains of fast-ripening rice. With this kind of rice, farmers could harvest two or three crops a year.

Rice provided more food per acre than other grains. With more food available, the population swelled. Between 750 and 1100, the population of China doubled from 50 million people to 100 million.

Reading Check Why was the shift to new types of rice important?

device, *n.,* machine

Farming Rice

During the Song dynasty, Chinese farmers began growing a new type of rice from Vietnam. In the 1100s, the government distributed instructions, similar to the ones to the left, to show people how to grow more rice. *Why might the government have issued instructions with drawings?*

⟶ **Simulation**

Farmers today harvest rice by hand.

my worldhistory.com

Simulation

521

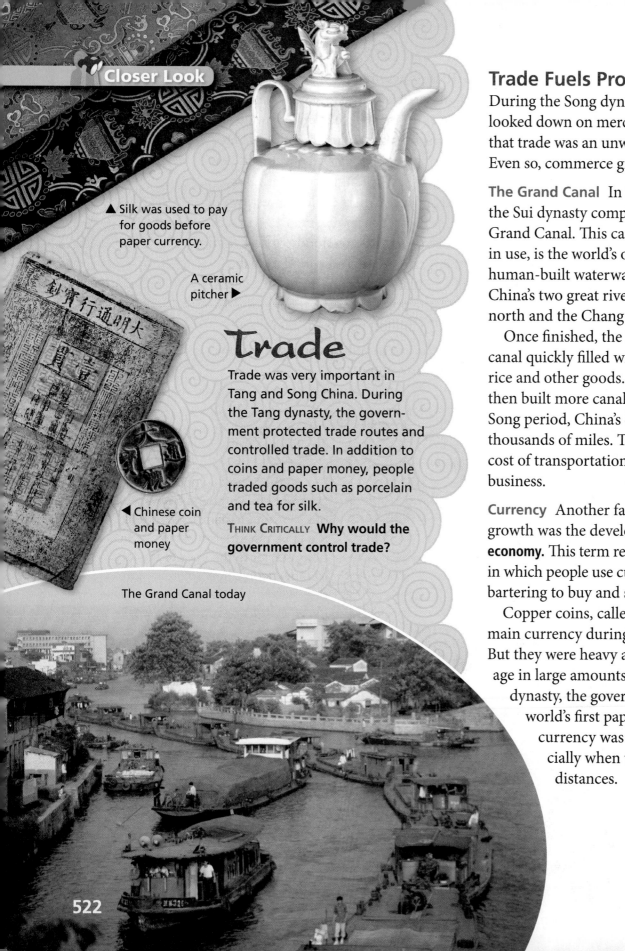

▲ Silk was used to pay for goods before paper currency.

A ceramic pitcher ▶

◀ Chinese coin and paper money

Trade

Trade was very important in Tang and Song China. During the Tang dynasty, the government protected trade routes and controlled trade. In addition to coins and paper money, people traded goods such as porcelain and tea for silk.

THINK CRITICALLY **Why would the government control trade?**

The Grand Canal today

Trade Fuels Prosperity

During the Song dynasty, many people looked down on merchants. They believed that trade was an unworthy profession. Even so, commerce grew to new levels.

The Grand Canal In the early 600s, the Sui dynasty completed work on the Grand Canal. This canal, which is still in use, is the world's oldest and longest human-built waterway. It connects China's two great rivers, the Huang in the north and the Chang in the south.

Once finished, the 1,100-mile-long canal quickly filled with barges carrying rice and other goods. The government then built more canals. By the end of the Song period, China's canals stretched for thousands of miles. These canals cut the cost of transportation and so promoted business.

Currency Another factor that helped fuel growth was the development of a **money economy.** This term refers to an economy in which people use currency rather than bartering to buy and sell goods.

Copper coins, called cash, were the main currency during the Tang dynasty. But they were heavy and hard to manage in large amounts. During the Song dynasty, the government issued the world's first paper currency. Paper currency was easy to use, especially when trading over long distances.

Expanding Industries When farmers grew more food than they needed, they could trade for craft items like pottery and cloth. As a result, many industries expanded. For example, the production of silk cloth rose during the Song dynasty. It was usually spun at home by women.

Another important industry was ceramics. During this time, China began to produce **porcelain,** a hard white pottery of extremely fine quality.

One of the biggest industries was iron production. Iron was essential in many industries, such as salt production. It was also used to make weapons, tools, nails, and even Buddhist statues.

The Growth of Trade With farms and factories producing more goods, trade increased. Canals and the use of money also promoted the growth of trade. A European visitor to China described trade on the Chang River: "In the total volume and value of the traffic on it, it exceeds all the rivers of the Christians put together plus their seas."

Reading Check How did the Grand Canal expand trade?

China's Golden Age

The Tang and Song eras represent a golden age for Chinese arts and literature. Some of the best-preserved Tang works are pottery figurines of horses, camels, and people. Many of these pieces demonstrate China's knowledge of other cultures. They show that Chinese people enjoyed music and games from Central Asia and India.

The Tang dynasty is also considered the greatest era of Chinese poetry. The famous poet Li Bai wrote in a playful, easygoing style. One of his favorite subjects was the beauty of nature.

Traditional arts were also valued during the Song dynasty. During the Song, architects designed magnificent Buddhist temples filled with statues. Potters turned clay into beautiful ceramic pieces. Artists created fine paintings in soft colors.

During the next dynasty, the Yuan, poets and artists continued to live at the emperor's court. However, the emperor was a Mongol. Many scholars decided to pursue the arts rather than work for the conquerors.

Reading Check What do pottery figures from the Tang dynasty show?

my World CONNECTIONS

The St. Lawrence Seaway spans more than **2,300** miles, connecting the Atlantic Ocean to the Great Lakes.

Section 1 Assessment

Essential Question

Key Terms

1. What is a bureaucracy?

2. Describe how scholar-officials qualified for government positions.

3. What term describes the growth of cities?

Key Ideas

4. Explain one reason for prosperity in Tang or Song China.

5. In what ways was the Song government a merit system?

Think Critically

6. **Analyze Cause and Effect** What caused the fall of the Tang dynasty?

7. **Draw Inferences** Why was paper money an improvement over coins?

What are the consequences of technology?

8. How did new technologies lead to prosperity in China? Go to your Student Journal to record your answer.

The Mongol Empire

Key Ideas
- The Mongols established the largest empire the world had ever seen.
- The Yuan rulers adopted many Chinese customs, but did not trust Chinese officials.
- The Mongol empire allowed trade to flourish along the Silk Road.

Key Terms • nomad • Mongol • steppe • khan

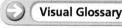 Visual Glossary

Reading Skill Sequence Take notes using the graphic organizer in your journal.

Genghis Khan ▼

Throughout its history, China has had to protect its borders from tribal **nomads,** or people who move from place to place at different times of the year. These nomads sometimes raided Chinese cities or even formed armies to invade China. In the 1200s, one of these peoples, the Mongols, conquered China and many other lands.

The Mongol Conquests

The **Mongols** were nomads who came from the steppes northwest of China. A **steppe** is a large, dry, grass-covered plain. Life on the steppes was difficult. The climate was harsh, and resources were limited. There, the Mongols herded sheep and became great horsemen.

Genghis Khan Mongols lived in clans led by a **khan,** or ruler. By 1206, a warrior had united the Mongol clans under his rule. He was known as Genghis Khan (GEN gis kahn), meaning "ruler of the universe."

After uniting the Mongols, Genghis turned to foreign conquest. He led his armies east into China. The Mongols broke through the Great Wall and destroyed many cities. By 1215, they had conquered most of the Jin kingdom that ruled northern China. Later, they swept across Central Asia and into Russia.

Military Victories Genghis was a highly effective military leader. He organized his troops in groups of 10, 100, 1,000, and 10,000 men. An officer chosen for his abilities led each group of fierce warriors. These fighters were expert horsemen who could fire arrows at a full gallop.

They moved fast, attacked swiftly, and terrorized enemies.

Genghis also used Chinese weapons. One was the catapult, a device that hurled rocks. The Mongols used it to break down city walls. They also used bombs made with gunpowder.

Genghis was ruthless in battle. He burned the cities of his enemies and left their bones piled on the ruins as a warning to others. Genghis once said,

66 The greatest joy a man can have is victory: to conquer one's enemy's armies, to pursue them, to deprive them of their possessions, to reduce their family to tears, [and] to ride on their horses 99

—Genghis Khan

Finally, Genghis maintained order among the Mongols. He banned theft and feuding. He also dictated harsh punishment, including death, for many crimes.

Mongols Build an Empire After the death of Genghis Khan in 1227, the Mongol empire continued to <u>expand</u>. Its armies conquered what was left of the Jin kingdom in 1234. Then they expanded to the west.

Genghis's grandson, Batu, led armies into Russia in 1236. Known as the Golden Horde, the Mongols ruled Russia for more than a century.

Mongol armies also took Persia, Mesopotamia, and Syria. In 1258, they sacked Baghdad and killed the Muslim caliph. The Mongols controlled the largest empire the world had ever known.

Reading Check How did the Mongols conquer northern China?

expand, *v.,* to grow, get bigger

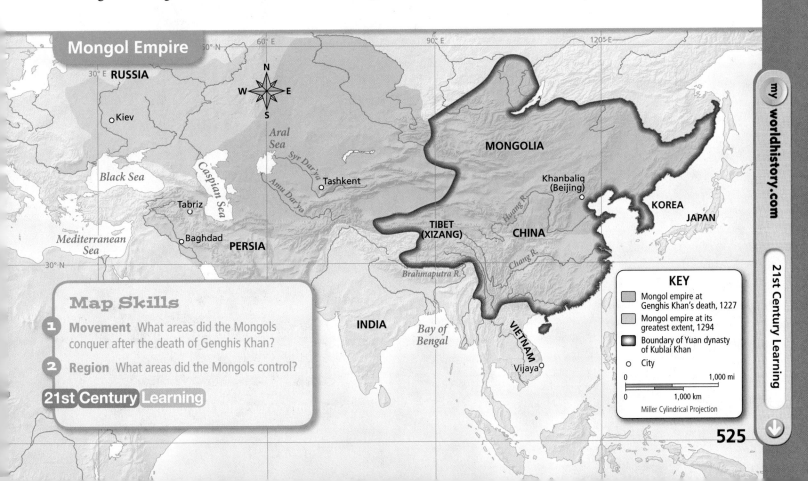

Mongol Empire

Map Skills

1 **Movement** What areas did the Mongols conquer after the death of Genghis Khan?

2 **Region** What areas did the Mongols control?

21st Century Learning

KEY
- Mongol empire at Genghis Khan's death, 1227
- Mongol empire at its greatest extent, 1294
- Boundary of Yuan dynasty of Kublai Khan
- City

0 — 1,000 mi
0 — 1,000 km
Miller Cylindrical Projection

Ruling the Empire

After Genghis Khan died, the Mongols divided their empire into four parts, called khanates. A descendant of Genghis ruled each khanate.

One khanate covered southern Central Asia. A second included northern Central Asia and Russia. The third, the land of the Il-Khans, stretched from modern Pakistan to Turkey. The fourth was the largest. It included China and Mongolia.

Outside China, the Mongols ruled through local officials. In Russia, local princes carried out Mongol laws and collected taxes. These princes later became Russia's rulers after the Mongols left.

In other areas, the Mongols ruled directly, but adapted to local culture. For example, the Il-Khans who ruled Muslim lands adopted the religion of Islam.

Reading Check How did the Mongols rule in the khanates?

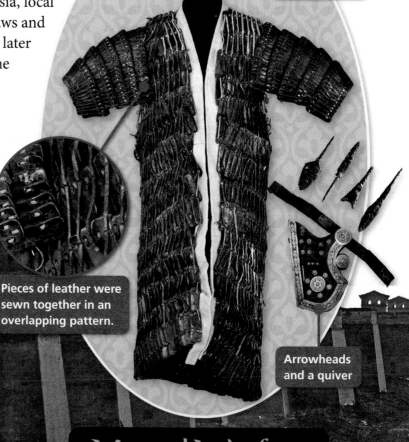

Mongols wore helmets of leather or iron.

Chinese cities were built with walls to repel attacks. ▼

Pieces of leather were sewn together in an overlapping pattern.

Arrowheads and a quiver

Genghis Khan

Mongol Warfare

Mongol warriors moved quickly, using their skills as horsemen to defeat their opponents. They traveled with two horses so they always had a fresh one and shot arrows at a full gallop.

526

The Yuan Dynasty

Before they could fully establish control over China, the Mongols had to complete their conquest of the Southern Song. In 1260, Genghis's grandson Kublai Khan took over northern China. He began a twenty-year effort to defeat the Song.

Completing the Conquest of China The many rivers and canals crossing southern China prevented the Mongols from moving quickly. Kublai Khan solved the problem by building a fleet. With thousands of ships, the Mongols were able to capture cities along southern China's rivers.

In 1279, the Mongols finally gained control of all of China. Kublai had already declared himself the ruler of a new dynasty, the Yuan (yooahn), in 1271. *Yuan* means "the origin," or "beginning."

Mongol Rule in China By declaring a new dynasty, Kublai showed his intention to honor some Chinese traditions. He kept much of the Song bureaucracy. He also adopted rituals of the Chinese court. In these ways, he kept symbols of Chinese royal power.

In other ways, however, Kublai changed China's government. He reduced the power of scholar-officials. He suspended the civil service exams and placed his own followers in office. Kublai also gave more power to regional officials.

Society in Yuan China Perhaps the greatest change under the Mongols was the creation of a new social order. Society was divided into four groups. At the top were the Mongols. Next came other foreigners. Then came the northern Chinese.

At the bottom were the recently conquered southern Chinese.

This social <u>structure</u> encouraged the Mongols to remain separate from the Chinese. Mongols were the favored group, while the Chinese had few rights or privileges.

To further limit Chinese influence, the Mongols welcomed foreigners in China. Turks and other Muslims were the largest group. They held key positions in the government. Many Tibetans were encouraged to spread their form of Buddhism across China. The Mongols also allowed Christian missionaries from Europe to preach in China.

Reading Check How did the Mongols change Chinese society?

structure, *n.,* organization

myWorld Activity
A Demand for Rights

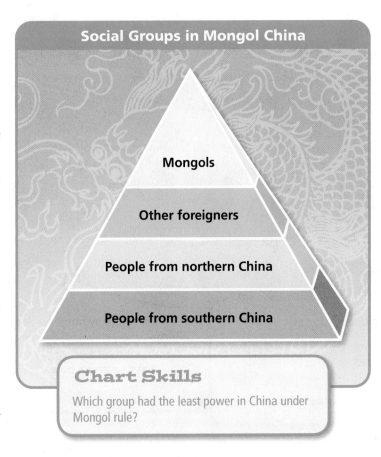

Social Groups in Mongol China

Mongols

Other foreigners

People from northern China

People from southern China

Chart Skills

Which group had the least power in China under Mongol rule?

Life in Yuan China

Under Mongol rule, peace and order returned to Asia. In the 1300s, a Muslim traveler named Ibn Battuta wrote of a journey he took to China. He was impressed by how easy it was to travel:

> 66 China is the safest and best regulated country for a traveller. A man may go by himself a nine month's journey, carrying with him large sums of money, without any fear on that account. 99

— Ibn Battuta, *Travels in Asia and Africa*

Revival of Trade The Mongols encouraged trade and commerce. Under the Yuan, merchants held a higher status in China than they had in earlier times. They were spared certain taxes they had paid during the Song dynasty.

The Mongols continued the sea trade begun under the Song. Many of the merchants who carried out this trade were Muslims from southwestern Asia.

They also reopened the ancient Silk Road across Central Asia. As you may recall, the Silk Road was an overland

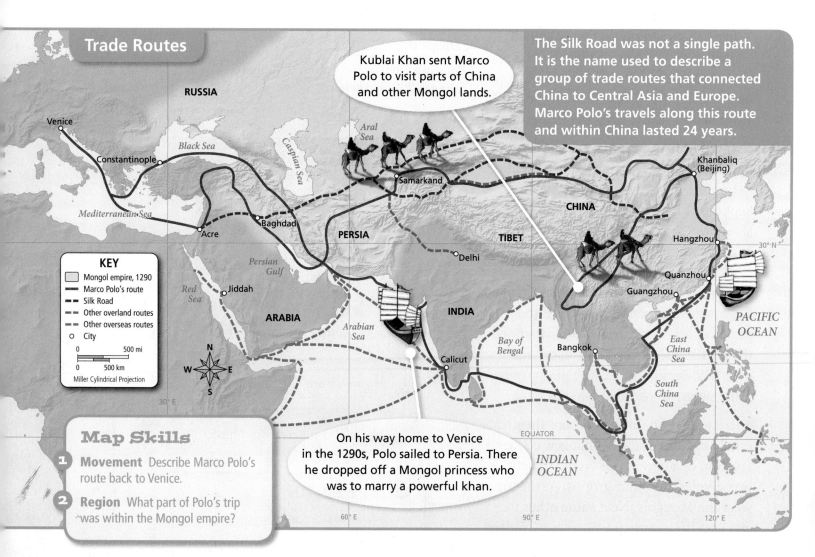

Trade Routes

Kublai Khan sent Marco Polo to visit parts of China and other Mongol lands.

The Silk Road was not a single path. It is the name used to describe a group of trade routes that connected China to Central Asia and Europe. Marco Polo's travels along this route and within China lasted 24 years.

RUSSIA

Venice

Black Sea

Constantinople

Caspian Sea

Aral Sea

Samarkand

Khanbaliq (Beijing)

CHINA

Mediterranean Sea

Acre

Baghdad

PERSIA

TIBET

Hangzhou

30° N

Delhi

Quanzhou

Guangzhou

KEY

Mongol empire, 1290
Marco Polo's route
Silk Road
Other overland routes
Other overseas routes
○ City

Red Sea

Jiddah

Persian Gulf

PACIFIC OCEAN

0   500 mi
0   500 km
Miller Cylindrical Projection

ARABIA

Arabian Sea

INDIA

N
W   E
S

Calicut

Bay of Bengal

Bangkok

East China Sea

South China Sea

EQUATOR

On his way home to Venice in the 1290s, Polo sailed to Persia. There he dropped off a Mongol princess who was to marry a powerful khan.

INDIAN OCEAN

0°

30° E

60° E

90° E

120° E

Map Skills

1 **Movement** Describe Marco Polo's route back to Venice.

2 **Region** What part of Polo's trip was within the Mongol empire?

trade route that linked China to Europe. It had been much used during the Han and Tang dynasties. But disorder and warfare in Central Asia had closed this route during the Song dynasty.

Under Mongol rule, traders once again took their caravans across the continent. They carried silk, porcelain, spices, and other luxury goods to southwest Asia and Europe. Traders carried ideas and inventions between the different lands as well.

Foreign Visitors The Silk Road provided a route for foreign travelers to enter China. The most famous European visitor was Marco Polo, a young man from Venice, Italy.

Polo journeyed to China with his father and uncle. He arrived in 1275 and stayed for 17 years. During this time, he was a favored guest of Kublai Khan. The ruler employed Polo as a diplomat and official, sending him on missions around the empire. As a result, Polo got a first-hand look at China.

After his return to Europe, Polo told stories of the places he saw. He described the splendor of Chinese cities and the wonders of Kublai Khan's court. He discussed the use of paper money, which was still unknown in Europe. And he told of an amazing kind of stone that burned. Today it is known as coal.

> **66** There is a sort of black stone, which is dug out of veins in the hillsides and burns like logs. . . . I assure you that, if you put them on the fire in the evening . . . they will continue to burn all night. **99**
>
> —*The Travels of Marco Polo*

Polo's book gave Europeans their first glimpse of China. Some readers doubted his fantastic tales. On his deathbed, Polo was asked to admit that he had made it all up. He replied that he had described only half of what he had seen.

Reading Check How did contact with people in other lands increase under the Mongols?

▲ Marco Polo's caravan

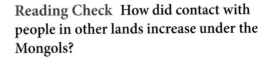

Section 2 Assessment

Essential Question

Key Terms

1. What is a nomad?
2. Who were the Mongols?
3. Describe the role of a khan.

Key Ideas

4. How were the Mongols able to conquer such a large empire?
5. Why did Mongol rulers adopt many Chinese customs?
6. Why did trade flourish along the Silk Road?

Think Critically

7. **Identify Bias** In what ways might Marco Polo's account of Kublai Khan's court have been biased?
8. **Make Inferences** Why did Europeans think Marco Polo made up his stories?

What are the consequences of technology?

9. How did military technology help the Mongols? Go to your Student Journal to record your answer.

The Ming Dynasty

Key Ideas

- The Ming sought to wipe out Mongol influence and restore Chinese rule.
- Ming rulers treated nearby lands as tributary states.
- After sponsoring a series of explorations, Ming rulers chose to reduce contact with the outside world.

Key Terms • despot • tribute • smuggler

 Visual Glossary

Reading Skill Summarize Take notes using the graphic organizer in your journal.

A statue from the Forbidden City ▼

Mongol rule weakened after the death of Kublai Khan in 1294. In the mid-1300s, China suffered through floods, disease, and famine. These hardships led to rebellion against the Mongols. In 1368, Chinese rule was restored under a new dynasty called the Ming.

The Ming Restore Chinese Power

Ming emperors tried to eliminate all traces of Mongol rule in China because they viewed the Mongols as foreigners. The founder of the Ming dynasty set the pattern for Ming government, which lasted until 1644.

Absolute Rule Zhu Yuan Zhang (joo yoo AHN jahng) joined the rebellion against the Mongols as a young man and became its leader. In 1368, he named himself emperor and took the name Hongwu, which means "vast military."

During his reign, Hongwu took several important steps. He moved the capital to Nanjing. He reversed Mongol trade policies. He also revived the civil service system and Confucian values.

Under Hongwu, China returned to strong, centralized rule. At first, Hongwu tried to rule in the interests of his people. Over time, however, he became a cruel despot. A **despot** is a tyrant or dictator. He trusted no one and made all decisions, large and small, himself.

Hongwu began to suspect others of plotting against him. He formed a secret police force to seek out his enemies. He had about 100,000 people arrested and executed for treason, or disloyal actions against the state.

Hongwu defended his harsh policy:

66 In the morning I punish a few; by evening others commit the same crime. I punish these in the evening and by the next morning again there are violations. . . . If I punish these persons, I am regarded as a tyrant. If I am lenient [soft] toward them, the law becomes ineffective, order deteriorates, and people deem me an <u>incapable</u> ruler. 99

—Hongwu

Yongle's Rule After Hongwu's death, his son Yongle (yong LEE) took power. Yongle continued his father's pattern of absolute rule. But he decided to move the capital from the southern city of Nanjing to Beijing in the north.

Yongle made this move for two reasons. One was to return the capital to China's northern heartland. The other was to strengthen the country's northern defenses against future Mongol invasion.

The new capital was built to impress visitors with the splendor of the Ming dynasty. At the heart of Beijing lay the Forbidden City, site of the emperor's palace. The design of the city was meant to reinforce the idea of China as the Middle Kingdom, or the center of the world. For many decades, this idea guided Ming rulers in their dealings with other countries.

Reading Check Why did Yongle move the capital to Beijing?

incapable, *adj.,* unskilled

Forbidden City

The Gate of Supreme Harmony ▼

Visitors passed through the Gate of Supreme Harmony to reach the Hall of Supreme Harmony. The hall included many throne rooms and was the heart of the Forbidden City. Visitors today can tour these buildings.

531

Ming Foreign Policy

For many years, Ming China acted forcefully on its view that it was the center of the world. Eventually, though, China turned inward and shut itself off from contact with other lands.

The Tributary System Yongle forced foreign countries to recognize China's power. Many countries sent tribute to China. **Tribute** is a payment or gift to a more powerful country. They did this to prevent attacks by China and win favor for their traders.

Ming China traded with other parts of Asia and eastern Africa. Foreign traders brought goods such as horses, spices, and silver from their lands. In return, they received silk, tea, porcelain, and other goods from China.

The system helped both China and the tributary states. China gained peaceful borders. With peace, Ming emperors could spend less money on armies and more on projects such as building canals. Tributary states benefited by getting goods they wanted without going to war.

The Voyages of Zheng He Between 1405 and 1433, Yongle sent an official named Zheng He (jung huh) to lead a series of sea voyages to demonstrate Chinese power and to win more tributary states.

A model of Zheng He's ship ▼

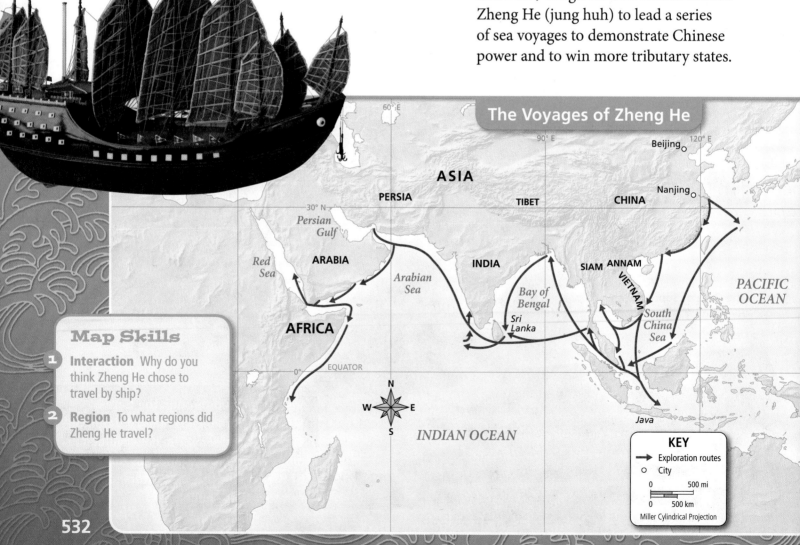

The Voyages of Zheng He

ASIA
PERSIA
Persian Gulf
Red Sea
ARABIA
Arabian Sea
AFRICA
TIBET
INDIA
Bay of Bengal
Sri Lanka
CHINA
Beijing
Nanjing
SIAM
ANNAM
VIETNAM
South China Sea
PACIFIC OCEAN
Java
EQUATOR
INDIAN OCEAN

KEY
→ Exploration routes
○ City
0 500 mi
0 500 km
Miller Cylindrical Projection

Map Skills

1. **Interaction** Why do you think Zheng He chose to travel by ship?

2. **Region** To what regions did Zheng He travel?

The fleet for the first voyage included more than 60 huge ships and 27,000 men. Zheng He traveled through Southeast Asia to the coast of India on this first trip. Later voyages went as far as the Persian Gulf and the east coast of Africa. Wherever Zheng went, he collected tribute for China.

China Turns Inward With Yongle's death, the voyages ended and China turned inward. China banned the building of large ships, overseas travel, and contact with most foreigners. Cost was almost certainly one reason. The voyages were very expensive and did not earn enough in trade or tribute to repay their costs.

More important was that scholar-officials believed that China had everything it needed. They saw foreigners as a threat to Chinese culture. They only allowed a few foreign traders to do business in certain cities under strict rules.

Meanwhile, fewer merchants used the overland Silk Road. After the Mongol empire weakened, the route became dangerous. Despite this, Chinese silk and porcelain remained in great demand.

Contact With Europe Portuguese sailors arrived in China in 1514. They refused to pay tribute and violated official limits on trade. Chinese officials at first saw Europeans as **smugglers,** or people who trade illegally. However, their silver was hard to resist and this trade grew.

End of the Ming Dynasty The despotism of Ming rulers led to corruption and rebellion. Like the Tang and Song, the Ming also fought invaders along the borders. To repel invasions, they rebuilt the Great Wall. But it was not enough. Protests in China and foreign invasion led to the fall of the dynasty in 1644.

Reading Check Why did the Ming rulers end the sea voyages?

myWorld Activity
Close the Doors

Zheng He is also known as Chengho. ▼

66 The countries beyond the horizon and from the ends of the earth have all become subjects. . . . We have crossed immense water spaces . . . and we have set eyes on barbarian regions far away . . . 99

—Zheng He

Section 3 Assessment

Key Terms
1. Describe a despot.
2. What is tribute?
3. What is a smuggler?

Key Ideas
4. Why did Hongwu restore the civil service?
5. How did tribute relate to trade?

Think Critically
6. **Make Inferences** Why were European traders considered smugglers?
7. **Identify Bias** Why did scholar-officials want to stop foreign trade?

Essential Question

What are the consequences of technology?

8. How did technology allow China to expand the tribute system? Go to your Student Journal to record your answer.

Chinese Society

Key Ideas
- China's technology and trade had a worldwide impact.
- Daoism, Buddhism, and Confucianism were influential belief systems in China.
- Some features of Chinese culture were important from the Tang dynasty through the Ming dynasty.

Key Terms
- compass
- block printing
- Daoism
- Buddhism
- Confucianism

 Visual Glossary

Reading Skill Identify Main Ideas and Details Take notes using the graphic organizer in your journal.

Longhua Pagoda in Shanghai ▼

During the Tang and Song dynasties, China developed the most advanced civilization in the world. China's technology and culture spread to other regions. Through the Ming era, trade and tribute promoted the flow of goods, technology, and ideas.

Technological Advances

The Chinese pioneered a number of key inventions during the Tang and Song dynasties. These inventions continued to be important to the Ming dynasty and, eventually, to the rest of Asia and Europe.

Shipbuilding and Navigation Chinese shipbuilding technologies were the most advanced in the world through the Ming dynasty. Huge ships, known as "junks," could hold as many as 500 people. These ships had multiple decks and masts (tall, vertical posts that carry sails on sailing ships). Rudders, or hinged boards at the back of the ships, made them easy to steer.

Chinese ships also had watertight compartments. If a leak occurred in one place, a section could be sealed off to prevent the ship from sinking. Marco Polo explained how this worked:

66 The sailors promptly find out where the breach is. Cargo is shifted from the damaged compartment into the neighboring ones; for the bulkheads [walls] are so stoutly [strongly] built that the compartments are watertight. The damage is then repaired and the cargo shifted back. 99

—*The Travels of Marco Polo*

Another important invention was the magnetic compass. A **compass** is a device with a magnetized piece of metal that points to the north. Chinese sailors used the compass to navigate open seas. It allowed them to travel to distant lands without getting lost. As a result, Chinese merchants opened up trade routes to India and Southeast Asia. Zheng He used this technology on his voyages.

Use of the magnetic compass also spread through Muslim lands to Europe. Arab and European sailors used compasses on their voyages by the 1200s.

Paper and Printing A Chinese court official invented paper in 105. Until that time, the Chinese wrote on strips of bamboo or silk.

By the 800s, the Chinese were making books using **block printing** in which workers carved text into blocks of wood. Each block was then covered with ink and pressed on paper to print a page.

Later, Chinese printers crafted movable type. Each piece of type had one character on it. The pieces could be <u>assembled</u> to print a page of text and then taken apart to be used again. With this system, printers no longer needed to carve a new block of text for every page of a book.

Printing lowered the cost of books during the Song dynasty. As a result, the number of schools rose. Literacy, or the ability to read and write, also increased. For the first time, common people could hope to become scholar-officials.

Use of paper traveled west to Muslim lands and then to Europe. Printing may have followed a similar path.

Some historians think that printing developed separately in Europe in the 1400s. Others think that Europeans may have gotten the idea from Chinese printed products. Either way, paper and printing made writing and publishing easier. As a result, more people could learn to read and get an education.

assemble, *v.,* to put together

A page from the earliest known printed book ▼

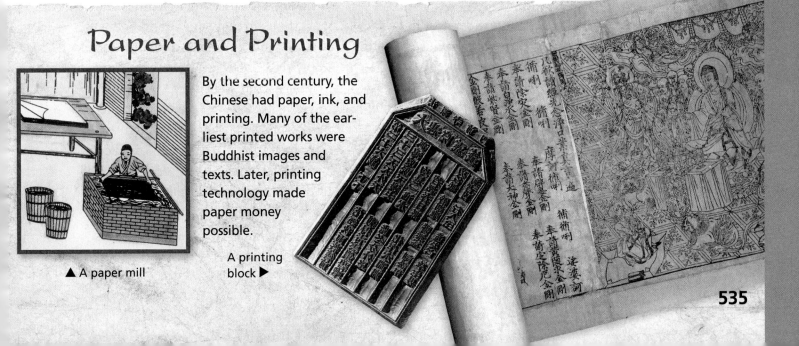

Paper and Printing

By the second century, the Chinese had paper, ink, and printing. Many of the earliest printed works were Buddhist images and texts. Later, printing technology made paper money possible.

▲ A paper mill

A printing block ▶

535

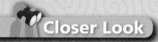
The Three Perfections

Educated and cultured people were expected to master the "three perfections" of painting, calligraphy, and poetry. The painting at the right shows all three. Red seals represent owners of the painting or those who admired it.

THINK CRITICALLY **How are the three perfections related?**

Gunpowder By the 900s, the Chinese discovered the mixture of ingredients we know today as gunpowder. They first used gunpowder in fireworks. By the Song era, however, they were using gunpowder to make bombs, rockets, and other weapons.

Like paper, gunpowder spread west to Muslim areas and, then, to Europe. Gunpowder was the Turks' secret weapon in their conquest of Constantinople. Like Muslims, Europeans were quick to put gunpowder to use in warfare.

Inventions Help Trade The Chinese developed other technologies that improved life and increased trade. In addition to the farming technology you read about, the Chinese developed water pumps for irrigation.

They also crafted a harness to control draft animals. A draft animal is used to pull a load, such as a wagon or a plow. As you have read, extra food from improved farming technology led to more trade.

Other inventions helped industry grow. Weaving and spinning machines allowed workshops to make more and better silk. Methods for making ceramics also improved. These goods were then traded inside and outside China.

Trade led to more creativity. Water pumps and wheelbarrows were used in building projects, such as in canal construction. Canals were used for inland trade. Increased trade led to the greater use of paper money.

Reading Check How was technology related to trade?

A stone used to mix ink ▶

A calligraphy brush, dating from before the Song dynasty ▶

Li Bai is one of the most famous Chinese poets.

66 To-night I stay at the Summit Temple.
Here I could pluck the stars with my hand,
I dare not speak aloud in the silence,
For fear of disturbing the dwellers of heaven.99
——Li Bai, "The Summit Temple"

Calligraphers must master more than 40,000 Chinese characters.

Chinese Arts and Culture

Some parts of Chinese culture were important for more than a thousand years. For example, craftsmen created trade goods that were valued around the world, including porcelain and silk. Scholars were also highly respected.

The Three Perfections From the Tang period through the Ming, scholars valued the "three perfections" of calligraphy, poetry, and painting. Scholars spent time perfecting their skills in these pursuits. They were also part of the examinations.

The Tang era is known as the peak of Chinese poetry. The Song era is famous for its painters. They created wonderful landscapes, which are images of scenery. Collectors sought out art from the best calligraphers.

Ceramics and Porcelain Ceramics and porcelain were important throughout much of Chinese history. Chinese porcelain became a <u>major</u> trade item that was prized around the world. Porcelain was thinner and stronger than other materials used for making plates, bowls, and vases. It was also beautiful, with a smooth white finish. Fancy porcelain plates are still known as "china."

The most famous Tang ceramics are figurines, which were often found in tombs. Song ceramics came in many different colors, from greens to blues to browns. Factories in different regions produced items of different colors.

During the Ming era, a town called Jingdezhen made the best porcelain in China. This porcelain, decorated with a blue glaze, was valued around the world.

major, *adj.,* important

Other Trade Items Silk was another highly valued trade item. Although silk had been produced since ancient times, it became a more organized industry. Factories improved the quality of silk and increased the amount of decoration on it.

Reading Check How was porcelain different from other ceramics?

Buddhist Art

▲ A Buddhist statue

◀ This cave is one of more than 500 in Dunhuang, located along the ancient Silk Road.

Religion and Thought

Three main belief systems shaped life in China from the Tang period to the Ming period: Daoism, Confucianism, and Buddhism. Each played an important role in Chinese culture.

Daoism **Daoism** is an ancient Chinese philosophy. Its basic teaching is that all things—earth, heaven, and people—should follow the Dao (dow). *Dao* means "the way." A person who follows the way will enjoy peace. For many Daoists, this meant leaving society to live close to nature. By the Tang period, Daoism had priests, temples, and monasteries.

Buddhism **Buddhism** is a religion based on the teachings of the Indian spiritual leader Siddhartha Gautama (sih DAHR tuh GOW tuh muh). He is also known as the Buddha (BOO duh), or "the Enlightened One." Gautama taught that life involves suffering. The way to ease suffering is to give up worldly desires and seek enlightenment, or perfect wisdom. Those who reach enlightenment enter nirvana, which is a state of complete peace. They also escape the endless cycle of suffering, death, and rebirth.

Buddhism reached China during the Han dynasty. It gained strength during the troubled times between the Han and Tang dynasties. Its appeal was based on the hope for an end to suffering.

Over time, Buddhism adapted and absorbed elements of Daoism. By the Tang dynasty, Buddhism had millions of followers in China. Temples and monasteries grew rich from donations.

Decline of Buddhism Some Chinese thinkers criticized Buddhism as a foreign religion. Other critics opposed Buddhists' withdrawal from the world. They believed that people should be involved in society and family life. Still others criticized the wealth and power of the monasteries.

At times, criticism led to persecution. The worst attacks came during the reign of Emperor Wuzong, a Daoist. In 845, Wuzong ordered the destruction of 4,600 Buddhist monasteries and 40,000 temples. Some 250,000 Buddhist monks and nuns were forced to give up religious life.

Buddhism never fully recovered from this attack. Although some Buddhist ideas remained important, Buddhism as a religion did not regain its popularity.

Confucianism Much of the opposition to Buddhism came from the followers of Confucianism. **Confucianism** is a system of moral behavior, based on the teachings of Confucius. It was an important belief system, especially for scholar-officials.

Confucius lived during a time of warfare and disorder in China. His philosophy was designed to restore peace and stability.

Confucius stressed the importance of virtue. He said that a wise ruler governed through moral example, not force. He taught that people could gain virtue through education.

Confucianism was also based on respect for family and the social order. Everyone had a role to play in society. As Confucius put it, "Let the prince be a prince, the minister a minister, the father a father, and the son a son." He taught that children should respect their parents.

Thought Systems and Religions

Daoism
- **Founder:** Laozi (500s B.C.)
- **Key Values:** Spiritual growth, harmony with nature
- **Influence in China:** Popular, but no government support

Buddhism
- **Founder:** Siddhartha Gautama (400s B.C.)
- **Key Values:** Spiritual enlightenment from within
- **Influence in China:** Most popular during the Tang dynasty

Confucianism
- **Founder:** Confucius (551–479 B.C.)
- **Key Values:** Order, harmonious relationships, respect for authority
- **Influence in China:** Backed by most dynasties, including the Song dynasty and the Ming dynasty

Chart Skills

1. Which thought system did the government support?

2. What are the key values of Daoism, Buddhism, and Confucianism?

539

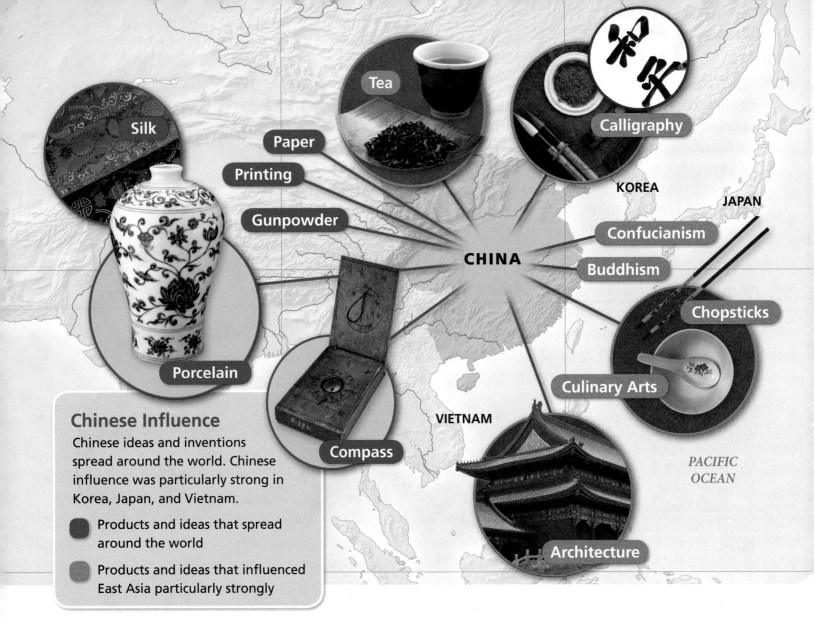

Chinese Influence

Chinese ideas and inventions spread around the world. Chinese influence was particularly strong in Korea, Japan, and Vietnam.

- Products and ideas that spread around the world
- Products and ideas that influenced East Asia particularly strongly

Silk

Paper

Printing

Gunpowder

Tea

Calligraphy

KOREA

JAPAN

Confucianism

Buddhism

Chopsticks

Culinary Arts

Porcelain

Compass

VIETNAM

Architecture

CHINA

PACIFIC OCEAN

Subjects should respect their rulers. Rulers should respect the nation. By following these roles and respecting social rank, the Chinese would maintain order.

Neo-Confucianism The growth of Buddhism caused Confucian scholars to think about religious questions. By the Song era, a new philosophy called Neo-Confucianism arose. The Neo-Confucians found new meanings in the writings of Confucius. In doing so, they answered questions about the meaning and purpose of life.

This form of Confucian thought showed the influence of Buddhism and Daoism. One famous Neo-Confucian, a scholar-official named Zhu Xi (joo shee), said that people should live according to the Dao. But he defined the Dao as a process of self-improvement and education, rather than as a retreat from society. The ideas of the Neo-Confucians had a great influence on China from the Song period onward.

Reading Check What were the teachings of the Neo-Confucians?

540

Chinese Influence Spreads

China had always been the largest, most influential country in East Asia. As a result, its civilization had great effects on smaller countries nearby. In addition, China manufactured more goods than any other country. Through trade, it influenced Central Asia and Europe.

The Impact of Chinese Thought Both Confucianism and Buddhism spread from China to nearby lands. Over time, the governments of Vietnam, Korea, and Japan all adopted practices that reflected Confucian ideas. For instance, scholar-officials ran their bureaucracies. The influence of Confucian ideas was particularly strong in Korea.

Buddhism also spread from China throughout East Asia. Buddhism arrived in Korea in the A.D. 300s. From there, it moved to Japan.

Chinese Culture Vietnam, Korea, and Japan also adopted many elements of Chinese culture. All three borrowed the Chinese writing system. In time, they adapted it to their needs. They imported Chinese styles of painting, music, and architecture. Both Korea and Japan built capital cities modeled on Changan.

Chinese culinary arts also spread throughout East Asia. Culinary arts are the skills involved in cooking and food preparation. Many countries adopted chopsticks as tools for cooking and eating. They borrowed the Chinese wok, a large round-bottomed pan used for frying and steaming foods. These countries also adopted the custom of drinking tea.

Trade and the West The Ming government tried to limit the influence of foreigners on China. Trade made that impossible. European merchants brought new goods and technologies to the Chinese. Missionaries brought Western Christianity. In turn, Chinese products and ideas spread to Europe.

Reading Check How did Chinese influence spread?

A figurine found in a tomb from the Tang period ▼

Section **4** Assessment

Essential Question

What are the consequences of technology?

Key Terms

1. How did the compass help sailors?
2. What are the main beliefs of Buddhism, Confucianism, and Daoism?

Key Ideas

3. How did Confucianism affect China's government?
4. Describe two Chinese technological advances.
5. What are the three perfections?

Think Critically

6. **Make Decisions** What Chinese technological advancement was most important? Why?
7. **Draw Conclusions** Why did China influence the countries around it?

8. How did Chinese technology affect the rest of the world? Go to your Student Journal to record your answer.

Chapter **17**
Chapter Assessment

Key Terms and Ideas

1. **Summarize** What was the role of **scholar-officials** in China?

2. **Describe** Describe Chang'an.

3. **Summarize** Why was China prosperous during the Tang and Song dynasties?

4. **Discuss** What was the significance of Genghis Khan?

5. **Recall** What goods were traded along the Silk Road?

6. **Explain** In what ways was Hongwu a **despot**?

7. **Discuss** How did China benefit from **tribute**?

8. **Compare and Contrast** How does **Buddhism** differ from **Confucianism**?

Think Critically

9. **Compare and Contrast** How was the Chinese government during the Yuan dynasty different than it was during the Tang, Song, and Ming dynasties?

10. **Decision Making** Which innovation—printing or fast-growing rice—do you think had a greater effect on Chinese civilization? Explain.

11. **Synthesize** How did improvements in farming lead to urbanization?

12. **Core Concepts: Money Management** How did the use of paper money affect trade in China?

Analyze Visuals

13. Describe the actions of the farmers in the picture to the right.

14. What do you think these instructions are trying to show?

15. In what ways does this picture show how technology improved methods for growing rice?

Essential Question

myWorld Chapter Activity

Trade in China Playing the role of a merchant, you will identify imports to and exports from China. Then make a shopping list of products you would like to buy. Make a commercial for your products and trade for the products you want to purchase.

21st Century Learning

Give an Effective Presentation

Choose one Chinese innovation from the Tang through Ming periods. Use the Internet to find more information about it. Design a presentation in which you answer the following questions: What problem did this innovation solve? How did this innovation work? How did this innovation affect the rest of the world?

Document-Based Questions

Success Tracker™
Online at myworldhistory.com

Use your knowledge of China in the Middle Ages and Documents A and B to answer Questions 1–3.

Document A

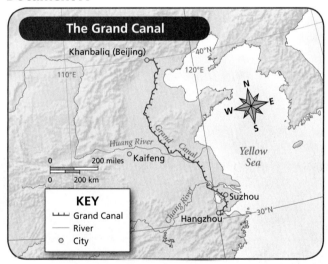

The Grand Canal

Khanbaliq (Beijing)
40°N
110°E
120°E
Huang River
Kaifeng
0   200 miles
0   200 km
Chang River
Grand Canal
Yellow Sea
Suzhou
Hangzhou
30°N

KEY
Grand Canal
— River
○ City

Document B

"[P]arallel to this great street, but at the back of the market places, there runs a very large canal, on the bank of which towards the squares are built great houses of stone, in which the merchants from India and other foreign parts store their wares, to be handy for the markets. In each of the squares is held a market three days in the week, frequented by 40,000 or 50,000 persons, who bring thither for sale every possible necessary of life, . . . "

1. What does the Grand Canal connect?
   A Kaifeng and Hangzhou
   B Kaifeng and the Yellow Sea
   C the Chang River and the Huang River
   D the east of China and the west of China

2. What were canals used for?
   A to transport the army
   B to transport goods for sale
   C to give fishermen access to the sea
   D to transport people from Kaifeng to the west of China

3. **Writing Task** In what ways did the Grand Canal improve life in China? Explain your answer.

myworldhistory.com

Self-Test

Japan Before Modern Times

? Essential Question

What distinguishes one culture from another?

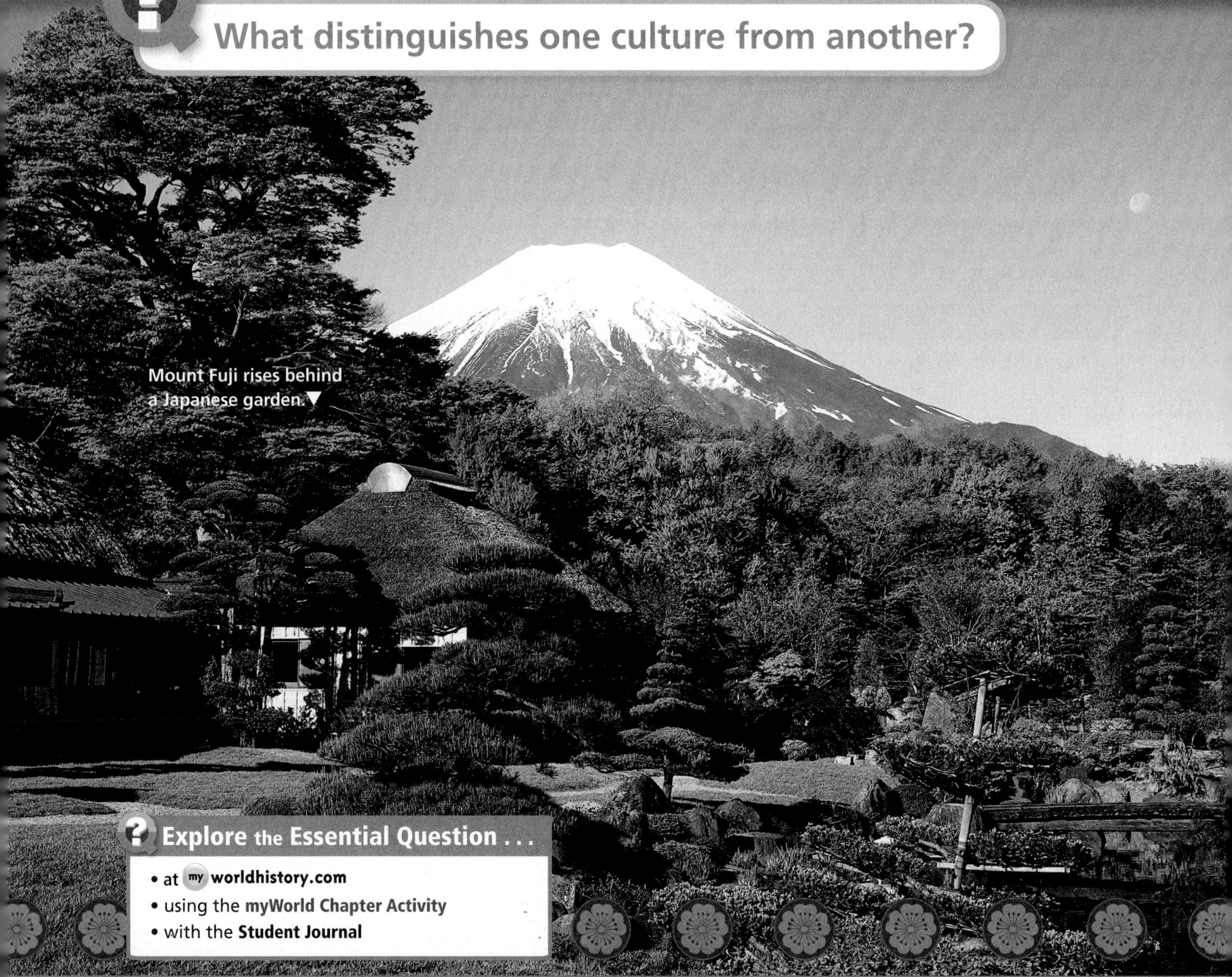

Mount Fuji rises behind a Japanese garden. ▼

? Explore the Essential Question . . .

- at **my** **worldhistory.com**
- using the **myWorld Chapter Activity**
- with the **Student Journal**

Key Dates in Japan Before Modern Times

538 Buddhism arrives in Japan.

794 The capital moves to Heian.

1185 Feudalism begins in Japan.

1274 The first Mongol invasion fails.

400 600 800 1000 1200 1400 1600

645 Taika Reform introduces new laws.

1600 Tokugawa Ieyasu unites Japan.

Murasaki Shikibu: Life Behind the Screen

This myStory is a fictionalized account of the life of Murasaki Shikibu, who appears in this chapter.

Lady Murasaki sat, deep in thought, behind a flowing silk screen. By appearances, she fit in with the other ladies of the empress's court at Heian. Her teeth were dyed black, her face was painted white, her hair fell all the way to the floor, and her robes were vividly colored. But she was not much like the other women. She was a famous writer.

As others gossiped or played games, she imagined new adventures for Genji, the hero of her stories. Suddenly, a red flower sailed over Lady Murasaki's screen and floated to the floor. She was fairly certain who delivered it—a man in court she didn't much like.

She was annoyed at stopping her own work, but she would be terribly rude if she didn't write a poem to thank him. With a sigh, Lady Murasaki picked up her brush and began to compose a poem in reply.

my worldhistory.com

Timeline/On Assignment

545

Murasaki listened as her brother learned Chinese. Her father wished that she were a boy because she was so smart.

Lady Murasaki preferred writing to interacting with others at court.

Murasaki kept a private diary about the silliness of life at court. She disliked the banquets, concerts, elaborate games, contests, back-stabbing gossip, and rivalries. She thought that strict rules about how men and women should interact at court were absurd. Everything had a symbolic meaning—a gesture, the details of an outfit, the color of the flower this man had dropped.

It bothered her that life at court was so fake, cut off from real problems. Once she described a picture competition as a "moment in the history of our country when the whole energy of the nation seemed to be concentrated upon the search for the prettiest method of mounting paper scrolls!"

For a woman so quiet that she seemed almost invisible, Murasaki Shikibu had many secrets. One was her real name. "Shikibu" refers to the government post her father held. He had arranged for her to come to court as lady-in-waiting to Akiko, the emperor's wife who was ten years her junior.

"Murasaki" comes from a main character in her masterpiece, *The Tale of Genji*. In it, she idealized Genji as "the Shining Prince." He was sensitive and a worthy friend, not like the rude men at court. His great love was a woman nicknamed Murasaki.

Murasaki is a plant that produces purple dye, and the woman reminded Genji of a purple flower. When the story became popular, people also began to call the author by the name Murasaki.

Lady Murasaki also tried to keep the secret that she could read and write in Chinese. Her father had not stopped her listening in on her brother's lessons in a language only men were supposed to know. Her father, though, wished she were a boy because he saw how smart she was. A woman could not use her learning to become a government official.

At court, Murasaki hid what she knew because people said "she will come to no good." It was not considered proper for a woman to read and write Chinese. She knew that other women whispered about her behind her back. They said, "It's because she goes on like this that she is so miserable. What kind of lady is it who reads Chinese books?"

Murasaki came to court as a star. Akiko was proud to have an accomplished writer among her attendants. When word leaked out that Murasaki also knew Chinese, the empress asked for lessons. But others were jealous. In her diary, Murasaki wrote, "to keep it secret we carefully chose times when the other women would not be present."

Court ladies sometimes passed their time playing a board game called go.

Lady Murasaki's tales were so popular that others sometimes sneaked into her room to steal a look at the next tale about Genji.

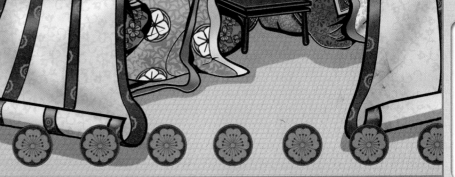

Although she recorded much about her daily life at court, Lady Murasaki had to be careful with her secrets and longed for acceptance. She confided in her diary, "There are ears everywhere. . . . I still fret over what others think of me."

And yet *The Tale of Genji* was popular even before she finished writing it. In fact, after dashing off her thank-you poem, she had to hurry back to her room. Certain ladies-in-waiting and courtiers had been stealing pages she hadn't even finished. They were anxious to discover what happened next.

Based on this story, how would you describe Heian court culture? As you read the chapter, think about what Murasaki's story tells you about life in Heian Japan.

 myStory Video

Learn more about Murasaki Shikibu and Japan before modern times.

my worldhistory.com

myStory Video

The Rise of Japan

| Key Ideas | • With limited land for agriculture, the people of Japan depended on the sea. | • The first Japanese rulers emerged through struggles among local clans. | • Under Prince Shotoku, Japan became a unified kingdom strongly influenced by China. |

Key Terms • archipelago • mainland • clan • kami • regent

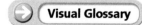 Visual Glossary

Reading Skill Sequence Take notes using the graphic organizer in your journal.

An actor portrays the sun goddess Amaterasu. ▼

Japan arose in the shadow of its powerful neighbor, China. Early Japanese culture and society often borrowed from China and its other neighbor, Korea. But Chinese and Korean cultures were not the only influences on Japan. Geography also had great effects on the island nation.

Geography of Japan

Japan is an **archipelago** (ahr kuh PEL uh go), or chain of islands. To Japan's west is the continent of Asia. To the east lies the broad Pacific Ocean. In ancient times, the Japanese believed that theirs was the first land to see the sun rise in the morning. They called their country *Nippon*, which means "land of the rising sun." In Japanese tradition, the Sun Goddess was the country's special protector.

Land and Climate Japan is made up of four large islands and thousands of smaller ones. Its total land area is about the size of the state of California. The archipelago is very long from north to south. Honshu (HAHN shoo), the main island, is much larger than the others.

Japan has many different climates. Heavy snows blanket the northernmost island of Hokkaido (hoh KY doh) in winter. The southern island of Kyushu (KYOO shoo) is almost tropical.

A ridge of volcanic mountains runs the length of the island chain. Mount Fuji is the highest peak. It rises more than 12,000 feet above sea level. Because of Mount Fuji's beauty, it has always been an important symbol for the Japanese people.

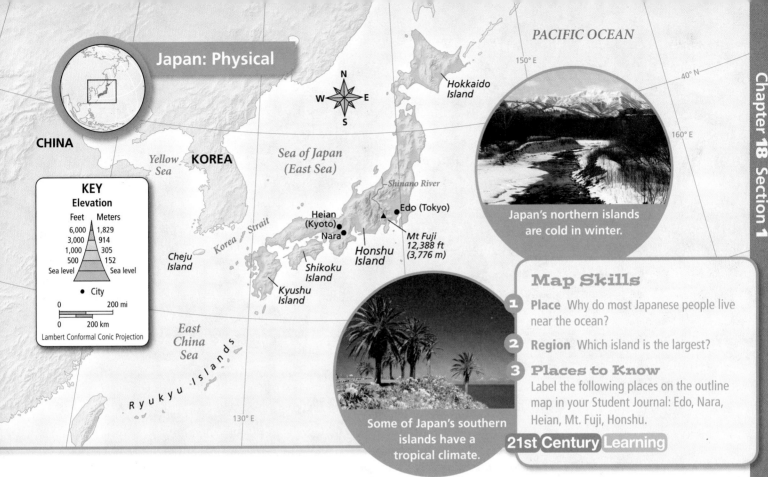

Japan: Physical

PACIFIC OCEAN

CHINA

KOREA

Yellow Sea

Sea of Japan (East Sea)

Hokkaido Island

Shinano River

Heian (Kyoto)

Nara

Edo (Tokyo)

Mt Fuji 12,388 ft (3,776 m)

Honshu Island

Shikoku Island

Kyushu Island

Cheju Island

Korea Strait

East China Sea

Ryukyu Islands

KEY
Elevation

Feet	Meters
6,000	1,829
3,000	914
1,000	305
500	152
Sea level	Sea level

● City

0   200 mi
0   200 km
Lambert Conformal Conic Projection

Japan's northern islands are cold in winter.

Some of Japan's southern islands have a tropical climate.

Map Skills

1 **Place** Why do most Japanese people live near the ocean?

2 **Region** Which island is the largest?

3 **Places to Know** Label the following places on the outline map in your Student Journal: Edo, Nara, Heian, Mt. Fuji, Honshu.

21st Century Learning

Japan is so mountainous that less than 15 percent of its land can be farmed. Most people live on plains or along the coastline. The Japanese take much of their food from the ocean. Their diets are rich in fish, shellfish, and seaweed. However, people grow food on the land that is available.

The Ring of Fire Japan sits at the border between two plates, or sections, of Earth's outer shell. The border forms part of the Ring of Fire. This region of volcanoes and earthquakes circles the Pacific Ocean.

Millions of years ago, the lava from erupting volcanoes slowly built up an underwater mountain range. In time, these mountains rose above the ocean's surface to create the islands of Japan. Mount Fuji last erupted in the early 1700s. Other volcanoes in Japan are still active.

The plates beneath Japan constantly push against each other. Whenever one of them suddenly shifts, an earthquake shakes Japan. Most of these earthquakes are small and harmless, but the big ones can be deadly.

Japan and Its Neighbors Korea and China are Japan's neighbors on the Asian mainland. A **mainland** is an area that is a part of a continent.

About 120 miles of ocean separates Korea from Japan. China is farther away. These distances discouraged frequent contact. Still, waves of <u>migrants</u> from the mainland crossed the water and settled in Japan. Over time, Japan felt the influence of Korean and Chinese cultures.

Reading Check What percentage of Japan's land is available for farming?

migrant, *n.*, a person who moves from one region to another

myworldhistory.com

Places to Know

THE AINU PEOPLE

Today's Ainu (EYE noo) people may be decendants of the Jomon people, who migrated to Japan some 11,000 years ago. They lived separately on Japan's northern islands until the 1900s. *Why do you think the Ainu lived separately?*

▲ Pottery from the Jomon period

Early History

The first groups of humans in Japan arrived many thousands of years ago. Historians have identified one culture group, the Jomon (JOH mon), by their distinctive pottery. The Jomon migrated to Japan some 11,000 years ago. They lived by hunting and fishing.

A Farming Culture By 250 B.C., a new group had appeared in Japan—the Yayoi (YAH yoy). They probably came from mainland Asia. In time, the Yayoi merged with or pushed out the Jomon. Unlike the Jomon, the Yayoi wove cloth and worked bronze and iron.

Most important, the Yayoi introduced the technique of growing rice in irrigated fields. Rice became Japan's most important crop. A diet based on seafood and rice helped boost the population.

The Yamato Clan Triumphs Local clans ruled Japan by the A.D. 200s. A **clan** is a group of people with a common ancestor. The head of a clan was also a religious leader. Part of his job was to show respect to the clan's kami so they would have good harvests. A **kami** (KAH mee) is a holy being that represents a spirit of nature, sacred place, ancestor, or clan in Japanese culture. Each clan also had its own land.

From the 200s to the 400s, warlike clans competed for land and power. The winner of this struggle was the Yamato clan from the plains of central Honshu.

Riding horses and fighting with swords and with bows and arrows, the Yamato first gained control over lands to the north and west. They eventually built a small state. Sometimes, they went to war against neighboring clans. More often, they made alliances through marriage or other ties.

The Yamato applied new technology in their territory. They used iron tools to till the land. They also found better ways to level and flood rice fields. These improvements added to their wealth and power.

Yamato emperors claimed descent from their kami, the Sun Goddess. Even today, Japan's imperial family traces its descent from the Sun Goddess and the Yamato clan. It is the world's oldest ruling royal family.

Reading Check How did the Yamato clan gain control of much of Japan?

Prince Shotoku Unites Japan

Even after the Yamato clan gained power, Japan was not fully united. Clan leaders saw little reason to obey a distant government. In 593, Prince Shotoku took power. He was not an emperor. Instead, he was a regent for the empress, his aunt. A **regent** is someone who governs a country in the name of a ruler who is unable to rule, often because of age.

Support for Buddhism Shotoku began the difficult task of uniting Japan. He had to strengthen the central government and reduce the power of clan leaders. One way he did this was by supporting Buddhism, which arrived from Korea in 538.

Shotoku hoped that the new religion would unite the Japanese people. However, clan leaders opposed the new religion because they were also religious leaders. If people stopped worshiping their kami, clan leaders would lose importance.

Guidelines for Government Japanese leaders also learned about Chinese government and the teachings of Confucius. Shotoku studied these. He believed that Confucianism, like Buddhism, could <u>unify</u> Japan. Shotoku's moral code is laid out in a document known as the Constitution of Seventeen Articles.

unify, *v.,* bring together

Emperor Akihito and Empress Michiko▼

551

Key Points from Prince Shotoku's Constitution

- When the people behave properly, the Government will be in good order.
- Deal impartially with the legal complaints that are submitted to you.
- Punish the evil and reward the good.
- When wise men are entrusted with office, the sound of praise arises. If corrupt men hold office, . . . disasters multiply.
- Decisions on important matters . . . should be discussed . . . with many people.

Adapted from *Japan: Selected Readings,* by Hyman Kublin

This document was not like modern constitutions. It was not a plan for government. Instead, it was a set of guiding principles for people, rulers, and the government itself. It was based on Confucian and Buddhist thought. The first article laid out the Confucian idea of harmony.

66 Harmony should be valued and quarrels should be avoided. . . . [W]hen the superiors are in harmony with each other and the inferiors are friendly . . . the right view of matters prevails. Then there is nothing that cannot be accomplished! 99

The second article called for respecting Buddhism. A later article said that clan heads should not be allowed to tax the people. That power, it suggested, belonged only to the central government.

Missions to China In 607, Shotoku sent official representatives to China to study arts and government. This was the first of several official missions to the Chinese mainland. A mission is a group of people sent to represent their country. The mission included scholars, artists, and Buddhist monks.

When they returned, these experts helped make Japan's government more like that of Tang China. For example, Japanese rulers began using a system of official ranks and duties like those in the Chinese court. Officials could be recognized by the color of their caps.

Reading Check What was the Constitution of Seventeen Articles?

552

Later Reforms

Prince Shotoku died in 622. Japan was still ruled by clans, but other reformers continued efforts to create a strong government. In 645, they began a program known as the Taika Reform. *Taika* means "great change."

The most important new laws said that all land belonged to the emperor and that everyone was his subject. Some clan leaders became local officials. They were responsible for collecting taxes, which were based on the number of people who lived in an area. These changes made Japan more like Tang China.

In 702, a new law code for the entire country made the leader of the Yamato clan the official emperor and said that he should be called "son of Heaven." The new laws also defined crimes and punishments. These criminal laws applied equally to everyone in Japan.

The rulers continued to strengthen their power. In 710 they built a new capital city at Nara.

Reading Check What does *taika* mean?

Borrowing From Neighbors

Chinese culture of the Tang dynasty strongly influenced Japan and Korea. As you learned, early Japanese rulers looked to China as a model for government. Japanese scholars organized an official history of Japan, just as Chinese rulers arranged histories of China. Japan also adopted the Chinese calendar.

In the time of the first Yamato emperor, Japanese had only been spoken, not written. Contact with the mainland changed that. Around 500, the Japanese began to adapt China's writing system. They used Chinese characters, with some changes, to write the Japanese language.

Japan and Korea also developed ties. Buddhist monks arrived in Japan from Korea in 538. Most Japanese practiced Shinto, a mix of ancient beliefs and traditions. Over time, this new faith would absorb many of the Shinto spirits and traditions. You will read more about these religions in Section 3.

Reading Check How did Buddhism arrive in Japan?

myWorld Activity
Guidelines for Government

tradition, *n.,* a practice or belief handed down from one generation to another

Section **1** Assessment

Essential Question

Key Terms

1. What is an archipelago?

2. What is the role of a kami in Japanese culture?

3. Use these words in a sentence: clan, mainland, and regent.

Key Ideas

4. Describe the geography of Japan.

5. Explain the significance of the Yamato clan.

6. How did Prince Shotoku try to unify Japan?

Think Critically

7. Analyze Cause and Effect How did Japanese emperors increase their power?

8. Draw Inferences Why did Japanese rulers send missions to China?

What distinguishes one culture from another?

9. What aspects of Chinese government and culture did the Japanese adopt? Go to your Student Journal to record your answer.

The Rise of the Samurai

Key Ideas
- As the power of the emperor faded, rival clans battled for control.
- Feudal Japan was marked by a strict social order and military values.
- After centuries of warfare, powerful rulers reunited Japan.

Key Terms
- figurehead
- shogun
- feudalism
- daimyo
- samurai
- bushido

 Visual Glossary

→ **Reading Skill Analyze Cause and Effect** Take notes using the graphic organizer in your journal.

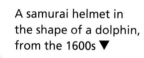
A samurai helmet in the shape of a dolphin, from the 1600s ▼

Prince Shotoku and other reformers tried to unify Japan. They had only limited success. Over time, the power of the emperor faded and Japan became a violent land ruled by rival warriors. Peace was only restored around 1600.

Shifts in Power

By tradition, each new Japanese emperor set up court in his own territory. Then, in 794, the imperial court settled in a new capital city, Heian (HAY ahn). The name meant "capital of peace and tranquility." It later became known as Kyoto. It was modeled after the Chinese city of Chang'an. Emperors lived in Heian for more than a thousand years. But during that time, their power began to shift into other hands.

The Imperial Court The imperial court was divided into different ranks, or levels, of nobles. Privileges and influence depended mainly on one's rank. Unlike China, Japan did not give out government jobs based on merit. Most officials were sons from noble families.

The emperor and nobles of the court appeared to live wonderful lives. Their nights and days were filled with dinner parties, dances, poetry contests, music, and religious rituals. They also produced magnificent art and literature. Among these nobles, the Fujiwara family stood out.

Rise of the Fujiwara By 860, the emperor was no longer the true ruler. The Fujiwara family was running the country. Behind the scenes, they controlled the government for some 300 years. The emperor was a **figurehead,** which means that he appeared to be in charge, but someone else was really in control.

The Fujiwara rose to power by having their daughters marry emperors. The sons of these marriages often became emperors. They made sure that members of the Fujiwara clan got high positions in the government.

In the late 800s, the Fujiwara moved closer to taking complete power. They persuaded several emperors to retire. The position of emperor went to the child who was next in line for the throne.

A Fujiwara leader then became regent for the child. He was now the power behind the throne. When the young emperor was finally old enough to rule, the leader became his advisor, thus holding on to power. The Fujiwara repeated this process again and again.

Fortunately for Japan, most of the Fujiwara were able rulers. But their long rule marked a shift in power. Japan remained unified, but the Fujiwara family was in charge, not the emperor. In addition, nobles came to own most of the land.

Reading Check How did the Fujiwara gain high positions in Japan's government?

my World CONNECTIONS

Kyoto was Japan's capital from **794** to **1868**. Washington, D.C., has been the capital of the United States since **1800**.

◀ Fujiwara no Moronaga plays a lute.

555

resent, *v.*, to be angry about something

Rival Clans Battle for Power

Outside the capital, other clans envied and <u>resented</u> the Fujiwara's power. Some clan leaders began to raise their own private armies. Those leaders became warlords. The warriors that they trained were fiercely loyal to their own clans, not to the Fujiwara or the emperor.

Military Leaders Gain Strength The most powerful of these warrior clans were the Taira (TY rah) and the Minamoto (mee nah MOH toh). They worked together just long enough to push the Fujiwara out of power. Then they turned against each other.

Over long years of war, power moved between the Taira and Minamoto clans. The violence eventually reached Kyoto.

In 1159, Minamoto forces stormed into the capital. They burned the emperor's palace and killed many court officials.

Japan had entered a long period of warfare and suffering. A poet expressed his sadness this way:

> 66 All hung about with cloud,
> The distant mountain meadows
> Are in autumn and
> All I do recall
> Is sadness 99
>
> —Saigyo, translated by Thomas McAuley

The First Shogun In 1185, Minamoto warriors defeated Taira forces in a final clash at sea. As a result, Minamoto Yoritomo (yoh ree TOH moh) became the most powerful person in Japan.

The Heiji scroll tells the story of the 1159 disturbance. In this scene, Minamoto forces capture the emperor.

Yoritomo wanted, and received, the title of **shogun** (SHOH gun), or supreme military commander. In the past, the emperor had granted the title to the leader of the imperial army. The position was supposed to be temporary, but Yoritomo intended to keep the title permanently. In theory, Yoritomo served as advisor to the emperor. In reality, he ruled Japan.

Reading Check How did Minamoto Yoritomo become shogun?

Feudalism in Japan

Yoritomo's rule did not end clan warfare in Japan. It marked the beginning of rule by local lords and their fighters. The central government became weak. Life was often lawless and violent under the shoguns. Local nobles owned much land and fought for power. The result was a new set of social, political, and economic relationships known together as feudalism.

A Strict Social Order **Feudalism** was a social system in which landowners granted people land or other rewards in exchange for military service or labor. Landowners, warriors, and peasants served one another's needs. This system spelled out relationships among those different classes of people.

In the Japanese feudal system, people had clearly defined roles. By the 1400s, protecting people had become the responsibility of **daimyo** (DY myoh), or local land-owning lords. Each daimyo relied on peasants to work the land. In exchange for a share of the crop, he promised to protect them.

The daimyo usually had a large wooden castle, surrounded by a strong wall. It offered some safety from attack. The daimyo also provided protection through a small army of **samurai** (SAM uh ry), or highly trained warriors. In Japanese, *samurai* means "those who serve." In exchange for their military service, the daimyo paid his samurai a salary.

Japanese Feudalism

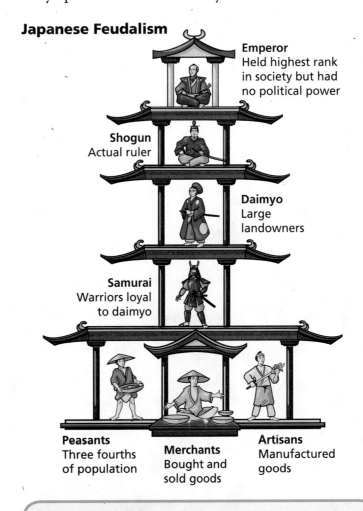

Emperor
Held highest rank in society but had no political power

Shogun
Actual ruler

Daimyo
Large landowners

Samurai
Warriors loyal to daimyo

Peasants
Three fourths of population

Merchants
Bought and sold goods

Artisans
Manufactured goods

Chart Skills

This diagram shows the various groups in Japanese feudal society and their relationships.

1. How might the daimyo have been a threat to the shogun?

2. To which group did most Japanese people belong?

myworldhistory.com

Primary Source

557

Samurai swords in
their sheaths

Samurai helmets were
often very elaborate. ▶

Closer Look

Samurai!

Samurai played an important role in feudal Japan. They were
proud warriors who protected their daimyo and fought to the
death for his honor. Although they worked hard to keep up
their fighting skills, samurai were born into their class.

A samurai's armor was made of small iron plates laced together
with silk or leather. His sword was sharp enough to lop off an
opponent's head in one blow.

THINK CRITICALLY What parts of a samurai's dress
were probably designed to scare opponents?

▲ Samurai battle on a bridge

The Code of Bushido Two ideals guided samurai warriors. One was loyalty to one's lord. The other was personal honor. These formed the heart of a code, or set of rules, called **bushido** (BOO shee doh)— "the way of the warrior." This strict code of conduct guided samurai behavior. It became an official code in the 1600s.

The code of bushido governed a samurai's life. He trained hard, fought bravely, and died with honor. To a skilled samurai, his sword was an extension of his arm. "A man born a samurai should live and die sword in hand," one warrior advised.

Under the code of bushido, loyalty to one's lord was more important than loyalty to family, religion, or even the emperor. If a samurai's lord was in danger, he would follow the lord, even if it meant certain death.

An old story relates a conversation between two samurai whose lord is losing a battle. "The general is surrounded by rebels," the first samurai reported. "It is hard to see how he can get away." The second samurai replied:

> 66 If he must die, I intend to share his fate and go with him to the underworld. 99
> —from *Tale of Mutsu*,
> translated by Helen Craig McCullough

Personal honor was also important. Riding into battle, a samurai shouted out his name and family. He wanted everyone to see his courage and skill. A samurai was also careful about his appearance. His robe, his armor, and even his horse reflected his pride.

Reading Check What two ideals guided samurai warriors?

Mongols Threaten Japan

Mongols took over China in the 1200s. Their ruler, Kublai Khan, sent officials to Japan to demand tribute. They said that there would be war if Japan did not pay for the Khan's friendship. The shogun's government sent the officials away.

The Mongols were terrifying warriors. They fought on horseback and had bombs that exploded with deafening bangs. In November 1274, the Khan sent hundreds of ships across the sea. They carried more than 25,000 troops, along with horses and weapons. This was the first experience Japanese warriors had with gunpowder weapons. Yet the samurai fought bravely and held off the invaders' first attack.

The invaders returned to their ships. That night, a fierce storm shattered them. Nearly 13,000 men drowned. Kublai Khan sent more officials to Japan to demand tribute. This time, the shogun had them beheaded on the beach.

In 1281, Kublai Khan tried again. This time his force was even larger—some 140,000 soldiers. The samurai held off the invaders for nearly two months.

The Japanese prayed to their gods, the kami, for help. A typhoon came roaring across the sea. A typhoon is a violent tropical storm. Thousands of Mongol and Chinese soldiers drowned. More were stranded on shore, where Japanese warriors killed them. The Japanese believed that the kami had sent the typhoon to save them. They called it *kamikaze* (kah muh KAH zee), or the "wind of the gods."

Reading Check How did the Japanese defeat the Mongols?

myWorld Activity
A Samurai Remembered

Samurai armor ▼

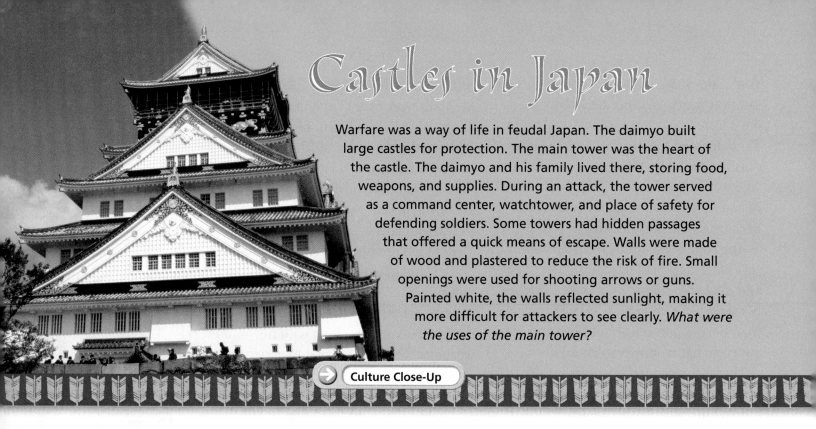

Castles in Japan

Warfare was a way of life in feudal Japan. The daimyo built large castles for protection. The main tower was the heart of the castle. The daimyo and his family lived there, storing food, weapons, and supplies. During an attack, the tower served as a command center, watchtower, and place of safety for defending soldiers. Some towers had hidden passages that offered a quick means of escape. Walls were made of wood and plastered to reduce the risk of fire. Small openings were used for shooting arrows or guns. Painted white, the walls reflected sunlight, making it more difficult for attackers to see clearly. *What were the uses of the main tower?*

Culture Close-Up

Japan Is Reunited

The end of the Mongol threat did not bring peace to Japan. With weak shoguns, the clans continued to fight among themselves. Centuries passed before Japan was unified again.

Strong Leaders Emerge During the 1400s and 1500s, Japan was controlled by daimyo who <u>constantly</u> fought for land and power. Historians call this violent period the "Era of the Warring States."

Finally, in the 1500s, three ambitious leaders managed to end the constant warfare. The first, Oda Nobunaga, worked all his life to bring Japan "under a single sword." Nobunaga did not fully succeed, but he reduced the power of the warlords.

The second great leader, Toyotomi Hideyoshi, unified Japan in 1590. He achieved peace only because the daimyo pledged loyalty to him. When Hideyoshi died, clans began to quarrel once more.

constantly, *adv.*, again and again without end

Tokugawa Ieyasu Brings Peace The third leader, Tokugawa Ieyasu (toh koo GAH wah ee YAY ah soo), united the country again in 1600. He took the title of shogun, then founded a new capital at Edo (present-day Tokyo). Ieyasu made laws that finally brought peace to Japan.

He ordered the daimyo to destroy their castles and spend much of the year in Edo, where he could watch them. When they left, they had to leave their families behind. Edo grew to be a huge city.

Ieyasu officially divided society into four classes: samurai, farmers, artisans, and merchants. Only samurai were allowed to own weapons. Farmers produced food. Artisans made the goods people needed, such as cloth, pottery, and weapons. Merchants traded goods.

Ieyasu's measures ended the violence at last. The Tokugawa family ruled a peaceful, unified Japan until 1868.

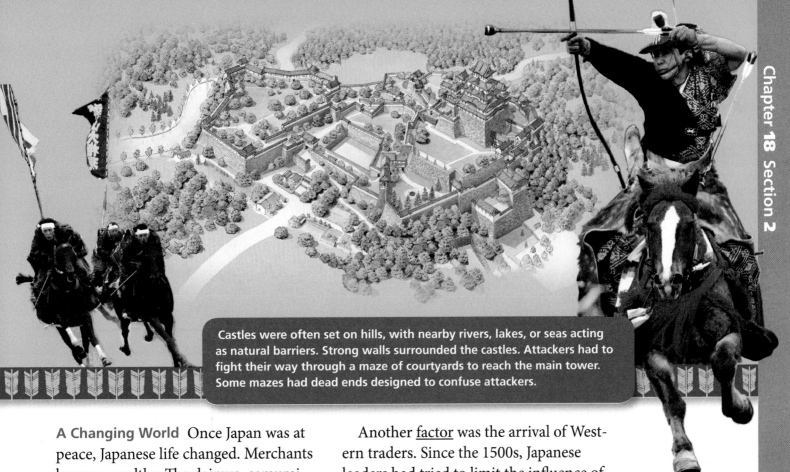

Castles were often set on hills, with nearby rivers, lakes, or seas acting as natural barriers. Strong walls surrounded the castles. Attackers had to fight their way through a maze of courtyards to reach the main tower. Some mazes had dead ends designed to confuse attackers.

A Changing World Once Japan was at peace, Japanese life changed. Merchants became wealthy. The daimyo, samurai, and peasants became less prosperous. Many samurai took government jobs, but others could not support themselves. Meanwhile, famines hurt peasants. Unrest among these groups led, in part, to the end of the Tokugawa shoguns.

Another <u>factor</u> was the arrival of Western traders. Since the 1500s, Japanese leaders had tried to limit the influence of Europeans and other outsiders. In 1853, however, American warships arrived and forced Japan to open trade. In 1868, the last shogun-led government fell.

factor, *n.*, cause

Reading Check How did the Tokugawa shoguns bring peace to Japan?

my worldhistory.com

Culture Close-Up

Section 2 Assessment

? Essential Question

What distinguishes one culture from another?

Key Terms

1. How were the daimyo related to feudalism?

2. Explain the code of bushido.

3. What were the duties of the samurai?

Key Ideas

4. Why were the Fujiwara important to the government in Japan?

5. What was the role of the emperor in feudal Japan?

6. What leaders brought peace to Japan?

Think Critically

7. **Analyze Cause and Effect** How did the rise of the Fujiwara lead to feudalism?

8. **Draw Inferences** Why did Tokugawa Ieyasu force the daimyo to leave their families in Edo?

9. How did the role of the Japanese emperor differ from the role of the Chinese emperor? Go to your Student Journal to record your answer.

Japanese Culture and Society

Key Ideas
- Literature, drama, and art flourished at the Heian court.
- Japanese culture emphasized the importance of family.
- Many Japanese people began to practice Buddhism by the Heian period, but the practice of Shinto continued.

Key Terms • Noh • Kabuki • consensus • Shinto • shrine • mantra

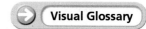 Visual Glossary

Reading Skill Identify Main Ideas and Details Take notes using the graphic organizer in your journal.

A statue near Kyoto shows Murasaki Shikibu, the subject of this chapter's myStory. ▼

China had a strong influence on Japan. But the Japanese added their own ideas and values to whatever they borrowed from China. The result was a country that shared much with its mainland neighbor but still had its own unique culture and society.

Japan Develops a Unique Culture

Many historians call the Heian period Japan's golden age. Lasting from 794 to 1185, it was a time of great cultural flowering in Japan.

Literature Nobles of the Heian court read classic works of Buddhism and Confucianism. They wrote journals, poems, and stories. Significantly, they wrote in a script called *kana*. It was adapted from Chinese characters. Each symbol represented a sound in Japanese. In the past, Japanese writers had used Chinese to tell their stories.

One lengthy story, *The Tale of Genji*, still entertains readers today. The story describes the romantic adventures of a prince named Genji. Murasaki Shikibu, the story's author, joined the Heian court around 1005 to serve the emperor's wife. There she wrote her tale, which is now praised as a great masterpiece of Japanese literature.

Many regard this work as the world's first novel. A novel is a long fictional story, often with a complex plot and many chapters. Murasaki's work, though fiction, has provided scholars with many details about life in the Heian court.

The Japanese Tea Ceremony

The tea ceremony, called *chanoyu,* became popular in the 1400s during the height of samurai culture. The ceremony shows harmony, cleanliness, tranquility, and respect. Today students learn the ceremony in school.

❶ The host prepares a tray with utensils and bowls and offers guests a snack. ❷ Then the host prepares the tea by whipping powdered green tea with hot water. ❸ Finally, the host serves the tea, but does not eat or drink. When guests finish, the tray and tools are removed from the room and the ceremony is over.

Art and Architecture Japanese artists and architects added their own ideas to styles borrowed from China. Heian artists admired Chinese scroll painting, but they developed scrolls with a distinctively Japanese style.

Homes of nobles looked similar in Japan and China. They included several buildings around a garden. But facing the garden, Japanese homes had sliding doors instead of fixed walls. In warm weather the doors were removed and the rooms became part of the garden.

The art of gardening also came from China. The Japanese garden usually had flowering trees and a small stream or pond. It might also have a teahouse. A practice borrowed from China, the formal tea ceremony was designed to calm the mind and heart.

Drama In the 1300s, well after the Heian period, a form of drama called Noh emerged in Japan. **Noh** was drama that appealed to the nobles and samurai. It is serious and intense. A Noh play takes place on a simple, almost bare stage. The players wear colorful costumes and masks. They dance and chant to the music of flutes and drums. Through movement and words, they tell a story.

The early 1600s saw the rise of a new form of drama, Kabuki. Like Noh, it uses music and dance to tell a story. Unlike Noh, **Kabuki** was drama aimed at farmers, merchants, and other common folk. Its stunning sets and flashy costumes excite the senses. During performances, viewers even yell out the names of favorite actors.

Reading Check What have scholars learned from *The Tale of Genji*?

emerge, *v.,* to develop

myWorld Activity
A Taste of Meditation

JAPANESE THEATER

Noh and Kabuki use music, dance, and colorful costumes to tell a story. But they have more differences than similarities. As you read, think about how each type of play would be to watch.

THINK CRITICALLY Which type of play would you prefer? Why?

NOH THEATER

Noh plays are performed on a bare stage with just a few props. One or two actors appear on the stage in brightly-colored costumes and expressive masks. The actors move slowly, playing out serious drama while a chorus chants in the background. Some scholars have compared Noh plays with those of the ancient Greeks.

KABUKI THEATER

Kabuki plays are perfomed on a large stage with a curtain that can be drawn to change scenery. Kabuki is often less serious than Noh and may include comedy. Actors use exaggerated poses and dance to tell a story. Kabuki actors are all men.

Japanese Society

The nobles at the Heian court enjoyed a life of luxury and leisure. Most other people in Japan did not. Yet as the economy grew, the lives of most Japanese improved. One thing that did not change was the society's shared values.

Family Loyalty and Harmony In Japan, family loyalty was a basic value. Following Shinto tradition, people honored their ancestors. The head of a family or clan put the welfare of the group ahead of other concerns. Individuals put family interests above personal interests.

This devotion to family remained strong through the feudal age and beyond. A modern historian wrote,

66 The keys to the continuity and toughness of Japanese society have been the family and traditional religion. The clan was the enlarged family, and the nation the most enlarged family of all. 99
—J. M. Roberts, *History of the World*

Confucianism also introduced the value of harmony to Japanese society. Concern for harmony led to the practice of seeking consensus. **Consensus** is agreement among the members of a group.

Economic Life Most people lived in rural areas, away from cities. Local daimyo kept order. Most rural people worked the land as tenant farmers. They paid rent with crops. As long as they kept up with the rent, the daimyo usually let them run their own affairs. A village assembly made most local decisions.

Despite the violence of the feudal age, Japan's economy grew. Farmers produced more crops, thanks to improved tools and techniques. Craftworkers made more goods to meet the demands of farmers, warriors, and wealthy daimyo. A merchant class arose to carry on the increased trade in goods. Merchants often set up markets near temples and within castle walls. Towns sprang up from these sites and along important travel routes.

Trade with China expanded as well. At first, Japan exported raw materials such as copper, pearls, and wood. In exchange for these items, Japan acquired books, silk, coins, and other manufactured goods. Then the Japanese began to make goods for export, including the world's finest swords. One shipment to China included 37,000 shiny samurai swords.

Status of Women Early in Japanese history, women headed clans and ruled as empresses. That changed, however, with the arrival of Confucianism. Men dominated Confucian relationships. A woman was expected to obey first her father and then her husband.

Some forms of Buddhism held a similar view of women. According to Buddhist scripture, or sacred writings, "no women are to be found" in paradise. Women were barred from some temples. As Murasaki Shikibu wrote in *The Tale of Genji*, "Whatever their station in life may be, women are bound to have a hard lot, not only in this life but in the world to come."

Reading Check How did most rural Japanese people make a living?

despite, *prep.*, even with or in spite of

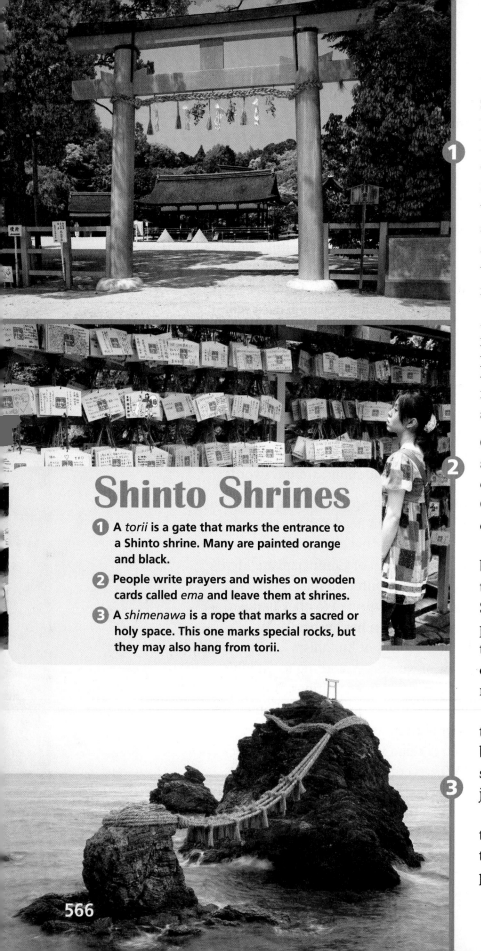

Shinto Shrines

1. A *torii* is a gate that marks the entrance to a Shinto shrine. Many are painted orange and black.

2. People write prayers and wishes on wooden cards called *ema* and leave them at shrines.

3. A *shimenawa* is a rope that marks a sacred or holy space. This one marks special rocks, but they may also hang from torii.

566

Shinto

Shinto is the traditional religion of Japan. It means "the way of the gods." After Buddhism entered Japan, many elements of Shinto merged into that new religion. Shinto lost many followers, especially in the cities. But it remained strong in rural areas. Today, Shinto and Buddhism exist side by side in Japan. Many Japanese think of themselves as followers of both religions.

Scholars believe that Shinto came into Japan with the Yayoi people. This religion had no founder. It had no scripture. It had no permanent set of gods. For centuries, it didn't even have a name. Yet it was a vital force in everyone's life.

Creation Myths Traditional Shinto stories describe how various aspects of Japanese life came to be. The Sun Goddess plays a central role in these creation stories.

One story explains how Japan came to be ruled by an emperor. It explains how the Sun Goddess and her brother, the Storm God, often quarreled. Each supported different clans who were fighting to rule Japan. The Sun Goddess won the conflict. She sent her grandson Ninigi to rule Japan.

The Sun Goddess gave Ninigi three treasures. The first, a bronze mirror, symbolized truth. The second, an iron sword, stood for wisdom. The third, a string of jewels, represented kindness.

Ninigi passed down all three treasures to his great-grandson Jimmu. According to myth, Jimmu became Japan's first emperor in 660 B.C. As a result, all Japanese emperors came to be thought of as living gods on Earth.

Honoring Local Spirits Under Shinto, each clan worshiped its own local kami. The Japanese believed that kami could be found in mountains, trees, rivers, and other natural objects. Through the kami, they learned proper behavior and values.

The Japanese built Shinto **shrines,** or places of worship, wherever they felt the power of kami. Thousands of such shrines still exist throughout Japan. Many people visit them each year. Shinto has grown and changed, but it still influences how the Japanese think and act.

Reading Check Where did the Japanese build Shinto shrines?

Japanese Buddhism

Buddhism originated in India. It attracted a large following in China and Korea before it appeared in Japan. As it spread, this religion changed to meet the needs of different peoples.

Spread of Buddhism When Buddhism arrived in Japan, some people opposed it. They feared that the new faith would offend the Shinto gods. Over time, more and more Japanese accepted the Buddha's teachings.

Yet even as the Japanese turned to Buddhism, they did not completely give up their Shinto beliefs. Buddhism was able to adapt to Japanese needs, in part, because it absorbed Shinto gods. But the appeal of its teachings also attracted many followers. Those teachings took several different forms.

Buddhism

1 Buddhist monks worship inside a temple in Tokyo, Japan.

2 The Golden Pavilion outside Kyoto is a Buddhist temple built in 1955. A retired shogun built the original building in 1394.

3 The Great Buddha Hall at the Todaiji Temple is the world's largest wooden building. Turn the page to learn more about the temple.

567

Mahayana School Long before it appeared in Japan, Buddhism had split into different schools of thought. The largest of these, and by far the most popular in Japan, is the Mahayana school. *Mahayana* means "Great Raft." The name refers to the Buddha's description of his teachings as a raft that carries people across the sea of life to enlightenment.

Mahayana Buddhism teaches that all living beings have the potential to be enlightened. No one is too bad or lowly to be saved. The central sutra (soo truh), or scripture, of the Mahayana school describes the Buddha's universal nature:

> 66 It is like unto a great cloud
> Rising above the world,
> Covering all things everywhere,
> A gracious cloud full of moisture;
> Lightning-flames flash and dazzle,
> Voice of thunder vibrates afar.
> Bringing joy and ease to all. 99
> —Lotus Sutra

THE GREAT BUDDHA OF NARA

The Great Buddha of Nara sits nearly 50 feet tall. It is part of the Todaiji Temple. The statue was built in the 700s, but it was repaired several times after it was damaged in fires and earthquakes.

The monks of the Todaiji Temple were very powerful when Nara was the capital. The emperor even moved the capital to escape their influence. *Why did the emperor move the capital?*

New Sects Emerge Within the Mahayana school, Buddhist monks in Japan founded different sects, or forms, of Buddhism. Each sect taught its own way to enlightenment.

One monk started the Shingon, or "true word," form of Buddhism in the 800s. Followers of the Shingon sect recited "true words" in the form of mantras. A **mantra** is a sacred word, chant, or sound that is repeated over and over to advance one's spiritual growth. This sect's focus on secret rituals attracted many followers among Japanese nobles.

Another sect, known as Pure Land Buddhism, centered on the concept of the bodhisattva (boh di SAHT vah), a merciful being who has <u>achieved</u> enlightenment but chooses to remain on Earth to help others. Pure Land Buddhism appealed to all classes, and it spread widely in the 1200s. Today, it remains the largest Buddhist sect in Japan.

Zen Buddhism Probably the most famous Buddhist sect is Zen. Known in China as *Chan,* this sect came to Japan in the 1100s. The central practice of Zen Buddhism is meditation.

For Zen followers, meditation means the emptying of the mind of thoughts in order to aid spiritual growth. The Buddha was thought to have achieved enlightenment through this form of meditation.

To find enlightenment through Zen Buddhism, individual efforts, not prayers or rituals, are required. That focus on self-control and discipline had great appeal among samurai. Samurai used Zen meditation to help them drive all fear of danger and death from their minds. These samurai had an advantage over more timid opponents in battle. Zen Buddhism also had a strong influence on Japanese art, especially Noh drama.

Reading Check What is the largest Buddhist sect in Japan?

achieve, *v.,* to succeed in gaining something, usually with effort

Inspired by Zen, rock gardens are designed for meditation. ▼

Section **3** Assessment

Essential Question
What distinguishes one culture from another?

Key Terms

1. How is Noh drama different from Kabuki?

2. What is consensus?

3. Describe the role of a mantra in Buddhism.

Key Ideas

4. Describe life at the Heian court.

5. What role does family play in the Shinto religion?

6. What are the teachings of the Mahayana School of Buddhism?

Think Critically

7. **Synthesize** Explain why people can follow both Buddhism and Shinto.

8. **Draw Conclusions** Why did Zen Buddhism appeal to samurai?

9. In what ways did Japanese artists and writers develop Japanese culture? Go to your Student Journal to record your answer.

Chapter **18**
Chapter Assessment

Key Terms and Ideas

1. **Describe** Describe Japan's geography and climate.
2. **Recall** What is an **archipelago**?
3. **Explain** What powers did **clan** leaders lose as a result of the Taika Reform?
4. **Summarize** What was the role of **samurai** in the Japanese feudal system?
5. **Recall** What is **Shinto**?

Think Critically

6. **Identify Main Ideas and Details** How was early Japanese society organized and ruled?
7. **Summarize** Describe how feudalism worked in Japan.
8. **Draw Conclusions** Why did Tokugawa Ieyasu change the role of the daimyo and samurai?
9. **Compare and Contrast** In what ways are Pure Land and Zen Buddhism different?
10. **Core Concepts: Cultural Diffusion and Change** What is cultural diffusion? How did Japanese people borrow parts of other cultures and then change them?

Analyze Visuals

11. What cultural influence came to Japan from Korea?
12. What cultural influence came to Japan from China?
13. Why were China and Korea able to influence Japan?
14. Which area influenced more aspects of Japan's culture?

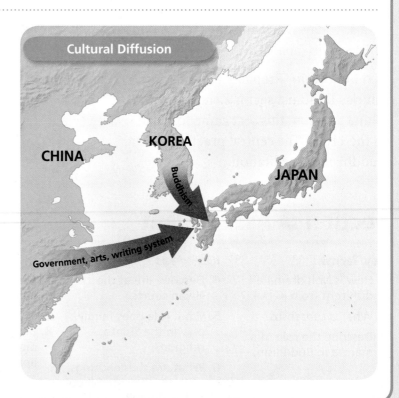

Cultural Diffusion

CHINA KOREA JAPAN

Buddhism

Government, arts, writing system

Essential Question

myWorld Chapter Activity

The Flow of Culture Explore how the Japanese adapted aspects of other cultures, added to them, and created a unique Japanese culture.

21st Century Learning

Develop Cultural Awareness

Japan has a rich cultural history. Describe the development of one aspect of Japanese culture chosen from the list below.
- Flower arranging
- The tea ceremony
- Painting
- Garden design
- Architecture

Document-Based Questions

Success Tracker™
Online at myworldhistory.com

Use your knowledge of Japan during the Heian era and Documents A and B to answer Questions 1–3.

Document A

"One has sent a friend a verse that turned out fairly well. How depressing when there is no reply-poem! Even in the case of love poems, people should at least answer that they were moved at receiving the message, or something of the sort; otherwise they will cause the keenest disappointment."

—Sei Shonagon, *The Pillow Book*

Document B

"[Lady Saisho] had a little fault in the colour combination at the wrist opening. When she went before the Royal presence to fetch something, the nobles and high officials noticed it. Afterwards Lady Saisho regretted it deeply. It was not so bad; only one colour was a little too pale."

—Murasaki Shikibu, *The Diary of Murasaki Shikibu*

1. What can be inferred from Document A?
   A Clothes were very important in Heian Japan.
   B Manners were very important in Heian Japan.
   C People did not expect a reply to a poem.
   D People did not like receiving poems.

2. What can be inferred from Document B?
   A Murasaki frowned upon Lady Saisho's mistake.
   B Appearances were not important at court.
   C Court ladies wore simple clothing.
   D Appearances were very important at court.

3. **Writing Task** Based on these documents, describe what was important at the Japanese court in the Heian era.

myworldhistory.com

Self-Test

571

Trade in Asia and Africa

Key Idea
- Trade was vital to the civilizations of Asia and Africa. Increased trade on Asia's Silk Road and along Africa's east coast had a lasting impact on societies.

During medieval times, different regions of Asia and Africa were linked by merchants who brought a variety of goods to far-away places. The following two documents describe this trade. The first excerpt was written by the Dutch monk William of Rubruck, who, in the 1250s, traveled as a missionary to the Mongol empire. He wrote about trade in what is now the Crimea, in Ukraine. In the early 1500s, Portuguese writer Duarte Barbosa traveled along the East African coast and around the Indian Ocean. In his memoirs, he described trade in these regions.

A Chinese sculpture of a trader on a camel

Read the text on the right. Stop at each circled letter. Then answer the question with the same letter on the left.

Ⓐ **Analyze Details** What does the mention of "Saint Clement"—also known as the Catholic pope Clement I—suggest about the writer?

Ⓑ **Summarize** In your own words, describe the movement and activity of merchants.

Ⓒ **Draw Inferences** How did travel and trade by water likely differ from travel and trade by land?

martyred, *v.,* killed for adhering to a belief
vair, *n.,* squirrel fur
minever, *n.,* a type of white fur
bark, *n.,* small sailing ship

Merchants in Asia

   ❝ So we made sail for the province of Gazaria, or Cassaria, which is about triangular in shape, having on its west side a

Ⓐ city called Kersona, where Saint Clement was <u>martyred</u>. . . . In the middle [of Gazaria] . . . is a city . . . and thither come all the merchants arriving from northern countries, and likewise those coming from [Russia] and the northern countries who wish to pass into Turkia. The latter carry <u>vair</u> and <u>minever</u>, and other costly furs: the others (the former)

Ⓑ carry cloths of cotton . . . silk stuffs and sweet-smelling spices. To the east of this province is a city called Matrica, where the river Tanais falls into the sea of Pontus. . . . [L]arge vessels do not enter it, but the merchants of Constantinople

Ⓒ who visit the said city of Matrica send their <u>barks</u> as far as the River Tanais to buy dried fish, such as sturgeon, barbell and tench, and other fishes in infinite varieties. ❞

—William of Rubruck, about 1255

Read the text on the right. Stop at each circled letter. Then answer the question with the same letter on the left.

D **Identify Main Ideas and Details** What products did African merchants bring with them to sell?

E **Draw Inferences** What is Barbosa saying about the value of some goods?

F **Summarize** In your own words, summarize Barbosa's description of East African trade.

Moors, *n.,* Arab and Berber conquerors of Spain

heathen, *n.,* uncivilized or nonreligious people

laden, *v.,* loaded, burdened

African Trade

❝ [T]hey came in small vessels named *zambucos* from the kingdoms of Quiloa (KIL wah), Mombaça (mahm BAH suh), and Melynde (MEE lind), bringing many cotton cloths, some spotted and others white and blue, also some of silk, and many small **D** beads, grey, red and yellow . . . from the great kingdom of Cambaya in other greater ships. And these wares the said <u>Moors</u> who came from Melynde and Mombaça . . . paid for in gold at such a price that those merchants departed well pleased; which **E** gold they gave by weight.

The Moors of Sofala kept these wares and sold them afterwards to the <u>Heathen</u> of the Kingdom of Benametapa, who came thither <u>laden</u> with gold which they gave in exchange for the said cloths without weighing it. These Moors collect also great store of ivory which they find [near] Çofala, and this also they sell in the Kingdom of Cambaya. . . . They clothe them- **F** selves from the waist down with cotton and silk cloths, and other cloths they wear over their shoulders like capes, and turbans on their heads. ❞

—Duarte Barbosa, about 1518, from *The Book of Duarte Barbosa,* edited by Mansel Longworth Dames

A modern market near Thies, Senegal

Analyze the Documents

1. **Compare** How does William of Rubruck's description of trade in Asia compare to Barbosa's description of merchants in Africa?

2. **Writing Task** Suppose that you are a tourist in the 1500s, exploring the regions described in these two documents. In your travel journal, write a page describing trade in each region.

Chart

Cultural Change

Your Mission In groups, create cause-and-effect charts about how trade affected, and was affected by, African and Asian civilizations. Each group will focus on one of three topics from the unit: geography, exploration and conquests, or power and government. Then it will draw a conclusion about how trade has helped change cultures.

Throughout history, trade has played a key role in the spread and blending of different cultures. Trade itself has been affected by geography, exploration and conquests, and power and government. Take geography, for example. In Africa, traders used camels to transport goods across the hot, dry sands of the Sahara. In Asia, China's Song dynasty built thousands of miles of canals to allow boats to ship trade goods among major rivers.

As you plan your chart and conclusion, think about the role trade has played in the histories of Africa and Asia. Remember, an event may have more than one cause or effect. Your chart should include all of the causes and effects that your group can brainstorm.

Go to myWorldHistory.com for help with this activity.

STEP 1

Identify Information.

Before you can create your chart, you need to know what information you want to present. For example, if your topic is geography, ask: How did geography affect people's lives? Your chart might show how mountains, rivers, and deserts affected trade routes. Take notes on possible causes and effects for your topic.

STEP 2

Create Your Chart.

After you have gathered information about your topic, think about how to show it on a cause-and-effect chart. For example, your chart might show how the gold and salt trades led to the development of African societies. Or it might show the effects of the Tang and Song dynasties on Chinese trade. Review your chart to be sure you have included main ideas and key details.

STEP 3

Present Your Chart and Conclusion.

After finishing your chart, prepare your conclusion. In your group, brainstorm the most important cultural changes related to your topic. Extend your earlier question: How did geography affect people's lives *then* and *now*? In your conclusion, remember to use cause-and-effect signal words, such as *because, due to, since, finally, then, so,* and *as a result*. Then present your chart and conclusion to the class.

myworldhistory.com
21st Century Learning

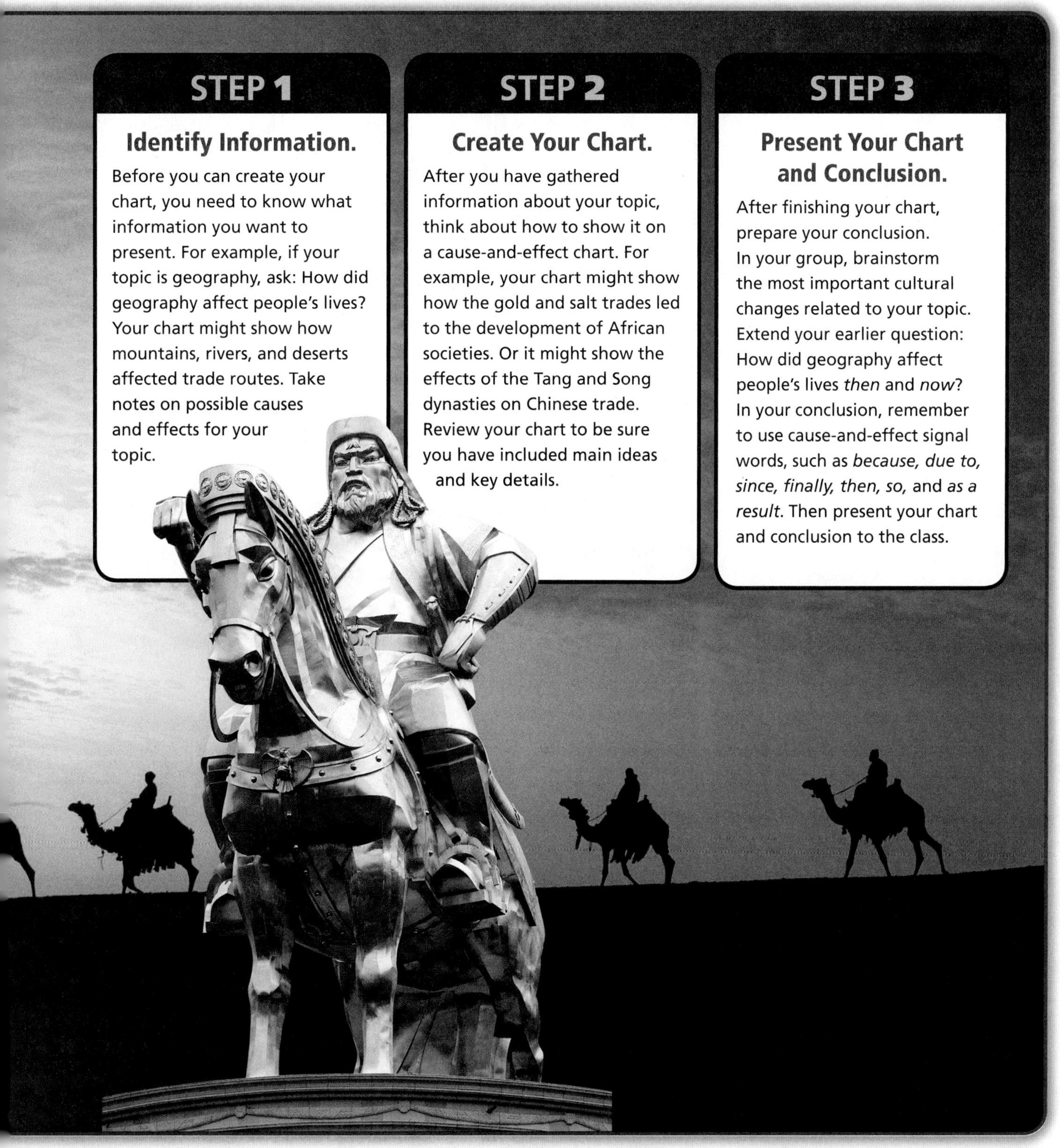

Civilizations of the Americas

North America

Atlantic Ocean

Pacific Ocean

Juanita (1400s) was a young Incan girl who was ritually buried on top of a Peruvian mountain.

Moctezuma I (1400s) was an Aztec leader who greatly expanded the Aztec empire.

South America

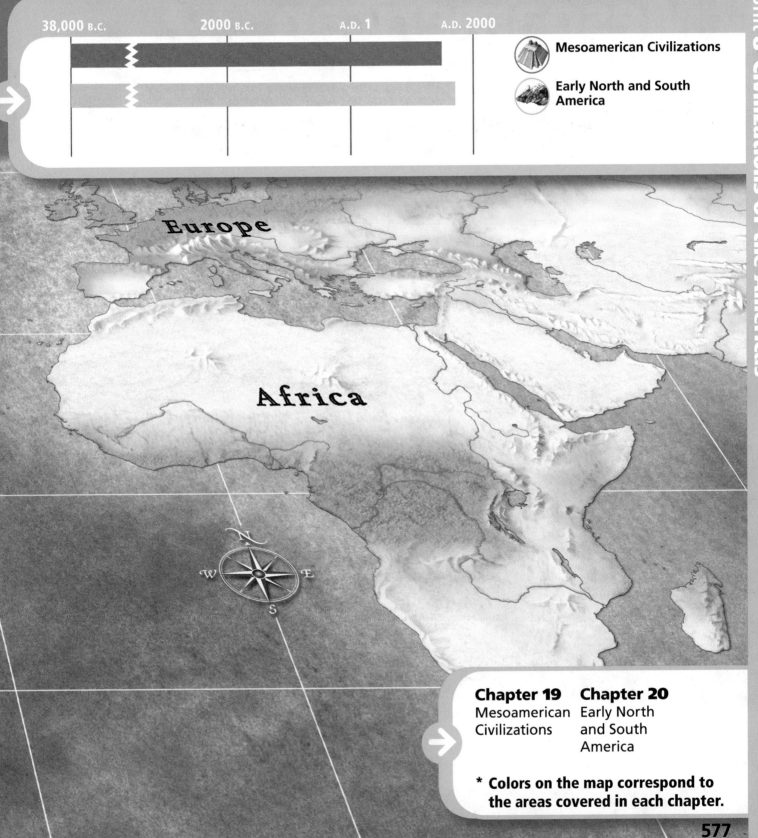

38,000 B.C.   2000 B.C.   A.D. 1   A.D. 2000

Mesoamerican Civilizations

Early North and South
America

Europe

Africa

N
W   E
S

Chapter 19   **Chapter 20**
Mesoamerican   Early North
Civilizations   and South
                America

* **Colors on the map correspond to
   the areas covered in each chapter.**

577

Mesoamerican Civilizations

? Essential Question

What distinguishes one culture from another?

▲ Ruins of a Maya palace, Palenque, Mexico

? Explore the Essential Question . . .

- at worldhistory.com
- using the **myWorld Chapter Activity**
- with the **Student Journal**

Key Dates for Mesoamerica

1200 B.C. Olmec civilization develops.

400 B.C. Olmec civilization disappears.

A.D. 250 Classic Maya civilization develops.

A.D. 1325 Aztecs found city of Tenochtitlan and begin to gain power.

1600 B.C.   800 B.C.   A.D. 1   A.D. 800   A.D. 1600

A.D. 900 Classic Maya civilization declines, but Maya culture survives.

A.D. 1521 Spanish conquer Aztecs.

Moctezuma Ilhuicamina:

He Frowned Like a Lord, He Pierces the Sky Like an Arrow

This is a fictionalized account of events in the life of Moctezuma Ilhuicamina, a real Aztec king who ruled during the mid-1400s.

The Aztec king paused on the shore of Lake Texcoco, close to a causeway, or raised roadway. The causeway led to the island city of Tenochtitlan (tay nawch TEE tlahn), his home. He turned to his army of warriors and their Chalco prisoners, and silence fell.

The king thought of his name: Moctezuma Ilhuicamina (mawk tay soo muh eel wee kuh MEE nuh), meaning "He Frowned Like a Lord, He Pierces the Sky Like an Arrow." He had indeed frowned like a lord and pierced the sky with his arrow—and it had struck the Chalco people. He had conquered the Chalco, just as he had done with the Otomi, Totonac, Huastec, and Zapotec. Their kings had bowed to him and agreed to his demands. Like the others, the Chalco would pay the empire a regular tribute of jade and cotton. For Huitzilopochtli (weet see loh PAWCH tlee), the bloodthirsty Aztec god of war, they would send a regular supply of prisoners.

my worldhistory.com

Timeline/On Assignment

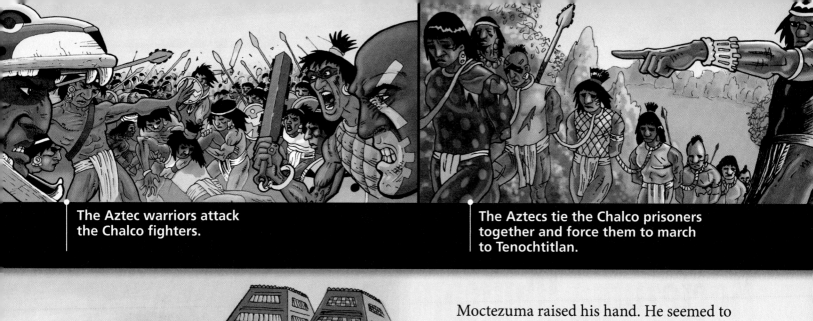

The Aztec warriors attack the Chalco fighters.

The Aztecs tie the Chalco prisoners together and force them to march to Tenochtitlan.

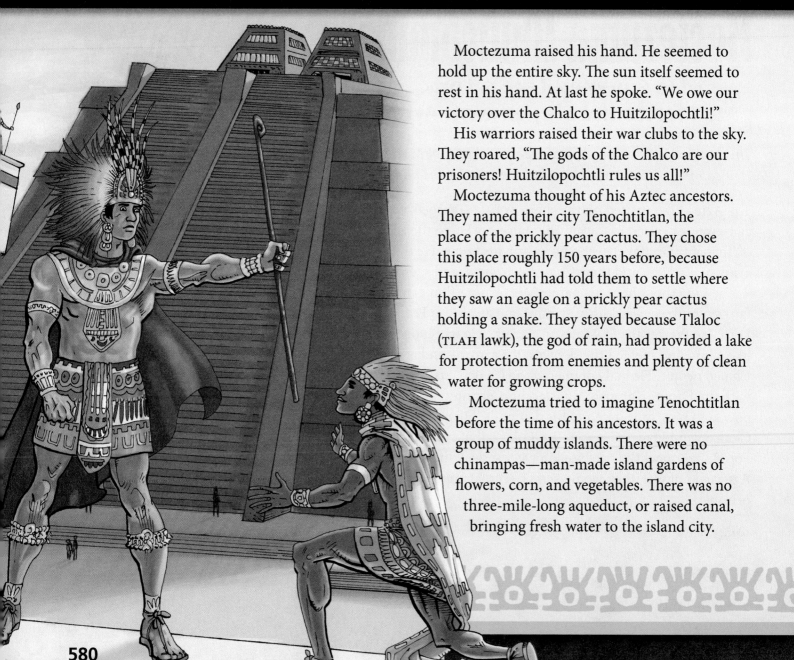

Moctezuma raised his hand. He seemed to hold up the entire sky. The sun itself seemed to rest in his hand. At last he spoke. "We owe our victory over the Chalco to Huitzilopochtli!"

His warriors raised their war clubs to the sky. They roared, "The gods of the Chalco are our prisoners! Huitzilopochtli rules us all!"

Moctezuma thought of his Aztec ancestors. They named their city Tenochtitlan, the place of the prickly pear cactus. They chose this place roughly 150 years before, because Huitzilopochtli had told them to settle where they saw an eagle on a prickly pear cactus holding a snake. They stayed because Tlaloc (TLAH lawk), the god of rain, had provided a lake for protection from enemies and plenty of clean water for growing crops.

Moctezuma tried to imagine Tenochtitlan before the time of his ancestors. It was a group of muddy islands. There were no chinampas—man-made island gardens of flowers, corn, and vegetables. There was no three-mile-long aqueduct, or raised canal, bringing fresh water to the island city.

On a marshy island in Lake Texcoco, Moctezuma's ancestors spotted an eagle holding a snake on a cactus. This was where their god, Huitzilopochtli, had told them to build their city.

As he neared the city gates he wondered if his ancestors would even recognize this magnificent city of Tenochtitlan.

He smiled as one of his warriors exclaimed, "Look at the squash on the chinampas! It is making me hungry for the feast."

Moctezuma turned to his warrior. "Our ancestors have pleased Tlaloc, our god of water." He stretched his arms wide, as if he could embrace the city. "It is because of Tlaloc that we have such plentiful food and clean water."

At sunset, Moctezuma stood with a nobleman and admired the Great Temple in the middle of Tenochtitlan. Moctezuma had ordered that the temple be made larger. "Our empire is growing because Huitzilopochtli and Tlaloc are pleased with us," he had told his engineers. "We must enlarge the temple to keep them happy."

Moctezuma was pleased to see the conquered Chalco prisoners hauling blocks of stone up the temple steps. The Chalco king was commanding the prisoners, just as Moctezuma had ordered.

"They would not cooperate were it not for your leadership," commented the nobleman standing with him. "Our Toltec forefathers would be proud of your majesty, O great lord."

Moctezuma looked down at the man. "We are not Toltecs."

The nobleman swallowed nervously. "I only meant that we are great warriors, O lord, just as they were."

Moctezuma nodded, and the nobleman relaxed. "I see your point. But we are more powerful than the Toltecs ever were. Our gods are stronger. We are better farmers. We are better warriors."

In this story, you read a fictionalized account of Moctezuma Ilhuicamina, a real Aztec king. Based on this story, what do you think distinguishes the cultures of Mesoamerica, or makes them different? As you read the chapter ahead, think about what Moctezuma's story tells you about life in the civilizations of Mesoamerica.

 myStory Video

Join Moctezuma Ilhuicamina as he tastes the fruit of victory.

Section 1
The Maya

Key Ideas

- After people in Mesoamerica learned to farm, civilizations developed in this region of tropical forest and highlands.

- In the Maya civilization, religion and government were closely related.

- The Maya developed a complex writing system and made advances in mathematics, science, and architecture.

Key Terms • obsidian • slash-and-burn agriculture • quetzal • drought • hieroglyphic • observatory

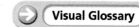 Visual Glossary

Reading Skill Sequence Take notes using the graphic organizer in your journal.

A massive Olmec sculpture, possibly the head of a ruler or god ▼

The oldest civilizations in the Americas formed in an area called Mesoamerica. Mesoamerica extends south from central Mexico into northern Central America. Several advanced cultures, including the Olmec (OHL mek), the Zapotec (ZAH poh tek), and the Maya (MY uh), developed there.

Migration to the Americas

The first people to settle in the Americas came from Asia. They arrived between about 40,000 and 15,000 years ago.

Some of these people probably came by land. Thousands of years ago, Earth's climate was very cold. Much of Earth's water was frozen into ice on land. As a result, sea levels were lower than they are now. Lower sea levels exposed the Bering Land Bridge. This was a strip of land connecting Asia to North America where Alaska is today. People may have crossed that land bridge into the Americas in search of food. Gaps in the ice sheets let them travel south.

Early settlers of the Americas may also have come from Asia by boat. These people would have paddled or sailed from place to place south of the ice sheets along the Pacific coast of the Americas.

However the first people arrived, their descendants spread throughout the Americas. Thousands of years ago, some of these people settled in Mesoamerica.

Reading Check When did people first arrive in the Americas?

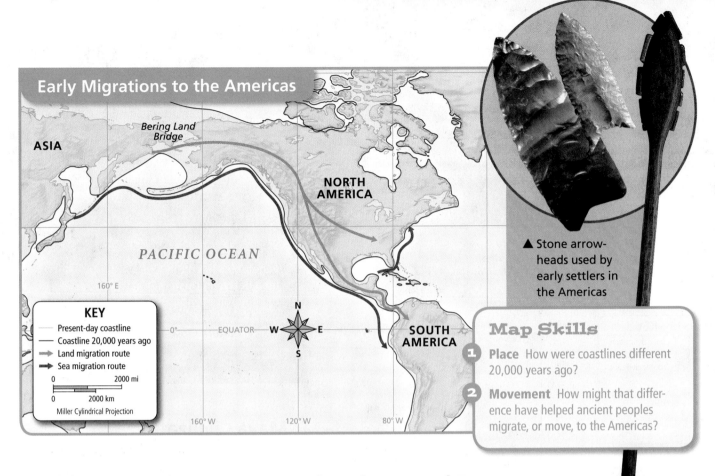

Early Migrations to the Americas

ASIA

Bering Land Bridge

NORTH AMERICA

PACIFIC OCEAN

160° E

SOUTH AMERICA

EQUATOR

160° W   120° W   80° W

KEY
- Present-day coastline
- Coastline 20,000 years ago
- Land migration route
- Sea migration route

0   2000 mi
0   2000 km
Miller Cylindrical Projection

▲ Stone arrowheads used by early settlers in the Americas

Map Skills

1 **Place** How were coastlines different 20,000 years ago?

2 **Movement** How might that difference have helped ancient peoples migrate, or move, to the Americas?

Geography of Mesoamerica

Highlands cover the south of Mesoamerica, and lowlands lie to the north. The highlands have warm temperatures year-round and rain from April to October. The lowlands have a hot, wet climate.

Ash from volcanoes in the highlands has produced rich soils. Volcanoes have also produced **obsidian,** or natural volcanic glass, a rock used in the past to make very sharp blades for spears and arrows.

Heavy rainfall in parts of the hot lowlands supports a <u>dense</u> rain forest. The soil in the rain forest is poor. However, the forest produced valuable resources, including plant foods and animals hunted for their meat, skin, or feathers.

Reading Check What resources are found in the highlands?

The Olmecs and Zapotecs

The Olmec people lived in the rain forest. Because the forest has poor soil, they used **slash-and-burn agriculture,** a farming method in which trees and other plants on a plot of land are cut down and burned. The ash fertilizes the soil.

After a few years, the soil would wear out. When that happened, farmers moved to a new plot and cleared it. They let the old fields rest and grow trees before clearing them again.

Olmec farmers grew corn and beans. They also planted tomatoes, squash, sweet potatoes, cotton, and peppers. As Olmec farmers learned to produce more food, the population grew. Over time, the Olmecs built cities. They set a pattern for future civilizations in Mesoamerica.

dense, *adj.,* thickly clustered

583

Maya Cities

At the center of Maya cities were impressive temple complexes with stepped pyramids and plazas where people could gather. Surrounding the temple complex were the palaces of nobles. Farther away were the houses and fields of the commoners.

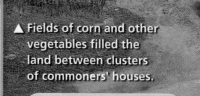

▲ Commoners' houses

Noble's palace ▶

▲ Fields of corn and other vegetables filled the land between clusters of commoners' houses.

→ Culture Close-Up

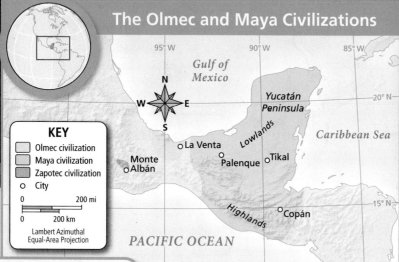

The Olmec and Maya Civilizations

KEY
- Olmec civilization
- Maya civilization
- Zapotec civilization
- ○ City

0   200 mi
0   200 km
Lambert Azimuthal
Equal-Area Projection

95° W   90° W   85° W

Gulf of Mexico

Yucatán Peninsula — 20° N

Caribbean Sea

Lowlands

La Venta
Palenque   ○Tikal
Monte Albán

Highlands   ○Copán — 15° N

PACIFIC OCEAN

Map Skills

1 **Region** Which Maya city was in the highlands?

2 **Location** Using the scale bar, find how far this city lay from the Caribbean coast.

3 **Places to Know!** Label the following places on the outline map in your Student Journal: Yucatán Peninsula, Gulf of Mexico, Caribbean Sea

21st Century Learning

The Olmecs are known for their art, including the huge heads they carved out of stone. These heads may portray Olmec rulers.

Olmec civilization lasted from about 1200 B.C. to about 400 B.C. Although their civilization ended, Olmec beliefs and practices helped shape the cultures of other Mesoamerican peoples.

One of those groups was the Zapotecs. They lived in the highlands southwest of the Olmecs. They built a beautiful hilltop city known today as Monte Albán (MAWN tay ahl BAHN). The Zapotecs developed what may have been the first system of writing in the Americas around 600 B.C.

Reading Check How did the Olmecs influence future civilizations?

Maya Civilization

The Maya lived in what are today Honduras, Guatemala, Belize, and the Yucatán Peninsula in Mexico. Like the Zapotecs, the Maya learned from the Olmecs. The earliest Maya cities developed at the time of the Olmecs. Between about A.D. 250 and 850, the Maya built great cities and made advances in science and art.

Maya Cities Archaeologists have learned much about the Maya by studying Maya cities such as Tikal (tee KAHL), Palenque (pah LENK ay), and Copán (koh PAHN). These cities had hundreds of buildings, including stone pyramids, temples, and palaces. In Maya cities, large, paved plazas were gathering places. Causeways, or raised roads, connected these plazas.

Most Maya people, however, did not live in the center of a city, near the major temples and palaces. Instead, most lived in farming villages surrounding a city.

584

The Maya built temples at the tops of pyramids. ▶

This carving from a temple at the Maya city of Copán shows kings of Copán.

Maya Society The Maya had complex societies. The three main groups were nobles, a middle class, and commoners.

The nobles were people born into powerful families. They included the king, high officials, and priests. Historians think that the nobles controlled the best land and the farmers who worked on it.

Most Maya were commoners who raised crops. Men worked in the fields and on the village buildings. Women raised children, tended gardens and farm animals, and cooked food. They also wove cloth and made pottery.

Lower-ranking lords and higher-ranking commoners formed a kind of middle class. Some were minor officials, soldiers, and scribes. Others were skilled craftworkers who served the nobles.

The basic social unit in Maya society was the extended family. Extended families often included an older couple, their children, and their grandchildren.

Extended families often lived in a group of simple houses around a central patio.

On days of major ceremonies, people gathered in cities for religious festivals. There, they saw great stone pyramids and temples and the palaces of the nobles.

Farming Nobles controlled large plots where corn was grown. Most families also had small plots of their own, where they grew fruit, beans, and other vegetables, and raised turkeys and ducks. The production of food on farms was at the center of the Maya <u>economy</u>.

Like the Olmecs, the Maya used slash-and-burn agriculture in the heavily forested lowlands. Near their cities, they also fertilized fields so that they could use them year after year. On the Yucatán Peninsula, there are few rivers, so the Maya got their water from sinkholes, or deep pits in the ground. They also built cisterns, or tanks, to hold rainwater.

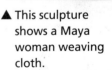

▲ This sculpture shows a Maya woman weaving cloth.

economy, *n.,* the system by which a country's people make a living

my worldhistory.com

Culture Close-Up

585

Trade Traveling merchants linked Maya cities together in a large trade network. Merchants traveled on footpaths or by canoe along the coast.

Merchants traded the natural resources of different Maya regions. Traders from farming villages traded food, cotton, and cacao beans, used to make chocolate. Those from the highlands traded obsidian, jade, and feathers from the **quetzal,** a colorful tropical bird. Traders from the coast brought salt, dried fish, and pearls. In fact, salt was used as currency, like money, in Tikal and other Maya cities.

Maya Government The Maya region contained dozens of independent city-states. Each Maya city-state had its own king. Usually, the kingship passed from a father to his son. Nobles helped run the government. Maya kings increased their power through warfare. Maya cities went to war to take captives. They also fought over control of trade routes and land.

Maya Religion The Maya were a deeply religious people who worshiped many gods. Most of these gods represented forces of nature, such as rain and lightning. Forces of nature often play a part in Maya myths, such as this creation myth:

The Maya and other Mesoamerican people prized the quetzal for its beautiful feathers.

66 First the earth was formed, the mountains and the valleys; the currents of water were divided, the rivulets [streams] were running freely between the hills, and the water was separated when the mountains appeared. 99

—From *Popol Vuh: Sacred Book of the Ancient Quiché Maya,* translated by Delia Goetz and Sylvanus G. Morley

The Maya believed that their priests and kings could communicate with the gods through religious rituals. Priests and kings performed many of these rituals in temples atop pyramids. Temples were built on pyramids so that they could be closer to the gods in heaven. Also, the towering pyramids were meant to show the power of the priests and kings.

Many Maya nobles were priests. Only nobles could become priests. Most kings served as priests before becoming king. Maya commoners feared displeasing priests or kings because they believed that their leaders could call on the gods to punish them.

The most startling Maya rituals were human sacrifice and bloodletting. People killed included prisoners of war, slaves, and even children. Priests also cut themselves and sacrificed their own blood. The Maya believed that these sacrifices were part of the natural cycle of death and rebirth. They saw it as a way to keep the gods satisfied and the universe in balance.

The Fall of the Maya Between A.D. 800 and 1000, many great Maya cities fell into ruin. Warfare was one cause. Drought may also have caused food shortages. **Drought** is a prolonged period of little or no rainfall.

Smaller Maya cities lasted another 600 years in the northern Yucatán Peninsula. These Maya traded with peoples such as the Aztecs. The Spanish conquered the Maya in the early 1500s, but the Maya people and language survive to this day.

Reading Check Why did the Maya build temples atop pyramids?

A Sacred Ball Game

Teams from Mesoamerican cities played a sacred ball game. The king whose team won was believed to have the gods' favor. The team that lost was sometimes sacrificed.

Players scored points by hitting balls through a stone hoop with their hips, thighs, and upper arms. ▶

The ball court was shaped like a short, wide letter H, with a hoop for each team in the middle.▼

◀ This photo shows the grassy ball court, surrounded by stone ramps and walls.

Maya Achievements

At their height, the Maya made many important achievements. They developed a complex writing system, created impressive works of art, and made important discoveries in astronomy and mathematics. Many of these achievements influenced other civilizations of Mesoamerica. Maya culture has also had a lasting influence on the cultures of Mexico and Central America.

Writing The Maya developed the most advanced writing system in the ancient Americas. This system used hieroglyphics. A **hieroglyphic**—also known as a glyph—is a symbol that stands for a word, idea, or sound. The Maya could combine 800 individual glyphs to form any word in their language. Writing enabled the Maya to preserve information that would otherwise be lost.

Maya books recorded Maya learning and beliefs. The Spanish destroyed most of them, but scholars have learned much from the few that survive. Carved glyphs have also been preserved on stone monuments called stelae. These carvings celebrate rulers and their deeds. Unfortunately, they reveal little about daily life.

Astronomy The Maya were excellent astronomers. Although they had no telescopes, they plotted the movements of the sun, moon, and planets. They used this information to predict events such as eclipses of the sun and moon.

Maya astronomers developed a complex system of calendars. They used a 260-day religious calendar and a 365-day solar calendar. The Maya used these calendars to plan religious festivals and seasonal farming tasks. They also used a 394-year calendar for historical dates.

my World CONNECTIONS

Like the Maya, U.S. astronomers use observatories, such as the one at Mount Graham, Arizona.

my worldhistory.com

Primary Source

587

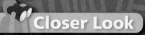

Maya Learning

Maya astronomers made careful observations of the movements of the sun and moon. Their observations were more accurate than those of European astronomers at that time. Maya mathematicians used these observations to develop a complex system of three calendars.

THINK CRITICALLY Why might astronomers need a good knowledge of mathematics?

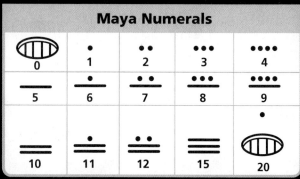

Maya Numerals

0	1	2	3	4
5	6	7	8	9
10	11	12	15	20

▲ Maya mathematicians used a numeral for zero long before Europeans did.

◄ This Maya calendar has three rings. The two small rings show the 20 days of each ritual "month" and the the 13 "months" of the ritual calendar. The larger ring shows the 365 days of the solar year.

▲ Maya astronomers used this observatory to view objects in the sky.

The Maya calculated dates using three calendars. ▶

Maya Calendars

	Ritual Year	Solar Year	Long Count Cycle
	260 days long	365 days long	394.3 solar years long
	Most common way to specify date	Specifies date within 52-solar-year calendar cycle	Specifies historic date
	Close to length of human pregnancy	Close to sun's movement and cycle of seasons	Mathematical cycle not linked to nature
	Used to time rituals and farming activity	Used to time farming activity	Used on monuments for historic dates
	73 ritual years in a calendar cycle	52 solar years in a calendar cycle	7.6 calendar cycles in each long-count cycle

myWorld Activity
The Human
Monument Game

Mathematics The Maya also developed an advanced system of numerals. This system, unlike that of Europeans at the time, included a numeral for zero. Zeros made calculation easier.

Architecture and Art The Maya created impressive architecture and art. All Maya cities contained pyramids, temples, and palaces. Pyramids, the largest buildings, rose hundreds of feet into the air. All had temples at the top. The Maya also built **observatories,** or buildings for observing the sky. Maya astronomers used observatories to follow the paths of the sun, moon, and other objects in the sky.

Maya temples, palaces, observatories, and plazas were made of large stone blocks. To build with such heavy material must have been extremely difficult. The Maya had no horses or oxen and no wheeled vehicles to help them haul the stone. They also lacked metal tools. So they had to cut the blocks using stone tools. Laborers then used their own strength to move the blocks into place.

Today, most Maya buildings are just plain, gray stone structures. But when they were built, they had elaborate decorations. Sculptures of kings, gods, jaguars, and other figures lined the walls. The buildings were also painted bright blue, green, yellow, and red.

Maya artists painted colorful murals on the walls of temples and palaces. Artists also created fine pottery. They crafted jewelry and masks from jade and pearls. Historians appreciate the art of the Maya stelae. These stone slabs are carved with writing about Maya history. They are monuments to the glory of Maya civilization.

Reading Check How did the Maya use their different calendars?

This Maya painting shows a mythical figure, the bird man, standing on a quetzal-feathered snake. ▶

Section 1 Assessment

Key Terms

1. Describe slash-and-burn agriculture.

2. How might drought have affected the Maya?

3. What are observatories, and how did the Maya use them?

Key Ideas

4. How did ancient farmers in the tropical lowlands of Mesoamerica cope with poor soils and thick forests?

5. How were Maya religion and government connected?

6. Describe some of the major accomplishments of the Maya.

Think Critically

7. **Summarize** How did the environment of the Maya affect their culture?

8. **Draw Inferences** How did Maya architecture reflect Maya religious beliefs?

? Essential Question

What distinguishes one culture from another?

9. How were the Olmec, Zapotec, and Maya cultures similar and different? Go to your Student Journal to record your answer.

The Aztecs

Key Ideas	• The Aztecs built a powerful empire through conquest.	• Aztec kings led a strong government and ruled a society organized into clearly defined social classes.	• The Aztec capital city, Tenochtitlan, featured advanced engineering and impressive architecture.

Key Terms • basin • chinampa • dike • absolute monarchy • aqueduct

 **Visual Glossary**

Reading Skill Summarize Take notes using the graphic organizer in your journal.

▲ A man performs a traditional Aztec dance.

A few hundred years after Maya civilization flourished, a new power emerged in central Mexico. In this section, you will learn about the Aztec empire and its civilization.

The Land of the Aztecs

The Aztec empire developed in the highlands of central Mexico. The highlands' geography was different from that of the Maya lowlands.

The Valley of Mexico A broad, high plateau stretches across the central highlands. Because of its high elevation, this plateau has cooler temperatures than the hot Maya lowlands. Volcanoes rise above the plateau. Some of the best farmland in this plateau is located in highland basins below volcanoes. A **basin** is a bowl-shaped area.

One of these basins—the Valley of Mexico—was the center of the Aztec empire. Fertile volcanic soils and water flowing from the mountains around it made the valley a good place to settle. At the center of the Valley of Mexico was a large lake, Lake Texcoco (tays кон koh).

Building a City The Aztecs came to the Valley of Mexico from the north during the 1200s. They first settled on a hill called Chapultepec but later moved to a small island in Lake Texcoco. There they built the city of Tenochtitlan. They built causeways to connect the island city to the lake shore.

This setting had several advantages. Although other city-states surrounded the island, the Aztecs could easily defend it from attack.

The water in the lake and the canals the Aztecs built made it easy to move goods and people. The lake was rich with fish and ducks. The land around the lake was ideal for farming.

The Aztecs added to their farmland by building **chinampas,** or artificial islands. Farming the chinampas helped the Aztecs feed a growing population.

Because the water of Lake Texcoco was at the bottom of a basin, it had no outlet that drained it. Over hundreds of years, it had become brackish, or partly salty. The Aztecs built a **dike**—a wall to hold back water—across the middle of the lake. Mountain streams brought fresh water to Tenochtitlan's side of the dike, which kept the brackish water away from the city.

Conquering an Empire Fierce warriors, the Aztecs began to take on their enemies in the early 1400s. The powerful Aztec army rarely suffered defeat. Soldiers swung heavy wooden clubs spiked with sharp obsidian blades. By 1440, the Aztecs ruled an empire that extended beyond the Valley of Mexico.

During the late 1400s, the Aztec empire continued to grow. By the early 1500s, the empire extended from central Mexico to Guatemala. Around ten million people lived within its borders.

By this time, the Valley of Mexico had become a great urban area of about one million people on and around Lake Texcoco. Goods and people from around the empire flowed into the valley. In the center of Lake Texcoco stood the rich island city of Tenochtitlan, with its magnificent pyramids and glittering palaces.

Reading Check What advantages did the Aztecs gain from living on an island?

BUILDING ISLANDS AND AN EMPIRE

The Aztecs built artificial islands called chinampas in Lake Texcoco. They farmed these islands to feed their capital, Tenochtitlan. The food from these islands helped them conquer first the valley around this lake, then an empire.

591

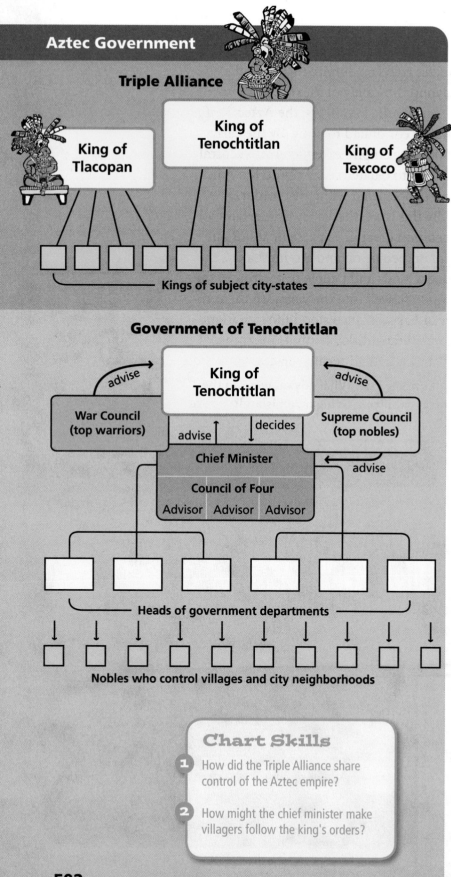

Aztec Government

Triple Alliance

King of Tenochtitlan

King of Tlacopan

King of Texcoco

└─ Kings of subject city-states ─┘

Government of Tenochtitlan

advise → King of Tenochtitlan ← *advise*

War Council (top warriors)

advise ↑ ↓ *decides*

Supreme Council (top nobles)

Chief Minister

advise

Council of Four

Advisor Advisor Advisor

└─ Heads of government departments ─┘

Nobles who control villages and city neighborhoods

Chart Skills

1 How did the Triple Alliance share control of the Aztec empire?

2 How might the chief minister make villagers follow the king's orders?

Aztec Government

The Aztec king, or the king of Tenochtitlan, was part of a Triple Alliance that included the the kings of Tlacopan and Texcoco. They agreed to support each other with troops and to share control of the Aztec empire. After 1428, the Aztec king was the most important ruler in the Triple Alliance. The Aztec king made all decisions having to do with war.

The three kings of the Triple Alliance controlled the kings of the city-states they conquered. These city-states had to send tribute, or regular payments of valuable goods, to the Triple Alliance kings.

Tribute goods ranged from clothing, food, and military supplies to jewelry, chocolate, quetzal feathers, and building materials. A Spanish visitor in the early 1500s wrote that "vast quantities" of tribute flowed into Tenochtitlan every day.

The Aztec king had total power over the people of Tenochtitlan. The Aztecs had an **absolute monarchy,** a system in which one person from a ruling family has unlimited powers.

When an Aztec king died, a Supreme Council of nobles chose a member of the ruling family as the new king. Sometimes kingship passed from father to son, but sometimes it passed to other blood relatives. Three councils advised the king. These included the Supreme Council that chose him and a War Council of warriors. The third, the Council of Four, was led by a chief minister who ran the everyday operations of the government. However, the king made all major decisions.

Reading Check Who chose the Aztec king?

Aztec Society

Aztec society revolved around farming, warfare, and religion. It also had a <u>rigid</u> class structure that shaped people's lives.

Religion The Aztecs worshiped many gods. They believed that the gods gave them life and controlled everything on Earth. The most important Aztec gods were Huitzilopochtli and Tlaloc. Aztecs believed that Huitzilopochtli brought success in battle and made the sun rise. Without human blood, they believed, Huitzilopochtli would grow weak, and the sun would disappear.

The Aztecs sacrificed thousands of victims every year, cutting out their hearts and offering them to Huitzilopochtli. Most victims were prisoners captured in war. The Aztecs also sacrificed young children to Tlaloc.

The Aztecs waged war partly to capture prisoners for sacrifice. The Aztecs also hoped to terrify conquered peoples, making them easier to control. Revolts were common in the Aztec empire, however.

Nobles and Commoners Like the Maya, the Aztecs had two classes: nobles and commoners. Nobles belonged to families descended from the first Aztec king. They lived in large homes and ate the best food. Many were government officials.

Nobles owned slaves. Some were commoners who had sold themselves into slavery to escape poverty. Other slaves were war captives. Slaves could marry and could buy their own freedom. The children of slaves were born free.

Most Aztecs were commoners. Commoners lived simply. Extended families lived in small houses around a shared courtyard. Commoners ate mainly corn, beans, and chili peppers.

rigid, *adj.*, inflexible, unchanging

myWorld Activity
Acrostic Visual Poems

The Great Temple

The drawing above is a reconstruction of the Templo Mayor (TEM ploh my OHR), or Great Temple, in Tenochtitlan. The stone serpent at the left lies in front of the temple's ruins today.

▲ The Aztecs created beautiful feather headdresses like the one above.

▲The Aztec Great Calendar Stone, above, measures 12 feet (3.6 meters) across. It shows the days and months of the Aztecs' 365-day solar calendar.

Agriculture and Economy For most commoners, life centered around farming or household duties. Men tended the fields, while women cooked, cleaned, and raised children. Aztec farmers planted corn and beans together, since they helped each other grow. Farmers also grew tomatoes, chili peppers, and squash, and they raised dogs and turkeys.

Some commoners worked as artisans. Artisans made fine craft goods for noble families, including jewelry and feather-decorated capes and headdresses.

The wealthiest commoners traveled the empire as traders. They traded Aztec craft goods for exotic feathers and precious stones. Trade let each town specialize in a particular craft. In each town, traders would <u>purchase</u> goods made in that town and sell goods made in other towns.

purchase, *v.,* to buy

Reading Check Why was warfare important to the Aztecs?

Aztec Achievements

You have read about the dike the Aztecs built across Lake Texcoco. The Aztecs made other achievements in engineering, urban planning, and the arts.

Engineering and Architecture The Aztecs designed and built an extraordinary capital city. Canals within the city and causeways across Lake Texcoco helped people move goods. The Aztecs built **aqueducts**—canals or pipes that carry fresh water—across Lake Texcoco from the hills surrounding the lake.

At the heart of Tenochtitlan was a large walled plaza. Palaces and temples surrounded the plaza. The largest structure was the Templo Mayor, or Great Temple.

Arts Jewelry was a specialty of Aztec craftsmen. Jewelers made rings, necklaces, and other jewelry from gold, silver, and semiprecious stones.

594

One of the finest forms of Aztec art was feather work. Specialists made fans, headdresses, capes, and shields from the brightly colored feathers of tropical birds.

The Aztecs also carved beautiful stone sculptures. One of the best-known examples is the great Aztec Calendar Stone.

The Oral Tradition The Aztecs did not have a well-developed writing system. They had symbols to represent some ideas, but not an actual written language. Oral, or spoken, language was more important to the Aztecs than writing.

The Aztecs were skilled orators, or public speakers. One of the titles of the Aztec king was "great speaker." Orators told stories from the past and legends of the gods. In this way they passed down Aztec history and religion from one generation to the next.

Poets were highly respected in Aztec society. Even kings composed poetry. The most famous of the poet kings was Nezahualcoyotl (nay sah wahl кон yohtl). In one of his poems, he reflects on the passing nature of life:

> 66Not forever on earth, only a little while.
>   Though jade it may be, it breaks;
>   though gold it may be, it is crushed;
>   though it be quetzal plumes, it shall
>   not last.
>   Not forever on earth, only a little while.99
>
> —Nezahualcoyotl

Historical Influence The Aztec empire fell in the 1500s to an alliance of European conquerors and native peoples who resented Aztec rule. Still, the Aztecs had a lasting impact. Tenochtitlan became Mexico City, the capital of Mexico. To this day, Mexicans cook with corn, beans, and chili. Words such as *chocolate, tomato,* and *avocado* passed from the Aztec language, Nahuatl, through Spanish and into English.

Reading Check Who preserved Aztec history?

Aztec jewelers made necklaces and other ornaments from gold, silver, and gemstones. ▼

Section 2 Assessment

Key Terms

1. Explain the importance of chinampas to the Aztecs.
2. What is an absolute monarchy?
3. Use the word *aqueduct* in a sentence about Tenochtitlan.

Key Ideas

4. What areas did the Aztec empire include?
5. How did nobles play a role in Aztec government?
6. How did people become slaves under the Aztecs?
7. What were some of the Aztecs' engineering accomplishments?

Think Critically

8. **Analyze Cause and Effect** Explain how tribute could have strengthened the Aztec empire and led to more conquests.
9. **Draw Conclusions** How did the Aztecs' location and environment help them conquer an empire?

Essential Question

What distinguishes one culture from another?

10. How was Aztec civilization similar to and different from Maya civilization? Go to your Student Journal to record your answer.

Chapter **19**

Chapter Assessment

Key Terms and Ideas

1. **Recall** Which Mesoamerican civilizations practiced **slash-and-burn agriculture?**

2. **Describe** How were the Mesoamerican highlands and lowlands different?

3. **Recall** Why were Maya priests powerful?

4. **Describe** Use the word **hieroglyphic** in a sentence describing Maya writing.

5. **Discuss** What was the significance of **quetzal** feathers in Mesoamerican civilizations?

6. **Explain** Why did the Aztecs build **chinampas?**

7. **Recall** Why did the Aztecs wage war?

8. **Explain** Why did the Aztecs build **dikes** and **aqueducts?**

9. **Discuss** How were the decisions of Aztec kings carried out?

10. **Describe** What were some impressive features of the Aztec capital, Tenochtitlan?

Think Critically

11. **Analyze Cause and Effect** How might ideas about city building or writing systems have spread from the Olmecs or Zapotecs to the Maya?

12. **Identify Evidence** How do the Maya calendars show the Maya's knowledge of mathematics?

13. **Synthesize** How did the Aztecs both adapt to the geography of their homeland and reshape that geography to meet their needs?

14. **Draw Inferences** What might explain why conquered peoples often rebelled against Aztec rule?

15. **Core Concepts: Political Systems** What were some similarities and differences between the political systems of the Maya and the Aztecs?

Analyze Visuals

Use the chart at right to answer the following questions.

16. Which part of this chart represents Moctezuma Ilhuicamina?

17. Which category in the chart represents traders who buy and sell goods in different parts of the empire?

18. Which category represents an official who controls a neighborhood of Tenochtitlan?

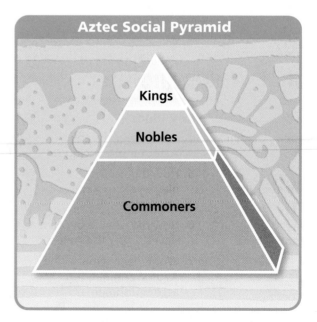

Aztec Social Pyramid

Kings

Nobles

Commoners

Essential Question

myWorld Chapter Activity

The myWorld Journal of History Follow your teacher's instructions to develop text and illustrations for an issue of a historical journal. Your special journal issue will cover the Maya, Zapotec, and Aztec civilizations of Mesoamerica.

21st Century Learning

Solve Problems

Working in small groups, list at least three different ways that scholars can learn about past cultures with few written records. Then think of ways that a scholar might try to learn why so many great Maya cities fell into ruin after A.D. 800. In a paragraph, explain what a scholar might try to find.

Document-Based Questions

Success Tracker™
Online at myworldhistory.com

Use your knowledge of Mesoamerican civilizations and Documents A and B to answer Questions 1–3.

Document A

" Among the treasures that were taken from the people of Yucatán in 1519 by the conqueror Hernán Cortés and his soldiers were some screenfold books, most likely Maya codices. . . . Martyr [a Spanish official] correctly speculated that the books contained information relating to laws, ceremonies, agriculture, computations [mathematics], and astronomy."

—from *Handbook to Life in the Ancient Maya World,* by Lynn V. Foster

Document B

" We found a large number of these books in these characters and, as they contained nothing in which there was not to be seen superstition and lies of the devil, we burned them all, which they regretted to an amazing degree and which caused them great affliction [suffering]."

—from Diego de Landa Calderón's *Relación de las cosas de Yucatán,* translated by Alfred M. Tozzer

1. What does Document A tell you about Maya books?
   A They were of little value.
   B They had information about mathematics.
   C They did not have information about mathematics.
   D The Spanish destroyed them.

2. Based on Document B, written by a Spanish priest, why might so few of these books survive?
   A Everyone thought they were evil.
   B They caused suffering for the Maya.
   C The Maya burned them.
   D The Spanish burned them.

3. **Writing Task** Write a paragraph from the perspective of a Maya person about the loss of these books.

my worldhistory.com

Self-Test

Early North and South America

How much does geography affect people's lives?

▲ Machu Picchu

? Explore the Essential Question . . .

- at **my** worldhistory.com
- using the **myWorld Chapter Activity**
- with the **Student Journal**

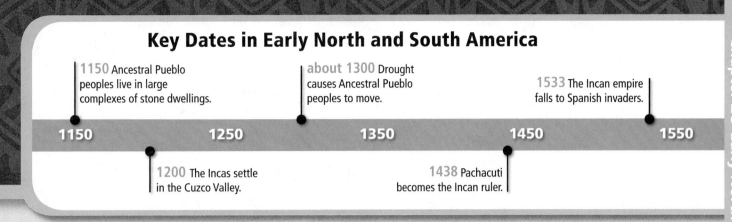

Key Dates in Early North and South America

1150 Ancestral Pueblo peoples live in large complexes of stone dwellings.

about 1300 Drought causes Ancestral Pueblo peoples to move.

1533 The Incan empire falls to Spanish invaders.

1150   1250   1350   1450   1550

1200 The Incas settle in the Cuzco Valley.

1438 Pachacuti becomes the Incan ruler.

The Incan Ice Maiden:
Frozen for Five Hundred Years

Details about the life of this Incan girl have been fictionalized.

A young Incan girl pulled her shawl closer to her body as she stumbled toward the peak of a tall mountain. The wind that whipped her face smelled of ash from a nearby erupting volcano. The ash had poisoned the water and killed crops below. People were starving, but she would help them. She would "live with the gods," making them happy and improving life for the people in the valley.

The girl had been climbing for hours since eating a meal of vegetables at a high mountain camp. She was tired. As she fell onto one knee, she felt a hand on her shoulder. An Incan priest put a flask to her lips and she tasted a sweet liquid that made her feel drowsy. She was relieved when the priest picked her up and carried her.

That girl climbed Mount Ampato in the 1400s. Fast forward to 1995, when an archaeologist and his assistant climbed that same mountain to investigate ancient Incan sites in the Andes. With snow and darkness falling, they saw red feathers sticking out of a ridge. It was a small gold statue. Nearby, they discovered a bundle containing the girl's body and other offerings.

myworldhistory.com

Timeline/On Assignment

Scared villagers watch the volcano as it spouts ash, ruining their crops and poisoning their water.

Juanita looks down at Cuzco, where she will be celebrated.

They called her Juanita, though it is a Spanish name rather than an Incan one. Science and educated guesses helped them to piece together her story. Juanita taught the scientists more about the Incas. Juanita's mummy bundle contained food, coca leaves, shells, pottery, and hair clippings, probably from her first haircut. Little statues in fine clothing were perhaps meant as companions for the girl in her journey beyond death, her life with the gods.

Juanita was about 13 years old when she died. She wore a brilliant red and white wool shawl, held with

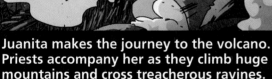

Juanita makes the journey to the volcano. Priests accompany her as they climb huge mountains and cross treacherous ravines.

A priest carries Juanita up Mount Ampato, a mountain near the volcano.

silver pins. The shawl covered a multicolored dress. Her long black braid was tied to a belt woven with geometric patterns. Her clothes told scientists that she probably came from a noble family, maybe even lived near Cuzco, the Incan capital.

Scientists could tell that Juanita had been healthy. Like all children chosen for such honor, she was physically perfect. She had nice teeth, high cheekbones, and lovely skin.

Juanita would have studied religion and learned to cook and to weave. Making beautiful cloth was a source of great pride to the Incas, and all women participated. Clothes showed status, and the nobles wore cloth of the finest fibers in rich colors, threads of gold and silver woven into the designs.

But why would the Incas offer a human child as a sacrifice? The Incas conducted many sacrifices, but they were usually guinea pigs or, for important occasions, llamas. It was only in an extreme situation that a child would be sacrificed. In Juanita's case, the erupting volcano caused starvation and death. The Incas believed that Juanita would stop the tragedy in the valley below when she joined the gods. It was an honor for Juanita to be selected.

Once Juanita was chosen, she probably traveled to Cuzco with its lavish temples. Other children joined her, but Juanita was the most important.

The children were sent from Cuzco with dancing and singing. From there, they trekked toward the mountain with priests and llamas carrying supplies. It might have taken weeks or months.

The ascent up the mountain was difficult, with the air becoming thinner as the children climbed higher. The priests and others built camps to rest.

On the final trip to the mountain peak, Juanita may have become dizzy and struggled to breathe. The priests gave her leaves to chew and a drink to make her tired and to stop any pain. Five hundred years later, Juanita helped modern people learn about her culture.

What does this story tell you about how geography affected the Incas? As you read on, think about what Juanita's story tells you about life in the Incan empire.

myStory Video

Learn more about the Incas.

Section 1

The Incas

Key Ideas
- The geography of the Andes shaped Incan civilization.
- The Incas had a highly organized government and society.
- The Incas' achievements in government, engineering, and the arts place them among the world's great civilizations.

Key Terms • Andes • terrace • quipu • hierarchy • ayllu • mita system  **Visual Glossary**

 Reading Skill Summarize Take notes using the graphic organizer in your journal.

This Incan doll was dressed to match the child with whom it was buried. ▼

Advanced civilizations arose throughout South America long before Europeans arrived in the 1500s. The greatest of these was the Incan empire. At its peak, it stretched 2,500 miles.

Geography Shapes Life

Many peoples lived in the Andes region before the Incas arrived. High mountains shaped the way of life for them and the Incas.

Life in the Andes The **Andes** (AN deez) are a mountain range along the western edge of South America. These huge mountains are a hard place for people to live. The slopes are rocky and steep. The climate is cold. Breathing is difficult because the air is thin at high elevations. The Incas and others before them adapted to these harsh conditions.

Other Geography A narrow desert lies between the Andes and the Pacific Ocean. The world's largest rain forest, the Amazon, lies to the east of the Andes. These provided resources for Andean people.

Andean Agriculture The first advanced cultures of South America appeared in the Andes region long before the Incas. As in other places, agriculture led to the growth of civilization. Andean peoples farmed lands along rivers. They also farmed the hillsides by cutting **terraces,** or strips of level land that are planted with crops. Irrigation canals carried water to terraces. With this technology, people grew more food, including corn, chili peppers, squash, beans, cotton, peanuts, and hundreds of types of potato.

Andean people hunted game on the mountain slopes and fished in the nearby ocean. Farmers raised llamas and alpacas, which are related to the camel. Andean people used llamas for meat and to carry large loads. Alpacas provided soft wool.

Reading Check How did the Incas change their environment?

The Incan Empire

The Incas built an empire in the 1400s and 1500s by taking over the lands of other peoples. Their success was partly due to their well-organized society.

The Incan Empire Grows Historians believe the Incas settled in the valley of Cuzco (KOOS koh), in present-day Peru, around 1200. Over the next 300 years, they built a great empire, led by a series of warrior-kings called Sapa Incas.

The greatest Sapa Inca was Pachacuti (pahch ah KOO tee), who took power in 1438. Under Pachacuti, the Incas built a powerful army. Marching into battle, soldiers often sang bloodthirsty songs to terrify their enemy. One such song began:

❝ We'll drink . . . from your skull,
From your teeth we'll make a necklace,
from your bones, flutes. ❞
 —Incan victory song

A strong army helped the Incas expand, but they preferred not to use it. Pachacuti offered peace and protection to those who agreed to join the empire. They kept their local rulers and customs. In return, they paid taxes in the form of labor and accepted Incan authority. Pachacuti ruled for more than 30 years.

A Strong Government Incan government was centered in Cuzco. Below the Sapa Inca, four governors each ruled a province. Below them, the administration was based on multiples of ten. Each village was divided into groups of ten families. Those were organized into larger groups of 100, 1,000, and 10,000 families. A government official was responsible for each group.

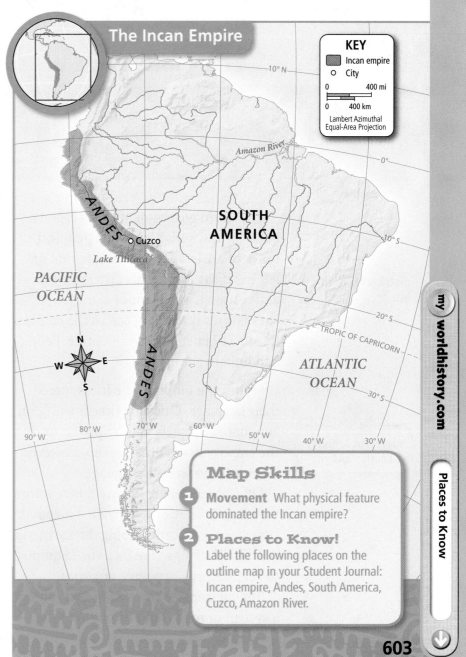

The Incan Empire

KEY

Incan empire
○ City

| 0 | 400 mi |
| 0 | 400 km |

Lambert Azimuthal
Equal-Area Projection

Map Skills

1 **Movement** What physical feature dominated the Incan empire?

2 **Places to Know!** Label the following places on the outline map in your Student Journal: Incan empire, Andes, South America, Cuzco, Amazon River.

603

Incan Engineering

The Incas' practical talents were clear in engineering and architecture. Their building skills were so great that the Incas are often compared to the ancient Romans. Many Incan buildings are still standing, having survived many centuries and many earthquakes. The Incas are also famous for their roads. They expanded the road system through the mountains, connecting and adding to those built by Andean peoples who came before them.

THINK CRITICALLY How did Incan engineers meet challenges of living in the Andes?

An Incan road leads up a mountain. Llamas and alpacas could navigate these steep roads.

Terraces turned mountainsides into usable fields.

distribute, *v.,* to give out

**myWorld Activity
A Knotty Problem**

The Incan government took responsibility for the well-being of its people. In times of crisis, such as a crop failure or natural disaster, officials <u>distributed</u> food and clothing. These goods came from storehouses spread out across the empire. But these benefits came at a price. People had little freedom.

Unifying the Empire The Incas forced their language, Quechua (KECH wuh), on conquered peoples. This helped to unify the empire. It was only spoken, however. There was no written language.

Official messengers sped reports across the empire. They often carried a **quipu** (KEE poo), a record-keeping device made of knotted strings. The Incas used quipus to keep records of people or goods.

The messengers traveled quickly along a system of roads built throughout the empire. Soldiers could also be sent along the roads to put down rebellions.

The End of the Empire The last great Sapa Inca, Huayna Capac (WY nuh kah PAHK), took power in 1493. By this time, the Incan empire stretched 2,500 miles from north to south. It may have included as many as ten million people who lived mostly in peace.

This time of peace did not last long. Huayna Capac died between 1525 and 1530 without arranging for a successor.

Two of Huayna Capac's sons fought to decide who would take his place. Their brutal civil war shattered the Incan world. The war had barely ended when Spanish soldiers invaded. The weakened empire fell to the invaders, called conquistadors.

Reading Check How did the Incan government respond to natural disasters?

604

Local people helped build bridges made from natural fibers.

Doors and windows in the shape of a trapezoid help buildings withstand earthquakes.

Incan Achievements

The Incas achieved great feats in architecture, astronomy, and metalwork.

Architecture The Incas were great architects. They built with huge stone blocks. They cut the blocks with great precision using only stone tools. Each stone fit in place perfectly. No <u>mortar</u> was needed to hold the blocks together. Many Incan buildings still stand after hundreds of years.

Incan cities were marvels of stone architecture. The Incan capital of Cuzco was filled with great palaces and temples. "Cuzco was grand and stately," wrote an early Spanish visitor. "It had fine streets . . . and the homes were built of solid stones, beautifully joined."

The Incas' greatest engineering feat was their road system. Incan roads stretched more than 15,000 miles across the empire. They crossed deserts, mountains, and jungles. They also spanned rivers on bridges that swung from cables. In some places, floating bridges rested on pontoons. Incan roads, often paved with stone, were very durable. Today, they can still be seen in parts of the Andes.

Arts and Crafts The Incas called gold the "sweat of the sun" and silver the "tears of the moon." With these metals, they crafted jewelry, dishes, statues, and wall decorations. Here is how a Spaniard described the Temple of the Sun in Cuzco:

> 66 The . . . doors were covered with sheets of [gold]. There was an image of the sun, of great size made of gold, beautifully wrought and set with precious stones. 99
>
> —Pedro de Cieza de León

mortar, *n.,* a cement mixture used to hold bricks together

605

Machu Picchu

Machu Picchu is a famous Incan site that sits high on a mountain ridge. It was a royal estate for Incan nobles that was forgotten by outsiders for more than 300 years. Local Peruvians used its terraces and aqueducts, but it was considered "undiscovered" until 1911 when a local guide showed the site to an American professor.

Incan nobles, like the one pictured here, probably stayed at Machu Picchu. ▶

The Incas valued textiles even more than gold. They wove richly colored and patterned cloth out of cotton, alpaca, and vicuña. Vicuña is an animal similar to the llama and the alpaca. Like the alpaca, it has rich, soft fur. Today, descendants of the Incas still produce beautiful textiles using ancient techniques and designs.

Science Like other ancient peoples, the Incas were skilled in astronomy. Astronomy is the study of stars, planets, and other heavenly bodies. The Incas made careful observations of the locations of different groups of stars. Many of the stars and planets were linked to gods and myths of their religion.

The Incas also studied movements of the sun and moon to develop calendars. These were used to decide when to plant crops or celebrate festivals. They knew which days of the year had the most and fewest hours of daylight and on which days daylight and night were equal.

Reading Check Why are the Incas known for their building?

Incan Society

Incan society was marked by strong government, religion, and a class system.

Social Order Incan society was divided into two large classes: nobles and commoners. Each class had its own hierarchy. A **hierarchy** is a system for ranking members of a group according to their importance.

The highest ranking nobles were close relatives of the ruling family. They lived in the finest houses, enjoyed the best food and clothes, and held the highest positions in government. The lower ranks of nobles held lower government positions. These included non-Incan local leaders.

Most non-Incan peoples were commoners. They were divided into categories based on age and gender. Each category had its own work and duties. For example, boys between the ages of 12 and 18 herded llamas and alpacas. Girls aged 9 to 12 gathered wild plants for dyes and medicines. Men aged 25 to 50 raised crops and served as soldiers.

Economy Incan society was organized into ayllus. The **ayllu** was a group of related families that pooled resources to meet people's needs. It owned and distributed land. The leader distributed food and materials to make sure that everyone received the goods they needed.

There was no money, so people paid taxes with labor. This was called the **mita system**. Under the Incas, the ayllu's land was divided into three parts: one for the government, one for the priests and gods, and one for the people.

Members of the ayllu farmed government and religious lands to pay the mita.

The government saved the crops for the army, times of famine, and ceremonies.

Incan Religion The Incas worshiped many gods. The most important was Inti, the sun god. The Incas believed they were descended from Inti. The Sapa Inca was honored as Inti's descendant and a living god. As long as they honored the Sapa Inca, conquered people were allowed to worship their own deities as well.

Reading Check How was land divided in the Incan empire?

This golden llama was buried as an offering to a mountain god. ▼

Textiles, or woven fabrics, were very important in Incan culture. Wealthy Incas wore brightly colored clothes such as these.

Section 1 Assessment

Key Terms
1. Describe the Andes.
2. What was the purpose of a quipu?
3. What was an ayllu?
4. Why was the mita paid with labor?

Key Ideas
5. How did the Incas grow crops in the Andes?
6. How did the Incas organize their empire?
7. Why was the road system important for unifying the Incan empire?

Think Critically
8. **Compare Viewpoints** How do you think conquered people felt about joining the Incan empire? Why?
9. **Make Decisions** What was the Incas' greatest achievement? Explain.

Essential Question
How much does geography affect people's lives?

10. In what ways were the Incas shaped by their environment? Go to your Student Journal to record your answer.

North American Cultures

A clay water vessel ▶

Key Ideas

- Much of our knowledge of early North American cultures comes from the archaeological evidence they left behind.
- Native American cultures were shaped by where people lived.
- There were many diverse native cultures in North America.

Key Terms
- artifact
- drought
- wigwam
- longhouse
- tepee
- igloo
- potlatch

→ **Visual Glossary**

 Reading Skill **Compare and Contrast** Take notes using the graphic organizer in your journal.

▲ These Native American cave drawings are found in Utah.

Native North Americans lived in places with very different landforms, weather, and vegetation. Each group developed a way of life that matched its resources, including unique beliefs, languages, and traditions. Historians divide later groups into ten culture areas. These are described in this section and shown on the map at the end.

Early North American Cultures

The first people to settle in the Americas came from Asia more than 15,000 years ago. Over time, people settled all over the Americas. Native North Americans did not leave written records. Even so, scientists have learned a lot about these peoples by studying artifacts. **Artifacts** are objects people make, such as tools, pottery, or jewelry. Scientists study them to figure out what crops Native Americans grew, what they hunted, what they wore, and what their homes were like.

The Ancestral Pueblo Several groups of people settled in the region that became the southwestern United States. They are called Ancestral Pueblo because they are the ancestors of people the Spanish later called the Pueblo peoples. Archaeologists also call them the Anasazi. They flourished for hundreds of years and built complex cultures.

At first, they dug houses into the ground. By 1150, they were building connected stone homes similar to apartment buildings. They had up to four stories and were sometimes built into the sides of cliffs.

Little rain fell in the Southwest, so the Ancestral Pueblo people had to use water wisely. For example, they dug ditches to carry water from streams to fields where they grew corn, beans, and squash.

Long droughts around 1300 made farming difficult. A **drought** (drowt) is a period of little or no rain. In response, Ancestral Pueblo groups left their villages and moved south. Some settled near rivers, where it was easier to farm. Others returned to hunting and gathering.

The Mississippians Another <u>complex</u> culture arose in the Mississippi River valley. It is known as Mississippian culture. Like the Ancestral Pueblo, the Mississippians lived in large communities and corn was their most important crop. Both cultures reached a peak between 1000 and 1300. But there were also big differences between these cultures.

The Mississippians are called mound builders because they made hills of earth near their villages for religious reasons. They respected the sun and their ancestors. Some mounds rose as high as 100 feet and covered many acres. Temples and priest-leaders' homes sat on the mounds.

Mississippian villages grew because of advances in farming. For example, they used tools such as hoes to help grow maize, another name for corn. The largest Mississippian town was Cahokia (kuh HOH kee uh), in today's state of Illinois. More than 10,000 people lived there.

complex, *adj.,* having many parts, advanced

Early North Americans

KEY
- Ancestral Pueblo culture area
- Mississippian culture area

0   400 mi
0   400 km
Albers Conic Equal-Area Projection

ATLANTIC OCEAN

PACIFIC OCEAN

Gulf of Mexico

Map Skills

Location Where did the Ancestral Pueblo live in relation to the Mississippians?

21st Century Learning

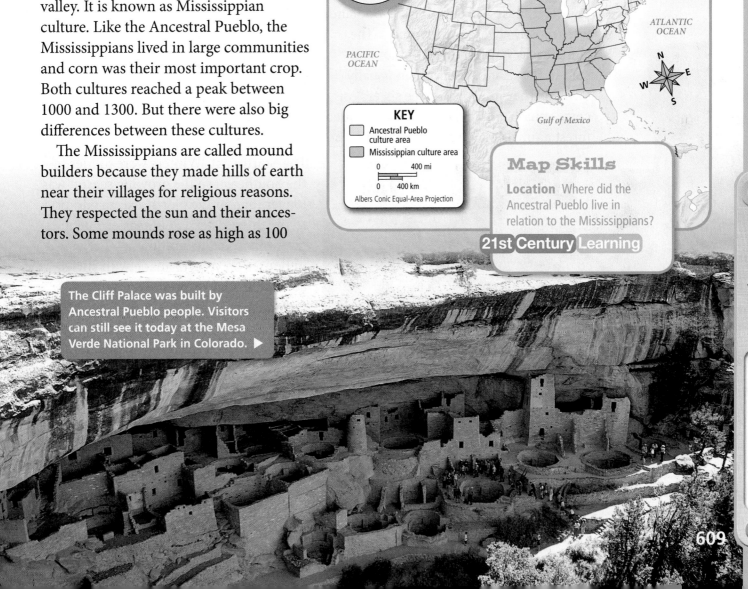

The Cliff Palace was built by Ancestral Pueblo people. Visitors can still see it today at the Mesa Verde National Park in Colorado. ▶

my worldhistory.com

21st Century Learning

Corn (1), beans (2), and squash (3) were known as "the three sisters" because they grew well together and were very important to many groups of Native Americans. *What do you think Native Americans ground with the mortar and pestle shown below?* ▼

As with the Ancestral Pueblo, a drought made it difficult for the Mississippians to grow their corn, beans, and squash. This led to violence between groups, so villagers surrounded their towns with thick walls made of logs and made alliances with other groups.

Reading Check **Why did the Ancestral Pueblo leave their villages?**

The Eastern Woodlands

By the 1500s, the Northeast and Southeast were home to groups called Eastern Woodlands peoples.

The Northeast The Northeast woodlands were mostly covered with forests. The climate was warm in the summer and cold in the winter. The women usually farmed. They grew "the three sisters" of corn, squash, and beans. The men hunted forest animals like deer and wild turkey.

The Three Sisters

Some fished from canoes made from tree trunks or birch bark.

Most people lived in a longhouse or a wigwam. A **wigwam** was a home formed by bending the trunks of young trees and tying them together to make a round frame. It was covered with bark or reed mats. A **longhouse** was similar, but rectangular. Each longhouse was home to several branches of an extended family.

In the 1500s, five groups in today's New York State formed the Iroquois League to end frequent wars among them. Each nation governed itself, but a joint council decided important matters. They agreed upon a constitution for the League:

66 Thus shall all Great Peace be established and hostilities shall no longer be known between the Five Nations but only peace to a united people. 99

—The Constitution of the Five Nations

The Southeast Winters were milder in the Southeast, so the growing season was longer than in the Northeast. In addition to the three sisters, Southeastern peoples grew tobacco and sunflowers. They lived in houses on stilts or made with sticks covered in clay or mud.

Some peoples of this region, such as the Natchez, followed Mississippian traditions. They lived in villages, built mounds, worshiped the sun, and had social classes.

Other groups lived in the forest, hunting and gathering. Social classes were less important for these groups.

Reading Check **What is a longhouse?**

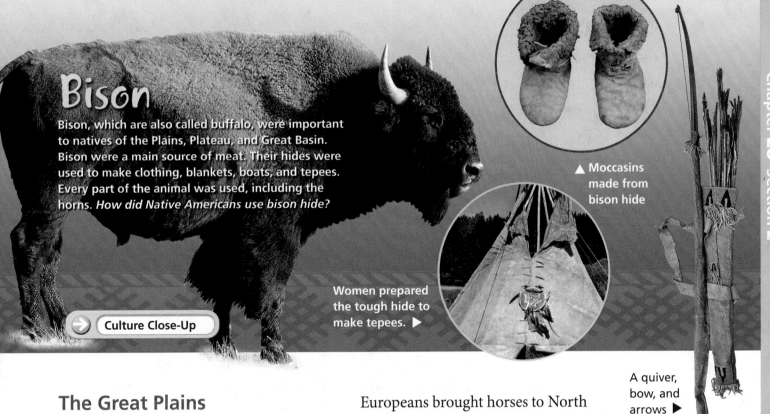

Bison

Bison, which are also called buffalo, were important to natives of the Plains, Plateau, and Great Basin. Bison were a main source of meat. Their hides were used to make clothing, blankets, boats, and tepees. Every part of the animal was used, including the horns. *How did Native Americans use bison hide?*

Culture Close-Up

▲ Moccasins made from bison hide

Women prepared the tough hide to make tepees. ▶

A quiver, bow, and arrows ▶

my **worldhistory**.com

Culture Close-Up

The Great Plains

Many Native American groups lived on a vast grassland called the Great Plains. It stretches across central North America. In 1500, the Plains were home to huge herds of bison. These animals were very important to the Native Americans who lived on the Plains.

Before the arrival of Europeans, many Plains peoples were farmers. They lived in villages along rivers. Their homes were large, round, and made from dirt and grass. They grew corn, beans, squash, sunflowers, and tobacco.

Bison hunts took place outside the planting and harvesting seasons. Men followed the bison on foot, shooting them with bows and arrows.

When the hunt was over, women prepared the animal skin, called the hide, to make leather. They made tools from bones and cooking pots from the stomachs. They used most other parts of the animal for food.

Europeans brought horses to North America. Hunting from horseback quickly became part of Plains life. Horses easily carried goods, allowing more groups to become migrants. That means that they moved from place to place rather than staying in villages.

Migrant groups lived in portable, cone-shaped homes called **tepees**. Some people used dogs to drag their tepees from place to place, but horses later took their place.

The Sun Dance was a religious ritual that took place during the spring or summer. The members of a tribe all gathered in one placc to watch warriors dance for several days without eating or drinking. They believed that these efforts would help the whole group in the coming year.

Many <u>distinct</u> groups lived on the Plains. They spoke many different languages, but they traded using a sign language developed for that purpose.

Reading Check How did the horse change life for the Plains peoples?

distinct, *adj.,* separate, diverse

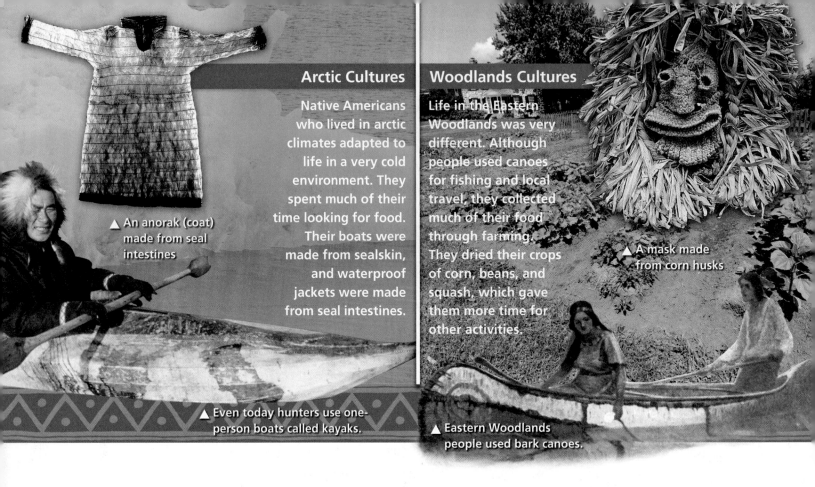

Arctic Cultures

Native Americans who lived in arctic climates adapted to life in a very cold environment. They spent much of their time looking for food. Their boats were made from sealskin, and waterproof jackets were made from seal intestines.

▲ An anorak (coat) made from seal intestines

▲ Even today hunters use one-person boats called kayaks.

Woodlands Cultures

Life in the Eastern Woodlands was very different. Although people used canoes for fishing and local travel, they collected much of their food through farming. They dried their crops of corn, beans, and squash, which gave them more time for other activities.

▲ A mask made from corn husks

▲ Eastern Woodlands people used bark canoes.

The North and Northwest

Northern North America includes three culture areas. They are the Arctic, the Subarctic, and the Pacific Northwest.

Arctic Cultures Arctic peoples live in a harsh environment. Winters are long, cold, snowy, and dark. The sun appears for only a few hours each day. Summer days are very long, but the season is short.

In southern Arctic areas, herds of caribou came to feed on summer plants. Arctic peoples used long summer days to gather as much food as possible. They hunted these caribou and moose.

Arctic people also hunted sea mammals such as seals, walrus, and whales. Hunters waited at seals' air holes or chased them in kayaks. They hunted whales using larger boats. From these animals, Arctic

people gained meat and materials for clothing and tools. They even used whale and seal oil to heat their homes.

Arctic people lived in several different types of homes. Some homes were built partly underground and covered with sod. Other homes were small, rounded structures covered with tree branches. Some lived in igloos during the winter. **Igloos** are domed houses made from blocks of snow. Those people usually lived in tents or underground homes during the summer.

Subarctic Cultures Subarctic cultures covered much of modern Canada and Alaska. Winters there are cold and summers short. The region has large forests and tundra. Food was scarce, but more easily <u>available</u> than in the Arctic.

available, *adj.,* able to be reached

612

The peoples of this region, like the Ojibwa, lived in small groups. They hunted animals like moose and elk. They also caught beaver and waterfowl, such as ducks. In the warmer months, they collected berries and other plant foods.

Some people lived in tents during the summer. In winter, people dug homes into the ground for protection from the wind. To stay warm, they wore fur clothing. They also used snowshoes and toboggans to move goods in the snow.

When Europeans arrived, Subarctic people traded pelts, or animal hides, for goods such as flour. Many Subarctic groups began spending more time hunting and preparing pelts. That allowed them to live in villages for more of the year rather than spending all their time collecting food.

Northwest Coast Peoples of the Northwest cultures lived along the coast of the Pacific Ocean. They had a rich and varied environment. The climate was neither very hot nor very cold. Forests provided plenty of game and plant foods.

Northwestern people cut down the large trees in these forests to make huge canoes. They took these canoes onto the nearby ocean to hunt seals, sea otters, and whales. They also caught fish, like salmon, and harvested shellfish.

Food was so plentiful in the Northwest that people did not need to farm. They also spent less time gathering, hunting, and storing food than other Native Americans. They were also able to settle in permanent communities.

Abundant food and permanent communities led to complex societies with social ranks. This means that some people and families had higher status, or social value, than others.

Dozens of related people may have lived in each large wooden family house. Set out in front of the family home was a totem (TOHT um) pole. This tall structure, made from a tree, was carved and painted to relate important events and individuals in a family's history.

Wealthy families hosted potlatches to mark important events. A **potlatch** was a ceremony in which a wealthy and high-ranking family had a feast and gave gifts to their guests. The ceremonies were also a time for telling stories about a family's history. In this way, a family's heritage was passed down from one generation to the next.

Reading Check What was the purpose of a totem pole?

The West and Southwest

Western North America included several Native American culture areas. The many environments led to diverse ways of life.

The Southwest The descendants of the Ancestral Pueblo settled in New Mexico. There, they built homes out of adobe, or dried mud. These homes had several stories. When Spaniards arrived in the region, they called the large structures *pueblos,* from the Spanish word for "town." Today, these peoples are called the Pueblos.

myWorld Activity
Create a School
Totem Pole

Totem poles are part of the culture of the Pacific Northwest.▼

613

Native American Dwellings

Native American dwellings reflect the different environments in which people lived. Each group adapted to use the materials available where they lived.

THINK CRITICALLY   What do these dwellings tell you about the region in which they are located?

A During the winter, Arctic peoples built igloos from blocks of snow.

B Longhouses were home to extended families in the Northeast.

C Wigwams were made from log poles covered with bark.

D Earth lodges had a log frame covered with branches and sod.

E People along the Northwest Coast built houses of cedar planks.

F Hogans were built in the Southwest with sticks and mud.

G Some homes in California were cedar poles covered with bark.

Like many native groups, the Pueblo peoples grew corn, beans, and squash. Some also grew cotton. The dry climate of this region continued to challenge them.

Other Southwestern Native Americans lived as hunter-gatherers. Peoples who lived near water built homes from logs. Other groups lived in wigwams or tepees.

Later, European settlers introduced sheep to the region. Some people, like the Navajo, began herding sheep. They used the wool to make blankets.

The Plateau and Great Basin The Plateau region was surrounded by mountains and had little rainfall. Many different cultures existed in the region. Most people in this area lived in permanent villages. They spent certain times of the year outside the villages gathering wild foods. The most important food was fish.

After horses came to North America, many shifted their way of life. The Nez Percé (nez purse), for example, began to live nomadically, following bison herds.

Some peoples lived in the region called the Great Basin. This desert area sits between the Rocky Mountains and the Sierra Nevada. Food was scarce in this hot, dry region.

People lived in small groups and moved often to find food. They ate mostly plants, though they also hunted small animals. In the 1600s, some groups began using horses and became more like the Plains peoples, hunting buffalo and living in tepees.

California As in the Plateau area, the California Native American groups were very diverse. There were many types of houses and ways of life. Most people were hunter-gatherers, though a few groups farmed. Many peoples who lived in California relied on acorns that they ground into flour.

Those living near water usually fished and lived in villages, while those in deserts moved around. Groups in California were also known for oral stories and poems.

Reading Check What is a pueblo?

my World CONNECTIONS

Spear tips found near Clovis, New Mexico, gave the earliest known North American culture its name, "Clovis culture."

Section 2 Assessment

Essential Question

Key Terms

1. How do historians use artifacts?

2. Describe a longhouse.

3. What happened at a potlatch?

Key Ideas

4. How does a wigwam compare to a longhouse?

5. What are two examples of how Native American groups adapted to their environment?

6. In which culture areas was farming important?

Think Critically

7. **Solve Problems** Why were both tepees and earth lodges used as housing on the Great Plains?

8. **Draw Conclusions** Why did some Native Americans develop farming while others did not?

How much does geography affect people's lives?

9. Choose one Native American culture region. How did geography affect the housing available there? Go to your Student Journal to record your answer.

Chapter Assessment

Key Terms and Ideas

1. **Describe** Describe the social hierarchy in the Incan empire.

2. **Summarize** Describe what an **ayllu** did.

3. **Recall** What is an **artifact?**

4. **Compare and Contrast** Compare a **tepee** to a **longhouse.**

5. **Explain** How did a **drought** affect the Ancestral Pueblo people?

Think Critically

6. **Problem Solving** How did the Incas build an empire in a difficult environment?

7. **Draw Inferences** Why did the Incas prefer not to use their army to expand their empire?

8. **Draw Conclusions** What was the purpose of the Mississippian mounds?

9. **Analyze Cause and Effect** How did horses change Native American Plains culture?

10. **Core Concepts: Geography's Five Themes** What is location? How did it influence Native Americans?

Analyze Visuals

11. Describe the actions of the Incas in this image.

12. What does this image tell you about Incan religion?

13. What does this image tell you about what was important to the Incas?

Essential Question

myWorld Chapter Activity

Where in the Americas? Investigate home sites and artifacts to learn about how Native American groups adapted to their environments. Analyze clues on each activity card to predict which region is represented on each activity card.

21st Century Learning

Develop Cultural Awareness

Choose one Native American group. Describe how they carry on their traditions today. Focus on one or two aspects of the group's culture, such as food or celebrations, that have been passed down from previous generations. Describe why each tradition or way of life began.

Document-Based Questions

Success Tracker™
Online at myworldhistory.com

Use your knowledge of the Incas and Documents A and B to answer Questions 1–3.

Document A

"In human memory, I believe that there is no account of a road as great as this, running through deep valleys, high mountains, banks of snow, torrents of water, living rock, and wild rivers. . . . In all places it was clean and swept free of refuse [trash], with lodgings, storehouses, Sun temples, and posts along the route. Oh! Can anything similar be claimed for . . . the powerful kings . . . ?"

—Pedro Cieza de León

Document B

"From the bridge floor up to the cables that serve as guard rails, they cover and intertwine the sides the whole length of the cables with branches; this makes two walls that serve more to keep those who cross from getting frightened than as a support. This construction makes these bridges strong and safe to cross for both men and beast carrying loads, although the bridges swing and sway."

—Father Bernabe Cobo

1. What did the author of Document A think about Incan roads?
   A Incan roads were very advanced.
   B Incan roads were very dirty.
   C Incan roads were not as great as European roads.
   D Incan roads should have had lodgings and storehouses.

2. Why did the Incas make walls on their bridges?
   A to prevent them from moving
   B to prevent people from falling
   C to allow horses to cross
   D to prevent people from becoming frightened

3. **Writing Task** Why were Europeans very impressed with the roads and bridges through the Andes?

myworldhistory.com

Self-Test

617

The Aztecs and the Incas

Key Idea
- The Aztecs and the Incas built highly advanced civilizations in the Americas.

Civilizations flourished in the Americas long before Europeans arrived. The Aztecs built a powerful empire through conquest. Their society was highly organized with a rigid class system and a strong government. The large capital city of Tenochtitlan showed Aztec skills in architecture and engineering. Like the Aztecs, the Incas also had an empire with well-engineered buildings and roads, as well as a complex political and religious system. Both societies worshiped many gods. Aztec religious ceremonies centered on the rain and the sun.

A modern illustration of Tenochtitlan

Read the text on the right. Stop at each circled letter. Then answer the question with the same letter on the left.

A **Analyze Cause and Effect** Why were the observers "astounded" by what they saw?

B **Draw Inferences** What characteristics of Aztec construction would make their towns and buildings "seem like an enchanted vision"?

C **Draw Conclusions** Why were these visions "never heard of, seen or dreamed of before"?

causeway, *n.,* a raised way across wet ground or water; highway

Amadis, *n.,* a fictional Spanish knight

vein, *n.,* a distinctive mode of expression; style

The Great City of Tenochtitlan

66 And when we saw all those cities and villages built in the water, and other great towns on dry land, and that straight
A and level <u>causeway</u> leading to Mexico, we were astounded. These great towns and . . . buildings rising from the water,
B all made of stone, seemed like an enchanted vision from the tale of <u>Amadis</u>. Indeed, some of our soldiers asked whether it was not all a dream. It is not surprising therefore that I should write in this <u>vein</u>. It was all so wonderful that I do not know how to describe this first glimpse of things
C never heard of, seen or dreamed of before. . . .

And when we entered the city of Iztapalapa, the sight of the palaces in which they lodged us! They were very spacious and well built, of magnificent stone, cedar wood, and the wood of other sweet-smelling trees, with great rooms and courts, which were a wonderful sight, and all covered with awnings of woven cotton. 99
—Bernal Díaz del Castillo, *The Conquest of New Spain,* late 1500s, translated by J. M. Cohen

Read the text on the right. Stop at each circled letter. Then answer the question with the same letter on the left.

D **Draw Conclusions** What do these lines indicate about the size of the Incan empire?

E **Analyze Details** What is the writer describing by using the phrase "stairways for giants"?

F **Summarize** In your own words, describe Incan tools and technology.

parched, *adj.,* deprived of moisture, dry

multitude, *n.,* a large number of people

precision, *n.,* a quality of being precise; accuracy

presiding, *v.,* holding authority

The Incan Empire

66 The age of the fifth Sun was the age of the glorious Inca empire,
D which stretched north, south, east and west . . . over coastal desert, frozen mountain and fertile valley, and dazzled with its imperial wonders: its network of roads, which allowed for good communications and the rapid movement of troops; its irrigation systems, which brought water to a <u>parched</u> earth; its agricultural terraces, climbing up the hillsides like stairways for
E giants, which produced not only enough food for the <u>multitude</u>, but a surplus; its monumental buildings, erected without the benefit of iron tools or the wheel, and constructed of stones . . .
F which interlock with such fine <u>precision</u> that barely a whisper can pass between them; its handicrafts in weaving and ceramics and jewelry and gold; and, <u>presiding</u> above it all, the High King himself, the Inca. **99**

—Diana Ferguson, *Tales of the Plumed Serpent,* 2000

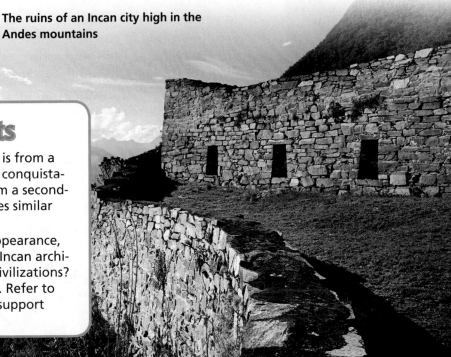

The ruins of an Incan city high in the Andes mountains

Analyze the Documents

1. **Draw Conclusions** The first passage is from a primary source written by a Spanish conquistador, while the second passage is from a secondary source. How are the two passages similar and different?

2. **Writing Task** What does the size, appearance, and engineering of both Aztec and Incan architecture suggest about life in these civilizations? Write your thoughts in a paragraph. Refer to one or both of these documents to support your ideas.

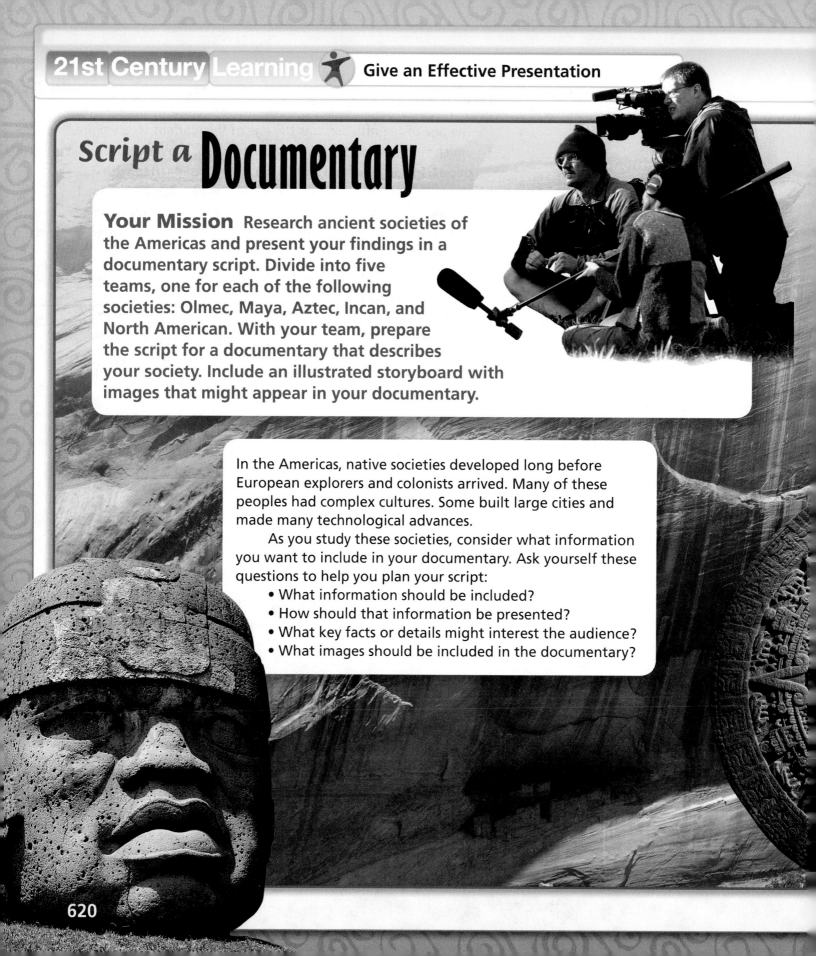

Script a Documentary

Your Mission Research ancient societies of the Americas and present your findings in a documentary script. Divide into five teams, one for each of the following societies: Olmec, Maya, Aztec, Incan, and North American. With your team, prepare the script for a documentary that describes your society. Include an illustrated storyboard with images that might appear in your documentary.

In the Americas, native societies developed long before European explorers and colonists arrived. Many of these peoples had complex cultures. Some built large cities and made many technological advances.

As you study these societies, consider what information you want to include in your documentary. Ask yourself these questions to help you plan your script:
- What information should be included?
- How should that information be presented?
- What key facts or details might interest the audience?
- What images should be included in the documentary?

STEP 1

Research Your Culture.

Go on a fact-finding mission about your team's society. Give each team member a topic to research, such as geography, belief systems, government, economics, culture, or science and technology. Once your group has gathered information and images about your society, begin planning your documentary. Consider how you will present your facts in an interesting and logical way.

STEP 2

Create Your Script and Storyboard.

Organize information about your society in a way that makes sense. You may wish to present information chronologically, or you might divide segments by topic. You may wish to have team members write the portion of the script that covers their topic. Then make a storyboard, or an illustrated mock-up of the images that might appear in your documentary.

STEP 3

Present Your Documentary.

A successful documentary explains facts about a topic in an interesting way. Review your script and storyboard to be sure you have included key information about your society. Before presenting your script to the class, rehearse it with your group. Be sure to decide which lines will be read by specific team members. Then read your script aloud and explain the images you've used on your storyboard.

my worldhistory.com

21st Century Learning

Europe in the Middle Ages

Henry II (1100s) was the king of England whose attempt to take more control over the Catholic Church led to the murder of Thomas Becket.

Joan of Arc (1400s) was a French teenager who led France to victories over the English army during the Hundred Years' War.

Atlantic Ocean

Charlemagne (700s–800s) was the powerful king of the Franks who was crowned emperor by Pope Leo III.

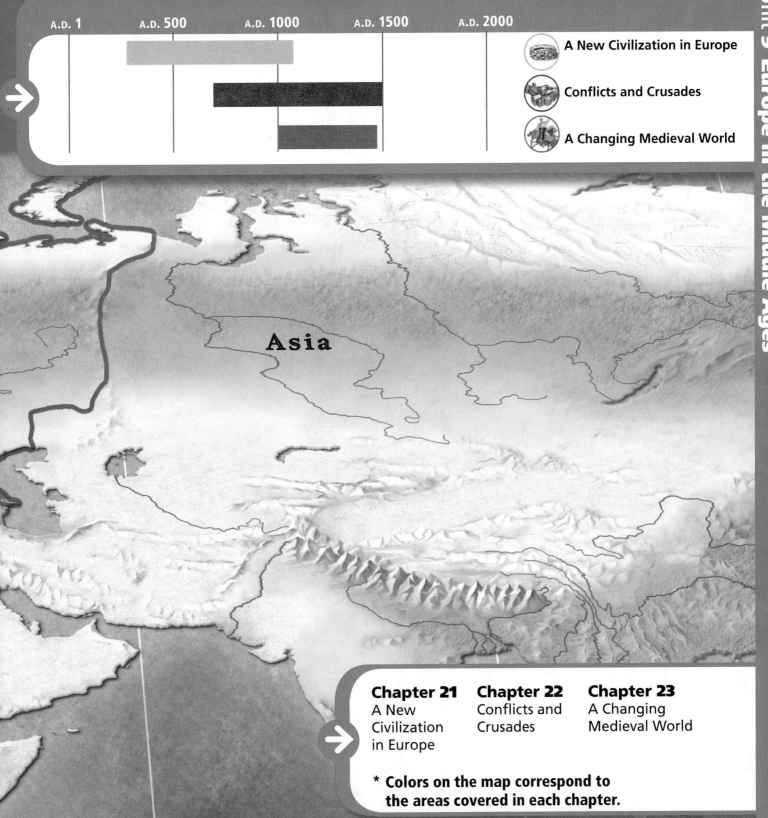

A.D. 1 — A.D. 500 — A.D. 1000 — A.D. 1500 — A.D. 2000

A New Civilization in Europe

Conflicts and Crusades

A Changing Medieval World

Asia

Chapter 21
A New
Civilization
in Europe

Chapter 22
Conflicts and
Crusades

Chapter 23
A Changing
Medieval World

* Colors on the map correspond to
  the areas covered in each chapter.

Unit 9 Europe in the Middle Ages

A New Civilization in Europe

Essential Question

What is power? Who should have it?

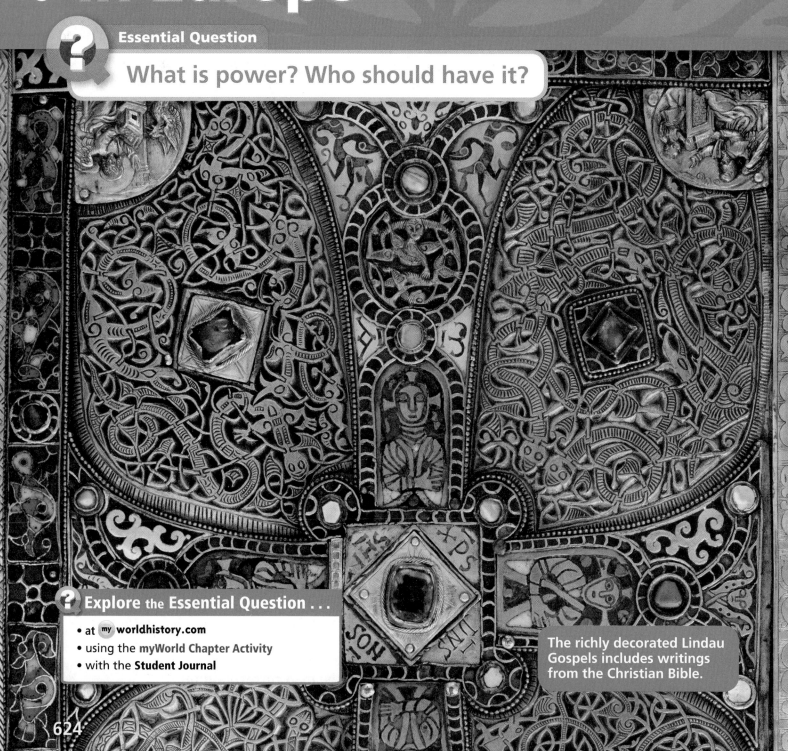

Explore the Essential Question . . .

- at **my worldhistory.com**
- using the **myWorld Chapter Activity**
- with the **Student Journal**

The richly decorated Lindau Gospels includes writings from the Christian Bible.

Early Middle Ages

486 Clovis defeats the last Roman army in Western Europe.

732 Charles Martel defeats Spanish Muslim invaders in the battle of Tours.

800 Pope Leo III crowns Charlemagne emperor.

450   550   650   750   850

529 Benedict of Nursia founds the first Benedictine monastery.

795 Vikings make their earliest known raid on Ireland.

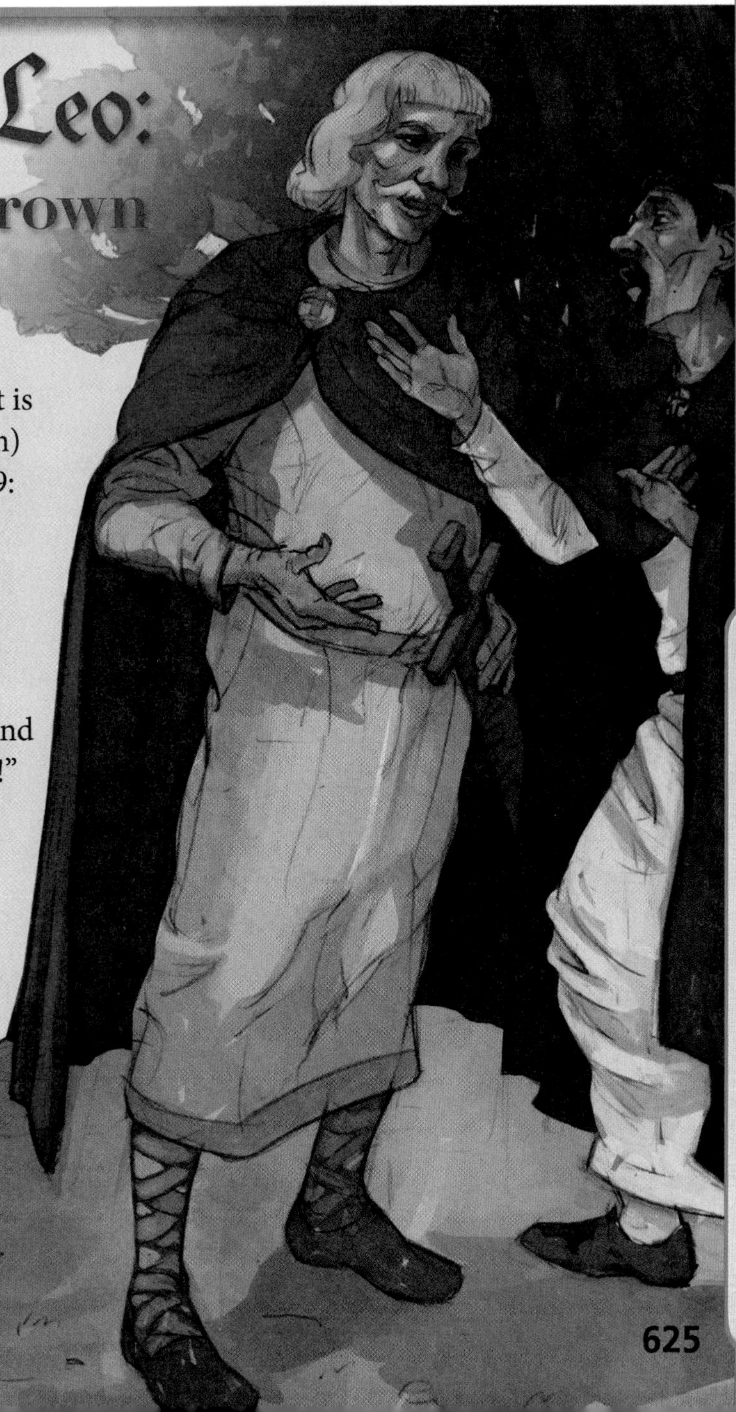

my worldhistory.com

Timeline/On Assignment

Charlemagne and Leo:
The Sword and the Crown

This myStory is a fictionalized account of events in the life of a real person from this chapter.

At his castle in Paderborn, deep in the heart of what is now Germany, King Charlemagne (SHAHR luh mayn) received a surprise visitor during the summer of 799: Pope Leo III, the leader of the Catholic Church. Leo had come seeking protection from his enemies in Rome, Italy.

"My enemies say I have committed terrible sins," Leo told Charlemagne, "but I have not! They threatened to gouge out my eyes and cut out my tongue, and they imprisoned me in a monastery. I had to escape!"

Charlemagne looked down at Leo from his full height of 6 feet, 3 inches. He rested his hand on the hilt of his sword. As the king of the Franks, he had used the sword for over thirty years, in battle after battle fought to extend his territory and power. These battles also increased Christianity's reach across Europe. With his sword, Charlemagne had become the most powerful ruler in Europe.

625

Leo told Charlemagne about his daring nighttime escape from the monastery where he was held prisoner by his enemies.

Now Leo was offering him something more than power. Charlemagne recalled how Leo had become pope after the death of Pope Adrian I. Adrian had been popular with the nobles who ruled Italy because he himself was a noble. Leo, however, was from a lower social class. Roman nobles who believed that the pope should be of noble birth were horrified at his rise to power.

As Charlemagne listened to Leo's tale of escape from his enemies, he realized that Leo needed him, and that he needed Leo. They could make a trade. When Leo asked for Charlemagne's protection to return to Rome, the king patted the hilt of his sword. "As a Christian, it is my duty to help defend the Church," he said. "But no mere king can restore order in Rome, the capital of the old Roman empire. Only a new Roman emperor can do that." So together, Leo and Charlemagne came up with a plan that would benefit them both.

Leo returned to Rome with an armed escort provided by Charlemagne. A few months later, Charlemagne himself traveled to Rome. In the presence of the great Frankish king, Leo's enemies did not dare bring any charges against the pope. Leo took an oath of innocence, and the nobles had to accept it. Now Charlemagne had shown that his power protected the leader of the Catholic Church.

A few days later, Charlemagne and Leo carried out the second part of their plan. On Christmas Day, Charlemagne attended a religious service with Leo. During the service, Charlemagne knelt in prayer. He bowed his head and closed his eyes. As he was doing so, Leo took a crown from the altar and placed it on Charlemagne's head. Everyone in the church cried out, acknowledging Charlemagne as the new emperor of the Romans.

Charlemagne knew that being named emperor did not give him any powers he did not already have. However, it gave him a prestige that no other Western European leader had. Leo had gained something, too: he had shown that only the pope had the right to name an emperor.

By crowning Charlemagne emperor, Leo risked starting a war with the Byzantine empire. Charlemagne knew that the Byzantine ruler, Empress Irene, might feel that he and Leo were attempting to take her throne. As Charlemagne felt the weight of the gold crown settle on his head, his

Charlemagne vowed to protect Leo. He sent Leo back to Rome with an escort of armed guards.

With Charlemagne at his side, Leo swore that he was innocent of the charges against him.

hand drifted down to the familiar hilt of his sword at his side. He wondered which would prove to be the most powerful: the sword of the king of the Franks, or the crown of the Roman emperor.

Based on this story, how do you think people in the Middle Ages struggled over power? As you read the chapter ahead, think about what Charlemagne and Leo's story tells you about life in medieval Europe.

myStory Video

Learn more about Charlemagne and Leo's story.

Europe in the Early Middle Ages

Key Ideas

- Europe's varied geography of plains, mountains, and rivers has attracted many different peoples.
- After the fall of Rome, Germanic tribes such as the Franks formed kingdoms.
- The Frankish emperor Charlemagne united a large part of Western Europe.

Key Terms • Middle Ages • medieval • topography • clergy

Visual Glossary

Reading Skill Sequence Take notes using the graphic organizer in your journal.

▲ Replica of an Anglo-Saxon helmet, A.D. 600s

A fter the western Roman empire collapsed, Western Europe began an era of social, political, and economic decline. But from the ruins of the Roman empire, a new European civilization emerged. Historians call this period between ancient times and modern times— roughly from A.D. 500 to 1500—the **Middle Ages.** Its culture is called **medieval** civilization, from the Latin words meaning "middle age."

The Geography of Europe

Geographers sometimes describe Europe as a "peninsula of peninsulas." A quick glance at a map of Europe explains why: Europe is a large peninsula that sticks out from the larger Eurasian landmass. Smaller peninsulas extend from the main European peninsula into the surrounding seas. In the north, the Scandinavian Peninsula divides the Atlantic Ocean and the Baltic Sea. In southern Europe, the Iberian, Italian, and Balkan peninsulas push into the Mediterranean Sea.

Mountains and Plains Europe's **topography,** or the physical features of its surface, is varied. Mountains edge much of the continent. To the north, a range of mountains runs along the Scandinavian Peninsula. The Alps form an arc of high mountains across southern Europe. To the west, the Pyrenees divide Spain and France. To the east, the Urals separate Europe and Asia.

Europe: Physical

ARCTIC OCEAN

Barents Sea

ARCTIC CIRCLE

Iceland

60° N

ATLANTIC OCEAN

50° N

SCANDINAVIAN PENINSULA

Ural Mountains

Volga R.

Baltic Sea

North Sea

Ireland

Great Britain

NORTH EUROPEAN PLAIN

Dnieper R.

Don R.

Caspian Sea

KEY
Elevation

Feet	Meters
6,000	1,829
3,000	914
1,000	305
500	152
Sea level	Sea level

0   400 mi

0   400 km

Lambert Conformal Conic Projection

Rhine R.

Loire R.

Alps

Carpathian Mountains

Danube R.

Caucasus Mountains

Black Sea

Pyrenees

Corsica

ITALIAN PENINSULA

BALKAN PENINSULA

ASIA

IBERIAN PENINSULA

Sardinia

Balearic Islands

Sicily

Crete

Mediterranean Sea

AFRICA

10° W   0°   10° E   20° E   30° E

The Alps in northern Italy

The Danube River valley

Map Skills

1 **Place** What peninsulas are labeled on this map?

2 **Region** How does elevation vary across Europe?

The North European Plain is the fertile heart of the continent. It stretches from the vineyards of France through the forests of Germany and into Eastern Europe. Some migrating peoples from Eastern Europe used this broad plain to travel west.

Europe's topography affects its climate. Except in the far north, moist westerly winds blow inland from the oceans, bringing rain. Those winds give most of Western Europe a relatively warm, moist climate year-round. However, mountains block the winds from reaching the Mediterranean countries. As a result, they have a Mediterranean climate, with hot, dry summers.

Waterways Europe's rivers flow from the central mountains and highlands. These rivers bring water to farmland and form natural boundaries. They make trade easier. Most early European cities formed near major rivers.

The longest rivers in Western Europe are the Rhine and the Danube. In Roman times, they marked the eastern and northern borders of the Roman empire. The Danube flows eastward across the broad central plains into Eastern Europe, emptying into the Black Sea. The Rhine runs northward through Germany and the Netherlands to the North Sea. Its waters carry fine soil that is deposited along the way, building up rich farmland.

Reading Check Why is Europe referred to as a "peninsula of peninsulas"?

629

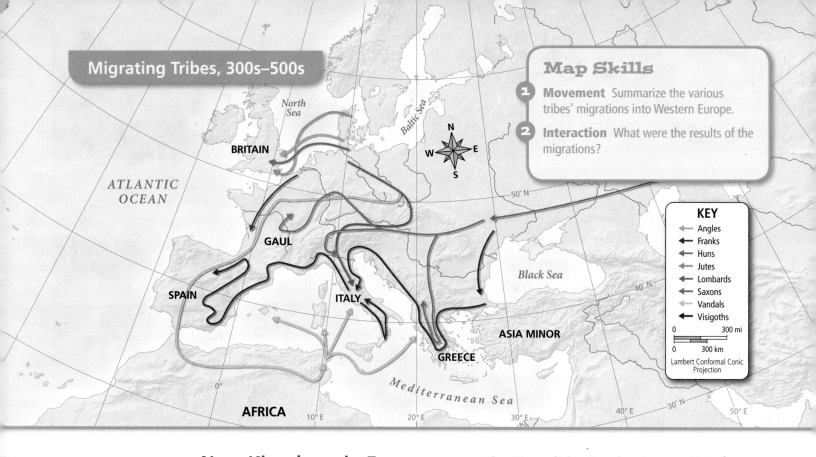

North
Sea

Baltic Sea

BRITAIN

ATLANTIC
OCEAN

50° N

GAUL

Black Sea

SPAIN

ITALY

40° N

ASIA MINOR

GREECE

Mediterranean Sea

AFRICA   10° E   20° E   30° E   40° E   50° E

0°

N
W   E
S

Map Skills

1 **Movement** Summarize the various tribes' migrations into Western Europe.

2 **Interaction** What were the results of the migrations?

KEY
← Angles
← Franks
← Huns
← Jutes
← Lombards
← Saxons
← Vandals
← Visigoths

0   300 mi
0   300 km
Lambert Conformal Conic
Projection

New Kingdoms in Europe

Over time, the favorable geography of Western Europe attracted different peoples into the region. The Huns and Germanic tribes began to migrate into the Roman empire by around A.D. 300. Some, such as the Lombards, settled in Europe's river valleys. Others, such as the Angles, Saxons, and Jutes, moved across the North Sea to the British Isles. These tribes divided Europe into a collection of small, warring kingdoms.

unite, *v.,* to bring together

◄ The Germanic tribes made detailed metalwork and jewelry such as the objects here. Clockwise from left: a buckle, a clasp, and a sword hilt

630

The Rise of the Franks In A.D. 486, the Frankish leader Clovis I defeated the last Roman army in Western Europe. Next, he took over several of the Germanic kingdoms. By the early 530s, the Franks controlled much of the land in Gaul (present-day France) and Germany. Although the Franks grew rich from their conquests, their central government did not last long. Eventually, the Frankish lands broke into smaller local kingdoms.

Charles Martel Takes Power In 717, a leader named Charles Martel—or Charles the Hammer—united the Frankish lands under his rule. His most important victory was the battle of Tours in 732, when he led Frankish warriors to defeat a Muslim army from Spain. The battle of Tours ended one of the last Muslim military invasions of Western Europe.

Frankish Kingdoms

Under leaders such as Clovis I and Charles Martel, the Franks became the most powerful of the many Germanic tribes that migrated into Western Europe.

▲ Charles Martel defeated a Muslim army at the battle of Tours in 732.

▲ Clovis I united the Frankish tribes. His lands were divided among his four sons after his death.

Muslim troops did not advance any farther into Western Europe, although they did rule most of what is now Spain.

Reading Check How did the Franks take power in Europe?

The Age of Charlemagne

In 768, Charles Martel's grandson—also named Charles—became king of the Franks. Today we call him Charlemagne (SHAHR luh mayn), or Charles the Great. By 800, Charlemagne had built an empire that stretched across what is now France, Germany, and Italy.

A Strong Ruler Charlemagne spent much of his 46-year reign fighting to increase his power and territory. He fought Saxons in the north, Avars and Slavs in the east, and Lombards in Italy. He fought Umayyad Muslims in Spain, but he also made alliances with other Muslim rulers. His military victories reunited much of the original western Roman empire.

Like other Germanic kings, Charlemagne appointed powerful nobles to rule local regions. He sent out officials to make sure that these nobles were ruling fairly and well.

Charlemagne thought that education could help unite his kingdom. Educated officials would be able to keep accurate records and write clear reports. Charlemagne encouraged the creation of schools. He himself studied widely, learning to read Latin and understand Greek.

Charlemagne and Christianity Charlemagne was a devout Christian. Many of his advisers were members of the **clergy,** or the group of people who are trained and ordained for religious services.

631

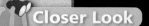
Charlemagne's Europe

Charlemagne spent his reign working to spread Christianity, preserve ancient knowledge, and support education. He also fought many wars to expand his power. By the time of his death, his empire included much of Western Europe.

THINK CRITICALLY How did Charlemagne use his power?

◄ Charlemagne as emperor

▲ Charlemagne's throne

Charlemagne's Empire, 814

KEY

Charlemagne's empire, 814

0   100   200 miles

0   100 200 kilometers

Lambert Conformal Conic Projection

North Sea

Saxons

Rhine R.

Aachen

50° N

Slavs

Seine R.   Paris   Verdun

Danube R.

Avars

Tours

Loire R.

Lombards

Po R.

Adriatic Sea

Atlantic Ocean

Rhône R.

Corsica

Rome

40° N

Mediterranean Sea

0°

10° E

N

▲ Charlemagne's armies fought Muslim soldiers in Spain.

Charlemagne admired learning. Here, he is shown with students at his Palace School.

On Christmas Day 800, Pope Leo III crowned Charlemagne as the emperor of the Romans.

myWorld Activity
Medieval Tic-Tac-Toe

Charlemagne wanted to create a unified Christian Europe. He worked closely with the Catholic Church to spread Christianity throughout Europe.

One person at Charlemagne's court described his religious habits in this way:

> 66 He cherished . . . the principles of the Christian religion. . . . Hence it was that he built the beautiful chapel at [Aachen, Germany], which he adorned with gold and silver. . . . He was a constant worshipper at this church as long as his health permitted, going morning and evening. 99
>
> — Einhard, *The Life of Charlemagne,* translated by Samuel Epes Turner

A New Emperor As you read in the myStory at the beginning of this chapter, Charlemagne helped protect Pope Leo III from enemies in Rome. In 800, the pope showed his thanks by crowning Charlemagne emperor.

The crowning of Charlemagne was very important. In the Christian Roman tradition begun by Constantine, the emperor had much authority over the Church. But by crowning Charlemagne, Pope Leo III established the idea that only the pope had the power to name an emperor. This strengthened the Church's power.

Leo's action angered the Byzantine empire and the Eastern Orthodox Church. The disagreement over who could crown an emperor worsened the split between the eastern and western Christian worlds.

Europe After Charlemagne After Charlemagne died in 814, his son Louis I took the throne. Louis' sons struggled among themselves for power. Finally, in 843, they agreed to the Treaty of Verdun, which split Charlemagne's empire into three parts.

Charlemagne left a lasting legacy in Europe. He extended Christianity into northern Europe and contributed to the blending of Germanic, Roman, and Christian traditions. He also set up strong, efficient governments. Later rulers looked to his example when they tried to strengthen their own kingdoms.

Reading Check How did Charlemagne extend his rule?

A gold-and-silver bust of Charlemagne ▼

Section 1 Assessment

Key Terms

1. What is topography?
2. What were the Middle Ages?
3. What role did the clergy have in Charlemagne's government?

Key Ideas

4. How did the Germanic tribes affect Europe?
5. How did Europe's geography attract people to different regions?
6. How did Charlemagne work to unite much of Western Europe?

Think Critically

7. **Summarize** Summarize the movement of people and the rise of kingdoms in early medieval Europe from the 300s to the 800s.
8. **Draw Conclusions** How did Charlemagne's rule affect medieval Europe?

? Essential Question

What is power? Who should have it?

9. How did different groups and individuals take power in early medieval Europe? Go to your Student Journal to record your answer.

The Spread of Christianity in Europe

Key Ideas

- Christian monks and nuns lived and worked in communities dedicated to spiritual goals.
- Missionaries spread Christian teachings throughout northern Europe.
- Through its teachings and sacraments, the Catholic Church became a center of authority in medieval Europe.

Key Terms
- monastery
- convent
- pagan
- missionary
- saint
- sacrament
- Christendom

→ (**Visual Glossary**)

Reading Skill Summarize Take notes using the graphic organizer in your journal.

Medieval nuns singing in a choir ▼

In an earlier chapter, you read that the Roman emperor Constantine ended the persecution of Christians in the A.D. 300s. At this time, most Christians lived in the Mediterranean region. During the Middle Ages, Christianity spread throughout much of Europe.

Monasteries and Convents

During the early Middle Ages, some Christian men and women chose lives of religious study and prayer. In time, those people formed monasteries and convents. A **monastery** is a secluded community where men called monks focus on prayer and scripture. A **convent** is a religious community for women known as nuns. Monks and nuns devote their lives to spiritual goals.

The Benedictine Rule The first Christian monasteries developed in Egypt in the A.D. 300s. Later, an Italian monk named Benedict established a new European version of monastic life. About 529, Benedict organized a monastery in central Italy. There, he created a series of rules for monastic life. In time, these rules—known as the Benedictine Rule—were adopted by monasteries and convents throughout Europe.

Under the Benedictine Rule, monastic life was a shared experience that balanced prayer and work. Monks and nuns made vows, or solemn promises, to live and worship within their communities for the rest of their lives. They also promised to obey their leaders, work for the good of their community, remain unmarried, and own nothing individually.

Daily Life in Monasteries The monastic day was busy—and long. It began early, with prayers before dawn, and ended late in the evening. Each day was divided into periods for worship, work, and study. Monks used chants to mark the canonical hours, or religious divisions, of the day.

Monasteries and convents were not only places where monks and nuns lived and prayed, but were also places of work and study. Many were self-contained communities that grew their own food. They made many of the things people needed in daily life. Monks worked in the monastery's gardens and workshops. They worked in libraries where they copied and illustrated religious manuscripts.

Early medieval Europe had no hospitals or public schools. As a result, monasteries and convents often provided basic health and educational services. Monks and nuns helped care for poor or sick people. They set up schools for children.

Monasteries and convents also helped keep ancient learning alive. Their libraries contained Greek and Roman works, which monks and nuns copied. Some monks and nuns wrote and taught Latin, which was the language of the Church and of educated people.

▲ Benedict (center, with beard) and other monks lived and worked in monasteries.

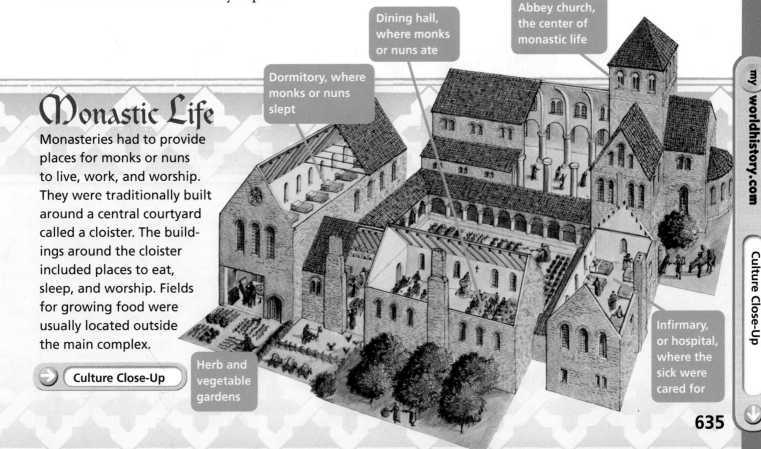

Monastic Life

Monasteries had to provide places for monks or nuns to live, work, and worship. They were traditionally built around a central courtyard called a cloister. The buildings around the cloister included places to eat, sleep, and worship. Fields for growing food were usually located outside the main complex.

→ **Culture Close-Up**

Dormitory, where monks or nuns slept

Dining hall, where monks or nuns ate

Abbey church, the center of monastic life

Herb and vegetable gardens

Infirmary, or hospital, where the sick were cared for

**myWorld Activity
Medieval Monastery**

One visitor to a medieval French monastery wrote the following:

> 66 For my part, the more attentively I watch them day by day, the more do I believe that they are perfect followers of Christ in all things. When they pray and speak to God in spirit and in truth, by their friendly and quiet speech to Him, as well as by their humbleness of demeanor, they are plainly seen to be God's companions and friends. . . . As I watch them, therefore, singing without fatigue from before midnight to the dawn of day, with only a brief interval, they appear a little less than angels, but much more than men. 99

—William of St. Thierry, Description of Clairvaux Abbey, about 1143

convert, *v.,* to bring over from one belief to another

Reading Check What services did monks and nuns provide?

The Conversion of Europe

When the Roman empire collapsed, Christianity had not spread far beyond the empire's borders. Many Europeans were pagans. A **pagan** is a follower of a polytheistic religion, or a religion with more than one god. During the early Middle Ages, Catholic missionaries traveled across Europe to <u>convert</u> pagans to Christianity. A **missionary** is a person who tries to convert others to a particular religion.

St. Patrick Converts Ireland One important early missionary was a man named Patrick. Some of the stories about Patrick are probably legendary, but we do know that Patrick was born in Britain in the late 300s. As a teenager, he was sold into slavery in Ireland. Patrick eventually escaped, but he later returned to Ireland to convert its people to Christianity.

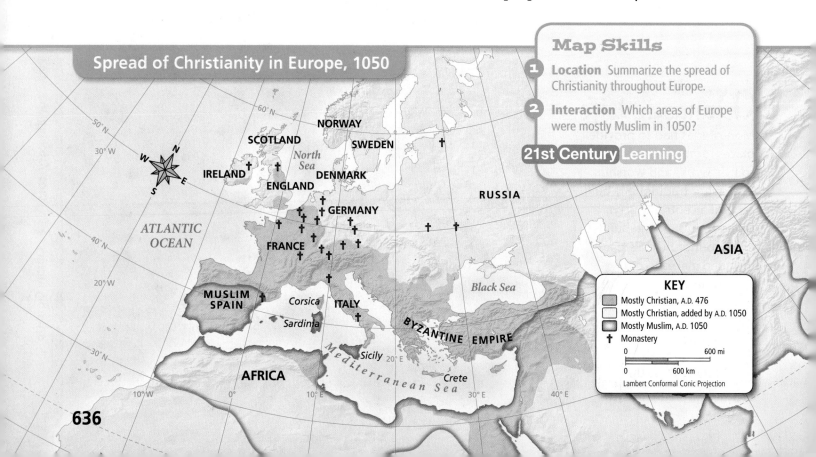

Spread of Christianity in Europe, 1050

Map Skills

1 **Location** Summarize the spread of Christianity throughout Europe.

2 **Interaction** Which areas of Europe were mostly Muslim in 1050?

21st Century Learning

NORWAY
SCOTLAND
SWEDEN
North Sea
IRELAND
DENMARK
ENGLAND
RUSSIA
GERMANY
ATLANTIC OCEAN
FRANCE
ASIA
Black Sea
MUSLIM SPAIN
Corsica
ITALY
Sardinia
BYZANTINE EMPIRE
Sicily
AFRICA
Mediterranean Sea
Crete

KEY
- Mostly Christian, A.D. 476
- Mostly Christian, added by A.D. 1050
- Mostly Muslim, A.D. 1050
- † Monastery

0   600 mi
0   600 km
Lambert Conformal Conic Projection

636

Patrick began his missionary work in northern and western Ireland. At first, Irish people resisted his teachings. But over time, he gained the trust and friendship of the local tribes. Many Irish people became Christians. In fact, Patrick and other early missionaries founded hundreds of Christian churches in Ireland. After Patrick's death, the Catholic Church recognized him as a **saint,** or an especially holy person.

Missionaries to Britain During the early Middle Ages, many missionaries were sent by popes, or the leaders of the Catholic Church. In 597, for example, Pope Gregory I sent a group of monks as missionaries to Britain. They were welcomed by the king of Kent, whose wife was already a Catholic. After the king converted to the new faith, his subjects followed his example. Over the next hundred years, most of Britain became Catholic as well.

Christianity Spreads Through Europe By the 700s and 800s, Catholic missionaries were working in other parts of Europe. In Eastern Europe, monks worked to convert Slavic peoples. In northern Europe, the British monk Boniface worked to establish the Catholic Church in Germany and the Netherlands.

Over time, the Catholic faith became part of everyday life in most parts of Europe. Daily life revolved around the Catholic calendar, which included many holidays, such as Easter, as well as local holy days dedicated to saints. The church became the center of European society as well as a place of worship.

Reading Check What did missionaries do?

A cross sits in front of the ruins of a medieval Irish monastery. ▼

Converting Europe

Missionaries, popes, and other Christians worked to spread Christianity throughout medieval Europe. By 1050, most of Europe was Christian.

▲ St. Patrick (at right)

▲ Pope Gregory I

▲ St. Boniface

myworldhistory.com
Primary Source

637

Illuminated Manuscripts

Some medieval monks spent their days copying ancient texts and creating illuminated manuscripts, or illustrated works. They decorated certain religious works with elaborate illustrations of biblical scenes or Christian concepts.

▲ A monk working on a manuscript

This illuminated manuscript from the 1100s shows hell (above) and heaven (right).

▲ The richly decorated cover of the Lindau Gospels, about 880, shows Jesus (center), angels (top), and figures from the Crucifixion (bottom).

▲ This medieval illustration shows the baptism of Jesus.

The Medieval Church

As Christianity spread, the Catholic Church gradually became a powerful force in Europe. Church leaders influenced not only the spiritual life of medieval Catholics, but also many aspects of secular, or nonreligious, life.

Catholic Teachings As you read in an earlier chapter, the Church taught that people should live lives based on the teachings of Jesus. Sins, such as stealing or doing harm to others, were violations of God's law. Catholics believed that the way people lived would affect what happened to their souls after death.

The concepts of heaven and hell were central to medieval Catholic beliefs.

Heaven was described as a perfect place of peace and beauty, where the souls of those who followed God's laws would go after death. Hell was described as a fiery place of punishment for sinners.

Catholics believed that the only way to avoid hell was to do good deeds, believe in Jesus, and participate in the sacraments. The **sacraments** are the sacred rites of the Christian Church, such as baptism and communion. Baptism is a rite that uses water as a sign of spiritual purification and admits a person to the Christian community. Communion is a rite in which people consume consecrated bread and wine, or bread and wine that has been made sacred and which Catholics believe thus becomes the body and blood of Jesus.

The Church's Power The pope and other Catholic leaders had significant influence in medieval Europe. Medieval Europeans believed that the Church was the highest authority and the guardian of God's truth. Because the Church controlled the administration of the sacraments, it could punish people by denying them the sacraments. Medieval Catholics believed that people who did not receive the sacraments would be condemned to hell.

The Church also controlled some land and wealth directly. The pope controlled vast lands in central Italy, and many high-ranking clergy were nobles who had their own territories and armies. Some wealthy monasteries held large areas of land.

Secular rulers sometimes struggled against the influence of the Church. For example, they argued over whether the pope or secular leaders had the right to choose local bishops.

Christendom Eventually, most peoples of Europe were united under the Catholic faith. Although Christians might speak

▲ Charlemagne built the Palatine Chapel in Aachen, Germany, as part of his palace.

different languages and follow different customs, they saw themselves as part of Christendom. **Christendom** is the large community of Christians spread across the world. The idea of Christendom gave the peoples of Europe a common identity and a sense of purpose. Over time, this sense of common purpose would bring some Christians into conflict with their pagan, Jewish, and Muslim neighbors.

Reading Check Why did the Catholic Church have great power over medieval life?

Section 2 Assessment

Key Terms

1. How do monasteries and convents differ?
2. What is a pagan?
3. List two examples of sacraments.

Key Ideas

4. How did missionaries help spread Christianity throughout Europe?
5. What did medieval monks and nuns do?
6. Why was the Catholic Church a center of authority?

Think Critically

7. **Draw Conclusions** How did monasteries help keep classical Greek and Roman civilization alive?
8. **Summarize** How did Christian teachings affect the lives of medieval Europeans?

Essential Question

What is power? Who should have it?

9. Describe the power of the Catholic Church in medieval Europe. Go to your Student Journal to record your answer.

Section 3
The Development of European Feudalism

Key Ideas

- Invasions by Vikings and other groups created disorder in Europe.
- Feudalism brought social and political order to Europe.
- Manorialism created many small, self-sufficient economic units.

Key Terms • vassal • fief • knight • chivalry • manor • serf

 (**Visual Glossary**)

Reading Skill Identify Main Ideas and Details Take notes using the graphic organizer in your journal.

 ▲ A Viking helmet, about 800–900

Charlemagne was able to unite much of Western Europe. After his death, however, his empire split apart. The collapse of Charlemagne's empire left Western Europe open to invasion. It also led to the development of a new system of life called feudalism.

A Violent Time

During the years between 800 and 1000, invaders threatened Western Europe from all directions. From the east came a people called the Magyars, who conquered what is now Hungary. They made fearsome raids into Germany, Italy, and other parts of Western Europe. From the south and east came Muslim soldiers from Spain, North Africa, and southwest Asia. In the late 800s, they conquered the island of Sicily, which became a thriving center of Muslim culture.

Viking Invasions The boldest and most successful invaders were the Vikings. They were from Scandinavia, a region of northern Europe that now includes Norway, Sweden, and Denmark. In the late 700s, Viking sailors began raiding monasteries in Scotland, England, and Ireland. Monasteries were ideal targets because they were often wealthy and poorly defended. Viking raiders also looted and burned farms and villages. They sailed up rivers into the heart of Europe, where they attacked villages and burned churches in Paris.

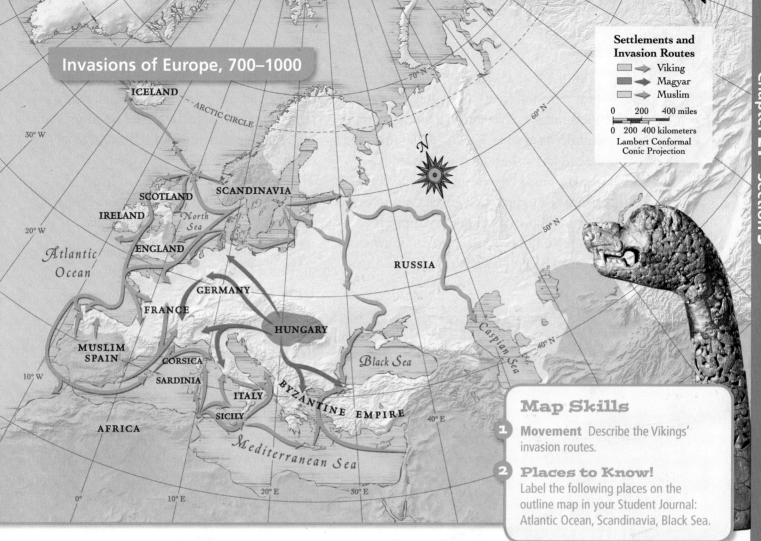

Invasions of Europe, 700–1000

ICELAND

ARCTIC CIRCLE

SCANDINAVIA

SCOTLAND

IRELAND

North Sea

ENGLAND

Atlantic Ocean

GERMANY

FRANCE

HUNGARY

RUSSIA

MUSLIM SPAIN

CORSICA

SARDINIA

Black Sea

Caspian Sea

ITALY

BYZANTINE EMPIRE

SICILY

AFRICA

Mediterranean Sea

Settlements and Invasion Routes

- Viking
- Magyar
- Muslim

0   200   400 miles
0   200   400 kilometers
Lambert Conformal Conic Projection

Map Skills

1 **Movement** Describe the Vikings' invasion routes.

2 **Places to Know!** Label the following places on the outline map in your Student Journal: Atlantic Ocean, Scandinavia, Black Sea.

Viking Exploration and Trade The Vikings were not just destructive raiders. They were also farmers, traders, and explorers who sailed throughout the North Atlantic Ocean. Some ventured into the Mediterranean Sea. Around the year 1000, Vikings established a short-lived colony in North America. They also settled in England, Ireland, northern France, and parts of Russia, where they mixed with the local populations. Viking travel in Russia helped open up trade routes between southwest Asia and Western Europe.

Reading Check What areas of Europe did the Vikings invade?

A Feudal Society

In the early Middle Ages, kings and emperors were too weak to protect their people from Magyar, Muslim, and Viking invasions. Instead, powerful local lords took over the responsibility of protecting people's homes and lands. The result was a system of feudalism that had some similarities to that of medieval Japan.

Lords and Vassals European feudalism was a system of rule in which powerful lords divided their lands among lesser lords, or **vassals.** In exchange for the land, a vassal pledged his service and <u>loyalty</u> to the more powerful lord.

▲ The carved head of a beast from a Viking ship

loyalty, *n.,* the state of being faithful

▲ A medieval seal shows a knight fighting a dragon.

In the feudal system, a powerful lord granted a **fief** (feef), or estate, to a vassal. Fiefs ranged in size from a few acres to hundreds of square miles. A fief included any towns or buildings on the land, as well as peasants to farm it. The lord also promised to protect the vassal. In return, the vassal provided military support and money or food for the lord. In many cases, a vassal had his own vassals below him.

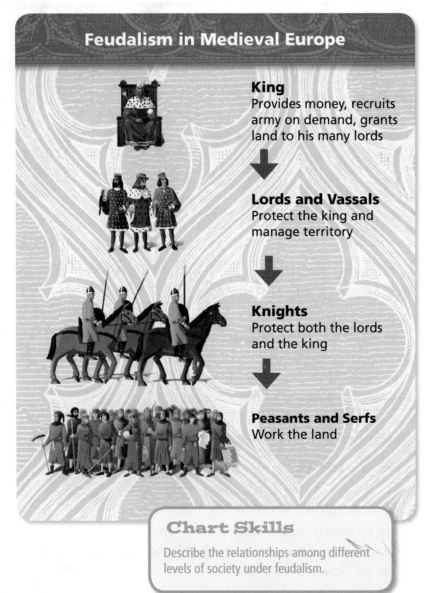

Feudalism in Medieval Europe

King
Provides money, recruits army on demand, grants land to his many lords

Lords and Vassals
Protect the king and manage territory

Knights
Protect both the lords and the king

Peasants and Serfs
Work the land

Chart Skills
Describe the relationships among different levels of society under feudalism.

Like Japanese daimyos, European lords built castles from which they ruled nearby lands. Over time, these castles became larger and grander, with high walls, towers, and drawbridges over wide moats. These castles were fortresses in times of war. When fighting broke out, local peasants took shelter behind castle walls.

Knights and Warfare For medieval lords and vassals, warfare was a way of life. Lords battled constantly for power. As a result, many boys and young men from noble families trained to become **knights,** or warriors mounted on horseback.

Around the age of seven, a boy who was to become a knight was sent to the castle of his father's lord. There, he learned how to fight and ride a horse. After years of training, he pledged his loyalty to the lord and became a knight.

Knights were expected to live by a code of conduct called **chivalry,** which required them to be brave, loyal, and generous. They had to fight fairly in battle. A medieval poet described the ideal knight:

> ❝ A knight there was, and that a worthy man,
> Who . . . vowed himself to chivalry,
> Honour and truth, freedom and courtesy . . .
> He was a very perfect gentle knight. ❞
>
> —Geoffrey Chaucer, *The Canterbury Tales*

During war, knights served their lords in battle. Knights usually fought on horseback. They used swords, axes, and lances, or long spears. Early medieval knights wore armor made of chain mail with thousands of small metal rings.

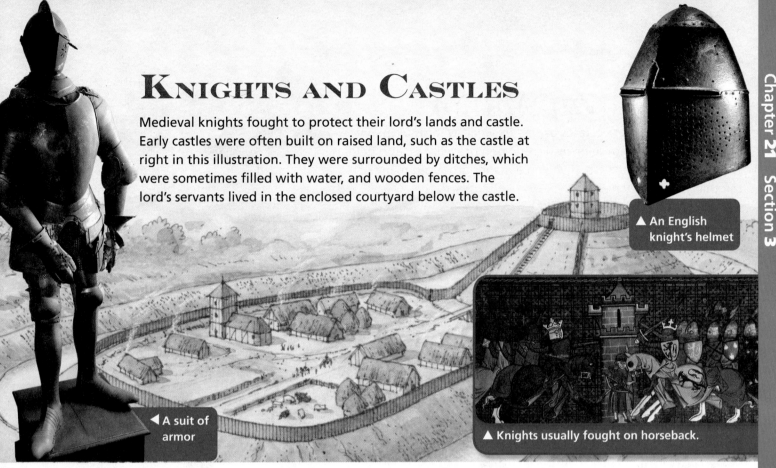

KNIGHTS AND CASTLES

Medieval knights fought to protect their lord's lands and castle. Early castles were often built on raised land, such as the castle at right in this illustration. They were surrounded by ditches, which were sometimes filled with water, and wooden fences. The lord's servants lived in the enclosed courtyard below the castle.

▲ An English knight's helmet

◄ A suit of armor

▲ Knights usually fought on horseback.

Later in the Middle Ages, knights wore heavy plate armor made of solid metal.

Comparing European and Japanese Feudalism European and Japanese feudalism shared some features. Both began during a time of violence and warfare. Both involved an exchange of land for services. Both knights and samurai were expected to follow codes of conduct that emphasized honor, bravery, and loyalty.

The two forms of feudalism had a major difference: religion. Most Europeans were Christian. Japanese feudalism was influenced by ideas from Buddhism, Shinto, and Confucianism. As a result, Europeans and Japanese had very different spiritual beliefs and views of the world.

Reading Check In what ways did lords have power over medieval life?

The Medieval Manor

The heart of the medieval economy was the **manor,** or the agricultural estate of a medieval lord. Manors were centered around the lord's house or castle. In addition to the lord's house, a manor usually included one or more villages and the surrounding fields and forests.

Peasants and Serfs Peasants made up the majority of the medieval population. Most people who lived and worked on a manor were peasants. Many of these peasants were **serfs,** or peasants who were legally bound to the lord's land. Serfs were not slaves who could be bought and sold, but they were not free. They could not leave the manor without the lord's permission. If the manor was given to a new lord, the serfs went along with it.

643

Closer Look

A Medieval Manor

Medieval manors were estates owned by wealthy lords. A manor included the lord's house or castle, one or more villages, and fields. The peasants and serfs who lived on a manor produced many of the things that they needed.

THINK CRITICALLY **How did manors shape medieval life?**

1. Manor house
2. Peasant fieldworkers
3. Mill
4. Sheep
5. Peasant house
6. Village church
7. Vegetable garden
8. Well

Life on the Manor Manors produced a wide range of goods and services, but they could not produce everything people needed. For that, people traveled to nearby market towns. Still, in the early Middle Ages, most peasants spent much of their lives in the places where they were born.

The peasants on a manor worked together to plant, care for, and harvest crops on the lord's lands. They generally worked about two or three days a week on the lord's land. At planting and harvest time they worked longer.

Peasants spent much of the remainder of their time growing crops for themselves and their families. They did so on land that the lord allowed them to use for this purpose. Peasants were also allowed to cut wood from the lord's forests to use for fuel and for building. They ground grain into flour at the lord's mill.

Peasants raised sheep, pigs, and cattle for meat. Women spun sheep's wool or linen fibers into thread. They wove woolen and linen cloth into clothing. Specialists such as carpenters and blacksmiths also lived and worked on the manor.

Managing the Manor In the early Middle Ages, the lord's wife ran the household. Because the lady was from a noble family, she probably was educated. She had learned Latin and her own language, as well as music, astronomy, and herbal remedies.

As the manor system developed during the Middle Ages, male officials gradually took over the running of the manor. The lord of the manor judged minor crimes and settled arguments among people on his manor. His officials looked after day-to-day affairs. The bailiff kept the estate's accounts and served as judge when the lord was away. The bailiff also collected taxes from the peasants, often in the form of farm products. Another official was the reeve, who was usually elected by the villagers. He had jobs such as repairing buildings and overseeing peasants at work.

Reading Check Why did ordinary people rarely leave the manor on which they lived?

my **World**
CONNECTIONS

Today, people move more often than in the Middle Ages. Nearly **12%** of Americans moved in **2008**.

myWorld Activity
Matching Game

Section **3** Assessment

Essential Question

Key Terms

1. What was a manor?

2. Did serfs or vassals have more power in medieval Europe?

3. What was a fief?

Key Ideas

4. What groups of invaders threatened Europe between 800 and 1000?

5. How were manors self-sufficient?

6. How did the concept of chivalry affect knights?

Think Critically

7. Compare and Contrast How were European and Japanese feudalism similar and different?

8. Synthesize How did feudalism shape medieval Europe?

What is power? Who should have it?

9. How did feudalism and the manor system affect the lives of people in medieval Europe? Go to your Student Journal to record your answer.

Chapter Assessment

Key Terms and Ideas

1. **Recall** What is a **missionary**?
2. **Discuss** How did Charlemagne expand his power and territory?
3. **Explain** What is a **monastery**?
4. **Describe** What was **manor** life like for **serfs** and peasants?
5. **Summarize** How did **missionaries** work to expand **Christendom**?
6. **Explain** Why was **chivalry** an important concept for medieval **knights**?
7. **Discuss** How did **vassals** serve more powerful lords?

Think Critically

8. **Draw Conclusions** How did Europe's geography affect the Viking, Magyar, and Muslim invasions between the years 800 and 1000?
9. **Summarize** How and why did Christianity spread through Europe during the early Middle Ages?
10. **Sequence** Put the following events in chronological order, beginning with the earliest: Charlemagne becomes emperor, Benedict organizes a monastery, Vikings establish a North American colony, and Clovis defeats a Roman army.
11. **Core Concepts: Political Structures** How was power distributed under feudalism?

Analyze Visuals

This painting from the 1800s shows Alcuin of York, a teacher and scholar at Charlemagne's court, giving several manuscripts to Charlemagne. Look at the painting and answer the following questions.

12. What does this painting suggest about Charlemagne's power?

13. Based on this painting and your reading, how did Charlemagne feel about education?

14. What evidence do you see of Charlemagne's religious beliefs?

Essential Question

myWorld Chapter Activity

A Knight's Journal Follow your teacher's instructions to role-play the journey of a medieval knight to the castle of the knight's new lord. Work with your group to collect information about manors, monasteries, villages, castles, and other aspects of medieval life. Then write and illustrate a journal describing the knight's journey.

21st Century Learning

Give an Effective Presentation

Write and illustrate a comic strip about a person, event, or topic from the chapter. Your comic strip does not need to be humorous, but it should clearly describe the topic you chose. Then present your comic strip to the class. Be sure to describe and explain your illustrations and text.

Document-Based Questions

Success Tracker™
Online at myworldhistory.com

Use your knowledge of the early Middle Ages and Documents A and B to answer Questions 1–3.

Document A

" The Muslims planned to go to Tours to destroy the Church of St. Martin, the city, and the whole country. Then came against them the glorious Prince Charles [Charles Martel], at the head of his whole force. He drew up his host, and he fought as fiercely as the hungry wolf falls upon the stag. By the grace of Our Lord, . . . he slew in that battle 300,000 men. . . . And what was the greatest marvel of all, he only lost in that battle 1500 men."

—Michel Pintoin, *The Chronicle of St. Denis*, 1400s

1. Why was the battle of Tours an important event in medieval European history?

   A It led to Charlemagne becoming emperor.

   B It ended a Muslim military advance into Western Europe.

   C It allowed Christian monks to travel to Tours.

   D It helped feudalism spread.

Document B

" He who swears [loyalty] to his lord ought always to have these six things in memory; what is harmless, safe, honorable, useful, easy, practicable. . . . [But] it is not sufficient to abstain from evil, unless what is good is done also. It remains, therefore, that in the same six things mentioned above he should faithfully counsel and aid his lord. . . . The lord also ought to act toward his faithful vassal [in the same way] in all these things."

—Bishop Fulrad of Chartres, letter to William V, Duke of Acquitaine, 1020

2. What is Bishop Fulrad describing in Document B?

   A the Benedictine Rule

   B the sacraments of the Catholic Church

   C the manor system economy

   D the obligations of vassal and lord under feudalism

3. **Writing Task** How did medieval kings and lords use their power? Answer in a short paragraph.

my worldhistory.com

Self-Test

Chapter 22

Conflicts and Crusades

Essential Question

How should we handle conflict?

Attack on Jerusalem during the Crusades, in this scene from a recent movie

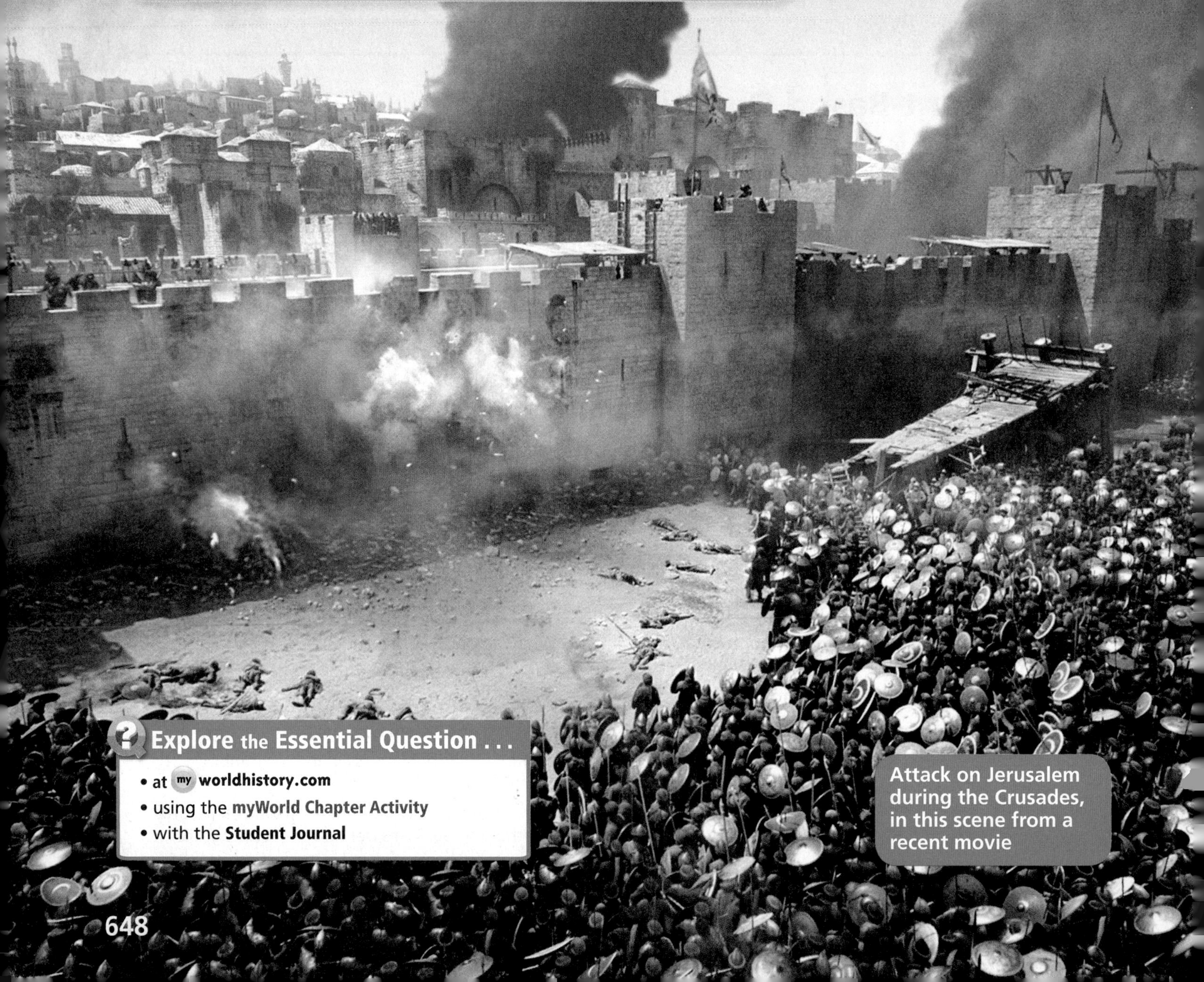

Explore the Essential Question . . .

- at my worldhistory.com
- using the **myWorld Chapter Activity**
- with the **Student Journal**

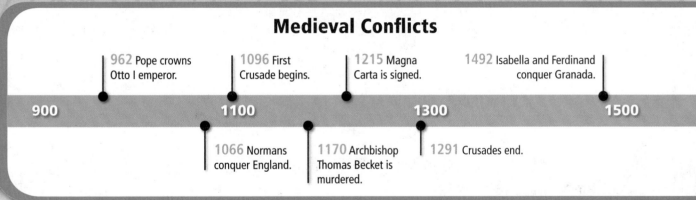

Medieval Conflicts

962 Pope crowns Otto I emperor.	1096 First Crusade begins.	1215 Magna Carta is signed.	1492 Isabella and Ferdinand conquer Granada.

900 — 1100 — 1300 — 1500

1066 Normans conquer England. 1170 Archbishop Thomas Becket is murdered. 1291 Crusades end.

Henry II's *Murderous Words*

This myStory is a fictionalized account of events in the life of real people from this chapter.

Music and laughter echoed through the castle, but this Christmas, in 1170, King Henry II of England was not in a festive mood. As Duke of Normandy, he controlled much land in France, and it was here, in one of his French fortresses, that he was celebrating the season, far from his troubles in England.

Henry watched silently as servants attended to diners in the Great Hall and his knights gorged on fine food and drink. In turn, his courtiers kept an eye on their king. They sensed that he was about to explode in fury.

Henry was large and athletic. His arrogance befitted someone who had been a well-educated, capable king since the age of 22. All who knew him feared the violence of his temper. During tantrums, Henry was known to froth at the mouth, hurl objects across the room, and even throw himself down to chew the rushes spread out on the floor.

Everyone in the castle hall knew that King Henry II was about to explode in fury.

my worldhistory.com

Timeline/On Assignment

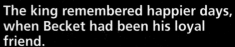
The king remembered happier days, when Becket had been his loyal friend.

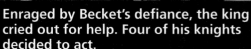
Enraged by Becket's defiance, the king cried out for help. Four of his knights decided to act.

This Christmas Henry had plenty to be angry about. His thoughts kept turning to his long feud with Thomas Becket, his former friend and chancellor, or chief minister. Brilliant, cheerful Becket had once been the king's faithful companion. In those early days of their friendship, Becket had been so much fun. Henry had taken him hunting, discussing matters of state as they rode through the countryside. The king often joined Becket for dinner, and even sent his son Henry to live with Becket for a time. The king had no better friend.

As chancellor, Becket devoted himself to Henry's main goal—strengthening the Crown, even if that meant defying the Church. All over Europe, a conflict between Church and state was raging, and King Henry was glad to have a close friend like Becket on his side.

But ever since Becket had been appointed archbishop of Canterbury, eight years earlier, the king's old friend had changed. Becket was now the most important bishop in England and took his new job seriously. When the king tried to limit the clergy's privileges, Becket defied the king's authority. Torn between duty and friendship, between loyalty to the Church and his friendship with the king, Becket had increasingly favored the Church.

Henry reacted first with disappointment, and then rage, as he watched his friend change. As king, Henry expected both obedience from his subjects and devotion from his friends. So he regarded Becket's behavior as the ultimate betrayal. Even now, at Christmas time, the season of goodwill, Henry's anger knew no bounds. In the midst of the feast, he stunned his courtiers into silence as he starting shouting about Becket's "treason." His outburst ended with a scream: "How can you all allow me, your king, to be treated with such contempt?"

What exactly did Henry mean by this? Four of his knights decided that they knew.

The knights slipped out of the Great Hall and mounted their horses. Reaching the French coast, they sailed across the channel to England, where they rode swiftly to Canterbury Cathedral. On the morning of December 29, they confronted Archbishop Becket in the cathedral and tried to drag him outside. Becket resisted with all his might. But it was four against one, and during the struggle, the knights struck him with their swords. The archbishop died later that afternoon.

When Henry heard of the murder, he was overcome with sorrow and regret. He realized that this had been the worst possible way to resolve their

On a cold December morning, the knights burst into Canterbury Cathedral.

They approached the archbishop with their swords drawn.

conflict. As the news spread, people condemned what Henry's knights had done. The king himself was blamed for the crime.

King Henry realized that he had to perform a public penance, or act of self-punishment, for his role in the murder. So the king walked in rags through the streets, kneeling before the people to beg forgiveness. Meanwhile, Canterbury became a shrine to the archbishop, as pilgrims arrived to honor the spot where he had been slain. Becket was transformed into a martyr, someone who dies for his beliefs. And despite his accomplishments, Henry II was condemned as the man whose angry words provoked the murder of Thomas Becket, minister of God.

Based on this story, how do you think Henry might have handled the conflict with his old friend Thomas Becket? As you read the chapter ahead, think about what Henry's story tells you about some of the conflicts of the Middle Ages.

→ myStory Video

Join Henry II and Thomas Becket as they argue about Church and state.

The king begged forgiveness.

651

Popes and Rulers

Key Ideas

- In the 1000s and 1100s, both the popes and the German emperors claimed authority in Europe.
- During the later Middle Ages, popes and monarchs competed for power.
- In England and France, strong monarchies emerged.

Key Terms • secular • excommunicate • pilgrimage

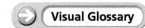 **Visual Glossary**

 Reading Skill Compare and Contrast Take notes using the graphic organizer in your journal.

▲ Otto III, grandson of Otto the Great, seated between officials of the Church (standing on the left) and the state

For centuries after the decline of Rome, people in Europe were still awed by the memory of the Roman empire. Churchmen and kings all claimed the authority of Rome. The Church continued to use Latin, the language of Rome. The popes governed the Church from Rome itself. At a time when Europe was split into hundreds of states, many longed for the political unity of the Roman empire.

As you have read, the Frankish king Charlemagne took the title of "emperor" in the year 800. He hoped to revive not only the Roman empire, but classical learning as well. Even though Charlemagne's empire did not last, later rulers pursued the same goals.

Reviving an Empire

After Charlemagne's empire collapsed, the eastern, German part of the kingdom was divided among a number of dukes. Following Germanic tradition, they chose one of their own to be king.

A German king known as Otto the Great increased his power by making alliances with other German nobles. In 962, he persuaded the pope to crown him emperor. By adopting this title, Otto was claiming to be the successor of Charlemagne.

Otto's empire included the land that came to be known as Germany, and also extended into Italian lands. In time, German

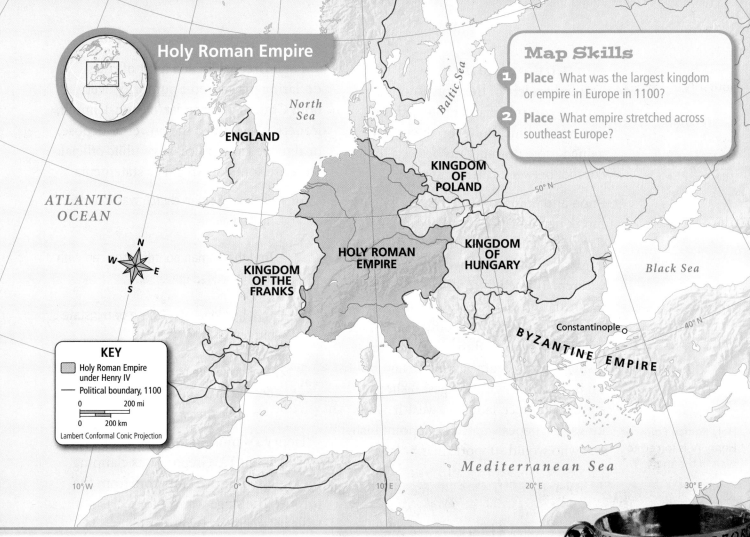

Holy Roman Empire

North Sea

ENGLAND

ATLANTIC OCEAN

Baltic Sea

KINGDOM OF POLAND

50° N

KINGDOM OF THE FRANKS

HOLY ROMAN EMPIRE

KINGDOM OF HUNGARY

Black Sea

Constantinople

40° N

BYZANTINE EMPIRE

KEY

Holy Roman Empire under Henry IV

Political boundary, 1100

0   200 mi

0   200 km

Lambert Conformal Conic Projection

Mediterranean Sea

10° W   0°   10° E   20° E   30° E

Map Skills

1 **Place** What was the largest kingdom or empire in Europe in 1100?

2 **Place** What empire stretched across southeast Europe?

emperors claimed authority over much of central and Eastern Europe. But their empire was not like an ancient empire, controlled by a single government. Instead, it was a collection of states ruled by princes who were loyal to the emperor.

Despite his limited power, Otto created a stable kingdom. His empire was prosperous and saw a great revival in the arts.

Like Charlemagne, Otto worked closely with the Church and strengthened the Church within his empire. In fact, the Church became so strong that eventually it rivaled the authority of the state.

After the death of Otto the Great, his empire continued to be ruled by his descendents, who became known as the Ottonian kings. The empire itself came to be called the Holy Roman Empire. The name of the empire showed that the German kings wanted to create a Christian, or holy, version of the Roman empire. In addition, by claiming to be Roman, the German kings were challenging the Byzantine rulers, who also called themselves Roman emperors.

Reading Check What was the Holy Roman Empire?

▲ Chalice made during the reign of the Ottonian kings

653

A Study in Conflict

The early rulers of the Holy Roman Empire controlled and protected the Church. In time, however, the popes gained more power. Thus began a long conflict between rulers and popes.

Pope and Emperor In 1073, an Italian monk named Hildebrand became Pope Gregory VII. Gregory believed that the emperor should not have power over the Church. This led to conflict with Henry IV, the Holy Roman emperor at the time.

Gregory insisted that only the Roman pontiff, or pope, had the right to choose bishops. This became an important political issue in the Middle Ages. Bishops controlled much land and wealth. Both kings and popes wanted to appoint bishops who would support their policies.

Holy Roman Emperor Henry IV is forced to wait in the snow. ▼

Pope Gregory issued a list of rules declaring his supreme <u>authority</u> over both Church and **secular,** or non-Church, leaders. He claimed the power to depose, or remove from office, any public official. Here are some of Gregory's statements.

> 66 1. That the Roman church was founded by God alone.
>
> 2. That the Roman pontiff alone can with right be called universal.
>
> 3. That he alone can depose or reinstate bishops. . . .
>
> 12. That it may be permitted to him to depose emperors. 99
>
> —Pope Gregory VII, *Dictatus Papae*

Henry IV must have been stunned by statement 12. Gregory was claiming the right to remove emperors from the throne! The stage was set for a clash of wills between the two men.

A Defiant Ruler The struggle began when Henry ignored the pope's rules. The emperor named his own bishop for the city of Milan, Italy. In response, Pope Gregory appointed a rival bishop. When Henry tried to remove Gregory from his position as pope, Gregory excommunicated Henry. To **excommunicate** means to exclude a person from a church or a religious community. The pope freed Henry's subjects from their feudal oaths of loyalty to the emperor.

Without the support of his subjects, Henry had no power. Desperate to end his excommunication, Henry visited the pope in an Italian castle. The pope kept

Henry waiting in the snow, outside the castle, for three days. Though the pope forgave Henry, their conflict continued. Henry later marched his army to Rome and forced the pope from the city.

The struggle between popes and rulers continued long after Gregory and Henry died. Eventually, in 1122, the Church and the Holy Roman Empire reached an agreement called the Concordat of Worms (kon KOR dat of vurmz). This agreement gave the Church the sole authority to appoint bishops. But it also allowed emperors to give fiefs, or grants of land, to bishops, in order to win their loyalty. Despite this agreement, conflicts between popes and rulers continued.

Reading Check How did Pope Gregory try to destroy Henry IV's authority?

Church and State in England

Elsewhere, similar conflicts were raging between Church and state. In England, a long struggle set King Henry II against his old friend, Thomas Becket, the archbishop of Canterbury.

Henry and Thomas Becket had once been allies. In 1162, King Henry appointed Becket to be the archbishop of Canterbury. Becket was now the most important bishop in the land.

Henry wanted to expand royal power. He thought that Becket would support his policies. But to the king's dismay, Becket grew more loyal to the Church than to the state. Becket resisted Henry's attempt to limit the power and independence of the Church. The struggle became so fierce that Becket excommunicated Henry.

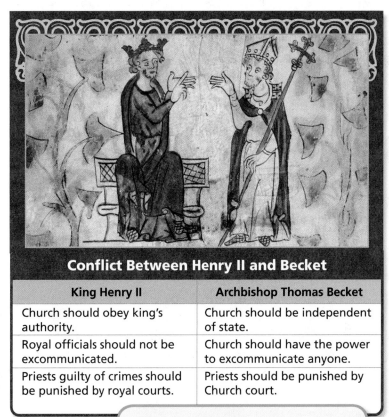

Conflict Between Henry II and Becket

King Henry II	Archbishop Thomas Becket
Church should obey king's authority.	Church should be independent of state.
Royal officials should not be excommunicated.	Church should have the power to excommunicate anyone.
Priests guilty of crimes should be punished by royal courts.	Priests should be punished by Church court.

Chart Skills

Why would the king want the right to punish priests who were guilty of crimes?

At last, Henry became so angry that he uttered words that he later regretted. As you read in the myStory for this chapter, some of his knights believed that the king was calling for Becket's death. They traveled to Canterbury and murdered the archbishop in the church itself.

The murder of an archbishop shocked Christendom. A shrine was set up where Becket had been killed. The cathedral of Canterbury became a destination of **pilgrimage**—a journey undertaken to worship at a holy place.

Reading Check Why was Thomas Becket murdered?

655

The Medieval Church

was rich, powerful, and well organized. The pope governed through a system of graded ranks known as a hierarchy (HI er ar kee).

THINK CRITICALLY **In what ways was the Church hierarchy like the feudal system?**

▲ The pope was the head of the Church.

Archbishops

◀ An archbishop ruled an important archdiocese, or religious district. He governed bishops.

Bishops

◀ A bishop supervised a diocese, usually a town district. He ordained new priests and ruled over court cases.

Priests

◀ A priest served in the local parish church and collected Church taxes.

Kings Grow Stronger

Between the 900s and 1200, there were few strong rulers in Europe. Political power lay with aristocrats, whose castles helped them control their lands. Then, in England and France, power began to shift into the hands of monarchs.

Increased Trade By the 1100s, trade was increasing throughout Europe. As trade boomed, kings benefited from taxes on the profits. The kings' new riches strengthened them politically.

King of France The ancestors of the French kings were merely aristocrats with little power. One family, the Capetians, (kuh PAY shunz) established their capital in Paris. Over time, their kingdom grew stronger. One Capetian ruler, King Philip II Augustus, came to the throne in 1180. He acquired large holdings of land. Royal documents refer to him with the new title of "King of France" rather than the old title of "King of the Franks."

Philip II created new officials to oversee justice. He also gained more control over the French Church.

Kingdom of England The roots of the kingdom of England reach back to a time before England existed. In the 400s, Germanic tribes began settling in the east of Britain. These tribes became known as Anglo-Saxons. Anglo-Saxon kingdoms formed, and the land <u>occupied</u> by these kingdoms became known as "England," or the land of the Angles.

During the 900s and 1000s, England became much more organized under a centralized government. A standardized system of coinage came into use throughout the kingdom.

By 1066, England was a stronger state. But despite the growing power of the English monarchy, the king was unable to resist an invasion led by a duke from northern France. In the next section, you will read about this invasion, which changed the history of Europe forever.

Reading Check Which states in Europe developed strong monarchies?

occupy, *v.,* to take up or fill up space

Section **1** Assessment

Key Terms

1. Use the following terms to describe the struggle between popes and rulers: secular, excommunicate, pilgrimage.

Key Ideas

2. What was the connection between ancient Rome and the Holy Roman Empire?

3. How did the popes try to control monarchs?

4. How did increased trade strengthen the power of the kings?

Think Critically

5. **Draw Inferences** Why did so many rulers try to claim the authority of ancient Rome?

6. **Draw Conclusions** Why did kings want the right to appoint bishops?

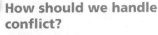

Essential Question

How should we handle conflict?

7. What mistakes did Henry II make in his conflict with the Church? Go to your Student Journal to record your answer.

Kings, Nobles, and the Magna Carta

Key Ideas

- The Norman Conquest transformed the history and culture of England.
- Magna Carta limited the monarch's power and helped establish rights that Americans enjoy today.
- Over time, England developed a representative government under a limited monarchy.

Key Terms
- Magna Carta
- common law
- habeas corpus
- writ
- parliament

→ **Visual Glossary**

Reading Skill Identify Main Ideas and Details Take notes using the graphic organizer in your journal.

The Normans attack London. ▼

On Christmas Day in 1066, William, Duke of Normandy, was about to be crowned king of England at Westminster Abbey, near London. But William and his Norman knights were nervous. They had just seized power and were afraid of an uprising. When the English crowds outside began to cheer, the Normans misunderstood and panicked. They attacked the people and set fire to nearby houses.

Inside the great coronation church, the ceremony continued. As the crown was placed on William's head, the firelight from the burning houses flickered over the church walls. It was a fitting coronation for a warlord who had gained power by sword and flame.

The Norman Conquest

William was descended from Viking raiders called Northmen, or Normans, who settled in northern France. This area of France came to be called Normandy, after the Normans. The dukes of Normandy became great feudal lords. They grew rich collecting taxes from traders who crossed their lands. In time, they wanted new lands to rule.

Norman Claims on England For some time, the Normans had been interested in the wealth of nearby England. Duke William of Normandy was related to the Anglo-Saxon king, Edward the Confessor. But Edward was a weak ruler. The real power in England was held by a noble family called the Godwins. Harold Godwin, Earl of Wessex, expected to inherit the throne.

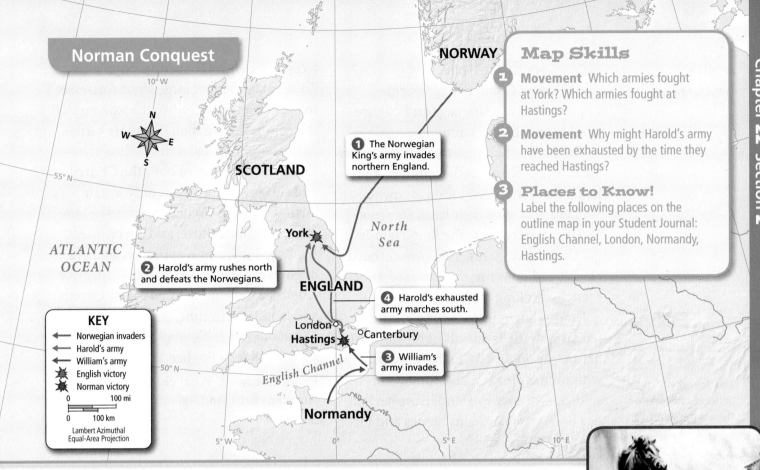

Norman Conquest

NORWAY

10° W

55° N

SCOTLAND

1 The Norwegian King's army invades northern England.

York

North Sea

2 Harold's army rushes north and defeats the Norwegians.

ATLANTIC OCEAN

ENGLAND

4 Harold's exhausted army marches south.

London

Hastings

Canterbury

50° N

3 William's army invades.

English Channel

KEY

← Norwegian invaders
← Harold's army
← William's army
✳ English victory
✳ Norman victory

| 0 | 100 mi |
| 0 | 100 km |

Lambert Azimuthal
Equal-Area Projection

Normandy

5° W   0°   5° E   10° E

Map Skills

1 **Movement** Which armies fought at York? Which armies fought at Hastings?

2 **Movement** Why might Harold's army have been exhausted by the time they reached Hastings?

3 **Places to Know!** Label the following places on the outline map in your Student Journal: English Channel, London, Normandy, Hastings.

As Edward lay dying, he supposedly promised the English Crown to Harold. But William, Duke of Normandy, claimed that Edward had already promised the Crown to him. The Norwegian king also claimed the English throne. So when Harold became king, he faced two strong and threatening rivals.

William the Conqueror In late September 1066, the Norwegian king landed his army in northern England. The English king, Harold, and his army rushed north and defeated the Norwegian invasion. But a few days after Harold's victory, William of Normandy invaded southern England. Harold was forced to march his exhausted army 250 miles south to confront William's forces.

On October 14, the two armies met near the village of Hastings, on the south coast of England. The English were on foot, fighting with swords and spears. The Normans' excellent cavalry and skilled archers easily defeated them. Harold and his brothers were killed in the battle, ending Anglo-Saxon rule in England.

The Norman duke William was now "the conqueror" of England. He and his army fought their way across the land, burning and looting. On Christmas Day 1066, William the Conqueror was crowned king of England in Westminster Abbey.

Reading Check What happened at the Battle of Hastings?

my worldhistory.com

Places to Know

▲ Duke William grabs a handful of English sand as his army comes ashore.

659

Norman England

transform, *v.,* to change

The Norman Conquest <u>transformed</u> England. English language and culture would never be the same.

The Battle of Hastings wiped out many great Anglo-Saxon noble families. There had been some 5,000 local landowners. William now gave their lands to about 180 Norman barons. The king's family got the largest shares. This concentrated wealth and power in the hands of a small French-speaking elite.

King William introduced a strong feudal system. As vassals of the king, the barons, or noblemen, had to support him with military service and supply him with soldiers. All over England, Norman barons built great castles as homes and fortresses to control the native population. These were the first large stone fortresses to appear in Britain since the Romans left the country more than 600 years earlier.

England now had a new ruling class. Everyone in power in both the Church and the government was of Norman birth. Latin and French became the languages of law, culture, and government. English would not reappear as a language of government for 300 years. Meanwhile, Anglo-Saxons maintained their customs and language. In time, Anglo-Saxon and Norman French blended together to create the modern English language.

Reading Check What changes did the Normans bring to England?

The Tower of London was one of the castles built to control England. ▼

Reenactors re-create the overwhelming power of the Norman cavalry.

Closer Look

NORMAN POWER

Like their Viking ancestors, the Normans were daring. They quickly conquered the English, who vastly outnumbered them. The Normans' organizational skills helped them rule England. Today, evidence of Norman power survives in their buildings and in the very language that we speak.

THINK CRITICALLY Study the chart of formal and informal language. Why is one set of words still considered more formal? In what situations would you use more formal language?

▲ The Normans built huge cathedrals like this one in Durham.

English Words That Came from Norman French

Government	Law	The Arts
council	court	art
country	judge	beauty
government	justice	color
nation	prison	fashion
parliament	verdict	music

Thanks to the Normans, English speakers can use two styles of speech. Formal speech includes words that come from Norman French—the language of aristocracy. Informal speech relies on words from Anglo-Saxon—the language of the people.

Formal (from the Norman French)	Informal (from the Anglo-Saxon)
inquire	ask
sovereign	king
relatives	kin
construct	build
demonstrate	show

SOURCE: *The Story of English*, Robert MacNeil

military, *adj.,* having to do with the armed forces

Limits on Royal Power

The Norman kings were always trying to strengthen the central government. But powerful feudal lords often opposed them. Kings had to ask their barons for money and soldiers to wage wars and crusades. In return, the barons could make demands on their king.

King John In 1199, a new ruler became king of England. As a descendant of William the Conqueror, King John also claimed Normandy in France. However, claiming and ruling were very different things. By 1204, John had lost control over most of his French lands. To get them back, he needed to raise an army. To raise that army, he needed money from taxes. His efforts to fund his army led to conflict with his barons over taxes and royal power.

King John reluctantly signs the Magna Carta. ▼

Signing Magna Carta By 1215, England's leaders had had enough of King John's high taxes and <u>military</u> failures. Rebellious barons forced the king to sign a document that promised them certain rights. This document came to be known as the **Magna Carta,** which is Latin for "Great Charter."

In the Magna Carta, King John agreed to recognize the rights of barons. He promised he would not collect more taxes without the approval of a council of barons and churchmen. He also promised to recognize the right of trial by jury. The charter stated that the king:

> 66 [will not] proceed against [the accused], or send others to do so, except according to the lawful sentence of his peers and according to the Common Law. 99
>
> —Magna Carta
> Translated by Xavier Hildegarde

The Magna Carta set a historic example. It made it clear that even a king must abide by the law of the land. Over time, the rights in the Magna Carta were extended to ordinary people. With only a few changes, they became part of English law. Later, other governments—including that of the United States—adopted its basic principles: rule of law, trial by jury, and the right of the people to have a voice in their laws and taxation.

English Law When the Magna Carta referred to "the law of the land," it meant English, rather than Roman, law. In many countries, medieval law was based on Roman law. In England, the law of the land was a mix of Norman French feudal law, Church law, and old Anglo-Saxon common law. **Common law** is a body of law that has developed from custom and from judges' decisions, rather than from laws passed by a lawmaking assembly.

An important legal practice to come out of English common law is known as **habeas corpus,** a Latin phrase that means "you shall have the body." Habeas corpus refers to a court order to bring an arrested person before a judge or court. A jailer who receives a **writ,** or court order, of habeas corpus must either release the prisoner or present a good reason for keeping that person in jail. The purpose of this writ is to prevent secret arrests and imprisonment without trial. However, throughout British and American history, the writ of habeas corpus has often been suspended during times of war.

Parliament During the 1200s, English kings began seeking advice from county representatives. This was the beginning of one of the oldest representative assemblies in Europe, the English Parliament. A **parliament** is an assembly of represen-

▲ Visitors studying a copy of the Magna Carta in England

tatives who make laws. At first, the king would call a meeting of Parliament when he needed to raise taxes. Eventually, Parliament became a true lawmaking body, divided into two houses. The House of Lords represented nobles. The House of Commons represented more ordinary people such as knights and town leaders.

Reading Check **What document limited the king's power?**

my World
CONNECTIONS

English common law provided the foundation for both U.S. federal law and the laws of most states.

Section 2 Assessment

Key Terms

1. Use the following terms to describe the struggle for power that developed between kings and nobles: Magna Carta, common law, habeas corpus, writ, parliament.

Key Ideas

2. What happened in 1066?

3. How was land ownership affected by the Norman Conquest?

4. What is the Magna Carta?

Think Critically

5. **Synthesize** Why would habeas corpus strengthen a free society?

6. **Make Inferences** Why did the Magna Carta help lay the foundation of democracy?

Essential Question

How should we handle conflict?

7. How did the barons resolve their conflict with King John? Go to your Student Journal to record your answer.

Religious Crusades

Key Ideas

- Europeans launched the Crusades to free the Holy Land from Muslim control.
- During the Crusades, persecution of Jews, Muslims, and Christian heretics increased.
- The Crusades failed but had lasting economic and cultural effects.

Key Terms • Crusades • heresy • Inquisition

 Visual Glossary

Reading Skill Sequence Take notes using the graphic organizer in your journal.

Medieval illustration showing the Turks destroying Peter the Hermit's army ▼

In March 1096, farmers in northern France paused in their plowing to listen to a distant roar. It was the sound of a vast crowd of people singing hymns and calling others to join them. The farmers watched the approaching mob of peasants, some 20,000 strong, led by a man dressed as a hermit. The farmers immediately knew who he was. For months, Peter the Hermit had been calling on all Christians to join his fight to free Jerusalem. His preaching had inspired thousands to follow him. Like so many others before them, the farmers left their fields and became part of Peter the Hermit's army.

The **Crusades,** a series of military campaigns to establish Christian control over the Holy Land, had begun. Over the next few centuries, wave after wave of peasants, soldiers, and kings would travel from Europe to the Middle East in pursuit of this goal. Their campaigns would reshape both Europe and the Middle East.

Call for a Crusade

The Crusades began with high hopes. One goal was to protect Christian pilgrims as they visited the Holy Land of Palestine. Muslim caliphs, or leaders, had generally allowed Christian pilgrims to visit holy places. But in the early 1000s, the Fatimid Arabs started destroying churches and killing pilgrims. Then, in 1071, Seljuk (SEL jook) Turks took over Jerusalem from the Fatimids. The Turks harassed pilgrims and marched on the Christian city of Constantinople. So the Byzantine emperor in Constantinople asked Pope Urban II for help.

The Pope's Call In 1095, Pope Urban II called for a crusade to free the Holy Land. He called on the "soldiers of Christ" to defend Constantinople and liberate Jerusalem from the Turks. People answered the pope's call with enthusiasm. Their slogan was "*Deus le veult!*" which means "God wills it!"

The Crusader's Creed Some religious leaders used feudal concepts to explain the idea of a holy war: Since Jesus was every Christian's Lord, Jesus' vassals were obliged to defend his lands and shrines. So a crusade was a just, or righteous, war.

The word *crusade* comes from the Latin word *crux,* or "cross." Crusaders sewed a cross on their clothing. They took a vow to make a pilgrimage to Jesus' tomb. Like other pilgrims, crusaders were promised forgiveness for sins.

People who "took the cross" made many sacrifices. Crusaders faced robbers, hunger, and disease before even encountering the enemy. Knights sold estates and borrowed money to pay for the long and dangerous trip. On his way to the Holy Land, one crusader, the French noble, Jean de Joinville, wrote:

> 66 I never once let my eyes turn back towards Joinville, for fear my heart might be filled with longing at the thought of my lovely castle and the two children I had left behind. 99
> —Jean de Joinville, *Life of Saint Louis*

Although many crusaders were members of the nobility, others hoped to gain land and wealth by joining the Crusades.

The First Crusade Perhaps as many as 150,000 people hurried to join. The first group of crusaders to leave for the Holy Land was a ragged mob of peasants led by Peter the Hermit. Peter's "army" of untrained men, women, and children was not prepared for the long journey to the Middle East. Most were killed by the Turks before ever reaching the Holy Land. More professional armies followed, traveling by land and sea.

Despite setbacks, the First Crusade was a military success. The crusaders had one important advantage—they took the Muslim kingdoms by surprise. The Muslims of the Middle East were too divided to resist. By 1099, the crusaders had captured Jerusalem and <u>established</u> four crusader states in the Holy Land. The crusaders also turned back the Turks' advance on Constantinople.

establish, *v.,* to set up

Reading Check Why did people join the Crusades?

◀ Medieval illustration of a praying knight. Many people hoped that crusading would cleanse them of their sins.

665

▲ A nineteenth-century depiction of Eleanor of Aquitaine, who participated in the Second Crusade

Second and Third Crusades

The crusader states were always on the defensive. In 1144, the Muslims counter-attacked and conquered the northern crusader state of Edessa. The fall of Edessa alarmed Europeans so much that the pope called for a second crusade.

Second Crusade King Louis VII of France and the German emperor orga-nized the Second Crusade. Other mon-archs, such as King Louis' wife, Eleanor of Aquitaine, also joined this crusade. But despite its powerful backing, the Second Crusade failed. There were sev-eral reasons for this failure. For example, the crusade's leaders argued. The crusad-ers, who often treated the Muslim major-ity of Palestine with disrespect and even cruelty, were unable to gain local support.

After the Second Crusade failed, the Muslim leader Saladin grew stronger. In 1187, Saladin recaptured Jerusalem.

"Crusade of the Kings" The fall of Jerusalem provoked the Third Crusade, which began in 1189. Because it was organized by the rulers of England, France, and Germany, it was called the "Crusade of the Kings." Richard I of England, called the "Lionheart," became leader of this crusade. He won important victories and developed a courteous rela-tionship with Saladin.

Saladin's noble character inspired respect, even from his enemies. One of Saladin's officials told how a terrified pris-oner was brought before Saladin:

66 The interpreter asked him [the prisoner]: 'What are you afraid of?' God inspired him to reply: 'At first I was afraid of seeing that face, but after seeing it and standing in his presence, I am sure that I shall see only good in it.' The Sultan was moved, pardoned him, and let him go free. 99
—Baha' ad-Din Ibn Shaddad

Saladin and Richard signed a truce that ended the Third Crusade. Christian pilgrims were free to travel, and Saladin agreed to respect crusader lands. But Jerusalem remained in Muslim hands.

Reading Check What did the Third Crusade fail to achieve?

THE Crusades

Waged over a span of 200 years, the Crusades were actually a series of short wars, most lasting no longer than three years. In between these wars, Muslims continued fighting the crusader states set up in the Holy Land. The clash between the Muslim and the Christian armies revealed differences in tactics and weaponry. *Which event provoked the Third Crusade?*

◄ Far left: The lightly clothed Turks rode fast Arabian horses. Speed and mobility gave them an advantage.

◄ Crusader knights wore heavy armor and rode large warhorses. Their cavalry charges were greatly feared.

1096–1099 First Crusade

1147–1149 Second Crusade

1189–1192 Third Crusade

1202–1204 Fourth Crusade

1217–1221 Fifth Crusade

1227–1229 Sixth Crusade

1248–1254 Seventh Crusade

1270–1272 Eighth Crusade

1050   1100   1150   1200   1250   1300

1099 Crusaders capture Jerusalem.

1144 Muslims capture Edessa.

1187 Saladin captures Jerusalem.

1212 The Children's Crusade fails.

1291 Last crusader state is defeated.

1204 Crusaders loot Constantinople.

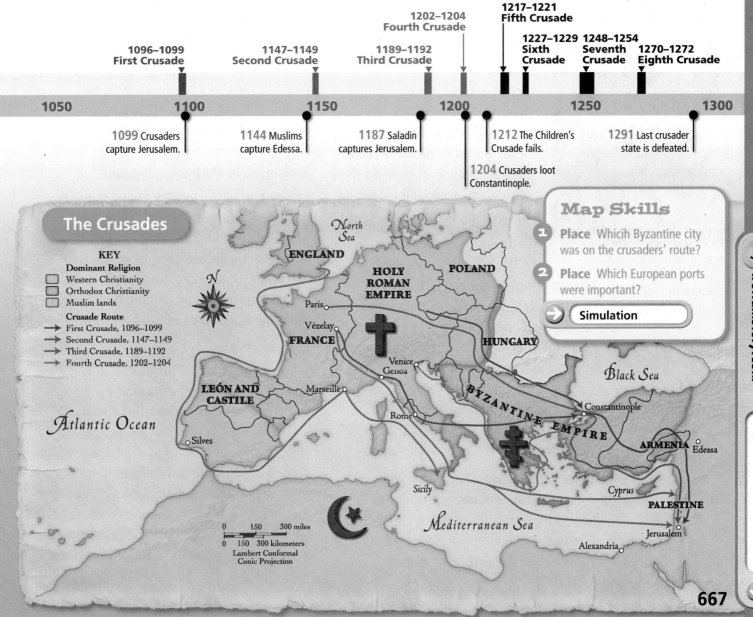

The Crusades

KEY

Dominant Religion
- Western Christianity
- Orthodox Christianity
- Muslim lands

Crusade Route
- → First Crusade, 1096–1099
- → Second Crusade, 1147–1149
- → Third Crusade, 1189–1192
- → Fourth Crusade, 1202–1204

North Sea
ENGLAND
POLAND
HOLY ROMAN EMPIRE
Paris
Vézelay
FRANCE
HUNGARY
Venice
Genoa
LEÓN AND CASTILE
Marseille
Rome
BYZANTINE EMPIRE
Black Sea
Constantinople
Atlantic Ocean
Silves
ARMENIA
Edessa
Sicily
Cyprus
PALESTINE
Mediterranean Sea
Jerusalem
Alexandria

0 150 300 miles
0 150 300 kilometers
Lambert Conformal Conic Projection

Map Skills

1. **Place** Which Byzantine city was on the crusaders' route?

2. **Place** Which European ports were important?

→ **Simulation**

my worldhistory.com

Simulation

Illustration from 1460, showing crusaders attacking Constantinople

Bronze horses looted from Constantinople

Fourth and Later Crusades

The Fourth Crusade embarrassed the pope who had launched it. The crusaders never reached the Holy Land. Instead, they tried to fund their campaign by looting Christian cities along the route.

Looting Constantinople In 1204, crusaders stormed Constantinople, the rich Byzantine capital. For three days, they smashed Christian icons, stole relics, and attacked women. The pope was furious. He wrote that crusaders who "should have used their swords against the infidel [unbeliever], have bathed those swords in the blood of Christians." The Byzantines never forgave the Catholic Christians.

Later Crusades In 1212, a popular crusading movement swept through France and Germany. The so-called Children's Crusade attracted poor people of all ages. Most never got farther than Italy.

Although several more crusades were launched, the crusaders were slowly forced out of the Holy Land. Finally, in 1291, Egyptian Muslims defeated the last crusader state.

The Muslim View Muslims in the Middle East were caught off guard by the first waves of crusaders. The Muslim world was too divided politically to organize a strong defense. Most Muslims regarded the crusaders as soldiers hired to win back Byzantine lands.

However, Muslim counterattacks became more successful. Like the crusaders, Muslims described their own campaigns in religious terms, as holy war.

Reading Check What important event happened during the Fourth Crusade?

Religious Persecutions

In Europe, the Crusades fueled dangerous passions. Religious fervor against Muslims led to brutal attacks against all whose beliefs differed from Church teachings. Soon after the First Crusade began, campaigns were launched against religious minorities in Europe itself.

Attacks on Jewish Communities Jewish groups were the first targets of attacks in Europe. Some Europeans already considered Jews to be enemies of Christianity, and used the Crusades as an excuse for violence. Mobs of Christian peasants turned on those Jews who would not instantly convert to Christianity. During the First Crusade, these mobs terrorized and slaughtered the Jewish communities along crusader routes to the Middle East.

The worst violence occurred in German cities along the Rhine River, such as Mainz and Cologne. Thousands of Jews killed themselves and their families to escape torture and murder. When the knights of the First Crusade took Jerusalem in 1099, they slaughtered Jews and Muslims alike.

A few Christian clergymen tried to protect the Jews. But the public mood led to more persecution in crusader countries. Jews were expelled from England in 1290, and from France in 1306.

Crusades Against Heretics Jews were not the only victims of religious persecution in Europe. Other targets included groups of Christians who followed various heresies. A **heresy** is a belief that is rejected by official Church teaching. Medieval Christians would not tolerate even minor differences in beliefs. Heretics were seen as "lost sheep," doomed for eternity. Many were considered dangerous, because their heretical ideas might influence others.

During this time, Christians fought holy wars against Muslims in Spain. ▼

Religious Campaigns in Europe

As the Crusades in the Middle East began, supporters of the Church began hunting down the "enemy within"—heretics and nonbelievers in Europe.

1096 Crusader armies attack Jews in Europe.

1147 Crusade against the pagan Wends in northern Germany begins.

1208 Pope launches Crusade against heretic Christians in southern France.

1240 Crusade against Orthodox Christians in Novgorod, Russia, begins.

1050	1100	1150	1200	1250

The French town of Carcassonne was a heretic stronghold.

Still from film of the crusade against Novgorod

669

At first, heretics were excommunicated. This was a serious punishment, because the Church was the center of medieval life. However, some heretics clung to their beliefs. The pope called on nobles to organize local crusades against them. In the Languedoc (lang DOK) region of southern France, entire communities of Christians were massacred or exiled for disagreeing with Church teachings.

region, *n.,* area of land

Accusations of heresy were used to destroy the Knights Templars, who had once been the military heroes of the Crusades. The Templars were an order of military monks approved by the Church in 1127. As warriors, they were greatly admired during the Crusades. However, they also set up an international banking system, which made them rich—and envied. The king of France, who owed them money, had their leaders arrested in 1307. The Templar leaders were accused of heresy, tortured, and burned alive.

The Inquisition In the 1200s, Pope Gregory IX created the **Inquisition,** a series of investigations designed to find and judge heretics. Accused heretics who did not cooperate were punished.

Heretics were punished in various ways. Minor differences in beliefs might be forgiven with a fast or a whipping. More serious accusations could lead to fines or imprisonment. If a heretic would not confess, often under torture, he or she was turned over to the civil authorities to be executed.

Reading Check: **What happened to Jewish communities during the Crusades?**

Effects of the Crusades

The Crusades failed to achieve their goal of forcing the Muslims out of the Holy Land. In addition, centuries of fighting weakened the Byzantine empire, which had protected Europe from Turkish invasion. However, the Crusades did have some lasting effects in Europe.

A Wider World The Crusades opened Europeans' eyes to the rest of the world. People who had never been farther from home than the next village suddenly saw new lands, peoples, and ways of life.

The Crusades may have encouraged Europeans to explore distant parts of the world. Some historians believe that the adventurous spirit of the Crusades helped lead to the great European voyages of discovery that began in the late 1400s.

◀ Knights Templars, like the one shown here, were heroes of the Crusades.

But after the Crusades, Templar leaders were burned as heretics. ▼

670

Trade With the East The Crusades brought wealth and trade to European port cities. Italian cities such as Venice and Genoa had always traded by sea. They were eager to supply the needs of the crusader states in the Holy Land. The crusader states were surrounded by hostile populations and had to depend on goods shipped from Europe. In the process, old trade routes between Europe and the Middle East were reopened. The merchants of Venice and Genoa also opened trading colonies in Egypt.

As trade routes reopened, trade increased. Crusaders returned home with silks, spices, and other exotic goods. Demand for these products at home encouraged European merchants to expand trade with Asia and to search for faster routes to China and India.

Cultural Exchange The Crusades led to cultural exchange between Europe and Muslim states. Europeans benefited greatly from this contact with the Middle East. The Crusades may have introduced Europeans to the Muslim hygienic practice of washing with soap. Scientific knowledge also expanded. Muslim medicine was more advanced than that of Europe. In addition, Muslims had preserved much ancient Greek and Roman knowledge that had been lost in Western Europe. This ancient wisdom, along with Muslim advances in science and medicine, now spread across Europe. This knowledge would one day help Europeans themselves make great advances in the sciences and the arts.

Reading Check Which Italian cities benefited from the Crusades and why?

An Italian merchant watches goods being loaded onto a ship. ▼

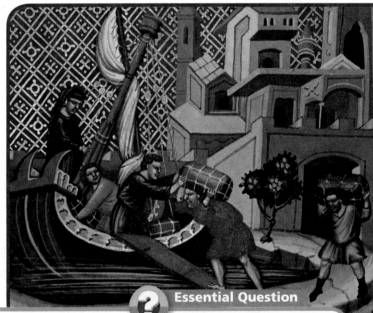

Section 3 Assessment

? Essential Question

How should we handle conflict?

Key Terms

1. Use the following terms to describe medieval conflicts and crusades: Crusades, heresy, Inquisition.

Key Ideas

2. Why did Pope Urban II call for a crusade?

3. Why did the Second Crusade fail?

4. What were some economic effects of the Crusades?

Think Critically

5. **Draw Conclusions** What were some unexpected results of the crusades?

6. **Make Inferences** Why were minorities in Europe persecuted during the Crusades?

7. Why did the conflicts known as the Crusades fail to achieve their goal? Go to your Student Journal to record your answer.

Section 4

Christians and Muslims in Spain

Key Ideas
- Muslims built a sophisticated society in medieval Spain.
- In the late Middle Ages, Christians drove Muslims and Jews from Spain and established a new kingdom.

Key Terms • Iberian Peninsula • Moors • Reconquista

 Visual Glossary

Reading Skill Summarize Take notes using the graphic organizer in your journal.

▲ A Muslim and a Christian playing music together, from a medieval manuscript

By the early 700s, Muslims ruled most of the **Iberian Peninsula,** the peninsula where present-day Spain and Portugal are located. Under Muslim rule, a culture of great diversity developed there. Muslim, Jewish, and Christian communities exchanged knowledge and customs. But the political situation on the peninsula was unstable. Christian kingdoms waged a long campaign against the Muslims. In 1492, Spain's multicultural society was finally swept away.

Spain Under Muslim Rule

As you have read in an earlier chapter, the Umayyad rulers of the Muslim empire were overthrown and murdered in A.D. 750. But one survivor fled to Spain. In 756, Abd al-Rahman established a new dynasty at Córdoba. The dynasty ruled most of Spain for nearly 300 years. A few small Christian kingdoms controlled the northern part of Spain.

Moorish Culture To European Christians, the Muslims in Spain were known as **Moors.** The Moors governed an extremely advanced, dynamic, and diverse society centered in what is now southern Spain. In Arabic, this region was called "al-Andalus," which became the modern name Andalusia.

In the tenth century, the Muslim capital of Córdoba was Europe's largest city. It may have been the most pleasant to live in, as well. It had many mosques, bookshops, and public baths. Houses had mosaic floors, gardens, and fountains. Its great library may have contained about 400,000 volumes.

Traders carried leather goods, silk cloth, and jewelry from Córdoba to markets in Europe. Moorish Spain was home to the Great Mosque of Córdoba and the Alhambra palace in Granada, two masterpieces of Muslim architecture.

A Multicultural Society The golden age of Moorish culture reached its peak in the 800s and 900s. Science and medicine were far more advanced in Muslim Spain than in the rest of Europe. Foreign students flocked to Córdoba. They studied philosophy, music, and medicine with Muslim and Jewish scholars.

Córdoba was home to two of the most famous philosophers of the Middle Ages. One was the Muslim legal scholar and judge Ibn Rushd, or Averroës. The other was the Jewish <u>legal</u> scholar Moses Maimonides (my MAHN nah deez).

By medieval standards, most of Spain's Muslim rulers were tolerant of Jews and Christians. The Quran encouraged tolerance, as all three religions worshiped one God. Muslim leaders wanted to create a prosperous, stable society. They accepted the religious diversity of their subjects. In fact, some Jews and Christians held high official positions. Non-Muslims had to follow certain rules and pay a special tax. Later Muslim rulers, however, were less tolerant. They imposed strict new rules. Christians could not carry Bibles in public. Jews also were persecuted.

Reading Check **Where was the heartland of Moorish Spain?**

legal, *adj.,* having to do with the law

Profits from the silk trade allowed Muslim rulers to build palaces like the Alhambra in Granada.▼

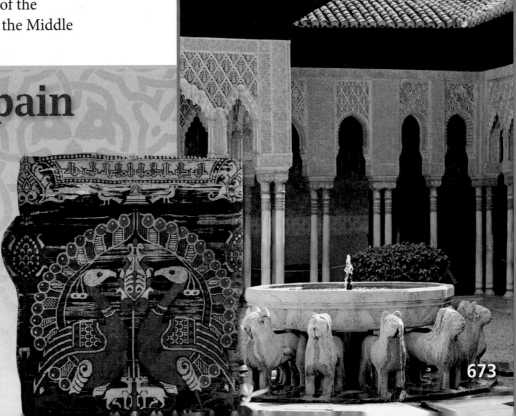

Muslim Spain

While most people in Europe were living in primitive conditions, the inhabitants of Muslim Spain were enjoying the comforts of an advanced civilization. Trade brought great wealth to cities like Córdoba and Granada.

Spanish Muslims were exporting silks like the one shown here. ▶

673

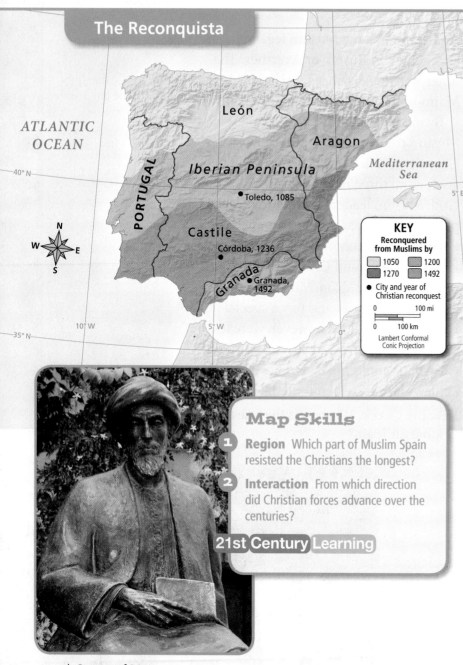

The Reconquista

ATLANTIC
OCEAN

León

Aragon

Iberian Peninsula

PORTUGAL

*Mediterranean
Sea*

40° N

• Toledo, 1085

5° E

Castile

Córdoba, 1236

•

Granada

• Granada,
1492

N
W E
S

10° W

5° W

0°

35° N

KEY
Reconquered
from Muslims by
☐ 1050 ☐ 1200
☐ 1270 ☐ 1492
● City and year of
Christian reconquest
0   100 mi
0   100 km
Lambert Conformal
Conic Projection

Map Skills

1 **Region** Which part of Muslim Spain resisted the Christians the longest?

2 **Interaction** From which direction did Christian forces advance over the centuries?

21st Century Learning

▲ Statue of Moses Maimonides, one of the Jewish scholars forced to leave Spain

The Reconquista

The decline of Muslim rule in Spain began in 1002 with a civil war. The Córdoba caliphate was split into small, weak kingdoms. In contrast, by 1050, the Christian kingdoms in northern Spain were more united. Long before the Crusades, popes urged Christians in

Spain to wage war against the Muslims. The movement to drive the Muslims from Spain was called the **Reconquista** (re kon KEES tah), or "Reconquest."

Military Campaigns The first major victory in the Reconquista was the capture of the city of Toledo in 1085. In 1139, a victory over the Muslims led to Portugal becoming a separate, Christian kingdom. Over time, the Christian kingdoms in Spain formed a powerful alliance against the Muslims. They attacked the Muslim city of Córdoba, which fell in 1236. Córdoba's Great Mosque became a Catholic cathedral.

By the middle of the 1200s, all that was left of Moorish Spain was the kingdom of Granada. By paying tribute, it managed to survive for a few hundred years more. However, most of Spain was now under Christian rule.

Uniting the Kingdoms In 1469, an important royal marriage took place. Ferdinand of Aragon married Isabella of Castile-León. Their marriage united Spain's largest Christian kingdoms. It laid the basis for a Spanish state.

Ferdinand and Isabella now concentrated on conquering Granada, the last Muslim territory. When the city fell in 1492, the pope was delighted. But the Catholic monarchs' crusade against the Muslims in Spain led to terrible persecutions of non-Christians.

Religious Persecutions Jewish people had lived quite peacefully in the Christian kingdoms until the late 1300s, when anti-Jewish attacks began. Thousands

674

died in massacres. Terrified, many Jews converted to Christianity. Isabella's reign, however, made life even more dangerous for Jews.

Isabella and Ferdinand were determined to unite Spain as a Catholic country. To do so, they brought in a Dominican friar named Torquemada (tor kay MAH duh) to head the Spanish Inquisition. The Inquisition had begun as a series of Church investigations to find and punish heretics. In Spain, it became a permanent institution. It used terror and torture against suspected Christian heretics. It also persecuted converts to Christianity who were suspected of maintaining their previous beliefs.

In 1492, Spain banished all Jews who refused to convert to Christianity. A few years later, Portugal did the same. Many Spanish Jews fled to Italy and the Ottoman empire. Later, the Muslims were also ordered to leave. The loss of these

▲ *Surrender of Granada,* by Francisco Pradilla y Ortiz, was painted in 1882.

two groups did great harm to Spain's economy and culture. Spain lost more than 160,000 of its people. But even those Jews and Muslims who had converted to Christianity and remained in Spain were not safe. Generations later, their families were still being persecuted for having a practicing Jewish or Muslim ancestor.

Reading Check What was the purpose of the Reconquista?

Section 4 Assessment

Key Terms

1. Use the following terms to describe Christians and Muslims in Spain: Iberian Peninsula, Moors, Reconquista.

Key Ideas

2. Why was culture in the Iberian Peninsula so diverse?

3. What was the first major event of the Reconquista?

4. What was the last Muslim kingdom in Spain?

Think Critically

5. **Synthesize** What connection do you see between the Crusades and the Reconquista?

6. **Draw Conclusions** Why do you think minorities were persecuted as Christian kingdoms united?

Essential Question

How should we handle conflict?

7. Why did religious intolerance lead to conflict in Spain? Go to your Student Journal to record your answer.

Chapter Assessment

Key Terms and Ideas

1. **Explain** Why was Henry IV **excommunicated** by Pope Gregory VII?

2. **Recall** What compromise was achieved by the Concordat of Worms?

3. **Explain** Why did the medieval German kingdom call itself the "Holy Roman Empire?"

4. **Describe** What is **habeas corpus**?

5. **Discuss** What effect did the **Magna Carta** have on the development of English government?

6. **Explain** Why did the pope call for the **Crusades**?

7. **Summarize** Why was the First Crusade so successful?

8. **Describe** Which monarchs completed the **Reconquista**?

Think Critically

9. **Draw Conclusions** Why were people afraid to be excommunicated?

10. **Draw Inferences** What role does habeas corpus play in protecting democratic freedom?

11. **Summarize** Why did minorities in Europe suffer during the Crusades?

12. **Core Concepts: Economic Basics** In what ways did the Crusades encourage trade?

Analyze Visuals

Identify the Christian and the Muslim warriors in this illustration. Then answer the following questions:

13. How do the clothes worn by the opposing forces differ?

14. What advantages might these clothes have given each side in battle?

15. What were the disadvantages of such clothing?

Essential Question
myWorld Chapter Activity

Filming the Middle Ages Follow your teacher's instructions to take the role of filmmakers directing films that explore the issues and disputes of the Middle Ages. Using the Activity Cards, along with Sections 1–4 and myworldhistory.com, you will create a storyboard for the main scenes of your film. Then you will develop a script for your storyboard and perform it for the class.

21st Century Learning
Develop Cultural Awareness

With a partner, search the Internet for information on how Jewish and Muslim historians today regard the Crusades. Present your findings to the class.

Document-Based Questions

Success Tracker™
Online at myworldhistory.com

Use your knowledge of the Middle Ages and Documents A and B to answer Questions 1–3.

Document A

" King John, when he saw that he was deserted by almost all, so that out of his regal [royal] superabundance of followers he scarcely retained seven knights, was much alarmed lest the barons would attack his castles and reduce them without difficulty."

—Roger of Wendover, *Flowers of History*

Document B

" If any one shall have been [dispossessed] by us, or removed, without a legal sentence of his peers, from his lands, castles, liberties, or lawful right, we shall straightway restore them to him."

—Magna Carta

1. In Document A, the writer describes King John as
   A confident of his power.
   B a very religious king.
   C angry with the barons.
   D fearful of the barons' power.

2. Document B, from the Magna Carta, shows that King John promised to
   A end legal abuses.
   B punish criminals.
   C attack the barons' castles.
   D give more lands to the barons.

3. **Writing Task** What do Documents A and B together reveal about the relationship between King John and the barons?

myworldhistory.com

Self-Test

Chapter 23

A Changing Medieval World

Essential Question

How are religion and culture connected?

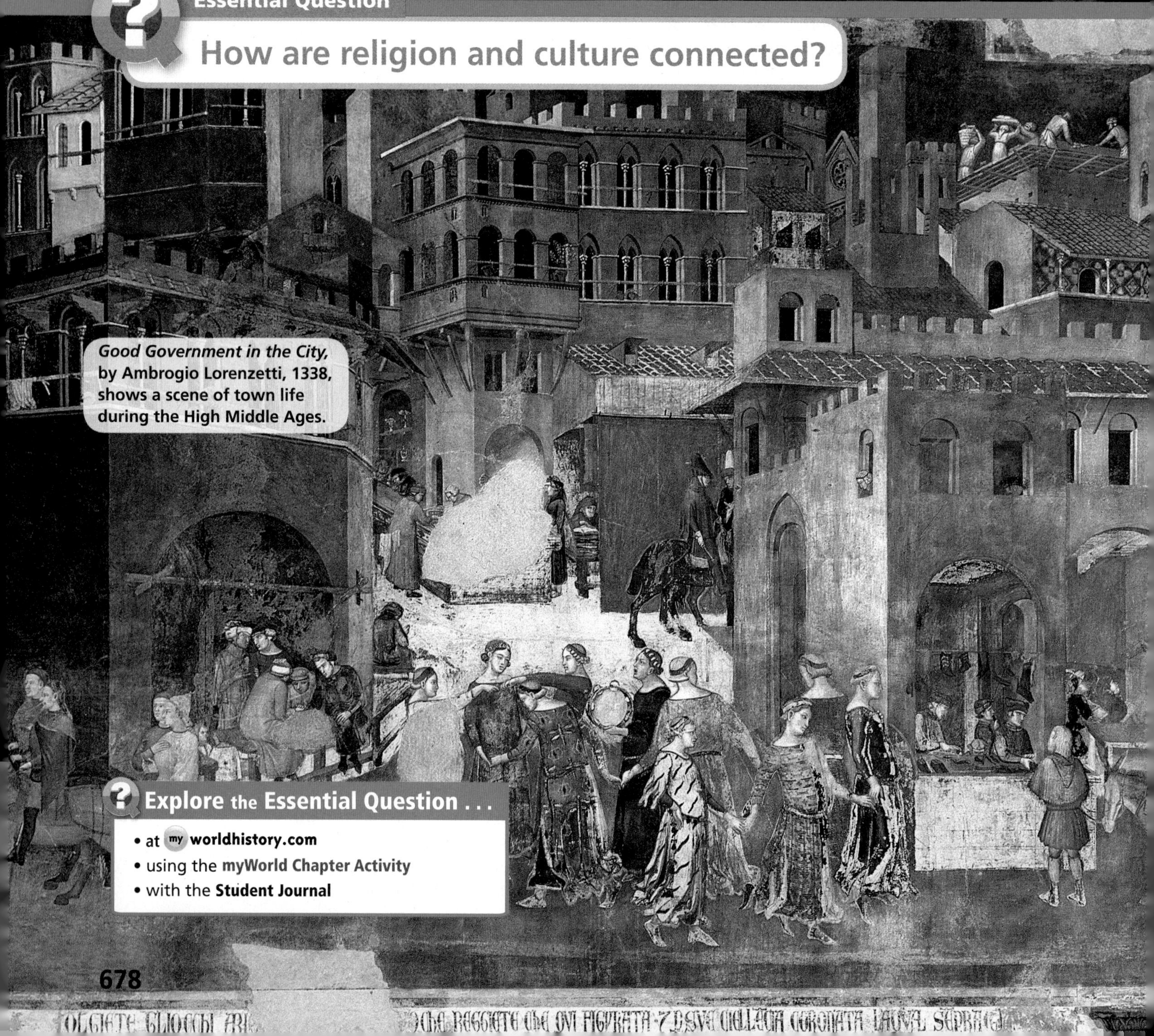

Good Government in the City, by Ambrogio Lorenzetti, 1338, shows a scene of town life during the High Middle Ages.

Explore the Essential Question . . .

- at my worldhistory.com
- using the **myWorld Chapter Activity**
- with the **Student Journal**

The High and Late Middle Ages

1088 University of Bologna is founded.

1337 The Hundred Years' War begins.

1381 Peasants revolt in England.

1000	1100	1200	1300	1400	1500

1209 The Franciscan order forms.

1347 Plague arrives in Europe.

1415 English win battle of Agincourt.

1429 Joan of Arc wins many victories.

Joan of Arc:
Voices of Victory

At 19 years old, Joan of Arc was in jail, a French girl imprisoned in a tower by English invaders. In this year of 1431, England and France were in the midst of a long war. Just when France seemed to be losing the war, Joan of Arc had emerged to lead the French to victory.

Joan was a devout Catholic. Since the age of 13, she had heard voices while praying, voices that she later claimed had come from Catholic saints. Europe in the late Middle Ages was a world dominated by religious faith. People believed that the Earth was a battleground of mysterious forces fighting for each person's soul. Sometimes these forces could make themselves seen and heard.

The voices told Joan that she had been chosen by God to play a role in the ongoing war between France and England. This conflict would later be known as the Hundred Years' War. Joan was to leave her family and village—and lead the French army to victory. It sounded impossible, even comical, for a teenage girl to lead an army.

myworldhistory.com

Timeline/On Assignment

Joan believed that holy voices were urging her to fight for France. When she was brought to the royal court, she offered the dauphin her help.

Joan was captured while protecting retreating French soldiers.

But Joan was stubborn and persuasive, and the French leaders were desperate.

Eventually, she was taken to meet the French dauphin, or prince. Having heard of her remarkable powers, the dauphin prepared a test for her. He hid himself among his courtiers to see if she could identify him. When Joan entered the room, she went straight to him. She told him that she would win victories for France and see him crowned king. The dauphin gave her the troops she requested.

Dressed in armor, Joan radiated courage. The French troops loved her, especially after her first battle, in which she freed the city of Orléans from an English siege. She later escorted the French prince to the cathedral of Reims to be crowned King Charles VII.

During her trial, Joan's clever answers amazed and frustrated her judges.

The people of Rouen wept for Joan as she was driven to her execution.

Joan dictated letters to be sent to the English, to show the strength of her will. "In God's name go back to your own lands," she ordered in one such letter, pressing her point hard. "I am a commander, and wherever I come across your troops in France, I shall make them go, whether willingly or unwillingly; and if they will not obey, I will have them wiped out. I am sent here by God the King of Heaven . . . to drive you entirely out of France."

English leaders worried as Joan won victory after victory. The determination of her own troops grew ever stronger as they watched Joan fight on—sometimes even after she had been wounded by arrows.

Her string of victories continued for a year, until she was captured in 1430 and imprisoned. The English handed her over to members of the Church who supported them politically. The English knew that if Joan described her religious experiences, the Church might condemn her for heresy—beliefs that did not agree with Church teaching. Heresy was a crime sometimes punishable by death.

With no lawyer or anyone to help her, Joan left her cell every morning and faced some 60 priests and bishops, who questioned her about her religious experiences and beliefs. They tried to trick her into saying that she knew God's mind. However, she cleverly avoided all their verbal traps.

"Does God hate the English?" one judge asked her.

Joan replied instantly: "Of the love or hate which God has for the English and of what He does to their souls, I know nothing. But I am well-assured they will be driven out of France."

For the five months of her trial in Rouen, Joan never wavered from her stance. But the outcome of the trial was never really in doubt, and she was found guilty and sentenced to death by burning.

It was 22 more years before the English were defeated. Meanwhile, Joan became a national heroine. Word of her bravery spread. Finally, in 1920, the Catholic Church made Joan of Arc a saint.

What does this story tell you about the role of religion in medieval life? As you read the chapter ahead, think about what Joan's story reveals about the culture of the Middle Ages.

 myStory Video

Join Joan of Arc as she fights for France.

my worldhistory.com

myStory Video

Section 1

Revival of Trade and Towns

Key Ideas
- Better farming techniques increased Europe's food supply and population.
- Expanding trade created wealth in the towns and led to the rise of banking.
- As towns and cities grew, guilds became important to the medieval economy.

Key Terms • crop rotation • fallow • three-field system • guild

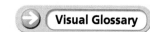
Visual Glossary

Reading Skill Compare and Contrast Take notes using the graphic organizer in your journal.

Peasants farming near Paris, from a French manuscript ▼

Picture yourself in this scene of life in the Middle Ages. At certain times of the year, you would have labored with your parents in fields that belonged to the local lord. Like most people of your age, you would not have attended school. You and your family would have lived without much hope of freedom or change.

But in the distance you might have glimpsed something that promised a better life—the walls of a town. In towns, peasants found more opportunity. Towns offered markets where peasants could sell crops. In towns, crops could also be traded for other goods. By the 1000s, the towns were growing richer as trade increased. The increase in trade was brought about, in part, by better ways of farming.

New Ways of Farming

From A.D. 1000 to 1300, the period known as the High Middle Ages, the number of people in Europe grew steadily. This population boom was fueled by an increase in food supplies that resulted from improvements in agriculture.

The Plow and the Horse Ever since Roman times, peasants had used wooden plows that only scratched the surface of the ground. These plows worked well on the thin soils of southern Europe. But new plows had iron blades that could cut through and turn over the thicker soils of northern Europe. With the iron plow, people could farm more land.

682

To pull this iron plow, farmers began using horses instead of oxen. Horses were faster and did more work for the amount of food they ate.

In order to use horses as <u>draft</u> animals, peasants developed a harness that helped horses pull heavier loads without injury. The increasing use of horseshoes protected horses' soft hooves.

Horse power and the new plow allowed peasants to cultivate more land. They cleared forests, planted new fields, and produced more food.

The Three-Field System Farmers also developed a system of **crop rotation,** the practice of changing the use of fields over time. In the early Middle Ages, peasants usually divided their farmland into two large fields. Each year, only one field was planted. The other was left **fallow,** or unplanted. The following year, the fallow one was planted. This process allowed the soil to recover some of its natural fertility.

Later, farmers developed a **three-field system** of crop rotation. In this system, a third of the land was planted with spring crops, such as oats and barley. A third was planted with winter crops, such as winter wheat and rye, and the final field was left fallow. The three-field system had great advantages. First, it increased the amount of land that could be planted each year. Second, it protected farmers from starvation if one of the crops failed.

Cistercians Expand Farming During the 1200s, an order of monks called the Cistercians (sis TUR shuns) helped expand farming in Europe. The Cistercians embraced poverty and simplicity. They sold surplus agricultural products, such as wool.

Many Cistercian monasteries were built in the countryside. With the help of peasants, Cistercians cut down forests, drained marshes, and brought huge areas of land under cultivation for the first time. By introducing sheep farming to many regions, the Cistercians increased wool production. This strengthened the textile, or cloth, industry and trade.

Food Fuels Growth Thanks to the new farming methods, the supply of grains increased. This helped feed the growing population in Europe. Scholars estimate that the population of Europe nearly doubled between A.D. 1000 and 1300, rising from 39 million to 74 million people. This surge in population transformed the medieval world.

Reading Check On what kind of food did the growing population of medieval Europe depend?

draft, *adj.,* drawing or pulling, as of a load

Modern Cistercian monks tend their kitchen garden in Italy.▼

Trade and Industry Grow

Population growth and advances in farming brought about important changes, especially in trade and industry. The medieval economy boomed.

Trade Revives As food became plentiful, surplus crops from one area were traded for surplus crops from another. Regions specialized in crops that grew best in particular climates and soils. In Spain, olive orchards supplied olive oil. In France, grapes were processed into wines. Surplus crops could also be traded for manufactured goods from distant lands.

Industry Thrives Some places became famous for a specific manufactured product. For example, the region of Flanders in northern Europe produced fine woolen cloth. This textile industry made northern towns rich. In southern Europe, Italian merchants set up a booming trade with the East.

As population and wealth increased, so did the demand for trade goods. The families of rich merchants and the nobility wanted expensive clothes, weaponry, and jewelry. The market for such goods encouraged specialization and long-distance trade.

Trade Goes Global In the early Middle Ages, trade networks had shrunk. Few people ventured far from their village. But after A.D. 1000, commerce revived.

Medieval Trade

The complex trade networks of Roman times had all but vanished by the early Middle Ages. Then, during the A.D. 1000s, improved farming methods led to an exchange of crops. The revival of trade transformed the medieval world. *Study the cartoons below. Why would trade have given townspeople more political power?*

Communities trade surplus goods.

Increased trade revives older towns and helps create new ones.

Peasants migrate to towns. Towns demand rights and independence from feudal lords.

Trade began tying Europe to the wider world, bringing the cultures of Europe, Asia, and Africa into contact once again.

The Crusades contributed to this revival of trade. Crusaders returned from the Holy Land with a taste for Asian spices, perfumes, silks, and other goods. Italian merchants worked to satisfy these tastes by importing trade goods from Asia in their ships.

Merchant Banking As trade increased, merchants needed to transfer large sums of money. Merchants often traveled long distances to buy and sell their goods. Such journeys were difficult and risky. A merchant carrying coins could lose a fortune through a shipwreck or a robbery.

Italian merchants solved this problem by creating a system that included bills of exchange. This was a system similar to the one used by Muslim traders. Bills of exchange allowed a merchant to deposit money in a bank in one city and withdraw money from a bank in a different city. Merchants no longer needed to carry money on dangerous journeys.

The banking system made many Italian families rich, especially in cities such as Florence. In Italy, banking also contributed to one of the most important developments of the High Middle Ages—the revival of towns and urban life.

Reading Check Why was there a need for a banking system?

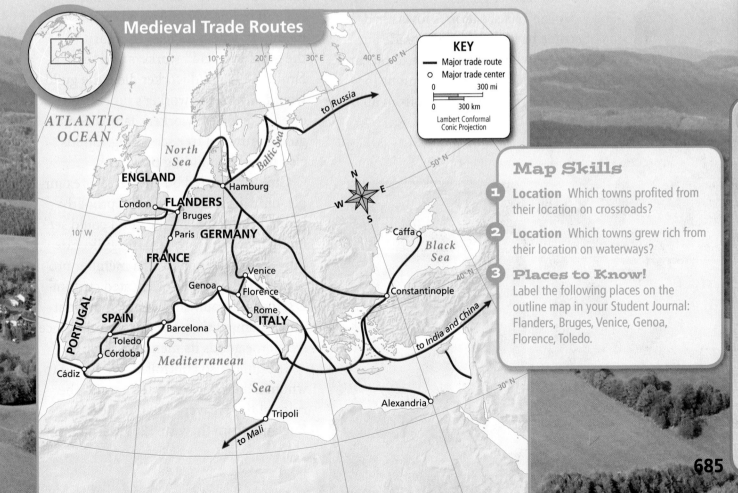

Medieval Trade Routes

KEY

— Major trade route
○ Major trade center

0   300 mi
0   300 km

Lambert Conformal Conic Projection

ATLANTIC OCEAN

North Sea

Baltic Sea

to Russia

ENGLAND

Hamburg

London   FLANDERS

Bruges

Paris   GERMANY

FRANCE

PORTUGAL

SPAIN

Toledo
Córdoba

Cádiz

Barcelona

Venice

Genoa

Florence

Rome

ITALY

Mediterranean Sea

Tripoli

to Mali

Caffa

Black Sea

Constantinople

to India and China

Alexandria

Map Skills

1 **Location** Which towns profited from their location on crossroads?

2 **Location** Which towns grew rich from their location on waterways?

3 **Places to Know!** Label the following places on the outline map in your Student Journal: Flanders, Bruges, Venice, Genoa, Florence, Toledo.

my worldhistory.com

Places to Know

Growing Towns

Throughout Europe, towns and cities had been in decay for centuries. Although trade between towns had never completely <u>ceased</u>, it had declined. But now, as trade revived, the older towns began to grow and new towns were built.

From Market Center to Busy Town

During the early Middle Ages, some towns held weekly markets where people from nearby villages could trade for food and other useful items.

In time, merchants and craftworkers—such as shoemakers, tailors, and metalworkers—set up shops in the towns. In some regions, merchants hired people to manufacture products such as woolen cloth or leather goods.

By the 1200s, Europe's towns had become bustling centers of trade and industry where people came to buy and sell goods. Some became famous for their great fairs. Merchants from all over Europe brought goods to sell at these fairs. Jugglers, musicians, and animal trainers came to entertain. In France during the 1100s and 1200s, fairs were held in the province of Champagne. At the Champagne fairs, cloth from northern Europe was exchanged for spices and objects from the Mediterranean.

Guilds As the demand for goods increased, the number of skilled craftworkers in towns grew. Artisans with the same skills often banded together to form guilds. A **guild** is a group of workers practicing the same craft, who have joined together to protect their economic interests. Merchants, grocers, and shoemakers—along with many other kinds of workers—all formed guilds.

Craft guilds were financed by their members, who paid fees. In return, the guild protected workers and their families. If a guild worker died, the guild would pay for the worker's funeral and often care for the worker's family. Some guilds provided free schooling. Guilds also financed building programs.

Guilds regulated businesses. For example, only those who had been properly trained and tested by the guild could set up their own businesses. The guild carefully controlled quality. If a member produced shoddy goods or cheated customers, the guild punished him. To prevent unfair competition, the guild set the price for all the goods its members sold.

The guild also controlled where and to whom a member could sell goods. The rules of the Weavers Guild in Beverley, England, from the year 1209 warned:

cease, *v.*, to stop

Below left: Modern shoppers around a medieval market building in Chichester, England

Right: A shopkeeper in medieval dress serves customers in an ancient market in Tallinn, Estonia.▼

66 Weavers . . . may sell their cloth to no foreigner, but only to merchants of the city. And if it happens that, in order to enrich himself, one of the weavers . . . wishes to go outside the city to sell his merchandise, he may be very sure that the honest men of the city will take all his cloth and bring it back to the city. . . . And if any weaver . . . sell his cloth to a foreigner, the foreigner shall lose his cloth. 99

—Beverley Town Documents

Freedom in the Air In the very local world of manors ruled by lords, towns offered new freedoms. Towns were often beyond the control of manorial lords. In some places, wealthy townsmen, not lords, controlled local governments.

The commerce of the towns brought increasing wealth and prosperity to society. Many townspeople grew rich through their labor. Rural peasants, many of whom lived in poverty, could not help but notice that towns offered a better life.

The towns' promise of freedom and prosperity was hard to resist. Peasants began deserting the rural manors, thus weakening the feudal system.

Peasants arriving in the towns must have been awed by their first view of urban life. Around the busy market-places, huge buildings were rising—houses, guildhalls, and mansions. But soaring even higher were the churches and cathedrals, whose spires drew the eye up toward heaven. The High Middle Ages was a time not only of economic growth, but of deep religious faith. In the next section, you will learn how this faith shaped the medieval world.

Reading Check Why was there more freedom in the towns than in rural areas?

myWorld Activity
Town and Country

Dancers celebrate in a medieval town, a detail of Lorenzetti's *Good Government in the City.* ▼

Section 1 Assessment

Essential Question
How are religion and culture connected?

Key Terms

1. For each key term, write a sentence explaining its importance to the revival of trade and towns: crop rotation, fallow, three-field system, guild.

Key Ideas

2. What caused the increase in food supply?

3. What goods were traded in the High Middle Ages?

4. How did trade help expand towns?

Think Critically

5. **Analyze Cause and Effect** How did increasing trade affect society?

6. **Draw Inferences** Why would the increase in trade have improved communication?

7. What effects did increasing wealth in towns have on church building? Go to your Student Journal to record your answer.

An Age of Faith

Key Ideas

- Religion dominated medieval society and culture.
- Religious faith shaped the art and architecture of the Middle Ages.
- Medieval universities were centers of both faith and learning.

Key Terms • mendicant order • university • natural law

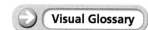 **Visual Glossary**

Reading Skill Summarize Take notes using the graphic organizer in your journal.

◄ Medieval rose made of gold— a symbol of Jesus' love and suffering

Religion shaped life in the Middle Ages. In the countryside, the pealing of church bells was one of the few sounds that echoed over the quiet fields. Country roads carried the traffic of pilgrims and crusaders on their way to worship sacred relics or fight in a holy war. In this age of devotion, even the natural world looked very different. A rose, for example, was much more than just a beautiful flower. To the medieval mind, it might symbolize some spiritual truth.

In the growing towns, too, the sights and sounds of faith were part of daily life. The streets were crowded with frequent processions—solemn lines of people walking to or from the churches. On holy days, in particular, the air smelled of incense and carried the sounds of religious chanting.

Forms of Devotion

Religion was so important in the Middle Ages that this period is sometimes called the Age of Faith. Throughout most of Western Europe, Roman Catholicism was the dominant form of Christianity. Christian Europe expressed its devotion to God through personal prayer and public worship.

Religious Orders In early Christianity, monks and nuns pursued personal salvation through prayer and meditation. They lived in monasteries that were often set in remote spots, cut off from contact with the world.

However, by the 1200s, monasteries played a more active role in the world. Monasteries were centers of agricultural production and owned large areas of land. Some monasteries were located in towns, where they provided education or charity to ordinary people.

Also in the 1200s, new forms of Christian community emerged. For example, the **mendicant orders** were founded to fight heresy and to preach to ordinary people. The mendicants, or beggars, owned no property. Mendicants survived by begging for food and drink.

St. Francis and St. Clare One of the best-known mendicant orders was founded by St. Francis of Assisi. As a young man, Francis was rich and spoiled. Then, he had a powerful religious experience. He felt called to live as simply as Jesus had lived. Francis believed that all nature was a reflection of God. Because of this, he felt compassion for all living things and referred to animals as his "brothers" and "sisters." An account of his life written after 1228 tells this story:

> 66 One day he came to a town called Alviano to preach the word of God. . . . The people became quiet and waited reverently, but a flock of swallows . . . continued to chatter away, making it impossible for the people to hear. Francis spoke to them, 'My sisters the swallows, it's my turn to speak now. . . . Listen to the word of God. Stay still and be quiet until it's over.' To the people's amazement, the little birds immediately stopped chattering and did not move until Francis had finished preaching. 99
> —Thomas of Celano,
> *First Life of Saint Francis*

Francis's pure and simple life of devotion attracted many followers. In 1209, he <u>established</u> the Franciscan order.

Women were also attracted to the kind of life preached by St. Francis. In 1212, a noblewoman later known as St. Clare of Assisi founded an order based on the teachings of St. Francis. Clare and her followers took a vow of poverty and aimed to live a life of devotion to God. Their order became known as the Poor Clares and spread first through Italy and then across Europe.

Reading Check What were the mendicant orders?

establish, *v.,* to set up

myWorld Activity
Faithful Observations

Medieval painting of St. Francis and St. Clare in the church of San Francesco, Assisi ▼

689

my worldhistory.com

Primary Source

▲ Fantastic creatures called gargoyles cover Gothic buildings.

Mystery plays like "The Flood," were performed on wagons that traveled to different locations in the town. ▼

Medieval Religion and Culture

Religion also had a great influence on the arts during the Middle Ages. The Church shaped cultural values and helped form codes of conduct.

Revival of Drama Since the fall of Rome, the Church had disapproved of drama because of its association with the pre-Christian world. Eventually, however, the Church allowed plays based on stories from the Bible. These "mystery plays" marked the revival of European drama.

New Architecture Religion also inspired some of the greatest architecture since ancient times. A new buildling style that came to be known as Gothic emerged. Gothic combined religious symbolism with engineering advances. Cathedrals built in the Gothic style were higher than any seen before in Western Europe.

Gothic was a revolutionary new architecture. Earlier churches were dark and gloomy. They had massive walls, thick columns, and narrow windows. By the mid-1100s, building technology had advanced. European architects found a way of concentrating the weight of the roof on certain points in the wall. This meant that huge areas of wall could now be opened up. Windows could be larger, filling buildings with light. This architectural breakthrough allowed masons to build stone structures that were spacious and airy.

Gothic churches first appeared in France, but they soon rose all over Europe. Rich townspeople funded their construction. The Gothic cathedral was a breathtaking sight. Rising high above the rooftops, it could be seen for miles.

The Church Shapes Chivalry The Church also influenced cultural values and social behavior. Medieval Europe was a place of almost constant conflict. In this violent world, a code of conduct known as chivalry helped control the behavior of knights. Some values of chivalry, such as bravery and loyalty to the king, were military and feudal in origin. However, the Church tried to shape chivalry to reflect Christian values of generosity, humility, and mercy. Knights were expected to defend the Church and to protect weaker members of society. While the conduct of knights was often far from chivalrous, the values of chivalry left a permanent mark on European manners.

Reading Check What was the purpose of chivalry?

A Gothic World

The high, soaring ceiling draws your eye up to heaven. Walls of glass surround you with the light of another world. The Gothic church offered worshipers a spiritual experience. It also combined sculpture, painting, music, and architecture to teach the lessons of Christianity. The new style spread from churches to guildhalls and palaces. By 1400, Europe was a Gothic world. *What features do you notice about the Gothic style?*

→ Culture Close-Up

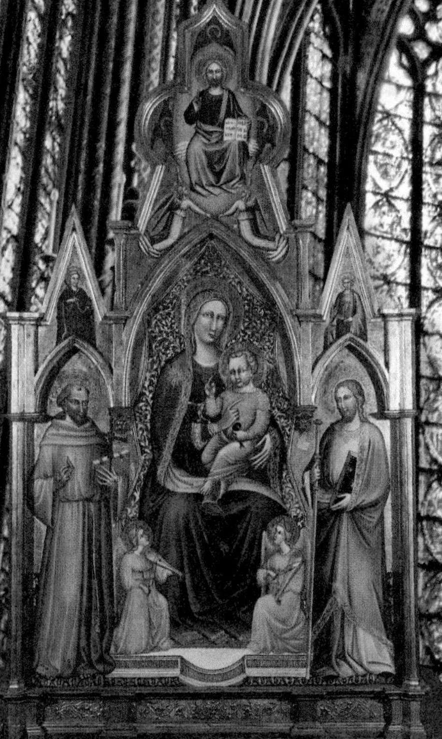

Italian Gothic altarpiece from the 1300s

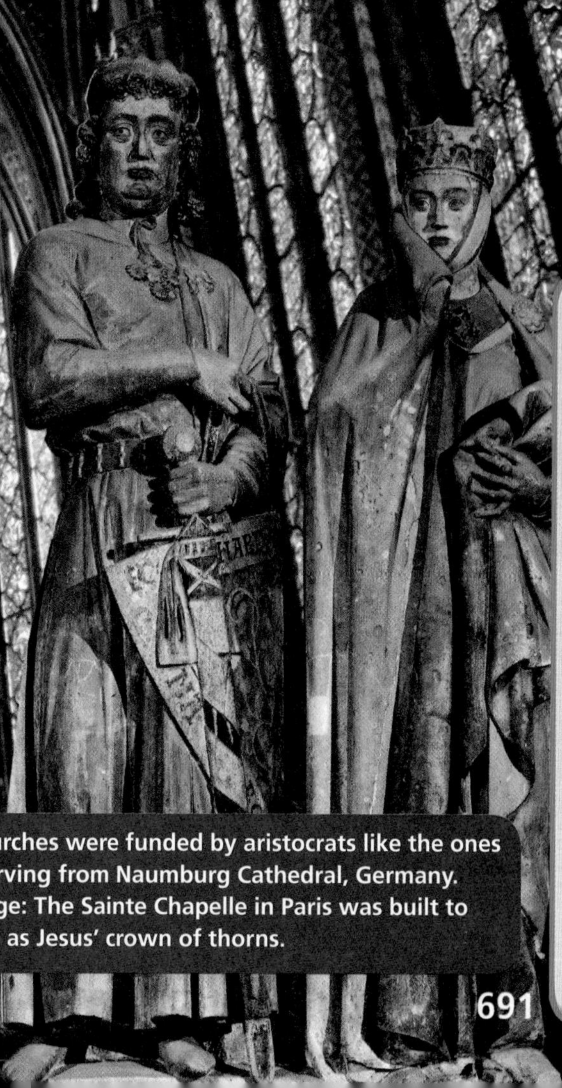

Many Gothic churches were funded by aristocrats like the ones shown in this carving from Naumburg Cathedral, Germany. Background image: The Sainte Chapelle in Paris was built to house relics such as Jesus' crown of thorns.

691

▲ Students listen to a professor at the University of Bologna.

The Growth of Learning

The High Middle Ages saw expansion not only in trade and culture but also in education. Once again, the Church influenced this growth of learning.

Medieval Universities Students were trained for the priesthood at schools attached to the cathedrals. Gradually, schools were set up to provide further education. These grew into **universities**— schools, or groups of schools, that train scholars at the highest levels.

The medieval university was itself a kind of guild. Professors and students organized to form the university. Classes were held in rented rooms or in churches. Books were expensive and were often rented or shared by students.

Despite these discomforts, there was a new excitement about learning. Many works of ancient Greece had been preserved in the Byzantine empire and in

The liberal arts taught at medieval universities formed the basis of liberal arts study today.

Muslim lands, where they had been studied by Arabic scholars. Copies of these books traveled to Europe, along with Arabic books of science and philosophy. Such books were added to the monastery libraries, which had preserved other works of classical learning.

Young men from all over Europe came to study at the universities of Bologna in Italy, Paris in France, and Oxford in England. They studied the "liberal arts," subjects such as grammar and logic, meant to develop their powers of reasoning. Although these students spoke different languages, communication was not a problem. The Church had preserved Latin as the language of learning. Students who spoke Latin could understand courses taught at any university.

Thomas Aquinas The universities attracted the best minds in Europe. One of the greatest medieval scholars was a professor at the University of Paris named Thomas Aquinas (uh KWEYE nus). He was deeply impressed by the writings of the ancient Greek philosopher Aristotle.

Aristotle had emphasized the use of human reason to discover knowledge. In contrast, many Church scholars emphasized faith as the path to truth. Aquinas wanted to show that there is no conflict between the two. He argued that both faith and reason come from God.

Aquinas believed in **natural law**. Unlike human-made law, natural law does not change over time or from one society to another. Aquinas believed that natural laws could be discovered through the power of human reason.

An Age of Confidence A growing confidence in human reason is one of the main features of the High Middle Ages. During this time, conditions in Europe improved <u>dramatically</u>. Towns grew, trade increased, and populations boomed. The universities created an educated class that helped run the Church and state.

Europe's growing prosperity influenced religious practices and attitudes. In art, painters began to show a more human Jesus—a Jesus who suffered, like ordinary human beings. The desire to help humanity, and to improve conditions in the world, influenced the formation of the new mendicant orders.

In the growing towns, soaring cathedrals expressed both the medieval devotion to God and a new confidence in human skills and abilities. Europeans felt great pride in these mighty symbols of faith and community.

But even in these centuries of confidence, Europeans remembered an even more ancient symbol—the wheel of fortune. At one turn of the wheel, fortune could make you rich and powerful. But another turn and the wheel could just as easily tumble you down into poverty and ruin. As the 1200s came to an end, there were signs that fortune's wheel was turning again. This time, it was spinning all Europe toward disaster.

dramatically, *adv.,* greatly

Reading Check How did universities develop?

Lady fortune spins the wheel. Who is about to fall? ▼

Section **2** Assessment

Key Terms

1. For each key term, write a sentence explaining its importance to the age of faith: mendicant order, university, natural law.

Key Ideas

2. How did the monks of the mendicant orders survive?

3. What were the mystery plays about?

4. Who were medieval schools meant to train?

Think Critically

5. Analyze Cause and Effect Why were the mendicant orders formed?

6. Synthesize How did Thomas Aquinas blend ancient and medieval thought?

Essential Question

How are religion and culture connected?

7. In what ways did religion affect culture in the Middle Ages? Go to your Student Journal to record your answer.

Breakdown of Medieval Society

Key Ideas	• Starvation and warfare shook the stability of medieval society.	• A terrible illness known as the Black Death spread across Europe in the 1300s.	• The Black Death helped destroy the medieval social order.

Key Terms • Hundred Years' War • bubonic plague • Black Death • Peasants' Revolt

 Visual Glossary

Reading Skill Analyze Cause and Effect Take notes using the graphic organizer in your journal.

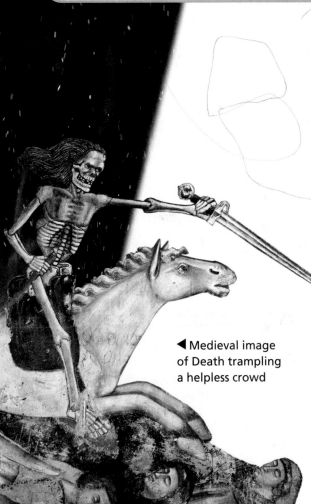

◀ Medieval image of Death trampling a helpless crowd

In the 1340s, rumors reached Europe about a terrifying illness in the Far East. These stories described a plague that was killing millions as it swept through China and India. Then, in 1347, ships began drifting into Italian ports filled with dead or dying crews. Very quickly, thousands in the port cities fell ill, often dying within days. From the ports, the plague spread inland. Soon, every corner of Europe was infected. With few people remaining healthy enough to grow food, medieval society was shaken. Villages were abandoned, as people tried to escape the disease. All lived in fear of human contact. For those who witnessed these terrifying events, it seemed that the end of the world had come.

Famine and Warfare

The plague was only one of a series of disasters to strike Europe in the 1300s. By 1300, Europe had enjoyed two centuries of economic growth. But now Europeans faced troubled times. A change in the weather may have played a part. From 1315 to 1317, it rained so much that crops were ruined. Cattle died of diseases brought on by the wet weather. In northern Europe, many people died of starvation, and the years became known as the Great Famine. A famine is a serious shortage of food. Europe had barely recovered from the famine when war broke out.

694

The Hundred Years' War The conflict began when Edward III of England claimed the throne of France. He was supported in this claim by the Flemish, whose textile industry depended on the wool exported from England to Flanders. The conflict between the kingdoms of England and France lasted from 1337 to 1453 and became known as the **Hundred Years' War.** Although few battles were fought during this war, rural areas in particular suffered as roaming armies destroyed crops and brought starvation to peasant communities.

In the early 1300s, England and France were becoming unified states, or nations. The Hundred Years' War increased the sense of patriotism that was developing in each kingdom. So the war was a new kind of conflict—a war between nations.

Lethal Weapons The English won key battles early in the war, partly because of a powerful weapon: the longbow. Arrows from the English longbow struck with great force, piercing the armor of French knights. In the battle of Crecy in 1346, the French army disintegrated under a thick rain of arrows. In the battle of Agincourt (AH jin cor), fought in 1415, the longbow brought the English another major victory. Thousands of French soldiers were massacred, and France lost important members of its nobility.

Soon, both sides were using even deadlier new weapons: guns and cannons. Guns shot through armor, and cannon blasts pierced even the strongest castle walls. Clearly, the age of knights and castles was ending.

▲ The English longbow varied in length from 5 to 7 feet. Arrows shot from such a weapon could reach a distance of about 500 yards. In the Middle Ages, the Welsh and the English were famous for their skill with the longbow.

Joan of Arc By the early 1400s, it appeared that France was losing the war. The tide was turned by a young peasant woman known as Joan of Arc, whom you read about in the myStory for this chapter. Joan claimed that voices from heaven had told her to dress in knight's clothing and lead the French army to victory. Joan led French soldiers against the English and won important victories. Joan was eventually captured by the English, tried for heresy, and burned at the stake. The French, who defeated the English after Joan's death, honor her today as a national heroine and saint.

Joan of Arc turned the fortunes of France during the Hundred Years' War. In 1453, England was finally defeated. However, the war had caused much suffering in France. During the early years of the war, the French suffered from the attacks of an even greater and <u>invisible</u> enemy— the plague.

invisible, *adj.,* not visible

Reading Check Who was Joan of Arc?

695

The Black Death

network, *n.*, a system that connects places or things

In 1347, ten years after the start of the Hundred Years' War, Europe was struck by a terrible epidemic, a disease that spreads quickly through a population. The epidemic was the **bubonic plague,** a deadly infection. Victims usually died within a few days, often in terrible agony, with their bodies covered in buboes, or swellings. At the time, people called the epidemic the Great Dying. Much later it came to be known as the **Black Death.** No one knew what caused the plague. It may have been carried by infected fleas that lived on rats. However, one form of the plague was transferred through the air and inhaled.

The Spread of the Disease The epidemic began in Central Asia. From there, it slowly spread along the trade networks that linked China, India, and the Middle East. Before reaching Europe, the Black Death had killed millions in Asia.

People infected with the plague rode merchant ships from the East to ports throughout Europe. The disease swept toward southern Europe from ports on the Black Sea, such as Caffa. First Italy, and then France, Spain, and England were struck. Travelers carried the plague up rivers and on overland trade routes, deep into the heart of Europe. In the decades that followed, the plague would often seem to ease, before returning with terrifying force.

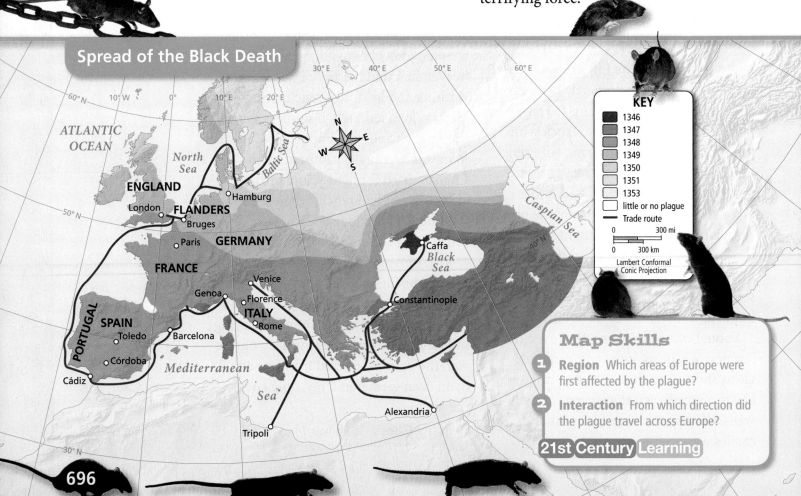

Spread of the Black Death

KEY
- 1346
- 1347
- 1348
- 1349
- 1350
- 1351
- 1353
- little or no plague
- — Trade route

0   300 mi
0   300 km

Lambert Conformal Conic Projection

ATLANTIC OCEAN

North Sea

Baltic Sea

ENGLAND

London

FLANDERS
Bruges

Hamburg

Paris

GERMANY

FRANCE

Venice

Genoa

Florence

ITALY
Rome

Caffa
Black Sea

Caspian Sea

Constantinople

PORTUGAL

SPAIN

Toledo

Córdoba

Cádiz

Barcelona

Mediterranean Sea

Alexandria

Tripoli

Map Skills

1 **Region** Which areas of Europe were first affected by the plague?

2 **Interaction** From which direction did the plague travel across Europe?

21st Century Learning

Closer Look

The Black Death

The plague arrived in Europe on merchant ships, traveling along the same trade routes that had made Europeans rich. After centuries of confidence and optimism, Europe was plunged into uncertainty and gloom. The plague transformed medieval culture, economy, and society.

THINK CRITICALLY **How might the plague have affected people's behavior and attitude to life?**

The triumph of Death, in which a figure representing death slays people of all social ranks, became a popular subject in art.

▲ Villages are abandoned.

▲ Population declines.

Wages rise.▲

▲ Feudalism is shaken.

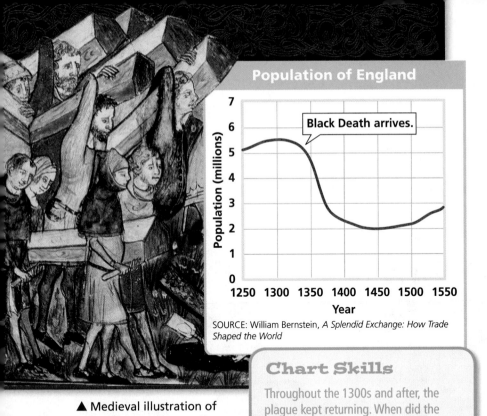

Population of England

Black Death arrives.

SOURCE: William Bernstein, *A Splendid Exchange: How Trade Shaped the World*

▲ Medieval illustration of villagers carrying coffins of plague victims

Chart Skills

Throughout the 1300s and after, the plague kept returning. When did the English population stop falling?

Giovanni Boccaccio lived through the plague in Florence and wrote a detailed account of what he saw:

   ❝ The plight of the lower and most of the middle classes was . . . pitiful to behold. Most of them remained in their houses, either through poverty or in hopes of safety, and fell sick by thousands. Since they received no care and attention, almost all of them died. Many ended their lives in the streets . . . many others who died in their houses were only known to be dead because the neighbours smelled their decaying bodies. Dead bodies filled every corner. ❞

—Giovanni Boccaccio, *The Decameron*

The plague slowly tore apart European society. All societies are based on human contact; but as the plague spread, fear of contact drove many into isolation. The rich fled the towns, often taking the town doctors with them. In the towns, entire families were wiped out. As many as one third of all Europeans—tens of millions of people—died between 1347 and 1352, when the first wave of the plague finally ran its course. Thousands of villages throughout Europe became ghost towns.

Search for Scapegoats In the midst of this mysterious horror, terrified people looked for scapegoats. Scapegoats are people who are blamed for a problem that they did not cause. Some Christians falsely accused the Jews of spreading the plague by poisoning wells. In many European towns, Jews were exiled or killed in anti-Jewish riots. In Strasbourg, the town council ordered that the city's 2,000 Jews convert to Christianity or be burned to death. The pope issued an order that Jews should not be killed or forced to convert. However, his order was widely ignored.

Reading Check What caused the Black Death?

Effects of the Black Death

The Black Death shook the medieval world. It hastened changes that were already underway and introduced disturbing new themes to European art.

A Culture of Despair Towns and the countryside lost vast numbers of people from every social rank: peasants, merchants, priests, scholars, nobles. A terrible gloom settled over the survivors. The art of the time reveals an obsession with death and disease.

Economic Changes With too few people to cultivate the land, much farmland reverted to pasture. Because so many peasants had died, manor lords were desperate for workers. Serfs who survived demanded wages for their work and left manors to work where wages were highest. In response to such changes, manor lords tried to limit the serfs' movements and freeze wages at pre-plague levels.

As social tensions rose, peasants and townspeople across Europe revolted. In 1381, English peasants mounted the **Peasants' Revolt,** killing lords and burning manors. Although such revolts were crushed, feudalism never recovered.

Effects on the Church The Black Death also affected the Church. England, for example, lost an estimated 40 percent of its clergy. The Church was forced to hire men who were often uneducated. This in turn encouraged a movement to reform Church practices.

Toward a New World In the pre-plague medieval world, everyone's place in society was fixed at birth. After the Black Death, Western Europeans were less tied to a stable social and spiritual community. As social tensions increased, serfs defied manorial lords, and many began criticizing medieval traditions. Throughout Western Europe, the shock of the Black Death hastened the end of the Middle Ages and the arrival of the modern world.

Reading Check What were the effects of the Black Death?

myWorld Activity
Dark Times

The plague inspired a new theme in Western art: the dance of Death. Here skeletons dance with churchmen and royalty. ▼

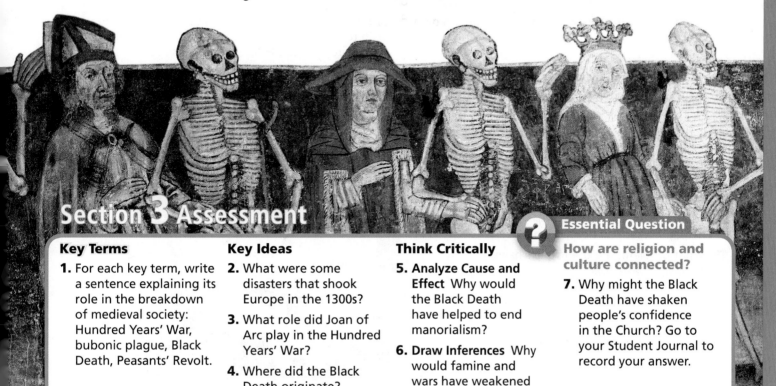

Section 3 Assessment

Key Terms

1. For each key term, write a sentence explaining its role in the breakdown of medieval society: Hundred Years' War, bubonic plague, Black Death, Peasants' Revolt.

Key Ideas

2. What were some disasters that shook Europe in the 1300s?

3. What role did Joan of Arc play in the Hundred Years' War?

4. Where did the Black Death originate?

Think Critically

5. **Analyze Cause and Effect** Why would the Black Death have helped to end manorialism?

6. **Draw Inferences** Why would famine and wars have weakened medieval society?

Essential Question

How are religion and culture connected?

7. Why might the Black Death have shaken people's confidence in the Church? Go to your Student Journal to record your answer.

Chapter Assessment

Key Terms and Ideas

1. **Discuss** How did new technology and **crop rotation** lead to an increase in population?
2. **Explain** What changes took place in economic life during the High Middle Ages?
3. **Recall** Why did townspeople form **guilds**?
4. **Summarize** Why did the growth of towns encourage the rise of the **mendicant orders**?
5. **Describe** In what ways did religious belief influence medieval art and architecture?

6. **Explain** How did **universities** develop?
7. **Recall** What weaponry became important during the **Hundred Years' War**?
8. **Explain** How did Joan of Arc change the course of the Hundred Years' War?
9. **Summarize** What was the significance of the **Peasants' Revolt**?

Think Critically

10. **Draw Inferences** Why did towns offer greater freedom?
11. **Analyze Cause and Effect** How do the great cathedrals reflect the prosperity and optimism of the 1200s?

12. **Draw Conclusions** What was the connection between international trade and the spread of the plague?
13. **Core Concepts: Economic Basics** How did changes in technology and agriculture affect the economy of Europe in the High Middle Ages?

Analyze Visuals

Study the medieval illustration of farming. Then answer the following questions:

14. The top image shows oxen pulling a plow. What kind of plow helped transform medieval farming?
15. Study the bottom image. What changes helped horses pull heavier loads?
16. What problems are the farmers having as they sow the seeds? How do they solve this problem?

Essential Question
myWorld Chapter Activity

Windows on the Middle Ages Follow your teacher's instructions to create stained-glass window designs. Using the Activity Cards, along with Sections 1–3 and myworldhistory.com, you will create images that show aspects of life during the High Middle Ages. You will then have a roundtable discussion of how Europe's fortunes rose and fell during the High Middle Ages.

21st Century Learning
Evaluate Web Sites

Work with a partner to explore the many Web sites that deal with life in the Middle Ages. Create an evaluation sheet, so that you can judge the effectiveness of each Web site. Evaluate each site in terms of design, organization, and information. Then compare your findings with those of others in the class.

Document-Based Questions

Use your knowledge of the Middle Ages and Documents A and B to answer Questions 1–3.

Document A

" I wish, my brother, that I had never been born, or at least had died before these times. . . . When has any such thing ever been heard or seen; in what annals has it ever been read that houses were left vacant, cities deserted, the countryside neglected, the fields too small for the dead to be buried, and a fearful and universal solitude over the whole earth?"

—Petrarch, letter to his brother from *The Black Death, 1347* by George Deaux

Document B

" All those who remained alive became rich, because the wealth of many remained to them."

—Anonymous author from Lucca, Italy, 1348, from *Daily Life During the Black Death* by Joseph Byrne

1. In Document A, the writer describes
   A the effects of war.
   B the effects of the plague.
   C the silence of a town on a holy day.
   D something he has never seen.

2. Document B reveals
   A the effects of the Hundred Years' War.
   B the effects of the growth of the towns.
   C the prosperity of the 1200s.
   D the effects of the plague.

3. **Writing Task** What do Documents A and B together reveal about changes in Europe during the 1300s?

The Crusades

Key Idea
- The Crusades were viewed very differently by Christians and by Muslims.

In a number of battles over nearly 200 years, Christian and Muslim armies fought for control of Jerusalem and the Holy Land. In the two excerpts below, both sides share some of their views about the Crusades. The first excerpt was written by Pope Gregory VII in 1074. In it, he reported that Muslims were killing Christians in the Holy Land. He called for a crusade to restore Christian control of the region. In the second excerpt, Beha-ad-Din (bee HAH ad din), a member of the Muslim army, describes the results of a battle fought in 1191. After the battle, King Richard I of England executed thousands of Muslim prisoners.

Pope Gregory VII

Read the text on the right. Stop at each circled letter. Then answer the question with the same letter on the left.

Ⓐ **Summarize** What does Gregory say is happening to Christians in the Holy Land?

Ⓑ **Draw Conclusions** According to Gregory, what should people do "to be recognized as Christians"?

Ⓒ **Identify Bias** Does the author show bias in the passage? If so, how?

pagan, *n.,* a follower of polytheism, a religion with more than one god

tyrannical, *adj.,* with absolute or brutal rule

liberate, *v.,* to free

Pope Gregory's Call for a Crusade

❝ [T]he bearer of this letter, on his recent return from across the sea, came to Rome to visit us. He repeated what we had heard from many others, that a <u>pagan</u> race had overcome the Christians and with horrible cruelty had devastated everything almost to the walls of Constantinople, and were now governing the conquered lands with <u>tyrannical</u> violence, and that they had slain many thousands of
Ⓐ Christians as if they were but sheep. If we love God and wish to be recognized as Christians, we should be filled with grief at the misfortune of this great [Greek] empire and the murder of so many Christians. But simply to grieve is not our whole duty. . . . [W]e should lay down our lives to <u>liberate</u>
Ⓑ them. . . . Know, therefore, that we are trusting in the mercy of God and in the power of his might and that we are striving in all possible ways and making preparations to render
Ⓒ aid to the Christian empire as quickly as possible. ❞

—Pope Gregory VII, 1074

Read the text on the right. Stop at each circled letter. Then answer the question with the same letter on the left.

D **Draw Inferences** What does this passage suggest about the Frankish army's devotion to the Christian faith?

E **Analyze Primary Sources** What does the writer mean by saying the Muslim prisoners' "martyrdom God had decreed for this day"?

F **Identify Bias** Does the author show bias in the passage? If so, how?

sultan, *n.,* a ruler of a Muslim state

Musulman, *adj.,* Muslim

martyrdom, *n.,* the suffering of death due to one's religious beliefs

decreed, *v.,* commanded

Massacre of Muslim Soldiers

❝ [King Richard I] came out on horseback with all the Frankish
D army, knights, footmen . . . and advanced to the pits at the foot of the hill . . . to which place he had already sent on his tents. The Franks, on reaching the middle of the plain . . . close to which place the <u>sultan's</u> advanced guard had drawn back, ordered all the <u>Musulman</u> prisoners, whose <u>martyrdom</u> God had
E <u>decreed</u> for this day, to be brought before him. They numbered more than three thousand and were all bound with ropes. The Franks then flung themselves upon them all at once and massacred them with sword and lance in cold blood. Our advanced guard had already told the Sultan of the enemy's movements and he sent it some reinforcements, but only after the massacre. . . .

    The motives of this massacre are differently told; according to some, the captives were slain by way of reprisal for the death of the Christians whom the Musulmans had slain. Others say that the king of England . . . thought it unwise to leave so many prisoners in the town after his departure. God alone
F knows what the real reason was. ❞

—Beha-ad-Din, account of the battle of Acre, 1191

An 1842 painting of a battle during the Crusades

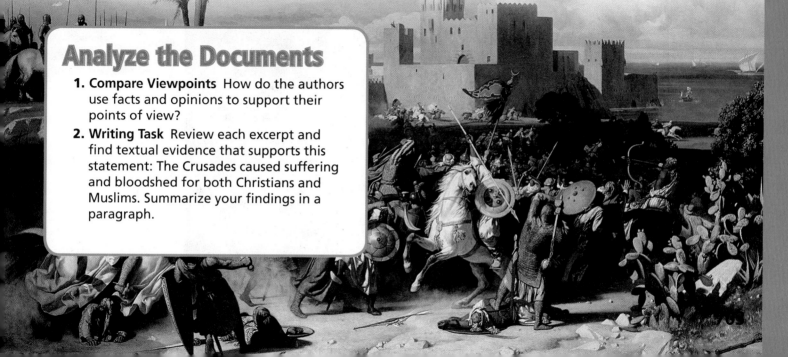

Analyze the Documents

1. **Compare Viewpoints** How do the authors use facts and opinions to support their points of view?

2. **Writing Task** Review each excerpt and find textual evidence that supports this statement: The Crusades caused suffering and bloodshed for both Christians and Muslims. Summarize your findings in a paragraph.

Make a Medieval Trivia Game

Your Mission Working in teams, you and your classmates will create medieval trivia games using information from the unit. Each team will make multiple-choice game cards with questions and answers relating to facts about the Middle Ages. Then trade cards with another team and take turns playing that team's game.

Europe changed in many ways during the Middle Ages. After the fall of Rome, new rulers rose to power. Christianity spread throughout Europe, and the Crusades resulted in years of war. Feudalism and the manor system brought order to medieval society, but farms and towns gradually changed as guilds formed and cities developed. The plague caused a drastic decline in population and a collapse of social order.

As you create your game cards, think about how to write effective trivia questions. You may want to include easier questions about important topics as well as more difficult questions about minor details.

STEP 1

Gather Information.

Work as a team to gather facts from the unit. You may wish to assign a member of your team to each chapter or section. As you gather information, consider how you will write questions and answers about each topic. Each of your questions should have four multiple-choice answers, so "yes" or "no" questions won't work.

STEP 2

Create Your Game.

After you have collected main ideas and key details from the unit, create ten numbered index cards. On one side of each card, write a question about the chapter. On the other side, write four multiple-choice answers, A through D. Make sure that only one answer is correct. Have a member of your team keep track of the correct answers. Review the unit carefully to be sure you have included important information on your cards.

STEP 3

Play the Game!

Once you have made all of your cards, play the game as a group. Make sure you have provided full and correct answers for each question. After you play the game, add any questions about important facts that you might have overlooked. Revise your cards as needed. Then trade game cards with another team and try to answer the questions the other team created. For every correct answer, each team scores two points. The team that scores the most points wins!

The Rise of Europe

North America

Pacific Ocean

Atlantic Ocean

Christopher Columbus (1400s) was an Italian navigator who sailed west across the Atlantic and reached the Americas.

N
W   E
S

South America

1000	1250	1500	1750	2000

The Renaissance

The Reformation

The Age of Exploration

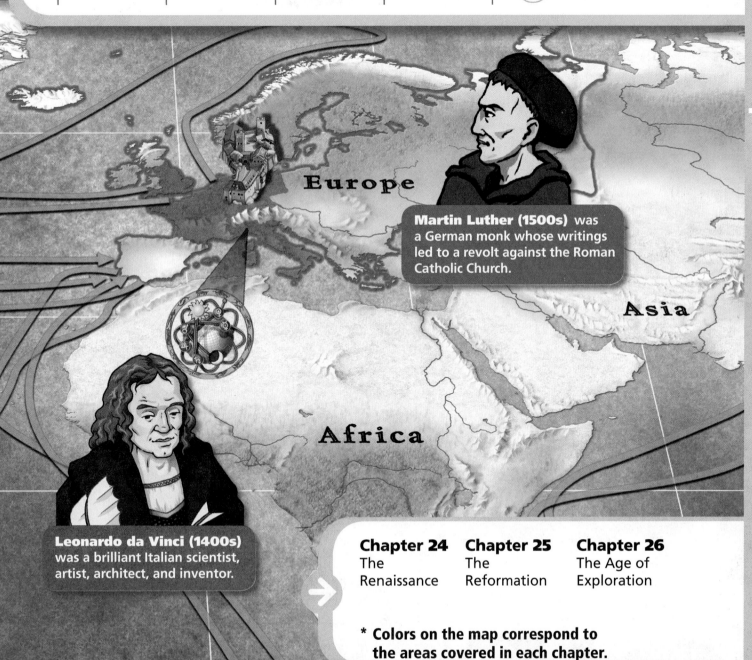

Europe

Martin Luther (1500s) was a German monk whose writings led to a revolt against the Roman Catholic Church.

Asia

Africa

Leonardo da Vinci (1400s) was a brilliant Italian scientist, artist, architect, and inventor.

Chapter 24
The Renaissance

Chapter 25
The Reformation

Chapter 26
The Age of Exploration

* Colors on the map correspond to the areas covered in each chapter.

707

Chapter 24

The Renaissance

Essential Question

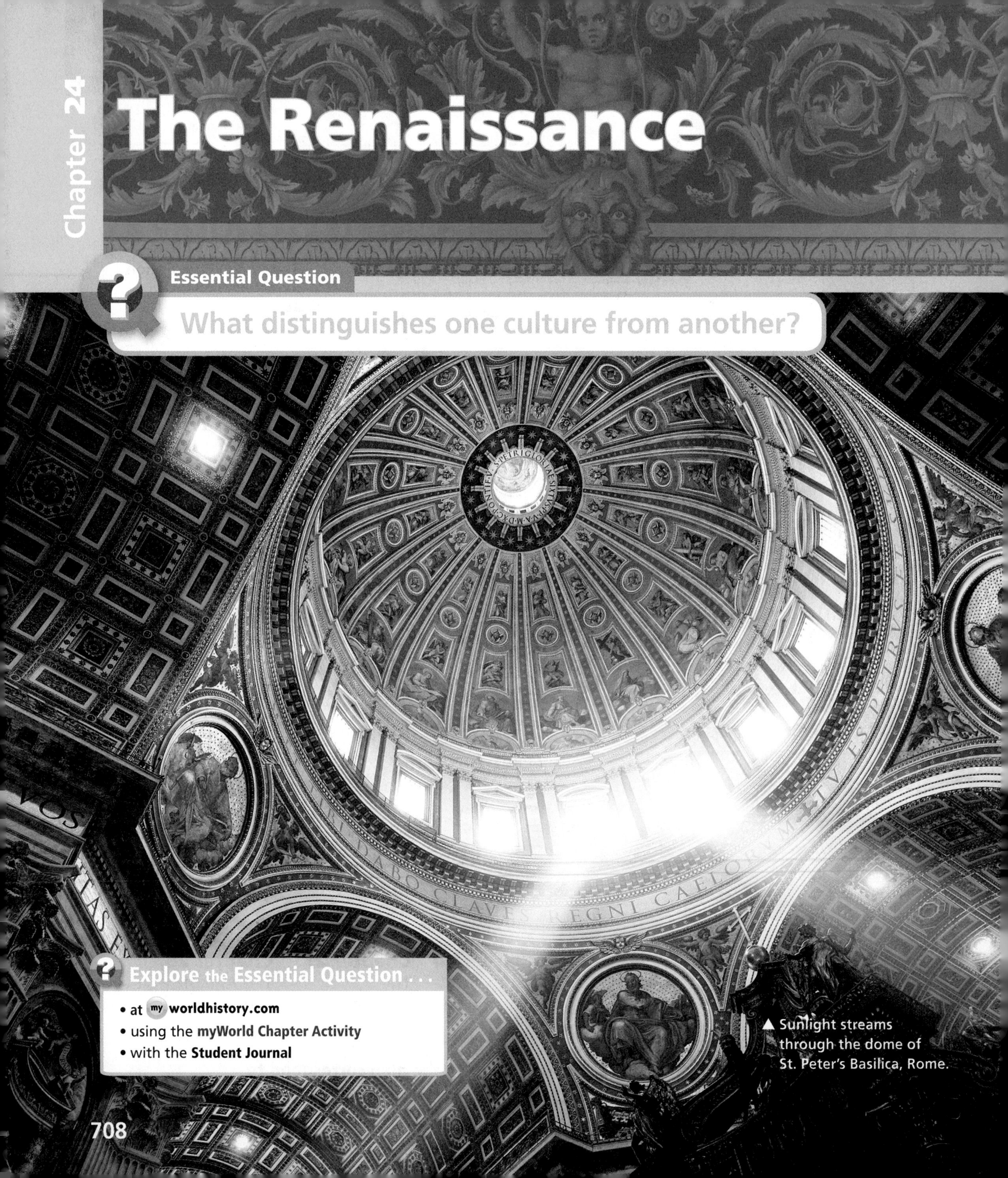

What distinguishes one culture from another?

Explore the Essential Question . . .

- at myworldhistory.com
- using the **myWorld Chapter Activity**
- with the **Student Journal**

▲ Sunlight streams through the dome of St. Peter's Basilica, Rome.

Renaissance Europe

1434 Cosimo de' Medici takes power in Florence.

1479 Lodovico Sforza seizes Milan.

1501 Cesare Borgia ends Spanish rule in southern Italy.

1509 Isabella d'Este rules Mantua.

1400

1500

1600

1452 Hapsburg rule of Holy Roman Empire begins.

1453 Fall of Constantinople

1492 The Reconquista is complete.

1588 Battle of the Spanish Armada

"So Many Things Unknown"

This story is based on events in the life of Leonardo da Vinci.

Leonardo da Vinci (1452–1519)—scientist, artist, architect, and inventor—was born at the right time in the right place: Renaissance Italy. In 1482, when he was 30 years old, Leonardo reached a turning point. After many years in Florence, he had completed an apprenticeship as an artist. He had begun to fill in the gaps in his education by studying the classics and the world around him. But to further his studies, Leonardo needed a friend in a high place. Though the most important man in Florence, Lorenzo de' Medici, was an distinguished arts patron—he was not the friend Leonardo was looking for.

Leonardo decided to leave Florence for Milan, a city-state 200 miles to the north. It was there that he began keeping his notebooks, exploring all areas of the natural world.

The heavens—or what we call outer space—were one of Leonardo's obsessions. In 1490, the powerful and corrupt Duke Sforza, Milan's ruler, invited all of Italy's elite to Milan for a great spectacle designed by Leonardo: The Feast of Paradise. Leonardo's task was to create the party's centerpiece, a clockwork-motion pageant called *The Masque of the Planets.*

my worldhistory.com — Timeline/On Assignment

Leonardo wanted to see how the human body worked from the inside, so he began dissecting dead bodies. He had to do this work secretly at night by candlelight.

In 1503, Leonardo began painting Mona Lisa, the wife of a Florentine banker. He kept the portrait with him until he died.

At the stroke of midnight, after the dancing and feasting, the duke stopped the music. He raised the curtain on Leonardo's latest creation: a gigantic revolving stage shaped like an enormous half egg.

Inside floated models of the sun, the moon, and the five planets known at that time. Earth was not considered a planet, and Uranus and Neptune hadn't been discovered yet.

Each planet revolved in its orbit, along with the signs of the zodiac illuminated by torches behind colored glass. Other torches flamed bright yellow, representing the stars. The effect was enchanting.

At age 38, Leonardo had made a name for himself. He had been promoted to what he considered the ideal job: *ingeniarius ducalis,* or engineer-architect to Duke Sforza of Milan.

Never had he enjoyed such financial stability. The duke gave him an entire wing of an old palace, opening onto the cathedral square, as a comfortable home and workshop. Best of all, he had plenty of spare time and the free run of the excellent library at the university. He had access to scholars and librarians. Some professors became his friends.

During his time in Milan, Leonardo was laboring on one of his most famous masterpieces, *The Last Supper,* painted on the wall of a monastery. He would paint for days without eating or drinking. Or he might study the mural for many hours, make a single brush stroke, and then leave.

Two years passed. Eventually he finished *The Last Supper,* but alas, his experimental use of oil paints on the dry plaster wall was a failure. The mural began deteriorating during his own lifetime.

Leonardo also devoted years of study to Duke Sforza's favorite project, a 24-foot-high bronze statue of the duke on horseback. Leonardo dissected horses to study their anatomy. He became an expert on horses. He was fascinated by the technological difficulty of making such a large statue. But the horse was never built. Why?

Because by that time, Leonardo was wrapped up in scientific investigations. "So many things unknown!" he wrote one day in his notebooks. What is milk? Why is the sky blue?

Leonardo painted two of the most well-known paintings in history—*The Last Supper* and *Mona Lisa.* But he devoted more time and energy to inventions and scientific investigations that he recorded in dozens of notebooks. His notebooks show a complex—and secretive—mind at work.

Leonardo often experimented with light and vision. He discovered that water bubbles can act like tiny prisms and separate light into different colors. At the time, people thought that the eye projected these different colors.

Unlike other scientists, Leonardo preferred to keep his scientific work hidden. (The notebooks were only published hundreds of years after his death.) He went out of his way to make the notebooks difficult to read by writing his notes in his famous mirror-image script. He sometimes wrote with his right hand, sometimes with his left.

There was just so much to be learned, so much to discover. "Obstacles cannot crush me," he proclaimed with resolve. "He who is fixed to a star does not change his mind."

Based on this story, what do you think distinguished the culture of Europe during the Renaissance? As you read the chapter ahead, think about what Leonardo's story tells you about life during the Renaissance.

 myStory Video

Join Leonardo in his studio.

The Masque of the Planets

The Origins of the Renaissance

Key Ideas	• During the Renaissance, economic and social changes began to break down the feudal order.	• The Renaissance began in Italian city-states that had become wealthy through trade and finance.

Key Terms • mercantile • Renaissance • patron

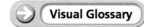 **Visual Glossary**

 **Reading Skill Analyze Cause and Effect** Take notes using the graphic organizer in your journal.

During the Middle Ages, life for most Europeans revolved around the manor and the Church. By the 1300s, however, new forces were at work that would bring considerable changes to Europe.

The Breakdown of the Feudal Order

As trade and industry grew, feudalism and manorialism weakened. A wealthy merchant in Scotland could now drink French wine, buy clothing made of Asian silk, and flavor his food with spices from Africa or India. In one Italian textile factory, there were 30,000 workers.

Urban Growth The labor force for this economic expansion came from migrants who moved from manors to towns. Peasants were drawn to towns by the promise of wages. Nobles were also attracted to towns for economic reasons. They saw opportunities to make money by buying property and holding public office.

In Italian cities, the rural nobility married into the mercantile middle class to form a new urban aristocracy. **Mercantile** means related to commerce or trade. This urban upper class kept its ties to the land but lived mainly in town. Instead of spending money on rural castles, the new nobility used its wealth to build beautiful homes in the city.

◀ Galileo may have conducted experiments on gravity from the Leaning Tower of Pisa.

Secular Learning For centuries, learning had been based in the Church. Even after universities sprang up in European cities, <u>theology</u> remained the most important course of study. In time, interest grew in secular subjects such as law, medicine, philosophy, engineering, and science.

Cultural Rebirth Around 1300, these different trends came together to begin the Renaissance. The **Renaissance** was a great cultural revival that swept through Europe from the 1300s through the 1500s. *Renaissance* is French for "rebirth."

Renaissance thinkers rediscovered the literature, art, and learning of ancient Greece and Rome. They looked to these classical cultures for models of how to live.

Reading Check What happened to feudalism in the 1300s?

Birthplace of the Renaissance

In England, France, and Spain, the feudal order defined the structure of life. In Italy, however, feudalism had never developed in the same way. This may help explain why Italy was the birthplace of the Renaissance.

Italian City-States By the 1300s, Italy was divided into several city-states. Because they were located near the Mediterranean Sea, the Italian city-states served as a natural crossroads between northern Europe and the lands of the Middle East and Africa. Merchants traveling on land and sea made the Italian peninsula a trading center. For this reason, Italy led medieval Europe in commercial growth.

theology, *n.*, study of religious faith, practice, and experience

A statue of Grand Duke Ferdinando I de' Medici, a member of one of Florence's most powerful ruling families ▼

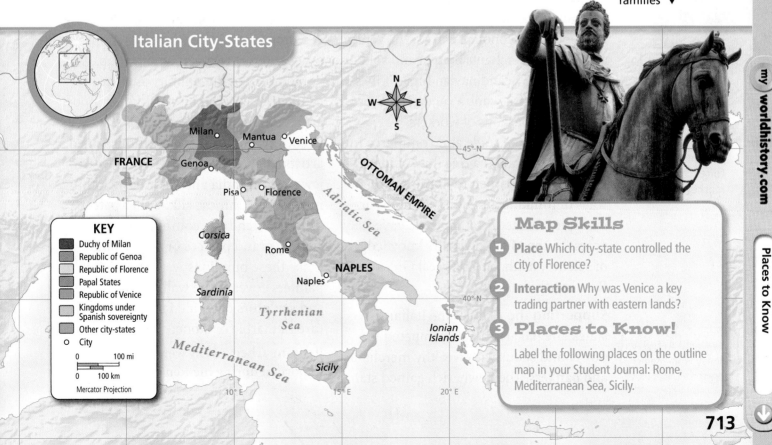

Italian City-States

KEY
- Duchy of Milan
- Republic of Genoa
- Republic of Florence
- Papal States
- Republic of Venice
- Kingdoms under Spanish sovereignty
- Other city-states
- ○ City

0   100 mi
0   100 km
Mercator Projection

FRANCE

Milan
Mantua
Venice
Genoa
Pisa
Florence
Corsica
Rome
NAPLES
Naples
Sardinia
Tyrrhenian Sea
Mediterranean Sea
Sicily
Adriatic Sea
OTTOMAN EMPIRE
Ionian Islands

45° N
40° N
10° E   15° E   20° E

Map Skills

1 **Place** Which city-state controlled the city of Florence?

2 **Interaction** Why was Venice a key trading partner with eastern lands?

3 **Places to Know!**

Label the following places on the outline map in your Student Journal: Rome, Mediterranean Sea, Sicily.

Italy: Renaissance Crossroads

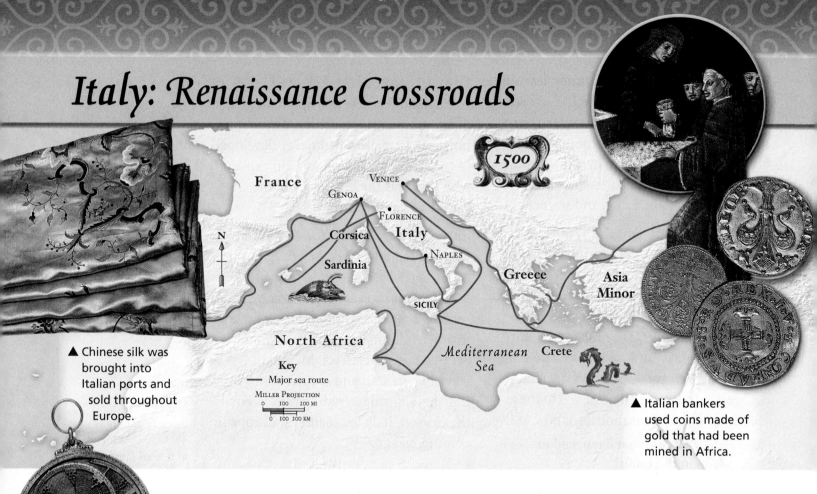

▲ Chinese silk was brought into Italian ports and sold throughout Europe.

Key
— Major sea route

MILLER PROJECTION
0   100   200 MI
0   100   200 KM

▲ Italian bankers used coins made of gold that had been mined in Africa.

▲ Italian sailors used instruments like the astrolabe to reach Asian markets.

myWorld Activity
Money From Medici

Many Italian city-states became thriving centers of economic activity. In Venice and Genoa, merchants bought and sold Indian spices, Scandinavian furs, Chinese silk, and English wool. Venetian shipyards employed thousands of workers.

The growth of trade and commerce in Italy also promoted a free flow of ideas. People began to open their minds to new ways of thinking and doing things. For example, contact through trade gave Italy access to the Muslim world's knowledge of science, math, and classical Greek and Roman scholarship.

Supporting the Arts In the Italian city-states, the old aristocrats competed for power and status with wealthy merchants and bankers. The newly rich gained status by becoming patrons of art and learning. A **patron** is someone who gives money or other support to a person or group.

Members of the nobility and the mercantile class used their wealth to support artists and to elevate their own status in society. Some patrons commissioned artists to paint portraits of them wearing jewels from India and their best clothing made from Chinese silk. Other patrons awarded architects commissions for designing grand palaces or public buildings. Once these buildings were completed, painters covered the walls with frescoes and sculptors decorated them with sculpture in marble or stone.

Reading Check Why were patrons important during the Renaissance?

714

Florence: Renaissance Center

Shipping through its port made Venice rich and cosmopolitan. Rome was the home of the powerful Catholic Church. However, it was the city of Florence that became the artistic center of the Renaissance.

Since ancient Roman times, Florence had been a major stop on trade routes. It was accessible from the Arno River or through passes in the Tuscan Apennines mountains. In addition to developing as a commerce center, Florence became known for its banking activity—even the pope kept his money there. Banking encouraged many other types of businesses such as silk manufacturing, the wool trade, and silver and gold crafts. Many of these groups established guilds.

One of the most powerful banking families in the city was the Medici (MED uh chee) family. Generations of Medicis were also patrons of the arts. Much of the art and architecture they commissioned was influenced by the grandeur they had seen while visiting aristocratic courts in France. The Medici also built many new churches in Florence and hired artists and sculptors to decorate them.

Lorenzo de' Medici, a major Florentine arts patron, understood the value of art to a city,

> 66 [I]t gave great luster to the state and this money seems to be well spent. 99
>
> —*Lorenzo de' Medici*

Florentine merchants also spent money on artistic projects. Artists were also sought after by guilds and <u>civic</u> groups. In this way, painters and sculptors worked alongside gold artists or stone carvers on larger projects such as cathedrals. As a result, Florence became a showcase of Renaissance art and architecture.

Reading Check How was Florence a center for Renaissance ideas?

civic, *adj.*, of or relating to citizenship or community affairs

This Renaissance portrait shows the elaborate dress and jewelry worn by the wealthy. ▼

Section 1 Assessment

Key Terms

1. Define each of the following key terms in a complete sentence: mercantile, Renaissance, patron.

Key Ideas

2. Describe the kinds of changes that took place in European cities and universities in the 1300s.

3. Why did Italy lead medieval Europe in commercial growth?

4. What economic activity was Florence known for?

Think Critically

5. **Analyze Cause and Effect** During the Renaissance, how did trade promote new ideas and learning?

6. **Synthesize** What characteristics helped Italy to become the birthplace of the Renaissance?

7. **Identify Evidence** What actions demonstrate that Lorenzo de' Medici was a patron of the arts?

? **Essential Question**

What distinguishes one culture from another?

8. How was the culture of Italian cities different from rural culture? How were the cultures of Venice and Florence different? Go to your Student Journal to record your answers.

New Ways of Viewing the World

Michelangelo's *David* ▶

Key Ideas	• Renaissance thinkers looked to classical learning for a deeper understanding of human life.	• Renaissance art treated both religious and secular themes in a new realistic style.

Key Terms • humanism • secularism • vernacular • individualism

 **Visual Glossary**

Reading Skill Compare and Contrast Take notes using the graphic organizer in your journal.

Thinkers during the Middle Ages concentrated on matters of faith and spirituality. Although much of the learning of the ancient Greek and Roman civilizations had been preserved, interest in it declined during that time. During the Renaissance, however, scholars considered this ancient heritage a foundation for the "new learning."

New Viewpoints

The new learning of the Renaissance suggested that human beings and the world deserved contemplation and study as much as matters of God and faith. This led to new ways of seeing the world and the role of humans in it. These new viewpoints include the three key Renaissance ideas: humanism, secularism, and individualism.

Humanism Knowledge of classical Greek and Roman thought did not suddenly come to light in the 1400s. Thinkers such as Petrarch (PEA trahrk) did much during the Renaissance to revive interest in classical learning. They applied what they learned about classical Greece and Rome to their own world. This new focus was called humanism, from the Latin word *humanitas*. **Humanism** was a cultural movement of the Renaissance based on the study of classical works.

◀ Michelangelo portrayed the Biblical figure of Leah in classical garments.

To humanists, learning led to a better earthly life rather than serving solely as preparation for eternity. Medieval thinkers had focused on spirituality and faith rather than self-worth.

Secularism The Renaissance marked a growing trend toward **secularism,** or the view that religion need not be the center of human affairs. People began to view life as an opportunity for enjoyment and pleasure. This contrasted with the medieval attitude of life as little more than a painful pilgrimage striving toward heaven. The growth of secularism was clear in writings that were intended to entertain or inform rather than to promote spirituality. One example was *The Decameron,* by Giovanni Boccaccio (bo CAH chee oh). This collection of tales, written in the mid-1300s, reflected the worldly views of Florentine society. It was written in the **vernacular,** or everyday spoken language of the people.

Another secular book was *The Prince* (1513), by Niccolò Machiavelli (mahk ee uh VEL ee). *The Prince* was a highly influential work of political thought in which Machiavelli described how leaders gain power, keep power, and lose power. He chose "to represent things as they are in real truth, rather than as they are imagined." Today, the word *Machiavellian* is used to describe someone who tries to achieve something by <u>manipulating</u> others. But Machiavelli was simply describing the realities of Renaissance politics.

manipulate, *v.,* to manage or utilize skillfully

The School of Athens

A The philosopher Socrates debating an issue

B Michelangelo as the philosopher Heraclitus

C Leonardo da Vinci as the philosopher Plato

D The philosopher Aristotle holding the *Ethics*

E Self-portrait of the artist Raphael Sanzio

my worldhistory.com   Culture Close-Up

Culture Close-Up

▲ In his fresco *The School of Athens* (1510–1511), Raphael uses human figures and architecture to represent philosophy. By portraying Renaissance figures as classical thinkers, he shows the importance of philosophy in Renaissance thought. *How does this work demonstrate human potential?*

Key Renaissance Events

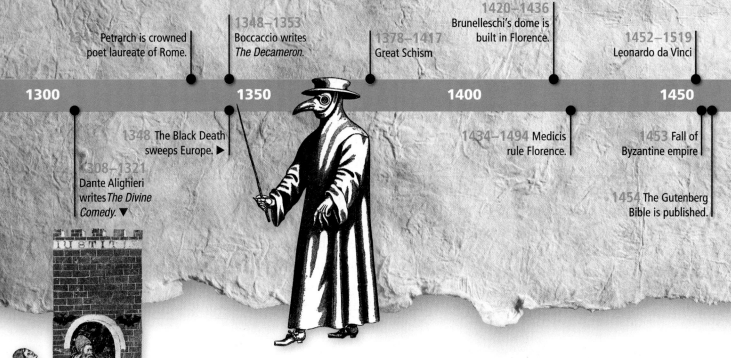

Petrarch is crowned poet laureate of Rome.

1348–1353 Boccaccio writes *The Decameron.*

1378–1417 Great Schism

1420–1436 Brunelleschi's dome is built in Florence.

1452–1519 Leonardo da Vinci

1300

1350

1400

1450

1348 The Black Death sweeps Europe. ▶

1308–1321 Dante Alighieri writes *The Divine Comedy.* ▼

1434–1494 Medicis rule Florence.

1453 Fall of Byzantine empire

1454 The Gutenberg Bible is published.

Individualism The third idea that defined Renaissance thought was **individualism,** the belief that the individual was more important than the larger community. During the medieval period, the individual's needs had been less significant than the needs of larger groups such as the residents of a manor. This concern for the worth of the individual was rooted in classical philosophy and reappeared in Renaissance thinking.

Protagoras (pro TA guh rus), the ancient Greek philosopher, voiced humanist ideas when he wrote, "Man is the measure of all things." Renaissance thinkers took this to mean that the individual is the ultimate judge of what is good or important. This was different from the typical attitude of medieval artists and architects who believed that they worked to glorify God rather than themselves.

Individualism freed Renaissance artists from an emphasis on sin and human imperfection. These painters, sculptors, architects, authors, poets, and composers began to explore the imagination and human potential. They came to value creativity for its own sake. Proud of their achievements, they signed their works and left records of their lives.

In turn, these artists' patrons encouraged them to take risks that expanded creative ideas even more. These risks led to exceptional efforts that brought <u>prestige</u> to both the artists and their patrons.

Reading Check **How did humanism differ from medieval ways of thinking?**

prestige, *n.,* respect and admiration from others

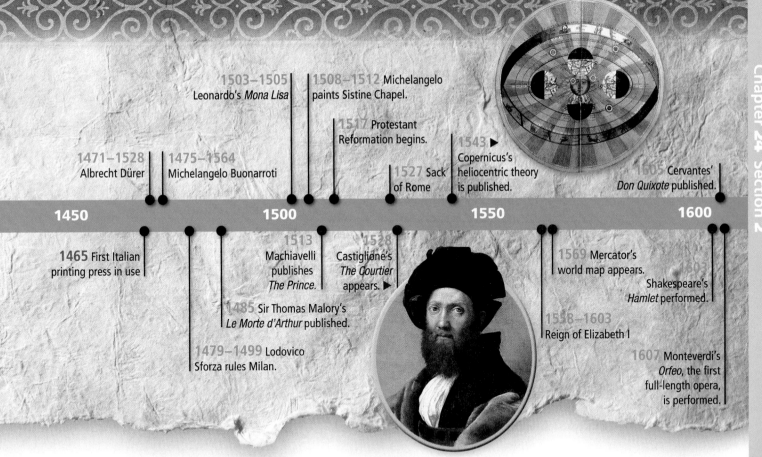

1471–1528 Albrecht Dürer

1475–1564 Michelangelo Buonarroti

1503–1505 Leonardo's *Mona Lisa*

1508–1512 Michelangelo paints Sistine Chapel.

1517 Protestant Reformation begins.

1527 Sack of Rome

1543 ▶ Copernicus's heliocentric theory is published.

1605 Cervantes' *Don Quixote* published.

1450   **1500**   **1550**   **1600**

1465 First Italian printing press in use

1513 Machiavelli publishes *The Prince*.

1528 Castiglione's *The Courtier* appears. ▶

1569 Mercator's world map appears.

Shakespeare's *Hamlet* performed.

1485 Sir Thomas Malory's *Le Morte d'Arthur* published.

1558–1603 Reign of Elizabeth I

1479–1499 Lodovico Sforza rules Milan.

1607 Monteverdi's *Orfeo*, the first full-length opera, is performed.

Changes in Daily Life

New views of the world also meant changes in daily life. During the Renaissance, more people learned to read and write, and a new calendar appeared.

Learning in the Vernacular In the Middle Ages, educated people spoke Latin. These people were generally men who had attended universities—women were excluded—to become physicians, lawyers, or priests. Ordinary people spoke in vernacular languages such as Italian or French.

By the time of the Renaissance, more books written in the vernacular were available. This led to an increase in literacy among ordinary people. In some homes, family members or tutors used printed books in the vernacular to teach children how to read and write.

Although there were learned women during the Middle Ages and the Renaissance, most young girls did not receive a formal education. Most of their education consisted of learning the skills needed to run a home and raise a family. A few boys could expect to learn to read and write. Some went on to university educations or to apprenticeships to acquire a craft.

A New Calendar During the Renaissance, people began to have a different perception of time. For centuries, people had marked off the year based on the seasons and the events in the church. The calendar commonly in use before the Renaissance was the Julian calendar established in ancient Rome by Julius Caesar.

myWorld Activity
Power Play

719

In the early 1560s, a commission headed by Pope Gregory XIII worked to correct inaccuracies found in the Julian calendar. It took the commission almost ten years to craft the Gregorian calendar, which we use today.

Not every nation adopted the Gregorian calendar immediately. Because the new calendar was formulated by a Catholic pope, some Protestant nations refused to adopt it. Catholic nations like France and Spain began using the calendar in 1582. Switzerland's adoption took place in stages, lasting from 1583 to 1812. Britain adopted the Gregorian calendar in 1752 and Greece followed only in 1923.

Reading Check Why did some European nations object to the Gregorian calendar?

New Directions in Art

New ways of thinking were also evident in Renaissance art. Art began to reflect a change in focus from religious devotion to worldly concerns.

Changing Content Medieval art generally had religious themes. Renaissance art often did as well, but with a twist. For example, Italian artist Benozzo Gozzoli (beh NOH tzoh goh TZOH lee) was commissioned by the Medici family to paint *The Journey of the Magi,* depicting the procession to visit the baby Jesus in Bethlehem. Gozzoli's work includes portraits of Medici family members dressed in rich garments as if they had attended the actual event.

Changing Styles

Compare the paintings of the Virgin Mary and the infant Jesus from the Middle Ages (left) and the Renaissance (right). *How do these differences reflect the spirit of the Renaissance?*

In the medieval painting, the human figures are unrealistic with unemotional faces. The Renaissance figures are tender and loving.

In the medieval painting, clothing is flat and one-dimensional, while in the Renaissance work, clothing has realistic folds and gathers.

In both paintings, the Christ child's gesture is affectionate, but the proportions are less realistic in the medieval painting.

Oil paint makes the Renaissance work appear three-dimensional, while the tempera colors of the medieval painting appear flat.

Increasingly, the subjects of Renaissance art were not religious at all. Greek and Roman mythology provided popular themes. The painting *The Birth of Venus* by Botticelli (boh tee CHEH lee) portrays an event in Greek mythology. In addition, individual portraits, usually of wealthy people, became popular, as did artists' self-portraits. Landscapes and scenes of daily life were also common.

Renaissance Realism Medieval painters and sculptors had celebrated the glory of God—not the human figure, as did ancient Greek and Roman artists. Just as Renaissance thinkers revived the wisdom of the ancient world, so Renaissance artists examined again classical art.

Renaissance art centered on realism and the living world. Artists used live models to draw or sculpt the human form—whether it was beautiful or grotesque. They depicted emotions ranging from bliss to grief. They were fascinated with nature and portrayed every detail of it.

For Renaissance painter and author Giorgio Vasari (vah SAH ree), merely copying reality was not enough.

66 He who has not drawn much nor studied the choicest ancient and modern works cannot . . . improve the things that he copies from life, giving them the grace and perfection in which art goes beyond the scope of nature. 99

—Giorgio Vasari, *The Lives of the Artists*

Renaissance artists took inspiration from classical ideas and added harmony, proportion, and a new realism. Renaissance art, ranging from architecture to furniture, celebrates these qualities.

Reading Check What subjects became popular for Renaissance painters?

▲ Oil paints were developed in the 1400s. Pigments came from ground berries, insects, or semiprecious stones. Brushes had animal hair for bristles.

Section 2 Assessment

Key Terms

1. Using complete sentences, explain how each of the following terms relates to a change that took place during the Renaissance: humanism, secularism, vernacular, individualism.

Key Ideas

2. What three ideas made up the new learning in the Renaissance?

3. How did the new ideas of the Renaissance change daily life?

4. What new materials did artists begin to use in the Renaissance?

Think Critically

5. **Draw Conclusions** Why did Renaissance artists favor realism in their work?

6. **Connect** Does the new learning of the Renaissance remain important to society today? Explain why or why not.

7. **Identify Evidence** What works of literature demonstrated the new trend toward secularism?

? Essential Question

What distinguishes one culture from another?

8. How did humanism differ from medieval education? How was Renaissance art different from medieval art? Go to your Student Journal to record your answers.

The Spread of New Ideas

Key Ideas
- Northern Renaissance thinkers promoted religious and social reforms.
- The development of printing increased literacy and helped spread new ideas.

Key Terms
- utopia
- satire
- engraving
- censor

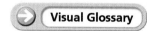

Visual Glossary

Reading Skill Identify Main Ideas and Details Take notes using the graphic organizer in your journal.

In the Middle Ages, information moved slowly. By the time of the Renaissance, however, ideas—like trade goods—moved more rapidly.

The Renaissance Moves North

Scholars traveled to Italy from all parts of Europe and took the new learning back to their home countries. As Renaissance ideas spread, northern European cities became important centers of humanist scholarship. Many northern scholars looked to the new learning to bring about reforms in the Church and in society.

More's *Utopia* One such reformer was Sir Thomas More, an English church leader and scholar. His best-known work is the book *Utopia* (1516). More coined the word *utopia* from the Greek words meaning "no place." It was the name he gave to his ideal society. Today, we use **utopia** to mean an imaginary, ideal place.

In More's book, Utopia is a community governed entirely by reason. Everyone is equal and there is no private property. Everyone receives a free education. This imaginary place offered a sharp contrast to corruption common in the Church and the government of the day. More wanted to suggest a better way to organize human affairs.

◀ Sir Thomas More and a copy of *Utopia* showing a map of the imaginary land and its language

Desiderius Erasmus Another important reformer was Desiderius Erasmus (ih RAZ mus), a Dutch scholar and lifelong friend of Thomas More. Erasmus believed that the life and lessons of Jesus should be the model for Church doctrine. But he claimed that the Church had abandoned Christian morality for empty rituals and ceremonies. Erasmus's most famous book, *In Praise of Folly,* used satire to criticize Church leaders and practices. **Satire** is a kind of writing that uses ridicule or sarcasm to criticize vice or folly. Erasmus wrote in the book's preface,

> 66 [H]e that spares no sort of men cannot be said to be angry with anyone in particular, but the vices of all. 99

> —Desiderius Erasmus, *In Praise of Folly*

The book's wit and bracing wisdom made it very popular during the Renaissance. Historians credit Erasmus with making humanism an international movement.

François Rabelais The French humanist François Rabelais (rab uh LAY) was a monk, a doctor, a scholar, and an author. In the books *Gargantua* and *Pantagruel,* he used humor and <u>exaggeration</u> to criticize traditions in religion, education, and politics. On the surface, these are comic tales of the giant Gargantua and his son Pantagruel. (The term *gargantuan,* meaning huge, comes from Rabelais' writings.) But Rabelais' characters also show the social upheaval that was occurring during the transition from feudalism to mercantilism.

Reading Check How did Erasmus and Rabelais use humor to state their ideas?

Gargantua Eats the Pilgrims

In Rabelais' tale, the giant Gargantua devours a huge salad concealing six religious pilgrims. To save themselves, the pilgrims hide in Gargantua's teeth. The giant then plucks them out with a toothpick. The scene is funny, but Rabelais is also portraying the pilgrims as powerless and fearful. In this way, the author makes fun of the medieval idea that going on pilgrimage makes a person special.

Northern Renaissance Artists

Much of northern Europe was still recovering from the ravages of the Black Death. Gradually, the prosperous cities of Flanders, France, Germany, Belgium, and England joined the cultural rebirth.

Painters in Flanders The Flemish painter Jan van Eyck (yahn van YK) dazzled the eye with his realistic scenes. In *The Arnolfini Portrait,* a mirror on the wall reflects the couple in the painting. Below the mirror, the artist noted "Jan van Eyck has been here. 1434."

Peter Paul Rubens—humanist, artist, and diplomat—blended Northern Renaissance realism with the classical influences of the Italian Renaissance artists. His paintings show his wide knowledge of mythology, the Bible, and classical history.

exaggeration, *n.,* overstatement for effect

723

▲ In Bruegel's *The Peasant Wedding*, the guests are served porridge carried on a door taken off its hinges. The man in the red jacket has brought his own spoon. *What other realistic details do you see?*

linen, *n.*, cloth made from the flax plant

724

Northern European artists like Pieter Bruegel (BROY gul) painted complex and realistic scenes of peasant life. Bruegel and many of his fellow artists found the new medium of oil paints perfect for trying to achieve realism in their works.

Leonardo of the North German artist Albrecht Dürer (DYOOR ur) is sometimes called the "Leonardo of the North" for his wide-ranging interests and great artistic skill. Following a trip to Italy in 1494, Dürer brought back many new painting and engraving techniques. **Engraving** is an art form in which the artist etches a design on a metal plate with a needle and acid. The image is then inked and the plate pressed on paper. Dürer's work helped spread Renaissance ideas to northern Europe.

Reading Check Why is Dürer called the Leonardo of the North?

The Printing Revolution

New developments promoted the spread of humanism. These included advances in printing and the expansion of literacy.

New Tools for Printing In the 1200s, block printing traveled from China to Europe by way of Muslim traders. In block printing, the text of a book page was carved into a block of wood. Block printing, however, was time-consuming and expensive. Wood blocks could only be used a few times and, if the block broke or wore down from printing, a new one had to be carved.

In the 1300s, Europeans learned to make paper out of <u>linen</u> rags. In the 1400s, they learned how to make oils for use in painting and then for printing inks. These improvements led to a communications revolution.

Gutenberg's Metal Type Around 1450, a German printer named Johann Gutenberg (YOH hahn GOOT un burg) invented movable metal type. With this method, individual letters formed in metal could be used again and again to form words, lines, and pages of text.

In 1455, Gutenberg published the Bible, an event that increased literacy as never before. Printed Bibles were less expensive than handwritten ones, and many people learned to read using Bibles they had at home. By 1490, printing presses were in use from London to Constantinople. By 1500, between 8 million and 20 million books had been printed in Europe.

Reading Check How did block printing differ from movable type?

Closer Look

Gutenberg's Press

With the introduction of the printing press, books could be printed inexpensively and in greater quantities. With more books available, more people began to learn to read. In addition to books, early newspapers appeared and people could learn about events in other parts of their country or the world. It was the dawn of the information age.

THINK CRITICALLY **How did Gutenberg's innovation change literacy?**

Gutenberg (right) and the press workers in his shop examine a newly printed sheet. The young man next to Gutenberg is probably an apprentice studying the trade of printing.

◀ This model of a printing press is similar to the kind used by Gutenberg.

Before printing, the printer puts each letter in a composing stick. The movable metal type letter is reversed from how it will read on the page. ▼

This early Bible was written and illustrated by hand. ▼

Gutenberg first printed the Bible. The words were made with movable type and the margins were decorated by hand. ▶

In the News

Modern newspapers began as broadsheets, or single printed sheets that sometimes combined text and illustrations in the form of woodcuts. Some broadsheets gave the news in verse. Newsbooks were multipage journals similar to today's magazines. *How did printing by hand affect the speed with which news reached readers?*

The big news in England in the 1600s was Prince Charles's return from exile (front) and the London plague of 1665 (behind). Below, a teen uses the latest technology to check news sites on the Internet.

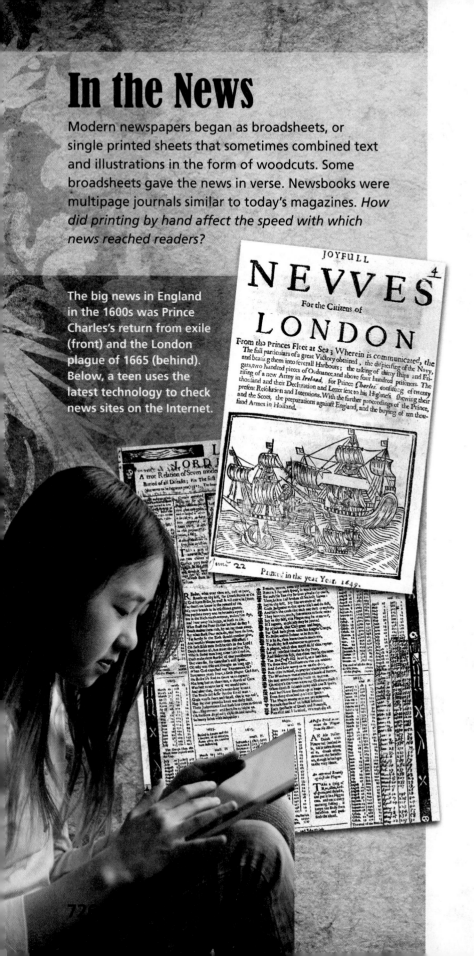

JOYFULL
NEVVES
For the Citizens of
LONDON

From tha Princes Fleet at Sea; Wherein is communicated, the full particulars of a great Victory obtained, the dispiersing of the Navy, and beati g them into severall Harbours; the taking of thirty ships and Fri-gats, two hundred pieces of Ordnance, and above four hundred prisoners. The rising of a new Army in *Ireland*, for Prince *Charles*, consisting of twenty thousand and their Declaration and Letter sent to his Higness, shewing their present Resolution and Intentions. With the further proceedings of the Prince, and the Scots, the preparations against England, and the buying of ten thou-sand Armes in Holland.

June 22

Printed in the year Yeat. 1649.

The Spread of Ideas

More reading materials encouraged more people to learn to read and write. However, the Catholic Church had strong ideas about what people should read.

Spread of Literacy Historians believe that literacy rates in medieval Europe were extremely low. Perhaps fewer than half of all men could read and maybe only one woman out of ten was literate. With the invention of mass printing, however, the literacy rate began to rise.

In addition to the Bible, people had other kinds of reading material. Printers published medical manuals and accounts of travelers. Governments used print to communicate with their subjects. People began to circulate broadsheets, or large printed sheets that often included wood-cut illustrations. These broadsheets were the earliest form of newspapers.

Rise of Censorship As the number of books increased, so did efforts to censor what people read. To **censor** means to remove material from published works or to prevent its publication. The idea of censorship goes back to ancient Rome when an official called a censor regulated public morals. Until modern times, people did not associate censorship with limits on individual freedom.

It was during the Renaissance that self-expression became associated with the freedom to form one's own opinion. For centuries, the Church had formed people's ideas. But with self-expression in books and broadsheets, people began to criticize institutions such as the Church.

The Church Reacts The Church took steps to address this growing criticism. In 1559, church officials published a list of prohibited books. This list served to guide censors whose job it was to approve or forbid works from being published. Censorship was seen as a way to reduce bad influences on people's morality. Some authors decided to prevent the risk of appearing on the list by changing their works before they were published. In this way, these authors acted as self-censors.

One of the most famous incidents of Church censorship involved the Italian astronomer Galileo. When he stated that the sun, not Earth, was the center of the solar system, Galileo violated church doctrine. In 1638, he was forced to recant, or withdraw his statements, and he spent the rest of his life under house arrest.

Reading Check What developments helped spread Renaissance ideas?

▲ This title page from the *Index of Prohibited Books* shows bearded men who look like scholars burning books.

myWorld Activity
To Censor or Not

Section 3 Assessment

Essential Question

What distinguishes one culture from another?

Key Terms

1. Explain how each of the following key terms relates to the spread of ideas during the Renaissance: utopia, satire, engraving, censor.

Key Ideas

2. What did many northern humanists try to do with Renaissance ideas?

3. Who invented the printing press?

4. How did the use of the printing press increase the spread of literacy?

Think Critically

5. **Synthesize** What developments in technology paved the way for Gutenberg's printing press?

6. **Draw Conclusions** Why did the Catholic Church try to censor books?

7. **Compare and Contrast** How were the writings of More, Erasmus, and Rabelais similar and different?

8. How did northern humanists differ from Italian humanists? How was the printing press different from the Chinese method of block printing? Go to your Student Journal to record your answers.

Section 4

The Legacy of the Renaissance

Key Ideas

- The art and architecture of the Renaissance helped shape Western ideas of form and beauty.
- Renaissance authors such as Dante, Shakespeare, and Cervantes created classics that are still read today.

Key Terms • proportion • linear perspective • sonnet • picaresque

 Visual Glossary

Reading Skill Summarize Take notes using the graphic organizer in your journal.

This Renaissance painting uses realistic perspective to depict a walkway with classical columns. ▼

During the Renaissance, Europeans began to think differently about themselves and the world. Their belief that people were capable of great things unleashed innovations in art, literature, science, mathematics, and exploration—ideas that remain today.

Renaissance Architecture

Renaissance architect Leon Alberti called architecture "a social art," meaning that it should blend beauty and usefulness for the improvement of society. Renaissance architects sought to adapt classical ideas to new needs.

An Ancient Legacy Renaissance architects modeled their works on the elements of classical Greek and Roman architecture—the column, the round arch, and the dome. Following principles of classical mathematics, they designed structures that were beautiful because of their harmony and proportion. **Proportion** is a way of balancing the parts of a design to make a pleasing whole.

Renaissance artists understood that classical architecture relied on simple geometric forms such as the circle and the square. They were also influenced by the works of the ancient builders of Egypt, Mesopotamia, Greece, and Rome.

728

Renaissance architects like Filippo Brunelleschi (broo nel LES kee) studied the proportions of ancient buildings. With what he learned, he built the dome of the Cathedral of Santa Maria del Fiore, a masterpiece of simple forms.

Brunelleschi is also credited with discovering the rules of **linear perspective,** a mathematical system for representing three-dimensional space on a flat surface. When transferred to art forms such as painting, this discovery introduced true realism in art on flat surfaces.

Reading Check What classical ideas influenced Renaissance architecture?

Renaissance Art

The phrases "Renaissance man" and "Renaissance woman" describe people who have many different kinds of talents. The phrase originated as a description for Leonardo da Vinci.

Leonardo da Vinci Leonardo was one of the most versatile artists of the Renaissance. He was talented at almost everything he tried—painting, drawing, engineering, architecture, and music. He wrote theories about painting, the flight of birds, and the human body. His ideas and curiosity seemed endless.

myWorld Activity
Draw in 3-D

A New Perspective

Before the 1400s, artists did not know how to show objects on flat surfaces the way the eye actually sees them. The discovery of perspective revolutionized art. Using simple geometry, Renaissance artists could finally reproduce the world as it really appeared.

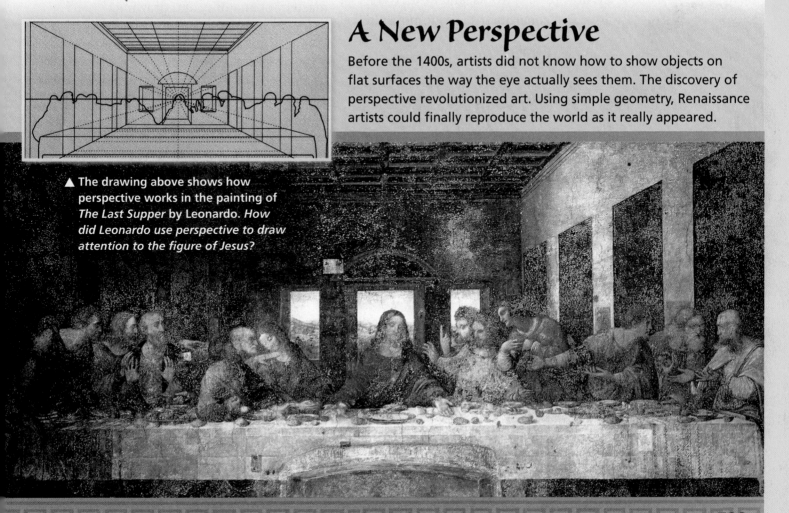

▲ The drawing above shows how perspective works in the painting of *The Last Supper* by Leonardo. *How did Leonardo use perspective to draw attention to the figure of Jesus?*

artificial, *adj.,* unnatural or human-made

Leonardo's best-known painting is the famous *Mona Lisa*. The woman in the portrait has a smile that has intrigued art lovers for centuries. For this painting, Leonardo invented a technique called sfumato (sfoo MAH toh), or "smoky" in Italian. This technique softens outlines and shadows to produce an effect of distance.

However, Leonardo wanted to master more than painting techniques. He was curious about almost every aspect of the natural world. He performed dissections of horses and human cadavers to learn how bones and muscles work. He experimented endlessly to discover how birds fly, how the eye works, and how rivers flow. To Leonardo, true wisdom resulted only from constant, careful observation: "All our knowledge has its origins in our perceptions."

Leonardo's studies of human anatomy were striking in their thoroughness and clarity. Not all of his conclusions were correct, but his research was centuries ahead of its time.

Michelangelo Another renowned Renaissance artist was Michelangelo Buonarroti, known as Michelangelo. He was a painter, sculptor, and architect as well as a poet. His works possess great energy and never seem <u>artificial</u>. The reality of his figures comes from his mastery of anatomy and drawing.

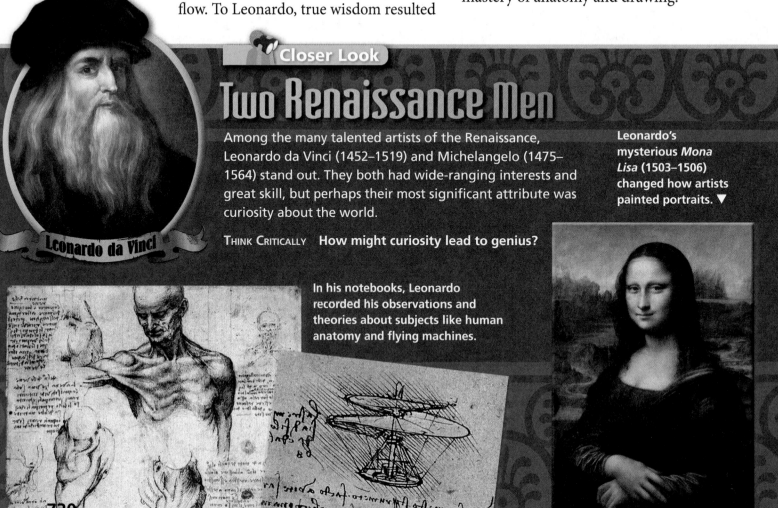

Closer Look

Two Renaissance Men

Among the many talented artists of the Renaissance, Leonardo da Vinci (1452–1519) and Michelangelo (1475–1564) stand out. They both had wide-ranging interests and great skill, but perhaps their most significant attribute was curiosity about the world.

THINK CRITICALLY **How might curiosity lead to genius?**

Leonardo da Vinci

In his notebooks, Leonardo recorded his observations and theories about subjects like human anatomy and flying machines.

Leonardo's mysterious *Mona Lisa* (1503–1506) changed how artists painted portraits. ▼

In the early 1500s, Pope Julius II, a patron of the arts, asked Michelangelo to paint the huge ceiling of the Sistine Chapel in the Vatican. His series of frescoes shows the biblical history of the world. It took four and a half years to complete and left Michelangelo partially crippled. On the rear wall of the chapel, Michelangelo painted *The Last Judgment*. This monumental work includes the artist's self-portrait in which, true to his nickname the "melancholy genius," Michelangelo looks sad and resigned. Today, millions of people travel to Italy each year to marvel at Michelangelo's works.

Renaissance Women Another part of the Renaissance legacy was the increasing number of women visible in politics and the arts. Queens such as Elizabeth I of England and Catherine de Médicis of France ruled with tolerance and courage.

The poet Laura Battiferri wrote verse in Italian. Painters like Artemisia Gentileschi and Sofonisba Anguissola introduced influential styles. Diana Mantuana, the first female Italian printmaker to sign her work, made engravings in order to support her architect husband.

Reading Check Which of the five senses did Leonardo think most important?

melancholy, *adj.*, depressed or sad

66 My beard turns up to heaven; my nape falls in
Fixed on my spine: my breast-bone visibly
Grows like a harp: a rich embroidery
Bedews my face from brush-drips, thick and thin. 99

—*Michelangelo, "On Painting the Sistine Chapel"*

◄ Michelangelo wrote a poem about the physical hardships of painting the ceiling of the Sistine Chapel. One of the most famous parts of this work is the extended fingers of the Biblical Adam and God.

Michelangelo

Michelangelo designed the dome of St. Peter's Basilica, Rome. ▶

◄ Michelangelo painted 12,000 square feet (1,100 square meters) of ceiling space in the Sistine Chapel between 1508 and 1512. An additional team of artists painted other parts of the chapel.

my worldhistory.com

Primary Source

731

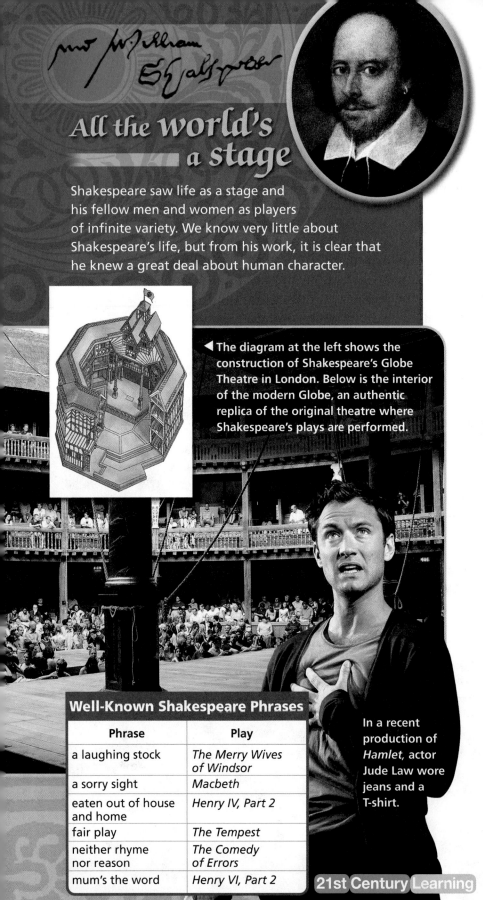

All the world's a stage

Shakespeare saw life as a stage and his fellow men and women as players of infinite variety. We know very little about Shakespeare's life, but from his work, it is clear that he knew a great deal about human character.

◀ The diagram at the left shows the construction of Shakespeare's Globe Theatre in London. Below is the interior of the modern Globe, an authentic replica of the original theatre where Shakespeare's plays are performed.

In a recent production of *Hamlet,* actor Jude Law wore jeans and a T-shirt.

Well-Known Shakespeare Phrases

Phrase	Play
a laughing stock	*The Merry Wives of Windsor*
a sorry sight	*Macbeth*
eaten out of house and home	*Henry IV, Part 2*
fair play	*The Tempest*
neither rhyme nor reason	*The Comedy of Errors*
mum's the word	*Henry VI, Part 2*

21st Century Learning

Renaissance Literature

Writers such as Dante, Petrarch, William Shakespeare, and Miguel de Cervantes continue to influence literature around the world.

Dante and Petrarch Dante Alighieri was born in Italy in the late 1200s. Although he wrote during the late Middle Ages, his ideas looked forward to those of the Renaissance. He is best known for *The Divine Comedy,* a long poem about an imaginary journey through hell and ending in heaven. Dante wrote the poem in Italian rather than in Latin. By writing in the vernacular, he helped shape Italian as a written language.

The Italian scholar and poet Francesco Petrarch is perhaps best known for his love poems to Laura, a woman who has never been identified. Petrarch also studied classical literature and sought to bring together the ideas of pagan classical culture and Christianity. For this reason, scholars consider him the founder of Renaissance humanism.

The Bard of Avon William Shakespeare was born in 1564 in the English town of Stratford-upon-Avon. Often called the Bard of Avon (*bard* means poet-singer), he is the world's best-known playwright. Shakespeare wrote 37 plays—comedies, histories, and tragedies such as *Romeo and Juliet* and *Hamlet.*

Shakespeare also wrote poems, most notably, sonnets. A **sonnet** is a poem of 14 lines with a fixed rhyming pattern. His work had a profound impact on the development of the English language.

Shakespeare is even more well-known for his examination of the many shades of human character. In the midst of the tragic play *Hamlet,* Shakespeare uses satire to mock human frailty,

> 66 What a piece of work is a man! how noble in reason! how infinite in faculty! in form and moving how express and admirable! in action how like an angel! in apprehension how like a god! the beauty of the world! the paragon [model of excellence] of animals! 99
>
> —*Hamlet,* Act II, Scene 2

Cervantes and His Knight Spanish author Miguel de Cervantes (sur VAHN teez) lived around the same time as Shakespeare. His 1605 novel *Don Quixote* follows the journey of a bumbling landowner (a "don," or Spanish nobleman) who believes it is his duty to become a knight and right every wrong.

Cervantes' novel is difficult to categorize. It combines the chivalric tale of honor with satire criticizing Spain's empire-building. The novel's style is known as picaresque. **Picaresque** refers to a series of comic episodes usually involving a mischievous character.

As the idealistic Don Quixote and his companion Sancho Panza travel around the countryside, they encounter many people and adventures. In one comic scene, Don Quixote tries to battle a windmill, thinking it is a gigantic enemy. The word *quixotic* commonly refers to any idealistic, but hopeless, endeavor.

Don Quixote was one of the first novels to portray many characters with different perspectives. Cervantes also shows in the novel that he is aware of the power of the printed word. *Don Quixote* continues to influence literature and arts of all kinds, from ballet to opera and film.

Reading Check Who was Shakespeare?

my World CONNECTIONS

In 1989, the foundations of the original Globe Theatre were discovered. An exact replica opened in 1997 with a production of Shakespeare's *Henry V.*

Section 4 Assessment

Essential Question
What distinguishes one culture from another?

Key Terms

1. Using complete sentences, explain how the following key terms relate to the Renaissance: proportion, linear perspective, sonnet, picaresque. You may combine related terms in a single sentence.

Key Ideas

2. What classical architectural features were used in Renaissance buildings?

3. What types of literature did William Shakespeare write?

4. What was Petrarch's goal for his writing?

Think Critically

5. **Analyze Cause and Effect** How did the techniques developed by Brunelleschi influence art and architecture?

6. **Synthesize** What characteristics did Leonardo da Vinci and Michelangelo have in common?

7. **Connect** How did Shakespeare and Dante influence modern languages?

8. How did Miguel de Cervantes draw on medieval culture to write his novel? How did the ideal of the Renaissance man differ from medieval ideals? Go to your Student Journal to record your answers.

Chapter Assessment

Key Terms and Ideas

1. **Discuss** How did **patrons** help encourage artistic achievement during the Renaissance?

2. **Explain** How did the growth of the **mercantile** class weaken the feudal order?

3. **Recall** What did **humanism** emphasize?

4. **Compare and Contrast** How was the Renaissance belief in individualism different from the values of the Middle Ages?

5. **Summarize** What did the technique of **linear perspective** help artists to accomplish?

6. **Recall** What types of works were published after the invention of the printing press?

7. **Explain** What was the purpose of the **satires** written by Erasmus and Rabelais?

8. **Describe** What did Dante's poem *The Divine Comedy* portray?

Think Critically

9. **Compare and Contrast** How was the upper class of Italy's city-states different from the old feudal upper class?

10. **Identify Evidence** Why do you think Lorenzo de' Medici believed it helped his public image to spend money on art and architecture?

11. **Synthesize** How did Renaissance art depict the influence of individualism?

12. **Analyze Cause and Effect** How did the ideas of the Renaissance spread to northern Europe?

13. **Draw Inferences** How would secularism and individualism affect the way people viewed the authority of the Catholic Church? Explain.

14. **Core Concepts: Trade** How did the growth of trade help promote the new ideas of the Renaissance?

Analyze Visuals

15. What does this map show?

16. What was significant about the cities of Paris, Cologne, Mainz, Nuremberg, Strasbourg, and Augsburg?

17. Were there more printing presses in the part of Italy north of Rome or south of Rome? What geographic reason might explain this pattern?

18. What might explain why London did not have a printing press until after 1471?

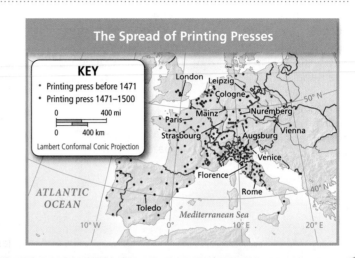

The Spread of Printing Presses

KEY
- Printing press before 1471
- Printing press 1471–1500

0   400 mi
0   400 km

Lambert Conformal Conic Projection

London   Leipzig
Cologne
50° N
Mainz   Nuremberg
Paris
Strasbourg   Augsburg   Vienna
Venice
Florence
40° N
ATLANTIC OCEAN   Rome
Toledo
Mediterranean Sea
10° W   0°   10° E   20° E

Essential Question
myWorld Chapter Activity

Make the Front Page Use this chapter's Activity Cards to analyze several changes that took place during the Renaissance. Think about the big ideas of humanism, individualism, secularism, the printing press, and linear perspective. If you were to make a newspaper front page, which would be your lead story? Work in groups to review the cards, talk about the stories, and create the front page of the newspaper *Changing Times.*

21st Century Learning
Develop Cultural Awareness

Artist's Web Page Research one of the artists mentioned in this chapter. Choose three or four works by that artist, and design a Web page to feature them. Include a short, one-paragraph introduction; a brief biogrgaphy of the artist; captions for each work of art; and a drawing or diagram of your page layout.

Document-Based Questions

Online at myworldhistory.com

Use your knowledge of the Renaissance and Documents A and B to answer Questions 1–3.

Document A

" I would have him more than passably learned in letters, at least in those studies which we call the humanities. Let him be conversant not only with the Latin language but with Greek as well. . . . Let him be versed in the poets, as well as in the orators and the historians, and let him be practiced also in writing verse and prose."

—Baldesar Castiglione, *The Book of the Courtier,* translated by Charles S. Singleton

Document B

" But 'tis a common proof,
That lowliness is young ambition's ladder,
Whereto the climber-upward turns his face;
But when he once attains the upmost round.
He then unto the ladder turns his back,
Looks in the clouds, scorning the base degrees
By which he did ascend."

—William Shakespeare, *Julius Caesar,* Act II, Scene 1

1. What types of writing does Castiglione want educated people to master?
   A prose and sermons
   B prose and poetry
   C legal documents and poetry
   D sermons and legal documents

2. Which phrase best summarizes the passage?
   A Ambition can make you forget who you are.
   B Take risks in life.
   C Always try to better yourself.
   D Avoid trying to be something you are not.

3. **Writing Task** How does each of these quotations show the influence of humanist ideas? Support your answer with specific details.

Chapter 25

The Reformation

Essential Question

How should we handle conflict?

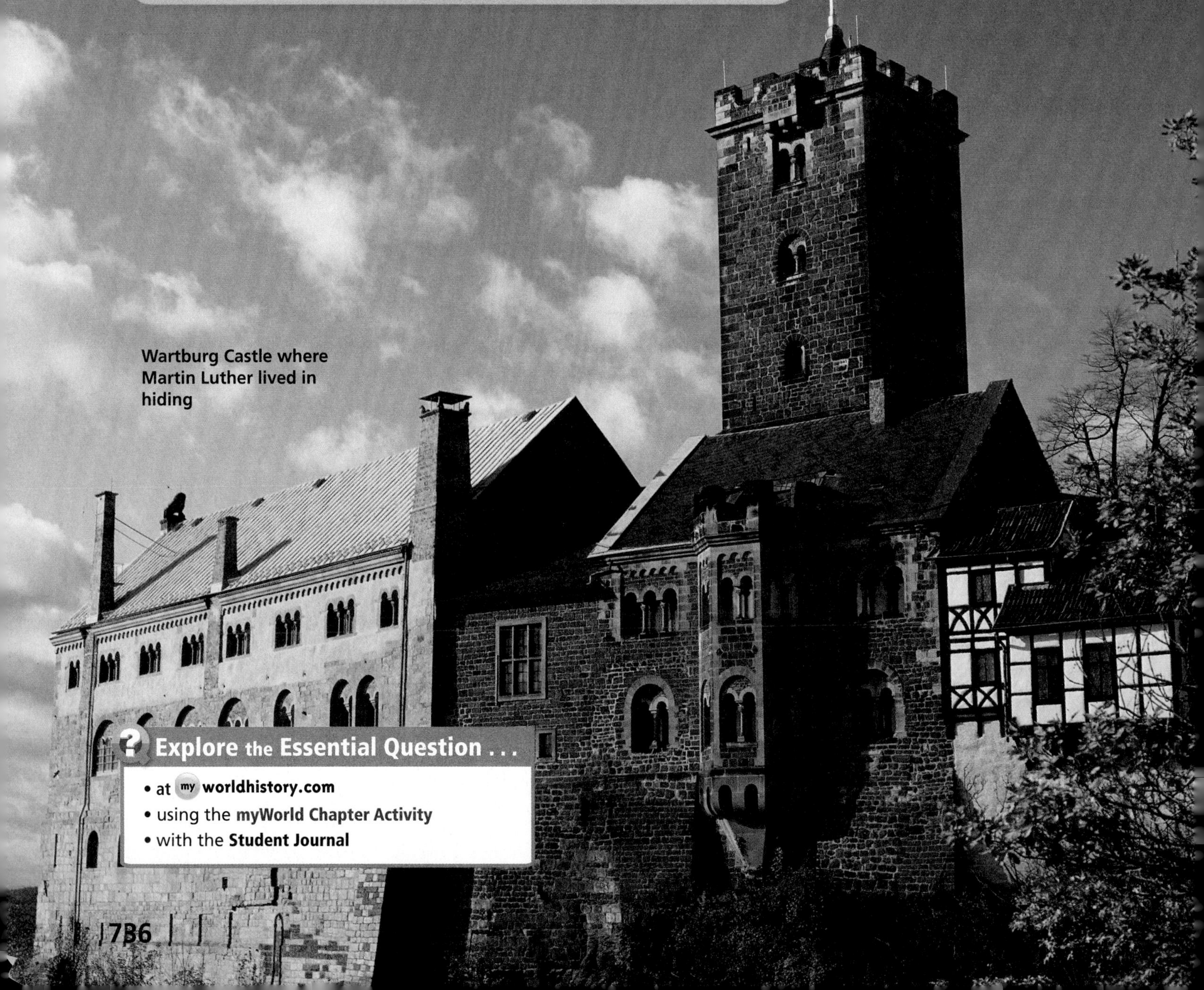

Wartburg Castle where Martin Luther lived in hiding

Explore the Essential Question . . .

- at my worldhistory.com
- using the **myWorld Chapter Activity**
- with the **Student Journal**

Reformation Europe

1517 Martin Luther writes 95 Theses.

1534 Luther publishes first Bible in German.

1545 Council of Trent begins.

| 1500 | 1525 | 1550 | 1575 | 1600 | 1625 |

1525–1526 William Tyndale publishes the New Testament in English.

1536 John Calvin publishes *The Institutes of Christian Religion*.

1618 Thirty Years' War begins.

Kidnapped!

This myStory is a fictionalized account of events in the life of Martin Luther.

It was a cool spring night in 1521, and the German monk Martin Luther was riding home from the imperial city of Worms. He had been summoned to Worms to a meeting of the diet (dee EHT), the German parliament. Officials wanted to question him about a list that he had nailed to the church door in Wittenberg back in 1517. That list—95 protests against the Catholic Church—had gotten him into a lot of trouble.

For hours, Luther had been questioned by the Holy Roman emperor and Catholic officials from Rome. He admitted that he had written certain books, but he refused to take back his accusations against the Church. No one could agree on how to punish the monk, so Luther was free to go.

myworldhistory.com

Timeline/On Assignment

Luther had been a law student but became a monk after surviving a thunderstorm.

The pope sent Luther a letter telling him to take back his criticisms of the Church. Luther refused. He and his students at the University of Wittenberg made a bonfire and threw in the pope's letter.

As he left Worms, Luther realized that he had just barely escaped being burned at the stake as an enemy of the Church. He had stood up to two of the most powerful men in the world, the Holy Roman emperor and the pope. He was free, but he was a marked man. His writings were to be burned, and anyone who helped him in any way was to be punished.

Defying the church authorities, one of Luther's friends agreed to accompany him home from Worms. As their cart rumbled over the rough roads of the dark forest, Luther and his friend began to doze. Suddenly, they heard the thunder of horses' hooves. Jolted awake, Luther was terrified and confused. Shouts rang out, calling "Halt!" Horses surrounded the cart. In the dim light of torches, Luther saw armor and swords pointing directly at him. He was clearly a target—but of what?

Rough hands pulled Luther down from the cart. He was dragged along and dumped on a horse with an empty saddle. In the flickering torchlight, he could see almost nothing. He barely had time to steady himself on the horse before they all galloped into the forest. The whole incident was over in a matter of minutes.

For three months, Luther was missing. At last, a friend received a letter with a strange clue:

At Worms, Luther defended himself against the greatest minds of the day. For hours, he had to answer questions about his ideas and his criticism of the Catholic Church.

Luther used his time in the castle to think about and write down all the ideas that he wanted to express about his beliefs.

> 66 Do not be anxious about me, for I am well. . . . in the region of the birds who sing beautifully on the trees, praising God night and day, with all their might. 99

In that same letter, Luther confirmed that he had been kidnapped—but by an unexpected friend and protector.

The night of the kidnapping, the soldiers took the frightened monk to a castle on a hill. This was Wartburg Castle, the home of Frederick the Wise, an important regional governor. Frederick had sent his soldiers to capture Luther to keep him safe from enemies. Frederick was motivated more by political ends than by religious belief, but his actions probably saved Luther's life.

Luther hid for months in the well-fortified Wartburg Castle, safe and sound, while others spread the rumor that he was dead. He disguised himself as Junker Jörg (YOONG ker yerg), or Knight George, complete with tunic, breeches, and sword. He grew a bushy beard and let his hair grow long.

The two rooms where he lived were simply furnished, with a fireplace to keep him warm, and a large table for writing. At night, the rooms were lit by candles. During the day, the sun streamed through the heavy glass windows. His rooms looked out on a spectacular view of the forest. Two servants brought him meals.

For hours every day, Luther sat at his desk thinking and writing. He struggled with how to express his ideas about church doctrine. He also began to translate the Bible's New Testament into German, using various ancient sources.

Luther's translation would encourage ordinary Germans to read and interpret Christian teachings for themselves. Indeed, more people wanted to learn how to read because there were books of all kinds in the language they spoke every day.

Luther's Bible translation also advanced the development of the German language. In addition, it spread literacy and education to German children. Thanks to the disappearance of a certain defiant monk, modern German culture began to take shape.

From what you just read, how do you think Luther handled conflict? As you read on, think about what Martin Luther's story tells you about the Reformation.

myStory Video

Join Luther in hiding.

my worldhistory.com

myStory Video

Section 1

The Origins of the Reformation

Key Ideas
- Martin Luther's protest against corruption in the Catholic Church set off the Protestant Reformations.
- John Calvin and other Reformation thinkers spread Protestant ideas throughout Europe.

Key Terms • Reformation • indulgence • recant • sect • predestination • theocracy

 Visual Glossary

 Reading Skill Analyze Cause and Effect Take notes using the graphic organizer in your journal.

The northern European humanists laid the foundation for the **Reformation,** a religious movement that gained momentum in the 1500s with the aim to reform the Catholic Church. Reformation thinkers changed European society in ways that are still felt today.

Luther Challenges the Church

An important leader of the Reformation was Martin Luther, a German monk. Luther was born in 1483, at a time of uneven prosperity and change in Germany. New universities were spreading the ideas of the northern European humanists. These thinkers had urged reform in the Church, but Luther offered a stronger challenge.

As a young man, Luther was caught one day in a thunderstorm. He vowed that if he lived through the storm, he would become a monk. Luther survived and, keeping his promise, entered a monastery.

Church Corruption In 1510, Luther visited Rome, the center of the Catholic Church. He was shocked by the corruption of the Roman clergy. The pope and high-ranking Church officials had become increasingly involved in politics. They also spent a great deal of time trying to raise money to complete construction of St. Peter's Basilica, the center of the Catholic church. Luther thought that they seemed more concerned with secular matters than with saving souls.

In this woodcut, the pope sells a letter of indulgence to the man at the right. ▼

Luther noted other problems as well. Many priests were poorly trained. Church leaders rose to power through wealth or political influence rather than because of their moral qualities. Some bishops lived far from their churches and often neglected their duties.

The Catholic Church also imposed taxes on its members. This money financed the construction of St. Peter's Basilica in Rome, as well as a rich lifestyle for the pope. The Church also raised money by selling **indulgences,** a kind of cancellation of punishment for sins that had been confessed and forgiven by God. Some priests promised that followers who contributed money or did good works would ensure that both they and their relatives would go to heaven.

Luther's 95 Theses Luther especially opposed the idea of indulgences. He reasoned that if people could buy indulgences, they might think they could buy God's forgiveness. Luther did not believe that salvation—given freely by God—should be entangled in a complex system of indulgences and good works. To Luther, faith, or trust, in God was all that was needed to gain salvation.

When a priest appeared in Wittenberg selling indulgences, an outraged Luther decided to act. "I am hotblooded by temperament," Luther said, "and my pen gets irritated easily." He wrote a list of theses, or arguments, against the sale of indulgences. In 1517, he posted the list on the door of the main church in Wittenberg.

temperament, *n.*, a specific person's way of behaving and thinking

Four Key Ideas From Luther's 95 Theses

1. The *Church* means "those who believe in Christ."

2. Though there may be hierarchies within the Church, no Christian is greater or more important than any other. All vocations are equal.

3. The Bible is the final authority for all Christians.

4. Men and women live by faith alone. No efforts or works, no matter how virtuous, are enough to save a person. Men and women are saved by the grace of God's love.

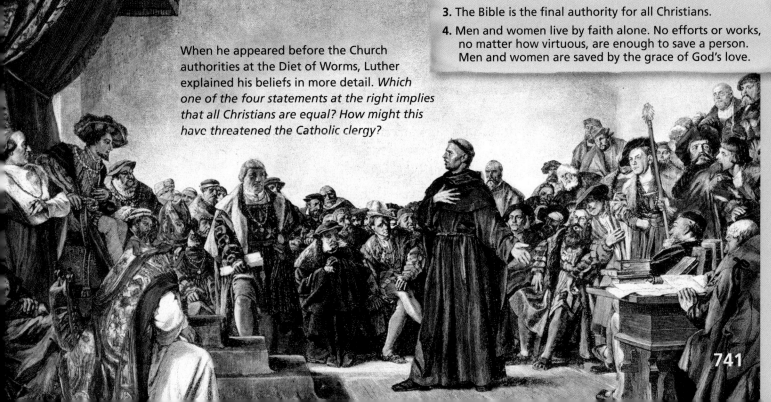

When he appeared before the Church authorities at the Diet of Worms, Luther explained his beliefs in more detail. *Which one of the four statements at the right implies that all Christians are equal? How might this have threatened the Catholic clergy?*

741

THE REFORMATION'S RIPPLE EFFECTS

Luther's criticism of the Catholic Church began with its sale of indulgences. In spite of threatening letters and trials, Luther refused to take back his objections. Following these events, Luther's reforming influence gradually rippled outward far beyond his home in northern Germany to other parts of Europe and England.

THINK CRITICALLY Why might Catholics have been unwilling to follow Luther?

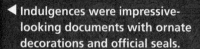

◀ Indulgences were impressive-looking documents with ornate decorations and official seals.

▲ This painting from the 1800s shows Luther throwing the pope's order to recant into a bonfire. The pope responded by expelling Luther from the Catholic Church.

The 95 Theses, as they became known, challenged the Church's authority and stressed the spiritual, inward character of the Christian faith. Thesis 37 targeted letters of indulgence, or pardon. "Every true Christian," Luther wrote, "whether living or dead, has part in all the blessings of Christ . . . and this is granted him by God, even without letters of pardon." In other words, God gave every true Christian salvation as a gift that did not need to be earned or bought.

The 95 Theses were soon translated into German and other languages. Due to the growing number of printing presses, copies quickly spread across Europe.

Many Church leaders saw the 95 Theses as an attack on the Church itself. In 1521, the pope excommunicated, or expelled, Luther from the Church.

myWorld Activity
Reformation News

The Diet at Worms Later that year, the Holy Roman emperor summoned Luther before a diet, or a meeting, in the city of Worms. There, he was put on trial and had to defend his writings. Luther was ordered to **recant,** or withdraw his words, but he declared,

> 66 If I were to revoke what I have written, what should I do....but strengthen this tyranny? I neither can nor will retract anything. 99
>
> —Martin Luther

The diet branded Luther an outlaw, but as you read in "Kidnapped!", he had powerful friends who protected him. Throughout Germany, thousands hailed Luther as a hero for his stand against corrupt Church practices and teachings.

Reading Check What prompted Luther to write the 95 Theses?

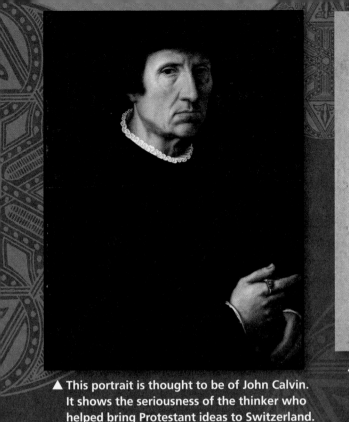

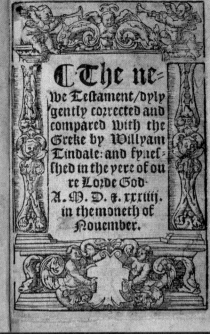

▲ This portrait is thought to be of John Calvin. It shows the seriousness of the thinker who helped bring Protestant ideas to Switzerland.

▲ William Tyndale's English translation of the New Testament greatly influenced the development of the English language. Because the spelling of names was not standardized at the time, Tyndale's last name appears in this 1534 edition as Tindall and Tindale.

The Reformation Grows

As Luther's ideas, or Lutheranism, spread, Protestant sects sprang up all over Europe. A **sect** is a subgroup of a major religious group. Protestants were people who protested against the authority of the Catholic Church. A French scholar named John Calvin was one of the most influential of the new Protestant leaders.

Calvin and Salvation John Calvin was born in France in 1509, a generation after Luther. Calvin had studied to be a priest in the Roman Catholic Church. But in the early 1530s, he declared himself a Protestant.

In 1536, Calvin published the *Institutes of Christian Religion* in which he set out the basic ideas of the Protestant faith. The *Institutes* became a foundation of Protestant thought.

One of Calvin's most influential teachings in the *Institutes* focused on the question of salvation. Like Luther, Calvin believed that salvation was gained through faith alone. Calvin also regarded the Bible as the sole source of religious truth.

In addition, Calvin supported the concept of **predestination,** the idea that God had long ago determined who would gain salvation. At that time, the Catholic Church and some other Protestant churches taught that people had free will to choose or reject the path to salvation.

Calvin taught that salvation was not a human choice, but a decision made by God from the beginning of time. No one, however, knows who God has chosen for salvation. Therefore, all people should lead God-fearing, religious lives. Calvin called this the "doctrine of the elect."

doctrine, *n.,* a set of principles or system of belief

743

Key Events
of the Reformation

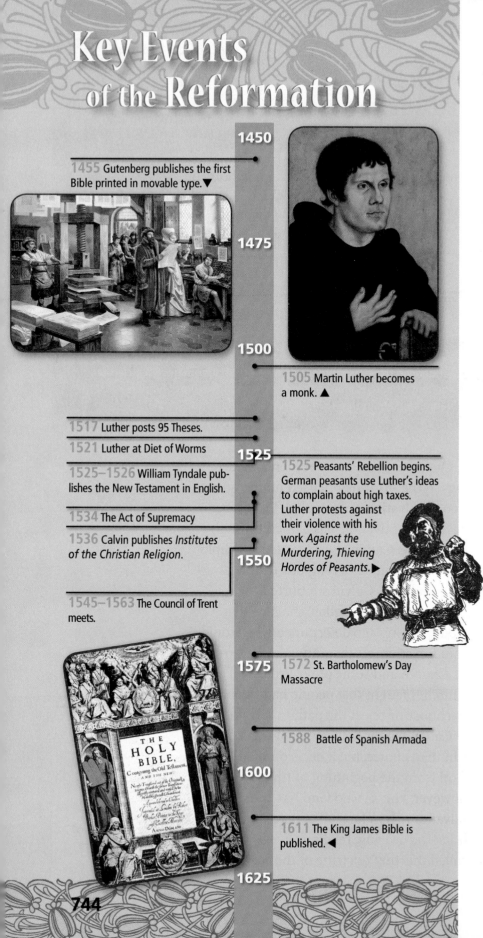

1450

1455 Gutenberg publishes the first Bible printed in movable type. ▼

1475

1500

1505 Martin Luther becomes a monk. ▲

1517 Luther posts 95 Theses.

1521 Luther at Diet of Worms

1525

1525–1526 William Tyndale publishes the New Testament in English.

1525 Peasants' Rebellion begins. German peasants use Luther's ideas to complain about high taxes. Luther protests against their violence with his work *Against the Murdering, Thieving Hordes of Peasants.* ▶

1534 The Act of Supremacy

1536 Calvin publishes *Institutes of the Christian Religion.*

1550

1545–1563 The Council of Trent meets.

1575

1572 St. Bartholomew's Day Massacre

1588 Battle of Spanish Armada

1600

1611 The King James Bible is published. ◀

1625

744

Calvin's "City of God" Calvin also applied his ideas to government. Many of the Protestant reformers had been accused of lawlessness, and Calvin came to their defense. He said that people were subject to both civil law and to the law of God. At the same time, rulers should not act as tyrants, but keep in mind the law of God. In this way, people who obeyed an earthly government were also following God's laws.

In the 1530s, Protestants in Geneva, Switzerland, invited Calvin to help them rule their city and reform their church. Calvin set up a theocracy in Geneva. A **theocracy** is a government ruled by religious leaders.

Calvin's goal was to found a "city of God." He stressed hard work, honesty, and morality. He imposed strict laws on people's behavior. To many Protestants, Geneva seemed a model community.

The Bible in Many Languages By the early 1500s, the Bible's New Testament had appeared in French, Spanish, Italian, and Dutch. Luther's German translation appeared in 1534 and would become highly influential in the development of the German language. It was now easier for most Europeans—not just scholars who read Latin—to read the Bible and think about its meaning.

The Protestant reformer William Tyndale translated the Greek New Testament into English. It was printed in Germany in 1525 and reached England in 1526. John Wycliffe, an English preacher and reformer, had translated parts of the Bible from Latin into English as early as 1382.

Tyndale was proud of his role in spreading God's word. He is said to have responded with strong words to a Catholic critic:

66 I defy the Pope. . . . If God spare my life [for] many years, I will cause a boy that driveth the plough, shall know more of the scripture than thou dost! 99

—William Tyndale,
from *John Foxe's Book of Martyrs*

After years of working in defiance of Catholic authorities, Tyndale had become an enemy of the Church. In 1536, he was working on a translation of the Old Testament in Antwerp (in present-day Belgium) and was invited to dine at the home of an English merchant. There, he was betrayed and turned over to the authorities. Tyndale was convicted as a heretic, strangled, and burned at the stake.

Reading Check How did John Calvin want to make Geneva a model community?

Comparing Catholicism and Lutheranism

	Catholicism	Lutheranism
Salvation	Faith and good works bring salvation.	Faith alone brings salvation.
Sacraments	Priests perform the seven sacraments, or rituals	Accepts some sacraments, but rejects others because they lack Biblical grounding
Church Leadership	The pope, together with the bishops	Elected councils
Importance of the Bible	Bible is one source of truth; Church tradition is another.	Bible alone is the source of truth.
Interpretation	Bible is interpreted by priests according to tradition and church leadership.	People read and interpret the Bible for themselves.

Chart Skills

Note the differences in the heads of the two churches. Why was this difference important?

21st Century Learning

Section 1 Assessment

Key Terms

1. Define each of the following key terms in a complete sentence: Reformation, indulgence, recant, sect, predestination, theocracy.

Key Ideas

2. Why did the sale of indulgences anger Luther?

3. What was the *Institutes of Christian Religion*?

4. How did the use of the printing press affect the Reformation?

Think Critically

5. **Draw Conclusions** Why did John Calvin believe that people should lead God-fearing, religious lives?

6. **Compare and Contrast** In what ways were the ideas of Luther and Calvin similar?

7. **Identify Evidence** What evidence convinced Luther that the Catholic Church needed to be reformed?

Essential Question

How should we handle conflict?

8. How did Luther express his conflict with the Church? How did the Church respond to Luther's actions? Go to your Student Journal to record your answers.

The Counter-Reformation

Key Ideas
- The Jesuits worked to reform and strengthen the Catholic Church.
- At the Council of Trent, Catholic leaders discussed ways to end corruption and reform Church doctrine.

Key Terms • Counter-Reformation • Jesuits • Council of Trent • ghetto

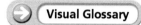 Visual Glossary

Reading Skill Summarize Take notes using the graphic organizer in your journal.

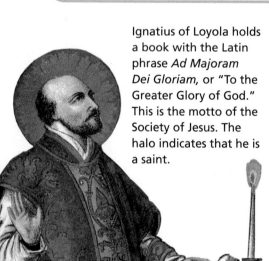

Ignatius of Loyola holds a book with the Latin phrase *Ad Majoram Dei Gloriam,* or "To the Greater Glory of God." This is the motto of the Society of Jesus. The halo indicates that he is a saint.

The Catholic Church was slow to respond to the Reformation. Within a few years, however, it had mounted a strong response to the Protestant challenge.

New Catholic Reformers

As Protestantism spread, the Catholic Church began its own reform movement. The movement to strengthen the teachings and structure of the Catholic Church was called the **Counter-Reformation.** During the Counter-Reformation, also known as the Catholic Reformation, reformers founded new religious orders, or groups with their own particular structure and purpose. They won respect by helping the poor, teaching, and leading spiritual lives. One such reformer was Ignatius of Loyola who founded the Society of Jesus, or the **Jesuits,** one of the most influential of the new religious orders.

Ignatius of Loyola In 1491, Ignatius of Loyola was born in northern Spain. As a young man, he entered military service and was seriously injured in battle. While recovering, Ignatius read about the lives of Jesus and the saints. Inspired, he vowed to lead a religious life.

Ignatius studied in Paris. There, with a small group of followers, he founded the Society of Jesus in 1534. Its goal was to defend and spread the Catholic faith throughout the world. The Society was organized like a military troop, with strict discipline. Ignatius was elected a "general" of the order, and members were organized into "companies." Recruits trained for years before joining the order.

The Jesuits' Influence The Jesuits helped end some of the corruption within the Catholic Church. Priests received stricter training. Jesuits also served the poor and helped the sick in hospitals. In addition, the Jesuits expanded the membership of the Church. Jesuit missionaries spread the Catholic faith to Africa, Asia, and the Americas. In Asia, the Jesuit Francis Xavier was said to have converted thousands of people to Catholicism.

The Jesuits also made important contributions in the field of education. They founded schools and universities and wrote numerous books on religion and secular topics like medicine. Their students included an emperor, dukes, and cardinals. The Jesuits also served as influential advisors to kings and popes.

Teresa of Avila During the Counter-Reformation, many Catholics experienced renewed feelings of faith. One of these was Teresa of Avila, a Spanish nun. Born into a wealthy family, Teresa entered the Carmelite convent at Avila in 1535, without her father's consent. Teresa lived an intensely spiritual life, often seeing visions she said were sent from God. She felt that convent life was not strict enough, so she founded her own order of nuns. They lived in <u>isolation</u>, completely dedicated to prayer and meditation. Teresa was widely honored for her efforts to reform Spanish convents and monasteries. She was declared a saint in 1622.

Reading Check Name three contributions of the Jesuits.

my **World**
CONNECTIONS

The Jesuits educate more than **46,000** students each year at **71** high schools, colleges, and universities in the United States.

isolation, *n.*, the condition of being alone

Jesuits in the World

Italian Jesuit missionary Matteo Ricci (left) introduced Christianity to China in the 1580s. Here, Ricci, a scholar of geography and astronomy, wears Chinese clothing and is surrounded by maps and navigational tools. Modern Jesuit schools encourage students to volunteer for reading programs and civic projects like trash collecting. *How do these photographs show Jesuit influence?*

747

The Council of Trent

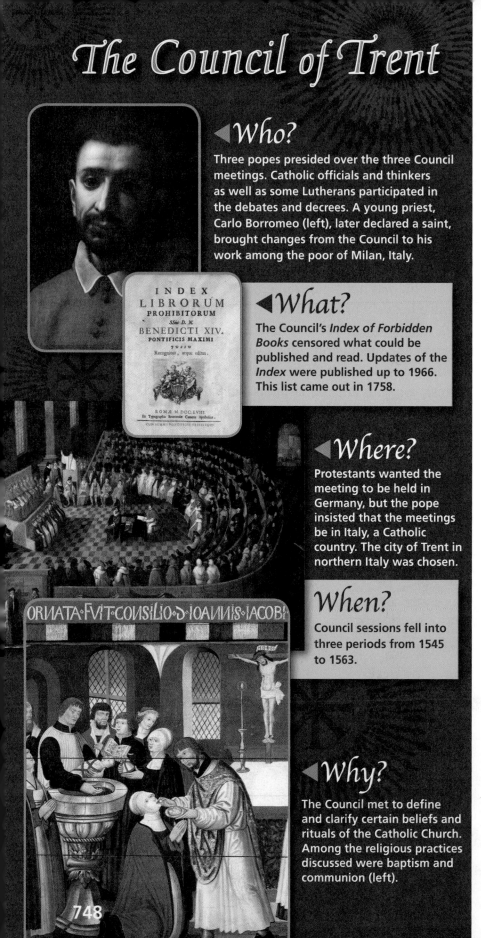

◄ Who?

Three popes presided over the three Council meetings. Catholic officials and thinkers as well as some Lutherans participated in the debates and decrees. A young priest, Carlo Borromeo (left), later declared a saint, brought changes from the Council to his work among the poor of Milan, Italy.

INDEX
LIBRORUM
PROHIBITORUM
SSmi D. N.
BENEDICTI XIV.
PONTIFICIS MAXIMI
jussu
Recognitus, atque editus.

ROMÆ M. DCC.LVIII.
Ex Typographia Reverendæ Cameræ Apostolicæ.
CUM SUMMI PONTIFICIS PRIVILEGIO.

◄ What?

The Council's *Index of Forbidden Books* censored what could be published and read. Updates of the *Index* were published up to 1966. This list came out in 1758.

◄ Where?

Protestants wanted the meeting to be held in Germany, but the pope insisted that the meetings be in Italy, a Catholic country. The city of Trent in northern Italy was chosen.

When?

Council sessions fell into three periods from 1545 to 1563.

ORNATA·FVIT·CONSILIO·D·IOANNIS·IACOBI

◄ Why?

The Council met to define and clarify certain beliefs and rituals of the Catholic Church. Among the religious practices discussed were baptism and communion (left).

748

The Church Responds

In 1545, Pope Paul III began a series of meetings known as the **Council of Trent.** During these meetings, Catholic leaders sought ways to revive the moral authority of the Catholic Church and to stop the spread of Protestantism. The Council of Trent took place at various times over the course of about 20 years. It was the high point of the Counter-Reformation.

Upholding Tradition At its meetings, the Council reaffirmed traditional Catholic doctrines that had been challenged by the Protestants. It rejected Luther's view of the Bible as the only source of truth. The Bible *and* church tradition, declared the Council, were equal sources of knowledge. While Luther said that faith is all that is needed for salvation, the Council said faith *plus* good works and receiving the sacraments are needed as well. Finally, the Council affirmed that people had free will. The Council of Trent also made sweeping reforms of Catholic practices and called for the education and training of priests.

The Inquisition The Church enforced the Council's decisions through the Inquisition. This institution was set up in the Middle Ages to combat heresy, or beliefs that clashed with Church teachings.

In 1492, the Spanish Inquisition forced Jews who refused to become Christians to leave the country. By the 1500s, Inquisitions existed in Portugal, Italy, and Spain. Powerful Inquisition officials often used torture to obtain confessions. Under the Inquisition, people suffered great cruelty and lost their religious freedoms.

Many of the Inquisition's policies came from Pope Innocent IV's papal order of 1252 which stated that heretics, or people accused of heresy, should be "forced" to confess. This statement encouraged torture and unjust imprisonment. This brutal policy had continued for centuries with judges seizing property, torturing, and condemning to death thousands of victims. Protestants living in Catholic lands were frequently the target of the Inquisition. However, even Church leaders and important nobles could be accused of heresy and forced to flee for their lives.

The Church also battled the spread of Protestant ideas by banning books. In 1557, the Inquisition published the first *Index of Forbidden Books,* a list of works that Catholics were forbidden to read. The list included books by Protestants such as Martin Luther, John Calvin, and William Tyndale.

Widespread Intolerance Both Catholics and Protestants were intolerant of each other. Catholics launched attacks against Protestants. Protestants destroyed Catholic churches and attacked priests.

Religious anxiety also brought a fear of witches, or people believed to be evil spirits. Between 1450 and 1750, tens of thousands of people, frequently women, died in witch hunts in Europe. Victims might also be beggars or outcasts.

Another group that suffered during this period were Jews. After being driven from Spain, many Jews went to Italy where they had prospered. However, by 1516, Jews in Venice were restricted to living and working in a separate quarter called a **ghetto.** This practice of keeping Jews separate from the population within walled areas spread to other parts of Europe. In some places, Jews were required to wear yellow identification badges if they traveled outside the ghetto.

Reading Check What was the purpose of the Inquisition?

myWorld Activity
Extra, Extra!

The hoods worn by Inquisitioners concealed their identities. ▶

Section 2 Assessment

Key Terms

1. For each of the key terms, write a complete sentence that explains its relationship to the Reformation: Counter-Reformation, Jesuits, Council of Trent, ghetto.

Key Ideas

2. During the Counter-Reformation, how did the Catholic Church gain more respect?

3. How did the Jesuits help end some of the corruption in the Catholic Church?

4. How did the Inquisition attempt to stop the spread of Protestantism?

Think Critically

5. **Draw Conclusions** How did Ignatius of Loyola use his military experience with the Jesuits?

6. **Compare Viewpoints** How did the religious views of the Council of Trent differ from those of Martin Luther?

7. **Make Decisions** Why did Ignatius decide to lead a religious life?

Essential Question

How should we handle conflict?

8. How did the Council of Trent attempt to stop the loss of church members to Protestantism? Did the Council's actions tend to decrease or increase conflict? Go to your Student Journal to record your answers.

The Reformation Divides Europe

<table>
<tr>
<td>Key Ideas</td>
<td>• The Reformation sparked conflicts between Protestant and Catholic regions of Europe.</td>
<td>• The Reformation had a long-term impact on government, society, and economics.</td>
</tr>
</table>

Key Terms • annulment • Act of Supremacy • Huguenots • edict • armada • federalism

 **Visual Glossary**

┼┼┼┼┼┼ **Reading Skill Sequence** Take notes using the graphic organizer in your journal.

Holbein's famous portrait shows Henry VIII as an imposing king. ▼

As the Protestant reform movement swept outward from Germany and Switzerland, ordinary people and their rulers were forced to take sides. The conflict between Catholics and Protestants resulted in bitter religious wars. These wars destroyed the religious unity that Europe had experienced under the Catholic Church's dominance.

Protestant Northern Europe

Germany was the birthplace of the Protestant faith. From northern Germany, Luther's followers took the faith to Sweden, Denmark, Norway, and Poland. Calvin's ideas spread to Switzerland, Scotland, and the Netherlands. In some places, the ideas of Luther and Calvin took hold peacefully. In other areas, religious conflict erupted.

The Reformation in England and Scotland In England, Luther's ideas were at first met with opposition. Henry VIII, the Catholic king of England, wrote a book criticizing Luther's beliefs. He was declared by the Church a "defender of the faith" for his words. Protestant reformers were burned at the stake or forced out of England.

In 1529, however, Henry VIII came into conflict with the pope. Henry wanted the pope to annul his marriage to Catherine of Aragon, as she had yet to give birth to a surviving male heir. An **annulment** is an official action canceling a marriage. The pope refused.

Religion in Europe

SWEDEN

SCOTLAND

*North
Sea*

IRELAND
(England)

DENMARK

*Baltic
Sea*

ENGLAND

Woodstock o o London

ATLANTIC
OCEAN

Münster o
o Wittenberg
o Wartburg

POLAND-
LITHUANIA

Paris o
Worms o
HOLY ROMAN
EMPIRE

o Augsburg

FRANCE

o Geneva
Trent

50° N

40° N

VENICE
o Venice

HUNGARY

Black Sea

PORTUGAL

SPAIN

Corsica

PAPAL
STATES

Rome o

Adriatic Sea

O T T O M A N   E M P I R E

NAPLES
(Spain)

Sardinia

M e d i t e r r a n e a n

Sicily

S e a

Map Skills

1 Place Which country was Anglican?

2 Places to Know!
Label the following places on the outline map in your Student Journal: England, Wittenberg, Scotland, Sweden, Paris, Spain, Geneva.

KEY

- Mainly Roman Catholic
- Mainly Anglican
- Mainly Lutheran
- Mainly Calvinist
- Eastern Orthodox
- Eastern Orthodox with Muslim minorities
- — Border as of 1600

0   400 mi

0   400 km

Lambert Conformal Conic Projection

Henry was furious at having his power limited by the pope. He decided to take the control of the English church away from the pope. Henry called Parliament into session and urged its members to pass a series of laws. These laws formed the Church of England, or the Anglican Church, and declared it to be independent of the Catholic Church. The archbishop of the Anglican Church annulled the king's marriage to Catherine, and Henry married Anne Boleyn in 1533. Parliament passed the **Act of Supremacy** in 1534, making the monarch the leader of the Church of England.

In Scotland, a <u>controversial</u> preacher named John Knox spread Calvin's ideas. Protestants there established the Church of Scotland, or Presbyterian Church, and the Scottish Episcopal Church.

Religious War in Germany Luther's ideas took hold in northern Germany but not in the south. In southern Germany, the Holy Roman emperor was Catholic and wanted his empire to be Catholic as well.

In 1547, the emperor initiated a crackdown against Protestants in Germany that resulted in religious war. The war ended in 1555 with the Peace of Augsburg. This treaty allowed each German ruler to decide which religion his realm would follow—Catholic or Lutheran.

Instead of a unified Catholic empire, Germany was now a group of independent regions with different religious traditions. Northern Germany was mostly Protestant, while most of southern Germany was Catholic.

Reading Check How did Henry VIII use Parliament for his own ends?

myWorld Activity
Life at Court

controversial, *adj.*, tending to cause dispute or disagreement

Chapter 25 Section 3

my worldhistory.com

Places to Know

Religious Conflict in Europe

Violence in the name of religion tore through Europe during the Reformation. Protestants pulled down statues in Catholic churches. Catholics and Protestants murdered each other. Wars of religion were launched throughout the continent in the 1500s and 1600s. People fought over beliefs, but their leaders were also fighting to expand their empires. *How might religion become involved with politics?*

◀ In 1572, French Catholics massacred thousands of Huguenots on St. Bartholomew's Day.

▲ Soldiers fighting in the wars of religion plundered villages throughout Northern Europe.

Catholic Southern Europe

Although Protestantism spread, the nations of southern Europe remained largely Catholic. Italy retained its Catholic faith. The powerful Catholic rulers of Spain became the main defenders of the Catholic Church in Europe. France remained Catholic, though not without friction from a growing number of French Protestants.

Religious Conflict in France At first, the Catholic king of France allowed **Huguenots,** or French Protestants, to worship freely. In 1534, however, the situation changed. Huguenots put up posters all over Paris—even on the king's bedroom door—denouncing the Catholic Church. The king ordered the arrest of hundreds of Protestants. Some were burned alive for their views.

By 1559, the French queen Catherine de' Medici arranged a marriage between her daughter Margaret and Henry of Navarre, the leader of the Huguenots. The marriage that was to have brought peace to the nation resulted in disaster.

In 1572, outraged anti-Protestants in Paris killed some 3,000 Huguenots in the St. Bartholomew's Day Massacre. After-ward, a French Protestant general said,

66 It was our wars of religion that made us forget our religion. 99

—General François de La Noue

Still, French Catholics refused to accept a Protestant king. Finally, in 1593, Henry converted to Catholicism in order to end resistance to his crowning as king. He became King Henry IV the following year. The civil war ended.

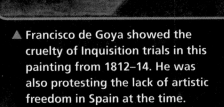

▲ Francisco de Goya showed the cruelty of Inquisition trials in this painting from 1812–14. He was also protesting the lack of artistic freedom in Spain at the time.

In 1572, 19 Catholics were hanged by Calvinists in Gorkum, Holland. The Catholics refused to give up their loyalty to the pope. ▶

Culture Close-Up

In 1598, Henry IV proclaimed the Edict of Nantes. An **edict** is an official public order made by a king or another authority. It made the Catholic Church the official church of France. But it also gave Huguenots the freedom to practice their own religion.

Spain and the Inquisition Unlike France, Spain did not allow Protestants to worship freely. Philip II, Spain's Catholic king, championed the Counter-Reformation as a way to force Catholicism on his people. He used the religious tribunal known as the Inquisition to bring suspects to trial for heresy. Although inquisitions had been known since medieval times, the Spanish Inquisition founded in 1478 was more feared than any previous church court. Among those tried and tortured were Protestants, Jews, and Muslim converts to Christianity.

In 1555, Philip inherited control of the Netherlands. Many of the Dutch had converted to Calvinism. Philip set up the Inquisition in the Netherlands to combat this Protestantism. The Dutch people rebelled, and Philip went to war. The fighting lasted more than 75 years. The mainly Calvinist Netherlands gained independence and became a major economic and military power.

When Henry VIII's daughter, Queen Elizabeth I, sent troops to aid the Dutch rebels, Philip responded with a sea attack on England. In 1588, King Philip sent an **armada,** or fleet of ships, to attack England. The English navy fought back and won. The Battle of the Spanish Armada ended Spain's domination of the seas.

myworldhistory.com

Culture Close-Up

753

Legacy of the Reformation

In spite of wars and division among Christians, Reformation ideas continue to influence modern society today.

Renewal and Reform: Luther and Calvin restated the basic ideas that Jesus had introduced among the early Christians. Their ideas also spurred the Catholic Church to reform itself. Institutions, both secular and religious, often seek periodic renewal and reform.

Freedom: Luther said that every Christian had an equal chance of salvation. His words suggested an equality among people that was not common at the time.

Progress: By encouraging people to read the Bible, Protestantism led to an increase in literacy and access to education. Some scholars believe that Protestant ideas also led to economic and scientific progress.

Tolerance: Protestants and Catholics eventually accepted different forms of worship. This led to an acceptance of differing opinions in nonreligious matters as well. This kind of tolerance is part of democratic values in nations such as the United States.

THINK CRITICALLY **How is tolerance a democratic value?**

The protestors above and below are exercising their right to voice their opinions. After the Reformation, ideas such as freedom of expression became more widespread.

The Thirty Years' War In spite of this loss, Philip was determined to restore Catholicism to other parts of Europe. His aggressiveness resulted in Spain joining in the Thirty Years' War.

This war, fought between 1618 and 1648, involved most of the major European powers. It began as a religious conflict between Protestants and Catholics. As time went on, however, the war developed into a political clash. Soldiers from many nations roamed northern Europe, stealing and burning towns and farms.

The Peace of Westphalia finally ended the war in 1648. The treaty allowed people to practice their own religion in private, even if it differed from the king's religion.

Reading Check What was the St. Bartholomew's Day Massacre?

Impact of the Reformation

Feudal Europe was a very different place from Europe of the 1600s. Under feudalism, Europe consisted of a few large kingdoms. By the late 1600s, Europe was a patchwork of hundreds of smaller, separate states.

In addition, the Reformation had ended the supremacy of the pope and the Catholic Church. Leaders needed new forms of government to meet the challenges of their developing nations.

Rulers Grow Stronger The wars of religion increased the authority of rulers outside the Church. Some of this authority included some control over religious affairs. The Peace of Westphalia, for example, had given rulers the right to determine their country's religion.

Catholicism, Lutheranism, and Calvinism all became recognized religions.

Sensing the treaty's threat to his authority, the pope declared it "null, void, <u>invalid</u>." However, it was a turning point in political and religious life in Europe.

Experiments in Self-Government

During this time, some Protestant nations moved toward self-government. One group of Dutch Protestants began to govern themselves guided by ideas of freedom and religious tolerance. In Geneva, Calvinist churches elected their own leaders, some of the earliest elected leaders in Europe.

Protestants also promoted civic participation, or regular people having a voice in government. Luther and Calvin both wrote about something similar when they encouraged people to interpret the Bible for themselves.

Protestant thinkers also crafted new ideas about government structure. The German Calvinist Johannes Althusius (al THOO sih us) thought that his city should be free to rule itself. He was influenced by Calvin's idea that churches should be subject to God's law alone, not to those of a government. Althusius developed the idea of **federalism,** a form of government in which power is shared between local and national levels. Federalist ideas would later influence the framers of the Constitution of the United States.

Economic and Social Effects Though it is still debated today, some scholars believe that Protestant ideas about self-government led to economic trends like free market capitalism. These ideas contributed to social changes such as greater access to education, increased literacy, and the growth of cities.

Reading Check **Name three effects of the Reformation.**

invalid, adj., without truth or unlawful

Section 3 Assessment

?

Essential Question

How should we handle conflict?

Key Terms

1. Define each of the following key terms in a complete sentence: annulment, Act of Supremacy, Huguenots, armada, federalism.

Key Ideas

2. How did Henry VIII come into conflict with the pope?

3. Why did Philip II send an armada to attack England?

4. How did the Thirty Years' War strengthen the monarchy?

Think Critically

5. Sequence List in chronological order by date the main legal decisions and treaties that contributed to the spread of Protestantism.

6. Analyze Cause and Effect What caused the St. Bartholomew's Day Massacre?

7. Categorize List three areas of European society strongly affected by the Reformation.

8. How did Henry of Navarre end civil war in France? How was the Thirty Years' War resolved? Go to your **Student Journal** to record your answers.

Chapter Assessment

Key Terms and Ideas

1. **Explain** How did priests use **indulgences** to raise money for the Church?

2. **Recall** What is **predestination**?

3. **Discuss** During the mid-1500s, was the city of Geneva, Switzerland, a **theocracy**? Explain.

4. **Compare and Contrast** How was the **Counter-Reformation** different from the Reformation?

5. **Summarize** What did the **Council of Trent** accomplish?

6. **Explain** Why did Henry VIII want an **annulment**?

7. **Describe** What happened to the **armada** that was sent by Philip II of Spain to attack England?

8. **Recall** Who was the first person to write about **federalism**?

Think Critically

9. **Identify Bias** Do you think the diet at Worms was biased? Explain.

10. **Draw Conclusions** Martin Luther was shocked to learn that many Catholic priests were poorly trained. Why might it be a problem for the Church to have uneducated priests?

11. **Draw Inferences** Jesuit missionaries spread the Catholic faith to distant lands. Why do you think they were so effective at spreading their beliefs?

12. **Analyze Cause and Effect** What caused Germany to become a group of independent states with different religious traditions?

13. **Compare and Contrast** During the Reformation, how did the treatment of Protestants differ in Spain and in France?

14. **Core Concepts: Cultural Diffusion and Change** What are two reasons why Reformation ideas spread throughout Europe?

Analyze Visuals

15. In this portrait of Teresa of Avila, what does her clothing reveal about her?

16. How does the painting portray Teresa of Avila as a scholar? Explain how her education might have affected her attempts at reform.

17. Judging from what you know of Teresa's life, what might she be writing?

18. Why do you think she is looking upward?

Essential Question

myWorld Chapter Activity

Guess Who Who's the mystery guest? In this activity, five classmates will use the Activity Cards to view portraits and learn biographical details about key people from this influential period. Then, they will be the contestants in a mock game show called Guess Who, and you will have a chance to guess their identities and maybe become a contestant yourself.

21st Century Learning

Give an Effective Presentation

Use the Internet to research one of the key historical figures mentioned in this chapter. Use your research on this person to incorporate related visuals. Then give a presentation about this person's life that uses these visuals. Also, write a two-page narration about the historical figure, a description of the visuals, and a summary that expresses your opinion of this person.

Document-Based Questions

Success **Tracker**™
Online at myworldhistory.com

Use your knowledge of the Reformation and Documents A and B to answer Questions 1–3.

Document A

"For people living today, the Protestant Reformation is three different stories, and each has an ending that would have saddened Martin Luther. It is, first of all, the story of the division of Western Christendom and the loss, probably forevermore, of its religious unity. . . . In the end the Lutheran banner would fly only over selected regions in northern Europe and America."

—Steven Ozment, *Protestants: The Birth of a Revolution* (1992)

Document B

Religions Practiced in European Countries Today (percentage of population)			
Country	Protestant	Catholic	Other*
France	2	83–88	10–15
Germany	34	34	32
Italy		90	10*
Netherlands	20	30	50
Norway	89	1	10
Switzerland	35	42	23
Spain		94	6*

* "Other" includes those who practice no religion; in Spain and Italy, includes Protestants.
SOURCE: *CIA World Factbook, 2009*

1. What does the author of Document A believe would have saddened Luther?

   A the design of the Lutheran banner

   B the divisions in Christianity

   C the churches in North America

   D the spread of Lutheranism

2. Which country above has the highest percentage of Protestants?

   A Germany

   B France

   C Italy

   D Norway

3. **Writing Task** Write a letter to Martin Luther that describes the effect that the Reformation still has on Europe today. Use details from the documents.

my worldhistory.com

Self-Test

The Age of Exploration

Essential Question

What are the consequences of trade?

The Padrão dos Descobrimentos, or Monument to the Discoveries, in Lisbon, Portugal ▼

Explore the Essential Question . . .

- at **my worldhistory.com**
- using the **myWorld Chapter Activity**
- with the **Student Journal**

The Age of Exploration

1400s Portuguese explore the coast of Africa.

1492 Columbus crosses the Atlantic.

1522 Magellan's expedition circumnavigates the globe.

1400   **1500**   **1600**   **1700**

1520s–1530s Spanish conquer Aztec and Inca empires.

1600s Europe adopts capitalism and mercantilism.

Journey Into Dark Waters

This fictionalized story is based on real events in the life of Columbus.

Protecting the page from a fine spray of salty seawater, Christopher Columbus wrote in his sea journal in 1492: "I set sail from Granada before sunrise." As captain of a fleet of three ships, the *Niña*, the *Pinta*, and the *Santa María*, Columbus looked ahead to a long journey.

Columbus wrote in his journal every day, no matter how rough the seas. Dipping his quill pen into ink every few words, he recorded the distance traveled that day and details about the wind and the weather. Columbus valued his journal so much that he had a plan should the ship go down. He would seal up the journal in a barrel and cast it into the sea, so that his words would wash ashore somewhere and live on, even if he was dead.

myworldhistory.com

Timeline/On Assignment

For years, Columbus begged King Ferdinand and Queen Isabella to finance his voyage.

Old sailors often told young men new to ocean voyages frightening tales of sea monsters and the boiling waters said to be near the equator.

Imagine the thoughts crossing Columbus's mind as he prepared to sail into an unknown world, commanding a tiny fleet of three fragile ships and about 90 men. If he felt scared, it was nothing compared to what his sailors felt.

Famously superstitious, sailors disliked the very idea of leaving sight of land, believing that in dark uncharted waters there lived sea monsters capable of swallowing entire ships. They feared tropical seas that were said to boil. All they had to look forward to were cramped quarters, poor food, and violent storms that might break up the ship or blow it off course. There was also the possibility of starvation, illness, and injury—and intense boredom.

For eight years, Columbus lived at the Spanish court, hoping to convince the king and queen to finance his "Enterprise of the Indies." When they finally agreed, Columbus expressed his gratitude,

66 Your Highnesses . . . took thought to send me, Christopher Columbus, to the said parts of [Asia], to see those princes and peoples and lands . . . and ordained that I should not go by land to the eastward, by which way it was the custom to go, but by way of the west, by which down to this day we do not know certainly that anyone has passed. . . . 99

To prepare for the voyage, Columbus studied the latest maps and honed his skills as a navigator. A friend praised Columbus's abilities, "There was never born a man so well equipped and expert in navigation as the said lord Admiral [Columbus]."

Like other Renaissance thinkers, Columbus wanted to know about the world around him. He read as much as he could and even mastered other languages to read important works. In one of his favorite books, *The Travels of Marco Polo*, Columbus had read about pearls, silks, ivory, pepper, nutmeg, and cloves. Like Marco Polo, he, too, was on the hunt for riches. Devoutly religious, Columbus also read the Bible, believing that it held geographic clues to legendary lands and riches.

Onboard ship, however, his crew did not always share his sense of adventure. As the weeks dragged on, the men grew restless. They worried about running out of food and water during the long voyage. Columbus tried to calm them by showing them the ship's log. However, the log he showed the crew was not the same as the private journal he kept to himself. The crew believed they had traveled fewer miles from home than they really had—Columbus hid the true distance from his men.

Columbus faced a mutiny of his men who became fearful as they sailed farther and farther from home with no sight of land.

The days at sea seemed endless. First, there were false reports of land . . . then no land at all . . . then more false reports. The crew grew so desperate that they vowed that if land was not sighted in three days, they would throw Columbus overboard and sail home without him. Columbus faced down the possible mutiny, or rebellion, by agreeing to turn around in three days if no land appeared.

Finally, on October 11, a green branch with flowers floated past the ship. Land ho! The ships had reached what we call today San Salvador, or Watling Island, in the Bahamas.

The next morning, Columbus put on his red silk jacket and went ashore. He was relieved and excited—he believed the riches of China awaited him. Columbus didn't realize that in spite of his skills as a navigator, he had made a big mistake. Still, it was an error that changed history.

From what you just read, can you predict how Columbus's voyages might affect trade? Think about the consequences of trade and exploration as you read the chapter.

myStory Video

Join Columbus as he sets sail to the other side of the world.

Section 1

The Voyages of Discovery

Key Ideas

- During the Renaissance, Europeans sought to profit from trade with Asian lands.

- New technologies made long ocean voyages possible.

- The voyages of Columbus and other explorers gave Europeans a new view of the world.

Key Terms • missionary • circumnavigate • cartography • caravel

 **Visual Glossary**

Reading Skill Analyze Cause and Effect Take notes using the graphic organizer in your journal.

This monument in Portugal shows Prince Henry the Navigator. ▼

Merchants had traded with Asia since ancient times. During the Crusades, Europeans brought back silks and jewels from Asia. For a time, the Black Death and the Mongol invasions had interrupted this trade. By the 1500s, traders were eager to return to Asia.

Some Motivations for Exploring

Renaissance merchants had grown wealthy trading goods imported from Asia. Other European nations wanted access to this trade without going through the Italians. They sought a sea route to Asia that bypassed Italian trade routes in the Mediterranean Sea.

The Search for Spices European traders had a new interest: the spice trade. Valuable spices were to be found in India, China, and the Spice Islands, or the Moluccas, a chain of islands in present-day Indonesia. There, traders could purchase spices such as peppers, cloves, nutmeg, and cinnamon—all in demand in Europe.

Winning Converts Another reason for exploring new lands was to win converts for Christianity. Ships' crews often included Christian **missionaries.** Missionaries are members of a religious order who encourage people to convert to a particular religion. Missionaries remained in these new lands to set up communities and schools.

Reading Check **What is the spice trade?**

762

Portugal Leads the Way

Portugal led the world in global exploration. It was the first European nation to acquire an overseas empire.

Prince Henry the Navigator Portuguese expansion began with the invasion of North Africa and the conquest of Ceuta in 1415. One of the most distinguished soldiers in that battle was Prince Henry, third son of King John I of Portugal. Around 1432, Prince Henry claimed for Portugal the rich islands of Madeira and the Azores. Known as Prince Henry the Navigator, he was also the first European to make contact with Africa for trade in ivory, gold, and slaves. Prince Henry is credited as well with sponsoring many explorers and training them in mapmaking, ship design, and navigation.

Part of Henry's mission in Africa was to drive out Muslims from North Africa and the Holy Land. As a devout Catholic, Henry wanted to recover Christian lands in the Mediterranean that had been taken by the Muslims. The Portuguese also hoped to convert Africans—most of whom practiced Islam or tribal religions—to Christianity. In addition, the Portuguese were looking for a faster sea route to Asia by sailing around Africa.

Dias Rounds the Cape In 1488, Bartolomeu Dias (bahr too loo MEE oo DEE us), a Portuguese captain, made a great discovery. Dias and his crew became the first Europeans to sail around the Cape of Good Hope at the southern tip of Africa. They proved that it was possible to reach the Indian Ocean by sea.

ivory, *n.,* a hard white substance from the tusk of an animal such as an elephant

Sails were made of a heavy woven linen called sailcloth.

The central mast was the tallest and held the largest sail.

The ship's pilot used the wheel on deck to turn the rudder and steer the ship.

Improved Ships Set Sail

By 1500, most explorers sailed in light, fast ships large enough to hold provisions for long voyages. Skilled sailors handled the ship's many sails to make the most of the wind. Ocean-going ships also had cannons and a company of marines for self-defense against pirates.

763

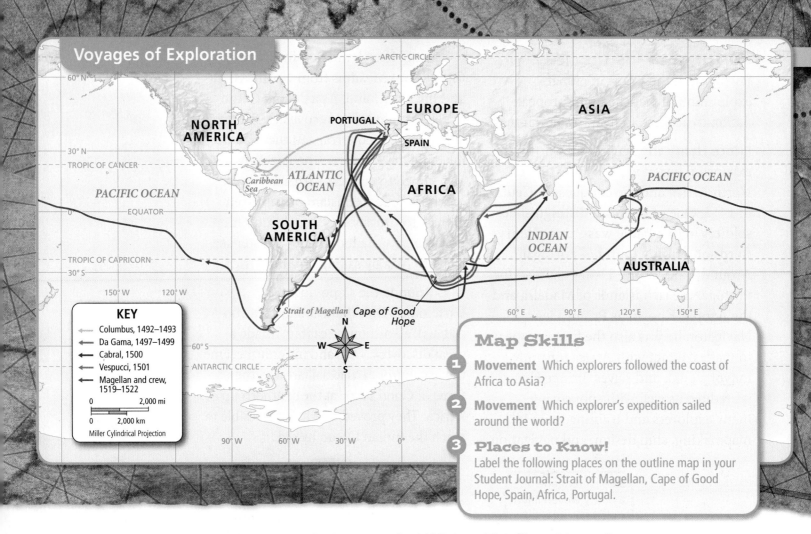

Voyages of Exploration

NORTH AMERICA

EUROPE

ASIA

PORTUGAL

SPAIN

ATLANTIC OCEAN

AFRICA

PACIFIC OCEAN

Caribbean Sea

PACIFIC OCEAN

EQUATOR

SOUTH AMERICA

INDIAN OCEAN

AUSTRALIA

TROPIC OF CANCER

TROPIC OF CAPRICORN

Strait of Magellan

Cape of Good Hope

ARCTIC CIRCLE

ANTARCTIC CIRCLE

KEY
- Columbus, 1492–1493
- Da Gama, 1497–1499
- Cabral, 1500
- Vespucci, 1501
- Magellan and crew, 1519–1522

0   2,000 mi
0   2,000 km

Miller Cylindrical Projection

Map Skills

1 **Movement** Which explorers followed the coast of Africa to Asia?

2 **Movement** Which explorer's expedition sailed around the world?

3 **Places to Know!**
Label the following places on the outline map in your Student Journal: Strait of Magellan, Cape of Good Hope, Spain, Africa, Portugal.

Da Gama's Round-Trip Route In 1497, Captain Vasco da Gama also sailed south from Portugal. In three months' time, his ships rounded the Cape of Good Hope and then sailed on to India. Da Gama returned with a cargo of spices that he sold at a huge profit. With the money, he outfitted a new fleet of cargo ships. He returned to India to seek more profit from the spice trade. Eventually, the Portuguese seized key ports in the Indian Ocean and established a vast trading empire. Da Gama confirmed Portugal's status as a world power.

Reading Check **How was exploration connected to trade?**

Finding New Routes

Portugal's sea captains left Europe and headed southward in their search for sea routes to Asia. Christopher Columbus, an Italian navigator, took a different route.

Columbus Sails West Like most well-educated Europeans, Columbus knew that Earth was a sphere. He reasoned that, by sailing west, he could reach the East Indies, a group of islands in Southeast Asia. But he made some errors.

First, Columbus underestimated the distance from Europe west to Asia. Also, no European knew at the time that two huge landforms—North America and South America—barred the way.

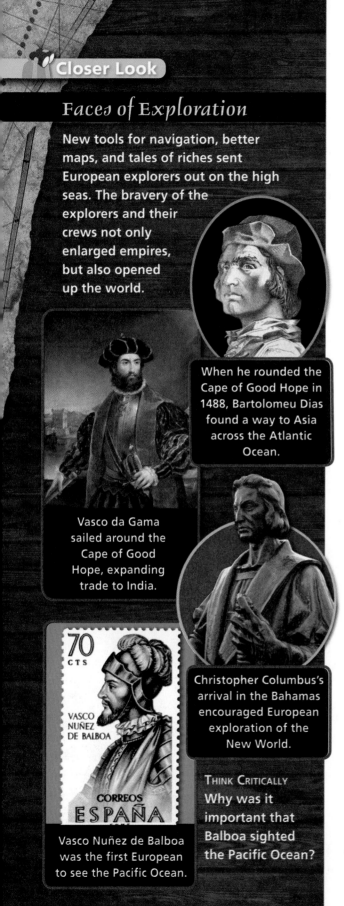

Closer Look

Faces of Exploration

New tools for navigation, better maps, and tales of riches sent European explorers out on the high seas. The bravery of the explorers and their crews not only enlarged empires, but also opened up the world.

When he rounded the Cape of Good Hope in 1488, Bartolomeu Dias found a way to Asia across the Atlantic Ocean.

Vasco da Gama sailed around the Cape of Good Hope, expanding trade to India.

70 CTS

VASCO NUÑEZ DE BALBOA

CORREOS

ESPAÑA

Vasco Nuñez de Balboa was the first European to see the Pacific Ocean.

Christopher Columbus's arrival in the Bahamas encouraged European exploration of the New World.

THINK CRITICALLY
Why was it important that Balboa sighted the Pacific Ocean?

With backing from Spain's monarchs, Columbus sailed in August 1492. His three ships made swift progress across the Atlantic and landed on an island in what are known today as the Bahamas. Columbus believed that he had reached lands just off the coast of China. He made three return voyages, but found no traces of the Asian mainland. Columbus died believing that these lands were the gateway to Asia.

Other Explorers Follow Inspired by Columbus and the Portuguese explorers, other nations sought new lands for trade. From its location on the North Sea, the Netherlands had long had access to European markets. Dutch merchants soon reached Asia, where they were especially successful in the East Indies spice trade. Dutch trading colonies sprang up in Suriname, South Africa, and in the Dutch East Indies (present-day Indonesia).

In 1500, Pedro Álvares Cabral, a Portuguese sea captain, led a fleet to the Indian Ocean. He sailed too far west and landed on the east coast of South America. He is credited as the discoverer of modern-day Brazil. In 1500, he reached India and loaded six ships with precious spices for a return voyage to Portugal.

Between 1497 and 1504, Amerigo Vespucci, an Italian navigator, made four voyages of exploration. He concluded that the lands Columbus called "the Indies" were, in fact, part of a "New World."

Vespucci's report was very popular in Europe. A German mapmaker named the newly encountered lands "America," a Latin version of Vespucci's first name.

myWorld Activity
A Memorable Map

Magellan's Feat In 1519, Ferdinand Magellan launched the most ambitious voyage of discovery. He set out from Spain to cross the Atlantic with five ships and a crew of more than 250. He hoped to find a western route to Asia.

Unlike Columbus, Magellan knew that a continent stood in his way. His fleet sailed south along the uncharted continent. For 38 days, Magellan and his weary crew navigated the <u>treacherous</u> waters. Finally, they threaded their way through a strait, or narrow channel, that led them to the Pacific Ocean. This channel was named the Strait of Magellan. The continent was South America, and Magellan's feat had confirmed that there was a southwest passage to Asia.

treacherous, *adj.,* dangerous or hazardous

Magellan continued north and sailed west across the Pacific Ocean. The journey used up all of the ships' food supplies. Many crew members died from a lack of certain nutrients such as vitamins in their diets. Crew member Antonio Pigafetta described the hardships of the voyage,

> 66 We ate biscuit [that had been reduced] to fistfuls of powder swarming with worms, for they had eaten the better part (it stank strongly of rat urine); and we drank yellow water that had been putrid for many days, and we also ate some ox hides . . . which had become hard because of the sun, rain, and wind. 99

—Antonio Pigafetta, *The First Voyage Around the World*

Magellan's voyage proved that there was a southwest passage to Asia around South America.

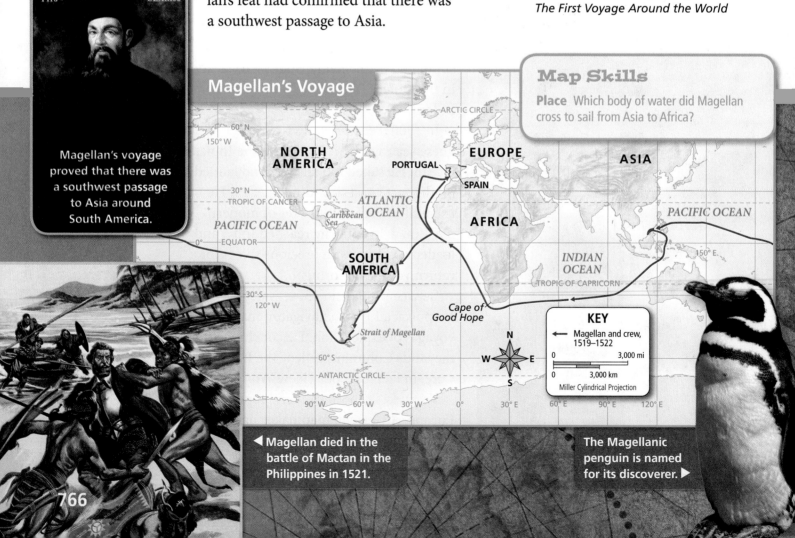

Magellan's Voyage

Map Skills

Place Which body of water did Magellan cross to sail from Asia to Africa?

KEY

← Magellan and crew, 1519–1522

0   3,000 mi
0   3,000 km
Miller Cylindrical Projection

◄ Magellan died in the battle of Mactan in the Philippines in 1521.

The Magellanic penguin is named for its discoverer. ►

766

Magellan next reached the Philippine Islands, claiming them for Spain. In 1521, he died in a battle with the islanders. In September 1522, three years after departing, the sole surviving ship of the fleet returned to Spain. Only 18 crew members survived. They had achieved the most difficult navigational feat of the age. They had **circumnavigated,** or sailed completely around, the world.

Reading Check **What is the significance of the Strait of Magellan?**

New Tools for Exploration

The voyages of exploration could not have been made without advances in sailing technology. These included improvements in mapmaking, navigation, and shipbuilding.

More Accurate Maps For 1,300 years, explorers had been guided by the works of the ancient Egyptian geographer Ptolemy. Crusaders and medieval traders also made maps. Though valuable, these early maps were inaccurate or incomplete.

During the Renaissance, mapmakers developed the science of making maps and globes, known as **cartography.** Those who made more accurate maps, atlases, and globes were called cartographers.

In 1569, Gerardus Mercator (juh RAHR dus mur KAY tur) discovered how to project the curved surface of the globe onto a flat page. His world map distorted the extreme northern and southern regions, but left the most traveled areas of the globe undistorted. Mercator projections, as these maps are called, continue to be used today.

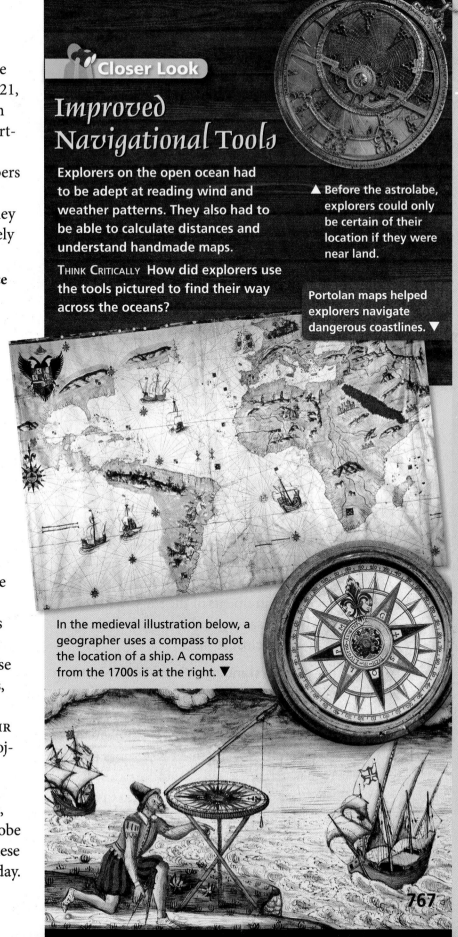

Closer Look

Improved Navigational Tools

Explorers on the open ocean had to be adept at reading wind and weather patterns. They also had to be able to calculate distances and understand handmade maps.

THINK CRITICALLY How did explorers use the tools pictured to find their way across the oceans?

▲ Before the astrolabe, explorers could only be certain of their location if they were near land.

Portolan maps helped explorers navigate dangerous coastlines. ▼

In the medieval illustration below, a geographer uses a compass to plot the location of a ship. A compass from the 1700s is at the right. ▼

767

New Views of the World

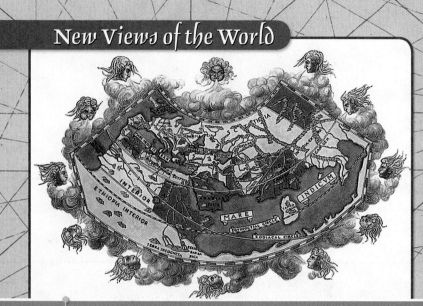

This map from the 1400s recreates the world map drawn around 150 A.D. by the ancient Egyptian geographer Ptolemy.

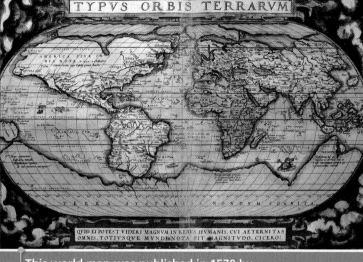

This world map was published in 1570 by Abraham Ortelius in the first modern atlas *Theatrum orbis terrarum (Theater of the World).*

Advances in Navigation The most commonly used navigational tool was the magnetic compass, used to show direction. This device was invented in China and came to Europe via the Silk Road traders. Navigators also used the astrolabe, which determined the ship's north-south position based on measurements of the stars. With these tools, sailors could navigate without being close to land.

Understanding Winds Understanding ocean winds was vital to European explorers. After much trial and error, mariners learned that winds were divided into zones and that these zones changed with the seasons. With this knowledge, they could map travel routes to catch the best winds. Explorers could also determine the best time of year to catch the winds for their voyages.

The Shipbuilding Revolution The Renaissance also launched a revolution in shipbuilding. Until the Middle Ages, rowers worked to move ships. These slow and heavy ships needed large crews, with many rowers. They were difficult to steer and best suited for calm seas.

European craftworkers developed new oceangoing ships. They modified a ship called a **caravel,** a small, narrow vessel with two or three masts and triangular sails. It was fast and easier to maneuver in different wind and sea conditions.

Wonders of the World The voyages of discovery revealed wonders and created excitement about the natural world. Explorers discovered the vastness of the African continent and the existence of North America and South America. "The hidden half of the globe is brought to light," rejoiced a scholar in 1493.

Modern maps such as the satellite map above clearly show geographic features such as mountains, lakes, deserts, and snowy regions.

Modern tools of mapmaking and exploration include space telescopes such as this one over North America.

Suddenly, even ordinary Europeans wanted to know about world geogaphy. Printers made cheap, portable atlases to meet the demand. Illustrated travel books became popular for those who wanted to read first-hand accounts of exploration on sea and land. An account of Magellan's voyage was published as early as 1523 and included interviews with the expedition's survivors.

Reading Check **Name three improvements in sailing technology.**

Section 1 Assessment

Key Terms

1. Define each of the following key terms in a complete sentence: missionary, circumnavigate, cartography, and caravel.

Key Ideas

2. Why did European nations embark on voyages of exploration?

3. What type of ship was best suited to long ocean voyages? Why?

4. How did the voyages of Columbus change Europeans' view of the world?

Think Critically

5. **Identify Evidence** What did Bartolomeu Dias and his crew prove when they sailed around the Cape of Good Hope?

6. **Categorize** What inventions helped sailors determine their location at sea?

7. **Compare and Contrast** How were the voyages of Columbus and Magellan similar and different?

Essential Question

What are the consequences of trade?

8. Who gained and who lost because of Italy's control of trade in the Mediterranean? What did Portugal gain by finding an ocean route to India? Go to your Student Journal to record your answers.

The Conquest of the Americas

| **Key Ideas** | • Spanish explorers defeated the Aztec and Incan empires. | • Conquest enriched Spain, but devastated the peoples of Mesoamerica and the Andes. |

Key Terms • conquistador • colonization • bullion • quipu • immunity

 Visual Glossary

┼┼┼┼┼┼ **Reading Skill Sequence** Take notes using the graphic organizer in your journal.

The meeting of Moctezuma and Cortés was a historic encounter between two cultures. ▼

At the time the Spanish explorers arrived, the Aztec leader Moctezuma ruled an empire that extended throughout Mexico. In South America, the Incan emperor Atahualpa (ah tuh WAHL puh) ruled more than 10 million people. These two empires were large and complex, but they were no match for the Spanish forces.

The Spanish Conquer Two Empires

The Spanish explorers and soldiers who conquered territory were known as **conquistadors.** Spain quickly began **colonization,** or the process of establishing settlements called colonies. Towns were settled and new governments were established. Spain's Caribbean colonies served as bases for conquering the mainland.

Cortés Defeats Moctezuma In 1519, Hernán Cortés sailed to Mexico to conquer the rich Aztec empire. He had fewer than 600 soldiers to counter Moctezuma's strong army. One of Cortés's advantages was his native interpreter, an Aztec woman named Malinche. Through her and a Spanish interpreter, the conquistador learned vital details about the Aztecs and their army.

This information helped Cortés form alliances with the Aztecs' enemies. Thousands of native warriors joined the Spaniards as they marched to Tenochtitlan, the Aztec capital. As you have read, Moctezuma and Cortés met on the outskirts of the grand imperial capital.

Though Moctezuma welcomed Cortés at first, tension mounted between the Aztecs and the Spaniards. A battle broke out, and Moctezuma was killed. By August 1521, the Aztecs had surrendered Tenochtitlan. A poem in the Aztec language of Nahuatl described the defeat:

66 Nothing but flowers and songs of sorrow / are left in Mexico /. . . . We are crushed to the ground; / we lie in ruins. 99

—unknown Aztec poet from *The Broken Spear* by Miguel León-Portilla

Atahualpa Falls Into Pizarro's Trap
Rumors of another golden empire drew Francisco Pizarro and a group of conquistadors to South America in the 1530s. It was a time of chaos for the Incas. The vast empire had split into factions and civil war erupted. Smallpox had arrived from Central America, killing thousands of Incas. Finally, a new emperor, Atahualpa, took the Incan throne.

Pizarro took advantage of the instability. He invited Atahualpa to a meeting and then threw him in prison. Atahualpa arranged for a ransom of almost 20 tons of gold and silver. This astonishing sum was said to be the largest ransom in history. Pizarro rejected Atahualpa's ransom and ordered the emperor killed.

Pizarro appointed a new Inca emperor who agreed to cooperate with the Spanish. Pizarro then marched to the Inca capital of Cuzco. In November 1533, his army took control of the city. The Inca empire was now in Spanish hands.

Reading Check How did Pizarro trap the emperor Atahualpa?

Empires of the Americas

Aztec serpent covered in turquoise

NORTH AMERICA

ATLANTIC OCEAN

TROPIC OF CANCER

Gulf of Mexico

Tenochtitlan

Caribbean Sea

EQUATOR

SOUTH AMERICA

PACIFIC OCEAN

Cuzco

TROPIC OF CAPRICORN

KEY
- Aztec empire, 1325–1521
- Inca empire, early 1400s–1533
- Spanish empire, 1600
- Portuguese empire, 1600
- Line of Demarcation
- Hernán Cortés, 1519–1521
- Francisco Pizarro, 1531

0   1,000 mi
0   1,000 km
Lambert Azimuthal Equal-Area Projection

Map Skills

1 **Region** How did the Line of Demarcation divide the territory of South America?

2 **Location** What advantage did Cuzco have as the Incan capital?

Incan ceremonial knife made of gold

771

myWorld Activity
Poem for Two Voices

The Impact of Conquest

Aztec lands then became part of New Spain and were renamed Mexico. Incan lands were claimed for Spain as the Viceroyalty of Peru. Both colonies brought great wealth to Spain. By contrast, the Aztecs and the Incas were <u>devastated</u>. Disease had wiped out millions of people. The destruction caused by warfare destroyed cultural artifacts like temples, paintings, carvings, and manuscripts.

devastate, *v.,* to bring to chaos, disorder, or ruin

The Treasure of Empire The Spanish monarch took one fifth of all the treasures taken by the conquistadors from these new colonies. The Incan writer Felipe Guamán Poma de Ayala described the conquistadors' search for treasure:

66 Every day they did nothing but think about the gold and silver and riches. They were like desperate men, foolish, crazy, their judgment lost with the greed for gold and silver. 99

—Felipe Guamán Poma de Ayala, *The First New Chronicle and Good Government*

Every year, ships filled with treasure sailed from the Americas to Europe. These ships carried mostly gold and silver bullion from the colonies' mines. **Bullion** is precious metals melted into bars. By 1660, 200 tons of gold and 18,000 tons of silver had been transported to Spain.

The Wealth of the Americas

Bolivia's Cerro Rico (far right), or Rich Mountain, is honeycombed with silver mines. During the colonial era, thousands of enslaved Native Americans and Africans mined about 45,000 tons of pure silver at Cerro Rico. This silver was minted into coins (center) and funded Spanish wars, shipbuilding, and the monarchy. Mining continues there today.

The seeds of the cacao tree (far left) are the source of cocoa and chocolate. The Toltec, Maya, and Aztec all cultivated cacao before Columbus arrived and took it back to Europe. By the 1600s, hot chocolate had become popular in Spain, France, Italy, and England.

Records of
Lost Worlds

Spanish priest Bernardino de Sahagún worked with native writers and painters on the *General History of the Things of New Spain,* an invaluable record of Aztec culture (right). Incan writer Felipe Guamán Poma de Ayala recorded the culture of his people in *The First Chronicle* (far right).

These Aztec boys are playing a game. The boy at the right is talking as shown by the speech scrolls near his mouth.

An Incan farmer uses a footplow to help sow seeds in this illustration from the 1600s.

In addition to bullion, Spanish fleets took back tons of dried insects valued for the red dye they produced. This insect, the cochineal (KAH chuh neel), feeds on cactus plants and produces a vibrant red dye. The Spanish had seen the red dye in woven garments in Mexico and Peru. It was a brighter red than that produced by European dyes. Cochineal red transformed the European textile industry.

However, not all these treasures reached Spain and Portugal. Some ships sank in storms or were raided by pirates. Attracted by New World wealth, other European nations also competed with Spain and Portugal and sent their own explorers to map and conquer colonies.

The Loss of People and Cultures Aztec and Incan gold and silver enriched the Spanish and Portuguese treasuries. However, it is impossible to measure how much evidence of native cultures

was lost. The conquistadors melted down carved gold ornaments, statues, and wall decorations. The cultures of the Aztecs and the Incas—as well as the collapsed culture of the Mayas—had all produced manuscripts recording religious or political aspects of their civilizations. The Spanish burned most of these manuscripts, considering them to be worthless, <u>pagan</u> scraps. At the same time, some Spaniards, such as Fray (Father) Bernardino de Sahagún, helped preserve native cultures and language in priceless documents like the *General History of the Things of New Spain.*

The conquistadors also wrecked Native American cities. In Tenochtitlan, the Spanish tore down the Templo Mayor and other Aztec buildings. On the ruins, the Spanish built their own capital, Mexico City. In Peru, Pizarro stripped all the riches from Incan cities like Cuzco.

pagan, *adj.,* related to a religion with many gods

my World
CONNECTIONS

The U.S. Post Office has issued more than **50** stamps with Hispanic themes, honoring athletes, explorers, musicians, and historical events.

Smallpox

People understood little about disease before the invention of the microscope. The Spanish did not know that they carried a contagious disease like smallpox in their bodies. The Aztec called the smallpox plague totomonjztli (toh toh mohn ZTEET lee) and wrote that it lasted 60 days.

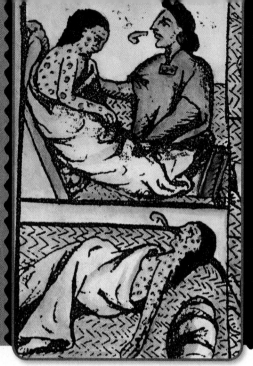

❝ The Plague Named Totomonjztli: Covered, mantled with pustules, very many people died of them. And very many were starved . . . [for] none could take care of [the sick]. . . . [M]any people were marred by [pustules] on their faces. . . . Some lost their eyes; they were blinded. ❞

—Fray Bernardino de Sahagún, *General History of the Things of New Spain*, **Book XII**

Eager to convert the natives to Catholicism, the Spaniards destroyed religious artifacts and temples related to the native religions. They also killed native priests.

In Peru, the Spanish encountered a unique recordkeeping tool called a quipu. A **quipu** is a series of knotted strings on which the Incas recorded information such as counts of people and goods and Incan history. The Spanish viewed the quipu with suspicion and destroyed many of them. However, they also found them surprisingly accurate and useful for dividing up the empire.

The presence of the Spanish also resulted in loss of life due to disease. Millions of natives died from smallpox or influenza. The natives died because they lacked **immunity,** or the ability of the body to fight a disease. The Spanish, by contrast, had built up resistance to smallpox, a disease that was common in Europe. Later epidemics killed even more, further weakening Aztec and Incan cultures.

Reading Check What is a quipu?

Incan men known as runners carried news stored on quipus from village to village. ▼

Cultural Blending

In Spanish America, the mix of diverse people gave rise to a new social structure. The blending of Native Americans, European peoples, and imported African slaves resulted in a culture unique to the Americas.

Native Influences Native culture that outlasted the Spanish conquest often influenced colonial life. The high level of Incan architecture impressed the Spanish. Native artisans and workers blended their own painting or carving styles with those of the Europeans. Colonists also learned to eat foods indigenous to the Americas or traveled in Indian-style canoes.

European Influences At the same time, European customs dominated the newly-conquered territories. The Spanish brought in their language, laws, and religion. They remade cities with buildings and homes in the Spanish style. Their Catholic churches were often built on top of Aztec or Incan temples.

Animals, such as sheep, pigs, goats, and cows, brought to the Spanish Americas changed eating habits. Animal husbandry, or the raising of and caring for livestock, continues to be an important occupation in the Americas. The Spanish also introduced the horse, an animal that transformed life by offering new means of transportation and new hunting options.

African Influences Other influences came with Africans imported as slaves to work the sugar plantations. They contributed African farming methods, new cooking styles, and different crops. African drama, dance, and songs became part of some Christian religious services. In Cuba, Haiti, and Brazil, Africans forged new religions that often blended African and Christian beliefs.

Reading Check How did new animals change life in the Americas?

De Elpañol y Meltifa Callifa

▲ This painting from the 1700s shows a family made up of a Spanish father, a Native American mother, and their mestizo, or mixed race, daughter.

Section 2 Assessment

Key Terms

1. For each of the key terms, write a complete sentence that explains its relationship to the Age of Exploration: conquistador, colonization, bullion, quipu, immunity.

Key Ideas

2. Which two American empires did the Spanish conquer?

3. What products from the Americas did Spanish ships carry to Spain in large quantities?

4. What caused many native people to die even after the fighting was over?

Think Critically

5. **Draw Inferences** Why did many native soldiers in Mexico decide to join forces with the Spanish conquistadors?

6. **Compare Viewpoints** Reread the quotation by Felipe Guamán Poma de Ayala. How did his viewpoint differ from that of the Spaniards he described?

7. **Identify Bias** Why did the Spanish destroy the temples, statues, and books of the people they conquered?

Essential Question

What are the consequences of trade?

8. What did the people of the Americas gain or lose from their dealings with the Spanish? Is it possible to have fair trade between a group of conquerors and the people they conquered? Explain. Go to your Student Journal to record your answers.

my worldhistory.com

Primary Source

The Growth of Trade

Key Ideas

- The voyages of discovery started a global exchange of people, goods, and ideas.

- European nations embraced the concept of mercantilism.

- Economic changes in Europe led to the development of capitalism.

Key Terms
- Columbian Exchange
- mercantilism
- capitalism
- inflation
- cottage industry
- traditional economy
- market economy

 Visual Glossary

Reading Skill Summarize Take notes using the graphic organizer in your journal.

The voyages of exploration linked the hemispheres. By the mid-1500s, the Atlantic Ocean had become a busy sea highway, populated with ships bearing explorers and settlers. It was also part of the global exchange network.

Wheat was originally cultivated southwestern Asia. The Spanish brought it to Mexico to make their traditional bread. ▼

The Columbian Exchange

Columbus's voyages linked the Americas to the rest of the world. People, plants, animals, diseases, and ideas from the Eastern Hemisphere, or the continents east of the Atlantic Ocean, changed the Americas. Plants, animals, and diseases from the Western Hemisphere, or the Americas, transformed the Eastern Hemisphere. The exchange of people, other living things, and ideas between the Eastern and Western hemispheres is called the **Columbian Exchange**.

Settlers Cross the Oceans Soon after the first wave of European settlers came enslaved Africans. These first migrations, or movements of people, were like waves on the ocean. A larger migration in the 1800s was more like a flood. More than 50 million people from all across Europe eventually settled in the Americas. People from Asia came to the Americas by the thousands, too, starting in the 1800s. The Americas continue to attract immigrants today. As a result, North America and South America have extremely diverse societies.

New Crops, New Foods Plants from the Americas altered worldwide eating habits and helped increase global population. One of the most important of these plants was maize, or corn. Corn harvests led to a population explosion in Africa and Asia. Peanuts became a <u>staple</u> crop in Africa, adding protein to soups or being pressed to make cooking oil. Other important food crops were potatoes, manioc, beans, and tomatoes.

Plants from the Eastern Hemisphere also changed life in the Americas. Once introduced in the Caribbean and Brazil, sugar cane, the plant that makes sugar, became a major profit source. As the raising of livestock increased, ranchers in the Americas depended on grains such as barley and oats. The Western Hemisphere was also transformed by new crops like rye, rice, grapes, bananas, and coffee.

staple, *adj.,* used or needed regularly

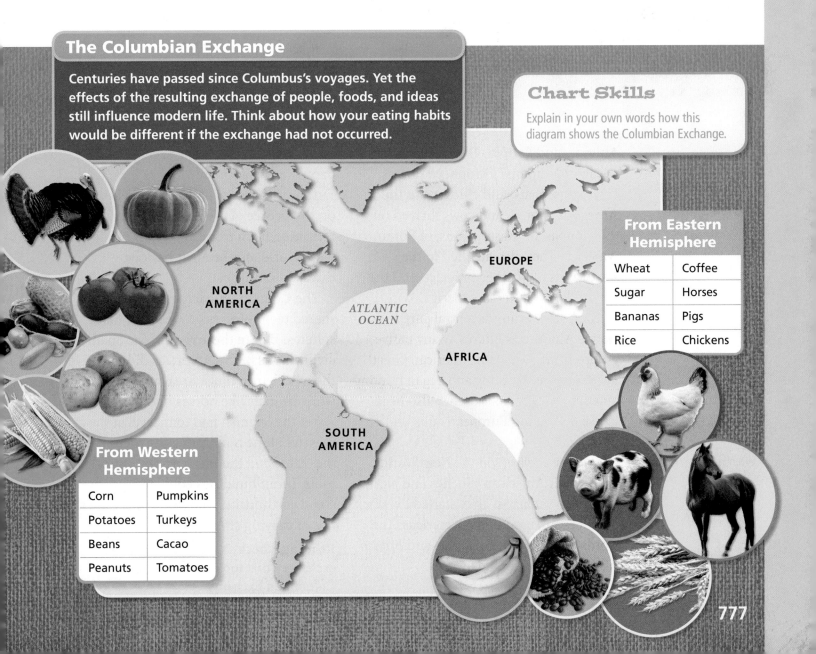

The Columbian Exchange

Centuries have passed since Columbus's voyages. Yet the effects of the resulting exchange of people, foods, and ideas still influence modern life. Think about how your eating habits would be different if the exchange had not occurred.

Chart Skills

Explain in your own words how this diagram shows the Columbian Exchange.

From Eastern Hemisphere

Wheat	Coffee
Sugar	Horses
Bananas	Pigs
Rice	Chickens

From Western Hemisphere

Corn	Pumpkins
Potatoes	Turkeys
Beans	Cacao
Peanuts	Tomatoes

Horses Arrive in the New World

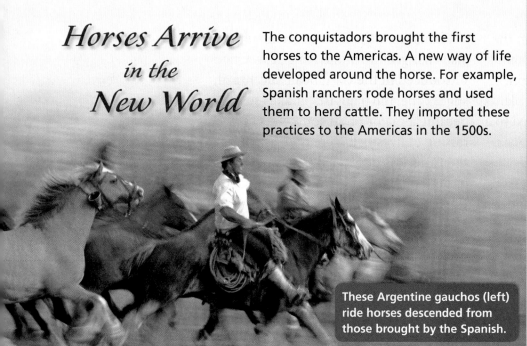

The conquistadors brought the first horses to the Americas. A new way of life developed around the horse. For example, Spanish ranchers rode horses and used them to herd cattle. They imported these practices to the Americas in the 1500s.

These Argentine gauchos (left) ride horses descended from those brought by the Spanish.

Above, horses are unloaded from Spanish ships arriving in the New World.

Animals and People On his second voyage, Columbus introduced horses, cows, pigs, goats, and chickens to the Americas. Horses and cows thrived on the pampas, or grassy plains, of South America. They also adapted to the scrublands of northern Mexico and the Great Plains of North America.

The horse became a central part of Native American cultures. Many native groups from the North American Great Plains stopped farming and began hunting buffalo from horseback. They also began to use horses and European guns in warfare.

The first cowboys in the New World were South American gauchos and North American vaqueros. They started livestock practices still used in the Americas. The words *rodeo, lariat, buckaroo,* and *bronco* are all Spanish ranching words.

Other Exchanges Some exchanges happened by accident. As you have read, European diseases had a deadly effect on the people of the Americas. Sailors returning from tropical regions in the New World also brought back new diseases to Europe.

The Columbian Exchange also led to shared technologies between the hemispheres. Before the arrival of the Spanish, civilizations in the Americas did not have the wheel, iron tools, firearms, or large work animals like horses or oxen.

Yet the Spanish had to marvel at the massive stone buildings constructed by the Aztec and the Incas without metal tools. Incan buildings could even withstand earthquakes due to advanced methods of carving stone.

Reading Check Name three kinds of exchanges that took place through the Columbian Exchange.

Mercantilism

As global trade changed, so did ways of doing business. These changes led to a new economic system known as mercantilism. **Mercantilism** is an economic policy that promotes strengthening a nation by expanding its trade. The goal is to bring as much wealth as possible into the country and make it powerful.

Trade and Wealth Mercantilists believed that the main goal of trade is to make a nation more powerful. Traders pursued this goal by selling goods in exchange for gold and silver. Money made from trading these precious metals paid for a powerful army and navy.

Mercantilists urged lawmakers to adopt policies to increase a nation's wealth. These policies were designed to regulate trade and to boost production. One English merchant explained mercantilism thus:

66 We must ever observe this rule: to sell more . . . yearly than we consume . . . in value. 99

—Thomas Mun,
England's Treasure by Foreign Trade

The Impact of Mercantilism Most European nations practiced mercantilism by the 1600s and the 1700s. They taxed imports to keep foreign goods out and to increase the market for domestic goods.

myWorld Activity
Mercantilism Mixer

Mercantilism in the Tea Trade

England's tea trade shows mercantilism at work. Buying and selling tea and tea tax revenues supported merchants, traders, and artists worldwide. *Describe four economic effects of the tea trade.*

21st Century Learning

England establishes tea plantations throughout its empire in Asia and Africa.

The British East India Company keeps tea prices high with its monopoly on the tea trade.

The British design faster ships to bring tea from China.

English porcelain and silver manufacturers export tea service items to the colonies and Europe.

English artists receive commissions to paint families drinking tea.

Tea Strengthens England's Economy

English tea drinkers begin to add sugar to their tea.

Sugar production in the Caribbean increases to meet demand.

British tea merchants open shops to sell imported tea to the public.

Tea drinking introduces new eating habits and new teatime foods.

TEA

779

Sugar
A Sweet Story of Capitalism

Sugar had been available in Europe in limited quantities since medieval times. By the 1600s, Europeans were demanding more sugar, and large sugar plantations in the Americas were supplying it. The sugar trade was part of a commercial cycle that included investment, land development, labor, and manufacturing. Profits from sugar could also be reinvested to keep the cycle going.

→ **Simulation**

2 Slaves in Brazil cultivate the sugar cane on plantations.

1 *Here, Captain, take this money I made from my last sugar sales and invest it in your next trip to Brazil.*

3 Stalks of the cut sugar cane are fed into a processor. Slaves turn the handle on the processor to crush the cane into raw sugar.

They also founded colonies. Colonies provided the raw materials that the home country made into products to sell to other countries. Colonies bought the home country's goods, but were not allowed to trade with other nations. In this way, the home country kept profits circulating within its own economy.

By buying and selling with other nations, mercantilist nations ensured that they would have access to growing markets and increasing revenue. When traders sold goods, buyers in other nations paid with gold and silver. This payment made the sellers' country richer and the buyers' country poorer—unless, they, too, did business in a mercantilist manner.

Reading Check How does mercantilism contribute to a nation's strength?

A Commercial Revolution

Expanded trade, an increased money supply, and overseas empire-building spurred the growth of capitalism. **Capitalism** is an economic system in which business is privately owned and operated for profit. Capitalism is also called the free market or free enterprise system.

The Price Revolution A free market is one in which sellers compete to supply goods to buyers who demand them. The interplay of supply and demand determines prices. In the 1500s, prices for food and other goods went up. At the same time, there was a sharp increase in the amount of money in circulation. A rise in prices and an increase in available cash leads to a situation called **inflation**.

4 The raw, processed sugar is poured into wooden barrels and loaded aboard merchant ships bound for Europe.

I love to use these elegant sugar tongs with my new china tea set. I also serve sugar cakes from the bakery at tea time.

This trip to Brazil was very successful, Mr. Merchant. Here are your profits—and I hope you'll invest again.

5 European households use sugar to sweeten coffee and tea and to flavor desserts.

6

Thanks, Captain! With these profits, I'm going to open a bakery to sell cakes and candies.

This historical period of runaway inflation in Europe is known as the price revolution.

There were two causes of this price revolution. One was rapid population growth. More people led to a demand for more food. However, farmers could not supply enough to keep up with the demand. As a result, food prices increased. For example, food was four to six times more expensive in England in 1640 than in 1500.

The second cause was the <u>enormous</u> flow of gold and silver from the Americas into Europe. These precious metals added to the money supply in Europe. People had more money, but there were fewer things, such as food, to buy. This worked to drive up prices.

Higher prices meant greater profits for landowners and merchants. They used the profits to invest in their businesses. Using capital, or money, to increase profits is a key part of capitalism.

Land, Crops, and Prices Another aspect of capitalism is the private ownership of land. In a capitalist economy, individuals rather than the government own the land and tools needed to grow crops. Individuals thus benefit not only from their crops and profitable harvests, but they may also buy and sell land for gain.

Under capitalism, farmers benefit by working for landowners and making wages that enable them to buy goods such as food and clothing. Some farmers saved money, purchased land, and became landowners themselves.

enormous, *adj.,* very large

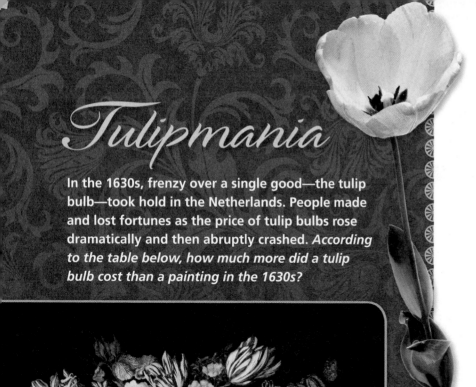

Tulipmania

In the 1630s, frenzy over a single good—the tulip bulb—took hold in the Netherlands. People made and lost fortunes as the price of tulip bulbs rose dramatically and then abruptly crashed. *According to the table below, how much more did a tulip bulb cost than a painting in the 1630s?*

At the height of the mania, paintings of tulips like the one above by Dutch master Joannes Busschaert were less expensive to buy than a single tulip bulb.

Prices in the Netherlands, 1630s

150 guilders	Average annual income
5,000 guilders	Price for a painting of tulips by a Dutch master
10,000 guilders	Cost of a luxurious Amsterdam estate house or A single tulip bulb

(100 guilders = approx. $12,500 in U.S. dollars today)

SOURCE: *The Tulip*, 1999

A modern tulip farm in the Netherlands

The price revolution benefited land-owners the most. Higher prices for crops meant higher profits. Because excess harvests from larger farms could bring in more profits, some landowners in Holland and England forced peasants off their land. They could then use all of these lands to raise sheep for the profit-able wool trade.

These economic changes ended what remained of the feudal system in the Netherlands and in England. Peasants no longer farmed the lord's land in exchange for part of the crop. Many moved to cities to find new ways to make a living.

Goods and Profits The price revolution also drove up prices for widely used goods, such as cloth. Like landowners, cloth merchants wanted to produce more and make larger profits.

In England, cloth merchants devised a clever system for making and selling cloth. They bought raw wool from sheep farmers at the cheapest prices they could find and took it to nearby villages. There, they paid families to spin and then weave the wool into cloth. When the cloth was ready, the merchants picked it up and took it to another location to be finished and dyed. Merchants then sold this cloth wherever prices were the highest. In this way, they produced cloth as cheaply as possible and then sold it for the greatest profit.

The people who wove this cloth worked in their own homes, called cot-tages, in a system known as **cottage indus-try.** They used their own equipment, and they often worked long hours.

For the first time, capital and labor became separated. This idea would be greatly expanded later in the huge capitalist-owned factories of the Industrial Revolution in the 1800s.

Gradually, capitalists also invested money in other developing industries. In England, they operated coal mines, iron-works, breweries, and shipyards. Dutch capitalists founded printing, diamond-cutting, sugar-refining, and even chocolate industries.

A Market Economy Over time, these changes in industry and agriculture transformed the English and Dutch economies. The Netherlands and England were the first European nations to move away from a traditional economy. A **traditional economy** is an economy in which the exchange of goods is based on custom or tradition. These practices are usually handed down from generation to generation without much change.

By contrast, a **market economy** is one in which prices and the distribution of goods are based on competition in a market. In a market economy, prices are not fixed by guilds, by the government, or by custom. Instead, forces of supply and demand set prices. A market economy requires private property ownership, a free market, and profit-making incentives.

Reading Check What is capitalism?

incentive, *n.,* something that leads to action

The Middle Class Grows

In Europe's growing cities, merchants and skilled workers thrived and became prosperous. This group became known as the middle class and included merchants, traders, and artisans. In contrast, hired laborers and servants in upper- and middle-class households often lived in crowded conditions on the edge of poverty. These economic changes took generations, even centuries, to reach all levels of European society. This was because so much of the population remained in rural areas.

Reading Check Who were members of the middle class?

Making lace was a common cottage industry as shown in this 1669–1670 painting by Johannes Vermeer. ▼

Section **3** Assessment

Key Terms

1. Define each of the following key terms in a complete sentence: Columbian exchange, mercantilism, capitalism, cottage industry, traditional economy, market economy.

Key Ideas

2. How did the Age of Exploration influence agriculture in the Eastern and Western hemispheres?

3. According to mercantilists, what was the main goal of trade?

4. How did capitalists tend to use their profits?

Think Critically

5. **Analyze Cause and Effect** How did the Columbian Exchange alter the way Native Americans of the Great Plains lived?

6. **Draw Conclusions** In a mercantilist system, would all nations be able to prosper? Explain.

What are the consequences of trade?

7. Who benefited more from mercantilism, European nations or their colonies? Explain. How did the rise in land prices cause benefits for some people and losses for others? Go to your Student Journal to record your answers.

Chapter Assessment

Key Terms and Ideas

1. **Explain** What advantages did the **caravel** have over older styles of ships?

2. **Recall** Whose expedition was the first to **circumnavigate** the globe?

3. **Describe** What were some of the hardships experienced by sailors during voyages of exploration?

4. **Explain** Why didn't the Aztecs and Incas have **immunity** to smallpox?

5. **Recall** Who were the **conquistadors**, and what did they do?

6. **Explain** How does a **cottage industry** work?

7. **Summarize** What was the **Columbian Exchange**?

8. **Discuss** In a **market economy,** what controls whether prices go up or down?

9. **Recall** What caused **inflation** during the 1500s and 1600s?

Think Critically

10. **Analyze Primary Sources** What did the European scholar quoted in Section 1 mean by saying "The hidden half of the globe is brought to light"?

11. **Compare and Contrast** How was the Portuguese approach to exploration different from the Spanish approach to exploration?

12. **Draw Conclusions** Do you think the Spanish leaders treated the Incan and Aztec leaders fairly? Explain.

13. **Draw Inferences** How would the destruction of their recorded history have changed Incan culture?

14. **Analyze Cause and Effect** How did the rise in land prices affect peasants in England and the Netherlands?

15. **Core Concepts: Economic Basics** How did the price revolution demonstrate the law of supply and demand?

Analyze Visuals

16. This Aztec artifact once held a pan of burning coals. Judging from its appearance, what is it made of?

17. This piece is called "Three Ages." How does it show three stages of human life?

18. Which layer do you think represents old age?

19. What stages of life seem to be missing? Explain.

Essential Question
myWorld Chapter Activity

Around the World in 1,000 Days Lights! Camera! Action! Your group will visit five exhibits posted around the classroom and discuss how to integrate what you learned into a documentary about Magellan's expedition. A discussion leader and a scribe will take notes on the exhibits you visit. Then, the group will use the notes and the visuals from the activity cards to produce a script and a documentary about Magellan's voyage.

21st Century Learning
Develop Cultural Awareness

Research the culture of either the Inca or the Aztec. Find out about their religion, technology, cities, economy, art, and social structure. Then, write a plan for a museum exhibit to teach younger students about this culture. Include photographs or drawings of the artifacts that would be on display; descriptions of the timelines, graphs, and biographies; and informative captions to explain the exhibits.

Document-Based Questions

Success Tracker™
Online at myworldhistory.com

Use your knowledge of the Age of Exploration and Documents A and B to answer Questions 1–3.

Document A

" And even before the Spaniards had risen against us, a pestilence first came to be [common]: the smallpox. . . . [I]t spread over the people as great destruction. . . . There was great havoc [chaos]. Very many died of it. They could not walk; they lay only in their resting places and beds."

—from *General History of the Things of New Spain,* Book XII, by Fray Bernardino de Sahagún, *c.*1579, translated by Arthur J. O. Anderson and Charles E. Dibble

Document B

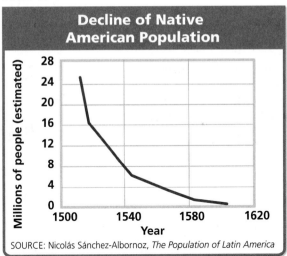

Decline of Native American Population

Millions of people (estimated)

SOURCE: Nicolás Sánchez-Albornoz, *The Population of Latin America*

1. According to Document A, how did the arrival of foreigners lead to instability?

   A by fighting native peoples

   B by bringing diseases to the Americas

   C by taking too much silver and gold from the Americas

   D by introducing Eastern Hemisphere crops to the Americas

2. According to the graph in Document B, how did the population of central Mexico change from the 1500s to 1600?

   A It doubled.

   B It increased ten times.

   C It decreased by half.

   D It decreased by about 25 million.

3. **Writing Task** Write a paragraph summarizing the way European colonization affected Native Americans, as shown by these two documents.

myworldhistory.com

Self-Test

Spanish Conquests in the Americas

> **Key Idea**
> • Europeans established empires during an age of worldwide exploration, discovery, and conquest.

S panish explorer Hernán Cortés traveled to Mexico in 1519 to conquer the rich Aztec empire. At first, he was able to convince many Aztec natives to become his allies. When he arrived in the Aztec capital city of Tenochtitlan, Aztec leader Moctezuma welcomed him graciously. Moctezuma apparently believed that the Spanish were descendants of an Aztec god. This meeting between Cortés and Moctezuma is described in the first excerpt. But Cortés and his soldiers soon attacked the Aztecs. The second excerpt gives a glimpse at how the Spanish were able to conquer the mighty Aztec empire.

A portrait of Moctezuma, 1800s

Read the text on the right. Stop at each circled letter. Then answer the question with the same letter on the left.

A **Analyze Primary Sources** Why does Moctezuma call Cortés "lord"?

B **Draw Conclusions** Why does Moctezuma say that the arrival of Cortés is "not a dream"?

C **Summarize** How did Cortés react to Moctezuma's speech?

weary, *adj.,* exhausted
canopy, *n.,* cloth covering

Moctezuma and Cortés Greet Each Other

❝ Then [Moctezuma] stood up to welcome Cortés; he came forward, bowed his head low and addressed him in these **A** words: 'Our lord, you are <u>weary.</u> The journey has tired you, but now you have arrived on the earth. . . . You have come here to sit on your throne, to sit under its <u>canopy</u>. . . .

B 'No, it is not a dream. I am not walking in my sleep. I am not seeing you in my dreams. . . . And now you have come out of the clouds and mists to sit on your throne again.

'. . . You have come back to us; you have come down from the sky. Rest now, and take possession of your royal houses. Welcome to your land, my lords!'

C . . . Cortés replied . . . 'Tell [Moctezuma] that we are his friends. There is nothing to fear. We have wanted to see him for a long time, and now we have seen his face and heard his words. Tell him that we love him well and that our hearts are contented.' ❞

—Moctezuma and Cortés, 1519, from *The Broken Spears: The Aztec Account of the Conquest of Mexico,* edited by Miguel León-Portilla

Read the text on the right. Stop at each circled letter. Then answer the question with the same letter on the left.

D **Analyze Details** What are people doing in the temple as the attack begins?

E **Draw Conclusions** How do you think Spanish weapons compared with Aztec weapons?

F **Draw Inferences** What was the result of the Spanish attack on the Aztecs?

fiesta, *n.,* a festival, celebration

fodder, *n.,* food given to animals

macana, *n.,* a wooden, swordlike weapon

treacherously, *adv.,* unreliably, marked by hidden dangers

Aztec Account of Spanish Attack

66 [T]he celebrants began to sing their songs. That is how they celebrated the first day of the <u>fiesta.</u> On the second day they

D began to sing again, but without warning they were all put to death. The dancers and singers were completely unarmed. . . .

The Spaniards attacked the musicians first, slashing at their hands and faces until they had killed all of them. The singers—and even the spectators—were also killed. This slaughter in the Sacred Patio went on for three hours. Then the Spaniards burst into the rooms of the temple to kill the others: those who were carrying water, or bringing <u>fodder</u> for the horses, or grinding meal, or sweeping, or standing watch over this work.

The king [Moctezuma] . . . protested: 'Our lords, that is

E enough! What are you doing? These people are not carrying shields or <u>macanas.</u> Our lords, they are completely unarmed!'

[The Spanish] . . . had <u>treacherously</u> murdered our people on the twentieth day after [Cortés] left for the coast. We allowed [Cortés] to return to the city in peace. But on the following day

F we attacked him with all our might, and that was the beginning of the war. 99

—Aztec account, 1519, from *The Broken Spears: The Aztec Account of the Conquest of Mexico,* edited by Miguel León-Portilla

Cortés attacks Tenochtitlán.

Analyze the Documents

1. **Synthesize** How does the wording of the second passage reveal the author's point of view?
2. **Writing Task** Moctezuma greets Cortés respectfully. How do you think he would have greeted other European explorers who arrived after Cortés? Explain your thoughts in a paragraph.

787

Debate
the Digital Future

Your Mission You will analyze the evolution of books from handwritten manuscripts and early printing to the Internet and modern electronic books. In groups, conduct a debate about printing and digital products. Then evaluate the pros and cons of modern digital products.

During the 1400s, Johann Gutenberg introduced to Europe the concept of movable type: metal letters and punctuation marks that can be arranged to form lines of text. Movable type made it possible to print books more rapidly than copying text by hand. Before the development of movable type, there were only a few thousand books in all of Europe. But by 1500, according to some estimates, millions of books had been printed. The new availability of printed books meant that more people learned how to read. These books exposed people to new ideas.

Your team should research the effects of movable type and printing, and then research modern digital products. As you plan your debate arguments, consider the challenges of technology and the pros and cons of digital products.

Go to myWorldHistory.com for help with this activity.

STEP 1

Research Print Technology.

Conduct research about the invention and effects of movable type. For instance, how did the invention of the printing press help spread literacy and new ideas? Then research how publishing has changed over time. Focus on facts about modern digital products and the ways that people access and read books, magazines, newspapers, and other publications.

STEP 2

Prepare and Conduct Your Debate.

In groups of four, debate this statement: The development of movable type caused more changes than the development of digital products. Two people should support the statement; the other two should oppose it. Be sure to research facts to back up your arguments. With your teacher as moderator, present your debate to classmates, who will take notes.

STEP 3

Evaluate the Pros and Cons of Digital Products.

What are the pros and cons of using digital products to access information? As a class, discuss the advantages and disadvantages of digital products and of printed products. Create a class list of these pros and cons. Do the advantages of digital products outweigh the disadvantages? Are digital products better than printed products for certain things?

Gutenberg's Metal Type Around 1450, a German printer named Johann Gutenberg (YOH hahn GOOT un burg) invented movable metal type. With this method, individual letters formed in metal could be used again and again to form words, lines, and pages of text.

In 1455, Gutenberg published the Bible, an event that increased literacy as never before. Printed Bibles were less expensive than handwritten ones, and many people learned to read using Bibles they had at home. By 1490, printing presses were in use from London to Constantinople. By 1500, between 8 million and 20 million books had been printed in Europe.

3 of 23

PORTABLE READER SYSTEM
PRS-505

MENU

The World: Political

ARCTIC OCEAN

GREENLAND
(Denmark)

ALASKA
(U.S.)

ARCTIC CIRCLE

Reykjavík ✪
ICELAND

80° N

60° N

C A N A D A

NORTH
AMERICA

Ottawa ✪

40° N

UNITED STATES

Washington, D.C. ✪

ATLANTIC
OCEAN

Rabat
MOROCCO

TROPIC OF CANCER

WESTERN SAHARA
(Morocco)

MEXICO

20° N

HAWAII
(U.S.)

Mexico
City ✪

CENTRAL AMERICA
AND THE CARIBBEAN
For detail, see map
North and South
America: Political.

WEST AFRICA
For detail, see map
Africa: Political.

PACIFIC
OCEAN

Caracas ✪
VENEZUELA

Georgetown ✪
Paramaribo ✪
FRENCH GUIANA
(France)

Bogotá ✪
COLOMBIA

0°   EQUATOR

Quito ✪
GALÁPAGOS
ISLANDS
(Ecuador)

ECUADOR

GUYANA
SURINAME

N

W   E

S

SAMOA

SOUTH
AMERICA

ATLANTIC

Apia ✪

COOK ISLANDS
(New Zealand)

PERU

Lima ✪

OCEAN

20° S

FRENCH POLYNESIA
(France)

Nuku'alofa ✪

TONGA

La Paz ✪
BOLIVIA

Sucre ✪

✪ Brasília

BRAZIL

TROPIC OF CAPRICORN

PITCAIRN ISLAND
(U.K.)

PARAGUAY

Asunción ✪

CHILE

KEY

- - - Disputed border
—— National border
✪ Capital city

Santiago ✪

Buenos
Aires ✪

URUGUAY

✪ Montevideo

40° S

ARGENTINA

FALKLAND ISLANDS
(U.K.)

160° W   140° W   120° W   100° W   80° W   60° W   40° W   20° W

60° S

SOUTHERN OCEAN

80° S

ANTARCTICA

20° E 40° E 60° E 80° E 100° E 120° E 140° E 160° E

SVALBARD
(Norway)

80° N

ARCTIC OCEAN

ROPE AND SOUTHWEST ASIA

etail, see maps Europe: Political
and Asia: Political.

ARCTIC CIRCLE

RUSSIA

60° N

⊕ Moscow

ASIA

Astana ⊕

KAZAKHSTAN

Ulaanbaatar ⊕

MONGOLIA

40° N

UZBEKISTAN Tashkent ⊕ ⊕ Bishkek
KYRGYZSTAN

TURKMENISTAN ⊕ Dushanbe
TAJIKISTAN

NORTH
KOREA

⊕ P'yongyang

Beijing ⊕ Seoul ⊕

SOUTH
KOREA

JAPAN

⊕ Tokyo

Ashgabat ⊕ ⊕ Tehran
Kabul ⊕

CHINA

TURKEY

⊕ Tunis
TUNISIA
⊕ Tripoli

IRAQ
Baghdad ⊕
Kuwait ⊕
KUWAIT
Manama ⊕
BAHRAIN
QATAR Doha ⊕
Riyadh ⊕ Abu Dhabi ⊕
⊕ Muscat

IRAN AFGHANISTAN Islamabad ⊕
Kathmandu ⊕ BHUTAN
PAKISTAN NEPAL ⊕ Thimphu
New Dhaka ⊕
Delhi ⊕

Cairo ⊕

LIBYA EGYPT

SAUDI
ARABIA OMAN

UNITED
ARAB
EMIRATES

INDIA

PACIFIC
OCEAN

⊕ Taipei

TAIWAN

TROPIC OF CANCER

20° N

AFRICA

GER Khartoum ⊕ ERITREA
CHAD SUDAN Asmara ⊕
N'Djamena ⊕

RIA CENTRAL
AFRICAN
REPUBLIC

⊕ Sanaa
YEMEN
⊕ Djibouti
DJIBOUTI
Addis Ababa ⊕

ETHIOPIA

BANGLADESH

MYANMAR ⊕ Hanoi
LAOS
⊕ Vientiane
Yangon ⊕ THAILAND VIETNAM
Bangkok ⊕ CAMBODIA
Phnom Penh ⊕

⊕ Manila

PHILIPPINES

MARSHALL
ISLANDS

⊕ Majuro

EROON
Bangui ⊕

SOMALIA

SRI
LANKA

REPUBLIC
OF THE
CONGO

UGANDA
Kampala ⊕ KENYA
Kigali ⊕ ⊕ Nairobi

⊕ Mogadishu

Colombo ⊕
Male ⊕
MALDIVES

BRUNEI

⊕ Bandar Seri Begawan

PALAU

⊕ Melekeok

Palikir ⊕

FEDERATED STATES
OF MICRONESIA

KIRIBATI

⊕ Tarawa

aville ⊕
DA RWANDA
ola) DEMOCRATIC
REPUBLIC OF
THE CONGO
anda

Bujumbura ⊕
BURUNDI
Dodoma ⊕ ⊕ Dar es Salaam
TANZANIA

SEYCHELLES

⊕ Victoria

Kuala Lumpur ⊕ MALAYSIA
Singapore ⊕ SINGAPORE

INDONESIA

⊕ Jakarta

NAURU ⊕ Yaren

EQUATOR

0°

PAPUA NEW
GUINEA

SOLOMON
ISLANDS

TUVALU

ANGOLA

MALAWI
ZAMBIA Lilongwe ⊕
Lusaka ⊕
Harare ⊕
ZIMBABWE

COMOROS

⊕ Moroni

Antananarivo ⊕

⊕ Dili
EAST TIMOR

⊕ Honiara

⊕ Port
Moresby

⊕ Funafuti

MOZAMBIQUE

NAMIBIA
indhoek ⊕ BOTSWANA
Gaborone ⊕
Pretoria ⊕
Bloemfontein ⊕
SOUTH
ape Town ⊕ AFRICA

⊕ Maputo
Mbabane ⊕
SWAZILAND
LESOTHO
Maseru

MADAGASCAR

MAURITIUS
⊕ Port Louis
RÉUNION
(France)

VANUATU
Port-Vila ⊕

FIJI
Suva ⊕

20° S

INDIAN
OCEAN

AUSTRALIA

NEW
CALEDONIA
(France)

0 2,000 mi

0 2,000 km

Robinson Projection

⊕ Canberra

NEW
ZEALAND

40° S

⊕ Wellington

20° E 40° E 60° E 80° E 100° E 120° E 140° E 160° E

60° S

SOUTHERN OCEAN

ANTARCTIC CIRCLE

80° S

ANTARCTICA

The World: Physical

160° W 140° W 120° W 100° W 80° W 60° W 40° W 20° W

80° N

Beaufort Sea

Yukon River

ARCTIC CIRCLE

Greenland

Baffin Island

60° N

Bering Sea

ROCKY MOUNTAINS

CANADIAN SHIELD

Hudson Bay

Labrador Sea

Icelar

Britis Isle

Aleutian Islands

NORTH AMERICA

Mackenzie R.

St. Lawrence River

GREAT PLAINS

Great Lakes

APPALACHIAN MTS.

40° N

Colorado R.

Missouri R.

Mississippi R.

ATLANTIC OCEAN

IBERI PENIN.

Rio Grande

Gulf of Mexico

TROPIC OF CANCER

West Indies

20° N

Hawaiian Islands

Caribbean Sea

Fout Djallo

PACIFIC OCEAN

Galápagos Islands

Orinoco R.

GUIANA HIGHLANDS

0°

EQUATOR

Amazon R.

N

W — E

S

POLYNESIA

AMAZON BASIN

A N D E S

SOUTH AMERICA

BRAZILIAN HIGHLANDS

KEY
Elevation

Feet	Meters
15,000	4,572
10,000	3,048
6,000	1,829
3,000	914
1,000	305
500	152
Sea level	Sea level

20° S

TROPIC OF CAPRICORN

0   1,000 mi

0   1,000 km

Robinson Projection

ATLANTIC OCEAN

PAMPAS

Río de la Plata

40° S

PATAGONIA

Cape Horn

160° W 140° W 120° W 100° W 80° W 60° W 40° W 20° W

60° S

SOUTHERN OCEAN

Drake Passage

ANTARCTIC CIRCLE

ANTARCTIC PENINSULA

Weddell Sea

80° S

ANTARCTICA

RCTIC OCEAN

ANDINAVIA

Baltic
Sea

NORTH EUROPEAN PLAIN

EUROPE

Black Sea

Mediterranean Sea

AHARA

AHEL

AFRICA

CONGO
BASIN

Cape of
od Hope

KALAHARI
DESERT

Kara
Sea

URAL MOUNTAINS

Ob River

Volga River

Aral
Sea

CAUCASUS
MTS

Caspian
Sea

IRANIAN
PLATEAU

Persian
Gulf

ARABIAN
PENINSULA

Red Sea

Nile R.

ETHIOPIAN
HIGHLANDS

Congo

Lake
Victoria

Serengeti
Plain

Zambezi R.

Madagascar

SIBERIA

Yenisey River

Lena River

CHERSKIY RANGE

ARCTIC CIRCLE

ASIA

ALTAY SHAN

TIAN SHAN

HINDU
KUSH

KUNLUN SHAN

PLATEAU
OF TIBET

HIMALAYAS

GOBI

Lake
Baikal

Amur River

Sea of
Okhotsk

Sea of
Japan
(East
Sea)

Hokkaido

Honshu

NORTH
CHINA
PLAIN

Huang R.

Chang R.

Yellow
Sea

East
China
Sea

DECCAN
PLATEAU

Arabian
Sea

Bay of
Bengal

Sri
Lanka

INDOCHINA
PENINSULA

South
China
Sea

Taiwan

TROPIC OF CANCER

Philippine
Sea

Philippine
Islands

Malay
Peninsula

Borneo

Sulawesi

Sumatra

Java Sea

Java

Lesser Sunda
Islands

New
Guinea

Arafura Sea

Coral Sea

**PACIFIC
OCEAN**

M I C R O N E S I A

M E L A N E S I A

**INDIAN
OCEAN**

AUSTRALIA

Great Sandy
Desert

Great Victoria
Desert

GREAT DIVIDING RANGE

TROPIC OF CAPRICORN

Tasman
Sea

New
Zealand

Tasmania

20° E   40° E   60° E   80° E   100° E   120° E   140° E   160° E

SOUTHERN OCEAN

ANTARCTIC CIRCLE

ANTARCTICA

80° N

60° N

40° N

20° N

0°

20° S

40° S

60° S

80° S

North and South America: Political

KEY
— National border
✪ Capital city
○ Other city

ASIA
ARCTIC OCEAN
Bering Strait
Bering Sea
Beaufort Sea
ALASKA (U.S.)
GREENLAND (Denmark)
Baffin Bay
EUROPE
Great Bear Lake
Great Slave Lake
Hudson Bay
Labrador Sea
CANADA
Lake Winnipeg
Great Lakes
Ottawa
Toronto
Chicago
UNITED STATES
San Francisco
New York City
Washington, D.C.
ATLANTIC OCEAN
Mississippi R.
Ohio R.
Los Angeles
Dallas
Rio Grande
HAWAII (U.S.)
TROPIC OF CANCER
MEXICO
Gulf of Mexico
Nassau
BAHAMAS
DOMINICAN REPUBLIC
PUERTO RICO (U.S.)
VIRGIN ISLANDS (U.S.)
ST. KITTS AND NEVIS
ANTIGUA AND BARBUDA
GUADELOUPE (France)
DOMINICA
MARTINIQUE (France)
ST. LUCIA
BARBADOS
ST. VINCENT AND THE GRENADINES
GRENADA
TRINIDAD AND TOBAGO
FRENCH GUIANA (France)
Havana
CUBA
JAMAICA
Kingston
Port-au-Prince
HAITI
Santo Domingo
Mexico City
Belmopan
BELIZE
GUATEMALA
HONDURAS
Guatemala
Tegucigalpa
Caribbean Sea
San Salvador
NICARAGUA
Caracas
EL SALVADOR
Managua
Panama
San José
VENEZUELA
Georgetown
Paramaribo
COSTA RICA
PACIFIC OCEAN
PANAMA
Bogotá
COLOMBIA
GUYANA
SURINAME
EQUATOR
Quito
ECUADOR
GALÁPAGOS ISLANDS (Ecuador)
Amazon R.
BRAZIL
São Francisco R.
Lima
PERU
La Paz
Brasília
Lake Titicaca
BOLIVIA
Sucre
Paraná R.
20° S
TROPIC OF CAPRICORN
CHILE
PARAGUAY
Rio de Janeiro
Asunción
São Paulo
0   1,000 mi
0   1,000 km
Azimuthal Equal-Area Projection
Santiago
URUGUAY
Montevideo
ATLANTIC OCEAN
Buenos Aires
Rio de la Plata
ARGENTINA
40° S
FALKLAND ISLANDS (U.K.)
Cape Horn
Tierra del Fuego

180°   160° W   140° W   120° W   100° W   80° W   60° W   40° W   20° W   0°

80° N
ARCTIC CIRCLE
60° N
40° N
20° N
0°
20° S
40° S

794

North and South America: Physical

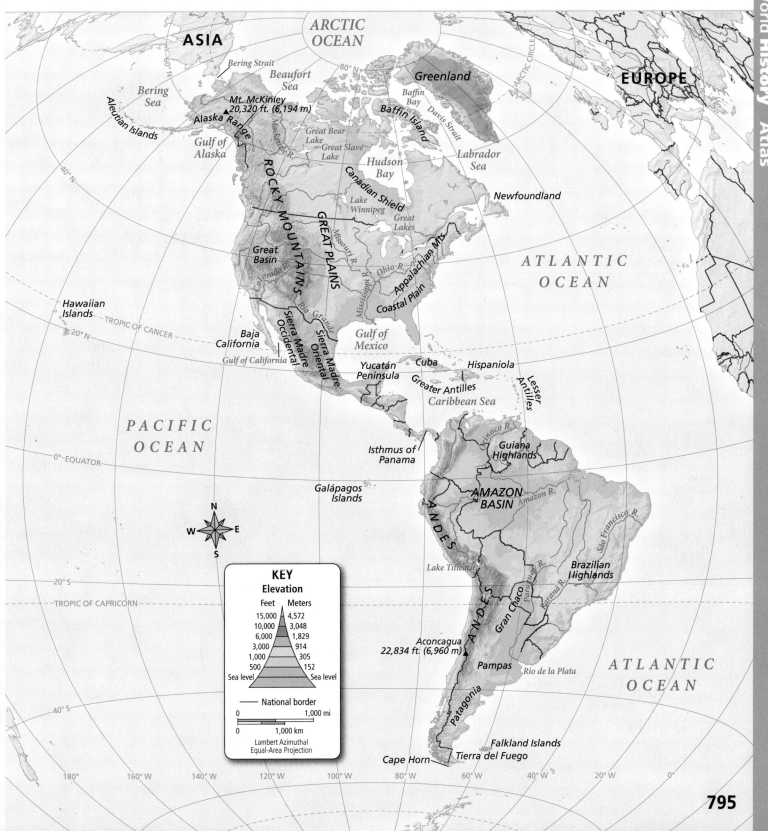

ASIA

ARCTIC OCEAN

EUROPE

Bering Strait

Beaufort Sea

Bering Sea

Greenland

Baffin Bay

Baffin Island

Davis Strait

Mt. McKinley
20,320 ft. (6,194 m)
Alaska Range

Aleutian Islands

Gulf of Alaska

Mackenzie R.

Great Bear Lake

Great Slave Lake

Hudson Bay

Labrador Sea

Newfoundland

ROCKY MOUNTAINS

Canadian Shield

Lake Winnipeg

Great Lakes

ATLANTIC OCEAN

GREAT PLAINS

Great Basin

Colorado R.

Missouri R.

Mississippi R.

Ohio R.

Appalachian Mts.

Coastal Plain

Hawaiian Islands

TROPIC OF CANCER

Baja California

Sierra Madre Occidental

Sierra Madre Oriental

Rio Grande

Gulf of Mexico

Gulf of California

Yucatán Peninsula

Cuba

Hispaniola

Greater Antilles

Lesser Antilles

Caribbean Sea

PACIFIC OCEAN

Isthmus of Panama

Orinoco R.

Guiana Highlands

0° EQUATOR

Galápagos Islands

AMAZON BASIN

Amazon R.

ANDES

São Francisco R.

Lake Titicaca

Brazilian Highlands

20° S

TROPIC OF CAPRICORN

Gran Chaco

Paraguay R.

Paraná R.

ANDES

Aconcagua
22,834 ft. (6,960 m)

Pampas

Río de la Plata

ATLANTIC OCEAN

Patagonia

Falkland Islands

40° S

Cape Horn

Tierra del Fuego

KEY
Elevation

Feet	Meters
15,000	4,572
10,000	3,048
6,000	1,829
3,000	914
1,000	305
500	152
Sea level	Sea level

National border

0   1,000 mi

0   1,000 km

Lambert Azimuthal
Equal-Area Projection

United States: Political

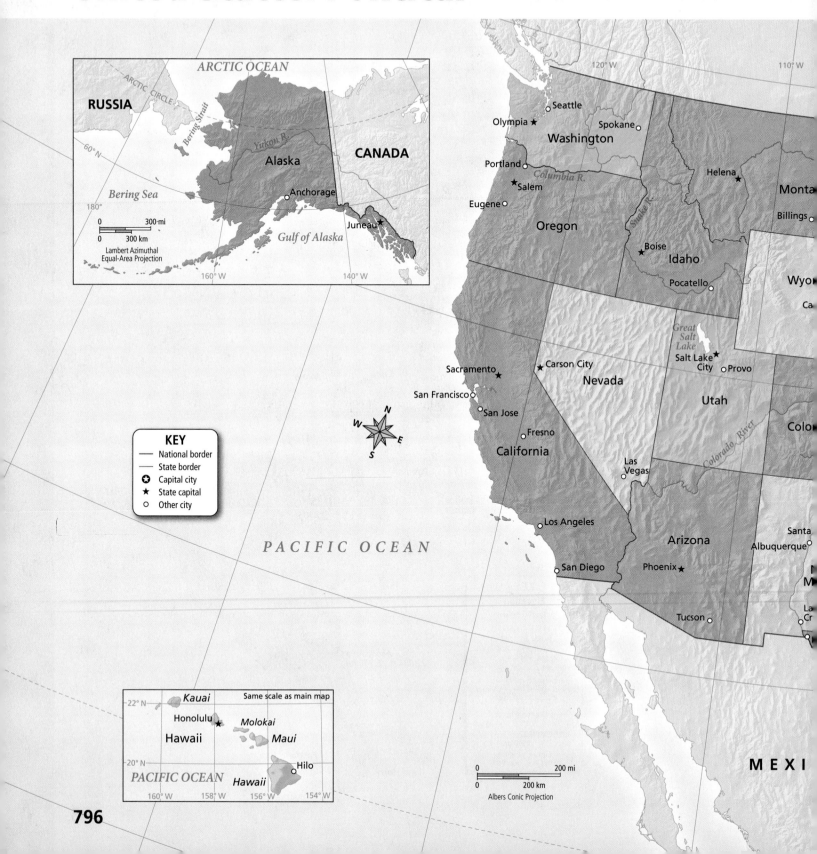

ARCTIC OCEAN

RUSSIA

ARCTIC CIRCLE

Bering Strait

60° N

Yukon R.

Alaska

CANADA

Bering Sea

180°

Anchorage

0   300 mi
0   300 km
Lambert Azimuthal
Equal-Area Projection

Gulf of Alaska

Juneau ★

160° W   140° W

KEY
— National border
— State border
✪ Capital city
★ State capital
○ Other city

120° W   110° W

Seattle ○
Olympia ★   Spokane ○
Washington

Portland ○
Columbia R.   Salem ★   Helena ★
Eugene ○   Mont

Oregon   Billings ○

Snake R.

Boise ★
Idaho

Wyo
Pocatello ○

Great
Salt
Lake   Ca

Salt Lake ★
City   City ○ Provo

Sacramento ★   ● Carson City   Utah
San Francisco ○   Nevada

San Jose ○   Colo
Colorado River

Fresno ○

California

Las
Vegas ○

Santa
Los Angeles ○   Arizona   Albuquerque ○

PACIFIC OCEAN

San Diego ○   Phoenix ★   M

La
Cr

Tucson ○

22° N   Kauai   Same scale as main map

Honolulu ★   Molokai

Hawaii   Maui

20° N   Hilo ○

PACIFIC OCEAN   Hawaii

160° W 158° W 156° W 154° W

0   200 mi
0   200 km
Albers Conic Projection

MEXI

796

CANADA

North Dakota

Bismarck★
Fargo○

Minnesota

South Dakota

Pierre★
Minneapolis○ St. Paul○

Sioux Falls○

Lake
Superior

Green
Bay○

Wisconsin

Madison★
Milwaukee○

Lake Michigan

Michigan

Grand
Rapids○
Lansing★
Detroit○

Lake
Huron

Lake Ontario

Lake Erie

Cleveland○

Maine

Augusta★

Vermont
Montpelier★
New
Hampshire

Portland○

Concord★

Boston★
Providence★
Rhode Island

New
York
Albany★

Rochester○

Buffalo○

Massachusetts

Hartford★
Connecticut

Nebraska

Omaha○
Lincoln★

Iowa

Missouri R.

Cedar
Rapids○
Des
Moines★

Illinois

Chicago○

Fort
Wayne○

Indiana

Indianapolis★

Springfield★

Ohio

Columbus★
Dayton○

Cincinnati○

Pennsylvania
Harrisburg★

Pittsburgh○

New York City

Trenton★
New Jersey

Philadelphia○

Dover★
Delaware

Baltimore○

West
Virginia

Washington,
D.C. Maryland

Annapolis○

Kansas

Topeka★
Kansas
City○

Wichita○

Arkansas River

Jefferson
City★
Missouri

St. Louis○

Ohio River

Louisville○

Kentucky

Frankfort★

Charleston★

Richmond★

Virginia

Norfolk○

Oklahoma

Oklahoma
City★

Tulsa○

Fort Smith○

Little Rock★

Arkansas

Red River

Nashville★
Tennessee

Knoxville○

Memphis○

Tennessee R.

North Carolina

Raleigh★

Charlotte○

Texas

Fort
Worth○ ○Dallas

San
Antonio○

Austin★

Houston○

Rio Grande

Shreveport○

Louisiana

Baton★
Rouge

Mississippi

Jackson★

Mississippi R.

Gulfport○
New Orleans○

Mobile○

Alabama

Birmingham○

Montgomery★

Atlanta★
Augusta○

Georgia

Columbus○

South Carolina

Columbia★

Charleston○

Savannah○

ATLANTIC
OCEAN

Tallahassee★

Jacksonville○

Florida

Orlando○

Tampa○

Gulf of Mexico

Miami○

Europe: Political

KEY
— National border
⊛ Capital city
○ Other city

0 ——— 200 mi
0 ——— 200 km
Lambert Conformal Conic Projection

ARCTIC OCEAN

Barents Sea

ARCTIC CIRCLE

ICELAND
Reykjavík

Lapland

FAROE ISLANDS
(Denmark)

White Sea

SWEDEN

FINLAND
Tampere

NORWAY

Bergen

Gulf of Bothnia

Helsinki
St. Petersburg

RUSSIA

20° W

60° N

70° N

North Sea

Oslo
Stockholm
Göteborg

Tallinn
Gulf of Finland
ESTONIA

Nizhni Novgorod

Glasgow

Riga
LATVIA

Moscow

Samara

IRELAND
Dublin
UNITED KINGDOM
Manchester
Birmingham

DENMARK
Copenhagen

LITHUANIA
Vilnius
KALININGRAD
(Russia)
Minsk

Volga R.

Baltic Sea

BELARUS

London

The Hague
NETHERLANDS
Amsterdam
Hamburg
Berlin

Warsaw

Kiev

English Channel

Brussels
BELGIUM
GERMANY
Frankfurt
LUXEMBOURG

POLAND

UKRAINE

Donets'k

ATLANTIC OCEAN

Paris

FRANCE
LIECHTENSTEIN

Prague
CZECH REPUBLIC
Vienna
Munich
SLOVAKIA
Bratislava
Budapest

MOLDOVA
Chişinău

Sea of Azov

Caspian Sea

10° W

Bern
SWITZERLAND
Lyon
Milan
SLOVENIA
Ljubljana
Zagreb
CROATIA
AUSTRIA
HUNGARY

Timişoara
Belgrade
ROMANIA
Bucharest
Constanţa

Black Sea

ASIA

Toulouse

SAN MARINO
BOSNIA AND HERZEGOVINA
Sarajevo
SERBIA
Priština

Danube R.

BULGARIA

Marseille

ANDORRA
MONACO
Corsica
ITALY
Rome
MONTENEGRO
Podgorica
Tirana
KOSOVO
Sofia
Skopje
MACEDONIA
Istanbul
TURKEY
Ankara

PORTUGAL
Madrid
Barcelona

Bay of Biscay

SPAIN
Lisbon
Seville

VATICAN CITY
Naples
ALBANIA

GREECE

GIBRALTAR
(U.K.)

Balearic Islands
Sardinia

M e d i t e r r a n e a n

Tyrrhenian Sea

Sicily

Ionian Sea

Athens

Valletta

MALTA

S e a

AFRICA

30° N

0°

10° E

20° E

30° E

40° E

798

Europe: Physical

ARCTIC OCEAN

Barents Sea

Kola Peninsula

White Sea

URAL MOUNTAINS

Iceland

Norwegian Sea

ARCTIC CIRCLE

70° N

Kjølen Mountains

SCANDINAVIAN PENINSULA

Gulf of Bothnia

Lake Ladoga

Northern Dvina R.

60° N

20° W

Faroe Islands

Shetland Islands

Lake Vänern

Gulf of Finland

Volga River

North Sea

Gotland

Baltic Sea

Jutland

Ireland

Great Britain

Sjælland

NORTH EUROPEAN PLAIN

Central Russian Upland

50° N

Thames R.

Elbe R.

Vistula R.

Oder R.

Volga River

English Channel

Seine R.

Rhine R.

Dnieper River

ATLANTIC OCEAN

10° W

Bay of Biscay

Loire R.

Danube R.

Dniester R.

Don River

Garonne R.

Massif Central

A L P S

Carpathian Mountains

Sea of Azov

Crimea

CAUCASUS MTS.

Mount Elbrus 18,510 ft (5,642 m)

Caspian Sea

Mont Blanc 15,781 ft (4,810 m)

Rhône R.

Po River

Dinaric Alps

Transylvanian Alps

Danube River

Black Sea

Pyrenees

Ebro R.

Douro R.

Apennines

Adriatic Sea

Balkan Mts.

Bosporus

ASIA

Meseta

IBERIAN PENINSULA

Tagus R.

Corsica

ITALIAN PENINSULA

BALKAN PENINSULA

Pindus Mts.

Dardanelles

Guadalquivir R.

Balearic Islands

Sardinia

Tyrrhenian Sea

Aegean Sea

Sicily

Ionian Sea

Peloponnisos

M e d i t e r r a n e a n

Maltese Islands

Crete

S e a

AFRICA

10° E

20° E

30° E

40° E

30° N

0°

KEY
Elevation

Feet	Meters
10,000	3,048
6,000	1,829
3,000	914
1,000	305
500	152
Sea level	Sea level

0   200 mi

0   200 km

Lambert Conformal Conic Projection

Africa: Political

KEY
— National border
-- Disputed border
✪ Capital city
○ Other city

EUROPE

ASIA

Mediterranean Sea

MADEIRA
(Portugal)

Strait of Gibraltar

Algiers ✪   Tunis ✪

TUNISIA   Tripoli ✪

Rabat ✪

Casablanca ○

MOROCCO

CANARY
ISLANDS
(Spain)

ALGERIA   LIBYA   EGYPT

Alexandria ○

Cairo ✪

Nile R.

Red Sea

WESTERN SAHARA
(under Moroccan control)

TROPIC OF CANCER

MAURITANIA   MALI   NIGER   CHAD   SUDAN   ERITREA

Nouakchott ✪   Khartoum ✪   Asmara ✪

CAPE
VERDE

Niger R.   *Blue Nile R.*   Gulf of Aden

Dakar   Niamey ✪   N'Djamena ✪

Praia ✪

SENEGAL   Bamako ✪   *Lake Chad*   DJIBOUTI

GAMBIA   BURKINA FASO   Kano ○   *White Nile R.*   Djibouti ✪

Banjul   BENIN   NIGERIA

Bissau   Ouagadougou ✪   Abuja ✪

GUINEA-   GUINEA   TOGO

BISSAU   Conakry ✪   IVORY   GHANA   Lagos ○   CAMEROON   Addis Ababa ✪

Freetown ✪   COAST   Porto-Novo ✪   CENTRAL AFRICAN   ETHIOPIA

SIERRA LEONE   Yamoussoukro ✪   Lomé ✪   REPUBLIC

Monrovia ✪   Abidjan ○   Accra ✪   Bangui ✪   *Lake Turkana*

LIBERIA   Yaoundé ✪   SOMALIA

Gulf of Guinea   Malabo ✪   UGANDA   KENYA   Mogadishu ○

EQUATORIAL GUINEA   Kisangani ○   Kampala ✪

SÃO TOMÉ AND PRÍNCIPE   *Congo R.*   RWANDA   Nairobi ✪

EQUATOR   São   Libreville ✪   Kigali ✪   *Lake Victoria*   Mombasa ○   Victoria ✪

Tomé   GABON   BURUNDI

CONGO   DEMOCRATIC   Bujumbura ✪   SEYCHELLES

Brazzaville ✪   REPUBLIC   Dodoma ✪   Zanzibar ○

CABINDA   Kinshasa ✪   OF THE CONGO   *Lake Tanganyika*   Dar es Salaam ○

(Angola)   TANZANIA

Luanda ✪   *Lake Nyasa*   Moroni ✪

ATLANTIC   Lubumbashi ○   COMOROS

OCEAN   ANGOLA   MALAWI

ZAMBIA   Lilongwe ✪

Lusaka ✪   *Zambezi R.*   MADAGASCAR   Antananarivo ✪

MOZAMBIQUE   MAURITIUS

Harare ✪   Port Louis ✪

NAMIBIA   ZIMBABWE   RÉUNION

(France)

TROPIC OF CAPRICORN   Windhoek ✪   BOTSWANA   *Mozambique Channel*

Gaborone ✪   Pretoria ✪   Maputo ✪

0   600 mi   *Limpopo R.*   Mbabane ✪

0   600 km   Johannesburg ○   SWAZILAND

Lambert Azimuthal Equal-Area Projection   Bloemfontein ○   Maseru ✪   Durban ○

LESOTHO

Cape Town ✪   SOUTH AFRICA

Cape of Good Hope   *Cape Agulhas*   INDIAN

OCEAN

800

Africa: Physical

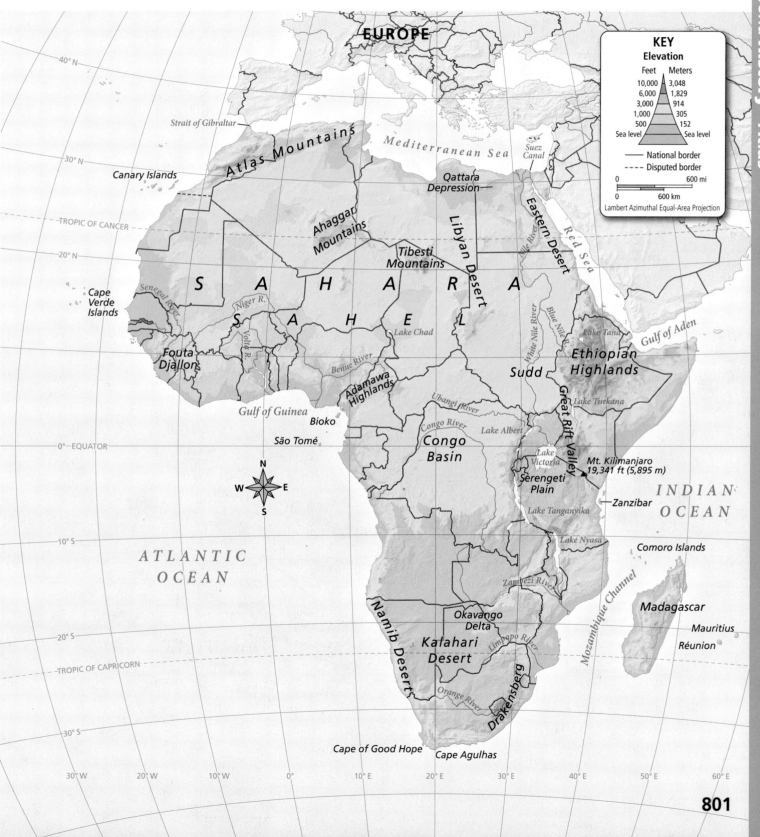

EUROPE

Strait of Gibraltar

Canary Islands

Atlas Mountains

Mediterranean Sea

Suez Canal

Qattara Depression

TROPIC OF CANCER

Ahaggar Mountains

Tibesti Mountains

Libyan Desert

Eastern Desert

Red Sea

20° N

S A H A R A

Cape Verde Islands

Senegal River

Niger R.

S A H E L

Lake Chad

White Nile River

Blue Nile R.

Nile River

Lake Tana

Gulf of Aden

Fouta Djallon

Volta R.

Benue River

Adamawa Highlands

Sudd

Ethiopian Highlands

Gulf of Guinea

Bioko

São Tomé

Ubangi River

Congo River

Lake Albert

Lake Turkana

0°—EQUATOR

Congo Basin

Lake Victoria

Great Rift Valley

Mt. Kilimanjaro 19,341 ft (5,895 m)

INDIAN OCEAN

Serengeti Plain

Zanzibar

N
W   E
S

Lake Tanganyika

10° S

ATLANTIC OCEAN

Lake Nyasa

Comoro Islands

Zambezi River

Mozambique Channel

Madagascar

Namib Desert

Okavango Delta

Kalahari Desert

Limpopo River

Mauritius

Réunion

20° S

TROPIC OF CAPRICORN

Orange River

Drakensberg

30° S

Cape of Good Hope

Cape Agulhas

30° W   20° W   10° W   0°   10° E   20° E   30° E   40° E   50° E   60° E

KEY
Elevation

Feet	Meters
10,000	3,048
6,000	1,829
3,000	914
1,000	305
500	152
Sea level	Sea level

National border
Disputed border

0   600 mi
0   600 km
Lambert Azimuthal Equal-Area Projection

Asia: Political

EUROPE

ARCTIC OCEAN

East Siberian Sea

Bering Sea

Barents Sea

Kara Sea

Laptev Sea

RUSSIA

St. Petersburg

Moscow

Nizhni Novgorod

Perm'

Samara

Yekaterinburg

Omsk

Novosibirsk

Astana

KAZAKHSTAN

Aral Sea

Lake Balkhash

Ob R.

Ob R.

Yenisey R.

Lena R.

Lena R.

Amur R.

Sakhalin Island

Kuril Islands

Sea of Okhotsk

Vladivostok

JAPAN

Tokyo

Osaka

PACIFIC OCEAN

Mediterranean Sea

Istanbul

Ankara

TURKEY

Black Sea

Caspian Sea

GEORGIA

Tbilisi

CYPRUS

Nicosia

ARMENIA

Yerevan

AZERBAIJAN

Baku

LEBANON

Beirut

SYRIA

Damascus

ISRAEL

Jerusalem

Amman

JORDAN

Baghdad

IRAQ

Kuwait

KUWAIT

SAUDI ARABIA

Mecca

Riyadh

BAHRAIN

Manama

QATAR

Doha

Abu Dhabi

UNITED ARAB EMIRATES

Muscat

OMAN

Sanaa

YEMEN

Red Sea

Gulf of Aden

SOCOTRA (Yemen)

AFRICA

TURKMENISTAN

Tehran

Ashgabat

IRAN

Mashhad

UZBEKISTAN

Bishkek

Tashkent

KYRGYZSTAN

TAJIKISTAN

Dushanbe

Almaty

AFGHANISTAN

Kabul

Islamabad

PAKISTAN

Karachi

New Delhi

NEPAL

Kathmandu

BHUTAN

Thimphu

BANGLADESH

Dhaka

INDIA

Ganges R.

Calcutta (Kolkata)

MYANMAR (BURMA)

Mumbai (Bombay)

Chennai (Madras)

Arabian Sea

Bay of Bengal

Andaman Sea

Yangon

MONGOLIA

Ulaanbaatar

CHINA

Beijing

Tianjin

NORTH KOREA

P'yongyang

Seoul

SOUTH KOREA

Yellow Sea

Shanghai

Wuhan

Huang R.

Chang R.

Chongqing

East China Sea

Ryukyu Islands

Taipei

TAIWAN

Guangzhou

Hong Kong

Hanoi

LAOS

Vientiane

South China Sea

Philippine Sea

Manila

PHILIPPINES

THAILAND

Bangkok

Phnom Penh

CAMBODIA

VIETNAM

Ho Chi Minh City

BRUNEI

Bandar Seri Begawan

MALAYSIA

Kuala Lumpur

Singapore

SINGAPORE

Borneo

INDONESIA

Sumatra

Sulawesi

New Guinea

Dili

EAST TIMOR

Timor

Jakarta

Java

Surabaya

SRI LANKA

Colombo

Male

MALDIVES

EQUATOR

INDIAN OCEAN

AUSTRALIA

ARCTIC CIRCLE

TROPIC OF CANCER

50° N

60° N

40° N

30° N

20° N

10° N

10° S

20° S

160° W

170° W

180°

170° E

160° E

150° E

140° E

130° E

120° E

110° E

100° E

90° E

80° E

70° E

60° E

50° E

KEY

- - - Disputed border
—— National border
⊛ Capital city
○ Other city

N
S
E
W

0   1,000 mi
0   1,000 km

Lambert Azimuthal Equal-Area Projection

Asia: Physical

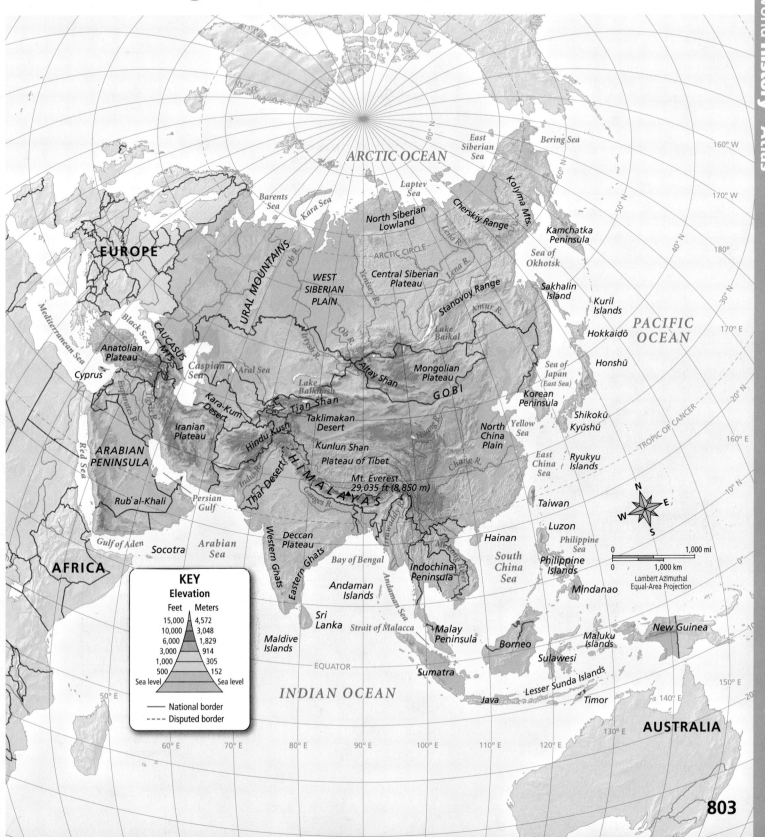

ARCTIC OCEAN

East Siberian Sea

Bering Sea

Barents Sea

Kara Sea

Laptev Sea

Cherskiy Range

Kolyma Mts.

North Siberian Lowland

Kamchatka Peninsula

EUROPE

URAL MOUNTAINS

ARCTIC CIRCLE

Ob R.

Lena R.

WEST SIBERIAN PLAIN

Central Siberian Plateau

Sea of Okhotsk

Yenisey R.

Sakhalin Island

Kuril Islands

Stanovoy Range

PACIFIC OCEAN

Mediterranean Sea

Black Sea

CAUCASUS MTS.

Anatolian Plateau

Caspian Sea

Aral Sea

Ob R.

Irtysh R.

Altay Shan

Lake Baikal

Amur R.

Hokkaidō

Honshū

Cyprus

Lake Balkhash

Tian Shan

Mongolian Plateau

GOBI

Sea of Japan (East Sea)

Kara-Kum Desert

Taklimakan Desert

Korean Peninsula

Shikoku

Kyūshū

Euphrates R.

Tigris R.

Iranian Plateau

Hindu Kush

Kunlun Shan

Plateau of Tibet

Huang R.

North China Plain

Yellow Sea

Ryukyu Islands

ARABIAN PENINSULA

Red Sea

Indus R.

Thar Desert

HIMALAYAS

Mt. Everest 29,035 ft (8,850 m)

Ganges R.

Chang R.

East China Sea

TROPIC OF CANCER

Rub' al-Khali

Persian Gulf

Taiwan

Gulf of Aden

Socotra

Arabian Sea

Deccan Plateau

Western Ghats

Eastern Ghats

Bay of Bengal

Irrawaddy R.

Andaman Sea

Indochina Peninsula

Mekong R.

Hainan

South China Sea

Luzon

Philippine Sea

Philippine Islands

Mindanao

N

W   E

S

AFRICA

Andaman Islands

Sri Lanka

Maldive Islands

Strait of Malacca

Malay Peninsula

Borneo

Sulawesi

Maluku Islands

New Guinea

0   1,000 mi

0   1,000 km

Lambert Azimuthal Equal-Area Projection

EQUATOR

Sumatra

Lesser Sunda Islands

Timor

INDIAN OCEAN

Java

AUSTRALIA

KEY
Elevation

Feet	Meters
15,000	4,572
10,000	3,048
6,000	1,829
3,000	914
1,000	305
500	152
Sea level	Sea level

——— National border

– – – Disputed border

160° W

170° W

180°

170° E

160° E

150° E

140° E

130° E

120° E

110° E

100° E

90° E

80° E

70° E

60° E

50° E

80° N

60° N

50° N

40° N

30° N

20° N

10° N

Australia and the Pacific

TROPIC OF CANCER

Philippine
Sea

NORTHERN
MARIANA
ISLANDS
(U.S.)

GUAM
(U.S.)

MARSHALL
ISLANDS

● Melekeok   Caroline Islands   ● Palikir   ☆ Majuro

PALAU

FEDERATED STATES
OF MICRONESIA

EQUATOR

☆ Tarawa

NAURU ☆ Yaren   K I R I B A T I

PAPUA
NEW GUINEA

SOLOMON
ISLANDS

TUVALU

TOKELAU
(New Zealand)

Timor
Sea

Arafura Sea

Port
Moresby

☆ Honiara

☆ Funafuti

SAMOA

Apia ☆

AMERICAN
SAMOA
(U.S.)

Cape
York
Peninsula

Coral
Sea

VANUATU

FIJI

NIUE
(New Zealand)

Kimberley
Plateau

Great Sandy
Desert

Great Dividing Range

Great Barrier Reef

● Port-Vila

Suva

NEW
CALEDONIA
(France)

☆ Nuku'alofa

COOK
ISLANDS
(New Zealand)

TROPIC OF CAPRICORN

AUSTRALIA

TONGA

PACIFIC
OCEAN

Gibson
Desert

Simpson
Desert

Great
Artesian
Basin

○ Brisbane

Great Victoria Desert

Darling River

Nullarbor Plain

Darling Range

Perth ○

Great
Australian
Bight

Adelaide ○

Murray
River

○ Sydney

☆ Canberra

○ Melbourne

Tasman Sea

○ Auckland

North
Island

Bass Strait

Cook Strait

NEW
ZEALAND

☆ Wellington

Tasmania

South Island

INDIAN OCEAN

☆ Hobart

○ Christchurch

● Dunedin

KEY
Elevation

Feet	Meters
6,000	1,829
3,000	914
1,000	305
500	152
Sea level	Sea level

— National border

☆ Capital city

○ Other city

0   600 mi

0   600 km

Mercator Projection

The Arctic

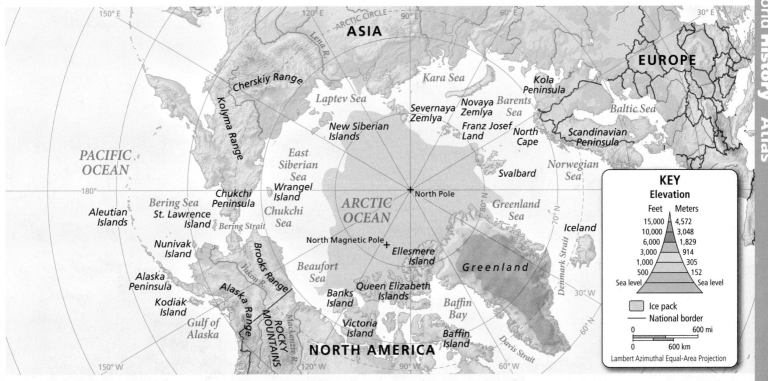

150° E · 120° E · ARCTIC CIRCLE · 90° E · 60° E · 30° E

ASIA

Lena R.

EUROPE

Cherskiy Range

Kara Sea

Kola Peninsula

Kolyma Range

Laptev Sea

Severnaya Zemlya

Novaya Zemlya

Barents Sea

Baltic Sea

New Siberian Islands

Franz Josef Land

North Cape

Scandinavian Peninsula

PACIFIC OCEAN

East Siberian Sea

Svalbard

Norwegian Sea

180°

Wrangel Island

ARCTIC OCEAN

North Pole

Greenland Sea

70° N

Chukchi Peninsula

Bering Sea

Chukchi Sea

Iceland

Aleutian Islands

St. Lawrence Island

Bering Strait

North Magnetic Pole +

Ellesmere Island

Greenland

Nunivak Island

Beaufort Sea

Alaska Peninsula

Brooks Range

Yukon R.

Banks Island

Queen Elizabeth Islands

Kodiak Island

Alaska Range

ROCKY MOUNTAINS

Mackenzie R.

Victoria Island

Baffin Bay

30° W

Gulf of Alaska

Baffin Island

150° W

120° W

90° W

60° W

Davis Strait

60° N

NORTH AMERICA

KEY

Elevation

Feet	Meters
15,000	4,572
10,000	3,048
6,000	1,829
3,000	914
1,000	305
500	152
Sea level	Sea level

Ice pack

National border

0 — 600 mi
0 — 600 km

Lambert Azimuthal Equal-Area Projection

Antarctica

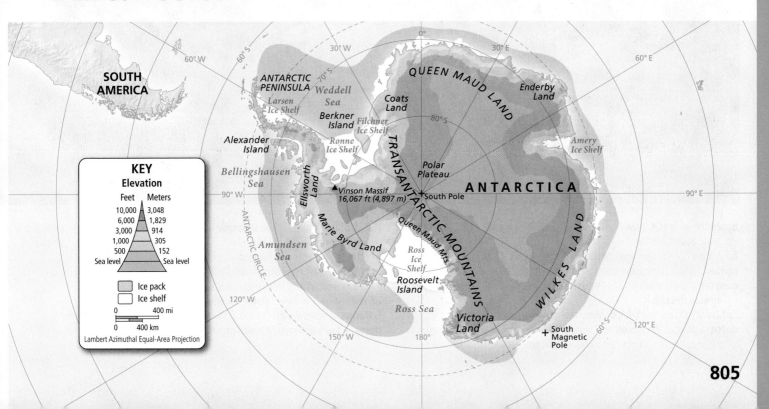

SOUTH AMERICA

60° W

60° S

30° W

0°

30° E

60° E

ANTARCTIC PENINSULA

70° S

Weddell Sea

QUEEN MAUD LAND

Enderby Land

Larsen Ice Shelf

Coats Land

Berkner Island

Filchner Ice Shelf

Alexander Island

Ronne Ice Shelf

80° S

Amery Ice Shelf

Bellingshausen Sea

Ellsworth Land

TRANSANTARCTIC MOUNTAINS

KEY

Elevation

Feet	Meters
10,000	3,048
6,000	1,829
3,000	914
1,000	305
500	152
Sea level	Sea level

Ice pack

Ice shelf

0 — 400 mi
0 — 400 km

Lambert Azimuthal Equal-Area Projection

90° W

▲ Vinson Massif 16,067 ft (4,897 m)

Polar Plateau

+ South Pole

ANTARCTICA

90° E

Marie Byrd Land

Queen Maud Mts.

WILKES LAND

ANTARCTIC CIRCLE

Amundsen Sea

Ross Ice Shelf

Roosevelt Island

120° W

120° E

Ross Sea

Victoria Land

+ South Magnetic Pole

150° W

180°

60° S

Landforms and Water Features

volcano

basin

mesa

plateau

butte

canyon

bay

strait

island

isthmus

peninsula

basin an area that is lower than surrounding land areas; some basins are filled with water

bay a part of a larger body of water that extends into the land

butte a small, high, flat-topped landform with cliff-like sides

canyon a deep, narrow valley with steep sides; often has a stream flowing through it

cataract a large waterfall or steep rapids

delta a plain at the mouth of a river, often triangular in shape, formed when material is deposited by flowing water

flood plain a broad plain on either side of a river, formed when sediment settles during floods

glacier a huge, slow-moving mass of snow and ice

hill an area that rises above surrounding land and has a rounded top; lower and usually less steep than a mountain

island an area of land completely surrounded by water

isthmus a narrow strip of land that connects two larger areas of land

mesa a high, flat-topped landform with cliff-like sides; larger than a butte

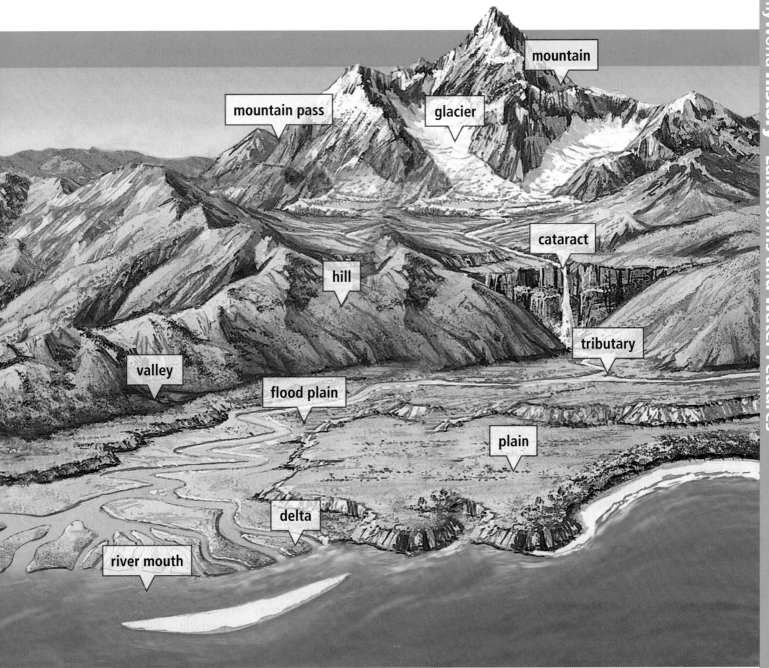

mountain a landform that rises steeply at least 2,000 feet (610 meters) above surrounding land; usually wide at the bottom and rising to a narrow peak or ridge

mountain pass a gap between mountains

peninsula an area of land almost completely surrounded by water and connected to the mainland by an isthmus

plain a large area of flat or gently rolling land

plateau a large, flat area that rises above the surrounding land; at least one side has a steep slope

river mouth the point where a river enters a lake or sea

strait a narrow stretch of water that connects two larger bodies of water

tributary a river or stream that flows into a larger river

valley a low stretch of land between mountains or hills; land that is drained by a river

volcano an opening in Earth's surface through which molten rock, ash, and gases from Earth's interior escape

Glossary

A

absolute location exact position on Earth in terms of longitude and latitude (p. 10)
ubicación absoluta posición exacta en la Tierra según la longitud y la latitud

absolute monarchy system of government in which the monarch has unlimited power over the government (p. 592)
monarquía absoluta sistema de gobierno en el que el poder del monarca es ilimitado

Academy school of philosophy founded by Plato (p. 345)
Academia escuela de filosofía fundada por Platón

acropolis "high city" in Greek; the upper part of an ancient Greek city, where public buildings and the city's defenses were located (p. 305)
acrópolis "ciudad alta" en griego; la parte elevada de una ciudad griega de la antigüedad, donde se ubicaban los edificios públicos y las defensas

Act of Supremacy the 1534 act that made the king of England the leader of the Church of England (p. 751)
Acta de Supremacía el acta de 1534 que convertía al rey en jefe de la Iglesia de Inglaterra

acupuncture therapy that uses needles to cure sickness and stop pain (p. 287)
acupuntura terapia que utiliza agujas para curar enfermedades y controlar el dolor

adapt change (p. 70)
adaptarse cambiar

ahimsa avoiding doing harm to any living thing (p. 216)
ahimsa evitar hacerle daño a un ser viviente

Alexandria city founded by Alexander the Great in Egypt (p. 336)
Alejandría ciudad fundada por Alejandro Magno en Egipto

ally independent state that works with other states to achieve a shared military or political goal (p. 118)
aliado estado independiente que colabora con otros estados para lograr un objetivo militar o político común

alphabet small set of letters or symbols, each of which stands for a single sound (p. 136)
alfabeto conjunto limitado de letras o símbolos, cada uno de los cuales representa un sonido

anatomy study of the structure of the body and its organs (p. 157)
anatomía estudio de la estructura del cuerpo y sus órganos

ancestor worship religious practice of honoring the spirits of the dead (p. 263)
culto de los ancestros práctica religiosa de honrar los espíritus de los muertos

Andes a mountain range that runs along the western edge of South America (p. 602)
Andes cadena montañosa que recorre el borde occidental de América del Sur

animism belief that the natural world is full of spirits (p. 75)
animismo la creencia de que la naturaleza está dotada de alma

annulment an official act ending a marriage (p. 750)
anulación decreto oficial de la terminación de un matrimonio

anthropology study of humankind in all aspects, especially development and culture (pp. 9, 58)
antropología estudio de todos los aspectos de la humanidad, especialmente el desarrollo y la cultura

aqueduct channel that moves water over a long distance (pp. 393, 594)
acueducto canal que transporta agua por largas distancias

Arabic numerals the system of writing numbers we use today (p. 472)
números arábigos sistema de escritura de números que usamos hoy en día

archaeologist scientist who studies human life in the past by examining the things that people left behind (p. 58)
arqueólogo científico que estudia la vida humana del pasado mediante el examen de los objetos que las personas dejaron

archaeology scientific study of ancient cultures through the examination of artifacts and other evidence (p. 9)
arqueología estudio científico de las culturas antiguas mediante el análisis de artefactos y otros tipos de evidencia

archipelago group of islands (p. 548)
archipiélago grupo de islas

aristocracy hereditary class of rulers, Greek for "rule by the best people" (p. 305)
aristocracia clase hereditaria de gobernantes, "gobierno por los mejores" en griego

armada a fleet of warships (p. 753)
armada una flota de barcos de guerra

artifact object made by a human being (pp. 6, 60, 608)
artefacto objeto hecho por un ser humano

artisan skilled worker who practices a handicraft (p. 146)
artesano trabajador especializado que ejerce un oficio manual

Augustus title used by Roman emperors meaning venerable or greatly honored person (p. 383)
Augusto título usado por los emperadores romanos, significa persona venerable o con muchos honores

authoritarian government in which all power is held by a single person or a small group (p. 23)
autoritario gobierno en el que todo el poder es ejercido por un individuo o grupo pequeño

ayllu in Incan society, a group of related families that pooled its resources to meet people's needs (p. 607)
ayllu en la sociedad inca, conjunto de familias emparentadas que juntaban sus recursos para satisfacer sus necesidades

B

baptism ritual cleansing by plunging into water (p. 403)
bautismo limpieza ritual que se realiza sumergiéndose en agua

barbarian word used by Greeks and Romans for all people who did not share their cultures (p. 416)
bárbaro término usado por los griegos y romanos para referirse a los pueblos que no compartían sus culturas

barracks military housing (p. 320)
barracas alojamientos militares

barter trading system in which people exchange goods directly without using money (p. 113)
trueque sistema de comercio en el cual las personas intercambian bienes directamente, sin usar dinero

basin bowl-shaped area (p. 590)
cuenca área en forma de cuenco o vasija

Battle of Marathon Greek victory over the Persian army that ended the First Persian War (p. 329)
Batalla de Maratón victoria griega sobre el ejército persa que terminó la Primera Guerra Médica

Battle of Salamis Greek victory over the Persian navy during the Second Persian War (p. 330)
Batalla de Salamina victoria griega sobre la armada persa durante la Segunda Guerra Médica

Bedouin Arab nomad (p. 451)
beduino nómada árabe

bias unfair preference for or dislike of something (p. 7)
prejuicio preferencia injusta o disgusto por algo

Black Death epidemic of the bubonic plague that killed as many as one third of all Europeans between 1347 and 1352 (p. 696)
Peste Negra epidemia de peste bubónica que causó la muerte de cerca de un tercio de la población europea entre 1347 y 1352

block printing early form of printing invented in China in which text was carved into a block of wood (p. 535)
impresión con bloques forma temprana de impresión inventada en China, en la que el texto se tallaba en un bloque de madera

bond certificate issued by a company or government promising to pay back borrowed money with interest (p. 37)
bono certificado emitido por una compañía o un gobierno que promete pagar el dinero prestado con intereses

Brahman in Hinduism, the supreme cosmic consciousness, spiritual force, or God (p. 215)
Brahman en la religión hindú, la conciencia cósmica suprema, fuerza espiritual, o Dios

Glossary (continued)

Brahmanism religion of Vedic India, based on priests and rituals, particularly sacrifices to the gods (p. 212)
brahmanismo religión de la India védica, basada en sacerdotes y rituales, especialmente sacrificios a los dioses

Brahmin member of the highest Indian caste grouping made up of priests (p. 209)
brahmán miembro de la casta más alta en la India, compuesta de sacerdotes

bubonic plague a deadly infection spread by fleas that live on rats (p. 696)
peste bubónica infección mortal propagada por las pulgas que habitan en las ratas

Buddhism religion that developed out of the teachings of Siddhartha Gautama, the Buddha (p. 538)
budismo religión que se desarrolló a partir de las enseñanzas de Siddhartha Gautama, el Buda

budget plan that shows income and expenses over a period of time (p. 36)
presupuesto plan que muestra los ingresos y los gastos para un período de tiempo

bullion precious metals melted into bars (p. 772)
lingotes metales preciosos fundidos en forma de barra

bureaucracy system of many government officials who carry out government rules and regulations (pp. 147, 236, 516)
burocracia sistema de numerosos funcionarios que ejecutan las normas y reglamentos del gobierno

bushido "the way of the warrior," a strict code of conduct that guided samurai behavior (p. 559)
bushido término japonés que significa "el camino del guerrero", código estricto de conducta que guiaba las acciones de los samuráis

Byzantine word used by historians to describe the eastern Roman empire after the fall of the western Roman empire (p. 432)
bizantino término usado por los historiadores para describir el Imperio Romano oriental después de la caída del Imperio Romano occidental

C

caliph title meaning "successor" in Arabic, used by leaders of the Muslim community who followed Muhammad (p. 463)
califa significa "sucesor" en árabe; título utilizado por los líderes de la comunidad musulmana, seguidores de Mahoma

calligraphy art of beautiful writing (p. 286, 473)
caligrafía arte de escribir con letra bella

capitalism economy based on the private ownership of property and the use of property to compete for profits or gains in a market (p. 780)
capitalismo economía que se basa en la propiedad privada y en el uso de la propiedad para competir por beneficios o ganancias en un mercado

caravan group of people traveling together (p. 495)
caravana grupo de personas que viajan juntas

caravel a small, light ship developed by the Portuguese that performed well on long voyages (p. 768)
carabela nave pequeña y ligera diseñada por los portugueses, especialmente efectiva en viajes largos

cartography the science of making maps and globes (p. 767)
cartografía técnica de trazar mapas y globos terráqueos

caste fixed social class into which a person is born (pp. 209, 504)
casta clase social fija en la que nace una persona

cataract group of rocky rapids (p. 144)
catarata formación de rápidos rocosos

cavalry soldiers who fight while riding horses (p. 124)
caballería soldados que combaten montados a caballo

censor to ban dangerous or offensive ideas, or remove material from published works or prevent its publication (pp. 277, 726)
censurar prohibir ideas peligrosas u ofensivas, o retirar materiales de obras publicadas o impedir su publicación

chaos total disorder and confusion (p. 260)
caos desorden y confusión totales

chinampa artificial island built by the Aztecs (p. 591)
chinampa isla artificial construida por los aztecas

chivalry code of conduct in medieval Europe that required knights to be brave, loyal, and honest (p. 642)
código de Caballería código de conducta en la Europa medieval que requería que los caballeros fueran valerosos, leales y honestos

chorus in ancient Greek drama, a group of people who commented on the action of a play and advised the characters (p. 342)
coro en el teatro griego de la antigüedad, grupos de personas que comentaban sobre la acción de la obra y aconsejaban a los personajes

Christendom large community of Christians spread across the world (p. 639)
cristiandad gran comunidad de cristianos extendida en el mundo entero

chronology list of events arranged in the order in which they occurred (p. 4)
cronología lista de sucesos organizados en el orden en que ocurrieron

circumnavigate to sail completely around (p. 767)
circunnavegar dar una vuelta completa en barco al rededor de algún lugar

citadel fortified area (p. 204)
ciudadela área fortificada

citizen legal member of a country or city-state (pp. 26, 304)
ciudadano miembro legal de un país o ciudad-estado

citizenship membership in a state or community which gives a person civil and political rights and obligations (pp. 243, 315)
ciudadanía membrecía en un estado o comunidad que confiere derechos y obligaciones civiles y políticos a las personas

city-state independent state consisting of a city and its surrounding territory (pp. 22, 112)
ciudad-estado estado independiente que consiste en una ciudad y el territorio aledaño

civic life activities having to do with one's society and community (p. 27)
vida cívica actividades relacionadas con nuestra sociedad o comunidad

civic participation taking part in government (p. 27)
participación cívica tomar parte en asuntos del gobierno

civil service the people who work for a government (p. 280)
servicio civil las personas que trabajan para un gobierno

civil war war between groups from the same country (p. 382)
guerra civil guerra entre grupos de un mismo país

civilization complex society that has cities, a well-organized government, and workers with specialized job skills (p. 93)
civilización sociedad compleja con ciudades, un gobierno organizado y trabajadores con destrezas especializadas

clan group of families with a common ancestor (pp. 72, 550)
clan grupo de familias con un ancestro común

clergy people who are trained and ordained for religious services (p. 631)
clero personas entrenadas y ordenadas para el servicio religioso

colonization establishment of new settlers and their culture in other territories (p. 770)
colonización establecimiento de nuevos pobladores y su cultura en otros territorios

colony group of people living in a new territory with ties to a distant state (p. 135)
colonia grupo de personas que viven en un nuevo territorio que tiene vínculos con un estado distante

Columbian Exchange exchange of people, plants and animals, and ideas between the Eastern Hemiphere and Western Hemisphere (p. 776)
intercambio colombino intercambio de personas, plantas, animales e ideas entre los hemispherios oriental y occidental

command economy economy in which the central government makes all basic economic decisions (p. 33)
economía dirigida sistema económico en el que el gobierno central toma todas las decisiones económicas básicas

commandment an order to do something (p. 174)
mandamiento una orden de hacer algo

commerce buying and selling of goods and services (p. 158)
comercio compra y venta de bienes y servicios

Glossary (continued)

common law a body of law that has developed from custom and from judges' decisions rather than from laws passed by a lawmaking assembly (p. 663)
derecho consuetudinario conjunto de leyes basadas en costumbres y decisiones judiciales, en vez de leyes aprobadas por una asamblea legislativa

communism political and economic system in which government owns all property and makes all economic decisions (p. 23)
comunismo sistema político y económico en el que el Estado posee toda la propiedad y toma todas las decisiones económicas

compass device with a magnetized piece of metal that points to the north, used for navigation (p. 535)
brújula instrumento con una pieza de metal imantada que señala el norte, usado en la navegación

compass rose diagram of a compass showing direction (p. 12)
rosa de los vientos diagrama de una brújula que indica la dirección

competition struggle among producers for consumers' money (p. 30)
competencia lucha entre los productores por el dinero de los consumidores

concrete building material made by mixing small stones and sand with limestone, clay, and water (p. 392)
concreto material de construcción fabricado mediante la mezcla de piedras pequeñas y arena con piedra caliza, arcilla y agua

Confucianism a belief system based on the ideas of the Chinese thinker Confucius (pp. 265, 539)
confucianismo sistema de creencias basado en la ideología del filósofo chino Confucio

conquistador Spanish soldier-explorer (p. 770)
conquistador soldado explorador de origen español

consensus agreement among the members of a group (p. 565)
consenso acuerdo entre los miembros de un grupo

constitution system of basic rules and principles by which a government is organized (pp. 21, 370)
constitución sistema de reglas y principios básicos que establece la organización de un gobierno

consul one of two top officials and military leaders in the Roman republic (p. 374)
cónsul uno de los dos altos funcionarios y líderes militares en la República romana

consumer person or business that buys, or consumes, products (p. 29)
consumidor persona o negocio que compra o consume productos

convent religious community for women known as nuns (p. 634)
convento comunidad religiosa para mujeres conocidas como monjas

conversion heartfelt change in one's opinions or beliefs, especially in religion (p. 405)
conversión cambio sincero de opiniones o creencias, especialmente en el campo religioso

cottage industy business that uses people who work at home with their own equipment (p. 782)
industria artesanal negocio que utiliza gente que trabaja en casa con su propio equipo

Council of Trent a series of meetings called in 1545, to find ways to revive the moral authority of the Catholic Church and stop the spread of Protestantism (p. 748)
Concilio de Trento una serie de reuniones que empezaron en 1545 para encontrar maneras de revivir la autoridad moral de la Iglesia Católica y detener el avance del protestantismo

Counter-Reformation a movement to strengthen the teachings and structure of the Catholic Church (p. 746)
contrarreforma movimiento para fortalecer las enseñanzas y estructura de la Iglesia Católica

covenant binding agreement (p. 171)
alianza pacto vinculante

credit arrangement in which a buyer can purchase something and pay for it over time (p. 37)
crédito arreglo que permite al consumidor comprar algo y pagarlo durante un plazo de tiempo

creed statement of beliefs (p. 436)
credo afirmación de creencias

crop rotation practice of changing the use of fields over time (p. 683)
rotación de cultivos práctica de alternar el uso que se le da a un campo de cultivo

crucifixion Roman method of execution by nailing a person to a wooden cross (p. 404)
crucifixión método romano de ejecución clavando a una persona a una cruz de madera

Crusades a series of military campaigns to establish Christian control over the Holy Land (p. 664)
Cruzadas serie de campañas militares para establecer el control cristiano de la Tierra Santa

cuisine style of food (p. 281)
cocina estilo de comida

cultural diffusion spread of cultural traits from one culture to another (pp. 46, 136)
difusión cultural propagación de los rasgos culturales de una cultura a otra

cultural hearth place where cultural traits begin and from which they spread to surrounding cultures and regions (p. 46)
corazón cultural lugar donde se originan los rasgos culturales y desde el que se difunden hacia las culturas y regiones aledañas

cultural landscape geographic area that has been shaped by people (p. 42)
paisaje cultural área geográfica moldeada por la gente

cultural trait idea or way of doing things that is common in a certain culture (pp. 42, 119)
rasgo cultural idea o manera de hacer las cosas que es común en una cultura determinada

culture beliefs, customs, practices, and behavior of a particular nation or group of people (pp. 42, 66)
cultura creencias, costumbres, prácticas y comportamientos de una nación o un grupo de personas determinado

culture region area in which a single culture or cultural trait is dominant (p. 42)
región cultural área en la que predomina una sola cultura o rasgo cultural

cuneiform Mesopotamian system of writing that uses triangular-shaped symbols to stand for ideas or things (p. 115)
cuneiforme sistema de escritura usado en Mesopotamia que emplea símbolos de forma triangular para representar ideas y objetos

currency money that is used as a medium of exchange, usually bills or coins (p. 129)
moneda corriente dinero que se usa como medio de intercambio, usualmente en forma de billetes y monedas

Cyrillic alphabet alphabet used mostly for Slavic languages such as Russian and Bulgarian, as well as for other languages (p. 443)
alfabeto cirílico alfabeto utilizado sobre todo para las lenguas eslavas, como el ruso, el búlgaro y otras más

D

daimyo local landowning lord in feudal Japan (p. 557)
daimyo señor terrateniente local en el Japón feudal

Dalit member of the lowest Indian caste grouping made up of people who did dirty or unpleasant jobs (p. 210)
dalit miembro de la casta más baja compuesta por personas dedicadas a trabajos sucios o desagradables

Daoism a philosophy of following the Dao, that is, the natural way of the universe (pp. 266, 538)
Taoísmo filosofía que sigue el Tao, es decir, el orden natural del universo

decimal system counting system based on units of ten (p. 245)
sistema decimal sistema para contar basado en unidades de diez

deify officially declare a person to be a god (p. 390)
deificar declarar oficialmente dios a una persona

Delian League military alliance led by Athens (p. 331)
Liga de Delos alianza militar liderada por Atenas

Delphic Oracle a priestess of Apollo believed by the ancient Greeks to predict the future (p. 340)
Oráculo de Delfos una sacerdotisa de Apolo que los griegos de la antigüedad creían capaz de predecir el futuro

delta a flat plain formed on the seabed where a river deposits material over many years (p. 145)
delta llanura plana que se forma en el lecho marino dende va río deposita sedimento a través de los años

demand desire for a particular good or service (p. 29)
demanda interés en un bien o servicio determinado

deez nut

Glossary (continued)

democracy form of government in which citizens hold political power (pp. 22, 314)
   democracia tipo de gobierno en el que los ciudadanos tienen el poder político

denomination religious group (p. 412)
   denominación grupo religioso

despot a tyrant or dictator (p. 530)
   déspota un tirano o dictador

dharma a person's duty or what is right for him or her (p. 216)
   dharma el deber de una persona o lo que es correcto para él o ella

Diaspora Jewish communities outside the ancient Jewish homeland, from a Greek word meaning dispersion, or scattering (p.184)
   Diáspora conjunto de comunidades judías que viven fuera de la antigua patria judía, viene de una palabra griega que significa dispersión

dike wall to hold back water (pp. 256, 591)
   dique muro construido para contener el agua

direct democracy government in which citizens take part directly in the day-to-day affairs of government (p. 317)
   democracia directa tipo de gobierno en el que los ciudadanos participan directamente en los asuntos diarios del gobierno

diversity cultural variety (p. 47)
   diversidad variedad cultural

domesticate change the growth of plants or behavior of animals in ways that are useful for humans (p. 83)
   domesticar cambiar el crecimiento de las plantas o la conducta de los animales de maneras que los hagan útiles para los seres humanos

drought long period of extremely dry weather (p. 609)
   sequía largo período de tiempo extremadamente seco

dynasty a series of rulers from the same family (pp. 147, 502)
   dinastía serie de monarcas pertenecientes a la misma familia

E

ebony black wood from West Africa (p. 163)
   ébano madera negra del África occidental

economics study of how people meet their wants and needs (p. 28)
   economía ciencia que estudia cómo la gente satisface sus deseos y necesidades

economy system that a community uses to produce and distribute goods and services (p. 91)
   economía sistema usado por una comunidad para producir y distribuir bienes y servicios

edict an official public order made by a king or other authority (p. 753)
   edicto orden pública oficial dada por un rey u otra autoridad

empire state containing several countries or territories (pp. 22, 118, 381)
   imperio estado que incluye a varios países o territorios

engraving an art form in which an artist etches a design on a metal plate with a needle and acid (p. 724)
   grabado forma artística en la que se graba un diseño en una placa de metal usando una aguja y ácido

enlightenment in Buddhism, a state of perfect wisdom (p. 221)
   iluminación en el budismo, un estado de sabiduría perfecta

environment surroundings (p. 70)
   medio ambiente lo que hay en los alrededores

envoy representative of a government sent to another country (p. 280)
   enviado representante de un gobierno ante otro gobierno

ephor man responsible for the day-to-day operation of the government in Sparta (p. 319)
   éforo hombre encargado de las operaciones cotidianas del gobierno en Esparta

epistle formal letter, several of which form part of the New Testament (p. 409)
   epístola carta formal; escritos que forman parte del Nuevo Testamento

established religion official religion supported by the government (p. 379)
religión establecida religión oficial apoyada por el gobierno

ethics beliefs about what is right and wrong (pp. 44, 170, 411)
ética creencias sobre el bien y el mal

ethnic group group of people who share a distinct culture, language, and identity (p. 505)
grupo étnico grupo de personas que comparten una cultura, un idioma y una identidad

excommunicate to exclude a person from a church or a religious community (p. 654)
excomulgar excluir a una persona de una iglesia o comunidad religiosa

exile separation from one's homeland (p. 184)
exilio separación de la patria

Exodus escape of the Israelites from slavery in Egypt (p. 173)
Éxodo huida de los israelitas de la esclavitud en Egipto

export good or service produced within a country and sold outside the country's borders (pp. 35, 133)
exportación bien o servicio que se produce en un país y se vende fuera de los límites del país

F

fallow unplanted land (p. 683)
barbecho tierra que se deja sin sembrar

federal system system of government in which power is divided among central, regional, and local governments (p. 24)
sistema federal sistema de gobierno en el que el poder se divide entre los gobiernos central, regional y local

federalism a form of government in which power is shared between local and national levels (p. 755)
federalismo forma de gobierno en la que el poder es compartido entre el nivel local y el nacional

Fertile Crescent a region with good conditions for growing crops that stretches from the Mediterranean coast east through Mesopotamia (modern Iraq) to the Persian Gulf (p. 110)
Creciente Fértil región con buenas condiciones para cultivos que se extiende desde las áreas de la costa del Mediterráneo, hacia el este por Mesopotamia (que hoy se conoce como Iraq) hasta el golfo Pérsico

feudalism a strict social system in which landowners grant people land or other rewards in exchange for military service or labor (p. 557)
feudalismo un sistema social estricto en el que los terratenientes dan a las personas tierras u otras recompensas a cambio de servicios militares o de trabajo

fief estate granted by a lord to a vassal (p. 642)
feudo propiedades otorgadas por un señor feudal a un vasallo

figurehead person who appears to be in charge when someone else is really in control (p. 555)
testaferro persona que aparenta estar a cargo cuando en realidad otra persona tiene el control

filial piety devotion of children to their parents (p. 265)
amor filial devoción de los hijos hacia sus padres

forum open area in a Roman city filled with public buildings, temples, and markets (p. 366)
foro área abierta en una ciudad romana llena de edificios públicos, templos y mercados

fossil preserved remains of ancient human, animal, or plant (p. 58)
fósil restos conservados de personas, animales o plantas de la antigüedad

free trade removal of trade barriers (p. 35)
libre comercio eliminación de las barreras comerciales

G

geologist scientist who studies the physical materials of the Earth itself, such as soil and rocks (p. 59)
geólogo científico que estudia los materiales físicos de la Tierra, como los suelos y las rocas

ghetto separate section of a city where members of a minority group are forced to live (p. 749)
gueto área separada de una ciudad donde se fuerza a vivir a los miembros de una minoría

815

Glossary (continued)

gladiator man who fought as part of public entertainment in ancient Rome (p. 398)
gladiador hombre que combatía en espectáculos públicos en la antigua Roma

Gospel one of the first four books of the New Testament that describe the life and teachings of Jesus (p. 409)
evangelio uno de los primeros cuatro libros del Nuevo Testamento, que describen la vida y las enseñanzas de Jesús

government group of people who have the power to make and enforce laws for a country or area (p. 20)
gobierno grupo de personas de un país o área que tienen el poder de crear y hacer cumplir las leyes

granary special building used to hold grain (p. 202)
granero edificio especial usado para almacenar granos

Great Schism split between the Eastern Orthodox and Roman Catholic churches in 1054 (p. 439)
Gran Cisma separación de la Iglesia Ortodoxa oriental y la Iglesia católica romana en 1054

Great Wall long wall running east and west along the Chinese empire's northern border (p. 275)
Gran Muralla China largo muro que recorre lo que fue la frontera norte del imperio chino en dirección este-oeste

Greco-Roman something that combines elements of Greek and Roman culture and traditions (pp. 395, 501)
greco-romano que combina elementos de las culturas y tradiciones griega y romana

Greek fire a chemical mixture that burned in water which was used by the Byzantine empire against enemy ships (p. 435)
fuego griego una mezcla química que ardía en el agua y era usada por el Imperio Bizantino contra los barcos enemigos

griot African musician-storyteller who uses music and stories to track heritage and record history as well as entertain (p. 499)
griot músico y narrador africano que usa canciones y cuentos para registrar la historia y la herencia cultural, además de entretener

guild association of people who have a common interest (p. 686)
gremio asociación de personas que comparten un interés común

guru thinker or teacher (p. 213)
gurú pensador o maestro

H

habeas corpus a court order to bring an arrested person before a judge or court (p. 663)
hábeas corpus orden judicial de llevar a una persona arrestada ante un juez o una corte

hajj pilgrimage made by Muslims to the holy city of Mecca (p. 456)
hajj peregrinación que realizan los musulmanes a la ciudad santa de La Meca

Hammurabi's Code a set of laws that governed life in the Babylonian empire (p. 121)
Código de Hamurabi conjunto de leyes que regían la vida en Babilonia

Hellenistic the form of Greek culture that emerged after Alexander's conquests (p. 337)
helenística la forma de cultura griega que surgió después de las conquistas de Alejandro

helot Messenian person forced to work as a lowly farmer by Sparta (p. 319)
ilota persona originaria de Mesenia forzada a trabajar como siervo agrícola en Esparta

heresy a belief that is rejected by official Church doctrine (p. 669)
herejía creencia rechazada por la doctrina oficial de la Iglesia

hierarchy system for ranking members of a group according to their importance (p. 606)
jerarquía sistema de rangos asignados a los miembros de un grupo según su importancia

hieroglyphic symbol that stands for a word, idea, or sound (pp. 152, 587)
jeroglífico símbolo usado para representar una palabra, idea o sonido

hijra Muhammad's migration with his followers from Mecca to Medina (p. 453)
hégira emigración de Mahoma con sus seguidores de La Meca a Medina

Hippocratic oath oath taken by medical students swearing to practice medicine in an ethical way (p. 349)
Juramento hipocrático juramento hecho por los estudiantes de medicina en el que prometen practicar su profesión de una manera ética

historian person who studies the past (p. 4)
historiador persona que estudia el pasado

historical map special-purpose map that provides information about a place at a certain time in history (p. 15)
mapa histórico mapa con el propósito particular de dar información acerca de un lugar en un momento determinado de la historia

Huguenot French Protestant (p. 752)
hugonote protestante francés

human–environment interaction how people affect their environment and how their environment affects them (p. 11)
interacción humanos–medio ambiente manera en la que los seres humanos influyen en su medio ambiente y viceversa

humanism a cultural movement of the Renaissance based on the study of classical works (p. 716)
humanismo movimiento cultural en el Renacimiento basado en el estudio de obras clásicas

Hundred Years' War destructive war between France and England that lasted from 1337 to 1453 (p. 695)
Guerra de los Cien años guerra cruenta entre Francia e Inglaterra que duró desde 1337 hasta 1453

hunter-gatherer person who lives by hunting animals and gathering plants (p. 64)
cazador-recolector persona que vive de la caza de animales y la recolección de plantas

hypothesis logical guess (p. 347)
hipótesis suposición lógica

Iberian Peninsula the peninsula where present-day Spain and Portugal are located (p. 672)
península Ibérica península en la que se ubican España y Portugal hoy en día

icon a holy image, usually a portrait of Jesus or a saint (p. 436)
ícono imagen sagrada, usualmente un retrato de Jesús o de un santo

iconoclast "image-breaker," person who opposed the use of icons in Christian worship (p. 437)
iconoclasta "destructor de imágenes", persona que se oponía al uso de íconos en el rito cristiano

igloo domed house made from blocks of snow by Native Americans who lived in the Arctic (p. 612)
iglú vivienda en forma de cúpula construida con bloques de nieve por los indígenas norteamericanos que habitan en el Ártico

immunity natural defense against disease (p. 774)
inmunidad defensa natural contra las enfermedades

import good or service sold within a country that is produced in another country (pp. 35, 133)
importación bien o servicio que se vende en un país pero se produce en otro

incentive factor that encourages people to behave in a certain way (p. 29)
incentivo factor que motiva a la gente a actuar de cierta manera

individualism the belief in the importance of the individual as opposed to the larger community (p. 718)
individualismo creencia en la importancia del individuo por encima de la comunidad

indulgence a kind of cancellation of punishment for sin (p. 741)
indulgencia una especie de anulación del castigo por los pecados cometidos

inflation general increase in prices (pp. 31, 415, 780, 987)
inflación alza general de los precios

Inquisition a series of investigations designed to find and judge heretics (p. 670)
Inquisición una serie de investigaciones diseñadas para encontrar y juzgar herejes

interdependence dependence by each country or group on the other (p. 159)
interdependencia dependencia de cada país o grupo entre sí

interest price paid for borrowing money (p. 37)
interés precio que se paga por el dinero prestado

interest group group that seeks to influence public policy on certain issues (p. 27)
grupo de interés grupo que busca influir en las políticas públicas en algunos asuntos

Glossary (continued)

investing act of using money in the hopes of making a future profit (p. 37)
invertir usar el dinero con la esperanza de obtener ganancias futuras

irrigate to supply water to (pp. 49, 112)
irrigar suministrar agua

ivory hard white material made from elephant tusks (p. 159)
marfil material blanco duro hecho de colmillos de elefante

J

Jesuits a religious order founded by Ignatius Loyola in 1534, also known as the Society of Jesus (p. 746)
jesuitas orden religiosa fundada por Ignacio de Loyola en 1534, también conocida como la Compañía de Jesús

judge in the Hebrew Bible, a leader who could rally the Israelites to defend their land (p. 182)
juez en la Biblia hebrea, se refiere a un líder que podía organizar a los israelitas para defender su tierra

justice fairness or fair treatment (p. 180)
justicia equidad o trato equitativo

Justinian's Code a law code published by the Byzantine emperor Justinian (p. 441)
Código de Justiniano un código de leyes publicado por el emperador bizantino Justiniano

K

Kaaba a shrine in Mecca that is the most important Islamic holy site (p. 453)
Kaaba santuario de La Meca que es el lugar sagrado más importante del Islam

kabuki Japanese drama aimed at farmers, merchants, and other common folk (p. 563)
kabuki tipo de teatro japonés dirigido a agricultores, comerciantes y a las personas comunes

kami god or spirit who represents a force of nature in the Japanese religion (p. 550)
kami divinidad o espíritu que representa una fuerza de la naturaleza en la religión japonesa

karma in Hinduism, the effect of a person's actions in this and in previous lives (p. 216)
karma en el hinduísmo, el efecto de las acciones de una persona en su vida actual y en las anteriores

key section of a map that explains the map's symbols and shading (p. 12)
leyenda sección de un mapa que explica el significado de sus símbolos y áreas sombreadas

khan Mongol ruler (p. 524)
kan gobernante mongol

kinship connection based on family relationships (p. 505)
parentesco conexión basada en relaciones de familia

knight warrior mounted on horseback (p. 642)
caballero guerrero montado a caballo

Kshatriya member of the second-highest Indian caste grouping, made up of rulers and warriors (p. 209)
chatría miembro de la segunda casta más alta en la India, compuesta de guerreros y gobernantes

L

labor specialization division of jobs and skills in a society (p. 491)
especialización laboral división de trabajos y destrezas en la sociedad

lacquer a protective coating made from the sap of a special tree (p. 286)
barniz capa protectora hecha de la savia de un árbol especial

Legalism an ancient Chinese philosophy stating that a strong leader and a strong legal system, not moral values, are needed to create social order (p. 276)
legismo antigua filosofía china según la cual se requiere de un líder y de un sistema legal fuertes, y no de valores morales, para mantener el orden social

legion basic unit of the Roman army, consisting of 4,500 to 5,000 heavily armed soldiers (p. 369)
legión unidad básica del ejército romano, formada por 4,500 a 5,000 soldados fuertemente armados

limited government government structure in which government actions are limited by law (p. 21)
gobierno limitado estructura gubernamental cuyas acciones están limitadas por la ley

lineage group of people descended from a common ancestor (p. 505)
linaje grupo de personas que descienden de un ancestro común

linear perspective a mathematical system for representing three-dimensional space on a flat surface (p. 729)
perspectiva lineal sistema matemático para representar el espacio tridimensional en una superficie plana

locator map section of a map that shows a larger area than the main map (p. 12)
mapa localizador sección de un mapa que amplía un área del mismo

loess a dustlike material that can form soil (p. 254)
loes material polvoroso que puede formar tierra

longhouse rectangular type of home built by northeastern Native Americans made from wood and bark or mats made of reeds (p. 610)
vivienda comunal casa de tipo rectangular construida por los indígenas norteamericanos del Noreste y hecha de madera y corteza o caña

lyric poetry poetic songs (p. 342)
poesía lírica canciones poéticas

M

magistrate government official who enforces the law (p. 371)
magistrado funcionario de gobierno encargado de hacer cumplir las leyes

Magna Carta a document that promised barons certain rights (p. 662)
Carta Magna documento que prometía a los barones ciertos derechos

Mahayana Buddhism Buddhist sect that focuses on the compassion of the Buddha (p. 227)
budismo mahayana secta budista que se concentra en la compasión de Buda

mainland area that is a part of a continent (p. 549)
tierra firme área que forma parte de un continente

Mandate of Heaven in ancient China, the right to rule given to a dynasty by Heaven, the highest force of nature (p. 258)
Mandato Celestial en la antigua China, derecho a gobernar concedido a una dinastía por el Cielo, la más alta fuerza de la naturaleza

maniple unit of 60 to 120 soldiers within a Roman legion that could act independently in battle (p. 369)
manípulo unidad de 60 a 120 soldados en una legión romana que podía actuar con independencia en la batalla

manor self-sufficient estate of a medieval lord (p. 643)
señorío propiedad autosuficiente de un señor medieval

mantra sacred word, chant, or sound that is repeated over and over to advance one's spiritual growth (p. 569)
mantra palabra, canto o sonido sagrado que se repite numerosas veces para ayudar al crecimiento espiritual

market organized way for producers and consumers to trade goods and services (p. 30)
mercado intercambio organizado de bienes y servicios entre productores y consumidores

market economy economy in which individual consumers and producers make all economic decisions (pp. 32, 783)
economía de mercado economía en la que los consumidores y los productores toman todas las decisiones económicas

martyr person who dies for his or her beliefs (p. 407)
mártir persona que muere por sus creencias

medieval from the Latin for "middle age," relating to the Middle Ages (p. 628)
medieval en latín significa "edad media", relacionado con la Edad Media

meditate calm or clear the mind, often by focusing on a single object (p. 221)
meditar calmar o aclarar la mente, con frecuencia mediante la concentración en un único objeto

mendicant order order founded to fight heresy and to preach to ordinary people (p. 689)
orden mendicante orden fundada para combatir la herejía y para predicar a la gente corriente

mercantile related to commerce or trade (p. 712)
mercantil referente al comercio o los negocios

819

Glossary (continued)

mercantilism economic policy in which a nation gains strength by controlling its trade, agriculture, industry, and money (p. 779)
mercantilismo política económica según la cual una nación se fortalece por medio del control de su comercio, agricultura, industria, y moneda

mercenary soldier who fights for pay rather than for his or her country (p. 419)
mercenario soldado que combate a cambio de dinero, en lugar de hacerlo por su país

merit system system in which people are hired and promoted based on talent and skills, rather than wealth or social status (p. 519)
sistema de mérito sistema en el que las personas son contratadas y ascendidas por su talento y destrezas, en lugar de por su riqueza o estatus social

Meroitic script one of the world's first alphabets, invented in ancient Nubia (p. 162)
escritura meroítica uno de los alfabetos más antiguos del mundo, inventado en la antigua Nubia

Mesopotamia wide, flat plain in between the Tigris and Euphrates rivers in present-day Irak (p. 110)
Mesopotamia planicie ancha situada entre los ríos Tigris y Eufrates en el Irak actual

metallurgy science that deals with extracting metal from ore and using it to create useful objects (p. 247)
metalurgia ciencia que se ocupa de la extracción de metales y su uso en la creación de objetos útiles

metic foreigner in a Greek city-state, often a merchant or artisan (p. 308)
meteco extranjero en una ciudad-estado griega, con frecuencia un mercader o artesano

Middle Ages period between ancient times and modern times, roughly from A.D. 500 to 1500 (p. 628)
Edad Media período entre la antigüedad clásica y los tiempos modernos, aproximadamente de 500 a 1,500 D.C.

migration movement of people from one place to another (p. 68)
migración desplazamiento de personas de un lugar a otro

military state society organized for the purpose of waging war (p. 319)
estado militarista sociedad organizada con el propósito de hacer la guerra

missionary someone who tries to convert others to a particular religion (pp. 442, 636, 762)
misionero alguien que intenta convertir a otras personas a una religión en particular

mita system Incan system for payment of taxes with labor (p. 607)
mita en el Imperio Inca, sistema de pago de impuestos por medio del trabajo

mixed economy economy that combines elements of traditional, market, and command economic systems (p. 33)
economía mixta economía que combina elementos de los sistemas económicos tradicional, de mercado y dirigido

moat trench filled with water as part of a fortification (p. 433)
foso trinchera llena de agua usada como parte de una fortificación

moksha liberation from reincarnation (p. 216)
moksha liberación de la reencarnación

monarchy form of government in which the state is ruled by a monarch (p. 23)
monarquía tipo de gobierno en el que el Estado está regido por un monarca

monastery secluded religious community (pp. 226, 634)
monasterio comunidad religiosa retirada

money economy economic system in which people use currency rather than bartering to buy and sell goods (p. 522)
economía monetaria sistema económico en el que las personas usan moneda corriente en lugar de trueque para comprar y vender bienes

Mongols nomads who came from the steppes northwest of China (p. 524)
mongoles nómadas que llegaron de las estepas al noroeste de China

monk man who dedicates himself to worshiping God (p. 502)
monje hombre que dedica su vida a la adoracion de Dios

monopoly single person or group who controls the production of a good or service (p. 285)
monopolio control de la producción de un bien o servicio por parte de una sola persona o grupo

monotheism belief in a single God (p. 170)
monoteísmo creencia en un solo dios

monsoon seasonal wind that brings rain to the Indian subcontinent during parts of the year (p. 201)
   monzón viento de estación que trae lluvia al subcontinente índico durante partes del año

Moors the Muslims in Spain (p. 672)
   moros musulmanes de España

mosaic design formed with small tiles of glass, stone, or pottery (p. 396)
   mosaico diseño formado usando pequeñas tejas de vidrio, piedra o cerámica

mosque Islamic house of worship (p. 458)
   mezquita lugar de culto islámico

movement how people, goods, and ideas get from one place to another (p. 11)
   movimiento manera en la que las personas, los bienes y las ideas van de un lugar a otro

mummy a body that has been preserved so it will not decompose (p. 151)
   momia cadáver preservado sin descomponerse

mythology collection of myths or stories that people tell about their gods and heroes (p. 338)
   mitología colección de mitos o historias que la gente cuenta sobre sus dioses o héroes

N

nation-state state that is independent of other states (p. 23)
   estado-nación estado que es independiente de otros

natural law idea that there are laws in nature that are basic to both the natural world and human affairs (p. 692)
   ley natural idea de que hay leyes en la naturaleza que son esenciales tanto para el mundo natural como para los seres humanos

natural resource useful material found in the environment (p. 490)
   recurso natural material útil que se encuentra en el medio ambiente

navigation art of steering a ship from place to place (p. 135)
   navegación arte de conducir un barco de un lugar a otro

New Testament writings that form part of the Christian Bible which tell the story of Jesus and his early followers (p. 408)
   Nuevo Testamento escritos incluidos en la Biblia cristiana que cuentan la historia de Jesús y sus primeros seguidores

nirvana a state of blissful peace without desire or suffering (p. 224)
   nirvana estado de paz beatífica sin deseo o sufrimiento

noh Japanese drama that appealed to the nobles and samurai (p. 563)
   noh tipo de teatro japonés que gustaba a los nobles y los samuráis

nomad person who moves from place to place without a permanent home (pp. 66, 524)
   nómada persona que se desplaza de un lugar a otro sin un hogar permanente

norm behavior that is considered normal in a particular society (p. 42)
   norma comportamiento que se considera normal en una sociedad determinada

numeral symbol used to represent a number (p. 245)
   número símbolo usado para representar una cantidad

O

oasis place in the desert where water can be found (p. 450)
   oasis lugar del desierto donde se halla agua

observatory building for observing the sky (p. 589)
   observatorio edificio usado para observar el cielo

obsidian natural volcanic glass used to make very sharp blades and heads for spears and arrows (p. 583)
   obsidiana cristal volcánico natural que se usaba para hacer cuchillos muy afilados y puntas de lanzas y flechas

official person who holds a government job (p. 279)
   funcionario persona que trabaja para el gobierno

oligarchy government in which a small group of people rule (p. 312)
   oligarquía tipo de gobierno en el que un grupo pequeño de personas tienen el poder

Glossary (continued)

Olympic games in ancient Greece, an athletic competition held every four years in honor of Zeus (p. 340)
Juegos olímpicos en la Grecia antigua, competición atlética celebrada cada cuatro años en honor a Zeus

opportunity cost cost of what you have to give up when making a choice (p. 29)
costo de oportunidad costo de lo que se pierde al elegir una opción

oracle bone animal bone or shell carved with written characters that was used to predict the future in ancient China (p. 257)
hueso oracular hueso animal o caparazón tallado con caracteres escritos que se usaba para predecir el futuro en la China antigua

oral tradition community's cultural and historical background, passed down in spoken stories and songs (pp. 9, 507)
tradición oral antecedentes culturales e históricos de una comunidad, transmitidos por cuentos hablados y canciones

oratory art of giving speeches (p. 397)
oratoria arte de dar discursos

orthodoxy traditional or established religious beliefs (p. 419)
ortodoxia creencias religiosas establecidas o tradicionales

P

pagan follower of a polytheistic religion (p. 636)
paganos seguidor de una religión politeísta

papyrus a writing surface similar to paper named after the papyrus reed that grew along the Nile River in ancient Egypt (p. 153)
papiro superficie para escribir similar al papel, nombrada así por los papiros, juncos que crecían en la ribera del río Nilo en el antiguo Egipto

parable story with a religious moral (p. 409)
parábola historia con una moraleja religiosa

parliament an assembly of representatives who make laws (p. 663)
parlamento asamblea de representantes encargados de hacer leyes

paterfamilias oldest man in a Roman family who had absolute power over his family (p. 376)
paterfamilias el hombre de más edad en una familia romana, que tenía poder absoluto sobre su familia

patriarchal society society in which men rule their families, and people trace their origins through male ancestors (p. 376)
sociedad patriarcal sociedad en la cual los hombres rigen las familias y las personas establecen sus orígenes a través de ancestros masculinos

patron someone who gives money or other support to a person or group (p. 714)
mecenas alguien que da dinero u otro tipo de apoyo a una persona o grupo

Pax Romana period of stability in the Roman empire (p. 391)
Paz Romana período de estabilidad del Imperio Romano

Peasants' Revolt unsuccessful revolt by peasants against feudal lords in England in 1381 (p. 699)
Rebelión de los campesinos fracasada revuelta de campesinos contra los señores feudales en Inglaterra en 1381

Peloponnesian League military alliance led by Sparta (p. 331)
Liga del Peloponeso alianza militar liderada por Esparta

period length of time singled out because of a specific event or development that happened during that time (p. 4)
período lapso de tiempo resaltado debido a un suceso o desarrollo específico que sucedió durante ese tiempo

phalanx Greek military formation of heavily armed foot soldiers who moved together as a unit (p. 313)
falange formación militar griega compuesta de soldados a pie fuertemente armados que se movían juntos como una unidad

pharaoh king of ancient Egypt (p. 147)
faraón rey del antiguo Egipto

philosophy general study of knowledge and the world; Greek for "love of wisdom" (p. 262)
filosofía estudio general sobre el conocimiento y el mundo; en griego significa "amor por la sabiduría"

picaresque a series of comic episodes usually involving a mischievous character (p. 733)
picaresca serie de episodios cómicos usualmente incluyen un personaje travieso

pictograph a picture that represents a word or idea (p. 257)
pictografía imagen que representa una palabra o idea

pilgrimage journey undertaken to worship at a religious place (p. 655)
peregrinaje viaje por devoción a un lugar sagrado

place mix of human and nonhuman features at a given location (p. 10)
lugar combinación de características humanas y no humanas en un sitio determinado

plateau large, mostly flat area that rises above the surrounding land (p. 488)
meseta gran extensión de terreno, generalmente plano, que se eleva sobre la tierra circundante

polis Greek city-state (p. 304)
polis ciudad-estado en Grecia

political party group that supports candidates for public offices (p. 27)
partido político grupo que apoya a los candidatos que postulan a cargos públicos

politics art and practice of government (p. 305)
política arte y práctica de gobernar

polyrhythmic drumming type of drumming that combines two or more different rhythms at the same time (p. 509)
percusión polirrítmica tipo de percusión que combina dos o más ritmos diferentes al mismo tiempo

polytheism worship of many gods or deities (pp. 114, 338)
politeísmo adoración de muchas deidades

pope leader of the Roman Catholic Church (p. 438)
papa líder de la Iglesia Católica Romana

populate to become an inhabitant of a place (p. 68)
poblar habitar un lugar

porcelain a hard white pottery of extremely fine quality (p. 523)
porcelana cerámica blanca y dura de muy alta calidad

potlatch feasting and gift-giving ceremony in northwestern Native American culture (p. 613)
potlatch ceremonia de festín y entrega de obsequios en la cultura indígena norteamericana del noroeste

predestination the idea that God had long ago determined who would gain salvation (p. 743)
predestinación idea de que Dios determinó hace mucho tiempo quién obtendrá la salvación

prehistory time before humans invented writing (pp. 5, 58)
prehistoria época anterior a la invención de la escritura

primary source information that comes directly from a person who experienced an event (p. 6)
fuente primaria información sobre un suceso que proviene directamente de una persona que experimentó el suceso

producer person or business that makes and sells products (p. 29)
productor persona o negocio que fabrica y vende productos

profit money a company has left over after subtracting the costs of doing business (p. 30)
ganancias dinero que sobra después que una compañía deduce los costos de operar el negocio

prophet person believed to be chosen by God to bring truth to the people (p. 177)
profeta persona de quien se cree ha sido elegida por Dios para enseñar la verdad a la gente

proportion using balanced or symmetric elements to form a pleasing design (p. 728)
proporción uso de elementos equilibrados o simétricos para formar un diseño agradable

proverb wise saying (p. 507)
proverbio dicho que contiene sabiduría

province territory that is under the control of a larger country (pp. 236, 281)
provincia territorio que se encuentra bajo la administración de un país más grande

pyramid structure with triangular sides (p. 154)
pirámide estructura con lados triangulares

Glossary (continued)

Q

quetzal colorful tropical bird (p. 586)
quetzal ave tropical colorida

quipu record-keeping device made of knotted strings, used by the Incas (pp. 604, 774)
quipu dispositivo usado por los incas para llevar registros con ayuda de cuerdas anudadas

Quran holy book of Islam (p. 454)
Corán libro sagrado del islam

R

rabbi Jewish religious teacher (p. 178)
rabino maestro espiritual de la religión judía

recant to withdraw or take back (p. 742)
abjurar retractarse de algo

recession zero or negative economic growth for six or more months in a row (p. 31)
recesión crecimiento cero o crecimiento económico negativo por un período continuo de seis meses o más

Reconquista movement to drive the Muslims from Spain (p. 674)
Reconquista movimiento para expulsar a los musulmanes de España

Reformation a religious movement that began in the 1500s to reform the Catholic Church (p. 740)
Reforma movimiento religioso iniciado en el siglo XVI para la reforma de la Iglesia Católica

regent someone who governs a country in the name of a ruler who is unable to rule, often because of age (p. 551)
regente alguien que gobierna un país cuando el gobernante no puede hacerlo, con frecuencia debido a su edad

region area with at least one unifying physical or human feature such as climate, landforms, population, or history (p. 11)
región área con al menos una característica física o humana que es unificadora, como el clima, los accidentes geográficos, la población o la historia

reincarnation rebirth of a soul in a new body (p. 216)
reencarnación renacimiento del alma en un nuevo cuerpo

relative location location of a place relative to another place (p. 10)
ubicación relativa ubicación de un lugar con respecto a otro

religion people's beliefs and practices about the existence, nature, and worship of a god or gods (pp. 44, 94)
religión creencias y prácticas de los seres humanos acerca de la existencia, la naturaleza y la adoración de un dios o dioses

Renaissance French for "rebirth"; refers to a period of cultural revival in Europe from the 1300s to the 1500s (p. 713)
Renacimiento se refiere a un período de revitalización cultural en Europa entre los siglos XIV y XVI.

representative democracy democracy in which people elect representatives to make the nation's laws (p. 317)
democracia representativa democracia en la que el pueblo elige representantes que redactan las leyes de la nación

republic form of government in which citizens have the right to vote and elect officials (p. 366)
república forma de gobierno en la que los ciudadanos tienen el derecho votar y elegir funcionarios

resource supply of something that can be used as needed (p. 93)
recurso existencia de algo que puede usarse según se necesite

resurrection coming back to life (p. 402)
resurrección retorno a la vida

revenue money earned by selling goods and services and by collecting taxes (p. 30)
ingreso dinero recaudado de la venta de bienes y servicios y de impuestos

revolution a complete change in ways of thinking, working, or living (p. 82)
revolución cambio completo en la forma de pensar, trabajar o vivir

righteousness acting or living in a way that is ethically right and obeys God's laws (p. 180)
rectitud cualidad de comportarse o vivir de una forma éticamente correcta y obedecer la ley de Dios

river system main river and all of the other rivers and streams that drain into it (p. 201)
sistema fluvial un río principal y los ríos y arroyos que desembocan en él

Romance language language that developed from Latin, such as French, Spanish, Portuguese, or Italian (p. 397)
lengua romance idioma que derivó del latín, como el francés, el español, el portugués o el italiano

rule of law idea that all members of a society—even the rich and powerful—must obey the law (p. 123)
imperio de la ley la idea de que todos los miembros de una sociedad, incluso los ricos y poderosos, deben obedecer la ley

S

Sabbath weekly day of rest (p. 181)
sabbat día de la semana establecido para el descanso

sacrament sacred rites of Christianity, such as baptism and communion (p. 638)
sacramento rito sagrado en el cristianismo, como el bautizo o la comunión

saint person believed to be especially holy (p. 637)
santo persona reconocida como especialmente sagrada

samurai highly trained Japanese warrior in feudal Japan (p. 557)
samurái guerrero altamente entrenado en el Japón feudal

sarissa 18-foot-long Macedonian pike (p. 335)
sarissa pica macedonia de 18 pies de largo

satire work of literature that makes fun of its subject, often mocking vice or folly (pp. 398, 723)
sátira obra literaria que se burla de su tema, con frecuencia los vicios o los absurdos de la vida

savanna parklike landscape of grasslands with scattered trees that can survive dry spells, found in tropical areas with dry seasons (p. 489)
sabana pradera con árboles dispersos que pueden sobrevivir periodos de sequía; se encuentra en las áreas tropicales que tienen estaciones secas

saving setting aside money for future use (p. 36)
ahorrar reservar dinero para el uso futuro

scale bar section of a map that shows how much distance on the map represents a given distance on the land (p. 12)
barra de escala sección de un mapa que indica la correspondencia entre las distancias que se muestran en el mapa y las distancias reales sobre del terreno

scarcity having a limited quantity of resources to meet unlimited wants (p. 28)
escasez tener una cantidad limitada de recursos para satisfacer un consumo ilimitado

scholar-official highly educated person who passed civil service examinations and worked in the government (p. 519)
mandarín persona con alto grado de educación que pasaba los exámenes del servicio civil y trabajaba para el gobierno

scholarship formal study and learning (p. 495)
erudición altos estudios y aprendizaje

science knowledge of the natural world (p. 48)
ciencia conocimientos sobre el mundo natural

Scripture sacred writing (p. 176)
Escritura texto sagrado

sculpture statue or other free-standing piece of art made of clay, stone, or other materials (p. 155)
escultura estatua u otra pieza de arte hecha de arcilla, piedra o materiales similares

secondary source information about an event that does not come directly from a person who experienced that event (p. 6)
fuente secundaria información sobre un suceso que no proviene directamente de una persona que experimentó el suceso

sect a subgroup of a major religious group (p. 743)
secta subgrupo de un grupo religioso mayor

secular nonreligious (p. 654)
laico no religioso

secularism the view that religion need not be the center of human affairs (p. 717)
laicismo la idea de que la religión no debe ser el centro de los asuntos humanos

seismometer a tool to measure earthquakes (p. 287)
sismómetro instrumento para medir terremotos

serf a peasant who is legally bound to live and work on land owned by a lord (p. 643)
siervo persona que está legalmente forzada a vivir y trabajar en la tierra de su señor

Glossary (continued)

Sharia Islamic law (p. 459)
sharia la ley islámica

Shia member of an Islamic religious group that supported Ali as the first caliph and now forms a minority of the world's Muslims (p. 463)
chií miembro de un grupo religioso islámico que apoyaba a Alí como primer califa y que ahora constituye una minoría de musulmanes

Shinto traditional religion that originated in Japan (p. 566)
sintoísmo religión tradicional que se originó en el Japón

shogun powerful Japanese military leader who often had more power than the emperor (p. 557)
shogun poderoso líder militar japonés que por lo general tenía más poder que el emperador

shrine place of worship (p. 567)
santuario lugar de veneración religiosa

Silk Road series of trade routes that crossed Asia (p. 280)
Ruta de la Seda red de rutas comerciales que atravesaban Asia

slash-and-burn agriculture farming method in which trees and other plants on a plot of land are cut down and burned and ash is used for fertilizer (p. 583)
agricultura de tala y quema método agrícola en el que los árboles y otras plantas de un terreno se cortan y queman, y la ceniza se usa como fertilizante

slavery ownership and control of other people as property (p. 308)
esclavitud control y propiedad de algunas personas por otras

smuggler person who trades illegally (p. 533)
contrabandista persona que comercia de forma ilegal

social class group of people living in similar economic conditions (p. 95)
clase social grupo de personas que tienen una condición económica similar

Socratic method form of teaching in which the teacher asks students question after question to force them to think more clearly (p. 345)
método socrático forma de enseñanza en la que el maestro hace preguntas a los estudiantes para obligarlos a pensar con más claridad

sonnet a poem of fourteen lines with a fixed rhyming pattern (p. 732)
soneto poema de catorce versos con un patrón de rima fijo

specialization act of concentrating on a limited number of goods or activities (pp. 30, 88)
especialización concentración en una cantidad limitada de bienes o actividades

standard of living level of comfort enjoyed by a person or society (p. 49)
nivel de vida nivel de comodidad que posee un individuo o una sociedad

standardize to set rules to make things more similar (p. 275)
estandarizar establecer normas para hacer cosas de manera más uniforme

standing army a permanent army of professional soldiers (p. 127)
ejército regular un ejército permanente compuesto por soldados profesionales

state region that shares a common government (p. 22)
estado región que tiene un gobierno común

stele grand stone pillar (pp. 131, 501)
estela gran pilar de piedra

steppe vast area of grasslands (p. 524)
estepa territorio extenso de llanuras

stock share of ownership in a company (p. 37)
acción porción de la propiedad de una compañía

stonetown word used to describe Swahili city–states and their multistoried stone houses (p. 503)
stonetown palabra usada para describir ciudades-estado suajilis y sus casas de piedra de varios pisos

strait narrow body of water that cuts through land, connecting two larger bodies of water (p. 432)
estrecho cuerpo de agua angosto que pasa por tierra para conectar a dos cuerpos de agua más grandes

strategy a long-term plan for achieving a goal (p. 235)
estrategia plan de largo plazo para obtener un objetivo

subcontinent a large landmass that is set apart from the rest of the continent (p. 200)
subcontinente territorio amplio que se distingue del continente al que pertenece

subject person under the rule of a monarch (p. 237)
súbdito persona gobernada por un monarca

Sudra member of the fourth-highest caste grouping, made up of farmers and people who did manual work (p. 209)
sudrá miembro de la cuarta casta más alta de la India, compuesta por agricultores y personas dedicadas al trabajo manual

Sufism an Islamic lifestyle that emphasizes controlling one's desires, giving up worldly attachments, and seeking nearness to God (p. 471)
sufismo un estilo de vida islámico que enfatiza el control de los propios deseos, renunciando a los apegos mundanos y buscando la cercanía a Dios

sultan title for a ruler of a Muslim country (p. 465)
sultán título de un gobernante de un país musulmán

Sunnah traditions believed by many Muslims to come from the prophet Muhammad (p. 455)
sunna tradiciones y enseñanzas que muchos musulmanes atribuyen al profeta Mahoma

Sunni member of an Islamic religious group that supported Abu Bakr as the first caliph and now form a majority of the world's Muslims (p. 463)
suní miembro de un grupo religioso islámico que apoyaba a Abu Bakr como el primer califa y que ahora constituye la mayoría de musulmanes del mundo

supply amount of a good or service that is available for use (p. 29)
oferta cantidad disponible de un bien o servicio

surplus extra (p. 88)
superávit excedente

synagogue Jewish house of worship (p. 186)
sinagoga casa de reunión y culto de las comunidades judías

T

Talmud collection of oral teachings and commentaries about the Hebrew Bible and Jewish law (p. 178)
Talmud colección de enseñanzas orales y comentarios sobre la Biblia hebrea y la ley judía

tariff tax on imports or exports (p. 35)
arancel impuesto a las importaciones o las exportaciones

technology tools and skills people use to meet their needs and wants (p. 64)
tecnología instrumentos y destrezas usados por las personas para satisfacer sus necesidades y deseos

tenant farmer person who pays rent, either in money or crops, to grow crops on another person's land (p. 308)
granjero arrendatario persona que paga renta, ya sea en dinero o cosecha, para poder cultivar en la tierra de otra persona

tepee portable, cone-shaped home made by Native Americans who lived on the Plains (p. 611)
tipi vivienda portátil de forma cónica usada por los indígenas norteamericanos que vivían en las Llanuras

terrace strip of level land cut into a slope that is planted with crops (p. 602)
terraza parcela de tierra nivelada que se corta en una colina y se cultiva

textile woven fabric (p. 469)
textil tejido

theocracy a government run by religious power (p. 744)
teocracia gobierno en el que rige el poder religioso

Theravada Buddhism Buddhist sect that focuses on the wisdom of the Buddha (p. 227)
budismo teravada secta budista que se concentra en la sabiduría de Buda

three-field system system of planting invented in the High Middle Ages which increased the amount of land that could be planted each year (p. 683)
rotación trienal sistema de siembra inventado en la Alta Edad Media, que incrementó la cantidad de tierras que podrían ser cultivadas cada año

timeline line marked off with a series of events and their dates (p. 4)
línea cronológica línea marcada con una serie de sucesos y sus fechas

toga garment that adult men wore wrapped around their bodies as a symbol of Roman citizenship (p. 371)
toga vestimenta que los hombres adultos usaban, envolviéndose en ella, como símbolo de ciudadanía romana

Glossary (continued)

tolerance willingness to respect different beliefs and customs (p. 239)
tolerancia voluntad de respetar costumbres y creencias diferentes

topography physical features of a place (p. 628)
topografía características físicas de un lugar

Torah first five books of the Hebrew Bible (p. 170)
Torá primeros cinco libros de la Biblia hebrea

trade exchange of goods and services in a market (p. 34)
comercio intercambio de bienes y servicios en un mercado

trade barrier something that keeps goods and services from entering a country (p. 35)
barrera comercial obstáculos para la entrada de bienes y servicios a un país

traditional economy economy in which people make economic decisions based on their customs and habits (pp. 32, 783)
economía tradicional economía en la que la gente toma decisiones económicas de acuerdo a sus costumbres y hábitos

trans-Saharan across the Sahara (p. 491)
trans-Sahariano a través del Sahara

tribute payment or gift to a stronger power (pp.128, 532)
tributo pago u obsequio a un poder mayor

Trinity the three persons, or forms, of God according to Christian belief: God the Father, Jesus the Son, and the Holy Spirit (p. 411)
Trinidad dícese de las tres personas o formas de Dios de acuerdo con las creencias cristianas: Dios padre, Dios hijo y Espíritu Santo

tyranny unjust use of power, or in ancient Greece a government run by a strong ruler (pp. 21, 314)
tiranía uso injusto del poder; en la antigua Grecia, el gobierno controlado por un gobernante firme

U

unitary system system of government in which a central government has the authority to make laws for the entire country (p. 24)
sistema unitario sistema de gobierno en el que un gobierno central tiene la autoridad de hacer leyes para todo el país

university school, or groups of schools, that trains scholars at the highest levels (p. 692)
universidad escuela o grupo de escuelas que imparte enseñanza académica a los niveles más altos

unlimited government government structure in which there are no effective limits on government actions (p. 21)
gobierno ilimitado estructura gubernamental en la que no existen límites sobre las acciones del gobierno

urbanization movement of people from rural to urban areas (p. 520)
urbanización desplazamiento de personas de las áreas rurales a las áreas urbanas

utopia an imaginary, ideal place (p. 722)
utopía lugar imaginario e ideal

V

Vaishya member of the third-highest Indian caste grouping, made up of landowners, bankers, and merchants (p. 209)
vaishia miembro de la tercera casta más alta de la India, compuesta por terratenientes, banqueros y comerciantes

vassals in medieval Europe, noblemen who received land from other noblemen in return for their services (p. 641)
vasallos en la Europa medieval, señores nobles que recibían terrenos de otros señores nobles a cambio de sus servicios

Veda collection of hundreds of sacred hymns composed by the Aryans of ancient India (p. 207)
Vedas colección de cientos de himnos sagrados compuestos por los arios de la antigua India

vernacular everyday spoken language (p. 717)
lengua vernácula idioma hablado en circunstancias informales

veto stop or cancel the action of a government official or body (p. 371)
vetar detener o cancelar las acciones de un funcionario o agencia de gobierno

villa large country home (p. 377)
villa casa de campo grande

W

warlord military ruler (p. 259)
    caudillo gobernante militar

Warring States Period a period from about 481 B.C.
to 221 B.C. of great conflict in ancient China (p. 260)
    Período de los Reinos Combatientes un período
de gran conflicto en la China antigua que abarca
aproximadamente de 481 A.C. a 221 A.C.

wigwam a home made by Northeastern Native
Americans formed by bending the trunks of young
trees and tying them together to make a round
frame covered with bark or reed mats (p. 610)
    wigwam vivienda de los indígenas
norteamericanos del noreste fabricada con troncos
de árboles jóvenes curvados y amarrados entre sí
para formar una estructura redonda cubierta con
corteza de árboles o caña

writ a court order (p. 663)
    mandato judicial la orden de una corte de justicia

Z

ziggurat brick, pyramid–shaped Mesopotamian
temple (p. 114)
    zigurat templo de Mesopotamia de forma
piramidal, hecho de ladrillo

Index

The letters after some page numbers refer to the following: *c* = chart; *g* = graph; *m* = map; *p* = picture; *q* = quotation.

A

Index (continued)

Index (continued)

Acknowledgments

The people who made up the **myWorld History team**—representing composition services; core design, digital, and multimedia production services; digital product development; editorial; materials management; marketing; and production management—are listed below.

Allysa Adams, Courtney Alexander, Leann Davis Alspaugh, Jose Arredondo, Sarah Aubry, Deanna Babikian, Pamela Bernstein, Paul Blankman, Alyssa Boehm, Dirk Bost, Brandon Bradley, Peter Brooks, Susan Brorein, Kathy Burnett, Megan Burnett, Jessica Chadbourn, Russell Chase, Ruth Hull Chatlien, Ryan Chavez, Melissa Chen, Lori-Anne Cohen, Neville Cole, Tom Columbus, Stephanie Corrigan, Tod Coyle, AnnMarie Coyne, Bob Craton, Brett Creane, Dana Damiano, Glenn Diedrich, Frederick Fellows, Jorgensen Fernandez, Thomas Ferreira, Andrea Frausto, Patricia Fromkin, Tom Gibbons, Andrea Golden, Marielle Guiney, Mary Ann Gundersen, Curt Green, Jeff Hall, Rebecca Hall, Christopher Harris, Susan Hersch, Paul Hughes, Katharine Ingram, Linda Johnson, Marian Jones, Nancy Jones, Judie Jozokos, Lynne Kalkanajian, Patrick Keithahn, Courtenay Kelley, Gina King, John Kingston, Kate Koch, Stephanie Krol, M. Monique Lawrence, Henry Lee, Martha Leibs, Ann-Michelle Levangie, Salena LiBritz, Cheryl Mahan, Dmitry Mangeym, Dominique Mariano, Courtney Markham, Candi McDowell, Constance J. McCarty, Rich McMahon, Natalie Moravek, Alison Muff, Karla Navarrete, Andrew Newcomb, Xavier Niz, Kathy Nordmeyer, Mark O'Malley, Jodie O'Rourke, Jen Paley, Charles E. Pederson, Gabriela Perez Fiato, Kasia Pilat, Judith Pinkham, Tero Potila, Aaron Price, Sareeka Rai, Robert J. Reed, Jennifer Reichlin, Vicki Riske, Rashid Ross, Alexandra Sherman, Owen Shows, Melissa Shustyk, Audrey Simon, Tony Smith, Ted Smykal, Emily Soltanoff, Sonia Soto, Mark Staloff, Mark Statkus, Helen C. Strahinich, Donald Suhr, Frank Tangredi, Dennis Tarwood, Simon Tuchman, Elizabeth Tustian, Merle Uuesoo, Srikant Veeraraghavan, Ryan Wendt, Dan Wilson, Jeanette Wollenhaupt, Heather Wright

Maps

XNR Productions, Inc.

Illustrations

Peter Bull, Kerry Cashman, Marcos Chin, Dave Cockburn, Rory Hensley, Kurt Huggins and Zelda Devon, Frank Ippolito, Jeremy Mohler, Goñi Montes, Craig Phillips, Tin Salamunic, Marc Scott

Photography
FRONT COVER B, Elenhil/iStockphoto; **RT,** Nefertiti Stephanie Pilick/dpa/Corbis; **RM,** Danny Lehman/Corbis; **RB,** The Bridgeman Art Library/Getty Images.
FRONTMATTER: Pages i–xxxi iii–v, Pearson Education; **vi, T,** ZZ/Alamy; **R,** GoGo Images Corporation/Alamy; **L,** Martin Gray/National Geographic Stock; **vii,** SuperStock/age fotostock; **viii,** Richard Hook/Dorling Kindersley; **ix,** Shutterstock, Inc.; **x,** Imagebroker/Photolibrary, New York; **xi,** Hemis/ Alamy; **xii,** Katja Kreder/Glow Images; **xiii,** Shutterstock, Inc.; **xiv,** Ancient Art & Architecture/DanitaDelimont.com; **xv,** John Warburton-Lee Photography/ Alamy; **xvii,** Chris Hellier/Corbis; **xviii,** JTB Photo/PhotoLibrary Group Ltd; **xix,** Harold R. Stinnette Photo Stock/Alamy; **xx,** The Art Archive/Gift of Mrs. William B. Miles/Museum of the City of New York/32.275.2; **xxi, L,** Bettmann/Corbis; **R,** Herwin Crasto/Reuters/Corbis; **xxv, MB,** Erich Lessing/Art Resource, NY; **R,** Shutterstock, Inc.; **xxvi, LB,** Paolo Koch/Photo Researchers, Inc.; **MB,** Museo Archeologico Nazionale, Naples, Italy/Alinari/The Bridgeman Art Library; **RB,** Karl Johaentges/age fotostock; **xxx, B,** The Granger Collection, New York.

CORE CONCEPTS: Pages xxxii–1, bkgrd, Image Source/Getty Images; **xxxii, R,** Digital Vision/Getty Images; **1, L, R,** Gavin Hellier/Getty Images; **2, RT,** Jim Zuckerman/Corbis; **LT,** Digital Vision/Getty Images; **B,** El Comercio Newspaper, Dante Piaggio/AP Images; **3, RT,** Photo courtesy of Brian McCray; **LT,** Ira Block/ National Geographic/Getty Images; **TM,** University of Oregon/AP Images; **4, LB,** The British Museum/Dorling Kindersley; **LB,** O. Louis Mazzatenta/ National Geographic Stock; **RB,** Ivonne Wierink/Shutterstock; **M,** Giles Stokoe/ Felix deWeldon/Dorling Kindersley; **5, RT,** Dagli Orti/Picture Desk, Inc./Kobal Collection; **M,** Andy Crawford/Dorling Kindersley, Courtesy of the University Museum of Archaeology and Anthropology, Cambridge; **RB,** Getty Images/De Agostini Editore Picture Library; **6, LB,** Bettmann/Corbis; **LM,** Bettmann/Corbis;

8, LT, Sean Hunter/Dorling Kindersley; **B,** Martin Gray/National Geographic Stock; **R,** Robert F. Sisson/National Geographic Society; **9, LB, O.** Louis Mazzatenta/National Geographic Stock; **LB,** Anders Ryman/Corbis. **10,** Saul Loeb/AFP/Getty Images; **18, RT,** Kim Sayer/Dorling Kindersley; **B,** Tom Sliter/ The Stennis Center for Public Service Leadership; **RT,** Phil Sandlin/AP Images; **19, LT,** Reuters/Hans Deryk; **RT,** Photo courtesy of Anne Marie Sutherland; **20, LB,** Art Resource/Musee du Louvre; **RB,** Spc Katherine M. Roth/HO/epa/ Corbis All Rights Reserved; **21, L,** Todd Gipstein/Corbis; **R,** Imaginechina via AP Images; **22, R,** Pool/Anwar Hussein Collection/Getty Images; **L,** Karel Prinsloo/ AP Images; **23,** John Leicester/AP Images; **24, T,** Kim Sayer/Dorling Kindersley; **M,** L. Clarke/Corbis; **B,** AP Photo/Douglas Healey; **25, M,** White House Photo Office; **T,** Wally McNamee/Corbis; **B,** The Collection of the Supreme Court of the United States; **26, B,** Jeff Greenberg/PhotoEdit; **T,** William Whitehurst/ Corbis; **27, RB,** Wally McNamee/Corbis; **28, LB,** LWA/Getty Images; **BM,** Ariel Skelley/Blend Images/Corbis; **BM,** fotog/Getty Images; **RB,** Getty Images; **29, RT,** Brigitte Sporrer/zefa/Corbis; **32, B,** Dennis MacDonald/PhotoEdit; **M,** Bruno Morandi/Age Fotostock; **33, T,** Reuters/KNS Korean News Agency; **34, B,** SuperStock/Age Fotostock; **35, LB,** The Seattle Times/Newscom; **RB,** Photo by Wang Kai/ChinaFotoPress/Newscom; **36, LB,** Ed Kashi/Corbis; **37, RT,** Hou Jun/Newscom; **40, B,** Interfoto/Alamy; **RT,** Sylvain Grandadam/age footstock; **LT,** © Dennis MacDonald/Alamy Images; **41, TM,** Photo courtesy of Joanna Baca; **RT,** © Rolf Nussbaumer Photography/Alamy Images; **RT,** Photo courtesy of Joanna Baca; **42, LT,** Gavin Hellier/Getty Images; **LB,** Pearson; **BM,** Pearson; **RB,** Pearson; **43, All,** Pearson; **46,** Stephane De Sakutin/AFP/Getty Images; **47, TM,** Dmitry Kosterev/Shutterstock; **RT,** Dave King/Dorling Kindersley; **RM,** Luchschen/Shutterstock; **BM,** Dorling Kindersley; **BM,** Owen Franken/Corbis; **RB,** James Marshall/Corbis; **48, L,** Alistair Duncan/Dorling Kindersley; **LB,** Michael Holford/Dorling Kindersley; **RB,** Bruce Forster/Dorling Kindersley\Courtesy of the National Historic Oregon Trail Interpretive Center; **49, LB,** Swim Ink 2, LLC/ Corbis; **RB,** Matthew Ward/Dorling Kindersley.

CHAPTER 1: Pages 54-77, 54, Robert Harding Picture Library Ltd./Alamy; **55,** Border Mike P Shepherd/Alamy; **59, M,** www.CartoonStock.com; **59, R,** James King Holmes/Photo Researchers; **59, L,** Scott Camazine/Photo Researchers, Inc.; **70, Inset,** Sisse Brimberg/National Geographic Stock; **62, TR,** David L. Brill; **58,** Colin Keates/Dorling Kindersley, Courtesy of the Natural History Museum, London; **61, B,** Richard T. Nowitz/Photo Researchers, Inc.; **61, T,** National Geographic/Getty Images; **61, M,** AFP/Getty Images; **62, TL,** Patrick Robert/Corbis; **62, TM,** Jack Maguire/Alamy; **62, B,** Andrew Woodley/ Alamy; **64,** Tom McHugh/Photo Researchers, Inc.; **65, B,** John Reader/Photo Researchers, Inc.; **65, T,** The Art Archive/National Anthropological Museum Mexico/Gianni Dagli Orti; **66,** John Reader/Photo Researchers, Inc.; **68,** Hamid Sardar/Corbis; **70, R,** Richard Hook/Dorling Kindersley; **70, L,** Lynton Gardiner/ Dorling Kindersley, Courtesy of The American Museum of Natural History; **71, L,** Malcolm McGregor/Dorling Kindersley; **71, R,** Dave King/Dorling Kindersley, Courtesy of the National Museum of Wales; **71, Bkgrnd,** The Art Archive; **73, Bkgrnd,** Photographer/National Geographic Society; **73, Inset,** (t) age fotostock/SuperStock; **73, Inset,** (b) Alberto Paredes/Alamy; **74, T,** Tomsich/ Photo Researchers, Inc.; **74, B,** Pascal Goetgheluck/Photo Researchers, Inc.; **76,** CartoonStock; **77,** Prehistoric/Getty Images.

CHAPTER 2: Pages 78-99, 78, Paolo Koch/Photo Researchers, Inc.; **83, T,** Juniors Bildarchiv/Alamy; **83, T4,** Juniors Bildarchiv/Alamy; **63,** Shutterstock, Inc.; **82,** Imagebroker/Alamy; **83, T1,** Shutterstock, Inc.; **83, T2,** Delphine Adburgham/Alamy; **83, T3,** imagebroker/Alamy; **83, T5,** Shutterstock, Inc.; **83, T6,** Shutterstock, Inc.; **83, BM,** Shutterstock, Inc.; **83, BL,** Shutterstock, Inc.; **83, BR,** Frank Lukasseck/Getty Images; **83,** Shutterstock, Inc.; **84, M,** Dave King/ Dorling Kindersley, Courtesy of The Museum of London; **84, B,** Shutterstock, Inc.; **84, T,** Ancient Art & Architecture/Danita Delimont; **86,** Sonia Halliday Photographs/Alamy; **87, BR,** Pictures of Record, Inc.; **87, M,** Chris Forsey/ Dorling Kindersley; **87, BL,** Marion Bull/Alamy; **87, T,** Gianni Dagli Orti/Corbis; **89,** Mike Cumberbatch/Alamy; **90,** The Art Archive/Archaeological Museum Baghdad/Gianni Dagli Orti; **91,** Nik Wheeler/Corbis; **92, BL,** The Art Archive/ Gianni Dagli Orti; **92, T,** Georg Gerster/Photo Researchers, Inc.; **92, BM,** The Art Archive/National Museum Karachi/Alfredo Dagli Orti; **92, BR,** The Art Archive/

Hunan Provincial Museum/Granger Collection; **95, T,** The Art Archive/Egyptian Museum Cairo/Dagli Orti; **95, M,** Bettmann/Corbis; **95, B,** PhotoEdit; **96, B,** Borromeo/Art Resource, NY; **96, M,** Emil von Maltitz/Alamy; **96, T,** Richard Hutchings/PhotoEdit; **97, L,** Royal Ontario Museum/Corbis; **97, M,** British Library/HIP/The Image Works; **97, R,** Pearson Education; **99, L,** Shutterstock, Inc.; **99, R,** Shutterstock, Inc.

UNIT 1 PRIMARY SOURCE: Pages 100-101, 100, AFP/Getty Images; **101,** Ancient Art & Architecture/Danita Delimont.

UNIT 1 CLOSER: Pages 102-103, 102, RB, British Museum/Art Resource, NY; **MR,** AAAC/Topham/The Image Works; **TL,** Exactostock/SuperStock; **102, RT,** Alamy Images; **102, Bkgrnd,** Shutterstock, Inc.; **103, Bkgrnd,** Design Pics Inc./Alamy; **103,B,** Uden Graham/Redlink/Corbis.

CHAPTER 3: Pages 106-139, 106 B, Age Fotostock/Superstock; **110, Bkgrnd,** Cheryl Diaz Meyer/Dallas Morning News/Corbis; **113, Inset,** The Art Archive/Musée du Louvre Paris/Gianni Dagli Orti; **115, T,** Dorling Kindersley; **115, Inset,** The Art Archive/Musée du Louvre Paris/Dagli Orti; **115, M,** The Art Archive/Musée du Louvre Paris/Gianni Dagli Orti; **116, T,** Dorling Kindersley; **118, LB,** Scala/Art Resource, NY; **119, Bkgrnd,** The Art Archive/Musée du Louvre Paris/Gianni Dagli Orti; **119, Inset,** The Art Archive/Archaeological Museum Baghdad/Gianni Dagli Orti; **120, L,** The Bridgeman Art Library; **120, R,** Mesopotamian/Louvre, Paris, France/Giraudon/The Bridgeman Art Library International; **121, Inset,** Louvre, Paris, France/The Bridgeman Art Library International; **122,** The Art Archive/Musée du Louvre Paris/Gianni Dagli Orti; **125, B,** The British Library/Photolibrary; **126, BM,** The Art Archive/British Museum/Alfredo Dagli Orti; **130,** Dorling Kindersley; **131, RB,** mtr/Shutterstock, Inc.; **133,** Ancient Art and Architecture Collection; **136, RT,** The Bridgeman Art Library International; **137, R,** Pearson.

CHAPTER 4: Pages 140-165, 140, nagelestock.com/Alamy; **144,** The Art Archive/Egyptian Museum Cairo/Gianni Dagli Orti; **146,** Paul Almasy/Corbis; **147,** The Art Archive/Luxor Museum, Egypt/Gianni Dagli Orti; **148,** The Art Archive/Egyptian Museum Cairo/Gianni Dagli Orti; **150, M,** The Art Archive/Egyptian Museum Cairo/Gianni Dagli Orti; **150, BR,** Dorling Kindersley; **150, BL,** Dorling Kindersley; **150, T,** SSPL/The Image Works; **150, Bkgrnd,** Shutterstock, Inc.; **151,** The Art Archive/Egyptian Museum Turin/Gianni Dagli Orti; **152,** The Art Archive/Musée du Louvre Paris/Gianni Dagli Orti; **153, R,** The Art Archive/Musée du Louvre Paris/Gianni Dagli Orti; **153, L,** DeA Picture Library/Art Resource, NY; **154, BL,** Shutterstock, Inc.; **154, T,** Shutterstock, Inc.; **154, BL,** The Art Archive/H.M. Herget/NGS Image Collection; **155, L,** The Art Archive/Dagli Orti; **155, R,** Richard Bonson/Dorling Kindersley; **155, Bkgrnd,** Shutterstock, Inc.; **156, T,** The Art Archive/Ragab Papyrus Institute Cairo/Gianni Dagli Orti; **156, BR,** Science Museum/SSPL/The Image Works; **156, BL,** SSPL/The Image Works; **156, Bkgrnd,** Shutterstock, Inc.; **157,** SSPL/The Image Works; **158,** Erich Lessing/Art Resource, NY; **159, RT,** SSPL/Science Museum/Art Resource, NY; **159, LB,** Shutterstock, Inc.; **159, LT,** Werner Forman/Topham/The Image Works; **160,** Biosphoto/Lorgnier Antoine/Peter Arnold, Inc.; **161,** Mary Evans Picture Library/Alamy; **162, ML,** imagebroker/Alamy; **162, T,** John Warburton-Lee Photography/Alamy; **162, B,** Bildarchiv Preussischer Kulturbesitz/Art Resource, NY; **162, MR,** Werner Forman/Topham/The Image Works; **163,** Topham/The Image Works; **164,** The Art Archive/Gianni Dagli Orti.

CHAPTER 5: Pages 166-189, 166, PhotoStock-Israel/Alamy; **166, Bkgrnd,** Shutterstock, Inc.; **166, Bkgrnd,** Shutterstock, Inc.; **167,** Border Shutterstock, Inc.; **168,** Border Shutterstock, Inc.; **170,** The Art Archive/Corbis; **172,** Private Collection/Look and Learn/The Bridgeman Art Library International; **173, TL,** The Art Archive/Private Collection/Gianni Dagli Orti; **173, TR,** Private Collection/Look and Learn/The Bridgeman Art Library International; **173, BL,** Private Collection/Look and Learn/The Bridgeman Art Library International; **173, BR,** Private Collection/Look and Learn/The Bridgeman Art Library International; **173, Bkgrnd,** Shutterstock, Inc.; **174,** The Granger Collection, New York; **175,** Private Collection/Look and Learn/The Bridgeman Art Library International; **176,** Israel images/Alamy; **177, T,** By kind permission of the Trustees of the Wallace Collection, London/Art Resource, NY; **177, B,** The Art Archive/St Pierre Church Moissac France/Gianni Dagli Orti; **177, M,** Victoria & Albert Museum, London, UK/The Bridgeman Art Library International; **177, Bkgrnd,** Shutterstock, Inc.; **177, Bkgrnd,** Shutterstock, Inc.; **178, R,** The Art Archive/Bodleian Library Oxford; **178, L,** Israel images/Alamy; **178, Bkgrnd,** Shutterstock, Inc.; **178, Bkgrnd,** Shutterstock, Inc.; **179, M,** Michael Newman/

PhotoEdit; **179, B,** Phil Schermeister/Corbis; **179, T,** Shutterstock, Inc.; **180, BL,** Shutterstock, Inc.; **180, TR,** Israel images/Alamy; **180, TL,** Photodisc/Getty Images, Inc.; **180, BR,** Bill Aron/PhotoEdit; **180, Bkgrnd,** Shutterstock, Inc.; **181,** Dorling Kindersley; **182,** Mary Evans Picture Library/The Image Works; **183,** SuperStock; **185, BR,** Sean Creech; **185, BM,** Nelson Hancock/Rough Guides/Dorling Kindersley; **185, TM,** Greg Balfour Evans/Alamy; **185, BL,** Bettmann/Corbis; **185, TL,** Photo by Anne Frank Fonds - Basel/Anne Frank House - Amsterdam/Getty Images; **185, M,** Mark Zylber/Alamy; **185, TR,** Pushkin Museum, Moscow, Russia/The Bridgeman Art Library International; **185, Bkgrnd,** Shutterstock, Inc.; **185, Bkgrnd,** Shutterstock, Inc.; **186, Bkgrnd,** Shutterstock, Inc.; **187,** Jeff Greenberg/The Image Works.

UNIT 2 PRIMARY SOURCE: Pages 190-191, 190, North Wind Picture Archives/Alamy; **191, B,** Alinari Archives/The Image Works.

UNIT 2 CLOSER: Pages 192-193, 192, T, Wayne Hutchinson/Alamy; **L,** Ira Lippke/Newscom; **RB,** AP Wide World Photo/John McConnico; **193, Bkgrnd,** America/Alamy.

CHAPTER 6: Pages 196-229, 196, Imagebroker/Photolibrary; **200,** commoner28th/Getty Images; **201, R,** Andy Crawford/Dorling Kindersley; **203, Bkgrnd,** Robert Harding Picture Library/SuperStock; **203, RB,** Jonathan Mark Kenoyer/Doranne Jacobson International Images/Courtesy Department of Archaeology and Museums, Government of Pakistan.; **203, TL,** The London Art Archive/Alamy; **204, Inset,** The Art Archive/National Museum Karachi/Alfredo Dagli Orti; **206, LB,** Indian School/India Office Library, London/Ann & Bury Peerless Picture Library/The Bridgeman Art Library International; **208,** Vivek Sharma/Alamy; **209, LB,** The Art Archive/National Museum Karachi/Alfredo Dagli Orti; **209, RT,** The Art Archive/National Museum Karachi/Dagli Orti; **210, LB,** Simon Bracken/Dorling Kindersley; **210, M,** Mark Edwards/Peter Arnold Inc.; **210, RB,** William Albert Allard/National Geographic Society; **210, RT,** Jim Zuckerman/Alamy; **211,** Villard/Sipa; **212, LB,** dbimages/Alamy; **213, TR,** Pep Roig/Alamy; **213, RB,** David Wells/Alamy; **213, B,** Dinodia Images/Alamy; **214, T,** Oriental Museum, Durham University, UK/The Bridgeman Art Library International; **215, L,** Réunion des Musées Nationaux/Art Resource, NY; **215, M,** The Art Archive/Musée Guimet Paris/Gianni Dagli Orti; **215, R,** The Cleveland Museum of Art, 2001, Purchase from the J. H. Wade Fund. 1930.331.; **216, BL,** Lynn Saville; **217,** Robert Harding Images/Masterfile; **218,** British Museum/Art Resource, NY; **219,** Keren Su/China Span/Alamy; **220,** Friedrich Stark/Alamy; **221,** The Art Archive/Musée Guimet Paris/Alfredo Dagli Orti; **222, T,** Christine Osborne; **222, Inset,** Hugh Sitton/Corbis; **223, RB,** Ray Moller/Dorling Kindersley, Courtesy of the Powell-Cotton Museum, Kent; **225, R,** Luca I. Tettoni/Corbis; **225, L,** Peter Brown/Alamy; **225, TR,** Friedrich Stark/Alamy; **225, LT,** Ben Pipe - Premium/Alamy; **227,** Photosindia.

CHAPTER 7: Pages 230-249, 230, Trans-World Photos/SuperStock; **232, B,** Nancy Carter/North Wind Picture Archives; **234,** Kamatís Potpourri; **235,** Burstein Collection/Corbis; **236,** Yogesh S. More/Age Fotostock; **237, R,** Indian School/National Museum of India, New Delhi, India/Giraudon/The Bridgeman Art Library International; **237, L,** Nikreates/Alamy; **238, M,** The British Library Board; **238, L,** Philip Baird/Anthropology, Archeology and Art; **238, R,** Mary Evans Picture Library/The Image Works; **239, R,** Sudharak Olwe/Dinodia Photo Library; **239, L,** Erich Lessing/Art Resource, NY; **240, Bkgrnd,** Paule Seux/Hemis/Corbis; **240, B,** Atlantide Phototravel/Corbis; **240, MR,** SEF/Art Resource, NY; **240, ML,** david pearson/Alamy; **240, TL,** Shutterstock, Inc.; **240, MM,** Joerg Boethling/Alamy; **240, TR,** Angelo Hornak/Corbis; **241,** age fotostock/SuperStock; **242,** Ancient Art & Architecture/Danita Delimont; **244, L,** Eddie Gerald/Alamy; **244, M,** The Art Archive/Bodleian Library Oxford/The Bodleian Library; **244, R,** Dorling Kindersley; **245, T,** The Trustees of the British Museum; **245, L,** Angelo Hornak/Alamy; **245, R,** Angelo Hornak/Alamy; **246, M,** Eye Ubiquitous/Alamy; **246, T,** British Library/HIP/The Image Works; **246, B,** Bob Daemmrich/PhotoEdit, Inc.; **247, T,** Luca Tettoni/Corbis.

CHAPTER 8: Pages 250-269, 250, The Art Archive/Hunan Provincial Museum/Granger Collection; **254,** The Art Archive/Musée Cernuschi Paris/Gianni Dagli Orti; **256,** Richard Swiecki/Corbis; **258,** The Art Archive/National Palace Museum Taiwan; **260, Bkgrnd,** Réunion des Musées Nationaux/Art Resource, NY; **261, L,** The Art Archive/Jean Vinchon Numismatist Paris/Gianni Dagli Orti; **261, R,** Erich Lessing/Art Resource, NY; **261, M,** Erich Lessing/Art Resource, NY; **262,** Dorling Kindersley; **262,** Ingram Publishing/Age Fotostock; **263, LB,** Look Die Bildagentur der Fotografen GmbH/Alamy; **263, L,** Ivy Close Images/Alamy;

851

Acknowledgments (continued)

264, RB, Chinatopix/AP Wide World Photos; 264, RT, Jacques Langevin/Sygma/Corbis; 264, Bkgrnd, Shutterstock; 266, M, Karl Johaentges/Age Fotostock; 266, TR, View Stock/Age Fotostock; 266, LT, AFP Photo/Frederic J. Brown/Newscom; 267, Inset, Look/Age Fotostock; 267, T, Look/Age Fotostock.

CHAPTER 9: Pages 270-291, 270, National Geographic Society; 274, Masterfile; 275, B, Tomb of Qin shi Huang Di, Xianyang, China/The Bridgeman Art Library International; 275, T, Ancient Art & Architecture/DanitaDelimont.com; 276, The Art Archive/BibliothËque Nationale Paris; 278, HIP/Art Resource, NY; 279, Panorama/The Image Works; 280, The Art Archive/Genius of China Exhibition; 281, Hemis/Alamy; 282, The Metropolitan Museum of Art/Art Resource, NY; 283, BR, Erich Lessing/Art Resource, NY; 283, T, The Granger Collection, New York; 283, BL, The Art Archive/Musée Cernuschi Paris/Gianni Dagli Orti; 284, ML, Maryann Frazier/Photo Researchers, Inc.; 284, BL, Keren Su/Corbis; 284, BM, Dex Image/Getty Images; 284, BR, Bibliotheque Municipale, Poitiers, France/Giraudon/The Bridgeman Art Library International; 284, T, Hunan Provincial Museum; 284, MR, The Art Archive/Victoria and Albert Museum London/Eileen Tweedy; 284, Bkgrnd, Shutterstock, Inc.; 285, The Art Archive/Musée Cernuschi Paris/Gianni Dagli Orti; 286, B, Alan Hills/The British Museum/Dorling Kindersley; 286, T, Werner Forman/Art Resource, NY; 287, Science Museum/The Image Works; 288, National Museum, Beijing, China/Erich Lessing/Art Resource, NY.

UNIT 3 PRIMARY SOURCE: Pages 290-291, 290, Yogesh S More/Age Fotostock/Photolibrary; 291, APIC/Getty Images.

UNIT 3 CLOSER: Pages 292-293, 292, LB, Gallo Images/Getty Images; 292, RB, Shutterstock, Inc.; 292, TL, Tim Gainey/Alamy; 293, RT, Peter Brown/Alamy; 293, Bkgrnd, Shutterstock, Inc.

CHAPTER 10: Pages 296-323, 296, AAAC/Topham/The Image Works; 296, Border Shutterstock, Inc.; 297, Border Museo Archeologico Nazionale, Naples, Italy/Alinari/The Bridgeman Art Library International; 300, B, SCPhotos/Alamy; 301, T, The Bridgeman Art Library International; 301, LB, © ian woolcock/Alamy Images; 302, L, Bibliotheque de la Sorbonne, Paris, France/Archives Charmet/The Bridgeman Art Library International; 302, R, PCL/Alamy; 303, Warner Bros./The Kobal Collection/Bailey, Alex; 304, T, Private Collection/Look and Learn/The Bridgeman Art Library International; 304, B, Katja Kreder/Glow Images; 306, Vanni Archive/Corbis; 307, Nick Nicholls/The British Museum/Dorling Kindersley; 308, Bkgrnd, Shutterstock, Inc.; 308, Bkgrnd, Shutterstock, Inc.; 309, L, Archives Larousse, Paris, France/Giraudon/The Bridgeman Art Library International; 309, R, Michael Yamashita/Corbis; 310, R, Ivor Kerslake/The British Museum/Dorling Kindersley; 310, LB, akg-images/Archives CDA/Guillo; 310, LT, Courtesy of Museum of Nacional de Arte de Catalunya; Ramon Manent/Corbis; 311, The Trustees of the British Museum; 312, Athens 2004/Alamy; 314, Private Collection/The Stapleton Collection/The Bridgeman Art Library International; 314, Border Shutterstock, Inc.; 315, Scala/Art Resource, NY; 316, T, akg-images/John Hios; 316, Border Shutterstock, Inc.; 318, Bkgrnd, Richard Garvey-Williams/Alamy; 318, De Agostini/Getty Images; 320, HIP/Art Resource, NY; 322, The Granger Collection, New York.

CHAPTER 11: Pages 324-533, 324, David Ball/Alamy; 325, Border Alexander Yu/Zotov/Shutterstock, Inc.; 325, T, Araldo de Luca/Corbis; 328, National Museums of Scotland/The Bridgeman Art Library International; 329, DACS/Giraudon/The Bridgeman Art Library International; 331, T, Private Collection/Archives Charmet/The Bridgeman Art Library International; 331, B, Ancient Art & Architecture/DanitaDelimont; 331, M, Reinhard Saczewski/Art Resource, NY; 334, Araldo de Luca/Corbis; 335, T, The Art Archive/Archaeological Museum Salonica/Gianni Dagli Orti; 336, Inset, Sandro Vannini/Corbis; 337, Erich Lessing/Art Resource, NY; 338, Private Collection/The Stapleton Collection/The Bridgeman Art Library International; 339, Araldo de Luca/Corbis; 340, Simela Pantzartzi/epa/Corbis; 341, R, Shutterstock, Inc.; 341, L, Michael Ciesielski/Alamy; 342, Robbie Jack/Corbis; 343, Ivy Close Images/Alamy; 344, Mary Evans Picture Library; 345, Jacques-Louis David (1748-1825), "The Death of Socrates. Oil on canvas, 51 x 77 1/4 in. (129.5 x 196.2 cm.). Signed and dated (lower left) L.D./MDCCLXXXVII; (on bench, at right) L. David. The Metropolitan Museum of Art, Catharine Lorillard Wolfe Collection, Wolfe Fund, 1931 (31.45). Photograph ©1980 The Metropolitan Museum of Art; 346, R, Bettmann/Corbis; 346, L, National Endowment for the Humanities/EDSITEment/Reconstructed from resources at The Perseus Project <http://www.perseus.tufts.edu/; 347, B, Bettmann/Corbis; 347, T, Matthias Kulka/Corbis; 348, Ancient Art & Architecture/Danita Delimont; 349, T, Gianni Dagli Orti/Corbis; 349, B, Shutterstock, Inc.; 350, B, The Metropolitan Museum of Art/Art Resource, NY; 350, MR, Hermitage, St. Petersburg, Russia/The Bridgeman Art Library International; 350, ML, Rob Howard/Corbis; 350, MM, Dorling Kindersley; 350, T, AP Photo/Hilti Foundation, Frederic Osada; 351, Araldo de Luca/Corbis; 352, Louvre, Paris, France/Giraudon/The Bridgeman Art Library International.

UNIT 4 PRIMARY SOURCE: Pages 354-355, 354, Ray Roberts/Alamy; 355, akg-images/Peter Connolly/The Image Works.

UNIT 4 CLOSER: Pages 356-357 356, R, Nobby Clark/Getty Images; 356, L, Richard Broadwell/Alamy; 357, L, Dorling Kindersley; 357, Bkgrnd, Shutterstock.

CHAPTER 12: Pages 360-385, 360, José Fuste Raga/Age Fotostock; 364, Snark/Art Resource NY; 365, Inset, Danilo Donadoni/Age footstock; 366, LB, Scala/Art Resource NY; 368, M, SuperStock; 368, Bkgrnd, Dorling Kindersley; 368, RB, Scala/Ministero per i Beni e le Attività Culturali/Art Resource, NY; 368, R, The Granger Collection, New York; 371, The Art Archive/Ca Rezzonico Museum Venice/Alfredo Dagli Orti; 373, R, Dorling Kindersley; 373, L, The Granger Collection, New York; 376, The Art Archive/Musée Archéologique Naples/Alfredo Dagli Orti; 377, R, Pearson; 377, L, The Metropolitan Museum of Art/Art Resource NY; 378, R, The Art Archive/Museo della Civilta Romana Rome/Dagli Orti; 378, Inset, Scala/Ministero per i Beni e le Attività Culturali/Art Resource, NY; 383, B, The Art Archive/Museo della Civilta Romana Rome/Alfredo Dagli Orti; 383, T, The Art Archive/Archaeological Museum Venice/Alfredo Dagli Orti; 383, M, Bildarchiv Preussischer Kulturbesitz/Art Resource, NY.

CHAPTER 13: Pages 386-421; 386, Tetra Images/Photolibrary New York; 386, Border Shutterstock, Inc.; 387, Border Shutterstock, Inc.; 389, Border Shutterstock, Inc.; 390, Asier Villafranca/Shutterstock, Inc.; 392, Elena Elisseeva/Shutterstock, Inc.; 393, L, imagebroker/Alamy; 393, R, Dorling Kindersley; 394, B, Christopher and Sally Gable/Dorling Kindersley; 394, T, Shutterstock, Inc.; 394, ML, Shutterstock, Inc.; 394, MR, Sylvia Cordaiy Photo Library Ltd/Alamy; 396, Erich Lessing/Art Resource, NY; 397, Pearson; 397, Border Shutterstock, Inc.; 397, Border Shutterstock, Inc.; 398, M, Archives Larousse, Paris, France/Giraudon/The Bridgeman Art Library; 398, B, Christi Graham and Nick Nicholls/The British Museum/Dorling Kindersley; 398, T, Bettmann/Corbis; 398, Border Shutterstock, Inc.; 400, L, Dorling Kindersley; 400, R, The Art Archive/Musée National de la voiture et du tourisme Compiègne/Gianni Dagli Orti; 400-401, Border Shutterstock, Inc.; 401, The Art Archive; 402, The Art Archive/Museo Capitolino Rome/Gianni Dagli Orti; 403, Border Shutterstock, Inc.; 403, Border Shutterstock, Inc.; 404, R, The Trustees of The British Museum/Art Resource, NY; 404, M, The Art Archive/Museum of Carthage/Gianni Dagli Orti; 404, L, The Art Archive/Musée du Louvre Paris/Gianni Dagli Orti; 404, Bkgrnd, Shutterstock, Inc.; 404, Border Shutterstock, Inc.; 404, Border Shutterstock, Inc.; 405, Shutterstock, Inc.; 407, The Art Archive/Archaeological Museum Split Croatia/Alfredo Dagli Orti; 408, Hill Street Studios/Getty Images, Inc.; 409, The Art Archive/Museo Tridentino Arte Sacra Trento/Alfredo Dagli Orti; 409, Border Shutterstock, Inc.; 410, Réunion des Musées Nationaux/Art Resource, NY; 410-411, Border Shutterstock, Inc.; 411, Erich Lessing/Art Resource, NY; 412, T, AFP/Getty Images; 412, BR, Mike Goldwater/Alamy; 412, BL, Jim West/Alamy; 412, Bkgrnd, Shutterstock, Inc.; 414, Ken Durden/Shutterstock, Inc.; 414, T, The Art Archive; 415, M, Réunion des Musées Nationaux/Art Resource, NY; 415, B, Illustration by - Wood Ronsaville Harlin, Inc.; 416, Erich Lessing/Art Resource, NY; 416, Border Shutterstock, Inc.; 416-417, Border Shutterstock, Inc.; 417, L, The Art Archive/Museo Capitolino Rome/Gianni Dagli Orti; 417, R, Shutterstock, Inc.; 418, TR, The Art Gallery Collection/Alamy; 418, TL, Erich Lessing/Art Resource, NY; 418, B, Raymond Delamarre/Archives Charmet/The Bridgeman Art Library, London/New York; 418, Bkgrnd, Shutterstock, Inc.; 420, Photolibrary New York.

UNIT 5 PRIMARY SOURCE: Pages 422-423, 422, Réunion des Musées/Nationaux/Art Resource, NY; 423, Ancient Art & Architecture/Danita Delimont.

UNIT 5 CLOSER: Pages 424-425, 424, LB, ColorBlind Images/Blend Images/Age Fotostock; 424, B, Inset, Hulton Archive Photos/Getty Images; 424, T, Claudia Veja/Alamy; 425, BR, Age Fotostock; 425, Bkgrnd, Picture Desk, Inc./Kobal Collection.

CHAPTER 14: Pages 428-445, 428, San Vitale, Ravenna, Italy/The Bridgeman

Art Library; **432,** The Art Archive/Museo Capitolino Rome/Alfredo Dagli Orti; **434, BL,** De Agostini/SuperStock; **434, TR,** The Granger Collection, New York; **434, TL,** Ancient Art & Architecture/DanitaDelimont; **434, BR,** Erich Lessing/ Art Resource, NY; **435,** The Board of Trustees of the Armouries/HIP/The Image Works; **436, B,** Erich Lessing/Art Resource, NY; **436, T,** The Metropolitan Museum of Art/Art Resource, NY; **437, L,** Directphoto.org/Alamy; **437, R,** Roger Cracknell 01/classic/Alamy; **438, B,** Buddy Mays/Alamy; **438, T,** Jonathan Little/ Alamy; **440,** The Art Archive/San Angelo in Formis Capua Italy/Alfredo Dagli Orti; **441, T,** Robert Harding Images/Masterfile; **441, B,** Harvey Lloyd/Getty Images; **442, L,** Mary Evans Picture Library/The Image Works; **442, R,** Massimo Listri/Corbis; **443,** DeA Picture Library/Art Resource, NY; **444,** The British Library/HIP/The Image Works.

CHAPTER 15: Pages 446-477, 446, JTB Photo Communications, Inc./Alamy; **450,** Tim E White/Alamy; **452,** Getty Images; **454,** Louise Batalla Duran/Alamy; **455, R,** Photolibrary New York; **455, L,** Réunion des Musées Nationaux/Art Resource, NY; **457, T,** Werner Forman/Art Resource, NY; **457, ML,** Photolibrary New York; **457, MM,** Chas Howson/The British Museum/Dorling Kindersley; **457, MR,** Louise Batalla Duran/Alamy; **457, B,** Suhaib Salem/Reuters Newmedia Inc./Corbis; **458,** World Religions Photo Library/Alamy; **460,** Private Collection/ The Bridgeman Art Library International; **462, AP,** Photo/Amr Nabil; **463,** akg-images/British Library; **464, L,** Ryan Rodrick Beiler/Alamy; **464, R,** mediacolor's/ Alamy; **465, L,** Private Collection/Archives Charmet/The Bridgeman Art Library International; **465, R,** The Art Archive/Bodleian Library Oxford; **466,** Kharidehal Abhirama Ashwin/Shutterstock, Inc.; **467, T,** PhotosIndia.com LLC/Alamy; **467, B,** akg-images/British Library; **468,** DeA Picture Library/Art Resource, NY; **470,** The Art Archive/National Museum Damascus Syria/Gianni Dagli Orti; **471, L,** The Granger Collection, New York; **471, R,** The Art Archive/Bodleian Library Oxford; **472, L,** The British Museum/HIP/The Image Works; **472, R,** The Art Archive/University Library Istanbul/Gianni Dagli Orti; **473, BL,** The Metropolitan Museum of Art/Art Resource, NY; **473, T,** Werner Forman/Art Resource, NY; **473, BR,** The Metropolitan Museum of Art/Art Resource, NY; **473, BM,** Werner Forman/HIP/The Image Works; **474, BL,** Alexander Ryabintsev/Shutterstock, Inc.; **474, ML,** Sailorr/Shutterstock, Inc.; **474, BR,** Naiyyer/Shutterstock, Inc.; **474, T,** Aztec Images/Alamy; **475, MR,** Massimiliano Lamagna/Shutterstock, Inc.; **477,** Rehman/Shutterstock, Inc.

UNIT 6 PRIMARY SOURCE: Pages 478-479, 478, North Wind Picture Archives/ Alamy; **479,** Photononstop/SuperStock.

UNIT 6 CLOSER: Pages 480-481, 480, B, Age Fotostock; **480, RT,** Andres Rodriguez/Alamy; **480, LT,** Dorling Kindersley; **480, LT,** Shutterstock, Inc.; **481, B,** katatonia82/Shutterstock, Inc.; **481, T,** Dorling Kindersley.

CHAPTER 16: Pages 484-511, 484, Dirk Bakker; **488,** Ariadne Van Zandbergen/Alamy; **489, TR,** Jon Arnold Images Ltd/Alamy; **489, TL,** Michael Dwyer/Alamy; **489, B,** Michael Nichols/National Geographic Society; **490, B,** Remi Benali/Panos Pictures; **490, Inset,** John Warburton-Lee Photography/ Alamy; **491,** CDA/Guillemot/akg-images/The Image Works; **492,** Sylvaine Poitau/ Alamy; **493, R,** Neil Cooper/Alamy; **493, Inset,** Greenshoots Communications/ Alamy; **494,** Cover of Sundiata by David Wisniewski. Copyright (c) 1992,by David Wisniewski. Reprinted by permission of Clarion Books/Houghton Mifflin Company. All rights reserved.; **495, R,** Alamy; **495, L,** The Granger Collection, New York; **498, BL,** Nik Wheeler/Corbis; **498, BR,** Sebastien Cailleux/Corbis; **498, M,** Bob Krist/Corbis; **498, T,** dbimages/Alamy; **498, Bkgrnd,** mediacolor's/ Alamy; **500,** Radu Sigheti/Reuters/Corbis; **502, ML,** The Art Archive/Marine Museum Lisbon/Gianni Dagli Orti; **502, MR,** Javed A Jafferji/Impact/HIP/The Image Works; **502, B,** J Marshall - Tribaleye Images/Alamy; **502, T,** Robert Harding Picture Library Ltd/Alamy; **504,** Florin Iorganda/Reuters/Corbis; **506, L,** Charles & Josette Lenars/Corbis; **506, M,** Ancestor screen "(duen fobara)", from Abonnema village, Nigeria. The Minneapolis Institute of Arts. The John R. Van Derlip Fund; **506, R,** Melanie Gaertner/Peter Arnold Inc.; **508, BR,** Dorling Kindersley, Courtesy of the Pitt Rivers Museum, University of Oxford; **508, BM,** John Elk III/Alamy; **508, T,** © H. Christoph/ullstein bild/The Image Works, Inc.; **508, ML,** Judith Miller/Dorling Kindersley/Jo De Buck; **508, MR,** Ray Moller/ Dorling Kindersley, Courtesy of the Powell-Cotton Museum, Kent; **508, BL,** GFC Collection/Alamy; **511,** The Granger Collection, New York.

CHAPTER 17: Pages 512-543, 512, John Warburton-Lee Photography/Alamy; **516, LB,** The Art Archive/National Palace Museum Taiwan; **517, RT,** The Art Archive/Genius of China Exhibition; **517, LB,** Royal Ontario Museum/Corbis;

519, RB, The Granger Collection, New York; **519, RT,** Bridgeman-Giraudon/Art Resource, NY; **519, M,** © Werner Forman Archive/Topham/The Image Works, Inc.; **521, Inset,** The Art Archive/Freer Gallery of Art; **521, B,** Nico Smit-2/Alamy; **522, LB,** Robert Harding Picture Library Ltd/Alamy; **522, MR,** The Trustees of The British Museum; **522, ML,** Private Collection/The Bridgeman Art Library International; **522, TL,** Images & Stories/Alamy; **522, TR,** The British Museum/ Art Resource, NY; **524, LB,** architectural i/Alamy; **526, Bkgrnd,** Demetrio Carrasc/Dorling Kindersley; **526, RM,** The Board of Trustees of the Royal Armouries; **526, BL,** Ms Pers.113 f.29 Genghis Khan (c.1162-1227) Fighting the Tartars, from a book by Rashid-al-Din (1247-1318) (gouache), Persian School, (14th century)/Bibliotheque Nationale, Paris, France/The Bridgeman Art Library International; **526, RRT,** James L. Stanfield/National Geographic Society; **526, RRB,** Dorling Kindersley, Courtesy of the Churchill College Archives, Cambridge University; **526, Inset, Bkgrnd,** Shutterstock; **526,** The Board of Trustees of the Royal Armouries; **528, Inset,** Shutterstock, Inc.; **529, Inset,** The Art Archive/Bibliothèque Nationale Paris; **530, LB,** John Henshall/Alamy; **531, T,** Dorling Kindersley; **531, B,** Shutterstock, Inc.; **532, LT,** PHOTOCOME-US/SIPA/Photocome/Sipa/NewsCom; **533, Inset,** AFP/Getty Images; **534, LB,** Shutterstock, Inc.; **535, RB,** British Library Board. All Rights Reserved (Picture number 1022251.611)/Dorling Kindersley; **535, Bkgrnd,** Shutterstock, Inc.; **536,** Burstein Collection/Corbis; **537, TR,** Laurence Pordes/Dorling Kindersley, Courtesy of The British Library; **537, RB,** Image Source/Getty Images; **537, L,** The Art Archive/British Library; **537, M,** Ashmolean Museum, University of Oxford, UK/Bridgeman Art Library International; **537, TM,** Alan Hills/The British Museum/Dorling Kindersley; **538, Inset,** © Henry Westheim Photography/ Alamy Images; **538, L,** Interfoto/Alamy; **539,** Mary Evans Picture Library; **540, CC,** © National Maritime Museum, London/The Image Works, Inc.; **540, TM,** Shutterstock, Inc.; **540, MR,** Barnabas Kindersley/Dorling Kindersley; **540, TR,** Shutterstock, Inc.; **540, BM,** Neg./Transparency no. 273708. Photo by H. S. Rice. Courtesy Dept. of Library Services, American Museum of Natural History.; **540, LB,** The Granger Collection, New York; **540, T3,** Tim Brightmore/Alamy; **540, B,** Shutterstock, Inc.; **540, ML,** Indianapolis Museum of Art, USA/Gift of Mr and Mrs Eli Lilly & J.W. Alsdorf/The Bridgeman Art Library International; **540, TL,** Images & Stories/Alamy; **541, R,** Panorama Media (Beijing) Ltd./Alamy; **542,** The Art Archive/Freer Gallery of Art.

CHAPTER 18: Pages 544-571, 544, Corbis RF/Age Fotostock; **548,** AP Photo/ Shizuo Kambayashi; **549, B,** amana images inc./Alamy; **549, T,** Radius Images/ Alamy Images; **550, T,** Robert Harding Picture Library Ltd/Alamy; **550, ML,** The Granger Collection, New York; **550, MR,** Kimball Art Museum. Fort Worth, TX/ Art Resource; **551,** Tim Graham/Getty Images; **552,** Howard Sochurek/Time Life Pictures/Getty Images; **554,** Werner Forman Art Resource, NY; **555,** Asian Art & Archaeology, Inc./Corbis; **556,** The Art Archive/The Granger Collection, New York; **558, T,** Dorling Kindersley; **558, TR,** The Granger Collection, New York; **558, Bkgrnd,** Réunion des Musées Nationaux/Art Resource, NY; **558, L,** Kyodo/AP Wide World Photos; **559,** Dorling Kindersley; **560,** Vidler Steve/ Age Fotostock; **561, Bkgrnd,** Dorling Kindersley; **563, LB,** Michael Boyny/ Photolibrary New York; **563, BM,** Douglas Williams/Photolibrary; **563, BR,** Axiom/Photolibrary; **564, TL,** Koichi Kamoshida/Getty Images; **564, TR,** Koichi Kamoshida/Getty Images; **564, TL,** The Granger Collection, New York; **564, BL,** The Granger Collection, New York; **564, BC,** Pacific Press Service/Alamy; **564, RB,** Bruno Vincent/Getty Images; **566, T,** Yoshitsugu Nishigaki/Photolibrary New York; **566, M,** Emilio Ereza/Age Fotostock; **566, B,** Dorling Kindersley; **567, T,** Can Balcioglu/Shutterstock, Inc.; **567, RB,** imagebroker/Alamy; **567, LB,** Neale Cousland/Shutterstock, Inc.; **568,** Dorling Kindersley; **569,** John Lander/Alamy.

UNIT 7 PRIMARY SOURCE: Pages 572-573, 572, Réunion des Musées Nationaux/Art Resource, NY; **573,** S.Nicolas/Age Fotostock.

UNIT 7 CLOSER: Pages 574-575 574, TR, Jon Arnold Images Ltd/Alamy; **574, MR,** Robert Harding Picture Library Ltd/Alamy; **574, RB,** Art Resource; **574, LB,** The Granger Collection, New York; **575, B,** Andrey Burmakin/Shutterstock, Inc.; **575, Bkgrnd,** JL Images/Alamy.

CHAPTER 19: Pages 578-597, 578, Matt Sjoberg/Photolibrary New York; **582,** Werner Foreman/Topham/The Image Works Credit Line: Werner Forman Archive/Anthropology Museum, Veracruz University, Jalapa; **583, L,** Kenneth Garrett/National Geographic Society; **583, R,** Michel Zabe/Conaculta-Inah-Mex Authorized reproduction by the Instituto Nacional de Antropologia e Historia/ Dorling Kindersley; **585, B,** Michel Zabe/Conaculta-Inah-Mex, Authorized reproduction by the Instituto Nacional de Antropologia e Historia/Dorling

Acknowledgments (continued)

Kindersley; **585, T,** Werner Forman/Art Resource, NY; **586,** Tony Crocetta/Age Fotostock; **587, BL,** The Art Archive/Bibliothèque de líAssemblée Nationale Paris/Gianni Dagli Orti; **587, T,** Jonathan Gordon/Alamy; **587, BR,** Danita Delimont/Alamy; **588, L,** Hemis/Alamy; **588, R,** Dorling Kindersley; **589,** The Art Archive/National Anthropological Museum Mexico/Gianni Dagli Orti; **590,** blickwinkel/Alamy; **591, B,** The Art Archive/Museo Ciudad Mexico/Alfredo Dagli Orti; **591, T,** South American Pictures; **592, L,** Shutterstock, Inc.; **592, R,** Shutterstock, Inc.; **592, M,** Shutterstock, Inc.; **593, T,** The Art Archive/Museo Ciudad Mexico/Gianni Dagli Orti; **593, B,** Peter Wilson/Conaculta-Inah-Mex. Authorized reproduction by the Instituto Nacional de Antropologia e Historia/ Dorling Kindersley; **594, L,** Jack Fields/Photo Researchers, Inc.; **594, R,** Jean-Pierre Courau/The Bridgeman Art Library International; **595,** The Art Archive/ Museo del Templo Mayor Mexico/Gianni Dagli Orti.

CHAPTER 20: Pages 598-617, 598, Kuttig - Travel/Alamy; **602,** Jorge Ianiszewski/Art Resource, NY; **604, R,** Jamie Marshall/Impact/HIP/The Image Works; **604, L,** Jeremy Horner/Corbis; **605, Inset,** Klaus Lang/Alamy; **605,** Rutahsa Adventures; **606,** Pies Specifics/Alamy; **606, Inset,** The Granger Collection, New York; **607, T,** The Trustees of the British Museum/Art Resource, NY; **607, B,** Werner Forman/Art Resource, NY; **608, B,** SuperStock; **608, T,** George H.H. Huey/Alamy; **609,** Alexey Stiop/Alamy; **610, B,** © North Wind Picture Archives/Alamy Images; **610, T,** Dorling Kindersley; **611, L,** SuperStock, Inc.; **611, MT,** Buffalo Bill Historical Center / The Art Archive/Art Resource, NY; **611, R,** Neg./Transparency no. 3273(3). (Photo by Lee Boltin). Courtesy Dept. of Library Services, American Museum of Natural History; **611, MB,** Nancy Carter/Photolibrary New York; **612, BR,** The Palma Collection/Getty Images; **612, BL,** © Accent Alaska.com/Alamy Images; **612, TL,** The Trustees of The British Museum/Art Resource, NY; **612, Bkgrnd,** (r) © Ilene MacDonald/Alamy Images; **612, TR,** Dave King/Dorling Kindersley, Courtesy of The American Museum of Natural History; **612, Bkgrnd,** (l) Shutterstock, Inc.; **613,** Gunter Marx/Alamy; **614, #4,** © Mike Booth/Alamy Images; **614, #1,** © Ton Koene/AGE Fotostock; **614, #2,** Danita Delimont/Getty Images; **614, #3,** © Ellen McKnight/ Alamy Images; **614, #5,** © age fotostock/SuperStock; **614, #6,** © Bill Bachmann/ The Image Works, Inc.; **614, #7,** M Timothy O'Keefe/Getty Images; **616,** Nick Saunders/Barbara Heller Photo Library, London/Art Resource, NY.

UNIT 8 PRIMARY SOURCE: Pages 618-619, 618, Schalkwijk/Art Resource, NY; **619,** Jason Rothe/Alamy.

UNIT 8 CLOSER: Pages 620-621, 620, T, Joe Vogan/Alamy; **620, B,** Werner Foreman/Topham/The Image Works; **620, Bkgrnd,** Shutterstock, Inc.; **621, R,** The Bridgeman Art Library/Getty Images; **621, L,** Photo Researchers, Inc.

CHAPTER 21: Pages 624-647, 624, The Pierpont Morgan Library/Art Resource, NY; **628,** The Art Archive/British Museum/Eileen Tweedy; **629, T,** Shutterstock, Inc.; **629, B,** Shutterstock, Inc.; **630, B,** Newscom; **630, TR,** The British Museum/ Art Resource, NY; **630, TL,** The British Museum/Art Resource, NY; **631, L,** The Art Archive/Bibliothèque Municipale de Toulouse/Kharbine-Tapabor/Coll. J. Vigne; **631, R,** The Granger Collection, New York; **632, TL,** The Gallery Collection/Corbis; **632, TR,** Bildarchiv Steffens/The Bridgeman Art Library International; **632, M,** Private Collection/Index/The Bridgeman Art Library International; **632, BL,** Bettmann/Corbis; **632, BR,** Bridgeman-Giraudon/ Art Resource, NY; **633,** Interfoto/Alamy; **634,** The Art Archive/British Library; **635, B,** Stephen Conlin/Dorling Kindersley; **635, T,** The Art Archive/Abbey of Monteoliveto Maggiore Siena/Alfredo Dagli Orti; **637, BL,** Huntington Library and Art Gallery, San Marino, CA, USA/The Bridgeman Art Library International; **637, BR,** The Granger Collection, New York; **637, BM,** The Art Archive/Palazzo Barberini Rome/Alfredo Dagli Orti; **637, T,** The Irish Image Collection/Design Pics/Corbis; **637, Bkgrnd,** Shutterstock, Inc.; **638, TL,** Trinity College, Cambridge, UK/The Bridgeman Art Library International; **638, TR,** The Pierpont Morgan Library/Art Resource, NY; **638, B,** Scala/Art Resource, NY; **638, MR,** Erich Lessing/ Art Resource, NY; **638, ML,** Erich Lessing/Art Resource, NY; **638, Bkgrnd,** Shutterstock, Inc.; **639,** The Art Archive/Gianni Dagli Orti; **640,** The Art Archive/ Historiska Muséet Stockholm/Gianni Dagli Orti; **641,** Universitetet Oldsaksamling Oslo; **642,** The Trustees of the British Museum/Art Resource, NY; **643, M,** Brian Delph/Dorling Kindersley; **643, RB,** HIP/Art Resource, NY; **643, RT,** The Board of Trustees of the Armouries/HIP/The Image Works; **643, L,** Jeff Greenberg/The Image Works; **646,** Reunion des Musee Nationaux/Art Resource, NY.

CHAPTER 22: Pages 648-677, 648, 20th Century Fox/The Kobal Collection;

652, Bayerische Staatsbibliothek, Munich, Germany/The Bridgeman Art Library International; **653,** Elio Ciol/Corbis; **654,** Private Collection/The Stapleton Collection/The Bridgeman Art Library International; **655,** The Art Archive/British Library; **656, B,** Bibliotheque Municipale, Rouen, France/ Lauros/Giraudon/The Bridgeman Art Library International; **656, ML,** Real Monasterio de El Escorial, El Escorial, Spain/Index/The Bridgeman Art Library International; **656, MR,** Canterbury Cathedral, Kent, UK/The Bridgeman Art Library International; **656, T,** Bibliotheque Municipale, Douai, France/Giraudon/ The Bridgeman Art Library International; **657, L,** The Art Archive/Bodleian Library Oxford; **657, R,** British Library, London, UK/The Bridgeman Art Library International; **658,** Private Collection/Look and Learn/The Bridgeman Art Library International; **659,** Private Collection/Look and Learn/The Bridgeman Art Library International; **660-661,** Charles and Josette Lenars/Corbis; **661,** Private Collection/Look and Learn/The Bridgeman Art Library International; **661, T,** Nigel Reed QEDimages/Alamy; **662,** Bettmann/Corbis; **663,** Mark Bassett/Alamy; **664,** Bibliotheque Nationale, Paris, France/The Bridgeman Art Library International; **665,** British Library, London, UK/British Library Board, All Rights Reserved/The Bridgeman Art Library International; **666,** National Museum Wales/The Bridgeman Art Library International; **667,** Private Collection/The Stapleton Collection/The Bridgeman Art Library International; **668, B,** Guido Baviera/Grand Tour/Corbis; **668, T,** The Art Archive/Bibliothèque de l'Arsenal Paris/Kharbine-Tapabor/Coll. Jean Vigne; **669, BL,** Chris Hellier/ Corbis; **669, BR,** Mosfilm/The Kobal Collection; **669, T,** Biblioteca Monasterio del Escorial, Madrid, Spain/Bildarchiv Steffens/The Bridgeman Art Library International; **670, L,** Peter Denni/Dorling Kindersley; **670, R,** Snark/Art Resource, NY; **671,** Biblioteca Nazionale, Turin, Italy/Index/The Bridgeman Art Library International; **672,** Monasterio de El Escorial, El Escorial, Spain/ Index/The Bridgeman Art Library International; **673, L,** Werner Forman/HIP/ The Image Works; **673, R,** Barry Mason/Alamy; **674,** Design Pics Inc./Alamy; **675,** Topham/The Image Works; **676,** Bibliotheque Nationale, Paris, France/The Bridgeman Art Library International.

CHAPTER 23: Pages 678-701, 678, Palazzo Pubblico, Siena, Italy/The Bridgeman Art Library International; **682,** Réunion des Musées Nationaux/ Art Resource; **683,** G Cargagna/Age Fotostock; **684, Bkgrnd,** Christian Handl/ Age Fotostock; **684, ML,** Museo Nazionale del Bargello, Florence, Italy/The Bridgeman Art Library International; **686, LB,** Colin Palmer Photography/ Alamy; **686, Inset,** Chris Fredriksson/Alamy; **687,** Palazzo Pubblico, Siena, Italy/ Alinari/The Bridgeman Art Library International; **688,** Réunion des Musées Nationaux/Art Resource, NY; **689,** Alinari/Art Resource, NY; **690, LB,** Imagestate Media Partners Limited - Impact Photos/Alamy; **690, LT,** Ewan Chesser/ Shutterstock, Inc; **691, Bkgrnd,** Yoshio Tomii/SuperStock; **691, LB,** Private Collection/Agnew's, London, UK/The Bridgeman Art Library International; **691, RB,** Erich Lessing/Art Resource, NY; **692,** Bildarchiv Preussischer Kulturbesitz/Art Resource, NY; **693,** Lauros/Giraudon/The Bridgeman Art Library; **694, LB,** The Art Archive/St Benedict Sacro Speco Subiaco Italy/Alfredo Dagli Orti **694, T,** Jeff Morgan 11/Alamy; **694, LT,** Shutterstock; **695, TR,** Charles Stirling/Alamy; **696, LT,** Shutterstock, Inc.; **696, BL,** Frank Greenaway/Dorling Kindersley; **696, BM,** Shutterstock, Inc.; **696, RM,** Shutterstock, Inc.; **696, RT,** Shutterstock, Inc.; **696, L,** Shutterstock, Inc.; **697, Bkgrnd,** Andy Williams/The Travel Library/Photolibrary; **697, Inset,** Bildarchiv Preussischer Kulturbesitz/Art Resource, NY; **698,** Snark/ Art Resource, NY; **699,** J.D. Dallet/Age Fotostock; **700,** The Print Collector/ Heritage/The Image Works.

UNIT 9 PRIMARY SOURCE: Pages 702-703, 702, Interfoto/Alamy; **703,** The Bridgeman Art Library/Getty Images.

UNIT 9 CLOSER: Pages 704-705, 704, RT, SuperStock; **704, RM,** The Art Archive/Gianni Dagli Orti; **704, LB,** Private Collection/The Stapleton Collection/ The Bridgeman Art Library International; **704, BR,** The Bridgeman Art Library International; **705, R,** The Gallery Collection/Corbis; **705, L,** Corbis; **705, M,** Science & Society Picture Library/Contributor/Getty Images.

CHAPTER 24: Pages 708-735, 708, Paul Hardy/Corbis; **712,** Kim Sayer/ Dorling Kindersley; **713,** Alinari Archives/Corbis; **714, B,** James Stevenson/ Dorling Kindersley, Courtesy of the National Maritime Museum, London; **714, ML,** Alan Hills/The British Museum/Dorling Kindersley; **714, MR,** The British Museum/Dorling Kindersley; **714, T,** The Art Archive/Archivio di Stato di Siena/Gianni Dagli Orti; **715,** Bronzino, Agnolo (1503-1572). Eleanora of

Toledo With Her Son Giovanni de Medici, ca. 1545. Oil on panel, 115 x 96 cm. Uffizi, Florence, Italy. Scala/Art Resource, NY.; **716, B,** Gianni Dagli Orti/Corbis; **716, T,** Scala/Ministero per i Beni e le Attività culturali/Art Resource, NY; **717,** Raphael, "The School of Athens," Vatican Museums, Rome, Italy, Scala/Art Resource, NY; **718, L,** Erich Lessing/Art Resource, NY; **718, R,** Bettmann/Corbis; **718-719, Bkgrnd,** Shutterstock, Inc.; **719, B,** Erich Lessing/Art Resource, NY; **719, T,** British Library, London, UK/Bridgeman Art Library; **720, L,** Scala/Art Resource, NY; **720, R,** Ali Meyer/Corbis; **721, B,** Andreas Von Einsiedel/Dorling Kindersley; **721, M,** Susanna Price/Dorling Kindersley; **721, T1,** Andy Crawford/Dorling Kindersley; **721, T2,** Susanna Price/Dorling Kindersley; **722, B,** Private Collection/The Stapleton Collection/The Bridgeman Art Library; **722, T,** The New York Public Library/Art Resource, NY; **723,** The Granger Collection, New York; **724,** Erich Lessing/Art Resource, NY; **725, BL,** Ancient Art & Architecture/www.DanitaDelimont.com; **725,** Border Shutterstock, Inc.; **725, BR,** Ellen Howdon/Dorling Kindersley, Courtesy of Glasgow Museum; **725, ML,** Dorling Kindersley, Courtesy of the Saint Bride Printing Library, London; **725, MR,** Dorling Kindersley, Courtesy of the London College of Printing; **725, T,** FPG/Getty Images, Inc; **726, Bkgrnd,** Shutterstock, Inc.; **726, BL,** © Christopher Stewart/Alamy Images; **726, BR,** The Art Archive; **726, T,** The Art Archive; **727,** Bibliotheque Nationale, Paris, France/The Bridgeman Art Library International; **728,** Hamburger Kunsthalle, Hamburg, Germany/The Bridgeman Art Library International; **729, B,** Santa Maria della Grazie, Milan/A.K.G., Berlin/SuperStock; **729, T,** Dorling Kindersley; **730, BL,** The Art Archive/Private Collection Italy/Gianni Dagli Orti; **730, BM,** Alinari Archives/Corbis; **730, BR,** Réunion des Musées Nationaux/Art Resource, NY; **730, T,** Mary Evans Picture Library; **731, BL,** Shutterstock, Inc.; **731, BR,** Stock Italia/Alamy; **731, TL,** Erich Lessing/Art Resource; **731, TR,** Scala/Art Resource, NY; **732, B,** Robbie Jack/Corbis; **732, ML,** Dorling Kindersley; **732, MR,** Bob Masters/Alamy; **732, T,** Lebrecht Music & Arts Photo Library.

CHAPTER 25: Pages 736-757, 736, JTB Photo/PhotoLibrary Group Ltd. **740,** Picture Desk, Inc./Kobal Collection; **741,** The Granger Collection, New York; **742, L,** The Bridgeman Art Library International; **742, R,** akg-images/The Image Works; **743, L,** The Art Archive/Musée Départemental des Vosges Epinal/Kharbine-Tapabor/Photo Prud'homme; **743, R,** HIP/Art Resource, NY; **744, TL,** The Bridgeman Art Library International; **744, LB,** Publiphoto/Photo Researchers, Inc.; **744, TR,** Interfoto/Alamy; **744, RB,** Lebrecht/The Image Works; **746,** The Print Collector/Heritage/The Image Works; **747,** Private Collection/The Bridgeman Art Library International; **747, R,** Jim West/Age Fotostock; **747, Bkgrnd,** Ajay Shrivastava/Shutterstock, Inc.; **747, M,** Myrleen Pearson/Alamy; **748, M,** Bonhams, London, UK/The Bridgeman Art Library; **748, B,** The Art Archive/Nationalmuseet Copenhagen Denmark/Alfredo Dagli Orti; **748, T, Inset,** Réunion des Musées Nationaux/Art Resource, NY; **748, B, Inset,** Bridwell Library; **749,** Science Museum/SSPL/The Image Works; **750,** Sunday Mirror/Topfoto/The Image Works; **752, R,** The Art Archive/Musée des Beaux Arts Lausanne/Alfredo Dagli Orti; **752, R,** akg-images; **752, Inset,** Mikhail/Shutterstock, Inc.; **753, R,** Spectrum Colour Library/HIP/The Image Works; **753, L,** Scala/Art Resource, NY; **753, Bkgrnd,** basel101658/Shutterstock, Inc.; **754, B,** Rena Schild/Shutterstock, Inc.; **754, LT,** Samuel Perry/Shutterstock, Inc.; **754, RT,** Ryan Rodrick Beiler/Shutterstock, Inc.; **754, TM,** Ryan Rodrick Beiler/Shutterstock, Inc.; **756,** akg-images.

CHAPTER 26: Pages 758-785, 758, Shutterstock, Inc.; **758, Bkgrnd,** Nikolay Okhitin/Shutterstock, Inc.; **759,** Border Molodec/Shutterstock, Inc.; **759,** Border Molodec/Shutterstock, Inc.; **760,** Border Molodec/Shutterstock, Inc.; **762,** Josep Pena Llorens/Shutterstock, Inc.; **763, B,** The Art Archive/Museo de la Torre del Oro Seville/Gianni Dagli Orti; **763, T,** Nata_Tata/Shutterstock, Inc.; **764, Bkgrnd,** Molodec/Shutterstock, Inc.; **764, Bkgrnd,** Molodec/Shutterstock, Inc.; **765, T,** Georgios Kollidas/Shutterstock, Inc.; **765, MT,** National Maritime Museum, London/The Image Works; **765, MB,** Nicola Asuni/Alamy; **765, BL,** The Granger Collection, New York; **765, Bkgrnd,** Ford Photography/Shutterstock, Inc.; **766, LT,** The Art Archive/Marine Museum Lisbon/Gianni Dagli Orti; **766, LB,** Private Collection/Look and Learn/The Bridgeman Art Library International; **766, R,** Luis César Tejo/Shutterstock, Inc.; **766, Bkgrnd,** Molodec/Shutterstock, Inc.; **767, T,** James Stevenson/Dorling Kindersley, Courtesy of the National Maritime Museum, London; **767, MB,** National Maritime Museum, Greenwich, London; **767, MT,** The Granger Collection, New York; **767, Bkgrnd,** Ford Photography/Shutterstock, Inc.; **767, B,** The Art Archive/Bibliothèque Nationale Paris; **768, L,** Sheila Terry/Photo Researchers; **768, R,** The Art Archive/Alfredo Dagli Orti; **768, Bkgrnd,** Betacam-SP/Shutterstock, Inc.; **769, L,** Map Resources/Shutterstock, Inc.; **769, R,** Neo Edmund/Shutterstock, Inc.; **769, Bkgrnd,** Betacam-SP/Shutterstock, Inc.; **770,** Michel Zabe/Art Resource, NY; **771, T,** Werner Forman/Art Resource, NY; **771, B,** Casadaphoto/Shutterstock, Inc.; **772, R,** The Granger Collection, New York; **772, L,** Mike Goldwater/Alamy; **772, M,** Jeff Rotman/Alamy; **773, L,** The Art Archive/Templo Mayor Library Mexico/Gianni Dagli Orti; **773, R,** The Granger Collection, New York; **774, B,** The Art Archive/Archaeological Museum Lima/Gianni Dagli Orti; **774, T,** The Granger Collection, New York; **775,** akg-images/Joseph Martin; **776,** John Warburton-Lee Photography/Alamy; **777, LTL,** Jeff Banke/Shutterstock, Inc.; **777, LTR,** Nikola Bilic/Shutterstock, Inc.; **777, LML,** SergioZ/Shutterstock, Inc.; **777, LMR,** Yellowj/Shutterstock, Inc.; **777, LBR,** Yasonya/Shutterstock, Inc.; **777, LBL,** James Clarke/Shutterstock, Inc.; **777, RT,** Lilya/Shutterstock, Inc.; **777, RML,** Michaela Stejskalova/Shutterstock, Inc.; **777, RMR,** Four Oaks/Shutterstock, Inc.; **777, RBR,** Andrey Kozachenko/Shutterstock, Inc.; **777, RBL,** Claire VD/Shutterstock, Inc.; **777, RBM,** eAlisa/Shutterstock, Inc.; **777, Bkgrnd,** Yuriy Chaban/Shutterstock, Inc.; **778, R,** Courtesy of the Bancroft Library, University of California, Berkeley.; **778, L,** Photolibrary New York; **779, RT,** Christopher Elwell/Shutterstock, Inc.; **779, RB,** Oleg Iatsun/Shutterstock, Inc.; **779, LB,** Berci/Shutterstock, Inc.; **779, Bkgrnd,** High Leg Studio/Shutterstock, Inc.; **779, LT,** Denis Barbulat/Shutterstock, Inc.; **780, Bkgrnd,** Apollofoto/Shutterstock, Inc.; **780, Bkgrnd,** Yuriy Chaban/Shutterstock, Inc.; **781, Bkgrnd,** High Leg Studio/Shutterstock, Inc.; **781, Bkgrnd,** Yuriy Chaban/Shutterstock, Inc.; **782, B,** Regien Paassen/Shutterstock, Inc.; **782, T,** Rob Byron/Shutterstock, Inc.; **782, M,** Christie's Images/Corbis; **782, Bkgrnd,** ussr/Shutterstock, Inc.; **783,** The Art Archive/Musée du Louvre Paris/Gianni Dagli Orti; **784,** Michel Zabé/Art Resource, NY.

UNIT 10 PRIMARY SOURCE: Pages 786-787, 786, Leemage/Lebrecht Music & Arts/Lebrecht Music & Arts; **787,** Getty Images/The Bridgeman Art Library International.

UNIT 10 CLOSER: Pages 788-789, 788, T, Dorling Kindersley; **788, B,** The Image Works; **789, B,** Vicki Beaver/Alamy; **789, T,** Age Fotostock.

Back Cover

T, César Crespo/Age Fotostock; **MT,** The Art Archive; **MB,** Toño Labra/Age Fotostock; **B,** The Art Archive.

Text Acknowledgements

Grateful acknowledgment is made to the following for copyrighted material:

Page 153 *Tale of Sinhue and Other Ancient Egyptian Poems* translated by R.B. Parkinson. Used by permission of Oxford University Press.

Page 168 & 169 Used from *Tanakh: The Holy Scriptures: The New JPS Translation to the Traditional Hebrew Text,* copyright © 1985 by The Jewish Publication Society, with the permission of the publisher.

Page 171 Used from *Tanakh: The Holy Scriptures: The New JPS Translation to the Traditional Hebrew Text,* copyright © 1985 by The Jewish Publication Society, with the permission of the publisher.

Page 174 Used from *Tanakh: The Holy Scriptures: The New JPS Translation to the Traditional Hebrew Text,* copyright © 1985 by The Jewish Publication Society, with the permission of the publisher.

Page 177 Used from *Tanakh: The Holy Scriptures: The New JPS Translation to the Traditional Hebrew Text,* copyright © 1985 by The Jewish Publication Society, with the permission of the publisher.

Page 179 Used from *Tanakh: The Holy Scriptures: The New JPS Translation to the Traditional Hebrew Text,* copyright © 1985 by The Jewish Publication Society, with the permission of the publisher.

Page 183 Used from *Tanakh: The Holy Scriptures: The New JPS Translation to the Traditional Hebrew Text,* copyright © 1985, by The Jewish Publication Society, with the permission of the publisher.

Page 189 Used from *Tanakh: The Holy Scriptures: The New JPS Translation to the Traditional Hebrew Text,* copyright © 1985 by The Jewish Publication Society, with the permission of the publisher.

Page 191 "Psalm 23 & 24" from *The Holy Bible: New Revised Standard Version.* Copyright © 1952 (2nd edition, 1971) by the Division of the Christian Education of the National Council of the Churches of Christ in the United States of America. All rights reserved.

Acknowledgments (continued)

Page 216 *Bhagavad-Gita,* translated by Barbara Stoller Miller, translation copyright © 1986 by Barbara Stoller Miller. Used by permission of Bantam Books, a division of Random House, Inc. Used by permission of The Estate of Barbara Miller Stoller.

Page 266 #s 8 (4.1 extract), 19 (6I.), 20 (1I.), 51 (5I.), 67 (9I.) from *Tao Te Ching* by Lao Tzu, A New English Version, with foreword and notes by Stephen Mitchell. Translation copyright © 1988 by Stephen Mitchell. Used by permission of Pan Macmillan, London.

Page 269 #s 8 (4.1 extract), 19 (6I.), 20 (1I.), 51 (5I.), 67 (9I.) from *Tao Te Ching* by Lao Tzu, A New English Version, with foreword and notes by Stephen Mitchell. Translation copyright © 1988 by Stephen Mitchell. Used by permission of Stephen Mitchell care of Michael Katz.

Page 269 #s 8 (4.1 extract), 19 (6I.), 20 (1I.), 51 (5I.), 67 (9I.) from *Tao Te Ching* by Lao Tzu, A New English Version, with foreword and notes by Stephen Mitchell. Translation copyright © 1988 by Stephen Mitchell. Used by permission of HarperCollins Publishers.

Page 269 #s 8 (4.1 extract), 19 (6I.), 20 (1I.), 51 (5I.), 67 (9I.) from *Tao Te Ching* by Lao Tzu, A New English Version, with foreword and notes by Stephen Mitchell. Translation copyright © 1988 by Stephen Mitchell. Used by permission of Pan Macmillan, London.

Page 271 *Records of the Grand Historian: Qin Dynasty* by Sima Qian, translated by Burton Watson. Copyright © The Chinese University of Hong Kong.

Page 277 *The Book of Lord Shang: A Classic of the Chinese School of Law* by Yang Shang, translated by Jan Julius Lodewijk Duyvendak. Copyright © London: Arthur Probsthain.

Page 280 *Records of the Grand Historian: Qin Dynasty* by Sima Qian, translated by Burton Watson. Copyright © The Chinese University of Hong Kong.

Page 283 *Pan Chao: Foremost Woman Scholar of China* translated by Nancy Lee Swann. Copyright © Center for Chinese Studies, The University of Michigan.

Page 285 *The History of the Former Han Dynasty* by Pan Ku, translated by Homer H. Dubs, Jen T'ai and P'an Lo-chi. Copyright © Waverly Press.

Page 289 *Records of the Grand Historian: Qin Dynasty* by Sima Qian, translated by Burton Watson. Copyright © The Chinese University of Hong Kong.

Page 323 *The World of the Ancient Greeks* by John Camp and Elizabeth Fisher. Copyright © Thames & Hudson.

Page 323 *A History of the Ancient Greeks* by Don Nardo. Copyright © Lucent Books.

Page 353 *A History of the Ancient Greeks* by Don Nardo. Copyright © Lucent Books.

Page 353 *The World of the Ancient Greeks* by John Camp and Elizabeth Fisher. Copyright © Thames & Hudson.

Page 361 *Cicero: A Portrait* by Elizabeth Rawson. Copyright © Cornell University Press.

Page 385 Used by permission of the publishers from *Diary and Autobiography of John Adams: Volume 2-Diary 1771-1781,* edited by L.H. Butterfield, Leonard C. Faber, and Wendell D. Garrett, pp. 1, 57, 58, Cambridge, Mass.: The Belknap Press of Harvard University, Copyright © 1961 by the Massachusetts Historical Society.

Page 389 "Acts 5: 22 & Acts 5: 23-25" from *The Holy Bible: New Revised Standard Version.* Copyright © 1952 (2nd edition, 1971) by the Division of the Christian Education of the National Council of the Churches of Christ in the United States of America. All rights reserved.

Page 390 *Ancient Roman Statutes* by Allan Chester Johnson, Paul Robinson Coleman-Norton and Frank Card Bourne. Copyright © University of Texas Press.

Page 404 "Matthew 22: 37-39" from *The Holy Bible: New Revised Standard Version.* Copyright © 1952 (2nd edition, 1971) by the Division of the Christian Education of the National Council of the Churches of Christ in the United States of America. All rights reserved.

Page 411 "Matthew 5: 3-6, Matthew 5: 43-44 & Matthew 7: 12" from *The Holy Bible: New Revised Standard Version.* Copyright © 1952 (2nd edition, 1971) by the Division of the Christian Education of the National Council of the Churches of Christ in the United States of America. All rights reserved.

Page 440 *Defense of Byzantine Africa from Justinian to the Arab Conquest* by Denys Pringle. Copyright © British Archaeological Reports.

Page 442 *The Russian Primary Chronicle* translated by Samuel Hazzard Cross and Olgred P. Sherbowitz-Wetzor. Copyright © Mediaeval Academy of America.

Page 448 *Travels in Asia and Africa 1325-1354* by Ibn Battuta, translator H.A.R. Gibb.

Page 449 *The Adventures of Ibn Battuta: A Muslim Traveler of the Fourteenth Century* by Ross E. Dunn. Copyright © University of California Press.

Page 452 Excerpt from "96:1-3" from *The Koran* translated by N.J. Dawood. Copyright © N.J. Dawood, 1956, 1959, 1966, 1968, 1974, 1990, 1993, 1997, 1999. All rights reserved. Used by permission of Penguin Books, Ltd.

Page 477 Excerpt from "39:28" from *The Koran* translated by N.J. Dawood. Copyright © N.J. Dawood, 1956, 1959, 1966, 1968, 1974, 1990, 1993, 1997, 1999. All rights reserved. Used by permission of Penguin Books, Ltd.

Page 496 *Travels in Asia and Africa 1325-1354* by Ibn Battuta, translator H.A.R. Gibb.

Page 507 "Anansi Folk Tale" from *The African Genius: An Introduction to African Social and Cultural History,* translated by Basil Davidson. Copyright © Little, Brown and Company. Used by permission.

Page 523 *The Cambridge Illustrated History of China* by Patricia Buckley Ebrey. Copyright © Cambridge University Press

Page 525 *The Mongol Conquests: Timeframe AD 1200-1300* by Time-Life Books.

Page 533 *1421: The Year China Discovered America* by Gavin Menzies. Copyright © Gavin Menzies.

Page 539 *The Analects of Confucius* translated by Arthur Waley. Copyright © Random House, Inc.

Page 543 *The Book of Ser Marco Polo, the Venetian, Concerning the Kingdoms and the Marvels of the East* by Henri Cordier, Marco Polo and Henry Yule.

Page 545 *The Tale of Genji* by Murasaki Shikibu, translated by Royall Tyler. Copyright © Royall Tyler.

Page 546 *Diary of Lady Murasaki* by Murasaki Shikibu, translated by Richard Bowring. Copyright © Richard Bowring.

Page 557 Excerpts from "WAKA 1484" from http://www.temcauley.staff. shef.ac.uk.poems.shtml translated by Thomas McAuley. Copyright © Thomas McAuley. Used by permission of Thomas McAuley.

Page 595 Excerpt from "Metaphysical and Theological Ideas of the Nahuas" by Miguel León-Portilla, translated by Jack Emory Davis from *Aztec Thought and Culture: Philosophy and Poetry.* Copyright © 1963 by The University of Oklahoma Press. Used by permission.

Page 709-711 Excerpted from *Leonardo da Vinci, Book 1* in *The Giants of Science Series* by Kathleen Krull. Copyright © 2005, Viking Children's Books. Used by permission of the author.

Page 755 *World Religions and Democracy* edited by Philip J. Costopoulos, Larry Diamond and Marc F. Plattner. Copyright © Johns Hopkins University Press.

Page 767 Excerpt from "Letter 136: Peter Martyr of Anghera in Milan to the Archbishop of Braga" from *Christopher Columbus: His Works, His Life, His Remains* by John Boyd Thacher. Copyright © G.P. Putnam's Sons.

Page 772 *The First New Chronicle And Good Government* by Felipe Guamán Poma De Ayala, translated by David L. Frye. Copyright © Hackett Publishing Company.

Page 774 Excerpt from "Chapter 29: The Plague Named Totomonjztil" from *Florentine Codex: General History Of The Things Of New Spain* by Fray Bernardino de Sahagún, translated by Arthur J. O. Anderson and Charles E. Dibble. Copyright © University of Utah Press.

Page 786 & 787 *The Broken Spears* by Miguel León-Portilla. Copyright © 1962, 1990 by Miguel León-Portilla. Expanded and updated edition © 1992 by Miguel León-Portilla. Used by permission of Beacon Press, Boston.

Page 786 & 787 *The Broken Spears* by Miguel León-Portilla. Copyright © 1962, 1990 by Miguel León-Portilla. Expanded and updated edition © 1992 by Miguel León-Portilla. Used with permission of Beacon Press, permission conveyed through Copyright Clearance Center, Inc.

Note: Every effort has been made to locate the copyright owner of material reproduced on this component. Omissions brought to our attention will be corrected in subsequent editions.